MW01630466

Welcome to

EXPECT EXCITEMENT!
EXPECT RESULTS!

"All my **students need** to know content that is based on the **California Standards.**"

Content that Reflects the California Standards

Holt Science and Technology, California Edition provides complete content coverage for earth, life, and physical sciences as described in the California Standards. Designed specifically for California middle school students, *Holt Science and Technology* was created with your classroom needs in mind.

Content that is balanced and focused

Holt Science and Technology, California Edition finds the right balance between the breadth and depth of content coverage. You'll notice that the narrative is content-rich, and the emphasis is on essential concepts as described in the California Standards. Understanding builds step-by-step, creating a solid foundation that allows students to gradually and successfully master the California Standards.

A text that motivates

Holt Science and Technology, California Edition motivates students through its visual impact and engaging writing style. Initially, concise, outline-style headings provide an easy-to-understand framework for the chapter narrative. The chapter flows in a clear, logical sequence and at a comfortable pace. The narrative itself uses friendly language that makes reading accessible and enjoyable without compromising the scope and range of coverage. Each lesson is divided into content blocks that facilitate understanding. Furthermore, the visuals are integrated into the narrative to maximize interest and comprehension. Because good artwork is like gold—hard to find and highly valued—we have included artwork and visuals with functionality, clarity, accuracy, and motivational value.

and

Builds

Lessons aligned with the California Standards

Holt Science and Technology, California Edition supports California Standards-based content. Correlations appearing in the chapter organizer, chapter and section openers, chapter and section reviews, and end-of-chapter features assist you in monitoring your students' progress on specific California Standards. (A complete correlation by Standard to textbook page number is provided on p. T20.) Every day and in every lesson, you can be confident your students are learning your state's standards. Whether you are introducing a lesson, teaching a concept, reviewing, or assessing—you will always know which California Standard is being addressed.

on Them, too.

For a complete listing of components for this program, see p. T24.

"I need a textbook that will engage and excite my students while they're learning."

A Text that Grabs and Holds

Can science be cool? With *Holt Science and Technology, California Edition,* science is always cool. Attention-getting features and headlines, such as **"Quakes and Shakes on Other Cosmic Bodies"** from the Earthquakes chapter, ignite student curiosity. Captivating scientific art makes California Standards-based content more accessible by visually representing scientific concepts and processes. High-quality scientific art has always been a tradition at Holt; *Holt Science and Technology* continues in this tradition to help students gain a true understanding of science.

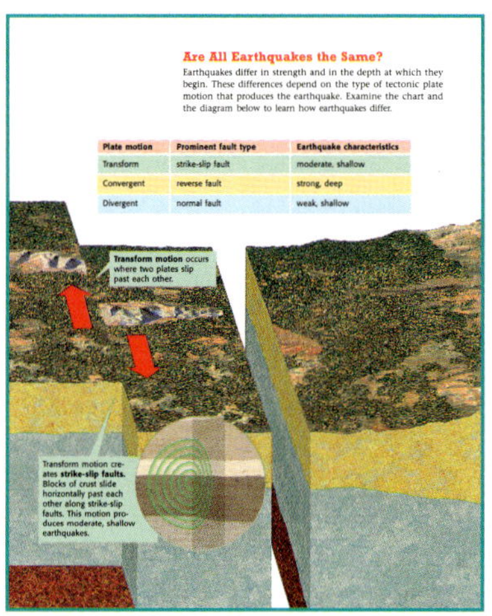

Are All Earthquakes the Same?

Earthquakes differ in strength and in the depth at which they begin. These differences depend on the type of tectonic plate motion that produces the earthquake. Examine the chart and the diagram below to learn how earthquakes differ.

Plate motion	Prominent fault type	Earthquake characteristics
Transform	strike-slip fault	moderate, shallow
Convergent	reverse fault	strong, deep
Divergent	normal fault	weak, shallow

Begins with a bang!

Each chapter begins with a brief introduction designed to pique students' interest. Here they may encounter a true story, such as **"This Really Happened!"** or a hypothetical situation that poses prereading questions.

Applies to real life

Some of your students may ask you why they are studying science. *Holt Science and Technology, California Edition* provides the answer with motivating activities, such as **Investigate!,** that connect concepts and principles to the real world. **BrainFood** feeds students' curiosity about the natural world around them.

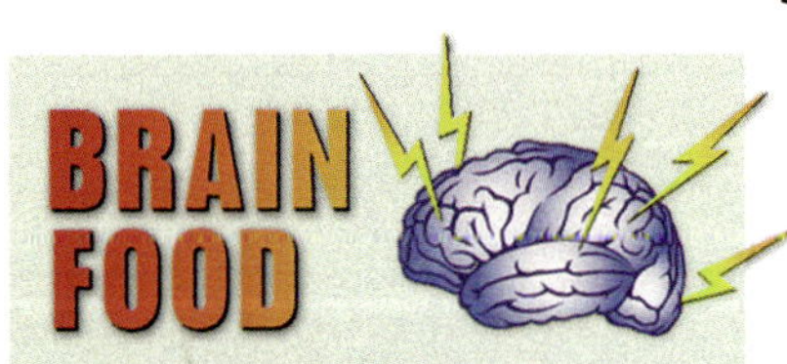

Anticipation

Imagine the thousands of lives that might have been saved if the people of St. Pierre could have predicted the eruption of Mount Pelée in 1902. Unfortunately, because volcanic eruptions are caused by processes deep within the Earth, they are very difficult to predict. See for yourself by creating your own volcano and then predicting its eruption.

Procedure

1. Tear off a sheet of **bathroom tissue,** and place 10 mL (2 tsp) of **baking soda** in the center of the tissue. Fold the corners of the tissue over the baking soda, and press the edges until the ends stay in place. Place the tissue packet in the middle of a large **plate** or **pan.**
2. Put some **modeling clay** around the top edge of a **funnel.** Turn the funnel upside down over the tissue packet in the bottom of the pan. The clay should form a watertight seal between the base of the funnel and the plate or pan. Press down to make a tight seal.
3. Add 50 mL (1/4 cup) of **vinegar,** two drops of **red food coloring,** and several drops of **liquid dish soap** to a 200 mL **beaker** or **measuring cup,** and stir.
4. Carefully pour the liquid into the spout of the upturned funnel. In your ScienceLog, record the time you began to pour.
5. Now predict how much time will elapse before your volcano erupts. Write your prediction in your ScienceLog.
6. When the volcano finally erupts, record the time again. How long did it take for your volcano to erupt? How close was your prediction?

Analysis

7. In what ways is your model volcano similar to a real one? In what ways is it different?
8. Based on the predictions of the entire class, what can you conclude about the accuracy of predicting volcanic eruptions?

Volcanoes 191

Your Students' Attention

Makes connections

In *Holt Science and Technology, California Edition,* **Connections** and **Across the Sciences** help students see the big picture by demonstrating the interrelatedness among the sciences and other disciplines. These features broaden students' perspectives as they make connections to life and physical sciences as well as to physics and chemistry. California Standards-based math is covered in the **MathBreak** in-text feature and in ***Math Skills for Science Worksheets,*** ultimately giving students a better understanding of science by asking them to apply math skills in a scientific context.

MATHBREAK

Moving Up the Scale

If the amount of energy released by an earthquake with a magnitude of 2.0 on the Richter scale is *n,* what are the amounts of energy

Links understanding to communication

Using scientific terminology can strengthen a student's grasp of science concepts. *Holt Science and Technology, California Edition* develops understanding of new words and concepts in a variety of ways. Vocabulary words are listed at the beginning of each section and are also highlighted in the narrative. If more support is needed, students have opportunities to review California Standards-based concepts, examine issues from different perspectives, or benefit from a different instructional approach with ***Reinforcement & Vocabulary Review Worksheets.***

Builds thinking and writing skills

Understanding is best reflected when students are able to express themselves through writing. To facilitate this, *Holt Science and Technology, California Edition* is loaded with a wide variety of writing opportunities—**Review** questions, expository writing assignments, **Homework,** research, and lab reports.

Brings focus to the Internet

While the text provides a solid foundation of scientific concepts, the Internet builds on that foundation by helping students and teachers stay abreast of new research and advancements. *Holt Science and Technology, California Edition* is the only California program that supplements California Standards-based content with up-to-date scientific information through NSTA's ***sci*LINKS**. To learn more about this groundbreaking service, see p. T17.

Labs to Make Learning

"I need a variety of fun yet meaningful lab activities that are cost effective."

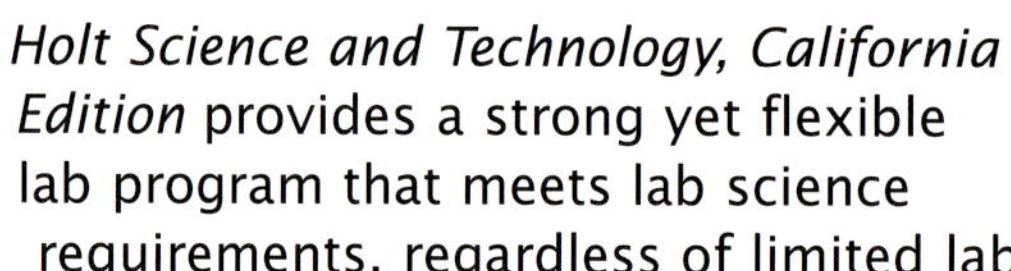

Holt Science and Technology, California Edition provides a strong yet flexible lab program that meets lab science requirements, regardless of limited lab equipment, time restrictions, or class management issues. All labs include clear procedures and demonstrate scientific concepts, theories, and principles while developing students' understanding of the scientific method. Each lab activity has been classroom tested and reviewed for reliability, safety, and efficient use of materials.

Built-in, flexible lab options

Holt Science and Technology, California Edition includes a wide range of lab options to enrich your classroom instruction. The lab activity **Investigate!** stimulates students' curiosity about upcoming scientific concepts in the chapter. **QuickLabs,** found throughout each chapter, are lab activities requiring minimal time and materials. In addition, **LabBook** icons appear at point-of-use, directing you and your students to appropriate labs at the back of the textbook. Praised by teachers for its convenience and flexibility, this feature enables you to control the context in which these labs are introduced.

QuickLab

Reaction to Stress

1. Make a pliable "rock" by pouring 60 mL (1/4 cup) of **water** into a **plastic cup** and adding 150 mL of **cornstarch,** 15 mL (1 tbsp) at a time. Stir well after each addition.

Through a variety of lab types within the LabBook—**Skill Builder, Inquiry, Discovery, Making Models,** and **Design Your Own**—students master prerequisite skills and knowledge before applying them to more complex scientific concepts. These labs provide students with opportunities to make observations, write hypotheses, and collect, analyze, and interpret data. They also sharpen investigative, logical- and critical-thinking, and problem-solving skills. Separate ***Datasheets for LabBook*** provides a convenient place for students to record their answers to the LabBook activities.

Turn to page 512 to build your own earthquake-safe building.

Lab manuals to meet every need

Wow your class with ***Whiz-Bang Demonstrations***—a rousing way to get students' attention at the beginning of your lesson. Students will find it hard to resist ***Labs You Can Eat,*** experiments that use food as materials. ***EcoLabs & Field Activities,*** a refreshing approach to experiments, address specific, ecological questions and increase environmental awareness. ***Inquiry Labs*** tap students' natural curiosity and creativity with a focus on the process of discovery.

Active and Meaningful

Time-saving tips and techniques

Lab Ratings for all labs make it easy for you to determine, at a glance, which lab is appropriate for your class. Aspects of each lab, such as teacher prep, student set-up, concept level, and clean up, are rated on a scale from easy to hard. **Demonstrations** are also provided so you have the option to demonstrate labs and procedures to the whole class.

> ***DEMONSTRATION***
>
> **Dissolution of Minerals** Limestone forms when calcium carbonate crystallizes out of ocean water. Students may not believe that water contains the chemical components of dissolved minerals. If you live in an area with hard water, have students observe ice melting in warm water.

Easy-to-order lab materials

Ordering lab materials is more efficient than ever with the *Holt Science and Technology* ***California Materials Ordering Software CD-ROM.*** This software, developed by Science Kit®, creates a "shopping list" of materials to order and their costs. The CD-ROM also lists required materials for every lab investigation in the program, including consumable and non-consumable kits.

***For a complete materials list, see page xxii in the* Annotated Teacher's Edition.**

"My teacher's edition should clearly organize all resources and provide techniques and tips."

A Well-organized Teacher's Edition

Each page in the *Annotated Teacher's Edition* features a reduced student page surrounded by a point-of-use lesson cycle consisting of teaching strategies, creative reinforcement, and thought-provoking extensions—all designed to help you teach to a wide variety of learning styles, ability levels, and interests.

Make the most of your daily lesson

With the wealth of program resources, you'll be glad to know we've included a convenient, time-saving guide suggesting how and when to use them. The **Chapter Organizer** serves as a visual master plan for integrating all labs, technology, and print resources. Because instructional time is so valuable, each section is organized according to time requirements. And you can quickly scan the correlations to the California Standards by section to see exactly which Standards are covered in each lesson. **Chapter Resources & Worksheets** also provide a reduced version of all available resources, categorized by **Visual Resources, Meeting Individual Needs, Review and Assessment, Lab Worksheets,** and **Applications & Extensions.** For in-depth, section-by-section information about the upcoming lesson, check out **Chapter Background.**

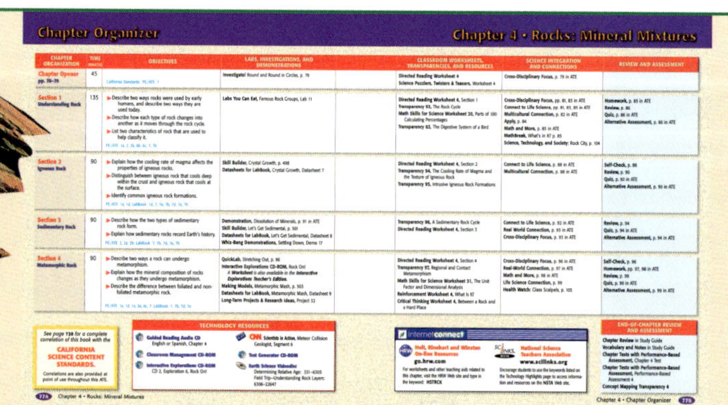
Chapter Organizer — Chapter 4 • Rocks: Mineral Mixtures

Keep the focus on the lesson

You can rely on an array of both traditional and new teaching strategies, reinforcement exercises, and extensions in the lesson cycle of the *Annotated Teacher's Edition*. The complete lesson cycle helps keep your students interested and involved.

- **Focus** explains the section concepts and objectives and includes a **Bellringer** activity for focusing students' attention at the beginning of class.
- **Motivate** captures students' attention with **Demonstrations, Activities,** and **Discussions.**
- **Teach** includes strategies such as **Meeting Individual Needs, Connections, Reading Strategy, Guided Practice,** and **Independent Practice. Using the Figure** helps you maximize the instructional value of in-text visuals.
- **Extend** enhances your lesson with a variety of intriguing activities. **Going Further** includes research activities, reports, and other projects designed to broaden students' knowledge. ***sci*LINKS** Internet references allow you to assign online activities when appropriate. **Homework,** available in every section, gives parents the opportunity to get involved.
- **Close** helps you check your students' comprehension of section content with **Quiz** and **Alternative Assessment.**

Keep your students on the right track

Misconception Alert highlights common misconceptions, allowing you to clear up misunderstandings before they hinder student learning. MISCONCEPTION ALERT

2

Volcanoes' Effects on Earth

NEW TERMS
shield volcano
cinder cone volcano
composite volcano
crater
caldera

OBJECTIVES
- Describe the effects that volcanoes have on Earth.
- Compare the different types of volcanoes.

The effects of volcanic eruptions can be seen both on land and in the air. Pyroclastic materials fall to the ground, causing great destruction, while ash and escaping gases affect global climatic patterns. Volcanoes also build mountains and plateaus that become lasting additions to the landscape.

An Explosive Impact

Because it is thrown high into the air, ash ejected during explosive volcanic eruptions can have widespread effects. The ash can block out the sun for days over thousands of square kilometers. Volcanic ash can blow down trees and buildings and can blanket nearby towns with a fine powder.

Flows As shown in **Figure 3,** clouds of hot ash can flow rapidly downhill like an avalanche, choking and searing every living thing in their path, as happened at Mount Peleé in 1902. Sometimes large deposits of ash mix with rainwater or the water from melted glaciers during an eruption. With the consistency of wet cement, the mixture flows downhill, picking up boulders, trees, and buildings along the way. More powerful than ordinary rivers, these mudflows move swiftly and cause immense damage.

Figure 3 During the 1991 eruption of Mount Pinatubo, in the Philippines, clouds of volcanic gases and ash sped downhill at up to 250 km/h.

Fallout As volcanic ash falls to the ground, the effects can be devastating. Buildings may collapse under the weight of so much ash. Ash can also dam up river valleys, resulting in massive floods. And although ash is an effective plant fertilizer, too much ash can smother crops, causing food shortages and loss of livestock.

Robot scientists? What will they think of next? Turn to Robot in the Hot Seat, on page 210, to get acquainted with this mechanical investigator.

Climatic Fluctuation In large-scale eruptions, volcanic ash, along with sulfur-rich gases, can reach the upper atmosphere. As the ash and gases spread around the globe, they can block out enough sunlight to cause the average global surface temperature to drop noticeably. The eruption of Mount Pinatubo in 1991 caused average global temperatures to drop by as much as 0.5°C. Although this may not seem like a large change in temperature, such a shift can disrupt climates all over the world. The lower average temperatures may last for several years, bringing wetter, milder summers and longer, harsher winters. Such changes in climate can cause worldwide food shortages that result in starvation and disease.

197

SECTION 2

Focus

Volcanoes' Effects on Earth

This section explores the effects of explosive eruptions. Students learn to identify different types of volcanoes and physical features created by volcanic activity, such as craters, calderas, and lava plateaus.

Bellringer

Write the following terms on the chalkboard:

shield volcano, cinder cone volcano, composite volcano, volcanic crater, caldera

Group students in threes, and have them look through the section to come up with a definition for each of the terms. Have them record their definitions and revise them after finishing the section.

1 Motivate

DISCUSSION

Have students discuss the most exciting images they've seen in movies and television programs featuring volcanoes. Have them describe what they think about volcanic eruptions in their ScienceLog so they can revisit these impressions after reading this section. Sheltered English

SCIENTISTS AT ODDS

Today most scientists believe that dinosaurs became extinct 65 million years ago because a large asteroid struck Earth. But a small group of volcanologists have a controversial hypothesis that the gases and ash released from a series of large volcanic eruptions may have caused the extinction. Encourage students to find out more about these theories.

READING STRATEGY

Prediction Guide Before reading the passage about the effects of explosive volcanic eruptions, have students respond to the following true/false statements:
- Ash flows can be more powerful than river floods. (true)
- Volcanic eruptions can affect the weather for many years. (true)

Directed Reading Worksheet 8 Section 2

SCLINKS TOPIC: Volcanic Effects GO TO: www.scilinks.org sciLINKS NUMBER: HSTE210

Section 2 • Volcanoes' Effects on Earth 197

Fuel your presentation

Fun features like WEIRD SCIENCE and Science Bloopers contain intriguing stories and information to get students thinking. Your students will laugh out loud at SCIENCE HUMOR and ponder fascinating facts in IS THAT A FACT!. Found on almost every page, these techniques will ignite class discussion.

"I would love to **streamline planning** so I can spend more time on what I do best—teaching."

Teaching Support that

Holt Science and Technology, California Edition takes the worry and work out of managing teaching resources. In this program, you will find a superb collection of time-saving teaching resources that can help you successfully streamline and orchestrate classroom instruction.

Sharpen your saw

The ***Professional Reference for Teachers*** provides current information about pertinent issues in science education today. In professional articles, many written by experts in the field of education, you can find out more about a variety of topics, including the National Science Education Standards, block scheduling, classroom management, teaching in an ESL classroom, and how gender impacts learning in the science classroom. A bibliography of books, lectures, magazines, and Web sites is included.

Manage your classroom resources

The ***Classroom Management CD-ROM*** (part of the ***One-Stop Planner CD-ROM***) organizes resources of time, energy, and equipment. **Lesson Plans** make it easy for you to know which resources work effectively with which concept, and can be edited to fit your needs. **Block Scheduling Lesson Plans** support various learning modalities and keep your students engaged during longer class periods. Other resources on the CD-ROM include student worksheets, Spanish transcripts of the text, assessment checklists and rubrics, correlations to the California Standards, lab inventory checklists, safety information, and more! All materials can be printed for your convenience.

Includes student worksheets

Visualize science concepts

Teaching Transparencies, with many images taken directly from the text, reinforce important science concepts and processes. Two ***Concept Mapping Transparencies*** are included for each chapter—a partial map transparency to use with your students as they progress through the chapter and a completed concept map to serve as an answer key. A correlation chart links transparencies across the sciences.

Makes Your Job Easier

Bellringer Transparency Masters, located on the ***Classroom Management CD-ROM*** (part of the ***One-Stop Planner CD-ROM***), help you focus students' attention quickly at the beginning of class and keep them focused while you are dealing with administrative demands.

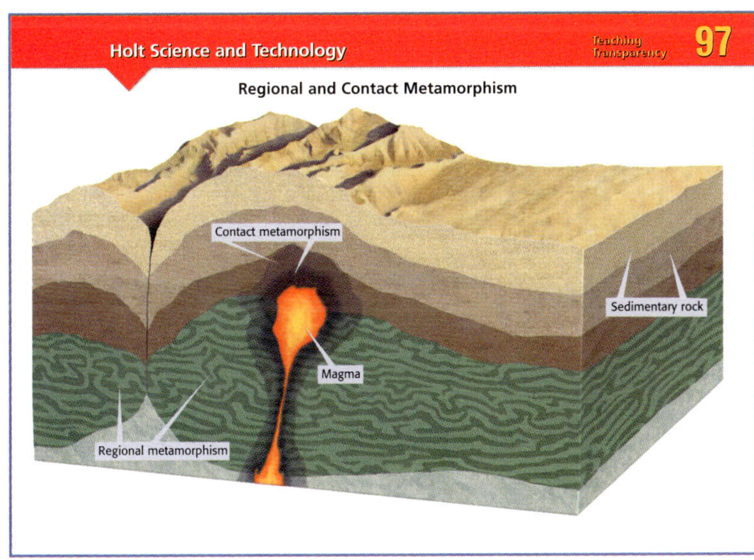

"I need a program that helps me teach today's students."

Giving Every Student

Holt Science and Technology, California Edition makes instruction accessible to all your students—English language learners, special needs students, those having difficulty mastering content, advanced learners, and students who need more practice or hands-on experience. A Sheltered English icon in the teacher's wrap alerts you to activities that are appropriate for English language learners. This program helps you teach today's students by giving you a variety of teaching tips, strategies, and resources in the *Annotated Teacher's Edition*.

Focus on reading

Reading Strategy emphasizes upcoming, key concepts in order to guide reading and ensure comprehension. ***Directed Reading Worksheets*** make reading an active process. These worksheets break lessons into small chunks, helping students stay focused. A variety of strategies and fun activities help students identify the main idea, then organize and synthesize supporting information. Other strategies develop students' abilities to retain and recall material.

Guided Reading Audio CD Program, available in both English and Spanish, provides students with a direct read of each chapter using instructional visuals as guideposts. Auditory learners, students with limited reading proficiency, or Spanish-speaking students receive the explanation they need from this alternative text format.

MEETING INDIVIDUAL NEEDS

Writing **Learners Having Difficulty** Have students copy descriptive phrases about the three types of volcanoes in their ScienceLog. Beside the entries, have them draw a cross section of each type of volcano. Students should find an example of each volcano type and write three paragraphs about each one. The paragraphs should describe how the volcano fits its category, detail its last eruption, and explain how the volcano's shape is linked to the way it erupted. Sheltered English

Provide universal access

Meeting Individual Needs in the teacher's wrap provides engaging demonstrations and hands-on activities to help different types of learners get a firmer grasp on California Standards-based content. **Reteaching** provides alternate methods of instruction for those students who need it. **Homework** options use a variety of teaching strategies to complement diverse learning styles.

a Chance

Approach learning from different angles

Cross-Disciplinary Focus facilitates interdisciplinary learning in the context of science. **Multicultural Connection** highlights important cultural issues relating to science. **Real-World Connection** links science to real-world applications, making science concepts relevant to students. **Group Activity** and **Cooperative Learning** contain group exercises and activities that are lesson-focused and facilitate peer education, communication, and teamwork.

In the Tule Lake region of northern California, volcanic eruptions created a rugged landscape of broken lava beds with glassy, splintery edges, deep trenches, and small lava caves where people can live—and hide.

In 1872, the United States and the Modoc Indians went to war. The Modocs set up a stronghold for 50 people in the jagged lava beds. The terrain was so hard to negotiate that the Modocs held off more than 1,000 federal troops for more than 5 months. Today, this area is part of Lava Beds National Monument.

to Succeed

"I want to make sure my students are learning the California Standards."

Assessment that Accurately Measures

In *Holt Science and Technology, California Edition,* you can assess your students' progress daily. The narrative engages students in a dialogue by asking questions. **What Do You Think?** assesses your students' prior knowledge of the science concepts in the upcoming chapter. After they finish the chapter, students can re-evaluate their prior knowledge in **Now What Do You Think?**—a great opportunity for students and parents to see how understanding has changed.

What Do You Think?

In your ScienceLog, try to answer the following questions based on what you already know:

1. What causes earthquakes?
2. Why are some earthquakes stronger than others?
3. Why do some buildings remain standing during earthquakes while others fall down?

Check progress

Self-Check encourages students to evaluate their own learning by answering questions found intermittently within the chapter. A page reference allows students to check their own answers. After reading each lesson, students explore, evaluate, and extend what they've learned through questions in the section **Review.** In the teacher's wrap, a **Quiz** provides an objective assessment of each lesson.

Chapter Highlights lists vocabulary and provides content summaries in a concise, visual format. This helps students organize their thoughts and synthesize information.

Study Guide contains blackline masters for Chapter Highlights and Chapter Reviews that will help students gear up for tests and quizzes.

Mastery of Standards-based Content

Chapter Review contains a variety of question types to help your students retain content, such as Using Vocabulary, Understanding Concepts, Concept Mapping, and Critical Thinking and Problem Solving. They are also correlated with learning objectives so you know what your students are learning.

Chapter Tests with Performance-Based Assessment include multiple-choice, concept-mapping, critical-thinking, interpreting graphics, math-in-science, and alternative assessment questions, to name a few. Questions have been carefully researched and developed to accurately measure your students' understanding of California Standards-based concepts and skills. Correlating test questions to learning objectives enables you to pinpoint what students are and aren't learning. You can be confident that your students will be prepared for **California Standards-based assessments.**

Alternative Assessment in the teacher's wrap provides you with different evaluation options, such as expository writing and concept mapping, to ensure a thorough assessment.

Create your own assessments

With the ***Test Generator CD-ROM with Testbuilder Software for Mac® and Win®*** (part of the ***One-Stop Planner CD-ROM***), you can create, revise, and edit quizzes, section and chapter reviews, or chapter tests, drawing from thousands of questions organized by chapter and linked to chapter objectives. Plus this special California Edition has test items that are correlated to the California Standards—making it easier for you to assess your students' learning of the Standards. It also includes performance-based assessment.

The ***Test Generator: Test Item Listing*** provides a printed copy of thousands of assessment items (including performance-based items) on the *Test Generator CD-ROM.* This handy guide allows you to preview test items before making selections.

Assessment Checklists & Rubrics, available on CD-ROM or as blackline masters, gives you guidelines for evaluating students' progress using a variety of assessment methods, including performance and portfolio assessment tools. You can also create a customized checklist for each class, helping you gather daily scores and determine grades.

"I don't have time to find and evaluate the technology resources out there."

Technology that Meets Your Goals

Holt Science and Technology, California Edition has done the legwork for you by providing an array of easy-to-use technology resources. These resources are fully integrated into each lesson so you can seamlessly introduce CD-ROM investigations and videodisc presentations as well as customize your lessons and provide thorough assessments. Whether you are preparing for class, delivering instruction, or having students interact with technology, this program provides the right combination of instructionally valuable technology resources to make your teaching more effective, efficient, and creative.

Teacher resources

The ***Classroom Management CD-ROM*** (part of the ***One-Stop Planner CD-ROM***) provides student resources and additional classroom management tools to help you organize your lessons. Also included on the ***One-Stop Planner CD-ROM*** is the ***Test Generator CD-ROM*** which allows you to create, revise, and edit quizzes, section and chapter reviews, and chapter tests. For more information, see pages T10 and T15.

Classroom resources

In ***CNN Presents: Science in the News*** videos, the CNN Turner Learning news teams bring to the classroom actual news coverage about scientists in action, and science and its impact on different cultures, technology, and the environment. Students can benefit because they relate what they are learning in the classroom to the real world. Each news segment has a related critical-thinking worksheet to enhance skill development.

The ***HRW Earth Science Videodisc with Image Directory*** motivates your students to take an interest in earth science by exposing them to over 1,800 multimedia images from the earth's core to outer space. The ***Science Discovery Videodisc Program*** contains stunning scientific images from the **Image and Activity Bank** as well as provides a fun means for solving scientific problems via the **Science Sleuths** series.

Student interactive resources

Holt Science and Technology, California Edition contains two valuable online resources that bring focus to the Internet. ***sci*LINKS,** a groundbreaking service developed by NSTA, integrates Internet technology into the science curriculum like never before. With *sci*LINKS, your students can access online educational resources that will help them review, extend, and enrich their knowledge about the topic at hand.

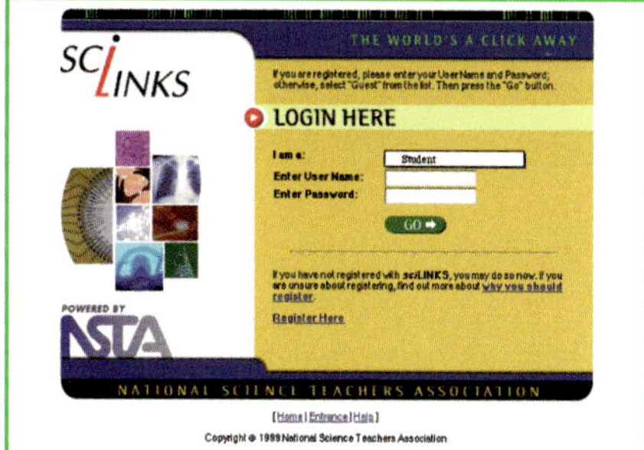

Here's how it works: Anytime students see a *sci*LINKS logo in the text, they can use the keyword to go to the *sci*LINKS Web site. They will be instantly linked to Internet resources with relevant content. The *sci*LINKS staff, consisting of teachers like you, reviews, monitors, and updates featured sites so you can rest assured that they contain appropriate and current information that will enhance student learning for years to come.

Your students can also enrich their knowledge by exploring the Internet through the **go.hrw.com** site, which links students to online chapter activities and resources.

and Expands Your Options

Develop your students' inquiry, analysis and decision-making skills with the ***Interactive Explorations CD-ROM Program.*** It invites your students to investigate science phenomena in a virtual lab setting not limited by time, scale, or availability of equipment.

With the ***Interactive Science Encyclopedia CD-ROM,*** your students have instant access to more than 3,000 cross-referenced science entries, in-depth articles, science fair project ideas, interactive activities, and projects.

EXPECT EXCITEMENT! EXPECT RESULTS!

California Science Content Standards

6TH GRADE
FOCUS ON
EARTH SCIENCE

Plate Tectonics and Earth's Structure

1. Plate tectonics explains important features of the Earth's surface and major geologic events. As the basis for understanding this concept, students know:

- **a.** the fit of the continents, location of earthquakes, volcanoes, and midocean ridges, and the distribution of fossils, rock types, and ancient climatic zones provide evidence for plate tectonics.
- **b.** the solid Earth is layered with cold, brittle lithosphere; hot, convecting mantle; and dense, metallic core.
- **c.** lithospheric plates that are the size of continents and oceans move at rates of centimeters per year in response to movements in the mantle.
- **d.** earthquakes are sudden motions along breaks in the crust called faults, and volcanoes/ fissures are locations where magma reaches the surface.
- **e.** major geologic events, such as earthquakes, volcanic eruptions, and mountain building result from plate motions.
- **f.** how to explain major features of California geology in terms of plate tectonics (including mountains, faults, volcanoes).
- **g.** how to determine the epicenter of an earthquake and that the effects of an earthquake vary with its size, distance from the epicenter, local geology, and the type of construction involved.

Shaping the Earth's Surface

2. Topography is reshaped by weathering of rock and soil and by the transportation and deposition of sediment. As the basis for understanding this concept, students know:

- **a.** water running downhill is the dominant process in shaping the landscape, including California's landscape.
- **b.** rivers and streams are dynamic systems that erode and transport sediment, change course, and flood their banks in natural and recurring patterns.
- **c.** beaches are dynamic systems in which sand is supplied by rivers and moved along the coast by wave action.
- **d.** earthquakes, volcanic eruptions, landslides, and floods change human and wildlife habitats.

Heat (Thermal Energy) (Physical Science)

3. Heat moves in a predictable flow from warmer objects to cooler objects until all objects are at the same temperature. As a basis for understanding this concept, students know:

- **a.** energy can be carried from one place to another by heat flow, or by waves including water waves, light and sound, or by moving objects.
- **b.** when fuel is consumed, most of the energy released becomes heat energy.
- **c.** heat flows in solids by conduction (which involves no flow of matter) and in fluids by conduction and also by convection (which involves flow of matter).
- **d.** heat energy is also transferred between objects by radiation; radiation can travel through space.

Energy in the Earth System

4. Many phenomena on the Earth's surface are affected by the transfer of energy through radiation and convection currents. As a basis for understanding this concept, students know:

- **a.** the sun is the major source of energy for phenomena on the Earth's surface, powering winds, ocean currents, and the water cycle.
- **b.** solar energy reaches Earth through radiation, mostly in the form of visible light.
- **c.** heat from Earth's interior reaches the surface primarily through convection.
- **d.** convection currents distribute heat in the atmosphere and oceans.
- **e.** differences in pressure, heat, air movement, and humidity result in changes of weather.

Ecology (Life Science)

5. Organisms in ecosystems exchange energy and nutrients among themselves and with the environment. As a basis for understanding this concept, students know:

- **a.** energy entering ecosystems as sunlight is transferred by producers into chemical energy through photosynthesis, and then from organism to organism in food webs.
- **b.** over time, matter is transferred from one organism to others in the food web, and between organisms and the physical environment.
- **c.** populations of organisms can be categorized by the functions they serve in an ecosystem.
- **d.** different kinds of organisms may play similar ecological roles in similar biomes.
- **e.** the number and types of organisms an ecosystem can support depends on the resources available and abiotic factors, such as quantity of light and water, range of temperatures, and soil composition.

Resources

6. Sources of energy and materials differ in amounts, distribution, usefulness, and the time required for their formation. As a basis for understanding this concept, students know:

- **a.** the utility of energy sources is determined by factors that are involved in converting these sources to useful forms and the consequences of the conversion process.
- **b.** different natural energy and material resources, including air, soil, rocks, minerals, petroleum, fresh water, wildlife, and forests, and classify them as renewable or nonrenewable.
- **c.** natural origin of the materials used to make common objects.

Investigation and Experimentation

7. Scientific progress is made by asking meaningful questions and conducting careful investigations. As a basis for understanding this concept, and to address the content of the other three strands, students should develop their own questions and perform investigations. Students will:

- **a.** develop a hypothesis.
- **b.** select and use appropriate tools and technology (including calculators, computers, balances, spring scales, microscopes, and binoculars) to perform tests, collect data, and display data.
- **c.** construct appropriate graphs from data and develop qualitative statements about the relationships between variables.
- **d.** communicate the steps and results from an investigation in written reports and verbal presentations.
- **e.** recognize whether evidence is consistent with a proposed explanation.
- **f.** read a topographic map and a geologic map for evidence provided on the maps, and construct and interpret a simple scale map.
- **g.** interpret events by sequence and time from natural phenomena (e.g., relative ages of rocks and intrusions).
- **h.** identify changes in natural phenomena over time without manipulating the phenomena (e.g., a tree limb, a grove of trees, a stream, a hillslope).

HOLT SCIENCE & TECHNOLOGY

Correlation to the California Science Content Standards

6TH GRADE
FOCUS ON EARTH SCIENCE

Plate Tectonics and Earth's Structure

	1	1a	1b	1c	1d	1e	1f	1g
Pupil's Edition	75, 135, 145–150, 155–157, 160–163, 166–168, 169, 170–171, 175, 181, 186–187, 196, 199, 201–204, 208–209, 301, 333, 336, 341, 343, 361, 378–379, 388, 471, 473, 476, LAB 508–509	88, 96, 143–150, 156–157, 160–163, 166–167, 168, 176, 181, 201–205, 208–209, 333, 336, 341, 343, 360–361, 471, 476, LAB 516	136–139, 142, 160–161, 181, 183, 186–187, 200, 203, 208, LAB 508	140, 150, 161, 204, 209, 361, LAB 508	88, 90, 96, 150, 166–171, 176, 186–187, 192–204, 208–209, LAB 498	96, 97, 99, 135, 151–157, 160–162, 166–169, 171, 186, 201–205, 208–209, 341, 375, 378–379, 388, 471, 473, 476, LAB 509, 516	150, 154, 160, 177	168–169, 172–174, 177–178, 181, 186–187, 204, LAB 514
Annotated Teacher's Edition	143, 148–150, 152–157, 167–168, 171, 175, 200–205, 343	80, 82–87, 90, 95–99, 143–144, 146, 148–150, 152–157, 201, 203, 205, 341	30, 136–139, 142, 181, 183	140, 142, 147, 149, 203	87, 97, 148, 166–168, 171, 175, 180, 192–194, 196–205	151–152, 155–157, 200–205	168, 175	172–174, 176, 178, 179, 180, 182–183, 189
Ancillaries	DRG 37–46, 47–54, 55–62, RVC 17–20, 21–22, 25–28, CTB 21–24, 25–28, 29–32, 49–52, LYE 76–79, IEC 87–96	DRG 21–28, 37–46, 47–54, 55–62, 97–108, RVC 17–20, 21–22, 25–28, CTB 21–24, 25–28, 29–32	DRG 37–46, RVC 17–20, CPS 11–12, CTB 21–24, LYE 61–65, 66–70	RVC 17–20	DRG 47–54, 55–62, RVC 21–22, CTB 25–28, 29–32, 89–92, LYE 76–79, WBD 29–30, IEC 27–37, 123–132	DRG 37–46, 47–54, 55–62, 97–108, RVC 25–28, CTB 21–24, 25–28, 29–32, LYE 66–70	LYE 71–75	DRG 47–54, RVC 21–22, CPS 11–12

Shaping the Earth's Surface

	2	2a	2b	2c	2d
Pupil's Edition	83–84, 86, 91, 94, 103, 192, 205, 247–258, 261–262, 270–271, 273, 276–298, 300–302, 376–377, 386–387, LAB 531, 533	247–254, 257, 270–271, 287, 289, 292	82, 94, 247–248, 250–257, 270–271, 273, 278, 292, 334	187, 256, 270, 273, 275–279, 281, 300–301, 303, 376–377, 383, 386–387	171, 174, 177–180, 186–187, 189, 192–193, 195–199, 202, 205, 208–209, 257, 295–298, 300–301, 375, 379, 386, 420
Annotated Teacher's Edition	92, 94, 192, 249–251, 253–254, 257, 260, 262, 276, 280–287, 290–294, 296–297	253–254, 257, 287, 290–291, 293	82, 92, 94, 248–249, 251, 253–255, 273, 341	276, 278–281, 377	169, 175, 193, 197, 200, 204, 295–297
Ancillaries	DRG 21–28, 73–80, 81–90, RVC 35–36, CPS 21–22, CTB 41–44, MSS 63–64, LYE 50–54, INQ 49–54, EFA 43–47, WBD 23–24, 32–34	DRG 73–80	DRG 73–80, RVC 33–36, MSS 63–64, WBD 23–24	DRG 81–90, CTB 41–44, INQ 49–54	DRG 47–54, 55–62, 73–80, CPS 15–16, 27–28, CTB 25–28, MSS 65–66, INQ 55–60, WBD 27–28, EOE 9

Heat (Thermal Energy) (Physical Science)

	3	3a	3b	3c	3d
Pupil's Edition	214–217, 219–230, 232, 236, 240–241, 243, 401, 403, 418, LAB 520, 522–523	96, 142, 216, 219–230, 232–233, 240–241, 276–277, 280, 300–301, 338, 374, 381, 383, 398–401, LAB 522	111, 231–232, 234, 237	221–223, 225, 227, 240–241, 401, 403, 418–419, LAB 522	223, 233, 401–403, 418–419, LAB 522
Annotated Teacher's Edition	219–220, 222, 225, 227–228, 230, 401, 403	227, 277	234	222, 225, 227, 401, 403	227, 401, 403
Ancillaries	DRG 63–72, RVC 27–30, CTB 33–36	DRG 109–116, RVC 27–30, CPS 27–28, CTB 33–36		DRG 63–72, RVC 27–30, CTB 33–36, 57–60	DRG 63–72, RVC 27–30, CTB 33–36, 57–60, EFA 56–59

Ancillary Product Codes

RVC Reinforcement & Vocabulary Review Worksheets, California Edition
CPS Critical Thinking & Problem Solving Worksheets, California Edition
CTB Chapter Tests with Performance-Based Assessment, California Edition
SSW Science Skills Worksheets
MSS Math Skills for Science
LYE Labs You Can Eat
INQ Inquiry Labs
EFA EcoLabs & Field Activities
WBD Whiz-Bang Demonstrations
IEC Interactive Explorations CD-ROM for Mac® and Win®
EOE CNN Presents Science in the News: Eye on the Environment

Energy in the Earth System

	4	4a	4b	4c	4d	4e
Pupil's Edition	18, 368–375, 380, 386–387, 400, 404–409, 418–419, 424, 431, 433–435, 453, 455, 457–459, 466, 470–473, 477, LAB 524	122, 248–249, 254, 337–338, 360, 365, 367–369, 372–375, 380, 382–383, 386–387, 400, 404–409, 415, 418–419, 424–425, 427, 430–433, 448–449, 459, 473	20, 203, 396–397, 399–400, 418, 453, 455, 466, 470, 472, 476–477, LAB 506	147, 150, 193, 203	338, 365, 367, 369, 370–373, 401, 403, 405–409, 418–419, 459, 477	372–373, 403, 425–441, 448–449, 454, 457, 466, 478
Annotated Teacher's Edition	20, 371–374, 405–406, 409, 425, 428–429, 431–432, 440–441, 470	335, 341, 366, 368–370, 373, 377, 379, 381–383, 409, 424, 428–429, 431, 458	20, 400, 459, 469	147	335, 370–373, 403, 406, 408–409	372, 404, 407, 408–409, 426, 428–432, 434–436, 438–441, 455, 458–459, 478
Ancillaries						RVC 53–56, EFA 60–65

Ecology (Life Science)

	5	5a	5b	5c	5d	5e
Pupil's Edition	28, 306, 308–315, 317–321, 324–325, 345–347, 461	306, 308–313, 315, 317, 321, 324–325	305–306, 309–315, 317–318, 321, 324–325, 389, 461	307, 309–321, 324–325, 344, 347	310–311, 315–316, 318, 325, 344, 460–468	273, 305, 308, 314–317, 319, 321, 324–325, 344–347, 373, 468, 476
Annotated Teacher's Edition	306–307, 309–321, 326	306–307, 309–313, 315–318, 320–321	306–307, 309–313, 315–321, 326	307, 309, 313, 317, 321	311, 347, 460, 462–464, 466–468	306, 308–309, 314–321, 346
Ancillaries	DRG 91–96, 97–108, RVC 37–40, CTB 45–48, EOE 3	DRG 91–96, RVC 37–40	RVC 37–40			

Resources

	6	6a	6b	6c
Pupil's Edition	62–63, 67–71, 74–76, 103, 108, 111–125, 128–129, 131, 154, 162, 263, 267, 270–272, 348–352, 362, 414	111–112, 115 125, 128–129, 154, 162, 232–237, 240–241, 272, 352, 412–414, 420, 472, 477	61–65, 67, 71, 74–76, 108–114, 117–120, 122–125, 128–129, 131, 154, 162, 258–260, 263–267, 270–271, 285, 348–352, 361–362, 414, 424	59, 71, 75, 80, 86, 99, 103, 105, 108, 110, 128, 130–131, 349, 351
Annotated Teacher's Edition	60–63, 68–71, 76, 111–115, 117, 120–125, 131, 162, 264, 350, 351, 421	111, 114, 116–117, 119–125, 162, 233–234, 350, 412, 421	60–67, 70, 76, 84, 108–110, 114, 117–121, 123–125, 131, 258–260, 262–264, 266–267, 349–352	68, 69–70, 80–81, 97–99, 104–105, 108–109, 130
Ancillaries	DRG 15–20, 29–36, RVC 13–16, CPS 7–8, EOE 21	DRG 29–36, CPS 7–8, EOE 10	DRG 29–36, 97–108, RVC 13–16, CPS 9–10	DRG 29–36

Investigation and Experimentation

	7	7a	7b	7c	7d	7e	7f	7g	7h
Pupil's Edition	7, 13–17, 23, 28, 36, 59, 66, 79, 96, 107, 113, 135, 141, 165, 171, 187, 191, 194, 200, 213, 215, 221, 242, 247, 259, 275, 283, 294, 305, 307, 331, 362, 365, 368, 379, 393, 406, 423, 427, 453, 457, LAB 486, 488, 490, 492, 494, 496, 498, 501, 503–504, 506, 508–509, 512, 514, 518, 520, 522–524, 526, 530–531, 533–534, 536, 538, 540, 542, 544, 546, 548, 550, 552, 555–556, 558–559, 562	15, 305, 351, LAB 486, 498, 512, 520, 526, 540, 546, 548, 559	7, 21, 23, 36, 59, 107, 113, 135, 165, 171, 191, 194, 200, 213, 215, 221, 242, 247, 275, 283, 294, 307, 351, 379, 393, 406, 423, 427, 445, 453, 457, LAB 486, 488, 490, 492, 494, 496, 498, 501, 503–504, 506, 508–509, 514, 518, 520, 522–524, 526, 530–531, 533, 538, 540, 542, 544, 546, 548, 550, 555–556, 559, 562	221, 307, LAB 514, 534, 538, 558	LAB 496, 498, 501, 503, 509, 520, 522, 526	21, 141, 165, 194, 215, 247, 275, 283, 294, 331, 351, 362, 365, 393, 406, 423, 453, 457, LAB 486, 488, 494, 498, 501, 503–504, 506, 509, 512, 514, 518, 520, 522, 524, 526, 530–531, 533–534, 536, 538, 540, 542, 544, 546, 548, 550, 558–559, 562	33, 37–39, 41–42, 44–49, 52–53, 55, 205, 458, LAB 490, 492, 516	209, LAB 514, 516, 530	199, 209, LAB 498, 501, 542, 558–559
Annotated Teacher's Edition	12–17, 34, 37, 61–62, 65, 84, 121, 172, 180, 213, 222, 228–229, 261, 332, 336, 341, 395, 400, 402, 426, 438, 443, 457	12–17, 228, 400	9, 18, 34, 37, 62, 84, 121, 229, 332, 395, 400, 402, 426, 443	371, 382, 466	12–17, 61, 180, 336	18–19, 21, 228, 395, 402	34, 39–40, 46–49, 141, 143–144, 149, 168, 292, 341		
Ancillaries	DRG 1–8, CPS 1–2, CTB 1–4, 69–134, LYE 50–84, INQ 44–54, 61–77, EFA 39–70, WBD 22–54, IEC 48–57, 133–142, EOE 4–5	DRG 1–8, CPS 1–2, 19–20, CTB 69–72, 93–96, 97–100, SSW 31–32, 33–34, LYE 66–70, 71–75, 76–79, INQ 49–54, 61–66, 72–77, EFA 43–47, 48–51, 52–55, 56–59, 60–65, EOE 3	DRG 1–8, CPS 1–2, 5–6, 19–20, CTB 69–112, 117–128, 133–134, LYE 50–65, 80–84, INQ 44–54, 61–77, EFA 39–70, WBD 22–54, IEC 133–142, EOE 4–5	SSW 63–65, 66–67, 68–71, MSS 63–64, LYE 50–54, 55–60, 66–70, 71–75, 76–79, EFA 39–42, 43–47, 48–51, 52–55	DRG 1–8, CTB 69–112, 125–128, 133–134, LYE 71–79, INQ 40–43, 61–66, EFA 52–55, WBD 25–29, 32–33, 35, 38–44, 46–54	DRG 1–8, 9–14, CTB 69–72, 77–80, 81–84, 93–96, 97–100, 105–108, 117–120, LYE 61–65, 80–84, EFA 39–42, 43–47, 48–51, 52–55, 56–59, 60–65, 66–70, WBD 30–31, 46–47, 48–49, 52–54	RVC 3–6, CTB 5–8, 129–132, INQ 40–43	CTB 1–4, EFA 39–42, 56–59	

Holt Science and Technology: Earth Science California Edition Components

H55667-8	Earth Science Pupil's Edition, CALIFORNIA EDITION
H55668-6	Earth Science Annotated Teacher's Edition, CALIFORNIA EDITION
H55669-4	Earth Science Study Guide, CALIFORNIA EDITION
H55689-9	Earth Science Study Guide Answer Key, CALIFORNIA EDITION
H55698-8	Earth Science Critical Thinking & Problem Solving Worksheets, CALIFORNIA EDITION
H55693-7	Earth Science Reinforcement & Vocabulary Review Worksheets, CALIFORNIA EDITION
H55674-0	Earth Science Science Puzzlers, Twisters & Teasers, CALIFORNIA EDITION
H55684-8	Earth Science Chapter Tests with Performance-Based Assessment, CALIFORNIA EDITION
H55697-X	Earth Science Directed Reading Worksheets, CALIFORNIA EDITION
H55678-3	Earth Science Directed Reading Worksheets Answer Key, CALIFORNIA EDITION
H55682-1	Earth Science Datasheets for LabBook, CALIFORNIA EDITION
H55679-1	Earth Science Datasheets for LabBook Answer Key, CALIFORNIA EDITION
H55673-2	Earth Science Test Generator: Test Item Listing, CALIFORNIA EDITION
H55683-X	Earth Science Teaching Transparencies with Concept Mapping Transparencies, CALIFORNIA EDITION
H55677-5	Earth Science Guided Reading Audio CD Program, CALIFORNIA EDITION
H55637-6	Guided Reading Audio CD Program, Spanish, CALIFORNIA EDITION
H54414-9	Labs You Can Eat
H54417-3	Whiz-Bang Demonstrations
H54419-X	Inquiry Labs
H54418-1	EcoLabs & Field Activities
H54421-1	Long-Term Projects & Research Ideas
H54426-2	Science Skills Worksheets
H54432-7	Math Skills for Science
H54422-X	Professional Reference for Teachers
H52947-6	Holt Anthology of Science Fiction
H55798-4	Assessment Checklists & Rubrics
H54424-6	Science Fair Guide
H54434-3	CNN Presents Science in the News: Video Library ▪ Scientists in Action ▪ Multicultural Connections ▪ Science, Technology & Society ▪ Eye on the Environment
H54439-4	Holt Science Posters
H56564-2	Earth Science One-Stop Planner CD-ROM: A Test Generator and Classroom Management CD-ROM for Mac® and Win®, CALIFORNIA EDITION
H55638-4	California Materials Ordering Software CD-ROM for Mac® and Win®
H55468-3	Interactive Explorations CD-ROM Program for Mac® and Win®
H05569-5	Science Discovery Videodisc Program, Complete Package
H05568-7	Science Sleuths
H05567-9	Image and Activity Bank
	Interactive Science Encyclopedia CD-ROM
0817239146	Windows®
0817239138	Macintosh®
H50784-7	HRW Earth Science Videodisc with Image Directory

CALIFORNIA

Earth Science

Annotated Teacher's Edition

HOLT, RINEHART AND WINSTON

A Harcourt Classroom Education Company

Austin • New York • Orlando • Atlanta • San Francisco • Boston • Dallas • Toronto • London

Staff Credits

Editorial

Robert W. Todd, Executive Editor

David F. Bowman, Managing Editor

Robert Tucek, Senior Editor

Leigh Ann Garcia, Timothy Pierce, Clay Walton

Annotated Teacher's Edition

Jim Ratcliffe, Bill Burnside, Kelly Graham

Ancillary Staff

Jennifer Childers, Senior Editor

Erin Bao, Kristen Karns, Andrew Strickler, Clay Crenshaw, Wayne Duncan, Molly Frohlich, Robin Goodman, Amy James, Monique Mayer, Traci Maxwell

Copyeditors

Steve Oelenberger, Copyediting Supervisor

Suzanne Brooks, Brooke Fugitt, Tania Hannan, Denise Nowotny

Editorial Support Staff

Christy Bear, Jeanne Graham, Rose Segrest, Tanu'e White

Editorial Permissions

Catherine J. Paré, Permissions Manager

Jan Harrington, Permissions Editor

Art, Design, and Photo

Book Design

Richard Metzger, Art Director

Marc Cooper, Senior Designer

David Hernandez, Designer

Alicia Sullivan (ATE), **Cristina Bowerman** (ATE), **Eric Rupprath** (Ancillaries)

Image Services

Elaine Tate, Art Buyer Supervisor

Erin Cone, Art Buyer

Photo Research

Jeannie Taylor, Senior Photo Researcher

Andy Christiansen, Photo Researcher

Photo Studio

Sam Dudgeon, Senior Staff Photographer

Victoria Smith, Photo Specialist

Design New Media

Susan Michael, Art Director

Design Media

Joe Melomo, Art Director

Shawn McKinney, Designer

Production

Mimi Stockdell, Senior Production Manager

Beth Sample, Production Coordinator

Suzanne Brooks, Sara Carroll-Downs

Media Production

Kim A. Scott, Senior Production Manager

Nancy Hargis, Production Supervisor

Adriana Bardin, Production Coordinator

New Media

Jim Bruno, Senior Project Manager

Lydia Doty, Senior Project Manager

Jessica Bega, Project Manager

Armin Gutzmer, Manager Training and Technical Support

Cathy Kuhles, Nina Degollado

Design Implementation and Production

Mazer Corporation

For permission to reprint copyrighted material, grateful acknowledgement is made to the following source: *sci*LINKS is owned and provided by the National Science Teachers Association. All rights reserved.

Printed in the United States of America
ISBN 0-03-055668-6
1 2 3 4 5 6 7 8 048 05 04 03 02 01 00 99

Acknowledgments

Chapter Writers

Kathleen Berry
Earth Science Teacher
Canon-McMillan Senior High School
Canon, Pennsylvania

Robert H. Fronk, Ph.D.
Chair of Science and Mathematics Education Department
Florida Institute of Technology
West Melbourne, Florida

Mary Kay Hemenway, Ph.D.
Research Associate and Senior Lecturer
Department of Astronomy
The University of Texas
Austin, Texas

Kathleen Kaska
Life and Earth Science Teacher
Lake Travis Middle School
Austin, Texas

Linda Ruth Berg, Ph.D.
Adjunct Professor–Natural Sciences
St. Petersburg Junior College
St. Petersburg, Florida

William G. Lamb, Ph.D.
Science Teacher and Dept. Chair
Oregon Episcopal School
Portland, Oregon

Peter E. Malin, Ph.D.
Professor of Geology
Division of Earth and Ocean Sciences
Duke University
Durham, North Carolina

Karen J. Meech, Ph.D.
Associate Astronomer
Institute for Astronomy
University of Hawaii
Honolulu, Hawaii

Robert J. Sager
Chair and Professor of Earth Sciences
Pierce College
Tacoma, Washington

Lab Writers

Kenneth Creese
Science Teacher
White Mountain Junior High School
Rock Springs, Wyoming

Linda A. Culp
Science Teacher and Dept. Chair
Thorndale High School
Thorndale, Texas

Bruce M. Jones
Science Teacher and Dept. Chair
The Blake School
Minneapolis, Minnesota

Shannon Miller
Science Teacher
Llano Junior High School
Llano, Texas

Robert Stephen Ricks
Special Services Teacher
Alabama State Department of Education
Montgomery, Alabama

James J. Secosky
Science Teacher
Bloomfield Central School
Bloomfield, New York

Academic Reviewers

Mead Allison, Ph.D.
Assistant Professor of Oceanography
Texas A & M University
Galveston, Texas

David M. Armstrong, Ph.D.
Professor of Biology
Department of EPO Biology
University of Colorado
Boulder, Colorado

Alissa Arp, Ph.D.
Director and Professor of Environmental Studies
Romberg Tiburon Center
San Francisco State University
Tiburon, California

Paul D. Asimow, Ph.D.
Postdoctoral Research Fellow
Lamont-Doherty Earth Observatory
Columbia University
Palisades, New York

Russell M. Brengelman, Ph.D.
Professor of Physics
Morehead State University
Morehead, Kentucky

John A. Brockhaus, Ph.D.
Associate Professor
Department of Geography and Environmental Engineering
United States Military Academy
West Point, New York

Peter E. Demmin, Ed.D.
Former Science Teacher and Department Chair
Amherst Central High School
Amherst, New York

Roy Hann, Ph.D.
Professor of Civil Engineering
Texas A & M University
College Station, Texas

Frederick R. Heck, Ph.D.
Professor of Geology
Ferris State University
Big Rapids, Michigan

Richard N. Hey, Ph.D.
Professor of Geophysics
Hawaii Institute of Geophysics and Planetology
University of Hawaii
Honolulu, Hawaii

John E. Hoover, Ph.D.
Associate Professor of Biology
Millersville University
Millersville, Pennsylvania

Robert W. Houghton, Ph.D.
Professor
Lamont-Doherty Earth Observatory
Columbia University
Palisades, New York

John L. Hubisz, Ph.D.
Professor of Physics
North Carolina State University
Raleigh, North Carolina

Steven A. Jennings, Ph.D.
Assistant Professor
Department of Geography & Environmental Studies
University of Colorado
Colorado Springs, Colorado

Eric Lee Johnson, Ph.D.
Assistant Professor of Geology
Central Michigan University
Mount Pleasant, Michigan

John Kermond, Ph.D.
Visiting Scientist
NOAA–Office of Global Programs
Silver Spring, Maryland

Zavareh Kothavala, Ph.D.
Postdoctoral Associate Scientist
Kline Geology Laboratory
Yale University
New Haven, Connecticut

Valerie Lang, Ph.D.
Project Leader of Environmental Programs
The Aerospace Corporation
Los Angeles, California

Duane F. Marble, Ph.D.
Professor Emeritus
Department of Geography and Natural Resources
Ohio State University
Columbus, Ohio

Joseph A. McClure, Ph.D.
Associate Professor
Department of Physics
Georgetown University
Washington, D.C.

Frank K. McKinney, Ph.D.
Professor of Geology
Appalachian State University
Boone, North Carolina

Joann Mossa, Ph.D.
Associate Professor of Geography
University of Florida
Gainesville, Florida

LaMoine L. Motz, Ph.D.
Coordinator of Science Education
Department of Learning Services
Oakland County Schools
Waterford, Michigan

Acknowledgments (cont.)

Barbara Murck, Ph.D.
Assistant Professor of Earth Science
Erindale College
University of Toronto
Mississauga, Ontario
CANADA

Hilary C. Olson, Ph.D.
Research Associate
Institute for Geophysics
The University of Texas
Austin, Texas

John R. Reid, Ph.D.
Professor Emeritus
Department of Geology and Geological Engineering
University of North Dakota
Grand Forks, North Dakota

Gary Rottman, Ph.D.
Associate Director
Laboratory for Atmosphere and Space Physics
University of Colorado
Boulder, Colorado

Dork L. Sahagian, Ph.D.
Professor
Institute for the Study of Earth, Oceans, and Space
University of New Hampshire
Durham, New Hampshire

Jack B. Swift, Ph.D.
Professor of Physics
The University of Texas
Austin, Texas

Lynne D. Talley, Ph.D.
Professor and Research Oceanographer
Scripps Institution of Oceanography
University of California, San Diego
La Jolla, California

Glenn Thompson, Ph.D.
Scientist
Geophysical Institute
University of Alaska
Fairbanks, Alaska

Martin VanDyke, Ph.D.
Professor of Chemistry Emeritus
Front Range Community College
Westminister, Colorado

Mollie Walton, Ph.D.
Scientist
U.S. Dept. of Agriculture–ARS
Jornada Experimental Range
Las Cruces, New Mexico

Thad A. Wasklewicz, Ph.D.
Assistant Professor of Geography
Colgate University
Hamilton, New York

Hans Rudolf Wenk, Ph.D.
Professor of Geology and Geophysical Sciences
University of California
Berkeley, California

Lisa D. White, Ph.D.
Associate Professor of Geosciences
San Francisco State University
San Francisco, California

Lorraine W. Wolf, Ph.D.
Associate Professor of Geology
Auburn University
Auburn, Alabama

Charles A. Wood, Ph.D.
Chairman and Professor of Space Studies
University of North Dakota
Grand Forks, North Dakota

Safety Reviewer

Jack Gerlovich, Ph.D.
Associate Professor
School of Education
Drake University
Des Moines, Iowa

Teacher Reviewers

Barry L. Bishop
Science Teacher and Dept. Chair
San Rafael Junior High School
Ferron, Utah

Daniel L. Bugenhagen
Science Teacher and Dept. Co-chair
Yutan Junior & Senior High School
Yutan, Nebraska

Yvonne Brannum
Science Teacher and Dept. Chair
Hine Junior High School
Washington District of Columbia

Kenneth Creese
Science Teacher
White Mountain Junior High School
Rock Springs, Wyoming

Linda A. Culp
Science Teacher and Dept. Chair
Thorndale High School
Thorndale, Texas

Alonda Droege
Science Teacher
Pioneer Middle School
Steilacom, Washington

Rebecca Ferguson
Science Teacher
North Ridge Middle School
North Richland Hills, Texas

Laura Fleet
Science Teacher
Alice B. Landrum Middle School
Ponte Vedra Beach, Florida

Jennifer Ford
Science Teacher and Dept. Chair
North Ridge Middle School
North Richland Hills, Texas

C. John Graves
Science Teacher
Monforton Middle School
Bozeman, Montana

Janel Guse
Science Teacher and Dept. Chair
West Central Middle School
Hartford, South Dakota

Gary Habeeb
Science Teacher
Sierra–Plumas Joint Unified School District
Downieville, California

Dennis Hanson
Science Teacher and Dept. Chair
Big Bear Middle School
Big Bear Lake, California

Norman Holcomb
Science Teacher
Marion Local Schools
Maria Stein, Ohio

Roberta Jacobowitz
Science Teacher
C.W. Otto Middle School
Lansing, Michigan

Tracy Jahn
Science Teacher
Berkshire Junior–Senior High School
Canaan, New York

David D. Jones
Science Teacher
Andrew Jackson Middle School
Cross Lanes, West Virginia

Howard Knodle
Science Teacher
Belvidere High School
Belvidere, Illinois

Michael E. Kral
Science Teacher
West Hardin Middle School
Cecilia, Kentucky

Kathy LaRoe
Science Teacher
East Valley Middle School
East Helena, Montana

Scott Mandel, Ph.D.
Director and Educational Consultant
Teachers Helping Teachers
Los Angeles, California

Jason Marsh
Science Teacher
Montevideo High and Country School
Montevideo, Minnesota

Acknowledgments continue on page 616

Contents in Brief

Contents

Contents

Unit 1 Introduction to Earth Science

Unit 2 ··· Earth's Resources

Contents

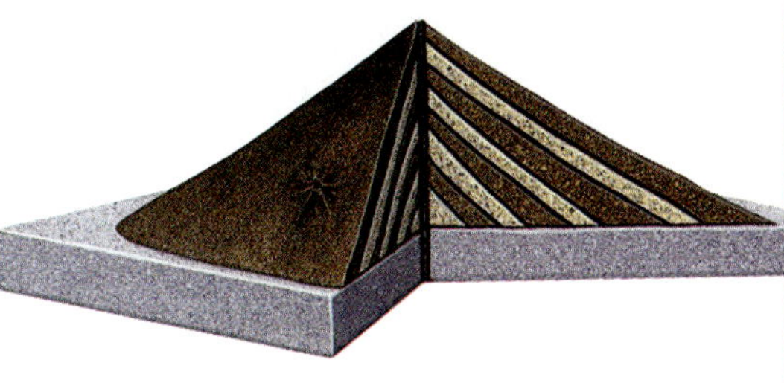

Contents

Contents

Contents

Unit 5 · · · Oceanography

CHAPTER 13

CHAPTER 14

Unit 6 ··· Weather and Climate

CHAPTER 

Contents

The more labs, the better!

Take a minute to browse the **LabBook** located at the end of this textbook. You'll find a wide variety of exciting labs that will help you experience science firsthand. But please don't forget to be safe. Read the "Safety First!" section before starting any of the labs.

Contents

CHAPTER 9
Heat and Heat Technology

CHAPTER 10
The Flow of Fresh Water

CHAPTER 11
Agents of Erosion and Deposition

CHAPTER 12
Interactions of Living Things

CHAPTER 13
Exploring the Oceans

CHAPTER 14
The Movement of Ocean Water

CHAPTER 15
The Atmosphere

CHAPTER 16
Understanding Weather

CHAPTER 17
Climate

Now is the time to Investigate!

Science is a process in which investigation leads to information and understanding. The **Investigate!** at the beginning of each chapter helps you gain scientific understanding of the topic through hands-on experience.

QuickLab

Not all laboratory investigations have to be long and involved.

The **QuickLabs** found throughout the chapters in this book require only a small amount of time and limited equipment. But just because they are quick, don't skimp on the safety.

Contents

MATH BREAK

Science and math go hand in hand.

The **MathBreaks** in the margins of the chapters show you many ways that math applies directly to science and vice versa.

APPLY

Science can be very useful in the real world.

It is interesting to learn how scientific information is being used in the real world. You can see for yourself in the **Apply** features. You will also be asked to apply your own knowledge. This is a good way to learn!

Connections

One science leads to another.

You may not realize it at first, but different areas of science are related to each other in many ways. Each **Connection** explores a topic from the viewpoint of another science discipline. In this way, areas of science merge to improve your understanding of the world around you.

environmental science CONNECTION

life science CONNECTION

Feature Articles

Feature articles for any appetite!

Science and technology affect us all in many ways. The following articles will give you an idea of just how interesting, strange, helpful, and action-packed science and technology are. At the end of each chapter, you will find two feature articles. Read them and you will be surprised at what you learn.

CAREERS

ACROSS THE SCIENCES

Science, Technology, and Society

EYE ON THE ENVIRONMENT

Eureka!

WATCH Health WATCH

SCIENTIFIC DEBATE

Science Fiction

WEIRD SCIENCE

Master Materials List

The following chart provides a comprehensive list of all the materials you would need in order to teach all of the labs and investigations in *Holt Science and Technology, Earth Science*.

For added convenience, Science Kit® provides materials-ordering software on CD-ROM designed specifically for *Holt Science and Technology*. This software allows you to create an electronic materials list, complete with item numbers. Using this software, you can order complete kits or individual items, quickly and efficiently.

For more information about this software, contact your HRW representative, call Science Kit® directly at 1-800-828-7777, or visit the Web site: www.sciencekit.com.

As you can see from the listings, *Holt Science and Technology* is designed around readily available materials and equipment, with an emphasis on economy. More specific materials lists and information can be found with the lab or investigation in this *Annotated Teacher's Edition*.

MATERIALS AND EQUIPMENT		QuickLab	Investigate!	LabBook
CONSUMABLE	**AMOUNT***	PAGE NO.	PAGE NO.	PAGE NO.
Aluminum foil, 2 × 8 cm	1			506
Aluminum foil, approx. 20 × 40 cm	1			498
Bag, paper lunch	1			534
Bag, plastic sealable sandwich	1			522, 526
Baking soda	15 mL			518
Baking soda	10 mL		191	
Balloon	1			550
Balloon, black	1		107	
Balloon, colored (not black or white)	3		107	
Balloon, white	1		107	
Bottle, soda, 2 L, with cap	1			526
Bottle, soda, 3 L (or jar)	1			501
Candle, birthday	1		393	
Card, index, 3 × 5 in	1			504, 546, 550, 556
Card, index, 3 × 5 in	5		305	
Cardboard, 1 × 1 cm	1			544
Cardboard, corrugated, 15 × 15 cm	4			559
Cardboard, corrugated 20 × 20 cm	2			544
Cardboard, corrugated, 20 × 20 cm (or plywood)	2			503
Cardboard, approx. 20 × 40 cm	1		135	
Carton, empty milk, 1/2 pint	1			522
Charcoal, activated	1/2 lb			526
Clay, modeling	2 sticks			503
Clay, modeling (3 colors)	2 sticks of each			486
Clay, modeling, (4 colors)	1 stick of each			509
Clothes hanger, plastic	1		165	
Clothes hanger, wire	1		165	
Container, empty milk, 1 gal	1			504
Cork	1			504
Cornstarch	150 mL	200		
Craft sticks	2			508
Cup, clear plastic, 9 fl oz	1			518
Cup, paper	5			548
Cup, plastic-foam	5	259		
Cup, plastic-foam	1		247	

* Amount is for one group of students.

MATERIALS AND EQUIPMENT		QuickLab	Investigate!	LabBook
CONSUMABLE *(CONTINUED)*	**AMOUNT***	PAGE NO.	PAGE NO.	PAGE NO.
Cup, plastic-foam with lid, small	1			523
Cup, plastic-foam, 9 fl oz	2			520
Cup, plastic-foam, large	1			523
Cup, plastic-foam, large	2			546
Detergent, dishwashing (powder or liquid)	40 mL			526
Detritus (cut up leaves and grass)	40 mL			526
Dowel, wood, approx. 20 cm	1		165	
Dowel, wood, 36 cm	1			544
Epsom salt	15 mL			498
Filters, coffee, cone-shaped (or plastic funnel)	1			546
Food coloring, any color	1 bottle			508
Food coloring, blue	1 bottle		365	542
Food coloring, red	1 bottle	406	191, 365	542, 546
Gelatin square, 8 × 8 cm	1			512
Gloves, protective	1		5	494, 540
Glue, white	1 bottle			504, 544
Gravel	2 lb		247	
Gravel	250 mL			501
Honey	1 jar	194		
Ice, shaved	150 mL			555
Limewater	1 L			518
Magazine	2			536
Marker, colored	1			498, 548
Marker, colored	1 pack		536	
Marker, permanent black	1			504, 506, 530, 534
Marker, transparency	1			492
Marshmallow	10			512
Mask, disposable filter	1	283		530
Match, long	1		423	
Napkin, paper	6		135	
Oil, light machine	1 small can	113		
Oil, light machine	15 mL			540
Paint, black tempera	1 container			559
Paint, light blue tempera	1 container			559
Paint, white tempera	1 container			559
Paper, adding machine, approx. 50 cm	1		135	
Paper, graph	1 sheet	307		516
Paper, tracing	1 sheet			492, 562
Paper clip	1		165	
Pencil, assorted colored	1 box		33	
Pencil, colored	3			486
Pencil, colored	4			509, 558
Pencil, colored (or marker)	2			490
Pencil, colored (red, orange, yellow)	3			516
pH test strips	6			526
Pinto beans	4–12 oz			534
Plastic tubing, 5 mm diam, 30 cm long (or clear inflexible plastic straws)	1			546
Plastic wrap, 30 × 20 cm	4			542
Plate, paper	1			512, 556
Poster board	1			536
Poster board, square, 5 × 5 cm	2			509

* Amount is for one group of students.

Master Materials List

MATERIALS AND EQUIPMENT		QuickLab	Investigate!	LabBook
CONSUMABLE *(continued)*	**AMOUNT***	**PAGE NO.**	**PAGE NO.**	**PAGE NO.**
Poster board strip, 5 × 15 cm	1			509
Potato	1			492
Rope, approx. 3 m	1	379		
Rope, approx. 30 cm	1		165	
Rubber band	1			520, 550
Salt	approx. 1 tbsp			542
Sand	4 oz	259		
Sand	250 mL			501
Sand	800 mL	294		
Sand	1/2 lb			526
Sand	1 lb	283		530, 531
Sand	10 lb			533
Sand	15 lb		247, 275	
Skewer, wooden	2			504
Soap, liquid dishwashing	1 small bottle		191	
Soil	250 mL			501
Soil, clay	40 mL			526
Soil, potting	4 oz	259		
Spoon, plastic	1		165	
Straw	1			550
Straw, flexible	1			518
Straw, straight plastic	1			556
Straw, straight plastic	2	194		548
String, 5 cm	1			544
String, 10 cm	1			488
String, approx. 25 cm	1	406		
String, 30 cm	1			520
String, approx. 40 cm	1			496
Tape, masking	1 roll		135	488, 498, 548, 550
Tape, transparent	1			504, 546, 550
Thread, white, 20 cm	1 spool			504
Tissue, bathroom	1 sheet		191	
Tissue, bathroom	2 sheets			518
Toothpick	10			512
Vinegar	40 mL			526
Vinegar	50 mL		191	
Vinegar	140 mL			518

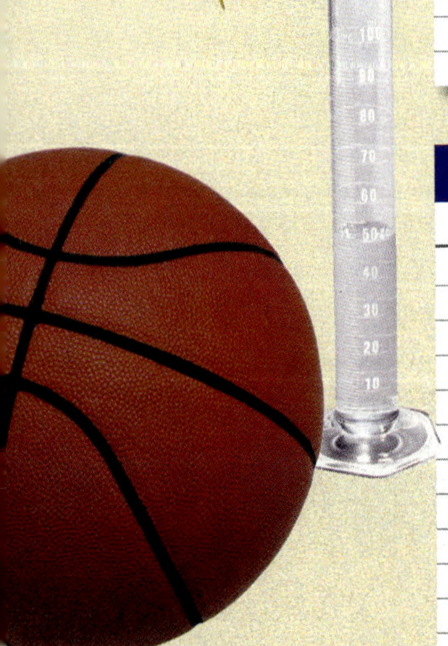

MATERIALS AND EQUIPMENT		QuickLab	Investigate!	LabBook
NONCONSUMABLE	**AMOUNT***	**PAGE NO.**	**PAGE NO.**	**PAGE NO.**
Balance, triple-beam, metric	1			496, 520, 522
Basketball	1			488
Beaker, 100 mL	1		393	555
Beaker, 250 mL	1	221	191	
Beaker, 400 mL	1			496, 498, 526
Beaker, 400 mL	2			524
Beaker, 400 mL	5			542
Beaker, 400 mL (or container)	1	294		
Beaker, 1000 mL	1	351		
Beaker, 1000 mL	2			526
Bottle, clear plastic, 64 fl oz	1		423	
Bottle, 16 fl oz	1			518

* Amount is for one group of students.

MATERIALS AND EQUIPMENT		QuickLab	Investigate!	LabBook
NONCONSUMABLE *(CONTINUED)*	**AMOUNT***	PAGE NO.	PAGE NO.	PAGE NO.
Bottle, small (vitamin)	1	406		
Bottle, soda, 2 L	1			504
Bowl, clear plastic, 12 oz	1	457		
Bowl, clear plastic, 3 gal	1	200	331	
Bowl, mixing, 3 gal	1			501
Box, cardboard, shallow (or lid)	1			530
Box, nontransparent (or pan), approx. 30 cm × 50 cm	1			486
Brick	3			531
Bucket, 5 gal	1			542
Bucket, 5 gal	2	215		
Calculator, scientific	1			506, 534
Can, coffee	1		5	550
Cardboard, approx. 10 × 10 cm	1		213	
Clay, modeling	1 stick		191	488, 504, 506, 518
Clay, modeling	1 lb			546, 548
Clay, modeling	2 lb			531, 538
Clay, modeling (4 colors)	1 stick of each		79	
Clothespin	1		247	
Coin	1			504, 518
Compass, drawing	1			514, 556
Compass, magnetic	1	36		490, 556
Container, clear plastic storage	1	141, 406		
Container, clear plastic storage with lid	1			492
Container, empty large margarine	3			531
Container, plastic (or jar or glass)	1	427		
Cup, plastic	1	200, 457	331	522
Cup, plastic	2	194		
Dropper	1	113		
Dropper pipet	1			501, 540
Erlenmeyer flask	1			526
Fan, electric	1	283		
Film canister	1	221		
Flashlight	1			488
Funnel, plastic	1		191	
Globe, world	1		453	
Gloves, heat-resistant	2			498, 506, 508, 524, 526, 542, 546, 555
Graduated cylinder, 100 mL	1			518, 520, 523, 524, 540, 555
Graduated cylinder, 100 mL	2	351		
Graduated cylinder, 1000 mL	1	351		531
Gravel	1/2 lb			526
Gravel	1 lb	283		531
Hair dryer	1			530
Hammer	1			526
Hole punch	1			504, 548
Hot plate	1			498, 523, 524, 526, 542, 546, 555
Hot plate	2			508
Iron filings	1/4 cup			494
Jar with 2 lids (one lid with a hole in its center), approx. 16 oz	1			506
Knife, plastic	1			486, 503, 509

* Amount is for one group of students.

Master Materials List

MATERIALS AND EQUIPMENT		QuickLab	Investigate!	LabBook
NONCONSUMABLE *(CONTINUED)*	AMOUNT*	PAGE NO.	PAGE NO.	PAGE NO.
Laboratory scoop, pointed	1			498
Lamp, with removable shade and 100 W bulb	1			506
Lamp, goose-neck with 60 W bulb	1		453	
Magnifying lens	1			498, 501, 526
Measuring tape, metric	1			488
Metal square, approx. 10 × 10 cm	1		213	
Meterstick	1			488
Mineral, biotite sample	1			494
Mineral, feldspar (pink) sample	1			494
Mineral, galena sample	1			494, 496
Mineral, graphite sample	1			494
Mineral, gypsum sample	1			494
Mineral, hematite sample	1			494
Mineral, hornblende sample	1			494
Mineral, magnetite sample	1			494
Mineral, muscovite sample	1			494
Mineral, pyrite sample	1			496
Mineral, quartz sample	1			494
Nail, approx. 1 in	1			526
Nail, approx. 2 in	12			520
Pan, aluminum pie	1		191, 393	540, 546
Pan, aluminum rectangular	1			508
Pan, aluminum rectangular	3			531
Penny	1	66		523
Petri dish	3	113		
Pin, bobby	2		135	
Pipe, PVC, 1.3 cm diam, approx. 20 cm long	1			486
Pitcher	1			546
Plastic-foam square, approx. 10 × 10 cm	1		213	
Plastic square, approx. 10 × 10 cm	1		213	
Plastic tubing, 5 mm diam, 1.5 m long	1			526
Protractor	1	294	165	488, 556
Putty, adhesive	1 package		393, 453	
Putty, plastic toy	1 ball	96		
Razor, safety	1			504
Ribbon, approx. 30 cm	1	379		
Ring stand	1			496
Ring stand with ring	1			526
Rock, approx. 10 cm diam.	1		213	
Rock, basalt sample	1			498
Rock, granite sample	1			498
Rock, limestone sample	1	113		
Rock, pumice sample	1			498
Rock, sandstone sample	1	113		
Rock, shale sample	1	113		
Rock, small, approx. 1/4 lb	1			556
Rolling pin, wood	1			509, 531
Rubber square, tan, approx. 15 × 15 cm	1			559
Ruler, metric	1	307		488, 490, 492, 504, 506, 508, 514, 516, 530, 531, 533, 538, 540, 546, 548, 555, 556, 558

* Amount is for one group of students.

MATERIALS AND EQUIPMENT		QuickLab	Investigate!	LabBook
NONCONSUMABLE *(CONTINUED)*	**AMOUNT***	PAGE NO.	PAGE NO.	PAGE NO.
Scale, spring	1			496
Scissors	1			501, 504, 526, 536, 538, 548, 550, 556
Sequin	1 small package			503
Shoe box with lid	1			538
Slides, microscope	10			494
Sock	1		5	
Spoon, plastic	1	200		
Spoon, plastic	2			526, 542
Spring toy, coiled	1	171	165	
Stapler	1			544, 556
Stapler (mini)	1			548
Stopper, rubber, 1 hole, with glass tube	1			526
Stopwatch	1	113		498, 504, 506, 523, 530, 531, 542
Streak plate	1			494
Test tube	1			498
Thermometer, Celsius	1	7, 457		498, 506, 520, 523, 546
Thermometer, Celsius	2	221	453	
Thermometer, Celsius	3			508
Thermometer, Celsius	4			559
Thermometer, Celsius	6		213	
Thumbtack	1			548
Thumbtack	5			504
Thumbtack (or pushpin)	1			556
Tissue box	1			518
Tongs	1			523, 524
Tongs, test-tube	1			498
Towel, small hand	1			531
Washtub, plastic	1		247, 275, 365	
Washtub, small plastic	1			533
Watch glass	1			524
Wood square, approx. 10 × 10 cm	1		213	
Wood square, approx. 15 × 15 cm	1			559
Wood, block, approx. 5 × 10 × 20 cm	4			508
Wood, block, approx. 5 × 10 × 20 cm	1	141		
Wood, block, approx. 8 × 3 × 3 cm	2		135	
Wood, block, approx. 35 × 10 × 5 cm	1		275	

* Amount is for one group of students.

Science & Math Skills Worksheets

The *Holt Science and Technology* program helps you meet the needs of a wide variety of students, regardless of their skill level. The following pages provide examples of the worksheets available to improve your students' science and math skills whether they already have a strong science and math background or are weak in these areas. Samples of assessment checklists and rubrics are also provided.

In addition to the skills worksheets represented here, *Holt Science and Technology* provides a variety of worksheets that are correlated directly with each chapter of the program. Representations of these worksheets are found at the beginning of each chapter in this Annotated Teacher's Edition.

Many worksheets are also available on the HRW Web site. The address is **go.hrw.com.**

Science Skills Worksheets: Thinking Skills

BEING FLEXIBLE

#1

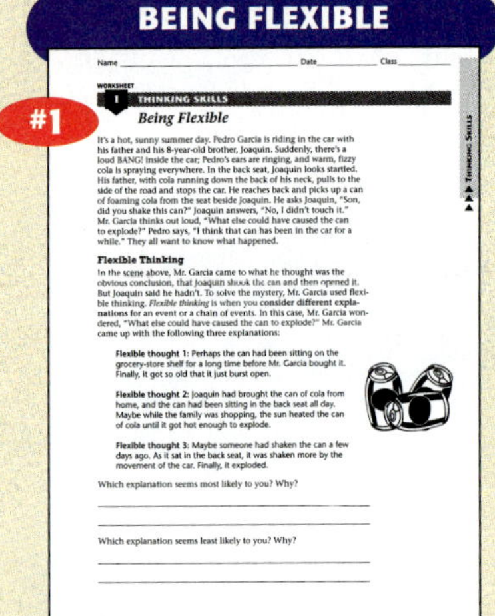

WORKSHEET 1 THINKING SKILLS

Being Flexible

USING YOUR SENSES

#2

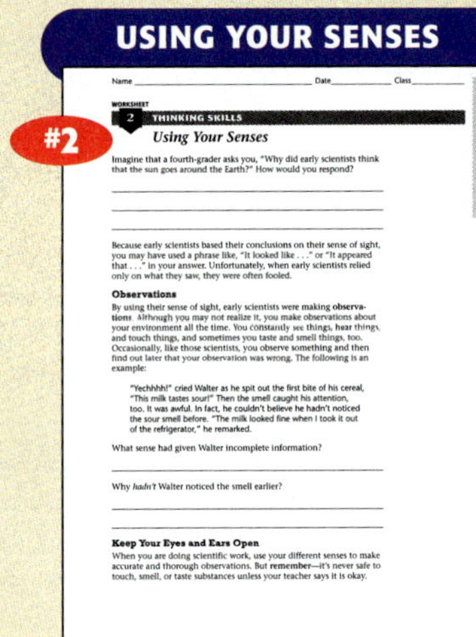

WORKSHEET 2 THINKING SKILLS

Using Your Senses

THINKING OBJECTIVELY

#3

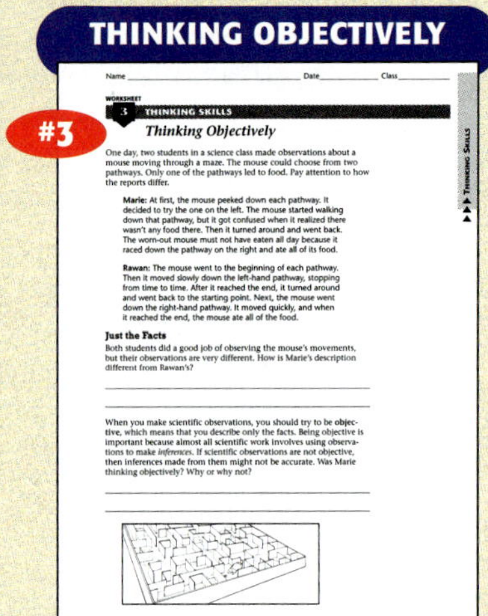

WORKSHEET 3 THINKING SKILLS

Thinking Objectively

UNDERSTANDING BIAS

#4

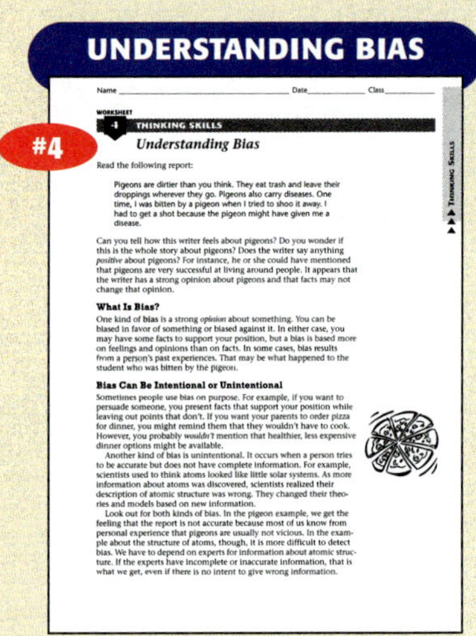

WORKSHEET 4 THINKING SKILLS

Understanding Bias

USING LOGIC

#5

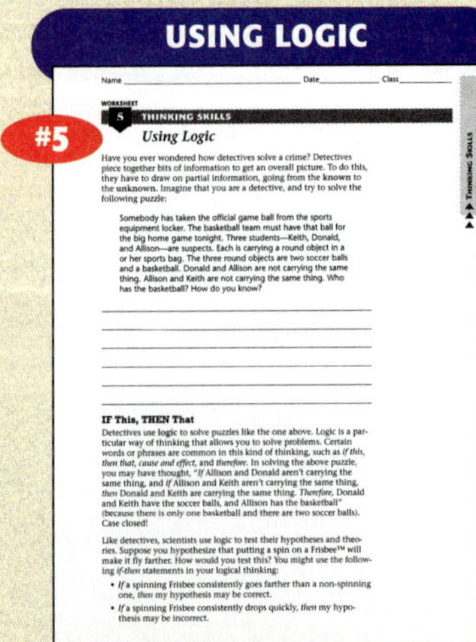

WORKSHEET 5 THINKING SKILLS

Using Logic

BOOSTING YOUR MEMORY

#6

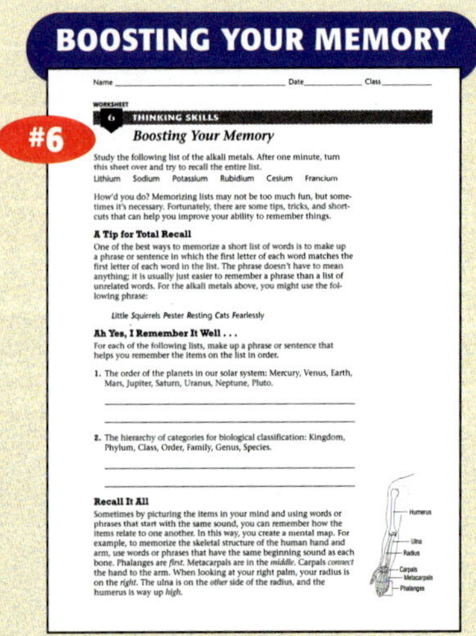

WORKSHEET 6 THINKING SKILLS

Boosting Your Memory

IMPROVING YOUR STUDY HABITS

#7

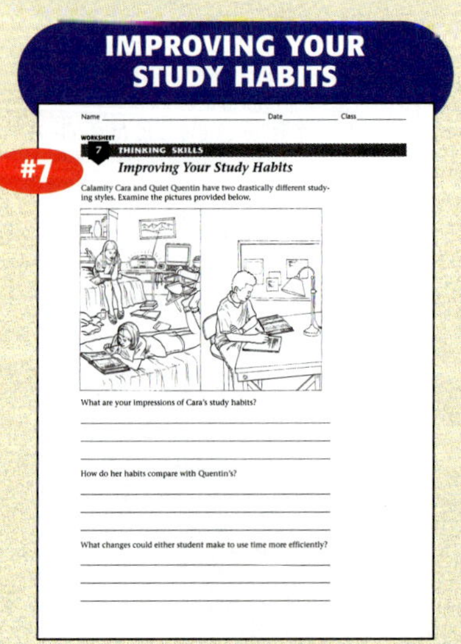

WORKSHEET 7 THINKING SKILLS

Improving Your Study Habits

READING A SCIENCE TEXTBOOK

#8

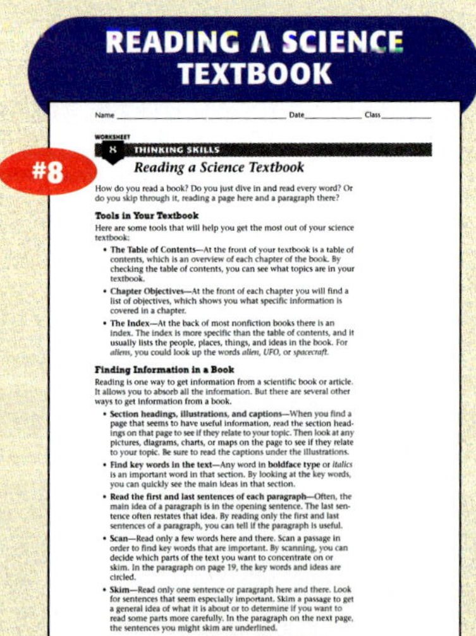

WORKSHEET 8 THINKING SKILLS

Reading a Science Textbook

Science Skills Worksheets: Experimenting Skills

SAFETY RULES!

#9

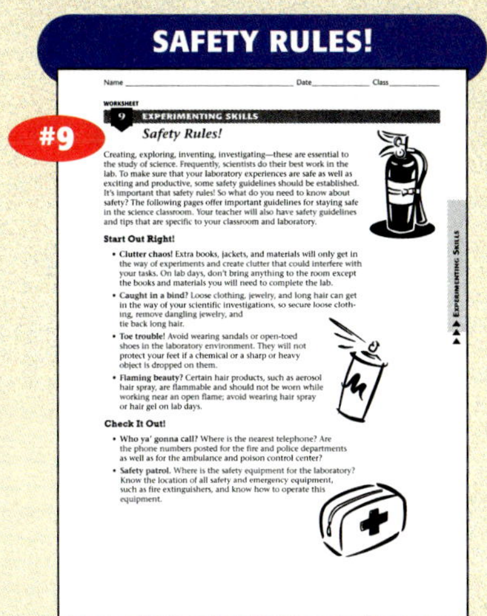

DOING A LAB WRITE-UP

#10

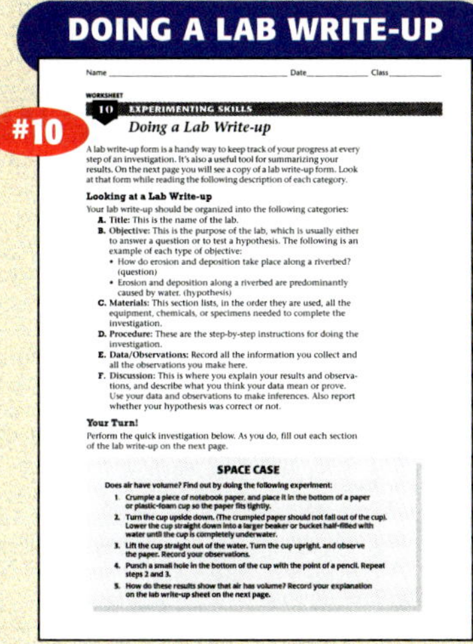

UNDERSTANDING VARIABLES

#11

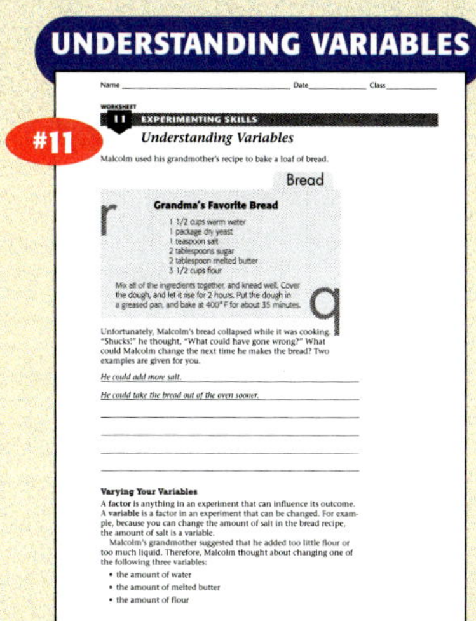

WORKING WITH HYPOTHESES

#12

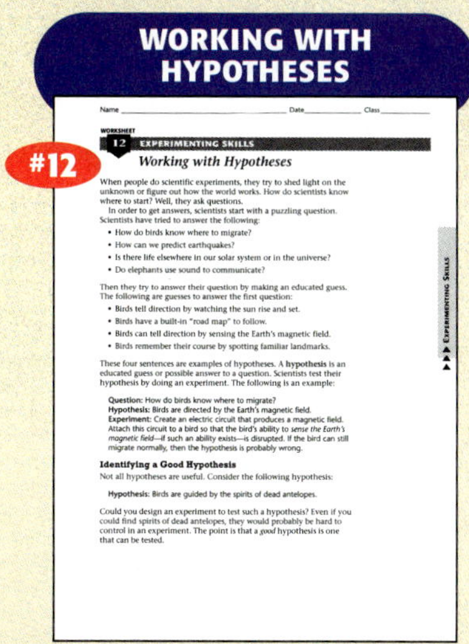

DESIGNING AN EXPERIMENT

#13

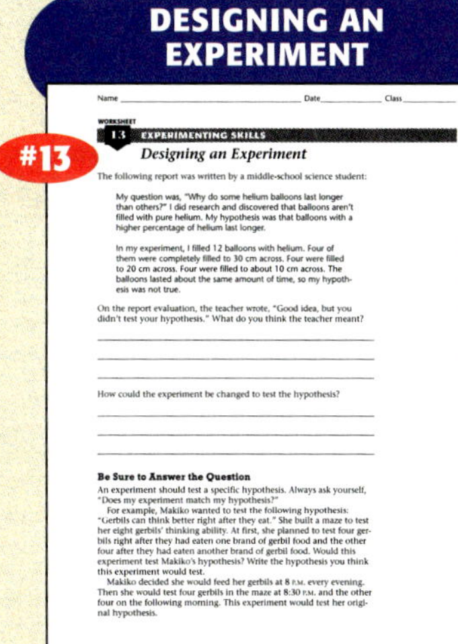

USING THE INTERNATIONAL SYSTEM OF UNITS (SI)

#14

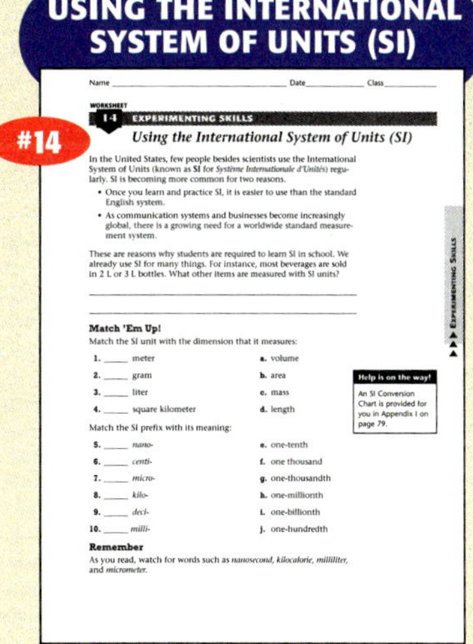

MEASURING

#15

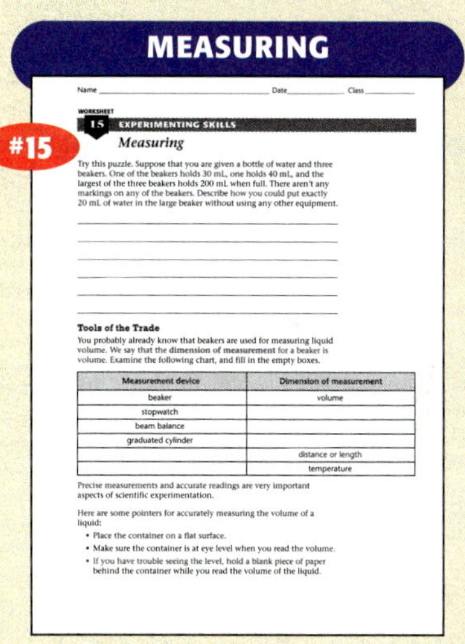

Science Skills Worksheets: Researching Skills

CHOOSING YOUR TOPIC

#16

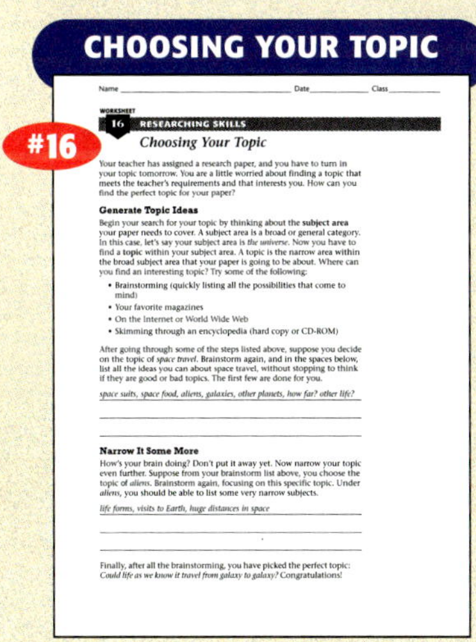

ORGANIZING YOUR RESEARCH

#17

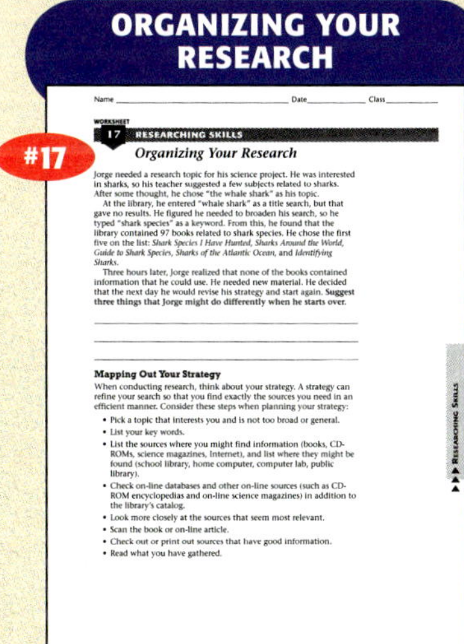

FINDING USEFUL SOURCES

#18

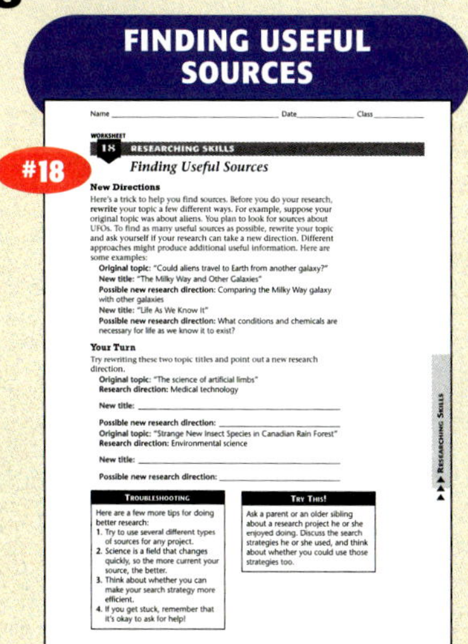

RESEARCHING ON THE WEB

#19

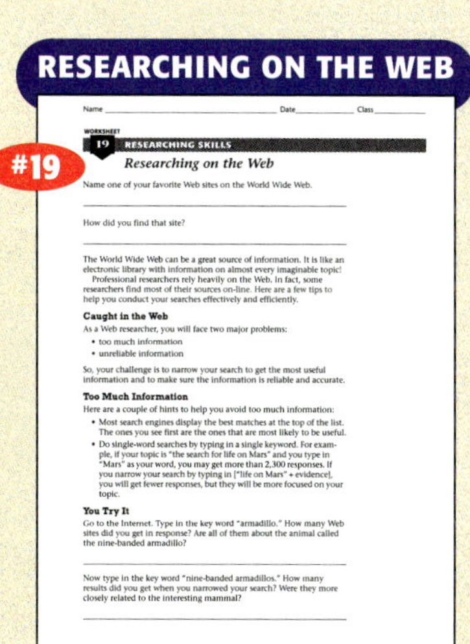

Science & Math Skills Worksheets (continued)

Science Skills Worksheets: Researching Skills (continued)

IDENTIFYING BIAS

#20

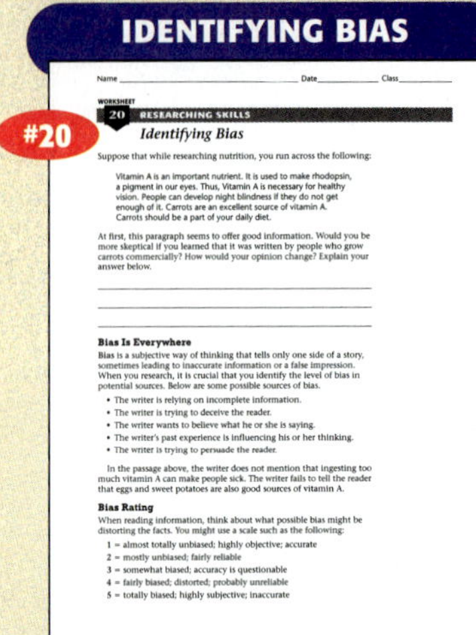
Worksheet 20 — RESEARCHING SKILLS — *Identifying Bias*

TAKING NOTES

#21

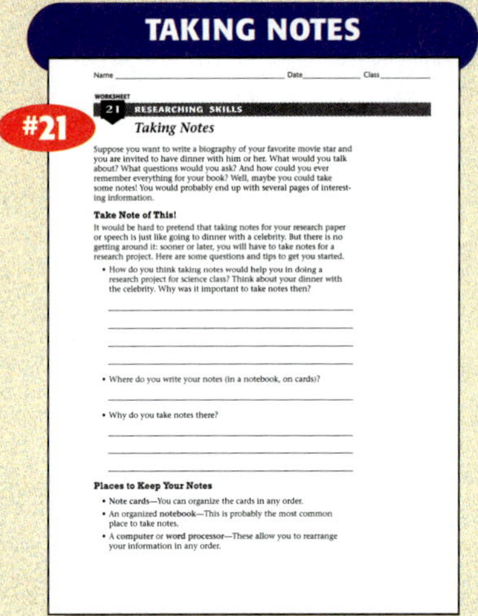
Worksheet 21 — RESEARCHING SKILLS — *Taking Notes*

SCIENCE WRITING

#22

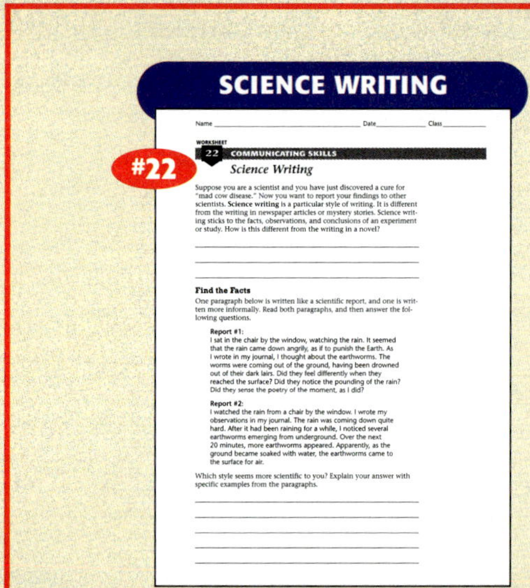
Worksheet 22 — COMMUNICATING SKILLS — *Science Writing*

Science Skills Worksheets: Communicating Skills

SCIENCE DRAWING

#23

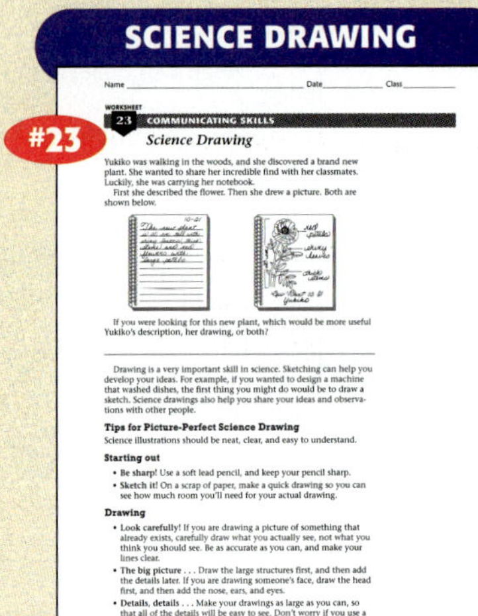
Worksheet 23 — COMMUNICATING SKILLS — *Science Drawing*

USING MODELS TO COMMUNICATE

#24

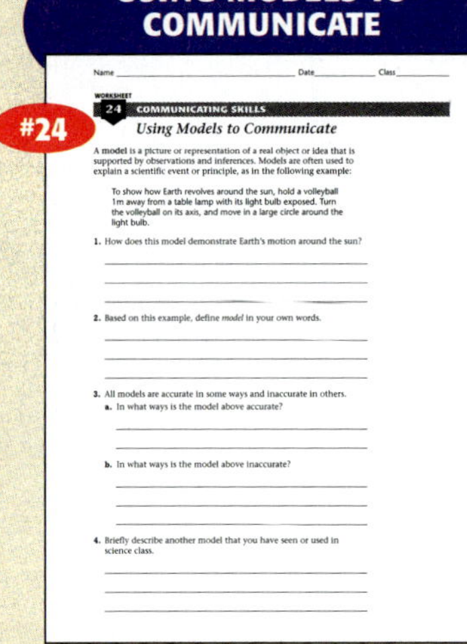
Worksheet 24 — COMMUNICATING SKILLS — *Using Models to Communicate*

INTRODUCTION TO GRAPHS

#25

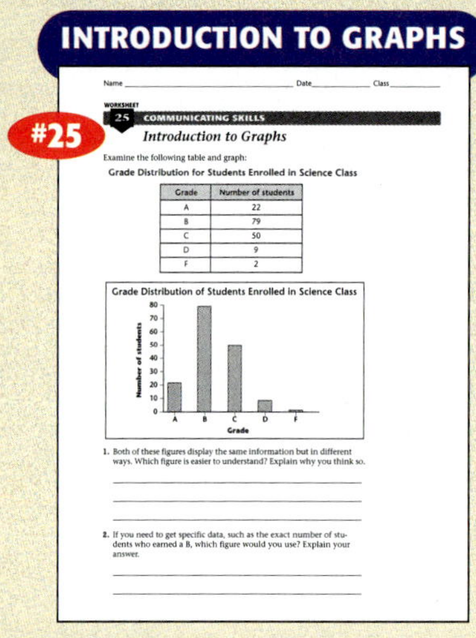
Worksheet 25 — COMMUNICATING SKILLS — *Introduction to Graphs*

GRASPING GRAPHING

#26

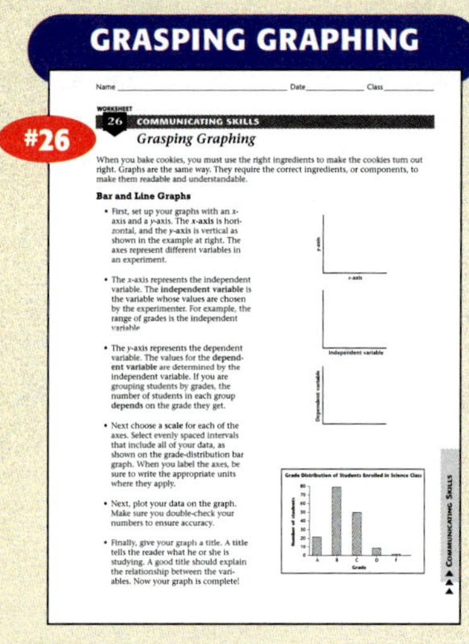
Worksheet 26 — COMMUNICATING SKILLS — *Grasping Graphing*

INTERPRETING YOUR DATA

#27

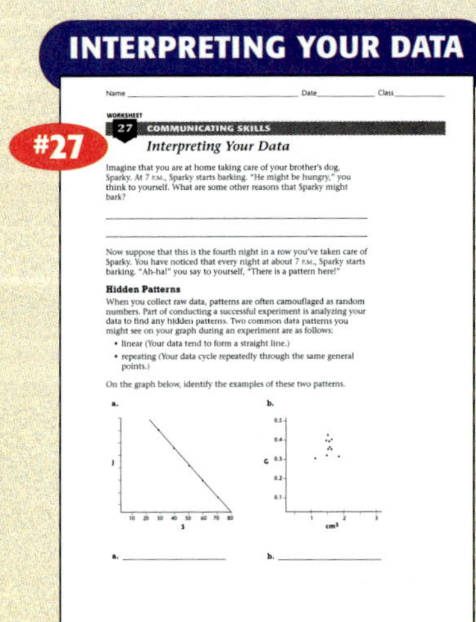
Worksheet 27 — COMMUNICATING SKILLS — *Interpreting Your Data*

RECOGNIZING BIAS IN GRAPHS

#28

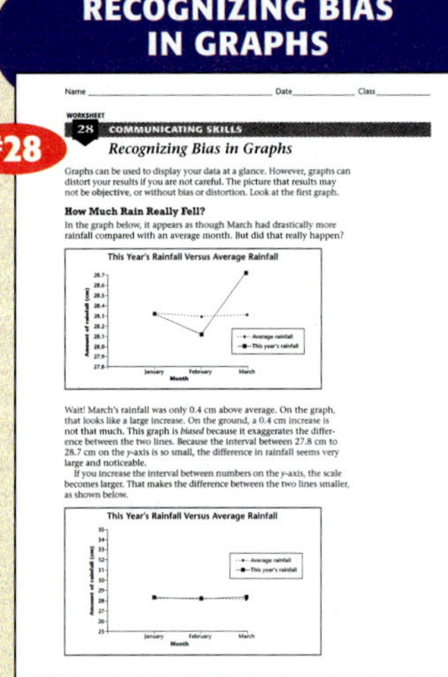
Worksheet 28 — COMMUNICATING SKILLS — *Recognizing Bias in Graphs*

MAKING DATA MEANINGFUL

#29

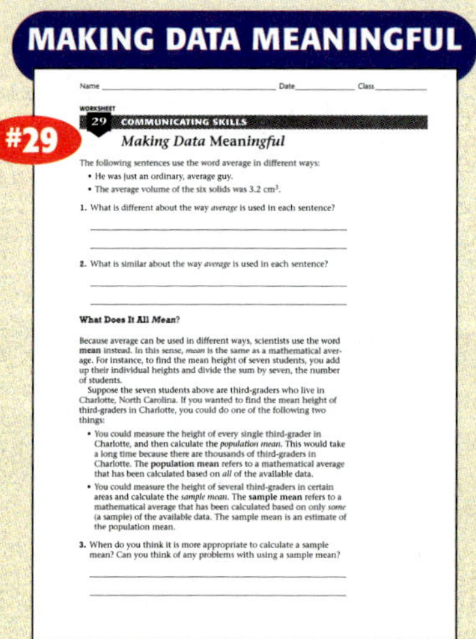
Worksheet 29 — COMMUNICATING SKILLS — *Making Data Meaningful*

HINTS FOR ORAL PRESENTATIONS

#30

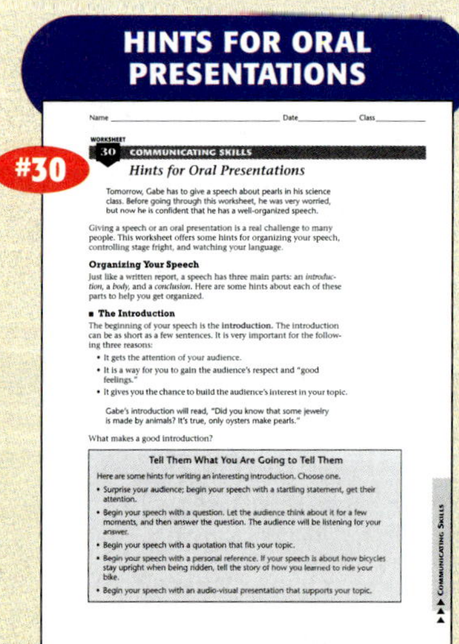
Worksheet 30 — COMMUNICATING SKILLS — *Hints for Oral Presentations*

Math Skills for Science

ADDITION AND SUBTRACTION

#1

#2

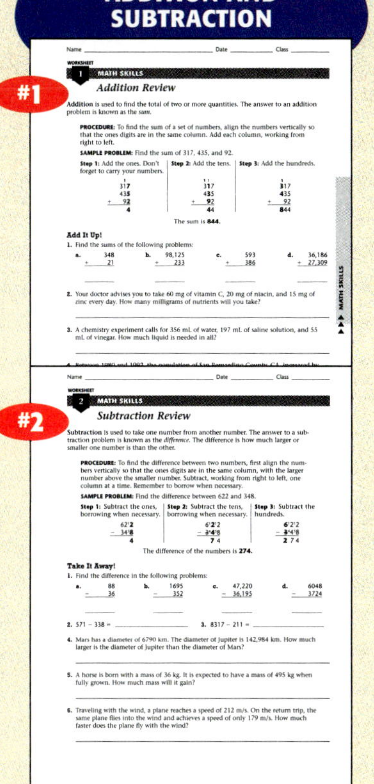

MULTIPLICATION

#3

#4

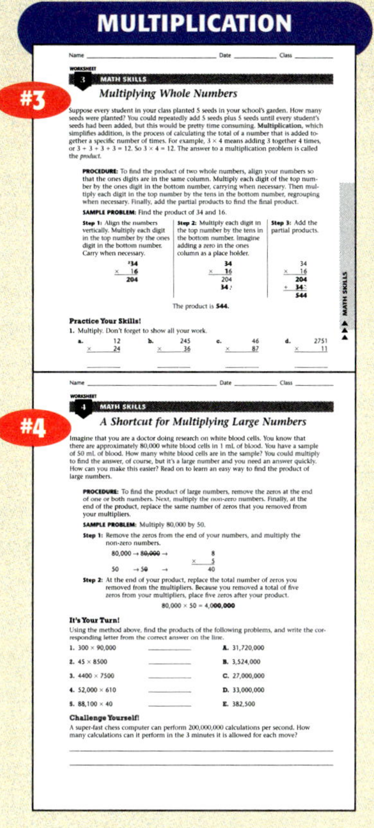

DIVISION

#5

#6

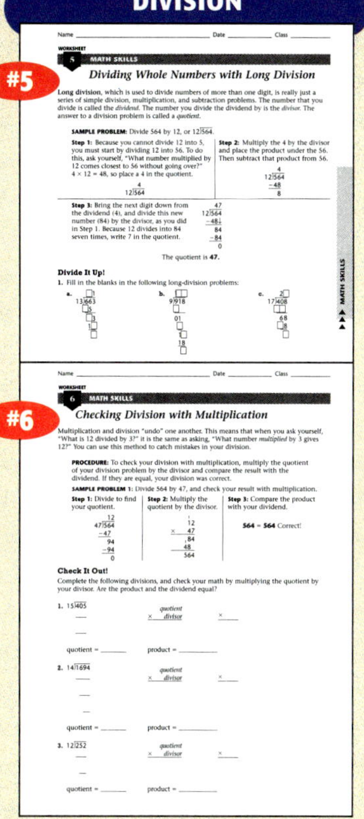

AVERAGES

#7

#8

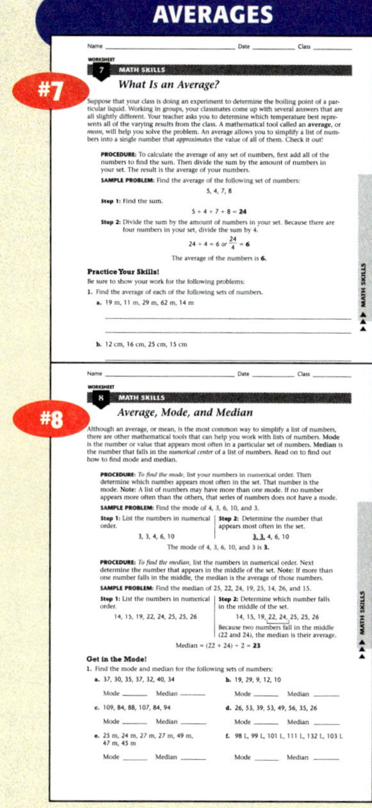

POSITIVE AND NEGATIVE NUMBERS

#9

#10

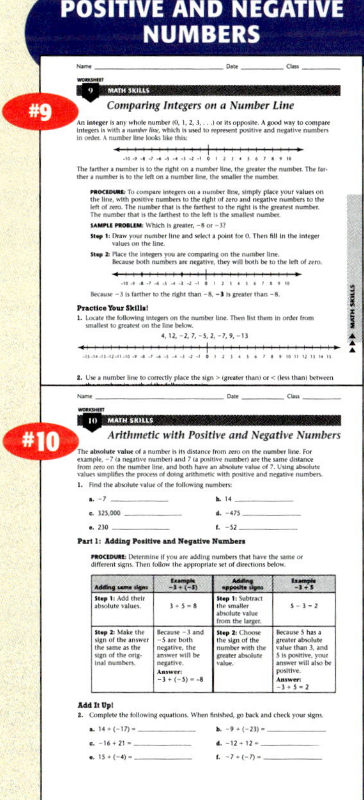

FRACTIONS

#11

#12

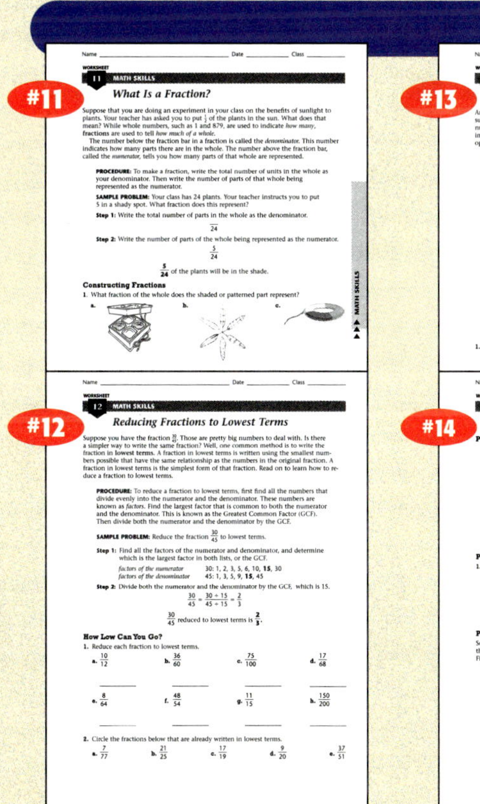

#13

#14

#15

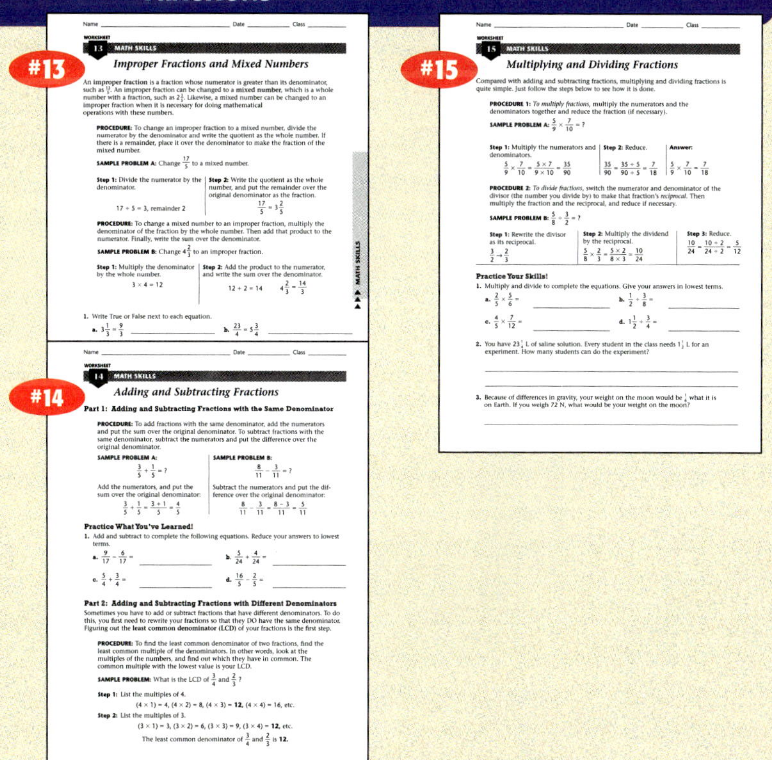

Science & Math Skills Worksheets (continued)

Math Skills for Science (continued)

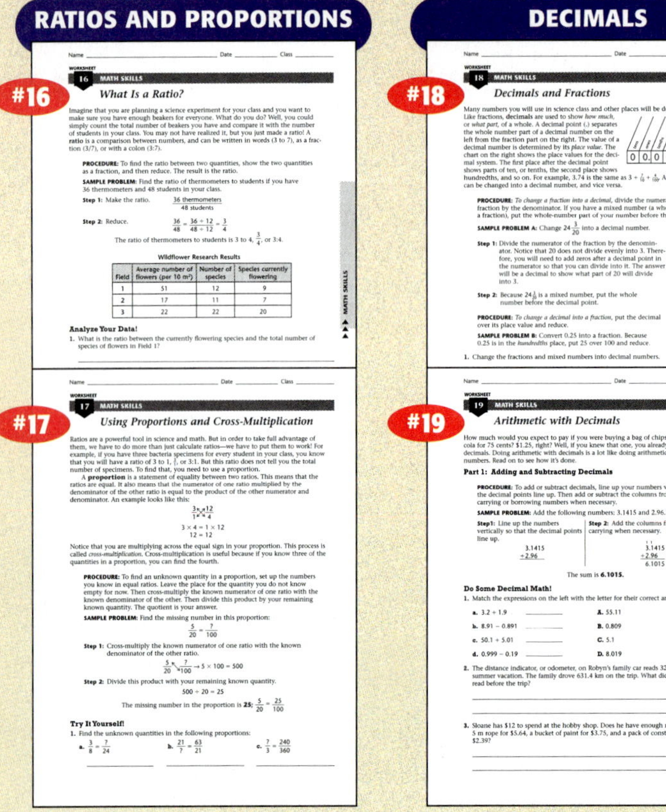

RATIOS AND PROPORTIONS

#16 What Is a Ratio?

#17 Using Proportions and Cross-Multiplication

DECIMALS

#18 Decimals and Fractions

#19 Arithmetic with Decimals

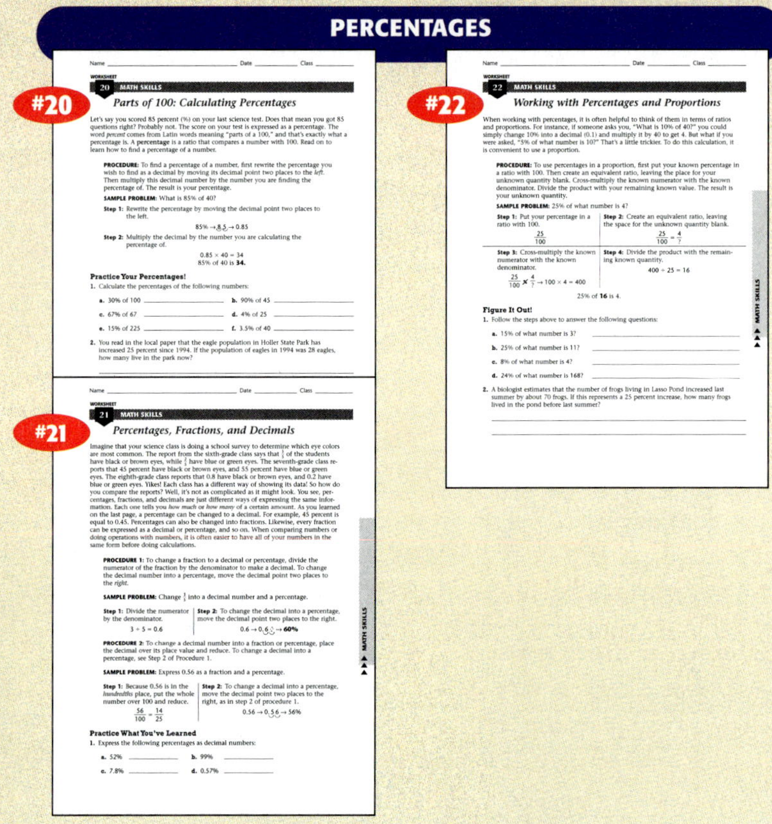

PERCENTAGES

#20 Parts of 100: Calculating Percentages

#21 Percentages, Fractions, and Decimals

#22 Working with Percentages and Proportions

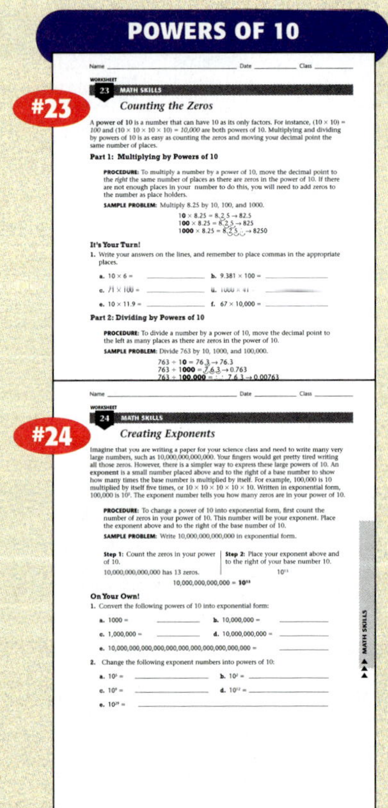

POWERS OF 10

#23 Counting the Zeros

#24 Creating Exponents

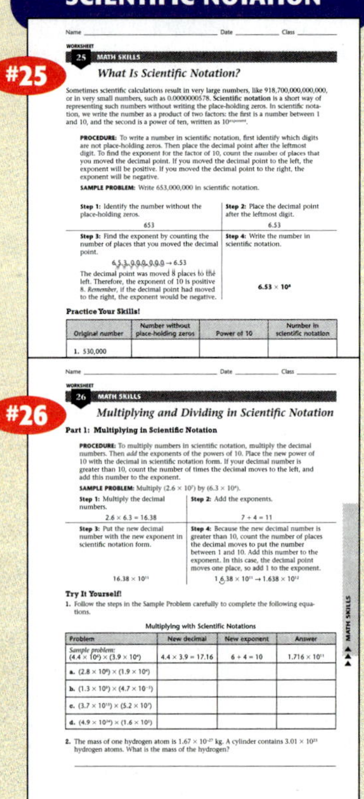

SCIENTIFIC NOTATION

#25 What Is Scientific Notation?

#26 Multiplying and Dividing in Scientific Notation

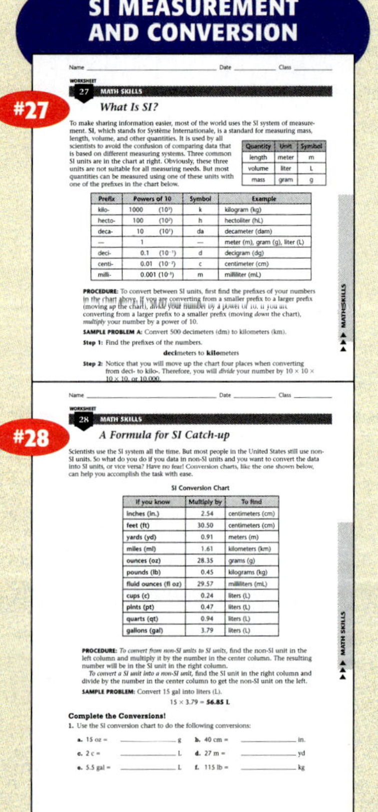

SI MEASUREMENT AND CONVERSION

#27 What Is SI?

#28 A Formula for SI Catch-up

Math Skills for Science (continued)

GEOMETRY

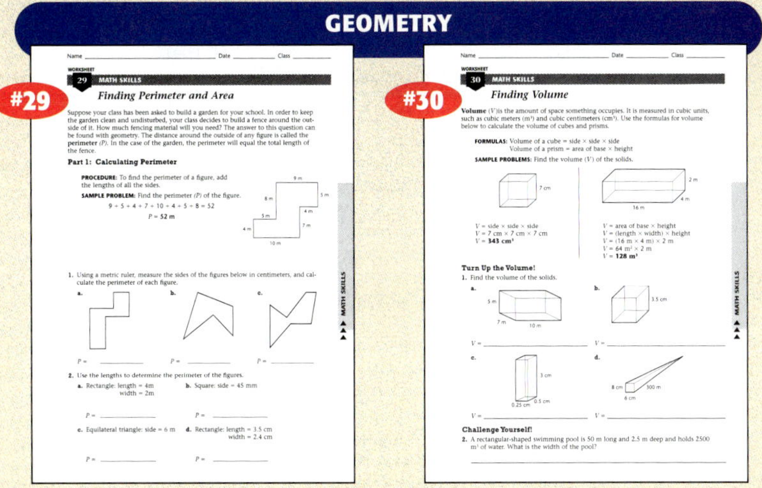

#29 Worksheet 29 Math Skills — *Finding Perimeter and Area*

Part 1: Calculating Perimeter

#30 Worksheet 30 Math Skills — *Finding Volume*

Turn Up the Volume!

Challenge Yourself!

THE UNIT FACTOR AND DIMENSIONAL ANALYSIS

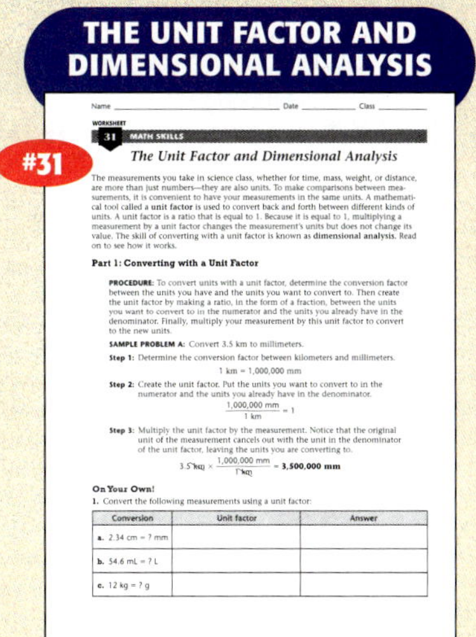

#31 Worksheet 31 Math Skills — *The Unit Factor and Dimensional Analysis*

Part 1: Converting with a Unit Factor

On Your Own!

MATH IN SCIENCE: INTEGRATED SCIENCE

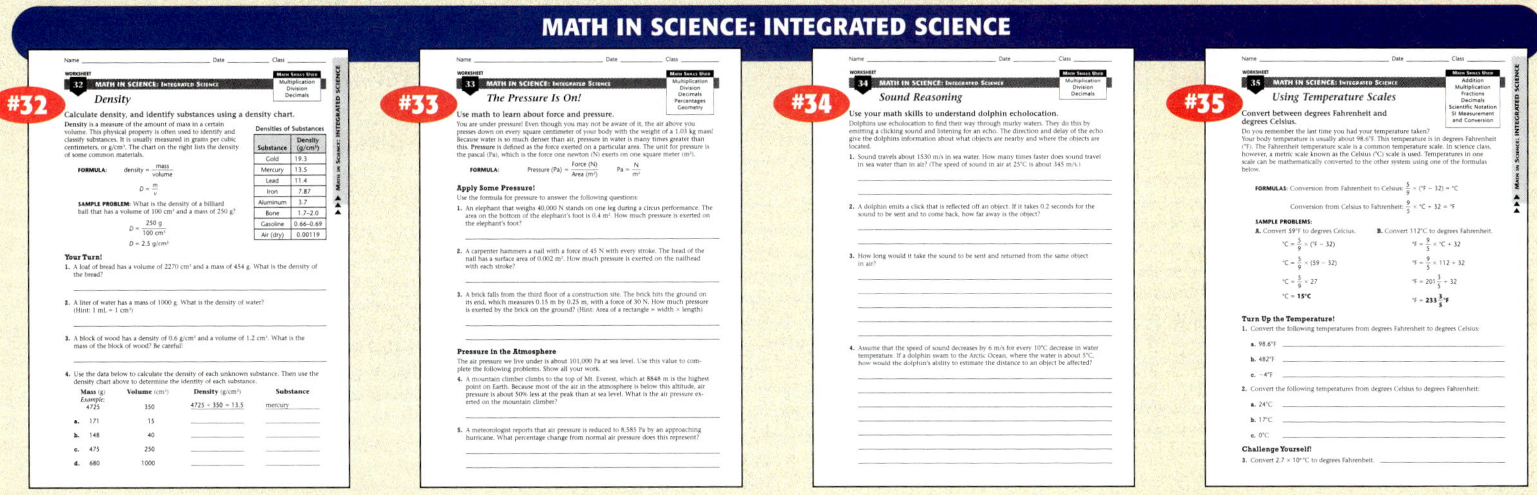

#32 Worksheet 32 Math in Science: Integrated Science — *Density*

Calculate density, and identify substances using a density chart.

#33 Worksheet 33 Math in Science: Integrated Science — *The Pressure Is On!*

Use math to learn about force and pressure.

#34 Worksheet 34 Math in Science: Integrated Science — *Sound Reasoning*

Use your math skills to understand dolphin echolocation.

#35 Worksheet 35 Math in Science: Integrated Science — *Using Temperature Scales*

Convert between degrees Fahrenheit and degrees Celsius.

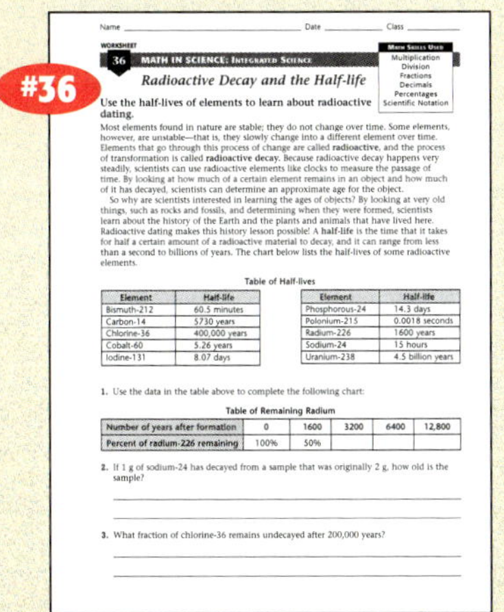

#36 Worksheet 36 Math in Science: Integrated Science — *Radioactive Decay and the Half-life*

Use the half-lives of elements to learn about radioactive dating.

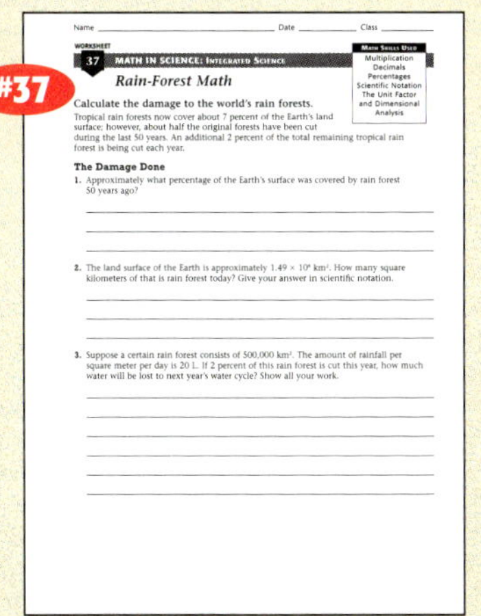

#37 Worksheet 37 Math in Science: Integrated Science — *Rain-Forest Math*

Calculate the damage to the world's rain forests.

Science & Math Skills Worksheets (continued)

Math Skills for Science (continued)

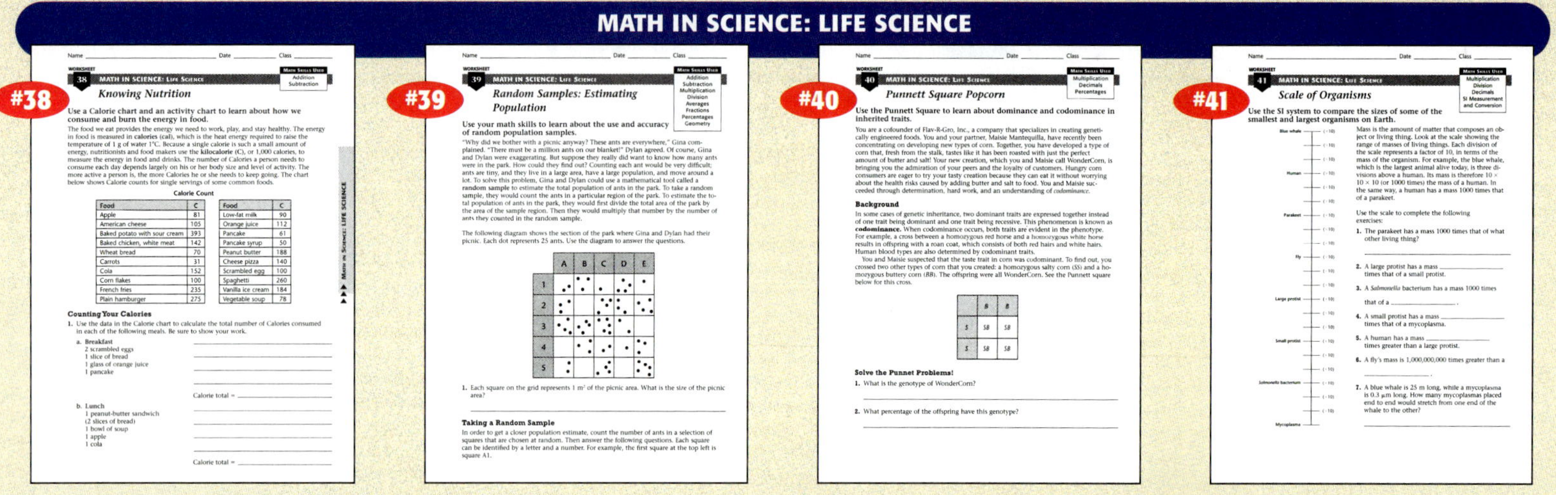

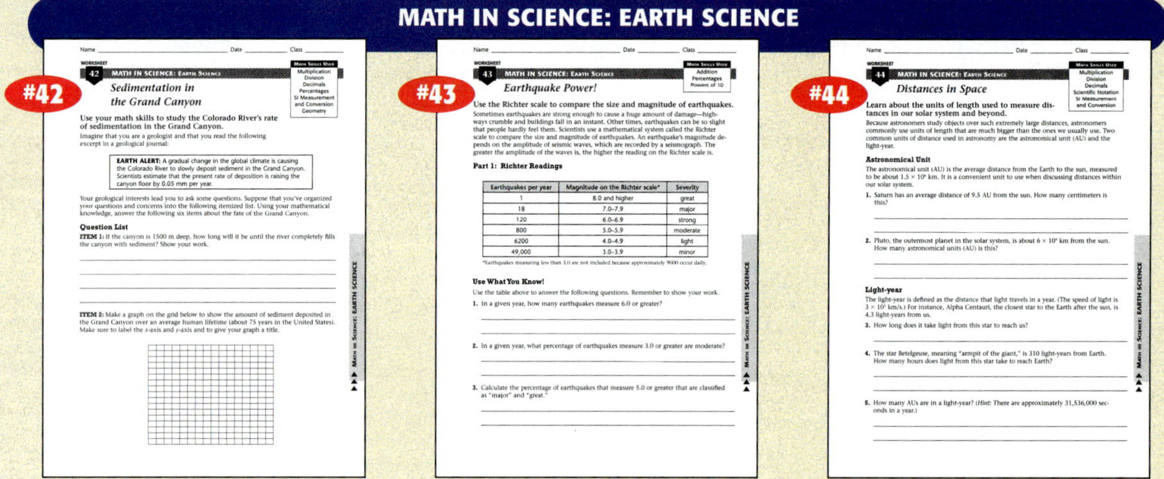

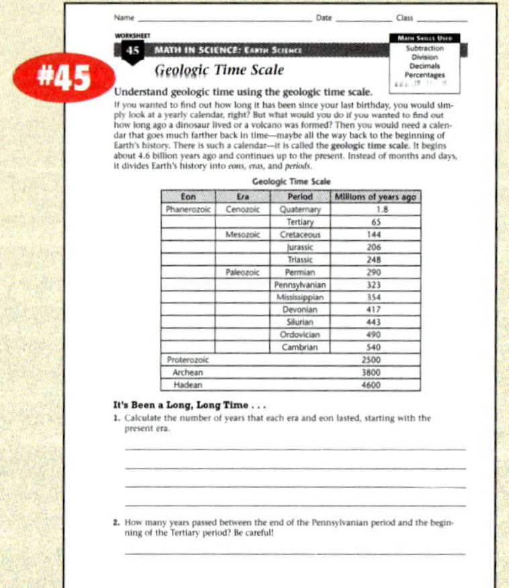

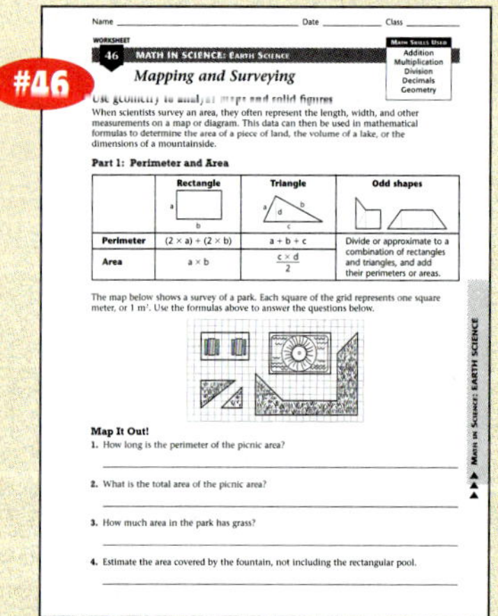

Math Skills for Science (continued)

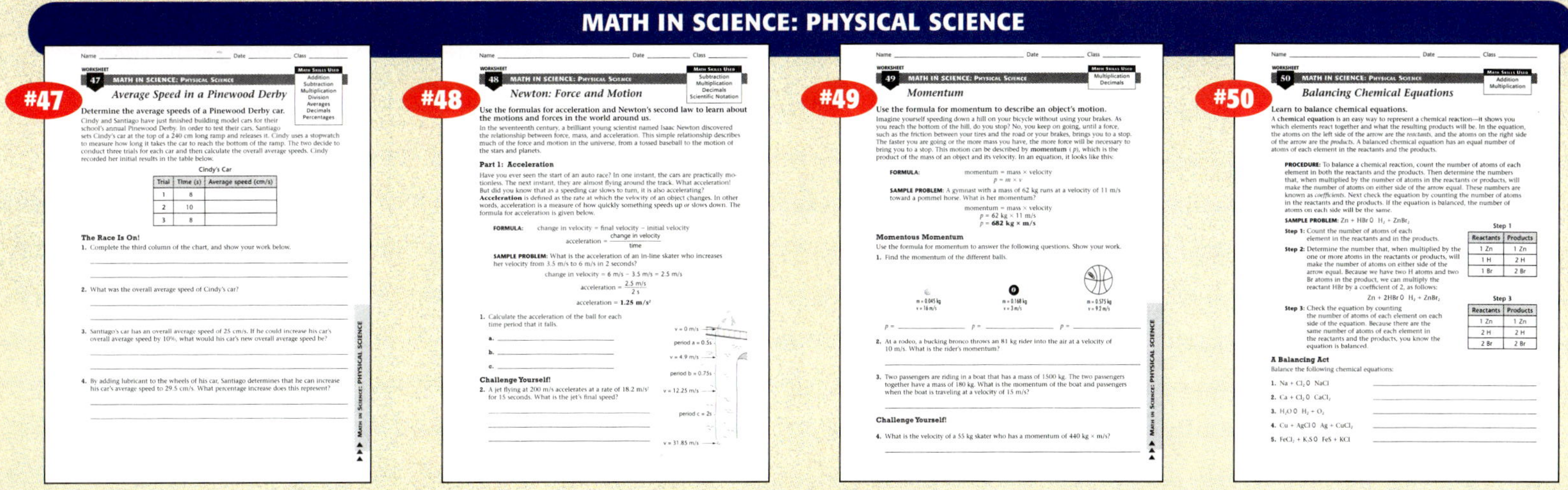

MATH IN SCIENCE: PHYSICAL SCIENCE

#47 Worksheet 47 — Math in Science: Physical Science — Average Speed in a Pinewood Derby

#48 Worksheet 48 — Math in Science: Physical Science — Newton: Force and Motion

#49 Worksheet 49 — Math in Science: Physical Science — Momentum

#50 Worksheet 50 — Math in Science: Physical Science — Balancing Chemical Equations

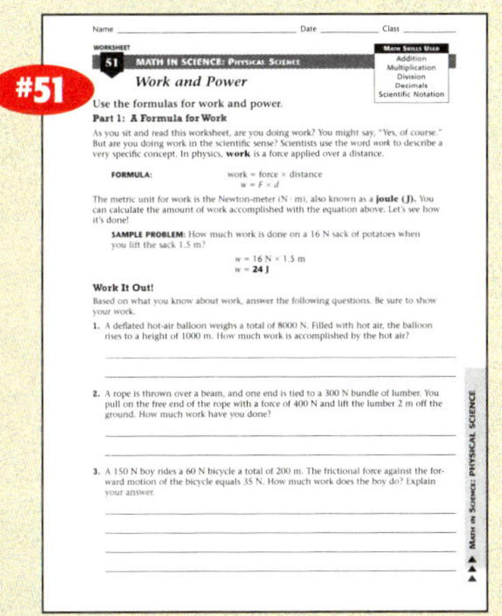

#51 Worksheet 51 — Math in Science: Physical Science — Work and Power

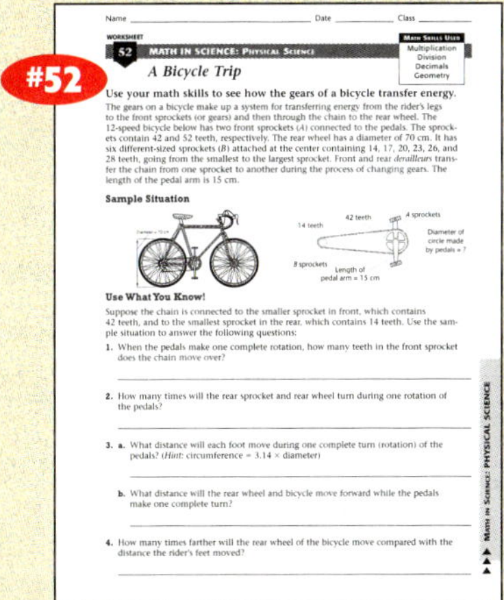

#52 Worksheet 52 — Math in Science: Physical Science — A Bicycle Trip

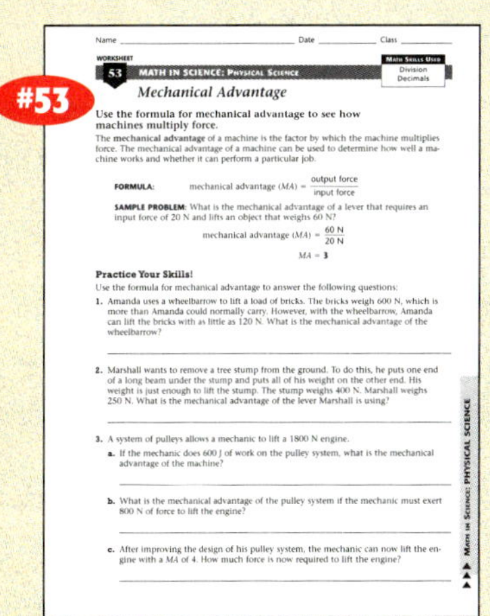

#53 Worksheet 53 — Math in Science: Physical Science — Mechanical Advantage

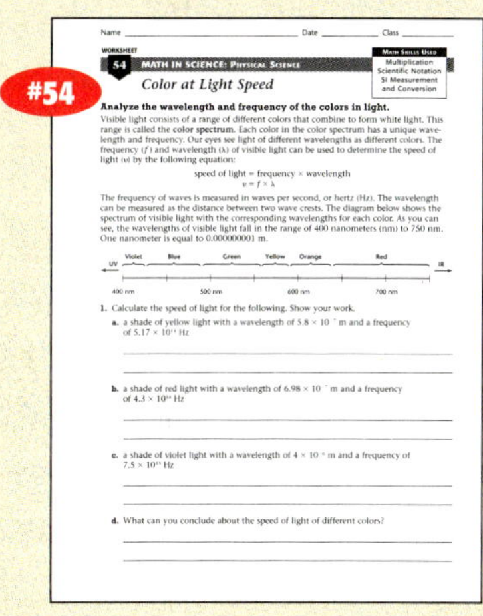

#54 Worksheet 54 — Math in Science: Physical Science — Color at Light Speed

Assessment Checklist & Rubrics

The following is just a sample of over 50 checklists and rubrics contained in this booklet.

RUBRICS FOR WRITTEN WORK

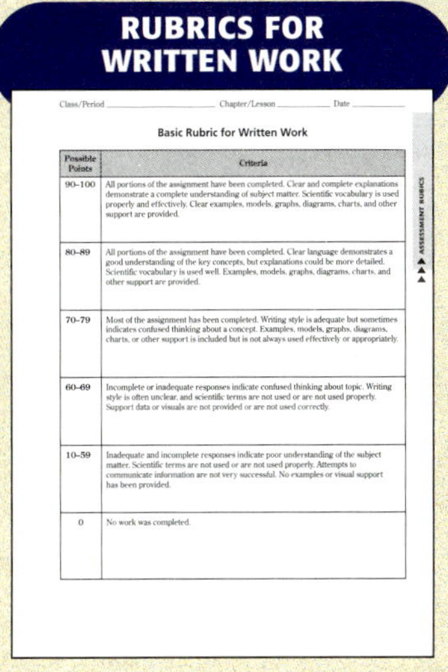

Basic Rubric for Written Work

RUBRIC FOR EXPERIMENTS

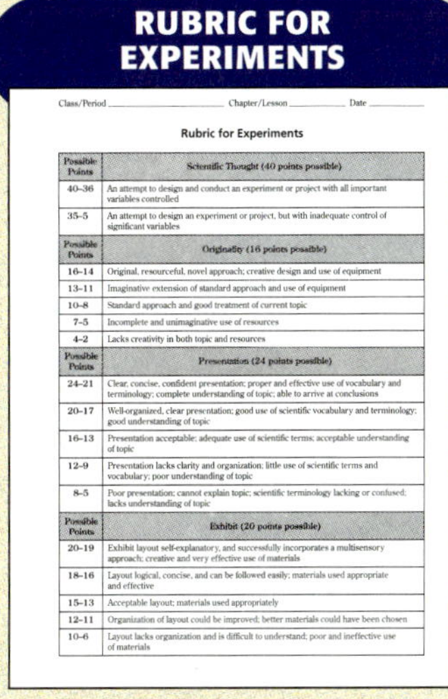

Rubric for Experiments

TEACHER EVALUATION OF COOPERATIVE LEARNING

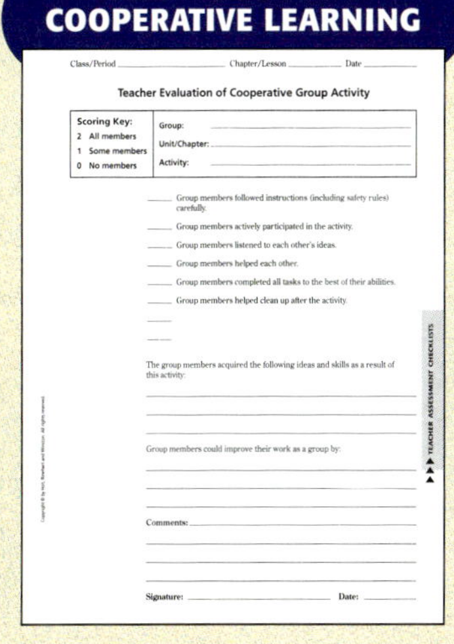

Teacher Evaluation of Cooperative Group Activity

TEACHER EVALUATION OF STUDENT PROGRESS

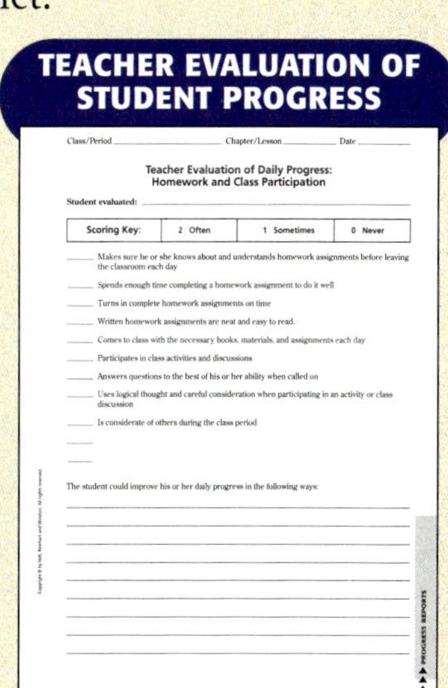

Teacher Evaluation of Daily Progress: Homework and Class Participation

TIMELINE

UNIT 1

Introduction to Earth Science

In this unit, you will start your own investigation of the planet Earth and of the regions of space beyond it. But first you should prepare yourself by learning about the tools and methods used by Earth scientists. As you can imagine, it is not easy to study something as large as the Earth or as far away as Venus. Yet that is what Earth scientists do. The timeline shown here identifies a few of the events that have helped shape our understanding of Earth.

1669
Nicolaus Steno accurately describes the process by which living organisms become fossils.

1758
Halley's comet makes a reappearance, confirming Edmond Halley's 1705 prediction. Unfortunately, the comet reappeared 16 years after his death.

1943
The volcano *Paricutín* grows more than 150 m tall during its first six days of eruption.

1960
The first weather satellite, *Tiros I*, is launched by the United States.

1962
By reaching an altitude of 95 km, the *X-15* becomes the first fixed-wing plane to reach outer space.

1896

The first modern Olympic Games are held in Athens, Greece.

1899

The Rosetta stone is discovered in Egypt. It enables scholars to decipher Egyptian hieroglyphics.

1906

Roald Amundsen determines the position of the magnetic north pole.

1922

Roy Chapman Andrews discovers fossilized dinosaur eggs in the Gobi Desert. They are the first such eggs to be found.

1970

The United States holds its first Earth Day on April 22. More than 20 million people participate in peaceful demonstrations to show their concern for the environment.

1990

The Hubble Space Telescope is launched into orbit. Three years later, faulty optics are repaired during a space walk.

1997

China begins construction of Three Gorges Dam, the world's largest dam. Designed to control the Yangtze River, the dam will supply 84 billion kilowatt-hours of hydroelectric power per year.

Chapter Organizer

CHAPTER ORGANIZATION	TIME MINUTES	OBJECTIVES	LABS, INVESTIGATIONS, AND DEMONSTRATIONS
Chapter Opener **pp. 4–5**	45	California Standards: PE/ATE 7, 7b	**Investigate!** A Little Bit of Science, p. 5
Section 1 **Branches of Earth Science**	45	▶ List major branches of Earth science. ▶ Identify branches of Earth science that are linked to other areas of science. ▶ Describe careers associated with different branches of Earth science. PE/ATE 7, 7b	**QuickLab,** How Hot is 300°C? p. 7
Section 2 **The Scientific Method in Earth Science**	120	▶ Explain the scientific method and how scientists use it. ▶ Apply the scientific method to an Earth science investigation. ▶ Identify the importance of communicating the results of a scientific investigation. ▶ Describe how scientific investigations often lead to new investigations. PE/ATE 7, 7a, 7b, 7d, 7e; LabBook 7, 7a, 7b, 7e	**Making Models,** Using the Scientific Method, p. 486 **Datasheets for LabBook,** Using the Scientific Method, Datasheet 1 **Whiz-Bang Demonstrations,** Tubby Terra, Demo 16
Section 3 **Life in a Warmer World–An Earth Science Model**	120	▶ Demonstrate how models are used in science. ▶ Compare mathematical models with physical models. PE/ATE 4, 4b, 7b, 7e	
Section 4 **Measurement and Safety**	120	▶ Explain the importance of the International System of Units. ▶ Determine appropriate units to use for particular measurements. ▶ Identify lab safety symbols and determine what they mean. PE/ATE 7, 7b	**Long-Term Projects & Research Ideas,** Project 29

See page **T20** *for a complete correlation of this book with the*

CALIFORNIA SCIENCE CONTENT STANDARDS.

Correlations are also provided at point of use throughout this ATE.

TECHNOLOGY RESOURCES

Guided Reading Audio CD
English or Spanish, Chapter 1

Classroom Management CD-ROM

Test Generator CD-ROM

Earth Science Videodisc
Introduction to Earth Science: 359–10426
Careers in Earth Science: 4875–10426

CNN. Scientists in Action, Exploring a Watery Cave, Segment 2

Multicultural Connections, Hopi Science, Segment 1

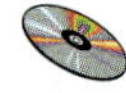

Science Discovery Videodiscs
Image and Activity Bank with Lesson Plans: Science and the Constitution, Models and Predictions

Chapter 1 • The World of Earth Science

CLASSROOM WORKSHEETS, TRANSPARENCIES, AND RESOURCES	SCIENCE INTEGRATION AND CONNECTIONS	REVIEW AND ASSESSMENT
Science Puzzlers, Twisters & Teasers, Worksheet 1 **Directed Reading Worksheet 1** **Science Skills Worksheet 8,** Reading a Science Textbook		
Directed Reading Worksheet 1, Section 1 **Math Skills for Science Worksheet 23,** Counting the Zeros **Math Skills for Science Worksheet 25,** What Is Scientific Notation? **Reinforcement Worksheet 1,** Scenes from the Earth	**Cross-Disciplinary Focus,** p. 7 in ATE **Real-World Connection,** p. 8 in ATE **Multicultural Connection,** p. 8 in ATE **MathBreak,** Lots of Zeros! p. 9 **Math and More,** p. 9 in ATE **Connect to Environmental Science,** p. 10 in ATE **Careers:** Geophysicist–Bob Grimm, p. 31	**Homework,** p. 9 in ATE **Review,** p. 11 **Quiz,** p. 11 in ATE **Alternative Assessment,** p. 11 in ATE
Directed Reading Worksheet 1, Section 2 **Transparency 85,** The Scientific Method **Problem Solving Worksheet 1,** Kryptonite!	**Cross-Disciplinary Focus,** p. 12 in ATE **Connect to Life Science,** p. 14 in ATE **Apply,** p. 15 **Connect to Physical Science,** p. 15 in ATE **Cross-Disciplinary Focus,** p. 16 in ATE	**Homework,** p. 13 in ATE **Review,** p. 17 **Quiz,** p. 17 in ATE **Alternative Assessment,** p. 17 in ATE
Directed Reading Worksheet 1, Section 3 **Math Skills Worksheet 17,** Using Proportions and Cross-Multiplication **Science Skills Worksheet 15,** Measuring	**Connect to Life Science,** p. 18 in ATE **Environmental Science Connection,** p. 20 **Cross-Disciplinary Focus,** p. 20 in ATE **Across the Sciences:** All the Earth's a Magnet, p. 30	**Homework,** p. 19 in ATE **Review,** p. 21 **Quiz,** p. 21 in ATE **Alternative Assessment,** p. 21 in ATE
Directed Reading Worksheet 1, Section 4 **Math Skills for Science Worksheet 27,** What Is SI? **Transparency 86,** Common SI Units **Transparency 176,** Weight and Mass Are Different **Science Skills Worksheet 9,** Safety Rules!	**Multicultural Connection,** p. 23 in ATE **Math and More,** p. 24 in ATE **Connect to Physical Science,** p. 24 in ATE	**Homework,** p. 24 in ATE **Review,** p. 25 **Quiz,** p. 25 in ATE **Alternative Assessment,** p. 25 in ATE

internetconnect

Holt, Rinehart and Winston On-line Resources

go.hrw.com

For worksheets and other teaching aids related to this chapter, visit the HRW Web site and type in the keyword: **HSTWES**

National Science Teachers Association

www.scilinks.org

Encourage students to use the keywords listed on the Technology Highlights page to access information and resources on the **NSTA** Web site.

END-OF-CHAPTER REVIEW AND ASSESSMENT

Chapter Review in Study Guide
Vocabulary and Notes in Study Guide
Chapter Tests with Performance-Based Assessment, Chapter 1 Test
Chapter Tests with Performance-Based Assessment, Performance-Based Assessment 1
Concept Mapping Transparency 1

Chapter Resources & Worksheets

Visual Resources

TEACHING TRANSPARENCIES

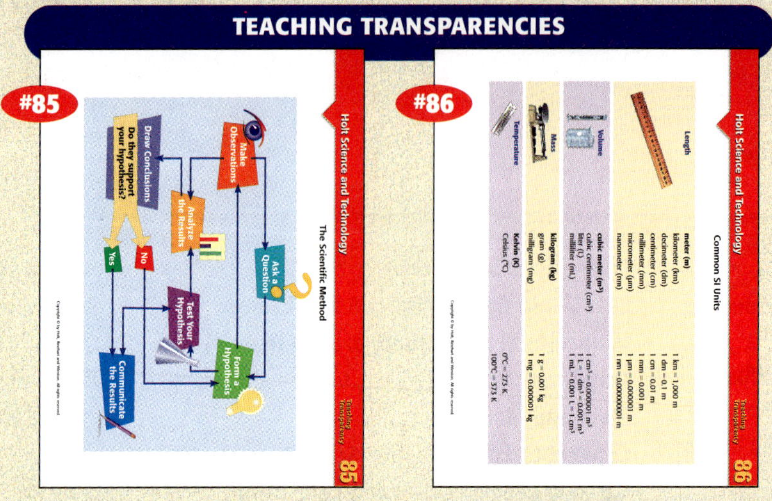

TEACHING TRANSPARENCIES

CONCEPT MAPPING TRANSPARENCY

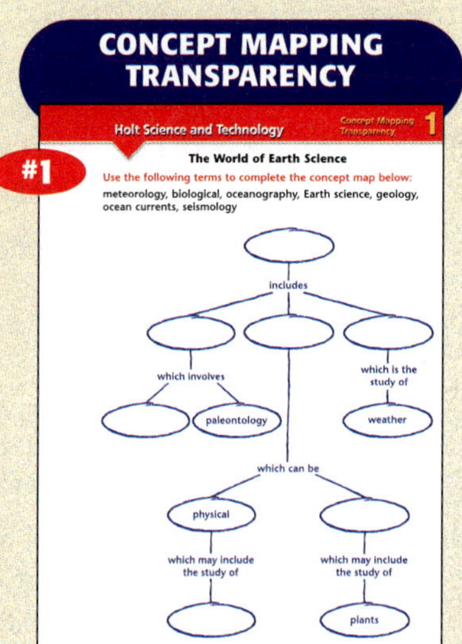

Meeting Individual Needs

DIRECTED READING

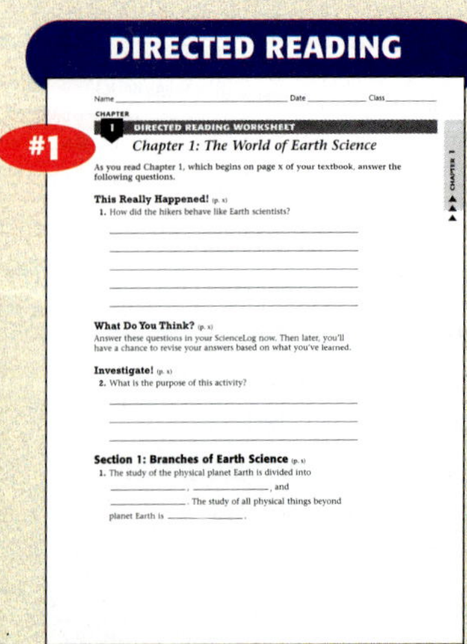

REINFORCEMENT & VOCABULARY REVIEW

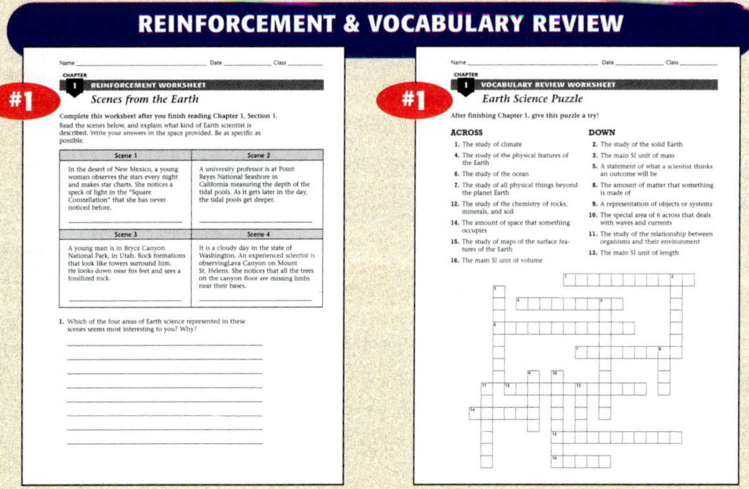

SCIENCE PUZZLERS, TWISTERS, & TEASERS

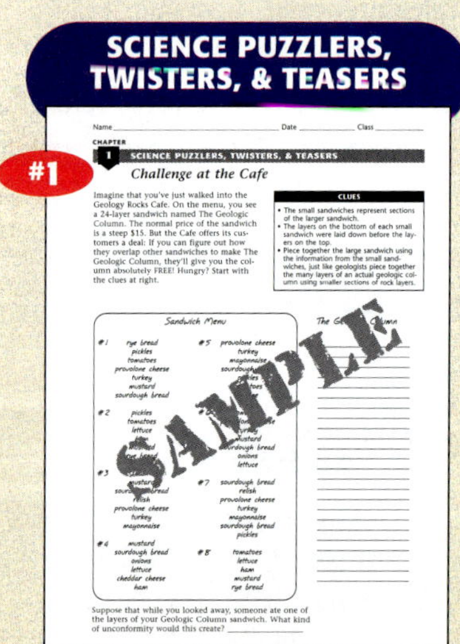

Chapter 1 • The World of Earth Science

Review & Assessment

STUDY GUIDE

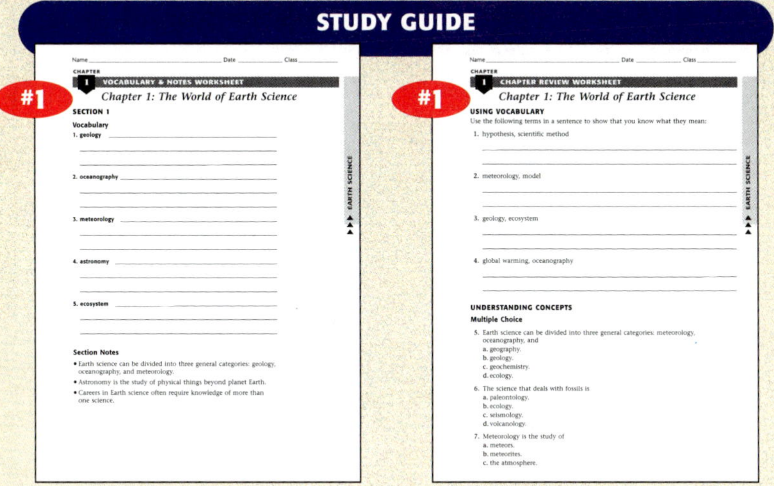
#1 VOCABULARY & NOTES WORKSHEET
Chapter 1: The World of Earth Science

#1 CHAPTER REVIEW WORKSHEET
Chapter 1: The World of Earth Science

CHAPTER TESTS WITH PERFORMANCE-BASED ASSESSMENT

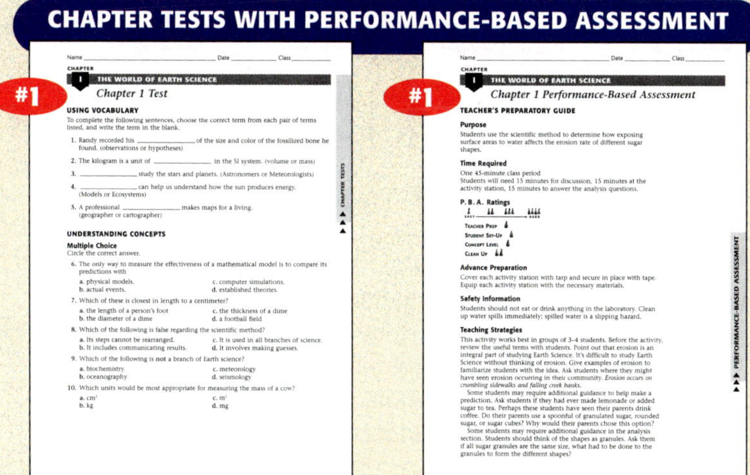
#1 THE WORLD OF EARTH SCIENCE
Chapter 1 Test

#1 THE WORLD OF EARTH SCIENCE
Chapter 1 Performance-Based Assessment

Lab Worksheets

WHIZ-BANG DEMONSTRATIONS

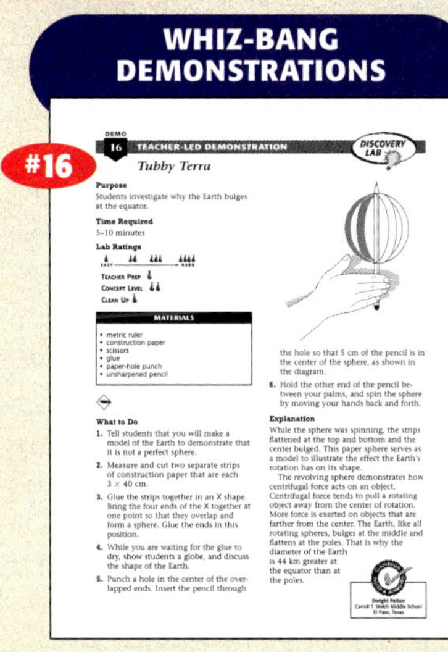
#16 TEACHER-LED DEMONSTRATION
Tubby Terra

LONG-TERM PROJECTS & RESEARCH IDEAS

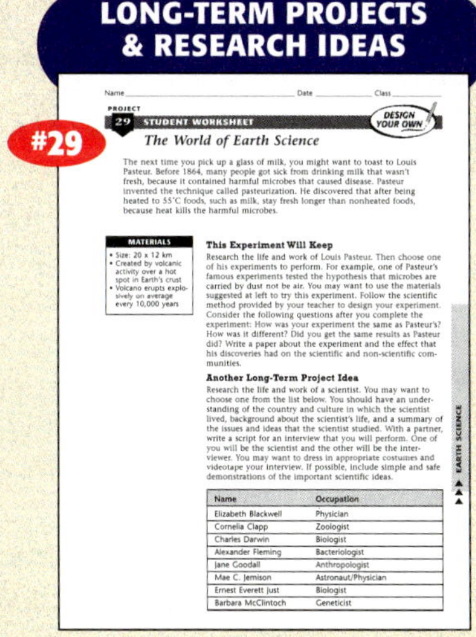
#29 STUDENT WORKSHEET
The World of Earth Science

DATASHEETS FOR LABBOOK

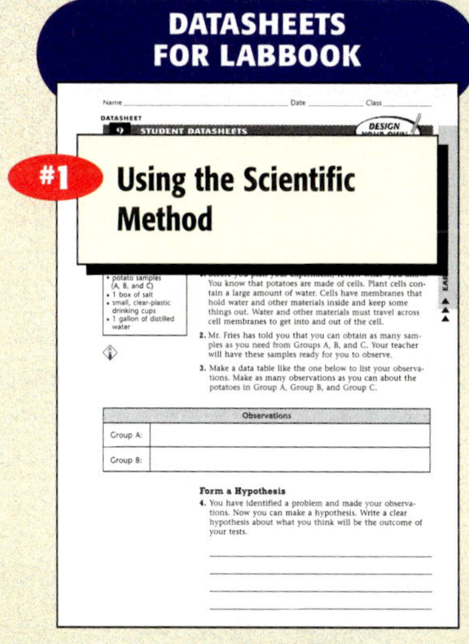
#1 Using the Scientific Method

Applications & Extensions

CRITICAL THINKING & PROBLEM SOLVING

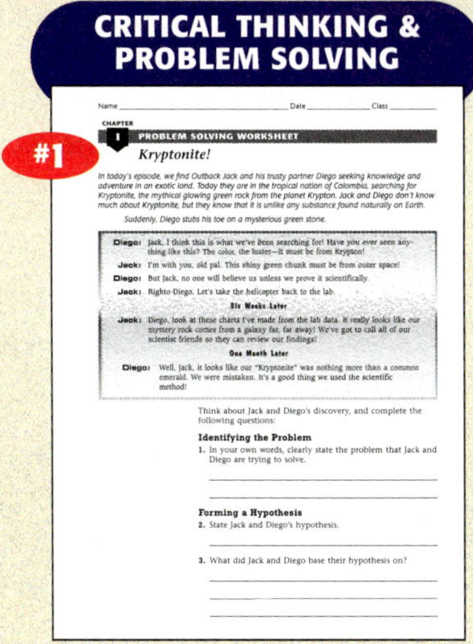
#1 PROBLEM SOLVING WORKSHEET
Kryptonite!

MULTICULTURAL CONNECTIONS

#1 Science in the News: Critical Thinking Worksheets
Segment 1
Hopi Science

SCIENTISTS IN ACTION

#2 Science in the News: Critical Thinking Worksheets
Segment 2
Exploring a Watery Cave

Chapter Background

Section 1

Branches of Earth Science

Volcanology and Seismology
Seismology and volcanology are separate branches of Earth science, but they are often studied together under the heading of geology. Earthquakes and volcanic activity are often connected. Earthquakes may give clues to impending eruptions, and movements of magma sometimes produce tremors. A volcanic eruption is accompanied by an almost continuous tremor.

Paleontology
From movies and TV, students might have the idea that there is a high demand for paleontologists. In truth there are currently relatively few positions available in the field. Most paleontologists work in related jobs, such as teaching. This allows them to pursue their research interests in the field.

Oceanography
Research organizations and industrial firms with interests in the ocean employ many oceanographers. These scientists must have at least a bachelor's degree with emphasis in geology, physics, chemistry, and biology. Most also have some specialized postgraduate training.

Meteorology and Doppler Radar
The National Weather Service has greatly improved the quality and reliability of forecasting with the use of Doppler weather surveillance radar. The radar bounces an electromagnetic signal off particles of water, ice, or dust in the atmosphere and measures the time it takes for the signal to return. If objects are moving, their speed can be determined by the time it takes two separate signals to return. Doppler technology can calculate both the direction and speed of severe storms. It also can identify the conditions leading to severe weather.

Section 2

The Scientific Method in Earth Science

Cooperation Between the Sciences
Before David Gillette and his team broke ground on their historic *Seismosaurus* dig, they used exhaustive high-tech sensing and mapping technology to locate the best places to dig. Gillette's team was helped by the technology and expertise of the Los Alamos National Laboratory, in New Mexico. The Los Alamos technology was developed for use in other fields of science, but paleontologists and physicists cooperated to make Gillette's dig a success.

- The ground-penetrating radar that helped paleontologists locate the bones of *Seismosaurus* was originally developed to locate 55 gal drums of hazardous waste beneath the soil.
- Magnetometry helped scientists identify the subtle variations in Earth's magnetic field that could be caused by buried bone.
- Radiation detectors measured radiation levels below the surface. Dinosaur bone can have as much as 100,000 times the uranium content of the surrounding rock.
- The underground location of the dinosaur bones was mapped using seismic waves. First a shotgun was fired into the Earth, and then the time it took for the waves to reach a receiving station was recorded.

IS THAT A FACT!

- A dowser also visited the site and tried his hand with a low-tech version of remote sensing.

SECTION 3

Life in a Warmer World—An Earth Science Model

▶ Revising the Model of the Solar System

Ptolemy (second century A.D.) is credited with developing the solar system model with Earth at its center. The sun, moon, and five visible planets moved around Earth in circular orbits. This model worked so well that astronomers used it to predict the positions of the known planets for many centuries.

- Nicolaus Copernicus (1473–1543) challenged Ptolemy's theory that the Earth was the center of the solar system and developed a model with the sun at the center. In this model, only the moon orbited Earth. Copernicus first presented his theory to friends in 1513. Only 30 years later, at the very end of his life, did Copernicus publish his complete theory.

IS THAT A FACT!

- Although Copernicus's model made it easier to explain the observed changes in the positions of the sun, moon, and planets, many people resisted the idea the model represented. They would not believe that Earth was not the center of *everything.*

▶ Early Flying Models

Some of the earliest pioneers in flight attempted to model the flight of birds. In the thirteenth century, Roger Bacon (c. 1220–1292) suggested that people could use wings like those of birds to fly. Two hundred years later, following Bacon's suggestions, Leonardo da Vinci (1452–1519) drew plans for a craft with flapping wings that would be operated by hand. The machine was referred to as an ornithopter. No one, including da Vinci, ever developed a successful ornithopter.

- Sir George Cayley (1773–1857) noticed that some birds could remain aloft for long periods of time without flapping their wings, so he took a different approach to human flight. He made a number of gliders with wings modeled after the wings of birds.
- The first successful glider flight was made in 1855 by Jean-Marie le Bris. The glider he designed was inspired by the albatross, a bird capable of soaring over the ocean for many hours without flapping its wings.

SECTION 4

Measurement and Safety

▶ Early Systems of Measurement

For many centuries, measurement was based on the human body. Egyptians defined a cubit as the distance between the elbow and the tip of the middle finger. A yard was the distance from the nose to the middle fingertip of an extended arm. The standard yard, still used today, was based on a measurement established by England's King Henry I (1068–1135).

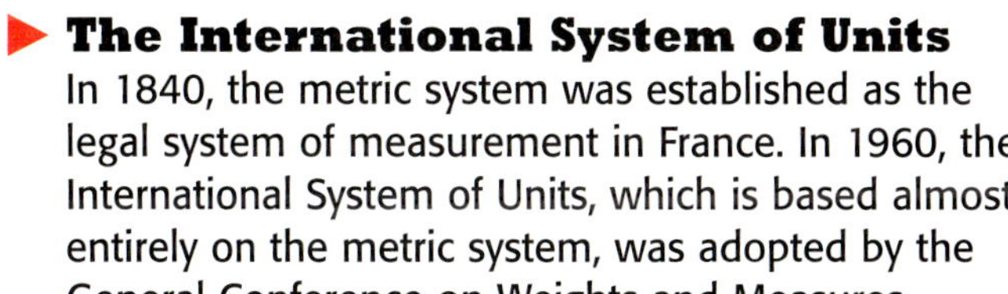

▶ The International System of Units

In 1840, the metric system was established as the legal system of measurement in France. In 1960, the International System of Units, which is based almost entirely on the metric system, was adopted by the General Conference on Weights and Measures.

For additional background resources, please refer to the ***HST Reference Library.***

CHAPTER 1

The World of Earth Science

Chapter Preview

Section 1
Branches of Earth Science
- Geology—Science that Rocks
- Oceanography—Water, Water Everywhere
- Meteorology—It's a Gas!
- Astronomy—Far, Far Away
- Special Branches of Earth Science

Section 2
The Scientific Method in Earth Science
- Steps of the Scientific Method
- Dino Discovery—A Case for the Scientific Method
- Case Closed?

Section 3
Life in a Warmer World—An Earth Science Model
- Types of Scientific Models
- The Greenhouse Effect—A Piece of the Global-Warming Model
- Testing the Global-Warming Model
- Using the Global-Warming Model

Section 4
Measurement and Safety
- Using the Same System
- Safety Rules!

Science Puzzlers, Twisters & Teasers Worksheet 1

Guided Reading Audio CD
English or Spanish, Chapter 1

CHAPTER 1 The World of Earth Science

This Really Happened!

The year was 1979. The place was a hot, wind-swept mesa in northwestern New Mexico. Two hikers were on their way to see some 1,000-year-old American Indian rock carvings on a sandstone cliff. Just before reaching the site, however, the hikers came across a row of several huge half-buried tailbones. What kind of animal could these bones possibly have come from? Judging by the size of the bones, the hikers guessed that they had belonged to some kind of dinosaur. What they didn't realize was just how important that dinosaur would turn out to be.

These hikers happened to stumble on their discovery, but their actions illustrate several qualities of Earth scientists. First, the hikers were observers. They did not simply trek right over the half-hidden bones without paying attention. Instead, they looked at the bones carefully. Earth scientists use observations as a primary tool in their work. The hikers' observations then led them to ask a question—what type of animal did these bones come from? Scientists also ask questions about things in nature they do not understand. Finally, the hikers guessed at what type of animal the bones might have come from. In a similar manner, scientists make educated guesses to answer the questions they ask. A scientist's guess is given a special name—*hypothesis.*

In this chapter you will learn how Earth scientists investigate the world we live in. You too can practice the things Earth scientists do as you begin your adventure through the world of Earth science.

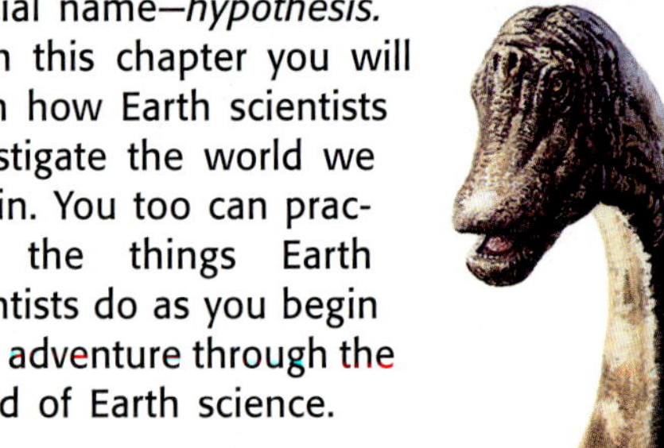

4

This Really Happened!

Tell students that as they read more of this chapter they will see how the scientific method solved the mystery of this dinosaur's identity.

What Do You Think?

In your ScienceLog, try to answer the following questions based on what you already know:

1. How many kinds of Earth scientists are there?
2. What is the scientific method?
3. What is the difference between a physical model and a mathematical model?

A Little Bit of Science

You are about to take a journey through the world of Earth science. While different scientists study many different things, they each encounter questions and problems that they try to answer and solve. Earth scientists must often rely on indirect measurements using tools to sense things that are beyond the reach of their own five senses. In this activity, you'll discover how limited senses can restrict your ability to learn about the unknown.

Procedure

1. Put on a pair of latex or plastic **gloves.** Make sure they are snug around your fingers.
2. Your teacher will supply you with a **coffee can** to which a **sock** has been attached. Do not look into the can.
3. Reach your gloved hand through the opening in the sock and into the can. You will be able to feel several objects inside the can.
4. Try to determine what the objects are by feeling them, moving them around, shaking the can, etc. Again, do not look into the can.
5. In your ScienceLog, make a list of the items that you think are in the can. State some reasons for your decisions.
6. Finally, pour the contents of the can onto your desk and see what was in the can.

Analysis

7. Were you correct in figuring out what was in the can?
8. Which items confused you? Why?
9. What characteristics of the objects were you not able to identify while they were in the can? Which of your five senses was needed to identify each of these characteristics?
10. What does the glove between your hand and the object represent? Explain.
11. How does this activity compare to the way scientists must study the Earth?

Going Further

Think about the types of things an Earth scientist might study. Would that scientist ever get to "open the can"? Explain.

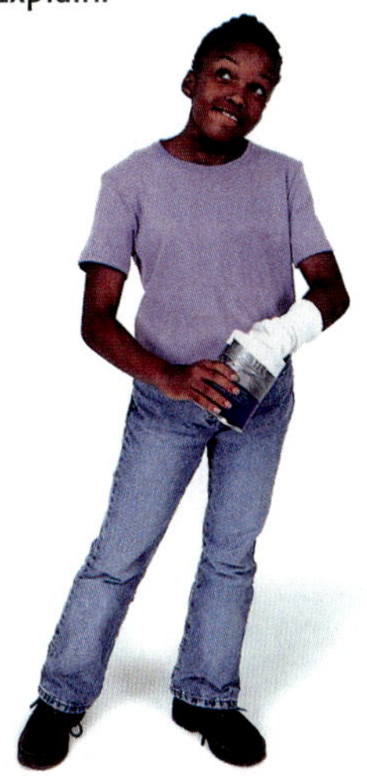

What Do You Think?

Accept all reasonable responses.

Students will have a chance to revise their answers in the Chapter Review under NOW What Do You Think?

Investigate!

MATERIALS

For Each Student:

- protective gloves
- coffee can
- sock
- various small items, such as nuts, washers, pencils, paper clips

Safety Caution: Be sure that students who may be allergic to latex do not use latex gloves for this activity.

Teacher Notes: You must prepare this activity ahead of time. Fill the cans with 4 or 5 small items. Try to choose some common and some uncommon items that would require more than one of the five senses to identify. To assemble each setup, cut the toe out of a sport sock, stretch the open toe around the open end of the coffee can, and use duct tape to secure the sock to the can, as shown in the photograph.

Directed Reading Worksheet 1

Science Skills Worksheet 8 "Reading a Science Textbook"

Answers to Investigate!

7. Answers will vary.
8. Answers will vary.
9. Answers will vary. Unidentifiable characteristics will most likely be characteristics that can be detected only by sight or smell.
10. A limit on a human sense. The sense of touch is limited when wearing the glove.
11. Scientists cannot always use all five senses when studying certain aspects of the Earth. Also, the senses that can be used are sometimes limited.

Answer to Going Further

No; there are some parts of the Earth that scientists cannot see. For example, even though scientists can create images of Earth's deep interior, they cannot look deep inside the Earth.

SECTION 1

Focus

Branches of Earth Science

This section shows how the branches of Earth science help us to understand and protect the Earth, survive its upheavals, and comprehend its place in the universe. It examines the fields of geology, oceanography, meteorology, and astronomy. Students also learn about ecology, geochemistry, geography, and cartography, which combine Earth science and other disciplines.

Bellringer

Tell students the following:

Imagine you are an Earth scientist, and you can travel wherever you want to on Earth. Name the aspects or features of Earth you would like to study. Explain where you would go and what you would do.

Have students write and illustrate their answers in their ScienceLog.

1 Motivate

ACTIVITY

Have students use dictionaries to determine the meaning of the following:

geo-
volcan-
paleo-
meteor-
ocean-
astro-

Ask students to build scientists' names by adding suffixes such as *-nomer, -ologist,* and *-ographer.* Have students describe what they think each scientist does based on the name. Sheltered English

1

NEW TERMS

geology
oceanography
meteorology
astronomy
ecosystem

OBJECTIVES

- List major branches of Earth science.
- Identify branches of Earth science that are linked to other areas of science.
- Describe careers associated with different branches of Earth science.

Branches of Earth Science

Planet Earth! How can anyone study something as large and complicated as our planet? One way is to divide the study of Earth into pieces. It's easier to study something large and complicated if you break it down into smaller, simpler things. Scientists divide the study of the physical planet Earth into three general categories—*geology, oceanography,* and *meteorology. Astronomy* is the study of all physical things beyond planet Earth. Let's take a look at each of these four sciences and at some of the people who work within them. Then we'll look at a few other areas of science that relate to these four.

Geology—Science that Rocks

Geology is the study of the solid Earth. Anything and everything that has to do with the solid Earth is part of geology. Most geologists specialize in a particular aspect of the Earth.

Would you like to put on an insulated suit and walk to the edge of a 1,000°C pool of lava? If so, you could be a *volcanologist,* a geologist who studies volcanoes. Are earthquakes more to your liking? Then you could be a *seismologist,* a geologist who studies earthquakes. How about digging up dinosaurs? You could be a *paleontologist,* a geologist who studies fossils. These are only a few of the careers you could have as a geologist.

Some geologists become highly specialized. For instance, geologist Robert Fronk, at the Florida Institute of Technology, explores the subsurface of Earth by scuba-diving in underwater caves in Florida and the Bahamas. Fronk says, "Bahamians call caves in the ocean floor 'blue holes.' This describes them well. From the surface, they are usually dark blue surrounded by bright white sand." Underwater caves often contain evidence that sea level was once much lower than it is now. They contain *stalagmites* and *stalactites,* as shown in **Figure 1.** These formations develop from minerals in dripping water in air-filled caves. When Fronk sees these kinds of geologic formations in underwater caves, he knows that the caves were once above sea level.

Figure 1 *Stalagmites grow upward from the floors of caves, and stalactites grow downward from the ceilings of caves. Both formations develop over millions of years in air-filled caves.*

6

Directed Reading Worksheet 1 Section 1

IS THAT A FACT!

Earth is estimated to be 4.6 billion years old. It travels around the sun at 29.79 km/s (18.5 mi/s). The Earth is not round; it is an oblate spheroid—flattened at the poles and bulging at the equator.

Oceanography—Water, Water Everywhere

Oceanography, which is the study of the ocean, is often divided into four areas: physical oceanography, biological oceanography, geological oceanography, and chemical oceanography. Physical oceanographers study things like waves and ocean currents. Biological oceanographers study the plants and animals that live in the ocean. Geological oceanographers study the ocean floor. Chemical oceanographers study natural chemicals and chemicals from pollution in the ocean.

Not long ago, people studied the ocean only from the surface. But as technology has advanced, scientists have worked with engineers to build miniature research submarines. Now oceanographers can go practically anywhere in the oceans. Below, oceanographer John Trefry talks about a trip he took in the minisub *Alvin.*

> *"We move through the darkness of the Pacific Ocean at a depth of almost one and a half miles [2.2 km] with the lights of the submersible shining on the glassy black rock that is new ocean crust. Then, in a magic moment, we can peer ahead through a small porthole at a 300°C [572°F] black smoker surrounded by an oasis of beautiful and exotic life-forms. The feeling of exhilaration inspires renewed wonderment and makes the many years of study in oceanography seem so satisfying and worthwhile. What a beautiful Earth! What a great career!"*

Trefry and other oceanographers have discovered one of the most exciting oceanographic finds of the twentieth century—the world of the black smokers. *Black smokers* are rock chimneys on the ocean floor that spew black clouds of minerals. Black smokers are a type of *hydrothermal vent,* which is a crack in the ocean floor that releases very hot water from beneath the Earth's surface. The minerals and hot water from these vents support a biological community like no other on Earth—one that does not depend on sunlight. Animals that call this community home include blood-red tube worms that are 3.5 m long, clams that are 30 cm in diameter, and blind white crabs.

QuickLab

How Hot Is 300°C?

1. Use a **thermometer** to measure the air's temperature in the room in degrees Celsius. Record your reading.
2. Hold the thermometer near a **heat source** in the room, such as a light bulb or a heating vent. Be careful not to burn yourself. Record your reading.
3. How do the temperatures you recorded compare with the 300°C temperature of the water from a black smoker? Write your answer and observations in your ScienceLog.

QuickLab

Answers to Quicklab

3. Answers will vary, but students should realize that the temperature of the water around a black smoker is much hotter than the temperatures they measured. Encourage students to speculate why the water temperature is 200°C above the boiling point of water at sea level. Students might conclude that the tremendous pressure at that depth raises the boiling point of water.

2 Teach

DISCUSSION

Invite students to speculate about what kind of scientist might answer each of the following questions. Discuss ways that scientists find answers to these questions.

- How can you tell when a volcano is going to erupt?
- What life-forms dwell on the ocean floor, 9.5 km down?
- Is Earth's atmosphere becoming warmer? How will this affect us?
- Are there deposits of oil, gas, gold, and silver still undiscovered in Earth's crust? How can they be reached?
- How many stars are there? Is there life on other planets?

Have students add their own questions to the discussion.

CROSS-DISCIPLINARY FOCUS

History Help students research the lives and contributions of the following Earth or space scientists:

- Hipparchus (developed the first system for identifying stars)
- James Hutton (father of modern geology)
- Galileo Galilei (refined the scientific method, astronomy)
- Inge Lehman (discovered the Earth's inner core)
- Robert Goddard (rocket science)
- Johannes Kepler (discovered elliptical orbits in the solar system)
- Wladimir Köppen (developed a climate classification system)
- George E. Hale (developed the Hale reflecting telescope)

2 Teach, continued

Real-World Connection

Ask students to describe their experiences with severe weather, such as tornadoes, hurricanes, or severe thunderstorms. What preparations did they make before the storm? What safety measures did they take during the storm? How did weather forecasters influence their behavior? What was the result of the storm in their community? Finally, discuss the information students get from meteorologists every day and how they use it.

Meeting Individual Needs

Learners Having Difficulty

Have students create concept-map posters for the four branches of Earth and space science and their subdivisions. Have them add illustrations, symbols, and photographs or headlines clipped from articles to provide visual information about each field. Sheltered English

Cultures all over the world observe animal behavior to predict the weather. Chinese farmers use this formula: If frogs croak on a fine day, it will rain in two days. If frogs croak after rain, there will be fine weather. It will continue to rain if frogs do not croak after many overcast days. Other cultures observe insect behavior: It will rain if ants travel in a straight line; it will be clear if the ants are scattered. Counting cricket chirps is a very reliable gauge to measure ambient temperature. Have students find out how other cultures observe animal behavior to predict the weather and use these methods to predict the weather for 1 week.

Meteorology—It's a Gas!

You might think that meteorology is the study of meteors. Not a bad guess, but not quite right. *Meteors* are the flashes of light seen when objects fall from space into our atmosphere. **Meteorology,** however, is the study of the entire atmosphere.

When you ask, "Is it going to rain today?" you are asking a meteorological question. One of the most common careers in meteorology is weather forecasting. Sometimes knowing what the weather is going to be like makes our lives more comfortable. And occasionally our lives depend on these forecasts.

Figure 2 *This satellite photo of Hurricane Andrew shows the storm at three different positions. You can trace Andrew's path from the Atlantic Ocean (right) to the Gulf of Mexico (left).*

Hurricanes In 1928, a major hurricane hit Florida and killed 1,836 people. In comparison, a hurricane of similar strength—Hurricane Andrew, shown in **Figure 2**—hit Florida in 1992, killing only 48 people. Why were there far fewer deaths in 1992? Two major reasons were hurricane tracking and weather forecasting.

Meteorologists began tracking Hurricane Andrew on Monday, August 17. By the following Sunday morning, most South Floridians had left the coast because the National Hurricane Center had warned them that Andrew was headed their way. Hurricane Andrew hit southern Florida early on Monday morning, August 24. The hurricane caused a lot of damage, but it killed very few people thanks to meteorologists' warnings.

Figure 3 *Too close for comfort? Not for Howard Bluestein and his tornado-chasing team. These meteorologists risk their lives to gather data.*

Tornadoes Another dangerous weather element is tornadoes. An average of 780 tornadoes touch down each year in the United States. What do you think about a meteorologist who chases tornadoes as a career? Howard Bluestein does just that. Bluestein predicts where tornadoes are likely to form and then drives to within a couple of kilometers of the site to gather data, as shown in **Figure 3.** By gathering data this way, scientists like Bluestein hope to understand tornadoes better. The better they understand them, the better they can predict how these violent storms will behave.

Is That a Fact!

Our planet has some extreme temperatures. A world record high temperature of 58°C (136°F) was recorded in El Azizia, Libya, in 1922. In 1983 in Vostok, Antarctica, a world record low temperature of −89°C (−192°F) was recorded.

Astronomy—Far, Far Away

How do you study things that are far away in space? That's a question that astronomers can answer. **Astronomy** is the study of all physical things beyond Earth. Astronomers study stars, asteroids, planets, and everything else in space.

Because most things in space are too far away to sense directly, astronomers depend on technology to help them study objects in space. Astronomers use a variety of instruments. Optical telescopes have been used for hundreds of years—Galileo built one in 1609. Astronomers still use optical telescopes to look into space, but they also use other types of telescopes. For example, the radio telescopes shown in **Figure 4** allow astronomers to study objects that are too far away to be seen using optical telescopes or that do not give off visible light.

Astronomers spend much of their time studying stars. Astronomers estimate that there are 100 billion billion stars in the sky. That's a lot of stars! Try the MathBreak at right to get an idea of how many stars there are.

The most familiar star in the universe is the sun, which is the closest star to Earth. Astronomers have studied the sun more than any other star. Astronomers have also studied planets that are close to Earth. **Figure 5** illustrates the sun, the Earth, and some nearby planets. Can you name these planets?

Figure 4 *These radio telescopes receive radio waves from space. Researchers use computers to turn the radio waves into visible data that they can study.*

Figure 5 *Astronomers know more about the sun and other nearby objects than they know about objects that are farther away in space.*

MATH BREAK

Lots of Zeros!

Astronomers estimate that there are more than 100 billion billion stars in the sky! One billion written out in numerals looks like this:

1,000,000,000

1. How many zeros do you need in order to write 100 billion billion in numerals? To find out, multiply 1 billion by 1 billion, then multiply your answer by 100. Count the zeros in the final answer.
2. Now time how long it takes you to count to 100. How long would it take you to count to 100 a billion billion times?

Using the Figure

Students are asked to name the planets shown in **Figure 5.** Moving away from the sun, they are: Mercury, Venus, Earth, Mars, Jupiter, and Saturn. Note that an asteroid belt is between Mars and Jupiter.

MATH and MORE

Explain that space science involves measuring extremely large distances. To express these enormous numbers, scientists use *scientific notation,* or powers of 10. Write on the board:

$10 = 10^1$

$100 = 10^2$

$1000 = 10^3$

Have students continue the table and explain the pattern. Ask students to express the following numbers using this type of notation:

1. 10,000°C (1.0×10^4°C)
2. 1,497,000 km (1.497×10^6 km)
3. 4,600,000,000 years (4.6×10^9 years)

Math Skills Worksheet 23 "Counting the Zeros"

Math Skills Worksheet 25 "What Is Scientific Notation?"

Homework

Research Ask students to learn about optical telescopes, liquid mirror telescopes, or radio telescopes. Have students draw the telescope and show its working parts. Ask them to write a brief explanation of how the telescope works and how it is used.

Answers to MATHBREAK

1. 20 zeros
2. Answers will vary, but counting one number per second, it will take more than 3 trillion years! The universe is thought to be only 10 billion to 15 billion years old.

3 Extend

CONNECT TO ENVIRONMENTAL SCIENCE

Many of the world's grassland ecosystems are endangered due to overgrazing. If too many animals graze the land, topsoil may dry out and be blown away. The result may be desertification—the dry grassland becomes a desert. Have students research how the Peace Corps or another organization attempts to control desertification around the world.

GOING FURTHER

Writing Ask students to imagine an exciting day in the life of an astronomer, a volcanologist, a meteorologist, or an oceanographer. Have them write a ScienceLog entry from the perspective of the scientist describing what happened to make the day exciting and why the scientist enjoys his or her job.

INDEPENDENT PRACTICE

Have students create an Earth Science Current Events scrapbook. Encourage creativity as they incorporate articles, illustrations, photographs, and original entries. The book can be organized by category in a three-ring binder, and students can add pages throughout the school year. Sheltered English

internetconnect

TOPIC: Branches of Earth Science
GO TO: www.scilinks.org
***sci*LINKS NUMBER:** HSTE005

TOPIC: Careers in Earth Science
GO TO: www.scilinks.org
***sci*LINKS NUMBER:** HSTE010

Special Branches of Earth Science

In addition to the main branches of Earth science, there are branches that depend more heavily on other areas of science. Earth scientists often find themselves in careers that rely on life science, chemistry, physics, and many other areas of science. Let's take a look at some Earth science careers with strong ties to other sciences.

Figure 6 *Because beavers spend time in water as well as on land, they share their ecosystem with many plants and animals, such as fishes, turtles, birds, reeds, and trees.*

Ecology It is difficult to understand the behavior of certain organisms without studying the relationships between these organisms and their surroundings. Ecologists study ecosystems, like the one in **Figure 6.** An **ecosystem** is a community of organisms and their nonliving environment. The principles of ecology are useful in many related fields, such as wildlife management, agriculture, forestry, and conservation. The science of ecology requires people trained in many disciplines, such as biology, geology, chemistry, climatology, mathematics, and computer technology.

Geochemistry As the name implies, geochemistry combines the studies of geology and chemistry. Geochemists, like the one in **Figure 7,** specialize in the chemistry of rocks, minerals, and soil. They study the chemistry of these materials to determine their economic value, interpret what the environment was like when they formed, and learn what has happened to them since they first formed.

Is there water on Mars? Turn to page 31 to see how one geophysicist is finding out.

Figure 7 *This geochemist is taking rock samples from the field so she can perform chemical analyses of them in her laboratory.*

10

MISCONCEPTION ALERT

Many people think that ecosystems exist somewhere "out there"—in open fields, quiet woods, and national parks. In fact, anywhere living things form a network of feeding, reproduction, and survival systems, an ecosystem exists. Ecosystems are found in cities and small towns, on school playgrounds, in backyards, and even in your body. Students who learn to observe carefully and patiently can learn a great deal about the ecosystems around them.

Environmental Science Humans have recently begun to examine their relationship with their surroundings, or *environment,* more closely. The study of how humans interact with the environment is called *environmental science.* As shown in **Figure 8,** one common task of an environmental scientist is trying to find out whether humans are damaging the environment. Pollution of the air, water, and land can harm natural resources, such as wildlife, drinking water, and soil. Environmental science, which relies on life science, chemistry, physics, and geology, is helping us to preserve Earth's resources and to use them more wisely.

Figure 8 *This environmental scientist is testing the effects of industry on the environment.*

Geography and Cartography Geographers, who are educated in geology, life science, and physics, study the surface features of the Earth. Cartographers make maps of those features. Have you ever wondered why our cities are located where they are? Often, the location of a city is determined by geography. Many cities, such as the one in **Figure 9,** were built near rivers, lakes, or oceans because boats were used for transporting people and items of trade. Rivers and lakes also provide communities with plenty of water for drinking and for raising crops and animals. We make maps to record the geography of our world. Maps help us keep track of natural resources and navigate the surface of the Earth.

Figure 9 *The easily accessible Mississippi River helped St. Louis become the large city it is today.*

REVIEW

1. List three major branches of Earth Science.
2. Name two branches of Earth science that rely heavily on other areas of science. Explain how the branches rely on the other areas of science.
3. List and describe three Earth-science careers.
4. **Inferring Relationships** If you were a *hydrogeologist,* what kind of work would you do?

Explore

Find and cut out a newspaper article about some topic in Earth science. After reading the article, classify it according to one of the following areas—geology, meteorology, oceanography, or astronomy.

4 Close

Quiz

1. Name three areas of specialization in geology and what each one focuses on. (volcanology—study of volcanoes; seismology—study of earthquakes; paleontology—study of fossils)
2. What new technology has expanded the study of the oceans in recent years? (the ability to travel to great depths in submersibles)
3. What tasks is a meteorologist likely to perform? (weather forecasting, climate study, hurricane tracking, tornado research)
4. Why is a radio telescope valuable to astronomers? (It enables them to see extremely distant stars and objects that do not give off visible light.)

Alternative Assessment

Have students work in small groups to prepare a poster ad to persuade students to choose one of the Earth or space sciences as a career. Posters should include an explanation of the field of study, a description of a job such scientists might tackle, and illustrations that show why that career is exciting. Have groups present their advertisements to the class.

Answers to Review

1. The preferred answer is geology, oceanography, and meteorology. Any other branches of Earth and space science should be accepted.
2. Answers will vary. Branches listed in the text include ecology, geochemistry, environmental science, geography, and cartography. Other branches not mentioned in the text are acceptable at the teacher's discretion. If branches are chosen from the text, explanations of how the branches rely on other areas should reflect the information given in the text.
3. Any of the careers listed in the text are acceptable. Descriptions should match the text. Other careers may be accepted.
4. A hydrogeologist is a geologist who studies water (*hydro-* refers to water).

Reinforcement Worksheet 1
"Scenes from the Earth"

SECTION 2

Focus

The Scientific Method in Earth Science

This section introduces the scientific method by following an actual paleontologist's discovery of a new type of dinosaur. The section also discusses the importance of sharing discoveries and information among scientists.

Bellringer

Pose the following question to your students:

How can paleontologists know what a dinosaur looked like, how it behaved, and what it ate based only on its fossilized skeleton?

Ask students to write their answers in their ScienceLog. Discuss their ideas.

1 Motivate

DISCUSSION

Ask students to think about "discoveries" they have made in their lives. Students may be surprised to learn that they make scientific discoveries every day. A student might say, for example, "I found out that if my brother sat on the see-saw opposite from me, I would go flying off." Tell students that discoveries are often made by accident but that a controlled experiment using the scientific method is necessary to explain observations. Have students identify the steps of the scientific method in the discoveries they have made. Sheltered English

Directed Reading Worksheet 1 Section 2

2

The Scientific Method in Earth Science

NEW TERMS

scientific method
observation
hypothesis

OBJECTIVES

- Explain the scientific method and how scientists use it.
- Apply the scientific method to an Earth science investigation.
- Identify the importance of communicating the results of a scientific investigation.
- Describe how scientific investigations often lead to new investigations.

Imagine that you are standing in a thick forest on the bank of a river. The sun is shining through the needles of the trees. You notice that the vegetation quickly becomes sparse not far from the river and that the land is much more open. Insects are buzzing, but no birds are flying because they don't yet exist. It is the Jurassic period, 150 million years ago.

Wading in the shallow water, several long-necked dinosaurs quietly munch on vegetation. As you peer through the trees, you spot a different type of dinosaur on the prowl for prey. It is about 12 m long and appears to weigh about 4 tons. It is an allosaur, the most common meat-eating predator of this time.

Suddenly you feel the ground begin to shake. The tremors are slight at first, but they grow stronger. You begin to hear a booming noise that accompanies the tremors. The allosaur stops and looks in the direction of the sound. Startled pterosaurs, winged reptiles, fly noisily by. The booming gets louder, and the tremors get stronger.

Suddenly you notice a creature's head looming over the treetops. The creature's head is so high that its neck must be 20 m long! Then the entire animal comes into view. You understand why the ground is shaking. The animal is *Seismosaurus hallorum* (SEIZ moh SAWR uhs hah LOHR uhm), the "earth shaker." You are looking at one of the largest dinosaurs known.

Seismosaurus hallorum

CROSS-DISCIPLINARY FOCUS

Language Arts As students read the description of a Jurassic period environment, have them pay particular attention to the language used to describe the scene. Ask them to analyze the description and hypothesize how scientists discovered what this environment was like. For example, what parts of the description could be learned from the fossil record? What parts are inferred from observations of living things today? Have students record their observations in their ScienceLog.

The scene you just witnessed is not based on imagination alone. Scientists have been studying dinosaurs for years. From the bits and pieces of information they gather about dinosaurs and their environment, scientists re-create what the Earth might have been like 150 million years ago. But how do scientists tell one dinosaur species from another? How do they know if they have discovered a new species? The answers to these questions are related to the methods that scientists use.

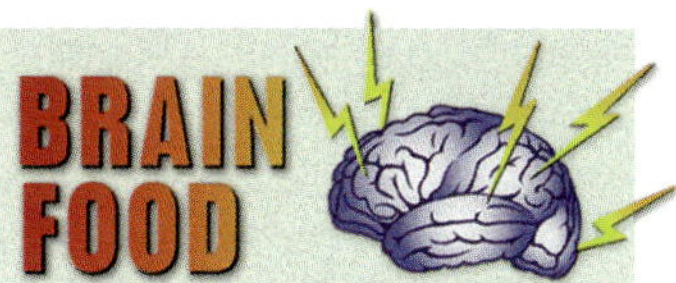

Several species of dinosaurs are claimed to be the largest known. So which is the largest? Good scientists look carefully at the information available and judge for themselves.

Steps of the Scientific Method

When scientists make observations about the natural world, they are often presented with a question or problem. But scientists don't just throw out random answers. Instead, they follow a series of steps called the *scientific method*. The **scientific method** is a series of steps that scientists use to answer questions and solve problems. The most basic steps are illustrated in **Figure 10.**

Although the scientific method has several distinct steps, it is not a rigid procedure. Scientists may use all of the steps or just some of the steps of the scientific method. They may even repeat some of the steps or do them in a different order. The goal of the scientific method is to come up with reliable answers and solutions. As long as scientists use the scientific method effectively, the overall result is the same—they gain more insight into the problems they investigate.

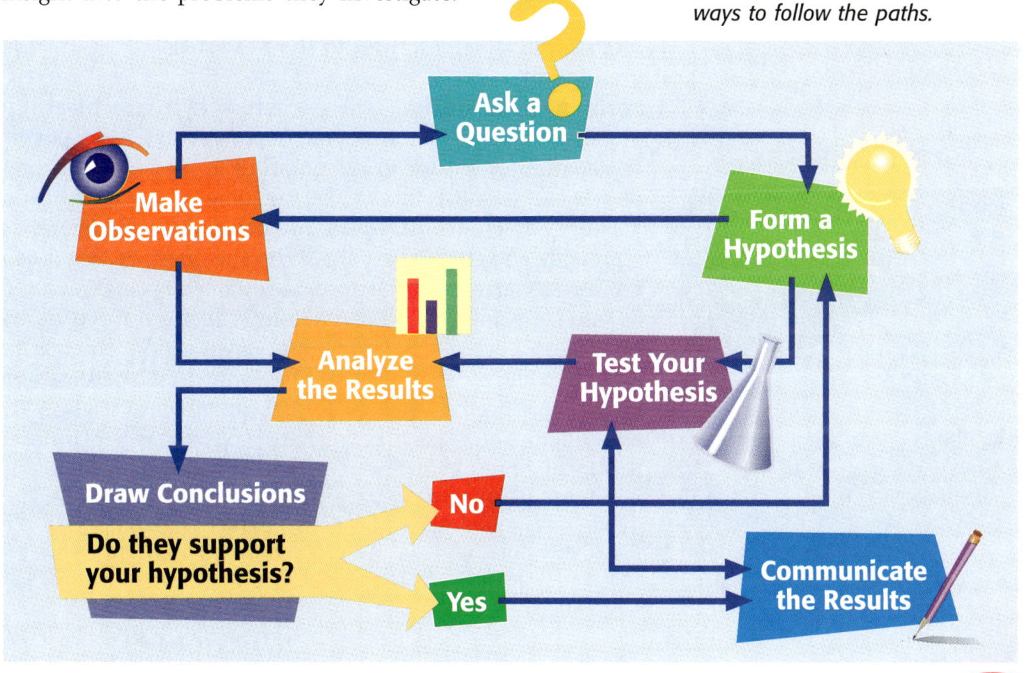

Figure 10 *The scientific method is illustrated in this flowchart. Notice that there are several ways to follow the paths.*

2 Teach

Group Activity

Have students work in small groups to solve an everyday problem using the scientific method. For example, students might devise a way to keep sandwiches in a sack lunch from being squashed in a backpack. Ask students to report on how they followed the six steps, and have them record their experimental processes and conclusions. Write the steps of the scientific method on the board, and point out different ways groups approached each step. Sheltered English

Homework

Using the Scientific Method Ask students to think of a question or a problem in their daily lives that they can answer by making observations, forming a hypothesis, testing the hypothesis, and analyzing the results. Set a time limit for students' observations, and have them share their results in a poster or written report.

Teaching Transparency 85 "The Scientific Method"

MISCONCEPTION ALERT

Ask students to define *observations*. Many may assume that observations only include phenomena they can see. In fact, observations are made using all the senses. Point out that many scientific observations must be made indirectly, for example, when studying Earth's deep interior, faraway stars, and magma chambers inside volcanoes.

2 Teach, continued

CONNECT TO LIFE SCIENCE

Fossils can tell a scientist many more things besides an animal's height or weight. In addition to bones, Gillette found many *gastroliths*—large stones found in the digestive system of some animals, particularly birds. *Seismosaurus* apparently swallowed the stones; once inside the digestive system, the stones ground up plant material that otherwise would have been too hard for *Seismosaurus* to digest!

DISCUSSION

How is the scientific method like detective work? Have students list the stages they think occur in a robbery investigation and match them to steps in the scientific method.

- Determine what happened, when, and where (state the problem).
- Gather clues (make observations).
- Determine suspects (form hypothesis).
- Interrogate suspects (test hypothesis).
- Analyze clues (analyze results).
- Solve the crime (draw conclusions).
- Arrest the alleged perpetrator (communicate results).

Dino Discovery—A Case for the Scientific Method

One of the first things a scientist does, even before starting an investigation, is make observations. An **observation** is any use of the senses to gather information. While observations can be made at any time, it is observations of objects and events in nature that lead to scientific investigations.

Remember the hikers at the beginning of this chapter and their discovery of dinosaur bones in the desert? Those hikers may have been the first to examine the bones, but they weren't the last. In May 1985, paleontologist David D. Gillette visited the site. Excited by what he saw, Gillette began to wonder what type of dinosaur these huge bones came from. As you will see, this started him on the path to using the scientific method.

Ask a Question

Ask a question that needs a scientific answer.

Ask a Question When scientists make observations, they often have questions that they would like answered. Good scientists recognize these questions as the potential beginning of an investigation. When scientists try to answer these questions, they begin to change from passive observer to active investigator.

Gillette may have asked, "What type of dinosaur did these bones come from?" He recognized this question as the beginning of a scientific investigation. Gillette knew that in order to answer this question, he would have to use the scientific method. So Gillette moved to the next step.

Form a Hypothesis

Propose a possible answer to the question.

Form a Hypothesis When scientists want to investigate a question, they form a *hypothesis*. A **hypothesis** is a possible explanation or answer to the question. It may be a statement of what a scientist thinks the outcome of an investigation will be. Sometimes called an *educated guess,* the hypothesis represents a scientist's best answer to the question. But it can't be just any answer. It has to be a testable explanation.

After making closer observations, Gillette realized he had never seen bones like these before. Based on his observations and on what he already knew, he formed a hypothesis—the bones came from a type of dinosaur unknown to science. This was Gillette's best testable explanation of what type of dinosaur the fossil bones came from. If correct, it would answer his question. To test his hypothesis, Gillette would have to do a lot of research.

SCIENTISTS AT ODDS

Paleontologist David Gillette named the dinosaur *Seismosaurus,* or earth shaker, because of its great size. No one doubts that *Seismosaurus* was very heavy, weighing more than 15 elephants. But there is debate about its length. Some paleontologists believe that it was the longest land animal that ever lived, measuring 45 to 50 m long. But other paleontologists say that *Seismosaurus* was only about 30 m long.

Scientists exploring the Texas Gulf Coast have discovered American Indian artifacts that are thousands of years old. The odd thing about it is that the artifacts were buried in the sea floor several meters below sea level. These artifacts were in-place, meaning that they had not been moved since they were originally buried. The *observation* is that there are American Indian artifacts several meters below sea level, and the *question* is, "Why are they there?" Your job is to *form a hypothesis* that answers this question. Remember, your hypothesis must be stated in such a way that it can be tested using the scientific method.

Test the Hypothesis Once a hypothesis is established, it must be tested. Scientists test hypotheses by gathering data that can help determine whether the hypotheses are valid or not. Often a scientist will run experiments to test a hypothesis.

To test a hypothesis, a scientist may conduct a controlled experiment. *A controlled experiment* is an experiment that tests only one factor at a time. By changing only one factor (the *variable*), scientists can see the results of just that one change. Experiments are often done in laboratories, where conditions are more easily controlled. Earth scientists, however, usually rely more heavily on observations to test their hypotheses. The Earth scientist's laboratory is the Earth itself, where variables cannot be easily controlled. Instead of trying to control nature, Earth scientists more often observe nature and collect large amounts of data to test their hypotheses.

To test his hypothesis, Gillette gathered all the data he could find. He took hundreds of measurements of the bones, carefully documenting their size and shape. He then compared his measurements with those of tailbones from known dinosaurs. He visited museums and talked with other paleontologists. His testing took more than a year to complete.

Analyze the Results Once scientists finish their tests, they must analyze the results. In this step, scientists often create tables and graphs to organize their data. When Gillette analyzed the results of the bone comparisons, he found that the bones of the mystery dinosaur were either too large or shaped too differently to have belonged to any of the dinosaurs he used for comparison.

Test the Hypothesis

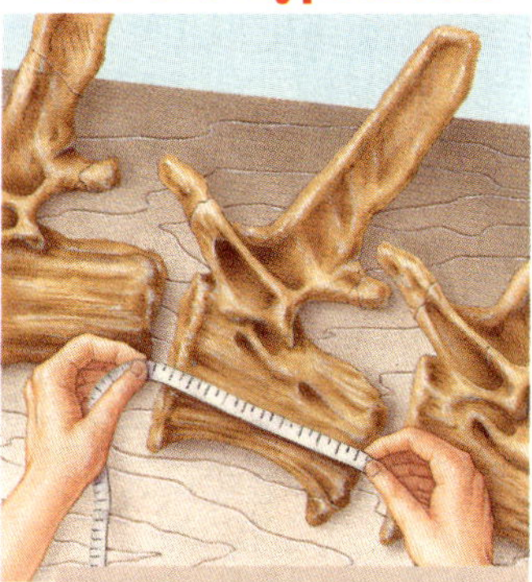

Test the hypothesis with observations or experiments.

Analyze the Results

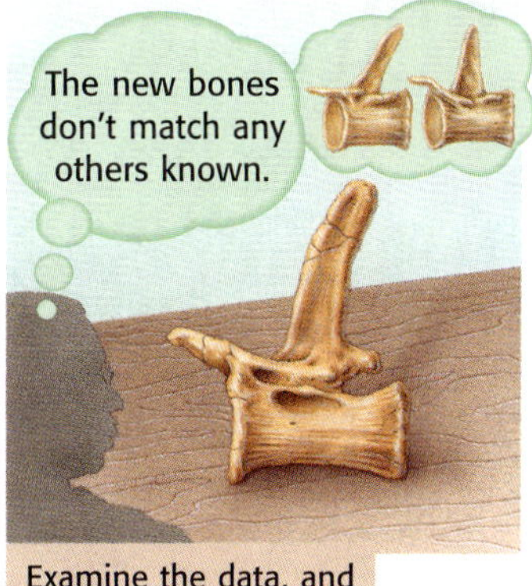

Examine the data, and look for patterns.

Answer to APPLY

Answers will vary. The most accepted hypothesis is that sea level has risen since the artifacts were originally placed. This hypothesis is testable through the analysis of other evidence that suggests sea level was once lower. For example, old river channels have been found below sea level in the same area as the artifacts.

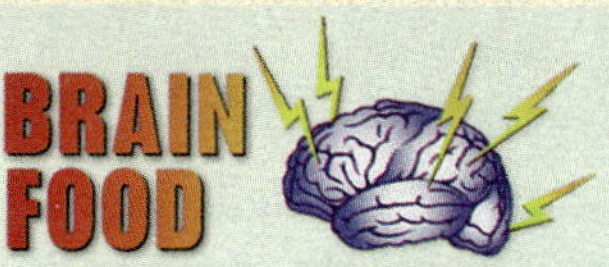

Sometimes scientists make new observations or discoveries while testing a hypothesis. These discoveries might require scientists to start over and rethink their original hypothesis. Ask students whether they think that the scientific method is a linear process or a complex circular one. Discuss how different steps could be connected.

MISCONCEPTION ALERT

Most people think of laboratories, bubbling test tubes, flashing screens, and white coats when they hear the word *experiment.* In Earth science, though, the laboratory is most often outdoors. Often, Earth science phenomena cannot be observed under controlled conditions—you can't make a volcano erupt at will. In these cases, Earth scientists make many observations and use statistics and long-term records to predict when an event, such as an eruption, will occur.

CONNECT TO PHYSICAL SCIENCE

Unearthing *Seismosaurus* took 7 years. The bones were so deeply embedded in sandstone that Gillette asked for help from the Los Alamos National Laboratory. The lab staff devised an experimental way to use ground-penetrating radar and magnetometers to pinpoint the location of bone inside solid rock. Although the laboratory helped locate the dinosaur, Gillette's team still put in many hard hours excavating the fossil with hammers, picks, and shovels.

3 Extend

Cross-Disciplinary Focus

Language Arts Communicating results, especially in writing, is an important part of science. Have students choose an important scientific discovery and then present those findings to their fellow scientists in class as if they were the discoverer. Students should write and read a brief speech describing their accomplishment. Encourage students to be creative as well as concise and clear in communicating their results. Sheltered English

Meeting Individual Needs

Advanced Learners Austrian-born philosopher Karl Popper once said, "A scientific idea can never be proven true, because no matter how many observations seem to agree with it, it may still be wrong." Discuss this statement with students, and ask them if they agree. Ask them to explain their reasoning.

Debate

Have students research the ways that the scientific method is applied by agribusinesses to increase the yield of their harvests. Suggest that students find out about tests in experimental plots and the genetic engineering of seeds. Students should also research the potential risks to human health and the environment that genetically engineered crops pose. Ask them to consider whether or not genetically engineered seeds should be patented and owned by private companies and what the rights of small farmers should be. Have student groups outline their positions and debate these topics in class.

Draw Conclusions

Decide if the original hypothesis is supported.

Communicate Results

Share your discoveries with other scientists.

Draw Conclusions Finally, after carefully analyzing the results of their tests, scientists must draw conclusions. Scientists must conclude whether the results supported the hypothesis. If the hypothesis was not supported, scientists may repeat the investigation to check for errors. Or they may ask new questions and form a new hypothesis.

Based on all his analyses, Gillette concluded that the eight bones found in New Mexico were indeed from a newly discovered dinosaur species that was probably 45 m long and weighed at least 100 tons. The creature certainly fit the name Gillette gave it—*Seismosaurus hallorum,* the "earth shaker."

Communicate Results Upon completing an investigation, scientists communicate their results. In this way, scientists share what they have learned with other scientists, who may want to repeat the investigation to see if they get the same results. Science depends on the sharing of information.

Scientists share information by publishing reports in scientific journals or by sharing their information over the Internet. Scientists also give lectures on the results of their scientific investigations at conferences, seminars, or other professional meetings. This method is appealing because it allows other scientists to ask questions directly to the scientist who performed the investigation.

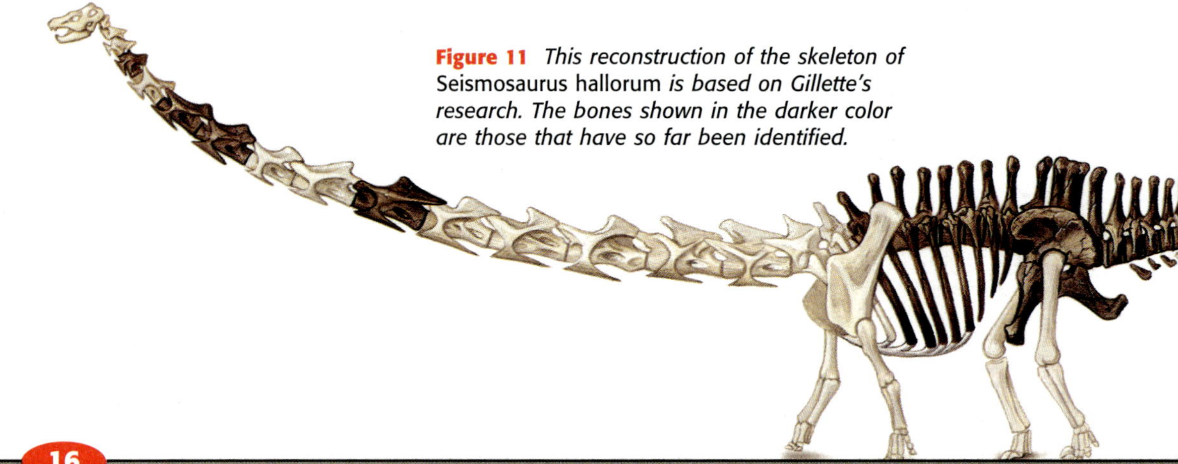

Figure 11 *This reconstruction of the skeleton of* Seismosaurus hallorum *is based on Gillette's research. The bones shown in the darker color are those that have so far been identified.*

16

Science Bloopers

In 1989, two scientists from the University of Utah held a press conference to announce that they accomplished nuclear fusion using a method called *cold fusion.* They claimed this would offer the world cheap, clean, and unlimited energy. Their press release went directly to the public, and their work was not first reviewed by other scientists. Within five weeks, scientists around the world discredited their work because the results could not be duplicated. Unable to provide data on how their apparatus created cold fusion, the two scientists were forced to withdraw their paper from a prestigious journal.

Gillette communicated his results by holding a press conference at the New Mexico Museum of Natural History and Science. There he announced his discovery of *Seismosaurus,* carefully answered questions, and defended his investigation. Gillette later submitted a report to the *Journal of Vertebrate Paleontology* that summarized his investigation. After two years of careful checking by other scientists, the journal published Gillette's report.

Case Closed?

All of the *Seismosaurus* bones that Gillette found have been dug up, but the *Seismosaurus* project continues in a laboratory phase as the remains of one of the largest dinosaurs ever discovered are still being studied. Like so many other scientific investigations, Gillette's work led to new problems to be explored using the scientific method.

Figure 12 *David Gillette continues to study the bones of* Seismosaurus *for new insights into the past.*

REVIEW

1. What is the scientific method? How do scientists use it?
2. After observing eight tailbones, Gillette hypothesized that they were from a newly discovered dinosaur species. What was his hypothesis based on?
3. Why do scientists communicate the results of their investigations?
4. **Applying Concepts** Why might two scientists develop different hypotheses based on the same observations?

To try your hand at using the scientific method, turn to page 486 in the LabBook.

4 Close

Quiz

1. Why is a hypothesis called an educated guess? Why must it be testable? (A hypothesis is a solution based on previous knowledge, so it is an educated guess. No conclusion can be reached if the hypothesis cannot be tested.)
2. What options does a scientist have if an experiment does not support a hypothesis? (A scientist could repeat the investigation to check for errors, ask new questions and form a new hypothesis, or simply communicate the results of the experiment.)
3. What would happen if scientists kept their experimental results secret? (Efforts and mistakes would be duplicated; there would be less scientific progress.)

PG 486

Using the Scientific Method

Alternative Assessment

PORTFOLIO

Have students write a detective story in which the detective solves a mystery using the scientific method. Encourage them to make the story flow naturally and to avoid merely listing steps in the process. Have students exchange stories and identify each of the steps used.

Problem Solving Worksheet 1
"Kryptonite!"

Answers to Review

1. It is a series of steps that scientists use to answer questions and solve problems. Scientists follow the steps of the scientific method to gain insights into the problems they investigate. (Answers that include only the definition of the scientific method are acceptable.)
2. the observation that the bones did not match tailbones of any dinosaur that he knew of
3. because science depends on the sharing of information
4. The scientists may have acquired different knowledge and points of view in their backgrounds.

Section 2 Review—California Standards: PE/ATE 7, 7a, 7b, 7d, 7e

SECTION 3

Focus

Life in a Warmer World—An Earth Science Model

This section discusses the importance of models in science and defines physical, mathematical, and conceptual models. Students will explore how a mathematical model is used to predict global warming. Students also see how models may be a limited but important tool for prediction.

Bellringer

Ask students to answer the following questions:

- Why is an airplane flight simulator a kind of model?
- What are some advantages to training pilots in a flight simulator rather than in a real airplane?

1 Motivate

ACTIVITY

Modeling a Human Leg On a table, place two half-meter lengths of lightweight wood, a metal hinge, screws, a screwdriver, and several large rubber bands. Ask students to help you use these materials to make a model of the human leg and to show how it works. Pose questions such as the following:

- In what ways would your model be like an actual leg?
- In what ways would it differ?
- For what purpose might you use the model?

Sheltered English

Directed Reading Worksheet 1 Section 3

3

NEW TERMS
global warming
model
theory

OBJECTIVES

- Demonstrate how models are used in science.
- Compare mathematical models with physical models.

Life in a Warmer World—An Earth Science Model

There has been a lot of talk lately about changes in Earth's climate. Some people think the world is getting dangerously warm; others say it is only a natural cycle. But what would happen if Earth's average surface-air temperature rose only a few degrees? Look at **Figure 13;** the answers might surprise you.

A worldwide increase in temperature is called **global warming.** Is global warming really happening? What would cause global warming? To answer these questions, many scientists are studying the concept of global warming. One way they study global warming is by making a model of it.

Figure 13 *A rise in Earth's average surface-air temperature would affect the world in many ways.*

Rotting Remains The rate of decay of plant and animal remains would increase if the Earth's temperature rose. This in turn would increase the amount of carbon dioxide (CO_2) released into the atmosphere. Later in this section, you will see that this is an important concern.

Ice Is Nice Warmer temperatures would mean that much of the sea ice near the North and South Poles would melt. Also, areas of the Earth that now have permanently frozen ground, such as some subpolar and mountainous regions, would thaw.

Rain, Rain, Go Away Overall, there would be more rain. This is because warmer air causes more evaporation from oceans, lakes, and streams. More water vapor in the atmosphere would lead to more rain. Some areas of the world might benefit from the extra water, but other areas might experience flooding and lose fertile soil.

Water, Water Everywhere As temperatures increased, the volume of the oceans would expand, causing sea level to rise. Melting ice would also add water, making sea level rise even more. In states such as Florida and New York, millions of people live in cities near the coast at an elevation of 8 m above sea level or less. If sea level rose only 8 m, these cities would be underwater!

18

CONNECT TO LIFE SCIENCE

One possible indicator of global warming is shorter winters. Scientists study plants in the Northern Hemisphere to see when their springtime growing season begins. Today, trees and grasses begin to sprout new leaves a full week earlier than they did just 20 years ago.

Section 3—California Standards: PE/ATE 4, 4b, 7b, 7e

Types of Scientific Models

You are probably familiar with many types of models—models of ships, cars, planes, buildings, and other objects. **Models** are representations of objects or systems. Models are used to represent things that are too small to see, such as atoms, or too large to completely see, like the Earth or the solar system. Models can also be used to explain the past and present as well as to predict the future. Scientific models come in three major types.

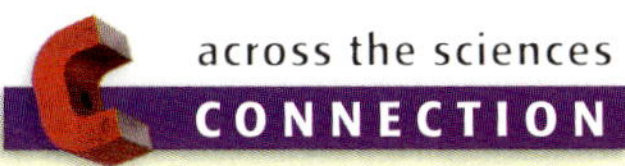

All the Earth's a magnet. Turn to page 30 to learn about Earth's magnetic field.

Physical Models Physical models are models that you can touch. Model airplanes, car kits, and dolls are all physical models. Physical models should look and act just like the real thing. For example, engineers put very accurate models of new airplanes in wind tunnels, as shown in **Figure 14,** to see how aerodynamic they are. It is safer and less expensive to discover problems with models than with real planes.

Figure 14 *Models of airplanes are tested in models of wind, as shown here by a prototype jet inside a wind tunnel.*

Mathematical Models Every day, people try to predict the weather. One way they do this is by making climate models, because weather patterns are part of the Earth's climate systems. Climate models, however, are not physical representations of climate. Instead, they are mathematical models. A mathematical model is made up of mathematical equations and data. Some mathematical models are so complex that only supercomputers can handle them. Climate models include information from meteorologists, oceanographers, and ecologists. These models are complicated, but then so is trying to predict the weather!

Conceptual Models The third type of model is a conceptual model, or system of ideas. These take the form of theories. A **theory** is a unifying explanation for a broad range of hypotheses and observations that have been supported by testing. Atomic theory and the big bang theory can be thought of as conceptual models. Conceptual models are composed of many hypotheses, each of which has found support through the scientific method.

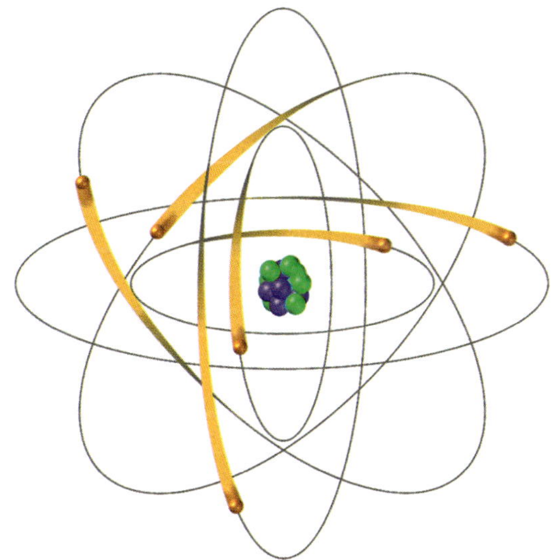

Figure 15 *Atoms are not really made up of tiny colored balls, but using a model like this helps scientists understand atoms.*

2 Teach

Activity

Display a variety of models of Earth, such as globes, political maps, satellite photos, and weather maps. Invite volunteers to describe each model, suggest uses for it, and compare and contrast it to another model. Sheltered English

Discussion

Use a model car and a map to discuss with students what a scale model is. A unit of measure in the model is equivalent to a larger or smaller unit of measure in the original. For example, in a model car, 1 cm might equal 15 cm on the actual vehicle. Point out the legend on the map, and ask students to explain how distance on the map relates to actual miles or kilometers.

MATH and MORE

Assign students to groups. Have each group select a large object to measure and record its dimensions. Have them plan a scale model of the object (suggest a one-tenth scale). Ask them to calculate the dimensions of their scale model and draw it. After the groups finish their drawings, discuss the methods they used to create their scale drawings. Have students devise strategies for creating more-accurate scale models, and have them work individually to create their own scale drawings.

Math Skills Worksheet 17 "Using Proportions and Cross-Multiplication"

Science Skills Worksheet 15 "Measuring"

Homework

Have students use the weather section of the newspaper to identify uses of physical, mathematical, and conceptual models. For example, a mathematical model may be used to predict how likely it is that it will rain on a certain day. A physical model, specifically a map, may be used to show the locations of pressure fronts or storms. A conceptual model may be used to explain long-term trends in the weather.

3 Extend

Cross-Disciplinary Focus

History From about A.D. 800 to 1250, Europe's climate was much milder than it is today. The milder climate could explain why Norse settlers migrated to Iceland, Greenland, and possibly even North America. Have students find out about the Norse expansion and what factors may have ended it.

Cooperative Learning

Ask students to create skits demonstrating the greenhouse effect, using the four stages in **Figure 16.** Students can choose to model the following:

- sunlight traveling to Earth
- heat radiating from Earth's surface
- greenhouse gases
- heat radiating back toward Earth

Sheltered English

Group Activity

Have students work with partners to create posters illustrating the factors that contribute to global warming. They will first need to research the effects of deforestation and air pollution on the carbon cycle. Stress that this visual aid will be a model that shows how the greenhouse effect works and how human activity contributes to it.

environmental science CONNECTION

The destruction of rain forests has been linked to increases in the greenhouse effect. Trees play a vital role in taking in carbon dioxide from the air, storing it, and releasing oxygen into the air. Without trees, more carbon dioxide would remain in the air, which would increase the greenhouse effect and possibly contribute to global warming.

The Greenhouse Effect—A Piece of the Global-Warming Model

All models have pieces. A model ship, for example, may contain hundreds of pieces that are glued together. Mathematical models also contain pieces. The pieces are numbers that represent pieces of information that describe real events. Thousands of these pieces may be used in a single model. The global-warming model is a mathematical model that depends on such information. One of the pieces used in the global-warming climate model is the *greenhouse effect.*

A greenhouse is a building made mostly of glass in which plants are grown. If you have been in a greenhouse, you know that it is usually warmer inside than outside. This is because sunlight not only heats the greenhouse directly after passing through the glass, but also reflects off the Earth's surface, producing heat that is trapped inside the greenhouse. The greenhouse effect, shown in **Figure 16,** works a lot like a greenhouse made of glass.

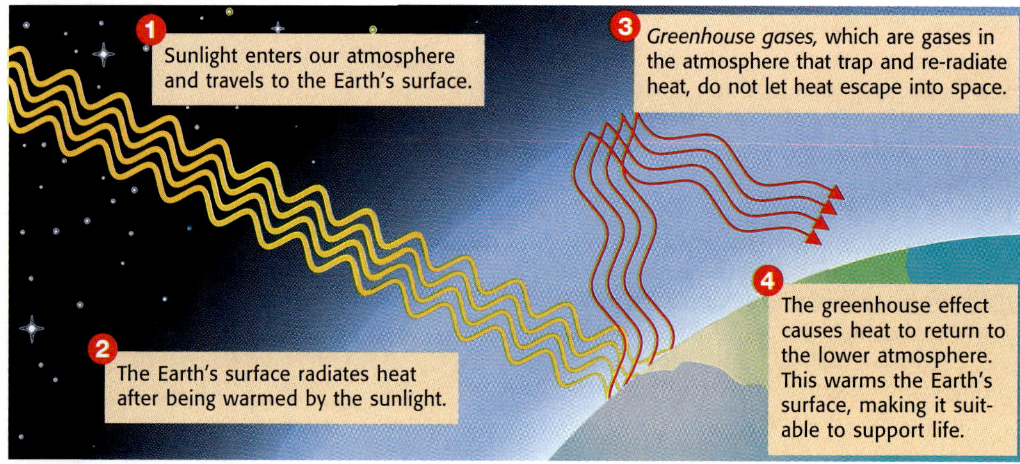

Figure 16 *The more greenhouse gases there are in the atmosphere, the greater the greenhouse effect is. When the amount of greenhouse gases increases, so does the temperature on Earth.*

Testing the Global-Warming Model

Models are used to try to explain the present. But how do we know if models are accurate? Physical, mathematical, and conceptual models can be tested. For instance, we can compare the model of a car with the real car. Similarly, we can compare our climate model's prediction of Earth's climate with Earth's actual climate. If the model can accurately explain the present, then we can be more confident that the model will be able to accurately predict the future.

20

Scientists at Odds

Some scientists fear that human actions, such as deforestation and the burning of fossil fuels, are causing Earth's temperatures to rise at an abnormally fast rate. Other scientists believe that Earth is simply in a normal temperature fluctuation (from colder to warmer temperatures) that lasts thousands of years.

Scientists have estimated the amount of carbon dioxide that has been added to the atmosphere over the last 100 years. The model should therefore be able to predict how much warmer the atmosphere is today than it was 100 years ago. Most climate models tell us that overall global warming due to increased greenhouse gases during the last 100 years should be between 0.5°C and 1.5°C. Now comes the test: How much global warming has actually taken place? The answer is 0.5°C. So far so good!

Using the Global Warming Model

Models are used to predict the future. Models are good for asking, "What if?"

These are the kinds of questions that many nations are asking as they enter the new millennium. The global-warming climate model can give them answers, but will these answers be accurate? The more complicated models are, the more careful scientists must be when using them to make predictions. Climate models are extremely complicated, so scientists often use words like *possible* and *probable* when making climate predictions. The only certain test of these models is the test of time.

REVIEW

1. How might a scientist use a model to test a new airplane design?
2. How are astronomers limited when they design models of the universe?
3. **Analyzing Relationships** Name one advantage of physical models and one advantage of mathematical models.

Explore

A scientist living at a research station in Antarctica has sent her daily activity log for the winter to her university. Every day for several months she observed that the sun was not visible in the sky.

1. Use a globe, a model of Earth, to demonstrate why the South Pole has such long winter nights.
2. While the South Pole was having long winter nights, what was going on at the North Pole?
3. Explain why a globe works as a model.

21

Answers to Review

1. Scientists could make a scale model of the proposed airplane and test it in a wind tunnel.
2. They cannot base everything in their model on what they can observe. The universe extends far beyond the limits of human perception.
3. Answers will vary. Physical models can often be more easily understood because they can be seen and touched. Mathematical models often better represent complex, large-scale phenomena.

4 Close

Quiz

1. What do scientists use models for? (to test hypotheses, explain events or behaviors, or predict future events or conditions)
2. How does a model help scientists predict that Earth's climate will continue to get warmer? (They measure changes in climate and other factors, such as global temperatures and CO_2 levels. Over time, they integrate the information into their model, see how the model compares with reality, and then make their predictions.)

Alternative Assessment

Making Models Have students construct a physical model. It could be a model of a room, a living thing, or a phenomenon, such as wave motion. Students should explain in writing what the model is and describe how it works and how it was constructed. They should also describe how the model can be used and what its limits are.

Answers to Explore

1. The South Pole has long winter nights because it faces away from the sun during winter.
2. The North Pole was having longer days. The North Pole faces the sun when the South Pole faces away from the sun.
3. A globe is a miniature version of the Earth that serves as a physical model.

SECTION 4

Focus

Measurement and Safety

This section introduces the International System of Units (SI), a unified global measurement system. Students explore the units and methods used to measure length, volume, mass, and temperature. Students also learn about lab safety and safety symbols and their meanings.

Bellringer

Ask students the following questions:

- What kinds of things would be best measured in millimeters? in meters? in kilometers?
- What kinds of things would be best measured in liters? in milliliters?
- What kinds of things would be best measured in milligrams? in grams? in kilograms?

Ask students to write their responses in their ScienceLog. Discuss their answers.

1 Motivate

DISCUSSION

Tell students that the SI system is based on the decimal system, just like our monetary system. Ask students the following questions:

How many pennies are in a dime? How many dimes are in a dollar? How many pennies are in 10 dollars?

Explain to students that the SI system uses different prefixes to move to larger or smaller units. Have students look at **Figure 17** and identify the prefixes and what they stand for.

4

Measurement and Safety

NEW TERMS

meter
volume
mass
temperature

OBJECTIVES

- Explain the importance of the International System of Units.
- Determine appropriate units to use for particular measurements.
- Identify lab safety symbols and determine what they mean.

Hundreds of years ago, different countries used different systems of measurement. These systems were developed from local customs and were often not interchangeable. At one time in England, the standard for an inch was three grains of barley placed end to end. Other standardized units of the modern English system, which is used in the United States, were once based on parts of the body, such as the foot. Such units were not very accurate because they were based on objects that varied in size.

Eventually people recognized that there was a need for a global measurement system that was simple and accurate. In the late 1700s, the French Academy of Sciences set out to develop that system. Over the next 200 years, the metric system, now called the International System of Units (SI), was refined.

Using the Same System

Today all scientists and almost all countries use the International System of Units. One advantage of using SI measurements is that it helps all scientists to share and compare their observations and results. Another advantage of SI is that all units are based on the number 10, which is a number that is easy to use in calculations. The table in **Figure 17** contains the commonly used SI units for length, volume, mass, and temperature.

Figure 17 *Prefixes are used with SI units to convert them to larger or smaller units. For example,* kilo *indicates 1,000 times, and* milli *indicates 1/1,000 times. The prefix used depends on the size of the object being measured.*

Common SI Units		
Length	**meter (m)**	
	kilometer (km)	1 km = 1,000 m
	decimeter (dm)	1 dm = 0.1 m
	centimeter (cm)	1 cm = 0.01 m
	millimeter (mm)	1 mm = 0.001 m
	micrometer (µm)	1 µm = 0.000001 m
	nanometer (nm)	1 nm = 0.000000001 m
Volume	**cubic meter (m^3)**	
	cubic centimeter (cm^3)	1 cm^3 = 0.000001 m^3
	liter (L)	1 L = 1 dm^3 = 0.001 m^3
	milliliter (mL)	1 mL = 0.001 L = 1 cm^3
Mass	**kilogram (kg)**	
	gram (g)	1 g = 0.001 kg
	milligram (mg)	1 mg = 0.000001 kg
Temperature	**Kelvin (K)**	
	Celsius (°C)	0°C = 273 K
		100°C = 373 K

Directed Reading Worksheet 1 Section 4

Math Skills Worksheet 27 "What Is SI?"

IS THAT A FACT!

If Earth were the size of a golf ball, the sun would be as large as a 3 m ball and would be located a football field's distance from Earth.

Length How thick is the ice sheet in **Figure 18**? To describe this length, an Earth scientist would probably use meters (m). A **meter** is the basic unit of length in the SI system. A meter is divided or multiplied by powers of 10 to produce the other SI units of length. If you divide 1 m into 100 parts, each part equals 1 cm. In other words, 1 cm is one-hundredth of a meter. If you divide 1 m into 1,000 parts, each part equals 1 mm. This means that 1 mm is one-thousandth of a meter. Although that seems pretty small, some objects are so tiny that even smaller units must be used. To describe the length of microscopic objects, micrometers (µm) or nanometers (nm) are used. Going the other way, 1,000 m is equal to one kilometer. **Figure 19** shows how the units of length relate to various objects.

Figure 18 *This scientist is measuring the thickness of an ice sheet. Which unit of length would best describe this length?*

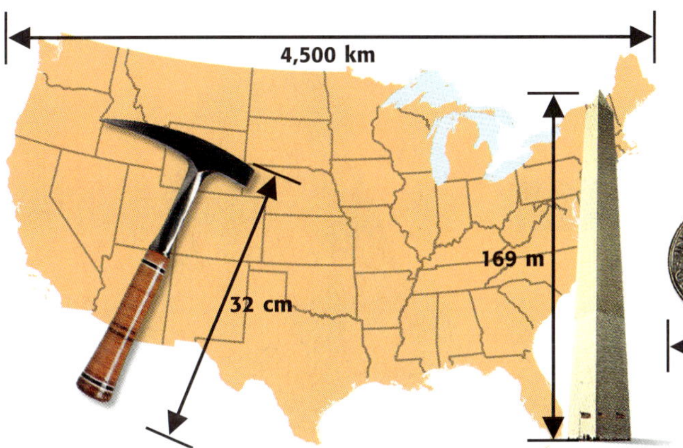

Figure 19 *The size of the object being measured determines which SI unit of length is used.*

Volume Imagine that you're a scientist who needs to move some fossils to a museum. How many fossils will fit into a crate? That depends on the volume of the crate and the volume of each fossil. **Volume** is the amount of space that something occupies, or, as in the case of the crate, the amount of space that something contains.

The volume of a liquid is often given in liters (L). Liters are based on the meter. A cubic meter (m^3) is equal to 1,000 L. In other words, 1,000 L of liquid will fit into a box 1 m on each side. You're probably more familiar with a 2 L soda bottle. Just like the meter, the liter can be divided into smaller units. A milliliter (mL) is one-thousandth of a liter and is equal to one cubic centimeter (1 cm^3). A microliter (µL) is one-millionth of a liter. Graduated cylinders are used to measure the volume of liquids.

Explore

Measure the width of your desk, but do not use a ruler or a tape measure. Pick an object to use as your unit of measurement. It could be a pencil, your hand, or anything else. Find how many units wide your desk is, and compare your measurement with those of your classmates. In your ScienceLog, explain why it is important to use standard units of measurement.

23

Science Bloopers

The meter was originally defined as one ten-millionth of the distance along the meridian running from the North Pole to the equator through Dunkirk, France, and Barcelona, Spain. French surveyors determined this length in 1798 after working for 6 years. Almost 100 years later, it was discovered that the surveyors had made an error of about 3.2 km in their measurement. Today, a meter is defined as the distance light travels in 1/299,792,458 of a second in a vacuum.

2 Teach

Multicultural CONNECTION

Before electricity and batteries, a variety of mechanical means were used to measure time. By 2000 B.C., the Egyptians had devised shadow clocks, or sundials, to measure time. By 1400 B.C., Egyptians were using water clocks, but they were imprecise. Around 300 B.C., the Greek inventor Ctesibius, of Alexandria, devised a much more precise water clock called a clepsydra. It measured a steady drip of water from a vessel that drove a mechanical device, indicating the hour. The water clock measured time in Egyptian hours, which changed in length according to the season. Encourage students to draw their own design for a clock that measures time in an uncommon way.

GUIDED PRACTICE

Have students make 3 × 5 in. cards with SI prefixes on one side and the values they designate on the other (for example, *deci-* = $\frac{1}{10}$, *kilo-* = 1,000). Students should use their cards to practice and build their familiarity with the prefixes and their values. Then have students arrange the following measurements in sequence from the shortest to the longest:

1. 3,000 mm, 0.5 km, 12 m, 1,000,000 nm, 15,000 cm
2. 8,500 cm, 250,000 mm, 0.25 km, 18 m

You may wish to provide similar practice with mass and volume quantities. Sheltered English

Teaching Transparency 86
"Common SI Units"

3 Extend

MATH and MORE

Give students the following dimensions for the crate in **Figure 20:**

volume: 40,392 cm^3

length: 51 cm

width: 33 cm

Test their comprehension of volume by asking them to calculate the height.

$\frac{40{,}392 \text{ cm}^3}{(51 \text{ cm} \times 33 \text{ cm})} = 24 \text{ cm}$

CONNECT TO PHYSICAL SCIENCE

Students often confuse mass and weight. Point out to students that mass is a measure of the amount of matter that makes up an object. Weight is expressed in newtons and measures the gravitational force between objects. If a given object has not lost or gained matter, its mass will be the same anywhere in the universe. The weight of an object, however, varies with gravity. Use the Teaching Transparency below to discuss this distinction with students.

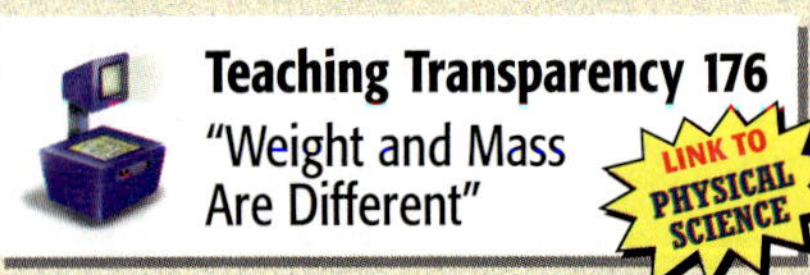

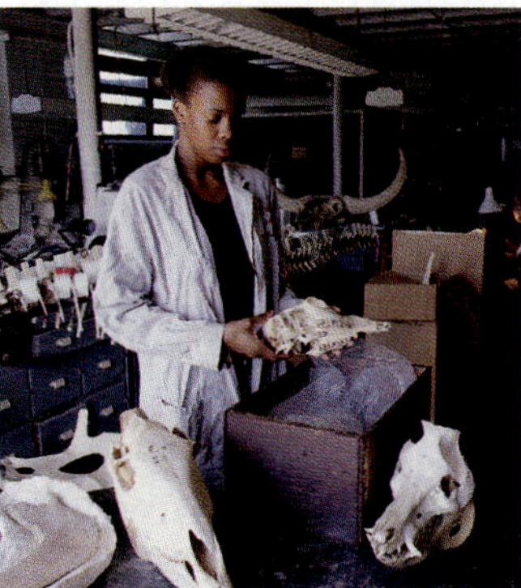

Figure 20 *The volume of the crate chosen by this scientist is just right for storing the fossil she is holding.*

The volume of a large solid object is given in cubic meters (m^3). The volumes of smaller objects, such as the crate in **Figure 20,** can be given in cubic centimeters (cm^3) or cubic millimeters (mm^3). To calculate the volume of a box-shaped object, multiply the object's length by its width by its height.

Objects like fossils and rocks have irregular shapes. If you multiplied only their length, width, and height, you would not get a very accurate measure of their volume. One way to determine the volume of an irregularly shaped object is to measure how much liquid the object displaces. The student in **Figure 21** is measuring the volume of a rock by placing it in a graduated cylinder that contains a known quantity of water. The rock causes the level of the water to rise. The student can find the volume of the rock by subtracting the volume of the water alone from the volume of the water and the rock.

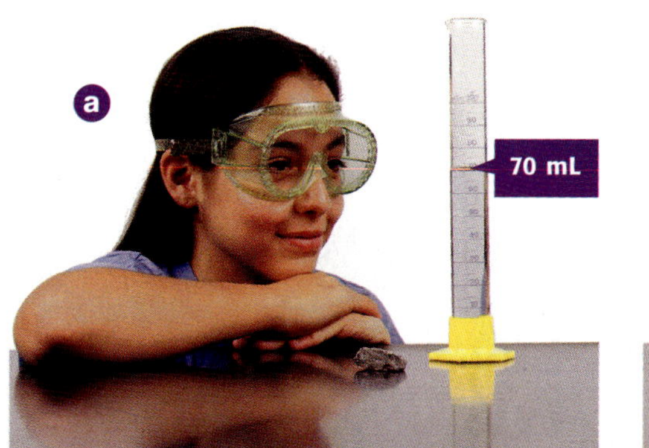

Figure 21 *This graduated cylinder contains 70 mL of water. After the rock was added, the water level moved to 80 mL. Because the rock displaced 10 mL of water, and because 1 mL = 1 cm^3, the volume of the rock is 10 cm^3.*

Mass How large of a boulder can a rushing stream move? That depends on the energy of the stream and the mass of the boulder. **Mass** is the amount of matter that something is made of. The kilogram (kg) is the basic unit for mass and is used to describe the mass of things like boulders. Many common objects are not so large, however. Grams (one-thousandth of a kilogram) are used to describe the mass of smaller objects. A medium-sized apple, for example, has a mass of about 100 g. The mass of very large objects is given in metric tons. A metric ton equals 1,000 kg.

24

Homework

Have students choose five photographs from magazines and label each with appropriate safety cautions. Students should use the safety symbols shown in this section. Ask students to explain to the class how each photo depicts a safety risk.

Sheltered English

SCIENCE HUMOR

Q: What happened when the inchworm went metric?

A: It became a centipede!

Temperature How hot is a lava flow? To answer this question, an Earth scientist would need to measure the temperature of the lava. **Temperature** is a measure of how hot (or cold) something is. You are probably used to describing temperature with degrees Fahrenheit (°F). Scientists use degrees Celsius (°C) and kelvins, which is the SI unit for temperature. The thermometer at right shows the relationship between °F and °C, the unit you will most often see in this book.

°F °C
212°F Water boils — 100°C Water boils
98.6°F Normal body temperature — 37°C Normal body temperature
32°F Water freezes — 0°C Water freezes

Safety Rules!

Earth science is exciting and fun, but it can also be dangerous. So don't take any chances! Always follow your teacher's instructions, and don't take short-cuts—even when you think there is little or no danger.

Before starting any science investigation, get your teacher's permission and read the lab procedures carefully. Pay particular attention to safety information and caution statements. The table below shows the safety symbols used in this book. Get to know these symbols and what they mean. Do this by reading the safety information starting on page 482. **This is important!** If you are still unsure about what a safety symbol means, ask your teacher.

Stay on the safe side by reading the safety information on page 482. **This is a must before doing any science activity!**

Safety Symbols		
Eye protection	Clothing protection	Hand safety
Heating safety	Electric safety	Sharp object
Chemical safety	Animal safety	Plant safety

REVIEW

1. What are two benefits of using the International System of Units?
2. Which SI unit best describes the volume of gasoline in a car?
3. **Doing Calculations** What is the minimum length and width (in meters) of a box that can contain an object 56 cm wide and 843 mm long?

25

4 Close

PG 482

Safety First!

Quiz

1. What is the basic SI unit for length? for mass? (meters; kilograms)
2. What are you determining when you calculate volume? (the amount of space something occupies or contains)
3. What are the first two steps to take before beginning any science investigation? (Get your teacher's permission; read the lab procedures carefully, paying particular attention to safety information and caution statements.)

Alternative Assessment

Concept Mapping Have students make a concept map of the common SI units shown in **Figure 17**.

Science Skills Worksheet 9 "Safety Rules!"

Answers to Review

1. It helps all scientists to share and compare observations and results, and all units are based on the number 10, which is a number that is easy to use in calculations.
2. liters or decimeters
3. length = 0.843 m, width = 0.56 m

Chapter Highlights

VOCABULARY DEFINITIONS

SECTION 1

geology the study of the solid Earth

oceanography the study of the ocean

meteorology the study of the entire atmosphere

astronomy the study of all physical objects beyond Earth

ecosystem a community of organisms and their nonliving environment

SECTION 2

scientific method a series of steps that scientists use to answer questions and solve problems

observation any use of the senses to gather information

hypothesis a possible explanation or answer to a question

Science Skills Worksheet 7 "Improving Your Study Habits"

Chapter Highlights

SECTION 1

Vocabulary

geology *(p. 6)*
oceanography *(p. 7)*
meteorology *(p. 8)*
astronomy *(p. 9)*
ecosystem *(p. 10)*

Section Notes

- Earth science can be divided into three general categories: geology, oceanography, and meteorology.
- Astronomy is the study of physical things beyond planet Earth.
- Careers in Earth science often require knowledge of more than one science.

SECTION 2

Vocabulary

scientific method *(p. 13)*
observation *(p. 14)*
hypothesis *(p. 14)*

Section Notes

- The scientific method is essential for proper scientific investigation.
- Different scientists may use the scientific method differently.
- The discovery of *Seismosaurus hallorum* as a new kind of dinosaur was made using the scientific method.
- When scientists finish investigations, it is important that they communicate the results to other scientists.

Labs

Using the Scientific Method *(p. 486)*

Skills Check

Math Concepts

CONVERTING SI UNITS Take another look at the SI chart on page 22. The SI units for most categories of measurement, such as length and mass, are all expressed in terms of a single unit. For example, the unit *centimeter* is expressed in terms of the unit *meter.* To write 50 cm in terms of meters, divide 50 by 100 (there are 100 cm in 1 m).

$$50\ \cancel{\text{cm}} \times \frac{1\ \text{m}}{100\ \cancel{\text{cm}}} = 0.5\ \text{m}$$

Visual Understanding

WHICH PATH SHOULD YOU FOLLOW? Review the flowchart on page 13. The scientific method can follow many paths. For example, a scientist may make observations before asking a question or after forming a hypothesis.

26

Lab and Activity Highlights

Using the Scientific Method PG 486

Datasheets for LabBook (blackline masters for this lab)

SECTION 3

Vocabulary

global warming *(p. 18)*
model *(p. 19)*
theory *(p. 19)*

Section Notes

- Models are used in science to represent physical things and systems.
- Typically, physical models represent objects, and mathematical models represent systems.
- Climate models are very complicated mathematical models.
- The global-warming model is a mathematical climate model.
- The greenhouse effect is an important part of the global-warming model.
- Scientists use models to explain the past and present as well as to predict the future.
- The only way to measure the accuracy of a climate model is to compare predictions based on the model with what actually occurs.

SECTION 4

Vocabulary

meter *(p. 23)*
volume *(p. 23)*
mass *(p. 24)*
temperature *(p. 25)*

Section Notes

- The International System of Units (SI) helps all scientists share and compare their work.
- The basic SI units of measurement for length, volume, and mass are the meter, cubic meter, and kilogram, respectively.
- To describe temperature, scientists use degrees Celsius (°C) and kelvins (K), which is the SI unit for temperature.

internet**connect**

GO TO: go.hrw.com

Visit the **HRW** Web site for a variety of learning tools related to this chapter. Just type in the keyword:

KEYWORD: HSTWES

GO TO: www.scilinks.org

Visit the **National Science Teachers Association** on-line Web site for Internet resources related to this chapter. Just type in the ***sci*LINKS** number for more information about the topic:

TOPIC	*sci*LINKS NUMBER
Branches of Earth Science	HSTE005
Careers in Earth Science	HSTE010
Using Models in Earth Science	HSTE015
Systems of Measurement	HSTE020

27

VOCABULARY DEFINITIONS, *continued*

SECTION 3

global warming a rise in average global temperatures

model a representation of an object or system

theory a unifying explanation for a broad range of hypotheses and observations that have been supported by testing

SECTION 4

meter the basic unit of length in the SI system

volume the amount of space that something occupies or the amount of space that something contains

mass the amount of matter that something is made of; its value does not change with the object's location

temperature a measure of how hot (or cold) something is

Vocabulary Review Worksheet 1

Blackline masters of these Chapter Highlights can be found in the **Study Guide.**

Lab and Activity Highlights

LabBank

Whiz-Bang Demonstrations, Tubby Terra, Demo 16

Long-Term Projects & Research Ideas, Project 29

Chapter Review Answers

Using Vocabulary

1. The scientific method involves forming a hypothesis that must be tested.
2. Models are used in meteorology to predict weather.
3. Geology can be part of studying an ecosystem.
4. Part of oceanography involves studying global warming because global warming may cause a rise in sea level.

Understanding Concepts

Multiple Choice

5. b
6. a
7. c
8. a
9. a
10. d
11. d
12. d
13. d

Short Answer

14. He compared the bones he found with similar bones from known dinosaurs. He could not find a match.
15. Answers may vary. Scientists use models to represent things that are too small or too large to see, to test designs without using the real thing, to test hypotheses, to explain the past, and to predict the future.
16. Sunlight not only heats the greenhouse directly after passing through the glass but also reflects off the Earth's surface, producing heat that is trapped inside the greenhouse.

Chapter Review

USING VOCABULARY

Use the following terms in a sentence to show that you know what they mean:

1. hypothesis, scientific method
2. meteorology, model
3. geology, ecosystem
4. global warming, oceanography

UNDERSTANDING CONCEPTS

Multiple Choice

5. Earth science can be divided into three general categories: meteorology, oceanography, and
   a. geography.
   b. geology.
   c. geochemistry.
   d. ecology.

6. The science that deals with fossils is
   a. paleontology.
   b. ecology.
   c. seismology.
   d. volcanology.

7. Meteorology is the study of
   a. meteors.
   b. meteorites.
   c. the atmosphere.
   d. maps.

8. Gillette's hypothesis was
   a. supported by his results.
   b. not supported by his results.
   c. based only on observations.
   d. based only on what he already knew.

9. Two of the most common greenhouse gases are water vapor (H_2O) and
   a. carbon dioxide (CO_2).
   b. krypton (Kr).
   c. radon (Rn).
   d. neon (Ne).

10. Over the past 100 years, the average temperature of Earth's atmosphere has risen about
   a. 10°C.
   b. 5°C.
   c. 1°C.
   d. 0.5°C.

11. The greenhouse effect is used to explain
   a. volcanoes.
   b. earthquakes.
   c. fossilization.
   d. global warming.

12. Global warming would cause
   a. some polar ice to melt.
   b. more rain.
   c. overall sea level to drop.
   d. Two of the above

13. An ecosystem can include
   a. plants and animals.
   b. weather and climate.
   c. humans.
   d. All of the above

Short Answer

14. How did Gillette determine that the dinosaur he found was new to science?
15. How and why do scientists use models?
16. Why is the temperature inside a greenhouse usually warmer than the temperature outside?

Chapter 1 Review—California Standards: PE/ATE Q1–4: 7; Q5–17: 5, 7

Concept Mapping

17. Use the following terms to create a concept map: Earth science, model, the scientific method, geology, hypothesis, meteorology, oceanography, observation, International System of Units.

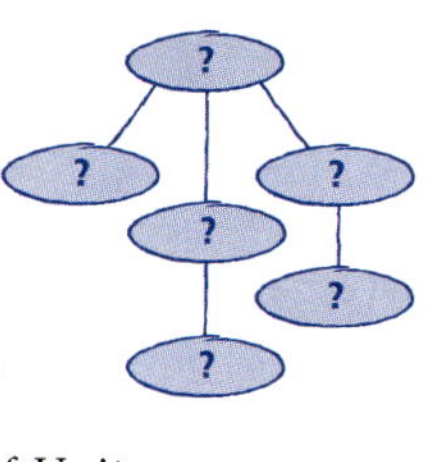

CRITICAL THINKING AND PROBLEM SOLVING

Write one or two sentences to answer the following questions:

18. A rock that contains fossil seashells might be studied by scientists in at least two branches of Earth science. Name those branches. Why did you choose those two?

19. Why might two scientists working on the same problem draw different conclusions?

20. The scientific method often begins with observation. How does observation limit what scientists can study?

21. Why are scientists so careful about making predictions from certain models, such as climate models?

MATH IN SCIENCE

22. Scientists often use scientific laws when constructing models. According to Boyle's law, for example, if you increase the pressure outside a balloon, the balloon will get smaller. This law is expressed as the following formula:

$$P_1 \times V_1 = P_2 \times V_2$$

If the pressure on a balloon (P_1) is one atmosphere (1 atm) and the volume of air in the balloon (V_1) is one liter (1 L), what will the volume be (in liters) if the pressure is increased to 3 atm?

INTERPRETING GRAPHICS

Examine the graph below, and answer the questions that follow.

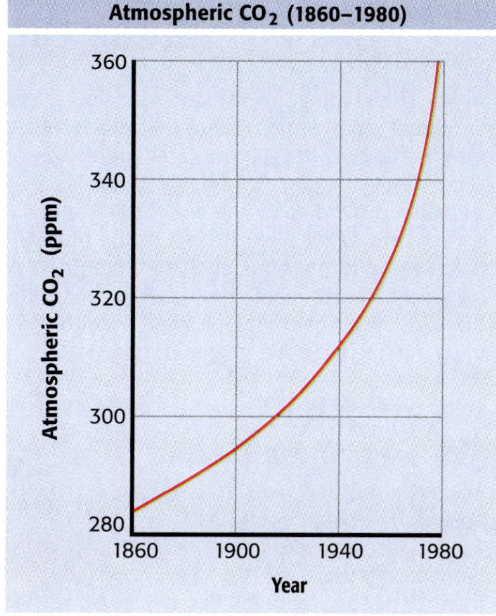

23. Has the amount of CO_2 in the atmosphere increased or decreased since 1860?

24. The line on the graph is curved. What does this mean?

25. Was the rate of change in the level of CO_2 between 1940 and 1960 higher or lower than it was between 1880 and 1900? How can you tell?

NOW What Do You Think?

Take a minute to review your answers to the ScienceLog questions on page 5. Have your answers changed? If necessary, revise your answers based on what you have learned since you began this chapter.

29

Concept Mapping

17. An answer to this exercise can be found at the end of this book.

Critical Thinking and Problem Solving

18. Geology and oceanography; it relates to geology because it is a rock and it contains fossils. It relates to oceanography because it is a rock formed in the ocean and it contains fossils of marine animals.
19. They may make different observations, form different hypotheses, test the same hypothesis differently, or analyze the results of their tests differently.
20. Observation limits what scientists can study because hypotheses can be supported only by observable phenomena.
21. They are careful because models are not the real thing—they only represent the real thing. For a model to be reliable, it must stand the test of time and repeated testing.

Math in Science

22. $\frac{1}{3}$ L

Interpreting Graphics

23. increased
24. The rate at which the amount of CO_2 in the atmosphere increases changes over time.
25. Higher; the graph's line curves more steeply between 1940 and 1960.

NOW What Do You Think?

1. There are many different kinds of Earth scientists. Although the text lists only three main branches of Earth science, Earth scientists specialize and study within many areas of science.
2. a series of steps that scientists use to answer questions and solve problems
3. A physical model is a physical representation of an object or system, while a mathematical model is made of formulas, numbers, and variables that represent an object or system.

Concept Mapping Transparency 1

Blackline masters of this Chapter Review can be found in the **Study Guide.**

Across the Sciences
All the Earth's a Magnet

Background

Geologists have known for a long time that a magnetic field surrounds the planet. Scientists suspected that the solid inner core had something to do with creating the magnetic field, but until recently they could only guess about the connection: the Earth is a huge electromagnet because the core rotates at a different speed than the mantle. The core rotates faster for the following reasons:

- The solid inner core, which is mostly iron, is surrounded by a liquid outer core, which means that it is possible for the inner core to rotate inside the outer core (not much friction exists between a solid and a liquid).
- Iron in the inner core is a conducting material, so it transmits billions of amps of electrical energy. This drives the core to rotate slightly faster than the mantle.

ACROSS THE SCIENCES

EARTH SCIENCE • LIFE SCIENCE

All the Earth's a Magnet

As you are reading this, you are spinning around at 1,670 km/h. Sound impossible? It's true. That's how fast Earth rotates on its axis. Deep inside the planet, Earth's core is also spinning. But did you know that Earth's inner core rotates *faster* than the rest of the planet? If you stood in the same spot on the equator for a year, Earth's inner core would travel more than 20 km farther than you would! But the inner core is 5,150 km below Earth's surface. What makes scientists think they know what's going on down there?

The Core of the Matter

Scientists start looking for answers by asking questions. For instance, scientists have wondered if there is some relationship between Earth's core and Earth's magnetic field. To build their hypothesis, scientists started with what they knew: Earth has a dense, solid inner core and a molten outer core. They then created a computer model to simulate how Earth's magnetic field is generated. The model predicted that Earth's inner core spins in the same direction as the rest of the Earth but slightly faster than the surface. If that theory is correct, it might explain how Earth's magnetic field is generated. But how could the researchers test the theory?

Because scientists couldn't drill down to the core, they had to get their information indirectly. They decided to track seismic waves created by earthquakes.

Catch the Waves

Scientists analyzed 30 years' worth of earthquake seismic data. They knew that seismic waves traveling through the inner core along a north-south path travel faster than waves passing through it along an east-west line. Scientists searched seismic data records to see if the orientation of the "fast path" for seismic waves changed over time. They found that in the last 30 years, the direction of the "fast path" for seismic waves had indeed shifted. This is strong evidence that Earth's core does travel faster than the surface, and it strengthens the theory that the spinning core creates Earth's magnetic field.

Now That We Know . . .

This discovery will lead to more research into how Earth's magnetic field changes and how the north and south poles "wander" and even occasionally reverse. The new information may also lead to a better understanding of the flow of planetary heat that moves the tectonic plates on Earth's surface.

Write About It

▶ Imagine what would happen if the magnetic poles were suddenly reversed or if magnetism disappeared completely. How would you be affected personally? How would it affect our civilization? Write a funny story describing a world with no magnetism.

30

Answers to Write About It

Stories will vary but could include the following information:

The Earth's magnetic field helps create the aurora borealis, or northern lights; makes compasses point north; and helps migratory animals keep their bearings. It also shields us from harmful solar radiation. Without a magnetic field, Earth probably could not support life as we know it.

CAREERS

GEOPHYSICIST

Bob Grimm is looking for water on Mars. Grimm is a geophysicist, a scientist who uses the science of physics to study Earth, its structure, and its atmosphere. Some geophysicists try to answer questions about the origin and history of Earth, while others use their knowledge of Earth to answer questions about other planets. One of those questions is whether there is water on Mars.

It isn't likely that humans will be living on Mars anytime soon, so why try to find water there? Bob Grimm explains the importance of his work this way: "It is only by questioning that we will learn, and I feel that by asking questions about outer space we will learn more about our own world. The information we obtain can give us valuable clues to the way our own planet works."

Probing Mars

Grimm isn't going to Mars in person. Instead, he and others are developing instruments to send to Mars to try to locate water beneath that planet's surface. These instruments work by reading patterns of electromagnetic waves reflected by formations beneath the surface. When electromagnetic waves hit something under the surface that conducts electricity, the pattern of the waves changes. By looking at the patterns in the waves as they are reflected back to the equipment, Grimm and others will be able to "see" what lies beneath Mars's surface. If there is underground water on Mars, it should show up as a change in the wave patterns.

Meanwhile, Back on Earth

The same procedures Grimm is using to find water on Mars can be used to locate objects, such as land mines, buried beneath the ground here on Earth. Standard metal detectors are useful, but they can't tell the difference between a mine and a piece of scrap metal. Along with electromagnetic pulses, Grimm uses imaging technologies similar to optical scanners to create images of objects buried beneath the ground. Once their location is pinpointed, mines can be safely removed or detonated.

An Interesting Career

Being a geophysicist has been rewarding for Grimm. "The sense of exploration really appeals to me," he explains. "It's like a hunt—I try to figure something out to bring some relationships together, and soon I have a story to tell!"

Think It Over

▶ Think of ways to locate objects buried more than 2 m below the surface. Could you use sound, light, X rays, or something else? What problems would you have to solve to make a useful detector to send to Mars?

▲ *The Surface of Mars*

CAREERS

Geophysicist–Bob Grimm

Background

Geophysics involves seismology, meteorology, and hydrology. Planetary geophysicists study many topics, from the shape of a planet's surface to the processes at work deep in its interior. They also study a planet's temperature variations, climatic patterns, volcanic activity, gravitational field, and magnetic field.

Sample Answer to Think It Over

Answers will vary. Students should discuss how wave energy can travel through a medium without disturbing it. A useful detector for the Martian surface would have to be lightweight and be able to withstand very cold temperatures and navigate on rugged terrain.

Chapter Organizer

CHAPTER ORGANIZATION	TIME MINUTES	OBJECTIVES	LABS, INVESTIGATIONS, AND DEMONSTRATIONS
Chapter Opener pp. 32–33	45	California Standards: PE/ATE 7f	**Investigate!** Follow the Yellow Brick Road, p. 33
Section 1 You Are Here	90	▶ Describe directions on a globe. ▶ Explain how a magnetic compass can be used to find directions on the Earth. ▶ Distinguish between true north and magnetic north. ▶ Distinguish between lines of latitude and lines of longitude on a globe or map. ▶ Explain how latitude and longitude can be used to locate places on Earth. PE/ATE 7, 7b, 7f; LabBook 7, 7b, 7e, 7f	**QuickLab,** Finding Directions with a Compass, p. 36 **Skill Builder,** Round or Flat? p. 488 **Datasheets for LabBook,** Round or Flat? Datasheet 2 **Design Your Own,** Orient Yourself! p. 490 **Datasheets for LabBook,** Orient Yourself! Datasheet 3
Section 2 Mapping the Earth's Surface	90	▶ Compare a map with a globe. ▶ Describe the three types of map projections. ▶ Describe recent technological advances that have helped the science of mapmaking progress. ▶ List the parts of a map. PE/ATE 7f	
Section 3 Topographic Maps	135	▶ Describe how contour lines show elevation and landforms on a map. ▶ List the rules of contour lines. ▶ Interpret a topographic map. PE/ATE 7f; LabBook 7, 7b, 7f	**Skill Builder,** Topographic Tuber, p. 492 **Datasheets for LabBook,** Topographic Tuber, Datasheet 4 **Inquiry Labs,** Looking for Buried Treasure, Lab 9 **Long-Term Projects & Research Ideas,** Project 30

See page **T20** *for a complete correlation of this book with the*

CALIFORNIA SCIENCE CONTENT STANDARDS.

Correlations are also provided at point of use throughout this ATE.

TECHNOLOGY RESOURCES

Guided Reading Audio CD
English or Spanish, Chapter 2

Classroom Management CD-ROM

Science Discovery Videodiscs
Image and Activity Bank with Lesson Plans: Remote Sensing

CNN **Multicultural Connections,** Mapping Asian Temples from Space, Segment 2

Test Generator CD-ROM

Chapter 2 • Maps as Models of the Earth

CLASSROOM WORKSHEETS, TRANSPARENCIES, AND RESOURCES	SCIENCE INTEGRATION AND CONNECTIONS	REVIEW AND ASSESSMENT
Directed Reading Worksheet 2 **Science Puzzlers, Twisters & Teasers,** Worksheet 2	**Cross-Disciplinary Focus,** p. 33 in ATE	
Transparency 87, Finding Direction on Earth **Directed Reading Worksheet 2,** Section 1 **Transparency 88,** Lines of Latitude **Transparency 88,** Lines of Longitude **Reinforcement Worksheet 2,** Where on Earth?	**Multicultural Connection,** p. 34 in ATE **Connect to Life Science,** p. 35 in ATE **Multicultural Connection,** p. 37 in ATE **Astronomy Connection,** p. 37	**Self-Check,** p. 36 **Homework,** p. 38 in ATE **Review,** p. 39 **Quiz,** p. 39 in ATE **Alternative Assessment,** p. 39 in ATE
Directed Reading Worksheet 2, Section 2 **Transparency 89,** Mercator Projection **Transparency 89,** Conic Projection **Transparency 89,** Azimuthal Projection **Transparency 6,** The Electromagnetic Spectrum **Math Skills for Science Worksheet 17,** Using Proportions and Cross-Multiplication **Critical Thinking Worksheet 2,** Shaping the World	**Cross-Disciplinary Focus,** p. 42 in ATE **Cross-Disciplinary Focus,** p. 43 in ATE **Connect to Life Science,** p. 43 in ATE **Math and More,** p. 44 in ATE **Multicultural Connection,** p. 44 in ATE **Apply,** p. 45 **Science, Technology, and Society:** The Lost City of Ubar, p. 54	**Self-Check,** p. 42 **Homework,** p. 42 in ATE **Review,** p. 45 **Quiz,** p. 45 in ATE **Alternative Assessment,** p. 45 in ATE
Directed Reading Worksheet 2, Section 3 **Reinforcement Worksheet 2,** Interpreting a Topographic Map **Math Skills for Science Worksheet 46,** Mapping and Surveying	**MathBreak,** Counting Contours, p. 47 **Connect to Oceanography,** p. 48 in ATE **Environmental Science Connection,** p. 49 **Careers:** Watershed Planner–Nancy Charbeneau, p. 55	**Self-Check,** p. 47 **Homework,** p. 47 in ATE **Review,** p. 49 **Quiz,** p. 49 in ATE **Alternative Assessment,** p. 49 in ATE

Holt, Rinehart and Winston On-line Resources

go.hrw.com

For worksheets and other teaching aids related to this chapter, visit the HRW Web site and type in the keyword: **HSTMAP**

National Science Teachers Association

www.scilinks.org

Encourage students to use the keywords listed on the Technology Highlights page to access information and resources on the **NSTA** Web site.

END-OF-CHAPTER REVIEW AND ASSESSMENT

Chapter Review in Study Guide
Vocabulary and Notes in Study Guide
Chapter Tests with Performance-Based Assessment, Chapter 2 Test
Chapter Tests with Performance-Based Assessment, Performance-Based Assessment 2
Concept Mapping Transparency 2

Chapter Resources & Worksheets

Visual Resources

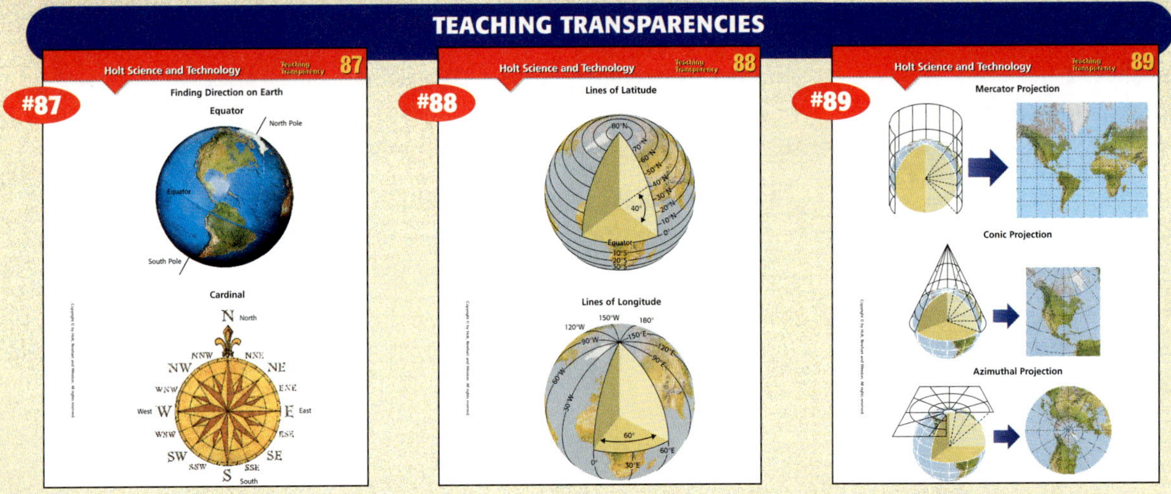

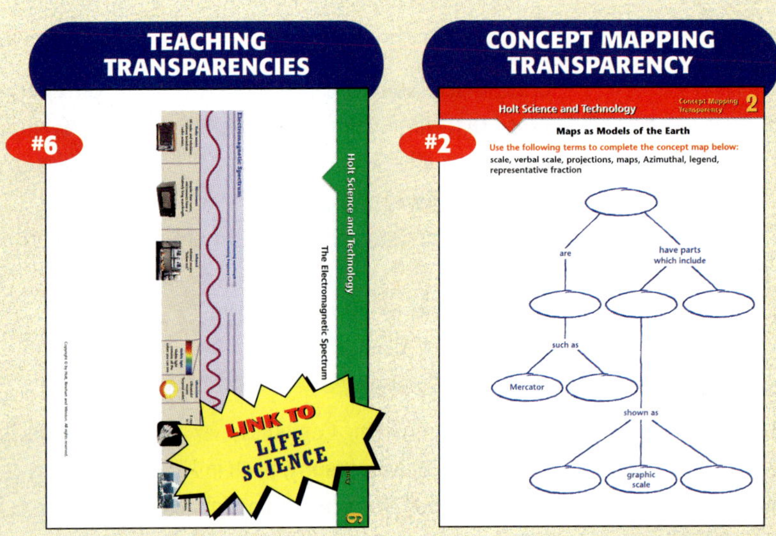

Meeting Individual Needs

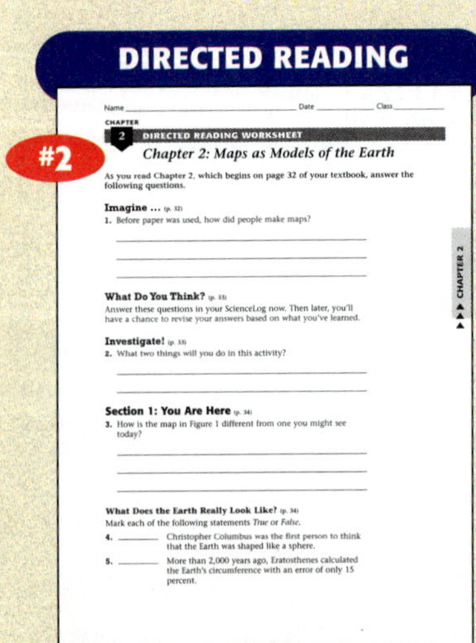

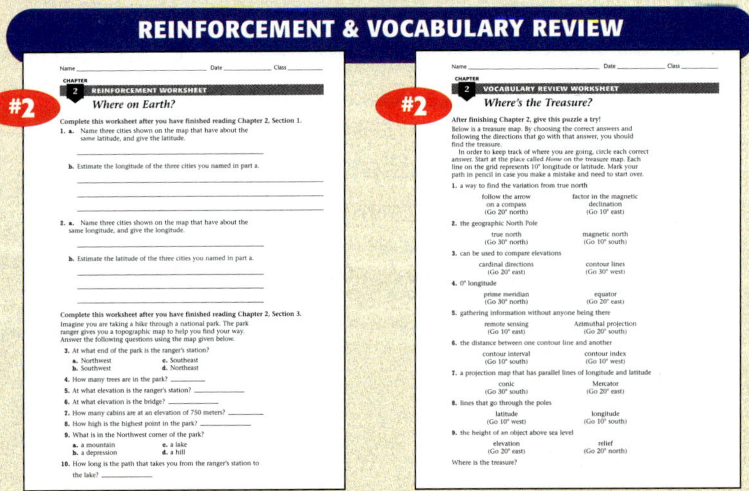

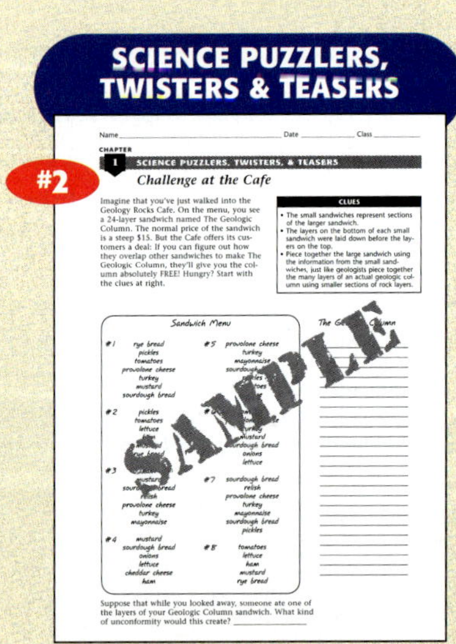

Chapter 2 • Maps as Models of the Earth

Review & Assessment

STUDY GUIDE

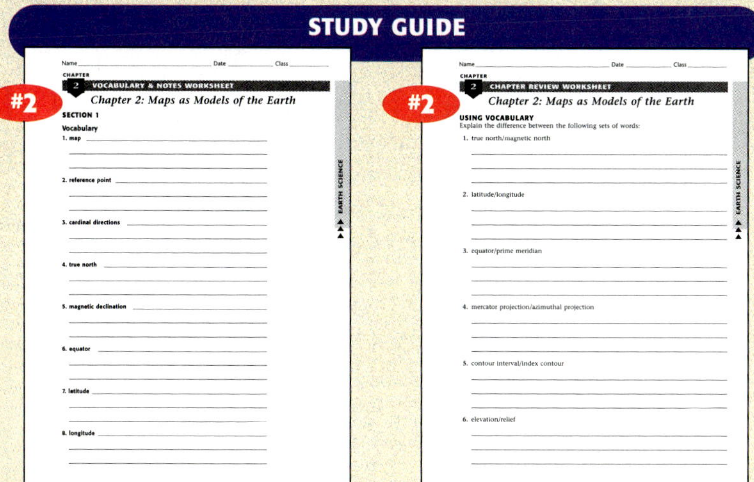

CHAPTER TESTS WITH PERFORMANCE-BASED ASSESSMENT

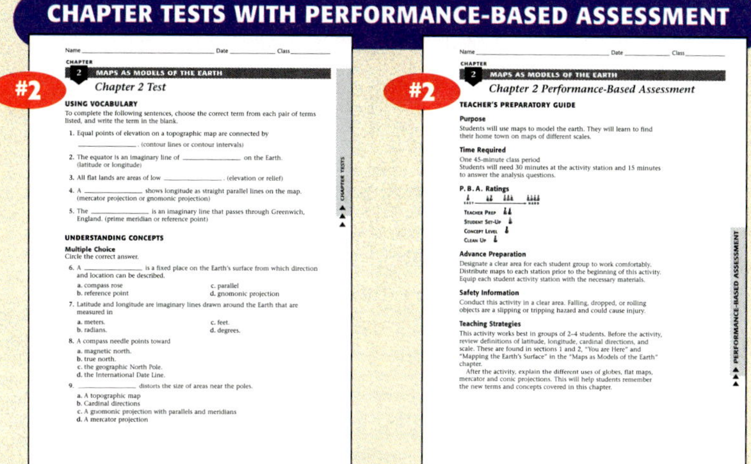

Lab Worksheets

INQUIRY LABS

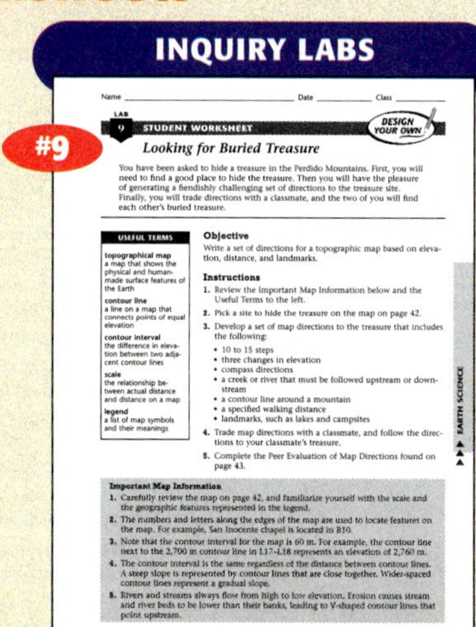

LONG-TERM PROJECTS & RESEARCH IDEAS

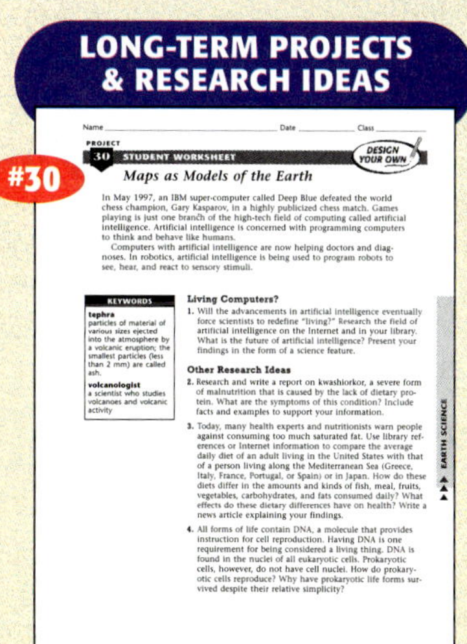

DATASHEETS FOR LABBOOK

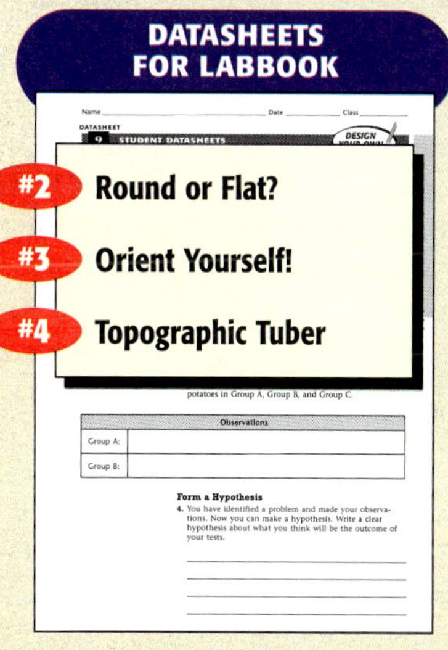

Applications & Extensions

CRITICAL THINKING & PROBLEM SOLVING

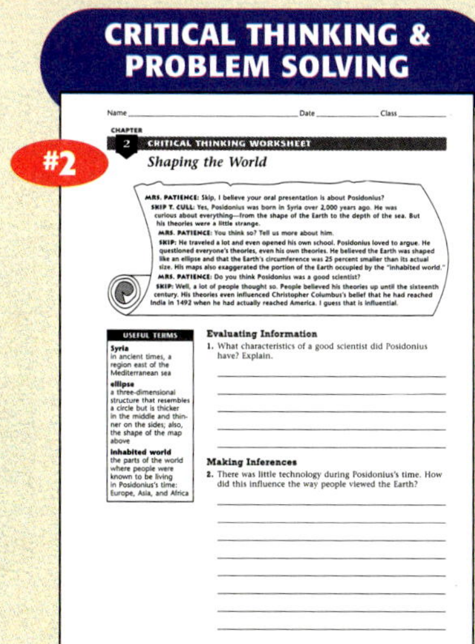

MULTICULTURAL CONNECTIONS

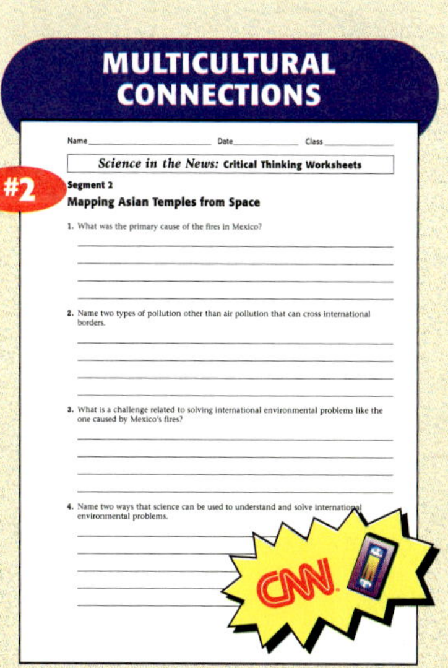

Chapter Background

SECTION 1

You Are Here

▶ Global Positioning Systems

During the 1970s, the U.S. Department of Defense developed the Global Positioning System (GPS) for use in aircraft navigation and missile guidance. The system uses a network of 25 satellites that continually transmit positioning information to receivers on Earth. The distance between a receiver and at least three satellites is used to compute the latitude and longitude coordinates of the receiver's position.

- In 1983, the system was made available to the public and has since been used for land, sea, and air navigation, surveying, geophysical exploration, and vehicle-location systems. The system can be highly accurate, making it possible to determine position to within less than 1 m. As the prices of some of the receivers have plummeted, the use of the GPS for recreational activities, such as boating, hiking, and hunting, has increased.

IS THAT A FACT!

- The first GPS receiver was about the size of a filing cabinet, but by 1989, manufacturers had perfected hand-held versions.

▶ Longitude

Because Earth rotates 360° every 24 hours, it turns 15° every hour. It is therefore possible to determine longitude at any place on the globe if the local time and the time at the prime meridian are known. Before the mid-eighteenth century, however, the unreliability of clocks—especially those aboard ships, where motion, temperature variation, and moisture could wreak havoc with a timepiece's workings—thwarted calculations of longitude. Many shipwrecks were caused because the ship captains could not accurately calculate their location.

- In 1707, inaccurate longitudinal information caused four ships in a British fleet to run aground, and 2,000 sailors died. The British Parliament addressed the problem by offering a large reward to anyone who could develop a method to accurately calculate longitude within half a degree. John Harrison (1693–1776), a self-taught clockmaker, developed a chronometer that remained accurate on rough seas and won the prize in 1763. More than 200 years later, astronaut Neil Armstrong gave credit to Harrison for the role he played in enabling exploration of Earth and in inspiring future generations to venture toward exploration of the moon.

SECTION 2

Mapping the Earth's Surface

▶ Gerardus Mercator

Gerardus Mercator was born Gerhard Kremer in 1512, in Rupelmonde, Flanders (present-day Belgium). At age 24, Mercator was a highly skilled engraver, calligrapher, and scientific-instrument maker. With two of his teachers, he made the first globe of Earth, in 1536–1537. A true Renaissance man, Mercator was a highly esteemed cartographer who also published a treatise on italic lettering, designed a grammar-school curriculum, taught mathematics, and conducted genealogical research for his patron, Duke Wilhelm of Cleve. He even attempted to write a chronology of the history of the world from the formation of Earth to 1568.

▶ Aerial Photographs

Aerial photographs used for mapping have been taken from mountaintops, airplanes, hot-air balloons, rockets, and satellites. Originally, the photographs were taken from various angles. Today, specialized cameras take pictures straight down, in sequences, and along predetermined lines. Each picture overlaps parts of the pictures taken before and after it. This is done because the least amount of

distortion is at the center of each photo. Together these photos produce an image with very little distortion. When used with specialized instruments, these photos can be used to produce a three-dimensional view of an area. From the three-dimensional model, land contours are plotted.

LANDSAT

Since the *LANDSAT* program began in 1972, a number of satellites have been deployed that carry remote sensing equipment. The equipment is designed to detect radiation in different bands of the electromagnetic spectrum. *LANDSATS 4* and *5* orbit Earth from pole to pole at an altitude of 705 km every 16 days. *LANDSAT* data are particularly useful for thematic mapping. For example, data from the blue-green spectral region are useful for distinguishing between coniferous and deciduous plants, while data from the thermal infrared range supply information about soil moisture.

Section 3

Topographic Maps

Inuit Relief Maps

The Inuit of Baffin Island were skilled mapmakers. They made permanent relief maps by carving coastal features into pieces of wood and walrus ivory. The Inuit also sewed small pieces of fur or driftwood to sealskin to represent islands. They measured distance on their maps not by miles but by "sleeps." This distance to a hunting ground, for example, would be measured by how many rest stops would be taken before reaching it.

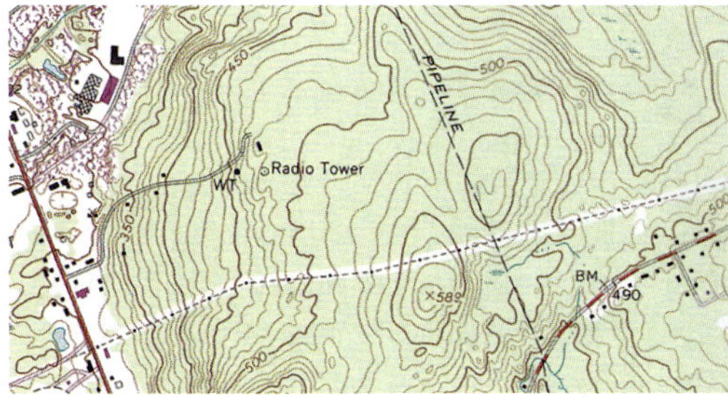

John Wesley Powell (1834–1902)

American geologist and surveyor John Wesley Powell headed an official expedition to the Grand Canyon in 1871. His purpose was to conduct a topographic survey to map "as broad a belt of country as it was possible" on both sides of the Colorado and Green Rivers. The expedition yielded meticulously detailed topographic maps for an area that had previously been described as the "great unknown." Those maps were instrumental to Powell's appointment in 1881 as director of the U.S. Geological Survey (USGS). As director, Powell aimed to create topographic maps for the entire country using very large scales, ranging from 6.4 km/2.5 cm for desert regions to 1.6 km/2.5 cm for densely populated areas. Powell insisted on including data concerning soils, springs, and other natural resources, which he felt were essential for making land-use decisions. The high-quality topographical maps created during Powell's administration set the standard for published topographic maps in the United States for many years to come.

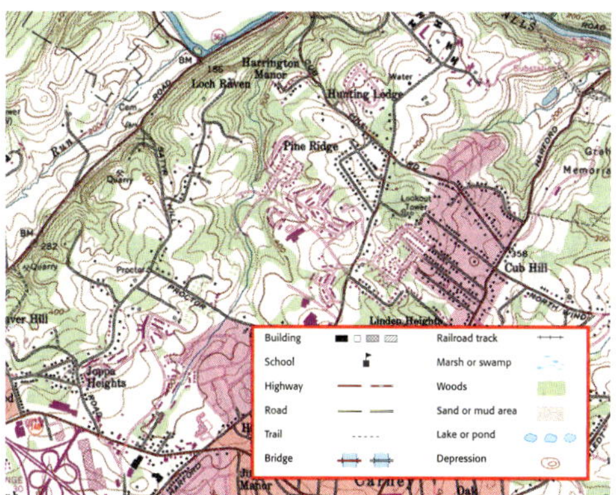

IS THAT A FACT!

- By the time Powell retired from the USGS, in 1894, about one-fifth of the United States had been mapped according to his standards. Powell told Congress that he expected the remainder of the task (excluding the mapping of Alaska) could be completed in 24 years. However, he vastly underestimated the undertaking; it was not until the 1980s that a full set of topographic maps was finally completed.

***For additional background resources, please refer to the* HST Reference Library.**

CHAPTER 2

Maps as Models of the Earth

Chapter Preview

Section 1
You Are Here
- What Does the Earth Really Look Like?
- Finding Direction on Earth
- Finding Locations on the Earth

Section 2
Mapping the Earth's Surface
- A Flat Sphere?
- Modern Mapmaking
- Information Shown on Maps

Section 3
Topographic Maps
- Elements of Elevation
- Reading a Topographic Map

Directed Reading Worksheet 2

Science Puzzlers, Twisters & Teasers Worksheet 2

Guided Reading Audio CD
English or Spanish, Chapter 2

CHAPTER 2

Maps as Models of the Earth

Imagine...

Imagine that friends from school are coming to visit you at home. You don't want them to get lost, so you decide to make a map. How would you make a map of where you live? Would you include everything in your neighborhood? What materials would you use to make your map?

The first mapmakers probably used sticks to scratch maps in the dirt. One of the oldest surviving maps is of an ancient city in Mesopotamia, which is in present-day Iraq. The nearly 5,000-year-old map was etched onto a clay tablet. The first paper map was printed in China in about A.D. 1155.

Babylonian plan of the world, seventh century B.C.

Genovese world map by Toscanelli, fifteenth century A.D.

During medieval times, maps of the known world produced by Europeans were often based on imagination, guesswork, and travelers' tales. At the center of the Earth was Europe. Areas that had not yet been visited and explored were sometimes filled in with scenes of mythical places and monsters.

Today computer technology and satellite images allow us to make maps that are extremely accurate. In this chapter you will learn about different types of maps, how these maps are represented, and what goes into making a map.

32

Imagine . . .

Mapmakers of medieval Europe relied on the writings of Roman scholars, such as Pliny the Elder (A.D. 23–79), to fill in unknown areas. Among Pliny's more bizarre writings were descriptions of the "Ear Islands," somewhere off the coast of Europe. The Ear Islanders, or "All-Ears," had giant ears to hear fish in the ocean. About 200 years later, the Roman scholar Gaius Julius Solinus wrote of lands peopled by horse-footed men, one-eyed men who drank from skulls, and "umbrella men" who had one foot large enough to shield their head from rain. Such fanciful beings and places, including the lost city of Atlantis, appeared on maps as late as the seventeenth century.

What Do You Think?

In your ScienceLog, try to answer the following questions based on what you already know:

1. Do all maps represent the world accurately?
2. How is information shown on maps?
3. What information must every map contain?

Follow the Yellow Brick Road

Have you ever been lost? Would a map have helped? Maps are the basic tools for visually presenting locations. Maps are necessary parts of your everyday life. They range from your teacher's seating chart of the class to the map of the United States hanging on your classroom wall. In this activity, you will draw and exchange maps with a partner. In doing so, you not only will learn how to read a map but also will make a map that someone else can read.

Procedure

1. With **colored pencils** and **paper,** draw a map illustrating how to get from your classroom to another location in your school, such as the restroom or the gym. Make sure you include enough information for someone unfamiliar with your school to find his or her way.
2. After you finish drawing your map, exchange maps with a partner. Study your classmate's map, and try to figure out where the map is leading you. Note what aspects of the map make it easy or difficult to read.

Analysis

3. Is your map an accurate representation of your school? Explain.
4. How do you think your map could be made better? What do you think is missing?
5. Compare your map with your partner's map. How are your maps alike? How are they different? What symbols does your map have in common with your partner's map?

Going Further

Perform the same activity, but this time walk the route before making the map, and make a mental note of landmarks and the distance between locations on the way. How does this improve your map? What additions would make your map easier to read?

What Do You Think?

Accept all reasonable responses.

Students will have a chance to revise their answers in the Chapter Review under NOW What Do You Think?

Investigate!

MATERIALS

- colored pencils
- paper

Teacher Notes: Before students start their maps, have them brainstorm to make a list of school landmarks and suggest that they use the location of these landmarks as reference points in their maps.

Answers to Investigate!

3. Answers will vary. Accept all reasonable responses.
4. Answers will vary. Accept all reasonable responses.
5. Answers will vary.

Answer to Going Further

Answers will vary.

Cross-Disciplinary Focus

History A simple map helped save countless lives during a London cholera epidemic in the mid-1800s. A physician named John Snow noticed that the Soho district seemed to be more severely afflicted than other parts of the city. He drew a large-scale map of Soho and marked each residence where someone had died. In time, it became clear that the highest concentration of deaths occurred near a certain public water pump. After the pump was disabled, no new cases of cholera developed in the area. Using his map, Snow discovered the link between cholera and the public water supply.

Section 1

Focus

You Are Here

This section opens with a discussion of the history of mapmaking. Students learn how to find directions on a globe by using reference points such as the North and South Poles and the equator. Students learn how a compass is used to find directions and how true north differs from magnetic north. The section closes with a discussion of lines of latitude and longitude and how they can be used to locate points on Earth's surface.

Bellringer

Ask students to draw a map from their homes to one of their favorite places. Have them clearly label all landmarks and include information that might be useful to someone using the map.

1 Motivate

Group Activity

Making Compasses This activity will work best when it is performed outside. Supply each group with a small bowl of water, a steel sewing needle, a magnet, and a 1 cm × 3 cm piece of tissue paper. Have students carefully rub the needle against the magnet in the same direction 40 times. Then have them float the paper on the surface of the water and place the needle on the paper. After a minute, allow students to observe other groups' bowls; all of the needles will be oriented in a north-south direction. Explain that they have all just created a simple compass, a device that changed the course of human history.

1

NEW TERMS

map	equator
reference point	latitude
cardinal directions	longitude
true north	prime meridian
magnetic declination	

OBJECTIVES

- Describe directions on a globe.
- Explain how a magnetic compass can be used to find directions on the Earth.
- Distinguish between true north and magnetic north.
- Distinguish between lines of latitude and lines of longitude on a globe or map.
- Explain how latitude and longitude can be used to locate places on Earth.

You Are Here

When you walk across the Earth's surface, the Earth does not appear to be curved. It looks flat. In the past, beliefs about the Earth's shape changed. Maps reflected the time's knowledge and views of the world as well as the current technology. A **map** is a model or representation of the Earth's surface. If you look at Ptolemy's world map from the second century, as shown in **Figure 1,** you probably will not recognize what you are looking at. Today satellites in space provide us with true images of what the Earth looks like. There is no guesswork involved. In this section you will learn how early scientists knew the Earth was round long before pictures from space were taken. You will also learn how to determine location and direction on the Earth's surface.

What Does the Earth Really Look Like?

The Greeks thought of the Earth as a sphere almost 2,000 years before Christopher Columbus made his voyage in 1492. The Greeks thought that the sphere was the most perfect form and that the Earth therefore had to be a sphere. Evidence based on observations supported the assumption. For example, the observation that a ship sinks below the horizon as it sails into the distance supported the idea of a round Earth. If the Earth were flat the ship would appear smaller as it moved away. Today we know the Earth is not a perfect sphere.

Figure 1 *This map shows what people thought the world looked like in the second century A.D. Can you recognize any continents or oceans?*

34

Multicultural Connection

The Chinese invented the magnetic compass in the third century B.C. The magnetic properties of lodestone, known today as magnetite, were well known to many ancient cultures. Lodestone was thought to have magical properties because it could attract metal. Early compasses consisted of a piece of lodestone on a card that was balanced on a pivot. The scale of the compass was marked with compass points at 15° increments. By the tenth century, the compass was standard equipment on Chinese sailing ships.

Section 1–California Standards: PE/ATE 7, 7b, 7f; LabBook: 7, 7b, 7e, 7f

Eratosthenes (ER uh TAHS thuh neez), a Greek mathematician, wanted to know how big the Earth was. In about 240 B.C., he calculated the Earth's circumference using geometry and observations of the sun. We now know his estimation was off by only 6,250 km, an error of 15 percent. That's not bad for someone who lived more than 2,000 years ago, in a time when computer and satellite technology did not exist!

Finding Direction on Earth

How would you give a friend from school directions to your home? You might mention a landmark, such as a grocery store or a restaurant, as a reference point. A **reference point** is a fixed place on the Earth's surface from which direction and location can be described.

Because the Earth is round, it has no top, bottom, or sides for people to use as reference points for determining locations on its surface. The Earth does, however, turn on its axis. The Earth's axis is an imaginary line that runs through the Earth. At either end of the axis is a geographic pole. The North and South Poles, as shown in **Figure 2**, are used as reference points when describing direction and location on Earth.

Figure 2 *Like the poles, the equator can be used as a reference. The equator is a circle halfway between the poles that divides the Earth into the Northern and Southern Hemispheres.*

Cardinal Directions North, south, east, and west are called **cardinal directions. Figure 3** shows these basic cardinal directions and various combinations of these directions. Using these directions is much more precise than using directions such as turn left, go straight, and turn right. Unfortunately for most of us, using cardinal directions requires the use of a compass.

Figure 3 *A compass rose helps you orient yourself on a map.*

2 Teach

Group Activity

Have students write a description of the route they take as they travel between home and school. Then have them rewrite the description using cardinal and intercardinal directions. Have pairs of students trade route descriptions and use a community map to check the accuracy of each other's maps.

Sheltered English

MISCONCEPTION ALERT

Students may be under the impression that Christopher Columbus discovered that Earth was round only after he safely made his voyage in 1492 without sailing off the edge of the world. In fact, Columbus, like most other educated people of his time, was well aware that Earth was not flat before he set out.

CONNECT TO LIFE SCIENCE

Magnetotactic bacteria use magnetic particles in their cytoplasm to align themselves with the Earth's magnetic field. North of the equator, the bacteria are north-seeking travelers. South of the equator, they are south-seeking travelers. At the equator, where the magnetic fields are at their weakest, the populations are mixed between north- and south-seeking bacteria.

IS THAT A FACT!

The orientation of maps with north at the "top" is arbitrary. For many centuries European maps placed east at the top to stress the importance of Jerusalem to their faith. The Chinese put the south at the top of their maps because nothing of interest to them was to the north.

WEIRD SCIENCE

Although globes are round, Earth is not a perfect sphere. Because Earth is a rotating body, it bulges at the equator and is slightly flattened at the poles. Earth's circumference measured pole to pole is 40,008 km, while its circumference around the equator is 40,075 km.

Teaching Transparency 87 "Finding Direction on Earth"

Directed Reading Worksheet 2 Section 1

2 Teach, continued

READING STRATEGY

Prediction Guide Before students read the following two pages, have them answer these true/false statements:

- Earth has four poles. (true)
- A compass is the only thing you need to find a location. (false)
- Imaginary lines drawn around Earth can be used to pinpoint locations. (true)

Sheltered English

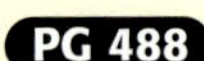

Round or Flat?

MISCONCEPTION ALERT

Explain that magnetic attraction occurs between the opposite poles of magnets. The north-seeking pole of a compass needle actually points to the south pole of Earth's magnetic field. What we call the Earth's magnetic north pole is actually the south pole of Earth's magnetic field. This can be easily demonstrated by placing the south pole of a bar magnet next to a compass. The compass needle will point toward the south pole of the bar magnet in the same way it tends to point toward the south pole of Earth's magnetic field, what we call magnetic north.

Answer to Self-Check

The Earth rotates around the geographic poles.

Orient Yourself!

QuickLab

Finding Directions with a Compass

1. This lab should be done outside. Hold a **compass** flat in your hand until the needle stops moving. Rotate the dial of the compass until the letter *N* on the case lines up with the painted or colored end of the needle.
2. While holding the compass steady, identify objects that line up with each of the cardinal points. List them in your ScienceLog.
3. See if you can locate objects at the various combinations of cardinal directions, such as SW and NE. Record your observations in your ScienceLog.

Using a Compass One way to determine north is by using a magnetic compass. The compass uses the natural magnetism of the Earth to indicate direction. A compass needle points to the magnetic north pole. The Earth has two different sets of poles—the geographic poles, which you learned about on the previous page, and the magnetic poles. As you can see in **Figure 4,** the magnetic poles have a slightly different location than the geographic poles.

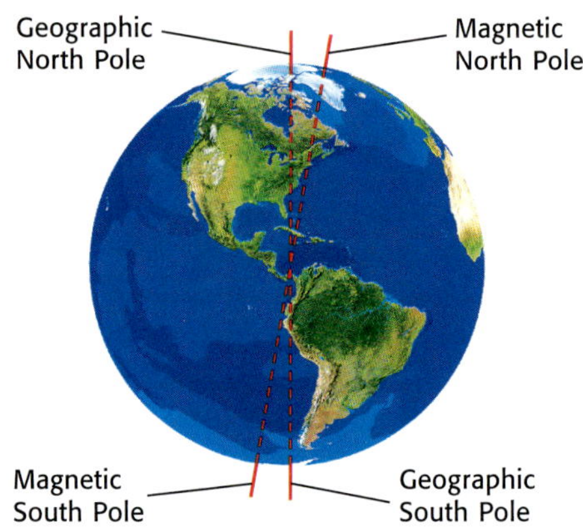

Figure 4 *Unlike the geographic poles, which are always in the same place, the magnetic poles have changed location throughout the history of the Earth.*

Self-Check

Does the Earth rotate around the geographic poles or the magnetic poles? *(See page 564 to check your answer.)*

It's better than a scavenger hunt! Interested? Turn to page 490 of your LabBook.

True North and Magnetic Declination Because the geographic North Pole never changes, it is called **true north.** The difference between the location of true north and the magnetic north pole requires that one more step be added to using a compass. Remember, a compass points to magnetic north, not geographic north. So when using a compass to map or explore the Earth's surface, you need to make a correction for the difference between geographic north and magnetic north. This angle of correction is called **magnetic declination.** Magnetic declination is measured in degrees east or west of true north.

Magnetic declination has been determined for different points on the Earth's surface. Once you know the declination for your area, you can use a compass to determine true north.

36

SCIENCE HUMOR

Before the seventeenth century, many sailors refused to transport onions and garlic because they believed they would destroy a compass's magnetic properties. In 1600, English physician and scientist William Gilbert set about testing the belief. He ate a quantity of garlic and then belched on a compass needle, which he had also rubbed with garlic juice. The compass' magnetic properties remained intact, and Gilbert proved, at least to himself, that the notion was unfounded.

This adjustment is like the adjustment you would make to the handlebars of a bike with a bent front wheel. You know how much you have to turn the handlebars to make the bike go straight.

As **Figure 5** shows, a compass needle at Pittsburgh, Pennsylvania, points 5° west of true north. At Savannah, Georgia, the compass needle lines up with true north, so the declination is 0°. At San Diego, California, the needle points 15° east of true north.

astronomy CONNECTION

There are ways you can find north without using a compass. In the morning, the sun rises in the east. In the evening, it sets in the west. If you point your right hand toward where you saw the sun rise in the morning and your left hand to where it sets at night, you will be facing north. "Right to rise, left to set" is a phrase that will help you remember not only what directions east and west are but also what direction north is.

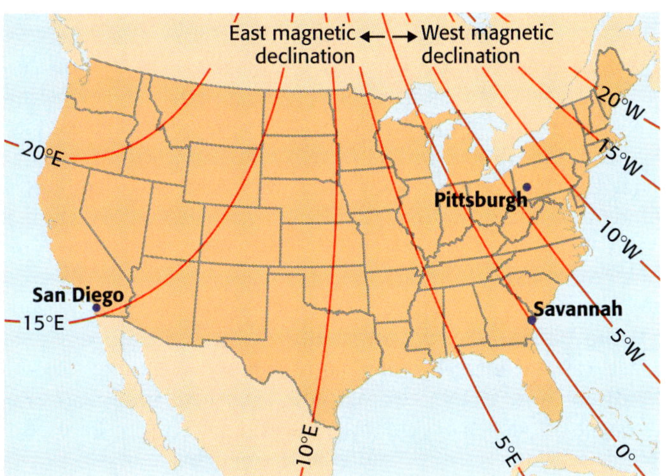

Figure 5 *The red lines on the map connect points with the same magnetic declination.*

Finding Locations on the Earth

The houses and buildings in your neighborhood all have addresses that identify their location. But how would you find the location of something on the Earth's surface that is much bigger, like a city or an island? These things can be given an "address" using *latitude* and *longitude.* Latitude and longitude are intersecting lines on a globe or map that allow you to find exact locations. They are used in combination to create global addresses. Read on to see how this system works.

Latitude Imaginary lines drawn around the Earth parallel to the equator are called lines of latitude, or *parallels.* The **equator** is a circle halfway between the poles that divides the Earth into the Northern and Southern Hemispheres. It represents 0° latitude. **Latitude** is the distance north or south, measured in degrees, from the equator, as shown in **Figure 6.** The North Pole is 90° north latitude, and the South Pole is 90° south latitude.

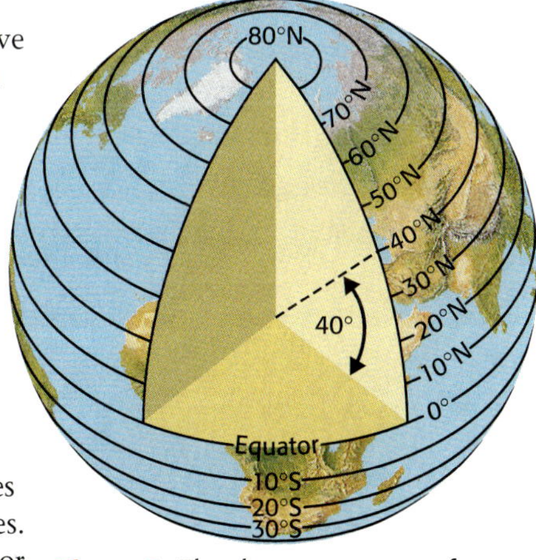

Figure 6 *The degree measure of latitude is the angle created by the equator, the center of the Earth, and the location on the Earth's surface.*

37

WEIRD SCIENCE

As the Earth rotates, both the geographic North Pole and the magnetic north pole move constantly. The geographic North Pole moves about 6 m on a 435-day cycle. This movement results from a wobble in the Earth's rotation. The magnetic north pole wanders because of changes in Earth's rotating iron core. The magnetic pole is currently moving northwest at an average rate of 10 km per year.

GROUP ACTIVITY

Finding True North For thousands of years, people have used the sun to determine true north. This activity is most accurate at midday, when the sun is at its southernmost point.

- At 11:30 A.M., have students insert a ruler in the ground and a pencil at the tip of the ruler's shadow.
- After 1 hour, have students insert another pencil where the tip of the ruler's shadow is now.
- Have students place a piece of string between the two pencils. The string will be an east-west line. Viewed with your back to the sun, the first pencil indicates west and the second indicates east.

Students can then use a protractor to position a north-south string perpendicular to the east-west string.

Matthew Henson (1866–1955), an African American member of Robert Peary's North Pole exploration team, was one of the first people believed to reach the geographic North Pole in 1909. Henson's knowledge of Arctic regions also helped him gain a position as an exhibit preparator at the American Museum of Natural History, in New York City. In 1944, Congress recognized Henson's contributions to polar exploration. Interested students may want to read Henson's autobiography, *A Negro Explorer at the North Pole.*

Teaching Transparency 88
"Lines of Latitude"

3 Extend

Going Further

Ask students to find out why the meridian passing through Greenwich, England, serves as the prime meridian. They should find that Greenwich was chosen as 0° by an international committee in 1884 in part because it was the site of Britain's Royal Greenwich Observatory, which had been important in developing time-keeping methods necessary for ship navigation. In addition, most of the world's shipping lines were already using Greenwich as the longitudinal baseline.

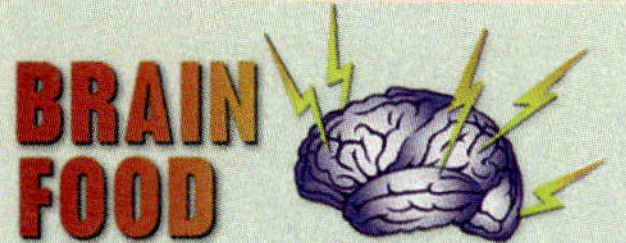

Before 1884, when Greenwich was established by international agreement as the prime meridian, there were no fewer than 13 "prime meridians" in use. Countries simply selected a meridian in their own country as the prime meridian; for example, Italy's prime meridian passed through Rome, and France's prime meridian passed through Paris. Discuss with students the benefits of the international standardization of the prime meridian.

Homework

Research Explain to students that longitude is directly related to time. Earth rotates 360° every 24 hours, turning 15° every hour. Earth can be divided into 24 meridians of 15° each. Have students find out how time in different parts of the world can be determined using lines of longitude and the local time at Greenwich.

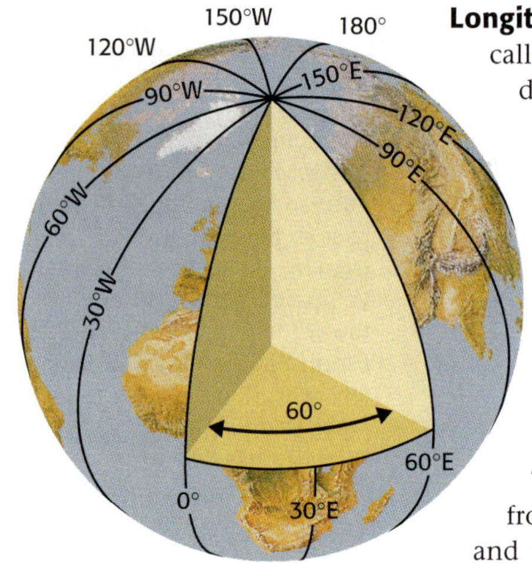

Figure 7 *The degree measure of longitude is the angle created by the prime meridian, the center of the Earth, and the location on the Earth's surface.*

Longitude Imaginary lines that pass through the poles are called lines of longitude, or *meridians*. **Longitude** is the distance east and west, measured in degrees, from the prime meridian, as shown in **Figure 7.** By international agreement, one meridian was selected to be 0°. The **prime meridian,** which passes through Greenwich, England, is the line that represents 0° longitude. Unlike lines of latitude, lines of longitude are not parallel. They touch at the poles and are farthest apart at the equator.

The prime meridian does not completely circle the globe like the equator does. It runs from the North Pole through Greenwich, England, to the South Pole. The 180° meridian lies on the opposite side of the Earth from the prime meridian. Together, the prime meridian and the 180° meridian divide the Earth into two equal halves—the Eastern and Western Hemispheres. East lines of longitude are found east of the prime meridian, between 0° and 180°. West lines of longitude are found west of the prime meridian, between 0° and 180°.

Using Latitude and Longitude Points on the Earth's surface can be located using latitude and longitude. Lines of latitude and lines of longitude intersect, forming a grid system on globes and maps. This grid system can be used to find locations north or south of the equator and east or west of the prime meridian.

Finding Your Way

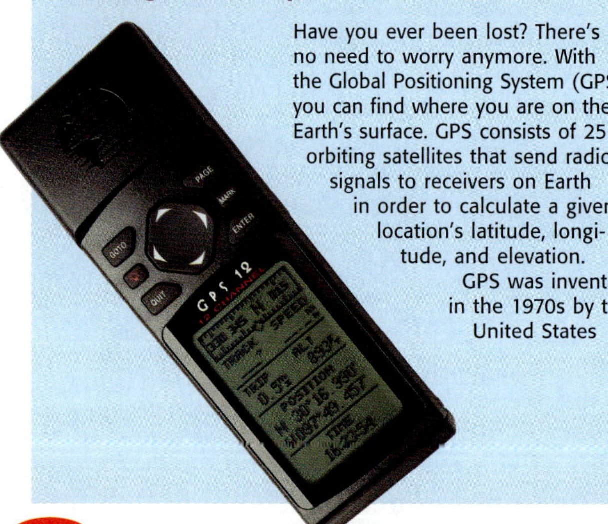

Have you ever been lost? There's no need to worry anymore. With the Global Positioning System (GPS), you can find where you are on the Earth's surface. GPS consists of 25 orbiting satellites that send radio signals to receivers on Earth in order to calculate a given location's latitude, longitude, and elevation.

GPS was invented in the 1970s by the United States Department of Defense for military purposes. During the last 20 years, this technology has made its way into the mainstream. Today, GPS is used in a variety of ways. Airplane and boat pilots use it for navigation, and industry uses include mining and resource mapping as well as environmental planning. Even some cars are equipped with a GPS unit that can display the vehicle's specific location on a computer screen on the dashboard.

38

internet connect

SCI LINKS. NSTA

TOPIC: Finding Locations on Earth
GO TO: www.scilinks.org
***sci*LINKS NUMBER:** HSTE030

TOPIC: Latitude and Longitude
GO TO: www.scilinks.org
***sci*LINKS NUMBER:** HSTE035

Students may believe that a compass is all you need to keep from getting lost outdoors. Point out that compasses are useful only when combined with the ability to read maps and to observe land features. Compasses can be used for orienting oneself and for taking bearings on landmarks for map triangulation.

Figure 8 shows you how latitude and longitude can be used to find the location of your state capital. First locate the star symbol representing your state capital on the appropriate map. Find the lines of latitude and longitude closest to your state capital. From here you can estimate your capital's approximate latitude and longitude.

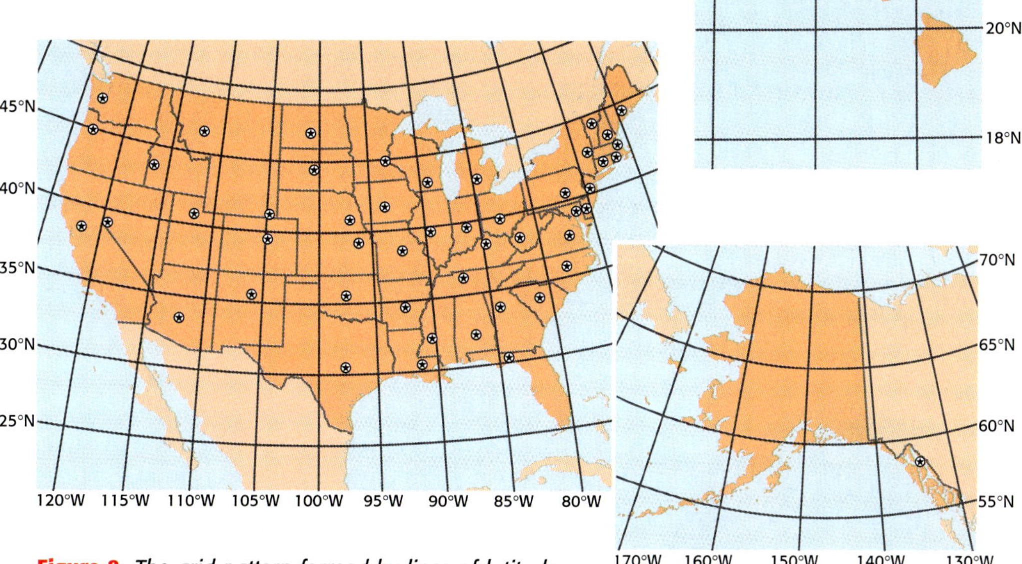

Figure 8 *The grid pattern formed by lines of latitude and longitude allows you to pinpoint any location on the Earth's surface.*

Explore

Use an atlas or globe to find the latitude and longitude of the following cities:
New York, New York
Sao Paulo, Brazil
Rome, Italy
Sydney, Australia
Madrid, Spain
Reykjavik, Iceland
Cairo, Egypt

REVIEW

1. Explain the difference between true north and magnetic north.
2. When using a compass to map an area, why is it important to know an area's magnetic declination?
3. In what three ways is the equator different from the prime meridian?
4. How do lines of latitude and longitude help you find locations on the Earth's surface?
5. **Applying Concepts** While digging through an old trunk, you find a treasure map. The map shows that the treasure is buried at 97° north and 188° east. Explain why this is impossible.

Answers to Review

1. Because the geographic North Pole never changes, it is called true north. Magnetic north refers to the magnetic north pole, which has changed throughout history.
2. Because the compass points to magnetic north, it is important to know the magnetic declination at your location. This will help you make corrections to adjust for the difference between true north and magnetic north.
3. Answers will vary.
4. Lines of latitude and lines of longitude form a grid system that can be used to find locations on the Earth's surface.
5. This is impossible because the greatest measure of latitude is 90° and the greatest measure of longitude is 180°.

4 Close

Quiz

1. Name three references that can be used to describe direction and location on Earth. (possible answers: North Pole, South Pole, the equator, lines of latitude and longitude)
2. What are lines of latitude and lines of longitude? (Lines of latitude are imaginary lines around Earth parallel to the equator, and they are used to measure a location's distance north or south of the equator. Lines of longitude are imaginary lines that run between the Earth's poles, and they are used to measure a location's distance east or west of the prime meridian.)

Alternative Assessment

Have students use a world map to plan an around-the-world trip in which they give their various destinations only in degrees of latitude and longitude. Have students trade their itinerary with a partner, and have each "decode" the other's trip.

Answers to Explore

New York, New York: 40°N, 74°W
Sao Paulo, Brazil: 23°S, 46°W
Rome, Italy: 41°N, 12°E
Sydney, Australia: 33°S, 151°E
Madrid, Spain: 40°N, 3°W
Reykjavik, Iceland: 64°N, 21°W
Cairo, Egypt: 30°N, 31°E

Teaching Transparency 88
"Lines of Longitude"

Reinforcement Worksheet 2
"Where on Earth?"

SECTION 2

Focus

Mapping the Earth's Surface

In this section, students compare the uses of maps and globes and explore the features of three common map projections. In addition, they learn the parts of a map and discover some of the technological advances that have influenced recent trends in cartography.

Bellringer

Display a world map, a map of your state, and a map of your community. Have students make a chart in which they list the similarities and differences between each map. Then have students suggest three uses for each map.

1 Motivate

DISCUSSION

Have students examine a globe and a Mercator projection of a world map. Point out to students that both are representations of Earth. Then challenge students to find examples of ways in which the two representations differ. If necessary, point out the relative difference in the size and shape of Greenland. Ask students how they might account for the discrepancies. Record students' ideas on the chalkboard, and tell them that in this section they will learn about some of the difficulties involved in making flat representations of Earth's curved surface.

Directed Reading Worksheet 2 Section 2

2

Mapping the Earth's Surface

NEW TERMS

Mercator projection
conic projection
azimuthal projection
aerial photograph
remote sensing

OBJECTIVES

- Compare a map with a globe.
- Describe the three types of map projections.
- Describe recent technological advances that have helped the science of mapmaking progress.
- List the parts of a map.

Models are often used to represent real objects. For example, architects use models of buildings to give their clients an idea of what a building will look like before it is completed. Likewise, Earth scientists often make models of the Earth. These models are globes and maps.

Because a globe is a sphere, a globe is probably the most accurate model of the Earth. Also, a globe accurately represents the sizes and shapes of the continents and oceans in relation to one another. But a globe is not always the best model to use when studying the Earth's surface. For example, a globe is too small to show a lot of detail, such as roads and rivers. It is much easier to show details on maps. Maps can show the entire Earth or parts of it. But how do you represent the Earth's curved surface on a flat surface? Read on to find out.

A Flat Sphere?

A map is a flat representation of the Earth's curved surface. However, when you transfer information from a curved surface to a flat surface, you lose some accuracy. Changes called distortions occur in the shapes and sizes of landmasses and oceans. These distortions make some landmasses appear larger than they really are. Direction and distance can also be distorted. Consider the example of the orange peel shown in **Figure 9.**

Figure 9 *If you remove the peel from an orange and flatten the peel, it will stretch and tear. The larger the piece of peel, the more its shape is distorted as it is flattened. Also distorted are distances between points on the peel.*

40

Q: What do you get when you cross a cowboy with a mapmaker?

A: a cowtographer

Mapmakers use map projections to transfer the image of Earth's curved surface onto a flat surface. No map projection of the Earth can represent the surface of a sphere exactly. All flat maps have some amount of distortion. A map showing a smaller area, such as a city, has much less distortion than a map showing a larger area, such as the entire world.

To understand how map projections are made, imagine the Earth as a transparent globe with a light inside. If you hold a piece of paper up against the globe, shadows appear on the paper that show markings on the globe, such as continents, oceans, lines of latitude, and lines of longitude. The way the paper is held against the globe determines the kind of projection that is made. The most common projections are based on three geometric shapes—cylinders, cones, and planes.

Mercator Projection A **Mercator projection** is a map projection that results when the contents of the globe are transferred onto a cylinder of paper, as shown in **Figure 10.**

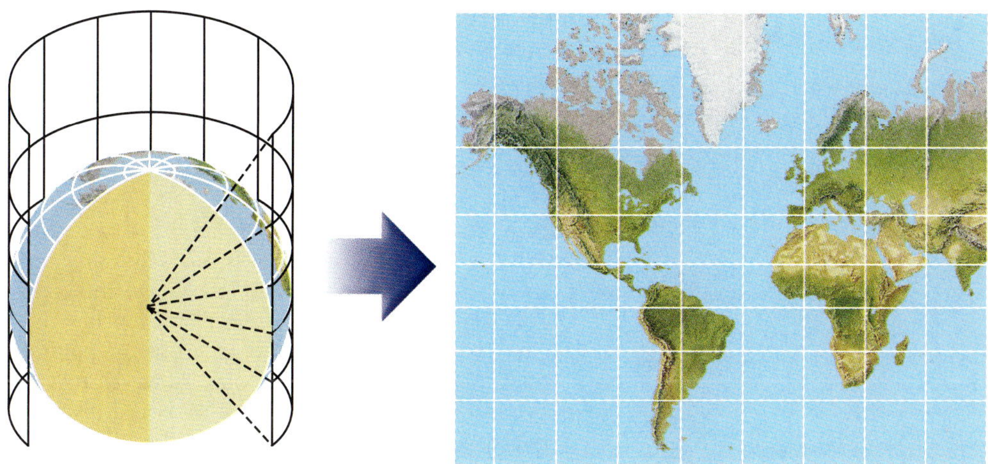

Figure 10 *A Mercator projection, though accurate near the equator, distorts distances between regions of land and distorts the sizes of areas near the poles.*

The Mercator projection shows the Earth's latitude and longitude as straight, parallel lines. Lines of longitude are plotted with an equal amount of space between each line. Lines of latitude are spaced farther apart north and south of the equator. This makes it easy to determine direction and measure latitude and longitude with a ruler. But remember, on a globe, lines of longitude are not parallel. They meet at the poles. Making the lines parallel widens and lengthens the size of areas near the poles. For example, on the Mercator projection in the map shown above, Greenland appears almost as large as Africa. Actually, Africa is 15 times larger than Greenland.

41

2 Teach

READING STRATEGY

Activity As students read about map projections, have them write down the name of each type of projection and a brief description of what the projection represents. Have students list the advantages or disadvantages of each type of projection. Sheltered English

MISCONCEPTION ALERT

The distortions of landmasses are not the only inaccuracies that occur on maps. When making maps for popular use, such as road maps, mapmakers routinely generalize them for both practical and aesthetic reasons. For example, when the size of a map's scale is reduced, two features (such as two lakes or two towns) might appear to be adjacent to each other. In this case, the mapmaker might move them slightly apart. Mapmakers sometimes also add details that may not really exist; for instance, meander loops might be added to a river or stream to make it look more realistic. Topographic maps, however, are made from aerial photographs and are extremely accurate.

Teaching Transparency 89
"Mercator Projection"

IS THAT A FACT!

In 1544, Gerardus Mercator was imprisoned on charges of treason. Apparently, his frequent absences from Flanders (now Belgium) to gather map data aroused the suspicions of authorities. He remained imprisoned for 7 months before his friends succeeded in clearing his name.

2 Teach, continued

Reading Strategy

Mnemonics Have students think of some rhymes to help them remember key points about the projections discussed in the text. You might suggest the following to help students get started:

"If you're traveling to the equator, you'll do well with Mercator;" "for east to west, conic is best;" "for a stroll at a pole, an azimuthal will help you stay in control." Sheltered English

Cross-Disciplinary Focus

History One of the earliest known maps was made by the Babylonians. It shows Babylon at the center, with Syria and other territories represented as a circular area surrounded by the Persian Gulf. This type of map is called a "wheel map." Many cultures in Arabian and European countries used wheel maps. Wheel maps reinforced the idea that a civilization was at the center of the universe. Ask students to draw a wheel map of the area where they live.

Answer to Self-Check

The measurements would be more accurate on a globe; there would be a certain amount of distortion on a world map.

Conic Projection A **conic projection** is a map projection that is made by transferring the contents of the globe onto a cone, as shown in **Figure 11.** This cone is then unrolled to form a flat plane.

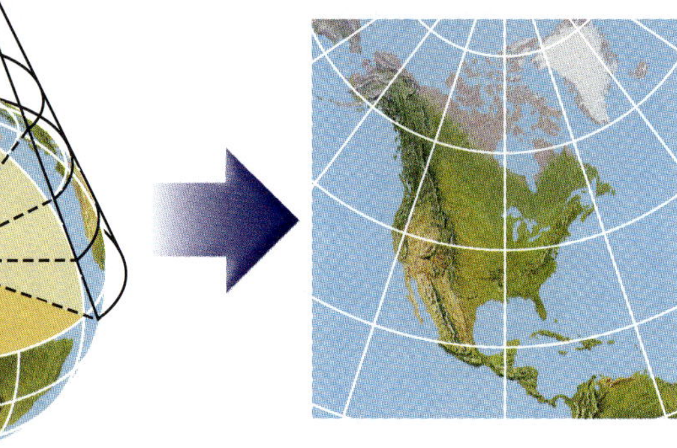

Figure 11 *A series of conic projections can be used to map a large area. Because each cone touches the globe at a different latitude, it reduces distortion.*

The cone touches the globe at one line of latitude. The line of latitude where the globe comes in contact with the cone is the only place where there is no distortion. Areas near the line of latitude where the globe and cone touch are distorted the least amount. Conic projections are best for mapping landmasses that have more area east to west, such as the United States, than north to south, such as South America, because distortion is limited along lines of longitude.

> **Self-Check**
>
> Imagine that you are assigned to measure distances between cities of the world. Will your measurements be more accurate if you use a globe or a world map? *(See page 564 to check your answer.)*

Azimuthal Projection An **azimuthal** (AZ i MYOOTH uhl) **projection** is a map projection that is made by transferring the contents of the globe onto a plane, as shown in **Figure 12.**

On an azimuthal projection, the plane touches the globe at only one point. Little distortion occurs at the point of contact, which is usually one of the poles. However, distortion of direction, distance, and shape increases as the distance from the point of contact increases. On azimuthal projections, true directions are shown from one central point to all other points.

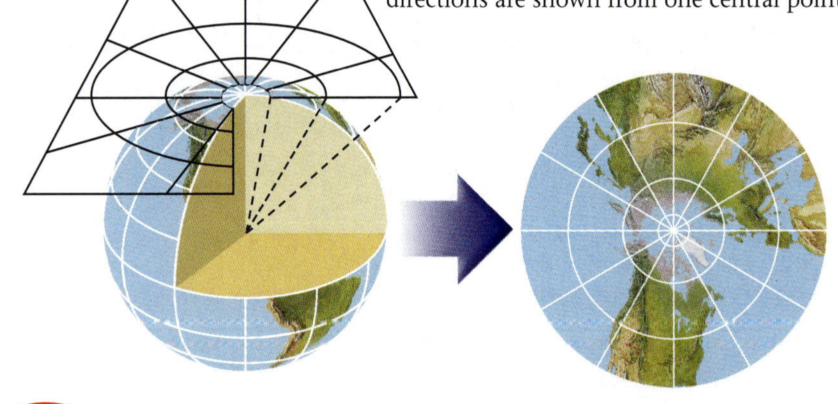

Figure 12 *This azimuthal projection is produced when points on the globe are projected onto a sheet of paper in contact with the North Pole.*

42

Homework

Have students make a chart listing the strengths and weaknesses of each of the three projections studied in this section. Then have them also research another projection, such as the Robinson projection. Have them add the strengths and weaknesses of that projection to their charts. At the bottom of the chart, have them explain why none of the projections is entirely free of distortions and inaccuracies.

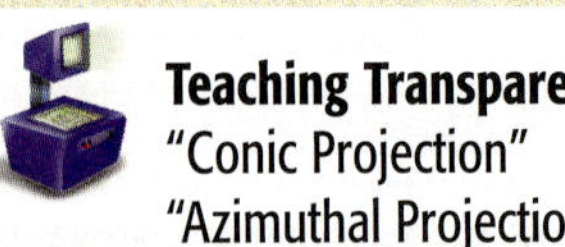

Teaching Transparency 89
"Conic Projection"
"Azimuthal Projection"

Modern Mapmaking

The science of mapmaking has changed more since the beginning of the 1900s than during any other time in history. This has been due to many technological advances in the twentieth century, such as the airplane, photography, computers, and space exploration.

Airplanes and Cameras The development of the airplane and advancements in photography have had the biggest effect on modern mapmaking. Airplanes give people a bird's-eye view of the Earth's surface. Improvements on the camera made it possible to take photographs of the land below. Photographs from the air are called **aerial photographs.** These photographs are important in helping mapmakers make accurate maps. **Figure 13** shows an example of an aerial photograph.

Figure 13 *What is this aerial photograph showing?*

Remote Sensing The combined use of airplanes and photography led to the science of remote sensing. **Remote sensing** is gathering information about something without actually being there. Remote sensing can be as basic as cameras in planes or as sophisticated as satellites with sensors that can sense and record what our eyes cannot see. Remotely-sensed images allow a mapmaker to map the surface of the Earth more accurately.

To learn more about current advances in mapmaking, turn to page 55.

We see only a small part of the sun's radiation. Radiation travels in waves of different lengths. The part of radiation we see is called visible light. Remote sensors on satellites can detect wavelengths that are longer and shorter than those of visible light. Satellites do not take photographs with film like cameras do. A satellite collects information about energy coming from the Earth's surface and sends it back to receiving stations on Earth. A computer is then used to process the information to create an image we can see, like the one shown in **Figure 14.**

Figure 14 *Satellites can detect objects the size of a baseball stadium. The satellite that took this picture was 220 km above the Earth's surface!*

Science Bloopers

During the complex process of compiling vast amounts of data from a number of different maps and sources, mistakes are sometimes made. Cartographers have wiped entire cities off maps accidentally! Canada's capital, Ottawa, for example, was once omitted from a Canadian tourist-office map. An official explanation that there was no direct air service between New York City and Ottawa failed to satisfy one Ottawa tourist bureau executive, who remarked irately, "Ottawa should be shown in any case, even if the only point of entry was by two-man kayak."

Using the Figure

Point out that **Figure 13** is an aerial photograph of Washington, D.C. See if students can identify the shadow of the Washington monument in the photo. What other features can they identify? The Russian Spin-2 satellite image in **Figure 14** is of Fulton County Stadium, in Atlanta, Georgia.

Cross-Disciplinary Focus

Language Arts Famous writers such as Anthony Trollope, Thomas Hardy, Sinclair Lewis, J. R. R. Tolkien, and Bernard Cornwall all drew maps to illustrate their works. Ask students to create a detailed map of an imaginary place. The maps must use all of the map elements shown in **Figure 15.** Students' maps can serve as inspiration for the setting of a short story.

Connect to Life Science

Data collected by remote sensing devices on satellites in the *LANDSAT* program are useful not only for making maps of physical features and landforms but also for determining the type and amount of vegetation in a certain area. Use Teaching Transparency 6 to show that *LANDSAT* satellites analyze the infrared range of the electromagnetic spectrum as well as visible light. Have interested students find out how remote sensors reveal vegetation cover and have been useful in the study of deforestation.

Teaching Transparency 6
"The Electromagnetic Spectrum"

LINK TO LIFE SCIENCE

3 Extend

MEETING INDIVIDUAL NEEDS

Learners Having Difficulty
Show students two maps with different representative fraction scales, such as a map of North America and a map of your community. Point out that the larger the denominator in a representative fraction scale, the smaller the scale of the map. You might clarify this by pointing out that $\frac{1}{4}$ of a pie is smaller than $\frac{1}{2}$ of a pie. Maps that show a large area, such as a continent, use a smaller scale and show less detail. Maps that show a smaller area, such as a town, can have a larger scale and show more detail. Discuss with students cases in which large-scale maps are the most useful and cases in which small-scale maps are most useful.
Sheltered English

MATH and MORE

Have students suppose that they want to use a map with a scale of 1:24,000 to estimate the length of a hike. On the map, the route measures 20 cm. Have students calculate the length of the hike in kilometers.

(20 cm × 24,000 = 480,000 cm;
480,000 cm ÷ 100 cm/m = 4,800 m;
4,800 ÷ 1,000 m/km = 4.8 km)

Math Skills Worksheet 17
"Using Proportions and Cross-Multiplication"

Information Shown on Maps

As you have already learned, there are many different ways of making maps. It is also true that there are many types of maps. You might already be familiar with some, such as road maps or political maps of the United States. But regardless of its type, each map should contain the information shown in **Figure 15.**

Figure 15 **Road Map of Connecticut**

Connecticut Road Map

Scale ONE CENTIMETER EQUALS ABOUT 4.6 KILOMETERS 1:460,000
ONE INCH EQUALS ABOUT 7.3 MILES

The **title** tells you what the map is about. The title will tell you what area is being shown on the map or give you information about the subject of the map.

A **map's scale** shows the relationship between the distance on the Earth's surface and the distance on the map. There are three ways a scale is shown on the map—verbal scale, graphic scale, and representative fraction.

A **graphic scale** is like a ruler. The distance on the Earth's surface is represented by a bar graph that shows units of distance.

A **verbal scale** is stated in words. It is a phrase that describes the measure of distance on the map relative to the distance on the Earth's surface.

A **representative fraction** is a fraction that shows the relationship between the distance on the map and the distance on the Earth's surface. It is unitless, meaning it stays the same no matter what units of measurement you are using. For example, say you are using a map with a representative fraction scale that is 1:24,000. If you are measuring distance on the map in centimeters, 1 cm on the map represents 24,000 cm on the Earth's surface. If the unit of measurement is an inch, then 1 in. on the map would represent 24,000 in. on the Earth's surface.

44

Multicultural CONNECTION

Maps made by Native Americans were similar to maps made by Europeans in that they included not only geographic information but also elements of their history, traditions, and mythology. Native American mapmakers also used standardized symbols to indicate roads, villages, rivers, and other physical features. The Aztec of central Mexico, for example, used rows of footprints to represent roads and swirling lines to indicate water. Aztec maps and mapmaking techniques were adapted by the Spanish, who explored and conquered the region.

Imagine that you are a trip planner for an automobile club. A couple of people come in who want to travel from Torrington, Connecticut, to Bristol, Connecticut. Using the map in Figure 15, describe the shortest travel route you would suggest they take between the two cities. List the roads they would take, the direction they would travel, and the towns they would pass through. Use the map scale to determine approximately how many miles there are between Torrington and Bristol.

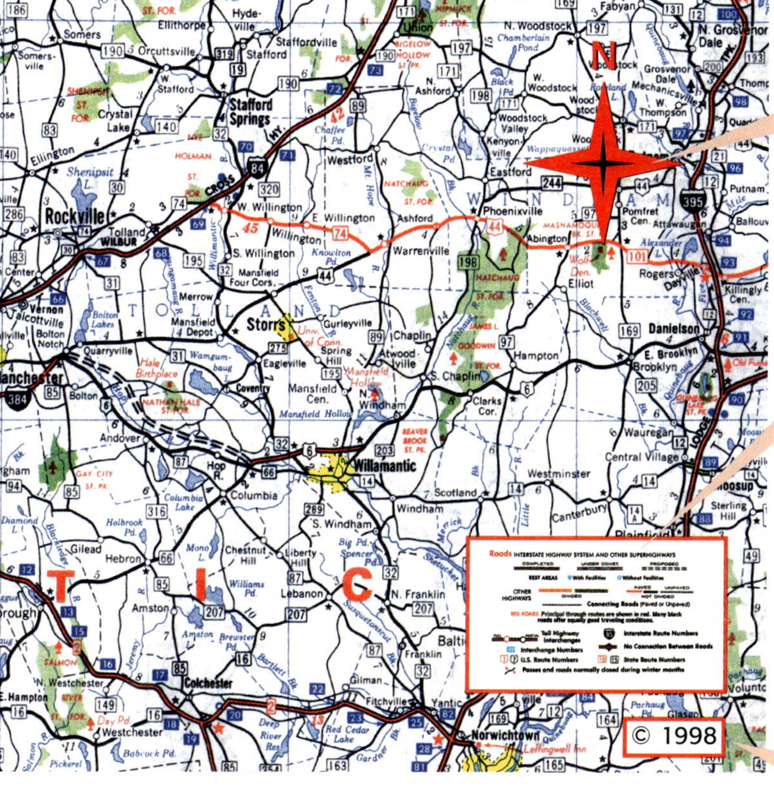

It is important to know direction on the map. One way to figure this out is to look at the compass rose. The **north arrow** shows you how the map is positioned in relation to true north.

Maps often use symbols for features such as highways and rivers. A **legend** is a list of the symbols used in the map and their explanations.

The **date** of a map is important because the Earth's surface is constantly changing. The date of a map tells you how old the information is.

REVIEW

1. A globe is a fairly accurate model of the Earth, yet it has some weaknesses. What is one weakness?
2. What is distortion on a map, and why does it occur?
3. What is remote sensing? How has it changed mapmaking?
4. **Summarizing Data** List five items found on maps. Explain how each item is important to reading a map.

45

Answers to Review

1. A globe is too small to show details, such as roads and rivers.
2. Distortions are changes in direction, distance, and the size and shape of landmasses that occur when information is transferred from a curved surface to a flat surface.
3. Remote sensing is the gathering of information about something without actually being there. Remote sensing has allowed mapmakers to map the surface of the Earth more accurately.
4. Title, scale, north arrow, legend, date; answers may vary.

4 Close

Quiz

1. Where is distortion found in a Mercator projection map? (near the poles)
2. How have photography and air travel contributed to the science of mapmaking? (Aircraft and satellites allow people to view Earth's surface from above; photography has improved the accuracy of maps.)
3. Why is it important for maps to have scales? (Map scales explain the relationship between distances as measured on the map and corresponding distances on Earth's surface.)

ALTERNATIVE ASSESSMENT

Desktop publishing software makes it easier for the noncartographer to create maps. Such maps often omit crucial elements, such as a scale, a date, or a compass rose. Have students bring in a map from a newspaper, a magazine, or an advertisement, and have them write a critique of the map's strengths and its shortcomings. Students may post the maps and critiques on a bulletin board.

Answers to APPLY

Answers may vary. Sample answer: The people would take State Road 8 south to U.S. Route 6 east to travel between Torrington and Bristol. This route would take them through Plymouth and Terryville before reaching Bristol. The trip is approximately 27 km.

Critical Thinking Worksheet 2
"Shaping the World"

Section 2 Review–California Standards: PE/ATE 7f

SECTION 3

Focus

Topographic Maps

In this section, students investigate how contour lines are used to show elevation and landforms on a topographic map. In addition, they learn how to read and interpret the features of a topographic map.

Bellringer

Have students examine the topographic map shown in **Figure 16.** Have them imagine that they are standing on the top of Campbell Hill. Students should describe in their ScienceLog what they see in each direction. Tell students that they will learn to read topographic maps, such as the ones in this section.

1) Motivate

ACTIVITY

Investigate Your Area If possible, obtain topographic maps of your area from the USGS. Display the maps for students to study. As a class, locate different landforms, such as lakes, mountains, and valleys. Discuss with students how contour intervals indicate changes in elevation.
Sheltered English

3

NEW TERMS
topographic map
elevation
contour lines
contour interval
relief
index contour

OBJECTIVES
- Describe how contour lines show elevation and landforms on a map.
- List the rules of contour lines.
- Interpret a topographic map.

Topographic Maps

Imagine that you are on an outdoor adventure trip. The trip's purpose is to improve your survival skills by having you travel across undeveloped territory with only a compass and a map. What kind of map will you be using? Well, it's not a road map—you won't be seeing a lot of roads where you are going. You will need a topographic map. A **topographic map** is a map that shows surface features, or topography, of the Earth. Topographic maps show both natural features, such as rivers, lakes and mountains, and features made by humans, such as cities, roads, and bridges. Topographic maps also show elevation. **Elevation** is the height of an object above sea level. The elevation at sea level is 0. In this section you will learn how to interpret a topographic map.

Elements of Elevation

The United States Geological Survey (USGS), a federal government agency, has made topographic maps for all of the United States. Each of these maps is a detailed description of a small area of the Earth's surface. Because the topographic maps produced by the USGS use feet as their unit of measure rather than meters, we will follow their example.

Contour Lines On a topographic map, contour lines are used to show elevation. **Contour lines** are lines that connect points of equal elevation. For example, one contour line would connect points on a map that have an elevation of 100 ft. Another line would connect points on a map that have an elevation of 200 ft. **Figure 16** illustrates how contour lines appear on a map.

Figure 16 *Because contour lines connect points of equal elevation, the shape of the contour lines reflects the shape of the land.*

46

Directed Reading Worksheet 2 Section 3

IS THAT A FACT!

The Ordnance Survey of Great Britain produces topographic maps with very large scales, ranging from 1:10,000 to 1:1,250. Such large scales permit a level of detail that extends to showing the location of public telephones, windmills, and large boulders!

Section 3–California Standards: PE/ATE 7f; LabBook: 7, 7b, 7f

Contour Interval The difference in elevation between one contour line and the next is called the **contour interval.** For example, a map with a contour interval of 20 ft would have contour lines every 20 ft of elevation change, such as 0 ft, 20 ft, 40 ft, 60 ft, and so on. A mapmaker chooses a contour interval based on the area's relief. **Relief** is the difference in elevation between the highest and lowest points of the area being mapped. Because the relief of a mountainous area is high, it might be shown on a map using a large contour interval, such as 100 ft. However, a flat area has low relief and might be shown on a map using a small contour interval, such as 10 ft.

The spacing of contour lines also indicates slope, as shown in **Figure 17.** Contour lines that are close together, with little space between them, usually show a steep slope. Contour lines that are spaced far apart generally represent a gentle slope.

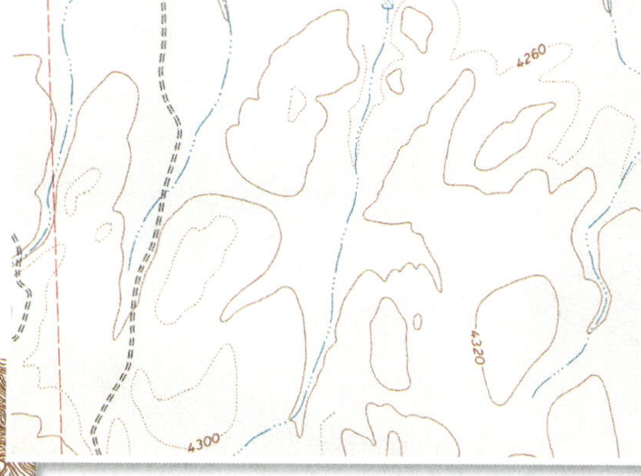

PIKES PEAK
Summit House
Water Tanks

Figure 17 *The portion of the topographic map on the left shows Pikes Peak, in Colorado. Notice how close together the contour lines are. The map above shows a valley in Big Bend Ranch State Park, in Texas. Notice the widely spaced contour lines.*

Index Contour On many topographic maps, the mapmaker uses an index contour to make reading the map a little easier. An **index contour** is a darker, heavier contour line that is usually every fifth line and that is labeled by elevation. Find an index contour on both of the topographic maps shown above.

Self-Check

If elevation is not labeled on a map, how can you determine if the mapped area is steep or not? *(See page 564 to check your answer.)*

MATH BREAK

Counting Contours

Calculate the contour interval for the map shown in Figure 16 on the previous page. (Hint: Find the difference between two bold lines found next to each other. Subtract the lower marked elevation from the higher marked elevation. Divide by 5.)

Homework

Have students write a fictitious journal from the perspective of a member of an expedition team. Every journal entry should include a description of the topography they encountered. Students should include a map in which they use the appropriate symbols and contour lines to show their route. This activity will take several days to complete. After the student explorers have "returned" from their expedition, they should present their map and read their journal entries to the class.

2 Teach

Discussion

Reproduce on the chalkboard a mountainous portion of one of the contour maps shown in the text. Discuss with students where the steepest slopes are (where the lines are closest together). Then change the contour interval by erasing every other contour line. Point out to students that the contour interval is now twice as large. Discuss with students the advantages and the disadvantages of a map with a larger contour interval. (The map may seem easier to read, but detail is lost.)

Reteaching

If students are having trouble understanding contour lines, use some modeling clay to make a landform. Ask a volunteer to hold a ruler vertically next to the landform while you use a plastic knife to mark off contour intervals around the landform. When you are finished, have students view the landform from the side so that they can see the uniformity of the contour intervals and from above so they can see how the intervals would appear on a topographic map. Then give pairs of students some modeling clay and invite them to try the same activity themselves. Sheltered English

Answers to Self-Check

If the lines are close together, then the mapped area is steep. If the lines are far apart, the mapped area has a gradual slope or is flat.

Answers to MATHBREAK

Sample answer:
500 ft − 450 ft = 50 ft
50 ft ÷ 5 = 10 ft
contour interval = 10 ft

3 Extend

Guided Practice

Display a portion of a topographic map and point to the following features. Have students identify them and describe what they indicate.

- index contour line (identifiable from its color and its label elevation; index contours make reading the map easier)
- steep slope (identifiable by the close spacing of the contour lines)
- gentle slope (identifiable because the contour lines are relatively far apart)
- river, lake, or pond (identifiable by shape and color)

Sheltered English

Group Activity

Have groups put together a contour-map-reading presentation for another class. Encourage them to make some handouts for the class about topographic maps and their uses and to include visual elements, such as a poster or a diagram, that highlight the features of topographic maps. Groups might finish their presentation with a quiz to assess how well they've explained the material.

Meeting Individual Needs

Advanced Learners Have students research orienteering and learn some of the techniques involved. Encourage students to explain or demonstrate for classmates such skills as how to set a map with a compass, how to determine bearings, and how to reconcile the differences between magnetic north, grid north, and true north.

Reading a Topographic Map

Topographic maps, like other maps, use symbols to represent parts of the Earth's surface. The legend from the USGS topographic map in **Figure 18** shows some of the common symbols used to represent certain features in topographic maps.

Different colors are also used to represent different features of the Earth's surface. In general, buildings, roads, bridges, and railroads are black. Contour lines are brown. Major highways are red. Cities and towns are pink. Bodies of water, such as rivers, lakes, and oceans, are shown in blue, and wooded areas are represented by the color green.

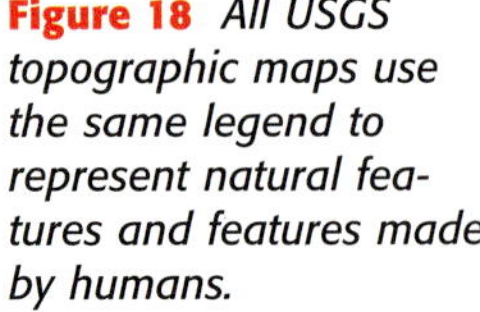

Figure 18 *All USGS topographic maps use the same legend to represent natural features and features made by humans.*

48

Connect to Oceanography

Oceanographers use contour maps to map the topography of the ocean floor. Traditionally, darker colors represent deeper depths, while lighter colors represent areas closer to the surface of the water. If possible, display an oceanographic map, and have students apply what they have learned about topographic maps to create a profile of a section of the ocean floor. Students should find similarities between the topography of the ocean floor and that of continental landmasses.

The Golden Rules of Contour Lines Contour lines are the key to interpreting the size and shape of landforms on a topographic map. When you first look at a topographic map, it might seem confusing. Accurately reading a topographic map requires training and practice. The following rules will help you understand how to read topographic maps:

1. Contour lines never cross. All points along a contour line represent a single elevation.

2. The spacing of contour lines depends on slope characteristics. Closely spaced contour lines represent a steep slope. Widely spaced contour lines represent a gentle slope.

3. Contour lines that cross a valley or stream are V-shaped. The V points toward the area of higher elevation. If a stream or river flows through the valley, the V points upstream.

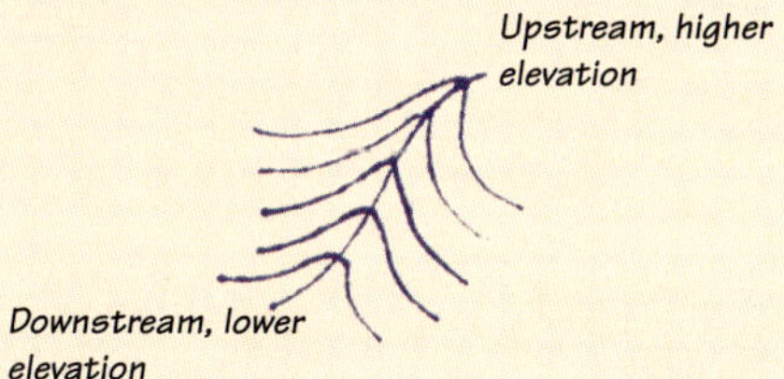

4. Contour lines form closed circles around the tops of hills, mountains, and depressions. One way to tell hills and depressions apart is that depressions are marked with short, straight lines inside the circle, pointing downslope toward the center of the depression.

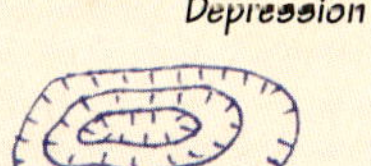

environmental science CONNECTION

State agencies, such as the Texas Parks and Wildlife Department, use topographic maps to plot the distribution and occurrence of endangered plant and animal species. By marking the location of endangered species on a map, these agencies can record and protect these habitats.

REVIEW

1. How do topographic maps represent the Earth's surface?
2. If a contour map contains streams, can you tell where the higher ground is even if all of the numbers are removed?
3. Why can't contour lines cross?
4. **Inferring Conclusions** Why isn't the highest point on a hill or a mountain represented by a contour line?

49

Answers to Review

1. Topographic maps use contour lines to show the surface features of Earth.
2. Yes; contour lines that cross a stream are V-shaped. The V points toward the area of higher elevation.
3. Contour lines cannot cross because they represent a certain elevation. If contour lines crossed, the point where the lines crossed would have two different elevations, which is impossible.
4. The highest point on a hill or mountain is a single point, not a group of points with the same elevation.

4 Close

PG 492

Topographic Tuber

Quiz

1. What is a contour interval on a topographic map? (the difference in elevation between one contour line and the next)
2. What do closely spaced contour lines on a topographic map indicate? (a steep area)
3. How does a topographic map indicate the direction that a stream flows ? (Streams flow downhill, or in the direction that elevation decreases. The V's point toward an area of higher elevation.)

Alternative Assessment

Photocopy a portion of a topographic map that shows a mountain. Distribute copies to students, and ask them to trace a route to the top. Then have them write a description of their "trail" that describes the length of the hike, at which elevations the trail is the steepest, and at which points the slope is gentle. Have them also discuss other features such as power lines or road crossings.

Reinforcement Worksheet 2
"Interpreting a Topographic Map"

Math Skills Worksheet 46
"Mapping and Surveying"

Section 3 Review–California Standards: PE/ATE 7f

Chapter Highlights

VOCABULARY DEFINITIONS

SECTION 1

map model or representation of the Earth's surface

reference point a fixed place on the Earth's surface used to describe direction and location

cardinal directions north, south, east, west

true north the geographic North Pole

magnetic declination the angle of correction for the difference between geographic north and magnetic north

equator an imaginary circle halfway between the poles that divides the Earth into the Northern and Southern Hemispheres

latitude the distance north or south from the equator; measured in degrees

longitude the distance east or west from the prime meridian; measured in degrees

prime meridian the line of longitude that passes through Greenwich, England; represents 0° longitude

SECTION 2

Mercator projection a map projection that results when the contents of the globe are transferred onto a cylinder

conic projection a map projection that is made by transferring the contents of the globe onto a cone

azimuthal projection a map projection that is made by transferring the contents of the globe onto a plane

aerial photograph a photograph taken from the air

remote sensing gathering information about something without actually being nearby

Chapter Highlights

SECTION 1

Vocabulary

map *(p. 34)*
reference point *(p. 35)*
cardinal directions *(p. 35)*
true north *(p. 36)*
magnetic declination *(p. 36)*
equator *(p. 37)*
latitude *(p. 37)*
longitude *(p. 38)*
prime meridian *(p. 38)*

Section Notes

- The North and South Poles are used as reference points for describing direction and location on the Earth.
- The cardinal directions—north, south, east, and west—are used for describing direction.
- Magnetic compasses are used to determine direction on the Earth's surface. The north needle on the compass points to the magnetic north pole.
- Because the geographic North Pole never changes location, it is called true north. The magnetic poles are different from the Earth's geographic poles and have changed location throughout the Earth's history.
- The magnetic declination is the adjustment or difference between magnetic north and geographic north.
- Latitude and longitude are intersecting lines that help you find locations on a map or a globe. Lines of latitude run east-west. Lines of longitude run north-south through the poles.

Labs

Round or Flat? *(p. 488)*
Orient Yourself! *(p. 490)*

SECTION 2

Vocabulary

Mercator projection *(p. 41)*
conic projection *(p. 42)*
azimuthal projection *(p. 42)*
aerial photograph *(p. 43)*
remote sensing *(p. 43)*

Section Notes

- A globe is the most accurate representation of the Earth's surface.
- Maps have built-in distortion because some information is lost when mapmakers transfer images from a curved surface to a flat surface.

Skills Check

Math Concepts

REPRESENTATIVE FRACTION One type of map scale is a representative fraction. A representative fraction is a fraction or ratio that shows the relationship between the distance on the map and the distance on the Earth's surface. It is unitless, meaning it stays the same no matter what units of measurement you are using. For example, say you are using a map with a representative fraction scale that is 1:12,000. If you are measuring distance on the map in centimeters, 1 cm on the map represents 12,000 cm on the Earth's surface. A measure of 3 cm on the map represents 12,000 × 3 cm = 36,000 cm on the Earth's surface.

Visual Understanding

THE POLES The Earth has two different sets of poles—the geographic poles and the magnetic poles. See Figure 4 on page 36 to review how the geographic poles and the magnetic poles differ.

INFORMATION SHOWN ON MAPS Study Figure 15 on pages 44 and 45 to review the necessary information each map should contain.

50

Lab and Activity Highlights

LabBook

Round or Flat? PG 488

Orient Yourself! PG 490

Topographic Tuber PG 492

Datasheets for LabBook (blackline masters for these labs)

SECTION 2

- Mapmakers use map projections to transfer images of the Earth's curved surface to a flat surface.
- The most common map projections are based on three geometric shapes—cylinders, cones, and planes.
- Remote sensing has allowed mapmakers to make more accurate maps.
- All maps should have a title, date, scale, legend, and north arrow.

SECTION 3

Vocabulary

topographic map *(p. 46)*
elevation *(p. 46)*
contour lines *(p. 46)*
contour interval *(p. 47)*
relief *(p. 47)*
index contour *(p. 47)*

Section Notes

- Topographic maps use contour lines to show a mapped area's elevation and the shape and size of landforms.
- The shape of contour lines reflects the shape of the land.
- The contour interval and the spacing of contour lines indicate the slope of the land.
- Like all maps, topographic maps use a set of symbols to represent features of the Earth's surface.
- Contour lines never cross. Contour lines that cross a valley or stream are V-shaped. Contour lines form closed circles around the tops of hills, mountains, and depressions.

Labs

Topographic Tuber *(p. 492)*

internetconnect

GO TO: go.hrw.com

Visit the **HRW** Web site for a variety of learning tools related to this chapter. Just type in the keyword:

KEYWORD: HSTMAP

GO TO: www.scilinks.org

Visit the **National Science Teachers Association** on-line Web site for Internet resources related to this chapter. Just type in the ***sci*LINKS** number for more information about the topic:

TOPIC: Finding Locations on the Earth	***sci*LINKS NUMBER:** HSTE030
TOPIC: Latitude and Longitude	***sci*LINKS NUMBER:** HSTE035
TOPIC: Mapmaking	***sci*LINKS NUMBER:** HSTE040
TOPIC: Topographic Maps	***sci*LINKS NUMBER:** HSTE045

51

Lab and Activity Highlights

LabBank

Inquiry Labs, Looking for Buried Treasure, Lab 9

Long-Term Projects & Research Ideas, Project 30

VOCABULARY DEFINITIONS, *continued*

SECTION 3

topographic map a map that shows the surface features of the Earth

elevation the height of surface landforms above sea level; the height of an object above sea level

contour lines lines that connect points of equal elevation

contour interval the difference in elevation between one contour line and the next

relief the difference in elevation between the highest and lowest points of an area being mapped

index contour a darker contour line that is usually every fifth line and is labeled by elevation

Vocabulary Review Worksheet 2

Blackline masters of these Chapter Highlights can be found in the **Study Guide.**

Chapter Review Answers

USING VOCABULARY

1. True north is the geographic North Pole. Magnetic north refers to the magnetic north pole, which changes.
2. Latitude is the distance north and south from the equator. Longitude is the distance east and west from the prime meridian. Both latitude and longitude are measured in degrees.
3. The equator is the imaginary circle halfway between the poles that divides the Earth into Northern and Southern Hemispheres and represents 0° latitude. The prime meridian represents 0° longitude.
4. A Mercator projection is a map projection made by transferring the contents of the globe onto a cylinder of paper. An azimuthal projection is a map projection made by projecting the contents of the globe onto a plane.
5. Contour interval is the difference in elevation between one contour line and the next. An index contour is a darker, heavier contour line that usually occurs every fifth line and is labeled.
6. Elevation is the height of an object above sea level. Relief is the difference in elevation between the highest and lowest points of the area being mapped.

UNDERSTANDING CONCEPTS

Multiple Choice

7. b
8. c
9. d
10. b
11. b
12. a
13. d
14. b
15. b
16. b

Chapter Review

USING VOCABULARY

Explain the difference between the following sets of words:

1. true north/magnetic north
2. latitude/longitude
3. equator/prime meridian
4. Mercator projection/azimuthal projection
5. contour interval/index contour
6. elevation/relief

UNDERSTANDING CONCEPTS

Multiple Choice

7. A point whose latitude is 0° is located on the
   a. North Pole.
   b. equator.
   c. South Pole.
   d. prime meridian.

8. The distance in degrees east or west of the prime meridian is
   a. latitude.
   b. declination.
   c. longitude.
   d. projection.

9. The needle of a magnetic compass points toward the
   a. meridians.
   b. parallels.
   c. geographic North Pole.
   d. magnetic north pole.

10. The most common map projections are based on three geometric shapes. Which of the following geometric shapes is not one of them?
    a. cylinder
    b. square
    c. cone
    d. plane

11. A Mercator projection is distorted near the
    a. equator.
    b. poles.
    c. prime meridian.
    d. date line.

12. What kind of scale is unitless?
    a. representative fraction
    b. verbal
    c. graphic
    d. mathematical

13. What is the relationship between the distance on a map and the actual distance on the Earth called?
    a. legend
    b. elevation
    c. relief
    d. scale

14. The latitude of the North Pole is
    a. 100° north.
    b. 90° north.
    c. 180° north.
    d. 90° south.

15. Widely spaced contour lines indicate a
    a. steep slope.
    b. gentle slope.
    c. hill.
    d. river.

52

Concept Mapping Transparency 2

Blackline masters of this Chapter Review can be found in the **Study Guide.**

Chapter 2 Review–California Standards: PE/ATE Q1–6: 7f; Q7–21: 7f

16. __?__ is the height of an object above sea level.
   a. Contour interval
   b. Elevation
   c. Declination
   d. Index contour

Short Answer

17. How can a magnetic compass be used to find direction on the Earth's surface?

18. Why is a map legend important?

19. Why does Greenland appear so large in relation to other landmasses on a map with a Mercator projection?

20. What is the function of contour lines on a topographic map?

Concept Mapping

21. Use the following terms to create a concept map: maps, legend, map projection, map parts, scale, cylinder, title, cone, plane, date, north arrow.

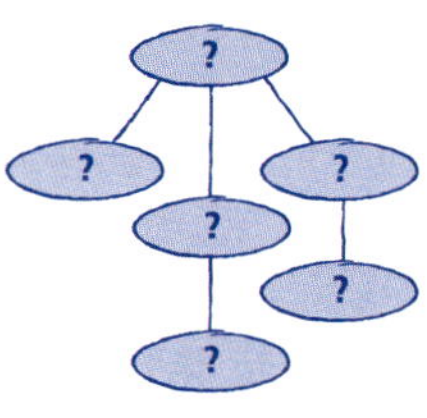

CRITICAL THINKING AND PROBLEM SOLVING

Write one or two sentences to answer the following questions:

22. One of the important parts of a map is its date. Why is this so important?

23. A mapmaker has to draw one map for three different countries that do not share a common unit of measure. What type of scale would this mapmaker use? Why?

24. How would a topographic map of the Rocky Mountains differ from a topographic map of the Great Plains?

MATH IN SCIENCE

25. A map has a verbal scale of 1 cm equals 200 m. If the actual distance between two points is 12,000 m, how far apart will they appear on the map?

26. On a topographic map, the contour interval is 50 ft. The bottom of a mountain begins on a contour line marked with a value of 1050 ft. The top of the mountain is within a contour line that is 12 lines higher than the bottom of the mountain. What is the elevation of the top of the mountain?

INTERPRETING GRAPHICS

Use the topographic map below to answer the questions that follow.

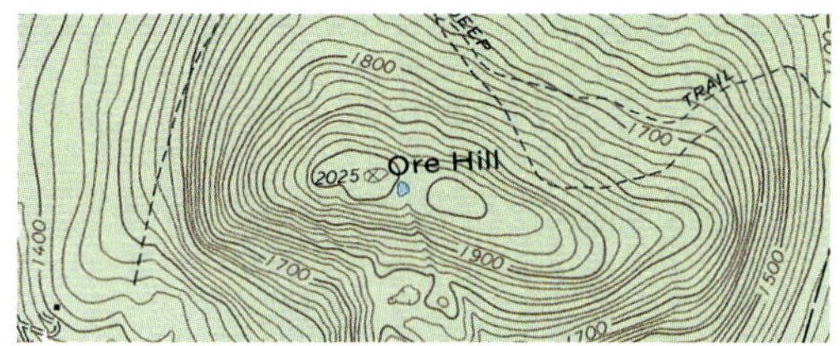

27. What is the elevation change between two adjacent lines on this map?

28. What type of relief does this area have?

29. What surface features are shown on this map?

30. What is the elevation at the top of Ore Hill?

NOW What Do You Think?

Take a minute to review your answers to the ScienceLog questions on page 33. Have your answers changed? If necessary, revise your answers based on what you have learned since you began this chapter.

Short Answer

17. The needle on a magnetic compass points to magnetic north, indicating the direction of the magnetic north pole. If you know an area's magnetic declination, you can determine true north.
18. A map legend is important because it defines the set of symbols used in the map.
19. Greenland appears large on a map with a Mercator projection because of distortion. Maps with a Mercator projection are increasingly distorted as the distance from the equator increases.
20. Contour lines on a topographic map show the elevation, the relief, and the shape of landforms.

Concept Mapping

21.  An answer to this exercise can be found at the end of this book.

Critical Thinking and Problem Solving

22. A date on a map is important because the Earth is constantly changing. The date shows you how old the information is. It might also show you what the landscape was once like.
23. The mapmaker should use a representative fraction. A representative fraction is unitless and could be used by all three countries. Furthermore, the countries could find out distances on the map using their own unit of measure.
24. A topographic map of the Rocky Mountains would show contour lines close together, indicating steep slopes, while a contour map of the Great Plains would show contour lines spaced far apart, indicating a flat or gradual slope.

Math in Science

25. 60 cm
26. 1,650 ft

NOW What Do You Think?

1. No; maps do not represent the world accurately because they are distorted.
2. Answers may vary. Sample answer: Symbols are used to show information on maps.
3. Every map must contain a title, legend, scale, date, and north arrow.

Interpreting Graphics

27. 20 ft
28. It has very high relief.
29. Two hills are shown on this map.
30. The elevation at the top of Ore Hill is 2,025 ft.

SCIENCE, TECHNOLOGY, AND SOCIETY

The Lost City of Ubar

Background

According to legend, Allah became displeased with the wickedness of the citizens of Ubar and buried the city under a wave of sand. Ubar remained lost for thousands of years until the coordinated efforts of filmmaker Nicholas Clapp, NASA scientist Dr. Ronald Blom, and a team of explorers uncovered the ruins in 1991.

Science, Technology, and Society

The Lost City of Ubar

Can you imagine tree sap being more valuable than gold? Well, about 2,000 years ago, a tree sap called frankincense was just that! Frankincense was used to treat illnesses and to disguise body odor. Ancient civilizations from Rome to India treasured it. While the name of the city that was the center of frankincense production and export had been known for generations—Ubar—there was just one problem: No one knew where it was! The name Ubar comes from Arab tradition, but the city's location had remained a mystery for more than 1,500 years. But now the mystery is solved. Using remote sensing, scientists have found clues hidden beneath desert sand dunes.

▲ *Trails and roads appear as purple lines on this computer-generated remote-sensing image.*

Using Eyes in the Sky

The process of remote sensing uses satellites to take pictures of large areas of land. The satellite records images as sets of data and then sends these data to a receiver on Earth. Then a computer processes the data and displays the images. These remote-sensing images can then be used to reveal differences unseen by the naked eye.

Remote-sensing images reveal modern roads as well as ancient caravan routes hidden beneath sand dunes in the Sahara Desert. But how could researchers tell the difference between the two? Everything on Earth reflects or radiates energy. Soil, vegetation, cities, and roads all emit a unique wavelength of energy. The problem is, sometimes modern roads and ancient roads are difficult to distinguish. The differences between similar objects can be enhanced by assigning natural or "false" color to an area and then displaying the area on a computer screen. Researchers used differences in color to distinguish between the roads of Ubar and modern roads. Decades of rubber tires cannot grind dirt and rock as fine as the hooves of camels can over hundreds of years. When researchers found ancient caravan routes and discovered that all the routes met at one location, they knew they had discovered the lost city of Ubar!

Continuing Discovery

Archaeologists continue to investigate the region around Ubar. They believe the great city may have collapsed into a limestone cavern beneath its foundation. Researchers are continuing to use remote sensing to study more images for clues to aid their investigation.

Think About It!

▶ Do modern civilizations value certain products or resources enough to establish elaborate trade routes for their transport? If so, what makes these products so valuable? Record your thoughts in your ScienceLog.

54

Answer to Think About It!

Students' answers will vary but may include the value modern civilizations place on paper currency, fossil fuels, or spices.

CAREERS

WATERSHED PLANNER

Have you ever wondered if the water you drink is safe, or what you could do to make sure it stays safe? As a watershed planner, **Nancy Charbeneau** identifies and solves land-use problems that may affect water quality.

Nancy Charbeneau enjoys using her teaching background in her current career as a watershed planner. A watershed is any section of land where runoff water drains into a stream, river, lake, or ocean. Charbeneau spends a lot of time writing publications and developing programs that explain the effects of land use on the quality of water.

Land is used in hundreds of ways. In urban areas, land is used for buildings and transportation. In rural areas, land is used for farming, ranching, and drilling. These land uses can have negative effects on water resources. Charbeneau produces educational materials to inform the public about threats to water quality.

Mapping the Problems

Charbeneau uses Geographic Information System (GIS) maps to determine types of vegetation and the functions of different sections of land. GIS is a computer-based tool that allows people to store, access, and display geographic information collected through remote-sensing field work, global positioning systems, and other sources. Maps and mapping systems play an important role in identifying land areas with water problems. Aerial photography as well as satellite and infrared imaging provide important information about topography, soil conditions, vegetation, and pollution.

Maps tell Charbeneau whether an area has problems with soil erosion that could threaten water quality. Often the type of soil plays an important role in erosion. Thin or sandy soil does not hold water well, allowing for faster runoff and erosion. Flat land with heavy vegetation holds more water and is less prone to sustain poor water quality due to erosion.

Understanding the Importance

Charbeneau's biggest challenge is raising awareness and increasing understanding of the link between land use and water quality. Many people who own land don't realize they could be using it in ways that damage their own drinking water. If a harmful substance is introduced into a watershed, it may contaminate an aquifer (underground stream) or a well. As Charbeneau puts it, "Most people want to do the right thing, but they need help identifying and implementing land management practices that will protect water quality but still allow them to earn a decent living off their land."

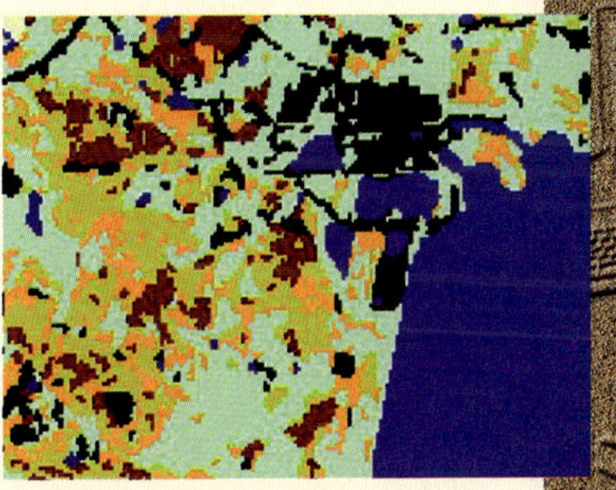

▲ *This GIS map shows the location of ground water in blue.*

Reading the Possibilities

▶ Map out your nearest watershed. Can you find any potential sources of contamination?

CAREERS

Watershed Planner—Nancy Charbeneau

Background

Nancy Charbeneau has undergraduate degrees in elementary education and biology and a master's degree in landscape architecture.

Charbeneau's experience as a teacher prepared her for the production of educational materials that alert the public to water-quality issues. Her degree in landscape architecture exposed her to the sophisticated mapping systems she uses as a watershed developer.

Answer to Reading the Possibilities

Answers will vary, depending on the topography and degree of urbanization of your region. Industrialized areas may have problems with groundwater pollution, while mountainous areas may have problems with erosion. Aerial photography, GIS, and infrared maps can reveal additional information about the vegetation and land use in a region.

TIMELINE

UNIT 2

Earth's Resources

In this unit, you will learn about the basic components of the solid Earth—rocks and the minerals from which they are made. The ground beneath your feet is a treasure-trove of interesting materials, some of which are very valuable. Secrets of the past are also hidden within its depths. This timeline shows some of the events that have occurred through history as scientists have come to understand more about our planet.

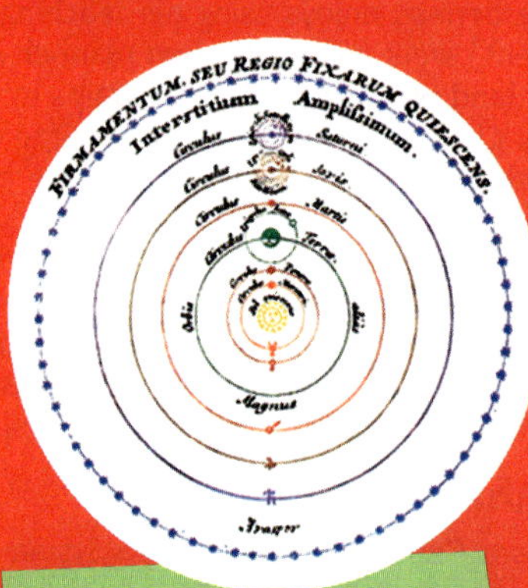

1533

Nicolaus Copernicus argues that the sun is the center of the universe rather than the Earth, as was commonly believed, but does not publish his findings for another 10 years.

1680

The dodo, a flightless bird, is driven to extinction by hunters. It is the first extinction of a species in recorded history.

1955

Using 1 million pounds of pressure and temperatures of more than 3,000°F, General Electric creates the first artificial diamonds from graphite.

1969

Apollo 11 astronauts Neil Armstrong and Edwin "Buzz" Aldrin bring 20 kg of moon rocks back to Earth.

1975

Junko Tabei becomes the first woman to successfully climb Mount Everest, 22 years after Edmund Hillary and Tenzing Norgay first conquered the mountain in 1953.

1735

George Brandt identifies a new element and names it cobalt. This is the first metal to be discovered since ancient times.

1848

Gold is discovered in California. Prospectors during the gold rush of the following year are referred to as "forty-niners."

1861

Fossil remains of *Archaeopteryx,* a possible link between reptiles and birds, are discovered in Germany.

1936

Hoover Dam is completed. This massive hydroelectric dam, standing more than 72 stories high, required 450,000 cement-truck loads of concrete to build.

1946

Willard F. Libby develops a method of dating prehistoric objects by using radioactive carbon.

1984

Russian engineers drill a borehole 12 km into the Earth's crust, three times deeper than the deepest mine shaft.

1997

Sojourner, a roving probe on Mars, investigates a Martian boulder nicknamed Yogi.

Chapter Organizer

CHAPTER ORGANIZATION	TIME MINUTES	OBJECTIVES	LABS, INVESTIGATIONS, AND DEMONSTRATIONS
Chapter Opener **pp. 58–59**	45	California Standards: PE/ATE 6c, 7, 7b, 7d	**Investigate!** Animal, Vegetable, or Mineral? p. 59
Section 1 **What Is a Mineral?**	90	▶ Explain the four characteristics of a mineral. ▶ Classify minerals according to the two major compositional groups. PE/ATE 6, 6b, 7, 7a, 7b, 7e	
Section 2 **Identifying Minerals**	90	▶ Classify minerals using common mineral-identification techniques. ▶ Explain special properties of minerals. ▶ Describe what makes a mineral crystal a gem. PE/ATE 6, 6b, 7; LabBook 7, 7b, 7d, 7e	**QuickLab,** Scratch Test, p. 66 **Skill Builder,** Mysterious Minerals, p. 494 **Datasheets for LabBook,** Mysterious Minerals, Datasheet 5 **Skill Builder,** Is It Fool's Gold?–A Dense Situation, p. 496 **Datasheets for LabBook,** Is It Fool's Gold?–A Dense Situation, Datasheet 6
Section 3 **The Formation and Mining of Minerals**	90	▶ Describe the environments in which minerals are formed. ▶ Compare and contrast the different types of mining. PE/ATE 6, 6b, 6c	**Long-Term Projects & Research Ideas,** Project 31

See page **T20** *for a complete correlation of this book with the*

CALIFORNIA SCIENCE CONTENT STANDARDS.

Correlations are also provided at point of use throughout this ATE.

TECHNOLOGY RESOURCES

Guided Reading Audio CD
English or Spanish, Chapter 3

Classroom Management CD-ROM

Test Generator CD-ROM

CNN **Eye on the Environment,** Greening Sudbury, Segment 12

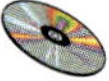

Earth Science Videodisc
Composition of the Earth: 32233–44060
Chemical Elements: 32234–37845
Minerals of the Earth's Crust: 37846–44060

Chapter 3 • Minerals of the Earth's Crust

	CLASSROOM WORKSHEETS, TRANSPARENCIES, AND RESOURCES	SCIENCE INTEGRATION AND CONNECTIONS	REVIEW AND ASSESSMENT
	Directed Reading Worksheet 3 **Science Puzzlers, Twisters & Teasers,** Worksheet 3		
	Directed Reading Worksheet 3, Section 1 **Transparency 90,** Gold Crystal Structure	**Connect to Life Science,** p. 60 in ATE **Life Science Connection,** p. 62 **Connect to Chemistry,** p. 62 in ATE **Multicultural Connection,** p. 62 in ATE **Holt Anthology of Science Fiction,** *The Metal Man*	**Homework,** p. 62 in ATE **Review,** p. 63 **Quiz,** p. 63 in ATE **Alternative Assessment,** p. 63 in ATE
	Directed Reading Worksheet 3, Section 2 **Reinforcement Worksheet 3,** Mystery Mineral **Transparency 91,** Mohs' Hardness Scale **Transparency 92,** Special Properties of Some Minerals **Reinforcement Worksheet 3,** The Mineral Quiz Show	**Multicultural Connection,** p. 66 in ATE **Real-World Connection,** p. 67 in ATE	**Review,** p. 67 **Quiz,** p. 67 in ATE **Alternative Assessment,** p. 67 in ATE
	Directed Reading Worksheet 3, Section 3 **Transparency 165,** Three Major Categories of Elements **Math Skills for Science Worksheet 21,** Percentages, Fractions, and Decimals **Critical Thinking Worksheet 3,** Mineral Hunt	**Connect to Life Science,** p. 69 in ATE **Cross-Disciplinary Focus,** p. 69 in ATE **Multicultural Connection,** p. 69 in ATE **MathBreak,** How Pure is Pure? p. 70 **Math and More,** p. 70 in ATE **Connect to Physical Science,** p. 70 in ATE **Multicultural Connection,** p. 70 in ATE **Weird Science:** Lightning Leftovers, p. 76	**Self-Check,** p. 69 **Review,** p. 71 **Quiz,** p. 71 in ATE **Alternative Assessment,** p. 71 in ATE

Holt, Rinehart and Winston On-line Resources

go.hrw.com

For worksheets and other teaching aids related to this chapter, visit the HRW Web site and type in the keyword: **HSTMIN**

National Science Teachers Association

www.scilinks.org

Encourage students to use the keywords listed on the Technology Highlights page to access information and resources on the **NSTA** Web site.

END-OF-CHAPTER REVIEW AND ASSESSMENT

Chapter Review in Study Guide
Vocabulary and Notes in Study Guide
Chapter Tests with Performance-Based Assessment, Chapter 3 Test
Chapter Tests with Performance-Based Assessment, Performance-Based Assessment 3
Concept Mapping Transparency 3

Chapter Resources & Worksheets

Visual Resources

TEACHING TRANSPARENCIES

#90 #91 #92

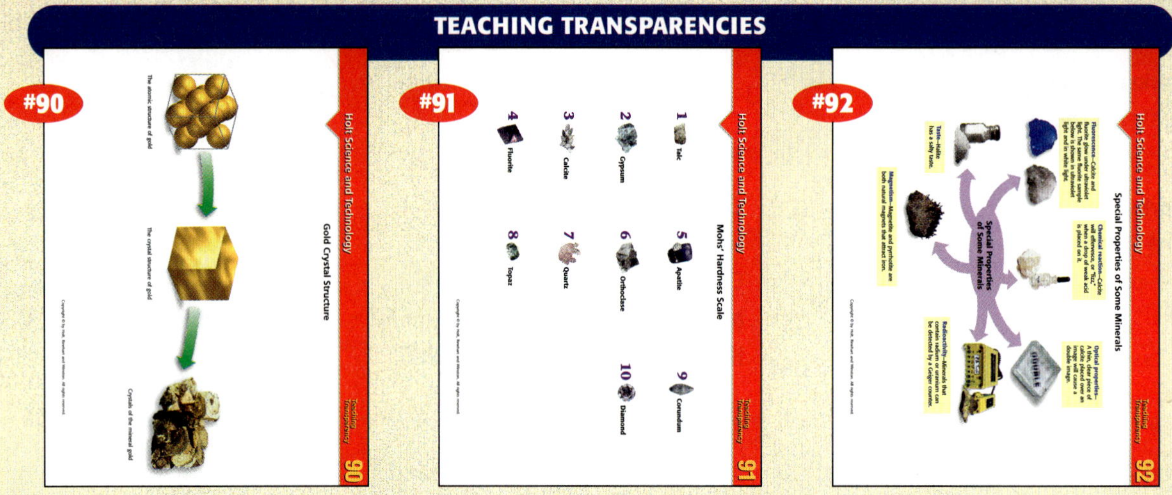

TEACHING TRANSPARENCIES

#165

CONCEPT MAPPING TRANSPARENCY

#3

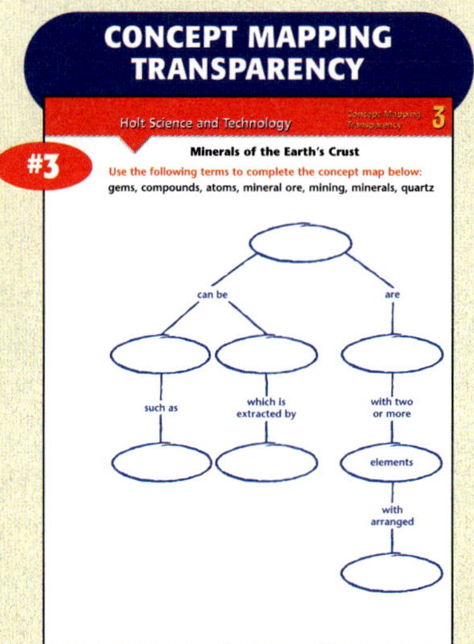

Meeting Individual Needs

DIRECTED READING

#3

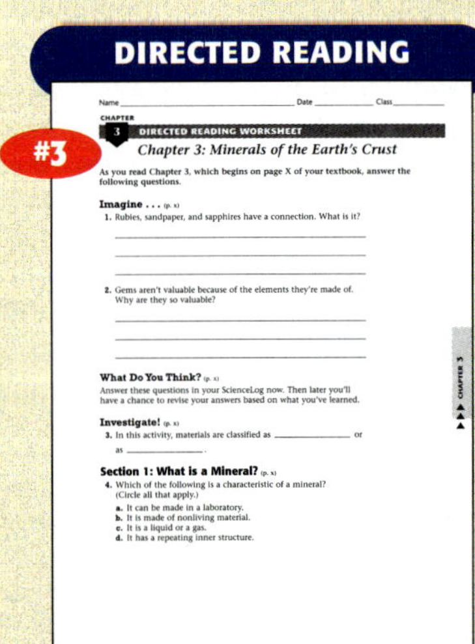

REINFORCEMENT & VOCABULARY REVIEW

#3 #3

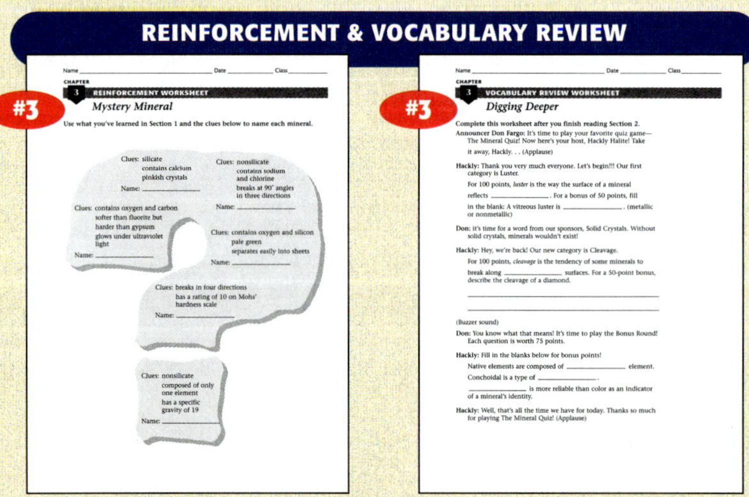

SCIENCE PUZZLERS, TWISTERS & TEASERS

#3

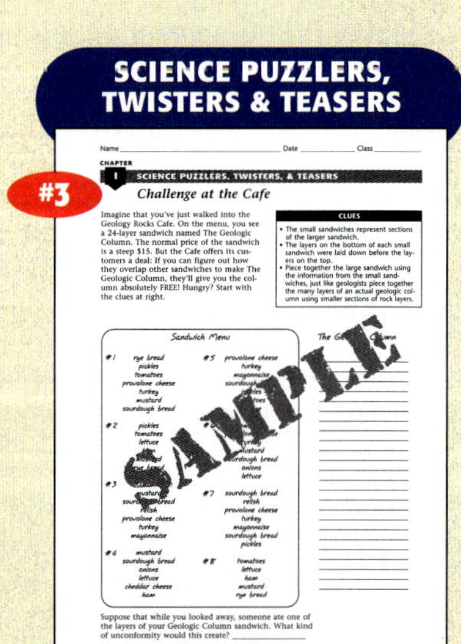

Chapter 3 • Minerals of the Earth's Crust

Review & Assessment

STUDY GUIDE

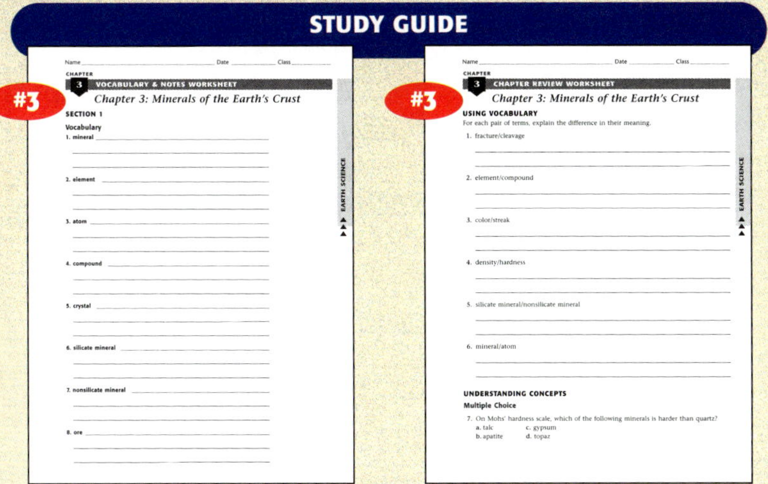

CHAPTER TESTS WITH PERFORMANCE-BASED ASSESSMENT

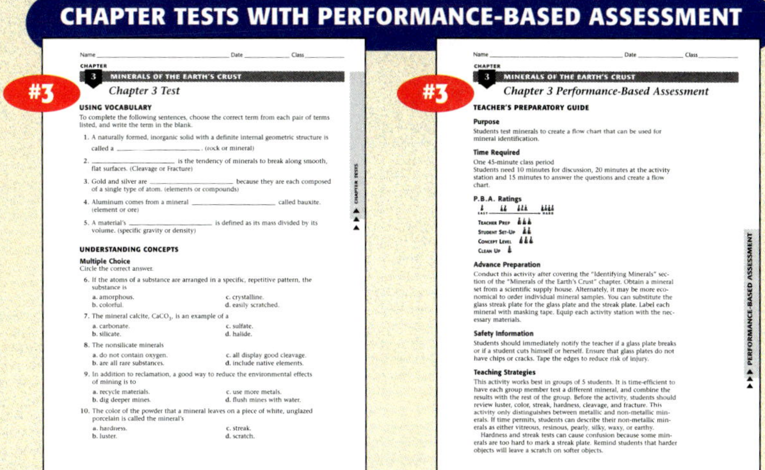

Lab Worksheets

LONG-TERM PROJECTS & RESEARCH IDEAS

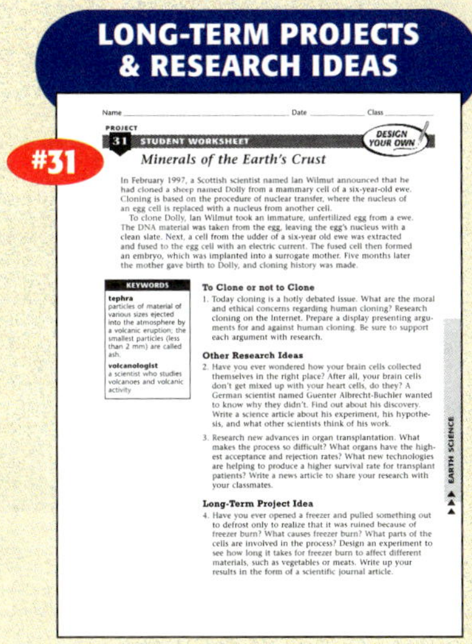

DATASHEETS FOR LABBOOK

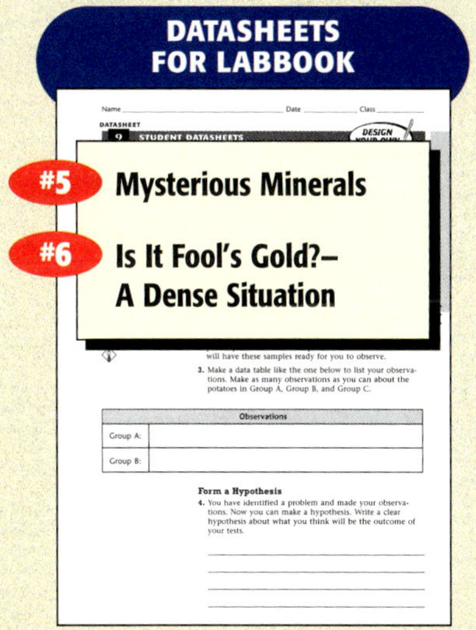

Applications & Extensions

CRITICAL THINKING & PROBLEM SOLVING

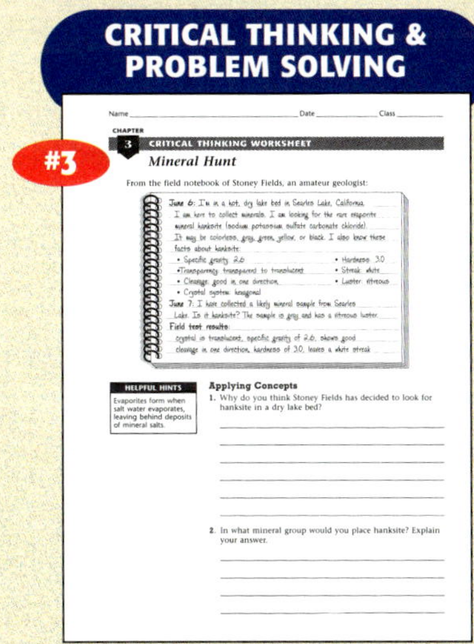

EYE ON THE ENVIRONMENT

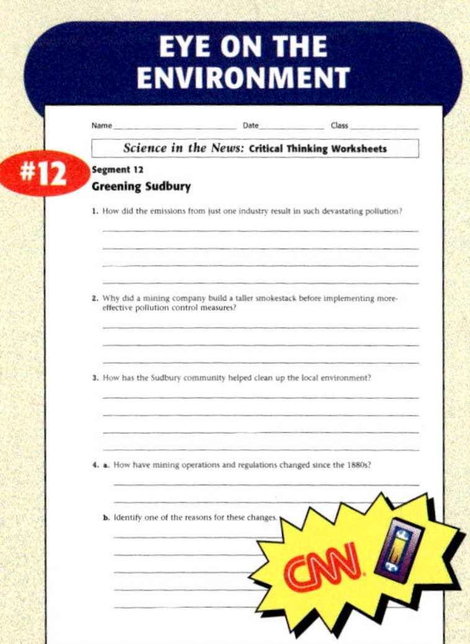

Chapter Background

Section 1

What Is a Mineral?

Crystal Structures

Minerals are composed of atoms that are arranged in repeating three-dimensional patterns. The basic building block of a mineral crystal is called a unit cell. A unit cell is the smallest three-dimensional arrangement of atoms that displays the basic form, or symmetry, of the crystal. Many unit cells stacked together form a crystal. For example, a crystal of halite is composed of unit cells of sodium and chlorine atoms arranged in a unique three-dimensional structure.

The Origins of Mineralogy

The founder of mineralogy is considered to be Georgius Agricola. His treatise on minerals, *De Re Metallica* (1556), recorded most of what was known about minerals at that time. The science of mineralogy advanced greatly when Rome de l'Isle, a French scientist, proposed the concept of the unit cell in 1772. He argued that the characteristics of mineral crystals could be explained only if they were composed of identical unit cells organized in a predictable way. Crystals are composed of unit cells much like a wall might be composed of bricks. After that discovery, the composition of mineral crystals was actively studied by many scientists.

Industrial Uses of Crystals

The properties of crystals make them useful in countless ways. The electronics industry uses quartz in the manufacture of radios, watches, microphones, and sonar transducers. Rubies are used in lasers and as ball bearings in record players and watches, while diamonds are used in industrial drills and saws.

IS THAT A FACT!

- Currently about 3,600 minerals have been identified, and about 50 new minerals are discovered each year.

Section 2

Identifying Minerals

Methods of Identifying Minerals

Scientists usually identify minerals using one of the following three methods.

- The *hand-specimen* method involves determining the color, luster, streak, cleavage, hardness, fluorescence, density, and magnetic qualities of a mineral.
- When geologists take samples back to the lab, they often use *petrographic microscopes* to identify minerals. These microscopes make it easier to identify minerals by the optical properties of their crystals. The image below is a photograph taken with a petrographic microscope of a metamorphic rock called *schist.* The clear mineral grains are quartz, and the more textured, colorful ones are muscovite mica.

- Geologists can analyze minerals at the atomic level by using *X-ray diffraction,* which measures the way crystal structures diffract X rays.

Mohs' Hardness Scale

Friedrich Mohs (1773–1839) was a mineralogist who lived in Vienna, Austria. In 1812, Mohs developed a method for identifying minerals based on their relative hardness. He proposed that a mineral's identity can be determined by comparing the mineral with several minerals of known hardness. A mineral can scratch another mineral of equal or lesser hardness, but it cannot scratch a mineral of greater hardness.

Gemstones

Of the 3,600 known minerals, only about 100 can be cut and polished to become gemstones. The definition of a gemstone is any naturally occurring mineral, rock, or organic material that, when cut and polished, is suitable for use as jewelry. Diamonds, emeralds, rubies, and topazes are usually referred to as precious stones. Amethysts, garnets, and jades are considered semiprecious. Materials such as coral, pearls, and amber are also considered gemstones, even though they form by organic processes.

- Many gems used in jewelry are imitations. For example, glass can be colored green to look like an emerald. Scientists also create some gems artificially. Synthetic rubies, for example, have the same chemical structure as natural rubies. However, a gemologist can identify synthetic rubies by the presence of curved growth striations and air pockets, which do not occur in natural rubies.

IS THAT A FACT!

- The largest gold nugget ever found had a mass of 71 kg! It was found in Australia on February 5, 1869.
- One of the world's largest rubies has a mass of 8,500 carats and is cut to resemble the Liberty Bell.

SECTION 3

The Formation and Mining of Minerals

Ancient Mines

The earliest evidence of mining dates to a 43,000-year-old iron mine in South Africa. Early iron miners were probably interested in the pigments associated with iron ores. The earliest metals used by neolithic people were gold and copper. Archaeological evidence indicates that the Egyptians mined copper and turquoise around 3400 B.C. Although most of the earliest mining was conducted on the surface, underground mining did occur by 1300 B.C. in Africa.

Intrusions and Mineral Formation

Plutons are bodies of igneous rock that cooled beneath the Earth's surface. They are composed of coarse-grained, interlocking crystals. A large area of exposed intrusive rock (greater than 100 km^2) is called a batholith. Large batholiths occur in British Columbia, Alaska, and in the Sierra Nevada.

- A pegmatite is a very coarse-grained intrusive rock formed from the fluid-rich magma that remains after the rest of a pluton has solidified. Pegmatites may contain minerals such as tourmaline, topaz, or beryl.

The Hope Diamond

The Hope diamond is a 45.5 carat blue diamond owned by the Smithsonian Institution since 1958. The fabled gem was originally 112 carats. It was mined in India, brought to France in 1668, sold to King Louis XIV, and named the French Blue. The gem was rumored to be cursed because it was allegedly stolen from a statue of the Hindu goddess Sita. Misfortune and tragedy seemed to befall those who came in contact with the stone. It was stolen in 1792 from Louis XVI and may have been depicted in an 1800 portrait of a Spanish queen. In 1830, a 45.5 carat cut diamond surfaced in London. Experts declared that it was the French Blue recut to hide its identity. The American Henry Hope bought it, and it has since been called the Hope diamond.

IS THAT A FACT!

- The Wieliczka Salt Mine, in Poland, has more than 200 km of tunnels and is carved entirely out of halite (rock salt). Rock salt has been mined there since the late thirteenth century. The mine contains a number of sculptures, statues, altars, and even a chapel—all carved from salt!

For additional background resources, please refer to the ***HST Reference Library.***

CHAPTER 3

Minerals of the Earth's Crust

Chapter Preview

Section 1
What Is a Mineral?
- Minerals: From the Inside Out
- Types of Minerals

Section 2
Identifying Minerals
- Color
- Luster
- Streak
- Cleavage and Fracture
- Hardness
- Density
- Special Properties

Section 3
The Formation and Mining of Minerals
- Mining
- The Value of Minerals
- Responsible Mining

Directed Reading Worksheet 3

Science Puzzlers, Twisters & Teasers Worksheet 3

Guided Reading Audio CD
English or Spanish, Chapter 3

CHAPTER 3

Minerals of the Earth's Crust

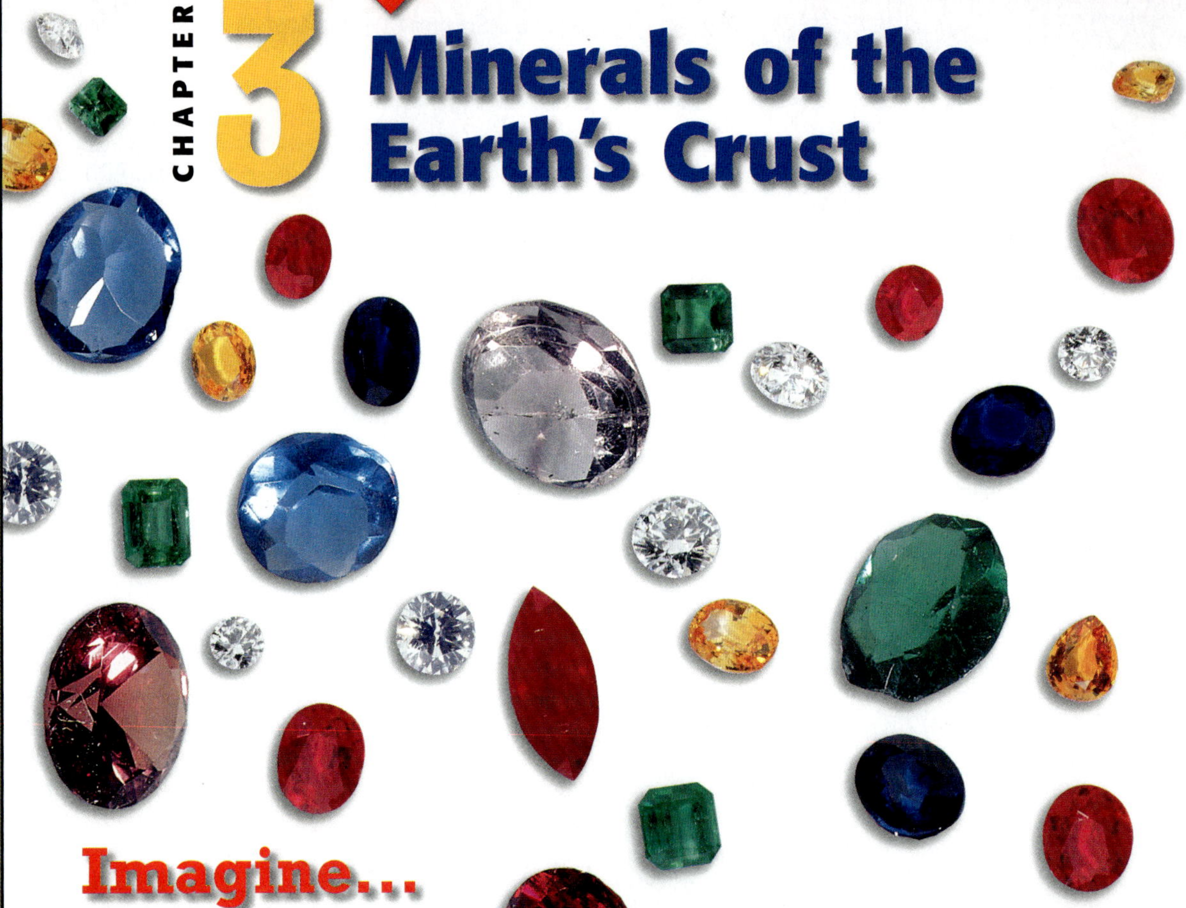

Imagine...

If you owned all of the jewels shown on this page, you would be a millionaire. These precious gems—diamonds, rubies, sapphires, and emeralds—are valued at anywhere from $1,000 to $50,000 per carat (1 carat = 200 mg).

You may not be surprised that precious gems are so expensive. But did you know that the value of these gems has little to do with what they're made of? For example, rubies and sapphires are two varieties of the same mineral that is used to make sandpaper. And diamonds are made of the same material as the graphite in your pencil. Unlike gems, however, a few handfuls of pencils will not make you rich.

Gems are valuable not because of the elements they contain but because of how their atoms are arranged. Under certain conditions, common atoms can be arranged into rare crystal forms. Gems are rare because the conditions that produce them exist in only a few places in the world. The crystals that form gems are prized for their durability, subtle colors, and translucent quality. When properly cut and polished, like the examples shown above, gems sparkle brilliantly.

58

Imagine . . .

Many students believe that gemstones like the ones shown on this page form their facets naturally. Students may be interested to learn that, by definition, gemstones must be cut. In fact, the rocks that the gemstones on this page were cut from probably looked pretty unremarkable to the untrained eye. Gemstones are cut with a grinding wheel embedded with tiny synthetic diamonds. Ask students to think about why gem cutters use diamonds to cut other gemstones.

What Do You Think?

In your ScienceLog, try to answer the following questions based on what you already know:

1. What is a mineral?
2. How do minerals form?

Investigate!

Animal, Vegetable, or Mineral?

All the gems shown on the previous page are *minerals.* More than 3,000 different minerals occur naturally on Earth, and gems make up a very small number of them. What is a mineral? Do the following investigation, and see if you can figure it out.

Procedure

1. In your ScienceLog, make two columns—one for minerals and one for nonminerals. Based on what you already know about minerals, classify *all* of the materials you see on this page into things that come from minerals and things that come from nonminerals.
2. Ask your classmates what ideas they have about the materials that make up the motorcycle. Take notes as you gather information. You can add the information to your list later.

Analysis

3. Based on your list, what kinds of materials made up most of the motorcycle—minerals or nonminerals?
4. Where do you think the minerals that make the metallic parts of the motorcycle come from?

59

What Do You Think?

Accept all reasonable responses.

Students will have a chance to revise their answers in the Chapter Review under NOW What Do You Think?

Investigate!

Teacher Notes: Display some photos of different types of motorcycles from magazines or books to help students make their classifications. Encourage them to take notes.

Materials shown on the student page that are minerals or are derived from minerals are as follows: sand, the glass headlight of the motorcycle, gems, and all the metal objects. All the plastic and rubber objects are not minerals.

Answers to Investigate!

3. Most of the materials are metals, which come from minerals.
4. Answers will vary. (Metals come from metal ore minerals, such as hematite, magnetite, beryl, and copper.)

internet connect

SCI LINKS NSTA

TOPIC: Gems
GO TO: www.scilinks.org
***sci*LINKS NUMBER:** HSTE055

TOPIC: Birthstones
GO TO: www.scilinks.org
***sci*LINKS NUMBER:** HSTE060

IS THAT A FACT!

The first motorcycles were a far cry from the powerful steel-and-chrome machines of today. The first motorcycle was invented in 1885 by German engineer and automobile pioneer Gottlieb Daimler, who attached a four-stroke gasoline engine to a wooden bicycle!

Chapter 3 Opener—California Standards: PE/ATE 6c, 7, 7b, 7d

SECTION 1

Focus

What Is a Mineral?

This section explores the nature of minerals by describing their four characteristics. Students learn that mineral crystals are generated by atomic structures, and they learn how to classify minerals in two major compositional groups—silicates and nonsilicates.

Bellringer

Display a piece of pencil lead (graphite) and a photograph of a diamond. Explain that both substances are composed of carbon. Ask students to brainstorm about how two substances with such different properties can form from atoms of the same element.

1 Motivate

GROUP ACTIVITY

Identifying Minerals Place an assortment of objects on a table. Possibilities include a piece of wood, a fossil, a piece of bone, a piece of granite, and a quartz crystal. Divide the class into groups of two or three students. Tell the students to examine the objects and to determine which ones are minerals by using the four questions on this page. Sheltered English

Directed Reading Worksheet 3 Section 1

1

What Is a Mineral?

NEW TERMS

mineral, element, atom, compound, crystal, silicate mineral, nonsilicate mineral

OBJECTIVES

- Explain the four characteristics of a mineral.
- Classify minerals according to the two major compositional groups.

Not all minerals look like gems. In fact, most of them look more like rocks. But are minerals the same as rocks? Well, not really. So what's the difference? For one thing, rocks are made of minerals, but minerals are not made of rocks. Then what exactly is a mineral? By asking the following four questions, you can tell whether something is a mineral:

Is it a solid? Minerals can't be gases or liquids.

Is it formed in nature? Crystalline materials made by people aren't classified as minerals.

Does it have a crystalline structure? Minerals are crystals, which have a repeating inner structure that is often reflected in the shape of the crystal. Minerals generally have the same chemical composition throughout.

Is it nonliving material? A mineral is inorganic, meaning it isn't made of living things.

A **mineral** is a naturally formed, inorganic solid with a crystalline structure. If you cannot answer "yes" to all four questions above, you don't have a mineral.

Minerals: From the Inside Out

Three of the four questions might be easy to answer. The one about crystalline structure may be more difficult. In order to understand what crystalline structure is, you need to know a little about the elements that make up a mineral. **Elements** are substances that cannot be broken down into simpler forms by ordinary chemical means. All minerals contain one or more of the 92 elements present in the Earth's crust.

60

CONNECT TO LIFE SCIENCE

Guide students in a discussion of the importance minerals have to life on Earth. Display a bone, a bottle of mineral supplements, and a plant. Ask students to brainstorm about how these objects are related to minerals. Explain to students that minerals, which are inorganic, provide essential nutrients to living things and are the building blocks of organisms.

- Bones are largely made of microscopic apatite crystals.
- Diatoms, which are microscopic organisms, have silica crystals in their cell walls.

Section 1—California Standards: PE/ATE 6, 6b, 7, 7a, 7b, 7e

Each element is made of only one kind of atom. An **atom,** as you may recall, is the smallest part of an element that has all the properties of that element. Like all other substances, minerals are made up of atoms of one or more elements.

Most minerals are made of compounds of several different elements. A **compound** is a substance made of two or more elements that have been chemically joined, or bonded together. Halite, for example, is a compound of sodium and chlorine, as shown in **Figure 1.** A few minerals, such as gold and silver, are composed of only one element. For example, pure gold is made up of only one kind of atom—gold.

Atoms within a mineral are arranged in specific patterns, as shown in **Figure 2.** When atoms are arranged in a pattern, they form crystals.

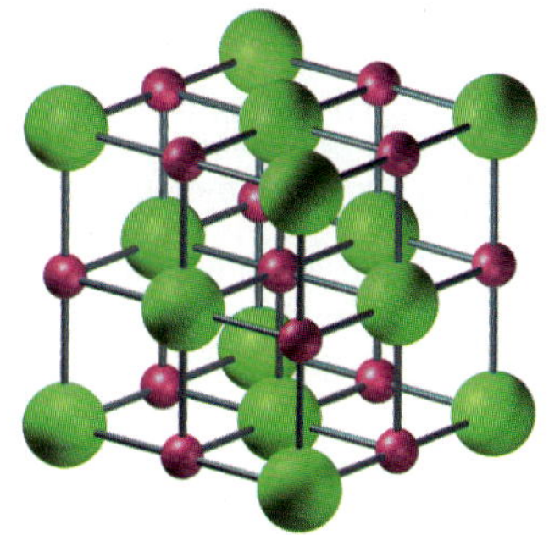

Figure 1 *Atoms of sodium and chlorine are joined together in a compound commonly known as rock salt, or the mineral halite.*

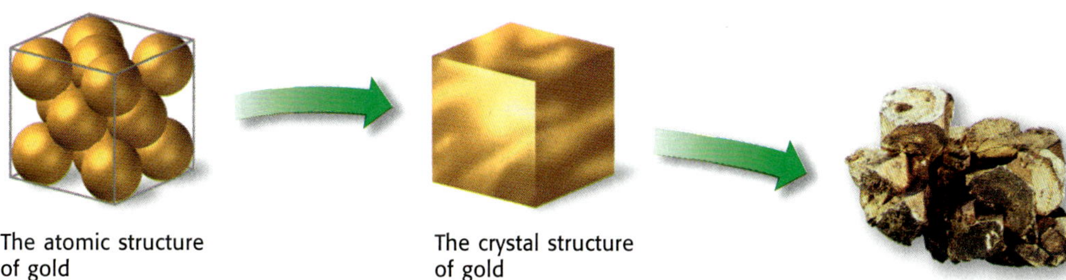

The atomic structure of gold

The crystal structure of gold

Crystals of the mineral gold

Figure 2 *The mineral gold is composed of gold atoms arranged in a crystalline structure.*

A mineral is made up of one or more crystals. **Crystals** are solid, geometric forms of minerals produced by a repeating pattern of atoms that is present throughout the mineral. A crystal's shape is determined by the arrangement of the atoms within the crystal. The arrangement of atoms in turn is determined by the kinds of atoms that make up the mineral. Each mineral has a definite crystalline structure. All of these structures can be grouped into six major classes according to the kinds of crystals they form. A chart of these six major crystal classes is shown below.

Crystal Classes

Isometric	Hexagonal	Tetragonal	Orthorhombic	Monoclinic	Triclinic

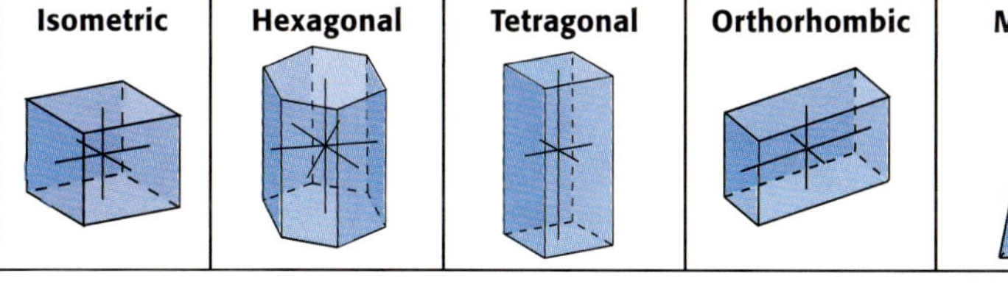

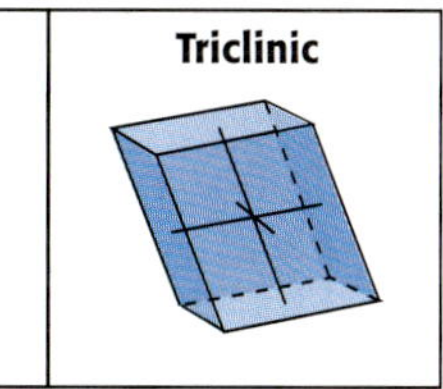

61

2 Teach

Discussion

Rocks and Minerals Students may benefit from a discussion of the differences between rocks and minerals. Stress that rocks are composed of minerals, but minerals are not composed of rock. It is possible for a rock to be made of just one mineral or many. Minerals should also not be confused with mineraloids. Mineraloids are similar to minerals, but they have no crystalline structure. Some common mineraloids are obsidian, limonite, flint, and opal. Sheltered English

Group Activity

Writing At the beginning of this section, give pairs of students an unknown mineral. Tell students that their goal will be to identify the mineral by the end of the chapter and to present a short report on it. Their reports should include the chemical formula of the mineral, detail the mineral's uses and properties, and explain what type of rock the mineral occurs in.

Teaching Transparency 90
"Gold Crystal Structure"

MISCONCEPTION ALERT

In much the same way that color is a deceptive guide to identifying minerals, crystal form is often a misleading physical property. The six crystal forms shown on this page represent the ideal atomic structures of different mineral groups. A large variety of complex crystal shapes can be generated by starting with a simple polyhedron, such as a cube. For example, the mineral fluorite belongs in the isometric (cubic) class but commonly forms octahedral-shaped crystals.

2 Teach, continued

Activity

Microscope Work Sand forms from the breakdown of rock over many years. Most sand is composed of the mineral quartz. Distribute magnifying lenses or microscopes to student groups, and invite them to examine samples of sand, rock salt, granulated salt, and sugar to compare the crystalline structure of each. Have students record what they see in their ScienceLog.

Using the Figure

After students study the examples shown in **Figure 3,** distribute samples of granite, feldspar, quartz, and mica to students for close examination. Encourage students to record their observations in their ScienceLog and to note differences and similarities. Sheltered English

Connect to Chemistry

The way atoms bond together gives a mineral its properties. For example, carbon atoms that are bonded in one way form graphite, which is commonly used for pencil lead, while carbon atoms that are bonded in another way form diamonds. Have students research the chemical composition and structure of different minerals and find out how the minerals are used. Ask students to make a model that shows the atomic structure of a unit cell of a simple mineral, such as halite, pyrite, galena, or quartz.

life science CONNECTION

Several species of animals have a brain that contains the mineral magnetite. Magnetite has a special property—it is magnetic. Scientists have shown that certain fish can sense magnetic fields because they have magnetite in their brain. The magnetite gives the fish a sense of direction.

Types of Minerals

Minerals can be classified by a number of different characteristics. The most common classification of minerals is based on chemical composition. Minerals are divided into two groups based on the elements they are composed of. These groups are the silicate minerals and the nonsilicate minerals.

Silicate minerals Silicon and oxygen are the two most common elements in the Earth's crust. Minerals that contain a combination of these two elements are called **silicate minerals.** Silicate minerals make up more than 90 percent of the Earth's crust—the rest is made up of nonsilicate minerals. Silicon and oxygen usually combine with other elements, such as aluminum, iron, magnesium, and potassium, to make up silicate minerals. Some of the more common silicate minerals are shown in **Figure 3.**

Feldspar The most common silicate mineral group in the crust is the feldspars. Feldspar minerals make up about half the Earth's crust, and they are the main component of most rocks on the Earth's surface. They contain the elements silicon and oxygen along with aluminum, potassium, sodium, and calcium. The pinkish crystals in the sample of granite shown below are feldspar.

Mica Mica minerals are shiny and soft, and they separate easily into sheets when they break. You can see one variety of mica in the granite sample. The two most common minerals of the mica group are *muscovite* and *biotite.* Muscovite is usually pale green, pale red, or clear, and biotite is brown or black.

Quartz Quartz (silicon dioxide, SiO_2) is the basic building block of many rocks. If you look closely at the piece of granite, you can see the quartz crystals. Even though there are many different forms of quartz, they all have the same chemical composition.

Figure 3 *Granite is a rock composed of various minerals, including feldspar, mica, and quartz.*

62

Multicultural Connection

The first recorded use of sandpaper dates to thirteenth-century China, when crushed seashells were bound to parchment with a natural adhesive from trees. Today sandpaper is made from aluminum oxide, garnet, or quartz. Interested students can make their own sandpaper at home and share it with the class.

Homework

Ask students to find four items in their home that are derived from minerals. Have them share their findings with the class on the following day. (Examples include table salt, composed of halite; pencil lead, composed of graphite; cooking pots, composed of iron, copper, or aluminum; and jewelry.)

Nonsilicate Minerals Minerals that do not contain a combination of the elements silicon and oxygen form a group called the **nonsilicate minerals.** Some of these minerals are made up of elements such as carbon, oxygen, iron, and sulfur. Below are several categories of nonsilicate minerals.

Native elements are minerals that are composed of only one element. About 20 minerals are native elements. Some examples are gold (Au), platinum (Pt), diamond (C), copper (Cu), sulfur (S), and silver (Ag).

Native copper

Carbonates are minerals that contain combinations of carbon and oxygen in their chemical structure. Calcite ($CaCO_3$) is an example of a carbonate mineral. We use carbonate minerals in cement, building stones, and fireworks.

Calcite

Halides are compounds that form when atoms of the elements fluorine (F), chlorine (Cl), iodine (I), or bromine (Br) combine with sodium (Na), potassium (K), or calcium (Ca). Halite (NaCl) is better known as rock salt. Fluorite (CaF_2) can have many different colors. Halide minerals are often used to make fertilizer.

Fluorite

Oxides are compounds that form when an element, such as aluminum or iron, combines chemically with oxygen. Corundum (Al_2O_3) is an oxide mineral. Magnetite (Fe_3O_4) is an important iron ore. Oxide minerals are used to make abrasives and aircraft parts. They are also used to give false teeth a natural color.

Corundum

Sulfates contain sulfur and oxygen (SO_4). The mineral gypsum ($CaSO_4 \cdot 2H_2O$) is a common sulfate. It makes up the white sand at White Sands National Monument, in New Mexico. Sulfates are used in cosmetics, toothpaste, and paint.

Gypsum

Sulfides are minerals that contain one or more elements, such as lead, iron, or nickel, combined with sulfur. Galena (PbS) is a sulfide. Sulfide minerals are used to make batteries, medicines, and electronic parts.

Galena

REVIEW

1. What are the differences between atoms, compounds, and minerals?
2. Which two elements are most commonly found in minerals?
3. How are silicate minerals different from nonsilicate minerals?
4. **Making Inferences** Explain why each of the following is not considered a mineral: a cupcake, water, teeth, oxygen.

3 Extend

Research

Writing From about 200 B.C. to A.D. 1700, alchemists explored the boundaries of chemistry and philosophy. They dedicated their lives to discovering a chemical reaction that would change common metals into precious gold and silver. Despite their unscientific methods, alchemists contributed a great deal to the development of the science we now call chemistry. Even Sir Isaac Newton devoted much of his life to pursuing alchemy. Challenge interested students to research the history of alchemy and to present a report to the class.

4 Close

Quiz

1. What is a mineral? (a naturally formed, inorganic solid with a crystalline structure)
2. What does a crystal's shape depend on? (the arrangement of the atoms within the crystal)

Alternative Assessment

Write the following mineral-group names on the board: silicates, native elements, carbonates, halides, oxides, sulfates, and sulfides. Have students match the following items with the mineral group from which they are derived: a copper penny (native elements); cement (carbonates); rock salt (halides); oxide sandpaper (oxides); toothpaste (sulfates); batteries (sulfides); sand (silicates).

Answers to Review

1. Compounds are composed of two or more atoms of different elements that are chemically bonded. Minerals consist of atoms or compounds arranged in a crystalline structure.
2. oxygen and silicon
3. Silicate minerals are made of combinations of the elements silicon and oxygen, and nonsilicate minerals are not.
4. A cupcake is not a mineral because it does not have a crystalline structure and it does not form in nature. Water is not a mineral because it does not have a crystalline structure and it is a liquid, not a solid. Teeth are not minerals because they are a living part of your body. Oxygen is not a mineral because oxygen atoms by themselves do not have a crystalline structure.

Section 1 Review—California Standards: PE/ATE 6b

SECTION 2

Focus

Identifying Minerals

In this lesson, students will learn some of the common techniques used to identify minerals. The section also examines some of the interesting properties of minerals, such as fluorescence, radioactivity, and magnetism.

Bellringer

Ask students to consider the question posed at the beginning of this section. Students should list as many phrases as they can to describe each mineral shown. Have students organize these phrases into different catagories, such as *color, shape,* and *luster.* Students can use these comparisons to determine whether or not the samples are actually the same mineral. (The mineral on the left is a yellow variety of garnet. The mineral on the right is a "diamond in the rough.")

1 Motivate

COOPERATIVE LEARNING

Ask students to work in small groups to determine a classification system for minerals based on observable physical properties. Give groups a number of minerals or photographs of a variety of minerals. Students should create a classification system based on observable differences and similarities among the samples. After groups have developed a classification system, give them several new samples, and have them place the samples in their classification scheme.

Directed Reading Worksheet 3 Section 2

2

NEW TERMS

luster, streak, cleavage, fracture, hardness, density

OBJECTIVES

- Classify minerals using common mineral-identification techniques.
- Explain special properties of minerals.
- Describe what makes a mineral crystal a gem.

Identifying Minerals

If you found the two mineral samples below, how would you know if they were the same mineral?

By looking at these photographs, you can easily see physical similarities in the two mineral crystals. But how can you tell whether they are the same mineral? Moreover, how can you determine the identity of a mineral? In this section you will learn about the different properties that can help you identify minerals.

Luster Chart

Metallic

Submetallic

Nonmetallic

Vitreous glassy, brilliant

Silky swirly, fibrous

Resinous plastic

Waxy greasy, oily

Pearly creamy

Earthy rough, dull

Color

When you see a mineral, its *color* is probably the first thing you notice. Minerals come in many different colors and shades. The same mineral can come in a variety of colors. For example, in its purest state quartz is clear. Quartz that contains small amounts of impurities, however, can be a variety of colors. Rose quartz gets its color from certain kinds of impurities. Amethyst, another variety of quartz, is purple because it contains other kinds of impurities.

Besides impurities, other factors can change the appearance of minerals. The mineral pyrite, often called fool's gold, normally has a golden color. But if pyrite is exposed to weather for a long period, it turns black. Because of factors such as weathering and impurities, color usually is not a reliable indicator of a mineral's identity. Although color can be helpful, other properties should be used to identify minerals.

Luster

The way a surface reflects light is called **luster.** When you say an object is shiny or dull, you are describing its luster. Minerals have metallic, submetallic, or nonmetallic luster. If a mineral is shiny, it may have either a glassy or a metallic luster. If the mineral is dull, its luster is either submetallic or nonmetallic. The different types of lusters are shown in the chart at left.

WEIRD SCIENCE

How can you tell a real diamond from a fake? A gem specialist uses specialized tools to distinguish real diamonds from impostors. But there are some tests that even an untrained person can conduct. One of the simplest is to try to pick up the stone in question with a moistened fingertip. Diamonds can be picked up this way; most other stones cannot.

Section 2—California Standards: PE/ATE 6, 6b, 7; LabBook: 7, 7b, 7d, 7e

Streak

The color of a mineral in powdered form is called the mineral's **streak.** To find a mineral's streak, the mineral is rubbed against a piece of unglazed porcelain called a streak plate. The mark left on the streak plate by the mineral is the streak. The color of a mineral's streak is not always the same as the color of the mineral sample, as shown in **Figure 4.** Unlike the surface of the mineral sample, the streak is not affected by weathering. For this reason, streak is more reliable than color as an indicator of a mineral's identity.

Figure 4 *The color of the mineral hematite may vary, but the streak is always red-brown.*

Cleavage and Fracture

Different types of minerals break in different ways. The way a mineral breaks is determined by the arrangement of its atoms. **Cleavage** is the tendency of some minerals to break along flat surfaces. Gem cutters take advantage of natural cleavage to remove flaws from certain minerals, such as diamonds and rubies, and to shape them into beautiful gemstones. **Figure 5** shows minerals with different cleavage patterns.

Fracture is the tendency of some minerals to break unevenly along curved or irregular surfaces. Minerals that display fracture are shown in the chart below.

Figure 5 *Cleavage varies with mineral type. Mica breaks easily into distinct sheets. Halite breaks at 90° angles in three directions. Diamond breaks in four different directions.*

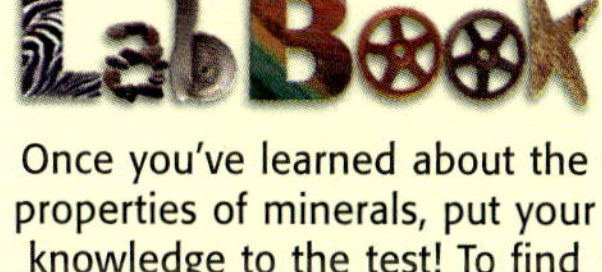

Once you've learned about the properties of minerals, put your knowledge to the test! To find out how, turn to page 494 in your LabBook.

2 Teach

Activity

Applying the Scientific Method
Before allowing students to test minerals themselves, go through the process with them to demonstrate how each identification step is performed. Use a few common minerals that have distinctly different characteristics, such as talc and quartz. Show students how each test is conducted, and discuss with them why every step is necessary to correctly identify a mineral. When students test the minerals, stress a systematic approach. Students should perform the same steps, in order, to each unknown sample. Caution students not to taste mineral samples. To satisfy their curiosity, provide table salt and explain that it is the mineral halite. With a magnifying glass, they should be able to see halite's cubic crystal form. Sheltered English

Misconception Alert

Students may believe that a specific mineral is always the same color. Explain to students that a mineral can occur in a range of colors. Labradorite can be yellow or dull gray. Quartz crystals range from clear to purple or brown to rose. Purple quartz is the gemstone known as *amethyst,* while yellow quartz is the gemstone *citrine*. Remind students that they must test all of a mineral's characteristics—color, luster, hardness, streak, cleavage, density, and fluorescence to determine its identity.

Is That a Fact!

During the black plague of the fourteenth century, opals developed a reputation for being unlucky gems. People observed that opals became brilliant when the wearer caught the fatal disease and then dulled when the person died!

Mysterious Minerals

TOPIC: Identifying Minerals
GO TO: www.scilinks.org
***sci*LINKS NUMBER:** HSTE065

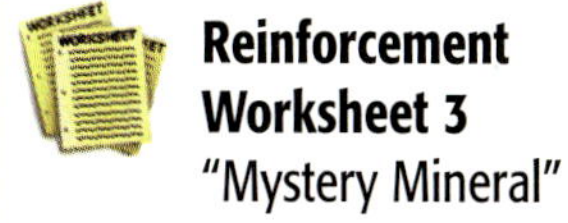

Reinforcement Worksheet 3
"Mystery Mineral"

3 Extend

READING STRATEGY

Mnemonics Have students create a mnemonic device that will help them learn Mohs' hardness scale. One example is **T**errible **G**iants **C**an **F**ind **A**lligators **O**r **Q**uaint **T**igers **C**onveniently **D**igestible. This will help students remember the minerals in order of hardness: **t**alc, **g**ypsum, **c**alcite, **f**luorite, **a**patite, **o**rthoclase feldspar, **q**uartz, **t**opaz, **c**orundum, and **d**iamond. Ask students to brainstorm for several mnemonic devices and share them with the class. Sheltered English

Jade is a mineral that has great importance in China. According to Chinese mythology, jade is a symbol of life and it possesses protective powers. Jade is actually the name given to two minerals—jadeite and nephrite—that rank between 6.5 and 7 on Mohs' hardness scale. Have students find out about the cultural significance of jade and how it was carved without metal tools.

QuickLab

MATERIALS

For Each Student:
- penny
- pencil

Answer to QuickLab

3. The penny is the hardest material of the three, followed by your fingernail and then the mineral graphite.

QuickLab

Scratch Test

1. You will need a **penny,** a **pencil,** and your **fingernail.** Which one of these three materials is the hardest?
2. Use your fingernail to try to scratch the graphite at the tip of a pencil.
3. Now try to scratch the penny with your fingernail. Which is the hardest of the three?

Hardness

Hardness refers to a mineral's resistance to being scratched. If you try to scratch a diamond, you will have a tough time because diamond is the hardest mineral. Talc, on the other hand, is one of the softest minerals. You can scratch it with your fingernail. To determine the hardness of minerals, scientists use *Mohs' hardness scale,* shown below. Notice that talc has a rating of 1 and diamond has a rating of 10. Between these two extremes are other minerals with progressively greater hardness. For example, calcite is harder than gypsum, and fluorite is harder than calcite.

To identify a mineral using Mohs' scale, try to scratch the surface of a mineral with the edge of one of the 10 reference minerals. If the reference mineral scratches your mineral, it is harder than your mineral. Continue trying to scratch the mineral until you find a reference mineral that cannot scratch your mineral. If the two minerals do not scratch each other, they have the same hardness.

Mohs' Hardness Scale

1 Talc
2 Gypsum
3 Calcite
4 Fluorite
5 Apatite
6 Orthoclase
7 Quartz
8 Topaz
9 Corundum
10 Diamond

Density

If you pick up a golf ball and a table-tennis ball, which will feel heavier? Although the balls are of similar size, the golf ball will feel heavier because it is denser, as shown in **Figure 6.** **Density** is the measure of how much matter there is in a given amount of space. In other words, density is a ratio of an object's mass to its volume. Density is usually measured in grams per cubic centimeter. Because water has a density of 1 g/cm^3, it is used as a reference point for other substances. The ratio of an object's density to the density of water is called the object's *specific gravity.* The specific gravity of gold, for example, is 19. This means that gold has a density of 19 g/cm^3. In other words, there is 19 times more matter in 1 cm^3 of gold than in 1 cm^3 of water. Most nonmetallic minerals have a specific gravity between 2.5 and 4. Specific gravity can be used to help determine a mineral's identity.

Figure 6 *Because a golf ball has a greater density than a table-tennis ball, more table-tennis balls are needed to balance the scale.*

66

Teaching Transparency 91
"Mohs' Hardness Scale"

Teaching Transparency 92
"Special Properties of Some Minerals"

Comparative Hardness Scale

Hardness	*Common material*
Less than 2.5	mineral that marks paper
2.5	fingernail
3	copper penny
5	steel knife blade
6.5	steel file

Special Properties

Some properties are particular to only a few types of minerals. The properties below can quickly help you identify the minerals shown. To identify some properties, however, you will need specialized equipment.

Fluorescence—Calcite and fluorite glow under ultraviolet light. The same fluorite sample below is shown in ultraviolet light and in white light.

Chemical reaction—Calcite will effervesce, or "fizz," when a drop of weak acid is placed on it.

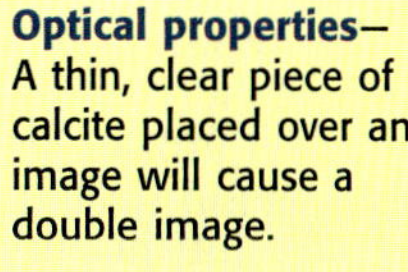

Optical properties—A thin, clear piece of calcite placed over an image will cause a double image.

Special Properties of Some Minerals

Radioactivity—Minerals that contain radium or uranium can be detected by a Geiger counter.

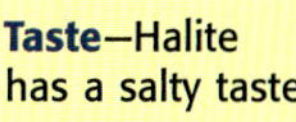

Taste—Halite has a salty taste.

Magnetism—Magnetite and pyrrhotite are both natural magnets that attract iron.

For a list of minerals and their properties, see page 588.

REVIEW

1. How do you determine a mineral's streak?
2. What is the difference between cleavage and fracture?
3. How would you determine the hardness of an unidentified mineral sample?
4. **Applying Concepts** Suppose you have two minerals that have the same hardness. Which other mineral properties would you use to determine whether the samples are the same mineral?

67

PG 496

Is It Fool's Gold?—A Dense Situation

Real-World Connection

Invite a jeweler to visit the class, and ask the jeweler to explain how gemstones are made into jewelry. The jeweler could bring in visual aids to help students understand how gems are located, mined, and prepared for commercial use.

4 Close

Quiz

1. Why is color not always a reliable way of identifying a mineral? (Factors such as weathering and the inclusion of impurities can affect the mineral's color.)
2. What property do minerals that glow under ultraviolet light display? (fluorescence)

Alternative Assessment

Have students prepare mineral identification cards for some of the most common minerals. They can list the words *color, luster, hardness, streak, cleavage and fracture,* and *density* on each card. For each card, ask them to fill in the properties of a common mineral. Students should write the name of the mineral on the back of the card and use the cards as study aids or assessment tools. Sheltered English

Answers to Review

1. Scrape the mineral across a ceramic streak plate. The color of the material that rubs off the mineral sample is the mineral's streak.
2. If a mineral has cleavage, it breaks along flat surfaces. Fracture is the way a mineral breaks along curved or irregular surfaces.
3. To determine the hardness of an unknown mineral sample, take a material of known hardness and try to scratch the unknown mineral with it. If the unknown mineral is scratched, try to scratch it with a material that has a lower hardness. Continue with this process until you know which materials are harder and which are softer than the unknown mineral sample. The hardness of the unknown mineral is between these two.
4. Answers will vary but should not include color.

Reinforcement Worksheet 3
"The Mineral Quiz Show"

Section 2 Review—California Standards: PE/ATE 6b

SECTION 3

Focus

The Formation and Mining of Minerals

This section discusses how minerals form deep within Earth's crust as well as close to the surface. Students will learn about different techniques used to mine minerals. This section concludes with a discussion of the value of mineral resources and the importance of ecologically responsible mining and reclamation.

Bellringer

Ask students to write briefly on this statement:

"The meek shall inherit the Earth but not the mineral rights."

Discuss students' responses, and ask them what they would do if valuable minerals were discovered on property they owned.

1 Motivate

DISCUSSION

Simulate the Gold Rush To simulate the excitement of the gold rush of 1849, make up a flyer that tells of a rich gold deposit found in a nearby area. Make copies and pass them out to students to read. Discuss with students what their reactions are to such an announcement. Then discuss the chaotic enthusiasm of the gold rush: from 1848 to 1860, the population in California grew from 14,000 to 380,000!

Directed Reading Worksheet 3 Section 3

3

The Formation and Mining of Minerals

NEW TERMS

ore
reclamation

OBJECTIVES

- Describe the environments in which minerals are formed.
- Compare and contrast the different types of mining.

Almost all known minerals can be found in the Earth's crust. They form in a large variety of environments under a variety of physical and chemical conditions. The environment in which a mineral forms determines the mineral's properties. Minerals form both deep beneath the Earth's surface and on or near the Earth's surface.

When a body of salt water, such as a lake or sea, dries up, minerals such as gypsum, anhydrite, and halite are left behind. As the salt water evaporates, these minerals crystallize, indicating where a body of salt water once existed.

Water that exists under ground is called ground water. Surface water and ground water carry dissolved minerals into lakes and seas, where they crystallize on the bottom. Minerals that form in this environment include calcite and quartz.

Changing conditions beneath the Earth's surface can alter the mineral composition of a preexisting rock. When changes in pressure, temperature, or chemical makeup alter a rock, *metamorphism* takes place. Minerals that form in metamorphic rock include calcite, garnet, graphite, hematite, magnetite, mica, and talc.

Heat and Pressure

68

WEIRD SCIENCE

Some of the greatest untapped sources of minerals are hydrothermal vents deep under the sea. These hydrothermal vents are called black smokers because they spew out hot, mineral-rich water that is almost black. As the hot water mixes with the cool ocean water, minerals crystallize and form nodules on the ocean floor. These mineral deposits contain significant amounts of manganese, copper, zinc, gold, and silver, but no one has figured out an economical way to mine them yet.

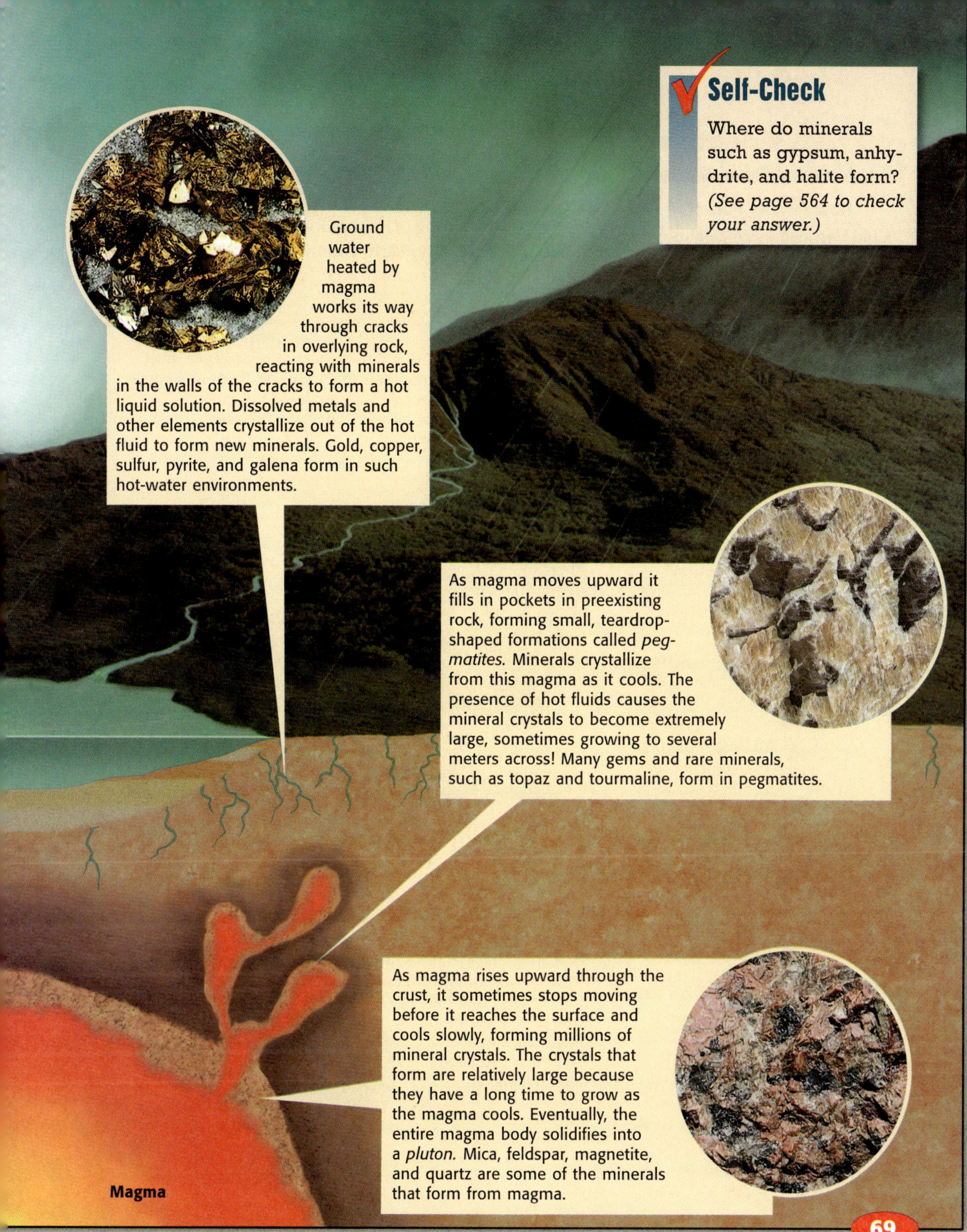
Ground water heated by magma works its way through cracks in overlying rock, reacting with minerals in the walls of the cracks to form a hot liquid solution. Dissolved metals and other elements crystallize out of the hot fluid to form new minerals. Gold, copper, sulfur, pyrite, and galena form in such hot-water environments.
As magma moves upward it fills in pockets in preexisting rock, forming small, teardrop-shaped formations called *pegmatites.* Minerals crystallize from this magma as it cools. The presence of hot fluids causes the mineral crystals to become extremely large, sometimes growing to several meters across! Many gems and rare minerals, such as topaz and tourmaline, form in pegmatites.
As magma rises upward through the crust, it sometimes stops moving before it reaches the surface and cools slowly, forming millions of mineral crystals. The crystals that form are relatively large because they have a long time to grow as the magma cools. Eventually, the entire magma body solidifies into a *pluton.* Mica, feldspar, magnetite, and quartz are some of the minerals that form from magma.
Magma

✓ Self-Check

Where do minerals such as gypsum, anhydrite, and halite form? *(See page 564 to check your answer.)*

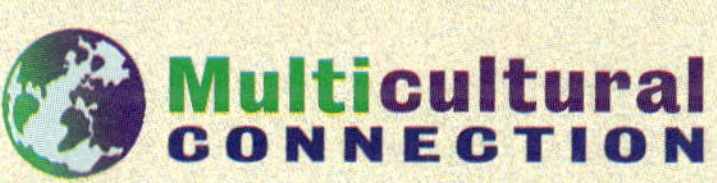

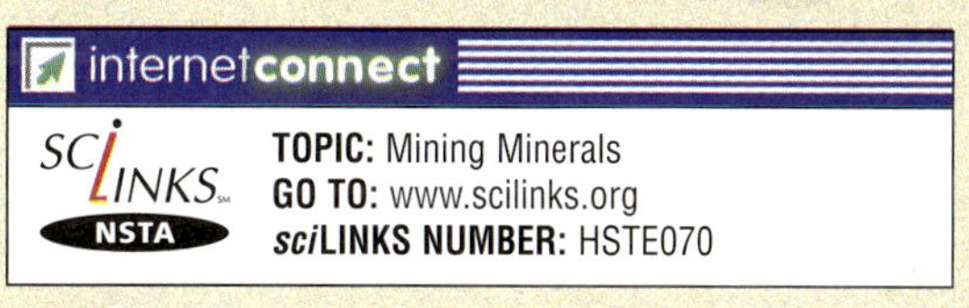

2 Teach

CONNECT TO LIFE SCIENCE

The Surface Environment and Mining (SEAM) program was established by the U.S. Forest Service in 1973 to address the issue of land reclamation in the wake of mining operations. Since then, this highly successful program has returned vast areas of land formerly used for mining to its original condition. The most recent SEAM projects can be researched on the Internet. To research local reclamation efforts, students could contact local conservation groups listed in the phone directory.

CROSS-DISCIPLINARY FOCUS

History Encourage students to learn more about the social and environmental effects of mining by having each student create a scrapbook detailing the history of a mining community. Students should research the history of a community from the discovery of ore to the present. Students' scrapbooks should include drawings and photographs showing changes in the community as well as text describing the history of the area. Have students focus on the types of ore extracted, the use and value of the ore in the world market, and the impact mining has had on the people and environment of the area. Possible communities include: Leadville, Colorado; Butte, Montana; and the Yanomami Indian tribes of Brazil and Venezuela. Have students share their scrapbooks with the class.

Multicultural CONNECTION

Halite, or rock salt, is perhaps the most important mineral to human civilization. The word *salt* is derived from the Latin word *sal.* Instead of money, Roman soldiers were paid their salary, or *salarium,* in salt. Have students research the Tibetan salt trade or the use of iodized salt to correct thyroid deficiencies.

internetconnect

SciLINKS NSTA

TOPIC: Mining Minerals
GO TO: www.scilinks.org
***sci*LINKS NUMBER:** HSTE070

Answer to Self-Check

These minerals form wherever salt water has evaporated.

3 Extend

MATH and MORE

To produce 1 metric ton of coal, up to 30 metric tons of earth must first be removed or stripped. Some strip mines produce up to 50,000 metric tons of coal a day. How many metric tons of earth could be removed in order to mine 50,000 metric tons of coal? (1,500,000 metric tons)

Answer to MATHBREAK

$\frac{18}{24} = \frac{3}{4} = 75\%$ pure

CONNECT TO PHYSICAL SCIENCE

Referring to the chart on the following page, discuss with students that minerals are valuable because of the properties of the elements that are in them. Elements can be divided into three major groups: *metals, nonmetals,* and *metalloids.* Use the Teaching Transparency below to discuss how the characteristics of each element group make the minerals they are found in useful to human cultures.

Teaching Transparency 165
"Three Major Categories of Elements"

Math Skills Worksheet 21
"Percentages, Fractions, and Decimals"

MATH BREAK

How Pure Is Pure?

Gold classified as 24-karat is 100 percent gold. Gold classified as 18-karat is 18 parts gold and 6 parts another, similar metal. It is therefore 18/24 or 3/4 pure. What is the percentage of pure gold in 18-karat gold?

Mining

Many kinds of rocks and minerals must be mined in order to extract the valuable elements they contain. Geologists use the term **ore** to describe a mineral deposit large enough and pure enough to be mined for a profit. Rocks and minerals are removed from the ground by one of two methods—surface mining or deep mining. The method miners choose depends on how far down in the Earth the mineral is located and how valuable the ore is. The two types of mining are illustrated below.

Surface mining is the removal of minerals or other materials at or near the Earth's surface. Types of surface mines include open pits, strip mines, and quarries. Materials mined in this way include copper and bauxite, a mixture of minerals rich in aluminum.

Deep mining is the removal of minerals or other materials from deep within the Earth. Shafts, tunnels, and other passageways must be dug underground to reach the ore. The retrieval of diamonds and coal commonly requires deep mining.

70

MISCONCEPTION ALERT

The mass of gems is measured using a unit called the *carat.* This should not be confused with the *karat* used to measure the purity of gold. A 1-carat diamond crystal has a mass of 200 mg. This is approximately the same as the mass of one children's aspirin. A one karat gold nugget is one twenty-fourth pure gold.

Multicultural CONNECTION

The mining of gold, copper, and iron in southeastern Africa helped build the empire of Great Zimbabwe, which arose during the mid-thirteenth century and lasted until about the middle of the fifteenth century. Invite students to find out more about mining techniques in Great Zimbabwe and about the Karanga people who ruled then.

The Value of Minerals

Many of the metals you are familiar with originally came from mineral ores. You may not be familiar with the minerals, but you will probably recognize the metals extracted from the minerals. The table at right lists some mineral ores and some of the familiar metals that come from them.

As you have seen, some minerals are highly valued for their beauty rather than for their usefulness. Mineral crystals that are attractive and rare are called gems, or gemstones. An example of a gem is shown in **Figure 7.** Gems must be hard enough to be cut and polished.

Common Uses of Minerals

Mineral	Metal	Uses
Chalcopyrite	copper	coins, electrical wire
Galena	lead	batteries, paints
Beryl	beryllium	bicycle frames, airplanes
Chromite	chromium	stainless steel, cast iron, leather tanners

Figure 7 *The Cullinan diamond is the largest, heaviest diamond ever found. Before the largest piece of it was placed in the royal scepter of the British crown jewels, it weighed 3,106 carats.*

Responsible Mining

Mining gives us the minerals we need, but it also creates problems. Mining destroys or disturbs the habitat of plants and animals. The waste products from a mine can get into water sources, polluting both surface water and ground water.

One way to reduce the harmful effects of mining is to return the land to its original state after the mining is completed. This process is called **reclamation.** Reclamation of mined public land has been required by law since the mid-1970s. But reclamation is an expensive and time-consuming process. Another way to reduce the effects of mining is to reduce our need for minerals. We can do this by recycling the mineral products we currently use, such as aluminum and iron. Mineral ores are *nonrenewable resources;* therefore, the more we recycle, the more we will have in the future.

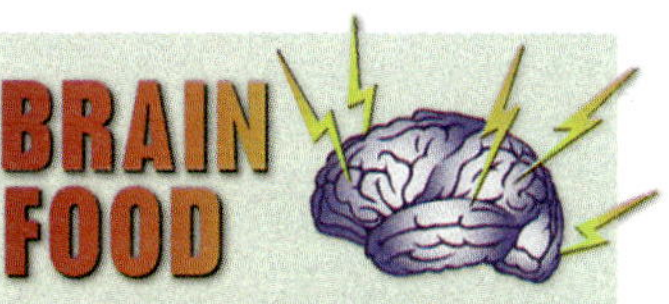

Both sapphires and rubies are forms of the mineral *corundum.* The difference in the color of the gems is caused by trace amounts of metals within the crystal structure of corundum. Sapphires are blue due to the presence of iron and titanium. Rubies are red due to the presence of chromium.

REVIEW

1. Describe how minerals form underground.
2. What are the two main types of mining?
3. **Analyzing Ideas** How does reclamation protect the environment around a mine?

Answers to Review

1. Answers will vary. Minerals form when magma cools and solidifies, when water evaporates from a lake or sea, when dissolved minerals crystallize on the bottom of lakes or seas, when changing temperature and pressure conditions in the Earth change preexisting rocks and new minerals form, and when dissolved minerals crystallize out of heated ground water.
2. surface mining and deep mining
3. Reclamation reduces the harmful effects of mining by returning the land to its original state.

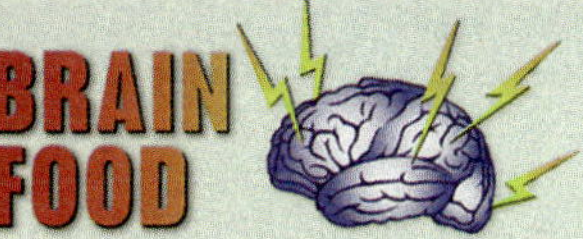

Scientists know that there are valuable deposits of minerals on other bodies in our solar system. Ask students to think about what issues should be considered before staking claims and mining other planets.

Quiz

1. Name three minerals that form in metamorphic rock. (possible answers: calcite, muscovite, chlorite, garnet, graphite, hematite, magnetite, and talc)
2. What is ore? (mineral deposits large enough and pure enough to be mined for profit)
3. How can mining cause water pollution? (The waste products from a mine can introduce toxic concentrations of elements in rivers, lakes, and ground water.)

Alternative Assessment

Concept Mapping Have students make a concept map in their ScienceLog of one mining process discussed in this section. Make sure students include each step in the process of mining. The first should be the search for the mineral or ore deposits. The final step should include information about the products that are manufactured with the mineral and the cleanup of the mine wastes.

Critical Thinking Worksheet 3
"Mineral Hunt"

Chapter Highlights

Vocabulary Definitions

Section 1

mineral a naturally formed, inorganic solid with a crystalline structure

element a pure substance that cannot be separated or broken down into simpler substances by ordinary physical or chemical means

atom the smallest particle into which an element can be divided and still retain all of the properties of that element

compound a pure substance composed of two or more elements that are chemically combined; forms when atoms of two or more different elements become chemically bonded

crystal the solid, geometric form of a mineral produced by a repeating pattern of atoms

silicate mineral a mineral that is made mostly of silica, a combination of the elements silicon and oxygen

nonsilicate mineral a mineral that does not contain compounds of silicon and oxygen

Section 2

luster the way the surface of a mineral reflects light

streak the color of a mineral in powdered form

cleavage the tendency of a mineral to break along flat, parallel surfaces

fracture the tendency of a mineral to break along curved or irregular surfaces

hardness the resistance of a mineral to being scratched

density the amount of matter in a given space; mass per unit volume

Chapter Highlights

SECTION 1

Vocabulary

mineral *(p. 60)*
element *(p. 60)*
atom *(p. 61)*
compound *(p. 61)*
crystal *(p. 61)*
silicate mineral *(p. 62)*
nonsilicate mineral *(p. 63)*

Section Notes

- A mineral is a naturally formed, inorganic solid with a definite crystalline structure.
- An atom is the smallest unit of an element that retains the properties of the element.
- A compound forms when atoms of two or more elements bond together chemically.
- Every mineral has a unique crystalline structure. The crystal class a mineral belongs to is directly related to the mineral's chemical composition.
- Minerals are classified as either silicates or nonsilicates. Each group includes different types of minerals.

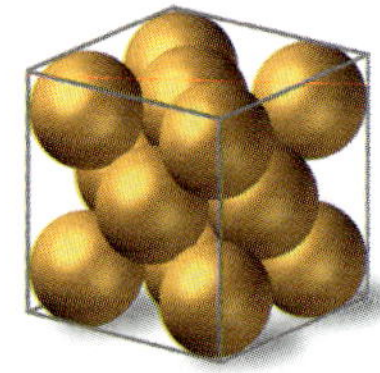
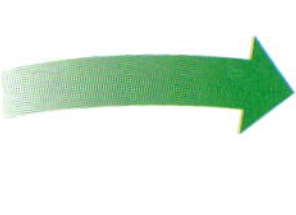

SECTION 2

Vocabulary

luster *(p. 64)*
streak *(p. 65)*
cleavage *(p. 65)*
fracture *(p. 65)*
hardness *(p. 66)*
density *(p. 66)*

Section Notes

- Color is not a reliable indicator for identifying minerals.
- The luster of a mineral can be metallic, submetallic, or nonmetallic.
- A mineral's streak does not necessarily match its surface color.
- The way a mineral breaks can be used to determine its identity. Cleavage and fracture are two ways that minerals break.

Skills Check

Math Concepts

THE PURITY OF GOLD The karat is a measure of the purity of gold. Gold that is 24 karats is 100 percent gold. But gold that is less than 24 karats is mixed with other elements, so it is less than 100 percent gold. If you have a gold nugget that is 16 karats, then 16 parts out of 24 are pure gold—the other 8 parts are composed of other elements.

24 karats = 100% gold
16 karats = 24 karats − 8 karats
$\frac{16}{24} = \frac{2}{3} = 0.67 = 67\%$ gold

Visual Understanding

ATOMIC STRUCTURE This illustration of the atomic structure of the mineral halite shows that halite is made of two elements—sodium and chlorine. The large spheres represent atoms of sodium, and the small spheres represent atoms of chlorine. The bars between the atoms represent the chemical bonds that hold them together.

72

Lab and Activity Highlights

Mysterious Minerals PG 494

**Is It Fool's Gold?—
A Dense Situation** PG 496

Datasheets for LabBook
(blackline masters for these labs)

SECTION 2

- Mohs' hardness scale provides a numerical rating for the hardness of minerals.
- The density of a mineral can be used to identify it.
- Some minerals have special properties that can be used to quickly identify them.

Labs

Mysterious Minerals *(p. 494)*

Is It Fools Gold?—A Dense Situation *(p. 496)*

SECTION 3

Vocabulary

ore *(p. 70)*

reclamation *(p. 71)*

Section Notes

- Minerals form in both underground environments and surface environments.
- Two main types of mining are surface mining and deep mining.
- Reclamation is the process of returning mined land to its original state.

internet**connect**

GO TO: go.hrw.com

Visit the **HRW** Web site for a variety of learning tools related to this chapter. Just type in the keyword:

KEYWORD: HSTMIN

GO TO: www.scilinks.org

Visit the **National Science Teachers Association** on-line Web site for Internet resources related to this chapter. Just type in the ***sci*LINKS** number for more information about the topic:

TOPIC: Gems	***sci*LINKS NUMBER:** HSTE055
TOPIC: Birthstones	***sci*LINKS NUMBER:** HSTE060
TOPIC: Identifying Minerals	***sci*LINKS NUMBER:** HSTE065
TOPIC: Mining Minerals	***sci*LINKS NUMBER:** HSTE070

Lab and Activity Highlights

LabBank

Long-Term Projects & Research Ideas, Project 31

VOCABULARY DEFINITIONS, *continued*

SECTION 3

ore a mineral deposit large enough and pure enough to be mined for a profit

reclamation the process of returning land to its original state after mining is completed

Vocabulary Review Worksheet 3

Blackline masters of these Chapter Highlights can be found in the **Study Guide.**

Chapter Review Answers

Using Vocabulary

1. If a mineral breaks along a curved or irregular surface, it has fracture. If a mineral breaks along flat surfaces, it has cleavage.
2. Elements are made of only one kind of atom, while compounds are made of two or more elements that are chemically bonded.
3. Streak is the color of a mineral in powdered form. The color of a mineral may change, but the mineral's streak is always the same.
4. The hardness of a mineral is its resistance to being scratched, while the density of a mineral is how much matter is packed into a certain volume.
5. Silicate minerals are made of silicon and oxygen compounds, while nonsilicate minerals are made of other compounds.
6. A mineral is made up of a particular arrangement of different kinds of atoms.

Understanding Concepts

Multiple Choice

7. d
8. a
9. d
10. d
11. d
12. b
13. d
14. b

Chapter Review

USING VOCABULARY

For each pair of terms, explain the difference in their meaning.

1. fracture/cleavage
2. element/compound
3. color/streak
4. density/hardness
5. silicate mineral/nonsilicate mineral
6. mineral/atom

UNDERSTANDING CONCEPTS

Multiple Choice

7. On Mohs' hardness scale, which of the following minerals is harder than quartz?
   a. talc
   b. apatite
   c. gypsum
   d. topaz

8. A mineral's streak
   a. is more reliable than color in identifying a mineral.
   b. reveals the mineral's specific gravity.
   c. is the same as a luster test.
   d. reveals the mineral's crystal structure.

9. Which of the following factors is **not** important in the formation of minerals?
   a. heat
   b. volcanic activity
   c. presence of ground water
   d. wind

10. Which of the following terms is **not** used to describe a mineral's luster?
    a. pearly
    b. waxy
    c. dull
    d. hexagonal

11. Which of the following is considered a special property that applies to only a few minerals?
    a. color
    b. luster
    c. streak
    d. magnetism

12. Which of the following physical properties can be expressed in numbers?
    a. luster
    b. hardness
    c. color
    d. reaction to acid

13. How many basic crystal classes are there?
    a. 3
    b. 10
    c. 5
    d. 6

14. Which of the following minerals would scratch fluorite?
    a. talc
    b. quartz
    c. gypsum
    d. calcite

Short Answer

15. Using no more than 25 words, define the term *mineral.*

16. In one sentence, describe how density is used to identify a mineral.

17. What methods of mineral identification are the most reliable? Explain.

Short Answer

15. A mineral is a naturally occurring inorganic solid with a crystalline structure.
16. Each mineral has its own unique density.
17. Answers will vary. Cleavage, hardness, and density are very reliable because they can be measured and do not change. Color and fracture are less reliable.

Chapter 3 Review—California Standards: PE/ATE Q7–18: 6, 6b

Concept Mapping

18. Use the following terms to create a concept map: minerals, oxides, nonsilicates, carbonates, silicates, hematite, calcite, quartz.

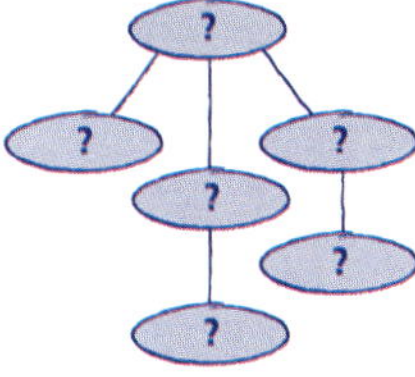

CRITICAL THINKING AND PROBLEM SOLVING

Write one or two sentences to answer the following questions:

19. Suppose you have three rings, each with a different gem. One has a diamond, one has an amethyst (purple quartz), and one has a topaz. You mail the rings in a small box to your friend who lives five states away. When the box arrives at its destination, two of the gems are damaged. One gem, however, is damaged much worse than the other two. What scientific reason can you give for the difference in damage?

20. While trying to determine the identity of a mineral, you decide to do a streak test. You rub the mineral across the plate, but it does not leave a streak. Does this mean your test failed? Explain your answer.

21. Imagine that you work at a jeweler's shop and someone brings in some "gold nuggets" that they want to sell. The person claims that an old prospector found the gold nuggets during the California gold rush. You are not sure if the nuggets are real gold. How would you decide whether to buy the nuggets? Which identification tests would help you decide the nuggets' identity?

22. Suppose that you find a mineral crystal that is as tall as you are. What kinds of environmental factors would cause such a crystal to form?

MATH IN SCIENCE

23. Gold has a specific gravity of 19. Pyrite's specific gravity is 5. How much denser is gold than pyrite?

24. In a quartz crystal there is one silicon atom for every two oxygen atoms. That means that the ratio of silicon atoms to oxygen atoms is 1:2. If there were 8 million oxygen atoms in a sample of quartz, how many silicon atoms would there be?

INTERPRETING GRAPHICS

Examine the photograph below of a garnet crystal, and answer the questions that follow.

25. List and describe three properties of this mineral.

26. Which crystal class do you think this mineral belongs to? Look at the chart of crystal classes at the beginning of Section 1.

NOW What Do You Think?

Take a minute to review your answers to the ScienceLog questions on page 59. Have your answers changed? If necessary, revise your answers based on what you have learned since you began this chapter.

75

Concept Mapping

18.  An answer to this exercise can be found at the end of this book.

Critical Thinking and Problem Solving

19. Each mineral has a different hardness. The hardest mineral was damaged the least. (The diamond will not be damaged, the topaz will be slightly damaged, and the amethyst will sustain the most damage.)
20. No; the test was actually successful. You learned that the unknown mineral has no streak and that it is harder than the streak plate. This clue will help you classify the mineral.
21. Students should suggest performing several tests to see whether the mineral is gold or not. Gold is very heavy and very soft, so one would start with density and hardness tests.
22. When magma contains a lot of hot fluids, very large crystals can grow.

Math in Science

23. Gold is $\frac{19}{5} = 3\frac{4}{5}$, or 3.8 times as dense as pyrite.
24. $\frac{8 \text{ million}}{2}$ = 4 million silicon atoms

Interpreting Graphics

25. It has a hexagonal crystal shape, red color, and glassy luster.
26. hexagonal

Concept Mapping Transparency 3

Blackline masters of this Chapter Review can be found in the **Study Guide.**

NOW What Do You Think?

1. A mineral is a naturally occurring inorganic solid that has a crystalline structure.
2. Answers will vary. Minerals form when salt water evaporates; they can crystallize out of a solution; and they form when magma solidifies.

Weird Science
Lightning Leftovers

Background

Silica, also known as silicon dioxide, SiO_2, is a compound of the two most common elements in the Earth's crust, silicon and oxygen. Silica can take a variety of forms. Crystalline forms include quartz, agate, and amethyst. Noncrystalline forms include obsidian, flint, and opal. Silica is the primary ingredient of most commercial glasses and ceramics and is also used in cements and mortars.

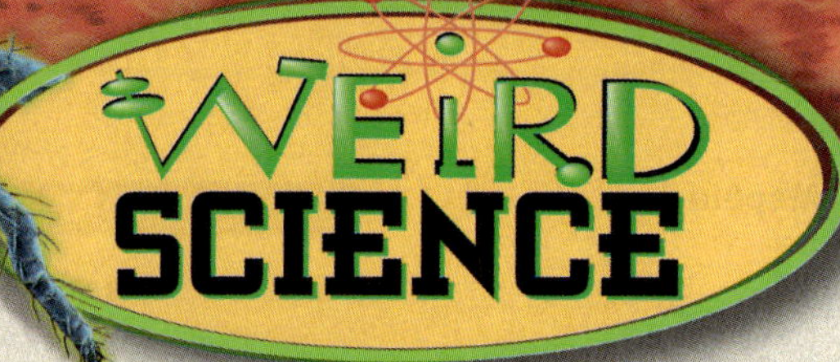

LIGHTNING LEFTOVERS

Without warning, a bolt of lightning lashes out from a storm cloud and strikes a sandy shoreline with a crash. Almost instantly, the sky is dark again—the lightning has disappeared without a trace. Or has it?

Nature's Glass Factory

Fulgurites are a rare type of natural glass formed when lightning strikes silica-rich minerals that occur commonly in sand, soil, and some rocks. *Tubular fulgurites* are found in areas with a lot of silica, such as beaches or deserts. Lightning creates a tubular fulgurite when a bolt penetrates the sand and melts silica into a liquid. The liquid silica cools and hardens quickly, leaving behind a thin glassy tube, usually with a rough outer surface and a smooth inner surface. Underground, a fulgurite may be shaped like the roots of a tree. It branches out with many arms that trace the zigzag path of the lightning bolt. Some fulgurites are as short as your little finger, while others stretch 20 m into the ground.

Underground Puzzles

So should you expect to run across a fulgurite on your next trip to the beach? Don't count on it. Scientists and collectors search long and hard for the dark glass formations, which often form with little or no surface evidence pointing to their underground location. Even when a fulgurite is located, removing it in one piece is difficult. They are quite delicate, with walls no thicker than 1–2 mm. Some of the largest fulgurites are removed from the ground in many pieces then glued back into their original shape.

Rock Fulgurites

Rock fulgurites are extremely rare, usually occurring only on high mountains. These oddities are created when lightning strikes the surface of a silica-rich rock. A rock fulgurite often looks like a bubbly glass case 1–3 mm thick around the rock. Lightning travels around the outside of the rock, fusing silica-rich minerals on its surface. Depending on which minerals melt, a rock fulgurite's color can range from glassy black to light gray or even bright yellow.

Find Out More

► Investigate how scientists studying the formation of fulgurites try to make lightning bolts strike a precise location to create a new fulgurite. You may also want to do some research to find out about companies that will *create* a fulgurite just for you!

◄ *A Tubular Fulgurite*

76

Sample Answer to Find Out More

To learn more about how fulgurites form, scientists have to get lightning to strike where they can observe it. To attract lightning, scientists attach long metal wires to a rocket that is then shot into storm clouds, triggering a huge electrical spark. The bolt of lightning travels down the wire and into the ground. There, it comes in contact with silica, forming a fulgurite, which scientists then study.

But scientific study is not the only reason to create a fulgurite: some companies sell custom-made fulgurites as natural works of art. You provide the sand, and they will fire the rocket and reel in a bolt of lightning, forming a fulgurite made just for you!

California Standards: PE/ATE 6, 6b

Science Fiction

"The Metal Man"

by Jack Williamson

In a dark, dusty corner of Tyburn College Museum stands a life-sized statue of a man. Except for its strange greenish color, the statue looks pretty ordinary. But if you look closely, you will marvel at the perfect detail of the hair and skin. You will also see a strange mark on the statue's chest, a dark crimson shape with six sides.

No one knows how the statue ended up in the dark corner. Everyone believes that the Metal Man is, or once was, Professor Thomas Kelvin of the Geology Department. Professor Kelvin had for many years spent his summer vacations along the Pacific coast of Mexico, prospecting for radium. Then at the end of one summer, Kelvin did not return to Tyburn. He had been more successful than he ever dreamed, and he had become very rich. But high in the mountains, he had also found something else . . .

Now there is only one person who knows what really happened to Professor Kelvin, and he tells the professor's story in "The Metal Man," by Jack Williamson. The tale involves Kelvin's expedition to search for the source of El Rio de la Sangre, the River of Blood, and the radium that makes the river radioactive. Did he find it? Is that what made Kelvin so rich? And what else did Professor Kelvin find there in the remote mountain valley?

Read for yourself the strange story of Professor Kelvin and the Metal Man in the *Holt Anthology of Science Fiction.*

77

Science Fiction
"The Metal Man"
by Jack Williamson

The Metal Man stands tall in the Tyburn College Museum, but it is no ordinary statue . . .

Teaching Strategy

Reading Level This compelling story will be a challenge for many students, but with some vocabulary help, they will enjoy this inventive work.

Background

About the Author Few people have had as long-lasting an impact on science fiction as Jack Williamson (1908–). This story, "The Metal Man," was first published in 1928—over 70 years ago! Although it was his very first short story, it is still a classic. Since then, Williamson has written dozens of science fiction novels, short-stories, other novels, and books about writing.

The term *science fiction* was not even around when Williamson began writing. Known as one of the great pioneers of science fiction, Williamson was the first to write about antimatter. In addition, he coined the terms *terraform* (in 1941) and *genetic engineering* (in 1951).

Williamson is also credited for legitimizing science fiction as a field worthy of literary attention. For this accomplishment, Williamson has received several awards. In 1976, he became the second person to win the Grand Master Nebula Award. In 1994, Williamson earned a lifetime achievement award from World Fantasy.

Further Reading

Wonder's Child: My Life in Science Fiction, Bluejay, 1985

The Best of Jack Williamson, Ballantine, 1978

The Pandora Effect, Ace Books, 1969

Chapter Organizer

CHAPTER ORGANIZATION	TIME MINUTES	OBJECTIVES	LABS, INVESTIGATIONS, AND DEMONSTRATIONS
Chapter Opener **pp. 78–79**	45	California Standards: PE/ATE 7	**Investigate!** Round and Round in Circles, p. 79
Section 1 **Understanding Rock**	135	▶ Describe two ways rocks were used by early humans, and describe two ways they are used today. ▶ Describe how each type of rock changes into another as it moves through the rock cycle. ▶ List two characteristics of rock that are used to help classify it. PE/ATE 1a, 2, 2b, 6b, 6c, 7, 7b	**Labs You Can Eat,** Famous Rock Groups, Lab 11
Section 2 **Igneous Rock**	90	▶ Explain how the cooling rate of magma affects the properties of igneous rocks. ▶ Distinguish between igneous rock that cools deep within the crust and igneous rock that cools at the surface. ▶ Identify common igneous rock formations. PE/ATE 1a, 1d; LabBook 1d, 7, 7a, 7b, 7d, 7e, 7h	**Skill Builder,** Crystal Growth, p. 498 **Datasheets for LabBook,** Crystal Growth, Datasheet 7
Section 3 **Sedimentary Rock**	90	▶ Describe how the two types of sedimentary rock form. ▶ Explain how sedimentary rocks record Earth's history. PE/ATE 2, 2a, 2b; LabBook 7, 7b, 7d, 7e, 7h	**Demonstration,** Dissolution of Minerals, p. 91 in ATE **Skill Builder,** Let's Get Sedimental, p. 501 **Datasheets for LabBook,** Let's Get Sedimental, Datasheet 8 **Whiz-Bang Demonstrations,** Settling Down, Demo 17
Section 4 **Metamorphic Rock**	90	▶ Describe two ways a rock can undergo metamorphism. ▶ Explain how the mineral composition of rocks changes as they undergo metamorphism. ▶ Describe the difference between foliated and non-foliated metamorphic rock. PE/ATE 1a, 1d, 1e, 3a, 6c, 7; LabBook 7, 7b, 7d, 7e	**QuickLab,** Stretching Out, p. 96 **Interactive Explorations CD-ROM,** Rock On! *A **Worksheet** is also available in the **Interactive Explorations Teacher's Edition.*** **Making Models,** Metamorphic Mash, p. 503 **Datasheets for LabBook,** Metamorphic Mash, Datasheet 9 **Long-Term Projects & Research Ideas,** Project 32

See page **T20** *for a complete correlation of this book with the*

CALIFORNIA SCIENCE CONTENT STANDARDS.

Correlations are also provided at point of use throughout this ATE.

TECHNOLOGY RESOURCES

Guided Reading Audio CD
English or Spanish, Chapter 4

Classroom Management CD-ROM

Interactive Explorations CD-ROM
CD 2, Exploration 6, Rock On!

CNN. **Scientists in Action,** Meteor Collision Geologist, Segment 6

Test Generator CD-ROM

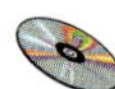
Earth Science Videodisc
Determining Relative Age: 331–6305
Field Trip–Understanding Rock Layers: 6306–22647

Chapter 4 • Rocks: Mineral Mixtures

CLASSROOM WORKSHEETS, TRANSPARENCIES, AND RESOURCES	SCIENCE INTEGRATION AND CONNECTIONS	REVIEW AND ASSESSMENT
Directed Reading Worksheet 4 **Science Puzzlers, Twisters & Teasers,** Worksheet 4	**Cross-Disciplinary Focus,** p. 79 in ATE	
Directed Reading Worksheet 4, Section 1 **Transparency 93,** The Rock Cycle **Math Skills for Science Worksheet 20,** Parts of 100: Calculating Percentages **Transparency 63,** The Digestive System of a Bird	**Cross-Disciplinary Focus,** pp. 81, 83 in ATE **Connect to Life Science,** pp. 81, 83, 85 in ATE **Multicultural Connection,** p. 82 in ATE **Apply,** p. 84 **Math and More,** p. 85 in ATE **MathBreak,** What's in It? p. 85 **Science, Technology, and Society:** Rock City, p. 104	**Homework,** p. 85 in ATE **Review,** p. 86 **Quiz,** p. 86 in ATE **Alternative Assessment,** p. 86 in ATE
Directed Reading Worksheet 4, Section 2 **Transparency 94,** The Cooling Rate of Magma and the Texture of Igneous Rock **Transparency 95,** Intrusive Igneous Rock Formations	**Connect to Life Science,** p. 88 in ATE **Multicultural Connection,** p. 88 in ATE	**Self-Check,** p. 88 **Review,** p. 90 **Quiz,** p. 90 in ATE **Alternative Assessment,** p. 90 in ATE
Transparency 96, A Sedimentary Rock Cycle **Directed Reading Worksheet 4,** Section 3	**Connect to Life Science,** p. 92 in ATE **Real World Connection,** p. 93 in ATE **Cross-Disciplinary Focus,** p. 93 in ATE	**Review,** p. 94 **Quiz,** p. 94 in ATE **Alternative Assessment,** p. 94 in ATE
Directed Reading Worksheet 4, Section 4 **Transparency 97,** Regional and Contact Metamorphism **Math Skills for Science Worksheet 31,** The Unit Factor and Dimensional Analysis **Reinforcement Worksheet 4,** What Is It? **Critical Thinking Worksheet 4,** Between a Rock and a Hard Place	**Cross-Disciplinary Focus,** p. 96 in ATE **Real-World Connection,** p. 97 in ATE **Math and More,** p. 98 in ATE **Life Science Connection,** p. 99 **Health Watch:** Glass Scalpels, p. 105	**Self-Check,** p. 96 **Homework,** pp. 97, 98 in ATE **Review,** p. 99 **Quiz,** p. 99 in ATE **Alternative Assessment,** p. 99 in ATE

internet connect

Holt, Rinehart and Winston On-line Resources

go.hrw.com

For worksheets and other teaching aids related to this chapter, visit the HRW Web site and type in the keyword: **HSTRCK**

National Science Teachers Association

www.scilinks.org

Encourage students to use the keywords listed on the Technology Highlights page to access information and resources on the NSTA Web site.

END-OF-CHAPTER REVIEW AND ASSESSMENT

Chapter Review in Study Guide
Vocabulary and Notes in Study Guide
Chapter Tests with Performance-Based Assessment, Chapter 4 Test
Chapter Tests with Performance-Based Assessment, Performance-Based Assessment 4
Concept Mapping Transparency 4

Chapter Resources & Worksheets

Visual Resources

TEACHING TRANSPARENCIES

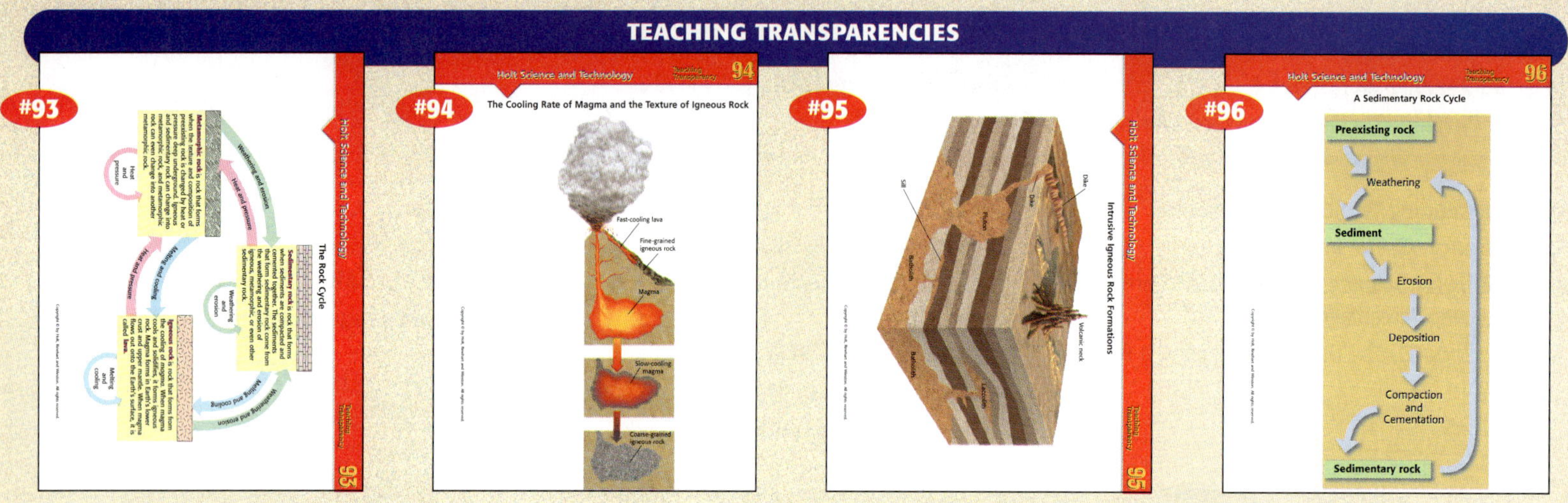

TEACHING TRANSPARENCIES

CONCEPT MAPPING TRANSPARENCY

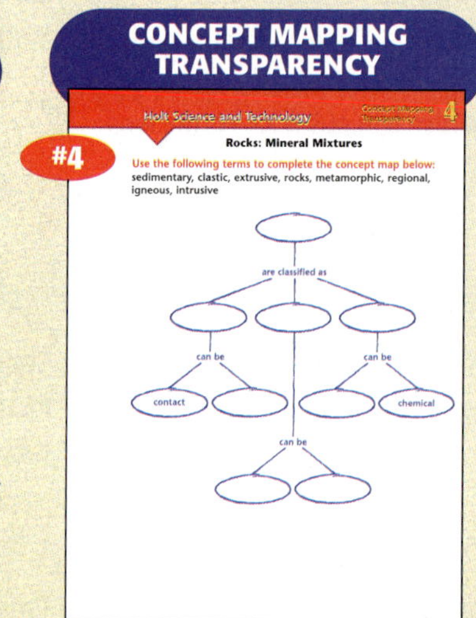

Meeting Individual Needs

DIRECTED READING

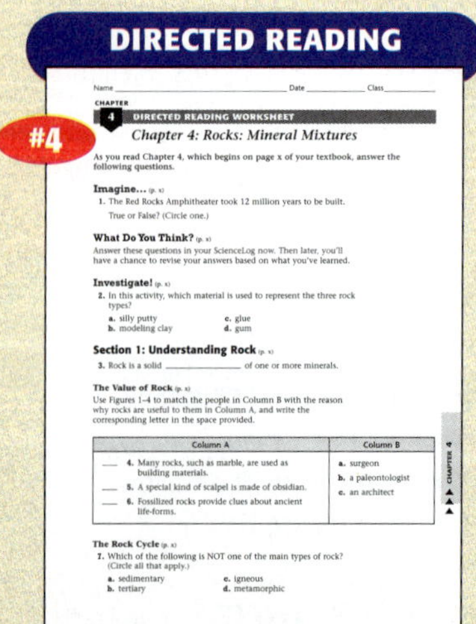

REINFORCEMENT & VOCABULARY REVIEW

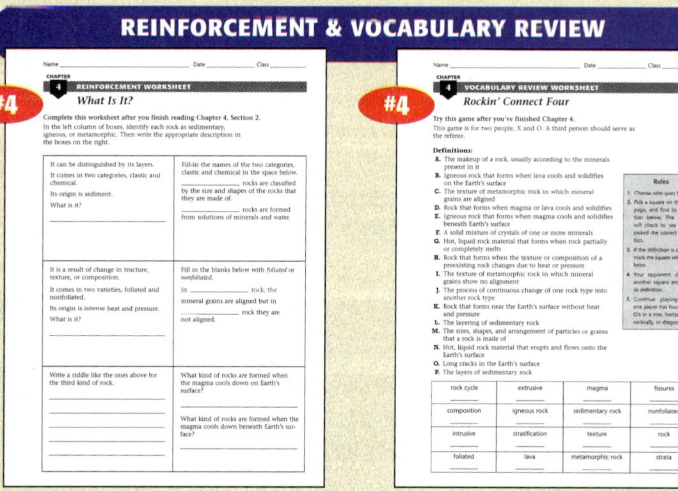

SCIENCE PUZZLERS, TWISTERS & TEASERS

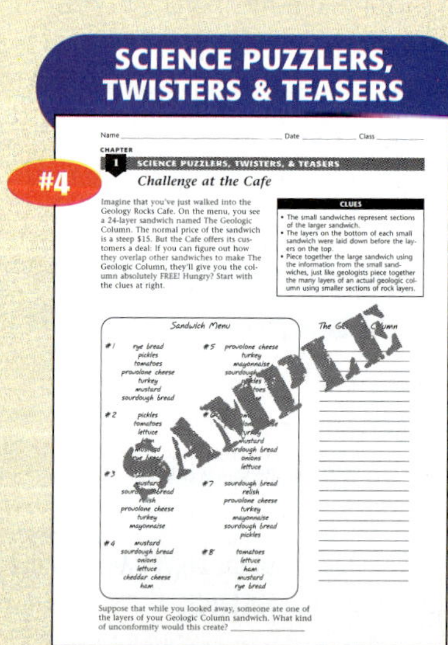

Chapter 4 • Rocks: Mineral Mixtures

Review & Assessment

STUDY GUIDE

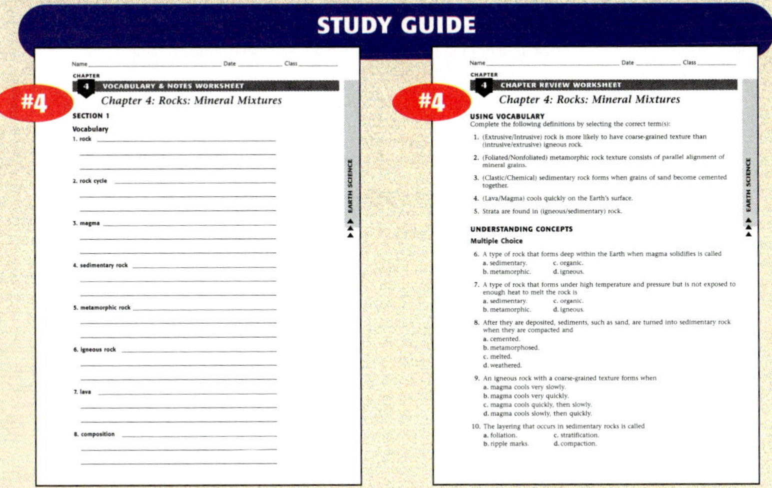

CHAPTER TESTS WITH PERFORMANCE-BASED ASSESSMENT

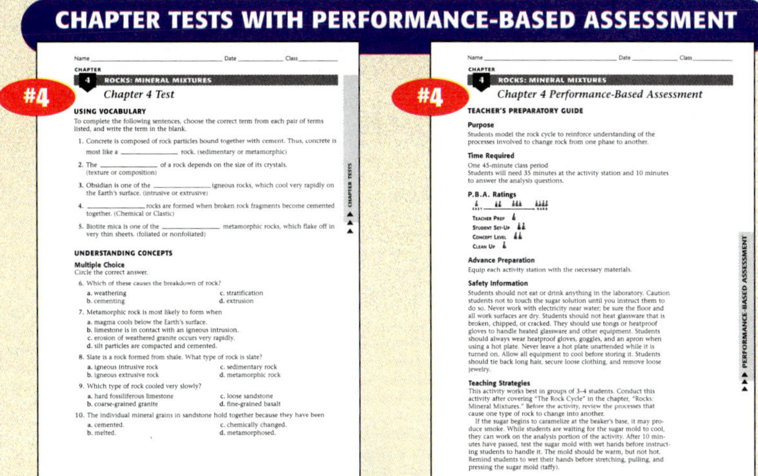

Lab Worksheets

LABS YOU CAN EAT

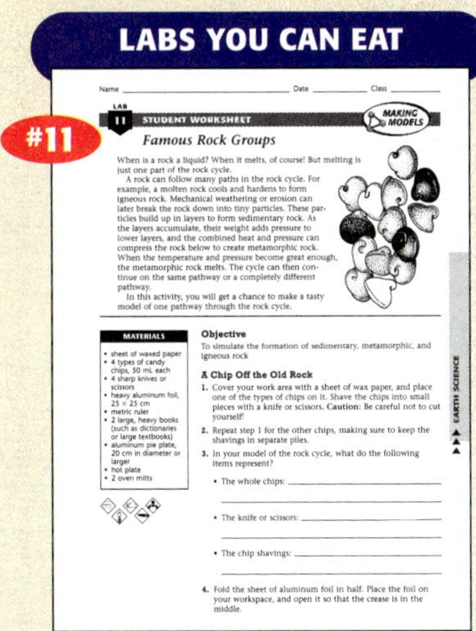

WHIZ-BANG DEMONSTRATIONS

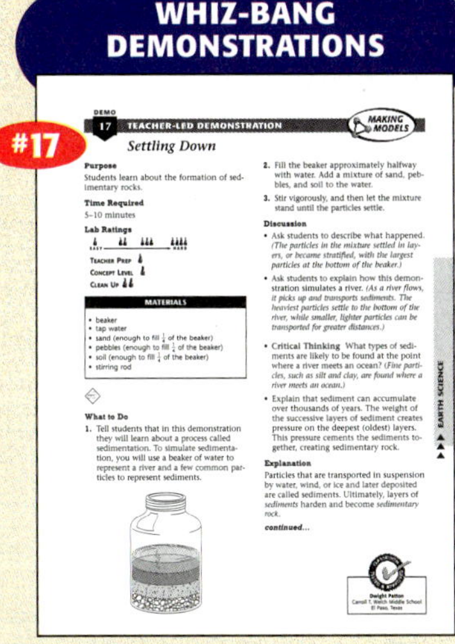

LONG-TERM PROJECTS & RESEARCH IDEAS

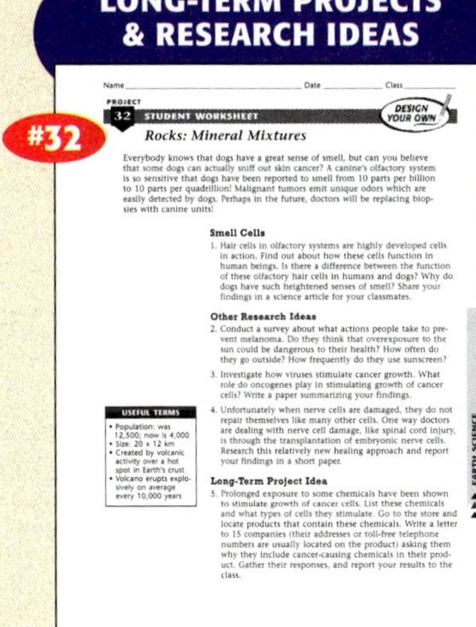

DATASHEETS FOR LABBOOK

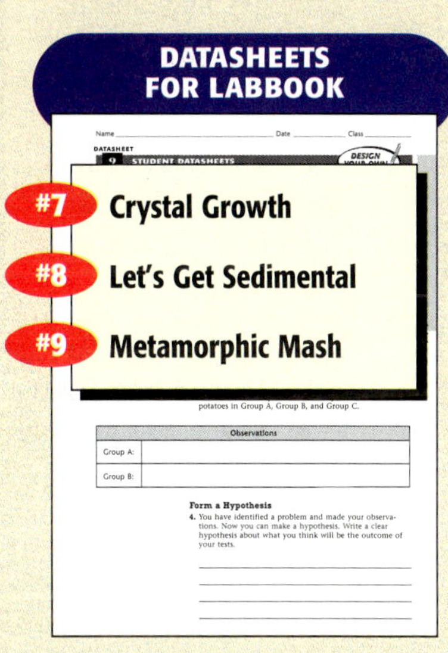

Applications & Extensions

CRITICAL THINKING & PROBLEM SOLVING

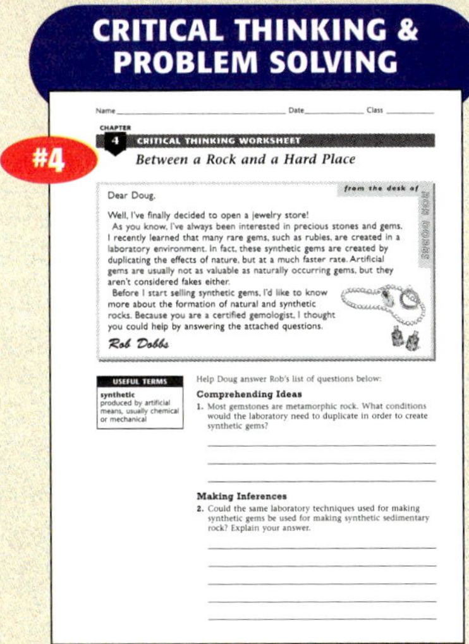

SCIENTISTS IN ACTION

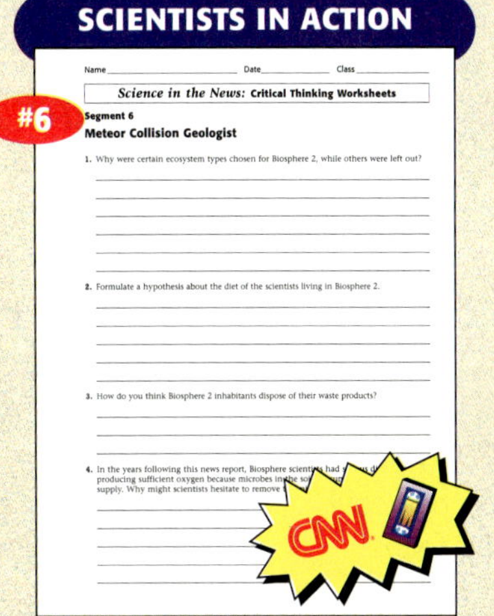

INTERACTIVE EXPLORATIONS

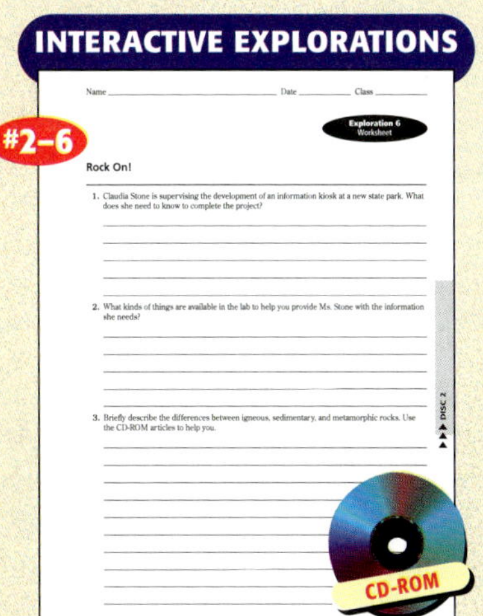

Chapter Background

Section 1

Understanding Rock

Rock Composition

This chapter focuses on the mineral composition of rock, not its bulk composition. These are two very different means of measuring rock composition.

- The *mineral composition* of a rock refers to the proportions of the different *minerals* in the rock and is usually expressed in percentages by volume. But not all rocks consist of minerals. For example, coal consists of organic matter and does not contain any minerals.

- The *bulk composition* of a rock is the sum of the different *elements* that make up the rock and is usually expressed in percentages by weight. Mineral composition is affected by bulk composition.

Is That a Fact!

- Although rocks contain many elements, the rocks in Earth's crust are nearly 94 percent oxygen by volume.
- Ninety-five percent of the outer 10 km of Earth is igneous and metamorphic rock.

- Although sedimentary rock makes up less than 5 percent of the Earth's crust, it is spread thinly over much of the planet's surface. Sedimentary rock covers 75 percent of the Earth's continental surfaces!

Section 2

Igneous Rock

The Great Dike of Rhodesia

Dikes can range in width from a few millimeters to thousands of meters. The Great Dike of Rhodesia, in Africa, is the largest known dike on Earth. It has an average width of 10 km and extends for almost 600 km.

Is That a Fact!

- A common name for quartz is rock crystal. Its name comes from the Greek word *krystallos,* meaning "ice."

Pumice

Some magmas contain dissolved gases such as carbon dioxide. When these gases come out of magma in the form of small bubbles, the magma greatly increases its volume, causing an enormous buildup of pressure. This results in a violent volcanic eruption. The result is a frothy-looking rock called pumice. Pumice is full of small holes called vesicles, where the trapped gases used to be. Depending on how much space is taken up by vesicles, some types of pumice can float in water!

- Pumice has a variety of industrial and household uses. Its abrasive qualities make it perfect for use in scouring and cleaning products. People use chunks of pumice in the bathtub to remove callouses from their feet.

Is That a Fact!

- Igneous rocks that form deep underground are called plutonic rocks, after Pluto, the god of the underworld in Roman mythology. Volcanic rocks are named after Vulcan, the Roman god of metalworking and fire.
- Although many people think of lava as a thin and runny liquid, lava flows are often quite viscous. Usually the temperature has cooled enough for crystals to begin forming, which can give lava a consistency similar to that of thick oatmeal.

SECTION 3

Sedimentary Rock

▶ Working with Clay

Clay is composed primarily of silicate minerals. Clays are easy to work with when they are wet because the tiny plate-shaped silicate crystals are trapped between water molecules. As the water evaporates, the silicates are cemented into place and the clay becomes brittle and difficult to work with.

IS THAT A FACT!

- Bentonite, a form of clay composed of very fine silicate crystals, has a wide variety of industrial applications. Some forms of bentonite can expand as much as 300 percent when mixed with water. Bentonite is used to make cat litter, to line artificial ponds, to remove impurities from wines and juices, to treat waste water, and in a variety of applications for oil drilling.
- The Mississippi River carries sediment from land as far away as the Appalachians and the Rocky Mountains. The Mississippi Delta, at the Gulf of Mexico, covers about 33,700 km^2. The delta has been forming for the last 2 million years.

SECTION 4

Metamorphic Rock

▶ Foliated Rocks

Foliated rocks develop during regional metamorphism. In slate, tiny flakes of mica line up into sheets. In some schists, mica forms dark or light layers, and the crystals are large enough to see. Gneiss has a coarse texture, and alternating layers are dominated by different minerals.

▶ Metamorphosis in a Lab

How do scientists determine the geologic history of a metamorphic rock? Geologists can estimate the temperature and pressure that metamorphosed a rock by simulating the process in a laboratory. When geologists know the chemical composition of certain minerals within a rock, they can subject a similar compound to a range of temperatures and pressures. By observing the laboratory results, they can make predictions about how similar materials behave in nature. Geologists can determine the temperature at which metamorphosis occurred within 20°C and the pressure within a fraction of a kilobar.

▶ Carrara Marble

In the mountains around Carrara, Italy, a marble prized for its purity has been mined for at least 2,000 years. Its whiteness is due to the lack of organic materials in the limestone from which it recrystallized. Carrara marble was used in the interior of the Parthenon, in Rome. It is also found in the Leaning Tower of Pisa, in the pavement of Saint Peter's Basilica, in Vatican City, and in the Kennedy Center, in Washington, D.C.

IS THAT A FACT!

- Metamorphic rocks are a challenge to study because they form within a wide range of heat and pressure. Scientists must distinguish between the geologic history of the metamorphic rock and the history of the igneous, sedimentary, or previously metamorphosed rocks it formed from. For the same reason, however, metamorphic rocks offer many important clues about tectonic activity in the Earth's past.

- Metamorphism occurs quickly at high temperatures, but it also occurs at temperatures that are surprisingly low. For example, clay minerals in mudstone and shale can begin to metamorphose at temperatures as low as 50°C! This reaction, however, takes many millions of years to occur.

For additional background resources, please refer to the **HST Reference Library.**

CHAPTER 4

Rocks: Mineral Mixtures

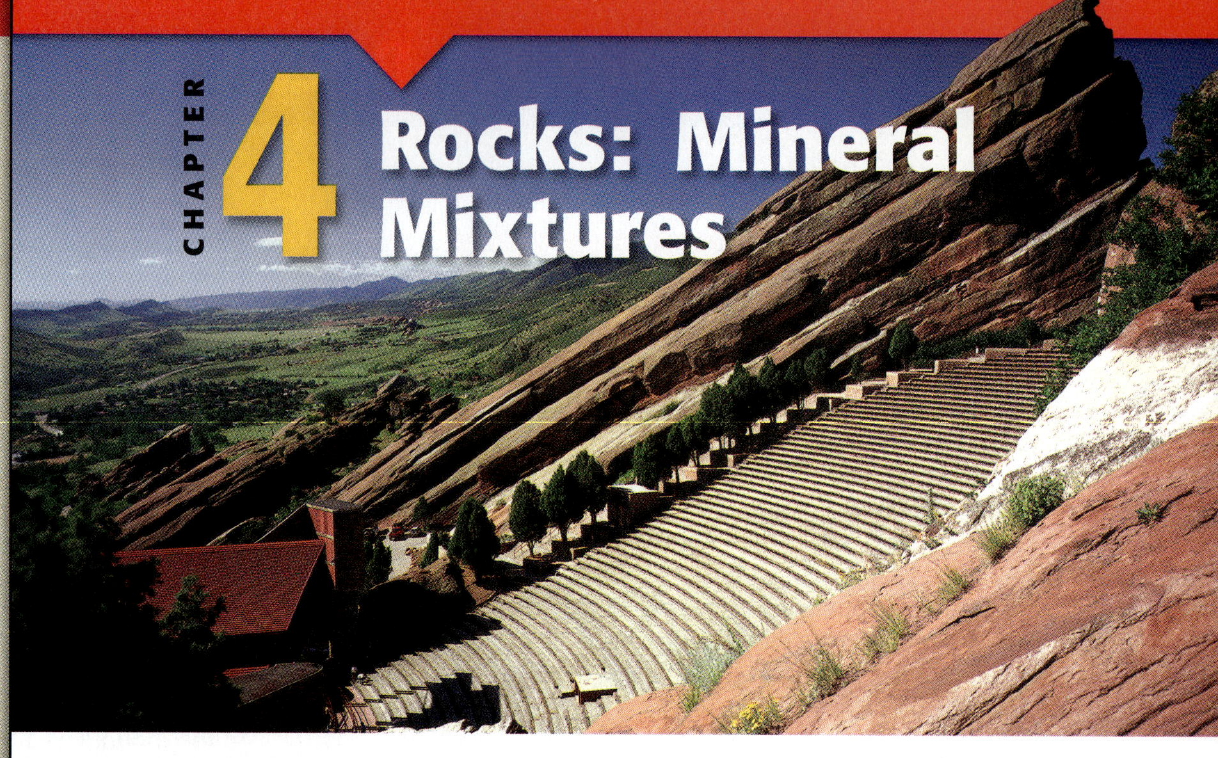

Imagine...

Imagine that you are an architect who has just been hired to design an amphitheater. The client wants the amphitheater to be big enough to host large concerts. In fact, she wants the amphitheater to seat an audience of 9,200. The client also wants excellent acoustics (sound qualities), and she wants it without a roof so the guests can enjoy the open air. She also wants the audience to be awed by two red sandstone formations that will tower 122 m above the stage.

You think about the design and come back with a plan that requires a minimum of 400 trillion metric tons of red sandstone for the walls and floor. You also estimate that it will take about 12 million years to form that much red sandstone. Sound ridiculous? Well, such an amphitheater actually exists.

Welcome to the Red Rocks Amphitheater just outside of Denver, Colorado. As you can see, this amphitheater was created by the forces of nature rather than by human hands. The amphitheater is a perfect place for a rock concert, and it is also a good place to start thinking about rocks. Exploring rocks will help you better understand the natural world. For example, what exactly is a rock? And how are rocks important to the study of Earth science? You will be able to answer these questions as you read this chapter.

78

Directed Reading Worksheet 4

Science Puzzlers, Twisters & Teasers Worksheet 4

Guided Reading Audio CD
English or Spanish, Chapter 4

Imagine . . .

The rocks of the Red Rocks Amphitheater formed many millions of years ago when Colorado lay beneath a warm inland sea. The sandstone of the Red Rocks area formed when sand settled to the bottom of that sea. The characteristic red color of the rock comes from the oxidation of iron-bearing minerals in the sediments. Over time, the sediments compacted and hardened. The water receded and the land dried. As tectonic forces pushed the Rocky Mountains up, the sandstone formations were tilted and eroded. As a result, some slabs of sandstone in the Red Rocks formation are nearly vertical!

What Do You Think?

In your ScienceLog, try to answer the following questions based on what you already know:

1. What is the difference between a rock and a mineral?
2. What are some modern uses of rock?
3. How does rock form?

Round and Round in Circles

The type of rock you can see at Red Rocks Amphitheater is one of three major types of rock found on Earth. In the pages that follow, you will learn the names of these rock types and how they actually form. But first do this activity to demonstrate one of the most important ideas about rock.

Procedure

1. Using several pieces of **modeling clay** of different colors, form as many tiny balls as you can from each piece. These will represent tiny pieces of rock or sand.
2. Gather all the tiny balls of clay together in one pile. With your hand, gently press down on the clay until the balls stick together. This mixture of minerals will represent *sedimentary rock*. In your ScienceLog, describe the properties of your new "rock." How is it different from the tiny balls of clay you started with?
3. Now press down on the clay a little harder, flattening the tiny balls. Fold the clay in half and press down some more. This is your second type of rock. This new "rock" will represent *metamorphic rock*. Describe how it was formed in your ScienceLog.
4. Now press the clay and roll it around your desktop. Kneed it like dough until the clay becomes one large mass of only one color. If you work the clay enough, it should start to feel a little warm. In this state, the clay represents hot, liquid rock material.
5. After your clay is warm and soft, form it into a rounded shape and let it cool and harden. This time the clay represents *igneous rock*. Describe how this "rock" is different from the first two you made.
6. Finally, break off bits of the "rock" and form tiny balls of clay. If you have time, go back to step 2.

Analysis

7. Review your descriptions of each type of "rock" in your ScienceLog. Which "rock" do you think resembles the rock that forms from erupting volcanoes?
8. In step 6 you were asked to go back to step 2. Explain how this activity can be described as a rock cycle.

79

What Do You Think?

Accept all reasonable responses.

Students will have a chance to revise their answers in the Chapter Review under NOW What Do You Think?

Investigate!

MATERIALS

For Each Group:

- modeling clay in a variety of colors

Teacher Notes: Remind students to write their observations in their ScienceLog after every step of the activity so that they will have accurate notes on the stages of the rock cycle.

The analogy in steps 4 and 5 is not exact, but students should realize that the softer, warmer clay represents a hot liquid. The igneous process can be demonstrated more accurately using candle wax. To show how igneous rock forms from the cooling of magma, melt the candle wax and then let it cool to its solid form. The liquid wax represents magma, and the solid wax represents igneous rock. A hot plate is recommended instead of an open flame to melt the wax.

The different mineral crystals that make up igneous rock would be best represented by different colors of clay, like the sedimentary "rock" in step 2.

Cross-Disciplinary Focus

History The amphitheater at Red Rocks was constructed during the Great Depression by the Civilian Conservation Corps (CCC). Have students research how these workers excavated the amphitheater out of solid rock. Suggest that students also find out more about a CCC project done in their county or state.

Answers to Investigate!

5. This "rock" is different from the other two in that it is all one color and has a different texture.
7. The last type of "rock" is most like the rock that is extruded from volcanoes because it flowed like lava.
8. One type of "rock" changes into another, and eventually becomes the original rock type.

SECTION 1

Focus

Understanding Rock

In this section students learn about the variety of ways rocks are used in human civilization. The section explains the rock cycle and introduces the three types of rock: igneous, sedimentary, and metamorphic. Students learn how each type of rock forms and that rocks are classified by texture and mineral composition.

Bellringer

Ask students to make a list of the ways rock is used in their life. Encourage them to think of imaginative answers.

(People use rock to sharpen knives; make gardens or borders in yards; produce fertilizer; carve statues; create jewelry; and construct buildings, roads, and sidewalks.)

Sheltered English

1) Motivate

ACTIVITY

Have students examine samples of various types of rock and take notes on their characteristics, such as texture, color, weight, and composition. Then divide the class into groups of four. Groups should hypothesize about how each rock formed and suggest three different uses for each type of rock.

Directed Reading Worksheet 4 Section 1

1

Understanding Rock

NEW TERMS

rock
rock cycle
magma
sedimentary rock
metamorphic rock
igneous rock
lava
composition
texture

OBJECTIVES

- Describe two ways rocks were used by early humans, and describe two ways they are used today.
- Describe how each type of rock changes into another as it moves through the rock cycle.
- List two characteristics of rock that are used to help classify it.

The Earth's crust is made up mostly of rock. But what exactly is rock? **Rock** is simply a solid mixture of crystals of one or more minerals. However, some types of rock, such as coal, are made of organic materials. Rocks come in all sizes—from pebbles to formations thousands of kilometers long!

The Value of Rock

Rock has been an important natural resource as long as humans have existed. Early humans used rocks as hammers to make other tools. They discovered that they could make arrowheads, spear points, knives, and scrapers by carefully hammering flint, chert, and obsidian rocks. See **Figure 1.** These rocks were shaped to form extremely sharp edges and points. Even today, obsidian is used to form special scalpels, as shown in **Figure 2.**

Rock has also been used for centuries to make buildings, roads, and monuments. **Figure 3** shows some inventive uses of rock by both ancient and modern civilizations. Buildings have been made out of marble, granite, sandstone, limestone, and slate. Modern buildings also use concrete, in which rock is an important ingredient. Concrete is one of the most common building materials used today.

Figure 1 *This stone tool was made and used more than 5,000 years ago.*

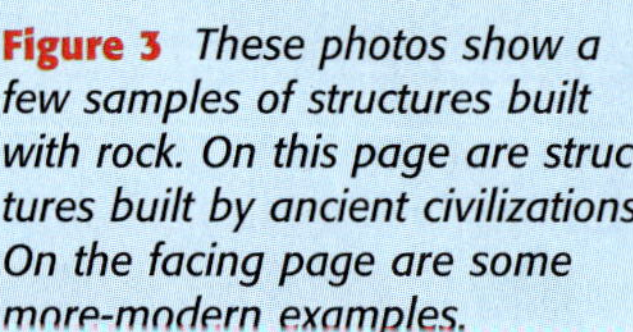

Figure 2 *This stone tool was made recently. It is an obsidian scalpel used in delicate operations.*

Pyramids at Giza, Egypt (3000 B.C.)

Macchu Pichu, Peru (A.D. 600)

Figure 3 *These photos show a few samples of structures built with rock. On this page are structures built by ancient civilizations. On the facing page are some more-modern examples.*

80

SCIENCE HUMOR

In 1976, Gary Dahl of California began marketing Pet Rocks. They came in a carrying case with a training manual and a pedigree that certified that they came from a California beach. In no time at all, more than 1 ton of the stones were sold. People held Pet Rock beauty contests and bought specialized foods and beds for them. There were even Pet Rock cemeteries!

Humans have a long history with rock. Certain types of rock have helped us to survive and to develop both our ancient and modern civilizations. Rock is also very important to scientists. The study of rocks helps answer questions about the history of the Earth and our solar system. Rocks provide a record of what the Earth and other planets were like before recorded history.

The fossils some rocks contain also provide clues about lifeforms that lived billions of years ago, long before dinosaurs walked the Earth. **Figure 4** shows how rocks can capture evidence of life that became extinct long ago. Without such fossils, scientists would know very little about the history of life on Earth. The answers we get from studying rocks often cause us to ask even more questions!

???

Is it possible to carve an entire city out of stone? Turn to page 104 to find out more.

BRAIN FOOD

Some meteorites are actually rocks that come from other planets. Below is a microscopic view of a meteorite that came from Mars. The tiny structures may indicate that microscopic life once existed on Mars.

Figure 4 *These fossilized remains of brachiopods were found on a mountaintop. Their presence indicates that what is now a mountaintop was once the bottom of a shallow sea.*

Exeter Cathedral, Exeter, England (A.D. 1120–1520)

LBJ Library, Austin, Texas (1972)

2 Teach

CROSS-DISCIPLINARY FOCUS

History Between A.D. 900 and 1400 the Anasazi Indians of the American Southwest carved small towns in cliff sides. In what is now Cambodia, a vast temple complex called Angkor was carved from brick, sandstone, and laterite in the twelfth century. In the 1300s, African traders built the Great Zimbabwe, an elaborate walled city guarded by huge monoliths. Have students write a report on one of these ancient sites.

MISCONCEPTION ALERT

The terms *rocks* and *rock formations* refer to the same material, but rock formations are large-scale bodies of rock, such as plutons, batholiths, and sedimentary strata, while rocks can be any size.

BRAIN FOOD

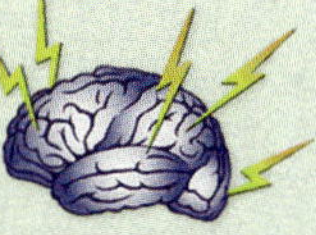

In 1996, scientists analyzed a meteorite from Mars and discovered possible microscopic fossils of primitive bacteria. The scientists also found organic molecules and mineral features that could indicate biological activity. When combined with other indirect evidence, this discovery raises the possibility that life once existed on Mars. But this evidence is hotly debated in the scientific community. Encourage students to learn more about the evidence for and against life on Mars.

CONNECT TO LIFE SCIENCE

European songbirds and jackdaws break the shells of snails by hammering them against rocks. Egyptian vultures break open ostrich eggs by grasping a pebble in their beak and pounding on the shell until it breaks. Have students research other animals that also use stones as tools, such as sea otters.

Students can then demonstrate for the class how these tools are used.

internet connect

TOPIC: Rocks and Human History
GO TO: www.scilinks.org
***sci*LINKS NUMBER:** HSTE080

TOPIC: Rock in Architecture
GO TO: www.scilinks.org
***sci*LINKS NUMBER:** HSTE085

2 Teach, *continued*

Using the Figure

Ask students to use the information in the rock-cycle illustration to draw a diagram of the rock cycle in their ScienceLog. The first step in the textbook illustration is the formation of sedimentary rock; ask students to begin their rock cycle with a different step. Encourage them to write a descriptive caption for every stage of the rock cycle.

Meeting Individual Needs

Students Having Difficulty

Have students prepare a *Rock Dictionary.* Ask them to list the three types of rock and the processes that occur in the rock cycle. Ask students to record the dictionary definition for each rock type or process and then define it in their own words. Encourage students to make up mnemonic devices, such as jokes or rhymes, to help them remember the meaning of each term.

Sheltered English

MISCONCEPTION ALERT

Rocks rarely undergo the complete process shown in the rock-cycle diagram. Sedimentary rocks can become igneous rocks, and metamorphic rocks can become sedimentary rocks. Some students may not realize the length of time it takes for changes to occur in the rock cycle. The process shown in the diagram can take billions of years.

Teaching Transparency 93
"The Rock Cycle"

The Rock Cycle

The rocks in the Earth's crust are constantly changing. Rock changes its shape and composition in a variety of ways. The way rock forms determines what type of rock it is. The three main types of rock are *igneous, sedimentary,* and *metamorphic.* Each type of rock is a part of the *rock cycle.* The **rock cycle** is the process by which one rock type changes into another. Follow this diagram to see one way sand grains can change as they travel through the rock cycle.

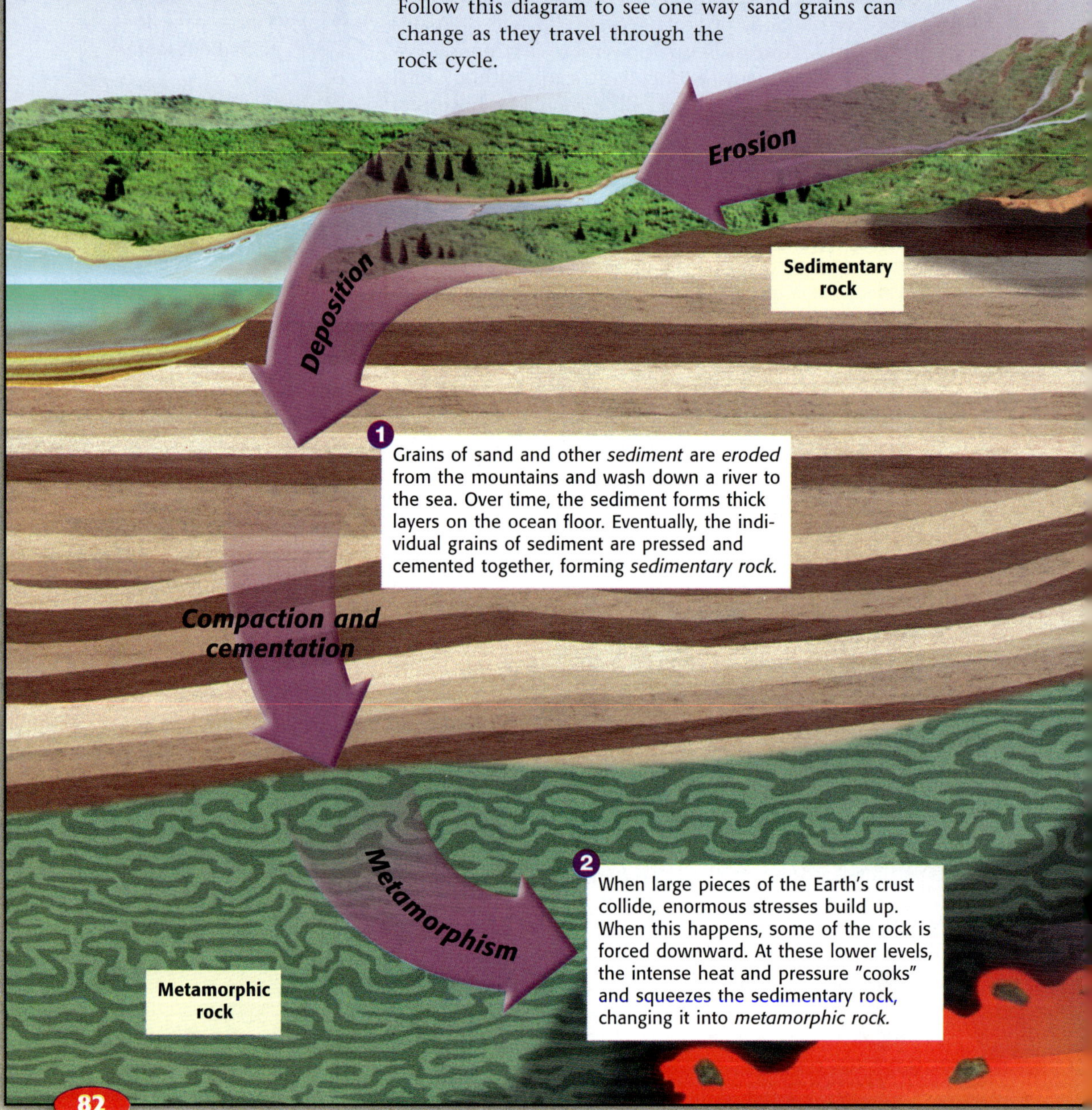

Erosion

Deposition

Sedimentary rock

1 Grains of sand and other *sediment* are *eroded* from the mountains and wash down a river to the sea. Over time, the sediment forms thick layers on the ocean floor. Eventually, the individual grains of sediment are pressed and cemented together, forming *sedimentary rock.*

Compaction and cementation

Metamorphism

Metamorphic rock

2 When large pieces of the Earth's crust collide, enormous stresses build up. When this happens, some of the rock is forced downward. At these lower levels, the intense heat and pressure "cooks" and squeezes the sedimentary rock, changing it into *metamorphic rock.*

82

Multicultural CONNECTION

The Islamic scholar Avicenna (980–1037) contributed immensely to our knowledge of medicine, astronomy, mathematics, and geology. In the *Book of Minerals* he described how rivers and seas laid down sediment that eventually became rock. Avicenna's theories contributed to the foundations of Western geology. Many of his controversial ideas did not gain acceptance in Europe until the 1600s. Encourage interested students to learn more about the life and work of Avicenna.

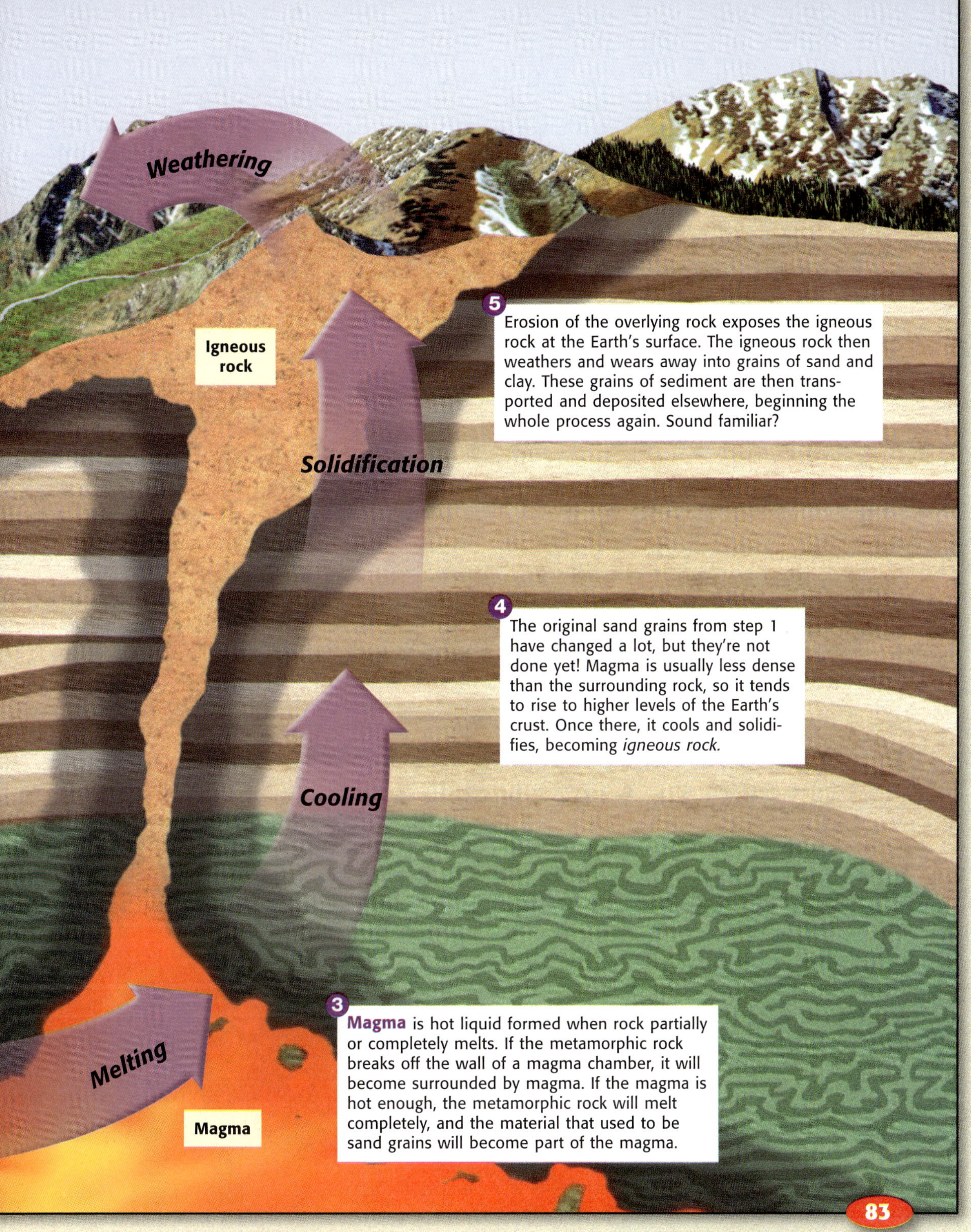

CONNECT TO LIFE SCIENCE

Many important substances on Earth follow cycles. Examples include water, nitrogen, sulfur, carbon, and phosphorous. Have students make a poster depicting the rock cycle and one other cycle in nature. Ask them to consider the ways that these cycles interact with each other.

CROSS-DISCIPLINARY FOCUS

Writing **Language Arts** Ask students to imagine being an ancient grain of sand on a beach. Have them write a letter to a young igneous rock describing their lifetime in the rock cycle. Students can share their letters with the class.

REAL-WORLD CONNECTION

Invite a local rock collector to address the class, and share his or her collection with the class. Tell the students to collect some rocks from their neighborhood for the collector to identify.

MISCONCEPTION ALERT

In some areas of the United States, especially in regions that experience long, cold winters, some people speak of rocks "growing." In the fall, farm fields are cleared of large rocks. The following spring, large rocks are found again in the fields and people say that the rocks have "grown" over the winter. In fact, when the ground freezes, it shifts and heaves, pushing buried rocks toward the surface.

IS THAT A FACT!

The space probes *Viking 1* and *Viking 2* provided detailed images of a gigantic volcano on Mars called Olympus Mons. The volcano is 25 km high, three times as high as Mount Everest. NASA scientists believe Olympus Mons is the largest volcano in the solar system.

Science Bloopers

In the Middle Ages, people believed that some rocks, called *eagle stones,* could reproduce. Scholars reported that the rocks crack like eggs and small stones pour out. Today, scientists call them *atetites,* or *clay-ironstone concretions.* Atetites have a shell of iron-rich clay that encloses smaller clay pebbles.

2 Teach, continued

Group Activity

Divide the class into small groups. Give each group samples of sandstone, limestone, and conglomerate. Number the samples. Provide a magnifying glass, a small dental pick, and paper towels to capture any pieces of rock that break off during the activity. Write the following instructions on the board:

1. Describe the color and texture of the specimen.
2. Using your unaided eye, examine the particles that make up the rock. Describe what you see.
3. Using the magnifying glass, try to identify the mineral composition of the specimen.
4. Use the dental pick to test the cohesiveness of the rocks, and record what you discover.
5. Try to classify each rock as fine-grained, medium-grained, or coarse-grained.

After groups have analyzed the rocks, discuss their findings.

Sheltered English

Now that you know something about the natural processes that make the three major rock types, you can see that each type of rock can become any other type of rock. This is why it is called a cycle—there is no beginning or end. All rocks are at some stage of the rock cycle and can change into a different rock type. **Figure 5** shows how the three types of rock change form.

Figure 5 **The Rock Cycle**

Sedimentary rock is rock that forms when sediments are compacted and cemented together. The sediments that form sedimentary rock come from the weathering and erosion of igneous, metamorphic, or even other sedimentary rock.

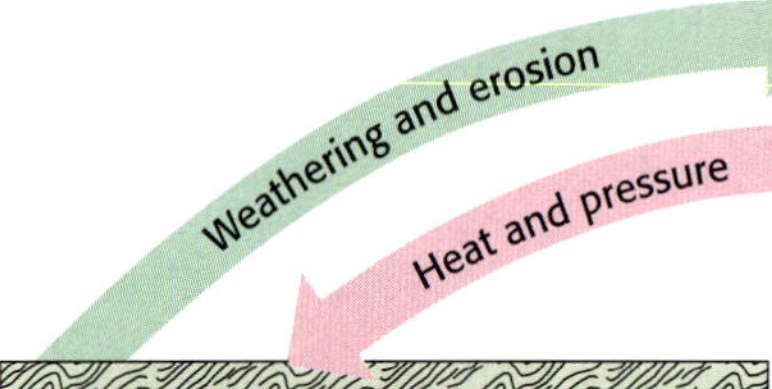

Weathering and erosion

Metamorphic rock is rock that forms when the texture and composition of a preexisting rock is changed by heat or pressure deep underground. Igneous and sedimentary rock can change into metamorphic rock, and metamorphic rock can even change into another metamorphic rock.

Heat and pressure

Melting and cooling

Heat and pressure

Igneous rock is rock that forms from the cooling of *magma.* When magma cools and solidifies, it forms igneous rock. Magma forms in Earth's lower crust and upper mantle. When magma flows out onto the Earth's surface, it is called **lava.**

Melting and cooling

Suppose you have an apple, a tomato, a peach, a kiwi fruit, a pineapple, a banana, a lemon, a cactus, a blue ball, a coconut, a brick, a sugar cube, a pair of sunglasses, and a garden hose. Use your imagination to invent three different ways to classify these objects into groups with similar characteristics. You may have as few as one group or as many as fourteen. What criteria did you use for each of your classification schemes? Which criteria would you use to classify rocks?

84

Answers to APPLY

Answers will vary. (These questions are intended to get the students to anticipate the content in the next two pages.)

Q: What happens to a small stone when it works up its courage?

A: It becomes a little boulder.

The Nitty-Gritty on Rock Classification

You now know that scientists classify all rock into three main types based on how they formed. But did you know that each type of rock is divided into even smaller groups? These smaller groups are also based on differences in the way rocks form. For example, all igneous rock forms when hot liquid cools and solidifies. But some igneous rocks form when lava cools on the Earth's surface, while others form when magma cools deep beneath the surface. Therefore, igneous rock is divided into two smaller groups, depending on how and where it forms. In the same way, sedimentary and metamorphic rocks are also divided into smaller groups. How do Earth scientists know how to classify different rocks? They study them in detail using two important criteria—*composition* and *texture*.

MATH BREAK

What's in It?

Assume that a granite rock you are studying is made of 30 percent quartz, 55 percent feldspar, and the rest biotite mica. What percentage of the rock is biotite mica?

Composition The minerals a rock is made of determine the **composition** of the rock. For example, a rock that is made up mostly of the mineral quartz will have a composition very similar to quartz. A rock that is made of 50 percent quartz and 50 percent feldspar will have a very different overall composition. Use this idea to compare the examples given in **Figure 6.**

Figure 6 *The overall composition of a rock depends on the minerals it contains.*

85

MATH and MORE

A percentage is a ratio that is expressed in terms of hundredths. When analyzing pure substances, percentage composition remains the same at any mass. For example, in terms of atomic mass, the percentage of oxygen atoms in water is 88.8 percent whether you are describing a single raindrop or an entire ocean.

Math Skills Worksheet 20
"Parts of 100: Calculating Percentages"

Answer to MATHBREAK

100 percent of rock − (30 percent quartz + 55 percent feldspar) = 15 percent biotite mica

CONNECT TO LIFE SCIENCE

Some birds swallow stones to help with digestion. The stones settle in a specialized stomach compartment called the gizzard. As seeds, stems, and leaves enter the gizzard, its strong muscles contract, and the stones grind up the tough cellulose fibers into pieces that are small enough to digest. To see how a gizzard functions, have students fill a small cloth bag with different-sized pebbles. Add some breakfast cereal and birdseed to the bag. Knead the bag to see what happens to the food. Tell students that some dinosaurs had gizzards as well.

Teaching Transparency 63
"The Digestive System of a Bird"

Homework

Illustration Have students make a poster that illustrates the rock cycle. Encourage them to cut out pictures from magazines of the different types of rock and processes in the rock cycle. For example, marble is a metamorphic rock that could be represented by a picture of a marble statue. Sheltered English

3 Extend

Research

Investigate Your Area Students can search the Internet to learn about nearby places that are good for rock hunting. Ask students to report their findings to the class.

4 Close

Quiz

1. Name four processes that change rock from one type to another. (weathering, changes in pressure, melting, and cooling)
2. What is the difference between magma and lava? (Magma is molten rock below the surface; lava is molten rock above the surface.)
3. What determines the texture of a rock? (the size, shape, arrangement, and composition of the rock's grains)

Alternative Assessment

Have students write a skit portraying the rock cycle. Roles can include the minerals that make up rock and the forces that affect them. To represent the forces—heat, pressure, erosion, and weathering—suggest that students create special costumes.

Texture The **texture** of a rock is determined by the sizes, shapes, and positions of the grains of which it is made. Rocks that are made entirely of small grains, such as silt or clay particles, are said to have a *fine-grained* texture. Rocks that are made of large grains, such as pebbles, are said to have a *coarse-grained* texture. Rocks that have a texture between fine- and coarse-grained are said to have a *medium-grained* texture. Examples of these textures are shown in **Figure 7.**

Figure 7 *These three sedimentary rocks are made up of grains of different sizes. Can you see the differences in their textures?*

Fine-grained

Siltstone

Medium-grained

Sandstone

Coarse-grained

Conglomerate

Each rock type has a different kind of texture. The texture of a rock is a good clue to how and where the rock formed. For example, the two rocks shown in **Figure 8** have textures that reflect how they formed. Both texture and composition are important characteristics that scientists use to understand the origin and history of rocks. Keep these characteristics in mind as you continue reading through this chapter.

Figure 8 *History is recorded in the texture of rock.*

This layered sandstone formed at the bottom of a river. You can see that the sediments from which it is made were deposited in layers.

This volcanic rock formed as a result of a violent eruption. The angular rock fragments were broken off a volcano during the eruption.

Review

1. List two ways rock is important to humans today.
2. What are the three major rock types, and how can they change from one type to another type?
3. How is lava different from magma?
4. **Interpreting Relationships** Explain how composition and texture are used to classify rock.

Answers to Review

1. Answers will vary.
2. The three major rock types are igneous, sedimentary, and metamorphic. Igneous rock forms when magma cools and solidifies. Sedimentary rock forms when sediments are cemented and compacted together or when minerals crystallize out of sea water. Metamorphic rock forms when the texture or mineral composition of a preexisting rock is changed by heat or pressure.
3. Magma is a hot liquid that exists underground. Lava is magma that erupts and flows onto the Earth's surface.
4. Texture and composition are used to understand the origin and history of rocks.

Section 1 Review—California Standards: PE/ATE 2, 6c

2

Igneous Rock

NEW TERMS
intrusive
extrusive

OBJECTIVES
- Explain how the cooling rate of magma affects the properties of igneous rock.
- Distinguish between igneous rock that cools deep within the crust and igneous rock that cools at the surface.
- Identify common igneous rock formations.

The word *igneous* comes from the Latin word for "fire." Magma cools into various types of igneous rock depending on the composition of the magma and the amount of time it takes the magma to cool and solidify. Like all other rock, igneous rock is classified according to its composition and texture.

Origins of Igneous Rock

Magma and lava solidify in the same way that water freezes. When magma or lava cools down enough, it solidifies, or freezes, to form igneous rock. The only difference between water freezing and magma freezing is that water freezes at 0°C and magma and lava freeze at between 700°C and 1,250°C.

There are three ways magma can form: when rock is heated, when pressure is released, or when rock changes composition. To see how this can happen, follow along with **Figure 9.**

Figure 9 *There are three ways a rock can melt.*

Temperature An increase in temperature deep within the Earth's crust can cause the minerals in a rock to melt. Different minerals melt at different temperatures. So depending on how hot a rock gets, some of the minerals can melt while other minerals remain solid.

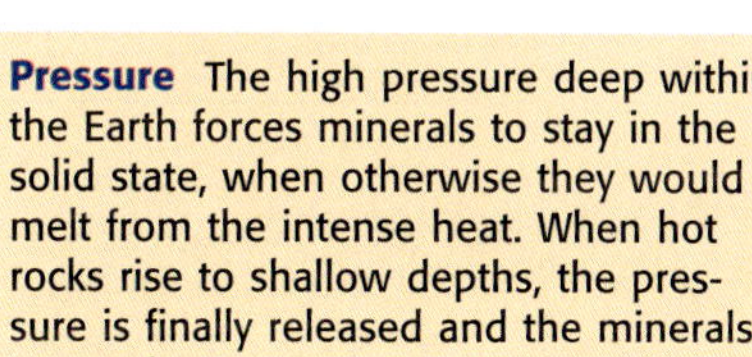

Pressure The high pressure deep within the Earth forces minerals to stay in the solid state, when otherwise they would melt from the intense heat. When hot rocks rise to shallow depths, the pressure is finally released and the minerals can melt.

Composition Sometimes fluids like water and carbon dioxide enter a rock that is slightly cooler than its melting temperature. When these fluids combine with the rock, they can lower the melting point of the rock enough for it to melt and form magma.

Surtsey is a volcanic island south of Iceland that people actually saw being born! In 1963, fishermen far out at sea saw jets of spray, steam, and lava shooting more than 30 m out of the ocean. One month later the volcano broke through the surface to form an island. By the time the eruptions ended, Surtsey covered an area of approximately 2.8 km^2. Seabirds started visiting, and tough grasses began to sprout. Today scientists think Surtsey may erode completely if the volcano doesn't erupt again.

SECTION 2

Focus

Igneous Rock

This section examines the relationship between magma and rock. It discusses how temperature, pressure, and composition affect the melting point of rock. Changes in all three of these conditions can occur simultaneously, interacting in complex ways. Students learn about the difference between felsic and mafic igneous rock as well as the difference between intrusive and extrusive igneous rock.

Bellringer

Pose the following question to students:

Do you think rocks that cooled and solidified from lava on Earth's surface would look different from those that cooled and solidified from magma inside the Earth? Why?

1 Motivate

Discussion

Ask students to talk about how volcanoes affect people and places. Discuss eruptions, lava flows, and ash clouds before asking students about the positive effects of volcanoes, such as land formation. Explain that lava and magma form land, and point out volcanic islands such as Hawaii and Iceland on a world map. Explain that volcanic soil is some of the most fertile soil in the world, which is why many populations are willing to live alongside potentially dangerous volcanoes.

Directed Reading Worksheet 4 Section 2

Section 2—California Standards: PE/ATE 1a, 1d; LabBook: 1d, 7, 7a, 7b, 7d, 7e, 7h

2 Teach

CONNECT TO LIFE SCIENCE

Until 1977, biologists thought few life-forms lived at ocean depths where sunlight does not reach. When scientists in the submersible *Alvin* explored the bottom of a deep ocean trench called the Galápagos Rift, they discovered structures called black smokers that release dissolved mineral compounds and heat into the water. Scientists were amazed to discover an entire ecosystem that did not depend on photosynthesis for energy. This discovery has led many scientists to speculate that life may also have evolved in the outer solar system—particularly in the subterranean oceans of Europa, one of Jupiter's moons. Have students research the bizarre life-forms that scientists found living around black smokers.

Multicultural CONNECTION

In the Tule Lake region of northern California, volcanic eruptions created a rugged landscape of broken lava beds with glassy, splintery edges, deep trenches, and small lava caves where people can live—and hide.

In 1872, the United States and the Modoc Indians went to war. The Modocs set up a stronghold for 50 people in the jagged lava beds. The terrain was so hard to negotiate that the Modocs held off more than 1,000 federal troops for more than 5 months. Today, this area is part of Lava Beds National Monument.

Composition and Texture of Igneous Rock

Look at the rocks in **Figure 10.** All of these are igneous rocks, even though they look very different from one another. These rocks differ from one another in what they are made of and how fast they cooled. Remember that igneous rocks are simply rocks that form as magma or lava cools. They are made of a variety of common minerals.

The light-colored rocks are not only lighter in color but also lighter in weight. These rocks are rich in elements such as silicon, aluminum, sodium, and potassium. These lightweight rocks are called *felsic*. The darker rocks are heavier than the felsic rocks. These rocks are rich in iron, magnesium, and calcium and are called *mafic*.

Figure 10 *Light-colored igneous rock generally has a felsic composition. Dark-colored igneous rock generally has a mafic composition.*

	Coarse-grained	Fine-grained
Felsic	 Granite	 Rhyolite
Mafic	 Gabbro	 Basalt

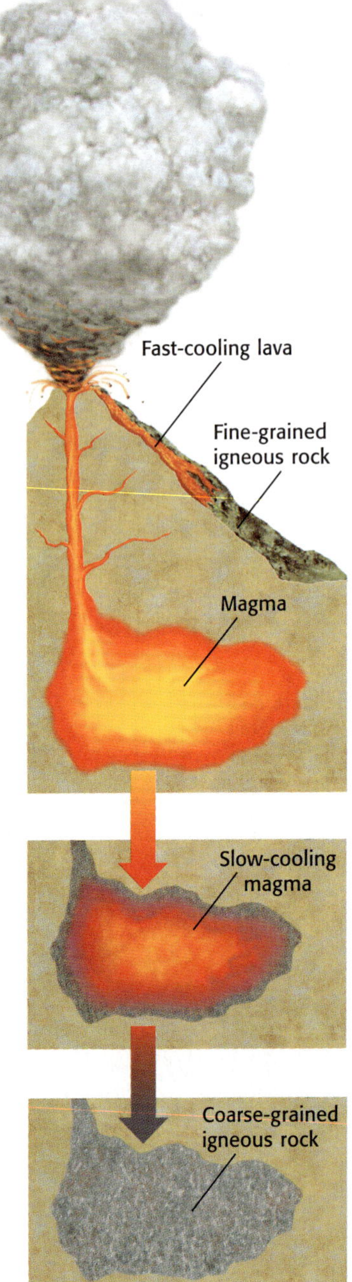

Figure 11 *The amount of time it takes for magma or lava to cool determines the texture of igneous rock.*

Now look at **Figure 11.** This illustration shows what happens to magma when it cools at different rates. The longer it takes for the magma or lava to cool, the more time mineral crystals have to grow. And the more time the crystals have to grow, the coarser the texture of the resulting igneous rock.

Self-Check

Rank the rocks shown in Figure 10 by how fast they cooled. Hint: Pay attention to their texture. *(See page 564 to check your answer.)*

88

Teaching Transparency 94
"The Cooling Rate of Magma and the Texture of Igneous Rock"

Answers to Self-Check

From fastest-cooled to slowest-cooled, the rocks in **Figure 10** are: basalt, rhyolite, gabbro, and granite.

Igneous Rock Formations

You have probably seen igneous rock formations that were caused by lava cooling on the Earth's surface. But not all magma reaches the surface. Some magma cools and solidifies deep within the Earth's crust.

Intrusive Igneous Rock When magma cools beneath the Earth's surface, the resulting rock is called **intrusive.** Intrusive rock usually has a coarse-grained texture. This is because it is well insulated by the surrounding rock and thus cools very slowly.

Intrusive rock formations are named for their size and the way in which they intrude, or push into, the surrounding rock. *Plutons* are large, balloon-shaped intrusive formations that result when magma cools at great depths. Because plutons are some of the most common intrusions, intrusive rocks are often called *plutonic rocks*. **Figure 12** shows an example of an intrusive formation that has been exposed on the Earth's surface. Some common intrusive rock formations are shown in **Figure 13.**

Figure 12 *Enchanted Rock, near Llano, Texas, is an exposed pluton made of granite.*

Figure 13 *Intrusive igneous rock formations occur in many different shapes and sizes. Dikes, plutons, and batholiths cut through existing rock formations. Sills and laccoliths intrude between layers of existing rock formations. Batholiths are the largest igneous formations of all.*

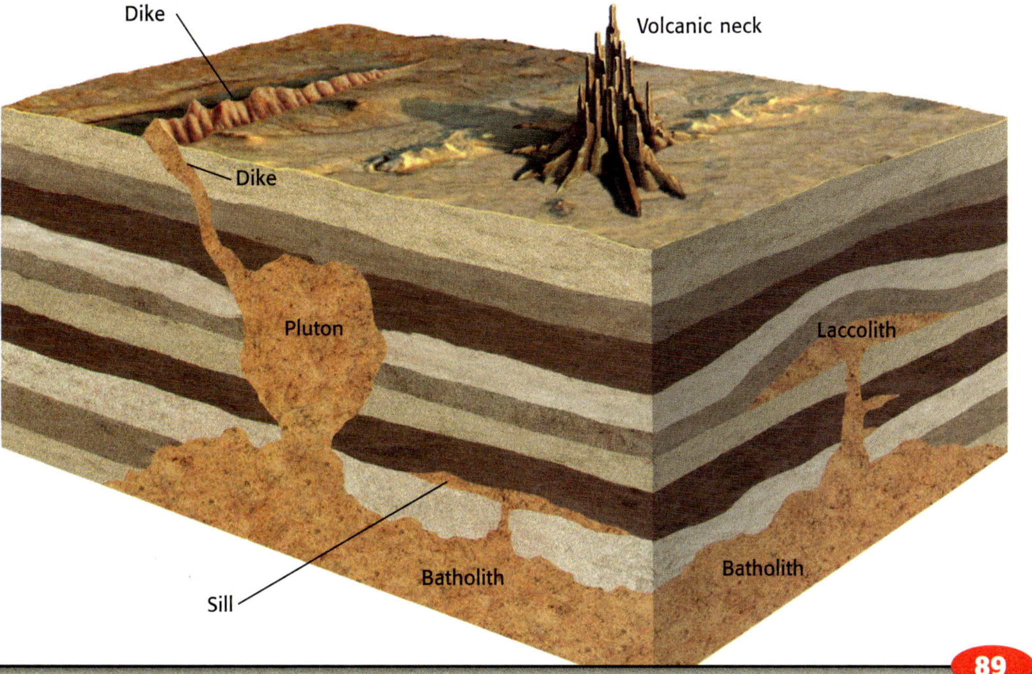

Meeting Individual Needs

Learners Having Difficulty
Ask students to compare the words *intrusive* and *extrusive* with the words *interior* and *exterior.* Have them brainstorm other words that use the prefixes *in-* and *ex-* to help them remember the meanings of these two terms. Sheltered English

Research

A volcanic neck is the hardened core of a volcano that is left behind after the volcano erodes away. They are strange and beautiful monuments to once-active volcanoes and are excellent examples of *intrusive* volcanic rocks. Ship Rock, a volcanic neck on a Navajo reservation in New Mexico, soars 518 m above the desert. Devils Tower National Monument, in Wyoming, rises 386 m.

Have students research one of these formations to learn how it formed. They could also explore stories or myths about volcanic necks.

Teaching Transparency 95
"Intrusive Igneous Rock Formations"

internetconnect

SCILINKS NSTA

TOPIC: Rock Formations
GO TO: www.scilinks.org
***sci*LINKS NUMBER:** HSTE095

Science Bloopers

In the eighteenth century some scholars thought lava formed when underground coal deposits caught fire. They believed that heat from the fires melted the surrounding rock, producing lava.

Scientists at Odds

Abraham Gottlob Werner was a geologist in the late eighteenth century who believed that layers of basalt found in sedimentary rock were sedimentary rocks that formed under the ocean. James Hutton opposed him vehemently, arguing that basalt and other igneous rocks formed by the cooling of magma.

3 Close

Quiz

1. Describe felsic and mafic rocks, and name three elements that occur in each type. (Felsic rock is lighter in color and weight; it is rich in silicon, sodium, and potassium. Mafic rock is darker and heavier; it is rich in iron, magnesium, and calcium.)
2. What is the difference between intrusive and extrusive rock? (Intrusive rock forms from magma that solidifies while still underground, while extrusive rock forms from magma that solidifies after it has reached the surface.)

Alternative Assessment

Have students create a model cross section that shows the formation of both intrusive and extrusive igneous rock. Supply students with several different colors of clay so they can color-code different formations, such as the magma source, dikes, sills, plutons, and the lava that forms extrusive rock. Sheltered English

Crystal Growth

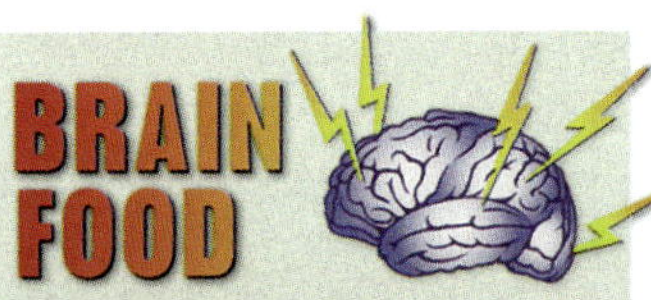

Violent volcanic eruptions sometimes produce a porous rock called pumice. Pumice is full of small holes once filled with trapped gases. Depending on how much space is taken up by these holes, some types of pumice can even float!

Extrusive Igneous Rock Igneous rock that forms on the Earth's surface is called **extrusive.** Most volcanic rock is extrusive. Extrusive rock cools quickly on the surface and contains either very small crystals or none at all. Look at **Figure 14** to see samples of some common extrusive rocks.

When lava erupts from a volcano, a formation called a *lava flow* is made. You can see an active lava flow in **Figure 15.** But lava does not always come from volcanoes. Sometimes lava erupts from long cracks in the Earth's surface called *fissures.* When a large amount of lava flows out of a fissure, it can cover a vast area, forming a plain called a *lava plateau.* Preexisting landforms are often buried by extrusive igneous rock formations.

Figure 14 *These are some common extrusive igneous rocks. All three formed from volcanic eruptions.*

Figure 15 *Below is an active basalt flow. When exposed to surface conditions, lava quickly cools and solidifies.*

Create crystals! To find out how, turn to page 498.

REVIEW

1. What two properties are used to classify igneous rock?
2. How does the cooling rate of lava or magma affect the texture of an igneous rock?
3. **Interpreting Illustrations** Use the diagram in Figure 13 to compare a sill with a dike. What makes them different from each other?

Answers to Review

1. texture and color (mineral composition)
2. When magma cools slowly, crystals have a long time to grow, so the igneous rock that forms is coarse-grained. When magma cools quickly, crystals have a short time to grow, so the igneous rock that forms is fine-grained.
3. Both a sill and a dike are sheetlike bodies of igneous rock. A sill intrudes rock parallel to the surrounding rock layers. A dike cuts across the surrounding rock layers.

3

Sedimentary Rock

NEW TERMS
strata
stratification

OBJECTIVES
- Describe how the two types of sedimentary rock form.
- Explain how sedimentary rocks record Earth's history.

Wind, water, ice, sunlight, and gravity all cause rock to *weather* into fragments. **Figure 16** shows how some sedimentary rocks form. Through the process of erosion, rock fragments, called sediment, are transported from one place to another. Eventually the sediment is deposited in layers. Sedimentary rock then forms as sediments become compacted and cemented together.

Origins of Sedimentary Rock

As new layers of sediment are deposited, the layers eventually become compressed, or compacted. The precipitation of new minerals forms a natural cement that binds the sediments together into sedimentary rock. Sedimentary rock forms at or near the Earth's surface, without the heat and pressure involved in the formation of igneous and metamorphic rocks. The physical features of sedimentary rock tell part of its history. The most noticeable feature of sedimentary rock is its layers, or **strata.** Road cuts and construction zones are good places to observe sedimentary rock formations, and as you can see in **Figure 17,** canyons carved by rivers provide some spectacular views.

Figure 16 A Sedimentary Rock Cycle

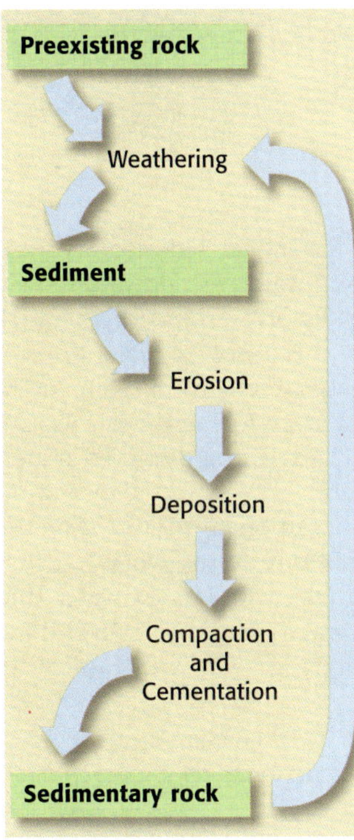

Figure 17 *Millions of years of erosion by the Colorado River have revealed the rock strata in the walls of the Grand Canyon. In some parts of the canyon, the river has cut to a depth of 1.6 km below the rim.*

91

SECTION 3

Focus

Sedimentary Rock

This section explores how sedimentary rock forms and how it accumulates in layers, or strata. Students distinguish between clastic and chemical sedimentary rock and learn how each forms.

Bellringer

Ask students to write about how layers in sedimentary rock are like the rings in a tree. How are they different? What information can geologists infer by examining sedimentary layers?

1 Motivate

DEMONSTRATION

Dissolution of Minerals

Limestone forms when calcium carbonate crystallizes out of ocean water. Students may not believe that water contains the chemical components of dissolved minerals. If you live in an area with hard water, have students observe ice melting in warm water. After the ice melts, there is a layer of fluffy calcium carbonate that forms at the bottom of the glass. If you live in an area with soft water, make hard water by dissolving a little baking soda (sodium bicarbonate) and calcium chloride in water. Then freeze it into ice cubes. Use these ice cubes for the demonstration.

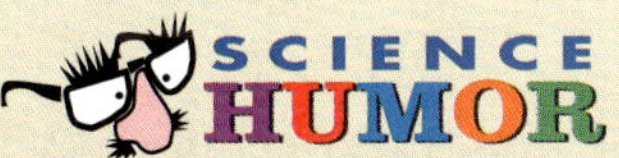

Q: What did the limestone rock say to the geologist?

A: Don't take me for granite.

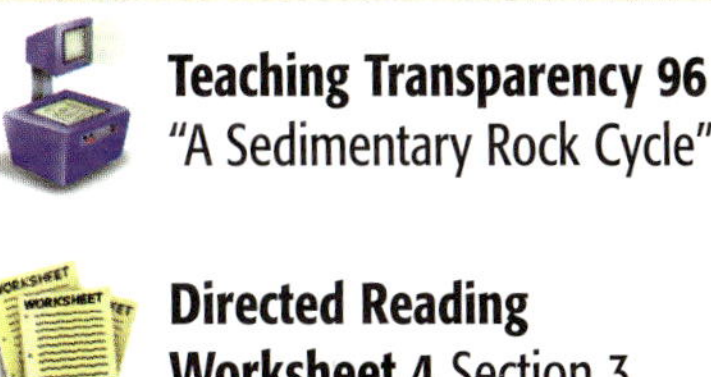

Teaching Transparency 96 "A Sedimentary Rock Cycle"

Directed Reading Worksheet 4 Section 3

Section 3—California Standards: PE/ATE 2, 2a, 2b; LabBook: 7, 7b, 7d, 7e, 7h

2 Teach

USING THE FIGURE

Point out that **Figure 19** illustrates part of a cyclical process. First rain falls to Earth, drenching the soil. Calcium and carbonate dissolve in the rainwater and are washed out to sea. As some of the sea water evaporates and returns to the atmosphere, the calcium and carbonate accumulate in the ocean. When the concentration of these two substances becomes high enough, the substances combine, forming crystals of calcium carbonate, $CaCO_3$. The calcium carbonate settles on the sea floor, where it begins to accumulate as a limestone deposit. If this limestone deposit is uplifted and becomes part of a continental landmass, the cycle will continue as erosion contributes calcium and carbonate to the ocean again. Sheltered English

CONNECT TO LIFE SCIENCE

Calcium carbonate is an important compound for many different animals. Many mollusks remove calcium and carbonate from the sea water and combine them in special tissues that then harden to form a calcium carbonate shell. When the mollusk dies, its shell either dissolves back into the water or becomes part of the sediment on the bottom of the ocean. If the shell is part of deposited sediment, it may become a fossil. Have students research the Mazon Creek deposits, in Kansas, or the Burgess Shale, in Canada, to learn more about these fossil beds.

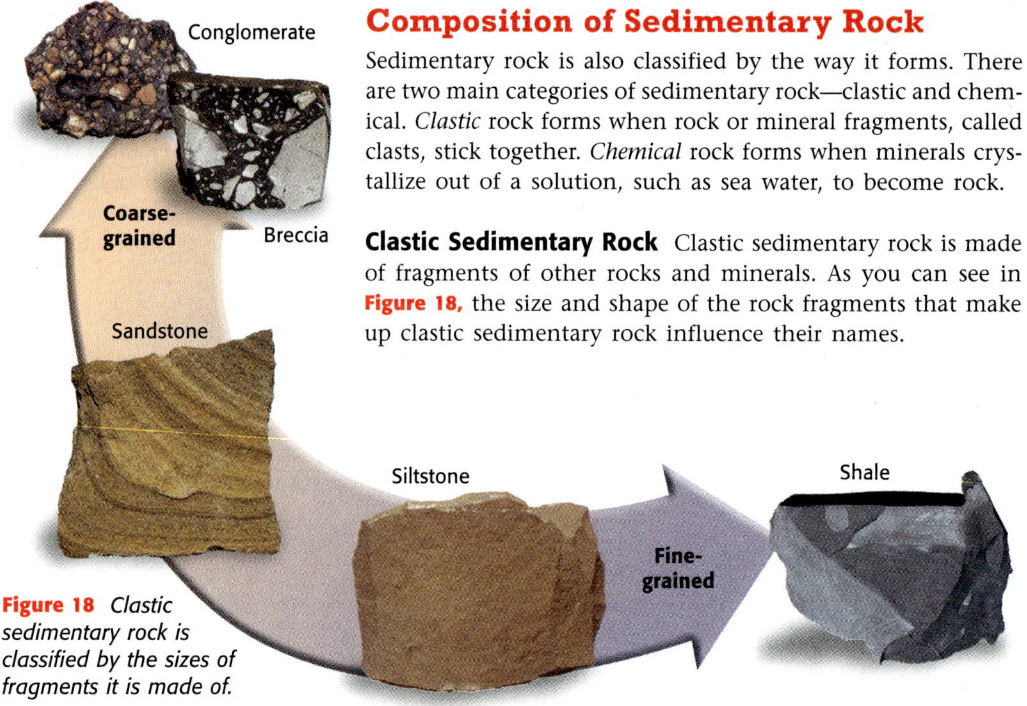

Figure 18 *Clastic sedimentary rock is classified by the sizes of fragments it is made of.*

Composition of Sedimentary Rock

Sedimentary rock is also classified by the way it forms. There are two main categories of sedimentary rock—clastic and chemical. *Clastic* rock forms when rock or mineral fragments, called clasts, stick together. *Chemical* rock forms when minerals crystallize out of a solution, such as sea water, to become rock.

Clastic Sedimentary Rock Clastic sedimentary rock is made of fragments of other rocks and minerals. As you can see in **Figure 18,** the size and shape of the rock fragments that make up clastic sedimentary rock influence their names.

Chemical Sedimentary Rock Chemical sedimentary rock forms from *solutions* of minerals and water. As rainwater slowly makes its way to the ocean, it dissolves some of the rock material it passes through. Some of this dissolved material eventually forms the minerals that make up chemical sedimentary rock. One type of chemical sedimentary rock, rock salt (NaCl), forms when water evaporates and leaves the dissolved material behind in the form of minerals.

Limestone is made of calcium carbonate ($CaCO_3$), or the mineral calcite. One kind of limestone forms when calcium and carbonate become so concentrated in the sea water that calcite crystallizes out of the sea water solution to form limestone, as shown in **Figure 19.**

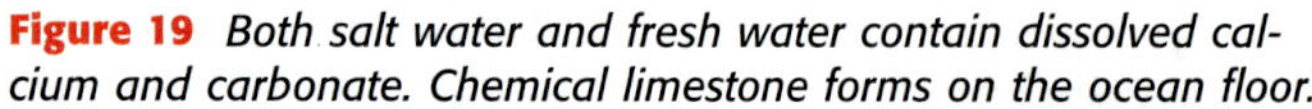

Figure 19 *Both salt water and fresh water contain dissolved calcium and carbonate. Chemical limestone forms on the ocean floor.*

92

SCIENTISTS AT ODDS

In the 1700s, the Neptunists and the Plutonists disagreed vehemently about how rocks form. Neptunists believed that all rocks developed from sediment laid down by a vast primordial ocean. The Plutonists believed rock formation was caused by heat from Earth's core. James Hutton's colleague, Sir James Hall, demonstrated the Plutonists' theories by melting rock in a furnace and letting it cool, showing how it changed from one form to another. This demonstration was a major victory for the Plutonists' arguments, but the debate raged for years until Charles Lyell synthesized both arguments in 1830 with *Principles of Geology*.

Most limestone forms from the remains of organisms, such as the shells of clams and the skeletons of tiny organisms called coral, that lived at the bottom of shallow seas. The shells or skeletons of these organisms are made of calcium carbonate, which comes from the sea water. This type of chemical sedimentary rock is forming even today. The remains of these sea animals are continuously accumulating on the ocean floor. Over time, these animal remains become cemented together to form *fossiliferous limestone.*

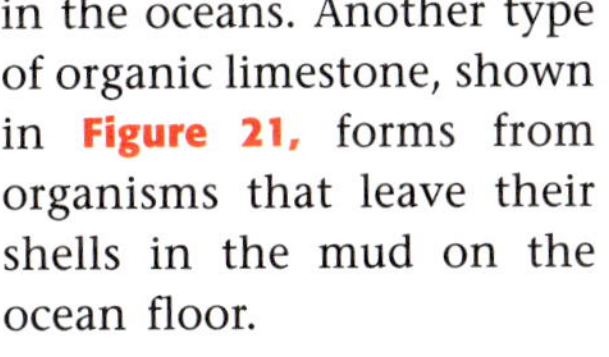

Figure 20 *One member of a coral colony is very small (left), but a colony of coral (center) is huge! Colonies of coral produced the Great Barrier Reef, which can be seen from orbiting satellites as a thin blue band (right).*

Fossils are the remains or traces of plants and animals that have been preserved in sedimentary rock. Fossils have given us enormous amounts of information about ancient life-forms and how they lived. Most fossils come from animals that lived in the oceans. Another type of organic limestone, shown in **Figure 21,** forms from organisms that leave their shells in the mud on the ocean floor.

Figure 21 *Shellfish, such as clams (left), get the calcium for their shells from sea water. When these organisms die, their shells collect on the ocean floor, eventually becoming rock (center). In time, huge rock formations result (right).*

93

Reteaching

Now that students have learned about both chemical and clastic sedimentary rock, have them refer back to **Figure 16.** It is a diagram of the clastic sedimentary rock cycle. Have students explain the steps of the cycle and then create a diagram that shows the chemical sedimentary rock cycle.

Real-World Connection

The most abundant material in toothpaste is water and the second-most abundant is chalk. Chalk is a sedimentary rock formed from the shells of ancient diatoms, and it is used as an abrasive to clean teeth.

Discussion

Chemical sedimentary rock can be divided into two categories: chemical and biochemical. Some rare forms of limestone are purely the result of a chemical process by which calcium carbonate precipitates out of sea water. But most limestones are biochemical because they form from the skeletons of marine organisms that extracted calcium and carbonate from sea water. Coal is also a biochemical sedimentary rock.

Cross-Disciplinary Focus

Fine Arts One type of printing used to reproduce fine art is called lithography. Lithography uses a flat piece of fine-grained, porous limestone. Interestingly, many important fossil beds were discovered while people quarried for lithographic limestone. The same qualities that make some limestone good for lithography also allow the preservation of extremely detailed fossils. Ask students to find out more about lithography and lithographic limestone beds around the world.

Is That a Fact!

The Great Barrier Reef, a long coral reef that lies off the northeastern coast of Australia, is the most massive structure ever built by living creatures. It is more than 2,000 km long and covers an area of 207,000 km^2.

Weird Science

The Bonneville Salt Flats, in Utah, are the remnants of a vast lake. After the last ice age, most of the lake drained quickly, but the remaining water slowly evaporated, leaving behind the salt flats. The Great Salt Lake is the largest of the few lakes left after Lake Bonneville evaporated.

3 Extend

Group Activity

Divide students into two groups to investigate sandstone, shale, and limestone. The first group should work together to learn how the rocks form. The second group should investigate how the rocks are used in industry, architecture, or the arts. Both could investigate rock formations that have become tourist attractions. Members of each group should prepare exhibits, posters, or models to demonstrate what they have learned.

4 Close

Quiz

1. How does chemical sedimentary rock form? (It forms when minerals crystallize out of water.)
2. What is stratification, and why is it important to Earth scientists? (Stratification is the layering of rock. It is important because it records many events in Earth's history as well as erosion and deposition rates.)

Alternative Assessment

Have students draw a picture of an environment that shows the source of sediments and where they are deposited. A second drawing should show what the environment will look like millions of years later after sedimentary rock has formed.

Let's Get Sedimental

Sedimentary Rock Structures

Many sedimentary rock features can tell you about the way the rock formed. The most characteristic feature of sedimentary rock is **stratification,** or layering. Strata differ from one another depending on the kind, size, and color of their sediment. The rate of deposition can also affect the thickness of the layers. Sedimentary rocks sometimes record the motion of wind and water waves on lakes, seas, rivers, and sand dunes. Some of these features are shown in **Figures 22** through **24.**

Figure 22 *When water and wind transport and deposit sediments, some unique patterns develop. A* ripple pattern *is made by flowing water and is preserved when the sediments become sedimentary rock.*

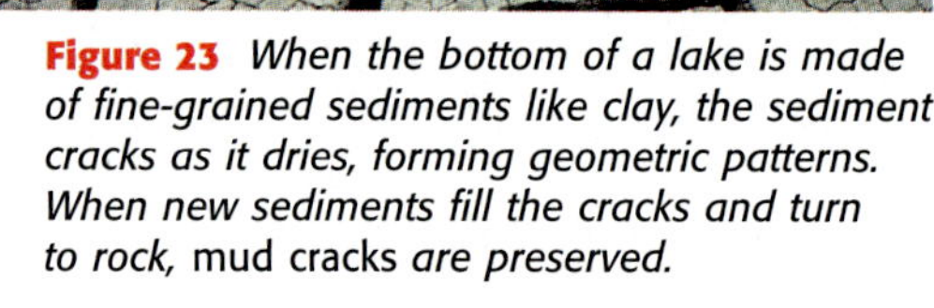

Figure 23 *When the bottom of a lake is made of fine-grained sediments like clay, the sediment cracks as it dries, forming geometric patterns. When new sediments fill the cracks and turn to rock,* mud cracks *are preserved.*

Figure 24 *Strata are not always parallel like the layers in a cake. Some strata are slanted. Wind caused these slanted deposits, called* cross-beds, *but water can also cause them.*

REVIEW

1. Describe the process by which clastic sedimentary rock forms.
2. List three sedimentary rock structures, and explain how they record geologic processes.
3. **Analyzing Relationships** Both clastic and chemical sedimentary rocks are classified according to texture and composition. Which property is more important for each sedimentary rock type? Explain.

94

Answers to Review

1. Clastic sedimentary rock forms when sediments become compacted and cemented together.
2. Three sedimentary structures are strata, ripple patterns, and mud cracks. Strata form when layers of sediment are deposited on top of each other. Ripple patterns form when sediments are shaped by flowing water before they turn into rock. Mud cracks form when fine-grained sediments dry and crack as water evaporates.
3. Texture is more important in classifying clastic sedimentary rock because clastic sedimentary rock is made of different sizes of sediments. Composition is more important in classifying chemical sedimentary rock because chemical sedimentary rock forms from different materials that crystallize out of solution.

4

Metamorphic Rock

NEW TERMS

foliated

nonfoliated

OBJECTIVES

- Describe two ways a rock can undergo metamorphism.
- Explain how the mineral composition of rocks changes as they undergo metamorphism.
- Describe the difference between foliated and nonfoliated metamorphic rock.

The word *metamorphic* comes from *meta,* meaning "changed," and *morphos,* meaning "shape." Remember, metamorphic rocks are those in which the structure, texture, or composition of the rock has changed. Rock can undergo metamorphism by heat or pressure acting alone, or by a combination of the two. All three types of rock—igneous, sedimentary, and even metamorphic—can change into metamorphic rock.

How, you may ask, can a metamorphic rock change into another metamorphic rock? The answer is that there are different kinds of metamorphism. A metamorphic rock can be changed again when even more heat and pressure are applied to it. You will learn more about this as you read on.

Origins of Metamorphic Rock

The texture or mineral composition of a rock can change when its surroundings change. If the temperature or pressure of the new environment is different from the one the rock formed in, the rock will undergo metamorphism.

Most metamorphic change is caused by increased pressure that takes place at depths greater than 2 km. At depths greater than 16 km, the pressure can be more than 4,000 times the pressure of the atmosphere! Look at **Figure 25.** This rock, called garnet schist, formed at a depth of about 30 km. Other types of schist form at much shallower depths.

The temperature at which metamorphism occurs ranges from 50°C to 1,000°C. At temperatures higher than 1,000°C, most rocks will melt. Metamorphism does not melt rock—when rock melts, it becomes magma and then igneous rock. In **Figure 26** you can see that this rock was deformed by intense pressure.

Figure 25 *Metamorphic rocks generally look as if they have been cooked and squeezed. At top is a metamorphic rock called garnet schist. At bottom is a microscopic view of a thin slice of a garnet schist.*

Figure 26 *In this outcrop, you can see an example of how sedimentary rock was deformed as it underwent metamorphism.*

95

Section 4

Focus

Metamorphic Rock

This section examines what happens when a rock metamorphoses. Changes in heat or pressure can alter a rock's chemical nature and physical structure. Students will learn how different types of metamorphism cause changes in a rock's texture and mineral composition.

Bellringer

Ask students to write a brief description of how cookies are made. Ask them to consider how the mixture of raw ingredients is like sedimentary rock. Ask them to describe how cookie dough metamorphoses when it is baked in an oven.

1 Motivate

Activity

Provide each student with pieces of red, yellow, green, and purple modeling clay. Have them flatten each piece, pile the pieces on top of each other, and press down on them firmly. Then have the students push inward on opposite sides of the stack or pull it gently so that the clay doesn't break apart. Explain that they will be learning how intense pressure and heat can cause rock to behave in similar ways.

Directed Reading Worksheet 4 Section 4

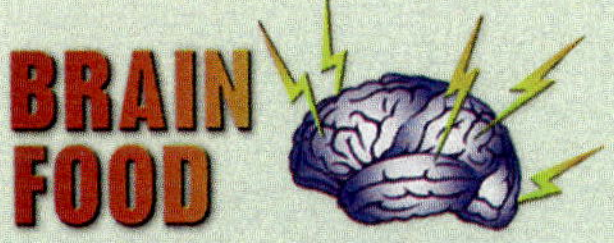

This rock in **Figure 25** is called garnet schist because it includes the mineral garnet. In the microscopic view, the brightly colored shapes are crystals of the mineral biotite mica, the black and white crystals are quartz, and the speckled grain in the upper right part of the circle is garnet. Have students compare the garnet schist with siltstone and shale, discussed in the sedimentary rock section. What is different? (Under high temperature and pressure conditions, both of these sedimentary rocks can become garnet schist.)

Section 4—California Standards: PE/ATE 1a, 1d, 1e, 3a, 6c, 7; LabBook: 7, 7b, 7d, 7e

2 Teach

QuickLab

MATERIALS
- paper
- black-ink pen
- plastic play putty

Answers to QuickLab

3. The "crystals" became stretched and deformed. The "granite" changed its shape because of the force applied to it.

Cross-Disciplinary Focus

Art Invite a potter to talk to the class about the processes involved in firing clay. Then have the class explore the different types of clay products that potters create (earthenware, stoneware, and ceramics) and the composition of the clays and glazes potters use.

Guided Practice

PORTFOLIO

As you discuss **Figure 27,** be sure students understand that a metamorphic rock's composition and the amount of heat and pressure it receives determine how much it deforms. Students should understand that the bulk composition of rock does not change during metamorphism unless fluids are introduced to the rock. However, the mineral composition of the rock may change as heat and pressure change. Ask students to think of some analogies for contact metamorphism (for example, an egg frying in a skillet). Have students draw rocks undergoing contact metamorphism. Have the class think of some analogies for regional metamorphism (for example, making toast). Then have students draw rocks undergoing regional metamorphism.

QuickLab

Stretching Out

How does pressure cause granite to undergo metamorphism? Try this:

1. Draw your version of a granite rock on a **piece of paper** with a **black-ink pen.** Be sure to include the outline of the rock, and fill it in with different crystal shapes.
2. Mash some **plastic play putty** over the "granite," and slowly peel it off.
3. After making sure that the outline of your "granite" has been transferred to the putty, push and pull on the putty. What happened to the "crystals"? What happened to the "granite"?

One way rock can undergo metamorphism is by coming into contact with magma. When magma moves through the crust, its heat flows into the surrounding rock and "cooks" it. The heat and fluids from the magma change some of the minerals in the surrounding rock into other minerals. The greatest change takes place where magma comes into direct contact with the surrounding rock. The effect of heat gradually lessens with distance from the magma. As you can see in **Figure 27,** *contact metamorphism* only happens next to igneous intrusions, so it affects small amounts of rock.

Rock can also undergo *regional metamorphism* when enormous pressure builds up in rock that is deeply buried under other rock formations, or when large pieces of the Earth's crust collide with each other. The pressure and increased temperature that exist under these conditions cause rock to become deformed and chemically changed. This kind of metamorphic rock is underneath most continental rock formations, as shown below.

Self-Check

How could a rock undergo both contact and regional metamorphism? *(See page 564 to check your answer.)*

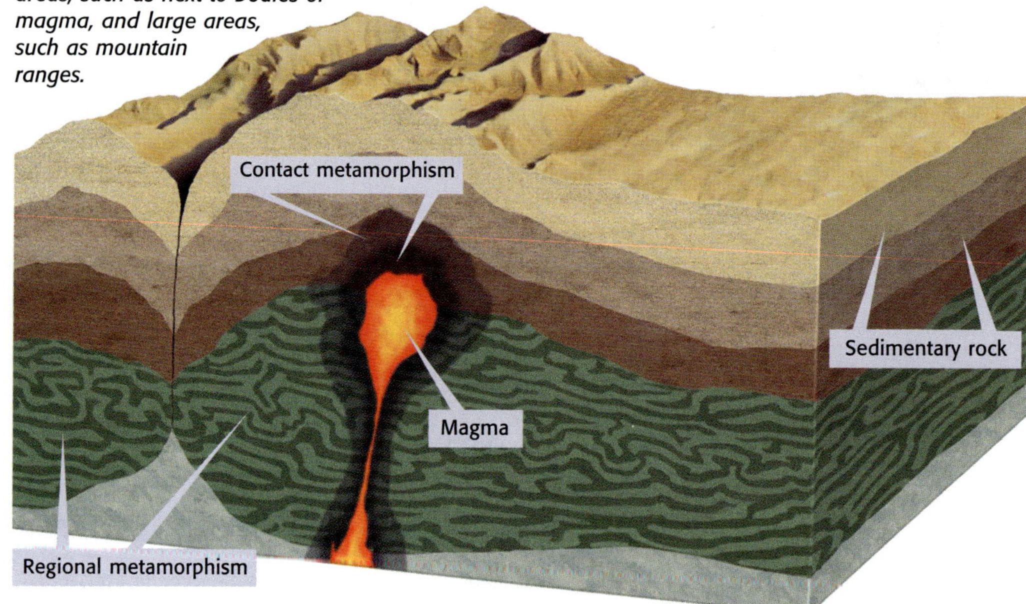

Figure 27 *Metamorphism occurs over small areas, such as next to bodies of magma, and large areas, such as mountain ranges.*

96

Answers to Self-Check

Answers will vary. Geologists have discovered that rocks can indeed undergo both regional and contact metamorphism. If a rock is buried and regionally metamorphosed when magma intrudes, the effects of contact metamorphism will be superimposed on the effects of regional metamorphism.

Is That a Fact!

The largest expanse of metamorphic rock in the world is the Canadian Shield, a huge horseshoe-shaped region encircling Hudson Bay. Covering about half of Canada, it is about 4,586,900 km^2 and is the source of more than 70 percent of the minerals mined in Canada.

Composition of Metamorphic Rock

When conditions within the Earth's crust change because of collisions between continents or the intrusion of magma, the temperature and pressure of the existing rock change. Minerals that were present in the rock when it formed may no longer be stable in the new environment. The original minerals change into minerals that are more stable in the new temperature and pressure conditions. Look at **Figure 28** to see an example of how this happens.

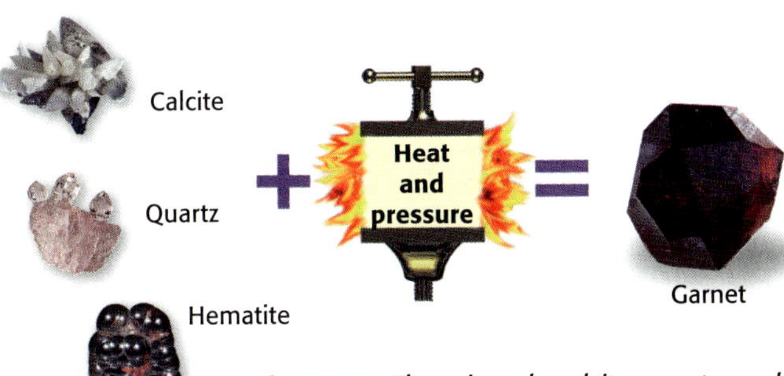

Figure 28 *The minerals calcite, quartz, and hematite combine and recrystallize to form the metamorphic mineral garnet.*

Explore

Did you know that you have a birthstone? Birthstones are gemstones, or mineral crystals. For each month of the year, there are one or two different birthstones. Find out which birthstone or birthstones you have by doing research in your school library or on the Internet. The names of birthstones are not usually the same as their actual mineral names. Find out which mineral is your birthstone. In what kind of rock would you likely find your birthstone? Why?

Many of these new minerals occur only in metamorphic rock. As shown in **Figure 29,** different metamorphic minerals reflect the different temperature and pressure conditions that existed when they formed. By knowing the temperature and pressure at which metamorphic minerals form, scientists can determine the depth and temperature at which recently exposed rock underwent metamorphism.

Figure 29 *Metamorphism can occur in many different environments. Temperature and pressure conditions, as well as the composition of the rock, determine which metamorphic minerals will form.*

97

ACTIVITY

Write the following metamorphic rock names on the board: gneiss, greenstone (greenschist), hornfels, marble, quartzite, schist, serpentinite, slate, and soapstone. Tell students that you're building a house and want to learn which of these rocks you should use.

Assign one of the rocks to each student. Have students learn everything they can about their rock, including its formation, appearance, locations, uses, and anything else they find interesting.

Have students working on the same rock form groups, pool their knowledge, and make a presentation about their rock to the class. At the end of each presentation, groups should suggest ways to use the rock in the house.

REAL-WORLD CONNECTION

Asbestos Removal Asbestos is an informal name for a group of fibrous minerals usually found in regionally metamorphosed rock. Manufacturers value these minerals because they resist burning and don't conduct heat or electricity easily. However, some kinds of asbestos fracture into tiny needles that can become airborne. This dust is linked to a lung disease called asbestosis. As a result, asbestos has been removed from many public places at great expense. Have students find out about the many uses for asbestos and any cleanup projects that are occurring in your area.

Homework

Making Models Have students make a model cross section of the Earth's crust. The model should include materials that represent magma, contact and regional metamorphic rocks, and sedimentary strata. Sheltered English

Answers to Explore

Answers will vary. (Many birthstones form in igneous and metamorphic rocks.)

Teaching Transparency 97 "Regional and Contact Metamorphism"

3 Extend

DISCUSSION

Display metamorphic rocks in groups of foliated rocks (slate, schist, phyllite, gneiss) and non-foliated rocks (quartzite, marble, hornfels, soapstone). Have students compare the rocks according to color, appearance, and composition. Explain that regional metamorphism tends to produce *foliated rocks,* while contact metamorphism tends to produce *nonfoliated rocks*. Ask students to predict what the terms mean then read this page to see if they were correct.

MATH and MORE

Metamorphic rock usually forms at depths greater than 16 km. To convert kilometers to miles, multiply the number of kilometers by 0.6. For example, 16 km multiplied by 0.6 is equal to 9.6 mi. Tell students that the continental crust can be up to 100 km thick. How many miles is that? (60 mi)

The crust under the ocean is about 5 km thick. How many miles is that? (3 mi)

Students might be interested in comparing these distances with the distance to a nearby town or landmark.

Math Skills Worksheet 31
"The Unit Factor and Dimensional Analysis"

LabBook PG 503
Metamorphic Mash

Reinforcement Worksheet 4
"What Is It?"

Figure 30 *The effects of metamorphism depend on the amount of heat and pressure applied to the rock. The more heat and pressure applied, the more intense the effects of metamorphism. Here you can see what happens to shale when it is exposed to more and more heat and pressure.*

Textures of Metamorphic Rock

As you know, texture helps to classify igneous and sedimentary rock. The same is true of metamorphic rock. All metamorphic rock has one of two textures—*foliated* or *nonfoliated.* **Foliated** metamorphic rock consists of minerals that are aligned and look almost like pages in a book. **Nonfoliated** metamorphic rock does not appear to have any regular pattern. Let's take a closer look at each of these types of metamorphic rock to find out how they form.

Foliated Metamorphic Rock Foliated metamorphic rock contains mineral grains that are aligned by pressure. Strongly foliated rocks usually contain flat minerals, like biotite mica. Look at the foliated metamorphic rock slate and the original sedimentary rock shale, shown in **Figure 30.** Shale consists of layers of clay minerals. When subjected to a small degree of heat and pressure, the clay minerals change into mica minerals and the shale becomes a fine-grained, foliated metamorphic rock called slate. What happens if the slate is then put under more heat and pressure?

Metamorphic rocks can become other metamorphic rocks if the environment changes again. With additional heat and pressure, slate can change into phyllite, another metamorphic rock. When phyllite is exposed to additional heat and pressure, it can change into a metamorphic rock called schist.

As the degree of metamorphism increases, the arrangement of minerals in the rock changes. With additional heat and pressure, coarse-grained minerals separate into bands in a metamorphic rock called *gneiss* (pronounced "nice").

LabBook

Wouldn't it be "gneiss" to make your own foliated rock? Turn to page 503 in your LabBook to find out how.

98

Homework

Investigate Your Area Have students look at stone buildings and houses around their town. Ask students to identify the rock used in construction as igneous, sedimentary, or metamorphic. Which rock type was most commonly used? Which was used least? Encourage students to find out the origin of rock used in buildings in your community.

WEIRD SCIENCE

When rocks metamorphose under high temperature and pressure, they become plastic and can be easily deformed. It is not unusual for spherical pebbles in a conglomerate to be stretched into ellipses more than 30 times their original diameter!

Nonfoliated Metamorphic Rock Nonfoliated metamorphic rocks are shown in **Figure 31.** Do you notice anything missing? The lack of aligned mineral grains makes them nonfoliated. They are rocks commonly made of only one, or just a few, minerals.

Sandstone is a sedimentary rock made of distinct quartz sand grains. But when sandstone is subjected to the heat and pressure of metamorphism, the spaces between the sand grains disappear as they recrystallize, forming quartzite. Quartzite has a shiny, glittery appearance. It is still made of quartz, but the mineral grains are larger. When limestone undergoes metamorphism, the same process happens to the mineral calcite, and the limestone becomes marble. Marble has larger calcite crystals than limestone. You have probably seen marble in buildings and statues.

The term *metamorphosis* means "change in form." When certain animals undergo a dramatic change in the shape of their body, they are said to have undergone a metamorphosis. As part of their natural life cycle, butterflies go through four stages of life. The first stage is when they are in the egg. After they hatch from an egg, they are in the larval stage, the form of a caterpillar. In the next stage they build a cocoon as a response to chemical changes in their body. This is called the pupal stage. When they finally emerge from their cocoon, they enter the adult stage of their life, complete with wings, antennae, and legs!

Figure 31 *Marble and quartzite are nonfoliated metamorphic rocks. As you can see in the microscopic views, none of the mineral crystals are aligned.*

REVIEW

1. What environmental factors cause rock to undergo metamorphism?
2. What is the difference between foliated and nonfoliated metamorphic rock?
3. **Making Inferences** If you had two metamorphic rocks, one with garnet crystals and the other with chlorite crystals, which one would have formed at a deeper level in the Earth's crust? Explain.

Going Further

Several types of minerals found in metamorphic rock, such as garnet, tourmaline, and serpentine, are used in sculpture and in jewelry making. Encourage students to choose one of these minerals, research it, and create a poster illustrating how it forms and what its uses are.

4 Close

Quiz

1. Explain what a regional metamorphic rock is. (A regional metamorphic rock has been changed by intense pressure and heat across great regions of the crust rather than by direct contact with magma.)
2. What does the composition of a metamorphic rock tell you about the rock's origin and formation? (Different metamorphic minerals indicate different temperature and pressure conditions that existed when they formed.)

Alternative Assessment

Have students prepare a lesson about this chapter to present to a second-grade class. They will need to prepare vocabulary lists, illustrations, and worksheets to help the younger students understand the types of rock, their uses, and how they form.

Answers to Review

1. increased pressure and increased temperature
2. The two types of rock differ in texture. Foliated metamorphic rock consists of minerals that are aligned and look like pages in a book. Nonfoliated metamorphic rock does not appear to have any regular pattern.
3. The rock with garnet crystals would have formed deeper in the Earth because the mineral garnet forms at a higher temperature and a higher pressure than the mineral chlorite.

Critical Thinking Worksheet 4 "Between a Rock and a Hard Place"

Interactive Explorations CD-ROM "Rock On!"

Section 4 Review—California Standards: PE/ATE 1e

Chapter Highlights

VOCABULARY DEFINITIONS

SECTION 1

rock a naturally formed solid mass made of one or more minerals or noncrystalline materials

rock cycle the continuous process by which one rock type changes into another rock type

magma the hot liquid that forms when rock partially or completely melts; may include mineral crystals

sedimentary rock rock that forms when sediments are compacted and cemented together or when minerals crystallize out of oceans and lakes

metamorphic rock rock that forms when the texture or composition of preexisting rock changes due to heat or pressure

igneous rock rock that forms when magma, lava, or pyroclastic material cools and solidifies

lava magma that erupts onto the Earth's surface

composition the makeup of a rock; describes either the minerals or elements present in it

texture the sizes, shapes, and arrangement of particles or grains that a rock is made of

SECTION 2

intrusive the type of igneous rock that forms when magma cools and solidifies beneath Earth's surface

extrusive the type of igneous rock that forms when lava or pyroclastic material cools and solidifies on the Earth's surface

Chapter Highlights

SECTION 1

Vocabulary

rock *(p. 80)*
rock cycle *(p. 82)*
magma *(p. 83)*
sedimentary rock *(p. 84)*
metamorphic rock *(p. 84)*
igneous rock *(p. 84)*
lava *(p. 84)*
composition *(p. 85)*
texture *(p. 86)*

Section Notes

- Rocks have been used by humans for thousands of years, and they are just as valuable today.
- Rocks are classified into three main types—igneous, sedimentary, and metamorphic—depending on how they formed.
- The rock cycle describes the process by which a rock can change from one rock type to another.
- Scientists further classify rocks according to two criteria—composition and texture.
- Molten igneous material creates rock formations both below and above ground.

SECTION 2

Vocabulary

intrusive *(p. 89)*
extrusive *(p. 90)*

Section Notes

- The texture of igneous rock is determined by the rate at which it cools. The slower magma cools, the larger the crystals are.
- Felsic igneous rock is light-colored and lightweight, while mafic igneous rock is dark-colored and heavy.
- Igneous material that solidifies at the Earth's surface is called extrusive, while igneous material that solidifies within the crust is called intrusive.

Lab

Crystal Growth *(p. 498)*

Skills Check

Math Concepts

MINERAL COMPOSITION Rocks are classified not only by the minerals they contain but also by the amounts of those minerals. Suppose a particular kind of granite is made of feldspar, biotite mica, and quartz. If you know that feldspar makes up 55 percent of the rock and biotite mica makes up 15 percent of the rock, the remaining 30 percent must be made of quartz.

55% feldspar		100% of granite
+ 15% biotite mica	or	− 55% feldspar
+ 30% quartz		− 15% biotite mica
= 100% of granite		= 30% quartz

Visual Understanding

PIE CHARTS The pie charts on page 85 help you visualize the relative amounts of minerals in different types of rock. The circle represents the whole rock, or 100%. Each part, or "slice," of the circle represents a fraction of the rock.

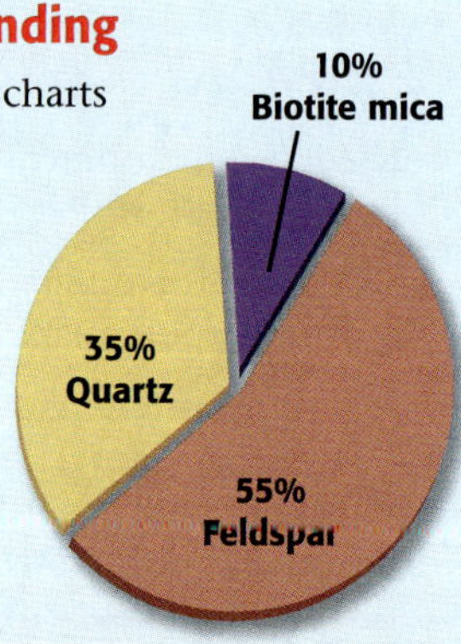

Lab and Activity Highlights

Crystal Growth PG 498

Let's Get Sedimental PG 501

Metamorphic Mash PG 503

Datasheets for LabBook
(blackline masters for these labs)

SECTION 3

Vocabulary

strata *(p. 91)*
stratification *(p. 94)*

Section Notes

- Clastic sedimentary rock is made of rock and mineral fragments that are compacted and cemented together. Chemical sedimentary rock forms when dissolved minerals crystallize out of a solution such as sea water.
- Sedimentary rocks record the history of their formation in their features. Some common features are strata, ripple marks, mud cracks, and fossils.

Lab

Let's Get Sedimental *(p. 501)*

SECTION 4

Vocabulary

foliated *(p. 98)*
nonfoliated *(p. 98)*

Section Notes

- One kind of metamorphism is the result of magma heating small areas of surrounding rock, changing its texture and composition.
- Most metamorphism is the product of heat and pressure acting on large regions of the Earth's crust.
- The mineral composition of a rock changes when the minerals it is made of recrystallize to form new minerals. These new minerals are more stable under increased temperature and pressure.
- Metamorphic rock that contains aligned mineral grains is called foliated, and metamorphic rock that does not contain aligned mineral grains is called nonfoliated.

Lab

Metamorphic Mash *(p. 503)*

internetconnect

GO TO: go.hrw.com

Visit the **HRW** Web site for a variety of learning tools related to this chapter. Just type in the keyword:

KEYWORD: HSTRCK

GO TO: www.scilinks.org

Visit the **National Science Teachers Association** on-line Web site for Internet resources related to this chapter. Just type in the ***sci*LINKS** number for more information about the topic:

TOPIC: Rocks and Human History — ***sci*LINKS NUMBER:** HSTE080
TOPIC: Rock in Architecture — ***sci*LINKS NUMBER:** HSTE085
TOPIC: Composition of Rock — ***sci*LINKS NUMBER:** HSTE090
TOPIC: Rock Formations — ***sci*LINKS NUMBER:** HSTE095
TOPIC: Petra: The Rock City — ***sci*LINKS NUMBER:** HSTE100

VOCABULARY DEFINITIONS, *continued*

SECTION 3

strata layers of sedimentary rock that form from the deposition of sediment

stratification the layering of sedimentary rock

SECTION 4

foliated the texture of metamorphic rock in which the mineral grains are aligned like the pages of a book

nonfoliated the texture of metamorphic rock in which mineral grains show no alignment

Vocabulary Review Worksheet 4

Blackline masters of these Chapter Highlights can be found in the **Study Guide.**

Lab and Activity Highlights

LabBank

Labs You Can Eat, Famous Rock Groups, Lab 11

Whiz-Bang Demonstrations, Settling Down, Demo 17

Long-Term Projects & Research Ideas, Project 32

Interactive Explorations CD-ROM

CD 2, Exploration 6, "Rock On!"

Chapter Review Answers

Using Vocabulary

1. Intrusive/extrusive
2. Foliated
3. Clastic
4. Lava
5. sedimentary

Understanding Concepts

Multiple Choice

6. d
7. b
8. a
9. a
10. c
11. b
12. c
13. b
14. c
15. b

Short Answer

16. Answers will vary. In the rock cycle, igneous, sedimentary, and metamorphic rock can change into other rock types through a variety of natural processes. All rock material, though it changes form, remains a part of the rock cycle.

Concept Mapping Transparency 4

Blackline masters of this Chapter Review can be found in the **Study Guide.**

Chapter Review

USING VOCABULARY

To complete the following sentences, choose the correct term from each pair of terms listed below:

1. __?__ igneous rock is more likely to have coarse-grained texture than __?__ igneous rock. (*Extrusive/intrusive* or *Intrusive/extrusive*)

2. __?__ metamorphic rock texture consists of parallel alignment of mineral grains. (*Foliated* or *Nonfoliated*)

3. __?__ sedimentary rock forms when grains of sand become cemented together. (*Clastic* or *Chemical*)

4. __?__ cools quickly on the Earth's surface. (*Lava* or *Magma*)

5. Strata are found in __?__ rock. (*igneous* or *sedimentary*)

UNDERSTANDING CONCEPTS

Multiple Choice

6. A type of rock that forms deep within the Earth when magma solidifies is called
   a. sedimentary. c. organic.
   b. metamorphic. d. igneous.

7. A type of rock that forms under high temperature and pressure but is not exposed to enough heat to melt the rock is
   a. sedimentary. c. organic.
   b. metamorphic. d. igneous.

8. After they are deposited, sediments, such as sand, are turned into sedimentary rock when they are compacted and
   a. cemented.
   b. metamorphosed.
   c. melted.
   d. weathered.

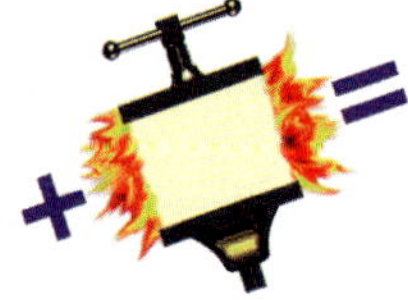

9. An igneous rock with a coarse-grained texture forms when
   a. magma cools very slowly.
   b. magma cools very quickly.
   c. magma cools quickly, then slowly.
   d. magma cools slowly, then quickly.

10. The layering that occurs in sedimentary rock is called
    a. foliation. c. stratification.
    b. ripple marks. d. compaction.

11. An example of a clastic sedimentary rock is
    a. obsidian. c. limestone.
    b. sandstone. d. marble.

12. A common sedimentary rock structure is
    a. a sill. c. cross-bedding.
    b. a pluton. d. a lava flow.

13. An example of mafic igneous rock is
    a. granite. c. quartzite.
    b. basalt. d. pumice.

14. Chemical sedimentary rock forms when
    a. magma cools and solidifies.
    b. minerals are twisted into a new arrangement.
    c. minerals crystallize from a solution.
    d. sand grains are cemented together.

15. Which of the following is a foliated metamorphic rock?
    a. sandstone c. shale
    b. gneiss d. basalt

Short Answer

16. In no more than three sentences, explain the rock cycle.

17. How are sandstone and siltstone different from one another? How are they the same?

102

18. In one or two sentences, explain how the cooling rate of magma affects the texture of the igneous rock that is formed.

Concept Mapping

19. Use the following terms to create a concept map: rocks, clastic, metamorphic, nonfoliated, igneous, intrusive, chemical, foliated, extrusive, sedimentary.

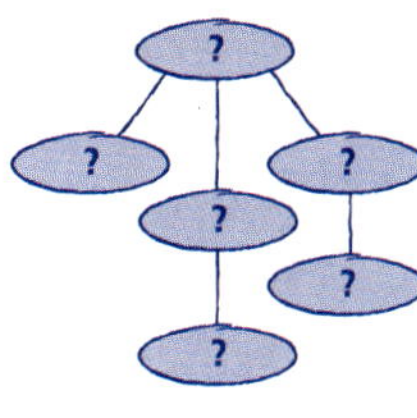

CRITICAL THINKING AND PROBLEM SOLVING

Write one or two sentences to answer the following questions:

20. The sedimentary rock coquina is made up of pieces of seashells. Which of the two kinds of sedimentary rock could it be? Explain.

21. If you were looking for fossils in the rocks around your home and the rock type that was closest to your home was metamorphic, would you find many fossils? Why or why not?

22. Suppose you are writing a book about another planet. In your book, you mention that the planet has no atmosphere or weather. Which type of rock will you not find on the planet? Explain.

23. Imagine that you want to quarry or mine granite. You have all of the equipment, but you need a place to quarry. You have two pieces of land to choose from. One piece is described as having a granite batholith under it, and the other has a granite sill. If both plutonic bodies were at the same depth, which one would be a better buy for you? Explain your answer.

MATH IN SCIENCE

24. If a 60 kg granite boulder were broken down into sand grains and if quartz made up 35 percent of the boulder's mass, how many kilograms of the resulting sand would be quartz grains?

INTERPRETING GRAPHICS

The curve on the graph below shows how the melting point of a particular rock changes with increasing temperature and pressure. Use the graph to answer the questions below.

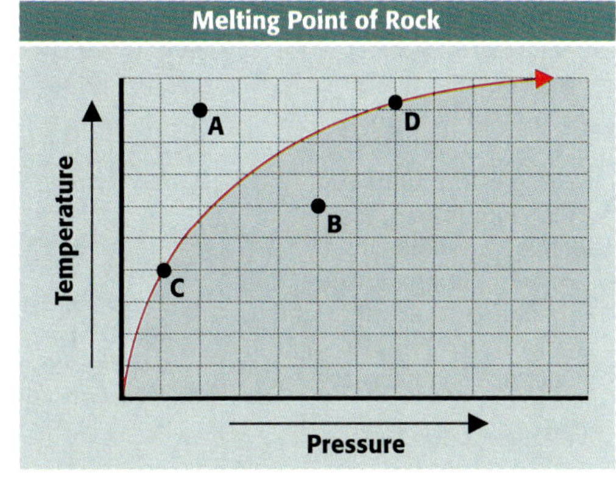

25. What type of material would you find at point **A** on the graph? Why?

26. What would you find at point **B**?

27. Points **C** and **D** represent different temperature and pressure conditions for a single, solid rock. Why does this rock have a higher melting temperature at point **D** than it does at point **C**?

NOW What Do You Think?

Take a minute to review your answers to the ScienceLog questions on page 79. Have your answers changed? If necessary, revise the answers based on what you have learned since you began this chapter.

17. Sandstone has a coarser-grained texture than siltstone. Both sandstone and siltstone are clastic sedimentary rocks.
18. When magma cools slowly, crystals have a long time to grow, so they grow to a much larger size than they do when magma cools quickly.

Concept Mapping

19. An answer to this exercise can be found at the end of this book.

Critical Thinking and Problem Solving

20. The seashells that make up coquina are made by shellfish that extract calcium and carbonate from sea water, so coquina is a chemical sedimentary rock. (Strictly speaking, the shell fragments are clasts because they are particles that have been deposited.)
21. You would not find many fossils where you lived because fossils are found in sedimentary rock, not metamorphic rock. (Occasionally, fossils are preserved in metamorphic rock that was once sedimentary rock.)
22. You will not find sedimentary rock because no weathering of rock can occur because there is no atmosphere.
23. The property with the batholith would be a better buy because batholiths are much bigger than sills.

Math in Science

24. 35% of 60 kg = 60×0.35 = 21 kg

Interpreting Graphics

25. The material at point A is magma. It is magma because everything above the curve on the graph is liquid.
26. igneous rock or solid rock
27. Although at point D the rock is at a higher temperature, it has much more pressure on it, which keeps it solid.

NOW What Do You Think?

1. Answers will vary. A mineral is an inorganic crystalline solid with a definite chemical composition. A rock is a solid mixture of one or more minerals, or organic materials like coal.
2. Answers will vary. Rocks are used as surgical blades and building materials and are studied to learn about the history of Earth and other planets.
3. Answers will vary. There are three ways a rock can form: when magma cools and solidifies, when sediments are deposited and cemented together (or minerals crystallize out of sea water), or when the composition or texture of a preexisting rock changes due to heat or pressure.

Chapter 4 Review—California Standards: PE/ATE Q20–23: 2, 6; Think: 6c

SCIENCE, TECHNOLOGY, AND SOCIETY

Rock City

Background

Just north of Petra is another huge temple, the magnificent El-Deir. This temple was carved from the mountainside, and it sits 1,200 m above the valley floor. Its facade is 50 m wide and 45 m tall, and its huge doorway is 8 m high.

TOPIC: Petra: The Rock City
GO TO: www.scilinks.org
***sci*LINKS NUMBER:** HSTE100

Science, Technology, and Society

Rock City

Today when we dig into a mountainside to build a highway or make room for a building, we use heavy machinery and explosives. Can you imagine doing the same job with just a hammer and chisel? Well, between about 300 B.C. and A.D. 200, an Arab tribe called the Nabataeans (nab uh TEE uhns) did just that. In fact, they carved a whole city—homes, storage areas, monuments, administrative offices, and temples—right into the mountainsides!

▲ *Petra's most famous building, the Treasury, was shown in the movie* Indiana Jones and the Last Crusade.

Rose-Red City

This amazing city in southern Jordan is Petra (named by the Roman emperor Hadrian Petra during a visit in A.D. 131). A poet once described Petra as "the rose-red city" because all the buildings and monuments were carved from the pink sandstone mountains surrounding Petra.

Using this reddish stone, the Nabataeans lined the main street in the center of the city with tall stone columns. The street ends at what was once the foot of a mountain but is now known as the Great Temple—a two-story stone religious complex larger than a football field!

The High Place of Sacrifice, another site near the center of the city, was a mountaintop. The Nabataeans leveled the top and created a place of worship more than 1,000 m above the valley floor. Today visitors climb stairs to the top. Along the way, they pass dozens of tombs carved into the pink rock walls.

Tombs and More Tombs

There are more than 800 other tombs dug into the mountainsides in and around Petra. One of them, the Treasury (created for a Nabataean ruler), stands more than 40 m high! It is a magnificent building with an elaborate facade. Behind the massive stone front, the Nabataeans carved one large room and two smaller rooms deeper into the mountain.

Petra Declines

The Nabataeans once ruled an area extending from Petra to Damascus. They grew wealthy and powerful by controlling important trade routes near Petra. But their wealth attracted the Roman Empire, and in A.D. 106, Petra became a Roman province. Though the city prospered under Roman rule for almost another century, a gradual decline in Nabataean power began. The trade routes by land that the Nabataeans controlled for hundreds of years were abandoned in favor of a route by the Red Sea. People moved and the city faded. By the seventh century, nothing was left of Petra but empty stone structures.

Think About It!

▶ Petra is sometimes referred to as a city "from the rock as if by magic grown." Why might such a city seem "magic" to us today? What might have encouraged the Nabataeans to create this city? Share your thoughts with a classmate.

104

Answer to Think About It!

Answers will vary. (Students can do research to find out more about Nabataean culture.)

California Standards: PE/ATE 6c

Health Watch

Glass Scalpels

Would you want your surgeon to use a scalpel that was thousands of years old? Probably not, unless it was a razor-sharp knife blade made of obsidian, a natural volcanic glass. Such blades and arrowheads were used for nearly 18,000 years by our ancestors. Recently, physicians have found a new use for these Stone Age tools. Obsidian blades, once used to hunt woolly mammoths, are now being used as scalpels in the operating room!

▲ *An obsidian scalpel can have an edge as fine as a single molecule.*

Obsidian or Stainless Steel?

Traditionally, physicians have used inexpensive stainless-steel scalpel blades for surgical procedures. Steel scalpels cost about $2 each, and surgeons use them just once and throw them away. Obsidian scalpels are more expensive—about $20 each—but they can be used many times before they lose their keen edge. And obsidian scalpel blades can be 100 times sharper than traditional scalpel blades!

During surgery, steel scalpels actually tear the skin apart. Obsidian scalpels divide the skin and cause much less damage. Some plastic surgeons use obsidian blades to make extremely fine incisions that leave almost no scarring. An obsidian-scalpel incision heals more quickly because the blade causes less damage to the skin and other tissues.

Many patients have allergic reactions to mineral components in steel blades. These patients often do not have an allergic reaction when obsidian scalpels are used. Given all of these advantages, it is not surprising that some physicians have made the change to obsidian scalpels.

A Long Tradition

Early Native Americans were among the first people to recognize that chipped obsidian has extremely sharp edges. Native Americans made obsidian arrowheads and knife blades by flaking away chips of rock by hand. Today obsidian scalpels are fashioned in much the same way by a *knapper,* a person who makes stone tools by hand. Knappers use the same basic technique that people have used for thousands of years to make obsidian blades and other stone tools.

Find Out for Yourself!

▶ Making obsidian blades and other stone tools requires a great deal of skill. Find out about the steps a knapper follows to create a stone tool. Find a piece of rock, and see if you can follow the steps to create a stone tool of your own. Be careful not to hit your fingers, and wear safety goggles.

105

Health Watch

Glass Scalpels

Background

Medical professionals use a variety of tools and treatments that rely on rocks and minerals. As students have learned in this chapter, every rock has unique properties that vary depending on its composition, its crystalline structure, and the conditions in which it formed. For example, obsidian's most prominent characteristic is the lack of a crystalline structure.

Students will know that diamonds are valuable gemstones, but they may be surprised that diamonds are frequently used in medicine. For example, dentists use drill bits coated with synthetic diamonds. Synthetic diamonds are used because they are much less expensive than their natural counterparts and are disposable. Diamonds are four times harder than the next hardest natural mineral.

California Standards: PE/ATE 6c

Chapter Organizer

CHAPTER ORGANIZATION	TIME MINUTES	OBJECTIVES	LABS, INVESTIGATIONS, AND DEMONSTRATIONS
Chapter Opener **pp. 106–107**	45	California Standards: PE/ATE 7, 7b	**Investigate!** What Is the Sun's Favorite Color? p. 107
Section 1 **Natural Resources**	90	▶ Determine how humans use natural resources. ▶ Contrast renewable resources with nonrenewable resources. ▶ Explain how humans can conserve natural resources. PE/ATE 6, 6b, 6c	
Section 2 **Fossil Fuels**	135	▶ Classify the different forms of fossil fuels. ▶ Determine how fossil fuels form. ▶ Identify where fossil fuels are found in the United States. ▶ Explain how fossil fuels are obtained. ▶ Identify problems with fossil fuels. ▶ List ways to deal with fossil-fuel problems. PE/ATE 3b, 6, 6a–6c, 7, 7b	**QuickLab,** Rock Sponge, p. 113 **Demonstration,** Simulating Reservoirs, p. 113 in ATE
Section 3 **Alternative Resources**	90	▶ Describe alternatives to the use of fossil fuels. ▶ List advantages and disadvantages of using alternative energy resources. PE/ATE 4a, 6, 6a, 6b, 7, 7b; LabBook 4b, 7, 7b, 7e	**Demonstration,** Calculating with Light, p. 118 in ATE **Interactive Explorations CD-ROM,** The Generation Gap *A **Worksheet** is also available in the **Interactive Explorations Teacher's Edition.*** **Skill Builder,** Make a Water Wheel, p. 504 **Datasheets for LabBook,** Make a Water Wheel, Datasheet 10 **Discovery Lab,** Power of the Sun, p. 506 **Datasheets for LabBook,** Power of the Sun, Datasheet 11 **Long-Term Projects & Research Ideas,** Project 33

See page **T20** for a complete correlation of this book with the

CALIFORNIA SCIENCE CONTENT STANDARDS.

Correlations are also provided at point of use throughout this ATE.

TECHNOLOGY RESOURCES

Guided Reading Audio CD
English or Spanish, Chapter 5

Classroom Management CD-ROM

Test Generator CD-ROM

Science Discovery Videodiscs
Image and Activity Bank with Lesson Plans: Energy Resources Tour
Science Sleuths: The Energy Mystery House

CNN. **Scientists in Action,** Forming the Future of Energy Efficiency, Segment 7
Science, Technology & Society, BioDiesel, Segment 6
Wind Power, Segment 14
Multicultural Connections, China's Solar Nomads, Segment 10

Interactive Explorations CD-ROM
CD 1, Exploration 6, The Generation Gap

Chapter 5 • Energy Resources

CLASSROOM WORKSHEETS, TRANSPARENCIES, AND RESOURCES	SCIENCE INTEGRATION AND CONNECTIONS	REVIEW AND ASSESSMENT
Science Puzzlers, Twisters & Teasers, Worksheet 5 **Directed Reading Worksheet 5**	**Connect to Geography,** p. 107 in ATE	
Directed Reading Worksheet 5, Section 1 **Transparency 70,** Practicing Conservation **Reinforcement Worksheet 5,** What Are My Resources?	**Connect to Life Science,** p. 109 in ATE **Apply,** p. 110 **Eye on the Environment:** Sitting on Your Trash, p. 130	**Review,** p. 110 **Quiz,** p. 110 in ATE **Alternative Assessment,** p. 110 in ATE
Directed Reading Worksheet 5, Section 2 **Transparency 98,** Porous Rocks Are Reservoirs for Fossil Fuels **Math Skills for Science Worksheet 20,** Parts of 100: Calculating Percentages **Transparency 99,** Formation of Coal **Reinforcement Worksheet 5,** If It's a Fossil, How Is It a Fuel?	**Chemistry Connection,** p. 112 **Multicultural Connection,** p. 112 in ATE **Real-World Connection,** p. 114 in ATE **Math and More,** Percent Carbon, p. 115 in ATE **Eureka!** Oil Rush! p. 131	**Review,** p. 114 **Review,** p. 117 **Quiz,** p. 117 in ATE **Alternative Assessment,** p. 117 in ATE
Directed Reading Worksheet 5, Section 3 **Math Skills for Science Worksheet 36,** Radioactive Decay and the Half-life **Transparency 100,** Generating Energy with Fission **Critical Thinking Worksheet 5,** Nature's Gold	**Math and More,** p. 119 in ATE **Physical Science Connection,** p. 120 **Cross-Disciplinary Focus,** p. 121 in ATE **MathBreak,** Miles per Acre, p. 124 **Multicultural Connection,** p. 124 in ATE	**Review,** p. 122 **Self-Check,** p. 123 **Homework,** p. 123 in ATE **Review,** p. 125 **Quiz,** p. 125 in ATE **Alternative Assessment,** p. 125 in ATE

END-OF-CHAPTER REVIEW AND ASSESSMENT

Chapter Review in Study Guide
Vocabulary and Notes in Study Guide
Chapter Tests with Performance-Based Assessment, Chapter 5 Test
Chapter Tests with Performance-Based Assessment, Performance-Based Assessment 5
Concept Mapping Transparency 5

Holt, Rinehart and Winston On-line Resources

go.hrw.com

For worksheets and other teaching aids related to this chapter, visit the HRW Web site and type in the keyword: **HSTENR**

National Science Teachers Association

www.scilinks.org

Encourage students to use the keywords listed on the Technology Highlights page to access information and resources on the **NSTA** Web site.

Chapter Resources & Worksheets

Visual Resources

TEACHING TRANSPARENCIES

#98 #99 #100

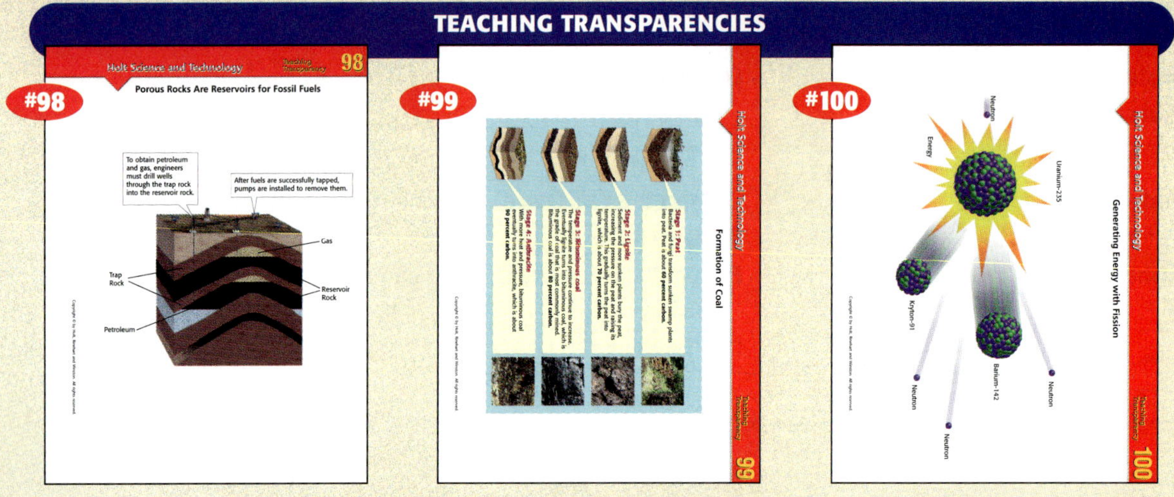

TEACHING TRANSPARENCIES

#70

CONCEPT MAPPING TRANSPARENCY

#5

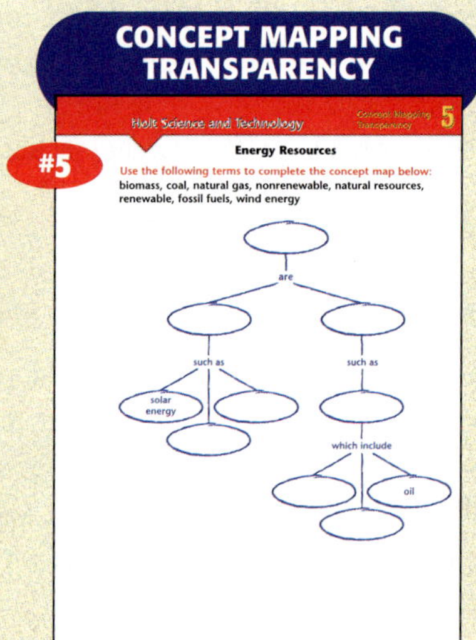

Meeting Individual Needs

DIRECTED READING

#5

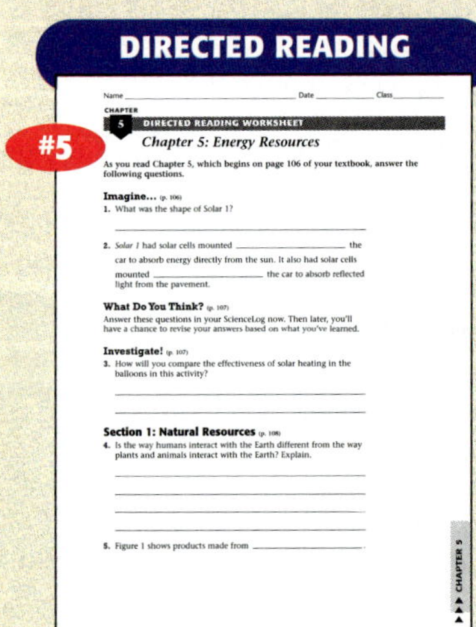

DIRECTED READING WORKSHEET

Chapter 5: Energy Resources

REINFORCEMENT & VOCABULARY REVIEW

#5

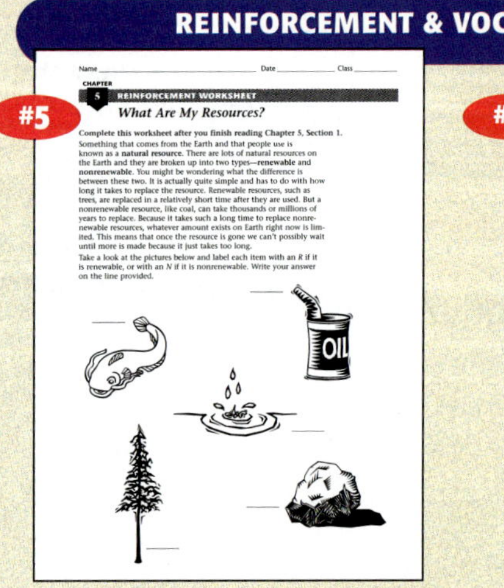

REINFORCEMENT WORKSHEET

What Are My Resources?

#5

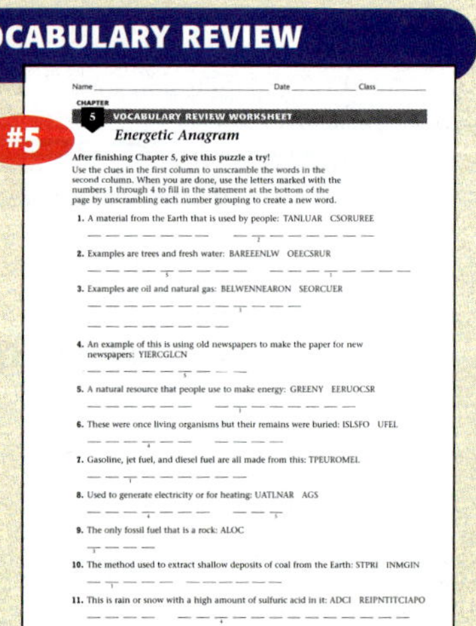

VOCABULARY REVIEW WORKSHEET

Energetic Anagram

SCIENCE PUZZLERS, TWISTERS & TEASERS

#5

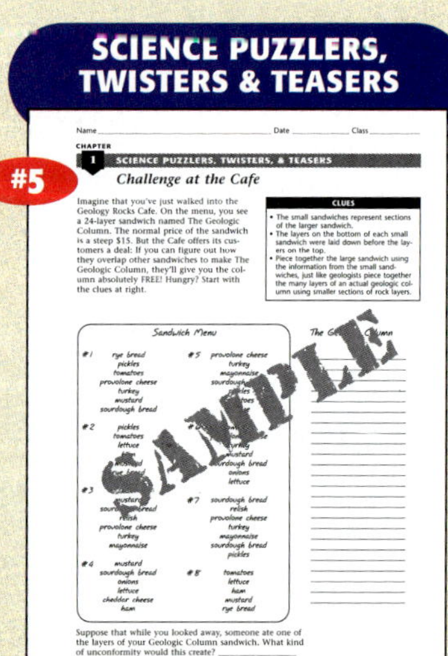

SCIENCE PUZZLERS, TWISTERS, & TEASERS

Challenge at the Cafe

Chapter 5 • Energy Resources

Review & Assessment

STUDY GUIDE

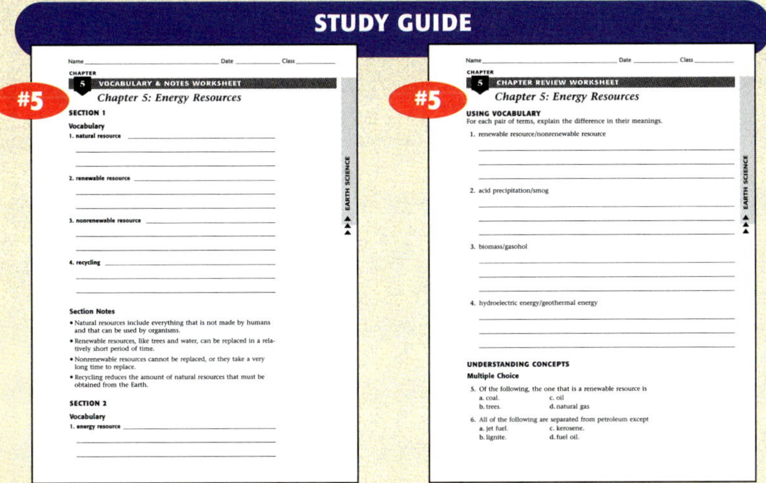
#5

CHAPTER 5 VOCABULARY & NOTES WORKSHEET

Chapter 5: Energy Resources

SECTION 1

Vocabulary

1. natural resource

2. renewable resource

3. nonrenewable resource

4. recycling

Section Notes

- Natural resources include everything that is not made by humans and that can be used by organisms.
- Renewable resources, like trees and water, can be replaced in a relatively short period of time.
- Nonrenewable resources cannot be replaced, or they take a very long time to replace.
- Recycling reduces the amount of natural resources that must be obtained from the Earth.

SECTION 2

Vocabulary

1. energy resource

#5

CHAPTER 5 CHAPTER REVIEW WORKSHEET

Chapter 5: Energy Resources

USING VOCABULARY

For each pair of terms, explain the difference in their meanings.

1. renewable resource/nonrenewable resource
2. acid precipitation/smog
3. biomass/gasohol
4. hydroelectric energy/geothermal energy

UNDERSTANDING CONCEPTS

Multiple Choice

5. Of the following, the one that is a renewable resource is
a. coal. c. oil
b. trees. d. natural gas
6. All of the following are separated from petroleum except
a. jet fuel. c. kerosene.
b. lignite. d. fuel oil.

CHAPTER TESTS WITH PERFORMANCE-BASED ASSESSMENT

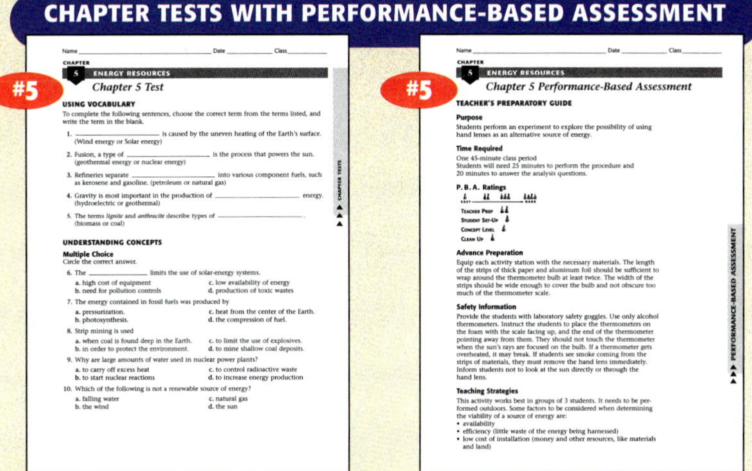
#5

CHAPTER 5 ENERGY RESOURCES

Chapter 5 Test

USING VOCABULARY

To complete the following sentences, choose the correct term from the terms listed, and write the term in the blank.

1. ______ is caused by the uneven heating of the Earth's surface. (Wind energy or Solar energy)
2. Fusion, a type of ______ is the process that powers the sun. (geothermal energy or nuclear energy)
3. Refineries separate ______ into various component fuels, such as kerosene and gasoline. (petroleum or natural gas)
4. Gravity is most important in the production of ______ energy. (hydroelectric or geothermal)
5. The terms *lignite* and *anthracite* describe types of ______. (biomass or coal)

UNDERSTANDING CONCEPTS

Multiple Choice

Circle the correct answer.

6. The ______ limits the use of solar-energy systems.
a. high cost of equipment c. low availability of energy
b. need for pollution controls d. production of toxic wastes
7. The energy contained in fossil fuels was produced by
a. pressurization. c. heat from the center of the Earth.
b. photosynthesis. d. the compression of fuel.
8. Strip mining is used
a. when coal is found deep in the Earth. c. to limit the use of explosives.
b. in order to protect the environment. d. to mine shallow coal deposits.
9. Why are large amounts of water used in nuclear power plants?
a. to carry off excess heat c. to control radioactive waste
b. to start nuclear reactions d. to increase energy production
10. Which of the following is not a renewable source of energy?
a. falling water c. natural gas
b. the wind d. the sun

#5

CHAPTER 5 ENERGY RESOURCES

Chapter 5 Performance-Based Assessment

TEACHER'S PREPARATORY GUIDE

Purpose

Students perform an experiment to explore the possibility of using hand lenses as an alternative source of energy.

Time Required

One 45-minute class period

Students will need 25 minutes to perform the procedure and 20 minutes to answer the analysis questions.

P. B. A. Ratings

Advance Preparation

Safety Information

Teaching Strategies

Lab Worksheets

LONG-TERM PROJECTS & RESEARCH IDEAS

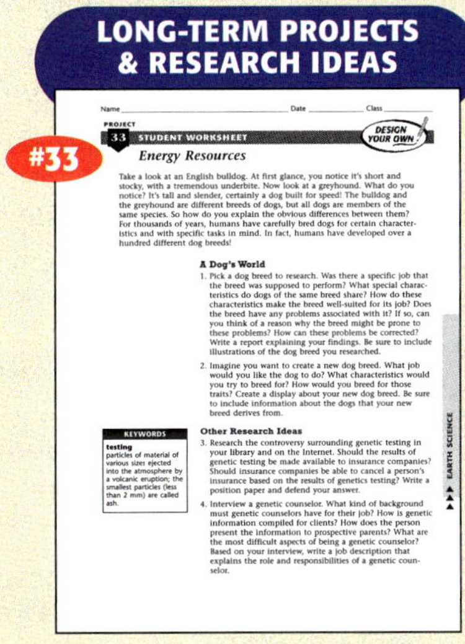
#33

PROJECT 33 STUDENT WORKSHEET

Energy Resources

A Dog's World

Other Research Ideas

DATASHEETS FOR LABBOOK

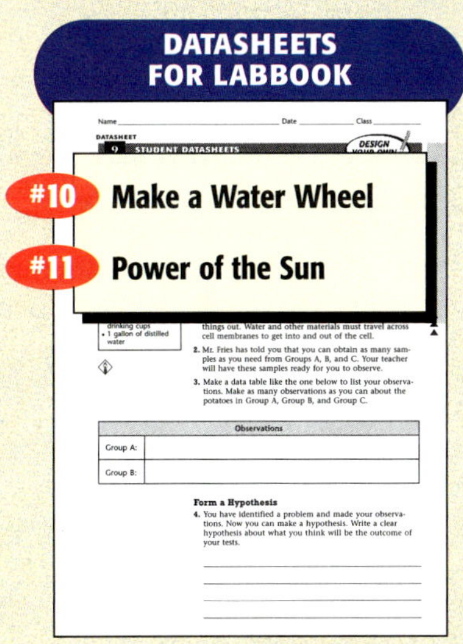
#10 Make a Water Wheel

#11 Power of the Sun

Applications & Extensions

CRITICAL THINKING & PROBLEM SOLVING

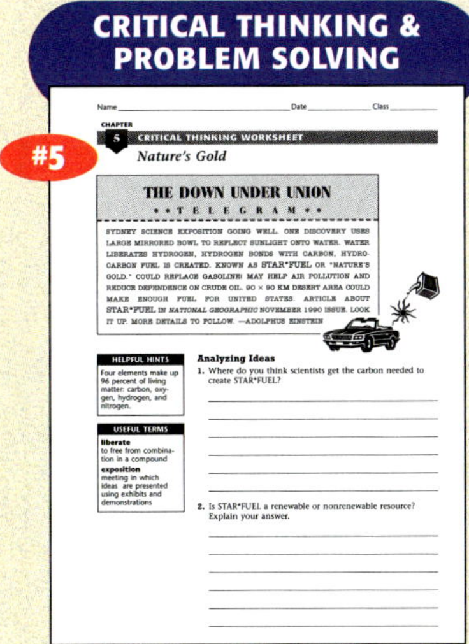
#5

CHAPTER 5 CRITICAL THINKING WORKSHEET

Nature's Gold

THE DOWN UNDER UNION

TELEGRAM

Analyzing Ideas

1. Where do you think scientists get the carbon needed to create STAR*FUEL?
2. Is STAR*FUEL a renewable or nonrenewable resource? Explain your answer.

MULTICULTURAL CONNECTIONS

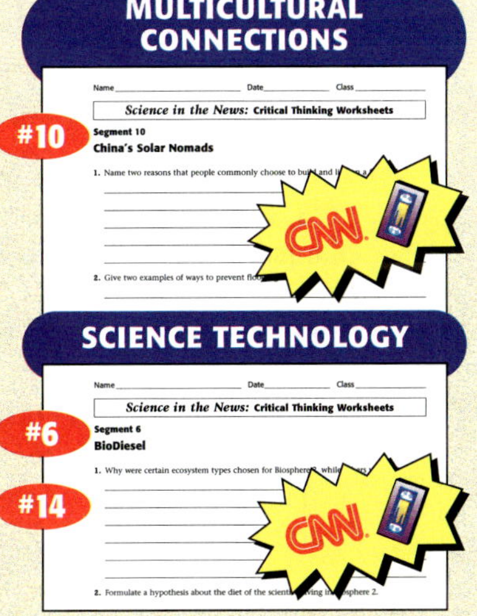
#10

Science in the News: Critical Thinking Worksheets

Segment 10

China's Solar Nomads

SCIENCE TECHNOLOGY

#6

#14

Science in the News: Critical Thinking Worksheets

Segment 6

BioDiesel

SCIENTISTS IN ACTION

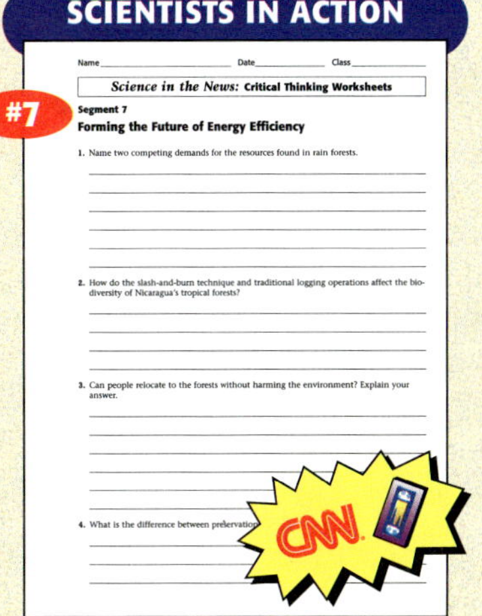
#7

Science in the News: Critical Thinking Worksheets

Segment 7

Forming the Future of Energy Efficiency

1. Name two competing demands for the resources found in rain forests.

INTERACTIVE EXPLORATIONS

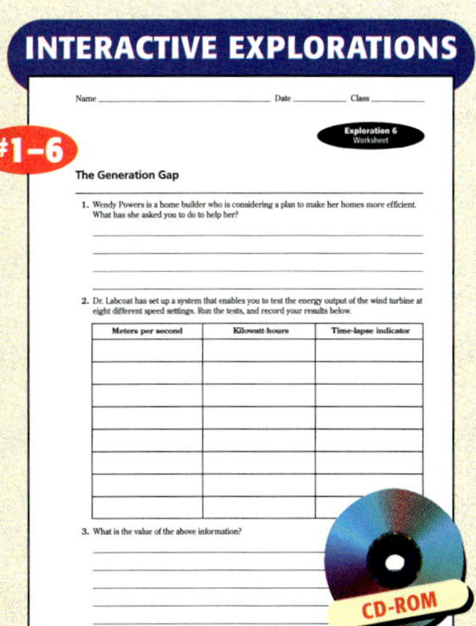
#1–6

Exploration 6 Worksheet

The Generation Gap

CD-ROM

Chapter Background

Section 1

Natural Resources

Interconnected Resources

The Earth's resources are intricately linked. For example, clearing trees affects the water quality downstream from a forest. We should pay attention not only to the rate at which we use natural resources but also to how our use affects other resources. The use of fossil fuels offers another example; fossil-fuel combustion adds enormous quantities of carbon dioxide, a greenhouse gas, to the atmosphere. Many scientists think that rising carbon dioxide levels are linked to the rising temperatures the Earth has experienced in recent years.

The Three Rs

During the past decade or so, environmentalists have encouraged consumers to consider the three Rs—reduce, recycle, and reuse—before buying to conserve Earth's natural resources, both renewable and nonrenewable.

- When buying new items, consumers who want to save money and conserve resources should buy in bulk or purchase products with minimal packaging. Washing and reusing plastic bags is another way to conserve petroleum-based natural resources. Use of cloth rags and napkins instead of paper towels and paper napkins is one way to reduce paper consumption. Glass and ceramic plates and cups and metal cutlery are more environmentally responsible than paper plates and plastic cups and utensils. Donating used items to charities and friends and family members is one way to recycle clothes, shoes, appliances, books, toys, and other such items.

Section 2

Fossil Fuels

Light Up Your Life

Before automobiles were invented and before electricity was discovered, one of the primary functions of fossil fuels was to provide light. Kerosene lamps became popular in the United States after the first oil well was drilled in 1859, in Pennsylvania. At the same time, use of coal gas and natural gas in lamps was increasing. Coal gas had been used in lamps as early as 1784. By the early 1800s, most cities in the United States and Europe had coal-gas streetlights. Electric lamps did not replace the gaslights until the early 1900s.

IS THAT A FACT!

- Ancient fossil reefs buried underground make excellent oil and gas reservoirs because the reefs are very porous. The productivity of the oil fields in Alberta, Canada, is due to the presence of Devonian reefs that are 408 million to 360 million years old.

"Rigs-to-Reefs"

Environmentalists usually consider offshore oil rigs to be detrimental to marine ecosystems because they disturb animal life and pose a risk of oil spills. Since 1979, however, obsolete oil rigs have become, many people believe, a welcome addition to these areas. In 1979, the Rigs-to-Reef program was initiated when a rig was moved from offshore Louisiana to a designated site off Florida to become an artificial reef. During the next 20 years, more than 500 platforms were relocated for the same purpose.

- Within 6 months of placement in a suitable marine area, a platform is covered with invertebrates and plants. These organisms attract other invertebrates and fish, forming the basis of a complex food chain. The open framework of the rig allows water to circulate and fish to swim freely through the structure. The marine animals and commercial and recreational anglers benefit from the artificial reefs. Some people remain concerned, however, about residual pollution from the submerged rigs.

Section 3

Alternative Resources

Chernobyl

The radioactive fallout from the 1986 Chernobyl nuclear accident affected people, livestock, and crops.

- Although only 31 people died, about 600,000 people were "significantly exposed" to the fallout. At least 50,000 people received 0.5 Gy of radiation. About 10,000 people were exposed to at least 1 Gy and suffered from radiation sickness. For comparison, a person undergoing a chest X ray is exposed to a maximum of 0.01 Gy.
- Livestock also suffered from the fallout. At least 86,000 head of cattle were evacuated from the area immediately after the accident. The sale of milk, meat, and many fruits and vegetables was banned in 1986 and 1987 in cities near Chernobyl. Many countries across Europe lost crops and other kinds of vegetation due to radioactive contamination.

Concentrating Solar Power Systems

Concentrating solar power systems harness solar energy by focusing reflected sunlight onto a receiver. The receiver absorbs the light and converts it into heat, which is then used to generate electricity.

- **Solar trough systems** consist of parabolic, mirrored troughs that focus sunlight onto oil-filled tubes at the troughs' focal points. The sunlight heats the oil, which then heats water. Steam from the heated water turns turbines in a generator to produce electricity.
- **Solar power towers** use thousands of mirrors to reflect sunlight onto a receiver that is mounted on a tall tower. The receiver contains salt that stores the solar energy as heat. The salt heats water, creating steam that turns turbines to produce electricity.
- **Solar dish systems** use circular mirrors arranged into the shape of a dish to concentrate solar energy onto a receiver. The receiver transfers the energy to an engine that generates electricity.

Geothermal Energy

Geothermal energy is tapped from places on Earth that experience high heat flow due to volcanic activity. It is currently used in Japan, parts of Russia, Iceland, Italy, New Zealand, and on the western coast of the United States.

- Iceland is the world leader in using geothermal energy for space heating. Over 85 percent of Icelanders use geothermal energy to warm their homes! The cost is only about one-third of what it would cost if they burned oil to power electric heaters. Industries in Iceland use geothermal energy because it is inexpensive, widely available, and very reliable.

Is That a Fact!

- Traditional fuels, such as wood and animal dung, are used to meet one-quarter of India's energy needs.

For additional background resources, please refer to the ***HST Reference Library.***

CHAPTER 5

Energy Resources

Chapter Preview

CHAPTER 5

Energy Resources

Imagine . . .

Imagine cruising down the highway faster than 100 km/h using only the power of the sun! Sound impossible? Well, it's not. Solar cars—cars that run exclusively on electricity converted from the sun's energy—have been around for years. Unlike driving gasoline-powered vehicles, driving these vehicles produces no air pollution, and the availability of the sun's energy isn't limited like gasoline. Scientists expect the sun to keep giving off energy for billions of years! Gasoline, on the other hand, comes from oil that we pump out of the Earth's crust. And most scientists think that oil will become scarce sometime in the twenty-first century.

So why don't you see solar cars zipping down the roads in your town every day after school? The main reason is that the technology still has a long way to go before solar cars will be practical. But the technology is becoming more advanced, and perhaps one day soon solar cars will be an option for motorists. Take a look at the variety of solar cars shown here, and prepare to learn how solar energy fits in with our wide assortment of energy resources.

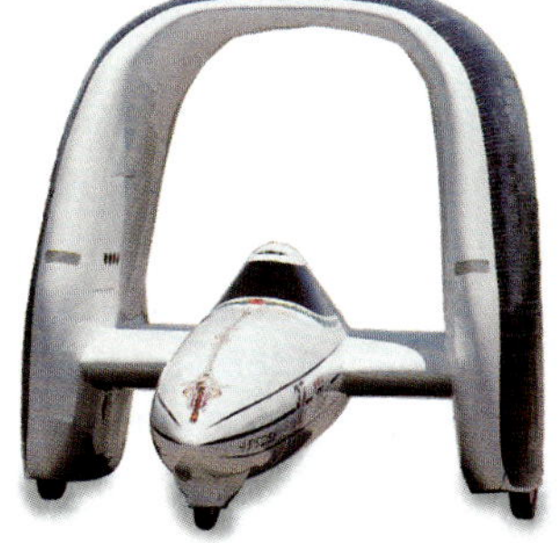

All over the world, car companies, universities, and experimental technologists are continuing to develop more-efficient solar cars.

Science Puzzlers, Twisters & Teasers Worksheet 5

Guided Reading Audio CD
English or Spanish, Chapter 5

Imagine . . .

Solar-powered vehicles use light to create electrical energy, which in turn provides power. Although electric vehicles, or EVs, may seem futuristic, they are already in use in California and Arizona. One example is the EV1, an EV that can travel between 80 km and 145 km on a single charge. The EV1's rechargeable battery contains slightly more than two-dozen 12 V modules capable of holding more than 16 kWh of energy.

What Do You Think?

In your ScienceLog, try to answer the following questions based on what you already know:

1. List four nonrenewable resources.
2. On which energy resources do humans currently depend the most?
3. What is the difference between a solar cell and a solar panel?

What Is the Sun's Favorite Color?

Are some colors better than others at absorbing the sun's energy? If so, how might this relate to collecting solar energy? Try the following activity to answer these questions.

Procedure

1. Obtain at least five **balloons** that are the same size and shape. One balloon should be white, and one should be black. The others can be whatever colors you can find.
2. Use **scissors** to cut at least half the stem off each of the balloons.
3. Place one large **ice cube** or several small cubes in each balloon. Each balloon should contain the same amount of ice.
4. Line the balloons up on a flat, uniformly colored surface that receives direct sunlight. Make sure that all the balloons receive the same amount of sunlight and that the openings in the balloons are not facing directly toward the sun.
5. Keep track of how much time it takes for the ice to melt completely in each of the balloons. You can tell how much ice has melted in each balloon by pinching the balloon's opening and then gently squeezing the balloon.

Analysis

6. In which balloon did the ice melt first? Why?
7. What color would you paint a device used to collect solar energy?

107

What Do You Think?

Accept all reasonable responses.

Students will have a chance to revise their answers in the Chapter Review under NOW What Do You Think?

Investigate!

MATERIALS

For Each Group:
- 5 different-colored round balloons
- scissors
- ice
- watch or clock with a second hand

Teacher Notes: Balloons must be identical except for color. Also note that one balloon in each group must be black and one must be white.

A single, large ice cube or several small cubes will work for this activity. Stress to students that they should not use too much ice or it will take too long to get results. You might have students mark their balloons with permanent markers before they add the ice so that each group is able to identify its balloons.

Answers to Investigate!

6. The ice in the black balloon melted first because the darker an object is, the more light energy it will absorb.
7. black

CONNECT TO GEOGRAPHY

Geography plays an important role in the use of alternative energy sources. For example, in the United States, using solar energy to generate electricity may be most practical in southern areas, which experience long hours of sunlight year-round.

Directed Reading Worksheet 5

Chapter 5 Opener–California Standards: PE/ATE 7, 7b

SECTION 1

Focus

Natural Resources

In this section, students learn the difference between renewable and nonrenewable resources. They also learn why conservation and recycling are important.

Bellringer

Display the following items:

a plastic sandwich bag, a piece of paper, a pencil, an empty soda can, a wooden match, a salt shaker, and some aquarium charcoal

Challenge students to determine what all of these items have in common. Lead students to conclude that all these items have their origin in natural resources. Sheltered English

1 Motivate

DISCUSSION

Kinds of Energy Have students brainstorm to form a list of different kinds of energy, including light energy, chemical energy, potential energy, kinetic energy, and thermal energy. Review the meaning of each term, if necessary. Now is also a good time to review or present the law of conservation of energy, which states that energy is never created or destroyed; it only changes from one form to another.

Directed Reading Worksheet 5 Section 1

1

NEW TERMS

natural resource
renewable resource
nonrenewable resource
recycling

OBJECTIVES

- Determine how humans use natural resources.
- Contrast renewable resources with nonrenewable resources.
- Explain how humans can conserve natural resources.

Natural Resources

Think of the Earth as a giant life-support system for all of humanity. The Earth's atmosphere, waters, and solid crust provide almost everything we need to survive. The atmosphere provides the air we need to breathe, distributes heat to maintain air temperatures, and produces rain. The oceans and other waters of the Earth provide food and needed fluids. The solid part of the Earth provides nutrients and minerals.

Interactions between the Earth's systems can cause changes in the Earth's environments. Organisms must adapt to these changes if they are to survive. Humans have found ways to survive by using natural resources to change their immediate surroundings. A **natural resource** is any natural substance, organism, or energy form that living things use. Few of the Earth's natural resources are used in their unaltered state. Most resources are made into products that make people's lives more comfortable and convenient, as shown in **Figure 1.**

Figure 1 *Lumber, gasoline, and electricity are all products that come from natural resources.*

108

internet connect

SCILINKS NSTA

TOPIC: Natural Resources
GO TO: www.scilinks.org
***sci*LINKS NUMBER:** HSTE105

IS THAT A FACT!

In 1998, people in the United States consumed nearly 583 billion liters of liquid fuel. More than 460 billion liters of this total was gasoline, which is used mostly in cars and trucks.

Section 1–California Standards: PE/ATE 6, 6b, 6c

Renewable Resources

Some natural resources are renewable. A **renewable resource** is a natural resource that can be used and replaced over a relatively short time. **Figure 2** shows several examples of renewable resources. Although many resources are renewable, humans often use them more quickly than they can be replaced. Trees, for example, are renewable, but humans are currently cutting trees down more quickly than other trees can grow to replace them.

Figure 2 *Fresh water, fish, and trees are just a few of the renewable resources available on Earth.*

Nonrenewable Resources

Not all of Earth's natural resources are renewable. A **nonrenewable resource** is a natural resource that cannot be replaced or that can be replaced only over thousands or millions of years. Examples of nonrenewable resources are shown in **Figure 3.** The amounts of nonrenewable resources on Earth are fixed with respect to their availability for human use. Once nonrenewable resources are used up, they are no longer available. Oil and natural gas, for example, exist in limited quantities. When these resources become scarce, humans will have to find other resources to replace them.

Figure 3 *Nonrenewable resources, such as coal, natural gas, and iron ore, can be replaced only over thousands or millions of years once they are used up.*

109

internetconnect

TOPIC: Renewable Resources
GO TO: www.scilinks.org
***sci*LINKS NUMBER:** HSTE110

TOPIC: Nonrenewable Resources
GO TO: www.scilinks.org
***sci*LINKS NUMBER:** HSTE115

2 Teach

READING STRATEGY

Prediction Guide Before students read this section, have them predict whether the following statements are true or false.

- Most of Earth's resources are used in their raw state. (false)
- Fish and trees are renewable resources. (true)
- Oil, gas, and coal are nonrenewable resources. (true)

MEETING INDIVIDUAL NEEDS

Learners Having Difficulty Provide students with two different-colored poster boards, scissors, glue or tape, and old magazines. Have students cut out pictures of products made from natural resources. Have them attach pictures of products made from renewable resources to one poster board and pictures of products made from nonrenewable resources to the other.

CONNECT TO LIFE SCIENCE

Reduce, Recycle, Reuse Round out your discussion of nonrenewable resources by introducing students to the three Rs of conservation. Use Teaching Transparency 70, "Practicing Conservation," as a guide.

Teaching Transparency 70 "Practicing Conservation"

LINK TO LIFE SCIENCE

Answers to APPLY

Answers to the first three questions will vary, depending on the items used. Answers to the fourth question might include reusing, recycling, and minimizing the use of products made from nonrenewable resources and renewable resources that are becoming more scarce.

3 Close

Quiz

1. Is the following statement true or false? Explain your answer.

   Sunlight is a natural resource. (True; light from the sun is an energy source that plants use to create food and that we can harness to do work.)

2. Explain the difference between conserving a resource and recycling it. (Conserving a resource means using it sparingly and not wasting it. Recycling refers to the use of products made from reprocessed used items.)

Alternative Assessment

Concept Mapping Have students use the following terms to construct a concept map:

use, disposal, recycling, nonrenewable resource, reuse, production, renewable resource

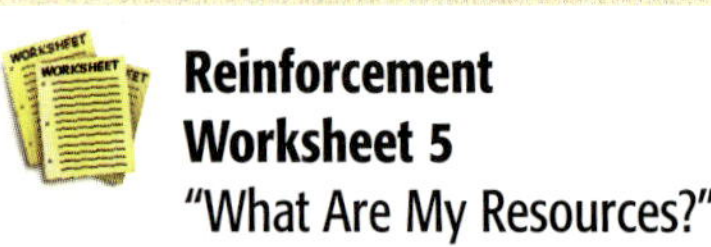

Reinforcement Worksheet 5
"What Are My Resources?"

Find five products in your home that were made from natural resources. List the resource or resources from which each product was made. Label each resource as renewable or nonrenewable.

Are the products made from mostly renewable or nonrenewable resources? Are those renewable resources plentiful on Earth? Do humans use those renewable resources more quickly than the resources can be replaced? What can you do to help conserve nonrenewable resources and renewable resources that are becoming more scarce?

Figure 4 *You can recycle many household items to help conserve natural resources.*

Conserving Natural Resources

Whether the natural resources we use are renewable or nonrenewable, we should be careful how we use them. To conserve natural resources, we should try to use them only when necessary. For example, leaving the faucet running while brushing your teeth wastes clean water. Turning the faucet on only to rinse your brush saves a lot of water that you or others need for other uses.

Another way to conserve natural resources is to recycle, as shown in **Figure 4. Recycling** is the use of used or discarded materials that have been reprocessed into new products. Recycling allows manufacturers to reuse natural resources when making new products. This in turn reduces the amount of natural resources that must be obtained from the Earth. For example, recycling aluminum cans reduces the amount of aluminum that must be mined from the Earth's crust to make new cans.

Sit on your trash! Turn to page 130 to find out how today's garbage becomes tomorrow's park benches.

REVIEW

1. How do humans use most natural resources?
2. What is the difference between renewable and nonrenewable resources?
3. Name two ways to conserve natural resources.
4. **Applying Concepts** List three renewable resources not mentioned in this section.

Answers to Review

1. by using products made from the resources
2. Renewable resources can be replaced over a relatively short time, while nonrenewable resources cannot be replaced or can be replaced only over thousands or millions of years.
3. using them only when necessary and recycling them
4. Answers will vary.

2

Fossil Fuels

NEW TERMS

energy resource, fossil fuel, petroleum, natural gas, coal, strip mining, acid precipitation, smog

OBJECTIVES

- Classify the different forms of fossil fuels.
- Determine how fossil fuels form.
- Identify where fossil fuels are found in the United States.
- Explain how fossil fuels are obtained.
- Identify problems with fossil fuels.
- List ways to deal with fossil-fuel problems.

Energy resources are natural resources that humans use to produce energy. There are many types of renewable and nonrenewable energy resources, and all of the energy released from these resources ultimately comes from the sun. The energy resources on which humans currently depend the most are fossil fuels. **Fossil fuels** are nonrenewable energy resources that form in the Earth's crust over millions of years from the buried remains of once-living organisms. Energy is released from fossil fuels when they are burned. There are many types of fossil fuels, which exist as liquids, gases, and solids, and humans use a variety of methods to obtain and process them. These methods depend on the type of fossil fuel, where the fossil fuel is located, and how the fossil fuel formed. Unfortunately, the methods of obtaining and using fossil fuels can have negative effects on the environment. Read on to learn about fossil fuels and the role they play in our lives.

Liquid Fossil Fuels—Petroleum

Petroleum, or crude oil, is an oily mixture of flammable organic compounds from which liquid fossil fuels and other products, such as asphalt, are separated. Petroleum is separated into several types of fossil fuels and other products in refineries, such as the one shown in **Figure 5.** Among the types of fossil fuels separated from petroleum are gasoline, jet fuel, kerosene, diesel fuel, and fuel oil.

Figure 5 *Fossil fuels and other products are separated from petroleum in a process called* fractionation. *In this process, petroleum is gradually heated in a tower so that different components boil and vaporize at different temperatures. Lighter components vaporize first and collect at the top of the tower, while heavier components vaporize last and collect at the bottom of the tower.*

IS THAT A FACT!

On January 10, 1901, oil from the famous Spindletop well near Beaumont, Texas, began to flow. In fact, the crude spewed higher than 90 m into the air! Caught off guard by the tremendous volume of petroleum, drillers took 9 days to cap the well.

SECTION 2

Focus

Fossil Fuels

In this section, students will learn how fossil fuels, such as petroleum, natural gas, and coal, form and where deposits of these fuels are found in the United States. Students will also learn about some of the ways we obtain fossil fuels and about the environmental problems associated with obtaining and using fossil fuels.

Bellringer

Pose this question on the board or an overhead projector:

What does the term *fossil fuels* imply about the source of these fuels? (The term *fossil fuels* implies that these fuels are derived from the remains of ancient life.)

1 Motivate

DISCUSSION

Fossil Fuel Use Lead students in a discussion about why fossil fuels, such as coal and gasoline, are so widely used as energy resources. (Answers may include their cost, widespread existence, and ease of use.)

Challenge them to think about what qualities a good fuel should have. (It should be abundant, affordable, easy to obtain, have a high ratio of energy to weight, be easy to transport, and produce little waste.)

Directed Reading Worksheet 5 Section 2

2 Teach

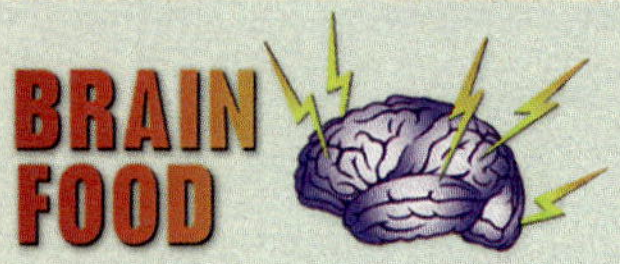

One characteristic all fossil fuels share is that they are formed from the remains of organisms that lived long ago. Over millions of years, plant and animal remains are buried by sediment and rock. As these remains get buried deeper underground, the high pressure and temperature slowly "cook" them. The result is solid, liquid, or gaseous mixtures that contain hydrocarbons—compounds containing only carbon and hydrogen. When hydrocarbons burn, or combine rapidly with oxygen, they release energy. The energy that originally formed the carbon-hydrogen bonds was captured by plants and incorporated into their tissues through photosynthesis.

Natural gas seeps were first discovered in ancient Persia (now Iran) between 6000 and 2000 B.C. Records from China indicate use of natural gas by 900 B.C. The Chinese drilled the first known natural gas well using bamboo poles and primitive drill bits. The well was 140 m deep. In Europe, natural gas was first discovered in England in 1659.

Petroleum and natural gas are both made of compounds called hydrocarbons. A *hydrocarbon* is an organic compound containing only carbon and hydrogen.

Gaseous Fossil Fuels—Natural Gas

Gaseous fossil fuels are classified as **natural gas.** Most natural gas is used for heating and for generating electricity. The stove in your kitchen may be powered by natural gas. Many motor vehicles, such as the van in **Figure 6,** are fueled by liquefied natural-gas. Vehicles like these produce less air pollution than vehicles powered by gasoline.

Methane is the main component of natural gas. But other natural-gas components, such as butane and propane, can be separated and used by humans. Butane is often used as fuel for camp stoves. Propane is often used as a heating fuel and as a cooking fuel, especially for outdoor grills.

Figure 6 *Vehicles powered by liquefied natural gas are becoming more common.*

Figure 7 *This coal is being gathered so that it may be burned in the power plant shown in the background. Burning coal provides energy that can be converted to electricity.*

Solid Fossil Fuels—Coal

The solid fossil fuel that humans use most is coal. **Coal** is a solid fossil fuel formed underground from buried, decomposed plant material. Coal, the only fossil fuel that is a rock, was once the leading source of energy in the United States. People burned coal for heating and transportation. Many trains in the 1800s and early 1900s were powered by coal-burning steam locomotives.

People began to use coal less because burning coal often produces large amounts of air pollution and because better energy resources were discovered. Coal is no longer used much as a fuel for heating or transportation in the United States. However, many power plants, like the one shown in **Figure 7,** burn coal to produce electricity.

IS THAT A FACT!

Methane, ethane, propane, and butane—four widely used hydrocarbons—differ in that they are each composed of increasing numbers of carbon and hydrogen atoms.

How Do Fossil Fuels Form?

All fossil fuels form from the buried remains of ancient organisms. But different types of fossil fuels form in different ways and from different types of organisms. Petroleum and natural gas form mainly from the remains of microscopic sea life. When these organisms die, their remains settle on the ocean floor, where they decay and become part of the ocean sediment. Over time, the sediment slowly becomes rock, trapping the decayed remains. Through physical and chemical changes, the remains become petroleum and gas over millions of years. Gradually, more rocks form above the rocks that contain the fossil fuels. Under the pressure of overlying rocks and sediments, the fossil fuels are squeezed out of their source rocks and into rocks with more pores. As shown in **Figure 8,** these porous rocks become reservoirs for petroleum and natural gas. The formation of petroleum and natural gas is an ongoing process. Part of the remains of today's sea life will probably become petroleum and natural gas millions of years from now.

Turn to page 131 to read about the nineteenth-century "oil rush" in the United States.

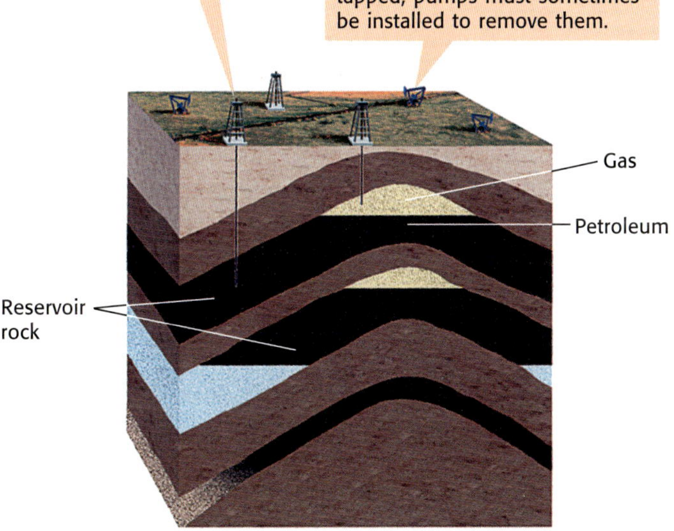

Figure 8 *Petroleum and gas rise from less-porous source rock into more-porous reservoir rock. Sometimes the fuels are trapped by overlying rock that has low porosity. Rocks that are folded upward are excellent fossil-fuel traps.*

QuickLab

Rock Sponge

What properties of reservoir rock allow oil and gas to be easily pumped from it? Investigate this question by trying the following activity:

1. Place samples of **sandstone, limestone,** and **shale** in separate **Petri dishes.**
2. Place 5 drops of light **machine oil** on each rock sample.
3. Observe and record the time required for the oil to be soaked up by each of the rock samples.
4. Which rock sample soaked up the oil fastest? Why?
5. Based on your findings, describe a property that allows for easy removal of fossil fuels from reservoir rock. Write your answers and observations in your ScienceLog.

DEMONSTRATION

MATERIALS

- clean, empty glass jar
- 100 mL each of rubbing alcohol, water, and vegetable oil
- red and blue food coloring

Simulating Reservoirs Petroleum does not fill all the available pore space in a subsurface reservoir. Some reservoirs contain thermal methane gas at great depths below the oil. Natural gas can be obtained through shallow drilling because it sits on top of the oil.

Tell students that the alcohol represents natural gas and that the cooking oil represents petroleum. Add a few drops of blue color to the water and a few drops of red color to the alcohol. Add the liquids to the jars in different sequences, and ask if this different treatment affects the final results. (no)

Sheltered English

QuickLab

MATERIALS

For Each Student:

- samples of sandstone, limestone, and shale
- Petri dishes
- light machine oil
- eyedropper

Answers to QuickLab

4. Answers will vary. The rock sample with the highest percentage of interconnected pore space should soak up the oil the fastest. Most reservoir rock is limestone that has many connected pores.
5. Oil and gas move easily through reservoir rock that has a high percentage of interconnected pore space. This allows for easy removal of liquid fossil fuels.

internetconnect

SCLINKS. NSTA

TOPIC: Fossil Fuels
GO TO: www.scilinks.org
***sci*LINKS NUMBER:** HSTE120

Teaching Transparency 98
"Porous Rocks Are Reservoirs for Fossil Fuels"

2 Teach, continued

Using the Figure

Have students refer to the diagram entitled "The Process of Coal Formation" to answer the questions below.

- What kinds of organisms play an important role in coal production? (bacteria, plants, and fungi)
- In a given area, which would be older: peat deposits or lignite deposits? (Lignite deposits; peat is an earlier stage of coal formation.)

Real-World Connection

Have students find out what fuel source is used to produce electricity in their community. If the community uses a combination of fuel sources, have students find the percentage of energy produced by each type. If fossil fuels are used, have students identify the fuel's source and explain how the fuel is transported to the power plant.

Independent Practice

Concept Mapping Have students construct concept maps that show the different methods of extraction used for various fossil fuels. Their maps should include the formation of the fuel, the location, and the extraction system. One type of fuel may have two or more locations and extraction methods. Encourage students to do additional research to complete their maps.

Coal forms differently from petroleum and natural gas. Coal forms underground over millions of years from decayed swamp plants. When swamp plants die, they sink to the bottom of the swamps. This begins the process of coal formation, which is illustrated below. Notice that the percentage of carbon increases with each stage. The higher the carbon content, the cleaner the material burns. However, all grades of coal will pollute the air when burned.

The Process of Coal Formation

Stage 1: Peat
Bacteria and fungi transform sunken swamp plants into peat. Peat is about **60 percent carbon.**

Stage 2: Lignite
Sediment and more sunken plants bury the peat, increasing the pressure on the peat and raising its temperature. This gradually turns the peat into lignite, which is about **70 percent carbon.**

Stage 3: Bituminous coal
The temperature and pressure continue to increase. Eventually lignite turns into bituminous coal, which is the grade of coal that is most commonly mined. Bituminous coal is about **80 percent carbon.**

Stage 4: Anthracite
With more heat and pressure, bituminous coal eventually turns into anthracite, which is about **90 percent carbon.**

REVIEW

1. Name a solid, liquid, and gaseous fossil fuel.
2. What component of coal-forming organic material increases with each step in coal formation?
3. **Comparing Concepts** What is the difference between the organic material from which coal forms and the organic material from which petroleum and natural gas mainly form?

114

Answers to Review

1. Answers will vary. The solid fossil fuel mentioned in this section is coal. Liquid fossil fuels mentioned in this section include gasoline, jet fuel, kerosene, diesel fuel, and fuel oil (petroleum is an acceptable answer). Gaseous fossil fuels mentioned in this section include methane, butane, and propane (natural gas is an acceptable answer).
2. carbon
3. Coal forms from buried, decayed swamp plants, while oil and natural gas form mainly from buried, decayed sea life.

Section 2 Mid-section Review—California Standards: PE/ATE 6, 6b

Where Are Fossil Fuels Found?

Fossil fuels are found in many parts of the world, both on land and beneath the ocean. As shown in **Figure 9,** the United States has large reserves of petroleum, natural gas, and coal. In spite of all our petroleum reserves, we import about one-half of our petroleum and petroleum products from the Middle East, South America, and Africa.

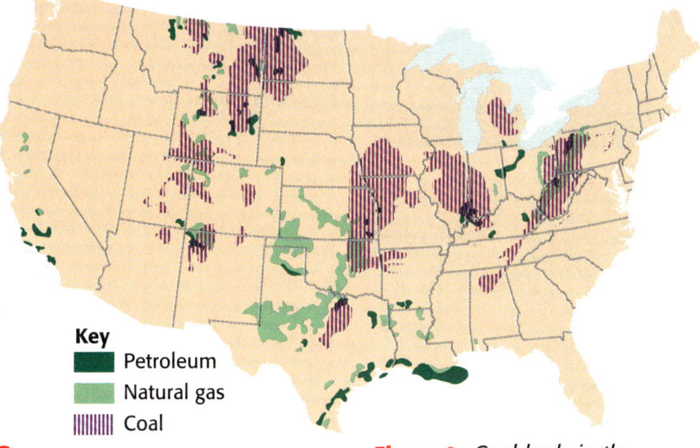

Figure 9 *Coal beds in the United States range in thickness from a few centimeters to nearly 50 m. Most oil and gas produced in the continental United States comes from California, Louisiana, and Texas. There are also large volumes of oil and gas in Alaska and offshore in the Gulf of Mexico.*

How Do Humans Obtain Fossil Fuels?

Humans use different methods to extract fossil fuels from the Earth's crust. These methods depend on the type of fuel being obtained and its location. Petroleum and natural gas are extracted by drilling wells into rock that contains these resources. Oil wells exist both on land and in the ocean. For offshore drilling, engineers mount drills on platforms that are secured to the ocean floor or float at the ocean's surface. **Figure 10** shows an offshore oil rig.

Coal is obtained either by mining deep beneath the Earth's surface or by strip mining. **Strip mining** is a process in which rock and soil are stripped from the Earth's surface to expose the underlying materials to be mined. Strip mining is used to mine shallow coal deposits. **Figure 11** shows a coal strip mine.

Figure 10 *Large oil rigs, some more than 300 m tall, operate offshore in many places, such as the Gulf of Mexico and the North Sea.*

Figure 11 *Strip miners use explosives to blast away rock and soil and to expose the material to be mined.*

115

Teaching Transparency 99
"Formation of Coal"

MATH and MORE

Percent Carbon A grade of coal with a higher percent carbon, such as anthracite, contains more usable energy than a grade with a lower percent carbon, such as lignite. To find the percent carbon in a coal sample, divide the mass of carbon by the total mass of a sample, and multiply the result by 100. If a 10 g coal sample has 8 g of carbon, the percent carbon is 8 divided by 10 times 100, or 80 percent.

What is the percent carbon in a 10 g coal sample if the mass of carbon is 6.5 g? (65 percent)

What is the percent carbon in a 10 g coal sample if the mass of carbon is 7.3 g? (73 percent)

What is the percent carbon in a 8 g coal sample if the mass of carbon is 5.6 g? (70 percent)

Math Skills Worksheet 20
"Parts of 100: Calculating Percentages"

Group Activity

Have students use encyclopedias, books, and Internet resources to find the location of fossil fuels worldwide. Then have them create a map illustrating the location of petroleum, natural gas, and coal. Tell them to label their maps clearly and to provide a key. Display the maps for the class to enjoy. Students should note the large volumes of oil in Alaska, the Gulf of Mexico, and the Middle East.

Sheltered English

3 Extend

DEBATE

Drilling in a Wildlife Refuge
The U.S. Fish and Wildlife Service, which administers Alaska's Arctic National Wildlife Refuge, states that its primary mandate is "to protect the wildlife and habitats of this area for the benefit of people now and in the future." The refuge's coastal plain is the calving ground for the Porcupine caribou herd, the most important land-based denning area for the entire Beaufort Sea polar bear population, home for 350 reintroduced musk oxen, and an important habitat for more than 180 bird species. Environmentalists claim that oil drilling on the refuge would bring pollution and disrupt the lives of the animals that use the coastal plain. Oil-industry executives say that they would drill on only 8 percent of the refuge—the 1.5-million-acre coastal plain; that oil revenues would benefit the state and federal governments; that more than 250,000 jobs would be created; and that importing foreign oil is too expensive.

Have students debate whether or not oil drilling should be allowed in Arctic National Wildlife Refuge.

Figure 12 *Acid precipitation can exist as rain, snow, mist, or any other form of precipitation. Acid precipitation can dissolve parts of statues (top) and kill trees (bottom).*

Problems with Fossil Fuels

Although fossil fuels provide energy for our technological world, the methods of obtaining and using them can have negative consequences. For example, some scientists think that the burning of fossil fuels is significantly increasing the amount of carbon dioxide in the atmosphere. It is possible that this increase in carbon dioxide is contributing to *global warming,* which is a rise in average global temperatures.

The burning of coal can cause damage to the environment in another way. When coal is burned, sulfur dioxide may be released. Sulfur dioxide combines with moisture in the air to produce sulfuric acid, which is one of the acids in acid precipitation. **Acid precipitation** is rain or snow that has a high acid content due mainly to air pollutants. Acid precipitation negatively affects wildlife, plants, buildings, and statues, as shown in **Figure 12.**

The mining of coal can also create environmental problems. Strip mining removes soil, which plants need for growth and some animals need for shelter. If land is not properly repaired afterward, strip mining can destroy wildlife habitats. Coal mines that are deep underground, such as the one shown in **Figure 13,** can be hazardous to the men and women working in them. Coal mining can also lower local water tables, pollute water supplies, and cause the overlying earth to collapse.

Figure 13 *Coal dust can damage the human respiratory system. And because coal dust is flammable, it increases the danger of fire and explosion in coal mines.*

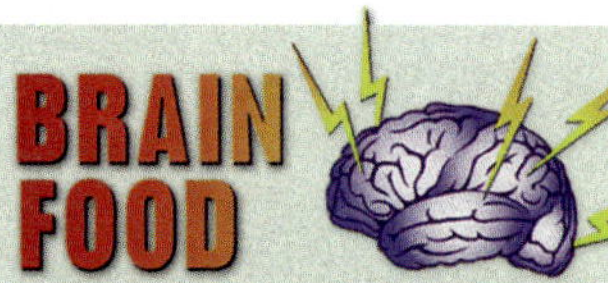

Although some countries have reduced their use of coal, the known coal reserves will last no more than 250 years at the present rates of coal consumption.

Obtaining petroleum can also cause environmental problems. In 1989, the supertanker *Exxon Valdez* spilled about 260,000 barrels of crude oil into the water when it ran aground off the coast of Alaska. The oil killed millions of animals and damaged the local fishing industry.

116

SCIENTISTS AT ODDS

One of the products of burning fossil fuels is carbon dioxide. Scientists recognize carbon dioxide as a greenhouse gas—a gas that traps heat and increases the temperature of the Earth's atmosphere. Most scientists agree that the global temperature is increasing. However, they have different opinions about the many possible ways rising carbon dioxide levels may be affecting the Earth's climate.

In addition to possibly contributing to global warming, burning petroleum products causes a big environmental problem called smog. **Smog** is a photochemical fog produced by the action of sunlight on air pollutants. Smog is particularly serious in places such as Denver and Los Angeles. In these cities, the sun shines most of the time, there are millions of automobiles, and surrounding mountains prevent the wind from blowing pollutants away. **Figure 14** shows a city with a smog problem. Smog levels in some cities, including Denver and Los Angeles, have begun to decrease in recent years.

Figure 14 *Smog reduces visibility and is dangerous to the human respiratory system.*

Dealing with Fossil-Fuel Problems

So what can be done to solve fossil-fuel problems? Obviously we can't stop using fossil fuels any time soon—we are too dependent on them. But there are things we can do to minimize the negative effects of fossil fuels. By traveling in automobiles only when absolutely necessary, people can cut down on car exhaust in the air. Carpooling, riding a bike, walking, and using mass-transit systems also help by reducing the number of cars on the road. These measures help reduce the negative effects of using fossil fuels, but they do not eliminate the problems. Only by using certain alternative energy resources, which you will learn about in the next section, can we eliminate them.

Figure 15 *Using mass transit or modes of transportation other than automobiles can help reduce air pollution due to burning fossil fuels.*

REVIEW

1. Name a state with petroleum, natural-gas, and coal reserves.
2. How do we obtain petroleum and natural gas? How do we obtain coal?
3. Name three problems with fossil fuels. Name three ways to minimize the negative effects of fossil fuels.
4. **Making Inferences** Why does the United States import petroleum from other regions even though the United States has its own petroleum reserves?

4 Close

Quiz

1. What is the relationship between petroleum and liquid fossil fuels? (Petroleum is the mixture of compounds from which liquid fossil fuels are separated.)
2. Explain why we use different methods to extract fossil fuels from the Earth's crust. (We use different methods because fossil fuels differ in their location and composition.)

Alternative Assessment

Have each student choose petroleum, natural gas, or coal. Instruct students to write the name of the fuel vertically down the center of a piece of ruled paper. Beginning with each letter in the fuel's name, have them write an adjective or a phrase that describes the fuel, how it forms, where it is found, how we use it, how we obtain it, where it forms, or problems associated with its use.

Reinforcement Worksheet 5
"If It's a Fossil, How Is It a Fuel?"

Answers to Review

1. Answers will vary. Use **Figure 9** to check answers.
2. We obtain petroleum and natural gas by drilling wells into rock that contains these resources. We obtain coal by mining.
3. Answers will vary. Problems include oil spills, loss of soil from strip mining coal, and the production of smog due to burning fossil fuels. Ways of minimizing negative effects include carpooling, riding a bike, walking, and using public transportation.
4. because it is currently cheaper to import petroleum from other regions and because there are fewer environmental regulations on petroleum production and transport in other regions

Section 2 Review—California Standards: PE/ATE 6, 6a, 6b

SECTION 3

Focus

Alternative Resources

In this section, students will learn about some of the alternatives to fossil fuels. The section also includes a discussion of the pros and cons of alternative energy sources.

Bellringer

Show students a picture of a wind farm, a solar energy facility, and a hydroelectric dam. Ask them which if any of these alternative energy facilities might be well suited to their community. Explain that the energy resources used in these facilities are just some of the alternatives to fossil fuels available.

1) Motivate

DEMONSTRATION

Calculating with Light Show students how solar cells can be used to power simple devices. Take a solar-powered calculator, and show students how the numbers fade out when the solar cells are covered. Ask students to name an application in which solar cells would be an effective way to provide energy.

Sheltered English

Directed Reading Worksheet 5 Section 3

3

NEW TERMS

nuclear energy
solar energy
wind energy
hydroelectric energy
biomass
gasohol
geothermal energy

OBJECTIVES

- Describe alternatives to the use of fossil fuels.
- List advantages and disadvantages of using alternative energy resources.

Alternative Resources

The energy needs of industry, transportation, and housing are increasingly met by electricity. However, most electricity is currently produced from fossil fuels, which are nonrenewable and cause pollution when burned. In the past, geologists have been able to find new fossil-fuel reserves to balance those being consumed. But this cannot go on forever. For people to continue their present lifestyles, new sources of energy must become available.

Splitting the Atom

Nuclear energy is an alternative source of energy that is derived from the nuclei of atoms. Most often it is produced by a process called *fission.* Fission is a process in which the nuclei of radioactive atoms are split, releasing energy, as shown in **Figure 16.** Nuclear power plants use radioactive atoms, such as uranium-235, as fuel. When fission takes place, a large amount of heat is given off. The heat is used to produce steam to run electric generators in the power plant.

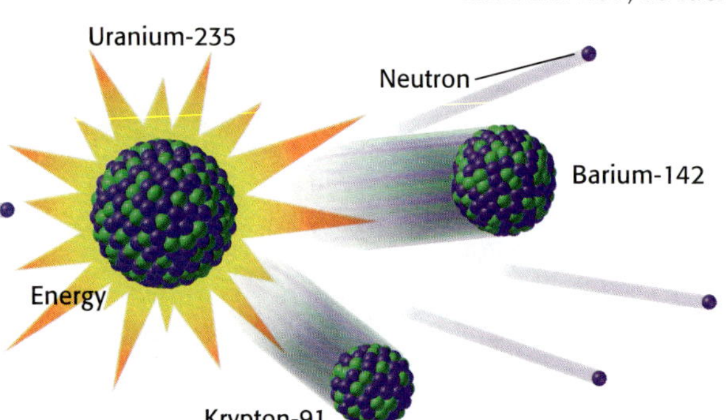

Figure 16 *The process of fission generates a tremendous amount of energy.*

There are more than 400 nuclear power plants in operation around the world. About 75 percent of France's electricity comes from nuclear energy, while less than 10 percent of the energy used in the United States comes from nuclear energy.

Pros and Cons Nuclear power plants provide alternative sources of energy without the problems that come with fossil fuels. So why don't we use nuclear energy instead of fossil fuels? Nuclear power plants produce dangerous wastes. The wastes are unsafe because they are radioactive. Radioactive wastes, such as the ones shown in **Figure 17,** must be removed from the plant and stored until they lose their radioactivity. But nuclear wastes can remain dangerously radioactive for thousands of years. A safe place must be found to store these wastes so that radiation cannot escape into the environment.

Figure 17 *The symbol on these barrels of nuclear waste represents radioactivity. Areas or objects marked with this symbol should be approached only after taking proper precautions.*

118

MISCONCEPTION ALERT

Although radioactive waste from nuclear power plants is dangerous, the plants themselves are safe as long as they are operated properly.

IS THAT A FACT!

Nuclear energy is the energy that exists in the bonds that hold together atomic nuclei. The breaking of these bonds, or nuclear fission, is what occurs at an uncontrolled rate in an atomic bomb. By contrast, the rate of fission in a nuclear power plant is carefully controlled.

Section 3—California Standards: PE/ATE 4a, 6, 6a, 6b, 7, 7b; LabBook: 4b, 7, 7b, 7e

Because nuclear power plants generate a lot of heat, large amounts of water are used in cooling towers, like the ones shown in **Figure 18,** to cool the plants. If a plant's cooling system were to stop working, the plant would overheat, and its reactor could possibly melt. Then a large amount of radiation could escape into the environment, as it did at Chernobyl, Ukraine, in 1986.

There is another type of nuclear energy that is potentially so abundant as to be considered inexhaustible. This energy is produced by *fusion*. Fusion is the joining of nuclei of small atoms to form larger atoms. This is the same process that is thought to produce energy in the sun.

The main advantage of fusion compared with fission is that fusion produces few dangerous wastes. The main disadvantage of fusion is that very high temperatures are required for the reaction to take place. No known material can withstand temperatures that high, so the reaction must occur within a special environment, such as a magnetic field. So far, fusion reactions have been limited to laboratory experiments.

Figure 18 *Cooling towers are one of many safety mechanisms used in nuclear power plants. Their purpose is to prevent the plant from overheating.*

Sitting in the Sun

When sunlight falls on your skin, the warmth you feel is part of solar energy. **Solar energy** is energy from the sun. Every day, the Earth receives more than enough solar energy to meet all of our energy needs. And since the Earth continuously receives solar energy, the energy is a renewable resource.

There are two common ways that we use solar energy. The use you are probably most familiar with is changing it directly into electricity. Sunlight can be changed into electricity by the use of solar cells. You may have used a calculator, like the one shown in **Figure 19,** that was powered by solar cells.

Figure 19 *This solar calculator receives all the energy it needs through the four solar cells located above its screen.*

2 Teach

Discussion

Nuclear Energy Use the following questions to stimulate a discussion on using nuclear energy to produce electricity.

- What is nuclear fission? How is fission used to generate electricity?
- Is nuclear energy currently being used?
- What are the advantages and disadvantages of nuclear fusion?

Reading Strategy

Mnemonics Provide students with the following mnemonic device to help them remember the difference between fission and fusion. "Atoms spl**i**t during f**i**ssion and **u**nite during f**u**sion." Sheltered English

MATH and MORE

Explain that a half-life is the time it takes for one half of a sample of radioactive material to decay. Have students graph radioactive decay over four half-lives of a hypothetical sample with a mass of 100 g and a half-life of 10,000 years.

Math Skills Worksheet 36 "Radioactive Decay and the Half-life"

Scientists at Odds

Fortunately, only a handful of accidents have occurred since we began using nuclear energy. In 1991, the International Atomic Energy Agency issued a report on the Chernobyl accident that concluded that "future increases over the natural incidence of cancers or heredity effects would be difficult to discern." In 1996, however, some cancer rates were 100 to 200 times higher than normal in areas contaminated by the fallout from the accident.

Teaching Transparency 100 "Generating Energy with Fission"

2 Teach, *continued*

Reading Strategy

Activity Before they read the information on solar cells and solar collectors, have students deduce whether each of the statements below is true or false. When students have finished reading these two pages, have them correct any wrong answers and rewrite the false statements to make them true.

- A solar cell produces only a very small amount of electricity. (true)
- Solar cells are not commonly used because they cause a great deal of pollution. (false)
- Solar panels have been used to heat houses and fuel aircraft and cars. (true)
- Solar collectors are usually white, fluid-filled boxes with glass tops. (false)
- Solar water heaters are most efficient in the far northern parts of the United States. (false)

physical science CONNECTION

Did you know that the energy from petroleum, coal, and natural gas is really a form of stored solar energy? All organisms ultimately get their energy from sunlight and store it in their cells. When ancient organisms died and became trapped in sediment, some of their energy was stored in the fossil fuel that formed in the sediment. So the gasoline that powers today's cars contains energy from sunlight that fell on the Earth millions of years ago!

A single solar cell produces only a tiny amount of electricity. For small electronic devices, such as calculators, this is not a problem because enough energy can be obtained with only a few cells. But in order to provide enough electricity for larger objects, such as a house, thousands of cells are needed. Has anyone tried this? They sure have. Many homes and businesses use solar panels mounted on their roof to provide much of their needed electricity. Solar panels are large panels made up of many solar cells wired together. **Figure 20** shows a building with solar panels.

Figure 20 *Although they are expensive to install, solar panels are good investments in the long run.*

Solar cells are reliable and quiet, have no moving parts, and can last for years with little maintenance. They produce no pollution during use, and pollution created by their manufacturing process is very low.

So why doesn't everyone use solar cells? The answer is cost. While solar energy itself is free, solar cells are relatively expensive to make. In a house built with enough solar panels to provide all needed electricity, the cost of the solar power system could account for one-third of the cost of the entire house. But in remote areas where it is difficult and costly to run electric wires, solar power systems can be a realistic option. In the United States today, tens of thousands of homes use solar panels to produce electricity.

Can you think of other places that you have seen solar panels? Take a look at **Figure 21.** There are even experimental solar-powered airplanes and cars, such as the cars you read about at the beginning of this chapter.

Figure 21 *Perhaps you have seen solar panels used in this manner in your town.*

120

MISCONCEPTION ALERT

Solar energy is for all practical purposes an inexhaustible source of energy. However, it is important to note that the sun doesn't shine 24 hours a day in most areas nor is it always directly overhead. Using solar energy efficiently depends on the time of day, local weather conditions, the time of year, and an area's latitude.

Another use of solar energy is direct heating through solar collectors. Solar collectors are dark-colored boxes with glass or plastic tops. Sun shines into the boxes, making the temperature inside very hot. Running through the boxes are liquid-filled tubes. As the liquid moves through the box, the liquid increases in temperature. A common use of solar collectors is heating water, as shown in **Figure 22.** Over 1 million solar water heaters have been installed in the United States. They are especially common in Florida, California, and some southwestern states.

As with solar cells, the problem with solar collectors is cost. But solar collectors quickly pay for themselves—heating water is one of the major uses of electricity in American homes. Also, solar collectors can be used to generate electricity.

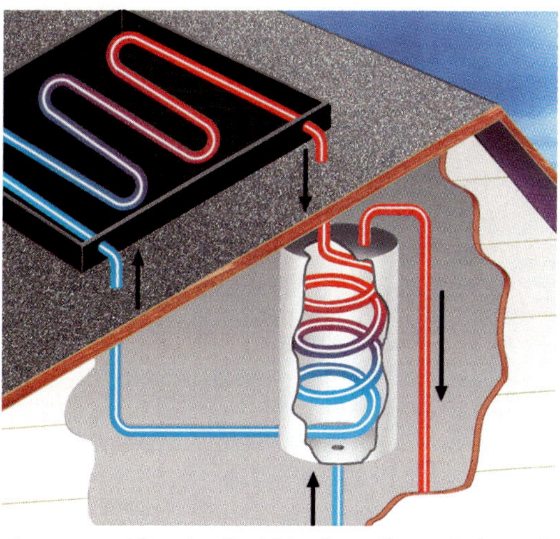

Figure 22 *After the liquid in the collector is heated by the sun, it is pumped through tubes that run through a water heater, causing the temperature of the water to rise.*

Large-Scale Solar Power So far you have seen how solar cells and solar panels can be used to generate electricity for a building or other solitary object. But what about providing solar energy for multiple objects? Experimental solar-power facilities, such as the one shown in **Figure 23,** have shown that this is a possibility. Facilities like this one are designed to use mirrors to focus sunlight onto coated steel pipes filled with synthetic oil. The oil is heated by the sunlight and is then used to heat water. The heated liquid water turns to steam, which is used to drive electric generators.

An alternative design for solar power facilities is one that uses mirrors to reflect sunlight onto a receiver on a central tower. The receiver captures the sunlight's energy and stores it in tanks of molten salt. The stored energy is then used to create steam, which drives a turbine in an electric generator. *Solar Two,* a solar-power facility designed in this manner, is capable of generating enough energy to power 10,000 homes in southern California.

Turn to page 506 to calculate the power of the sun.

Figure 23 *This solar facility in the Mojave Desert has 1,926 sun-tracking mirrors called* heliostats.

121

Guided Practice

Put the statements below on an overhead transparency in the order shown. Prompt students to sequence the statements to explain how the solar facility in the Mojave Desert works.

- The oil is heated and in turn heats water. (3)
- Computer-guided mirrors collect solar energy. (1)
- The heated water turns into steam, which is used to turn generators that produce electricity. (4)
- Mirrors focus sunlight onto pipes that are filled with oil. (2)

Activity

MATERIALS

For Each Group:
- small piece of cheese
- aluminum foil
- round metal bowl
- masking tape

Safety Caution: Warn students not to stare at reflected sunlight for long periods of time.

Solar Cooker Have students line the bowl with aluminum foil, shiny side up. Tell them to make the foil as smooth as possible and then tape it in position. Have them place the piece of cheese in the center of the bowl's base and place the "cooker" facing the sun. (To get the best results, this should be done at about noon on a very sunny day.) Have students observe what happens to the cheese (it melts) and how long it takes to happen. Have them write their observations in their ScienceLog. Explain to students that the aluminum foil reflects the sun's rays and concentrates them on the piece of cheese. The heat warms the cheese and eventually melts it. Sheltered English

Cross-Disciplinary Focus

Geography Have students use their knowledge of climate zones and geography to identify places on Earth where using solar energy holds great promise. (Locations include the southwestern United States, Latin America, and parts of Asia and Africa, among others.)

Power of the Sun

2 Teach, *continued*

USING THE FIGURE

Draw students' attention to **Figures 24** and **25,** and ask the following questions:

- What happens when wind passes over the blades of the turbines? (The blades spin due to the force of the wind.)
- What is an advantage of having wind turbines mounted on towers? (Answers may vary. One advantage is that the land under the towers can be used for other purposes.)

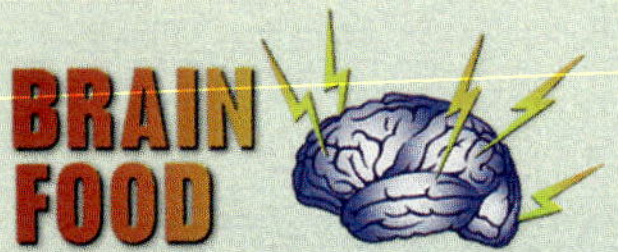

Wind turbines in the United States currently produce about 3 billion kilowatt-hours of electricity annually. According to the National Wind Technology Center, the United States has the ability to use the wind to produce more electricity than our country currently uses! North Dakota alone experiences enough steady wind to supply about a third of the nation's electricity needs.

Figure 24 *Windmills like this one are still common in rural areas of the United States.*

Capture the Wind

Wind is created indirectly by solar energy through the uneven heating of air. There is a tremendous amount of energy in wind, called **wind energy.** You can see the effects of this energy unleashed in a hurricane or tornado. Wind energy can also be used productively by humans. Wind energy can turn a windmill, pumping water or producing electricity. Small windmills, like the one shown in **Figure 24,** have been generating electricity in the United States since the 1920s.

Today, fields of modern wind turbines—technological updates of the old windmills—generate significant amounts of electricity. Clusters of these turbines are often called wind farms. Wind farms are located in areas where winds are strong and steady. Most of the wind farms in the United States are in California. The amount of energy produced by California wind farms could power all of the homes in San Francisco. Scientists have determined that portions of 37 states in the United States have enough wind to support commercial wind farms.

There are many benefits of using wind energy. Wind energy is renewable. Wind farms can be built in only 3–6 months. Wind turbines produce no carbon dioxide or other air pollutants during operation. The land used for wind farms can also be used for other purposes, such as cattle grazing, as shown in **Figure 25.** However, the wind blows strongly and steadily enough to produce electricity on a large scale only in certain places. Currently, wind energy accounts for only a small percentage of the energy used in the United States.

Figure 25 *Wind turbines take up only a small portion of the ground's surface. This allows the land on wind farms to be used for more than one purpose.*

REVIEW

1. Briefly describe two ways of using solar energy.
2. In addition to multiple turbines, what is needed to produce electricity from wind energy on a large scale?
3. **Analyzing Methods** Nuclear power plants are found in many places in the United States. But they are rarely found in the middle of deserts or other extremely dry areas. If you were going to build a nuclear plant, why would you not build it in the middle of a desert?

122

Answers to Review

1. Change it directly into electricity, or use it to heat objects directly.
2. strong, steady wind
3. Large amounts of water are needed to cool the plants so they don't overheat. Deserts and other dry areas may not have large or steady enough water supplies.

Section 3 Mid-section Review—California Standards: PE/ATE 6, 6a

Hydroelectric Energy

The energy of falling water has been used by humans for thousands of years. Water wheels, such as the one shown in **Figure 26,** have been around since ancient times. In the early years of the Industrial Revolution, water wheels provided energy for many factories. More recently, the energy of falling water has been used to generate electricity. Electricity produced by falling water is called **hydroelectric energy.**

Hydroelectric energy is inexpensive and produces little pollution, and it is renewable because water constantly cycles from the ocean to the air, to the land, and back to the ocean. But like wind energy, hydroelectric energy is not available everywhere. Hydroelectric energy can be produced only where large volumes of falling water can be harnessed. Huge dams, like the one in **Figure 27,** must be built on major rivers to capture enough water to generate significant amounts of electricity. There are many hydroelectric dams around the world, but the production of hydroelectric energy can be greatly increased. There are many places in the world where large volumes of falling water are not currently being used to generate electricity.

Figure 26 *Falling water turns water wheels, which turn giant millstones used to grind grain into flour.*

Turn to page 504 to make your own water wheel.

Figure 27 *Falling water turns huge turbines inside hydroelectric dams, generating electricity for millions of people.*

Increased use of hydroelectric energy could reduce the demand for fossil fuels, but there are trade-offs. Construction of the large dams necessary for hydroelectric power plants often destroys other resources, such as forests and wildlife habitats. For example, hydroelectric dams on the Lower Snake and Columbia Rivers in Washington disrupt the migratory paths of local populations of salmon and steelhead. Large numbers of these fish die each year because their life cycle is disrupted. Dams can also decrease water quality and create erosion problems.

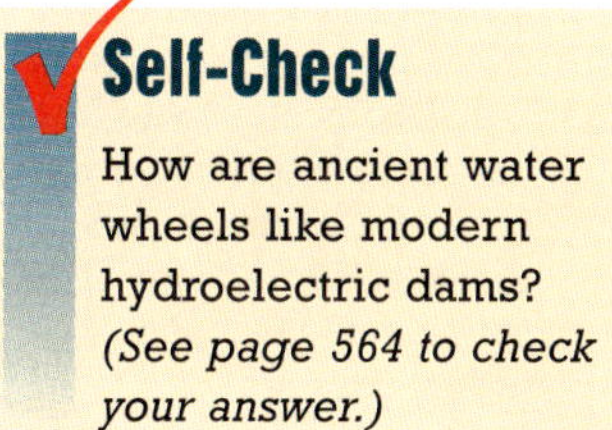

Self-Check

How are ancient water wheels like modern hydroelectric dams? *(See page 564 to check your answer.)*

Prediction Guide Before students read this page, ask them to decide whether the following statements are true or false:

- Moving water can be used to produce electricity. (true)
- Water wheels were once used to power cars and other vehicles. (false)
- Hydroelectric energy is a nonrenewable natural resource. (false)
- Hydroelectric power plants can disrupt forests, streams, and other types of ecosystems. (true)

PG 504

Make a Water Wheel

Homework

Poster Project Have students research how the moving water of ocean waves and tides can be used to generate electricity. Have them present their information as a poster with labeled diagrams.

Answer to Self-Check

Both devices harness energy from falling water.

IS THAT A FACT!

Both hydroelectric dams and wind turbines supply electricity, but how? They use a device called a *generator* to convert kinetic energy (the energy of motion) into electrical energy (the energy of moving electrons).

2 Teach, continued

Meeting Individual Needs

Writing **Advanced Learners** Have students research and prepare reports on biomass fuels. Students might choose to research the use of lumber industry wastes, agricultural wastes, organic municipal wastes, food processing wastes, aquatic plants and algae, and municipal sewage.

In the Bolivian highlands of South America, the llama is a traditional beast of burden, but it is also a source of meat, wool, and leather, and its dung is a source of biomass fuel. In the deserts of Arabia, the nomadic Bedouin use camel dung as fuel, and the nomads of eastern and northeastern Tibet and Nepal use yak dung as fuel. Dried yak dung is the main fuel available on the treeless Tibetan plateaus.

Answers to MATHBREAK

2.5 acres

Critical Thinking Worksheet 5 "Nature's Gold"

Interactive Explorations CD-ROM "The Generation Gap"

Powerful Plants

Plants are similar to solar collectors, absorbing energy from the sun and storing it for later use. Leaves, wood, and other parts of plants contain the stored energy. Even the dung of plant-grazing animals is high in stored energy. These sources of energy are called biomass. **Biomass** is organic matter that contains stored energy.

Biomass energy can be released in several ways. The most common is the burning of biomass. Approximately 70 percent of people living in developing countries heat their homes and cook their food by burning wood or charcoal. In the United States this number is about 5 percent. United Nations scientists estimate that the burning of wood and animal dung accounts for approximately 14 percent of the world's total energy use.

Figure 28 *In many parts of the world where firewood is scarce, people burn animal dung for energy. This woman is preparing cow dung that will be dried and used as fuel.*

MATH BREAK

Miles per Acre

Imagine that you own a car that runs on alcohol made from corn that you grow. You drive your car about 15,000 miles in a year, and you get 240 gallons of alcohol from each acre of corn that you process. If your car gets 25 mi/gal, how many acres of corn would you have to grow to fuel your car for a year?

Plant material can also be changed into liquid fuel. Plants containing sugar or starch, for example, can be made into alcohol. The alcohol is burned as a fuel or mixed with gasoline to make a fuel mixture called **gasohol.** An acre of corn can produce more than 1,000 L of alcohol. But in the United States we use a lot of fuel for our cars. It would take about 40 percent of the entire United States corn harvest to make enough alcohol to make just 10 percent of the fuel we use in our cars!

Biomass is obviously a renewable source of energy, but producing biomass requires land that could be used for growing food. And it takes about 10 times as much land to grow biomass fuel as land required by solar cells to produce the same amount of electricity.

Q: What kind of plants can't photosynthesize?

A: power plants

Deep Heat

Imagine being able to tap into the energy of the Earth. In a few places this is possible. This type of energy is called geothermal energy. **Geothermal energy** is energy produced by heat within the Earth's crust.

In some locations, rainwater penetrates porous rock near a source of magma. The heat from the magma heats the water, often turning it to steam. The steam and hot water escape through natural vents, like the one in **Figure 29,** or through wells drilled into the rock. The steam and water contain geothermal energy. Some geothermal power plants, such as The Geysers, in northern California, use primarily steam to generate electricity. This process is illustrated in **Figure 30.** In recent years, geothermal power plants that use primarily hot water instead of steam have become more common.

Geothermal energy can also be used as a direct source of heat. In this process, hot water and steam are used to heat a fluid that is pumped through a building in order to heat it. Buildings in Iceland are heated in this way from the country's many geothermal sites.

Figure 29 *Natural holes in the Earth's surface allow hot water and steam to escape from the Earth's crust.*

Figure 30 How a Geothermal Power Plant Works

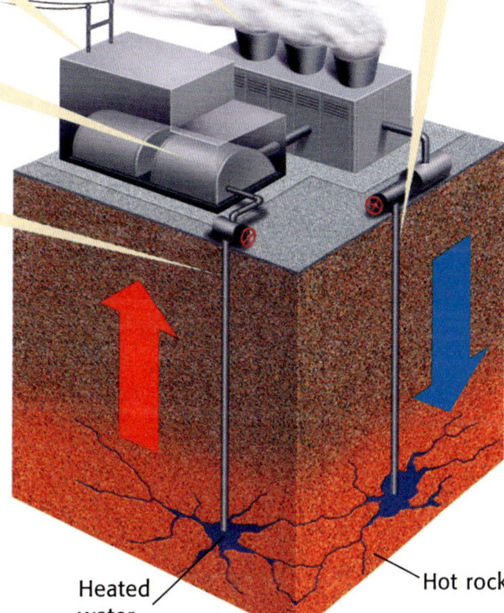

REVIEW

1. Where is the production of hydroelectric energy practical?
2. Name two ways to release biomass energy.
3. Describe two ways to use geothermal energy.
4. **Summarizing Data** List four energy alternatives to fossil fuels, and give one advantage and one disadvantage of each alternative.

3 Extend

GOING FURTHER

Writing | Have students find out what fuels are used in your area. Ask them to find out if there are presently any alternative energy resources that are being used or could be used in your area. Have them find out how the costs of these alternatives would compare with those of the fuels currently used. Have students share their findings in a brief report.

4 Close

Quiz

1. Compare and contrast fission and fusion. (Both are atomic reactions that generate vast amounts of energy. Fission, which is presently used to generate energy, is the splitting of an atom. Fusion is the joining of atoms.)
2. How are plants used to produce energy? (Burning wood, crops, and alcohol made from plants are some ways plants are used to produce energy.)

ALTERNATIVE ASSESSMENT

Have students compile a table that lists each fuel mentioned in this chapter and the advantages and disadvantages of using each.

Answers to Review

1. where there are large volumes of falling water
2. Answers may vary. Methods given in text are burning biomass and converting plant material to alcohol that can be burned.
3. Steam and hot water containing geothermal energy can be used to generate electricity. Steam and hot water containing geothermal energy can be used as a direct source of heat.
4. Answers will vary. Any four of the six alternative energy resources featured in this section are acceptable, as are reasonable alternatives not mentioned in this section.

Section 3 Review—California Standards: PE/ATE 6, 6a, 6b

Chapter Highlights

Vocabulary Definitions

Section 1

natural resource any natural substance, organism, or energy form that living things use

renewable resource a natural resource that can be used and replaced over a relatively short time

nonrenewable resource a natural resource that cannot be replaced or that can be replaced only over thousands or millions of years

recycling the use of used or discarded materials that have been reprocessed into new products

Section 2

energy resource a natural resource that can be converted by humans into other forms of energy in order to do useful work

fossil fuel a nonrenewable energy resource that forms in the Earth's crust over millions of years from the buried remains of once-living organisms

petroleum an oily mixture of flammable organic compounds from which liquid fossil fuels and other products are separated; crude oil

natural gas a gaseous fossil fuel

coal a solid fossil fuel formed underground from buried, decomposed plant material

strip mining a process in which rock and soil are stripped from the Earth's surface to expose the underlying materials to be mined

acid precipitation precipitation that contains acids due to air pollution

smog a photochemical fog produced by the action of sunlight on air pollutants

Chapter Highlights

SECTION 1

Vocabulary

natural resource *(p. 108)*
renewable resource *(p. 109)*
nonrenewable resource *(p. 109)*
recycling *(p. 110)*

Section Notes

- Natural resources include everything that is not made by humans and that can be used by organisms.
- Renewable resources, like trees and water, can be replaced in a relatively short period of time.
- Nonrenewable resources cannot be replaced, or they take a very long time to replace.
- Recycling reduces the amount of natural resources that must be obtained from the Earth.

SECTION 2

Vocabulary

energy resource *(p. 111)*
fossil fuel *(p. 111)*
petroleum *(p. 111)*
natural gas *(p. 112)*
coal *(p. 112)*
strip mining *(p. 115)*
acid precipitation *(p. 116)*
smog *(p. 117)*

Section Notes

- Fossil fuels, including petroleum, natural gas, and coal, form from the buried remains of once-living organisms.
- Petroleum and natural gas form mainly from the remains of microscopic sea life.
- Coal forms from decayed swamp plants and varies in quality based on its percentage of carbon.
- Petroleum and natural gas are obtained through drilling, while coal is obtained through mining.
- Obtaining and using fossil fuels can cause many environmental problems, including acid precipitation, water pollution, smog, and the release of excess carbon dioxide.

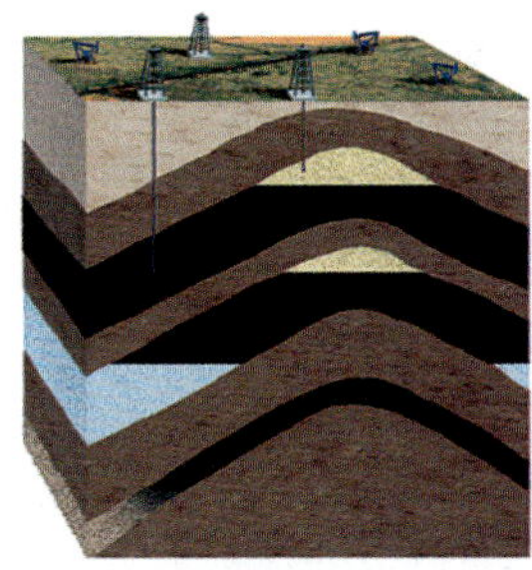

Skills Check

Math Concepts

THE CARBON CONTENT OF COAL Turn back to page 114 to study the process of coal formation. Notice that at each stage, 10% more of the organic material becomes carbon. To calculate the percentage of carbon present at the next stage, just add 10%, or 0.10. For example:

peat → lignite
60% → 70%
$0.60 + 0.10 = 0.70$, or 70%

Visual Understanding

NO DIRECT CONTACT Take another look at Figure 22 on page 121. It is important to realize that the heated liquid inside the solar collector's tubes never comes in direct contact with the water in the tank. Cold water enters the tank, receives heat from the hot, coiled tube, and leaves the tank when someone turns on the hot-water tap.

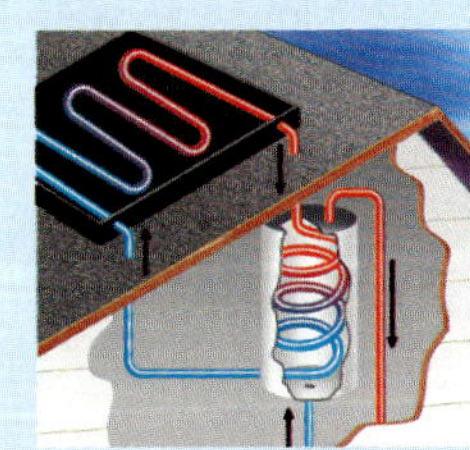

126

Lab and Activity Highlights

LabBook

Make a Water Wheel PG 504

Power of the Sun PG 506

Datasheets for LabBook (blackline masters for these labs)

SECTION 3

Vocabulary

nuclear energy *(p. 118)*
solar energy *(p. 119)*
wind energy *(p. 122)*
hydroelectric energy *(p. 123)*
biomass *(p. 124)*
gasohol *(p. 124)*
geothermal energy *(p. 125)*

Section Notes

- Nuclear energy is most often produced by fission.
- Radioactive wastes and the threat of overheating in nuclear power plants are among the major problems associated with using nuclear energy.
- Solar energy can be converted to electricity by using solar cells.
- Solar energy can be used for direct heating by using solar collectors.
- Solar energy can be converted to electricity on both a small and large scale.
- Although harnessing wind energy is practical only in certain areas, the process produces no air pollutants, and land on wind farms can be used for more than one purpose.
- Hydroelectric energy is inexpensive, renewable, and produces little pollution. However, hydroelectric dams can damage wildlife habitats, create erosion problems, and decrease water quality.
- Plant material and animal dung that contains plant material can be burned to release energy.
- Some plant material can be converted to alcohol. This alcohol can be mixed with gasoline to make a fuel mixture called gasohol.
- Geothermal energy can be harnessed from hot, liquid water and steam that escape through natural vents or through wells drilled into the Earth's crust. This energy can be used for direct heating or can be converted to electricity.

Labs

Make a Water Wheel *(p. 504)*
Power of the Sun *(p. 506)*

internetconnect

GO TO: go.hrw.com

Visit the **HRW** Web site for a variety of learning tools related to this chapter. Just type in the keyword:

KEYWORD: HSTENR

GO TO: www.scilinks.org

Visit the **National Science Teachers Association** on-line Web site for Internet resources related to this chapter. Just type in the ***sci*LINKS** number for more information about the topic:

TOPIC: Natural Resources	***sci*LINKS NUMBER:** HSTE105
TOPIC: Renewable Resources	***sci*LINKS NUMBER:** HSTE110
TOPIC: Nonrenewable Resources	***sci*LINKS NUMBER:** HSTE115
TOPIC: Fossil Fuels	***sci*LINKS NUMBER:** HSTE120

127

VOCABULARY DEFINITIONS, *continued*

SECTION 3

nuclear energy the form of energy associated with changes in the nucleus of an atom; an alternative energy resource

solar energy energy from the sun

wind energy energy in wind

hydroelectric energy electricity produced by falling water

biomass organic matter, such as plants, wood, and waste, that contains stored energy

gasohol a mixture of gasoline and alcohol that is burned as a fuel

geothermal energy energy resulting from the heating of the Earth's crust

Vocabulary Review Worksheet 5

Blackline masters of these Chapter Highlights can be found in the **Study Guide.**

Lab and Activity Highlights

LabBank

Long-Term Projects & Research Ideas, Project 33

Interactive Explorations CD-ROM

CD 1, Exploration 6, "The Generation Gap"

Chapter Review Answers

Using Vocabulary

1. An energy resource is a resource that humans can use to produce energy, while a natural resource is any natural substance, organism, or energy form that living things use.
2. Acid precipitation is formed from the mixing of air pollutants with precipitation, while smog is produced by the action of sunlight on air pollutants.
3. Biomass is organic matter that contains stored energy, while gasohol is a fuel made from plant biomass.
4. Hydroelectric energy is harnessed from falling water, while geothermal energy is harnessed from steam and hot liquid water escaping from the Earth's crust.

Understanding Concepts

Multiple Choice

5. b
6. b
7. b
8. c
9. d
10. a
11. a
12. d
13. c
14. c

Short Answer

15. so we won't use them up faster than they can be replaced
16. Air pollutants mix with moisture in the air, producing acids. These acids fall with rain or snow as acid precipitation.
17. Solar cells are relatively expensive to make.

Chapter Review

USING VOCABULARY

For each pair of terms, explain the difference in their meanings.

1. natural resource/energy resource
2. acid precipitation/smog
3. biomass/gasohol
4. hydroelectric energy/geothermal energy

UNDERSTANDING CONCEPTS

Multiple Choice

5. Of the following, the one that is a renewable resource is
   a. coal.
   b. trees.
   c. oil.
   d. natural gas.

6. All of the following are separated from petroleum except
   a. jet fuel.
   b. lignite.
   c. kerosene.
   d. fuel oil.

7. Which of the following are components of natural gas?
   a. gasohol
   b. methane
   c. kerosene
   d. gasoline

8. Peat, lignite, and anthracite are all stages in the formation of
   a. petroleum.
   b. natural gas.
   c. coal.
   d. gasohol.

9. Which of the following factors contribute to smog problems?
   a. high numbers of automobiles
   b. lots of sunlight
   c. mountains surrounding urban areas
   d. all of the above

10. Which of the following resources produces the least pollution?
    a. solar energy
    b. natural gas
    c. nuclear energy
    d. petroleum

11. Nuclear power plants use a process called ___?___ to produce energy.
    a. fission
    b. fusion
    c. fractionation
    d. None of the above

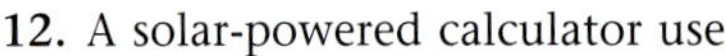

12. A solar-powered calculator uses
    a. solar collectors.
    b. solar panels.
    c. solar mirrors.
    d. solar cells.

13. Which of the following is a problem with using wind energy?
    a. air pollution
    b. amount of land required for wind turbines
    c. limited locations for wind farms
    d. none of the above

14. Dung is a type of
    a. geothermal energy.
    b. gasohol.
    c. biomass.
    d. None of the above

Short Answer

15. Since renewable resources can be replaced, why do we need to conserve them?
16. How does acid precipitation form?
17. If sunlight is free, why is electricity from solar cells expensive?

128

Chapter 5 Review—California Standards: PE/ATE Q1–4: 6b; Q5–18: 6, 6a, 6b, 6c

Concept Mapping

18. Use the following terms to create a concept map: fossil fuels, wind energy, energy resources, biomass, renewable resources, solar energy, nonrenewable resources, natural gas, gasohol, coal, oil.

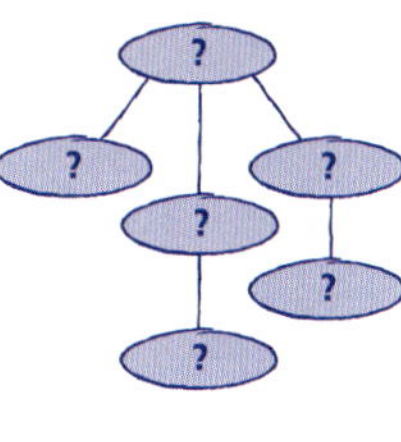

CRITICAL THINKING AND PROBLEM SOLVING

Write one or two sentences to answer the following questions:

19. How would your life be different if all fossil fuels suddenly disappeared?
20. Are fossil fuels really nonrenewable? Explain.
21. What solutions are there for the problems associated with nuclear waste?
22. How could the problems associated with the dams in Washington and local fish populations be solved?
23. What limits might there be on the productivity of a geothermal power plant?

MATH IN SCIENCE

24. Imagine that you are designing a solar car. If you mount solar cells on the underside of the car as well as on the top in direct sunlight, and it takes five times as many cells underneath to generate the same amount of electricity generated by the cells on top, what percentage of the sunlight is reflected back off the pavement?

INTERPRETING GRAPHICS

The chart below shows how various energy resources meet the world's energy needs. Use the chart to answer the following questions:

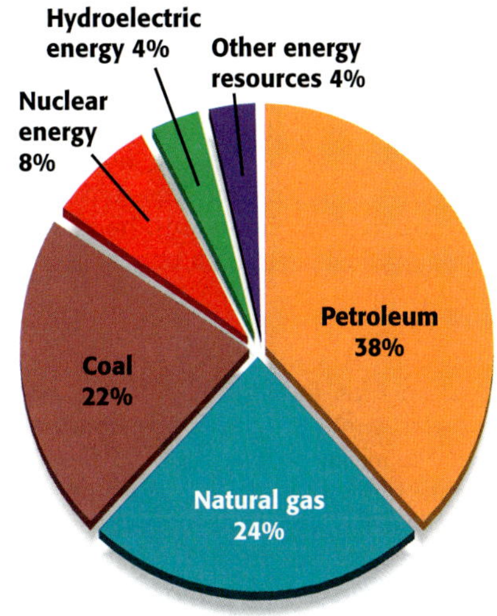

25. What percentage of the world's total energy needs is met by coal? by natural gas? by hydroelectric energy?
26. What percentage of the world's total energy needs is met by fossil fuels?
27. How much more of the world's total energy needs is met by petroleum than by natural gas?

NOW What Do You Think?

Take a minute to review your answers to the ScienceLog questions on page 107. Have your answers changed? If necessary, revise your answers based on what you have learned since you began this chapter.

129

Concept Mapping

18. An answer to this exercise can be found at the end of this book.

Critical Thinking and Problem Solving

19. Answers will vary. Answers should discuss using alternative energy resources.
20. Answers will vary. We label certain resources as nonrenewable because it takes so long for them to be replenished. Fossil fuels (and many other nonrenewable resources) are renewable in the sense that they will probably be renewed in the future. But they cannot be renewed in time for us to count on them as energy resources.
21. Answers will vary. Answers may discuss storing nuclear waste in safe areas or minimizing the use of nuclear energy to avoid producing more radioactive waste.
22. Answers will vary. Answers may discuss modifying the dams to allow fish populations to migrate, decreasing erosion, and improving water quality. Encourage students to research the problems at a library or on the Internet.
23. Answers will vary. Answers may discuss the amount of water and steam available, the amount of energy needed to remove enough steam and water from the ground, and the number of vents the plant uses.

Math in Science

24. 20%

Interpreting Graphics

25. 22%; 24%; 4%
26. 84%
27. 14%

NOW What Do You Think?

1. Answers will vary. Sample answer: coal, petroleum, iron ore, diamonds
2. fossil fuels
3. A solar cell is an individual cell that converts light into electrical energy, while a solar panel is a panel composed of many solar cells wired together.

Concept Mapping Transparency 5

Blackline masters of this Chapter Review can be found in the **Study Guide.**

Chapter 5 Review—California Standards: PE/ATE Q19–23: 6, 6a, 6b; Q25–27: 6; Think: 6, 6a, 6b

Eye on the Environment

Sitting on Your Trash

Background

Petroleum is not important just as a fuel source. It also plays several vital roles in the production and recycling of plastics. First, petroleum is the main component of plastics. Second, petroleum is often used as fuel to provide the energy used in the manufacture of plastic products. If these products are recycled, the melting and reshaping processes require heat and electricity, which may come from the burning of petroleum fuels.

Teaching Strategy

Does your school recycle? If not, work with students to find out how to start a recycling program in your school. This would be a good opportunity to work with other schools in your district by setting up a districtwide program if you don't already have one. If you do have a recycling program, do some research to find out how much is recycled at your school and other schools in your district. Encourage students to recycle at home if they don't already.

Eye on the Environment

Sitting on Your Trash

Did you know that the average person creates about 2 kg of waste every day? About 7 percent of this waste is composed of plastic products that can be recycled. Instead of adding to the landfill problem, why not recycle your plastic trash so you can sit on it? Well you can, you know! Today plastic is recycled into products like picnic tables, park benches, and even high-chairs! But how on Earth does the plastic you throw away become a park bench?

Sort It Out

Once collected and taken to a recycling center, plastic must be sorted. This process involves the coded symbols that are printed on every recyclable plastic product we use. Each product falls into one of two types of plastic—*polyethylene* or *polymer.* The plastic mainly used to make furniture includes the polyethylene plastics called *high density polyethylene,* or HDPE, and *low density polyethylene,* or LDPE. These are items such as milk jugs, detergent bottles, plastic bags, and grocery bags.

Grind It and Wash It

The recycling processes for HDPE and LDPE are fairly simple. Once it reaches the processing facility, HDPE plastic is ground into small flakes about 1 cm in diameter. In the case of LDPE plastic, which are thin films, a special grinder is used to break it down. From that point on, the recycling process is pretty much the same for LDPE and HDPE. The pieces are then washed with hot water and detergent. In this step, dirt and things like labels are removed. After the wash, the flakes are dried with blasts of hot air.

Recycle It!

Some recycling plants sell the recycled flakes. But others may reheat the flakes, change the color by adding a pigment, and then put the material in a *pelletizer.* The little pellets that result are then purchased by a company that molds the pellets into pieces of plastic lumber. This plastic lumber is used to create flowerpots, trash cans, pipes, picnic tables, park benches, toys, mats, and many other products!

From waste…

to plastic lumber…

to a park bench!

Can You Recycle It?

▶ The coded symbol on a plastic container tells you what type of plastic the item is made from, but it doesn't mean that you can recycle it in your area. Find out which plastics can be recycled in your state.

130

Answer to Can You Recycle It?

Answers will vary.

California Standards: PE/ATE 6c

Eureka!

Oil Rush!

You may have heard of the great California gold rush. In 1849, thousands of people moved to the West hoping to strike gold. But you may not have heard about another rush that followed 10 years later. What lured people to northwestern Pennsylvania in 1859? The thrill of striking oil!

Demand for Petroleum

People began using oil as early as 3000 B.C., and oil has been a valuable substance ever since. In Mesopotamia, people used oil to waterproof their ships. The Egyptians and Chinese used oil as a medicine. It was not until the late 1700s and early 1800s that people began to use oil as a fuel. Oil was used to light homes and factories.

Petroleum Collection

But what about the oil in northwestern Pennsylvania? Did people use the oil in Pennsylvania before the rush of 1859? Native Americans were the first to dig pits to collect oil near Titusville, Pennsylvania. Early settlers used the oil as a medicine and as a fuel to light their homes. But their methods for collecting the oil were very inefficient.

The First Oil Well

In 1859, "Colonel" Edwin L. Drake came up with a better method of collecting oil from the ground. Drilling for oil! Drake hired salt-well drillers to burrow to the bedrock where oil deposits lay. But each effort was unsuccessful because water seeped into the wells, causing them to cave in. Then Drake came up with a unique idea that would make him a very wealthy man. Drake suggested that the drillers drive an iron pipe down to the bedrock 21.2 m below the surface. Then they could drill through the inner diameter of the pipe. The morning after the iron pipe was drilled, Drake woke to find that the pipe had filled with oil!

Oil City

Within 3 months, nearly 10,000 people rushed to Oil City, Pennsylvania, in search of the wealth that oil promised. Within 2 years, the small village became a bustling oil town of 50,000 people! In 1861, the first gusher well was drilled nearby, and some 3,000 barrels of oil spouted out daily. Four years later, the first oil pipeline carried crude oil a distance of 8 km.

▲ *Edwin Drake (right) and his friend Peter Wilson (left) in front of Drake Oil Well, near Titusville, Pennsylvania*

Find Out for Yourself!

▶ Drake's oil well was the first well used to collect oil from the ground. Research the oil wells today. How are they similar to Drake's well?

131

Answer to Find Out for Yourself!

Today's oil wells are somewhat similar to Drake's oil well in that they also use a metal pipe. First a hole, or *well bore,* is drilled into the ground. The equivalent of Drake's metal pipe is a metal pipe, or *casing,* that is inserted into the well bore. Cement is pumped through the casing until it reaches the top of the hole by filling the narrow space between the well bore and the casing. Once the cement dries, the casing is bonded to the well bore and prevents the contamination of oil, gas, and water resources that otherwise might flow through the oil well.

Eureka!

Oil Rush!

Background

Until 1880, people in the United States relied on vegetable and animal oils to light their homes. The production of oil products from these sources was time-intensive and costly. Whales, in particular, became rare because they were hunted for their oils during the nineteenth century.

Drake's well ushered in the modern era of the petroleum industry. His drilling methods allowed oil to be collected quickly and inexpensively. By 1900, nearly 64 million barrels of oil had been collected in the United States. Many of Drake's original techniques have been adapted and are still being used today.

In 1896, the first offshore oil drilling operations were started off the coast of California. The operations opened new and potentially lucrative opportunities to oil speculators. By 1938, the first oil platform had been built off the Louisiana coast.

Some experts wonder whether we will face an oil shortage in the near future. Fewer and fewer oil reserves are being discovered. Some people wonder if the recently discovered oil deposits in the Caspian Sea may be fostering the last great oil rush.

Encourage students to consider alternative sources of energy. For example, they may want to investigate the use of solar energy to power cars and heat homes.

California Standards: PE/ATE 6, 6b, 6c

TIMELINE

UNIT 3

The Restless Earth

In this unit, you will learn about the Earth's internal structure. Many mysteries remain because we cannot see very far inside the Earth. The deepest holes we can dig barely scratch the planet's surface. If the Earth were an orange, our attempts to dig into it would not even break through the peel. One way scientists can learn about the Earth's interior is by studying earthquakes and volcanoes. This timeline shows some of the events that have occurred as scientists have tried to understand our dynamic Earth.

1864
Jules Verne's *A Journey to the Center of the Earth* is published. In this fictional story, the heroes enter and exit the Earth through volcanoes.

1883
Krakatau erupts, killing 36,000 people.

1966
A worldwide network of seismographs is established.

1979
Volcanoes are discovered on Io, one of Jupiter's moons.

1980
Mount St. Helens erupts.

1896

Henry Ford builds his first car.

1906

San Francisco burns in the aftermath of an earthquake.

1912

Alfred Wegener proposes his continental-drift theory.

1935

Charles Richter devises a system of measuring the strength of earthquakes.

1951

Color television is introduced in the United States.

1982

Compact discs (CDs) and compact-disc players are made available to the public.

1994

An eight-legged robot named *Dante II* descends into the crater of an active volcano in Alaska.

1997

The population of the Caribbean island of Montserrat dwindles to less than half its original size as frequent eruptions of the Soufriere Hills volcano force evacuations.

Chapter Organizer

CHAPTER ORGANIZATION	TIME MINUTES	OBJECTIVES	LABS, INVESTIGATIONS, AND DEMONSTRATIONS
Chapter Opener pp. 134–135	45	California Standards: PE/ATE 1, 1e, 7, 7b	**Investigate!** Continental Collisions, p. 135
Section 1 Inside the Earth	90	▶ Identify and describe the layers of the Earth by what they are made of. ▶ Identify and describe the layers of the Earth by their physical properties. ▶ Define *tectonic plate.* ▶ Explain how scientists know about the structure of Earth's interior. PE/ATE 1b, 1g, 3a, 7, 7e, 7f	**QuickLab,** Floating Mountains, p. 141 **Labs You Can Eat,** Rescue Near the Center of the Earth, Lab 13 **Whiz-Bang Demonstrations,** Thar She Blows! Demo 18
Section 2 Restless Continents	90	▶ Describe Wegener's theory of continental drift, and explain why it was not accepted at first. ▶ Explain how sea-floor spreading provides a way for continents to move. ▶ Describe how new oceanic crust forms at mid-ocean ridges. ▶ Explain how magnetic reversals provide evidence for sea-floor spreading. PE/ATE 1, 1a, 7f	**Labs You Can Eat,** Cracks in the Hard-Boiled Earth, Lab 14
Section 3 The Theory of Plate Tectonics	90	▶ Describe the three forces thought to move tectonic plates. ▶ Describe the three types of tectonic plate boundaries. ▶ Explain how scientists measure the rate at which tectonic plates move. PE/ATE 1, 1a, 1c–1f, 4c, 6, 6a, 6b, 7f; LabBook 1, 1b, 1c, 7, 7b	**Demonstration,** p. 147 in ATE **Making Models,** Convection Connection, p. 508 **Datasheets for LabBook,** Convection Connection, Datasheet 12 **Labs You Can Eat,** Dough Fault of Your Own, Lab 15
Section 4 Deforming the Earth's Crust	90	▶ Describe major types of folds. ▶ Explain how the three major types of faults differ. ▶ Name and describe the most common types of mountains. ▶ Explain how various types of mountains form. PE/ATE 1, 1a, 1e, 1f, 6, 6a, 6b; LabBook 1, 1e, 7, 7b, 7d, 7e	**Demonstration,** p. 151 in ATE **Making Models,** Oh, the Pressure! p. 509 **Datasheets for LabBook,** Oh, the Pressure! Datasheet 13 **Long-Term Projects & Research Ideas,** Project 35

See page **T20** *for a complete correlation of this book with the*

CALIFORNIA SCIENCE CONTENT STANDARDS.

Correlations are also provided at point of use throughout this ATE.

TECHNOLOGY RESOURCES

Guided Reading Audio CD
English or Spanish, Chapter 6

Classroom Management CD-ROM

Earth Science Videodiscs

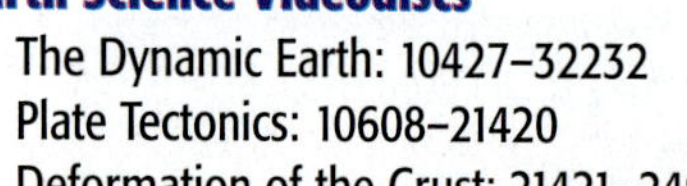
The Dynamic Earth: 10427–32232
Plate Tectonics: 10608–21420
Deformation of the Crust: 21421–24901

CNN **Scientists in Action,** Studying Sea Floor Tectonics, Segment 10

Test Generator CD-ROM

Chapter 6 • Plate Tectonics

CLASSROOM WORKSHEETS, TRANSPARENCIES, AND RESOURCES	SCIENCE INTEGRATION AND CONNECTIONS	REVIEW AND ASSESSMENT
Directed Reading Worksheet 6 **Science Puzzlers, Twisters & Teasers,** Worksheet 6		
Transparency 101, The Composition of the Earth **Directed Reading Worksheet 6,** Section 1 **Transparency 102,** The Earth's Crust, Lithosphere, and Asthenosphere **Transparency 103,** Tectonic Plates **Transparency 103,** Close-up of a Tectonic Plate **Reinforcement Worksheet 6,** The Layered Earth **Critical Thinking Worksheet 6,** Planet of Waves	**Math and More,** p. 137 in ATE **Connect to Physical Science,** p. 137 in ATE **MathBreak,** Using Models, p. 138 **Connect to Physical Science,** p. 138 in ATE **Life Science Connection,** p. 139 **Cross-Disciplinary Focus,** p. 140 in ATE **Multicultural Connection,** p. 141 in ATE	**Review,** p. 142 **Quiz,** p. 142 in ATE **Alternative Assessment,** p. 142 in ATE
Directed Reading Worksheet 6, Section 2 **Transparency 33,** Evolution of the Galápagos Finches **Transparency 104,** The Breakup of Pangaea	**Connect to Life Science,** p. 144 in ATE **Connect to Physical Science,** p. 145 in ATE **Physical Science Connection,** p. 146	**Review,** p. 146 **Quiz,** p. 146 in ATE **Alternative Assessment,** p. 146 in ATE
Teaching Transparencies 105–107 **Directed Reading Worksheet 6,** Section 3 **Math Skills for Science Worksheet 4,** A Shortcut for Multiplying Large Numbers **Reinforcement Worksheet 6,** A Moving Jigsaw Puzzle	**Cross-Disciplinary Focus,** p. 148 in ATE **Math and More,** p. 149 in ATE **Science, Technology, and Society:** Living on the Mid-Atlantic Ridge, p. 162 **Scientific Debate:** Continental Drift, p. 163	**Homework,** p. 149 in ATE **Review,** p. 150 **Quiz,** p. 150 in ATE **Alternative Assessment,** p. 150 in ATE
Directed Reading Worksheet 6, Section 4	**Cross-Disciplinary Focus,** p. 152 in ATE **Connect to Life Science,** p. 153 in ATE **Apply,** p. 154 **Multicultural Connection,** pp. 155, 157 in ATE **Connect to Astronomy,** p. 155 in ATE	**Homework,** p. 152 in ATE **Self-Check,** p. 153 **Review,** p. 157 **Quiz,** p. 157 in ATE **Alternative Assessment,** p. 157 in ATE

Holt, Rinehart and Winston On-line Resources

go.hrw.com

For worksheets and other teaching aids related to this chapter, visit the HRW Web site and type in the keyword: **HSTTEC**

National Science Teachers Association

www.scilinks.org

Encourage students to use the keywords listed on the Technology Highlights page to access information and resources on the **NSTA** Web site.

END-OF-CHAPTER REVIEW AND ASSESSMENT

Chapter Review in Study Guide
Vocabulary and Notes in Study Guide
Chapter Tests with Performance-Based Assessment, Chapter 6 Test, Performance-Based Assessment 6
Concept Mapping Transparency 6

Chapter Resources & Worksheets

Visual Resources

TEACHING TRANSPARENCIES

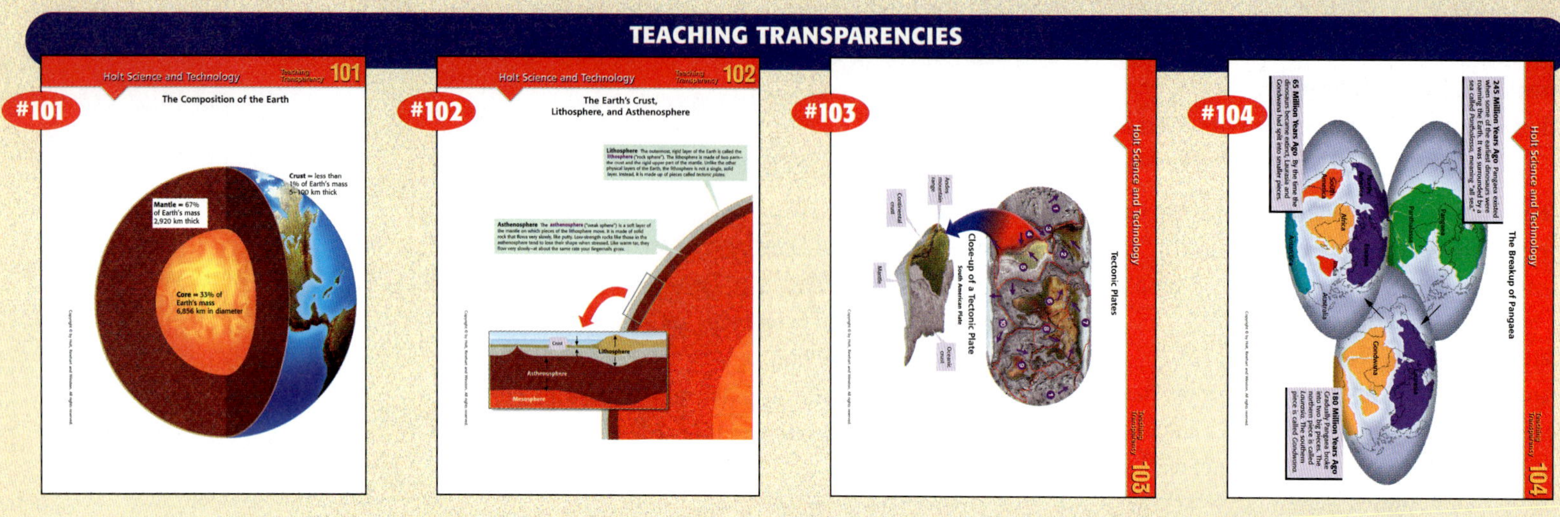

TEACHING TRANSPARENCIES

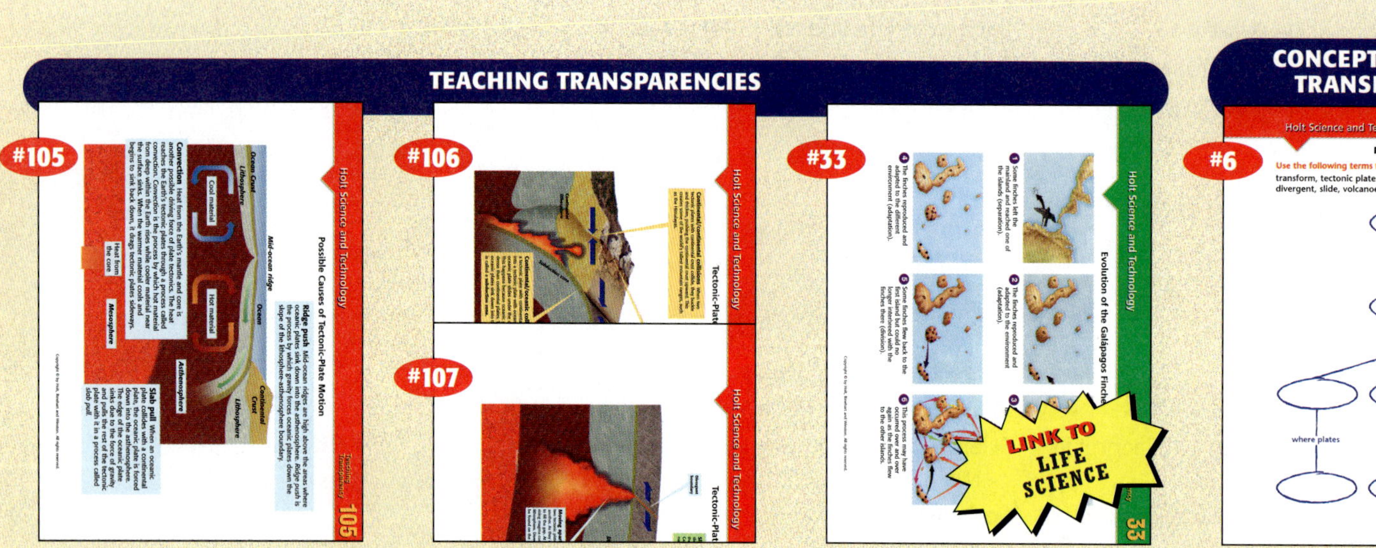

CONCEPT MAPPING TRANSPARENCY

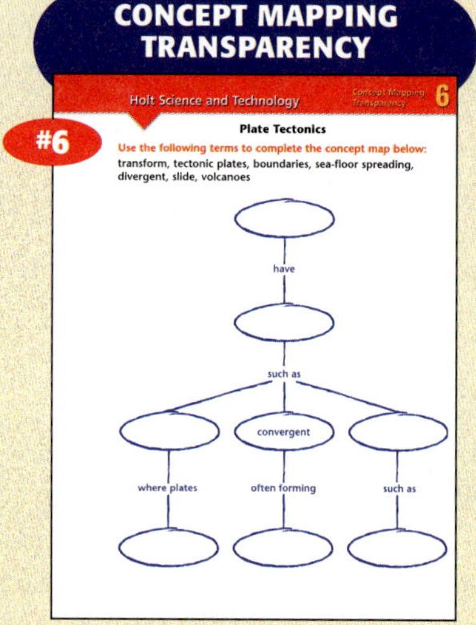

Meeting Individual Needs

DIRECTED READING

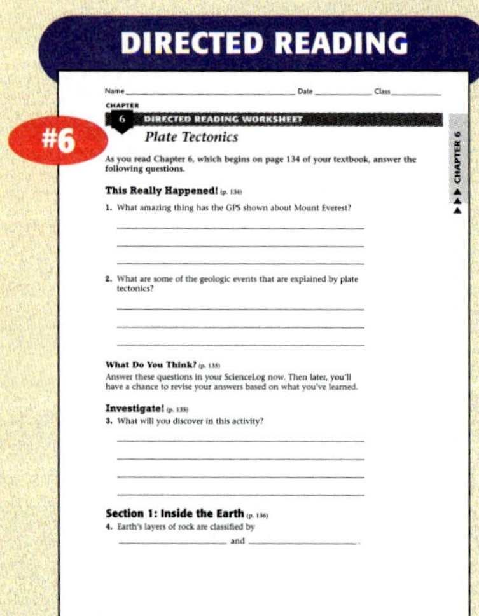

REINFORCEMENT & VOCABULARY REVIEW

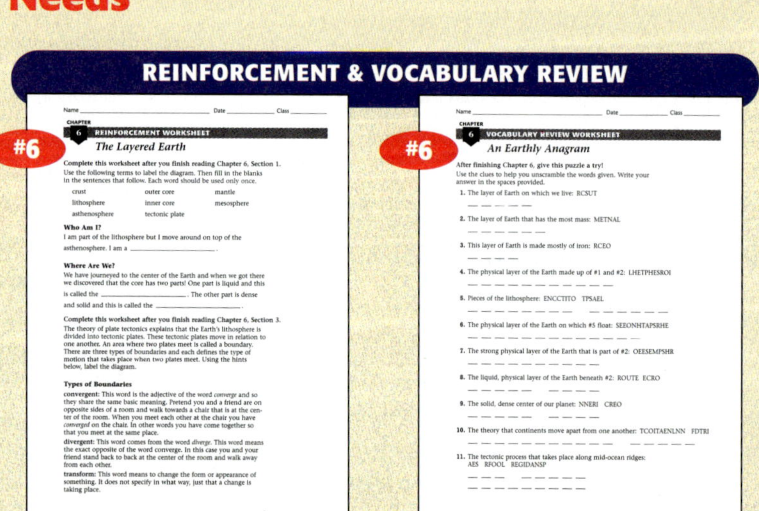

SCIENCE PUZZLERS, TWISTERS & TEASERS

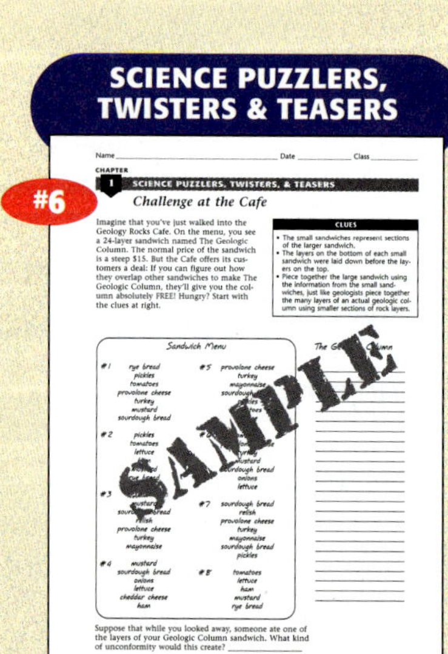

Review & Assessment

STUDY GUIDE

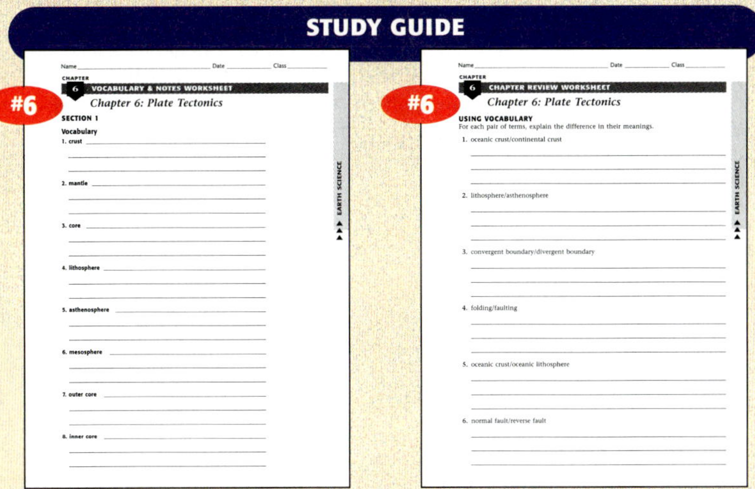
#6 — Chapter 6 Vocabulary & Notes Worksheet: *Chapter 6: Plate Tectonics*

Section 1 Vocabulary: 1. crust 2. mantle 3. core 4. lithosphere 5. asthenosphere 6. mesosphere 7. outer core 8. inner core

#6 — Chapter Review Worksheet: *Chapter 6: Plate Tectonics*

Using Vocabulary: For each pair of terms, explain the difference in their meanings.

1. oceanic crust/continental crust
2. lithosphere/asthenosphere
3. convergent boundary/divergent boundary
4. folding/faulting
5. oceanic crust/oceanic lithosphere
6. normal fault/reverse fault

CHAPTER TESTS WITH PERFORMANCE-BASED ASSESSMENT

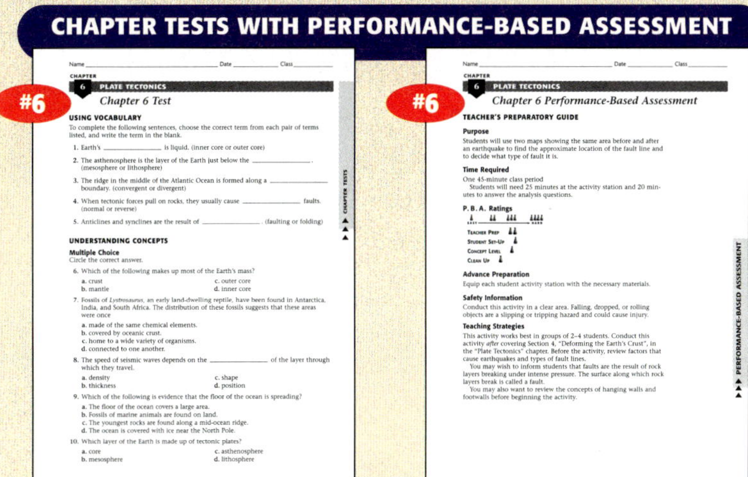
#6 — Plate Tectonics: *Chapter 6 Test*

#6 — Plate Tectonics: *Chapter 6 Performance-Based Assessment*

Lab Worksheets

LABS YOU CAN EAT

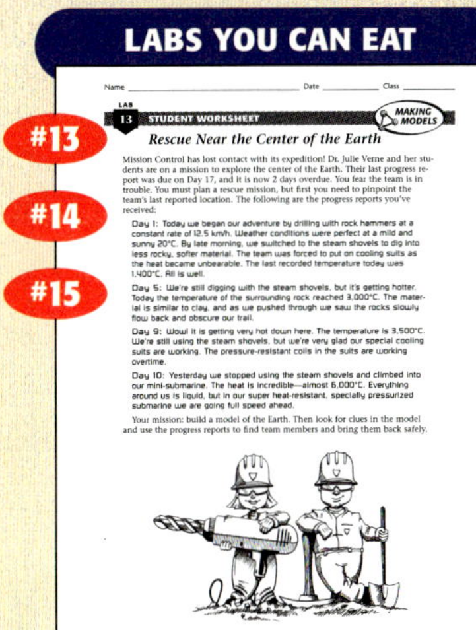
#13 — Lab 13 Student Worksheet (Making Models): *Rescue Near the Center of the Earth*

#14

#15

WHIZ-BANG DEMONSTRATIONS

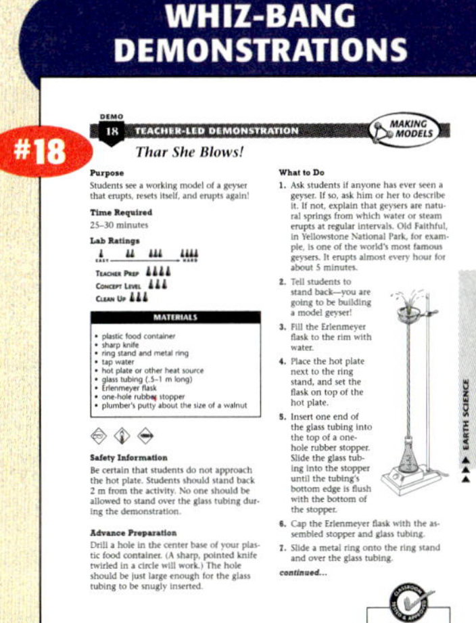
#18 — Demo 18 Teacher-Led Demonstration (Making Models): *Thar She Blows!*

LONG-TERM PROJECTS & RESEARCH IDEAS

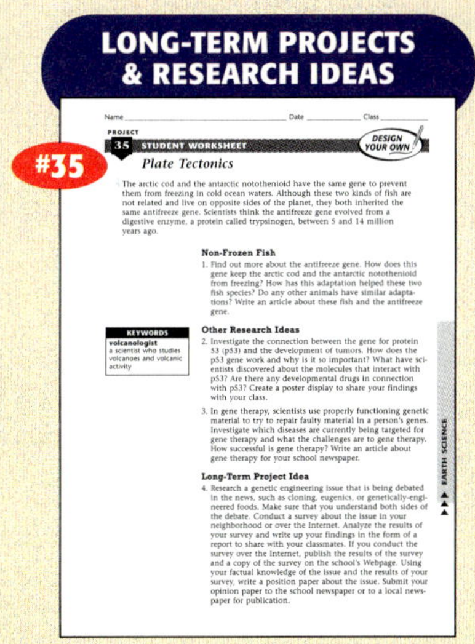
#35 — Project 35 Student Worksheet (Design Your Own): *Plate Tectonics*

DATASHEETS FOR LABBOOK

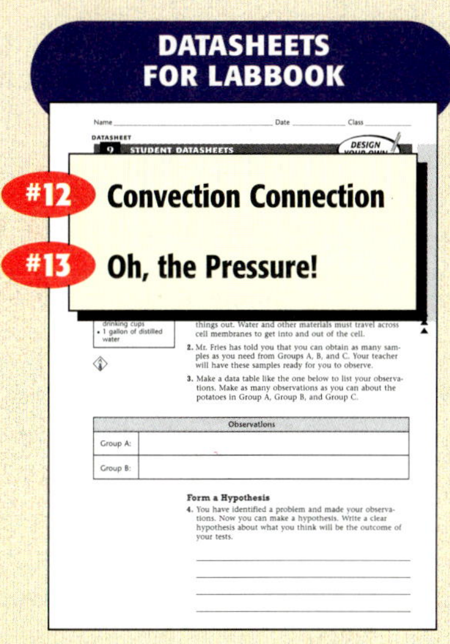
#12 Convection Connection

#13 Oh, the Pressure!

Applications & Extensions

CRITICAL THINKING & PROBLEM SOLVING

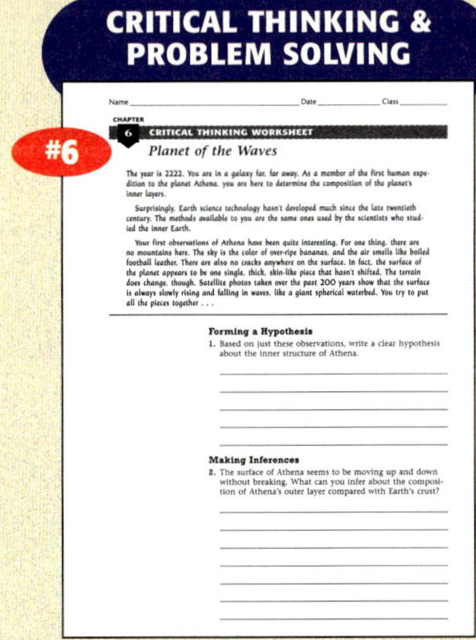
#6 — Chapter 6 Critical Thinking Worksheet: *Planet of the Waves*

SCIENTISTS IN ACTION

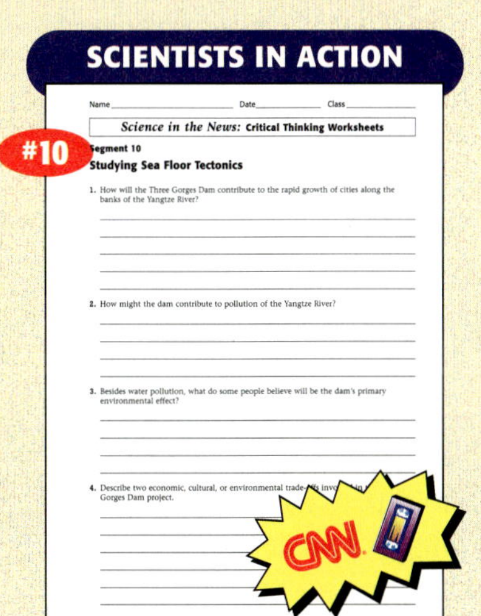
#10 — *Science in the News:* Critical Thinking Worksheets — Segment 10: Studying Sea Floor Tectonics

1. How will the Three Gorges Dam contribute to the rapid growth of cities along the banks of the Yangtze River?
2. How might the dam contribute to pollution of the Yangtze River?
3. Besides water pollution, what do some people believe will be the dam's primary environmental effect?
4. Describe two economic, cultural, or environmental trade-offs involved in the Three Gorges Dam project.

Chapter Background

Section 1

Inside the Earth

▶ Continents and the Earth's Crust

Continents are large, continuous landmasses composed of crust that is generally much older than the surrounding oceanic crust. The core of a continent, called a craton, is generally composed of ancient, crystalline igneous and metamorphic rock. Cratons are relatively thick and make up the most stable part of continents. They range from 200 million to 3.9 billion years of age.

▶ Heat Within the Earth

The Earth's internal heat contributes to the process of differentiation—the division of the Earth into layers with distinct characteristics. This heat has three main sources:

- the decay of radioactive elements
- the differentiation of the Earth's interior
- leftover energy from the accretion and compression of particles that coalesced to form Earth

▶ Earth's Inner Core

Research conducted in 1996 suggests that the solid inner core of the Earth spins faster than the rest of the planet. This 2,456 km wide ball of hot iron moves at a speed that would allow it to lap Earth's surface once every 400 years. This information may give scientists clues about how the Earth formed.

- The Earth's outer core is a hot, electrically conducting liquid thought to be continuously moved by convection. This layer's conductivity combines with the differential spin of the Earth's inner core to create powerful electric currents that, in turn, generate the Earth's magnetic field.

IS THAT A FACT!

- Earth's magnetic poles have reversed more than 177 times in the last 85 million years. The most recent switch occurred within the last 2 million years. With complex computer models, scientists are beginning to understand how this process happens, but they are still unable to predict the next time the poles will reverse or how life on Earth will be affected by this change.

Section 2

Restless Continents

▶ Continental Drift: An Old Idea

The idea that the continents were once joined together was not a new idea in Alfred Wegener's time. In 1620, Francis Bacon noted that the continents seemed to fit together like a jigsaw puzzle, but no one could understand how they moved. In 1858, a French scientist named Antonio Snider-Pellegrini cited fossil evidence that suggested the continents had been joined. Wegener's studies in 1915 were the first exhaustive research on the topic, combining evidence from many disciplines. In 1958, an American geologist named Frank Taylor pointed out geologic similarities between South America and Africa. But neither scientist could explain how the continents had separated, and their observations were dismissed. It was not until the discovery of sea-floor spreading that the continental drift hypothesis was accepted.

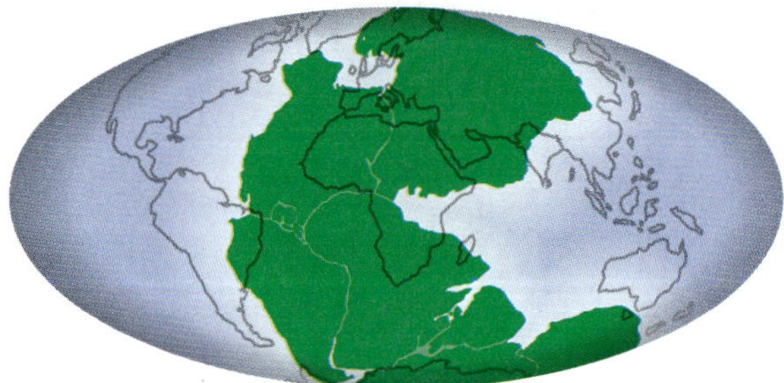

▶ Testing the Continental Drift Hypothesis

After sea-floor spreading was discovered in the 1960s, research groups tested Wegener's hypothesis using as many methods as possible:

- The edges of continental slopes were mapped with sonar and shown to fit together even better than the coastlines did.

- New radiometric dating methods showed that rocks in corresponding parts of Africa and South America formed at the same time.
- The dating of igneous rocks around mid-ocean ridges showed a symmetrical pattern, with older rocks located farther away from the rifts. Few rocks older than 180 million years were discovered on the ocean floor. This indicates that the oceanic lithosphere is continuously recycled.
- Scientists found that zones of magnetic reversals also followed a symmetrical pattern on either side of mid-ocean ridges, matching the pattern revealed by the ages of those rocks.
- The magnetic reversals recorded horizontally in the ocean floor matched those recorded in vertical sequences of lava flows on continents.

Harry Hammond Hess (1906–1969)

Henry Hess was an American geologist who proposed the idea of sea-floor spreading in 1960, thus playing a key role in developing the theory of plate tectonics. Hess suggested that convection within the Earth was continuously creating new ocean floor at the mid-ocean ridges. He also theorized that rocks would be older at increasing distances from these ridges, an expectation confirmed by research beginning in 1963. Hess also correctly explained the subduction of oceanic crust beneath less dense continental crust.

SECTION 3

The Theory of Plate Tectonics

Trenches

Where an oceanic plate subducts under another tectonic plate, a long, steep-sided trench forms on the sea floor. On average, subduction trenches are 2,000–4,000 m lower than the rest of the ocean floor. Nevertheless, some animals are capable of living in the cold, pressurized depths of ocean trenches, including species of sea cucumbers, sea anemones, and marine worms.

IS THAT A FACT!

- The Mariana Trench, which is 2,500 km long and 11,035 m below sea level at its deepest, is the deepest known point on Earth. This trench is located where the Pacific plate is subducted beneath the Philippine plate.

SECTION 4

Deforming the Earth's Crust

Fault Versus Fold

Tectonic activity exerts a tremendous amount of pressure on crustal rocks; whether they bend or break depends on several factors:

- type of stress—If stress is applied gradually, rocks often fold; if stress is applied suddenly, rocks tend to fault.
- composition of rock—Brittle rocks, such as sandstone, tend to break; ductile (easily bent) rocks, such as shale, tend to fold.
- temperature—As the temperature at the point of stress increases, rocks are more likely to fold rather than fault.

For additional background resources, please refer to the ***HST Reference Library.***

CHAPTER 6

Plate Tectonics

CHAPTER 6

Plate Tectonics

This Really Happened!

It was a grueling climb to the top of Mount Everest. The temperature was well below freezing, and the blinding snow made it difficult to see. These harsh conditions and the extreme altitude are what make Mount Everest one of the most difficult mountains to climb. But these conditions did not stop a professional mountain climber by the name of Wally Berg. He was on a mission—a scientific mission that had been years in the planning.

Once at the top of the world's highest mountain, some 8,848 m high, Wally began drilling a hole in the rock. At this altitude the air is so thin that even easy tasks are difficult to accomplish. Wally brought bottles of oxygen with him to make his breathing easier.

Why did Wally drill a hole in Mount Everest? He needed the hole in order to secure a special device that receives and records signals from a network of satellites called the Global Positioning System (GPS).

GPS can pinpoint the exact location of these special receivers over long periods of time. In analyzing GPS data, scientists found out that Mount Everest not only is moving but also is growing taller every year. Over a year's time, the mountain moves northeast about 27 mm and grows from 3 to 5 mm taller!

Why is Mount Everest moving and growing? The answer is *plate tectonics.* Plate tectonics is also the reason why California has so many earthquakes and why volcanoes are found all around the rim of the Pacific Ocean. Get ready to learn much more about plate tectonics in this chapter.

134

This Really Happened!

Mount Everest is part of the Himalaya mountain range. Thirty-five of the highest peaks in the world are in the Himalayas. The Himalayas and Hindu Kush form a chain of mountains 3,862 km in length. These relatively young mountains began to form about 40 million years ago when the Indian plate collided with the Eurasian plate.

Directed Reading Worksheet 6

Science Puzzlers, Twisters & Teasers Worksheet 6

Guided Reading Audio CD
English or Spanish, Chapter 6

What Do You Think?

In your ScienceLog, try to answer the following questions based on what you already know:

1. Why do entire mountain ranges move?
2. How do mountains form?

Continental Collisions

Believe it or not, continents not only move but also sometimes crash into each other. For the past 40 to 60 million years, the Indian subcontinent has been colliding with the Eurasian continent. As these continents push against each other, they buckle and bend. As a result, the Himalaya Mountains, where Mount Everest is located, are still forming today. In this investigation you will create a model to help explain how the Himalaya Mountains formed.

Procedure 

1. Cut a 7 cm long slit in a large piece of **cardboard** about 6 cm from one edge of the cardboard. Cut the slit wide enough so that a 50 cm long strip of **adding-machine paper** will feed through it.
2. Use **tape** to secure a small **wood block** next to the slit, between the slit and the edge of the cardboard. Tape another small **wood block** to one end of the adding-machine paper. Both blocks should be parallel to each other.
3. Cut eight identical strips about 8 cm wide and 15 to 20 cm long from several **paper napkins.**
4. Stack the napkin strips on top of each other.
5. Place the napkin strips on the adding-machine paper next to the wood block.
6. Attach the napkin strips to the adding-machine paper using two **bobby pins,** one at each end of the strips.
7. Push the end of the adding-machine paper through the slit in the cardboard until the napkin strips rest against the wood block you attached to the cardboard. Hold the cardboard at about eye level, and pull gently and slowly downward on the paper strip.

Analysis

8. What happens as the paper napkin strips come in contact with the block of wood?
9. What happens as you continue to pull downward on the strip of paper?
10. How does this model represent what is happening between India and Eurasia?

What Do You Think?

Accept all reasonable responses.

Students will have a chance to revise their answers in the Chapter Review under NOW What Do You Think?

Investigate!

MATERIALS

For Each Student:
- cardboard
- adding-machine paper
- tape
- two small wood blocks
- paper napkins
- two bobby pins

Safety Caution: Remind students to review all safety cautions and icons before beginning this lab activity.

Answers to Investigate!

8. They begin to crumple up.
9. The napkins make folds that become squeezed together.
10. The stationary block represents the Eurasian continent, while the moving block represents the Indian continent crashing into the Eurasian continent. The folded and crumpled napkins represent the Himalaya Mountains, which formed as a result of the collision between these two continents.

IS THAT A FACT!

Variations in the Earth's surface, such as tall mountains, seem enormous from our vantage point. But when you consider the Earth as a whole, the mountain heights and ocean depths are just tiny bumps and scratches on the planet's surface. If you had a model of the Earth the size of a beach ball and you rubbed your hand over the surface, you would barely feel the changes in elevation.

SECTION 1

Focus

Inside the Earth

This section describes the classification of the Earth according to composition (crust, mantle, and core) and according to physical structure (lithosphere, asthenosphere, mesosphere, outer core, and inner core). Students then learn about *tectonic plates*. The section concludes with a discussion of how scientists study seismic waves to map the Earth's interior.

Bellringer

On the board or an overhead projector, pose the following question to your students at the beginning of class:

If you journeyed to the center of the Earth, what do you think you would see along the way?

Have students draw an illustration of their journey in their ScienceLog. Sheltered English

1) Motivate

COOPERATIVE LEARNING

Pose the following situation to small groups of students for discussion: Measurements show that the land west of the San Andreas Fault, in California, is moving toward the northwest at a rate of 5 cm per year relative to the land east of the fault. What forces do you think cause this movement? Where do these forces come from? When groups agree on a hypothesis, have them create illustrations or a model they can use to explain their theory to the class.

1

NEW TERMS

crust, mantle, core, lithosphere, tectonic plates, asthenosphere, mesosphere, outer core, inner core

OBJECTIVES

- Identify and describe the layers of the Earth by what they are made of.
- Identify and describe the layers of the Earth by their physical properties.
- Define *tectonic plate.*
- Explain how scientists know about the structure of Earth's interior.

Inside the Earth

The Earth is not just a ball of solid rock. It is made of several layers with different physical properties and compositions. As you will discover, there are two ways scientists think about the Earth's layers—by their *composition* and by their *physical properties.*

The layers of the Earth are made of different mixtures of elements. This is what is meant by differences in composition. Many of the Earth's layers also have different physical properties. Physical properties include temperature, density, and ability to flow. Let's first take a look at the composition of the Earth.

The Composition of the Earth

The Earth is divided into three layers—the *crust, mantle,* and *core*—based on what each one is made of. The lightest materials make up the outermost layer, and the densest materials make up the inner layers. This is because lighter materials tend to float up, while heavier materials sink. First let's take a look at the outer layer, the Earth's crust.

The Crust The **crust** is the outermost layer of the Earth. Ranging from 5 to 100 km thick, it is also the thinnest layer of the Earth. And because it is the layer we live on, we know more about this layer than we know about the other two.

There are two types of crust—continental and oceanic. *Continental crust* has a composition similar to granite. It has an average thickness of 30 km. In some mountainous areas continental crust is as much as 100 km thick. *Oceanic crust* has a composition similar to basalt. It is generally between 5 and 8 km thick. Because basalt is denser than granite, oceanic crust is denser than continental crust.

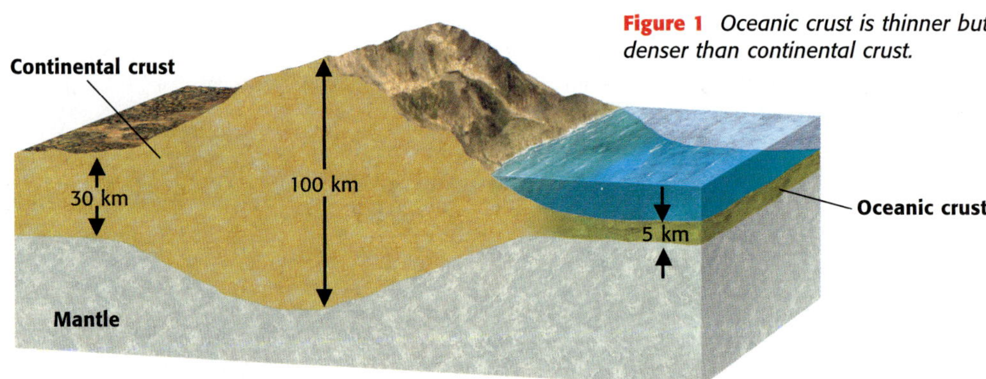

Figure 1 *Oceanic crust is thinner but denser than continental crust.*

136

Teaching Transparency 101 "The Composition of the Earth"

Directed Reading Worksheet 6 Section 1

Section 1–California Standards: PE/ATE 1b, 1c, 1g, 3a, 7, 7e, 7f

The Mantle The **mantle** is the layer of the Earth between the crust and the core. Compared with the crust, the mantle is extremely thick. The mantle is about 2,900 km thick and contains most of the Earth's mass.

No one has ever seen what the mantle really looks like. It is just too far down to drill for a sample. Scientists must infer what the composition and other characteristics of the mantle are from observations they make on the Earth's surface. In some places mantle rock has been pushed up to the surface by tectonic forces, allowing scientists to observe the rock directly.

As you can see in **Figure 2,** one place scientists look is on the ocean floor, where molten rock from the mantle flows out of active volcanoes. These underwater volcanoes are like windows through the crust into the mantle. The "windows" have given us strong clues about the composition of the mantle. Scientists have learned that the mantle's composition is similar to that of the mineral olivine, which has large amounts of iron and magnesium compared with other common minerals.

Figure 2 *Volcanic vents on the ocean floor, such as this one off the coast of Hawaii, allow magma to escape from the mantle beneath oceanic crust.*

The Core By studying the different layers that make up the Earth, geologists can get an idea of which elements each is made of. They think that the Earth's *core* is made mostly of iron, with smaller amounts of nickel and possibly some sulfur and oxygen. The **core** extends from the bottom of the mantle to the center of the Earth. The diameter of the core is about 6,856 km. As you can see in **Figure 3,** at 6,787 km, the diameter of the planet Mars is slightly smaller than that of the Earth's core.

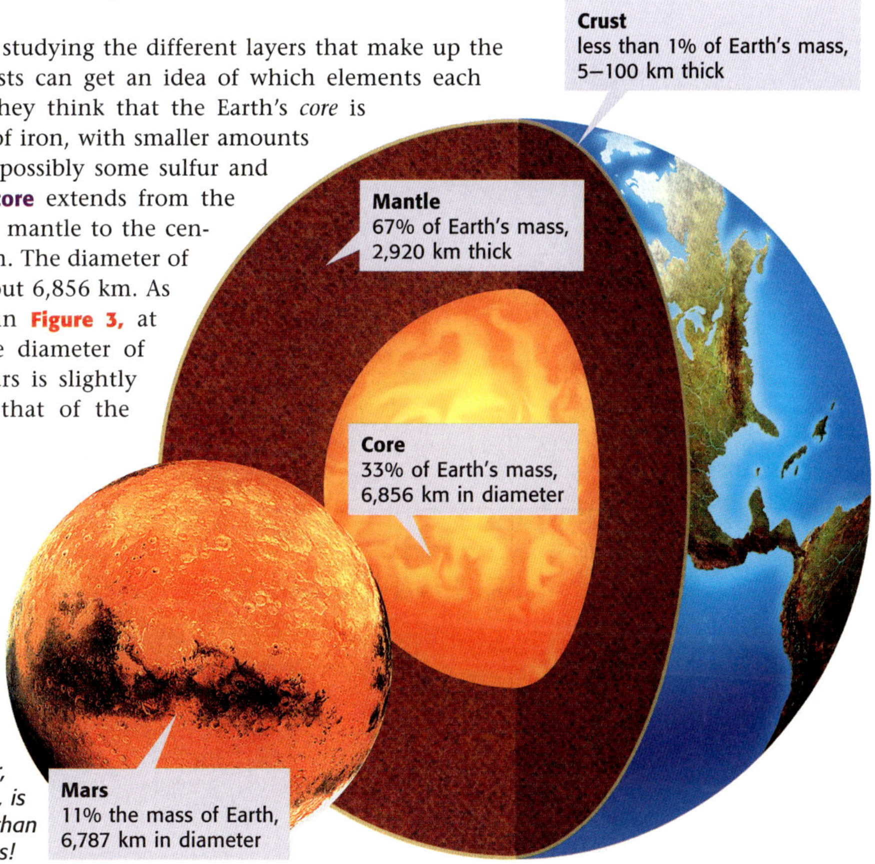

Crust
less than 1% of Earth's mass, 5–100 km thick

Mantle
67% of Earth's mass, 2,920 km thick

Core
33% of Earth's mass, 6,856 km in diameter

Mars
11% the mass of Earth, 6,787 km in diameter

Figure 3 *The Earth is made up of three layers, as shown here. The inner layer, called the core, is slightly larger than the planet Mars!*

137

2 Teach

Using the Figure

Discuss scale models with students, and point out that the illustrations showing cross sections of the Earth in Sections 1 and 2 are drawn to scale. These include **Figures 1, 3, 6, 12,** and **13.** Have students identify illustrations in the text that are not drawn to scale.

MATH and MORE

Tell students to assume that the average thickness for the crust is 50 km, and have them calculate how much thicker the mantle is than the crust. Invite volunteers to write their calculations on the board. (2,900 km ÷ 50 = 58 km; the mantle is 58 times thicker than the crust.)

CONNECT TO PHYSICAL SCIENCE

Use **Figure 3** to discuss the relationship between mass, volume, and density. Notice that the Earth's core, although similar in size (volume) to the planet Mars, is much more massive than Mars. This is because the Earth's core is very dense compared with the core of Mars. The Earth's core is composed mostly of iron, which is much denser than the mantle and crustal rocks that make up the rest of the Earth.

IS THAT A FACT!

Two lines of evidence indicate that Earth's core is a mixture of iron and nickel. The core's density, which is similar to a mixture of iron and nickel, was determined by studying the way seismic waves travel through it. The Earth's magnetic field also suggests this composition.

Explain the differences between radius, diameter, and thickness. In **Figure 3,** the crust and mantle are shells measured by their thickness. The core is a sphere, so it is measured by its diameter or radius. Note that the radius of a shell is always larger than its thickness, as can be shown using the diagram on the following two pages.

2 Teach, continued

READING STRATEGY

Prediction Guide Before students read this page, ask them the following question: If you could burrow to the center of the Earth, what would you expect to happen to the pressure, the temperature, and the solidity of matter? Each successive layer will:

a. become hotter, have higher pressure, and become more liquid

b. become cooler, have higher pressure, and become harder

c. become hotter, have lower pressure, and become more liquid

d. become hotter and have higher pressure; the solidity of layers will depend on temperature and pressure

(answer: d)

CONNECT TO PHYSICAL SCIENCE

The composition of the core is probably similar throughout. Why, then, is part of the core liquid and the rest solid? You would think that if the outer core were hot enough to be in a liquid state, the inner core would be at least as hot if not hotter. The difference in physical states is due not to temperature but to differences in pressure. Even though the inner core is extremely hot, the high pressure keeps the material in a solid state. The outer core, on the other hand, has less pressure. The pressure in the outer core is just low enough that the hot iron can stay in a liquid state.

MATH BREAK

Using Models

Imagine that you are building a model of the Earth that is going to have a radius of 1 m in diameter. You find out that the average radius of the Earth is 6,378 km and that the thickness of the lithosphere is about 150 km. What percentage of the Earth's radius is the lithosphere? How thick (in centimeters) would you make the lithosphere in your model?

The Structure of the Earth

So far we have talked about the composition of the Earth. Another way to look at how the Earth is made is to examine the physical properties of its layers. The Earth is divided into five main physical layers—the *lithosphere, asthenosphere, mesosphere, outer core,* and *inner core.* As shown below, each layer has its own set of physical properties.

Lithosphere The outermost, rigid layer of the Earth is called the **lithosphere** ("rock sphere"). The lithosphere is made of two parts—the crust and the rigid upper part of the mantle. Unlike the other physical layers of the Earth, the lithosphere is not a single, solid layer. Instead, it is made up of pieces called *tectonic plates.*

Asthenosphere The **asthenosphere** ("weak sphere") is a soft layer of the mantle on which pieces of the lithosphere move. It is made of solid rock that flows very slowly, like putty. Low-strength rocks like those in the asthenosphere tend to lose their shape when stressed. Like warm tar, they flow very slowly—at about the same rate your fingernails grow.

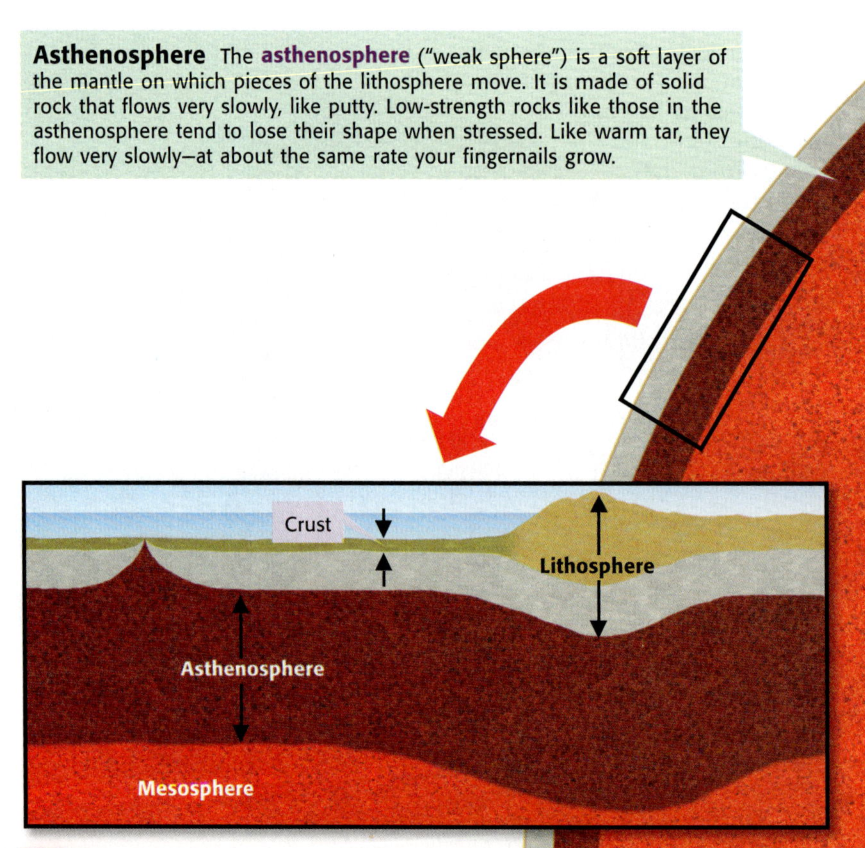

Answers to MATHBREAK

$\frac{150 \text{ km}}{6{,}378 \text{ km}} = 0.0235 = 2.35\%$

$2.35\% \times 1.00 \text{ m} = 0.0235 \text{ m}$, or 2.35 cm

Be sure students understand that the two systems of naming Earth's layers describe different properties. *Crust, mantle,* and *core* describe differences in chemical makeup; *lithosphere, asthenosphere, mesosphere, outer core,* and *inner core* describe differences in temperature and pressure and, therefore, physical properties.

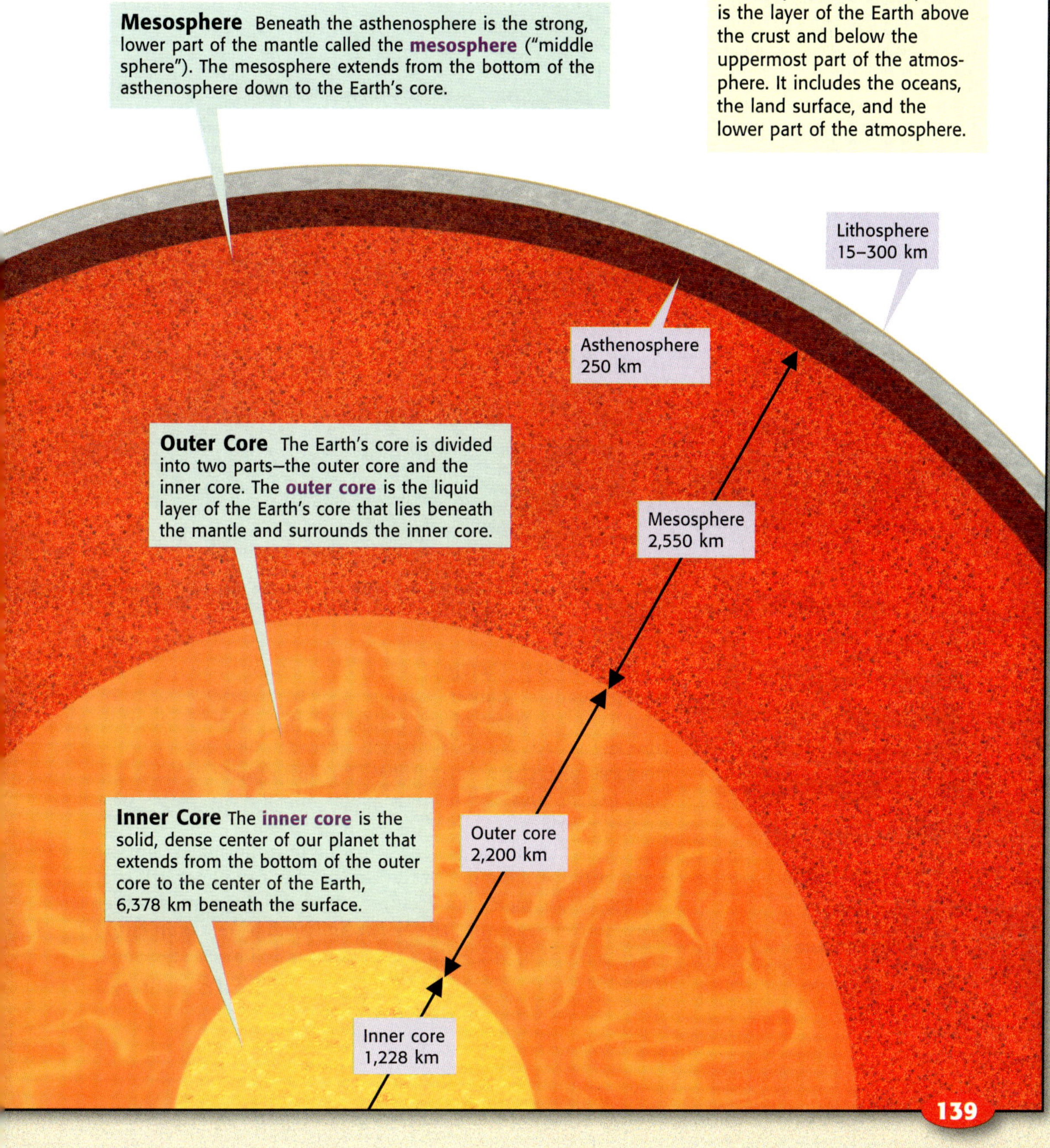

Mesosphere Beneath the asthenosphere is the strong, lower part of the mantle called the **mesosphere** ("middle sphere"). The mesosphere extends from the bottom of the asthenosphere down to the Earth's core.

Scientists call the part of the Earth where life is possible the *biosphere.* The biosphere is the layer of the Earth above the crust and below the uppermost part of the atmosphere. It includes the oceans, the land surface, and the lower part of the atmosphere.

Lithosphere 15–300 km

Asthenosphere 250 km

Outer Core The Earth's core is divided into two parts—the outer core and the inner core. The **outer core** is the liquid layer of the Earth's core that lies beneath the mantle and surrounds the inner core.

Mesosphere 2,550 km

Inner Core The **inner core** is the solid, dense center of our planet that extends from the bottom of the outer core to the center of the Earth, 6,378 km beneath the surface.

Outer core 2,200 km

Inner core 1,228 km

139

IS THAT A FACT!

The center of the Earth's core is hotter than the surface of the sun! The temperature of Earth's inner core reaches 6,000°C. The photosphere of the sun, which we see as its surface, has a temperature of 5,500°C. The sun's core temperature, however, is 15,000,000°C.

READING STRATEGY

Mnemonics Encourage students to look up and learn the meanings of the following prefixes:

litho- rock (solid)
astheno- weak (flows)
meso- middle

By associating the prefix with the meaning, students may find it easier to remember the physical characteristics and locations of the Earth's layers. Sheltered English

USING THE FIGURE

Have students read about each layer in the illustration on these two pages. Ask students to sketch a simple model of the layers on scratch paper and label each layer "solid," "liquid," or "viscous." As they work from the outside in, what pattern do they notice? (solid, viscous, solid, liquid, solid)

Ask students to explain why inner layers, although very hot, are not all liquid. (Although the Earth's inner layers are very hot, the pressure exerted on them is so great that they cannot exist as liquid.)

Teaching Transparency 102 "The Earth's Crust, Lithosphere, and Asthenosphere"

TOPIC: Composition of the Earth
GO TO: www.scilinks.org
***sci*LINKS NUMBER:** HSTE155

TOPIC: Structure of the Earth
GO TO: www.scilinks.org
***sci*LINKS NUMBER:** HSTE160

2 Teach, *continued*

CROSS-DISCIPLINARY FOCUS

Language Arts *Tectonic* comes from the Greek word *tektonikos,* meaning "of a builder." Ask students to consider how this meaning is appropriate for tectonic plates. In what ways are tectonic plates responsible for building the Earth's surface?

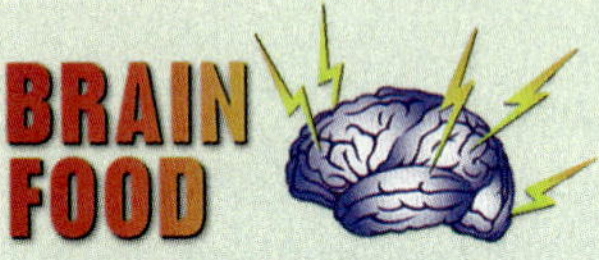

The deepest hole ever drilled into the continental crust was in the Kola Peninsula, in Russia, in 1984. It was 12,226 m deep! It is very difficult to drill much deeper than that because the deeper you go, the hotter it gets. If you drill too deep, the hot rock flows around the drill bit, filling the hole faster than it can be drilled.

Have students calculate the depth, in kilometers, of the deepest human-made hole. Did it extend to the asthenosphere? (12.2 km; no)

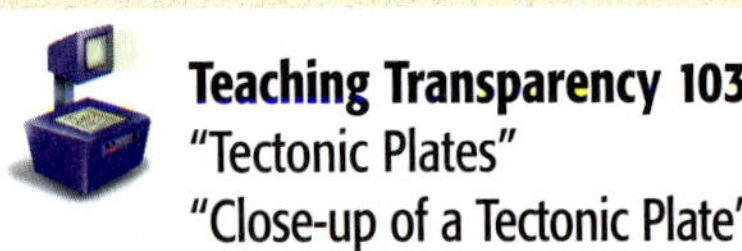

Teaching Transparency 103
"Tectonic Plates"
"Close-up of a Tectonic Plate"

Tectonic Plates

Tectonic plates are pieces of the lithosphere that move around on top of the asthenosphere. But what exactly does a tectonic plate look like? How big are tectonic plates? How and why do they move around? To answer these questions, start by thinking of the lithosphere as a giant jigsaw puzzle.

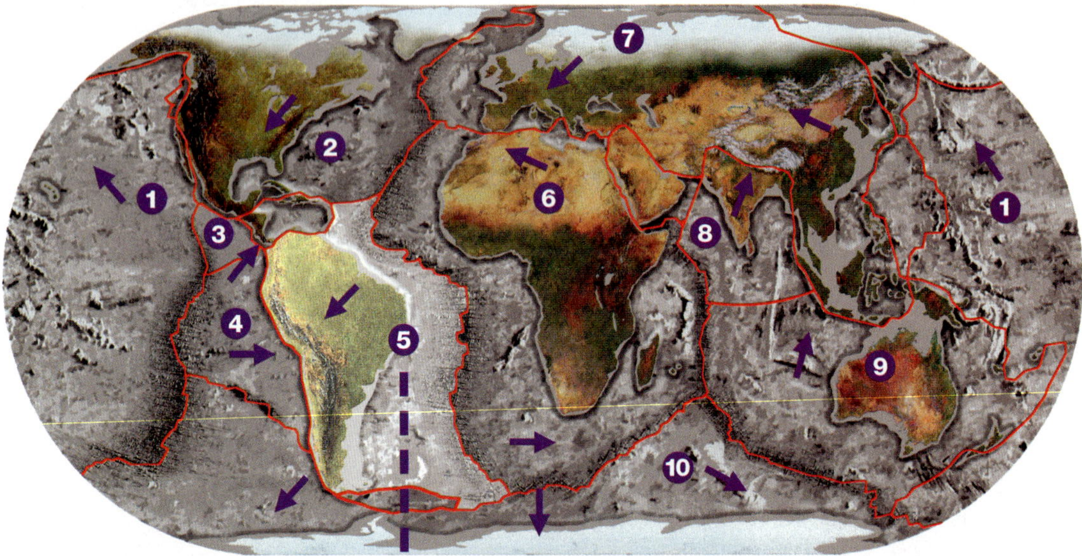

Figure 4 *Tectonic plates fit together like the pieces of a jigsaw puzzle. On this map, the relative motions of some of the major tectonic plates are shown with arrows.*

Major Tectonic Plates

1. Pacific plate
2. North American plate
3. Cocos plate
4. Nazca plate
5. South American plate
6. African plate
7. Eurasian plate
8. Indian plate
9. Australian plate
10. Antarctic plate

A Giant Jigsaw Puzzle Look at the world map above. All of the plates have names, some of which you may already be familiar with. Some of the major tectonic plates are listed in the key at left. Notice that each tectonic plate fits the other tectonic plates that surround it. The lithosphere is like a jigsaw puzzle, and the tectonic plates are like the pieces of a jigsaw puzzle.

You will also notice that not all tectonic plates are the same. Compare the size of the North American plate with that of the Cocos plate. But tectonic plates are different in other ways too. For example, the North American plate has an entire continent on it, while the Cocos plate only has oceanic crust. Like the North American plate, some tectonic plates include both continental *and* oceanic crust.

MISCONCEPTION ALERT

Be sure students realize that tectonic plates are not always neatly divided along continental lines. For example, the North American plate includes the North American continent, Greenland, half of Iceland, and part of Eurasia. All six of the Earth's large continental plates contain a continent and a large section of oceanic lithosphere. Some of the smaller tectonic plates contain only oceanic crust.

A Tectonic Plate Close Up What would a tectonic plate look like if you could lift it out of its place? **Figure 5** shows what the South American plate might look like if you could. Notice that this tectonic plate consists of both oceanic and continental crust, just like the North American plate.

The thickest part of this tectonic plate is on the South American continent, under the Andes mountain range. The thinnest part of the South American plate is at the Mid-Atlantic Ridge.

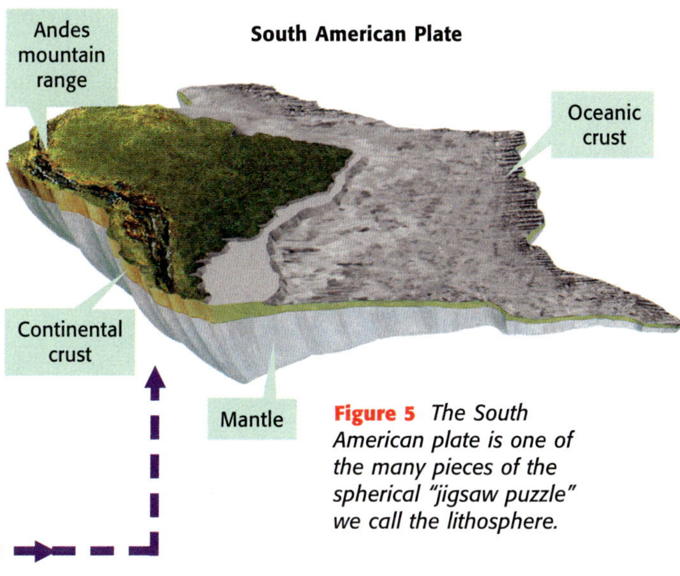

Figure 5 *The South American plate is one of the many pieces of the spherical "jigsaw puzzle" we call the lithosphere.*

Tip of the Iceberg If you could look at a tectonic plate from the side, you would see that mountain ranges are like the tips of icebergs—there is much more material below the surface than above. Mountain ranges that occur in continental crust have very deep roots relative to their height. For example, the Rocky Mountains rise less than 5 km above sea level, but their roots go down to about 60 km *below* sea level.

But if continental crust is so much thicker than oceanic crust, why doesn't it sink down below the oceanic crust? Think back to the difference between continental and oceanic crust. Continental crust stands much higher than oceanic crust because it is both thicker and less dense. Both kinds of crust are less dense than the mantle and "float" on top of the asthenosphere, similar to the way ice floats on top of water.

QuickLab

Floating Mountains

1. Take a large **block** of wood and place it in a clear plastic **container.** The block of wood represents the mantle part of the lithosphere.
2. Fill the container with **water** at least 10 cm deep. The water represents the asthenosphere. Use a ruler to measure how far the top of the wood block sits above the surface of the water.
3. Now try loading the block of wood with several different **wooden objects,** each with a different weight. These objects represent different amounts of crustal material loaded onto the lithosphere during mountain building. Measure how far the block sinks under each different weight.
4. What can you conclude about how the tectonic plate reacts to increasing weight of crustal material?
5. What happens to a tectonic plate when the crustal material is removed?

3 Extend

QuickLab

MATERIALS
- block of wood
- plastic container
- water
- wooden objects

Teacher Notes: In step 3, the wooden objects should each weigh less than the original wooden block. Explain to students that removing the wooden objects is analogous to large-scale erosion of crustal materials.

Answers to QuickLab

4. As a tectonic plate is weighed down with crustal material, it sinks lower into the asthenosphere.
5. When the weight is removed, the tectonic plate rises back up to its former level.

Group Activity

Pair students with a partner, and have them plan and build a three-dimensional model of a tectonic plate on the asthenosphere. Students might use materials such as cardboard, wood, and clay. Remind students to label the continental crust, oceanic crust, and lithosphere, as well as any surface topographical features, such as mountain ranges. When models are complete, have students display them and give a brief presentation to the class. Sheltered English

The contact between the crust and the mantle is called the Mohorovičić discontinuity, or the Moho. The discontinuity is caused by a density difference between the crust and the mantle. The discontinuity was discovered by a Croatian geologist named Andrija Mohorovičić. While investigating a 1909 earthquake in Croatia, he noticed there had been two sets of seismic waves. He theorized that the existence of these two sets was caused by a density difference between the crust and the mantle. Further studies indicated that the discontinuity is found worldwide. Have interested students find out more about the Moho and Gutenberg discontinuities.

Reinforcement Worksheet 6
"The Layered Earth"

4 Close

Using the Figure

The key for **Figure 6** shows the speeds of only one type of seismic wave—the compression, or P wave. P waves can travel through both liquids and solids and thus can travel through the liquid outer core, unlike other seismic waves.

Quiz

1. The crust is the Earth's only solid layer. (false)
2. The inner core of the Earth is solid and made primarily of iron. (true)
3. Temperature and pressure increase toward the center of the Earth. (true)
4. The asthenosphere is the thinnest layer. (false)

Alternative Assessment

Have students write a story describing their own "journey to the center of the Earth," or they may choose to write a travel guide that describes the experience of traveling through Earth's different layers. Have students draw and color-code a model of Earth to include with their project. Emphasize that this model must show layers defined by chemical composition (crust, mantle, core) and by physical traits (lithosphere, asthenosphere, mesosphere, outer core, and inner core.)

Problem Solving Worksheet 6
"Planet of Waves"

Mapping the Earth's Interior

How do we know all these things about the deepest parts of the Earth, where no one has ever been? Scientists have never even drilled through the crust, which is only a thin skin on the surface of the Earth. So how do we know so much about the mantle and the core?

Would you be surprised to know that the answers come from earthquakes? When an earthquake occurs, vibrations called seismic waves are produced. *Seismic waves* are vibrations that travel through the Earth. Depending on the density and strength of material they pass through, seismic waves travel at different speeds. For example, a seismic wave traveling through solid rock will go faster than a seismic wave traveling through a liquid.

When an earthquake occurs, *seismographs* measure the difference in the arrival times of seismic waves and record them. Seismologists can then use these measurements to calculate the density and thickness of each physical layer of the Earth. **Figure 6** shows how one kind of seismic wave travels through the Earth.

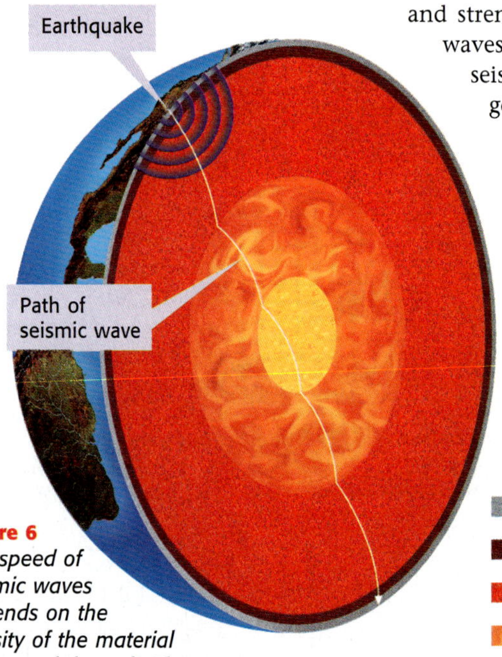

Earthquake
Path of seismic wave

Lithosphere 7–8 km/second
Asthenosphere 7–11 km/second
Mesosphere 11–13 km/second
Outer core 7–10 km/second
Inner core 11–12 km/second

Figure 6 *The speed of seismic waves depends on the density of the material they travel through. The denser the material, the faster seismic waves move. Another property of seismic waves is that when they change speed, they also change direction.*

Review

1. What is the difference between continental and oceanic crust?
2. How is the lithosphere different from the asthenosphere?
3. How do scientists know about the structure of the Earth's interior? Explain.
4. **Analyzing Relationships** Explain the difference between the crust and the lithosphere.

142

Answers to Review

1. Oceanic crust is thin and dense compared with continental crust. Continental crust and granite have a similar composition, and oceanic crust and basalt have a similar composition.
2. The lithosphere is rigid and is divided into tectonic plates. The asthenosphere is a layer of soft mantle material that flows very slowly.
3. Scientists measure the different speeds at which seismic waves travel through different parts of the Earth. This indicates the density and thickness of each layer the waves pass through.
4. The crust and the lithosphere are the outermost layers of the Earth, but the lithosphere includes the crust and the rigid, uppermost part of the mantle.

Section 1 Review–California Standards: PE/ATE 1b

2

Restless Continents

NEW TERMS
continental drift
sea-floor spreading

OBJECTIVES
- Describe Wegener's theory of continental drift, and explain why it was not accepted at first.
- Explain how sea-floor spreading provides a way for continents to move.
- Describe how new oceanic crust forms at mid-ocean ridges.
- Explain how magnetic reversals provide evidence for sea-floor spreading.

Take a look at **Figure 7.** It shows how continents would fit together if you removed the Atlantic Ocean and moved the land together. Is it just coincidence that the coastlines fit together so well? Is it possible that the continents were actually together sometime in the past?

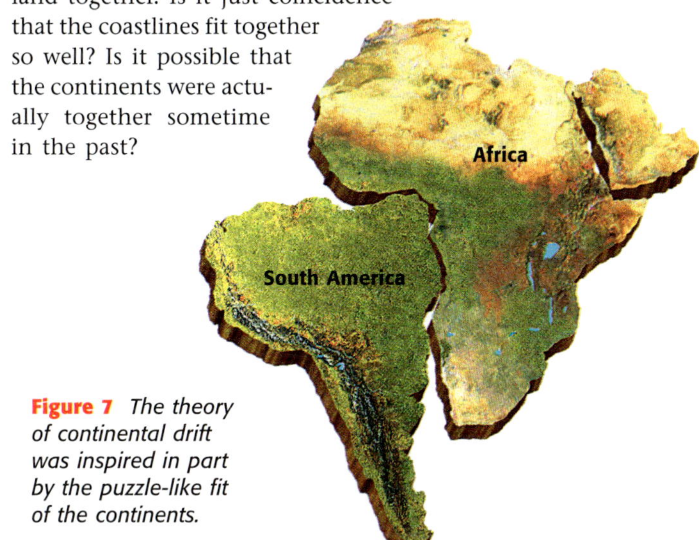

Figure 7 *The theory of continental drift was inspired in part by the puzzle-like fit of the continents.*

Wegener's Theory of Continental Drift

One scientist who looked at the pieces of this puzzle was Alfred Wegener. In the early 1900s he wrote about his theory of *continental drift*. **Continental drift** is the theory that continents can drift apart from one another and have done so in the past. This theory seemed to explain a lot of puzzling observations, including the very good fit of some of the continents.

Continental drift also explained why fossils of the same plant and animal species are found on both sides of the Atlantic Ocean. Many of these ancient species could not have made it across the Atlantic Ocean. As you can see in **Figure 8,** without continental drift, this pattern of fossil findings would be hard to explain. In addition to fossils, similar types of rock and evidence of the same ancient climatic conditions were found on several continents.

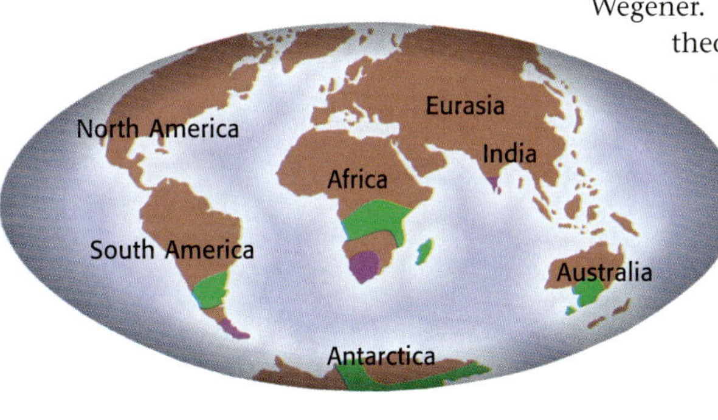

Mesosaurus

Glossopteris

Figure 8 *Fossils of* Mesosaurus, *a small, aquatic reptile, and* Glossopteris, *an ancient plant species, have been found on several continents.*

143

Section 2

Focus

Restless Continents

This section explains how, over millions of years, continents have moved to their present locations. Students learn about continental drift—the theory that the Earth's continents were originally united as the giant landmass called Pangaea and have since drifted apart. The section explains that support for this theory came when mid-ocean ridges were discovered. In turn, the phenomenon of sea-floor spreading was evidenced by the record of reversals of the Earth's magnetic field present in oceanic crust.

Bellringer

Ask students to explain why the following statement is true or false:

The United States is moving westward.

1 Motivate

Discussion

Show students a map of the world and demonstrate how the continents seem to fit together, as shown in **Figure 7.** Ask them to help you write a list of other evidence that supports Wegener's theories. (Students might suggest similar fossils on continents that were once joined, similar rock strata and crust thickness, or the continuity of ancient geologic features, such as mountain chains or faults.)

Is That a Fact!

By the time Alfred Wegener was 32, he had set a world record for balloon flight, earned a doctorate in astronomy, made two meteorological expeditions to Greenland, and written the paper that was the main catalyst for the greatest geologic insight of the twentieth century.

In **Figure 7,** the southern tips of South America and Africa do not touch, while **Figure 8** indicates that they did touch in the past. According to one interpretation, the southern tip of South America was wrapped around the southern tip of Africa when the two continents were together.

Directed Reading Worksheet 6 Section 2

Section 2–California Standards: PE/ATE 1, 1a, 7f

2 Teach

Guided Practice

Have students work in small groups to create a model of Pangaea. Provide each group with two world maps. With pencils, students can mark hypothetical glacial grooves extending from the poles of both maps. Have them cut the continents out of one map and treat them as puzzle pieces, seeing how they best fit together. Refer to both the complete and the altered maps, and help students explain and demonstrate how each continent moved from its original position. Sheltered English

Connect to Life Science

Before Pangaea broke up, dinosaurs roamed the entire continent. The populations were very widespread. As Pangaea began to break up, the populations of dinosaurs were fragmented and isolated on the new continents. The fossil record indicates that dinosaurs began to evolve divergently as a result. By the time dinosaurs became extinct, about 65 million years ago, there was great diversity among the different dinosaurs. Use the Teaching Transparencies listed below to discuss natural selection and the breakup of Pangaea. Have groups of students research different dinosaurs that lived after the breakup of Pangaea and speculate why these dinosaurs evolved the way they did.

Teaching Transparency 33 "Evolution of the Galápagos Finches"

Teaching Transparency 104 "The Breakup of Pangaea"

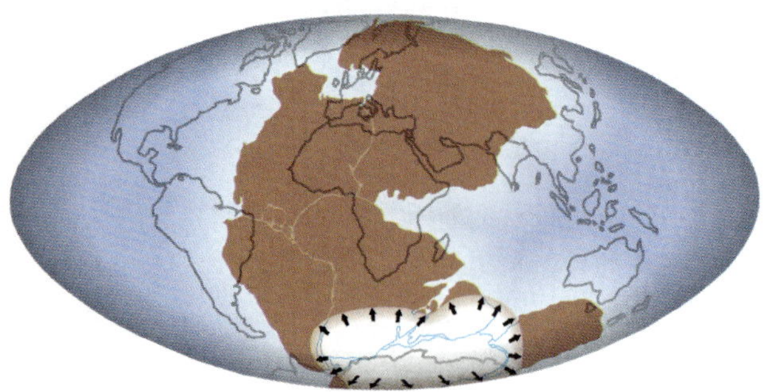

Figure 9 *The arrows show the direction ancient glaciers traveled when the continents were joined together.*

Continental drift also explained puzzling evidence left by ancient glaciers. Glaciers cut grooves in the ground that indicate the direction they traveled. When you look at the placement of today's continents, these glacial activities do not seem to be related. But when you bring all of these continental pieces back to their original arrangement, the glacial grooves fit together! **Figure 9** shows how they would look. You can imagine a huge ice sheet expanding in all directions from the center of this giant landmass.

The Breakup of Pangaea

Wegener studied many observations before establishing his theory of continental drift. He thought that all the separate continents of today were once joined in a single landmass that he called *Pangaea,* which is Greek for "all earth." As shown in **Figure 10,** almost all of Earth's landmasses were joined together in one huge continent 245 million years ago.

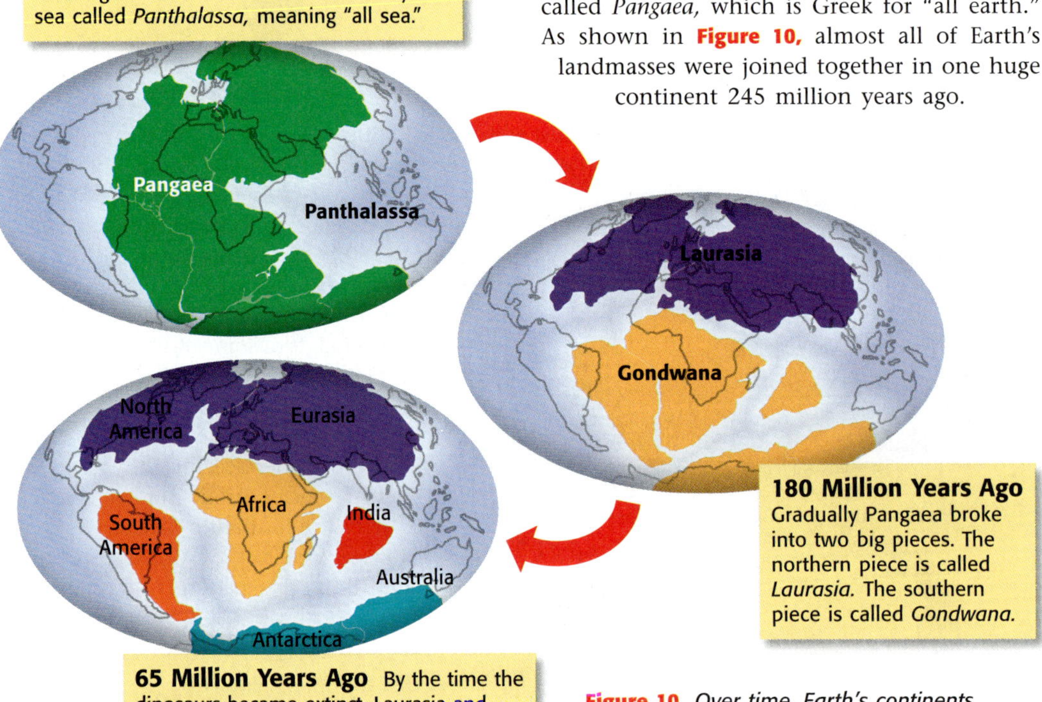

Figure 10 *Over time, Earth's continents have changed shape and traveled great distances.*

144

Misconception Alert

Pangaea was not the only supercontinent that existed. Some 500 million years before Pangaea began to form, another supercontinent dominated the globe—Rodinia. Some scientists speculate that the formation of supercontinents occurs as a cycle of accretion and breakup. If this is true, there may have been as many as 10 different supercontinents in the last 3 billion years and there may be more in the future!

Sea-Floor Spreading

When Wegener put forth his theory of continental drift, many scientists would not accept his theory. What force of nature, they wondered, could move entire continents? In Wegener's day, no one could answer that question. It wasn't until many years later that new evidence provided some clues.

In **Figure 11** you will notice that there is a chain of submerged mountains running through the center of the Atlantic Ocean. The chain is called the Mid-Atlantic Ridge, part of a worldwide system of ocean ridges. Mid-ocean ridges are underwater mountain chains that run through Earth's ocean basins.

Figure 11 *The Mid-Atlantic Ridge is part of the longest mountain chain in the world.*

Mid-ocean ridges are places where sea-floor spreading takes place. **Sea-floor spreading** is the process by which new oceanic lithosphere is created as older materials are pulled away. As tectonic plates move away from each other, the sea floor spreads apart and magma rises to fill in the gap. Notice in **Figure 12** that the crust increases in age the farther it is from the mid-ocean ridge. This is because new crust continually forms from molten material at the ridge. The oldest crust in the Atlantic Ocean is found along the edges of the continents. It dates back to the time of the dinosaurs. The newest crust is in the center of the ocean. This crust has just formed!

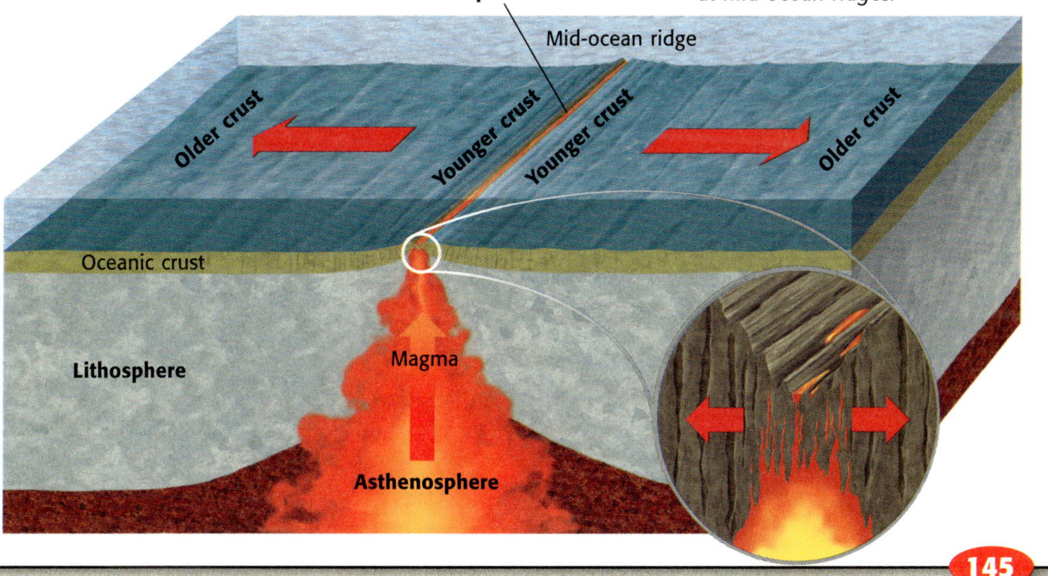

Figure 12 *Sea-floor spreading creates new oceanic lithosphere at mid-ocean ridges.*

145

3 Extend

Using the Figure

Have students use **Figure 12** to explain the forces that pull rocks outward from mid-ocean ridges. Guide their explanations by asking the following questions:

- Why does molten rock from the mantle come to the surface at the ridges?
- Why does the ocean floor spread apart at the ridges?
- Why is rock at the ridge "new" rock?

Stress that mid-ocean ridges are not always in the middle of an ocean. Have students compare the locations of mid-ocean ridges in **Figure 4.**

Connect to Physical Science

Explain that researchers used sonar to discover that the ocean floor is not flat. In the 1950s, scientists broadcast sound waves toward the sea floor and measured how long it took the waves to return. The echoes revealed the existence of oceanic valleys and mountains. In short, the ocean floors turned out to be as varied as the continents! What amazed scientists most was the chain of undersea mountains snaking thousands of kilometers around the globe, the mid-ocean ridge.

Science Bloopers

Before the discovery of the Mid-Atlantic Ridge, many scientists thought that a land bridge had once connected South America and Africa. Despite the fact that there was no evidence to support it, the popular land-bridge theory was used to explain why the fossil record was similar on both continents.

Scientists at Odds

Many geologists ridiculed Wegener's theories because they had been taught that continents and ocean basins were fixed in their positions. These scientists knew of no force that could move an entire continent, and they discounted the overwhelming evidence that continental drift had occurred.

4 Close

BRAIN FOOD

Why is the south pole of the bar magnet in **Figure 13** located at the Earth's north pole during "normal polarity"? Explain to students that magnetic attraction occurs between the opposite poles of magnets. The north-seeking pole of a compass needle actually points to the south pole of Earth's magnetic field. Thus, during periods of "normal polarity" what we call the Earth's magnetic north pole is actually the south pole of Earth's magnetic field. This concept can be easily demonstrated by placing the south pole of a bar magnet next to a compass. The compass needle will point toward the south pole of the bar magnet in the same way it tends to point toward the south pole of Earth's magnetic field, what we call magnetic north.

Quiz

1. If the Earth's crust is growing at mid-ocean ridges, why doesn't the Earth itself grow larger? (because crust is also subducted)
2. What was Pangaea? (the large landmass that later broke up to form two supercontinents and then fragmented further to form the six continents of today)

Alternative Assessment

Writing Have students write a paragraph explaining how sea-floor spreading causes continents to move apart. Students should also include a diagram of this process.

physical science CONNECTION

You may already be familiar with how magnets work—if you place the north pole of a magnet next to the north pole of another magnet, the two magnets repel each other. What you may not know is that all matter has the property of magnetism, though in most cases it is very weak compared with that of magnets. This explains why researchers have been able to levitate a frog—by creating a very strong magnetic field beneath it!

Magnetic Reversals

Some of the most important evidence of sea-floor spreading comes from magnetic reversals recorded in the ocean floor. Throughout Earth's history, the north and south magnetic poles have changed places many times. When Earth's magnetic poles change place, this is called a *magnetic reversal.*

The molten rocks at the mid-ocean ridges contain tiny grains of magnetic minerals. These mineral grains act like compasses. They align with the magnetic field of the Earth. Once the molten rock cools, the record of these tiny compasses is literally set in stone. This record is then carried slowly away from the spreading center as sea-floor spreading occurs. As you can see in **Figure 13,** when the Earth's magnetic field reverses, a new band is started, and this time the magnetic mineral grains point in the opposite direction. The new rock records the direction of the Earth's magnetic field. This record of magnetic reversals was the final proof that sea-floor spreading does occur.

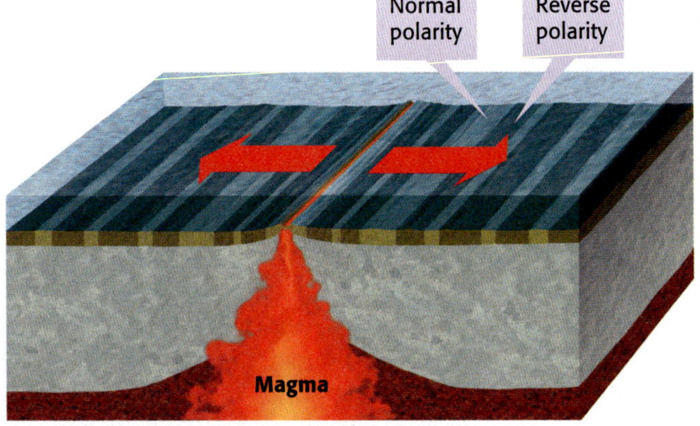

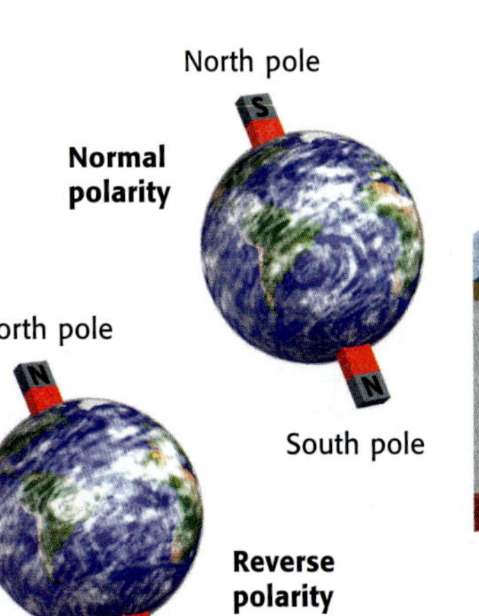

Figure 13 *Magnetic reversals in oceanic crust are shown here in light and dark blue. The dark blue stripes represent periods when magnetic north was true north. The light blue stripes represent periods when magnetic north was at the South Pole.*

REVIEW

1. List three puzzling occurrences that the theory of continental drift helped to explain, and describe how it explained them.
2. Explain why Wegener's theory of continental drift was not accepted at first.
3. **Identifying Relationships** Explain how the processes of sea-floor spreading and magnetic reversal produce bands of oceanic crust that have different magnetic polarities.

Answers to Review

1. Occurrences include the puzzle-like fit of the continents, the fit of glacial grooves, the occurrence of plant and animal fossils of the same species on different continents, the distribution of rock types and ancient climatic zones; continental drift explained that these coincidences exist because at one time all the continents were joined together in one large landmass.
2. Wegener's theory of continental drift described the movement of continents but did not explain what forces of nature moved them.
3. During sea-floor spreading, new oceanic crust forms on either side of the mid-ocean ridge. The changing polarity of the Earth's magnetic poles causes the new oceanic crust to have alternating bands of normal and reverse polarity.

Section 2 Review–California Standards: PE/ATE 1, 1a

3 The Theory of Plate Tectonics

NEW TERMS

plate tectonics
convergent boundary
subduction zone
divergent boundary
transform boundary

OBJECTIVES

- Describe the three forces thought to move tectonic plates.
- Describe the three types of tectonic plate boundaries.
- Explain how scientists measure the rate at which tectonic plates move.

The proof of sea-floor spreading supported Wegener's original idea that the continents move. But because both oceanic and continental crust appear to move, a new theory was devised to explain both continental drift and sea-floor spreading—the theory of *plate tectonics*. **Plate tectonics** is the theory that the Earth's lithosphere is divided into tectonic plates that move around on top of the asthenosphere. So what causes tectonic plates to move?

Possible Causes of Tectonic Plate Motion

An incredible amount of energy is needed to move something as massive as a tectonic plate! We still don't know exactly why tectonic plates move as they do, but recently scientists have come up with some possible answers, as shown in **Figure 14.** Notice how all three are driven by the force of gravity.

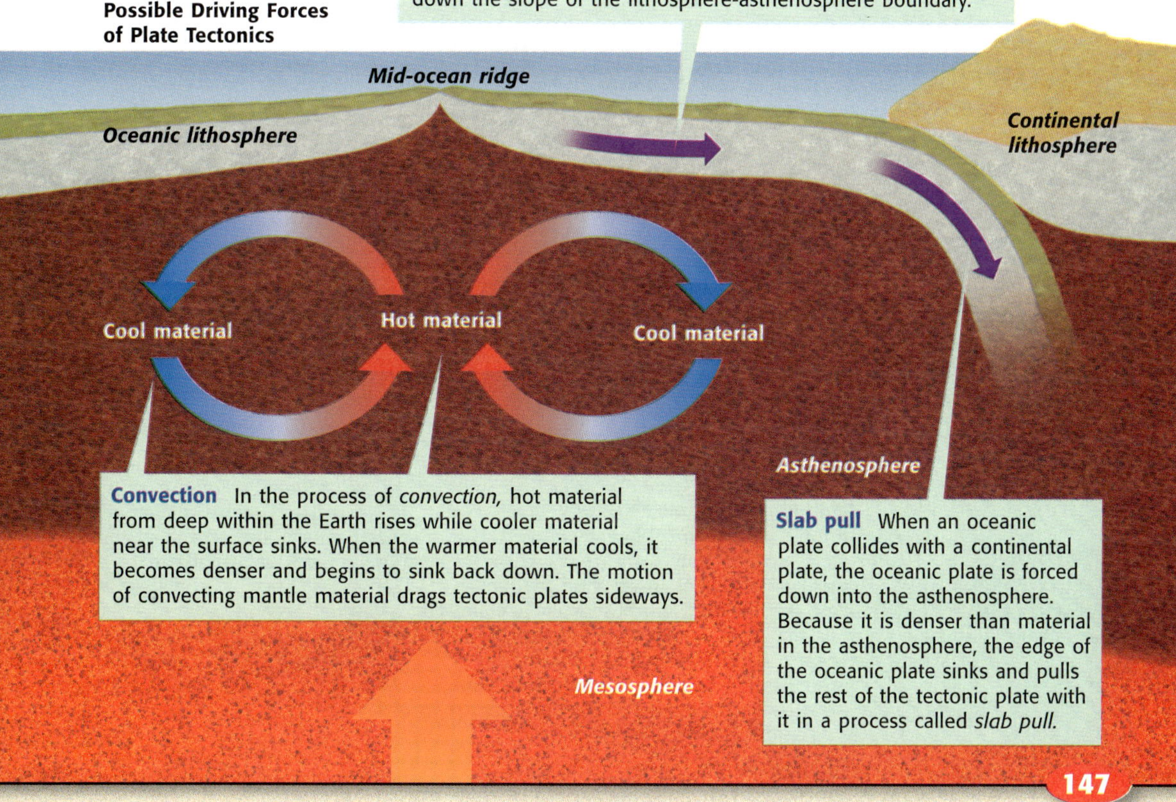

Figure 14 Three Possible Driving Forces of Plate Tectonics

Ridge push At mid-ocean ridges, the oceanic lithosphere is higher than it is where it sinks beneath continental lithosphere. *Ridge push* is the process by which an oceanic plate slides down the slope of the lithosphere-asthenosphere boundary.

Convection In the process of *convection,* hot material from deep within the Earth rises while cooler material near the surface sinks. When the warmer material cools, it becomes denser and begins to sink back down. The motion of convecting mantle material drags tectonic plates sideways.

Slab pull When an oceanic plate collides with a continental plate, the oceanic plate is forced down into the asthenosphere. Because it is denser than material in the asthenosphere, the edge of the oceanic plate sinks and pulls the rest of the tectonic plate with it in a process called *slab pull.*

147

SECTION 3

Focus

The Theory of Plate Tectonics

This section discusses the plate tectonic model of Earth's crustal movements. Students learn about possible causes of some plate movements: convection within the mantle, ridge push at mid-ocean ridges, and slab pull at subduction zones. It also describes the types of plate boundaries and how scientists use GPS satellites to track plate motion.

Bellringer

Have students calculate the number of years that it took New York and the west coast of Africa to reach their current locations, 676,000,000 cm apart, if the sea floor is spreading an average of 4 cm a year. (Students will calculate that the Atlantic Ocean has been spreading apart for about 169 million years. Point out that this is fairly close to the estimate of when the breakup of Pangaea began 180 million years ago.)

1 Motivate

DEMONSTRATION

Discuss **Figure 14** with students, and point out how the movement of tectonic plates is driven by the force of gravity. In *slab pull* and *ridge push,* gravity pulls the oceanic plate downward because it is more dense than the continental lithosphere. In *convection,* hot material rises because it is less dense than cooler material, which sinks.

IS THAT A FACT!

Convection currents circulate material deep inside the Earth in a long, slow movement. The material cools near the surface and then sinks again into the depths. A single particle takes hundreds of millions of years to make a complete circle.

Teaching Transparency 105 "Possible Causes of Tectonic Plate Motion"

Directed Reading Worksheet 6 Section 3

2 Teach

MEETING INDIVIDUAL NEEDS

Advanced Learners Challenge students to explain why continental/oceanic and oceanic/oceanic convergent boundaries result in subduction, whereas continental/continental convergent boundaries build mountains. Then have them:

- create an illustrated chart showing the five types of boundary movements
- write captions explaining both how the boundaries move and the forces responsible for their movement

DISCUSSION

Ask students to imagine trying to push a heavy crate along a concrete sidewalk. When you start to push, the box doesn't move. But as you push harder, the box finally slips a little and then stops again. Tectonic plates tend to move in similar jerks and jolts. When they move with a sudden jerk, an earthquake occurs. Sheltered English

INDEPENDENT PRACTICE

Have students refer back to **Figure 4** to locate examples of different types of tectonic plate boundaries given in **Figure 15.** (Teaching Transparencies 106 and 107 reproduce **Figure 15** for classroom use.) Test students' understanding of tectonic plate boundaries by asking them to identify which kind of boundary each red line in **Figure 4** represents.

Convection Connection

Tectonic Plate Boundaries

All tectonic plates have boundaries with other tectonic plates. These boundaries are divided into three main types depending on how the tectonic plates move relative to one another. Tectonic plates can collide, separate, or slide past each other. **Figure 15** shows some examples of tectonic plate boundaries.

Convergent Boundaries When two tectonic plates push into one another, the boundary where they meet is called a **convergent boundary.** What happens at a convergent boundary depends on what kind of crust—continental or oceanic—the leading edge of each tectonic plate has. As you can see below, there are three types of convergent boundaries—continental/continental, continental/oceanic, and oceanic/oceanic.

Figure 15 *This diagram shows five tectonic plate boundaries. Each pair of arrows shows the relative movement of the tectonic plates. Notice that there are three types of convergent boundaries.*

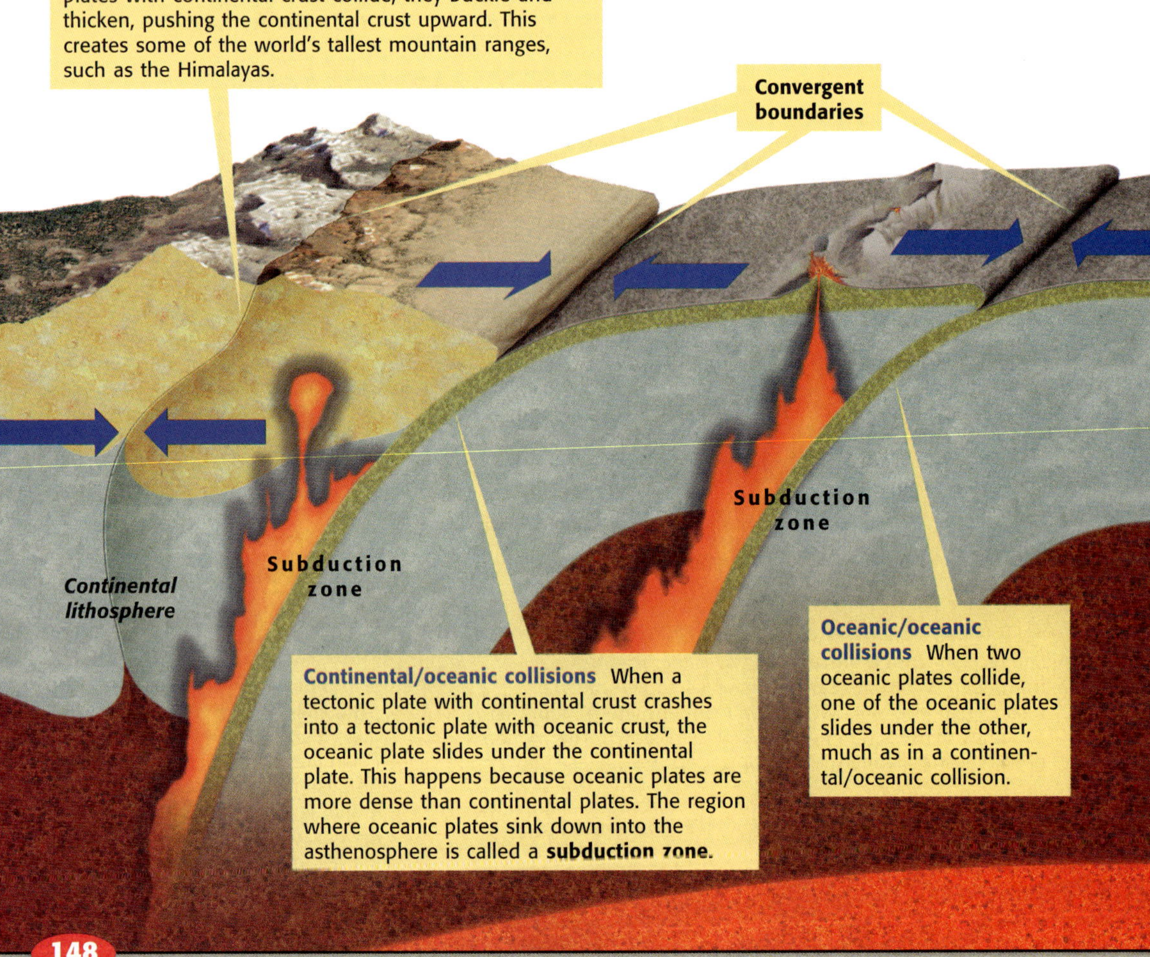

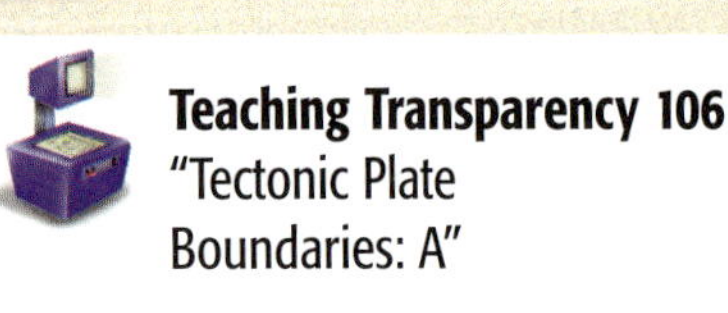

Teaching Transparency 106 "Tectonic Plate Boundaries: A"

Teaching Transparency 107 "Tectonic Plate Boundaries: B"

CROSS-DISCIPLINARY FOCUS

Writing **Language Arts** Have students write a short story about a rock, from its formation from magma at an oceanic ridge to its subduction at a tectonic plate boundary.

Divergent Boundaries When two tectonic plates move away from one another, the boundary between them is called a **divergent boundary.** Remember sea-floor spreading? The mid-ocean ridges that mark the spreading centers are the most common type of divergent boundary. Remember, divergent boundaries are where new oceanic lithosphere forms.

Transform Boundaries When two tectonic plates slide past each other, the boundary between them is called a **transform boundary.** The San Andreas Fault, in southern California, is a good example of a *transform boundary.* This fault marks the place where the Pacific plate and the North American plate slide past each other.

What is it like living on top of a mid-ocean spreading center? To find out how plate tectonics affects Icelanders, turn to page 162.

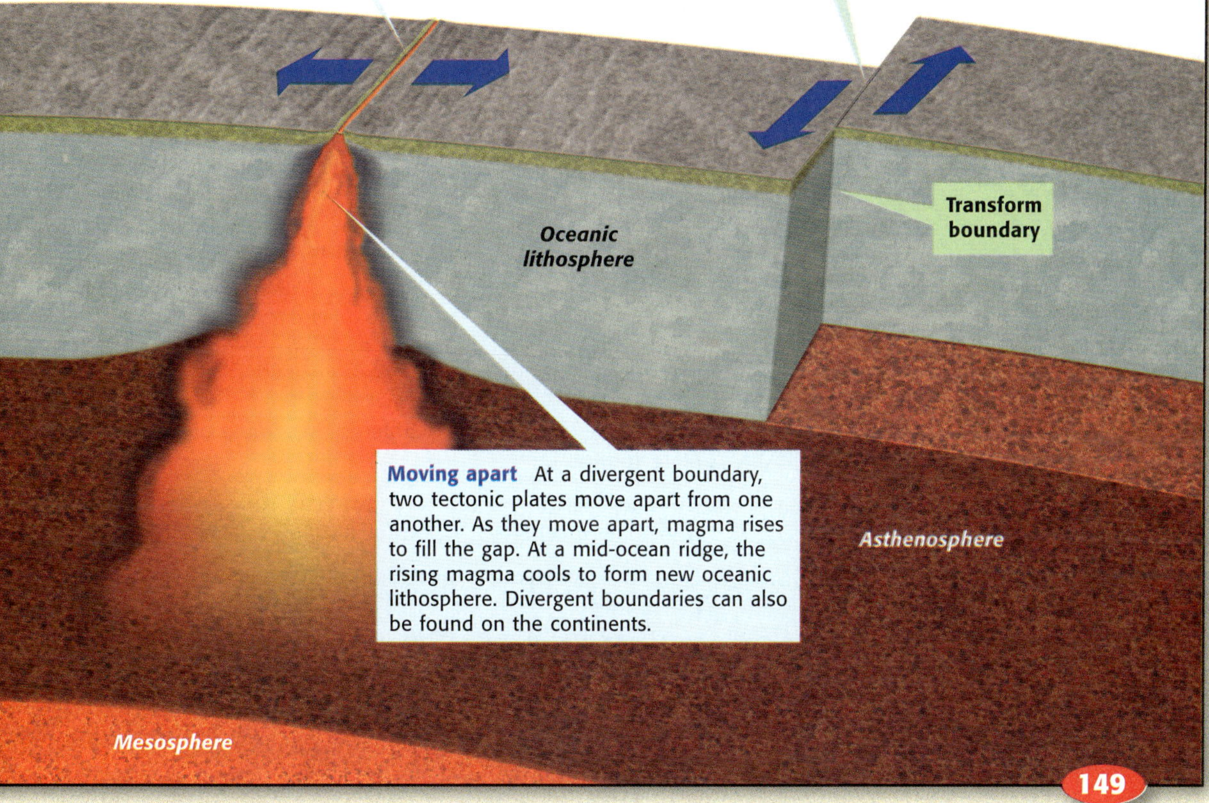

149

3 Extend

Group Activity

Challenge students to model the types of movement at each type of plate boundary. Have them work in pairs with materials they have chosen. Possible materials include sheets of foam padding, cardboard, modeling clay, or phone books.

As students demonstrate plate movements, they should be prepared to explain the composition of each plate and the differences between the forces at work.
Sheltered English

Independent Practice

Writing Tell students to hypothesize about what kinds of geologic features occur at different types of plate boundaries. Then have them compare a topographic world map with the tectonic plate map in **Figure 4.** Encourage them to do library and Internet research to find out if their hypotheses were correct. Suggest that they summarize their findings in a brief report.

MATH and MORE

The distance between New York and Paris changes every year. Currently, the two cities are moving apart by about 2 cm per year. This may not sound like much, but have students calculate the increase in distance in 1 million years. (20 km)

How much will the distance increase in 100 million years? (2,000 km)

Math Skills Worksheet 4
"A Shortcut for Multiplying Large Numbers"

Homework

PORTFOLIO **Writing Assignment** Alfred Wegener wrote, "If it turns out that sense and meaning are now becoming evident in the whole history of the Earth's development, why should we hesitate to toss the old views overboard?" Ask students to think about why the acceptance of new ideas in science is a slow process. Ask students to explain why continental drift and another controversial theory took a long time to be accepted.

4 Close

Quiz

1. Why are there several categories of convergent plate boundaries? (Plates that are pushed together behave differently, depending on their composition and density.)
2. Tell where you would expect to see the following features:
   a. tall, wrinkled mountains in the middle of a continent (convergent continental/continental boundary)
   b. a long parallel ridge on the ocean floor surrounded by parallel zones of magnetic reversal (divergent boundary)
3. Explain the process of subduction. (A denser oceanic plate is forced beneath a less-dense oceanic or continental plate at a convergent boundary. Gravity pulls the oceanic plate into the asthenosphere, where it begins to melt.)

Alternative Assessment

Have students work with a group or a partner to make models of different kinds of tectonic plate boundaries using modeling clay. Have students label their models, add appropriate surface features, and explain the processes responsible for the features.
Sheltered English

Figure 16 *The image above shows the orbits of the GPS satellites. Known as a "constellation," this group of satellites helps to measure the movement of tectonic plates on Earth.*

Tracking Tectonic Plate Motion

Just how fast do tectonic plates move? The answer to this question depends on many factors, such as the type of tectonic plate, the shape of the tectonic plate, and the way it interacts with the tectonic plates that surround it. Tectonic movements are generally so slow and gradual that you can't see or feel them—they are measured in centimeters per year.

As you have seen, one exception to this rule is the San Andreas Fault, in California. The San Andreas Fault is a part of the transform boundary between the Pacific plate and the North American plate. The two tectonic plates do not slide past each other smoothly or continuously. Instead, this movement happens in jerks and jolts. Sections of the San Andreas fault remain stationary for years and then suddenly shift several meters, causing an earthquake.

Large shifts that occur at the San Andreas fault can be measured right on the surface. Unfortunately for scientists, most movements of tectonic plates are very difficult to measure.

Scientists use a network of satellites called the *Global Positioning System* (GPS), shown in **Figure 16,** to measure the rate of tectonic plate movement. Radio signals are continuously beamed from satellites to GPS ground stations, which record the exact distance between the satellites and the ground station. Over time, these distances change slightly. By recording the time it takes for the GPS ground stations to move a given distance, scientists can measure the rate of motion of each tectonic plate.

REVIEW

1. List and describe three possible driving forces of tectonic plate motion.
2. How do the three types of convergent boundaries differ from one another?
3. Explain how scientists measure the rate at which tectonic plates move.
4. **Identifying Relationships** When convection takes place in the mantle, why does cooler material sink, while warmer material rises?

Reinforcement Worksheet 6
"A Moving Jigsaw Puzzle"

internet**connect**
SCILINKS NSTA
TOPIC: Tectonic Plates
GO TO: www.scilinks.org
***sci*LINKS NUMBER:** HSTE165

Answers to Review

1. Ridge push occurs when an oceanic plate slides down the tilted slope of the lithosphere/asthenosphere boundary. Slab pull occurs when the sinking edge of an oceanic plate pulls the rest of the plate down with it into the subduction zone. Convection occurs when hot mantle material in the asthenosphere convects, dragging the tectonic plate sideways.
2. Convergent boundaries can occur between two oceanic plates, two continental plates, or between an oceanic and a continental plate.
3. They measure tectonic plate movement by using a network of satellites to track the movement of GPS ground stations over long periods of time.
4. Cooler material sinks because it is denser than warmer material.

Section 3 Review–California Standards: PE/ATE 1, 1a, 1c, 4c

Deforming the Earth's Crust

NEW TERMS

stress, compression, tension, fault, folding, normal fault, reverse fault, strike-slip fault

OBJECTIVES

- Describe major types of folds.
- Explain how the three major types of faults differ.
- Name and describe the most common types of mountains.
- Explain how various types of mountains form.

Have you ever tried to bend something, only to have it break? Try this: take a long, uncooked piece of spaghetti, and bend it very slowly, and only a little. Now bend it again, but this time much farther and faster. What happened to it the second time? How can the same material bend at one time and break at another? The answer is that the *stress* you put on it was different. **Stress** is the amount of force that is put on a given material. The same principle works on the rocks in the Earth's crust. The conditions under which a rock is stressed determine its behavior.

Rocks Get Stressed

When rock changes its shape due to stress, this reaction is called *deformation*. In the example above, you saw the spaghetti deform in two different ways—by bending and by breaking. The same thing happens in rock layers. Rock layers can bend when certain types of stress are placed on them. But when other kinds of stress are placed on them, they break. Rocks can deform due to the forces of plate tectonics.

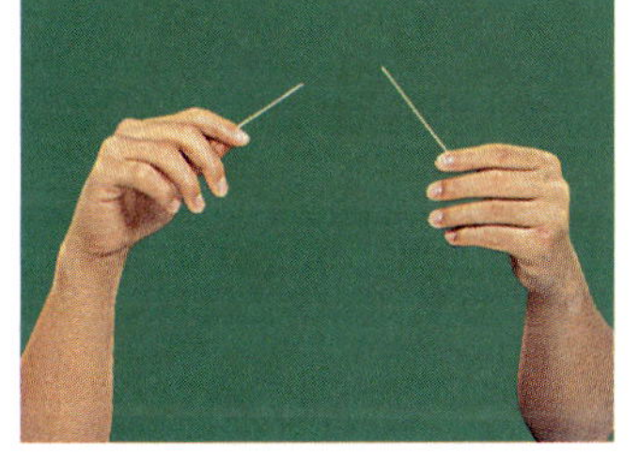

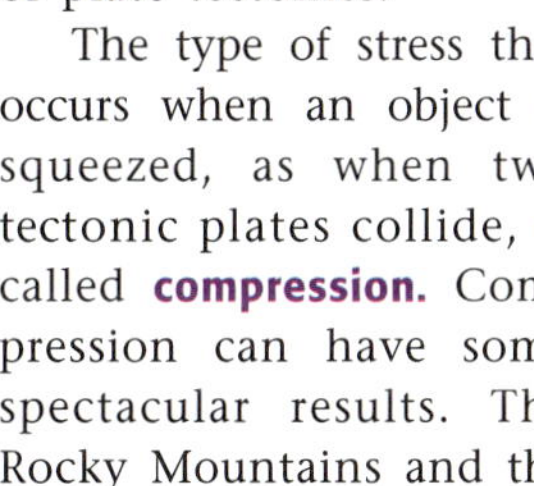

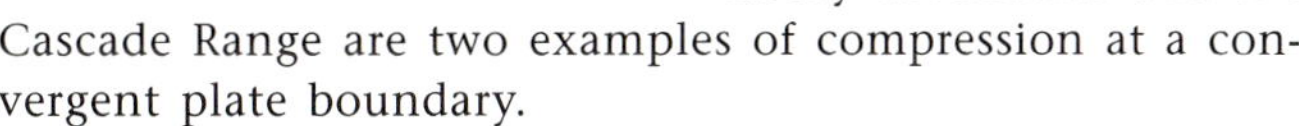

Figure 17 *Materials react to different types of stress in different ways.*

The type of stress that occurs when an object is squeezed, as when two tectonic plates collide, is called **compression.** Compression can have some spectacular results. The Rocky Mountains and the Cascade Range are two examples of compression at a convergent plate boundary.

Another form of stress is *tension.* **Tension** is stress that occurs when forces act to stretch an object. As you might guess, tension occurs at divergent plate boundaries, when two tectonic plates pull away from each other. In the following pages you will learn how these two tectonic forces—compression and tension—bend and break rock to form some of the common landforms you already know.

LabBook

After you've read about how tectonic forces cause rocks to bend and break, you may want to create some stress of your own. To find out how, turn to page 509 in your LabBook.

151

SECTION 4

Focus

Deforming the Earth's Crust

This section explores effects of tectonic forces on the Earth's crust. Students learn how stress on rock causes it to fold or fault in various ways. The section then discusses how different types of mountains form from the action of tectonic forces and volcanic activity.

Bellringer

Display photographs of several types of mountains. Have students write a description of each example and suggest how it might have formed.

1 Motivate

DEMONSTRATION

Display two thin strips of modeling clay, one frozen and one at room temperature. Have a volunteer demonstrate what happens when the warm clay is bent. (It folds.)

Ask students to predict what will happen to the frozen clay when a force is applied to it. Provide protective gloves, and have a second volunteer attempt to bend the frozen clay. (It should break.)

Discuss factors that affect the way a rock reacts to stress. (temperature, composition, amount and type of force applied)

Oh, the Pressure!

Directed Reading Worksheet 6 Section 4

Science Bloopers

In the 1800s, some scientists believed mountains formed as the result of Earth's shrinking. The theory proposed that Earth had once been a ball of semimolten rock; as it cooled, it shrank and wrinkles formed on the surface, much as an apple skin wrinkles as the fruit dries. This popular theory was not discarded until the structure and age of the Earth were better understood in the twentieth century.

Section 4–California Standards: PE/ATE 1, 1a, 1e, 1f, 6, 6a, 6b; LabBook: 1, 1e, 7, 7b, 7d, 7e

2 Teach

READING STRATEGY

Activity As students read this section, have them sketch the following examples in their ScienceLog:

- folds that illustrate anticlines and synclines
- a fold that illustrates a monocline
- a normal fault
- a reverse fault
- a strike-slip fault

Have students label each sketch clearly, provide a caption, and draw arrows showing the direction of the forces causing the deformation. Sheltered English

CROSS-DISCIPLINARY FOCUS

Geography Plate tectonics play an important role in the formation of most mountain ranges. Mountain ranges in turn influence the weather around them. Because mountains are high, they influence the flow of air in a region, causing a rain shadow effect. Have interested students select a mountain range and learn more about how it affects the weather in its area. Tell students they should find out what rain shadows are and give a few geographic examples of them. Students should also explore how a certain mountain range supports a variety of ecosystems.

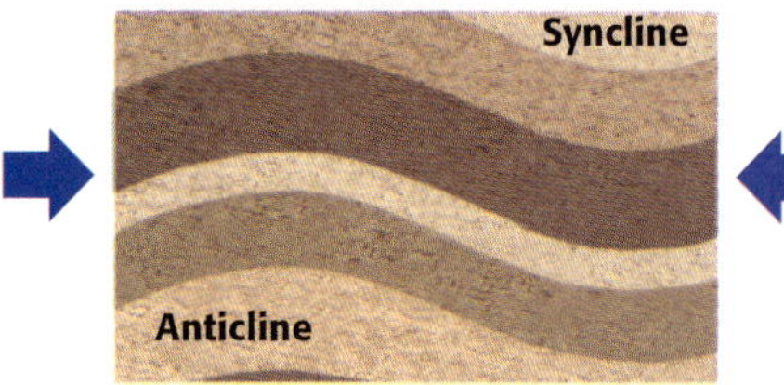

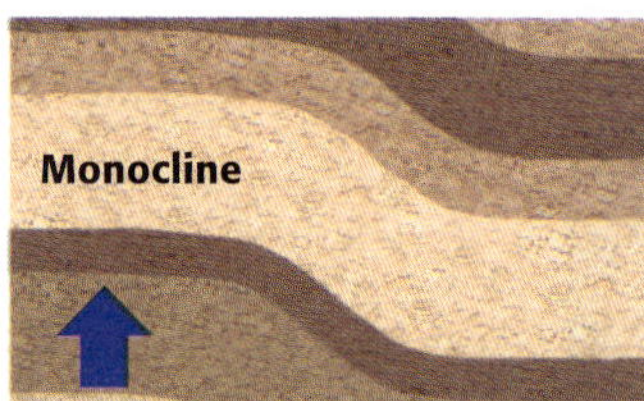

Figure 18 *When two tectonic forces compress rock layers, they can cause the layers to bend and fold.* Anticlines *and* synclines *form when horizontal stress acts on rock. Monoclines form when vertical stress acts on rock.*

Folding

Folding occurs when rock layers bend due to compression of the Earth's crust. We assume that all sedimentary rock layers started out as horizontal layers. So when you see a fold, you know that compression has taken place. Depending on how the rock layers deform, different types of folds are made. **Figure 18** shows the two most common types—*anticlines* and *synclines*.

Another type of fold is a *monocline*. In a monocline, rock layers are folded so that both ends of the fold are still horizontal. Imagine taking a stack of paper and laying it on a table top. Think of all the sheets of paper as different rock layers. Now put a book under one end of the stack. You can see that both ends of the sheets are still horizontal, but all the sheets are bent in the middle.

Folds can be large or small. Take a look at **Figure 19.** The largest folds are measured in kilometers. They can make up the entire side of a mountain. Other folds are still obvious but much smaller. Note the size of the pocket knife in the smaller photo. Now look at the smallest folds. You would measure these folds in centimeters.

Figure 19 *Folds vary greatly in size. The larger photo at left shows mountain-sized folds in the Rocky Mountains.*

152

Homework

Making Models Have students select a topographic feature in your state that resulted from the deformation of the Earth's crust and find out about how it formed. Tell them to choose appropriate materials and create a model of the formation. Point out that they may need to create a cutaway view to show layers within the formation. Finally, ask students to write labels explaining the formation's features and the tectonic forces that caused them.

Faulting

While some rock layers bend and fold when stress is applied, under other conditions rock layers break. At first the rocks will only bend slightly. But if the stress is great enough, the rocks can eventually break. The surface along which rocks break and slide past each other is called a **fault.** The blocks of crust on each side of the fault are called *fault blocks.*

If a fault is not vertical, it is useful to distinguish between its two sides—the *hanging wall* and the *footwall.* **Figure 20** shows the difference between a hanging wall and a footwall. Depending on how the hanging wall and footwall move relative to each other, one of two main types of faults can form.

Figure 20 *The position of a fault block determines whether it is a hanging wall or a footwall.*

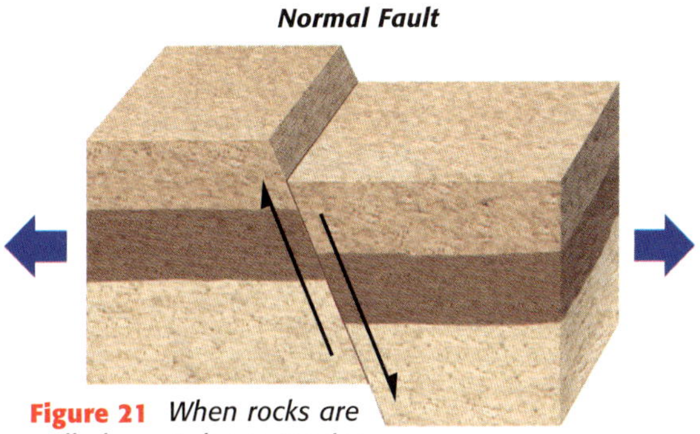

Normal Faults A *normal fault* is shown in **Figure 21.** The movement of a **normal fault** causes the hanging wall to move down relative to the footwall. Normal faults usually occur when tectonic forces cause tension that pulls rocks apart.

Normal Fault

Figure 21 *When rocks are pulled apart due to tension, normal faults often result.*

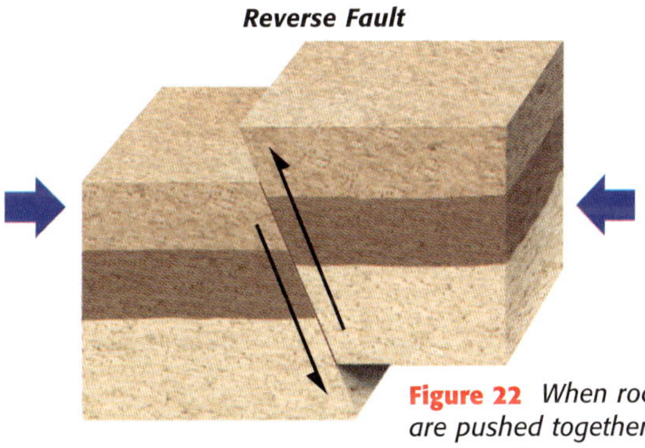

Reverse Faults A *reverse fault* is shown in **Figure 22.** The movement of a **reverse fault** causes the hanging wall to move up relative to the footwall—the "reverse" of a normal fault. Reverse faults usually happen when tectonic forces cause compression that pushes rocks together.

Reverse Fault

Figure 22 *When rocks are pushed together by compression, reverse faults often result.*

Self-Check

How is folding different from faulting? *(See page 564 to check your answer.)*

IS THAT A FACT!

Thrust faults are large-scale, low-angle reverse faults caused by the collision of tectonic plates. They are an example of what can happen when stress (compression) is applied to the crust. Large-scale folding can also result from compression.

Answers to Self-Check

When folding occurs, sedimentary rock strata bend but do not break. When faulting occurs, sedimentary rock strata break along a fault and the fault blocks on either side move relative to each other.

RETEACHING

Have students refer to **Figure 20** while you give this explanation of hanging walls and footwalls: When a fault occurs at an angle, the hanging wall is the block above the fault surface, while the footwall is the block below it. Have students identify both the hanging walls and the footwalls in **Figures 21** and **22.** Point out that either side can be higher; it is the orientation of the fault-plane that matters.

DISCUSSION

Refer to **Figure 21,** and point out that in a normal fault the hanging wall moves downward. Ask students to describe the tectonic force that causes this type of fault movement. (tension or stretching from plate movements pulling rocks apart)

Invite a volunteer to use **Figure 22** to discuss the forces that cause reverse faults. (When plate movements squeeze rocks together, compression forces the hanging wall up and the footwall down.)

Sheltered English

CONNECT TO LIFE SCIENCE

Point out that living at high altitudes places stress on organisms. This stress has led to the evolution of various adaptations. For example, because there is less oxygen at high altitudes, some animals that live on mountains produce more red blood cells. This makes the blood more efficient at delivering oxygen to body tissues. Have students find out about adaptations of other organisms to life in high-altitude environments.

Activity

Making Models Have students use two blocks of wood to model the three types of fault movements. Tell students to sand one side of each block until it is smooth and to score another side until it is rough.

Inform students that the San Andreas Fault is a strike-slip fault. As they demonstrate the strike-slip movement, have them:

- slide smooth wood surfaces together
- slide rough wood surfaces together
- compare the amounts of resistance
- explain why movement at a strike-slip fault causes earthquakes

It is important that students understand the relationship between strike-slip faults and the transform boundaries where tectonic plates meet. Some transform boundaries are actually systems of hundreds or thousands of strike-slip faults. Shown in **Figure 24,** the San Andreas Fault is an example of a particularly large strike-slip fault located between the Pacific and North American plates. In addition to the San Andreas Fault, a number of other strike-slip faults make up this transform boundary. Such large-scale strike-slip faults are often called transform faults. Strike-slip faults are not always associated with tectonic plate boundaries, however.

Figure 23 *The photo at top left is a normal fault. The photo at top right is a reverse fault. Can you tell which kind of tectonic stress—compression or tension—must have acted on the rocks in each photo?*

Telling the Difference It's easy to tell the difference between a normal fault and a reverse fault in diagrams with arrows. But what about the faults in **Figure 23**? You can certainly see the faults, but which one is a normal fault, and which one is a reverse fault? In the top photo, one side has obviously moved relative to the other. You can tell this is a normal fault by looking at the sequence of sedimentary rock layers. You can see by the relative positions of the two dark layers that the hanging wall has moved down relative to the footwall.

Figure 24 *In this photo of the San Andreas fault, you can see how the course of two river channels changed when the fault moved. The land at the top moved to the right relative to the land at the bottom.*

Strike-Slip Faults A third major type of fault is shown in **Figure 24.** **Strike-slip faults** occur when opposing forces cause rock to break and move horizontally. If you were standing on one side of a strike-slip fault looking across the fault when it moved, the ground on the other side would appear to move to your left or right.

Natural gas is used in many homes and factories as a source of energy. Some companies explore for sources of natural gas just as other companies explore for oil and coal. Like oil, natural gas travels upward through rock layers until it hits a layer through which it cannot travel and becomes trapped. Imagine that you are searching for pockets of trapped natural gas. Would you expect to find these pockets associated with anticlines, synclines, or faults? Explain your answer in your ScienceLog. Include drawings to help in your explanation.

154

Answers to APPLY

Pockets of natural gas would tend to get trapped in anticlines and faults because impermeable layers in these structures can seal off upward movement of the gas. In a syncline, the natural gas will still travel upward along the bottom of an impermeable layer.

Plate Tectonics and Mountain Building

You have just learned about several ways the Earth's crust changes due to the forces of plate tectonics. When tectonic plates collide, land features that start out as small folds and faults can eventually become great mountain ranges. The reason mountains exist is that tectonic plates are continually moving around and bumping into one another. As you can see in **Figure 25,** most major mountain ranges form at the edges of tectonic plates.

When tectonic plates undergo compression or tension, they can form mountains in several different ways. Let's take a look at three of the most common types of mountains—*folded mountains, fault-block mountains,* and *volcanic mountains.*

Folded Mountains *Folded mountains* form when rock layers are squeezed together and pushed upward. If you take a pile of paper on a table top and push on opposite edges of the pile, you will see how a folded mountain forms. You saw how these layers crunched together in Figure 18. **Figure 26** shows an example of a folded mountain range that formed at a convergent boundary.

Figure 25 *Most of the world's major mountain ranges form at tectonic plate boundaries. Notice that the Appalachian Mountains, however, are located in the middle of the North American plate.*

Figure 26 *Once as mighty as the Himalayas, the Appalachians have been worn down by hundreds of millions of years of weathering and erosion.*

BRAIN FOOD

By now you know that plate tectonics is the force that creates the world's highest mountains, but did you know that plate tectonics is also responsible for creating some of the lowest places on Earth? It's true. When one tectonic plate is subducted beneath another, a deep valley called a *trench* forms at the boundary. The Mariana trench is the deepest point in the oceans—10,924 m below sea level!

155

IS THAT A FACT!

The Sierra Nevada, in California, and the Teton Range, in Wyoming, are examples of fault-block mountains. The Appalachian Mountains, in eastern North America, are an example of folded mountains.

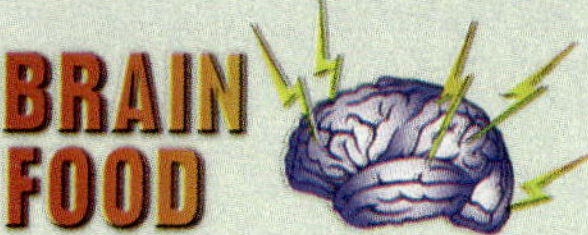

BRAIN FOOD

Ask students to write a one page paper explaining their thoughts on the following quote:

"What we have been pleased to call 'solid Earth' is not as solid as we thought. It is energetic, dynamic, and fundamentally restless."

—Jonathan Weiner, *Planet Earth*

Multicultural CONNECTION

By the twelfth century, Chinese scientists recognized the fact that some mountains had been elevated from the ocean floor and that fossils were the remains of organisms that lived in the distant past. Chinese scientists discovered these facts more than 700 years before European scientists. Have interested students research some of the other early advances of Chinese geologists.

CONNECT TO ASTRONOMY

Earth is not the only place with mountains. Astronomers give extraterrestrial mountains the name "mons," while extraterrestrial mountain ranges are called either "montes" or "highlands." Encourage students to find out more about the formation of mountains on Mercury, Mars, Earth's moon, or one of the moons of Jupiter or Saturn. Have students compare the mountains they study with mountains on Earth.

3 Extend

Reteaching

After students have read this section, invite volunteers to sketch examples of each type of mountain on the board. Ask other students to explain how each mountain type forms. Have them refer to the diagram and add labels and arrows to show the direction of forces at work. Sheltered English

Activity

Tell students to locate photographs of mountains in magazines, books, or the Internet. Have them cut out, copy, or print these images and mount them on paper. Then have them write the type of mountain and a description of how it formed on a card and tape the card to the back of the photo.

Number and post the photos around the room so that students can view the "gallery" and write their own guesses about each mountain. Have students check their guesses against the cards.

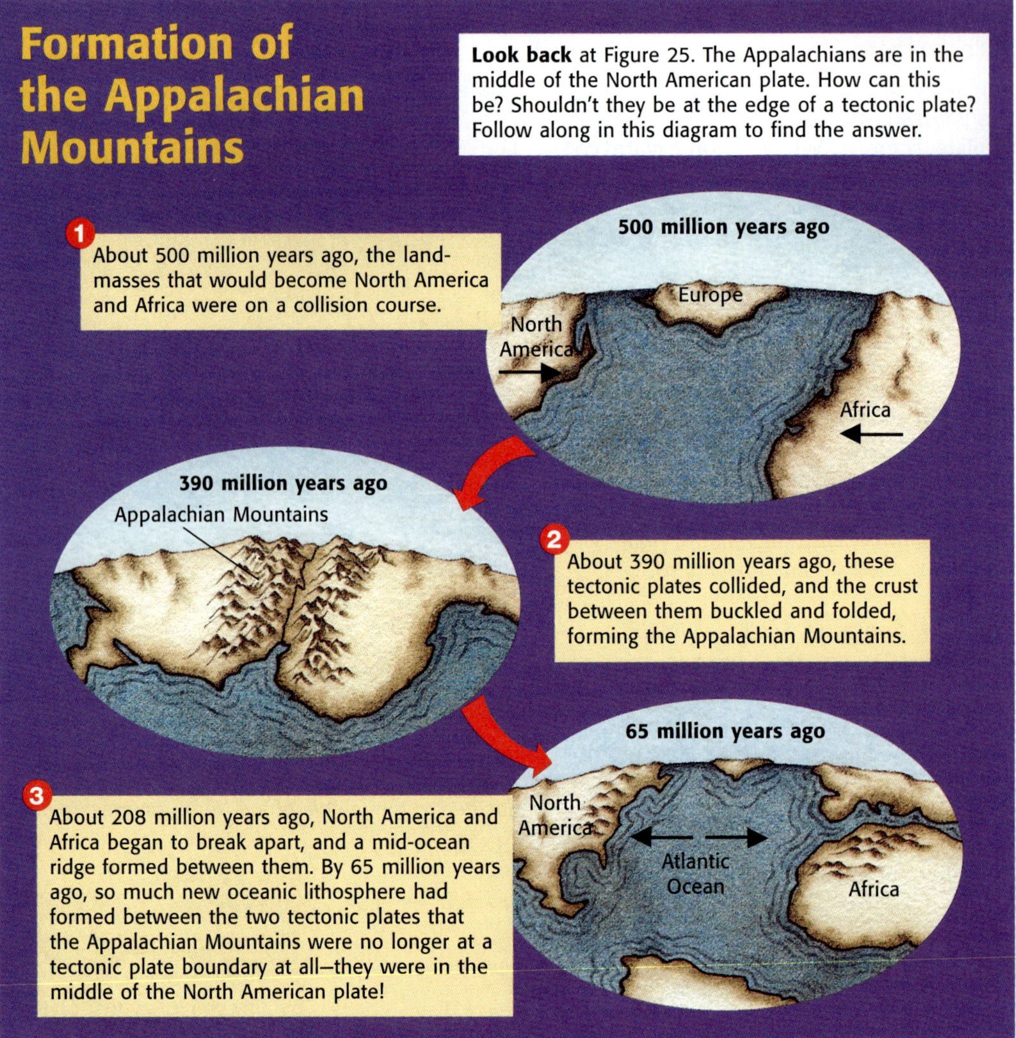

Figure 27 *When the crust is subjected to tension, the rock can break along a series of normal faults, resulting in fault-block mountains.*

Fault-Block Mountains Where tectonic forces put enough tension on the Earth's crust, a large number of normal faults can result. *Fault-block mountains* form when this faulting causes large blocks of the Earth's crust to drop down relative to other blocks. **Figure 27** shows one way this can happen.

156

Is That a Fact!

When the Appalachian Mountains formed, they were probably very similar to the Himalayas. The Appalachians were of a comparable height and must have been characterized by frequent seismic activity. The Appalachians are about 350 million years older than the Himalayas, however, and have been worn down steadily by weathering and erosion over hundreds of millions of years.

When sedimentary rock layers are tilted up by faulting, they can produce mountains with sharp, jagged peaks. As you can see in **Figure 28,** the Tetons of western Wyoming are a spectacular example of this type of mountain.

Figure 28 *The Tetons formed as a result of tectonic forces that stretched the Earth's crust, causing it to break in a series of normal faults. Compare this photo with the illustration in Figure 27.*

Volcanic Mountains Most of the world's major volcanic mountains are located at convergent boundaries. Most volcanic mountains tend to form over the type of convergent boundaries that include subduction zones. There are so many volcanic mountains around the rim of the Pacific Ocean that early explorers named it the *Ring of Fire*. **Figure 29** shows an active volcano of the Ring of Fire.

Volcanic mountains form when molten rock erupts onto the Earth's surface. Unlike folded and fault-block mountains, volcanic mountains form from new material being added to the Earth's surface.

Figure 29 *A recent lava flow shows up starkly against the snow on Mount St. Helens, a mountain that formed from volcanic activity. Many of the mountains in the Cascade Range formed in this way.*

REVIEW

1. What is the difference between an anticline and a syncline?
2. What is the difference between a normal fault and a reverse fault?
3. Name and describe the tectonic force that forms folded mountains.
4. Name and describe the tectonic force that forms fault-block mountains.
5. **Making Predictions** If a fault occurs in an area where rock layers have been folded, which type of fault is it likely to be? Why?

Answers to Review

1. An anticline is a fold shaped like an upside-down bowl, while a syncline resembles a bowl that is right side up.
2. In a normal fault the hanging wall moves down relative to the footwall. In a reverse fault the hanging wall moves up relative to the footwall.
3. Folded mountains form when compression acts on rock strata (such as when two continental plates collide) so that the layers of rock are pushed up into huge folds.
4. Fault-block mountains form when tension pulls rock apart, causing a large number of normal faults to form. When some of these fault blocks drop down relative to others, fault-block mountains form.
5. A reverse fault is likely to form because both reverse faults and folding occur in areas where compression takes place.

4 Close

Quiz

1. What three features form when rock layers bend? (anticlines, synclines, and monoclines)
2. How do fault blocks move in a strike-slip fault? (They slide past each other in a horizontal direction.)

Alternative Assessment

PORTFOLIO

Have students choose a mountain range and research it in the library or on the Internet. Then ask students to identify in writing the relationship between the mountain range and the forces that created it. Students can summarize their findings in a letter informing scientists living in the 1700s how mountains form and what causes earthquakes.

Multicultural Connection

Although cultures living in mountainous regions are some of the world's most impoverished populations, they inhabit remarkably diverse ecosystems and have developed innovative technologies to live at high altitudes, where resources may be scarce. Encourage students to learn about a culture living in the Andes, the Himalayas, the Alps, or the Appalachians. Students should give a presentation about the culture they studied and conclude with a round-table discussion of the problems and opportunities mountain cultures face.

Chapter Highlights

Vocabulary Definitions

Section 1

crust the thin, outermost layer of the Earth, or the uppermost part of the lithosphere

mantle the layer of the Earth between the crust and the core

core the central, spherical part of the Earth below the mantle

lithosphere the outermost, rigid layer of the Earth that consists of the crust and the rigid, uppermost part of the mantle

asthenosphere the partially molten layer of the upper mantle on which the tectonic plates of the lithosphere move

mesosphere literally, the "middle sphere"–the rigid, lower part of the mantle between the asthenosphere and the outer core

outer core the liquid layer of the Earth's core between the mesosphere and the inner core

inner core the solid, dense, spherical center of the Earth

tectonic plates huge pieces of the lithosphere that move around on top of the asthenosphere

Section 2

continental drift the theory that continents can drift apart from one another and that they have done so in the past

sea-floor spreading the process by which new oceanic crust forms at mid-ocean ridges as tectonic plates are pulled away from each other

Vocabulary Review Worksheet 6

Chapter Highlights

Section 1

Vocabulary

crust *(p. 136)*
mantle *(p. 137)*
core *(p. 137)*
lithosphere *(p. 138)*
asthenosphere *(p. 138)*
mesosphere *(p. 139)*
outer core *(p. 139)*
inner core *(p. 139)*
tectonic plates *(p. 140)*

Section Notes

- The Earth is made of three basic compositional layers—the crust, the mantle, and the core.
- The Earth is made of five main structural layers—lithosphere, asthenosphere, mesosphere, outer core, and inner core.
- Tectonic plates are large pieces of the lithosphere that move around on the Earth's surface.
- Knowledge about the structure of the Earth comes from the study of seismic waves caused by earthquakes.

Section 2

Vocabulary

continental drift *(p. 143)*
sea-floor spreading *(p. 145)*

Section Notes

- Wegener's theory of continental drift explained many puzzling facts, including the fit of the Atlantic coastlines of South America and Africa.
- Today's continents were originally joined together in the ancient continent Pangaea.
- Some of the most important evidence for sea-floor spreading comes from magnetic reversals recorded in the ocean floor.

Skills Check

Math Concepts

MAKING MODELS Suppose you built a model of the Earth that had a radius of 100 cm (diameter of 200 cm). The radius of the real Earth is 6,378 km, and the thickness of its outer core is 2,200 km. What percentage of the Earth's radius is the outer core? How thick would the outer core be in your model?

$$\frac{2{,}200 \text{ km}}{6{,}378 \text{ km}} = 0.34 = 34\%$$

$$34\% \text{ of } 100 \text{ cm} = 0.34 \times 100 \text{ cm} = 34 \text{ cm}$$

Visual Understanding

SEA-FLOOR SPREADING This close-up view of a mid-ocean ridge shows how new oceanic lithosphere forms. As the two tectonic plates pull away from each other, magma fills in the cracks that open between them. When this magma solidifies, it becomes the newest part of the oceanic plate.

158

Lab and Activity Highlights

Convection Connection PG 508

Oh, the Pressure! PG 509

Datasheets for LabBook (blackline masters for these labs)

SECTION 3

Vocabulary

plate tectonics *(p. 147)*
convergent boundary *(p. 148)*
subduction zone *(p. 148)*
divergent boundary *(p. 149)*
transform boundary *(p. 149)*

Section Notes

- The processes of ridge push, convection, and slab pull provide some possible driving forces for plate tectonics.
- Tectonic plate boundaries are classified as convergent, divergent, or transform.
- Data from satellite tracking indicate that some tectonic plates move an average of 3 cm a year.

Labs

Convection Connection *(p. 508)*

SECTION 4

Vocabulary

stress *(p. 151)*
compression *(p. 151)*
tension *(p. 151)*
folding *(p. 152)*
fault *(p. 153)*
normal fault *(p. 153)*
reverse fault *(p. 153)*
strike-slip fault *(p. 154)*

Section Notes

- As tectonic plates move next to and into each other, a great amount of stress is placed on the rocks at the boundary.
- Folding occurs when rock layers bend due to stress.
- Faulting occurs when rock layers break due to stress and then move on either side of the break.
- Mountains are classified as either folded, fault-block, or volcanic, depending on how they form.
- Mountain building is caused by the movement of tectonic plates. Different types of movement cause different types of mountains.

Labs

Oh, the Pressure! *(p. 509)*

internetconnect

GO TO: go.hrw.com

Visit the **HRW** Web site for a variety of learning tools related to this chapter. Just type in the keyword:

KEYWORD: HSTTEC

GO TO: www.scilinks.org

Visit the **National Science Teachers Association** on-line Web site for Internet resources related to this chapter. Just type in the ***sci*LINKS** number for more information about the topic:

TOPIC	*sci*LINKS NUMBER
Composition of the Earth	HSTE155
Structure of the Earth	HSTE160
Tectonic Plates	HSTE165
Faults	HSTE170
Mountain Building	HSTE175

159

Lab and Activity Highlights

LabBank

Whiz-Bang Demonstrations, Thar She Blows! Demo 18

Labs You Can Eat
- Rescue Near the Center of the Earth, Lab 13
- Cracks in the Hard-Boiled Earth, Lab 14
- Dough Fault of Your Own, Lab 15

Long-Term Projects & Research Ideas, Project 35

VOCABULARY DEFINITIONS, *continued*

SECTION 3

plate tectonics the theory that the Earth's lithosphere is divided into tectonic plates that move around on top of the asthenosphere

convergent boundary the boundary between two colliding tectonic plates

subduction zone the region where an oceanic plate sinks down into the asthenosphere at a convergent boundary, usually between continental and oceanic plates

divergent boundary the boundary between two tectonic plates that are moving away from each other

transform boundary the boundary between two tectonic plates that are sliding past each other

SECTION 4

stress the amount of force placed on a given material

compression stress that occurs when opposing forces apply pressure to a given material

tension stress that occurs when opposing forces act to stretch a given material

folding the bending of rock layers due to pressure caused by movements in the Earth's crust

fault a break in the Earth's crust along which two blocks of the crust slide relative to each other due to tectonic forces

normal fault a fault in which the hanging wall moves down relative to the footwall

reverse fault a fault in which the hanging wall moves up relative to the footwall

strike-slip fault a fault in which the two fault blocks move past each other horizontally

Blackline masters of these Chapter Highlights can be found in the **Study Guide.**

Chapter Review Answers

Using Vocabulary

1. Oceanic crust is a relatively thin, dense layer of crust underneath the oceans that has a composition similar to that of basalt. Continental crust is a relatively thick, light-weight layer of crust that makes up the Earth's continents and has a composition similar to that of granite.
2. *Lithosphere* means "rock sphere" and is the rigid outer layer of the Earth. *Asthenosphere* means "weak sphere" and is the soft, partially molten layer of the mantle below the lithosphere.
3. At a convergent boundary, two tectonic plates collide; at a divergent boundary, two tectonic plates pull apart.
4. Folding occurs when tectonic forces bend rock layers; faulting occurs when tectonic forces break rock.
5. Oceanic crust is crust under the oceans. Oceanic lithosphere includes oceanic crust and the rigid part of the mantle that lies below it.
6. Normal faults occur when the hanging wall moves down relative to the footwall, and reverse faults occur when the hanging wall moves up relative to the footwall.

Understanding Concepts

Multiple Choice

7. c
8. b
9. a
10. c
11. c
12. b
13. b
14. c
15. a
16. c
17. a

Chapter Review

USING VOCABULARY

For each pair of terms, explain the difference in their meanings.

1. oceanic crust/continental crust
2. lithosphere/asthenosphere
3. convergent boundary/divergent boundary
4. folding/faulting
5. oceanic crust/oceanic lithosphere
6. normal fault/reverse fault

UNDERSTANDING CONCEPTS

Multiple Choice

7. The part of the Earth that is a liquid is the
   a. crust.
   b. mantle.
   c. outer core.
   d. inner core.

8. The part of the Earth on which the tectonic plates are able to move is the
   a. lithosphere.
   b. asthenosphere.
   c. mesosphere.
   d. subduction zone.

9. The ancient continent that contained all the landmasses is called
   a. Pangaea.
   b. Gondwana.
   c. Laurasia.
   d. Panthalassa.

10. The type of tectonic plate boundary involving a collision between two tectonic plates is
    a. divergent.
    b. transform.
    c. convergent.
    d. normal.

11. The type of tectonic plate boundary that sometimes has a subduction zone is
    a. divergent.
    b. transform.
    c. convergent.
    d. normal.

12. The San Andreas fault is an example of a
    a. divergent boundary.
    b. transform boundary.
    c. convergent boundary.
    d. normal boundary.

13. When a fold is shaped like an arch, with the fold in an upward direction, it is called a(n)
    a. monocline.
    b. anticline.
    c. syncline.
    d. decline.

14. The type of fault in which the hanging wall moves down relative to the footwall is called
    a. strike-slip.
    b. reverse.
    c. normal.
    d. fault block.

15. The type of mountain involving huge sections of the Earth's crust being pushed up into anticlines and synclines is the
    a. folded mountain.
    b. fault-block mountain.
    c. volcanic mountain.
    d. strike-slip mountain.

16. Continental mountain ranges are usually associated with
    a. divergent boundaries.
    b. transform boundaries.
    c. convergent boundaries.
    d. normal boundaries.

17. Mid-ocean ridges are associated with
    a. divergent boundaries.
    b. transform boundaries.
    c. convergent boundaries.
    d. normal boundaries.

160

Short Answer

18. A tectonic plate is a large piece of the lithosphere that moves around on top of the asthenosphere.
19. Wegener's theory did not explain the driving force responsible for continental drift.
20. Stress occurs in the Earth's crust because the crust is a part of all tectonic plates, and tectonic plates are constantly colliding, pulling apart, and sliding past each other.

Chapter 6 Review–California Standards: PE/ATE Q1–6: 1a, 1b; Q7–21: 1, 1a, 1b, 1c, 1e, 1f

Short Answer

18. What is a tectonic plate?

19. What was the major problem with Wegener's theory of continental drift?

20. Why is there stress on the Earth's crust?

Concept Mapping

21. Use the following terms to create a concept map: sea-floor spreading, convergent boundary, divergent boundary, subduction zone, transform boundary, tectonic plates.

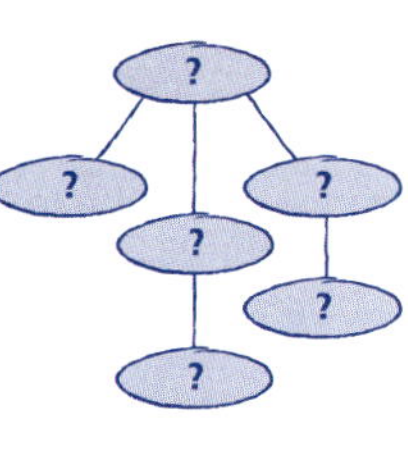

CRITICAL THINKING AND PROBLEM SOLVING

Write one or two sentences to answer each of the following questions:

22. Why is it necessary to think about the different layers of the Earth in terms of both their composition and their physical properties?

23. Folded mountains usually form at the edge of a tectonic plate. How can you explain old folded mountain ranges located in the middle of a tectonic plate?

24. New tectonic plate material continually forms at divergent boundaries. Tectonic plate material is also continually destroyed in subduction zones at convergent boundaries. Do you think the total amount of lithosphere formed on Earth is about equal to the amount destroyed? Why?

MATH IN SCIENCE

25. Assume that a very small oceanic plate is between a mid-ocean ridge to the west and a subduction zone to the east. At the ridge, the oceanic plate is growing at a rate of 5 km every million years. At the subduction zone, the oceanic plate is being destroyed at a rate of 10 km every million years. If the oceanic plate is 100 km across, in how many million years will the oceanic plate disappear?

INTERPRETING GRAPHICS

Imagine that you could travel to the center of the Earth. Use the diagram below to answer the questions that follow.

Composition	Structure
Crust (50 km)	Lithosphere (150 km)
Mantle (2,900 km)	Asthenosphere (250 km)
	Mesosphere (2,550 km)
Core (3,428 km)	Outer core (2,200 km)
	Inner core (1,228 km)

26. How far beneath Earth's surface would you have to go to find the liquid material in the Earth's core?

27. At what range of depth would you find mantle material but still be within the lithosphere?

NOW What Do You Think?

Take a minute to review your answers to the ScienceLog questions on page 135. Have your answers changed? If necessary, revise your answers based on what you have learned since you began this chapter.

Concept Mapping

21. An answer to this exercise can be found at the back of this book.

Critical Thinking and Problem Solving

22. Some layers of the Earth (such as the inner and outer cores) have the same composition but different physical properties.

23. At the time they formed, the folded mountains must have been on the edge of a tectonic plate. New material was later added to the tectonic plate, causing the folded mountains to be more centrally located.

24. Answers will vary. The amount of crust formed is roughly equal to the amount of crust destroyed globally. If this were not true, the Earth would be either expanding or shrinking.

Math in Science

25. In 1 million years, the tectonic plate grows 5 km on one side but shrinks by 10 km on the other side. Every 1 million years, the tectonic plate shrinks by 5 km. In 20 million years, the tectonic plate will disappear entirely.

rate of tectonic plate destruction:
$5 \text{ km/y} - 10 \text{ km/y} = -5 \text{ km/y}$

The tectonic plate will completely disappear in:
$\frac{100 \text{ km}}{5 \text{ km/y}} = 20$ million years

Interpreting Graphics

26. 150 km + 250 km + 2,550 km = 2,950 km

27. between 50 and 150 km

Now What Do You Think?

1. Mountain ranges move because they are part of tectonic plates, which move around on top of the asthenosphere.
2. Mountains can form in three main ways: when rock layers are folded as tectonic plates collide; when the crust is stretched due to tension, forming a large number of normal faults; and when volcanoes form as molten rock erupts onto the Earth's surface.

Concept Mapping Transparency 6

Blackline masters of this Chapter Review can be found in the **Study Guide.**

Chapter 6 Review–California Standards: PE/ATE Q22–24: 1, 1a, 1b, 1e; Q25: 1, 1a; Q26–27: 1b; Think: 1, 1e

Science, Technology, and Society

Living on the Mid-Atlantic Ridge

Background

Geothermal energy is a clean natural resource that is relatively easy to harness. Before converting to geothermal energy, Reykjavik, Iceland's capital, was one of the most polluted cities in the world. The city relied on imported fossil fuels, so heating costs were very high. Today Reykjavik has better air quality than any large city in Europe. Electricity costs in Iceland are among the lowest in the world and have attracted foreign investment projects in the power-intensive industries.

Science, Technology, and Society

Living on the Mid-Atlantic Ridge

Imagine living hundreds of miles from other people on an icy outcrop of volcanic rock surrounded by the cold North Atlantic Ocean. How would you stay warm? For the people of Iceland, this is an important question that affects their daily life. Iceland is a volcanic island situated on the Mid-Atlantic Ridge, just south of the Arctic Circle. Sea-floor spreading produces active volcanoes, earthquakes, hot springs, and geysers that make life on this island seem a little unstable. However, the same volcanic force that threatens civilization provides the heat necessary for daily life. Icelanders use the geothermal energy supplied by their surroundings in ways that might surprise you.

▲ *The Blue Lagoon in Iceland is the result of producing energy from water power.*

Let's Go Geothermal!

Geothermal literally means "earth heat," *geo* meaning "earth" and *therme* meaning "heat." Around the ninth century A.D., Iceland's earliest settlers took advantage of the Earth's heat by planting crops in naturally heated ground. This encouraged rapid plant growth and an early harvest of food. In 1928, Iceland built its first public geothermal utility project—a hole drilled into the Earth in order to pump water from a hot spring. After the oil crisis of the 1970s, geothermal-energy projects were built on a grand scale in Iceland. Today 85 percent of all houses in Iceland are heated by geothermal energy. Hot water from underground pools is pumped directly to houses, where it is routed through radiators to provide heat.

Geothermal water is also pumped to homes to provide hot tap water. This natural source meets all the hot-water needs for the city of Reykjavik, with a population of about 150,000 people!

There are still other uses for this hot water. For example, it is used to heat 120 public swimming pools. Picture yourself swimming outside in naturally hot water during the dead of winter! Greenhouses, where fruits and vegetables are grown, are also warmed by this water. Even fish farming on Iceland's exposed coastline wouldn't be possible without geothermal heat to adjust the water temperature. In other industries, geothermal energy is used to dry timber, wool, and seaweed.

Power Production

Although hydropower (producing energy from water power) is the principal source of electricity in Iceland, geothermal energy is also used. Water ranging in temperature from 300–700°C is pumped into a reservoir, where the water turns into steam that forces turbines to turn. The spinning motion of these turbines generates electricity. Power generation from geothermal sources is only about 5–15 percent efficient and results in a very large amount of water runoff. At the Svartsengi power plant, this water runoff has created a beautiful pool that swimmers call the Blue Lagoon.

Going Further

▶ Can you think of other abundant clean-energy resources? How could we harness such sources?

162

Answers to Going Further

Such possible energy sources are wind and solar power. Experiments are being done to harness wave power and temperature-gradient power in the oceans. It is important that students realize the consequences of rampant consumption of fossil fuels and learn from Iceland's model of using alternative, clean energy resources. Students should realize, however, that geothermal energy is not a practical option in most parts of the world.

California Standards: PE/ATE 1, 1a, 1e, 6, 6a, 6b

SCIENTIFICDEBATE

Continental Drift

When Alfred Wegener proposed his theory of continental drift in the early 1900s, many scientists laughed at the idea of continents plowing across the ocean. In fact, many people found his theory so ridiculous that Wegener, a university professor, had difficulty getting a job! Wegener's theory jolted the very foundation of geology.

Alfred Wegener (1880–1930)

Wegener's Theory

Wegener used geologic, fossil, and glacial evidence gathered on opposite sides of the Atlantic Ocean to support his theory of continental drift. For example, Wegener recognized geologic similarities between the Appalachian Mountains, in eastern North America, and the Scottish Highlands, as well as similarities between rock strata in South Africa and Brazil. He believed that these striking similarities could be explained only if these geologic features were once part of the same continent.

Wegener proposed that because they are less dense, continents float on top of the denser rock of the ocean floor. Although continental drift explained many of Wegener's observations, he could not find scientific evidence to develop a complete explanation of how continents move.

The Critics

Most scientists were skeptical of Wegener's theory and dismissed it as foolishness. Some critics held fast to old theories that giant land bridges could explain similarities among fossils in South America and Africa. Others argued that Wegener's theory could not account for the tremendous forces that would have been required to move continents such great distances. Wegener, however, believed that these forces could be the same forces responsible for earthquakes and volcanic eruptions.

The Evidence

During the 1950s and 1960s, discoveries of sea-floor spreading and magnetic reversal provided the evidence that Wegener's theory needed and led to the theory of plate tectonics. The theory of plate tectonics describes how the continents move. Today geologists recognize that continents are actually parts of moving lithosphere plates that float on the asthenosphere, which consists of molten magma.

Like the accomplishments of so many scientists, Wegener's accomplishments went unrecognized until years after his death. The next time you hear a scientific theory that sounds far out, don't underestimate it. It may be proven true!

Also an Astronomer and Meteorologist

Wegener had a very diverse background in the sciences. He earned a Ph.D. in astronomy from the University of Berlin. But he was always very interested in geophysics and meteorology. His interest in geophysics led to his theory on continental drift. His interest in meteorology eventually led to his death. He froze to death in Greenland while returning from a rescue mission to bring food to meteorologists camped on a polar icecap.

On Your Own

▶ Photocopy a world map. Carefully cut out the continents from the map. Be sure to cut along the line where the land meets the water. Slide the continents together like a jigsaw puzzle. How does this relate to the tectonic plates and continental drift?

163

Teaching Strategy

The formation of new hypotheses is an essential part of scientific inquiry. Yet scientists are often met with opposition when they challenge conventional theories of the world around us. Encourage students to investigate other scientists whose theories were believed to be absurd during their lifetime. Students may want to explore the controversial theories of Copernicus, Mendel, or Darwin or explore some modern controversies in the scientific community.

Answers to On Your Own!

The coastlines of most continents make a rough fit, especially those of South America and Africa. In the case of South America and Africa, this implies that the two continents were once joined. One would then look for other evidence of continental drift by looking for similarities in the rocks of each continent in the places where they would have been next to each other long ago.

Chapter Organizer

CHAPTER ORGANIZATION	TIME MINUTES	OBJECTIVES	LABS, INVESTIGATIONS, AND DEMONSTRATIONS
Chapter Opener pp. 164–165	45	California Standards: PE/ATE 7, 7b, 7e	**Investigate!** Bend, Break, or Shake, p. 165
Section 1 What Are Earthquakes?	90	▶ Determine where earthquakes come from and what causes them. ▶ Identify different types of earthquakes. ▶ Describe how earthquakes travel through the Earth. PE/ATE 1, 1a, 1d–1g, 2d, 7f	**Demonstration,** Faults and Earthquakes, p. 167 in ATE **QuickLab,** Seismic Waves in Class? p. 171
Section 2 Earthquake Measurement	120	▶ Explain how earthquakes are detected. ▶ Demonstrate how to locate earthquakes. ▶ Describe how the strength of an earthquake is measured. PE/ATE 1g, 2d, 7; LabBook 1g, 7, 7b, 7c, 7e, 7g	**Skill Builder,** Earthquake Waves, p. 514 **Datasheets for LabBook,** Earthquake Waves, Datasheet 15
Section 3 Earthquakes and Society	120	▶ Explain earthquake hazard. ▶ Compare methods of earthquake forecasting. ▶ List ways to safeguard buildings against earthquakes. ▶ Outline earthquake safety procedures. PE/ATE 1, 1d, 1f, 1g, 2d, 7, 7d; LabBook 7, 7a, 7e	**Design Your Own,** Quake Challenge, p. 512 **Datasheets for LabBook,** Quake Challenge, Datasheet 14 **Whiz-Bang Demonstrations,** When Buildings Boogie, Demo 19
Section 4 Earthquake Discoveries Near and Far	90	▶ Describe how seismic studies reveal Earth's interior. ▶ Summarize seismic discoveries on other cosmic bodies. PE/ATE 1, 1a, 1b, 1g	**Demonstration,** Mapping with Seismic Waves, p. 182 in ATE **Long-Term Projects & Research Ideas,** Project 36

See page **T20** *for a complete correlation of this book with the*

CALIFORNIA SCIENCE CONTENT STANDARDS.

Correlations are also provided at point of use throughout this ATE.

TECHNOLOGY RESOURCES

Guided Reading Audio CD
English or Spanish, Chapter 7

Classroom Management CD-ROM

CNN **Scientists in Action,** Earthquake Architect, Segment 11

Test Generator CD-ROM

Chapter 7 • Earthquakes

Classroom Worksheets, Transparencies, and Resources	Science Integration and Connections	Review and Assessment
Directed Reading Worksheet 7 **Science Puzzlers, Twisters & Teasers,** Worksheet 7		
Directed Reading Worksheet 7, Section 1 **Transparency 108,** Elastic Rebound **Transparency 193,** Transverse and Longitudinal Waves **Transparency 109,** Primary Wave **Transparency 109,** Secondary Wave **Transparency 109,** Time-Distance Graph of P and S Waves	**Cross-Disciplinary Focus,** p. 166 in ATE **Multicultural Connection,** p. 167 in ATE **Cross-Disciplinary Focus,** p. 169 in ATE **Multicultural Connection,** p. 169 in ATE **Physics Connection,** p. 170 **Connect to Physical Science,** p. 170 in ATE	**Homework,** pp. 167, 168 in ATE **Self-Check,** p. 169 **Review,** p. 171 **Quiz,** p. 171 in ATE **Alternative Assessment,** p. 171 in ATE
Transparency 110, Finding an Earthquake's Epicenter **Directed Reading Worksheet 7,** Section 2 **Reinforcement Worksheet 7,** Complete a Seismic Story **Math Skills for Science Worksheet 43,** Earthquake Power!	**Multicultural Connection,** p. 172 in ATE **MathBreak,** Moving Up the Scale, p. 174	**Review,** p. 174 **Quiz,** p. 174 in ATE **Alternative Assessment,** p. 174 in ATE
Directed Reading Worksheet 7, Section 3 **Math Skills for Science Worksheet 5,** Dividing Whole Numbers with Long Division	**Cross-Disciplinary Focus,** p. 176 in ATE **Math and More,** p. 176 in ATE **Connect to Life Science,** p. 177 in ATE **Apply,** p. 180 **Weird Science:** Can Animals Predict Earthquakes? p. 188 **Eye on the Environment:** What Causes Such Destruction? p. 189	**Self-Check,** p. 176 **Homework,** pp. 178, 179 in ATE **Review,** p. 180 **Quiz,** p. 180 in ATE **Alternative Assessment,** p. 180 in ATE
Transparency 111, Discoveries in Earth's Interior **Directed Reading Worksheet 7,** Section 4 **Critical Thinking Worksheet 7,** Nearthlings Unite!		**Homework,** p. 182 in ATE **Review,** p. 183 **Quiz,** p. 183 in ATE **Alternative Assessment,** p. 183 in ATE

Holt, Rinehart and Winston On-line Resources

go.hrw.com

For worksheets and other teaching aids related to this chapter, visit the HRW Web site and type in the keyword: **HSTEQK**

National Science Teachers Association

www.scilinks.org

Encourage students to use the keywords listed on the Technology Highlights page to access information and resources on the **NSTA** Web site.

End-of-Chapter Review and Assessment

Chapter Review in Study Guide
Vocabulary and Notes in Study Guide
Chapter Tests with Performance-Based Assessment, Chapter 7 Test
Chapter Tests with Performance-Based Assessment, Performance-Based Assessment 7
Concept Mapping Transparency 7

Chapter Resources & Worksheets

Visual Resources

TEACHING TRANSPARENCIES

#108 #109 #110 #111

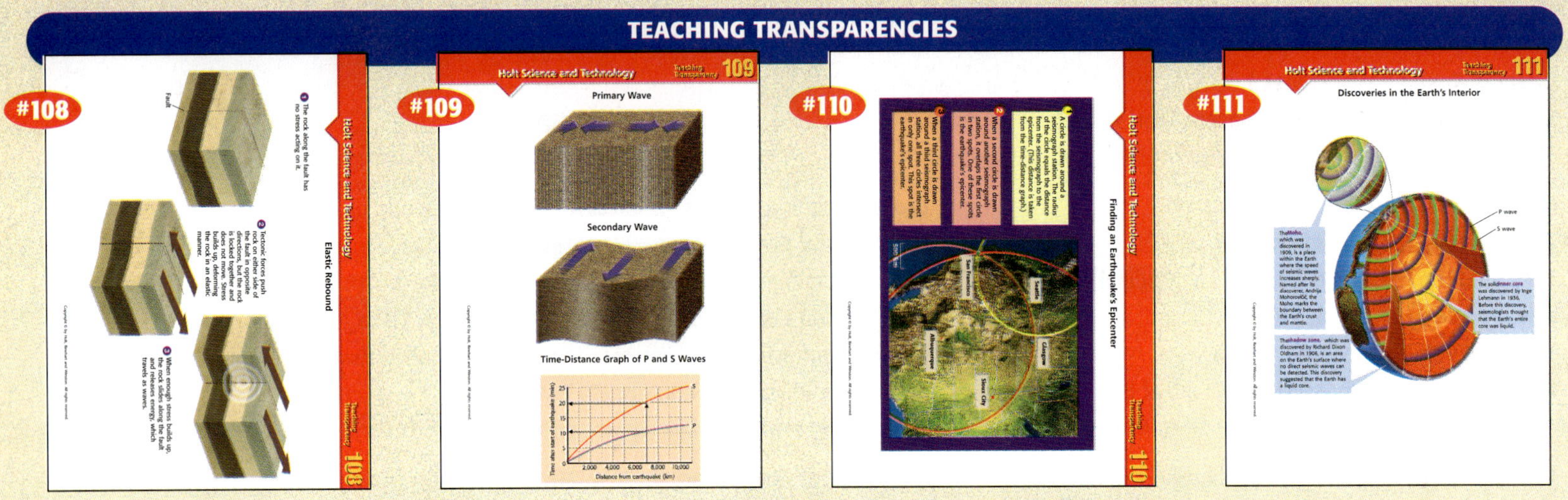

TEACHING TRANSPARENCIES

#193

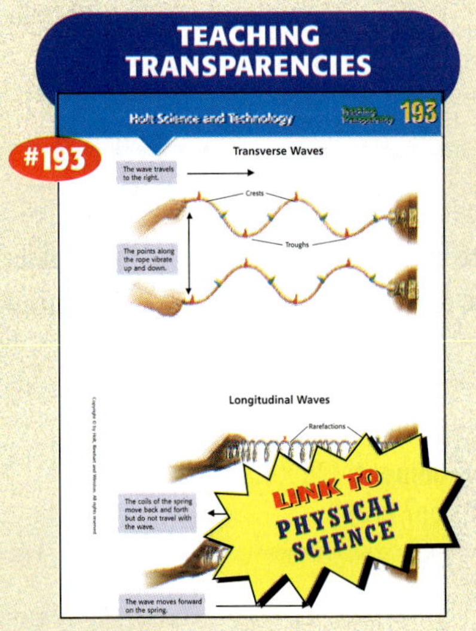

CONCEPT MAPPING TRANSPARENCY

#7

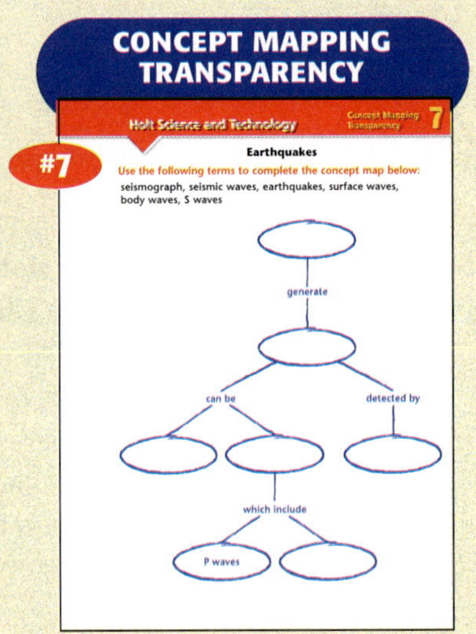

Meeting Individual Needs

DIRECTED READING

#7

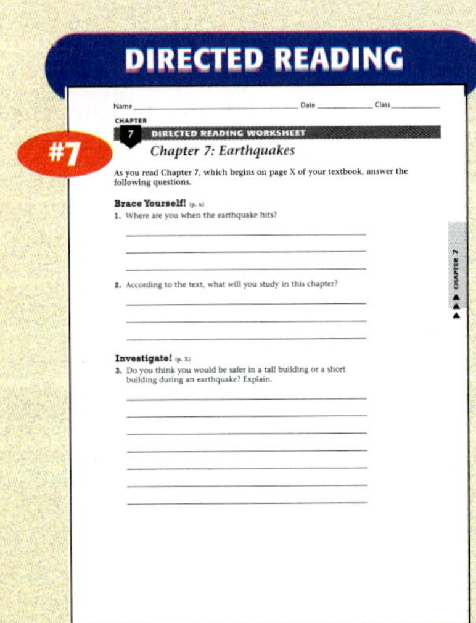

REINFORCEMENT & VOCABULARY REVIEW

#7

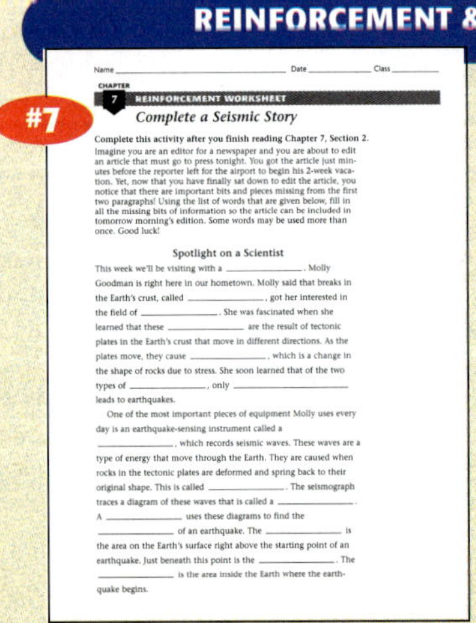

#7

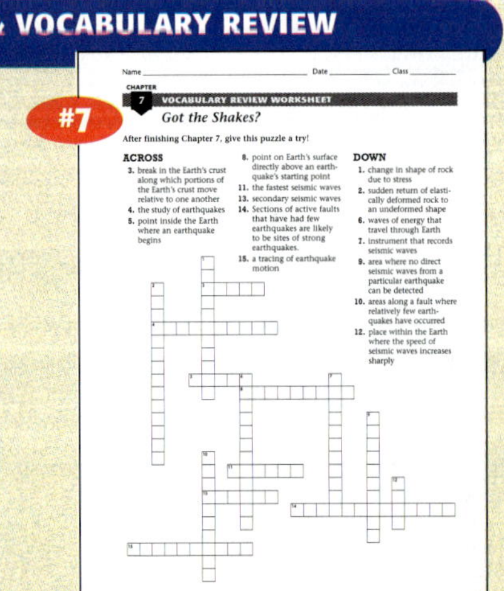

SCIENCE PUZZLERS, TWISTERS & TEASERS

#7

SCIENCE PUZZLERS, TWISTERS, & TEASERS

Challenge at the Cafe

SAMPLE

Chapter 7 • Earthquakes

Review & Assessment

STUDY GUIDE

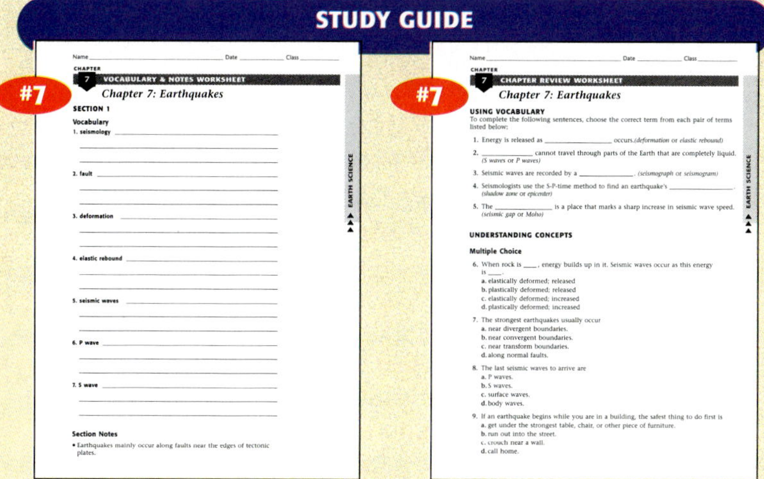
#7 VOCABULARY & NOTES WORKSHEET — *Chapter 7: Earthquakes*

#7 CHAPTER REVIEW WORKSHEET — *Chapter 7: Earthquakes*

CHAPTER TESTS WITH PERFORMANCE-BASED ASSESSMENT

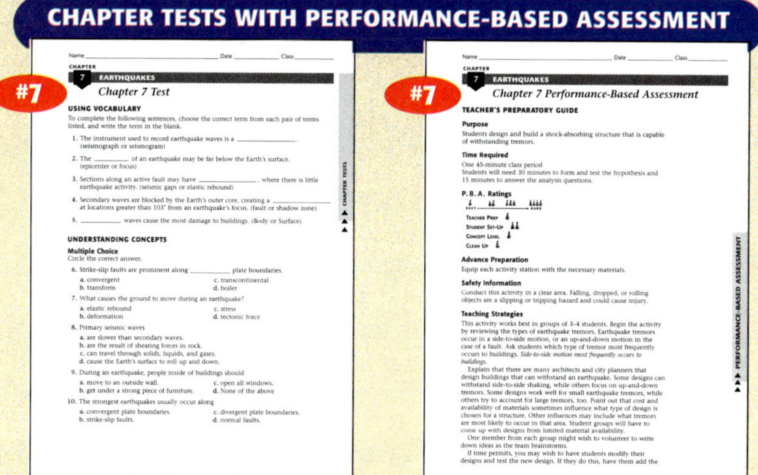
#7 EARTHQUAKES — *Chapter 7 Test*

#7 EARTHQUAKES — *Chapter 7 Performance-Based Assessment*

Lab Worksheets

WHIZ-BANG DEMONSTRATIONS

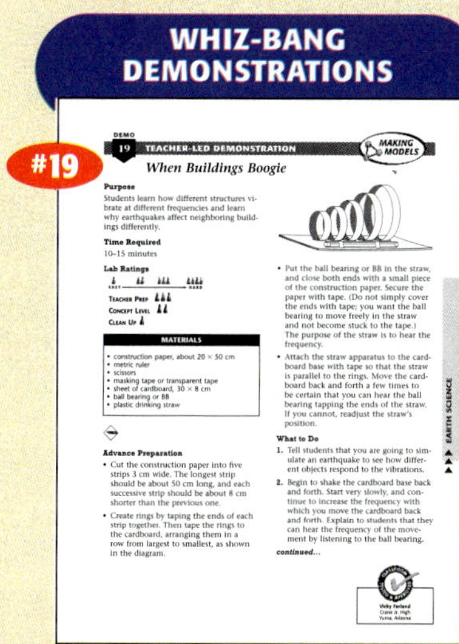
#19 TEACHER-LED DEMONSTRATION — *When Buildings Boogie*

LONG-TERM PROJECTS & RESEARCH IDEAS

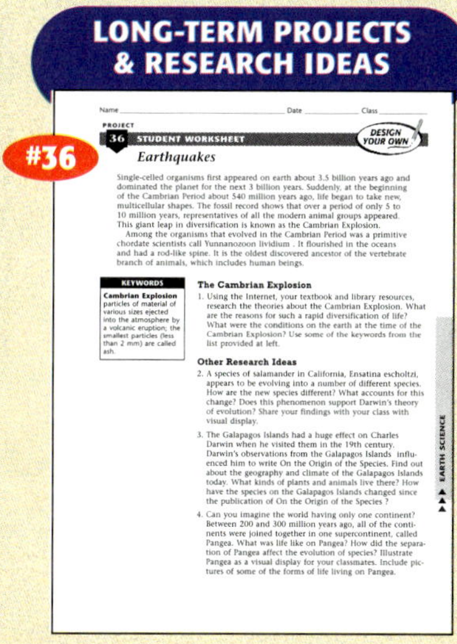
#36 STUDENT WORKSHEET — *Earthquakes*

DATASHEETS FOR LABBOOK

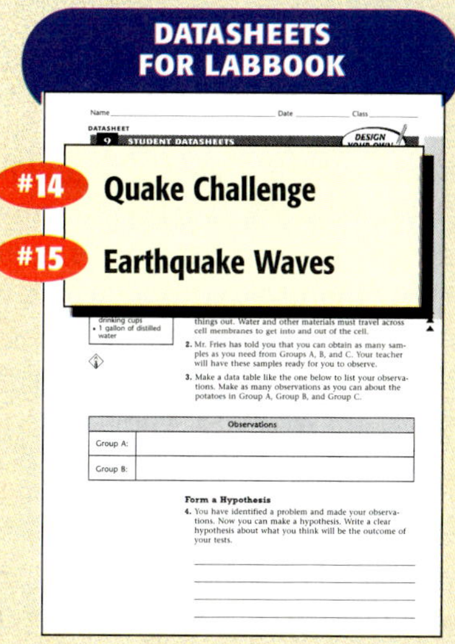
#14 Quake Challenge

#15 Earthquake Waves

Applications & Extensions

CRITICAL THINKING & PROBLEM SOLVING

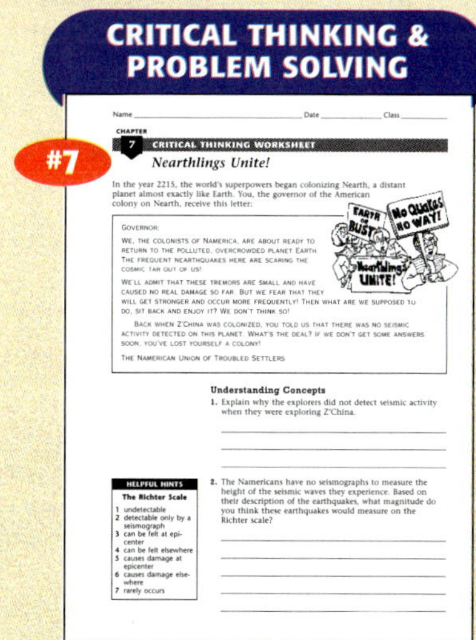
#7 CRITICAL THINKING WORKSHEET — *Nearthlings Unite!*

SCIENTISTS IN ACTION

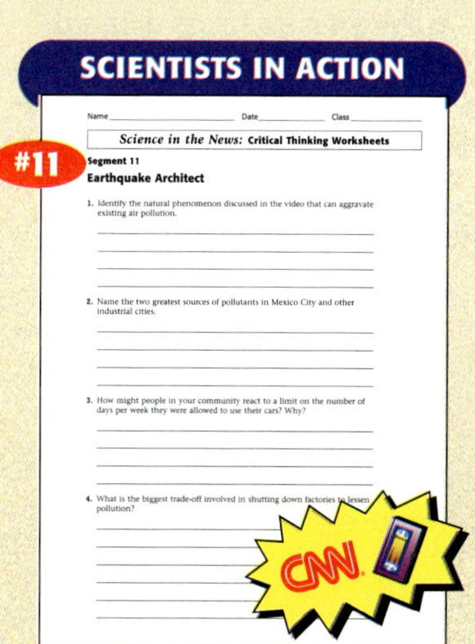
#11 *Science in the News:* Critical Thinking Worksheets — Segment 11 — Earthquake Architect

Chapter Background

Section 1

What Are Earthquakes?

Earthquake Origins

Shallow earthquakes are those that originate within about 60 km of Earth's surface. Intermediate-depth earthquakes are those that originate between depths of about 60 km and 300 km. Deep earthquakes are those that originate below 300 km.

- Tectonic activity is not the only source of earthquakes. Earthquakes can also be caused by volcanic eruptions and by the impacts of cosmic bodies. These earthquakes, however, are less common than those occurring along faults.

The New Madrid Earthquakes

Eyewitnesses to the 1811–1812 earthquakes in New Madrid, Missouri, reported seeing bright flashes of light and a dull glow in the sky over a wide area. Reeking sulfurous odors also accompanied the quakes. Many survivors were convinced that the quakes were a heavenly sign meant to frighten the local citizens back to church. As a result, church attendance in the area skyrocketed between 1811 and 1812!

The Punishment of Loki

In Scandinavian mythology, earthquakes are believed to be caused by the clever prankster Loki. The gods decided to punish Loki when they discovered that he killed Balder, the god of light and joy. Loki was chained in a deep cave, and a huge, poisonous snake was hung above him. As the poison from the snake's fangs dripped down, Loki's sister tried to protect him by catching the poison in a cup. Sometimes, however, a drop of poison would splash Loki, causing him unbearable pain. At those times he would pull so violently on his chains that the ground above would tremble.

IS THAT A FACT!

- In 1755, in Lisbon, Portugal, an earthquake occurred that killed an estimated 60,000 people. It was this tragedy that resulted in an analytic and systematic approach to studying earthquakes, the basis of seismology.

Section 2

Earthquake Measurement

Magnitude Versus Intensity

Earthquakes can be measured by magnitude or intensity. An earthquake's magnitude is a quantitative measurement of its strength. The Richter scale is used to measure magnitude. Intensity is a qualitative measurement of an earthquake's effect in a particular area. The Modified Mercalli Intensity scale is used to assess an earthquake's intensity. This scale incorporates observations of the earthquake's effects at a particular location. Although an earthquake may have different intensities at different locations, it has only one magnitude.

Seismic Rock

In 1992, a British rock group caused some miniature earthquakes at one of their concerts! Scientists were at first mystified by the seismic events they recorded. Upon investigating the tremors, however, researchers at the Global Seismology Research Group, in Scotland, discovered that the energy patterns of the tremors matched those of certain hit songs and were generated by the foot stomping of the more than 30,000 fans at a nearby stadium!

IS THAT A FACT!

- One of the best structures for resisting damage from earthquakes is a wood-framed building. Wood-framed buildings are not very rigid and can therefore flex quite a bit without collapsing.
- The strongest earthquake recorded to date occurred in Chile in 1960. It measured 9.5 on the Richter scale. This is equivalent to detonating more than 1 billion tons of TNT!

Section 3

Earthquakes and Society

▶ Magnetometers

Magnetometers are devices that measure changes in the Earth's magnetic field, which can be indicative of an upcoming quake. Elastic strain can cause slight magnetic variations in the rock. Detecting these variations can help seismologists predict earthquakes.

▶ Survival of Structures

The ability of a structure to withstand a quake depends on a variety of factors, including the composition of the ground on which the structure stands. Structures built on waterlogged or unconsolidated sediment, such as sand, are more likely to suffer intense damage than structures built on bedrock.

IS THAT A FACT!

- Sand boils are common during earthquakes that occur in areas with unconsolidated sediments. Loose, sandy sediments behave like a fluid as the ground moves. This condition can create a miniature "geyser" that spews buried debris from beneath the Earth's surface.
- In 1975, scientists successfully predicted a major earthquake in Haicheng, China. Officials issued a warning in the preceding months because the land and ground water levels shifted, people reported strange animal behavior, and scientists noted many tremors. People were ordered to evacuate after an increase in tremors. The next day, a 7.3 magnitude quake shook the area. This successful prediction probably saved thousands of lives.

Section 4

Earthquake Discoveries Near and Far

▶ Sunquakes

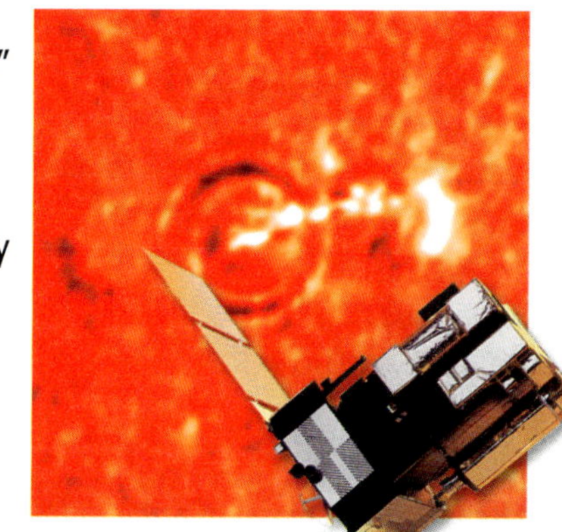

The waves generated by "sunquakes" resemble those produced when an object is dropped into a standing body of water. Unlike water ripples, however, in which a series of waves travels at constant velocity, a single series of solar seismic waves may vary in velocity from 35,400 km/h to 402,300 km/h. "Sunquakes" release enormous amounts of energy. Scientists estimate that a "sunquake" observed in 1996 released an incredible amount of energy—equivalent to covering Earth's land masses with a meter-deep pile of dynamite and detonating it all at once!

▶ The Passive Seismic Experiment

The passive seismic experiment, conducted via the *Apollo 11–16* space missions, produced some significant information about the moon. The experiment suggested that the moon has three distinct layers—a crust, a mantle, and a small, dense core. The studies also suggest that most significant "moonquakes" originate within the moon's mantle; few start in the crust. On Earth, most significant quakes originate in the crust.

IS THAT A FACT!

- The average "moonquake" is about one-millionth as strong as the average earthquake.

For additional background resources, please refer to the ***HST Reference Library.***

CHAPTER 7

Earthquakes

Chapter Preview

Section 1
What Are Earthquakes?
- Where Do Earthquakes Occur?
- What Causes Earthquakes?
- Are All Earthquakes the Same?
- How Do Earthquakes Travel?

Section 2
Earthquake Measurement
- Locating Earthquakes
- Measuring Earthquake Strength

Section 3
Earthquakes and Society
- Earthquake Hazard
- Earthquake Forecasting
- Earthquakes and Buildings
- Are You Prepared for an Earthquake?

Section 4
Earthquake Discoveries Near and Far
- Discoveries in Earth's Interior
- Quakes and Shakes on Other Cosmic Bodies

Directed Reading Worksheet 7

Science Puzzlers, Twisters & Teasers Worksheet 7

Guided Reading Audio CD
English or Spanish, Chapter 7

CHAPTER 7 Earthquakes

Tokyo
Kobe

Brace Yourself!

Imagine visiting Kobe, Japan. The date is January 17, 1995. It's early in the morning—5:46 A.M. to be exact—and you're in a taxi on the Hanshin Expressway. The expressway is elevated, supported by a long row of large columns. All of a sudden, you feel the taxi start to shake. The driver slows down. You watch a truck pass you. It looks like it is out of control. Suddenly the truck disappears! The taxi stops. You look out the window to see what is going on. The superhighway is twisting like a giant snake. The shaking lasts for less than a minute. The part of the highway that you are on seems to be in one piece, but for nearly half a mile in front of you, the expressway has collapsed. It looks as if something jerked the ground right out from under it, snapping the support columns like twigs. You now know why the truck disappeared, and you feel very lucky the taxi stopped in time.

The event you just imagined witnessing was the Great Hanshin earthquake. It killed 5,500 people and left 300,000 others homeless. Nearly 200,000 buildings were destroyed. While the earthquake tremor lasted less than a minute, terrible disasters continued afterward. Natural gas lines that ruptured and kerosene stoves that were crushed started huge fires. Pipes carrying the water that would have been used to put out the fires were broken, so the fires burned for days. Kobe was devastated, with damage totaling more than $100 billion.

In this chapter, you will learn what causes earthquakes and how earthquakes work. You will also learn how they affect our lives. There is much that we can do with the knowledge we gain from studying earthquakes. Think about what you could do with this knowledge as you learn about one of the most powerful parts of nature.

164

Brace Yourself!

The Great Hanshin earthquake brought back memories of another destructive quake that rocked Japan. In 1923, the Great Kanto earthquake destroyed much of Tokyo and the surrounding area; 143,000 people died, mostly as a result of fires. The quake shook the ground so hard that potatoes were pushed up out of the soft soil.

Earthquakes are common on the small island nation of Japan due to tectonic activity along subduction trenches just off the eastern coast, where one tectonic plate moves beneath another. Movement along faults at this convergent plate boundary causes earthquakes.

Chapter 7 Opener–California Standards: PE/ATE 7, 7b, 7e

What Do You Think?

In your ScienceLog, try to answer the following questions based on what you already know:

1. What causes earthquakes?
2. Why are some earthquakes stronger than others?
3. Why do some buildings remain standing during earthquakes while others fall down?

Bend, Break, or Shake

If you were in a building during an earthquake, how would you want the building to respond to the ground's movement? What would you want the building to be made of? How would you want it to be constructed?

To answer these questions, you need to know how building materials behave during earthquakes. Do different materials react differently to the ground's movement? Try this activity to find out.

Procedure

1. Gather all (or most) of the following items: a piece of **rope** or **cord** about 30 cm long, a **wooden stick** about the size of a pencil, a large **paper clip**, a **plastic spoon**, a **wire clothes hanger**, a **plastic clothes hanger**, and a **spring**.
2. Using the straight edge of a **protractor**, draw a straight line on a sheet of **paper**. Measure the following angles from the line, and draw them on the paper: 20°, 45°, and 90°.
3. Put on your goggles and gloves. Using the angles that you drew as a guide, try bending each item 20° and then releasing it (you should still hold the item in your hands as you stop bending it). What happens? Does it break? If it bends, what happens when you stop bending it? Does it stay bent? Does it return to its original shape? Write your observations in your ScienceLog.
4. Repeat step 3, but this time bend each item 45°. Now repeat the test, this time bending each item 90°.
5. In your ScienceLog, make three lists: one for materials that broke, one for materials that stayed bent, and one for materials that bent and then returned to their original shape.

Analysis

6. How do the materials' responses to bending compare?
7. In earthquake-prone areas, engineers use building materials that move with the ground as it shakes but that do not break or bend permanently. Based on this knowledge, which materials from this experiment would you want building materials to behave like? Which materials would you not want building materials to behave like? Explain.

Going Further

Name some building materials that might behave like each of the lab materials. For example, wooden beams might behave like the stick.

What Do You Think?

Accept all reasonable responses.

Students will have a chance to revise their answers in the Chapter Review under NOW What Do You Think?

Investigate!

MATERIALS

For Each Group:

- piece of rope or cord about 30 cm long
- small wooden stick flexible enough to bend
- large metal paper clip
- plastic spoon, knife, or fork
- wire clothes hanger
- plastic clothes hanger
- small spring
- gardening gloves *(1 pair per student)*
- protractor *(1 per student)*
- sheet of paper *(1 per student)*

Safety Caution: Remind students to review all safety cautions and icons before beginning this lab activity.

Teacher Notes: Assist students who have difficulty manipulating the protractor or provide them with paper on which the angles have already been drawn.

Answers to Investigate!

6. Answers will vary depending on the materials used and on the strength of the materials.
7. Desirable building materials would behave like the materials that did not bend permanently or break. Undesirable building materials behave like those that bent permanently or broke. Engineers use materials that move with the ground during an earthquake without bending permanently or breaking.

Answer to Going Further

Accept all reasonable responses. Wooden beams might behave like the stick or the plastic utensils. Steel and iron beams might behave like the wire clothes hanger and the paper clip.

Section 1

Focus

What Are Earthquakes?

This section discusses seismic events known as earthquakes. Students learn where earthquakes most commonly occur and what causes them. The section also covers different kinds of earthquakes and discusses how earthquakes travel as waves of energy through the Earth.

Bellringer

Ask students to write a few sentences in their ScienceLog describing what they think an earthquake is. Ask volunteers to read their descriptions. Students can review what they wrote after completing this section. Sheltered English

1 Motivate

Discussion

Explain to students that *seismos* is a Greek word meaning "to shake." Have students make a list of all the words that contain the root *seis-*. (These include *seismology, seismologists, seismic, seismographs*, and *seismograms*.) Have students who are learning English copy the words onto a sheet of paper and consult a dictionary to divide each word into its proper parts. Then have students define each word part and write a definition of each complete term using the meanings of its parts. Sheltered English

Directed Reading Worksheet 7 Section 1

1

NEW TERMS

seismology, fault, deformation, elastic rebound, seismic waves, P waves, S waves

OBJECTIVES

- Determine where earthquakes come from and what causes them.
- Identify different types of earthquakes.
- Describe how earthquakes travel through the Earth.

What Are Earthquakes?

The word *earthquake* defines itself fairly well. But there is more to an earthquake than just ground shaking. In fact, there is a branch of Earth science devoted to earthquakes called seismology (siez MAHL uh jee). **Seismology** is the study of earthquakes. Earthquakes are complex, and they present many questions for *seismologists*, the scientists who study earthquakes. Although much about earthquakes is unknown, seismologists have found some answers to the following questions.

Where Do Earthquakes Occur?

Most earthquakes take place near the edges of tectonic plates. *Tectonic plates* are giant masses of solid rock that make up the outermost part of the Earth. **Figure 1** shows the Earth's tectonic plates and the locations of recent major earthquakes recorded by scientists. Note the high number of earthquakes near plate boundaries.

Tectonic plates move in different directions and at different speeds. Two plates can push toward each other or pull away from each other. They can also slip past each other like slow-moving trains traveling in opposite directions.

As a result of these movements, numerous features called faults exist in the Earth's crust. A **fault** is a break in the Earth's crust along which blocks of the crust slide relative to one another. Earthquakes occur along faults due to this sliding.

Faults occur in many places, but they are especially common near the edges of tectonic plates where they form the boundaries along which the plates move. This is why earthquakes are so common near plate boundaries.

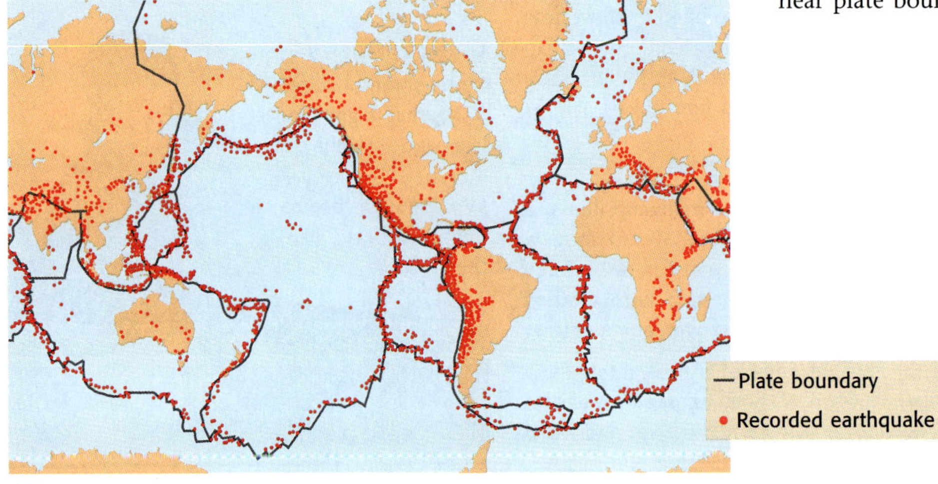

Figure 1 *The largest and most active earthquake zone lies along the plate boundaries surrounding the Pacific Ocean.*

166

Cross-Disciplinary Focus

History Until the seventeenth century, many people believed that earthquakes were caused by large, restless creatures beneath the Earth's surface. Aristotle was one of the first to attribute earthquakes to Earth processes. He hypothesized that earthquakes were caused by strong winds blowing through a myriad of caverns deep in the Earth's interior. It wasn't until the late 1700s that scientists began a systematic study of earthquakes. As recently as the late 1800s, scientists did not know the true cause of most earthquakes.

Section 1–California Standards: PE/ATE 1, 1a, 1d, 1e, 1f, 1g, 2d, 7f

What Causes Earthquakes?

As tectonic plates push, pull, or scrape against each other, stress builds up along faults near the plates' edges. In response to this stress, rock in the plates deforms. **Deformation** is the change in the shape of rock in response to stress. Rock along a fault deforms in mainly two ways—in a plastic manner, like a piece of molded clay, or in an elastic manner, like a rubber band. Plastic deformation, which is shown in **Figure 2,** does not lead to earthquakes.

Elastic deformation, however, does lead to earthquakes. While rock can stretch farther than steel without breaking, it will break at some point. Think of elastically deformed rock as a stretched rubber band. You can stretch a rubber band only so far before it breaks. When the rubber band breaks, it releases energy, and the broken pieces return to their unstretched shape.

Like the return of the broken rubber-band pieces to their unstretched shape, **elastic rebound** is the sudden return of elastically deformed rock to its undeformed shape. Elastic rebound occurs when more stress is applied to rock than the rock can withstand. During elastic rebound, rock releases energy that causes an earthquake, as shown in **Figure 3.**

Figure 2 *This photograph, taken in Hollister, California, shows how plastic deformation along the Calaveras Fault permanently bent a wall. No major earthquakes have occurred since the wall was built.*

Figure 3 *Elastic rebound releases energy waves that cause earthquakes.*

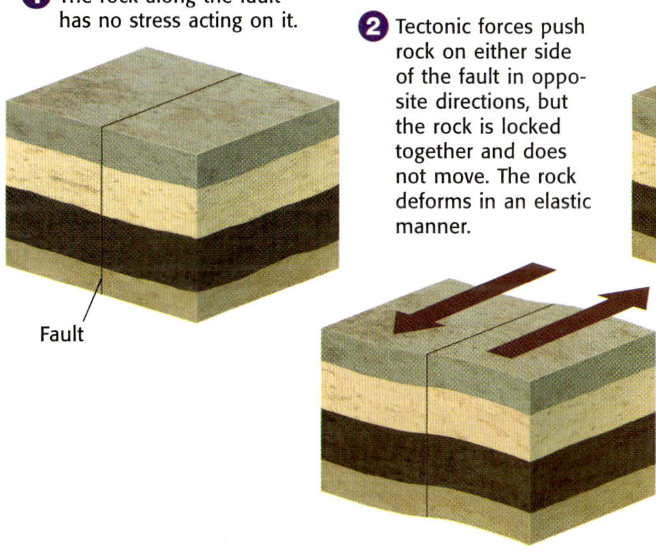

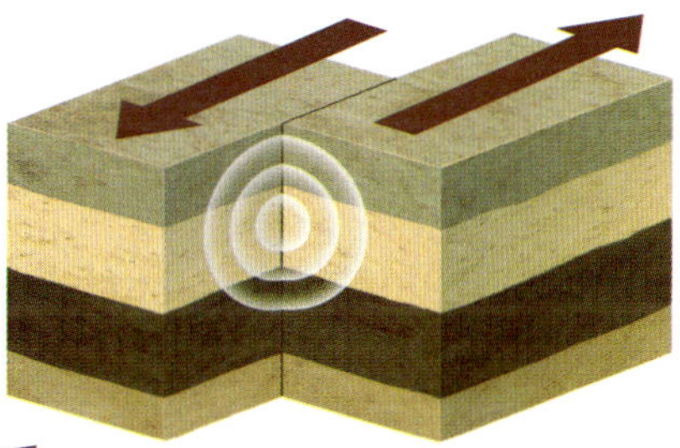

2 Teach

Demonstration

Faults and Earthquakes Use two smooth wooden blocks to demonstrate how blocks of crust move along a fault. Glue coarse sandpaper onto one side of each block. Firmly slide the sandpaper-covered sides against each other until there is a sudden movement. Explain that this is how rock slides along a fault during elastic rebound. As the rock slides, it releases energy that travels as waves. Sheltered English

Misconception Alert

Earthquakes are not a rare phenomenon. In fact, more than 3 million earthquakes happen each year, about one every 10 seconds! Most earthquakes are too weak to be felt by humans. The Ring of Fire, a volcanic zone which lies along the plate boundaries surrounding the Pacific Ocean, is also the world's largest and most active earthquake zone.

Homework

Mapping Encourage students to create an earthquake map using data from Internet sites that contain a log of the time and location of earthquakes around the world. This will help students understand that earthquakes occur every day and that they occur mainly near plate boundaries. This activity could become an ongoing investigation in which students could keep records of earthquakes over the course of the school year.

Multicultural Connection

Many different cultures have myths about earthquakes. According to Japanese mythology, earthquakes are caused by the *namazu,* a giant catfish that lives in mud beneath the Earth. Kamisha, a brave warrior, protects Japan from earthquakes by using divine powers to trap the *namazu* under an enormous rock. Earthquakes occur when Kamisha lets his guard down and allows the *namazu* to thrash about. Encourage students to research other cultural myths about earthquakes and to share their research with the class. Students can also write their own legend about the origin of earthquakes.

Teaching Transparency 108
"Elastic Rebound"

2 Teach, continued

Using the Figure

Each circle in the illustration is a magnified view of a fault at the edge of a tectonic plate. In fact, large systems of multiple faults define the boundaries between plates. The sliding of crust along these faults and the overall movement of crust along plate boundaries are similar. For example, the block of crust to the right of the reverse fault moves down relative to the block to the left of the fault. Similarly, the plate to the right of the convergent plate boundary moves down relative to the plate to the left of the boundary.

Group Activity

Forces and Faults For each pair of students, obtain a pair of wooden blocks. Ask students to demonstrate normal-fault movement by sliding the top block down relative to the bottom block. To show a reverse fault, students slide the top block up relative to the bottom block. Have them slide the blocks horizontally to demonstrate a strike-slip fault. Make sure students see how divergent, convergent, and transform motion cause the different types of fault movement.

Reading Strategy

Mnemonics A footwall is the rock beneath an inclined fault. Using these mnemonic devices, students can remember the difference between a normal fault and a reverse fault by noting the movement of the footwall.

FUN **F**ootwall **U**p is **N**ormal

FDR **F**ootwall **D**own is **R**everse

Are All Earthquakes the Same?

Earthquakes differ in strength and in the depth at which they begin. These differences depend on the type of tectonic plate motion that produces the earthquake. Examine the chart and the diagram below to learn how earthquakes differ.

Plate motion	Prominent fault type	Earthquake characteristics
Transform	strike-slip fault	moderate, shallow
Convergent	reverse fault	strong, deep
Divergent	normal fault	weak, shallow

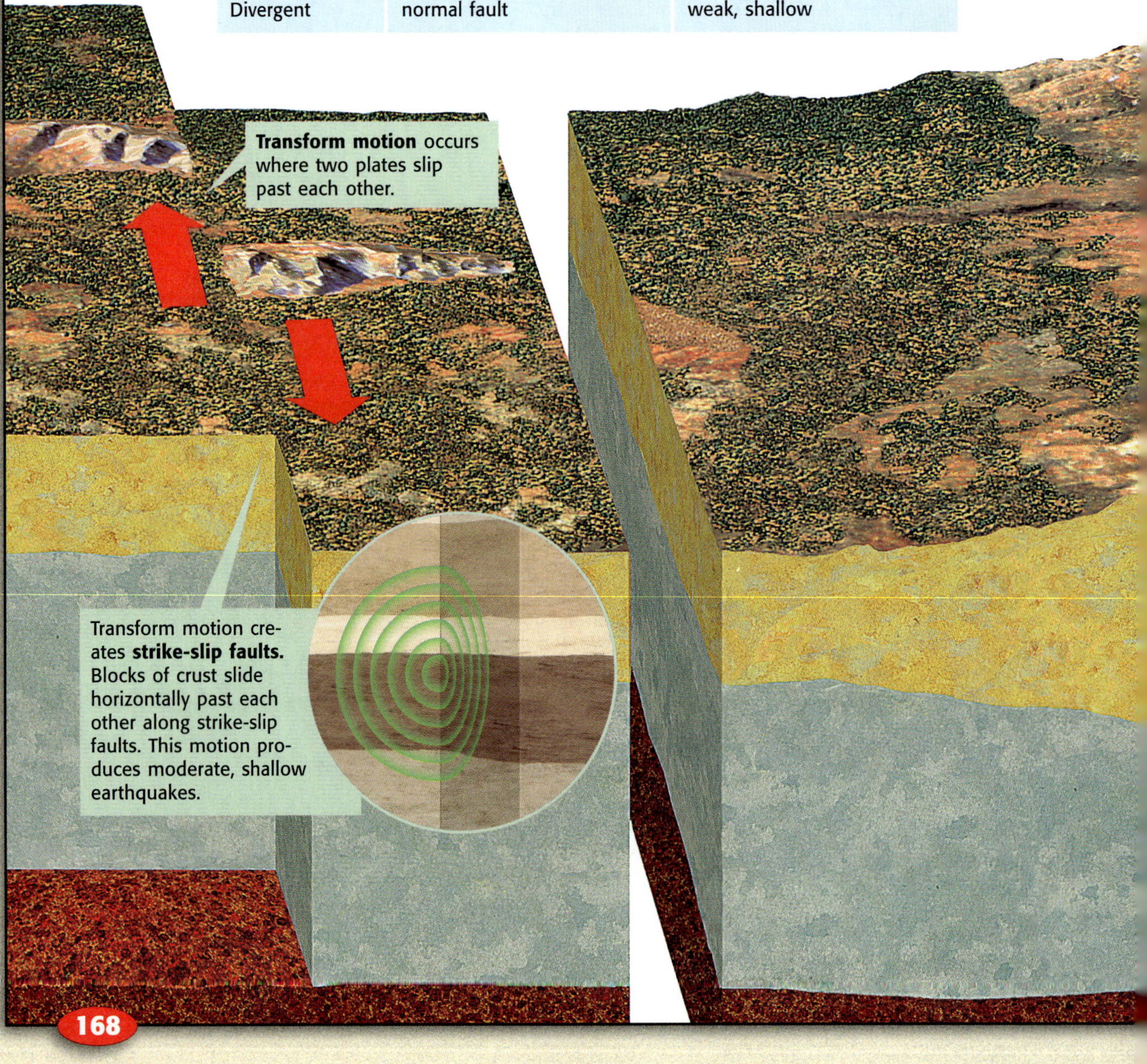

Transform motion occurs where two plates slip past each other.

Transform motion creates **strike-slip faults.** Blocks of crust slide horizontally past each other along strike-slip faults. This motion produces moderate, shallow earthquakes.

168

Homework

Ask students to draw the three types of faults illustrated on these pages. Students should label each fault, state the type of plate motion that creates each fault, and write a brief description of the earthquakes associated with each type of fault.

Encourage students to locate an example of each type of tectonic plate boundary on a map. (An example of a transform plate boundary could include the San Andreas Fault, in California; an example of a convergent plate boundary is off the west coast of South America —convergent motion created the Andes; an example of a divergent plate boundary is the Mid-Atlantic Ridge, on the bottom of the Atlantic Ocean.) Sheltered English

Self-Check

Name two differences between the results of convergent motion and the results of divergent motion. *(See page 564 to check your answer.)*

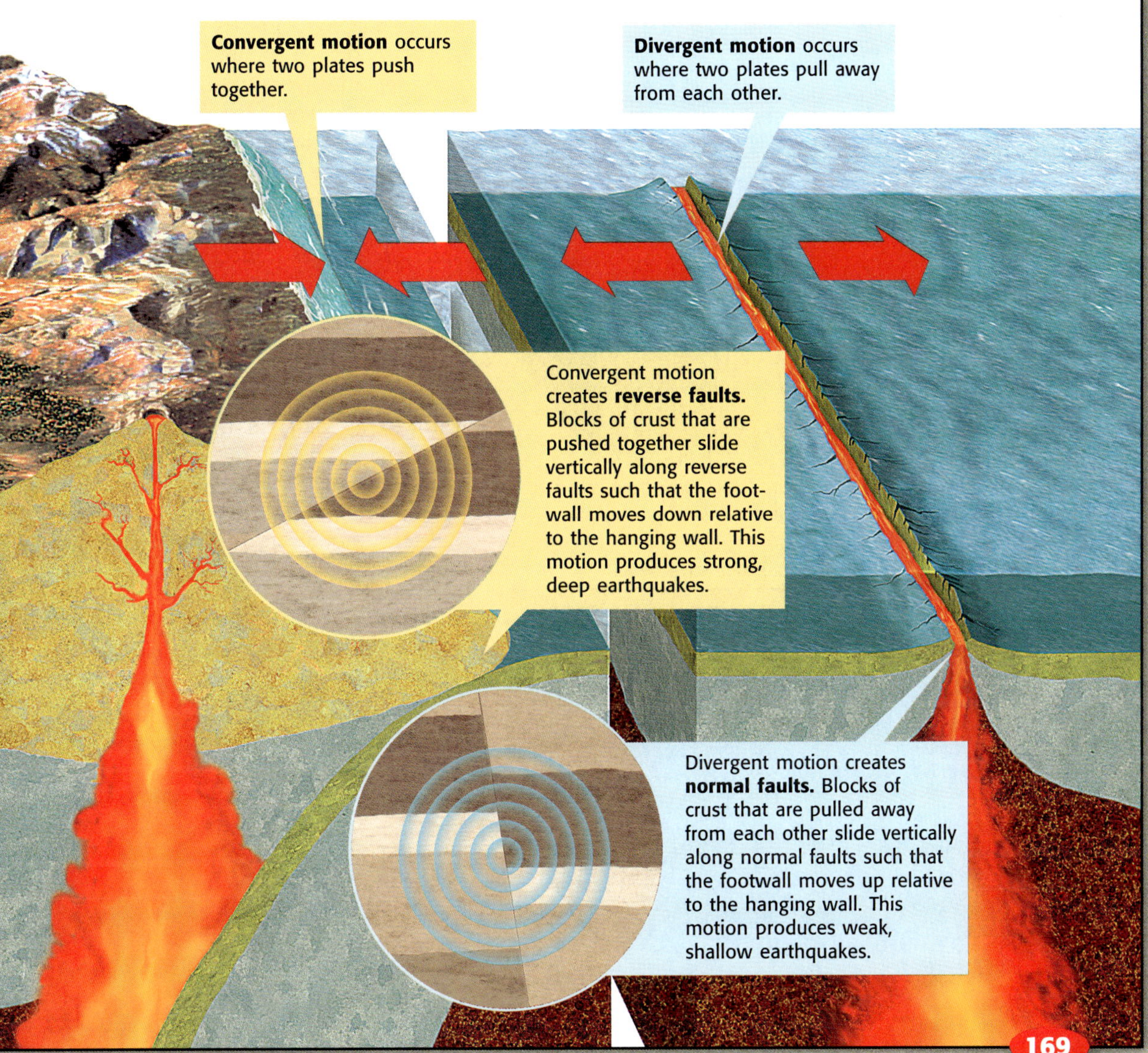

Answers to Self-Check

Convergent motion creates reverse faults, while divergent motion creates normal faults. Convergent motion produces deep, strong earthquakes, while divergent motion produces shallow, weak earthquakes.

Cross-Disciplinary Focus

Writing **Language Arts** John James Audubon was in Kentucky during the New Madrid earthquakes. He wrote that "the ground rose and fell in successive furrows like the ruffled waters of a lake. The earth waved like a field of corn before a breeze." After sharing this quote with the class, ask students to use similes and metaphors to write their own description of an earthquake.

Multicultural Connection

American Indian legends refer to the unstable crust in the New Madrid area. One story describes how Chief Reelfoot of the Chickasaw tribe kidnapped a bride from the Choctaw tribe. Just as the Chief and his bride were about to be married, a great earthquake caused the ground under them to collapse. The entire wedding party was drowned as a river flooded the area, forming Reelfoot Lake, in Tennessee. The lake was indeed formed by the New Madrid earthquakes.

Weird Science

Many people assume that major earthquakes in the United States occur only on the West Coast. However, major quakes have occurred in South Carolina and Missouri—far from any active plate boundaries. The four major tremors of the 1811–1812 earthquakes in New Madrid, Missouri, were so intense that, according to reports, they altered the flow of the Mississippi River and rang church bells in Boston, Massachusetts! The cause of these quakes baffled scientists until the late 1970s, when scientists found a series of faults deep beneath sediment deposited by the Mississippi River. The area is still seismically active, and large quakes may still occur.

3 Extend

Meeting Individual Needs

Learners Having Difficulty
Tell students that the *P* in P waves and the *S* in S waves each stand for two descriptive words. The letters describe how each type of wave affects rock; *P* stands for *pressure,* and *S* stands for *shear. P* also stands for *primary,* while *S* stands for *secondary.* This scheme describes the arrival times of each type of wave—P waves always arrive first, and S waves always arrive second.
Sheltered English

Connect to Physical Science

Use Transparency 193 to discuss the differences between P waves (longitudinal) and S waves (transverse). Have students create a labeled poster of S waves and identify the trough, crest, wave period, wavelength, and wave height. Then have students make a list of the differences between P waves and S waves. Lists should include but are not limited to the following:

- P waves travel faster than S waves
- P waves travel through solids, liquids, and gases; S waves cannot travel through materials that are completely liquid.
- P waves move rock back and forth between a squeezed and stretched position, while S waves shear rock back and forth.

Teaching Transparency 193
"Transverse and Longitudinal Waves"
LINK TO PHYSICAL SCIENCE

physics CONNECTION

All types of waves share basic features. Understanding one type of wave, such as seismic waves, can help you understand many other types, such as light waves and water waves. Some scientists study a branch of physics that deals only with waves—wave mechanics.

How Do Earthquakes Travel?

Remember that rock releases energy when it springs back after being deformed. This energy travels in the form of seismic waves. **Seismic waves** are waves of energy that travel through the Earth. Seismic waves that travel through the Earth's interior are called *body waves.* There are two types of body waves: P waves and S waves. Seismic waves that travel along the Earth's surface are called *surface waves.* Different types of seismic waves travel at different speeds and move the materials that they travel through differently.

P Is for Primary If you squeeze an elastic material into a smaller volume or stretch it into a larger volume, the pressure inside the material changes. When you suddenly stop squeezing or stretching the material, it springs briefly back and forth before returning to its original shape. This is how P waves (pressure waves) affect rock, as shown in **Figure 4. P waves,** which travel through solids, liquids, and gases, are the fastest seismic waves. Because they are the fastest seismic waves and because they can move through all parts of the Earth, P waves always travel ahead of other seismic waves. Because P waves are always the first seismic waves to be detected, they are also called *primary* waves.

Direction of wave travel

Figure 4 *P waves move rock back and forth between a squeezed position and a stretched position as they travel through it.*

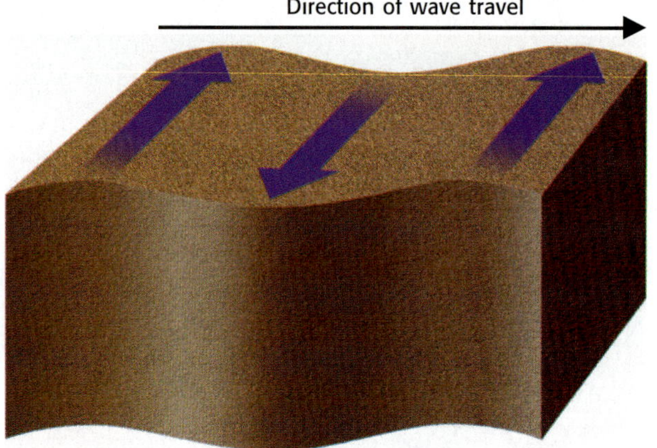

Figure 5 *S waves shear rock back and forth as they travel through it.*

S Is for Secondary Rock can also be twisted. When rock is released after being twisted, S waves are created. **S waves,** or shear waves, are the second-fastest seismic wave. S waves shear rock back and forth, as shown in **Figure 5.** *Shearing* stretches parts of rock sideways from other parts.

170

internet connect

TOPIC: What Is an Earthquake?
GO TO: www.scilinks.org
***sci*LINKS NUMBER:** HSTE180

Unlike P waves, S waves cannot travel through parts of the Earth that are completely liquid. Also, S waves are slower than P waves and always arrive second; thus, they are also called *secondary* waves. The graph in **Figure 6,** which is called a *time-distance graph,* compares the speeds of P waves and S waves.

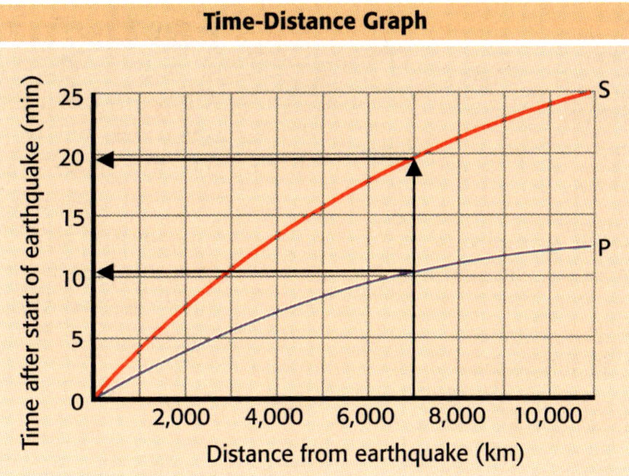

Figure 6 *As you can see, it takes S waves nearly 20 minutes to travel 7,000 km, while it takes P waves less than 11 minutes to travel the same distance.*

Surface Waves Surface waves move the ground up and down in circles as the waves travel along the surface. This is shown in **Figure 7.** Many people have reported feeling like they were on a roller coaster during an earthquake. This feeling comes from surface waves passing along the Earth's surface. Surface waves travel more slowly than body waves but are more destructive. Most damage during an earthquake comes from surface waves, which can literally shake the ground out from under a building.

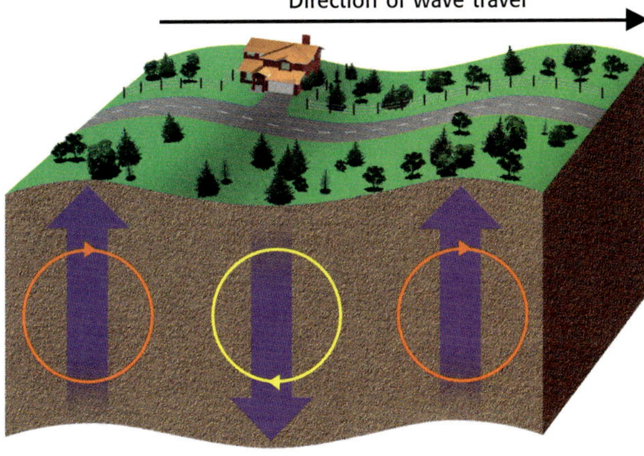

Figure 7 *Surface waves move the ground much like ocean waves move water particles.*

REVIEW

1. Where do earthquakes occur?
2. What directly causes earthquakes?
3. Arrange the types of earthquakes caused by the three plate-motion types from weakest to strongest.
4. **Using Graphics** Refer to Figure 6. How long does it take S waves to travel 1,500 km?

QuickLab

Seismic Waves in Class?

1. Stretch a **spring toy** lengthwise on a **table.**
2. Hold one end of the spring while a partner holds the other end. Push your end toward your partner's end, and observe what happens.
3. Repeat step 2, but this time shake the spring from side to side.
4. Which type of seismic wave is represented in step 2? in step 3?

Answers to Review

1. Answers may vary slightly. Most earthquakes take place near the edges of tectonic plates.
2. Answers may vary slightly. Rock releasing energy during elastic rebound.
3. Earthquakes caused by divergent motion are weakest; earthquakes caused by transform motion are moderate; and earthquakes caused by convergent motion are strongest.
4. about 6 minutes

4 Close

Quiz

1. What is a fault? (A fault is a break in the Earth's crust along which blocks of the crust slide relative to one another.)
2. Name two ways in which rock along a fault deforms in response to stress. (in a plastic manner, like a piece of molded clay, or in an elastic manner, like a rubber band)

Alternative Assessment

Concept Mapping Have students create a concept map explaining the relationship between tectonic plate motion, earthquake characteristics, and fault types.

QuickLab

MATERIALS

For Each Pair:

- small metal or plastic spring toys

Answer to QuickLab

4. P waves are represented in step 2, and S waves are represented in step 3.

Teaching Transparency 109
"Primary Wave"
"Secondary Wave"
"Time-Distance Graph of P and S Waves"

SECTION 2

Focus

Earthquake Measurement

In this section students learn how seismographs are used to detect and locate earthquakes. This section explains the difference between an earthquake's focus and its epicenter. Students will also learn how the Richter scale is used to measure the strength of earthquakes.

Bellringer

Ask students to create a qualitative scale for gauging earthquake intensity. Students should use brief phrases to describe the effects of very minor to extreme earthquakes. Discuss the advantages and disadvantages of their finished scale. Tell them that they will learn about a quantitative scale for earthquake measurement in this chapter.

1) Motivate

ACTIVITY

Ask students to close their eyes. Tell them that you will move to some part of the room and snap your fingers. When they hear you snap, have them point to where they think you are standing. Have them keep their eyes closed while you return to the front of the room. Ask the class to locate where you were standing, and have a helper stand in that spot. Ask students how they were able to pinpoint your location. Explain that when an earthquake occurs, it is noted at seismic stations around the world. By comparing the time it took the tremors to reach each station, the earthquake's origin can be pinpointed.

2

Earthquake Measurement

NEW TERMS

seismograph, epicenter, seismogram, focus

OBJECTIVES

- Explain how earthquakes are detected.
- Demonstrate how to locate earthquakes.
- Describe how the strength of an earthquake is measured.

After an earthquake occurs, seismologists try to find out when and where it started. Earthquake-sensing devices enable seismologists to record and measure seismic waves. These measurements show how far the seismic waves traveled. The measurements also show how much the ground moved. Seismologists use this information to pinpoint where the earthquake started and to find out how strong the earthquake was.

Figure 8 *The line in a seismogram traces the movement of the ground as it shakes. The more the ground moves, the farther back and forth the line traces.*

Locating Earthquakes

How do seismologists know when and where earthquakes begin? They depend on earthquake-sensing instruments called seismographs. **Seismographs** are instruments located at or near the surface of the Earth that record seismic waves. When the waves reach a seismograph, the seismograph creates a seismogram, such as the one in **Figure 8.** A **seismogram** is a tracing of earthquake motion created by a seismograph.

Seismologists use seismograms to calculate when an earthquake started. An earthquake starts when rock slips suddenly enough along a fault to create seismic waves. Remember the time-distance graph in Figure 6? Seismologists find an earthquake's start time by comparing seismograms to the time-distance graph and noting the difference in arrival times of P waves and S waves.

Seismologists also use seismograms to find an earthquake's epicenter. An **epicenter** is the point on the Earth's surface directly above an earthquake's starting point. A **focus** is the point inside the Earth where an earthquake begins. **Figure 9** shows the relationship between an earthquake's epicenter and its focus.

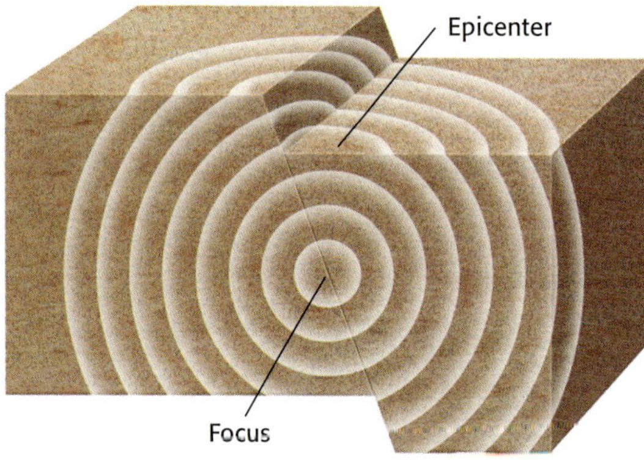

Figure 9 *An earthquake's epicenter is on the Earth's surface directly above the earthquake's focus.*

172

Multicultural CONNECTION

A Chinese man named Chang Heng designed the first earthquake detector around A.D. 132. It was a bronze urn decorated with six dragons' heads. Each head held a bronze ball in its mouth. A pendulum was suspended inside the urn. During a tremor, the urn would strike the pendulum, causing one of the balls to drop into the open mouth of a bronze toad below. The ball would make a loud noise, signaling the occurrence of an earthquake. By noting which ball fell, people could determine the direction of the earthquake's epicenter. Have students design an earthquake detector and bring it to class.

Section 2–California Standards: PE/ATE 1g, 2d, 7; LabBook: 1g, 7, 7b, 7c, 7e, 7g

Perhaps the most common method by which seismologists find an earthquake's epicenter is the *S-P-time method.* When using the S-P-time method, seismologists begin by collecting several seismograms of the same earthquake from different locations. Seismologists then place the seismograms on the time-distance graph so the first P waves line up with the P-wave curve and the first S waves line up with the S-wave curve. This is shown in **Figure 10.**

After the seismograms are placed on the graph, seismologists can see how far away from each station the earthquake was by reading the distance axis. After seismologists find out the distances, they can find the earthquake's epicenter as shown below.

Plotting Seismograms on a Time-Distance Graph

Time after start of earthquake (min): 0, 5, 10, 15, 20, 25

Distance from earthquake (km): 2,000, 4,000, 6,000, 8,000, 10,000

A, B, C, S, P

Figure 10 *Seismograms are lined up so that the first P wave and the first S wave line up with the correct curves. Seismologists subtract a wave's travel time (read from the vertical axis) from the time that the wave was recorded. This determines when the earthquake started. The distance of the stations from the epicenter is read from the horizontal axis.*

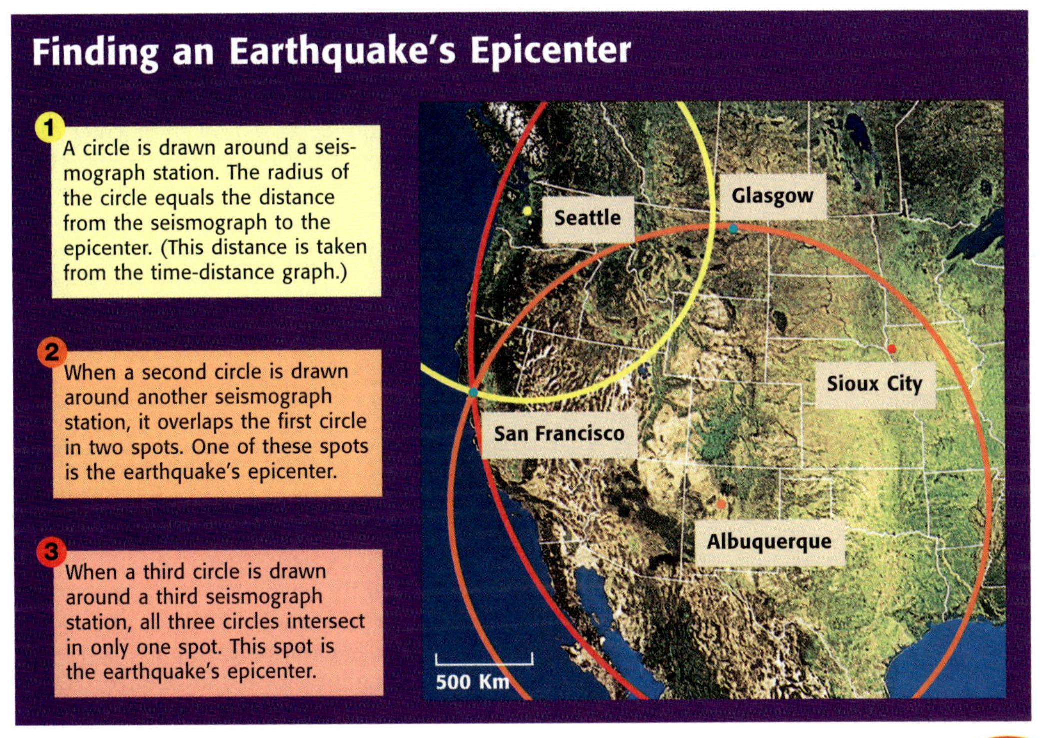

173

2 Teach

USING THE FIGURE

Explain to students that in **Figure 10** the seismograms are the blue, wavy lines that extend vertically. The seismograms read from bottom to top; seismic activity at bottom of seismogram was recorded before seismic activity at the top. The large "wiggles" that line up with the P-wave curve are P waves, and the large "wiggles" that line up with the S-wave curve are S waves.

Earthquake Waves

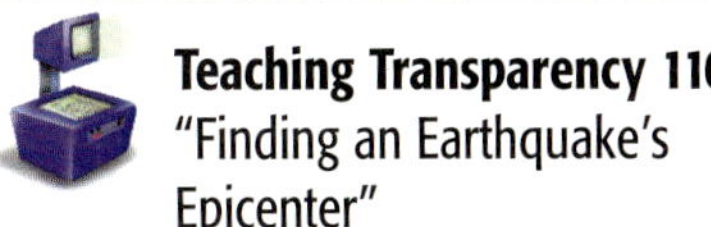

Teaching Transparency 110 "Finding an Earthquake's Epicenter"

Directed Reading Worksheet 7 Section 2

Reinforcement Worksheet 7 "Complete a Seismic Story"

SCIENTISTS AT ODDS

When Charles Richter was a 27-year-old graduate student, he was working on a catalog of earthquakes in southern California. He wanted to find an objective way to compare earthquakes. Up to that point, geologists used the Mercalli scale to classify earthquakes. Giuseppe Mercalli developed the scale in 1902 to describe the intensity of earthquakes. The Mercalli scale was based on the observations of people who witnessed an earthquake and on the damage it caused. Richter wanted to devise a more objective, quantitative measure of earthquake strength. This desire led him to develop the Richter scale in 1935, which is based on measurements from seismographs.

3 Close

Quiz

1. How is an earthquake's epicenter related to its focus? (The epicenter is the point on the Earth's surface directly above the focus, which is where the earthquake begins.)
2. As seismic waves travel farther, what happens to the difference in arrival times of P and S waves? (It increases.)

Alternative Assessment

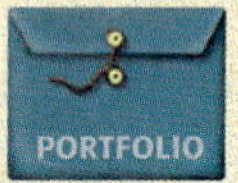

Have students identify 10 recent earthquakes with a magnitude greater than 5.0 on the Richter scale. Students can compile their findings in a table that includes the epicenter and the magnitude of the quake, the damage it caused, and any other interesting information about the quake. Challenge students to find trends in the data.

Answers to MATHBREAK

Answers should be close to those below and should follow rules of significant digits:

The energy released by earthquake with a magnitude of 3.0 is about 31.7*n*. The energy released by earthquake with a magnitude of 4.0 is about 1,000*n*. The energy released by earthquake with a magnitude of 5.0 is about 31,900*n*. The energy released by earthquake with a magnitude of 6.0 is about 1,010,000*n*.

Math Skills Worksheet 43
"Earthquake Power!"

Measuring Earthquake Strength

"How strong was the earthquake?" is a common question asked of seismologists. This is not an easy question to answer. But it is an important question for public officials, safety organizations, and businesses as well as seismologists. Fortunately, seismograms can be used not only to determine an earthquake's epicenter and its start time but also to find out an earthquake's strength.

The *Richter scale* is a commonly used tool for measuring earthquake strength. It is named after Charles Richter, an American seismologist who developed the scale in the 1930s. Richter used the same type of seismograph to record seismograms from numerous earthquakes. He then plotted the maximum height of each seismogram and found that the heights varied dramatically. The smallest height that he could measure was between 0.1 mm and 0.3 mm, and the greatest height that he could measure was more than 100 mm. After some trial and error, Richter created the scale that was later named after him. A modified version of the Richter scale is shown at left.

Modified Richter Scale

Magnitude	Estimated Effects
2.0	can be detected only by seismograph
3.0	can be felt at epicenter
4.0	felt by most in area
5.0	causes damage at epicenter
6.0	causes widespread damage
7.0	causes great, widespread damage

There is a pattern in the Richter scale relating an earthquake's magnitude and the amount of energy released by the earthquake. Each time the magnitude increases by 1 unit, the amount of energy released becomes 31.7 times larger. For example, an earthquake with a magnitude of 5.0 on the Richter scale will release 31.7 times as much energy as an earthquake with a magnitude of 4.0 on the Richter scale. An earthquake with a magnitude of 6.0 releases 31.7 × 31.7—or about 1,000 times—as much energy as an earthquake with a magnitude of 4.0 does. Try the MathBreak at left to see if you understand the relationship between strength and magnitude on the Richter scale.

MATH BREAK

Moving Up the Scale

If the amount of energy released by an earthquake with a magnitude of 2.0 on the Richter scale is *n*, what are the amounts of energy released by earthquakes with the following magnitudes in terms of *n*: 3.0, 4.0, 5.0, and 6.0? (Hint: The energy released by an earthquake with a magnitude of 3.0 is 31.7*n*.)

REVIEW

1. What is the difference between a seismogram and a seismograph?
2. How many seismograph stations are needed to use the S-P-time method? Why?
3. **Doing Calculations** If the amount of energy released by an earthquake with a magnitude of 7.0 on the Richter scale is *x*, what is the amount of energy released by an earthquake with a magnitude of 6.0 in terms of *x*?

174

Answers to Review

1. A seismograph is an instrument that records seismic waves. A seismogram, which is created by a seismograph, is a tracing of the ground's motion during an earthquake.
2. Three; two seismograph stations can narrow the location of the earthquake to two possible locations. Adding a third enables scientists to determine which of the two locations is correct.
3. $\frac{x}{31.7}$

3

Earthquakes and Society

NEW TERMS

gap hypothesis

seismic gap

OBJECTIVES

- Explain earthquake hazard.
- Compare methods of earthquake forecasting.
- List ways to safeguard buildings against earthquakes.
- Outline earthquake safety procedures.

Earthquakes are a fascinating part of Earth science, but they are very dangerous. Seismologists have had some success in predicting earthquakes, but simply being aware of earthquakes is not enough. It is important for people in earthquake-prone areas to be prepared.

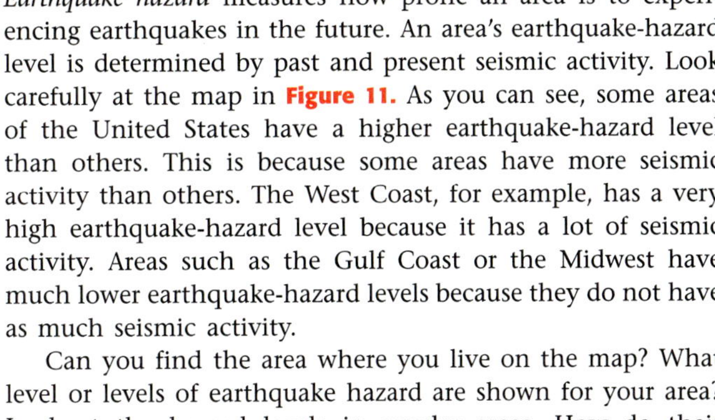

Earthquake Hazard

Earthquake hazard measures how prone an area is to experiencing earthquakes in the future. An area's earthquake-hazard level is determined by past and present seismic activity. Look carefully at the map in **Figure 11.** As you can see, some areas of the United States have a higher earthquake-hazard level than others. This is because some areas have more seismic activity than others. The West Coast, for example, has a very high earthquake-hazard level because it has a lot of seismic activity. Areas such as the Gulf Coast or the Midwest have much lower earthquake-hazard levels because they do not have as much seismic activity.

Can you find the area where you live on the map? What level or levels of earthquake hazard are shown for your area? Look at the hazard levels in nearby areas. How do their hazard levels compare with your area's hazard level? What could explain the earthquake-hazard levels in your area and nearby areas?

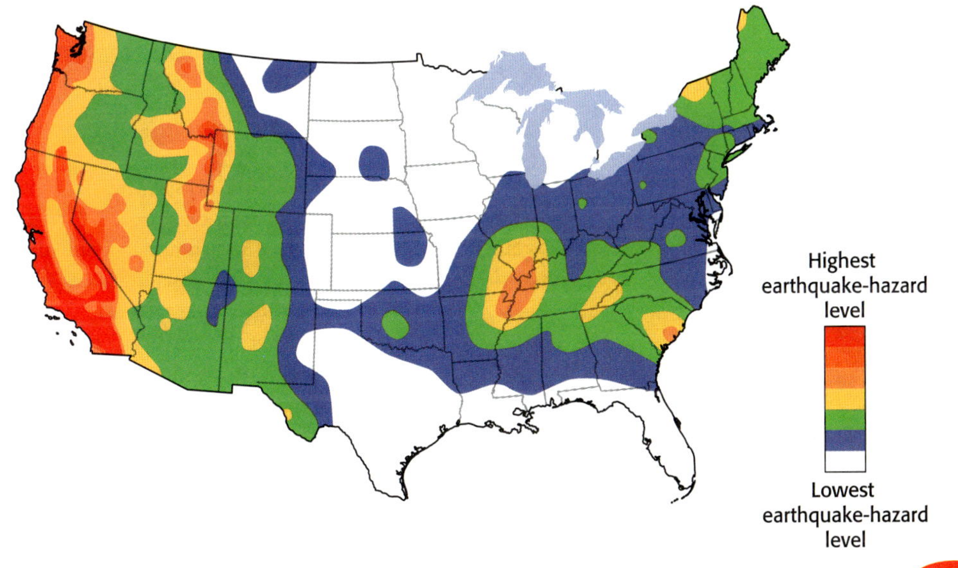

Figure 11 *This is an earthquake-hazard map of the continental United States. It shows various levels of earthquake hazard for different areas of the country.*

SECTION 3

Focus

Earthquakes and Society

In this section students learn how earthquake hazard is determined. The section explores the methods seismologists use to predict when and where earthquakes will occur. Students learn about the technologies used to reinforce buildings against earthquakes. The section concludes with a discussion of earthquake safety procedures.

Bellringer

If any of your students have experienced an earthquake, have them write a short paragraph in their ScienceLog describing how they felt and what they did to protect themselves during the quake. Have students who have not experienced a quake write a paragraph describing what they *think* they would do during a moderate earthquake.

1 Motivate

Have students examine **Figure 11.** Challenge them to explain why the West Coast has such high levels of earthquake hazard. If they need a hint, have them look again at **Figure 1,** in Section 1. (The correct explanation is that there is a tectonic plate boundary along the western coast of the United States.)

Directed Reading Worksheet 7 Section 3

IS THAT A FACT!

On March 27, 1964, an earthquake with a magnitude of 9.1 occurred in southern Alaska. The earthquake, which is the strongest recorded earthquake in North America, lasted for about 4 minutes. When it was over, about 215,000 km^2 of land had been either raised or lowered. In some areas, the land was raised as much as 10 m. The port on Montague Island was raised 10 m, stranding ships that had been docked in the port. After the earthquake, four tsunamis swept the coastline, adding to the destruction.

Section 3–California Standards: PE/ATE 1, 1d, 1f, 1g, 2d, 7, 7d; LabBook: 7, 7a, 7e

2 Teach

Reading Strategy

Prediction Guide Have students determine whether the following statements are true or false before they read the rest of this section:

- Hundreds of thousands of earthquakes that occur each year are not felt by people. (true)
- During an earthquake, rigid pipelines for natural gas and water are more resistant to damage than flexible pipelines are. (false)
- Because earthquakes are unpredictable, people cannot prepare for them. (false)

Cross-Disciplinary Focus

Art Have students find out what has been done to protect sculptures from earthquake damage at the J. Paul Getty Museum, in Malibu, California, or at another museum in an earthquake-prone area.

Answer to Self-Check

120

MATH and MORE

Have students use **Figure 12** to convert the average number of minor earthquakes that occur each year to the number that occur each day. (49,000 quakes a year ÷ 365 days a year = 134 quakes a day)

Math Skills Worksheet 5 "Dividing Whole Numbers with Long Division"

Earthquake Forecasting

Predicting when and where earthquakes will occur and how strong they will be is a very difficult task. Earthquakes are perhaps the most unpredictable part of Earth science. However, by closely monitoring active faults and other areas of seismic activity, seismologists have discovered some patterns in earthquakes that allow them to make some broad predictions.

Worldwide Earthquake Frequency (Based on Observations Since 1900)

Descriptor	Magnitude	Average occurring annually
Great	8.0 and higher	1
Major	7.0–7.9	18
Strong	6.0–6.9	120
Moderate	5.0–5.9	800
Light	4.0–4.9	about 6,200
Minor	3.0–3.9	about 49,000
Very minor	2.0–2.9	about 365,000

Figure 12 *Generally, with each step down in earthquake magnitude, the number of earthquakes per year is about 10 times greater.*

Strength and Frequency As you learned earlier, earthquakes vary in strength. And you can probably guess that earthquakes don't occur on a set schedule. But what you may not know is that the strength of earthquakes is related to how often they occur. The chart in **Figure 12** provides more detail on this relationship.

This relationship between earthquake strength and frequency is also observed on a local scale. For example, each year approximately 10 earthquakes occur in the Puget Sound area of Washington with a magnitude of 4 on the Richter scale. Over this same time period, approximately 100 earthquakes occur in the same area with a magnitude of 3. This means that 10 times as many earthquakes with a magnitude of 3 occur in this area as earthquakes with a magnitude of 4. Scientists use these statistics to make predictions about the strength, location, and frequency of future earthquakes.

Can animals predict earthquakes? To decide for yourself, turn to page 188 to read about links between animal behavior and earthquakes.

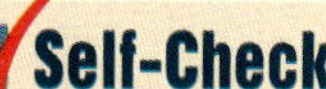

Self-Check

According to the chart above, about how many earthquakes with a magnitude between 6.0 and 6.9 occur annually? *(See page 564 to check your answer.)*

The Gap Hypothesis Another method of predicting an earthquake's strength, location, and frequency is based on the gap hypothesis. The **gap hypothesis** states that sections of active faults that have had relatively few earthquakes are likely to be the sites of strong earthquakes in the future. The areas along a fault where relatively few earthquakes have occurred are called **seismic gaps.**

176

Science Bloopers

In 1989, Iben Browning, a self-taught climatologist, predicted that a large earthquake would occur near New Madrid, Missouri. He based his prediction on the fact that the gravitational pull of the sun and the moon on the area would be very strong on December 3, 1990. Seismologists dismissed his prediction, but after the story made the news, public interest increased. As the date approached, schools in New Madrid were dismissed and emergency personnel were prepared. Some residents left town, while other people flocked to New Madrid to experience a major earthquake. The much-awaited day passed without the slightest tremor.

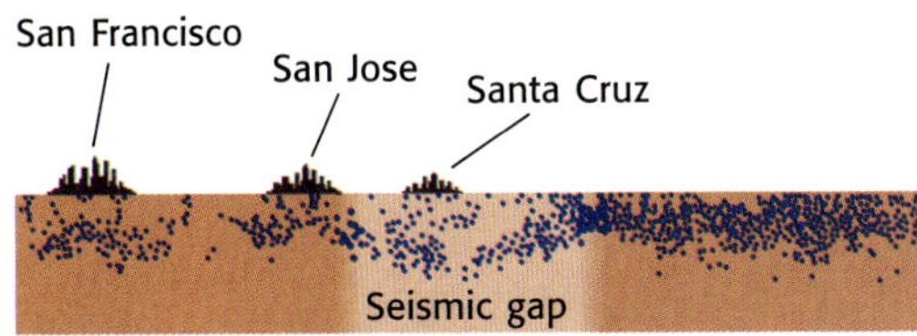

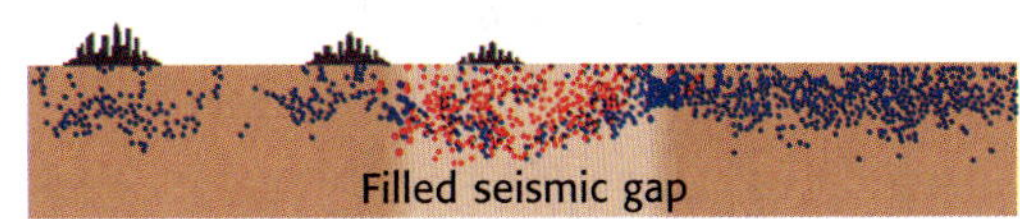

Figure 13 *This diagram shows a cross section of the San Andreas Fault. Notice the highlighted seismic gap before the 1989 earthquake. Note how the gap was filled by the 1989 earthquake and its* aftershocks, *which are weaker earthquakes that follow stronger earthquakes.*

The gap hypothesis helped seismologists forecast the approximate time, strength, and location of the 1989 Loma Prieta earthquake in the San Francisco Bay area. The seismic gap that they identified is illustrated in **Figure 13.** In 1988, seismologists predicted that over the next 30 years there was a 30 percent chance that an earthquake with a magnitude of at least 6.5 would fill this seismic gap. Were they correct? The Loma Prieta earthquake, which filled in the seismic gap in 1989, measured 7.1 on the Richter scale. That's very close, considering how complicated the forecasting of earthquakes is.

Earthquakes and Buildings

Much like a judo master knocks the feet out from under his or her opponent, earthquakes shake the ground out from under buildings and bridges. Once the center of gravity of a structure has been displaced far enough off the structure's supporting base, most structures simply collapse.

Figure 14 shows what can happen to buildings during an earthquake. These buildings were not designed or constructed to withstand the forces of an earthquake. Similar collapses can occur on bridges, highway overpasses, gas and water pipelines, and dams.

Figure 14 *These cars are pinned under the second story of the apartment buildings that they were parked beside. An earthquake shook the ground floor out from under the second story, which then collapsed.*

177

MEETING INDIVIDUAL NEEDS

Advanced Learners Have interested students research the various types of instruments used to detect seismic activity including tiltmeters, gravimeters, strainmeters, magnetometers, and laser range finders. Students' findings should include illustrations and detailed descriptions of how the instruments work.

CONNECT TO LIFE SCIENCE

References to observing animal behavior to predict earthquakes date back 3,000 years in Chinese literature. This behavior includes dogs howling, chickens leaving their roosts, fish thrashing about in ponds, and snakes awakening from hibernation to leave their holes. The Chinese government monitors animal behavior as part of an early warning system for earthquakes. On February 4, 1975, the Chinese government issued an earthquake warning based on observations of strange animal behavior in Liaoning province. The warning indicated that there would be a major earthquake that night. More than 3 million people were evacuated from their homes. At 7:36 P.M., an earthquake with a magnitude of 7.3 occurred. Many buildings were destroyed, but only about 300 people were killed. Tens of thousands of people may have been saved because the government paid attention to animal behavior.

Science Bloopers

In 1976, scientists forecasted a major quake for the Kwangtung province, in China. Thousands of people evacuated their homes for more than 2 months. Finally, people were allowed to return. Shortly after people returned to their homes, two earthquakes and many aftershocks occurred in the region.

Q: What do you get when a cow is caught in an earthquake?

A: a milkshake

3 Extend

Using the Figure

Have students answer the following questions using the illustrations on this page:

- How are the mass damper system and the active tendon system alike? (In both systems, motion sensors detect movement and send this information to a computer. The computer signals devices that counteract the movement of the structure.)
- What is a base isolator? (a shock absorber that prevents seismic waves from traveling through a structure)
- What advantage do flexible pipes have over rigid metal pipes during an earthquake? (Flexible pipes twist and bend more readily than metal pipes, which tend to snap when subjected to significant seismic tremors.)

Debate

Nuclear Waste: Is Any Area Seismically Stable? Scientists must consider the geologic stability of potential sites for nuclear waste facilities. Have students research and debate the issue of nuclear waste disposal. Have them consider that there are few viable options for the disposal of the world's nuclear waste. Remind them that no one can be sure that an area will be seismically stable over the thousands of years it takes for nuclear waste to decay.

Answers to Explore

Accept all reasonable responses.

Explore

Research a tall building to find out how its structure is reinforced. Would any of the building's reinforcements safeguard it against earthquakes? Has an earthquake occurred in the building's area since the building was constructed? If so, how well did the building withstand the shaking?

People have learned a lot from building failure during earthquakes. Architects and engineers use the newest technology to design and construct buildings and bridges to better withstand earthquakes. Study this diagram carefully to learn about some of this modern technology.

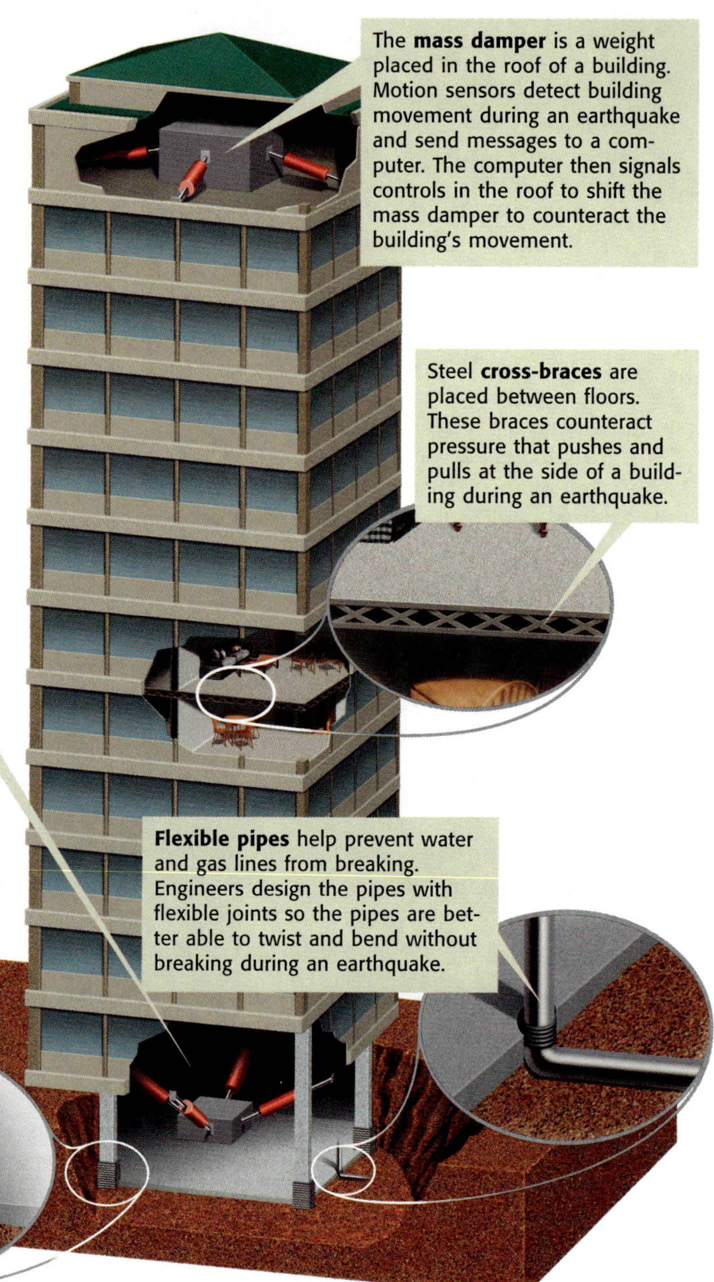

178

Homework

Investigate Your Area Have students conduct a survey of their home and make a list of at least five things that should be altered to ensure minimal damage should an earthquake occur. Changes might include reinforcing the foundation, adding steel support bars to unsupported areas of the building, bolting refrigerators and tall bookshelves to the walls, reinforcing old walls with plywood, securing water heaters, and replacing rigid pipes with flexible pipes. Suggest that students also include a floor plan that shows safe and unsafe places and possible escape routes.

Are You Prepared for an Earthquake?

If you live in an earthquake-prone area or ever plan to visit one, there are many things you can do to protect yourself and your property from earthquakes. Plan ahead so you will know what to do before, during, and after an earthquake. Stick to your plan as closely as possible.

Turn to page 512 to build your own earthquake-safe building.

Before the Shaking Starts The first thing you should do is safeguard your house against earthquakes. For example, put heavier objects on lower shelves so they do not fall on anyone during the earthquake. You can also talk to adults about having your home reinforced. Make a plan with others (your family, neighbors, or friends) to meet somewhere after the earthquake is over. This way someone will know you are safe. During the earthquake, waterlines, power lines, and roadways may be damaged. Therefore, you should store nonperishable food, water, a fire extinguisher, a flashlight with batteries, and a first-aid kit in a place you can access after the earthquake.

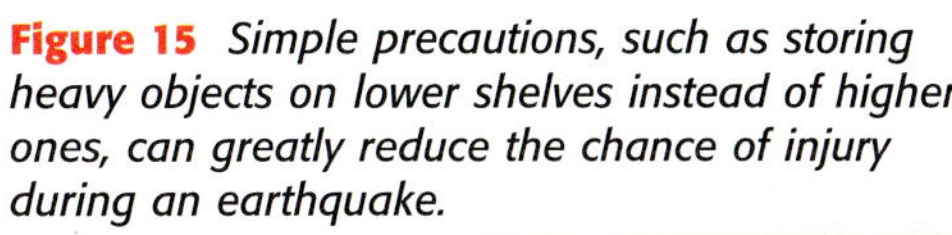

Figure 15 *Simple precautions, such as storing heavy objects on lower shelves instead of higher ones, can greatly reduce the chance of injury during an earthquake.*

When the Shaking Starts The best thing to do if you are indoors is to crouch or lie face down under a table or desk in the center of a room, as shown in **Figure 16.** If you are outside, lie face down away from buildings, power lines, and trees, and cover your head with your hands. If you are in a car on an open road, you should stop the car and remain inside.

You finally make it to a World Series game, but the game is called halfway through. Is it rain? Hardly. Turn to page 189 to find out what happens.

Figure 16 *These students are participating in an earthquake drill. If an earthquake occurs during class, these students will know what to do.*

PG 512

Quake Challenge

Activity

Earthquake Kit Collect the following items: bottled water, nonperishable foods, a flashlight, batteries, a bucket, rubber gloves, safety goggles, a first-aid kit, money, an electric can opener, a few perishable food items, a small TV (not battery-operated), a battery-operated radio, clean rags, tissues and toilet paper, a deck of playing cards, and a blanket. Have students take turns deciding which items would be useful should a severe earthquake occur in your area. Use questions to help students realize that electricity and fresh water may not be available for some time after the quake.
Sheltered English

Going Further

People on the highest floors of tall buildings often feel minor tremors that go unnoticed by people on the ground. Tall buildings exaggerate minor tremors. Demonstrate this concept by holding a meterstick upright by the end and shaking it back and forth. Tell students to observe the difference in movement between the top and the bottom of the meterstick.

Weird Science

Engineers have devised giant shock absorbers for buildings. The shock absorbers contain a ferrofluid solution that becomes rigid in a magnetic field. When an earthquake occurs, a computer controls electromagnets in the shock absorbers to dampen the vibrations.

internetconnect

TOPIC: Earthquakes and Society
GO TO: www.scilinks.org
***sci*LINKS NUMBER:** HSTE190

Homework

Presentation Have students create a poster to promote earthquake safety. Posters should focus on one of the following: preparing for an earthquake, what to do during an earthquake, or what to do after an earthquake. Students can create a display to educate the school about earthquake safety.

4 Close

Quiz

1. What is the gap hypothesis? (The gap hypothesis states that sections of active faults that have had relatively few earthquakes are likely to be the sites of strong earthquakes in the future.)
2. Why should you lie under a table or desk during an earthquake? (The table or desk might prevent falling objects from hitting you and causing injury.)
3. What are aftershocks? (weaker earthquakes that follow stronger earthquakes)

Alternative Assessment

Ask students to write a description of the hazards they might face if an earthquake occurred when they were in each of the following situations:

- asleep in bed (collapsing building)
- at the beach (tsunamis)
- snow skiing (avalanche)

Group Activity

Have small groups research how to make a building earthquake-proof. They should consider the site for the building and brainstorm about ways to protect the building. They can illustrate their best ideas and use descriptive labels to show how their building works. Have groups present their ideas to the class.

Answer to APPLY

Answers will vary but should reflect some precautions and procedures mentioned in this section.

After the Shaking Stops Being in an earthquake is a startling experience. Afterward, you should not be surprised to find yourself and others puzzled about what happened. You should try to calm down, get your bearings, and remove yourself from immediate danger, such as downed power lines, broken glass, and fire hazards. Be aware that there may be aftershocks. Recall your earthquake plan, and follow it through.

REVIEW

1. How is an area's earthquake hazard determined?
2. Which earthquake forecast predicts a more precise location—a forecast based on the relationship between strength and frequency or a forecast based on the gap hypothesis?
3. Describe two ways that buildings are reinforced against earthquakes.
4. Name four items that you should store in case of an earthquake.
5. **Using Graphics** Would the street shown in the photo at left be a safe place during an earthquake? Why or why not?

You are at home reading the evening news. On the front page you read a report from the local seismology station. Scientists predict an earthquake in your area sometime in the near future. You realize that you are not prepared.

Make a detailed outline of how you would prepare yourself and your home for an earthquake. Then write a list of safety procedures to follow during an earthquake. When you are done, exchange your work with a classmate. How do your plans differ from your classmate's? How might you work together to improve your earthquake safety plans?

180

Answers to Review

1. by past and present seismic activity
2. a forecast based on the gap hypothesis
3. Describing any two features from this section (mass damper, cross braces, active tendon system, flexible pipes, and base isolators) is acceptable. Students may also describe features they learn about through additional research.
4. Answers will vary. Students may list some items not mentioned in the textbook. Items mentioned in this section include nonperishable food, water, a fire extinguisher, a flashlight with batteries, and a first-aid kit.
5. No; you would be very close to tall buildings that could collapse during the earthquake.

Section 3 Review–California Standards: PE/ATE 1d, 1g, 2d

4

Earthquake Discoveries Near and Far

NEW TERMS
Moho
shadow zone

OBJECTIVES
- Describe how seismic studies reveal Earth's interior.
- Summarize seismic discoveries on other cosmic bodies.

The study of earthquakes has led to many important discoveries about the Earth's interior. Seismologists learn about the Earth's interior by observing how seismic waves travel through the Earth. Likewise, seismic waves on other cosmic bodies allow seismologists to study the interiors of those bodies.

Discoveries in Earth's Interior

Have you ever noticed how light bends in water? If you poke part of a pencil into water and look at it from a certain angle, the pencil looks bent. This is because the light waves that bounce off the pencil bend as they pass through the water's surface toward your eye. Seismic waves bend in much the same way as they travel through rock. Seismologists have learned a lot about the Earth's interior by studying how seismic waves bend.

P wave
S wave

The **Moho,** which was discovered in 1909, is a place within the Earth where the speed of seismic waves increases sharply. Named after its discoverer, Andrija Mohorovičić, the Moho marks the boundary between the Earth's crust and mantle.

The solid **inner core** was discovered by Inge Lehmann in 1936. Before this discovery, seismologists thought that the Earth's entire core was liquid.

The **shadow zone,** which was discovered by Richard Dixon Oldham in 1906, is an area on the Earth's surface where no direct seismic waves from a particular earthquake can be detected. This discovery suggested that the Earth has a liquid core.

181

SCIENTISTS AT ODDS

Until Inge Lehmann published her paper titled "P′" in 1936, most seismologists thought that the Earth's core was entirely liquid. Lehmann's work proved that the Earth's core had two parts—an outer, liquid part and an inner, solid part. She came up with her idea partly by calculating the time it took waves to pass through the Earth's core. Her discovery was based on observations of the reflection and refraction of seismic waves generated by deep-focus earthquakes.

SECTION 4

Focus

Earthquake Discoveries Near and Far

In this section students learn how seismic evidence led to important discoveries about the Earth's interior. Students also learn about seismic activity on the moon, Mars, and the sun.

Bellringer

Ask students to brainstorm about what activities in their town might cause seismic "noise" that interferes with studying earthquakes in the same way that wind on Mars interfered with studying "marsquakes." (Traffic, trains, and construction all cause vibrations in the ground.)

1 Motivate

USING THE FIGURE

Use the figure on this page and Teaching Transparency 111 to help students understand why it took scientists so long to discover the cause of some earthquakes and to understand how the structure of the Earth's interior affects the way seismic waves travel.

Teaching Transparency 111 "Discoveries in Earth's Interior"

Directed Reading Worksheet 7 Section 4

internet**connect**

TOPIC: Earthquake Discoveries Near and Far
GO TO: www.scilinks.org
***sci*LINKS NUMBER:** HSTE195

2 Teach

DEMONSTRATION

Mapping with Seismic Waves Place a clear, shallow glass pan containing 3 to 5 cm of water on an overhead projector. Turn on the projector, and produce waves by touching the surface of the water with your finger. Students will see the waves radiate from the point where you touched the water. Tell students that these waves simulate those that radiate out from an earthquake's epicenter. Next place a solid object, such as a coffee cup, in the pan. Repeat the demonstration, and ask students to describe what happens to the waves when they encounter the object. (Students should see that the solid object deflects the waves.)

Explain that this is similar to what happens to seismic waves as they pass through the Earth. As seismic waves encounter different zones of Earth's interior, their paths change.

3 Extend

RESEARCH

Have students find out about other hypotheses regarding the origin of the moon. Have students make written evaluations of the strengths and weaknesses of these hypotheses. Tell them to base their evaluations on their understanding of the scientific method.

BRAIN FOOD

Many scientists think part of the moon was once part of the Earth. It is thought that when the Earth was almost entirely molten, a Mars-sized object collided with the Earth, knocking off part of Earth's mantle. The mantle material and material from the impacting body then began orbiting the Earth. Eventually, the orbiting material joined to form the moon.

Quakes and Shakes on Other Cosmic Bodies

Seismologists have taken what they have learned from earthquakes and applied it to studies of other cosmic bodies, such as planets and moons. They have been able to learn about the interiors of these cosmic bodies by studying how seismic waves behave within them. The first and perhaps most successful seismic test on another cosmic body was on Earth's moon. Other studies have taken place on Mars, and even the sun's seismicity has been studied via satellite.

The Moon In July 1969, humans set foot on the moon for the first time. They brought with them a seismograph. Not knowing if the moon was seismically active, they left nothing to chance—they purposely crashed their landing vehicle back into the moon's surface after they left to create artificial seismic waves. What happened after that left seismologists astonished.

If the lander had crashed into the Earth, the equivalent seismograms would have lasted 20–30 seconds at most. The surface of the moon, however, vibrated for more than an hour and a half! At first scientists thought the equipment was not working properly. But the seismograph recorded similar signals produced by meteoroid impacts and "moonquakes" long after the astronauts had left the moon. **Figure 17** shows the nature of these seismic events, which were observed remotely from Earth. Based on these long-lasting seismic events and other studies of seismic waves on the moon, scientists think that the material in the moon's interior has different properties than the moon's surface material.

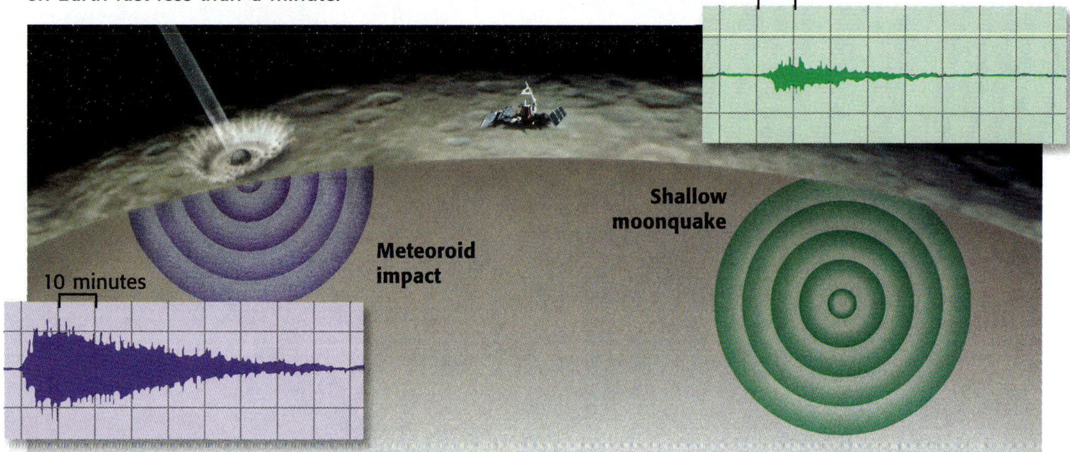

Figure 17 *These seismograms show that seismic waves in the moon last longer than they do in the Earth. Seismic waves from a shallow "moonquake" last 50 minutes. Seismic waves from a meteoroid impact last an hour and a half. Similar disturbances on Earth last less than a minute.*

182

Homework

Research Have interested students find out more about "moonquakes" and the Apollo space missions such as the passive seismic experiment. Students could learn more about other cosmic bodies to find out if there are new discoveries about their seismic activity.

IS THAT A FACT!

"Moonquakes" fall into three categories: deep quakes, which might result from the gravitational pull of Earth; shallow quakes, which may be caused by the heating and cooling of the moon's surface; and quakes caused by the impact of objects with the moon's surface.

Mars In 1976, a space probe called *Viking 1* allowed seismologists to learn about seismic activity on Mars. The probe, which was controlled remotely from Earth, landed on Mars and conducted several experiments. A seismograph was placed on top of the spacecraft, a model of which is shown in **Figure 18,** to measure seismic waves on Mars. However, as soon as the craft landed, the seismograph began to shake. Scientists immediately discovered that Mars is a very windy planet, and the seismograph worked mainly as a wind gauge!

Although the wind on Mars interfered with the seismograph, the seismograph recorded seismograms for months. During that time, only one possible "marsquake" shook the seismograph harder than the wind did. Seismic activity is just one of several aspects of Mars that scientists study. Several projects are currently underway to study Mars's water supply, wind, soil, atmosphere and climate, and many other aspects of the planet.

Figure 18 *Scientists attempted to obtain Martian seismic data with a seismograph on top of* Viking I.

The Sun Seismologists have also studied seismic waves on the sun. Because humans cannot directly access the sun, scientists study it remotely by using a satellite called *SOHO*. Information gathered by *SOHO* has shown that solar flares produce seismic waves. *Solar flares* are powerful nuclear explosions in the sun. The seismic waves that result cause "sunquakes," which are similar to earthquakes but are generally much stronger. For example, a moderate sunquake detected by *SOHO* in 1996 was equivalent to an earthquake with a magnitude of 11.3. This sunquake, which is shown in **Figure 19** beneath an image of *SOHO,* released more than 1 million times as much energy as the Great Hanshin earthquake mentioned at the beginning of this chapter!

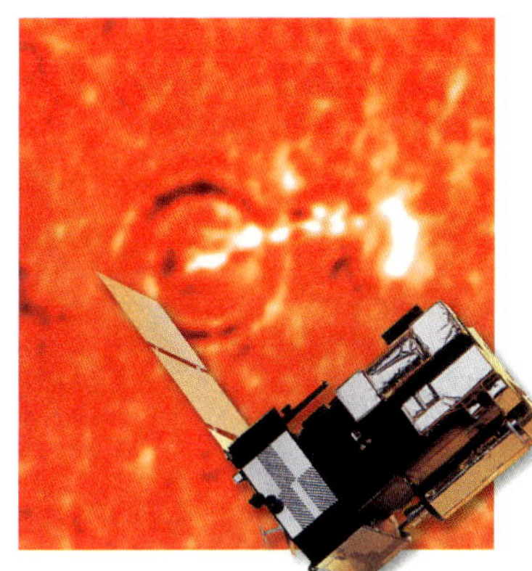

Figure 19 SOHO *detects "sunquakes" that dwarf the greatest earthquakes in history.*

REVIEW

1. What observation of seismic-wave travel led to the discovery of the Moho?
2. Briefly describe one discovery seismologists have made about each of the following cosmic bodies: the moon, Mars, and the sun.
3. **Interpreting Graphics** Take another look at the figure on the first page of Section 4. Why don't S waves enter the Earth's outer core?

4 Close

Quiz

1. Name three features in the Earth's interior that were discovered by studying seismic waves. (the Moho, the inner core, and the shadow zone)
2. What is the shadow zone? What does it tell scientists about Earth's interior? (The shadow zone is an area on the Earth's surface that does not receive seismic waves from a particular earthquake. It tells scientists that at least part of the Earth's core is liquid.)
3. How do "sunquakes" compare with earthquakes? ("Sunquakes" are much stronger than earthquakes.)

ALTERNATIVE ASSESSMENT

Have students read sections of Jules Verne's *A Journey to the Center of the Earth.* Ask them to write short stories about traveling through the Earth's interior based on what they now know about the Earth's structure.

Critical Thinking Worksheet 7
"Nearthlings Unite!"

Answers to Review

1. a sharp increase in the speed of seismic waves; the bending of seismic waves; a change in the direction of seismic waves
2. Answers will vary. Check students' answers against information in the text. Possible answers include:
   - Seismic waves last a lot longer on the moon than they do on Earth.
   - Mars is not very seismically active.
   - "Sunquakes" are generally a lot stronger than earthquakes.
3. because S waves cannot travel through parts of the Earth that are completely liquid

Section 4 Review–California Standards: PE/ATE 1b

Chapter Highlights

Vocabulary Definitions

Section 1

seismology the study of earthquakes

fault a break in the Earth's crust along which blocks of the crust slide relative to one another

deformation the change in the shape of rock in response to stress

elastic rebound the sudden return of elastically deformed rock to its undeformed shape

seismic waves waves of energy that travel through the Earth

P waves the fastest type of seismic wave; can travel through solids, liquids, and gases; also known as pressure waves and primary waves

S waves the second-fastest type of seismic wave; cannot travel through materials that are completely liquid; also known as shear waves and secondary waves

Section 2

seismograph an instrument located at or near the surface of the Earth that records seismic waves

seismogram a tracing of earthquake motion created by a seismograph

epicenter the point on the Earth's surface directly above an earthquake's starting point

focus the point inside the Earth where an earthquake begins

Chapter Highlights

SECTION 1

Vocabulary

seismology *(p. 166)*
fault *(p. 166)*
deformation *(p. 167)*
elastic rebound *(p. 167)*
seismic waves *(p. 170)*
P waves *(p. 170)*
S waves *(p. 170)*

Section Notes

- Earthquakes mainly occur along faults near the edges of tectonic plates.
- Elastic rebound is the direct cause of earthquakes.
- Earthquakes differ depending on what type of plate motion causes them.
- Seismic waves are classified as body waves or surface waves.
- Body waves travel through the Earth's interior, while surface waves travel along the surface.
- There are two types of body waves: P waves and S waves.

SECTION 2

Vocabulary

seismograph *(p. 172)*
seismogram *(p. 172)*
epicenter *(p. 172)*
focus *(p. 172)*

Section Notes

- Seismographs detect seismic waves and record them as seismograms.
- An earthquake's focus is the underground location where seismic waves begin. The earthquake's epicenter is on the surface directly above the focus.
- Seismologists use the S-P-time method to find an earthquake's epicenter.
- Seismologists use the Richter scale to measure an earthquake's strength.

Labs

Earthquake Waves *(p. 514)*

Skills Check

Math Concepts

EARTHQUAKE STRENGTH The energy released by an earthquake increases by a factor of 31.7 with each increase in magnitude. The energy released decreases by a factor of 31.7 with each decrease in magnitude. All you have to do is multiply or divide.

If magnitude 4 releases energy y, then:

- magnitude 5 releases energy $31.7y$
- magnitude 3 releases energy $\frac{y}{31.7}$

Visual Understanding

TIME-DISTANCE GRAPH Note on the time-distance graph in Figure 10 that the difference in arrival times between P waves and S waves increases with distance from the epicenter.

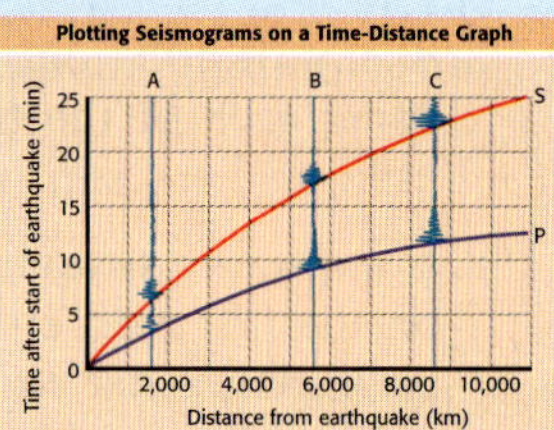

184

Lab and Activity Highlights

Earthquake Waves PG 514

Quake Challenge PG 512

Datasheets for LabBook
(blackline masters for these labs)

SECTION 3

Vocabulary

gap hypothesis *(p. 176)*
seismic gap *(p. 176)*

Section Notes

- Earthquake hazard measures how prone an area is to experiencing earthquakes in the future.
- Some earthquake predictions are based on the relationship between earthquake strength and earthquake frequency. As earthquake frequency decreases, earthquake strength increases.

- Predictions based on the gap hypothesis target seismically inactive areas along faults for strong earthquakes in the future.
- An earthquake usually collapses a structure by displacing the structure's center of gravity off the structure's supporting base.
- Buildings and bridges can be reinforced to minimize earthquake damage.
- People in earthquake-prone areas should plan ahead for earthquakes.

Labs

Quake Challenge *(p. 512)*

SECTION 4

Vocabulary

Moho *(p. 181)*
shadow zone *(p. 181)*

Section Notes

- The Moho, shadow zone, and inner core are features discovered on and inside Earth by observing seismic waves.
- Seismology has been used to study other cosmic bodies.
- Seismic waves last much longer on the moon than they do on Earth.
- Based on early seismic studies, Mars appears much less active seismically than the Earth.
- "Sunquakes" produce energy far greater than any earthquakes we know of.

internetconnect

GO TO: go.hrw.com

Visit the **HRW** Web site for a variety of learning tools related to this chapter. Just type in the keyword:

KEYWORD: HSTEQK

GO TO: www.scilinks.org

Visit the **National Science Teachers Association** on-line Web site for Internet resources related to this chapter. Just type in the ***sci*LINKS** number for more information about the topic:

TOPIC	*sci*LINKS NUMBER
What Is an Earthquake?	HSTE180
Earthquake Measurement	HSTE185
Earthquakes and Society	HSTE190
Earthquake Discoveries Near and Far	HSTE195

185

Lab and Activity Highlights

LabBank

Whiz-Bang Demonstrations, When Buildings Boogie, Demo 19

Long-Term Projects & Research Ideas, Project 36

VOCABULARY DEFINITIONS, *continued*

SECTION 3

gap hypothesis states that sections of active faults that have had relatively few earthquakes are likely to be the sites of strong earthquakes in the future

seismic gap an area along a fault where relatively few earthquakes have occurred

SECTION 4

Moho a place within the Earth where the speed of seismic waves increases sharply; marks the boundary between the Earth's crust and mantle

shadow zone an area on the Earth's surface where no direct seismic waves from a particular earthquake can be detected

Vocabulary Review Worksheet 7

Blackline masters of these Chapter Highlights can be found in the **Study Guide.**

Chapter Review Answers

Using Vocabulary

1. elastic rebound
2. S waves
3. seismograph
4. epicenter
5. Moho

Understanding Concepts

Multiple Choice

6. a
7. b
8. c
9. a
10. c
11. d

Short Answer

12. Generally, with each step down in earthquake magnitude, the number of earthquakes per year is 10 times greater.
13. Answers will vary. Students may consider leaving a car to avoid impending danger, such as the car falling off a cliff or being crushed by a tall, heavy object nearby.
14. Answers may vary slightly. Oldham discovered that no seismic waves were detected in the shadow zone. If the outer core were not liquid, seismic waves would not change direction the way they do when they encounter the core. S waves would pass through the core, and P waves would not change direction as drastically as they do. If the outer core were solid, P waves and S waves would be detected in the shadow zone.

Chapter Review

USING VOCABULARY

To complete the following sentences, choose the correct term from each pair of terms listed below:

1. Energy is released as __?__ occurs. *(deformation* or *elastic rebound)*
2. __?__ cannot travel through parts of the Earth that are completely liquid. *(S waves* or *P waves)*
3. Seismic waves are recorded by a __?__. *(seismograph* or *seismogram)*

4. Seismologists use the S-P-time method to find an earthquake's __?__. *(shadow zone* or *epicenter)*
5. The __?__ is a place that marks a sharp increase in seismic wave speed. *(seismic gap* or *Moho)*

UNDERSTANDING CONCEPTS

Multiple Choice

6. When rock is __?__, energy builds up in it. Seismic waves occur as this energy is __?__.
   a. elastically deformed; released
   b. plastically deformed; released
   c. elastically deformed; increased
   d. plastically deformed; increased

7. The strongest earthquakes usually occur
   a. near divergent boundaries.
   b. near convergent boundaries.
   c. near transform boundaries.
   d. along normal faults.

8. The last seismic waves to arrive are
   a. P waves.
   b. S waves.
   c. surface waves.
   d. body waves.

9. If an earthquake begins while you are in a building, the safest thing to do first is
   a. get under the strongest table, chair, or other piece of furniture.
   b. run out into the street.
   c. crouch near a wall.
   d. call home.

10. Studying earthquake waves currently allows seismologists to do all of the following *except*
    a. determine when an earthquake started.
    b. learn about the Earth's interior.
    c. decrease an earthquake's strength.
    d. determine where an earthquake started.

11. If a planet has a liquid core, then S waves
    a. speed up as they travel through the core.
    b. maintain their speed as they travel through the core.
    c. change direction as they travel through the core.
    d. cannot pass through the core.

Short Answer

12. What is the relationship between the strength of earthquakes and earthquake frequency?

Chapter 7 Review–California Standards: PE/ATE Q1–5: 1b, 1g; Q6–15: 1, 1a, 1b, 1d, 1e, 1g, 2d

13. You learned earlier that if you are in a car during an earthquake and are out in the open, it is best to stay in the car. Briefly describe a situation in which you might want to leave a car during an earthquake.

14. How did Richard Oldham discover that the outer core of the Earth was liquid?

Concept Mapping

15. Use the following terms to create a concept map: focus, epicenter, earthquake start time, seismic waves, P waves, S waves.

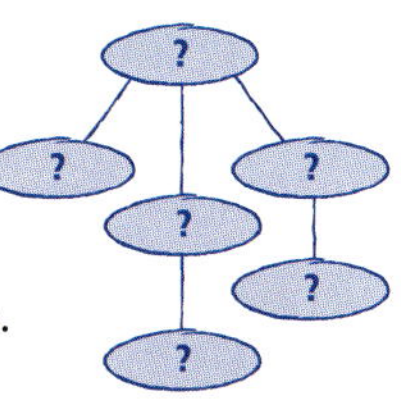

CRITICAL THINKING AND PROBLEM SOLVING

Write one or two sentences to answer the following questions:

16. How might the wall in Figure 2 appear if it had deformed elastically instead of plastically?

17. Why do strong earthquakes occur where there have not been many recent earthquakes? (**Hint:** Think about what gradually happens to rock before an earthquake occurs.)

18. What could be done to solve the wind problem with the seismograph on Mars? Explain how you would set up the seismograph.

MATH IN SCIENCE

19. Based on the relationship between earthquake magnitude and frequency, if 150 earthquakes with a magnitude of 2 occur in your area this year, about how many earthquakes with a magnitude of 4 should occur in your area this year?

INTERPRETING GRAPHICS

The graph below illustrates the relationship between earthquake magnitude and the height of the tracings on a seismogram. Charles Richter initially formed his magnitude scale by comparing the heights of seismogram readings for different earthquakes. Study the graph, and then answer the questions that follow.

Seismogram Height vs. Earthquake Magnitude

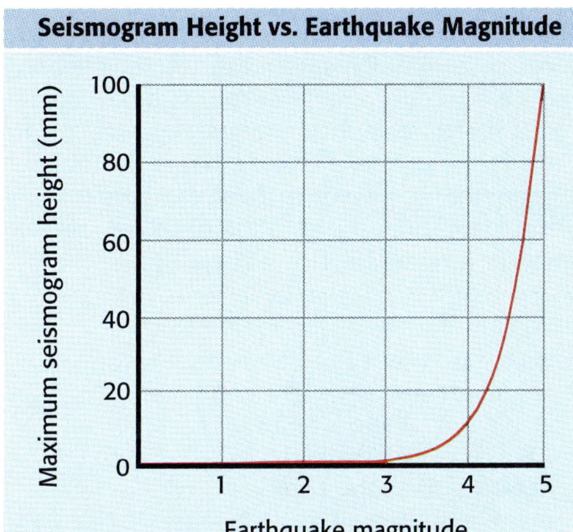

20. What would the magnitude of an earthquake be if the height of its seismogram readings were 10 mm?

21. Look at the shape of the curve on the graph. What does this tell you about the relationship between seismogram heights and earthquake magnitudes? Explain.

NOW What Do You Think?

Take a minute to review your answers to the ScienceLog questions on page 165. Have your answers changed? If necessary, revise your answers based on what you have learned since you began this chapter.

Concept Mapping

15. An answer to this exercise can be found at the end of this book.

Critical Thinking and Problem Solving

16. If the wall in Figure 2 had deformed elastically instead of plastically, it might appear broken or cracked.

17. Strong earthquakes occur where there have not been many recent earthquakes because a lot of elastic deformation builds up along active faults where rock has not moved for awhile. The more deformation that builds up, the more energy the rock releases when it finally slips along the fault.

18. Answers will vary. One solution might be to place the seismograph in a hole or depression that is shielded from wind.

Math in Science

19. one or two

Interpreting Graphics

20. 4

21. Answers will vary slightly. The relationship is not linear; it is logarithmic. Students should recognize that seismogram heights increase at a larger rate with each increase in earthquake magnitude.

NOW What Do You Think?

1. Elastic rebound along active faults is the direct cause of most earthquakes. Answers that attribute earthquakes to tectonic-plate movement or the movement of rock along faults are acceptable. Less appropriate answers may attribute earthquakes to volcanic eruptions, impact by cosmic bodies, or explosions.
2. Answers will vary. Earthquake strength varies according to the type of tectonic-plate motion that causes them. Also, some earthquakes are stronger than others because more elastic deformation builds up along certain faults or parts of faults than along others.
3. It depends on how they are built. Some buildings are reinforced to withstand earthquakes better than other buildings do.

Concept Mapping Transparency 7

Blackline masters of this Chapter Review can be found in the **Study Guide.**

Chapter 7 Review–California Standards: PE/ATE Q16–18: 1, 1g, 2d; Q19: 1g, Think: 1d, 1g, 2d

Weird Science
Can Animals Predict Earthquakes?

Background

There have been many studies on the different types of animal responses to the geophysical environment. Most of these studies illustrated that the behavior of living organisms is affected by electromagnetic fields. Studies have been performed on how migrating birds find their way and how fish navigate. Fish such as catfish and sharks utilize electroreceptors to detect objects around them and as a means of communication. Even earthworms respond to changes in Earth's magnetic field.

An American geologist named Jim Berkland has been a strong proponent of using animals to predict earthquakes. It is likely that students pursuing further research in this area will encounter his name often. Berkland has predicted a few earthquakes by observing animal behavior. However, he does not always correctly predict the magnitude of the earthquakes.

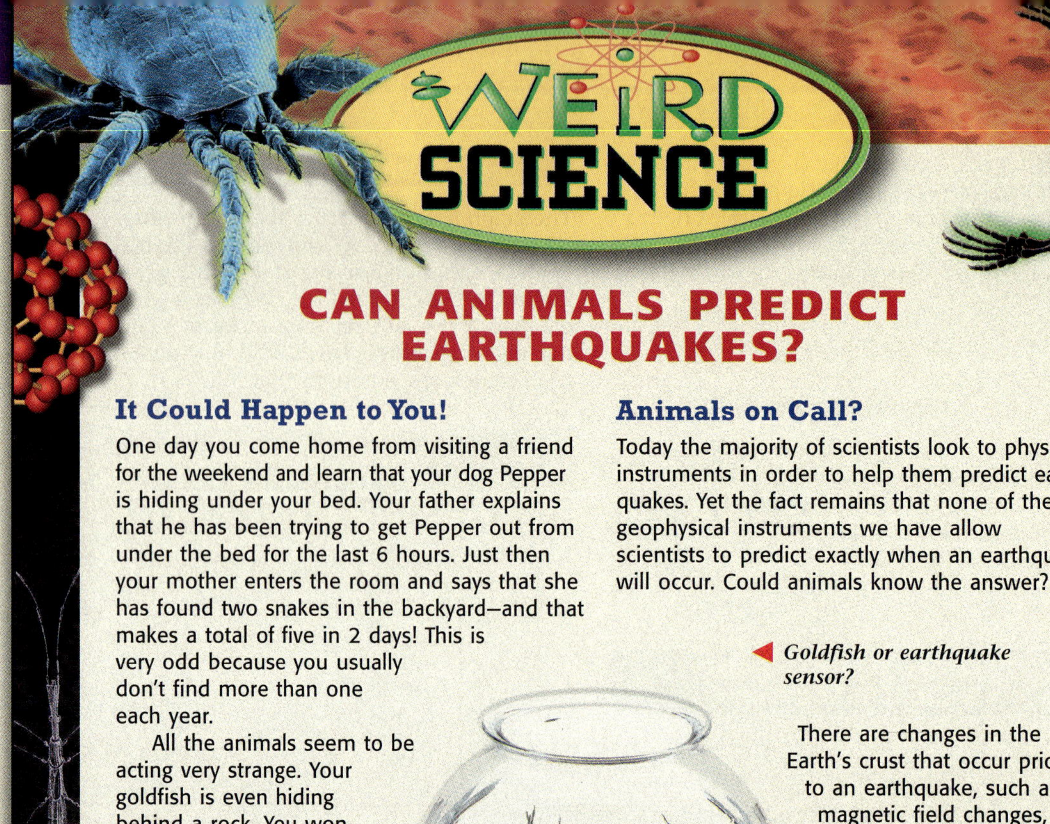

CAN ANIMALS PREDICT EARTHQUAKES?

It Could Happen to You!

One day you come home from visiting a friend for the weekend and learn that your dog Pepper is hiding under your bed. Your father explains that he has been trying to get Pepper out from under the bed for the last 6 hours. Just then your mother enters the room and says that she has found two snakes in the backyard—and that makes a total of five in 2 days! This is very odd because you usually don't find more than one each year.

All the animals seem to be acting very strange. Your goldfish is even hiding behind a rock. You wonder if there is some explanation.

What's Going On?

So what's your guess? What do you think is happening? Did you guess that an earthquake is about to occur? Well, if you did, you are probably right!

Publications from as far back as 1784 record unusual animal behavior prior to earthquakes. Some examples included zoo animals refusing to go into their shelters at night and domestic cattle seeking high ground. Other animals, like lizards, snakes, and small mammals, evacuate their underground burrows, and wild birds leave their usual habitats. All of these events occurred a few days, several hours, or a few minutes before the earthquakes happened.

Animals on Call?

Today the majority of scientists look to physical instruments in order to help them predict earthquakes. Yet the fact remains that none of the geophysical instruments we have allow scientists to predict exactly when an earthquake will occur. Could animals know the answer?

◀ *Goldfish or earthquake sensor?*

There are changes in the Earth's crust that occur prior to an earthquake, such as magnetic field changes, subsidence (sinking), tilting, and bulging of the surface. These things can be monitored by modern instruments. Many studies have shown that electromagnetic fields affect the behavior of living organisms. Is it possible that animals close to the epicenter of an earthquake are able to sense changes in their environment? Should we pay attention?

You Decide

▶ Currently, the United States government does not fund research that investigates whether animals can predict earthquakes. Have a debate with your classmates about whether the government should fund such research.

188

Answer to You Decide

Encourage students to understand both sides of this debate. Because government funding is limited, using these funds for one area of study could result in a reduction in the funding for other areas. Would students be willing to fund a study about animals predicting earthquakes if it meant decreasing the funding toward finding a cure for AIDS? Would it be better to require states in seismically active areas to fund this research themselves, either publicly or privately? Ask students to come up with solutions.

EYE ON THE ENVIRONMENT

What Causes Such Destruction?

At 5:04 P.M. on October 14, 1989, life in California's San Francisco Bay Area seemed as normal as ever. The third game of the World Series was underway in Candlestick Park, now called 3Com Park. While 62,000 fans filled the park, other people were rushing home from a day's work. By 5:05 P.M., however, things had changed drastically. The fact sheet of destruction looks like this:

Injuries:	3,757
Deaths:	68
Damaged homes:	23,408
Destroyed homes:	1,018
Damaged businesses:	3,530
Destroyed businesses:	366
Financial loss:	over $6 billion

The Culprit

The cause of such destruction was a 7.1 magnitude earthquake that lasted for 20 seconds. Its epicenter was 97 km south of San Francisco in an area called Loma Prieta. The earthquake was so strong that people in San Diego and western Nevada (740 km away) felt it too. Considering the earthquake's high magnitude and the fact that it occurred during rush hour, it is amazing that more people did not die. However, the damage to buildings was widespread—it covered an area of 7,770 km^2. And by October 1, 1990, there had been more than 7,000 aftershocks of this quake.

Take Heed

Engineers and seismologists had expected a major earthquake, so the amount of damage they saw from this earthquake was no surprise. But experts agree that if the earthquake were of a higher magnitude or centered closer to Oakland, San Jose, or San Francisco, the damage would have been much worse. They are concerned that people who live in these areas aren't paying attention to the warning this earthquake represents.

Many people have a false sense of security because their buildings withstood the quake with little or no damage. But engineers and seismologists agree that the only reason the buildings survived was because the ground motion in those areas was fairly low.

Tomorrow May Be Too Late

Many buildings that withstood this earthquake were poorly constructed and would not withstand another earthquake. Experts say there is a 50 percent chance that one or more 7.0 magnitude earthquakes will occur in the San Francisco Bay Area in the next 30 years. And the results of the next quake could be much more devastating if people don't reinforce their buildings before it's too late.

▲ *Notice the different levels of destruction for various buildings on the same street.*

On Your Own

▶ Research the engineering innovations for constructing bridges and buildings in areas with seismic activity. Share your information with the class.

EYE ON THE ENVIRONMENT

What Causes Such Destruction?

Answers to On Your Own

Students' answers will vary. However, some of the design features that engineers and architects use to make buildings that better withstand earthquakes are as follows: the mass damper, the active tendon system, base isolators, cross-braces, and flexible pipes.

- **Mass Damper:** The mass damper is a 6-ton weight built into the top of the building. Motion sensors detect swaying and send a message to a computer system. The computer system then directs hydraulic actuators to shift the weight of the mass damper in order to counteract the building's movement during an earthquake or high winds.
- **Active Tendon System:** Similar to the mass damper system, but the damper is located at the base of the building.
- **Base Isolators:** Base isolators act as shock absorbers against the force of an earthquake. Each base isolator (approximately 60 cm tall and 60 cm wide) consists of layers of rubber and steel wrapped around a lead core. This arrangement of materials absorbs the energy of seismic waves that would otherwise travel up through the building.
- **Cross-Braces:** Cross-braces lend strength by counteracting the push-and-pull pressures that occur at the sides of a building during an earthquake. These cross-braces are made of steel, which is strong but flexible enough to stretch considerably before breaking.
- **Flexible Pipes:** The swaying and rocking of a building during an earthquake can cause pipes to break. Pipes with flexible joints are better able to bend without breaking during an earthquake.

California Standards: PE/ATE 2d

Chapter Organizer

CHAPTER ORGANIZATION	TIME MINUTES	OBJECTIVES	LABS, INVESTIGATIONS, AND DEMONSTRATIONS
Chapter Opener pp. 190–191	45	California Standards: PE/ATE 7, 7b	**Investigate!** Anticipation, p. 191
Section 1 Volcanic Eruptions	90	▶ Distinguish between nonexplosive and explosive volcanic eruptions. ▶ Explain how the composition of magma determines the type of volcanic eruption that will occur. ▶ Classify the main types of lava and volcanic debris. PE/ATE 1, 1d, 2, 2d, 4c, 7, 7b	**QuickLab,** Bubble, Bubble, Toil and Trouble, p. 194
Section 2 Volcanoes' Effects on Earth	90	▶ Describe the effects that volcanoes have on Earth. ▶ Compare the different types of volcanoes. PE/ATE 1d, 2d; LabBook 1a, 1e, 7f, 7g	**Discovery Lab,** Some Go "Pop," Some Do Not, p. 516 **Datasheets for LabBook,** Some Go "Pop," Some Do Not, Datasheet 16 **Whiz-Bang Demonstrations,** How's Your Lava Life? Demo 21
Section 3 What Causes Volcanoes?	135	▶ Describe the formation and movement of magma. ▶ Identify the places where magma forms. ▶ Explain the relationship between volcanoes and plate tectonics. ▶ Summarize the methods scientists use to predict volcanic eruptions. PE/ATE 1, 1a–1e, 1g, 2, 2d, 4, 4c, 7, 7b, 7f; LabBook 7, 7b, 7e	**QuickLab,** Reaction to Stress, p. 200 **Interactive Explorations CD-ROM,** What's the Matter? *A **Worksheet** is also available in the **Interactive Explorations Teacher's Edition.*** **Skill Builder,** Volcano Verdict, p. 518 **Datasheets for LabBook,** Volcano Verdict, Datasheet 17 **Labs You Can Eat,** Hot Spots, Lab 16 **Whiz-Bang Demonstrations,** What Makes a Vent Event? Demo 20 **Long-Term Projects & Research Ideas,** Project 37

See page **T20** *for a complete correlation of this book with the*

CALIFORNIA SCIENCE CONTENT STANDARDS.

Correlations are also provided at point of use throughout this ATE.

TECHNOLOGY RESOURCES

Guided Reading Audio CD
English or Spanish, Chapter 8

Classroom Management CD-ROM

Interactive Explorations CD-ROM
CD 1, Exploration 4, What's the Matter?

CNN **Scientists in Action,** Volcano Hunters, Segment 13

Test Generator CD-ROM

Earth Science Videodisc
Volcanoes: 28244–32232

Chapter 8 • Volcanoes

CLASSROOM WORKSHEETS, TRANSPARENCIES, AND RESOURCES	SCIENCE INTEGRATION AND CONNECTIONS	REVIEW AND ASSESSMENT
Directed Reading Worksheet 8 **Science Puzzlers, Twisters & Teasers,** Worksheet 8	**Cross-Disciplinary Focus,** p. 191 in ATE	
Directed Reading Worksheet 8, Section 1 **Transparency 163,** Summarizing the Changes of State	**Connect to Life Science,** p. 193 in ATE **Multicultural Connection,** p. 193 in ATE **Connect to Physical Science,** p. 194 in ATE **Life Science Connection,** p. 196 **Across the Sciences:** Europa: Life on a Moon? p. 211	**Review,** p. 196 **Quiz,** p. 196 in ATE **Alternative Assessment,** p. 196 in ATE
Directed Reading Worksheet 8, Section 2 **Transparency 112,** Three Types of Volcanoes **Problem Solving Worksheet 8,** Eruption Disruption **Transparency 113,** The Formation of a Caldera **Reinforcement Worksheet 8,** A Variety of Volcanoes	**Cross-Disciplinary Focus,** p. 198 in ATE **Astronomy Connection,** p. 199 **Science, Technology, and Society:** Robot in the Hot Seat, p. 210	**Review,** p. 199 **Quiz,** p. 199 in ATE **Alternative Assessment,** p. 199 in ATE
Transparency 114, The Formation of Magma **Directed Reading Worksheet 8,** Section 3 **Math Skills for Science Worksheet 35,** Using Temperature Scales **Transparency 115,** A Mantle Plume and a Hot Spot **Reinforcement Worksheet 8,** Tectonic Plate Movement	**Cross-Disciplinary Focus,** p. 201 in ATE **MathBreak,** How Hot Is Hot? p. 202 **Real-World Connection,** p. 202 in ATE **Chemistry Connection,** p. 205 **Apply,** p. 205	**Self-Check,** p. 201 **Homework,** pp. 202, 204 in ATE **Review,** p. 205 **Quiz,** p. 205 in ATE **Alternative Assessment,** p. 205 in ATE

Holt, Rinehart and Winston On-line Resources

go.hrw.com

For worksheets and other teaching aids related to this chapter, visit the HRW Web site and type in the keyword: **HSTVOL**

National Science Teachers Association

www.scilinks.org

Encourage students to use the keywords listed on the Technology Highlights page to access information and resources on the **NSTA** Web site.

END-OF-CHAPTER REVIEW AND ASSESSMENT

Chapter Review in Study Guide
Vocabulary and Notes in Study Guide
Chapter Tests with Performance-Based Assessment, Chapter 8 Test
Chapter Tests with Performance-Based Assessment, Performance-Based Assessment 8
Concept Mapping Transparency 8

Chapter Resources & Worksheets

Visual Resources

TEACHING TRANSPARENCIES

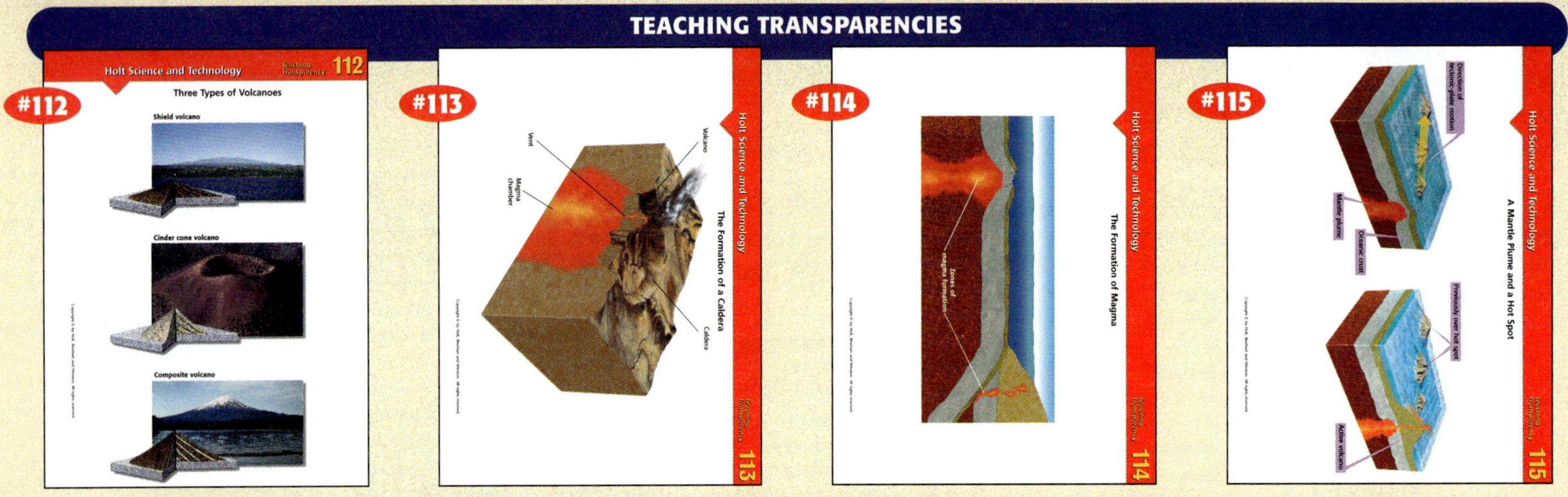

TEACHING TRANSPARENCIES

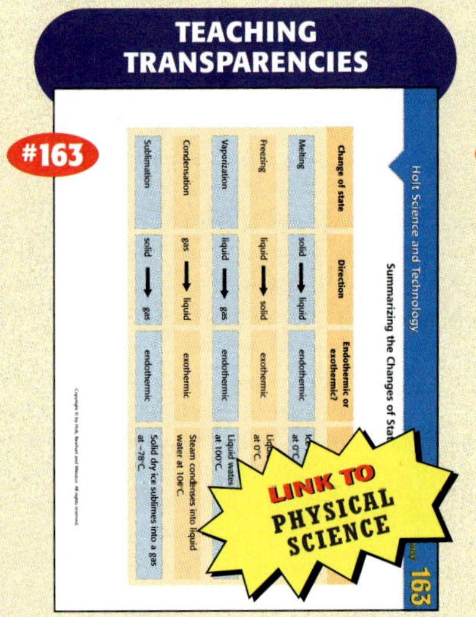

CONCEPT MAPPING TRANSPARENCY

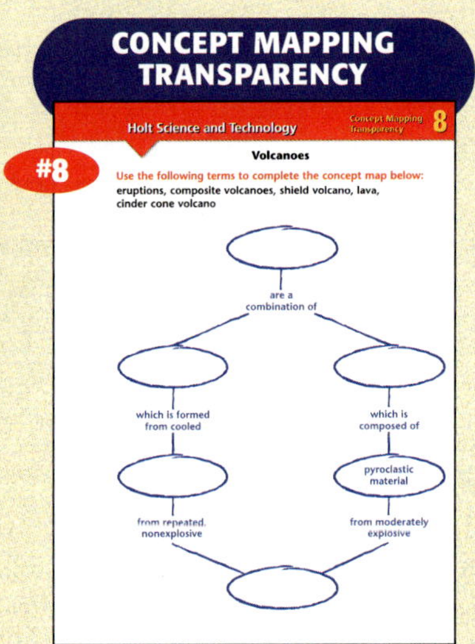

Meeting Individual Needs

DIRECTED READING

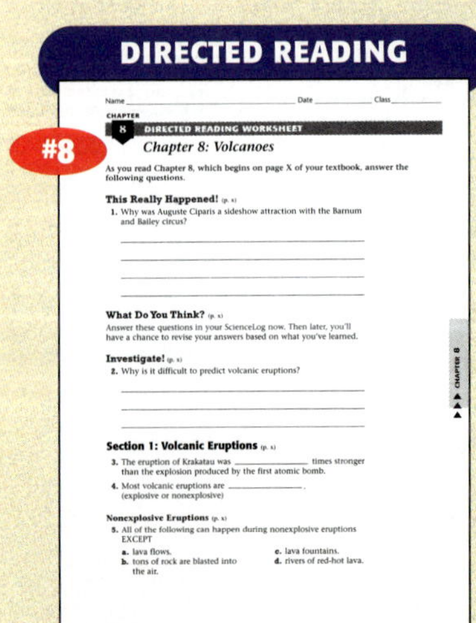

REINFORCEMENT & VOCABULARY REVIEW

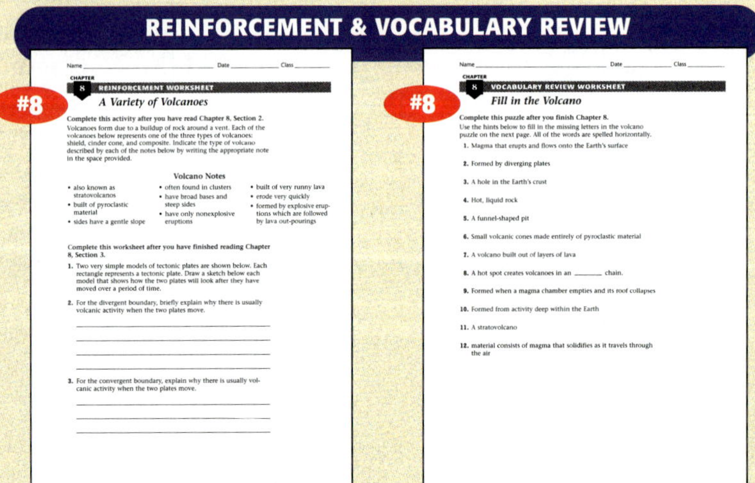

SCIENCE PUZZLERS, TWISTERS & TEASERS

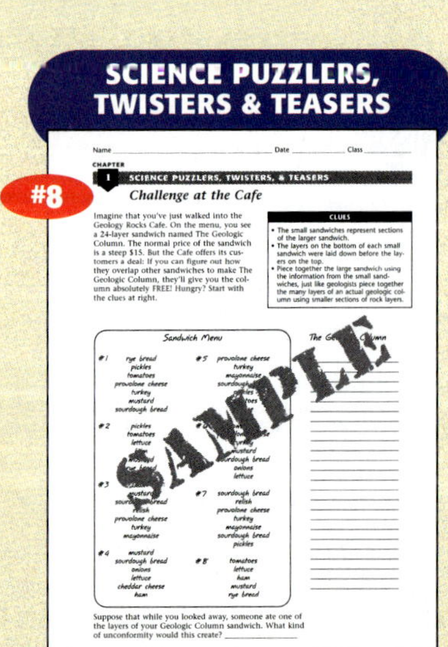

Review & Assessment

STUDY GUIDE

#8 #8

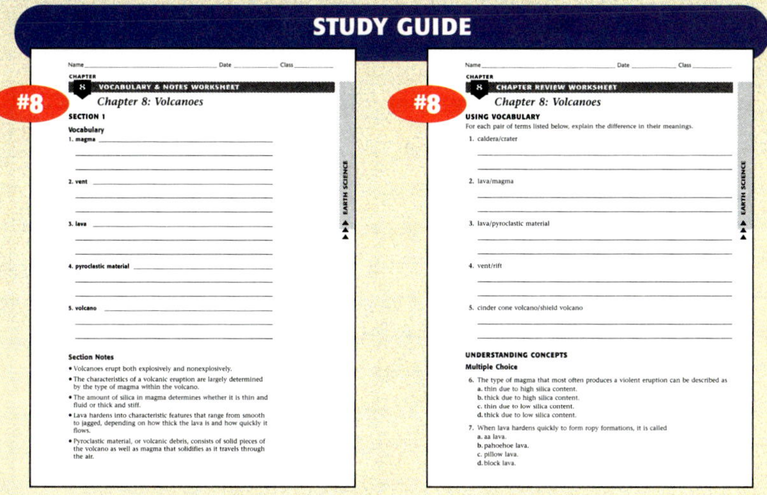
Vocabulary & Notes Worksheet — Chapter 8: Volcanoes

Chapter Review Worksheet — Chapter 8: Volcanoes

CHAPTER TESTS WITH PERFORMANCE-BASED ASSESSMENT

#8 #8

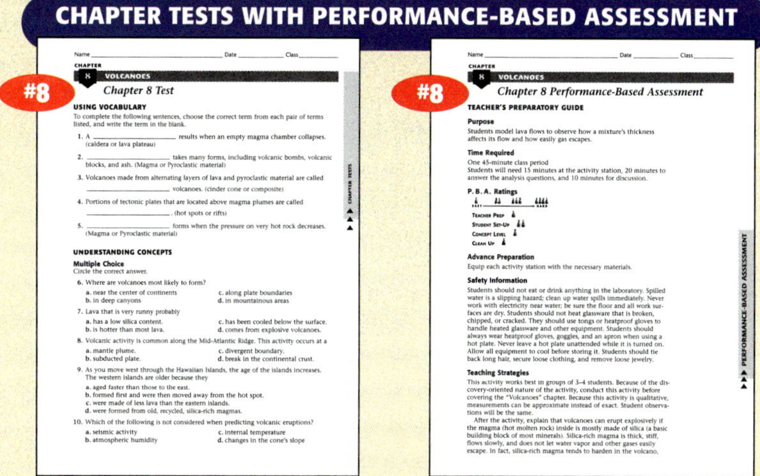
Volcanoes — Chapter 8 Test

Volcanoes — Chapter 8 Performance-Based Assessment

Lab Worksheets

LABS YOU CAN EAT

#16

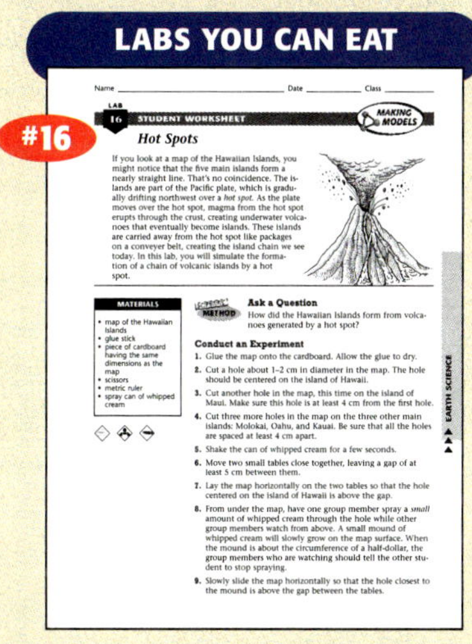
Student Worksheet — Hot Spots

WHIZ-BANG DEMONSTRATIONS

#20 #21

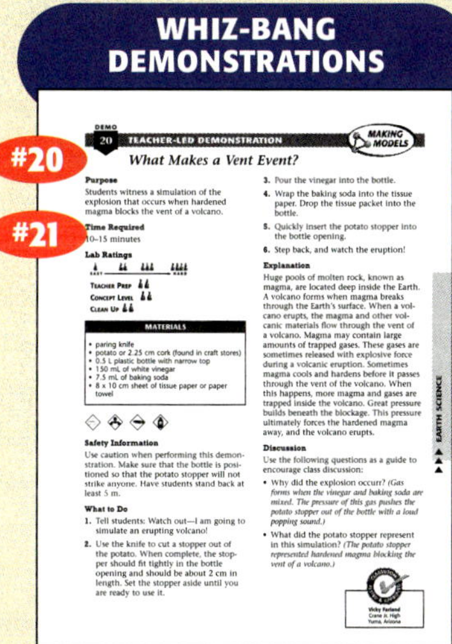
Teacher-Led Demonstration — What Makes a Vent Event?

LONG-TERM PROJECTS & RESEARCH IDEAS

#37

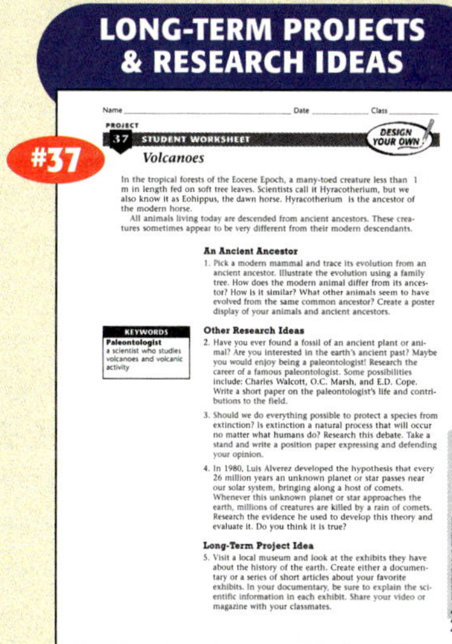
Student Worksheet — Volcanoes

DATASHEETS FOR LABBOOK

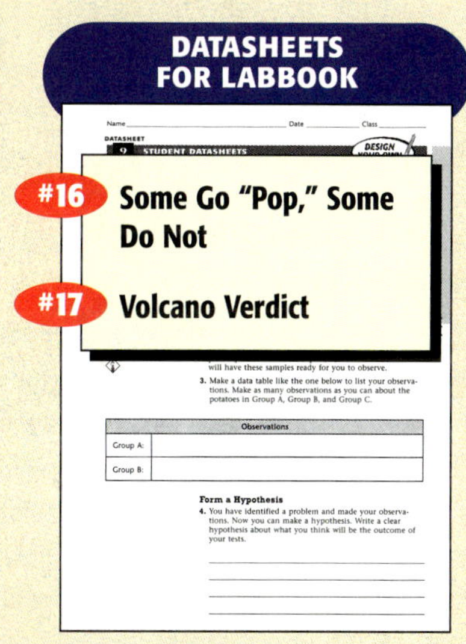
#16 Some Go "Pop," Some Do Not

#17 Volcano Verdict

Applications & Extensions

CRITICAL THINKING & PROBLEM SOLVING

#8

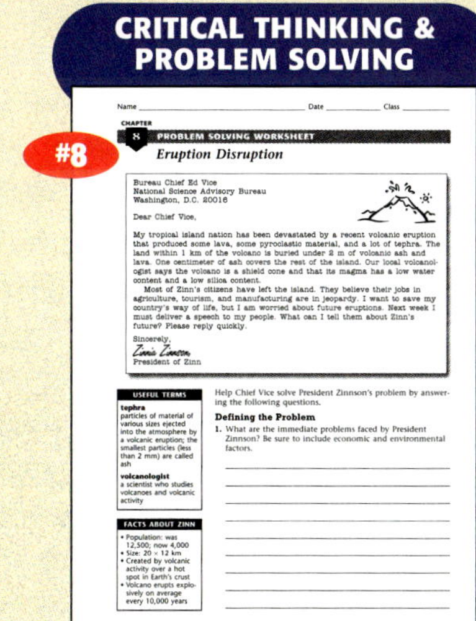
Problem Solving Worksheet — Eruption Disruption

SCIENTISTS IN ACTION

#13

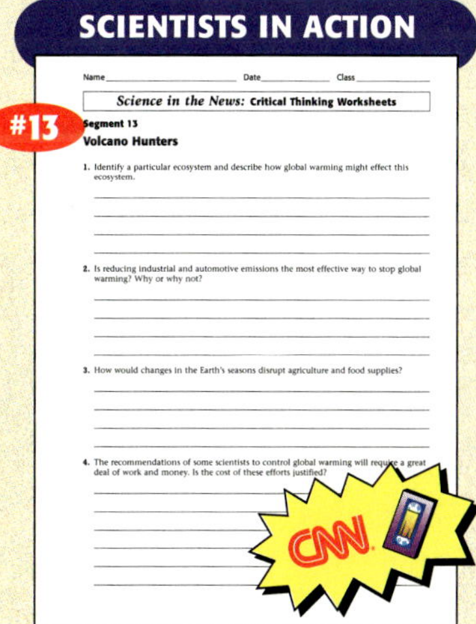
Science in the News: Critical Thinking Worksheets — Segment 13 — Volcano Hunters

INTERACTIVE EXPLORATIONS

#1–4

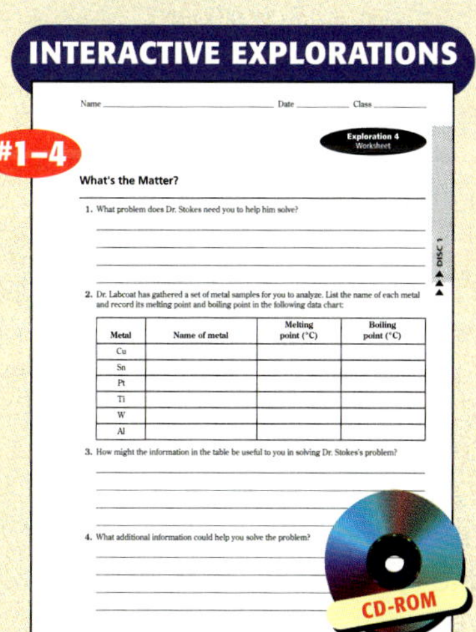
Exploration 4 Worksheet — What's the Matter?

Chapter Background

Section 1

Volcanic Eruptions

▶ Mining in Subduction Zones
Mining can be very productive in regions where subduction creates volcanoes. In the magma chamber that feeds a volcano, trace amounts of metals such as copper, gold, silver, lead, and zinc are dissolved in the magma. On its way upward, the magma undergoes physical and chemical changes that sometimes produce hot, ore-bearing fluids. Under the right temperature and pressure conditions, these fluids concentrate the metals, which then precipitate out of the solution, forming mineral veins. **Figure 2** shows the volcanic structures that may lead to mineral deposits.

▶ The Origin of Volcanic Terms
Many terms for nonviolent eruptions are Hawaiian. Drops of liquid lava that blow into fine spiky strands are called *Pele's hair,* after the Hawaiian goddess of fire. *Limu o Pele,* or "Pele's seaweed," is the term for delicate, translucent sheets of spatter filled with tiny glass bubbles.

- The terms for violent eruptions, however, are generally not Hawaiian. *Nuée ardente,* French for "burning cloud," is a hot mass of volcanic gases, ash, and debris that is expelled explosively and then travels at hurricane speeds down a mountainside.

IS THAT A FACT!

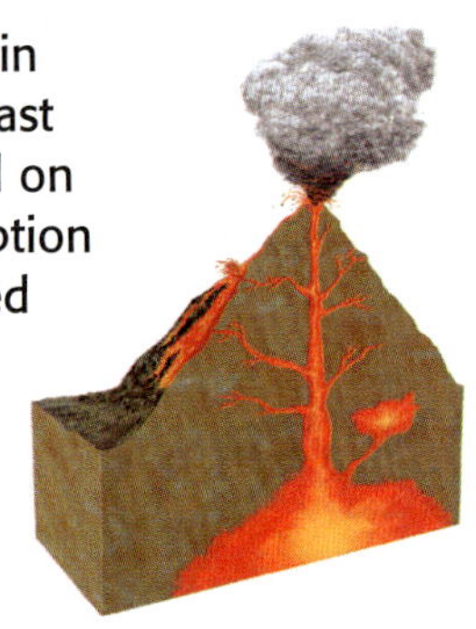

- The Tambora volcano eruption in Indonesia is the largest in the last 200 years. The volcano erupted on April 10 and 11, 1815. The eruption and the resulting tsunamis killed more than 10,000 people. Ash covered so much land that farmland was devastated; disease and famine killed 82,000 more.
- During the Tambora eruption, so much ash was thrown into the atmosphere that weather patterns were affected worldwide. Scholars believe the eruption caused the "Year Without a Summer" in 1816, when snow fell in New England in July.

Section 2

Volcanoes' Effects on Earth

▶ The Krakatau Explosion
When the island of Krakatau, in Indonesia, exploded in 1883, it caused a shockwave that sped around the world seven times. The volcano ejected about 18 km^3 of volcanic material into the air. One ash cloud reached 80 km high, and the explosion was heard in Australia, nearly 2,000 km away. As a result of the explosion, the volcano collapsed and the island lost 21 km^2 of land. Before the eruption, Krakatau had been 450 m high. After the eruption, all that was left was a caldera lying as deep as 275 m below the ocean!

- After the eruption, Krakatau's magma chamber was not gone. In 1927, a cloud of sulfur and ash rose from the water above the volcano. It was the beginning of Anak Krakatau, or "Child of Krakatau," which rose from the original volcano's crater. By 1960, Anak Krakatau was 166 m high, and it continues to grow.

Fighting Lava with Water

Most attempts to divert lava away from homes and towns have failed. However, when lava flows in Iceland threatened to engulf a seaport and its harbor, the townspeople decided on a unique approach. Using oceangoing firefighting boats, they pumped icy water from the bay onto the oncoming lava. The water cooled the lava fast enough to divert the flow. Hawaiians have tried to divert lava flows this way but with little success.

IS THAT A FACT!

- When lava flows in a defined channel, a crust forms on the surface. If the crust remains stationary while the lava below is still flowing, a lava tube or a lava cave several kilometers long can result.

SECTION 3

What Causes Volcanoes?

Merapi, "Mountain of Fire"

There are more active volcanoes in Indonesia than anywhere else on Earth—130! Perhaps the most dangerous volcano is called Merapi, or "Mountain of Fire," on the island of Java. Since 1548, Merapi has erupted violently 68 times. In 1998, it became active again, and people began to evacuate. Scientists are worried about the city of Yogyakarta, which lies just 70 km north of the volcano and is home to about 500,000 people. A large eruption could completely destroy it.

Predicting the Mount Pinatubo Eruptions

Perhaps the most successful prediction of a volcanic eruption was on Mount Pinatubo, in the Philippine Islands. When Pinatubo became active in March and April 1991, scientists rushed to the area and quickly established monitoring systems. Groups of scientists from the Philippines and the United States distributed a five-level alert system to civil defense and local officials. Evacuations began when an eruption appeared imminent (Level 4 alert); ultimately, more than 100,000 people evacuated the area. There were enormous losses of land, housing, and crops, but because of the preparations and warnings, there were only 700 deaths.

- Pinatubo was what geologists call a well-behaved volcano. It behaved as the geologists predicted, becoming increasingly active and then exploding. Most volcanoes are not so well behaved. For example, the same monitoring methods have been much less successful on Montserrat, in the Caribbean.

IS THAT A FACT!

- The youngest Hawaiian "island," Loihi, is 3,500 m above the ocean floor, but it must grow almost 1 km before coming out of the ocean. That, scientists say, could take more than 20,000 years.
- Native Hawaiians believed that Pele, the fire goddess, was responsible for volcanic activity on the islands. According to their tradition, Pele lives in the active crater of Kilauea. When angered, she stamps her feet, causing earthquakes and sending forth lava. Legend maintains that she appears as an old woman just before an eruption.

For additional background resources, please refer to the **HST Reference Library.**

CHAPTER 8

Volcanoes

Chapter Preview

Section 1
Volcanic Eruptions
- Nonexplosive Eruptions
- Explosive Eruptions
- Cross Section of a Volcano
- Magma
- What Erupts from a Volcano?

Section 2
Volcanoes' Effects on Earth
- An Explosive Impact
- Different Types of Volcanoes
- Craters and Calderas
- Lava Plateaus

Section 3
What Causes Volcanoes?
- The Formation of Magma
- Where Volcanoes Form
- Hot Spots
- Predicting Volcanic Eruptions

Directed Reading Worksheet 8

Science Puzzlers, Twisters & Teasers Worksheet 8

Guided Reading Audio CD
English or Spanish, Chapter 8

CHAPTER 8 Volcanoes

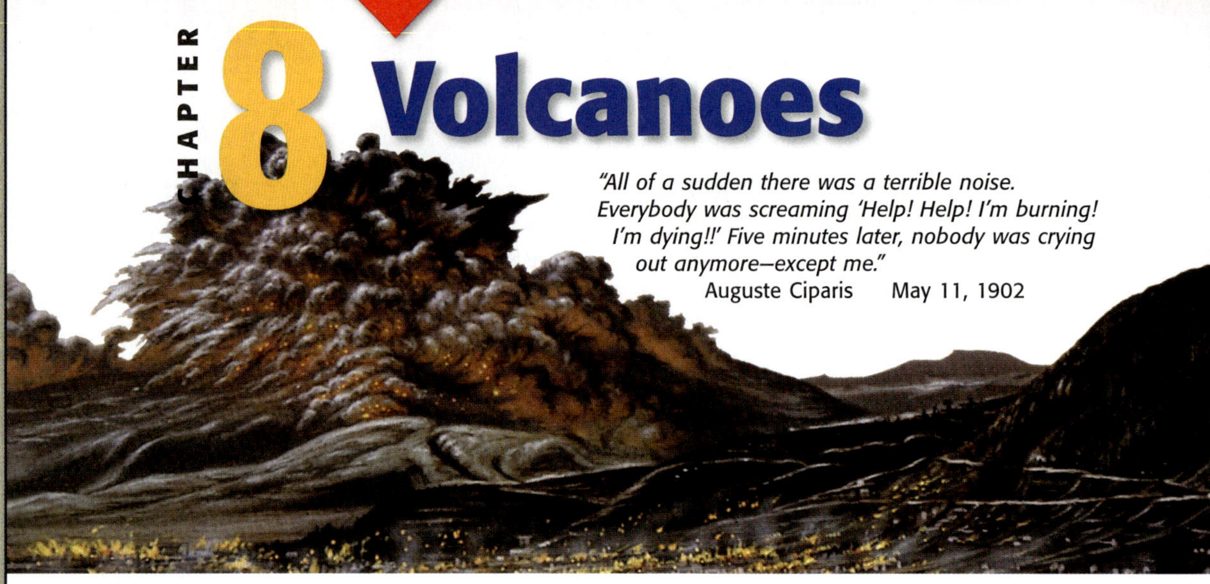

"All of a sudden there was a terrible noise. Everybody was screaming 'Help! Help! I'm burning! I'm dying!!' Five minutes later, nobody was crying out anymore—except me."
Auguste Ciparis May 11, 1902

This Really Happened!

Auguste Ciparis was a condemned man. He was sentenced to be executed for murder in the town of St. Pierre, on Martinique, a small volcanic island in the Caribbean Sea. On the morning of May 8, 1902, Ciparis sat in jail waiting for his breakfast. As he waited, disaster struck the town—a disaster that killed thousands of people.

That morning, one of the island's volcanoes, Mount Pelée, erupted in a series of explosions. The eruption sent a fiery cloud of volcanic debris, superheated steam, and toxic gases through the town. Everyone in St. Pierre, nearly 30,000 people, died. Everyone, that is, except Auguste.

Auguste had survived the deadliest volcanic eruption of the century. Underground in his dungeon, Auguste had been sheltered from the worst of the fiery fallout. Auguste cried out for help for four days before rescuers found him. He was exhausted and badly burned, but alive.

Spared from execution, Auguste joined the Barnum & Bailey circus as a sideshow attraction. Known as the Prisoner of St. Pierre, Auguste was hired to tell his tale and show off his burns in a replica of the dungeon that had saved his life.

190

This Really Happened!

Students might note that the circus poster lists the casualties of the St. Pierre eruption as 40,000 rather than 30,000, as stated in the text. The lower number is a more recent and accurate count. The temperature of the fiery cloud that overtook St. Pierre is estimated to have been between 700°C and 1,000°C. Scientists know this because although windows were deformed, copper telephone wires did not melt. The temperature was high enough to soften glass but not to melt copper.

What Do You Think?

In your ScienceLog, try to answer the following questions based on what you already know:

1. What causes a volcanic eruption?
2. What is lava, and how does it form?

Investigate!

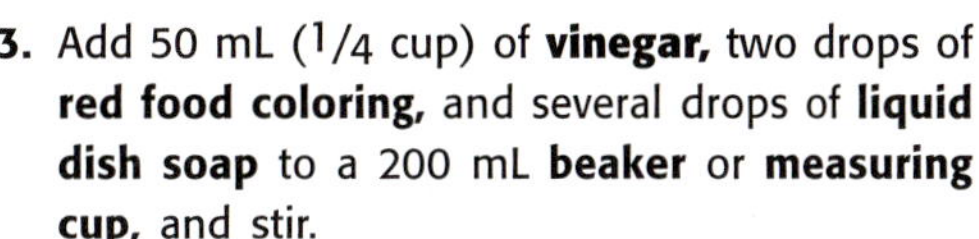

Anticipation

Imagine the thousands of lives that might have been saved if the people of St. Pierre could have predicted the eruption of Mount Pelée in 1902. Unfortunately, because volcanic eruptions are caused by processes deep within the Earth, they are very difficult to predict. See for yourself by creating your own volcano and then predicting its eruption.

Procedure

1. Tear off a sheet of **bathroom tissue,** and place 10 mL (2 tsp) of **baking soda** in the center of the tissue. Fold the corners of the tissue over the baking soda, and press the edges until the ends stay in place. Place the tissue packet in the middle of a large **plate** or **pan.**
2. Put some **modeling clay** around the top edge of a **funnel.** Turn the funnel upside down over the tissue packet in the bottom of the pan. The clay should form a watertight seal between the base of the funnel and the plate or pan. Press down to make a tight seal.
3. Add 50 mL (1/4 cup) of **vinegar,** two drops of **red food coloring,** and several drops of **liquid dish soap** to a 200 mL **beaker** or **measuring cup,** and stir.
4. Carefully pour the liquid into the spout of the upturned funnel. In your ScienceLog, record the time you began to pour.
5. Now predict how much time will elapse before your volcano erupts. Write your prediction in your ScienceLog.
6. When the volcano finally erupts, record the time again. How long did it take for your volcano to erupt? How close was your prediction?

Analysis

7. In what ways is your model volcano similar to a real one? In what ways is it different?
8. Based on the predictions of the entire class, what can you conclude about the accuracy of predicting volcanic eruptions?

191

What Do You Think?

Accept all reasonable responses.

Students will have a chance to revise their answers in the Chapter Review under NOW What Do You Think?

Investigate!

MATERIALS

- bathroom tissue
- baking soda
- large plate or pan
- modeling clay
- funnel
- vinegar
- red food coloring
- liquid dishwashing soap
- 200 mL beaker or measuring cup
- stirring stick

Safety Caution: Students should wear safety goggles and aprons during this activity.

Teacher Notes: Students should be able to compare their predictions with the time of eruption.

Answers to Investigate!

7. **Similarities:** A buildup of pressure below the surface causes an eruption. Magma and the vinegar/dishwashing soap mixture are both liquids. The sides of a volcano and the funnel and modeling clay are solids.

   Differences: The materials are different. The temperature and pressure in a real volcano are much higher than those produced in the model.
8. Eruptions are very difficult to predict. As in the experiment, you can know that an eruption will occur in the near future, but it may be impossible to predict the exact moment of eruption.

CROSS-DISCIPLINARY FOCUS

History Some explosive eruptions produce great amounts of ash. In this type of eruption, whole cities can be buried suddenly, with little advance warning. These sealed-off cities provide archaeologists with an opportunity to study the day-to-day life of a past culture. One famous example is Pompeii, where an eruption buried the Italian city in A.D. 79. Archaeologists made fascinating discoveries, such as perfectly preserved frescoes and ovens with bread still in them. Have interested students find out more about archaeological studies at cities such as Pompeii or Cerran, El Salvador.

Chapter 8 Opener–California Standards: PE/ATE 7, 7b

Section 1

Focus

Volcanic Eruptions

In this section, students learn about explosive and nonexplosive eruptions and about how the composition of magma affects these eruptions. Students learn to identify the internal structure of a volcano and the types of lava and pyroclastic material produced in an eruption.

Bellringer

Ask students to create a labeled drawing in their ScienceLog that illustrates what happens when a volcano erupts. Then have students sketch a design for a model that would simulate a volcanic eruption. Have students share their ideas with the class. Sheltered English

1 Motivate

Activity

Have students write a letter to a friend from a fictional survivor of the St. Pierre eruption described at the beginning of this chapter. Have students describe what the volcano was like hours before the eruption, the eruption itself, and the aftermath. Students can then exchange letters.

Directed Reading Worksheet 8 Section 1

1

NEW TERMS

magma, lava, vent, volcano, pyroclastic material

OBJECTIVES

- Distinguish between nonexplosive and explosive volcanic eruptions.
- Explain how the composition of magma determines the type of volcanic eruption that will occur.
- Classify the main types of lava and volcanic debris.

Volcanic Eruptions

Think about the force of the explosion produced by the first atomic bomb used in World War II. Now imagine an explosion 10,000 times stronger, and you get an idea of how powerful a volcanic eruption can be. This was the size of the explosion that occurred in Indonesia when the Krakatau volcano erupted in 1883. The eruption of Krakatau was so powerful that it was heard 4,000 km away.

Fortunately, few volcanoes give rise to explosive eruptions like that of Krakatau, which killed 36,000 people. Most eruptions are of a nonexplosive variety. You can compare these two types of eruptions for yourself by looking at the photographs on this and the next page.

Nonexplosive Eruptions

When people think of volcanic eruptions, they often imagine rivers of red-hot lava, called *lava flows*. Lava flows come from nonexplosive eruptions. Relatively calm outpourings of lava, like the ones shown below, can release a huge amount of molten rock. Some of the largest mountains on Earth grew from repeated lava flows over hundreds of thousands of years.

Sometimes nonexplosive eruptions can spray lava into the air. Lava fountains, such as this one, rarely exceed a few hundred meters in height. Most of the lava falls back to the ground while still molten.

In this nonexplosive eruption, a continuous stream of lava pours quietly from the crater of Kilauea, in Hawaii.

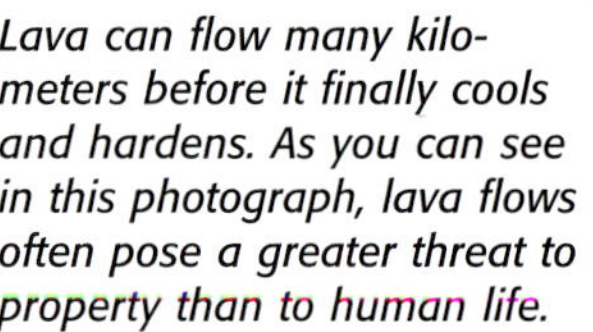

Lava can flow many kilometers before it finally cools and hardens. As you can see in this photograph, lava flows often pose a greater threat to property than to human life.

192

Misconception Alert

Although explosive volcanoes get the most attention, nonexplosive extrusions play a much more significant role in shaping our world. For instance, much of the ocean floor is covered by basaltic pillow lava, and nonexplosive volcanoes formed many of the Pacific islands.

Is That a Fact!

The volcano Mauna Kea is the tallest mountain in the world. It rises 4 km above sea level, and its slopes descend 5 km below the ocean. Hawaii's mass depresses the ocean floor another 8 km. This makes the volcano 17 km tall, almost twice the height of Mount Everest!

Section 1–California Standards: PE/ATE 1d, 2, 2d, 4c, 7, 7b

Explosive Eruptions

In an explosive volcanic eruption, clouds of hot debris and gases shoot out from the volcano, often at supersonic speeds. Instead of producing lava flows, molten rock is blown into millions of pieces that harden in the air, as shown in **Figure 1.** The dust-sized particles can circle the globe for years in the upper atmosphere, while larger pieces of debris fall closer to the volcano.

In addition to shooting molten rock into the air, an explosive eruption can blast millions of tons of solid rock from a volcano. In a matter of minutes, an explosive eruption can demolish rock formations that took thousands of years to accumulate. Thus, a volcano may actually shrink in size rather than grow from repeated eruptions.

Figure 1 *In what resembles a nuclear explosion, volcanic debris rockets skyward during an eruption of Mount Redoubt, in Alaska.*

After an explosive eruption, thick, gooey lava slowly oozes from the Soufriere Hills volcano, in Montserrat, hardening to form a dome-shaped mass. Molten rock rising up from below causes the dome to expand. If enough lava hardens to plug the volcano, the molten rock below has nowhere to go. Pressure then mounts until it is great enough to cause another explosive eruption.

This photograph shows part of the blast area from the 1980 eruption of Mount St. Helens, in Washington. In minutes, the explosive eruption flattened and scorched 600 km² of forest. Notice how the downed trees clearly show the direction of the blast (from left to right).

Multicultural CONNECTION

The Klickitat tribe of the Pacific Northwest had two names for Mount St. Helens. The first name was Loo-Wit, which referred to a lovely maiden who changed into a beautiful white mountain. Their other name was Tah-one-lat-clah, or "fire mountain," indicating their knowledge that the volcano was prone to eruptions. Ask students why they think the tribe had two very different names for Mount St. Helens. Have students research other American Indian names and legends for volcanic peaks in North America.

2 Teach

CONNECT TO LIFE SCIENCE

Nonexplosive volcanoes, like Kilauea, on the island of Hawaii, may produce several different lava flows during an eruption. If these flows surround an area of forest, they create an island in a sea of lava. Hawaiians call such areas *kipukas,* or "islands of survival." Over the last 20 years, biologists have studied populations of animals isolated in kipukas and have found interesting evidence for evolution. Picture-wing drosophila flies have exhibited changes that ultimately could produce new species. Suggest that students find out more about kipukas and the research being conducted at such sites.

COOPERATIVE LEARNING

Have groups prepare and present a mock radio program about a volcanic eruption of one of the following volcanoes:

Mount St. Helens, Vesuvius, Mount Pinatubo, or Nevada del Ruiz

Group members will research the event together. Two will write the script. One student could produce sound effects. One student will be the moderator, and two will be on-the-spot reporters. The remaining students will play people directly affected by the eruption (teachers, students, store owners, and rescue personnel). Make sure students describe the event from the first signs of volcanic activity to the aftermath. Sheltered English

2 Teach, *continued*

QuickLab

MATERIALS

- water
- honey
- 2 small drinking cups
- 2 straws

Answers to QuickLab

3. Answers will vary.
4. The honey is thicker, so the air bubbles move much more slowly than in water.
5. Because the honey is thicker than water, it traps more air bubbles. Magma that is thicker will trap more gases, which creates a buildup of pressure. The more pressure that builds up, the more violent the volcanic eruption will be.

CONNECT TO PHYSICAL SCIENCE

Use Teaching Transparency 163 to discuss changes of state in magma. When water or carbon dioxide are part of minerals in a rock, they are in the solid state. When rock melts to form magma, it changes to liquid. When this happens, the water and carbon dioxide dissolved in the magma are also liquid. When temperature and pressure conditions allow, water and carbon dioxide in the magma solution exsolve, or vaporize, changing from liquid to gas. This greatly increases the volume of the magma and often results in violent eruptions. When the magma erupts on the surface, it cools and solidifies, changing from a liquid to a solid state.

Teaching Transparency 163
"Summarizing the Changes of State"
LINK TO PHYSICAL SCIENCE

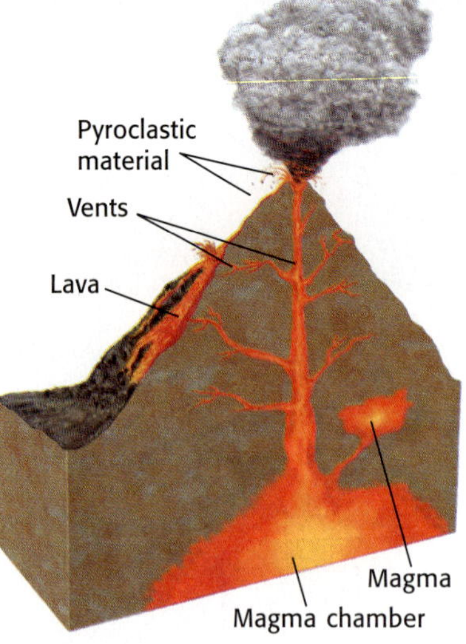

Figure 2 *Volcanoes form around vents that release magma onto the Earth's surface.*

Cross Section of a Volcano

Whether they produce explosive or nonexplosive eruptions, all volcanoes share the same basic features. **Figure 2** shows some of the features that you might see if you could look inside an erupting volcano. Deep underground, the driving force that creates volcanoes is hot, liquid material known as **magma.** Magma collects in *magma chambers* as deep as 160 km below the surface. From there, the magma rises through holes in the Earth's crust called **vents.** Magma that erupts and flows onto the Earth's surface is called **lava.** Magma that erupts as fragments of molten material that solidify in the air is called *pyroclastic material.* **Pyroclastic material** includes magma and fragments of rock that are blasted into the air during violent volcanic eruptions. A vent or a group of vents combined with the buildup of lava or pyroclastic material on the Earth's surface is a **volcano.**

QuickLab

Bubble, Bubble, Toil and Trouble

With a few simple items, you can easily discover how the consistency of a liquid affects the flow of gases. You will need **water, honey,** two small **drinking cups,** and two **straws.**

1. Fill one cup halfway with water and the other cup halfway with honey.
2. Using one of the straws, blow into the water and observe the bubbles.
3. Take the other straw and blow into the honey. What happens?
4. How does the honey behave differently from the water?
5. How do you think this difference relates to volcanic eruptions?

Magma

By comparing the composition of magma from different types of eruptions, scientists have made an important discovery—the composition of the magma determines whether a volcanic eruption is nonexplosive, explosive, or somewhere in between.

Water A volcano is more likely to erupt explosively if its magma has a high water content. The effect water has on magma is similar to the effect carbon dioxide gas has in a can of soda. When you shake the can up, the carbon dioxide that was dissolved in the soda is released, and because gases need much more room than liquids, a great amount of pressure builds up. When you open the can, soda comes shooting out. The same phenomenon occurs with explosive volcanic eruptions. The more water magma contains, the greater the pressure is and the greater the chances are that a violent explosion will occur.

Silica Explosive eruptions are also caused by magma that contains a large percentage of silica (a basic building block of most minerals). Silica-rich magma has a thick, stiff consistency. It flows slowly and tends to harden in the volcano's vent. This plugs the vent, resulting in a buildup of pressure as magma pushes up from below. If enough pressure builds up, an explosive eruption results. Thick magma also prevents water vapor and other gases from easily escaping. Magma that contains a smaller percentage of silica has a thinner, runnier consistency. Gases escape this type of magma more easily, making it less likely that explosive pressure will build up.

MISCONCEPTION ALERT

It may seem illogical that water makes magma more likely to explode. Explain that magma contains water and that the water is dissolved in the magma. When the water changes from liquid to steam, its volume increases dramatically. This change causes pressure that, when released, creates a great deal of explosive force. Discuss what would happen if students boiled water in a pot with a tight lid. Have them think of other examples where water can be an explosive force, such as in a car's radiator or in popcorn.

What Erupts from a Volcano?

Depending on how explosive a volcanic eruption is, magma erupts as either lava or pyroclastic material. The composition of both lava and pyroclastic material differs from that of magma because much of the magma's gases is released in an eruption. Nonexplosive eruptions produce mostly lava. Explosive eruptions produce mostly pyroclastic material. Over many years, a volcano may alternate between eruptions of lava and eruptions of pyroclastic material. Eruptions of lava and pyroclastic material may also occur as separate stages of a single eruption event.

Fire and ice! A phrase to describe volcanoes? That depends on where they are. Turn to page 211 to find out more.

Lava Lava is magma that flows onto the Earth's surface. Like magma, lava ranges in consistency from thick to thin. Blocky lava is so thick in consistency that it barely creeps along the ground. Other types of lava, such as *pahoehoe* (pah HOY HOY), *aa* (AH ah), and *pillow lava,* are thinner in consistency and produce faster lava flows. These types of lava are shown in the photographs below.

Blocky lava *is cool, stiff lava that cannot travel far from the erupting vent. Blocky lava usually oozes from a volcano only after an explosive eruption has released much of the gas pressure from the magma chamber. As shown here, blocky lava forms jumbled heaps of sharp-edged chunks.*

Pahoehoe *lava flows slowly, like wax dripping from a candle, forming a glassy surface with rounded wrinkles. This lava gets its name from the Hawaiian word for "ropy" because its surface resembles coils of rope.*

Aa *is a Hawaiian word that refers to a type of lava that has a jagged surface. This slightly stiffer lava pours out quickly and forms a brittle crust. The crust is torn into jagged pieces as the molten lava underneath continues to move. Aa is named after the sound you would make if you were to walk across this type of lava barefoot.*

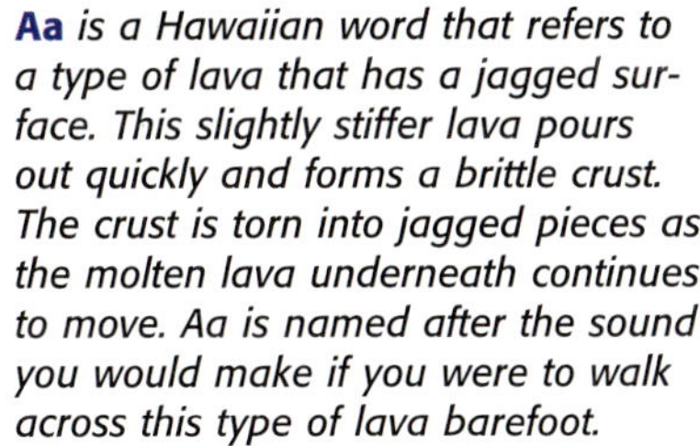

Pillow lava *forms when lava erupts underwater. As you can see here, it forms rounded lumps that are the size and shape of pillows. Pillow lava has a rounded shape because contact with water causes rapid cooling of the lava's surface.*

195

WEIRD SCIENCE

Lava cools very slowly not only because it is very hot to start with but also because it is a good insulator. When a Mexican lava flow in 1952 stopped, it was 10 m thick. In 1956, four years later, the lava still steamed when it rained.

READING STRATEGY

Mnemonics The word *pyroclastic* has two parts: *pyro,* Greek for "fire," and *clastic,* Greek for "broken." Other words that include *pyro-* are *pyrotechnics,* which describes "fire art," or fireworks, and *pyrometer,* a thermometer that measures temperatures too high for a mercury thermometer. Have students invent other words that include the prefix *pyro-*. Sheltered English

DISCUSSION

Discuss with students the differences between a *direct relationship* and an *inverse relationship.* Explain that when they push a swing, it goes higher and faster. This is a direct relationship. To illustrate an inverse relationship, explain that when they push down on one end of a seesaw, the other end rises. Then ask students to think about the role of water and silica in magma. Discuss them in terms of how they have a *direct relationship* with an explosion: as the amount of water or silica increases, the possibility of explosion also increases. Then discuss the way that silica affects lava's speed and consistency in terms of their *inverse relationship:* as the amount of silica increases, the speed of the lava decreases, and vice versa. Sheltered English

GROUP ACTIVITY

Introduce the concept of viscosity by having students describe the observable differences in flow rate as you pour molasses or honey, water, and vegetable oil down a gently sloping cookie sheet. (They should observe that the molasses or honey flows slowest, oil flows somewhat faster, and water flows very fast.)

Explain to students that viscosity is a liquid's resistance to flow. Honey has a high viscosity, so it flows very slowly. Water has a low viscosity, so it flows easily. Ask the students how magma's composition affects its viscosity. (The more silica that is present in magma, the greater its viscosity.)

TOPIC: Volcanic Eruptions
GO TO: www.scilinks.org
*sci*LINKS NUMBER: HSTE205

3 Extend

GOING FURTHER

Writing *Lahar* is an Indonesian term for a particularly deadly kind of pyroclastic flow. A lahar is a flow of water-saturated volcanic debris with a consistency of wet cement that races down the slope of a volcano. The water usually comes from snow that originally topped the volcano but that was instantly melted by the eruption. When Nevada del Ruiz erupted in Colombia, its lahar killed more than 25,000 people. Have students research and report on lahars from two eruptions.

4 Close

Quiz

1. Describe the lava flow from a nonexplosive eruption. (a calm stream that can flow for hundreds of kilometers)
2. Describe an explosive eruption. (Ash, hot debris, gases, and chunks of rock spew from the volcano.)
3. Define *blocky* lava, *pahoehoe* lava, and *aa* lava. (*blocky* lava: cool, stiff lava that doesn't travel very fast; *pahoehoe* lava: flows quickly and forms a wrinkled surface, looks like coiled rope; *aa* lava: flows slowly and forms a brittle, jagged crust.

ALTERNATIVE ASSESSMENT

Provide cornstarch, salt, and water to make a natural paste. Then have students experiment with the ingredients in order to create representations of the types of lava discussed in the chapter.

Pyroclastic material Pyroclastic material refers to the rock fragments created by explosive volcanic eruptions. Pyroclastic material is produced when magma explodes from a volcano and solidifies in the air. It is also produced when existing rock is shattered by powerful eruptions. It comes in a variety of sizes, from boulders the size of houses to particles so small they can remain suspended in the atmosphere for years. The photographs on this page show four major kinds of pyroclastic material: volcanic bombs, volcanic blocks, lapilli (luh PILL ee), and volcanic ash.

Volcanic blocks *are the largest pieces of pyroclastic material. They consist of solid rock blasted out of the volcano.*

Volcanic bombs *are large blobs of magma that harden in the air. The flattened, elongated shape of the bomb shown here resulted from the magma's spinning through the air as it cooled. Volcanic bombs are more than 64 mm in diameter.*

Lapilli, *which means "little stones" in Italian, are pebble-like bits of pyroclastic material between 2 and 64 mm in diameter. Both lapilli and volcanic bombs are solid when they hit the ground, although they may still be red hot.*

Volcanic ash *consists of particles that are less than 2 mm in diameter. Volcanic ash forms when the gases in stiff magma expand rapidly and the walls of the gas bubbles explode into tiny glasslike slivers.*

life science CONNECTION

Why do people choose to live near potentially explosive volcanoes? One reason is that these volcanoes provide some of the most productive farmland in the world. Volcanic rocks contain almost all of the elements plants need to grow, though it may take hundreds or even thousands of years for volcanic rock to break down into usable soil nutrients. On the other hand, the ash from a single explosive eruption can greatly increase the fertility of soil in only a few years and can keep the soil fertile for centuries.

REVIEW

1. Is a nonexplosive volcanic eruption more likely to produce lava or pyroclastic material? Explain.
2. If a volcano contained magma with small proportions of water and silica, would you predict a nonexplosive eruption or an explosive one? Why?
3. **Making Inferences** Pyroclastic material is classified primarily by the size of the particles. What is the basis for classifying lava?

196

Answers to Review

1. A nonexplosive eruption is more likely to produce lava than pyroclastic material because lava is thin and runny compared with pyroclastic material.
2. A nonexplosive eruption should result. Water turns to steam, which builds up a great amount of pressure, leading to explosive eruptions. Silica-rich magma is thick, allowing it to trap volcanic gases, such as steam, causing explosive eruptions.
3. Lava is classified according to how it flows. Blocky lava is thickest and flows very slowly because it is mostly solidified. Aa lava is still thick but is made of smaller blocks and thus flows faster than blocky lava. Pahoehoe lava is thin and runny, and it flows quickly, forming a ropy texture. Pillow lava forms under water.

Section 1 Review–California Standards: PE/ATE 1, 1d

2

Volcanoes' Effects on Earth

NEW TERMS
shield volcano
cinder cone volcano
composite volcano
crater
caldera

OBJECTIVES
- Describe the effects that volcanoes have on Earth.
- Compare the different types of volcanoes.

The effects of volcanic eruptions can be seen both on land and in the air. Pyroclastic materials fall to the ground, causing great destruction, while ash and escaping gases affect global climatic patterns. Volcanoes also build mountains and plateaus that become lasting additions to the landscape.

An Explosive Impact

Because it is thrown high into the air, ash ejected during explosive volcanic eruptions can have widespread effects. The ash can block out the sun for days over thousands of square kilometers. Volcanic ash can blow down trees and buildings and can blanket nearby towns with a fine powder.

Figure 3 *During the 1991 eruption of Mount Pinatubo, in the Philippines, clouds of volcanic gases and ash sped downhill at up to 250 km/h.*

Flows As shown in **Figure 3,** clouds of hot ash can flow rapidly downhill like an avalanche, choking and searing every living thing in their path, as happened at Mount Peleé in 1902. Sometimes large deposits of ash mix with rainwater or the water from melted glaciers during an eruption. With the consistency of wet cement, the mixture flows downhill, picking up boulders, trees, and buildings along the way. More powerful than ordinary rivers, these mudflows move swiftly and cause immense damage.

Fallout As volcanic ash falls to the ground, the effects can be devastating. Buildings may collapse under the weight of so much ash. Ash can also dam up river valleys, resulting in massive floods. And although ash is an effective plant fertilizer, too much ash can smother crops, causing food shortages and loss of livestock.

Climatic Fluctuation In large-scale eruptions, volcanic ash, along with sulfur-rich gases, can reach the upper atmosphere. As the ash and gases spread around the globe, they can block out enough sunlight to cause the average global surface temperature to drop noticeably. The eruption of Mount Pinatubo in 1991 caused average global temperatures to drop by as much as 0.5°C. Although this may not seem like a large change in temperature, such a shift can disrupt climates all over the world. The lower average temperatures may last for several years, bringing wetter, milder summers and longer, harsher winters. Such changes in climate can cause worldwide food shortages that result in starvation and disease.

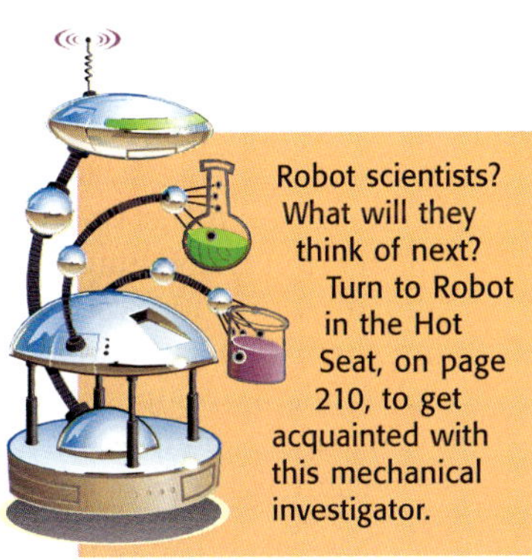

Robot scientists? What will they think of next? Turn to Robot in the Hot Seat, on page 210, to get acquainted with this mechanical investigator.

197

SECTION 2

Focus

Volcanoes' Effects on Earth

This section explores the effects of explosive eruptions. Students learn to identify different types of volcanoes and physical features created by volcanic activity, such as craters, calderas, and lava plateaus.

Bellringer

Write the following terms on the chalkboard:

shield volcano, cinder cone volcano, composite volcano, volcanic crater, caldera

Group students in threes, and have them look through the section to come up with a definition for each of the terms. Have them record their definitions and revise them after finishing the section.

1 Motivate

Discussion

Have students discuss the most exciting images they've seen in movies and television programs featuring volcanoes. Have them describe what they think about volcanic eruptions in their ScienceLog so they can revisit these impressions after reading this section. Sheltered English

Scientists at Odds

Today most scientists believe that dinosaurs became extinct 65 million years ago because a large asteroid struck Earth. But a small group of volcanologists have a controversial hypothesis that the gases and ash released from a series of large volcanic eruptions may have caused the extinction. Encourage students to find out more about these theories.

Reading Strategy

Prediction Guide Before reading the passage about the effects of explosive volcanic eruptions, have students respond to the following true/false statements:

- Ash flows can be more powerful than river floods. (true)
- Volcanic eruptions can affect the weather for many years. (true)

Directed Reading Worksheet 8 Section 2

internet connect
SCILINKS NSTA
TOPIC: Volcanic Effects
GO TO: www.scilinks.org
*sci*LINKS NUMBER: HSTE210

Section 2–California Standards: PE/ATE 1d, 2d; LabBook: 1a, 1e, 7f, 7g

2 Teach

PG 516

Some Go "Pop," Some Do Not

MEETING INDIVIDUAL NEEDS

Learners Having Difficulty Have students copy descriptive phrases about the three types of volcanoes in their ScienceLog. Beside the entries, have them draw a cross section of each type of volcano. Students should find an example of each volcano type and write three paragraphs about each one. The paragraphs should describe how the volcano fits its category, detail its last eruption, and explain how the volcano's shape is linked to the way it erupted. Sheltered English

MEETING INDIVIDUAL NEEDS

Advanced Learners In 1943, Dominic Pulido, a farmer in central Mexico, was working in his cornfield when the ground began to tremble and a noise like thunder filled the air. Pulido discovered a fissure in the field about 0.5 m deep. The ground began to swell and formed a mound 2.5 m high! A volcano named Paricutín was being born. In one year, the cinder cone volcano grew to 334 m high! Encourage students to read *Hill of Fire,* by Thomas P. Lewis, and write a book report about it.

Teaching Transparency 112 "Three Types of Volcanoes"

Problem Solving Worksheet 8 "Eruption Disruption"

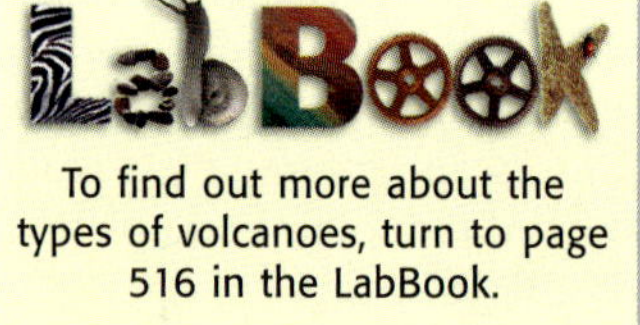

To find out more about the types of volcanoes, turn to page 516 in the LabBook.

Different Types of Volcanoes

The lava and pyroclastic material that erupt from volcanoes create a variety of landforms. Perhaps the best known of all volcanic landforms are the volcanoes themselves. Volcanoes result from the buildup of rock around a vent. Three basic types of volcanoes are illustrated in **Figure 4.**

Figure 4 Three Types of Volcanoes

Shield volcano

Shield volcanoes are built out of layers of lava from repeated nonexplosive eruptions. Because the lava is very runny, it spreads out over a wide area. Over time, the layers of lava create a volcano with gently sloping sides. Although their sides are not very steep, shield volcanoes can be enormous. Hawaii's Mauna Kea, the shield volcano shown here, is the largest mountain on Earth. Measured from its base on the sea floor, Mauna Kea is taller than Mount Everest, the tallest mountain on land.

Cinder cone volcano

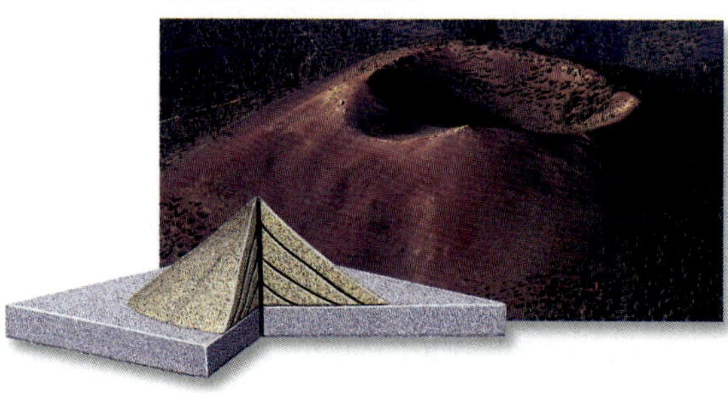

Cinder cone volcanoes are small volcanic cones made entirely of pyroclastic material from moderately explosive eruptions. The pyroclastic material forms steeper slopes with a narrower base than the lava flows of shield volcanoes, as you can see in this photo of the volcano Paricutín, in Mexico. Cinder cone volcanoes usually erupt for only a short time and often occur in clusters, commonly on the sides of shield and composite volcanoes. They erode quickly because the pyroclastic particles are not cemented together by lava.

Composite volcano

Composite volcanoes, sometimes referred to as *stratovolcanoes,* are one of the most common types of volcanoes. They form by explosive eruptions of pyroclastic material followed by quieter outpourings of lava. The combination of both types of eruptions forms alternating layers of pyroclastic material and lava. Composite volcanoes, such as Japan's Mount Fuji, shown here, have broad bases and sides that get steeper toward the summit.

CROSS-DISCIPLINARY FOCUS

History One of World War II's fiercest battles was fought on the volcanic island of Iwo Jima. More than 6,000 Allied soldiers and 20,000 Japanese soldiers died fighting for an island about 8 km long and 4 km wide. Have students research the battle of Iwo Jima and prepare a map to show why this volcanic island was difficult to capture.

IS THAT A FACT!

The fastest lava flow recorded moved at a speed of 60 km/h—about the same speed as a champion thoroughbred racehorse.

Craters and Calderas

At the top of the central vent in most volcanoes is a funnel-shaped pit called a **crater.** (Craters are also the circular pits made by meteorite impacts.) The photograph of the cinder cone on the previous page shows a well-defined crater. A crater's funnel shape results from explosions of material out of the vent as well as the collapse of material from the crater's rim back into the vent. A **caldera** forms when a magma chamber that supplies material to a volcano empties and its roof collapses. This causes the ground to sink, leaving a large, circular depression.

Volcano
Caldera
Vent
Magma chamber

Figure 5 *A caldera forms when enough magma is ejected from a magma chamber that the ground above collapses to fill the empty space. Calderas are generally much larger than volcanic craters.*

Lava Plateaus

The most massive outpourings of lava do not come from individual volcanoes. Most of the lava on Earth's continents erupts from long cracks, or *fissures,* in the crust. In this nonexplosive type of eruption, runny lava pours from a series of fissures and may spread evenly over thousands of square kilometers. The resulting landform is known as a *lava plateau.* **Figure 6** shows a portion of the Columbia River Plateau, a lava plateau that formed about 15 million years ago in what is now the northwestern United States.

Figure 6 *This formation in the Columbia River Plateau reveals rock layers that were created by a series of large lava flows.*

astronomy CONNECTION

Have you ever noticed the dark patches on the moon? Early astronomers thought these areas were bodies of water. Astronomers now know that these areas are basins filled with dark solidified lava. They formed in much the same way as Earth's lava plateaus.

REVIEW

1. Briefly explain why the ash from a volcanic eruption can be hazardous.
2. Why do cinder cone volcanoes have narrower bases and steeper sides than shield volcanoes?
3. **Comparing Concepts** Briefly describe the difference between a crater and a caldera.

199

Answers to Review

1. Answers will vary. Volcanic ash is hazardous when it dams rivers, causing floods, and when it smothers crops, resulting in food shortages.
2. Shield volcanoes are made of lava flows, which are thin and runny, and spread out over large areas. Cinder cone volcanoes are made of pyroclastic material, which is thick and piles up around the volcano.
3. A crater forms when the rock around the main vent of a volcano is blasted out in an explosive eruption, forming an inverted cone-shaped depression. Most volcanoes have craters at their summits. A caldera forms when the magma chamber that feeds a volcano empties. When this happens, the roof of the magma chamber collapses, forming a circular depression. Calderas are usually much larger than craters.

Research

Have students form pairs and search books, magazines, or Internet sites for pictures of craters, calderas, and lava plateaus. Have pairs use their findings to make a model of one of these features. Sheltered English

3 Close

Quiz

1. Describe the shapes of shield, cinder cone, and composite volcanoes. (shield volcano: broad area with gentle shallow slopes; cinder cone volcano: generally smaller, steeper, more angled sides; composite volcano: high, covers less area than shield volcanoes, has sides that become steeper as they near the crater)
2. What causes a caldera? (A volcano's magma chamber empties, causing the ground above it to collapse.)
3. What is a lava plateau? (a layered formation caused when lava erupts from long cracks, or fissures, and covers a wide area)

Alternative Assessment

Have students draw a poster of an explosive volcano. Have them incorporate flows, fallout, and a crater or caldera. Students must label and write a caption for all the volcano's parts.

Teaching Transparency 113
"The Formation of a Caldera"

Reinforcement Worksheet 8
"A Variety of Volcanoes"

SECTION 3

Focus

What Causes Volcanoes?

In this section, students learn how magma forms and how pressure and heat affect the temperature at which rocks melt. The section draws a connection between volcanic activity and tectonic movement and concludes with a discussion of the challenges involved in predicting eruptions.

Bellringer

Ask students to imagine they live on a volcanic island. Have them list in their ScienceLog the signals that would tell them the volcano was about to erupt.

1 Motivate

DISCUSSION

Have students brainstorm about measures a community could take to protect citizens from a volcanic eruption and then write their ideas in their ScienceLog. Have them compare their suggestions with the information they learn in the chapter.
Sheltered English

Teaching Transparency 114
"The Formation of Magma"

Directed Reading Worksheet 8 Section 3

3

NEW TERMS
rift hot spot

OBJECTIVES
- Describe the formation and movement of magma.
- Identify the places where magma forms.
- Explain the relationship between volcanoes and plate tectonics.
- Summarize the methods scientists use to predict volcanic eruptions.

What Causes Volcanoes?

Scientists have learned a great deal over the years about what happens when a volcano erupts. Many of the results are dramatic and immediately visible. Unfortunately, understanding what causes a volcano to erupt in the first place is much more difficult. Scientists have no way of seeing firsthand what is going on deep within the Earth. They must rely on models based on rock samples and other data that provide insight into volcanic processes. Because it is so difficult to "see" what is going on deep inside the Earth, there are many uncertainties about why volcanoes form.

The Formation of Magma

You learned in the previous section that volcanoes form by the eruption of lava and pyroclastic material onto the Earth's surface. But the key to understanding why volcanoes erupt is understanding how magma forms. As you can see in **Figure 7**, all volcanoes begin when magma collects in pockets in the deeper regions of the Earth's crust and in the uppermost layers of the mantle, the zone of intensely hot and pliable rock between the Earth's crust and the core. This zone of magma formation is between 25 and 160 km below the surface.

Although hot and pliable, the rock of the mantle is considered a solid. But the temperature of the mantle is high enough to melt almost any rock, so why doesn't it melt? The answer has to do with pressure. The weight of the rock above the mantle exerts a tremendous amount of pressure. This pressure keeps the atoms of mantle rock tightly packed, preventing the rock from changing into a liquid state. An increase in pressure raises the melting point of most materials.

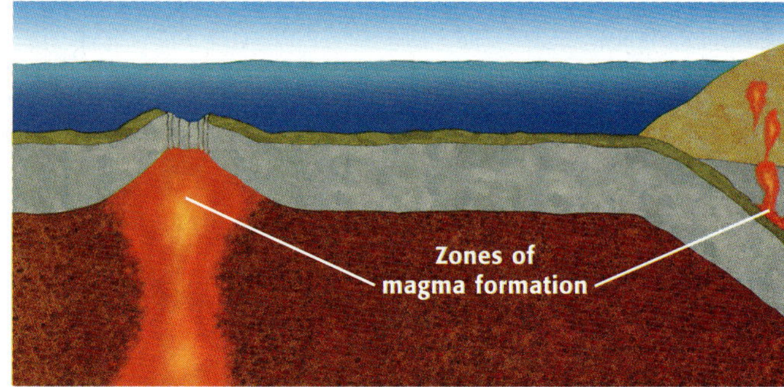

Figure 7 *Magma forms below the Earth's surface in a region that includes the lower crust and part of the upper mantle.*

QuickLab

Reaction to Stress

1. Make a pliable "rock" by pouring 60 mL (1/4 cup) of **water** into a **plastic cup** and adding 150 mL of **cornstarch,** 15 mL (1 tbsp) at a time. Stir well after each addition. (The mixture should be hard to stir, but not powdery.)
2. Pour half of the cornstarch mixture into a **clear bowl.** Carefully observe how the "rock" flows. Be patient—this is a slow process!
3. Scrape the rest of the "rock" out of the cup with a **spoon.** Observe the behavior of the "rock" as you scrape.
4. What happened to the "rock" when you let it flow by itself? What happened when you put stress on the "rock"?
5. How is this pliable "rock" similar to the rock of the upper part of the mantle?

QuickLab

MATERIALS
- water
- plastic cup
- cornstarch
- stirring stick
- clear bowl
- spoon

Answers to QuickLab

4. When left alone, the "rock" flowed like a liquid but very slowly. When pressure was applied by the spoon, the "rock" broke, acting like a solid.
5. Because of the high pressure, the mantle is a solid. But over long periods of time, the mantle flows, acting more like a liquid.

Section 3–California Standards: PE/ATE 1, 1a, 1b, 1c, 1d, 1e, 1g, 2, 2d, 4, 4c, 7, 7b; LabBook: 7, 7b, 7e

As you can see in **Figure 8,** rock melts and forms magma when the temperature of the rock increases or when the pressure on the rock decreases. Because the temperature of the mantle is relatively constant, a decrease in pressure is usually what causes magma to form. In some cases, the magma melts the solid rock above it to make its way upward. In other cases, the magma rises through existing cracks and fissures in the overlying rock.

Once formed, the magma rises toward the surface of the Earth because it is less dense than the surrounding rock. Magma is commonly a mixture of liquid and solid mineral crystals and is therefore normally less dense than the completely solid rock that surrounds it. Like air bubbles that form on the bottom of a pan of boiling water, magma will rise toward the surface.

Not all magma makes it all the way to the Earth's surface to form a volcano. Stiff magma often cools and solidifies while still in the Earth's crust.

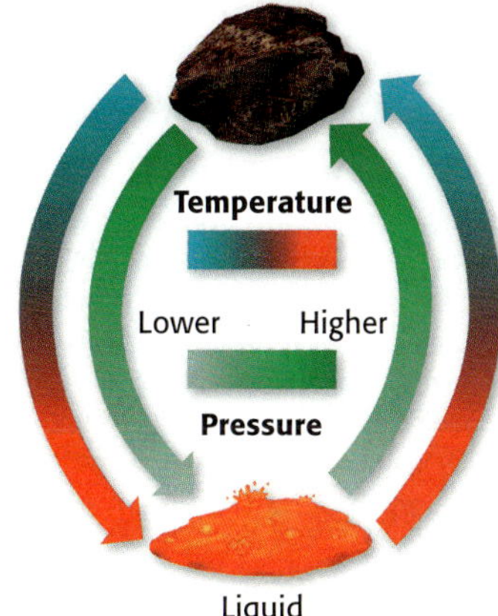

Figure 8 *This diagram shows how both pressure and temperature affect the formation of magma within the mantle.*

Self-Check

1. What two factors may cause solid rock to become magma?
2. Where does magma form?

(See page 564 to check your answers.)

Where Volcanoes Form

The locations of volcanoes around the globe provide clues to how volcanoes form. The world map in **Figure 9** shows the location of the world's active volcanoes on land. It also shows tectonic plate boundaries. As you can see, a large number of the volcanoes lie directly on tectonic plate boundaries. In fact, the plate boundaries surrounding the Pacific Ocean have so many volcanoes that these boundaries together are called the *Ring of Fire.*

Why are most volcanoes on tectonic plate boundaries? These boundaries are where the plates either collide with one another or separate from one another. In these zones of weakness, it is easier for magma to travel upward through the crust. In other words, the boundaries are where the action is!

Figure 9 *Tectonic plate boundaries are likely places for volcanoes to form. The Ring of Fire contains nearly 75 percent of the world's active volcanoes on land.*

2) Teach

BRAIN FOOD

Igneous rocks form when either magma or lava cools and solidifies. If they are from the same source, often the only difference between the two is the rate at which they cool. Because magma is underground, it cools much more slowly than lava. A molten rock that cools slowly generally has larger crystals than one that cools faster.

How could scientists use this information to study an igneous outcrop? (By studying mineral crystal size and type, scientists can determine the origin of igneous rock.)

CROSS-DISCIPLINARY FOCUS

Geography Point out to students that most volcanic activity takes place on the ocean floor, where vast amounts of lava rise through rifts or volcanoes at diverging plate boundaries. Ask students to identify a spot where plates are diverging. (Sample answer: the mid-Atlantic Ridge)

What plates are diverging along the mid-Atlantic Ridge? (the North American and Eurasian plates)

What landmass formed by volcanic activity along this diverging plate boundary? (the island of Iceland)

Then point out to students that Iceland is merely a visible part of the mid-Atlantic Ridge. Also explain that volcanic eruptions along diverging tectonic plates are generally much less violent than volcanoes typical of convergent boundaries.

IS THAT A FACT!

Kilauea, in Hawaii, is one of the most studied volcanoes in the world. It has been erupting regularly since 1983. Every day, enough lava to pave a two-lane road 32 km long pours from the volcano.

Answers to Self-Check

1. Solid rock may become magma when pressure is released, when the temperature rises above its melting point, or when its composition changes.
2. Magma forms in the lower crust and upper mantle, at depths between 25 and 160 km.

2 Teach, continued

REAL-WORLD CONNECTION

Writing Earthquake tremors are often a warning signal that a volcano is about to erupt. In the months before the explosive eruption of Mount St. Helens, small earthquakes, which grew in number and intensity, shook the area. On March 27, 1980, the volcano began venting steam and ash. Geologists had set up seismometers to record the frequency, location, and magnitude of the quakes. Electronic surveying equipment employed laser beams to measure ground swelling as the lava dome rose. Tiltmeters measured changes in the mountain's slope. Steam gauges recorded water temperatures, pH levels, and amounts of suspended minerals in the waters around the volcano. Gas sensors on the ground and in aircraft monitored hydrogen, carbon dioxide, and sulfur dioxide levels that might signal the movement of magma toward the surface. Have students write a report about predicting the Mount St. Helens eruption and the eruption itself.

Answer to MATHBREAK

$°F = \frac{9}{5} \times 1{,}400°C + 32 = 2{,}552°F$

Math Skills Worksheet 35 "Using Temperature Scales"

internetconnect

SCILINKS NSTA

TOPIC: What Causes Volcanoes?
GO TO: www.scilinks.org
***sci*LINKS NUMBER:** HSTE215

TOPIC: The Ring of Fire
GO TO: www.scilinks.org
***sci*LINKS NUMBER:** HSTE220

MATHBREAK

How Hot Is Hot?

Inside the Earth, magma can reach a burning-hot 1,400°C! You are probably more familiar with Fahrenheit temperatures, so convert 1,400° Celsius to degrees Fahrenheit by using the formula below.

$$°F = \frac{9}{5}°C + 32$$

What is the magma's temperature in degrees Fahrenheit?

When Tectonic Plates Separate When two tectonic plates separate and move away from each other, a *divergent boundary* forms. As the tectonic plates separate, a deep crack, or **rift,** forms between the plates. Mantle material then rises to fill in the gap. Because the mantle material is closer to the surface, the pressure on it becomes less. This decrease in pressure causes the mantle rock below the rift to partially melt and become magma.

Because magma is less dense than the surrounding rock, it rises up through the rift. As the magma rises, it cools down, and the pressure on it decreases. So even though it becomes cooler as it rises, it remains molten because of the reduced pressure. By the time the magma spills out onto the Earth's surface as lava, it may have decreased in temperature by as much as 800°C.

Magma continuously rises up through the rift between the separating plates and creates new crust. Although a few divergent boundaries exist on land, most are located on the ocean floor, where they produce long mountain chains called mid-ocean spreading centers, or mid-ocean ridges. **Figure 10** shows the process of forming such an underwater mountain range at a divergent boundary.

Figure 10 How Magma Forms at a Divergent Boundary

As the tectonic plates separate, a rift forms. Mantle material rises to fill the space opened by the separating tectonic plates. As the pressure decreases, the mantle begins to melt.

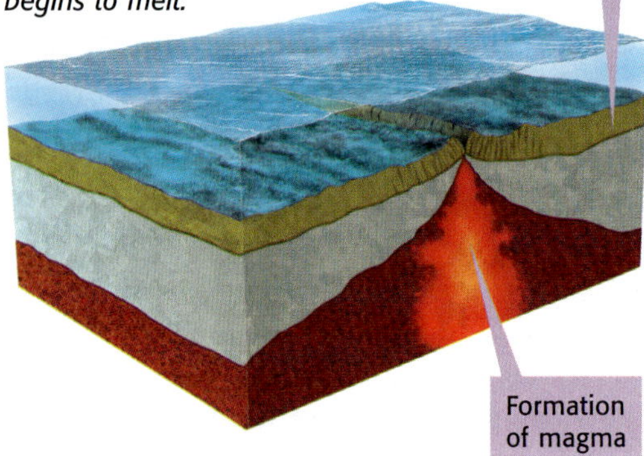

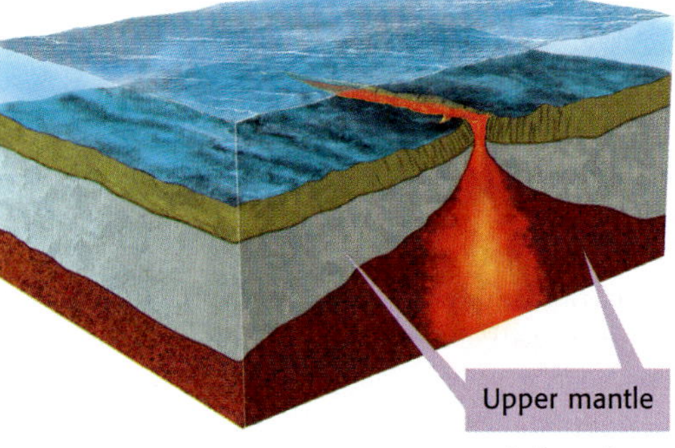

Because magma is less dense than the surrounding rock, it rises toward the surface, where it forms new crust on the ocean floor.

202

Homework

Debate How reliable are volcano warnings? An estimated 500 million people around the world live either on or near a volcano, and each year more than 100 volcanoes erupt on Earth. The potential for an eruption to affect a large number of people is great. Scientists are using tools such as seismographs, laser range finders, and satellites to learn more about volcanoes and volcanic eruptions, but they are still not able to accurately predict volcanic eruptions. Encourage students to research the recent advances in volcano-eruption prediction and debate whether scientists will ever be able to make accurate predictions, and what kinds of technology would make this possible.

When Tectonic Plates Collide If you slide two pieces of notebook paper into one another on a flat desktop, the papers will either buckle upward or one piece of paper will move under the other. This gives you an idea of what happens when tectonic plates collide. The place where two tectonic plates collide is called a *convergent boundary.* The movement of one tectonic plate under another is called *subduction,* shown in **Figure 11.** Convergent boundaries are commonly located where oceanic plates collide with continental plates. The oceanic crust is denser and thinner and therefore is subducted underneath the continental crust.

Oceanic crust contains water, which lowers the melting point of rocks it comes in contact with. As the descending oceanic crust scrapes past the continental crust, it sinks deeper and deeper into the mantle, getting hotter and hotter. As it does so, the pressure on the oceanic crust increases as well. The combination of increased heat and pressure causes the water contained in the oceanic crust to be released. The water then mixes with the mantle rock, causing it to melt.

On its way to the surface, heat from rising magma may cause some of the overlying continental crust (rich in silica) to melt and become part of the magma. The silica from the continental crust then becomes part of a gooey, silica-rich lava that is likely to cause an explosive eruption when it finally reaches the surface.

Figure 11 How Magma Forms at a Convergent Boundary

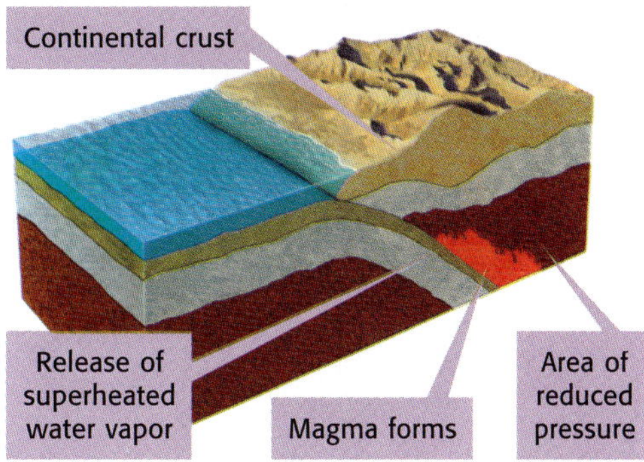

When an oceanic plate and a continental plate converge, the denser oceanic plate is subducted. As the subducted plate moves downward, the rock melts and forms magma.

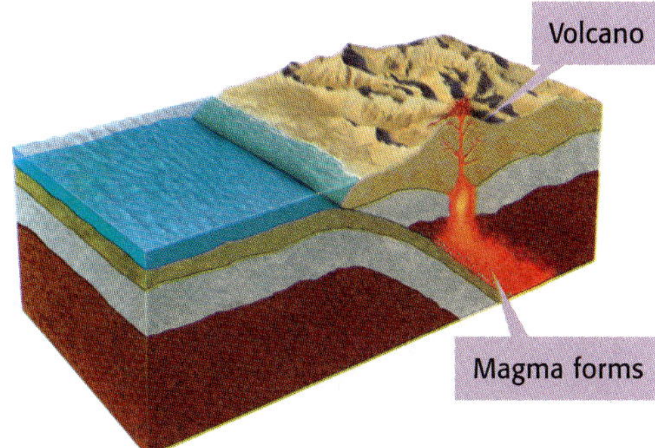

When magma is less dense than the surrounding rock, it rises toward the surface.

Hot Spots

Not all magma develops along tectonic plate boundaries. For example, the Hawaiian Islands, some of the most well-known volcanoes on Earth, are nowhere near a plate boundary. The volcanoes of Hawaii and several other places on Earth are caused by **hot spots.** Hot spots are places within tectonic plates that are directly above columns of rising magma, called *mantle plumes,* that begin deep in the Earth, possibly at the boundary between the mantle and the core. Scientists are not sure what causes these plumes, but some think that a combination of heat conducted upward from the core and heat from radioactive elements keeps the plumes rising.

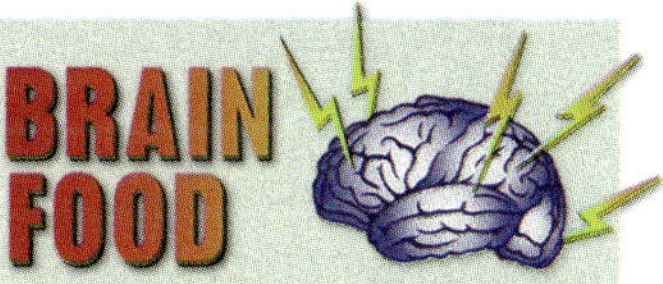

There are 10 times as many active volcanoes at the bottom of the ocean as there are on land. The ocean floor, roughly three-fourths of the Earth's surface, was produced primarily by volcanic activity.

IS THAT A FACT!

In the Caribbean, a submarine volcano named Kick'em Jenny is gaining a very bad reputation. As one sailboat captain said, "Kick'em Jenny . . . has a reputation of kicking up a nasty sea." Between 1986 and 1996, the volcano grew over 50 m; its top is now only 200 m below sea level. It's close enough to the surface that eruptions can cause waves and turbulence in the sea. Volcanologists are concerned that a large eruption could cause devastating tsunamis throughout the Caribbean.

GUIDED PRACTICE

Have students study **Figure 11,** in which a continental plate and an oceanic plate coverge. Ask which plate is more dense. (oceanic)

Explain that when an oceanic plate sinks, or *subducts,* beneath another tectonic plate the scraping, pushing, and jostling may cause earthquakes and tsunamis.

Ask what kind of tectonic plate contains more water. (oceanic)

Have students explain how water content affects magma formation. (The more water that is present in mantle rock the more likely it is to melt.)

Have students explain how magma forms when these two tectonic plates converge. (The subducted oceanic plate moves downward, and the high water content and increased temperature cause the rock to melt and form magma.)

Refer to a physical map to point out the deep trenches that form around the edges of the oceans, where oceanic and continental plates collide. These trenches are the deepest parts of the ocean floor.

RETEACHING

Be sure students understand that a hot spot remains relatively stationary and that volcanic activity occurs as a tectonic plate moves over a hot spot. You might compare a hot spot to a candle flame and a tectonic plate to a piece of paper passing over the flame. Sheltered English

Interactive Explorations CD-ROM "What's the Matter?"

3 Extend

Cooperative Learning

More than 30 earthquakes a year are caused by the movement of magma beneath Mount Rainier, in Washington State. It is the second most seismically active volcano in the Cascade Range, after Mount St. Helens. Because the area around Mount Rainier is so heavily populated, an eruption would endanger thousands of people and destroy property worth millions of dollars. Many groups of people are studying Mount Rainier and preparing for a possible eruption.

Divide the class into groups and give the following assignments:

- **Research Group** Members investigate the volcano's history to determine why it has been ranked as a "decade volcano."
- **Early-Warning Group** Members research how the volcano's activity is being monitored with scientific equipment and other methods.
- **Washington State Emergency Management Agency (WaSEMA) Group** Members find out how this state organization plans to help people in case of an eruption.
- **Schools, Police, and Fire Group** This group investigates how local agencies would design a plan for warning and a plan for the aftermath of an eruption.

After the groups research their areas, have them make presentations using posters, models, maps, and graphs.

PG 518
Volcano Verdict

Figure 12 *A plume of hot mantle rock flows slowly upward through the mantle. As the tectonic plate moves slowly over the hot spot, a chain of volcanic islands forms.*

A hot spot often produces a long chain of volcanoes. This is because the mantle plume stays in the same spot, while the tectonic plate above moves over it. The Hawaiian Islands, for example, are riding on the Pacific plate, which is moving slowly to the northwest. **Figure 12** shows how a hot spot creates a volcano in an island chain. Each of the islands was once an erupting volcano situated directly over the hot spot.

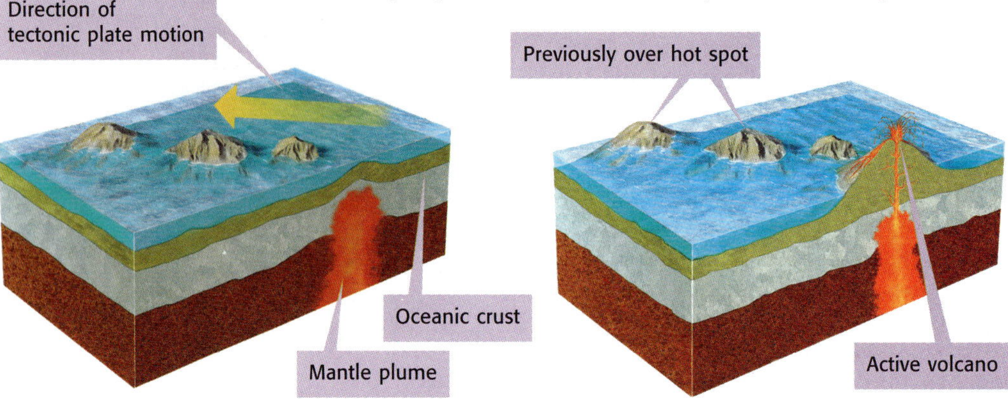

Figure 13 *Seismographs help scientists determine when magma is moving beneath a volcano.*

How do poisonous gases help scientists predict eruptions? Turn to page 518 in the LabBook to find out.

Predicting Volcanic Eruptions

It is one thing to know where volcanoes occur, but it is quite another thing to predict when they might erupt. To help predict volcanic eruptions, scientists classify volcanoes based on their eruption histories and on how likely it is that they will erupt again. *Extinct* volcanoes are those that have not erupted in recorded history and probably never will again. *Dormant* volcanoes are those that are not currently erupting but have erupted at some time in recorded history. *Active* volcanoes are those that are in the process of erupting or that show signs of erupting in the very near future.

When it comes to predicting eruptions, the dormant and active volcanoes keep scientists guessing. However, scientists have found certain clues that reveal when a volcano is likely to erupt. For example, most active volcanoes produce small earthquakes as the magma within them moves upward and causes the surrounding rock to shift. Just before an eruption, the number and intensity of the small earthquakes increase, and the occurrence of quakes may be continuous. These earthquakes are measured with a *seismograph,* as shown in **Figure 13.**

Measurements of a volcano's slope also give scientists clues with which to predict eruptions. For example, bulges in the volcano's slope may form as magma pushes against the inside of the volcano. By attaching an instrument called a *tiltmeter* to the surface of the volcano, scientists can detect small changes in the angle of the slope.

204

Teaching Transparency 115
"Mantle Plume and a Hot Spot"

Reinforcement Worksheet 8
"Tectonic Plate Movement"

Homework

There are volcanic hot spots in Yellowstone Park, Easter Island, Baja California, Hawaii, the Marquesas, the Canary Islands, Cameroon, Iceland, the Galápagos Islands, and the Samoan Islands. Have each student prepare a report on a hot spot, using maps, models, and details of the hot spot's history.

The outflow of volcanic gases from a volcano can also help scientists predict eruptions. As magma rises, the pressure from trapped volcanic gases builds. The pressure may reach a point where it breaks small holes in the rock, allowing the gases to escape through the sides of the volcano. Some scientists think that the ratio of certain gases, especially that of sulfur dioxide (SO_2) to carbon dioxide (CO_2), is important in predicting eruptions. They know that when this ratio changes, it is an indication that things are changing in the magma chamber down below, which means an eruption may not be far away! As you can see in **Figure 14,** collecting this type of data is often dangerous.

Some of the newest methods scientists are using to predict volcanic eruptions rely on satellite images. Many of these images record infrared radiation, which allows scientists to measure changes in temperature over time. They are taken from satellites orbiting more than 700 km above the Earth. By analyzing images taken at different times, scientists can determine if the site is getting hotter as magma pushes closer to the surface.

Figure 14 *As if getting this close to an active volcano is not dangerous enough, the gases that are being collected here are extremely poisonous.*

chemistry CONNECTION

Ground water can seep through cracks and pores in the rocks of an active volcano, where it is heated by the underlying magma and reacts with volcanic gases to form sulfuric acid. The acid turns solid rock into soft clay and weakens the sides of a volcano. This can cause parts of the volcano to collapse, producing avalanches, mudflows, or even eruptions.

REVIEW

1. How does pressure determine whether the mantle is solid or liquid?
2. Describe a technology scientists use to predict volcanic eruptions.
3. **Interpreting Illustrations** Figure 9, shown earlier in this chapter, shows the locations of active volcanoes on land. Describe where on the map you would plot the location of underwater volcanoes and why. (Do not write in this book.)

APPLY

Although scientists have learned a lot about volcanoes, they cannot predict eruptions with total accuracy. Sometimes there are warning signs before an eruption, but often there are none. Imagine that you are the mayor of a town near a large volcano, and a geologist warns you that an eruption is probable. You realize that ordering an evacuation of your town could be an expensive embarrassment if the volcano doesn't erupt. But if you decide to keep quiet, people could be in serious danger if the volcano does erupt. Considering the social and economic consequences of your decision, your job is perhaps even more difficult. What would you do?

RESEARCH

The International Association of Volcanology and Chemistry of the Earth's Interior (IAVCEI) has declared 15 volcanoes to be "decade volcanoes," or volcanoes that pose enough danger that they warrant focused scientific attention. Have students prepare reports on the decade-volcano program. They may research IAVCEI's criteria, the designated volcanoes, a particular volcano's history, and monitoring and research of the volcano.

4 Close

Quiz

1. What conditions make magma rise? (when magma is less dense than the surrounding rock and when it has a conduit to move up through)
2. Define a rift. (a series of deep cracks that occur where tectonic plates separate)

ALTERNATIVE ASSESSMENT

Post a map of the world on the bulletin board that shows the location of tectonic plates. Have volunteers use pins and string to outline the plates on the map. Have other students use flagged pins to mark the location of the volcanoes they learned about in this chapter. Then pair students, and have partners explain how tectonic plate boundaries and volcanoes are related. Each partner should evaluate the other's understanding by assessing their descriptions of rifts, converging tectonic plates, diverging tectonic plates, subduction, hot spots, and magma formation.

Answers to Review

1. Where there is enough pressure on the mantle, the atoms in the rock are forced to stay close together, keeping it solid. Where this pressure is released, mantle rock melts.
2. Answers will vary but should include a discussion of one of the following: measuring changes in the frequency of small earthquakes near the volcano; measuring changes in the slope of the volcano; measuring changes in the ratios of different volcanic gases over time; and measuring changes in how much heat escapes a volcano by using infrared satellite images.
3. Underwater volcanoes should appear along the southern margin of the Pacific plate because most volcanic activity happens at tectonic plate boundaries.

Chapter Highlights

VOCABULARY DEFINITIONS

SECTION 1

magma the hot liquid that forms when rock partially or completely melts; may include mineral crystals

vent a hole or crack in the Earth's crust through which magma rises to the surface

lava magma that erupts onto the Earth's surface

pyroclastic material magma and fragments of rock that are ejected into the atmosphere during a violent volcanic eruption

volcano a mountain that forms when lava or pyroclastic material builds up around a volcanic vent

SECTION 2

shield volcano a large, gently sloped volcano that forms from repeated, nonexplosive eruptions of lava

cinder cone volcano a small, steeply sloped volcano that forms from moderately explosive eruptions of pyroclastic material

composite volcano a volcano made of alternating layers of lava and pyroclastic material; also called *stratovolcano*

crater a funnel-shaped pit around the central vent of a volcano

caldera a circular depression that forms when a magma chamber empties and causes the ground above to sink

Chapter Highlights

SECTION 1

Vocabulary

magma *(p. 194)*
vent *(p. 194)*
lava *(p. 194)*
pyroclastic material *(p. 194)*
volcano *(p. 194)*

Section Notes

- Volcanoes erupt both explosively and nonexplosively.
- The characteristics of a volcanic eruption are largely determined by the type of magma within the volcano.
- The amount of silica in magma determines whether it is thin and fluid or thick and stiff.
- Lava hardens into characteristic features that range from smooth to jagged, depending on how thick the lava is and how quickly it flows.
- Pyroclastic material, or volcanic debris, consists of solid pieces of the volcano as well as magma that solidifies as it travels through the air.

SECTION 2

Vocabulary

shield volcano *(p. 198)*
cinder cone volcano *(p. 198)*
composite volcano *(p. 198)*
crater *(p. 199)*
caldera *(p. 199)*

Section Notes

- The effects of volcanic eruptions are felt both locally and around the world.
- Volcanic mountains can be classified according to their composition and overall shape.
- Craters are funnel-shaped pits that form around the central vent of a volcano. Calderas are large bowl-shaped depressions formed by a collapsed magma chamber.

Skills Check

Math Concepts

CONVERTING TEMPERATURE SCALES So-called low-temperature magmas can be 1,100°C. Just how hot is such a magma? If you are used to measuring temperature in degrees Fahrenheit, you can use a simple formula to find out.

$$°F = \frac{9}{5}°C + 32$$

$$°F = \frac{9}{5}(1{,}100) + 32$$

$$°F = 1{,}960 + 32 = 1{,}992$$

$$1{,}992°F = 1{,}100°C$$

Visual Understanding

CALDERAS Calderas are caused by the release of massive amounts of magma from beneath the Earth's surface. When the volume of magma decreases, it no longer exerts pressure to hold the ground up. As a result, the ground sinks, forming a caldera.

Lab and Activity Highlights

Some Go "Pop," Some Do Not PG 516

Volcano Verdict PG 518

Datasheets for LabBook (blackline masters for these labs)

SECTION 2

- In the largest type of volcanic eruption, lava simply pours from long fissures in the Earth's crust to form lava plateaus.

Labs

Some Go "Pop," Some Do Not *(p. 516)*

SECTION 3

Vocabulary

rift *(p. 202)*

hot spot *(p. 203)*

Section Notes

- Volcanoes result from magma formed in the mantle.
- When pressure is reduced, some of the solid rock of the already hot mantle melts to form magma.
- Because it is less dense than the surrounding rock, magma rises to the Earth's surface. It either erupts as lava or solidifies in the crust.
- Most volcanic activity takes place along tectonic plate boundaries, where plates either separate or collide.
- Volcanoes also occur above hot spots in the mantle. As a tectonic plate moves over the hot spot, a chain of volcanic islands forms.
- Volcanic eruptions cannot be predicted with complete accuracy. But scientists now have several methods of forecasting future eruptions.

Labs

Volcano Verdict *(p. 518)*

internetconnect

GO TO: go.hrw.com

Visit the **HRW** Web site for a variety of learning tools related to this chapter. Just type in the keyword:

KEYWORD: HSTVOL

GO TO: www.scilinks.org

Visit the **National Science Teachers Association** on-line Web site for Internet resources related to this chapter. Just type in the ***sci*LINKS** number for more information about the topic:

TOPIC: Volcanic Eruptions **_sci_LINKS NUMBER:** HSTE205
TOPIC: Volcanic Effects **_sci_LINKS NUMBER:** HSTE210
TOPIC: What Causes Volcanoes? **_sci_LINKS NUMBER:** HSTE215
TOPIC: The Ring of Fire **_sci_LINKS NUMBER:** HSTE220

207

Vocabulary Definitions, *continued*

Section 3

rift a zone of thin, fractured lithosphere that forms between tectonic plates as they separate

hot spot a place within a tectonic plate that sits directly above a rising column of magma called a mantle plume

Vocabulary Review Worksheet 8

Blackline masters of these Chapter Highlights can be found in the **Study Guide.**

Lab and Activity Highlights

LabBank

Whiz-Bang Demonstrations
- How's Your Lava Life? Demo 21
- What Makes a Vent Event? Demo 20

Labs You Can Eat, Hot Spots, Lab 16

Long-Term Projects & Research Ideas, Project 37

Interactive Explorations CD-ROM

CD 1, Exploration 4, "What's the Matter?"

Chapter Review Answers

USING VOCABULARY

1. A caldera forms when the roof of a magma chamber collapses. A crater forms when the material above the main vent of a volcano is blasted out.
2. Magma is hot, liquid material. Lava is magma that flows out onto the Earth's surface.
3. Lava is mostly liquid and is thin and runny. Lava flows out of a volcanic vent onto the ground. Pyroclastic material is mostly solid rock and is blasted into the air in a violent volcanic eruption.
4. A vent is a hole in the Earth's surface that allows lava or pyroclastic material to erupt. A rift is a long, deep crack in the Earth's surface that forms when tectonic plates separate.
5. A shield volcano forms when both lava erupts and spreads out over large areas. A cinder cone volcano forms when pyroclastic material erupts and piles up around the volcanic vent.

UNDERSTANDING CONCEPTS

Multiple Choice

6. b
7. b
8. b
9. d
10. b
11. c
12. b

Short Answer

13. Answers will vary but should include two of the following: measuring changes in the frequency of small earthquakes near the volcano; measuring changes in the slope of the volcano; measuring changes in the ratios of different volcanic gases over time; and measuring changes in how much heat escapes a volcano by using infrared satellite images.

Chapter Review

USING VOCABULARY

For each pair of terms listed below, explain the difference in their meanings.

1. caldera/crater
2. lava/magma
3. lava/pyroclastic material
4. vent/rift
5. cinder cone volcano/shield volcano

UNDERSTANDING CONCEPTS

Multiple Choice

6. The type of magma that often produces a violent eruption can be described as
   a. thin due to high silica content.
   b. thick due to high silica content.
   c. thin due to low silica content.
   d. thick due to low silica content.

7. When lava hardens quickly to form ropy formations, it is called
   a. aa lava.
   b. pahoehoe lava.
   c. pillow lava.
   d. blocky lava.

8. Volcanic dust and ash can remain in the atmosphere for months or years, causing
   a. decreased solar reflection and higher temperatures.
   b. increased solar reflection and lower temperatures.
   c. decreased solar reflection and lower temperatures.
   d. increased solar reflection and higher temperatures.

9. Mount St. Helens, in Washington, covered the city of Spokane with tons of ash. Its eruption would most likely be described as
   a. nonexplosive, producing lava.
   b. explosive, producing lava.
   c. nonexplosive, producing pyroclastic material.
   d. explosive, producing pyroclastic material.

10. Magma forms within the mantle most often as a result of
    a. high temperature and high pressure.
    b. high temperature and low pressure.
    c. low temperature and high pressure.
    d. low temperature and low pressure.

11. At divergent plate boundaries,
    a. heat from the Earth's core produces mantle plumes.
    b. plates are subducted, causing magma to form.
    c. tectonic plates move apart.
    d. hot spots produce volcanoes.

12. A theory that helps to explain the causes of both earthquakes and volcanoes is the theory of
    a. subduction.
    b. plate tectonics.
    c. climatic fluctuation.
    d. mantle plumes.

Short Answer

13. Briefly describe two methods that scientists use to predict volcanic eruptions.

14. Describe how differences in magma affect volcanic eruptions.

15. Along what types of tectonic plate boundaries are volcanoes generally found? Why?

16. Describe the characteristics of the three types of volcanic mountains.

14. Magma that has a high water and silica content will more likely produce a violent volcanic eruption than magma that has a low water and silica content. Water turns to steam, which builds up a great amount of pressure, which leads to explosive eruptions. Silica makes magma thick, allowing it to trap volcanic gases such as water (steam).
15. Volcanoes are generally found along convergent boundaries because in a subduction zone, oceanic crust is forced downward, which adds water to the mantle. The addition of water lowers the mantle rock's melting point. This melted mantle becomes magma that rises to the surface to form volcanoes.
16. Cinder cones are made from a pyroclastic eruption, are small, and have steep sides. Shield volcanoes are made of lava that runs over great distances before it solidifies, making very large, gently sloped volcanoes. Composite volcanoes are made of both

Chapter 8 Review–California Standards: PE/ATE Q1–5: 1d; Q6–17: 1, 1a, 1b, 1d, 1e, 1g, 2d

Concept Mapping

17. Use any of the terms from the vocabulary lists in Chapter Highlights to construct a concept map that illustrates the relationship between types of magma, the eruptions they produce, and the shapes of the volcanoes that result.

CRITICAL THINKING AND PROBLEM SOLVING

Write one or two sentences to answer the following questions:

18. Imagine that you are exploring a volcano that has been dormant for some time. You begin to keep notes on the types of volcanic debris you encounter as you walk. Your first notes describe volcanic ash, and later your notes describe lapilli. In what direction would you most likely be traveling—toward or away from the crater? Explain.

19. Loihi is a future Hawaiian island in the process of forming on the ocean floor. Considering how this island chain formed, tell where you think the new volcanic island will be located and why.

20. What do you think would happen to the Earth's climate if volcanic activity increased to 10 times its current level?

MATH IN SCIENCE

21. Midway Island is 2,400 km northwest of Hawaii. If the Pacific plate is moving to the northwest at 6 cm per year, how long ago was Midway Island located over the hot spot that formed it?

INTERPRETING GRAPHICS

The following graph illustrates the average change in temperature above or below normal for a community over several years.

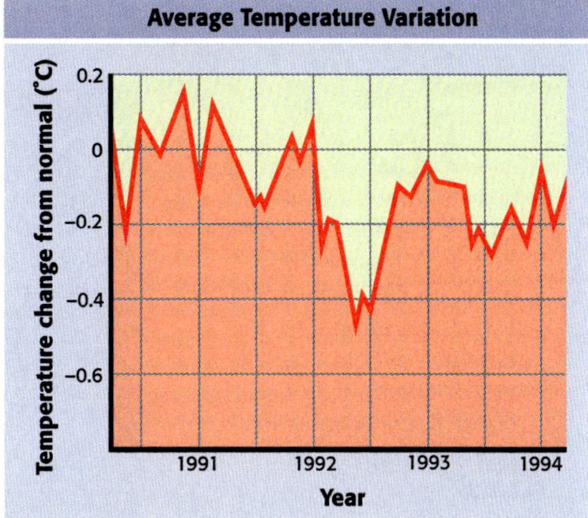

22. If the variation in temperature over the years was influenced by a major volcanic eruption, when did the eruption most likely take place? Explain.

23. If the temperature were plotted only in yearly intervals rather than several times per year, how might your interpretation be different?

NOW What Do You Think?

Take a minute to review your answers to the ScienceLog questions on page 191. Have your answers changed? If necessary, revise your answers based on what you have learned since you began this chapter.

lava and pyroclastic material. Composite volcanoes have large, gently sloping bases and steep sides.

Concept Mapping

17. An answer to this exercise can be found at the end of this book.

Critical Thinking and Problem Solving

18. You would be traveling toward the volcano because the larger the pyroclastic material is, the closer it will be to the vent. It takes more energy to move larger rocks than it does to move smaller rocks.

19. The new island will be located southeast of Hawaii because the hot spot stays in the same place, while the Pacific plate moves above it toward the northwest.

20. The overall surface temperature of the Earth would decrease because all the volcanic ash in the atmosphere would block out much of the sun's energy.

Math in Science

21. 1 km = 1,000 m = 100,000 cm
2,400 km = 240,000,000 cm
240,000,000/6 cm per year = **40,000,000 years**

Interpreting Graphics

22. The eruption probably happened in 1992 because that year had the lowest temperature below normal. The volcanic ash that is erupted into the atmosphere blocks the sunlight, lowering temperature.

23. If the temperature were plotted in only yearly intervals, it would look as if 1993 or 1994 had the lowest temperatures. This would mean that the eruptions happened in 1993 or 1994 instead of 1992.

NOW What Do You Think?

1. A volcanic eruption is caused when pressure forces magma to rise toward the Earth's surface. If there is a vent or opening for the magma to escape through, it is extruded as lava in a volcanic eruption.
2. Lava is magma that has been extruded on the Earth's surface. Magma forms when rock melts due to changes in the composition of the rock, decreases in the pressure that it is subjected to, or an increase in temperature.

Concept Mapping Transparency 8

Blackline masters of this Chapter Review can be found in the **Study Guide.**

Chapter 8 Review–California Standards: PE/ATE Q18–20: 1, 1a, 1e, 2d; Q21: 1, 1c, 1e, 7g; Q22–23: 2d, 7g, 7h; Think: 1, 1d, 1e

Science, Technology, and Society

Robot in the Hot Seat

Teaching Strategies

After its mission was completed, the *Dante II* robot was put on display at the Carnegie Science Center in Pittsburgh. The exhibit included information on *Dante II*'s expedition as well as general information on robotics. Have students construct an exhibit for the classroom that serves the same purpose.

You may wish to have students investigate other current applications of robotic technology. For instance, robots are used extensively in industry to perform repetitive or dangerous tasks.

Science, Technology, and Society

Robot in the Hot Seat

Scientists have to be calm, cool, and collected to study volcano craters. But the cooled magma of a crater's floor isn't the most hospitable location for scientific study. What kind of daredevil would run the risk of creeping along a crater floor? A volcanologist like *Dante II,* that's who!

Hot Stuff

A volcano crater may seem empty after a volcano erupts, but it is in no way devoid of volcanic information. Gases hissing up through the crater floor give scientists clues about the molten rock underneath, which may help them understand how and why volcanoes erupt repeatedly. But these gases may be poisonous or scalding hot, and the crater's floor can crack or shift at any time. Over the years, dozens of scientists have been seriously injured or killed while trying to explore volcano craters. Obviously, volcanologists needed some help studying the steamy abyss.

▲ *Dante II*

Getting a Robot to Take the Heat

Enter *Dante II,* an eight-legged robot with cameras for eyes and computers for a brain. In 1994, led by a team of scientists from NASA, Carnegie Mellon University, and the Alaskan Volcano Observatory, *Dante II* embarked on its first mission. It climbed into a breach called Crater Peak on the side of Mount Spurr, an active volcano in Alaska. Anchored at the crater's rim by a strong cable, *Dante II* was controlled partly by internal computers and partly by a team of scientists. The team communicated with the robot through a satellite link and Internet connections. *Dante II* moved very slowly, taking pictures and collecting scientific data. It was equipped with gas sensors that provided continuous readings of the crater gases. It performed the tasks human scientists would, letting the humans keep their cool.

Mission Accomplished?

During its expedition, *Dante II* encountered large rocks, some of which were as big as the robot itself. In addition, *Dante II* slipped and fell, damaging one of its legs, while climbing out of the volcano. Its support cable broke, and it eventually had to be rescued by a helicopter. Despite these obstacles, *Dante II* was able to gather valuable data from the volcano's crater.

Dante II's mission also met one of NASA's objectives: to prove that robots could be used successfully to explore extreme terrain, such as that found on planetary surfaces. *Dante II* paved the way for later robotic projects, such as the exploration of the surface of Mars by the *Sojourner* rover in 1997.

Write About It

▶ Write a proposal for a project in which a robot is used to explore a dangerous place. Don't forget to include what types of data the robot would be collecting.

210

Answers to Write About It

Accept all reasonable responses. Students may propose that a robot be used to explore a mine, a site contaminated with hazardous waste, or an extraterrestrial environment.

EARTH SCIENCE • LIFE SCIENCE

Europa: Life on a Moon?

Smooth and brownish white, one of Jupiter's moons, Europa, has fascinated scientists and science-fiction writers for decades. More recently, scientists were excited by tantalizing images from the Galileo Europa Mission. Could it be that life is lurking (or sloshing) beneath Europa's surface?

An Active History

Slightly smaller than Earth's moon, Europa is the fourth largest of Jupiter's moons. It is unusual among other bodies in the solar system because of its extraordinarily smooth surface. But the ridges and brownish channels that crisscross Europa's smooth surface may tell a unique story—the surface appears to be a slushy combination of ice and water. Some scientists think that the icy ridges and channels are ice floes left over from ancient volcanoes that erupted water! The water flowed over Europa's surface and froze, like lava flows and cools on Earth's surface.

A Slushy Situation

Scientists speculate that Europa's surface consists of thin tectonic plates of ice floating on a layer of slush or water. These plates, which would look like icy rafts floating in an ocean of slush, have been compared to giant glaciers floating in polar regions on Earth.

Where plates push together, the material of the plates may crumple, forming an icy ridge. Where plates pull apart, warmer liquid mixed with darker silicates may erupt toward the surface and freeze, forming the brownish icy channels that create Europa's cracked cue-ball appearance.

Life on Europa?

These discoveries have led scientists to consider an exciting possibility: Does Europa have an environment that could support primitive life-forms? In general, at least three things are necessary for life as we know it to develop—water, organic compounds (substances that contain carbon), and heat. Europa has water, and organic compounds are fairly common in the solar system. But does it have heat? Europa's slushy nature suggests a warm interior. One theory is that the warmth is the result of Jupiter's strong gravitational pull on Europa. Another theory is that warmth is brought to Europa's surface by convection heating.

So does Europa truly satisfy the three requirements for life? The answer is still unknown, but the sloshing beneath Europa's surface has sure heightened some scientists' curiosity!

If You Were in Charge . . .

▶ If you were in charge of NASA's space-exploration program, would you send a spacecraft to look for life on Europa? (Remember that this would cost millions of dollars and would mean sacrificing other important projects!) Explain your answer.

◀ *Europa looks like a cracked cue ball.*

211

Across the Sciences
Europa: Life on a Moon?

Teaching Strategies

The latest information about Europa can be found at the NASA Web site. You could ask students to compare Europa with Callisto or Gamymede, which some scientists believe could also support life.

Answers to If You Were in Charge . . .

Accept all reasonable answers. Factors that students should consider are the tremendous costs associated with sending astronauts on long-term space travel—food, fuel, water, oxygen, wastes, safety—and finding people who can make the trip. Even if the spaceship were unmanned, the cost of one or more sophisticated probes or explorer craft would be hundreds of millions or billions of dollars. To pay for a project of that nature, taxes would have to be raised or money would have to be taken from other government programs, such as health care, defense spending, environmental protection, or law enforcement.

Chapter Organizer

CHAPTER ORGANIZATION	TIME MINUTES	OBJECTIVES	LABS, INVESTIGATIONS, AND DEMONSTRATIONS
Chapter Opener pp. 212–213	45	California Standards: PE/ATE 7, 7b	**Investigate!** Some Like It Hot, p. 213
Section 1 **Temperature**	90	▶ Describe how temperature relates to kinetic energy. ▶ Give examples of thermal expansion. ▶ Compare temperatures on different temperature scales. PE/ATE 3, 3a, 7, 7b, 7e	**Demonstration,** p. 214 in ATE **QuickLab,** Hot or Cold? p. 215 **Whiz-Bang Demonstrations,** Cool It, Demo 52
Section 2 **What Is Heat?**	90	▶ Define heat as the transfer of energy between objects at different temperatures. ▶ Compare methods of heating. ▶ Describe how specific heat capacity makes substances change temperature at different rates. ▶ Calculate energy transferred by heat. ▶ Explain the differences between temperature, thermal energy, and heat. PE/ATE 3, 3a, 3c, 3d, 7, 7b, 7c; LabBook 3, 3a, 3c, 3d, 7, 7a, 7b, 7d, 7e	**Demonstration,** p. 220 in ATE **QuickLab,** Heat Exchange, p. 221 **Demonstration,** Convection Currents, p. 222 in ATE **Discovery Lab,** Feel the Heat, p. 520 **Datasheets for LabBook,** Feel the Heat, Datasheet 18 **Design Your Own,** Save the Cube! p. 522 **Datasheets for LabBook,** Save the Cube! Datasheet 19 **Making Models,** Counting Calories, p. 523 **Datasheets for LabBook,** Counting Calories, Datasheet 20
Section 3 **Matter and Heat**	90	▶ Identify three states of matter. ▶ Explain how heat affects matter during a change of state. ▶ Describe how heat affects matter during a chemical change. PE/ATE 3, 3a, 7, 7b	**Demonstration,** p. 228 in ATE **Labs You Can Eat,** Baked Alaska, Lab 22
Section 4 **Heat Technology**	90	▶ Analyze several kinds of heating systems. ▶ Describe how a heat engine works. ▶ Explain how a refrigerator keeps food cold. ▶ Give examples of some effects of heat technology on the environment. PE/ATE 3, 3a, 3b, 6a	**EcoLabs & Field Activities,** Energy-Efficient Home, EcoLab 19 **Long-Term Projects & Research Ideas,** Project 60

See page **T20** *for a complete correlation of this book with the*

CALIFORNIA SCIENCE CONTENT STANDARDS.

Correlations are also provided at point of use throughout this ATE.

TECHNOLOGY RESOURCES

Guided Reading Audio CD English or Spanish, Chapter 9

Classroom Management CD-ROM

CNN **Eye on the Environment,** Geothermal Energy, Segment 22

Test Generator CD-ROM

Chapter 9 • Heat and Heat Technology

CLASSROOM WORKSHEETS, TRANSPARENCIES, AND RESOURCES	SCIENCE INTEGRATION AND CONNECTIONS	REVIEW AND ASSESSMENT
Science Puzzlers, Twisters & Teasers, Worksheet 9 **Directed Reading Worksheet 9**		
Directed Reading Worksheet 9, Section 1 **Transparency 116,** Three Temperature Scales **Math Skills for Science Worksheet 35,** Using Temperature Scales	**MathBreak,** Converting Temperatures, p. 217 **Math and More,** p. 217 in ATE **Science, Technology, and Society:** The Deep Freeze, p. 242	**Review,** p. 218 **Quiz,** p. 218 in ATE **Alternative Assessment,** p. 218 in ATE **Homework,** p. 218 in ATE
Directed Reading Worksheet 9, Section 2 **Transparency 117,** Reaching Thermal Equilibrium **Transparency 118,** Conduction **Transparency 118,** Convection **Critical Thinking Worksheet 9,** Try and Try Again **Math Skills for Science Worksheet 38,** Knowing Nutrition **Reinforcement Worksheet 9,** Feel the Heat	**Apply,** p. 222 **Connect to Life Science,** p. 222 in ATE **Connect to Astronomy,** p. 223 in ATE **Weather Connection,** p. 224 **Cross-Disciplinary Focus,** p. 224 in ATE **MathBreak,** Calculating Energy Transfer, p. 225 **Math and More,** p. 225 in ATE **Cross-Disciplinary Focus,** p. 225 in ATE **Cross-Disciplinary Focus,** p. 226 in ATE	**Homework,** pp. 220, 225 in ATE **Review,** p. 223 **Self-Check,** p. 227 **Review,** p. 227 **Quiz,** p. 227 in ATE **Alternative Assessment,** p. 227 in ATE
Transparency 119, Models of a Solid, a Liquid, and a Gas **Transparency 120,** Changes of State for Water **Directed Reading Worksheet 9,** Section 3	**Connect to Earth Science,** p. 228 in ATE **Life Science Connection,** p. 230 **Across the Sciences:** Diaplex, p. 243	**Self-Check,** p. 229 **Review,** p. 230 **Quiz,** p. 230 in ATE **Alternative Assessment,** p. 230 in ATE
Directed Reading Worksheet 9, Section 4 **Transparency 121,** Solar Heating Systems **Transparency 192,** Energy Conversions in a Car Engine	**Cross-Disciplinary Focus,** pp. 231, 234, 236 in ATE **Oceanography Connection,** p. 234 **Real-World Connection,** p. 235 in ATE **Connect to Physical Science,** p. 235 in ATE **Environmental Science Connection,** p. 237	**Homework,** p. 232 in ATE **Review,** p. 237 **Quiz,** p. 237 in ATE **Alternative Assessment,** p. 237 in ATE

Holt, Rinehart and Winston On-line Resources

go.hrw.com

For worksheets and other teaching aids related to this chapter, visit the HRW Web site and type in the keyword: **HSTHOT**

National Science Teachers Association

www.scilinks.org

Encourage students to use the keywords listed on the Technology Highlights page to access information and resources on the **NSTA** Web site.

END-OF-CHAPTER REVIEW AND ASSESSMENT

Chapter Review in Study Guide
Vocabulary and Notes in Study Guide
Chapter Tests with Performance-Based Assessment, Chapter 9 Test, Performance-Based Assessment 9
Concept Mapping Transparency 9

Chapter Resources & Worksheets

Visual Resources

TEACHING TRANSPARENCIES

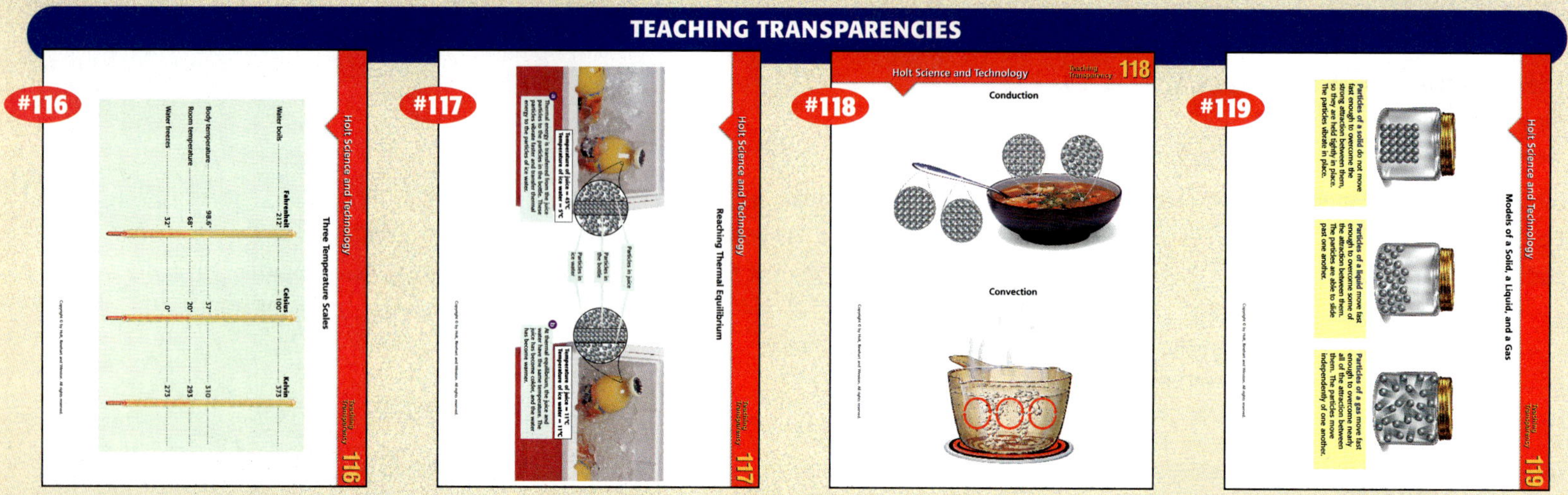

TEACHING TRANSPARENCIES

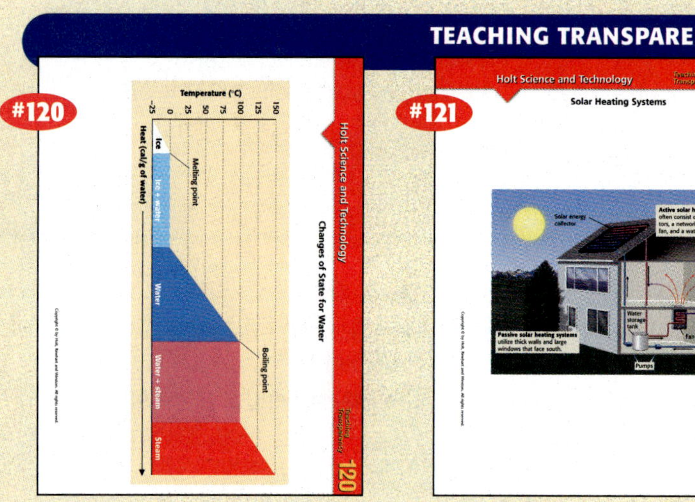

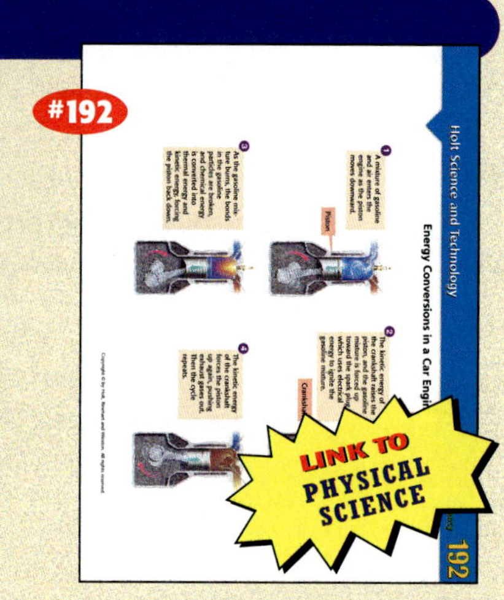

CONCEPT MAPPING TRANSPARENCY

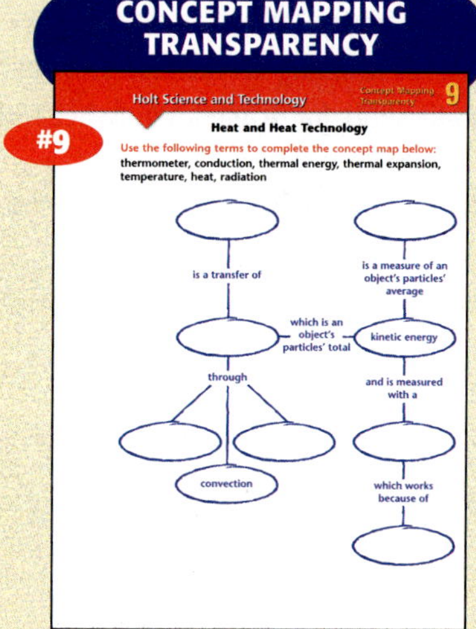

Meeting Individual Needs

DIRECTED READING

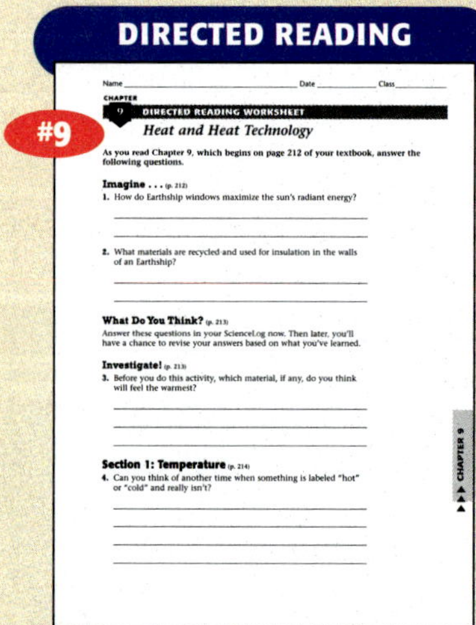

REINFORCEMENT & VOCABULARY REVIEW

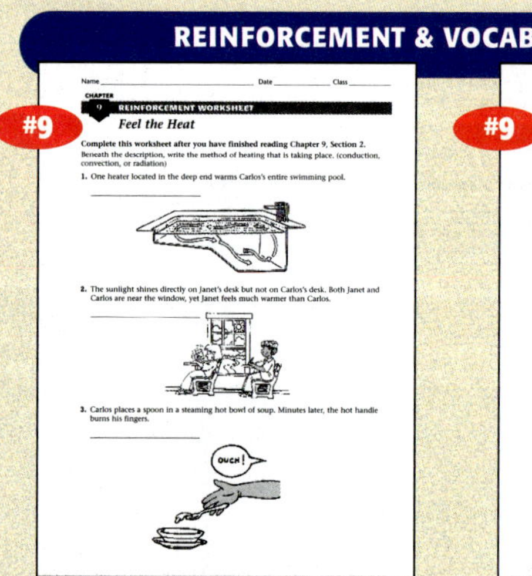

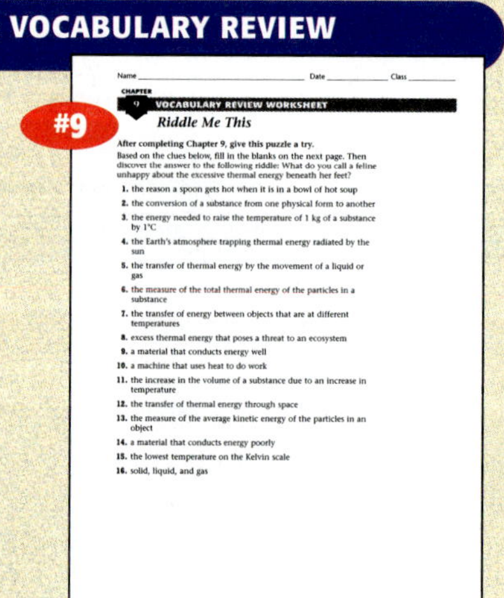

SCIENCE PUZZLERS, TWISTERS & TEASERS

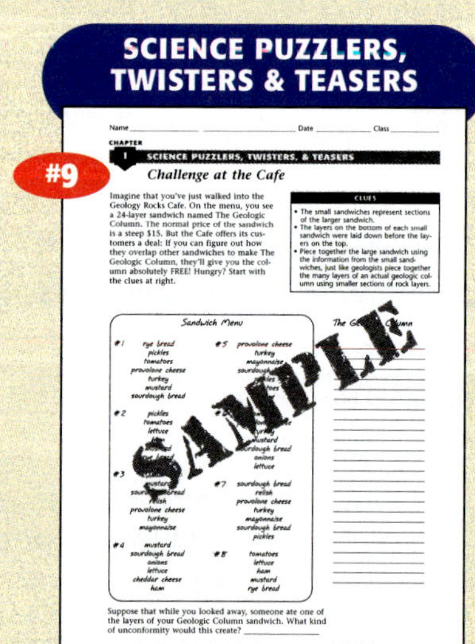

Chapter 9 • Heat and Heat Technology

Review & Assessment

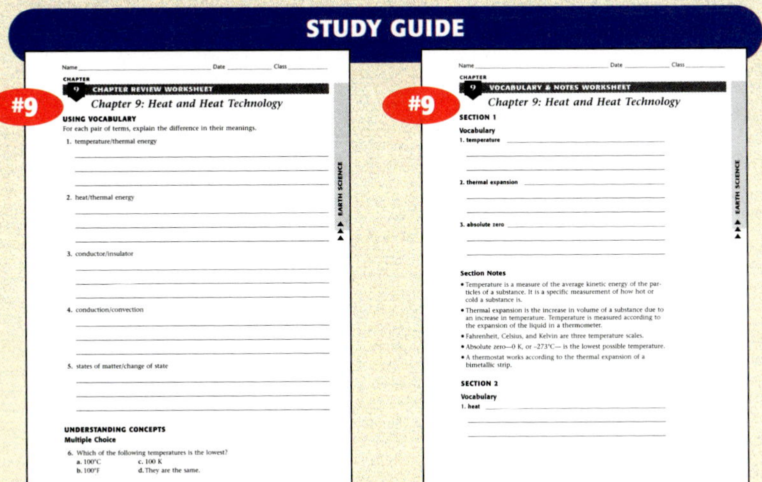

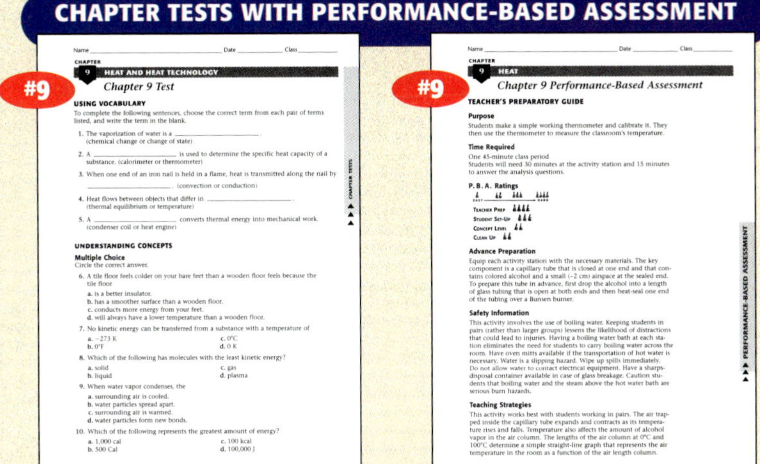

Lab Worksheets

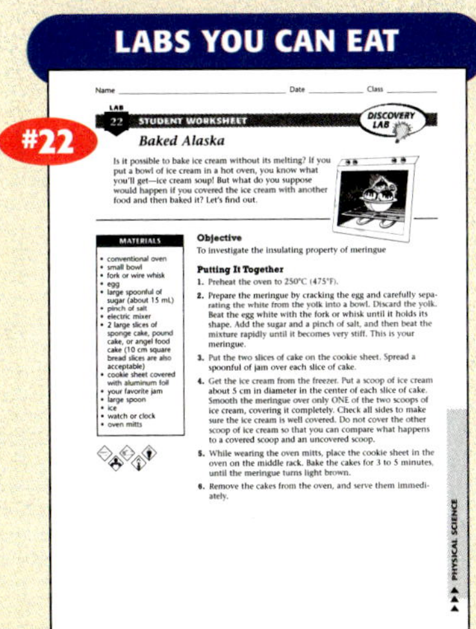

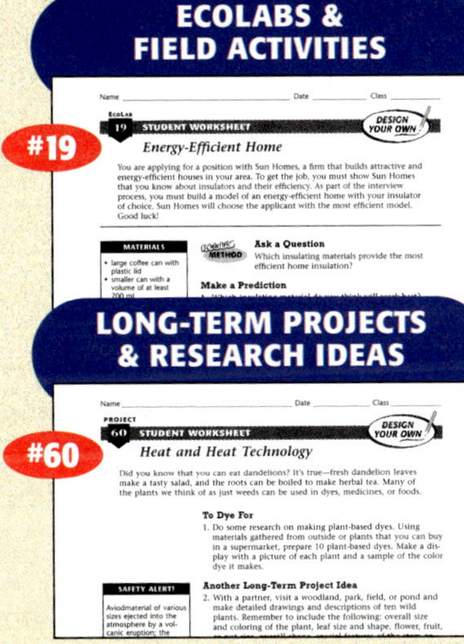

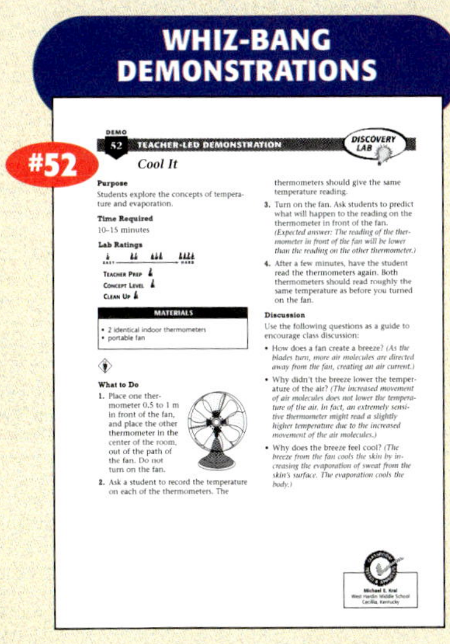

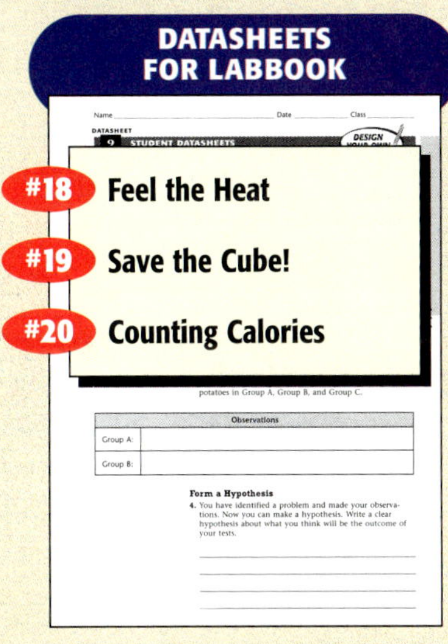

Applications & Extensions

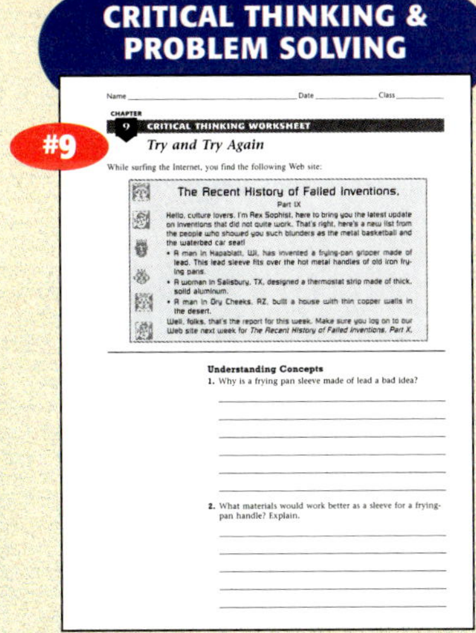

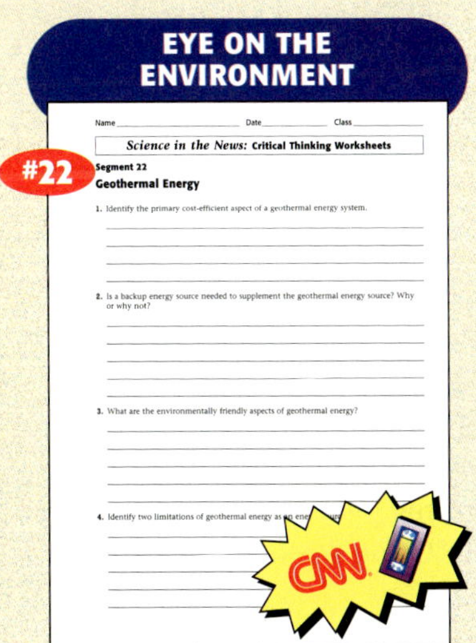

Chapter Background

Section 1

Temperature

Temperature Scales

Daniel Gabriel Fahrenheit (1686–1736) developed the first mercury thermometer in 1714. His scale used the temperature of a brine solution of ice and salt as 0°. He chose 30° for the freezing temperature of water and 90° for the temperature of the human body. These were later adjusted to 32° and 98.6°.

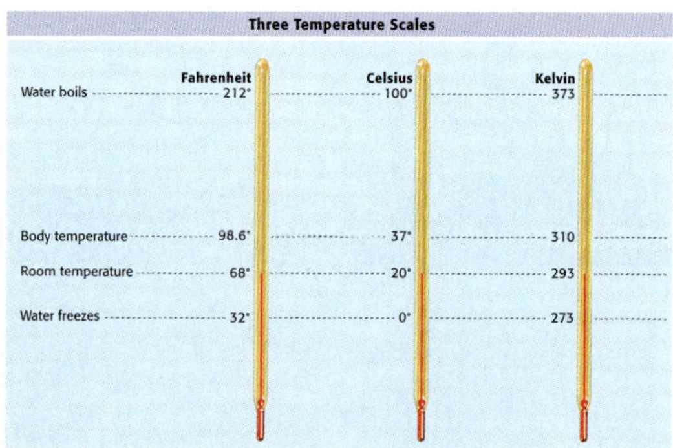

- Anders Celsius (1701–1744) developed the centigrade temperature scale using two physical properties of pure water as his standards. The modern Celsius scale assigns 0° to the freezing point of pure water and 100° to the boiling point of pure water. The Celsius scale has been adopted for use by the scientific community.
- In 1848, British physicist and mathematician William Thomson (1824–1907), later Lord Kelvin, developed the absolute temperature scale. Using J. A. C. Charles's (1746–1823) work with gases, Kelvin realized that a gas decreased by $\frac{1}{273}$ of its volume for each Celsius-degree decrease in temperature. Kelvin theorized that a substance would lose all energy at a temperature of −273°C, so he assigned that point a value of zero on his scale.

Is That a Fact!

- In 1933, a new international temperature scale based on the thermodynamic, or Kelvin, scale was adopted by 31 nations. This new scale uses the property of electrical resistivity in platinum wire as the standard for temperatures between −190°C and 660°C. From 661° to 1063°C, the melting point of gold is used.

Section 2

What Is Heat?

Ideas About Heat

A scientist from the eighteenth century would have defined heat as an invisible and weightless fluid that soaks into an object when the object is heated and leaves an object as it cools.

- Benjamin Thompson (1753–1814), also known as Count von Rumford, a British physicist, noticed that metal became very hot during the boring process in cannon making. He set up an experiment to find out why the cannons became hot when they were bored.
- In his experiment, Thompson encased the cannon form in a wooden barrel filled with water. After hours of drilling, the water began to boil. When the drilling stopped, the water stopped boiling. When the drilling began again, the water once again boiled. This result seemed to contradict the scientific belief that heat was a material substance.
- Because there was no source of heat, Thompson decided that heat was actually a form of energy supplied by the work of the horses turning the drill. Thompson reasoned that the drilling caused the molecules in the cannon to vibrate faster and that the cannon's molecules caused the water molecules to vibrate faster. When the drilling stopped, the source of energy also stopped.

Is That a Fact!

- How much energy does the human body radiate in 1 second? It uses as much as a 60 W light bulb.

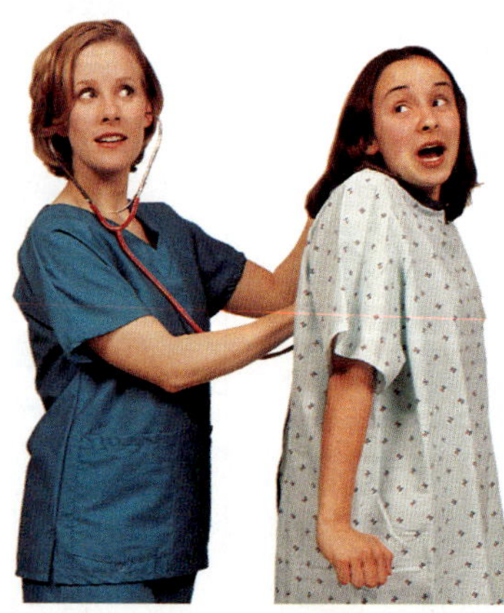

Section 3

Matter and Heat

Water and Heat

When thermal energy is added to substances, they expand. When thermal energy is subtracted, they contract. Water behaves this way until it reaches the temperature range between 4°C and 0°C. In this range, water expands as it cools and freezes, making its solid form less dense than its liquid form.

Latent Heat

The amount of thermal energy that is lost or gained during a phase change is called latent heat. During a phase change, there is no change in temperature. The energy that is absorbed or released is used to recreate or to break physical bonds.

IS THAT A FACT!

- More than 2 million joules of thermal energy are lost from a mammal's body as 1 L of perspiration is evaporated.

Section 4

Heat Technology

Central Heating

Central-heating systems that used hot water were developed in the 1800s. The first successful central-heating system, used in 1835, relied on warm air. In 1850, steam heating was developed.

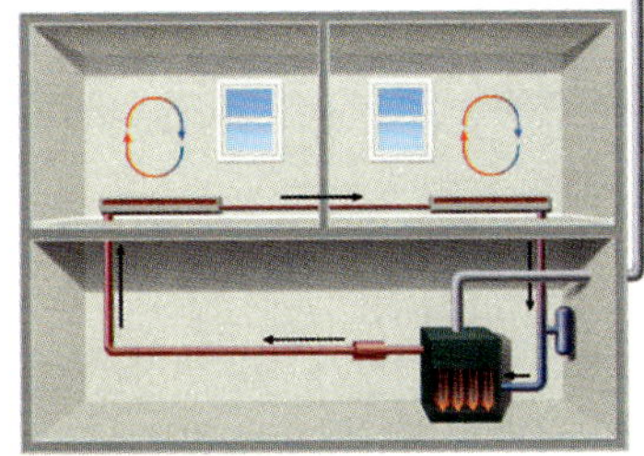

- Radiant heating refers to systems in which floors, walls, and ceilings are used as radiant heating units. When floors and walls are used, steam or hot-water pipes are placed in the floors or the walls during the construction of the building.
- Radiant heating can be provided by electrical resistance. If electrical resistance is used, the panels containing coils are placed in the baseboard or the ceiling.

Steam Engines

Hero of Alexandria (first century A.D.) invented a type of steam engine, but the French physicist Denis Papin (c. 1647–1712) developed the first piston steam engine in 1690. Thomas Savery (c. 1650–1715) and Thomas Newcomen (1663–1729) made improvements on Papin's design, but it was James Watt (1736–1819) who produced the modern steam engine.

Internal Combustion Engines

Jean Joseph Etienne Lenoir (1822–1900) is given credit for inventing the first practical internal combustion engine. Nikolaus August Otto (1832–1891) and Rudolf Diesel (1858–1913) also did extensive work with internal combustion engines. Gottlieb Daimler (1834–1900) assisted Otto with this engine. Daimler, who developed both two- and four-cycle engines, patented his own engine in 1887.

- Karl Benz (1844–1929), a German engineer, developed a two-cycle internal combustion engine and a light four-cycle engine. In 1886, Benz patented a vehicle that had his engine.
- Benz and Daimler, who worked independently of each other and who never met, were each credited with building the first automobile.

IS THAT A FACT!

- Heating, cooling, and breathing produce hazardous waste gases and vapors. An adequate ventilation system provides about 280 to 850 L of outside air per minute for each person in a room.

For additional background resources, please refer to the ***HST Reference Library.***

Heat and Heat Technology

Chapter Preview

Section 1
Temperature
- What Is Temperature?
- Measuring Temperature
- More About Thermal Expansion

Section 2
What is Heat?
- Heat Is a Transfer of Energy
- Methods of Heating
- How Much Heat?
- The Differences Between Temperature, Thermal Energy, and Heat

Section 3
Matter and Heat
- States of Matter
- Changes of State
- Heat and Chemical Changes

Section 4
Heat Technology
- Heating Systems
- Heat Engines
- Cooling Systems
- Heat Technology and Thermal Pollution

Science Puzzlers, Twisters & Teasers Worksheet 9

Guided Reading Audio CD
English or Spanish, Chapter 9

CHAPTER 9 Heat and Heat Technology

Strange but True!

Would you want to live in a house without a heating system? You could if you lived in an Earthship! Earthships are the brainchild of Michael Reynolds, an architect in Taos, New Mexico. These ultra-modern housing structures are designed to make the most of our planet's most abundant source of energy, the sun.

Each Earthship is custom-built to take full advantage of passive solar heating opportunities. For example, large windows face south in order to maximize the amount of radiant energy—energy from the sun—the house receives. Each home is partially buried in the ground, with the excavated soil piled almost to the roof. The energy-absorbing soil helps to keep the energy that comes in through the windows inside the house.

In many traditional houses, the outer walls are too thin and lightweight to absorb radiant energy. But Reynolds designs the outer walls of Earthships to be massive and thick. The walls are sometimes filled with crushed aluminum cans packed tightly together. For especially large projects, Reynolds uses stacks of old automobile tires filled with dirt. These materials absorb the sun's energy during daylight hours and naturally heat the house from the walls inward. Air pockets between the packed cans and the dirt filling the tires provide extra insulation. As a result, a lot of energy is prevented from leaving the house, even as the sun goes down and the outside air grows cold. Because

212

Strange but True!

One of the main purposes of housing is to provide shelter from the elements. The inside climate must be kept comfortable when the outside climate is not. Traditional houses accomplish this at high energy costs. The thermal mass of an Earthship's walls is used to store thermal energy and to regulate temperature for the living area.

an Earthship can maintain a steady temperature around 15°C (about 60°F), it can keep its occupants comfortable through all but the coldest winter nights.

Technology that keeps you warm or cool can be very important. In this chapter, you'll learn about temperature and heat, how different materials transfer energy, and how heat technology is used in everyday life.

What Do You Think?

In your ScienceLog, try to answer the following questions based on what you already know:

1. How do you measure how hot or cold an object is?
2. What makes an object hot or cold?
3. How can heat be used in your home?

Some Like It Hot

Sometimes you can tell the relative temperature of something by touching it with your hand. But how well does your hand work as a thermometer? In this activity, you will find out!

Procedure

1. Gather small pieces of the following materials from your teacher: **metal, wood, plastic foam, rock, plastic,** and **cardboard.**
2. Allow the materials to sit untouched on a table for several minutes.
3. Put your hands palms down on each of the various materials. Compare how warm or cool the materials feel.
4. In your ScienceLog, list the materials in order from coolest to warmest. Compare your results with those of your classmates.
5. Based on your discussion, arrange the materials in order from coolest to warmest.

6. Place a **thermometer strip** on the surface of each material. In your ScienceLog, record the temperature of each material.

Analysis

7. Which material felt the warmest?
8. Which material had the highest temperature?
9. Why do you think some materials felt warmer than others?
10. Was your hand a good thermometer? Why or why not?

213

What Do You Think?

Accept all reasonable responses.

Students will have a chance to revise their answers in the Chapter Review under NOW What Do You Think?

Investigate!

MATERIALS

For Each Group:

- small pieces of metal, wood, plastic foam, rock, plastic, cardboard
- thermometer strip (You can use bulb thermometers, but liquid crystal thermometer strips or cards available from a science store or supply house may measure temperature on the materials more accurately.)

Answers to Investigate!

7. Answers will vary but students may say that the plastic foam felt the warmest.
8. Students should find that the materials were all about the same temperature.
9. Answers will vary, but students may conclude that the material something is made of determines how warm or cold it feels.
10. Students will probably conclude that their hands were not a good thermometer because some materials felt warmer than others, even though they were all about the same temperature.

IS THAT A FACT!

In the mid-1800s, in some warm parts of the United States, people built houses that had a "dog run" to help cool the house. The simplest of these homes consisted of two rooms separated by a hallway (the dog run) that ran from the front of the house all the way through to the back. A wide porch stretched across the front. Later designs included rooms and a second story. The dog run was an efficient way of cooling the house because it allowed the breeze to blow between the two parts of the building and create air flow.

Directed Reading Worksheet 9

SECTION 1

Focus

Temperature

This section explains temperature and how it is measured. Students learn how temperature relates to kinetic energy. They will explore thermal expansion and learn how to convert between the three temperature scales.

Bellringer

Write the following on the board:

The temperature of boiling water is 100° on the Celsius scale and 212° on the Fahrenheit scale.

Look at each of the following temperatures carefully, and decide whether you think that it is hot or cold:

60°F, 60°C, 37°F, 37°C, 0°C, 100°F, and 70°F

Write your responses in your ScienceLog.

1) Motivate

DEMONSTRATION

Using a metal ball-and-ring set, demonstrate how the ball easily slips through the ring. Be sure to use tongs or protective gloves. Heat the ball for a minute or two, then try to pass the ball through the ring. Ask students to theorize why the ball no longer passes through the ring. Next heat the ring and pass the ball through it. Ask students to theorize why the ball again passed through the ring. (The ball expanded when it was heated and would not fit through the ring. When the ring was heated, the ring expanded enough to allow the ball to pass through.)

1

NEW TERMS

temperature
thermal expansion
absolute zero

OBJECTIVES

- Describe how temperature relates to kinetic energy.
- Give examples of thermal expansion.
- Compare temperatures on different temperature scales.

Temperature

You probably put on a sweater or a jacket when it's cold outside. Likewise, you probably wear shorts in the summer when it gets hot. But how hot is hot, and how cold is cold? Think about how the knobs on a water faucet are labeled *H* for hot and *C* for cold. But does only hot water come out when the hot-water knob is on? You may have noticed that when you first turn on the water it is warm or even cool. Are you being misled by the label on the knob? The terms *hot* and *cold* are not very scientific terms. If you really want to specify how hot or cold something is, you must use temperature.

What Is Temperature?

You probably think of temperature as a measure of how hot or cold something is. But scientifically, **temperature** is a measure of the average kinetic energy of the particles in an object. Using temperature instead of words like *hot* or *cold* reduces confusion. The scenario below emphasizes the importance of communicating about temperature. You can learn more about hot and cold comparisons by doing the QuickLab on the next page.

Students often think that heat and temperature are the same. Stress that temperature is the measure of the average kinetic energy of the molecules in a substance. Heat is the transfer of thermal energy between objects that are at different temperatures. These concepts are covered in Section 2 of this chapter.

Temperature Depends on the Kinetic Energy of Particles All matter is made of particles—atoms or molecules—that are in constant motion. Because the particles are in motion, they have kinetic energy. The faster particles move, the more kinetic energy they have. What does temperature have to do with kinetic energy? Well, as described in **Figure 1,** the more kinetic energy the particles of an object have, the higher the temperature of the object.

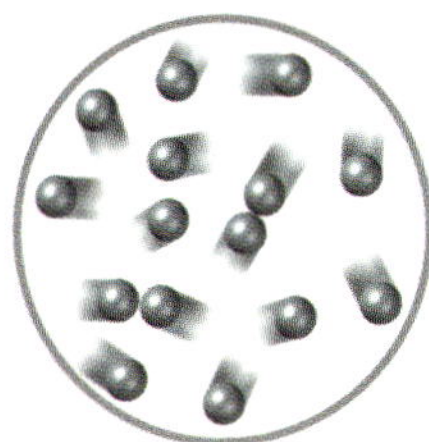

Figure 1 *The gas particles on the right have more kinetic energy than those on the left. So the gas on the right is at a higher temperature.*

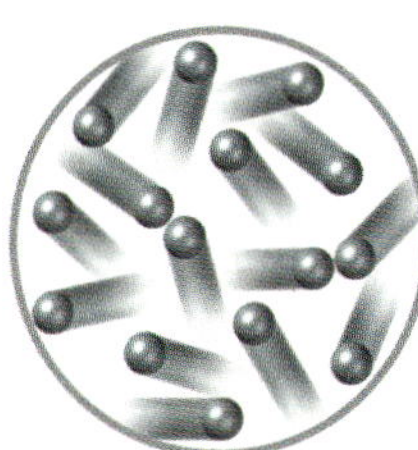

Temperature Is an Average Measure Particles of matter are constantly moving, but they don't all move at the same speed and in the same direction all the time. Look back at Figure 1. As you can see, the motion of the particles is random. The particles of matter in an object move in different directions, and some particles move faster than others. As a result, some particles have more kinetic energy than others. So what determines an object's temperature? An object's temperature is the best approximation of the kinetic energy of the particles. When you measure an object's temperature, you measure the average kinetic energy of the particles in the object.

The temperature of a substance is not determined by how much of the substance you have. As shown in **Figure 2,** different amounts of the same substance can have the same temperature. However, the total kinetic energy of the particles in each amount is different. You will learn more about that kind of total kinetic energy in the next section.

Figure 2 *Even though there is more tea in the teapot than in the mug, the average kinetic energy, and therefore the temperature, of the tea in the mug is the same as that of the tea in the teapot.*

QuickLab

Hot or Cold?

1. Put both your hands into a **bucket of warm water,** and note how it feels.
2. Now put one hand into a **bucket of cold water** and the other into a **bucket of hot water.**
3. After a minute, take your hands out of the hot and cold water, and put them back in the warm water.
4. Can you rely on your hands to determine temperature? In your ScienceLog, explain your observations.

2 Teach

Discussion

In any object, there are always a few particles moving very slowly and a few particles moving very quickly, but most of the particles are moving about the same speed. Speed and kinetic energy are related, so temperature and average particle speed are related. If the temperature is high, the particles are moving quickly on average. If the temperature is low, the particles are moving slowly on average. Discuss this simple relationship with students. It will help them understand many of the effects associated with temperature differences and temperature changes.

QuickLab

MATERIALS

For Class or Small Groups:
- bucket of warm water
- bucket of cold water
- bucket of hot water

Safety Caution: Caution students to wear safety goggles and an apron when doing this activity.

Answer to QuickLab

4. Students should observe that the warm water felt warmer to the hand that had been in the cold water and cooler to the hand that had been in the hot water. Students should conclude that their hands are not reliable temperature indicators.

Science Bloopers

When Anders Celsius invented his temperature scale, he set the freezing point of water as 100° and the boiling point of water at 0°. Apparently, the person who made thermometers for Celsius got the two numbers reversed, and ever since 0° has been the freezing point of water, and 100° has been the boiling point of water.

Is That a Fact!

There are five temperature scales used today: Fahrenheit, Celsius, Kelvin, the international thermodynamic temperature scale, and Rankine. Scientists use the Celsius and Kelvin scales almost exclusively.

2 Teach, continued

Using the Figure

Ask students to use the figure of the **Three Temperature Scales** on this page to determine human body temperature on the Kelvin scale (310 K), the Celsius scale (37°C) and the Fahrenheit scale (98.6°F).

At what temperature does water boil on the Celsius scale? (100°C) on the Kelvin scale? (373 K)

Discussion

The Fahrenheit scale defines the freezing point of water as 32°F. By the time 0°F is reached, the temperature is well below the freezing point of water. Human body temperature is 98.6°F. Discuss with the class what would happen if normal human body temperature suddenly shot up to 98.6°C. Would air temperatures of 70–75°C feel comfortable? Why do doctors worry more about a fever of a couple of degrees Celsius than a fever of a couple of degrees Fahrenheit?

Teaching Transparency 116
"Three Temperature Scales"

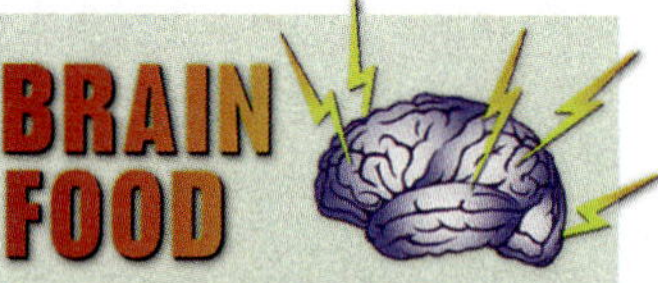

The Earth's coldest temperature on record occurred in Vostok Station, Antarctica. In 1983, the temperature dropped to –89°C (about –192°F). The Earth's hottest temperature on record occurred in 1922 in a Libyan desert. A scorching temperature of 58°C (about 136°F) was recorded—in the shade!

Measuring Temperature

How would you measure the temperature of a steaming cup of hot chocolate? Would you take a sip of it or stick your finger into it? Probably not—you would use a thermometer.

Using a Thermometer Many thermometers are thin glass tubes filled with a liquid. Mercury and alcohol are often used in thermometers because they remain liquids over a large temperature range. Thermometers can measure temperature because of thermal expansion. **Thermal expansion** is the increase in volume of a substance due to an increase in temperature. As a substance gets hotter, its particles move faster. The particles themselves do not expand; they just spread out so that the entire substance expands. Different substances expand by different amounts for a given temperature change. When you insert a thermometer into a hot substance, the liquid inside the thermometer expands and rises. You measure the temperature of a substance by measuring the expansion of the liquid in the thermometer.

Temperature Scales Temperature can be expressed according to different scales. Notice how the same temperatures have different readings on the three temperature scales shown below.

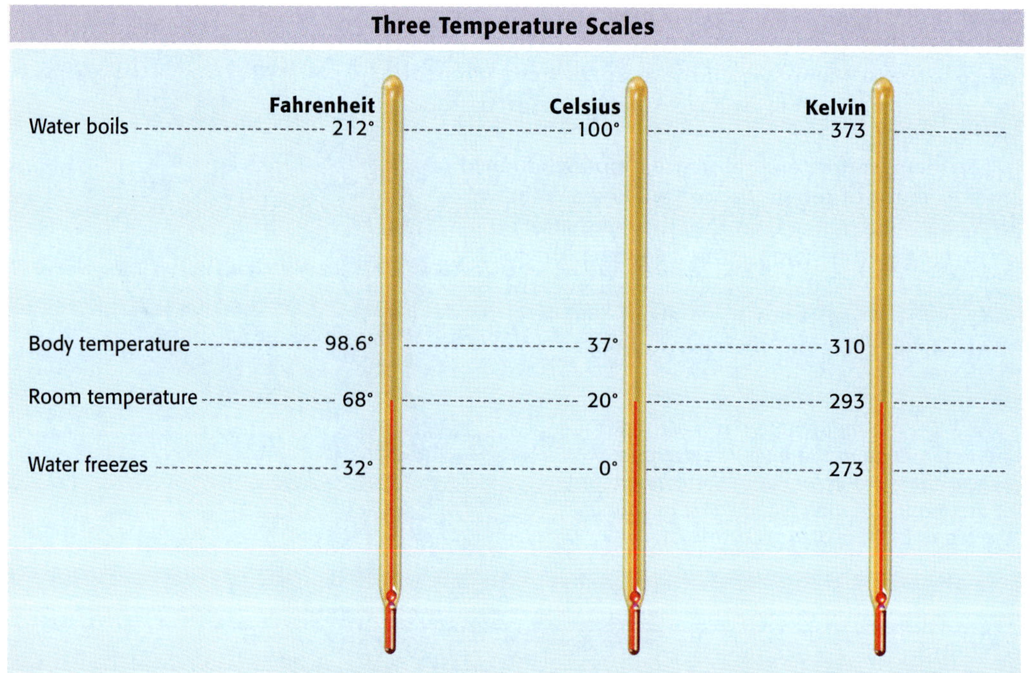

216

When you hear a weather report that gives the current temperature as 65°, chances are you are given the temperature in degrees Fahrenheit (°F). In science, the Celsius scale is used more often than the Fahrenheit scale. The Celsius scale is divided into 100 equal parts called degrees Celsius (°C) between the freezing point and boiling point of water. A third scale, called the Kelvin (or absolute) scale, is the official SI temperature scale. The Kelvin scale is divided into units called kelvins (K)—not degrees kelvin. The lowest temperature on the Kelvin scale is 0 K, which is called **absolute zero.** It is not possible to reach a temperature lower than absolute zero. In fact, temperatures within millionths of a kelvin above absolute zero have been achieved in laboratories, but absolute zero itself has never been reached.

As shown by the thermometers illustrated on the previous page, a given temperature is represented by different numbers on the three temperature scales. For example, the freezing point of water is 32°F, 0°C, or 273 K. As you can see, 0°C is actually a much higher temperature than 0 K, but a change of 1 K is equal to a change of 1 Celsius degree. In addition, 0°C is a higher temperature than 0°F, but a change of 1 Fahrenheit degree is *not* equal to a change of 1 Celsius degree. You can convert from one scale to another using the simple equations shown below. After reading the examples given, try the MathBreak on this page.

What can you do at temperatures near absolute zero? Turn to page 242 and find out!

To convert	Use this equation:	Example
Celsius to Fahrenheit °C ⟶ °F	$°F = \left(\frac{9}{5} \times °C\right) + 32$	Convert 45°C to °F. $°F = \left(\frac{9}{5} \times 45°C\right) + 32 = 113°F$
Fahrenheit to Celsius °F ⟶ °C	$°C = \frac{5}{9} \times (°F - 32)$	Convert 68°F to °C. $°C = \frac{5}{9} \times (68°F - 32) = 20°C$
Celsius to Kelvin °C ⟶ K	$K = °C + 273$	Convert 45°C to K. $K = 45°C + 273 = 318\ K$
Kelvin to Celsius K ⟶ °C	$°C = K - 273$	Convert 32 K to °C. $°C = 32\ K - 273 = -241°C$

MATH BREAK

Converting Temperatures

Use the equations at left to answer the following questions:

1. What temperature on the Celsius scale is equivalent to 373 K?
2. Absolute zero is 0 K. What is the equivalent temperature on the Celsius scale? on the Fahrenheit scale?
3. Which temperature is colder, 0°F or 200 K?

3 Extend

RESEARCH

Encourage students to research the lives and work of Anders Celsius, Gabriel Fahrenheit, William Rankine, and William Thomson (Lord Kelvin). Students can present their findings on posters, by writing a story or skit, or in a report.

PORTFOLIO

MATH and MORE

When solving equations, it is important to follow the order of operations. Remind students to do what is inside the parentheses first, then multiply or divide from left to right, and finally add or subtract from left to right.

Have students do the following conversion problems:

- Normal body temperature is 98.6°F. Marie has a temperature of 38.5°C. Does Marie have a fever? (yes; 38.5°C = 101.3°F)
- The temperature tonight is supposed to be 265 K. Will water left in a bucket outside freeze? (yes; 265 K = −8°C, which is below water's freezing point, 0°C)

Math Skills Worksheet 35 "Using Temperature Scales"

internet**connect**

TOPIC: Thermal Expansion
GO TO: www.scilinks.org
***sci*LINKS NUMBER:** HSTE560

Answers to MATHBREAK

1. 100°C
2. −273°C; −523.4°F
3. 200 K is colder

4 Close

Quiz

1. Most substances _____ when they are cooled. (contract)
2. The common temperature scale used by most Americans is the _____ scale. (Fahrenheit)
3. Scientists use either the _____ scale or the _____ scale. (Celsius, Kelvin)
4. Temperature _____ as average kinetic energy decreases. (decreases)

Alternative Assessment

Ask students to theorize why large buildings and sidewalks are constructed with expansion joints. (to allow for thermal expansion)

Ask them to explain what would happen in hot or cold weather if there were no expansion joints.

Answer to Explore

When students start to move around faster, ask how this is like an increase in kinetic energy. (Like atoms of a heated substance, they are moving faster.) When they move faster, what else happens? (They need more room.)

Homework

Writing | Have students explain how they could measure temperature if they were given a thermometer without marks on it. Remind students that water would help them with their measurements.

Figure 3 *The concrete segments of a bridge can expand on hot days. When the temperature drops, the segments contract.*

More About Thermal Expansion

Have you ever gone across a highway bridge in a car? You probably heard and felt a *"Thuh-thunk"* every couple of seconds as you went over the bridge. That sound occurs when the car goes over small gaps called expansion joints, shown in **Figure 3.** These joints keep the bridge from buckling as a result of thermal expansion. Recall that thermal expansion is the increase in volume of a substance due to an increase in temperature.

Thermal expansion also occurs in a thermostat, the device that controls the heater in your home. Inside a thermostat is a bimetallic strip. A *bimetallic strip* is made of two different metals stacked in a thin strip. Because different materials expand at different rates, one of the metals expands more than the other when the strip gets hot. This makes the strip coil and uncoil in response to changes in temperature. This coiling and uncoiling closes and opens an electric circuit that turns the heater on and off in your home, as shown in **Figure 4.**

Figure 4 **How a Thermostat Works**

a As the room temperature drops below the desired level, the bimetallic strip coils up, and the glass tube tilts. A drop of mercury closes an electric circuit that turns the heater on.

b As the room temperature rises above the desired level, the bimetallic strip uncoils. The drop of mercury rolls back in the tube, opening the electric circuit, and the heater turns off.

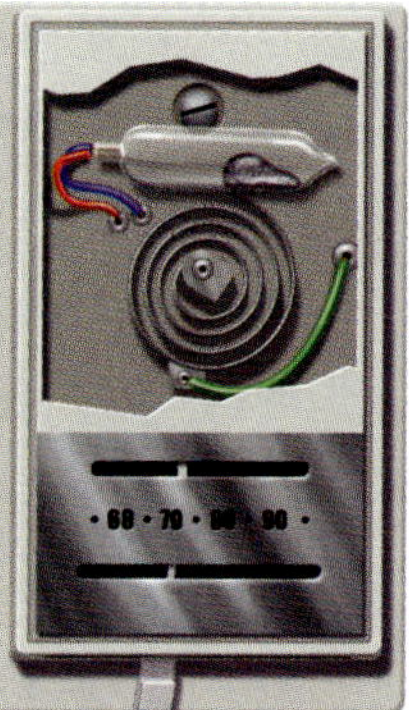

Explore

Stand in a huddle with three or four classmates. Have another classmate lay down a piece of string in a circle around you. Without holding on to each other, start moving around inside the circle. Gradually increase your kinetic energy. Did you have to move outside the string as you started to move faster? How is this like thermal expansion?

Review

1. What is temperature?
2. What is the coldest temperature possible?
3. Convert 35°C to degrees Fahrenheit.
4. **Inferring Conclusions** Why do you think heating a full pot of soup on the stove could cause the soup to overflow?

Answers to Review

1. Temperature is a measure of how hot or cold an object is. Specifically, temperature is a direct measure of the average kinetic energy of the particles in an object.
2. The coldest possible temperature is absolute zero (0 K or −273°C).
3. $°F = (\frac{9}{5} \times °C) + 32$
   $°F = \frac{9}{5} \times 35°C + 32$
   $°F = 95$, or 95°F
4. The soup could overflow its pot as it cooks on the stove because of thermal expansion. The soup will expand in volume as its temperature increases. If the cold soup is too close to the top of a pot, it will likely overflow as it expands.

2

What Is Heat?

NEW TERMS

heat
thermal energy
conduction
conductor
insulator
convection
radiation
specific heat capacity

OBJECTIVES

- Define heat as the transfer of energy between objects at different temperatures.
- Compare methods of heating.
- Describe how specific heat capacity makes substances change temperature at different rates.
- Calculate energy transferred by heat.
- Explain the differences between temperature, thermal energy, and heat.

It's time for your annual physical. The doctor comes in and begins her exam by looking down your throat using a wooden tongue depressor. Next she listens to your heart and lungs. But when she places a metal stethoscope on your back, as shown in **Figure 5,** you jump a little and say, "Whoa! That's cold!" The doctor apologizes and continues with your checkup.

Why did the metal stethoscope feel cold? After all, it was at the same temperature as the tongue depressor, which didn't make you jump. What is it about the stethoscope that made it feel cold? The answer has to do with how energy is transferred between the metal and your skin. In this section, you'll learn about this kind of energy transfer.

Heat Is a Transfer of Energy

You might think of the word *heat* as having to do with things that feel hot. But heat also has to do with things that feel cold—like the stethoscope. In fact, heat is what causes objects to feel hot or cold or to get hot or cold under the right conditions. **Heat** is the transfer of energy between objects that are at different temperatures.

Why do some things feel hot, while others feel cold? When two objects at different temperatures come in contact, energy is always transferred from the object with the higher temperature to the object with the lower temperature. When the doctor's stethoscope touches your back, energy is transferred from your back to the stethoscope because your back has a higher temperature (37°C) than the stethoscope (probably room temperature, 20°C). So to you, the stethoscope is cold, but compared with the stethoscope, you are hot! You'll learn about why the tongue depressor didn't feel cold a little later in this section.

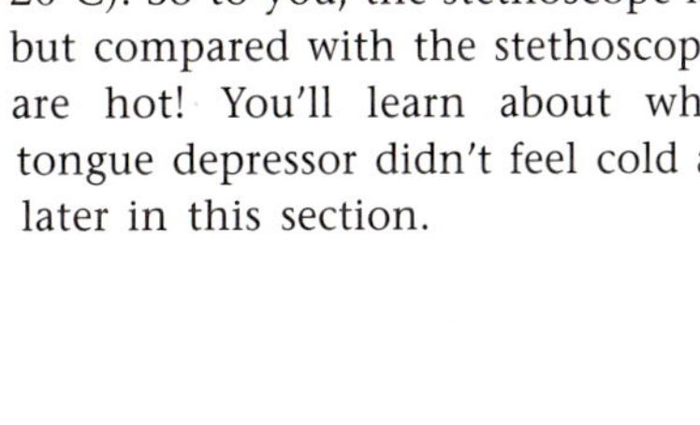

Figure 5 *The reason the metal stethoscope feels cold is actually because of heat!*

SECTION 2

Focus

What Is Heat?

In this section, students learn that heat is the transfer of energy between objects at different temperatures. They also learn the three methods of heating objects and how to calculate heat using specific heat capacity. Finally, they learn about the differences between temperature, thermal energy, and heat.

Bellringer

Have students imagine the following:

You walk into the bathroom in your bare feet. The temperature there is 23°C. You step onto the tile floor, and it feels very cold. Quickly, you step onto the throw rug in front of the sink, which feels warmer.

Ask students to answer these questions in their ScienceLog:

Is the floor really colder than the rug? Why do they seem to be at different temperatures when your bare feet touch them?

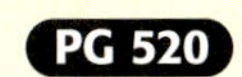

Feel the Heat

Directed Reading Worksheet 9 Section 2

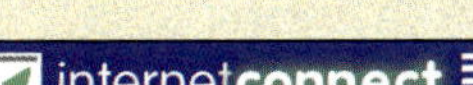

TOPIC: What Is Heat?
GO TO: www.scilinks.org
KEYWORD: HSTE565

MISCONCEPTION ALERT

Students often believe that if an object feels cooler to the touch than other objects in the same room, then it must have a lower temperature. For example, a bowl of cotton balls and several metal spoons left in the freezer overnight will have the same temperature, but the spoons will seem to have a much lower temperature. In fact, the cotton balls and the spoons are the same temperature. They feel different because of the rate at which each transfers thermal energy to its surroudings.

Section 2–California Standards: PE/ATE 3, 3a, 3c, 3d, 7, 7b, 7c; LabBook: 3, 3a, 3c, 3d, 7, 7a, 7b, 7d, 7e

1 Motivate

DEMONSTRATION

Place three objects with similar masses, such as a rock, a block of brass, and a block of steel, in boiling water. After 2 minutes, remove each object from the boiling water and immediately place it on a block of wax. When the objects have cooled, remove them from the block of wax. Measure the depth of the indentation made by each object on the wax. Ask the students to explain the different measurements. (Each object had a different amount of thermal energy.)

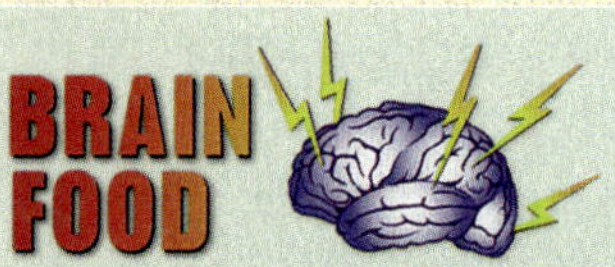

If you put an ice cube into a thermos of liquid nitrogen, energy is transferred from the ice cube to the liquid nitrogen—the ice cube heats the liquid nitrogen!

2 Teach

READING STRATEGY

Prediction Guide Before students read the section about heat and thermal energy, ask them whether the following statements are true or false.

- Thermal energy depends partly on the temperature of a substance. (true)
- At thermal equilibrium, two substances in contact may have the same temperature but not the same thermal energy. (true)
- A cup of water at 283 K and a pot of water at 283 K have the same thermal energy. (false)

Heat and Thermal Energy If heat is a process of energy transfer, what form of energy is being transferred? The answer is thermal energy. **Thermal energy** is the total kinetic energy of the particles that make up a substance. Thermal energy depends partially on temperature. An object at a high temperature contains more thermal energy than the same-sized object at a lower temperature. Thermal energy also depends on how much of a substance you have. As described by **Figure 6,** the more moving particles there are in a substance, the greater the thermal energy of the substance.

When you hold an ice cube in your hand, thermal energy is transferred from your hand to the ice cube. As a result, the ice cube's thermal energy increases, and it starts to melt. At the same time, your hand's thermal energy decreases. The particles in the surface of your skin start moving slower, and the surface temperature of your skin drops slightly. That's why ice makes your hand feel cold!

Figure 6 *Although both soups are at the same temperature, the soup in the pan has more thermal energy than the soup in the bowl.*

Reaching the Same Temperature Take a look at **Figure 7.** When objects at different temperatures come in contact, energy will always be transferred from the higher-temperature object to the lower-temperature object until both objects reach the same temperature. This point is called *thermal equilibrium* (EE kwi LIB ree uhm). When objects are at thermal equilibrium, no net change in either object's thermal energy occurs. Although one object may have more thermal energy, both objects have the same temperature.

Figure 7
Reaching Thermal Equilibrium

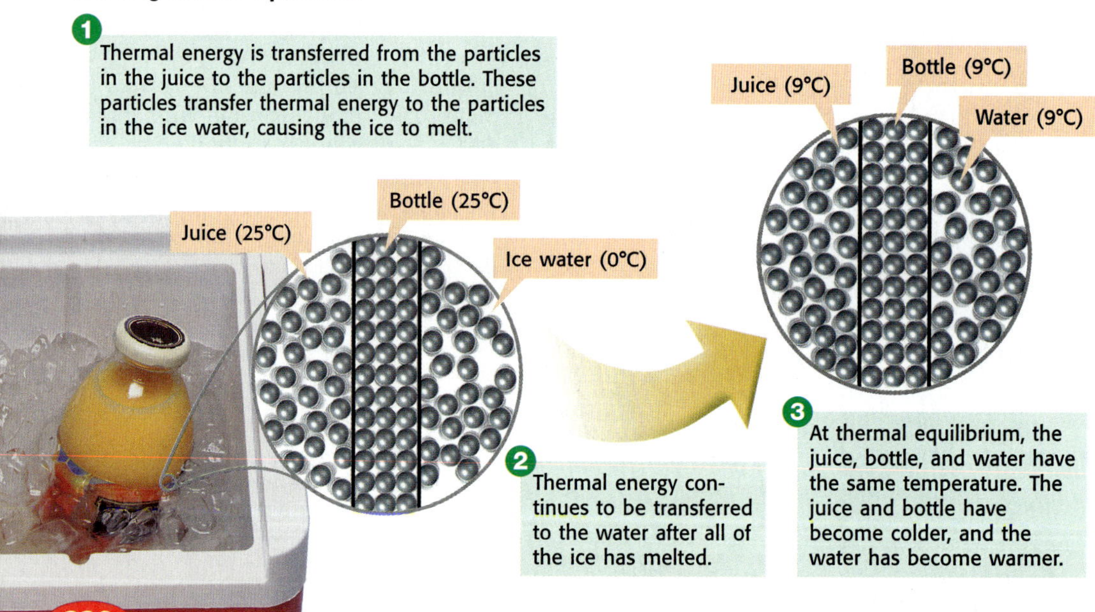

220

Homework

Ask students this question:

When energy has been transferred by heat, what happens to it? Explain your answer. (Energy transferred by heat moves from a higher-temperature object to a lower-temperature object. The thermal energy of the lower-temperature object increases, as does its temperature. The thermal energy of the higher-temperature object decreases, as does its temperature.)

Methods of Heating

So far you've read about several examples of how heat is a process of energy transfer: stoves transfer energy to substances in pots and pans, you can adjust the temperature of your bath water by adding cold or hot water to the tub, and the sun warms your skin. In the next couple of pages you'll learn about three methods of heating: *conduction, convection,* and *radiation.*

Conduction Imagine that you put a cold metal spoon in a bowl of hot soup, as shown in **Figure 8.** Soon the handle of the spoon warms up—even though it is not in the soup! The entire spoon gets warm due to conduction. **Conduction** is the transfer of thermal energy from one substance to another through direct contact. Conduction can also occur within a substance, such as the spoon in Figure 8.

How does conduction work? As substances come in contact, particles collide, and thermal energy is transferred from the higher-temperature substance to the lower-temperature substance. Remember that particles of substances at different temperatures have different average kinetic energy. So when particles collide, higher-kinetic-energy particles transfer kinetic energy to lower-kinetic-energy particles. This makes some particles slow down and other particles speed up until all particles have the same average kinetic energy. As a result, the substances have the same temperature.

Figure 8 *The end of this spoon will warm up because conduction, the transfer of energy through direct contact, occurs all the way up the handle.*

QuickLab

Heat Exchange

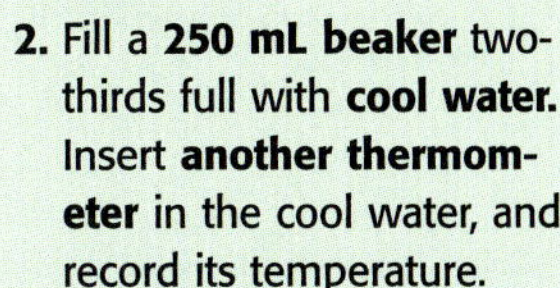

1. Fill a **film canister** with **hot water.** Insert the **thermometer apparatus** prepared by your teacher. Record the temperature of the water.
2. Fill a **250 mL beaker** two-thirds full with **cool water.** Insert **another thermometer** in the cool water, and record its temperature.
3. Place the canister in the cool water. Record the temperature measured by each thermometer every 30 seconds.
4. When the thermometers read nearly the same temperature, stop and graph your data. Plot temperature (*y*-axis) versus time (*x*-axis).
5. In your ScienceLog, describe what happens to the rate of energy transfer as the two samples of water get closer in temperature.

QuickLab

MATERIALS

For Each Group:
- film canister
- 2 thermometers
- 250 mL beaker
- hot and cool water
- graph paper

Safety Caution: Remind students to handle thermometers carefully. Caution students to wear safety goggles during this activity.

Teacher Notes: Prepare the film canister lids in advance. Make a hole in each canister lid with an awl or a pair of sharp scissors. The thermometer should fit tightly enough in the lid that water will not drip out when the assembly is turned upside down. (One-hole stoppers can also be used.)

Students should graph both sets of data on the same grid. You may wish to assist students in adjusting the scales of their graph to show all their data.

Answers to QuickLab

5. Answers will vary, but students should see that the rate of energy transfer decreases as the two water samples approach the same temperature.

Teaching Transparency 117
"Reaching Thermal Equilibrium"

Teaching Transparency 118
"Conduction"

SCIENCE HUMOR

Q: Why did the music teacher bring a metal pole to orchestra rehearsal?

A: He wanted the orchestra to have a good conductor.

IS THAT A FACT!

Special ceramic tiles were created for use on the underside of the space shuttle. These tiles transfer so little energy that one side can be exposed to a welder's torch while the other side remains cool to the touch.

2 Teach, continued

Answer to APPLY

The drink holder is an insulator because it does not conduct energy very well. It protects the can, which is a conductor, from energy that transfers from the warmer air to the cooler can.

DEMONSTRATION

Convection Currents Fill a 250 mL beaker about two-thirds full of water. Place the beaker on a hot plate turned on low or medium. Roll some very small pieces of aluminum foil into small, tightly packed balls. Drop the foil balls into the water, and direct students to observe what happens to the balls as the water warms up. Ask students what the movement of the foil balls suggests about the movement of water within the beaker. (The circulation of the foil balls suggests that the water in the beaker is circulating too.)

Then ask what method of heating is shown in this demonstration. (convection)

CONNECT TO LIFE SCIENCE

Convection currents caused by the uneven heating of Earth's surface are responsible for Earth's winds, weather patterns, and ocean currents. Without these currents, Earth's climates would be very different, and life on Earth might be much more difficult.

Teaching Transparency 118 "Convection"

Conductors	Insulators
Curling iron	Flannel shirt
Iron skillet	Oven mitt
Cookie sheet	Plastic spatula
Copper pipes	Fiberglass insulation
Stove coils	Ceramic bowl

Substances that conduct thermal energy very well are called **conductors.** For example, a metal spoon in a bowl of hot soup is a conductor, as is the metal in a doctor's stethoscope. Energy is transferred rapidly from your higher-temperature skin to the room-temperature stethoscope. That's why the stethoscope feels cold. Substances that do not conduct thermal energy very well are called **insulators.** For example, the wooden tongue depressor in the doctor's office is an insulator. It has the same temperature as the doctor's stethoscope, but the tongue depressor doesn't feel cold. That's because thermal energy is transferred very slowly from your tongue to the wood. You can compare some typical conductors and insulators in the chart at left.

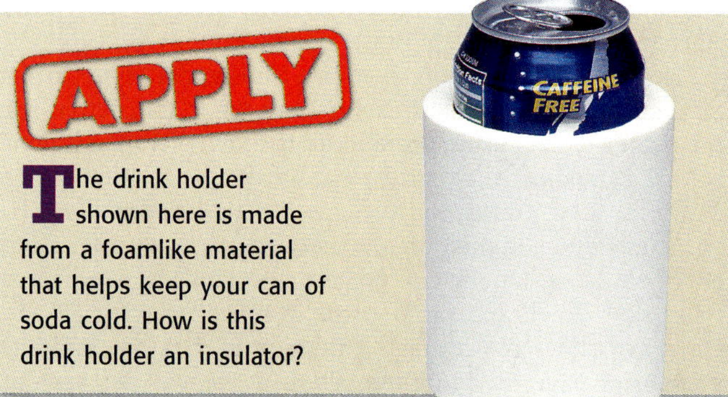

APPLY

The drink holder shown here is made from a foamlike material that helps keep your can of soda cold. How is this drink holder an insulator?

Convection When you boil a pot of water, like the one shown in **Figure 9,** the water moves in roughly circular patterns due to convection. **Convection** is the transfer of thermal energy by the movement of a liquid or a gas. The water at the bottom of a pot on a stove burner becomes hot due to contact with the pot itself (conduction). As a result, the hot water becomes less dense because its higher-energy particles have spread apart. The warmer water rises through the denser, cooler water above it. At the surface, the warm water begins to cool, and the lower-energy particles move closer together, making the water denser. The denser, cooler water sinks back to the bottom, where it will be heated again. This circular motion of liquids or gases due to density differences that result from temperature differences is called a *convection current.*

Figure 9 *The repeated rising and sinking of water during boiling is due to convection.*

Science Bloopers

The use of glass fibers goes back to the ancient Egyptians, but making useful fiberglass was hard to do. Then, in 1932, as a researcher was trying to weld glass blocks together, a burst of compressed air accidentally hit some molten glass. The burst blew the molten glass into very fine glass fibers. This accident led to one of today's most common insulating materials, fiberglass.

Radiation Unlike the two other methods of heating, radiation does not involve an energy transfer between particles of matter. **Radiation** is the transfer of thermal energy through space. For example, you can light a match simply by holding it near a flame. The flame will radiate energy toward the unlit match and light it. Another example of radiation is shown in **Figure 10.**

Radiation provides much of the energy we use on Earth. The sun's radiant energy is absorbed by objects. As a result, the kinetic energy of the particles in objects increases. That's why you feel warm when you stand in the sunshine. You might be surprised to learn that Earth is such a livable place because of radiation and the *greenhouse effect.* The Earth's atmosphere acts like a greenhouse, trapping thermal energy radiated by the sun. The greenhouse effect, illustrated in **Figure 11,** is essential in maintaining Earth's moderate temperatures. Some scientists warn against excessive greenhouse gases (water vapor, carbon dioxide, and methane) in the atmosphere because trapping too much thermal energy might make the Earth too warm. However, if it were not for the greenhouse effect, the Earth would be a cold, lifeless planet.

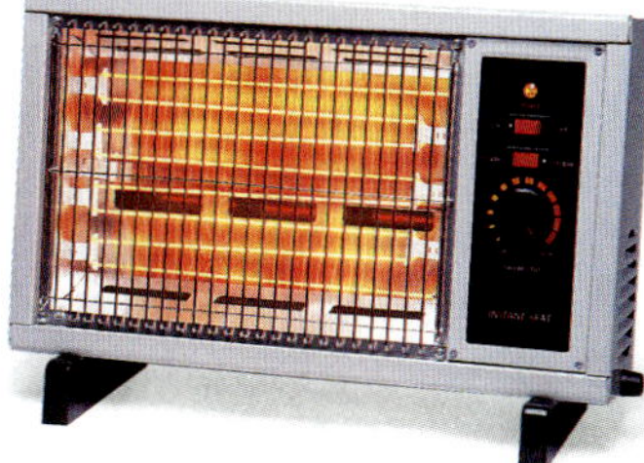

Figure 10 *The hot coils of a portable heater radiate thermal energy. You can feel the warmth of the heater even when you're standing away from it.*

Figure 11 The Greenhouse Effect

a Sunlight streams through the atmosphere and heats the Earth.

b The Earth radiates thermal energy, some of which escapes into space.

c Greenhouse gases trap some of the thermal energy near the Earth's surface.

REVIEW

1. What is heat?
2. Explain how radiation is different from conduction and convection.
3. **Applying Concepts** Why do many metal cooking utensils have wooden handles?

Quick—the ice is melting! Turn to page 522 in the LabBook and attempt to save the cube!

USING THE FIGURE

Draw students attention to **Figure 11.** Ask students why they think clouds would keep an area of Earth from heating up as much as it would on a clear day. (Clouds prevent some radiation from reaching Earth.)

Then ask what would happen if greenhouse gases kept most of the thermal energy that reaches Earth from escaping into space. (Earth would gradually warm up.) Sheltered English

CONNECT TO ASTRONOMY

The very dense atmosphere of Venus is composed mostly of carbon dioxide. The high amount of carbon dioxide results in a greenhouse effect that traps most of the thermal energy from sunlight. The surface temperature of Venus is therefore the hottest of any planet in the solar system. It remains at about 460°C—hot enough to melt zinc metal.

PG 522

Save the Cube!

TOPIC: Methods of Heating
GO TO: www.scilinks.org
KEYWORD: HSTE570

Answers to Review

1. Heat is the transfer of energy between objects that are at different temperatures. Energy is always transferred from an object with a higher temperature to an object with a lower temperature.
2. Radiation is different from conduction and convection in that it does not involve energy transfer among particles of matter. Radiation is the transfer of energy through space. The sun heats Earth by radiation.
3. Sample answer: Many metal cooking utensils have wooden handles because wood is an insulator. When you are preparing hot food, a wooden handle will prevent the thermal energy of the food from being conducted to your hand.

2 Teach, continued

USING THE TABLE

Have students study the table of **Specific Heat Capacities of Some Common Substances** found on this page. Then ask the following questions:

- If you have a sample of each substance in the following pairs, which will become hotter faster: some silver coins or water (silver coins); a copper pan on a hot stove or its wooden handle (pan); a car's aluminum door handle sitting in the hot summer sun or the windshield (the windshield).
- Explain why auto makers now use aluminum-cast engines instead of iron-cast engines. (Aluminum has a higher specific heat capacity than iron.)
- Explain why water is used as a coolant. (Water has a very high specific heat capacity.)
- Why would you want to put cloth-covered cushions on wood patio furniture in the summer? (Cloth has a higher specific heat capacity than wood.)

CROSS-DISCIPLINARY FOCUS

Home Economics When an apple pie is taken from the oven, the crust cools faster than the filling. Ask students to compare the specific heat capacity of the crust with that of the filling.

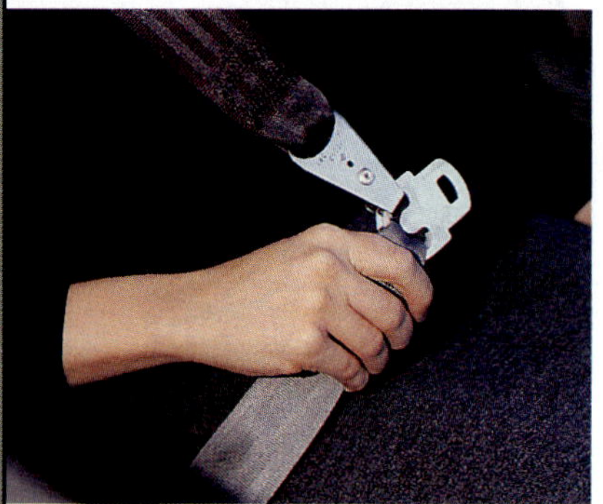

Figure 12 *The metal part of a seat belt gets hot faster than the cloth part because metal and cloth are affected differently by heat.*

How Much Heat?

On a hot summer day, have you ever tried to fasten your seat belt in a car, only to be shocked at how hot the metal seat-belt latch felt? The cloth part of a seat belt, shown in **Figure 12,** isn't nearly so hot. Even when the car is left in the sunlight for a short time, the metal part is always hotter than the cloth part. How does the metal get hot faster than the cloth? In order to explain this difference, you must consider how different substances are affected by heat.

Specific Heat Capacity Because the cloth and metal that make up the seat belt are different substances, they are affected by heat differently. The same amount of thermal energy transferred to or away from the two substances will result in different temperature changes for each substance. **Specific heat capacity** is the amount of energy needed to change the temperature of 1 kg of a substance by 1°C. Look at the table below. The metal part of a seat belt has a lower specific heat capacity than does the cloth part. That means that it takes less energy to change the temperature of the metal than it takes to change the temperature of the cloth. As a result, the metal part of a seat belt will get hotter faster than the cloth part when a car is left in the sunlight. In addition, the metal will cool off faster than the cloth part when the car is left in the shade.

Specific heat capacity is a characteristic property of a substance. That means no matter how much of a substance you have, it will always have the same specific heat capacity. In addition, every substance has a unique specific heat capacity. So you could identify a substance by determining its specific heat capacity. Check out the specific heat capacities for various substances in the table below.

Water has a higher specific heat capacity than land has. This difference affects the climate of different areas on Earth. Climates in coastal areas are moderated by the ocean. Because of water's high specific heat capacity, the ocean retains a lot of thermal energy. So even in the winter, when inland temperatures drop, coastal areas stay moderately warm. Because water does not heat up as easily as land does, oceans can help to keep coastal areas cool during the summer when inland temperatures soar.

Specific Heat Capacities of Some Common Substances

Substance	Specific heat capacity (J/kg•°C)	Substance	Specific heat capacity (J/kg•°C)
Lead	128	Metal of seat belt	500
Gold	129	Glass	837
Mercury	138	Aluminum	899
Wood	176	Cloth of seat belt	1,340
Silver	234	Steam	2,010
Copper	387	Ice	2,090
Iron	448	Water	4,184

224

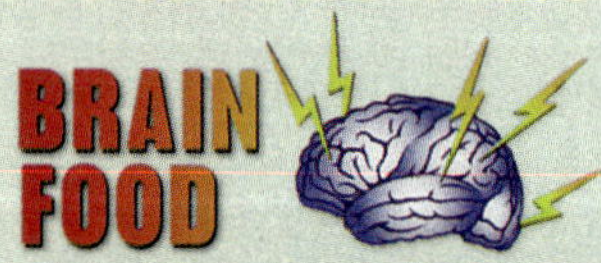

Challenge students to explain whether water would be a good insulator for a home with passive solar heating, such as the Earthship that students read about in the chapter opener.

Calculating Heat How much energy is required to heat a cup of water to make tea? Unlike temperature, energy transferred by heat cannot be measured directly. So in order to answer this question, you have to consider the thermal energy of the water and the change in the water's temperature. Because thermal energy is related to the number of particles in an object, you must consider the water's mass. In addition, you must consider the water's specific heat capacity. In general, if you know the mass of a substance, how much the substance's temperature changed when it was heated, and the substance's specific heat capacity, you can use the equation below to find out how much energy was transferred to the substance.

$$\text{Energy transferred (J)} = \text{specific heat capacity (J/kg•°C)} \times \text{mass (kg)} \times \text{change in temperature (°C)}$$

Using this equation and the data shown in **Figure 13,** you can find out how much energy was transferred to the water in the cup. The steps below show you how this is done. This equation can also help you find out how much energy is transferred when a substance cools down, or decreases in temperature. Energy is transferred away from a substance as it cools down. As a result, the value for energy transferred is negative because the difference in temperature is negative. You can practice using this equation in the MathBreak at right.

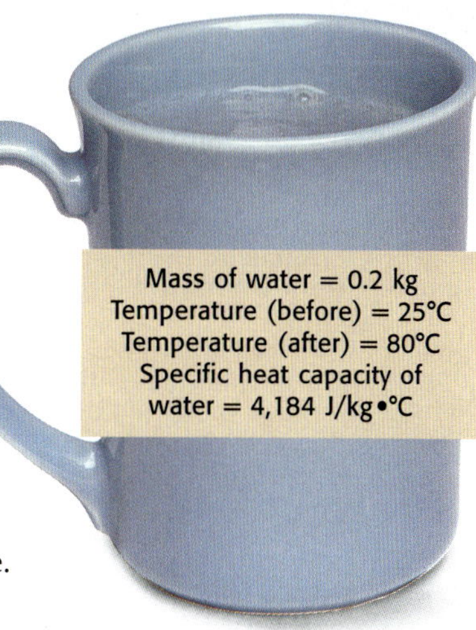

Mass of water = 0.2 kg
Temperature (before) = 25°C
Temperature (after) = 80°C
Specific heat capacity of water = 4,184 J/kg•°C

Figure 13 *Information used to calculate the energy transferred to the water is shown above.*

1 Write down what you know.

Specific heat capacity of water = 4,184 J/kg•°C
Mass of water = 0.2 kg
Change in temperature = (80°C − 25°C) = 55°C

2 Substitute the values into the equation.

Energy transferred = specific heat capacity × mass × change in temperature
= 4,184 J/kg•°C × 0.2 kg × 55°C

3 Solve and cancel units.

Energy transferred = 4,184 J/~~kg~~•~~°C~~ × 0.2 ~~kg~~ × 55~~°C~~
= 4,184 J × 0.2 × 55
= 46,024 J

MATH BREAK

Calculating Energy Transfer

Use the equation at left to solve the following problems:

1. Imagine that you heat 2 L of water to make pasta. The temperature of the water before is 40°C, and the temperature after is 100°C. How much energy is transferred to the water? (Hint: 1 L of water = 1 kg of water.)
2. Suppose you put a glass filled with 180 mL of water into the refrigerator. The temperature of the water before going into the refrigerator is 25°C, and the temperature after is 10°C. How much energy was transferred away from the water as it became colder?

Answers to MATHBREAK

1. Energy transferred = specific heat capacity × mass × change in temperature
   Energy transferred = 4,184 J/kg•°C × 2 kg × 60°C
   Energy transferred = 502,080 J
2. Energy transferred = 4,184 J/kg•°C × 0.180 kg × (−15°C)
   Energy transferred = −11,297 J

MATH and MORE

Have students calculate the following problems.

- How much energy would be transferred if 50 kg of gold cools from 50°C to 20°C? 129 J/kg•°C × 50 kg × (−30°C) = −193,500 J
- How much energy would be needed to raise the temperature of 20 kg of iron from 30°C to 100°C? 448 J/kg•°C × 20 kg × 70°C = 627,200 J

CROSS-DISCIPLINARY FOCUS

History Iced tea was invented in 1904 at the World's Fair in St. Louis, Missouri. A tea plantation owner was giving away free samples of his hot tea. When a heat wave hit St. Louis, no one wanted hot tea. To get people to drink his tea, the owner dumped ice into it and served it cold. "Iced tea" was an immediate success.

WEIRD SCIENCE

A paper cup can be used to boil water. The water removes the thermal energy—water boils at 100°C—from the paper before the cup reaches its kindling temperature (more than 230°C).

Homework

Concept Mapping Have students use the concept of specific heat capacity to explain in a concept map why coastal cities have milder temperatures year-round than inland cities.

3 Extend

RESEARCH

Have students find out how insulating materials are rated. Ask them to research what the R-values are based on and what R-values are recommended for homes in your geographic area.

GOING FURTHER

A typical use of calorimetery is to figure out how much energy is transferred in a chemical reaction. When acids and bases react with each other, there is less chemical potential energy in the bonds of the products than in the bonds of the reacting acid and base molecules. Because energy is conserved, energy will be transferred to the reaction's environment.

Have students propose a way to use water to calculate the change in chemical potential energy. (Perform the reaction in water. Measure the mass of the water and the temperature increase to calculate the amount of energy transferred to the water.)

Counting Calories

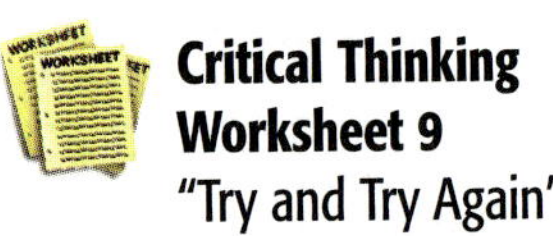

Critical Thinking Worksheet 9
"Try and Try Again"

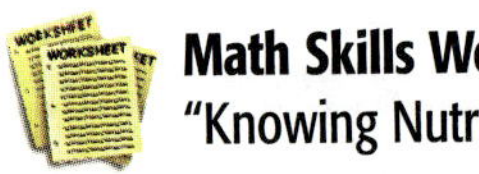

Math Skills Worksheet 38
"Knowing Nutrition"

Build your own calorimeter! Try the lab on page 523 of the LabBook.

Calorimeters When one object transfers thermal energy to another object, the energy lost by one object is gained by the other object. This phenomenon is the key to how a *calorimeter* (KAL uh RIM uh ter) works. Inside a calorimeter, shown in **Figure 14,** thermal energy is transferred from a known mass of a test substance to a known mass of another substance, usually water. Water is used in calorimeters because its specific heat capacity is well known. If a hot test substance is placed inside the calorimeter's inner container of water, the substance transfers energy to the water until thermal equilibrium is reached. By measuring the temperature change of the water and using water's specific heat capacity, you can determine the exact amount of energy transferred by the test substance to the water. You can then use this amount of energy, the test substance's change in temperature (its temperature before being placed in the water – the thermal equilibrium temperature), and the mass of the test substance to calculate the specific heat capacity of the substance.

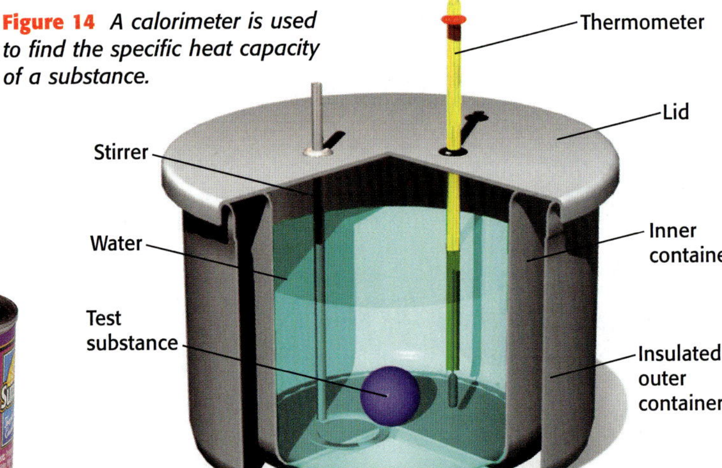

Figure 14 *A calorimeter is used to find the specific heat capacity of a substance.*

Figure 15 *A serving of this fruit contains 120 Cal (502,080 J) of energy that will be transferred to your body when you eat it.*

Calories and Kilocalories Energy transferred by heat can be expressed in units called calories. A *calorie (cal)* is the amount of energy needed to change the temperature of 0.001 kg of water by 1°C. Therefore, 1,000 calories are required to change the temperature of 1 kg of water by 1°C. One calorie is equivalent to 4.184 J. Another unit used to express energy transferred by heat is the *kilocalorie (kcal),* which is equivalent to 1,000 calories. The kilocalorie can also be referred to as the *Calorie* (with a capital *C*). Calories are the units listed on food labels, such as the label shown in **Figure 15.**

226

CROSS-DISCIPLINARY FOCUS

Health Have students examine the nutrition information labels from several packages of prepared foods or snacks to determine the number of kilocalories (Calories) contained in one serving. One Calorie is 1000 calories. One calorie can also be defined as the amount of energy needed to change the temperature of 1g of water by 1°C. Then have students calculate the number of joules of energy that would be transferred to their body by eating one serving of each of the foods.

The Differences Between Temperature, Thermal Energy, and Heat

So far in this chapter, you have been learning about some concepts that are closely related: temperature, heat, and thermal energy. But the differences between these concepts are very important.

Temperature Versus Thermal Energy Both temperature and thermal energy involve kinetic energy. Temperature is the average kinetic energy of an object's particles, and thermal energy is the total kinetic energy of an object's particles. While thermal energy varies with the mass of an object, temperature does not. A drop of boiling water has the same temperature as a pot of boiling water, but the pot has more thermal energy because there are more particles.

Self-Check

How can two substances have the same temperature but different amounts of thermal energy? *(See page 564 to check your answer.)*

Thermal Energy Versus Heat Heat and thermal energy are not the same thing; heat is a transfer of thermal energy. Objects contain thermal energy, but they do not contain heat. Heating transfers thermal energy from one object to another. The table below summarizes the differences between temperature, thermal energy, and heat.

Temperature	Thermal energy	Heat
A measure of the average kinetic energy of the particles in a substance	A measure of the total kinetic energy of the particles in a substance	The transfer of energy between objects that are at different temperatures
Expressed in degrees Fahrenheit, degrees Celsius, or kelvins	Expressed in joules	Cannot be measured directly; energy transferred expressed in joules or calories
Does not vary with the mass of a substance	Varies with the mass and temperature of a substance	Varies with the mass, specific heat capacity, and temperature change of a substance

REVIEW

1. Why do some substances get hotter faster than others?
2. How are temperature and heat different?
3. **Applying Concepts** Examine the photo at right. How do you think the specific heat capacities for water and air influence the temperature of a swimming pool and the area around it?

227

Answers to Review

1. It depends on the substance's specific heat capacity. A substance with a low specific heat capacity gets hotter (and cooler) faster than one with a high specific heat capacity.
2. Temperature is a measure of the average kinetic energy of particles in a substance. Heat is the transfer of energy between objects that are at different temperatures and must be calculated, not measured.
3. Sample answer: Water has a higher specific heat capacity than air. The water takes longer to warm than the surrounding air, so water may feel cool even when it is hot outdoors. In addition, it will stay warmer longer.

4 Close

Answer to Self-Check

Two substances can have the same temperature but different amounts of thermal energy because temperature, unlike thermal energy, does not depend on mass. A small amount of a substance at a particular temperature will have less thermal energy than a large amount of the substance at the same temperature.

Quiz

Ask students whether the following statements are true or false.

1. Heat is the transfer of energy between two objects with different temperatures. (true)
2. Conduction is the heating method that occurs in fluids. (false)
3. Convection currents result from temperature differences in liquids and gases. (true)
4. Radiation is the means by which the energy from the sun is transferred to Earth. (true)
5. Water warms up and cools down more slowly than land because water has a lower specific heat capacity than land. (false)

Alternative Assessment

Concept Mapping Have the students construct a concept map using the following terms:

temperature, thermal energy, heat, conduction, radiation, convection, solids, liquids, gases, vacuum

Reinforcement Worksheet 9
"Feel the Heat"

SECTION 3

Focus

Matter and Heat

In this section, students learn how substances change from state to state and how heat affects matter during state changes. They also learn how heat affects matter during chemical changes.

Bellringer

Ask students to predict what changes would occur if they added an equal number of ice cubes to a glass of cold water and a glass of warm water. Ask them to explain their answer.

1 Motivate

DEMONSTRATION

On an overhead projector, place a beaker half-full of very hot water. Place a second beaker half-full of very cold water next to the first. Before turning on the projector, ask students to watch the screen. As you drop food coloring into each beaker, have students describe what they see happening in the beaker. Ask them these questions:

From your observations, which beaker contained the hotter water? How did you come to this conclusion? Predict what will happen to the molecules of a liquid if more thermal energy is added.

Teaching Transparency 119 "Models of a Solid, a Liquid, and a Gas"

Teaching Transparency 120 "Changes of State for Water"

3

Matter and Heat

NEW TERMS

states of matter
change of state

OBJECTIVES

- Identify three states of matter.
- Explain how heat affects matter during a change of state.
- Describe how heat affects matter during a chemical change.

Have you ever eaten a frozen juice bar outside on a hot summer day? It's pretty hard to finish the entire thing before it starts to drip and make a big mess! The juice bar melts because the sun radiates energy to the air, which transfers energy to the frozen juice bar. The energy absorbed by the juice bar increases the kinetic energy of the molecules in the juice bar, which starts to turn to a liquid. In this section, you'll learn more about how heat affects matter.

States of Matter

The matter that makes up a frozen juice bar has the same identity whether the juice bar is frozen or has melted. The matter is just in a different form, or state. The **states of matter** are the physical forms in which a substance can exist. As you learned in the last two sections, matter consists of particles—atoms or molecules—that can move around at different speeds. The state a substance is in depends on how fast its particles are moving. The three most familiar states of matter are solid, liquid, and gas, as shown in **Figure 16.** You may recall that thermal energy depends partly on the kinetic energy of the particles that make up a substance. So if you have equal masses of a substance in its three states, the substance will have the most thermal energy as a gas and the least thermal energy as a solid. That's because the particles move around fastest in a gas.

Figure 16 Models of a Solid, a Liquid, and a Gas

Particles of a solid do not move fast enough to overcome the strong attraction between them, so they are held tightly together. The particles vibrate in place.

Particles of a liquid move fast enough to overcome some of the attraction between them. The particles are able to slide past one another.

Particles of a gas move fast enough to overcome nearly all of the attraction between them. The particles move independently of one another.

228

Directed Reading Worksheet 9 Section 3

CONNECT TO EARTH SCIENCE

Life on Earth would end if there were no water. Water occurs in three states—solid, liquid, and gas—and all three are critical to survival. Even though water vapor (a gas) is invisible, it is just as important as the water we can see.

Section 3–California Standards: PE/ATE 3, 3a, 7, 7b

Changes of State

When you melt cheese to make a cheese dip, like that shown in **Figure 17**, the cheese changes from a solid to a thick, gooey liquid. A **change of state** is the conversion of a substance from one physical form to another. A change of state is a *physical change*, a change that affects one or more physical properties of a substance without changing the identity of the substance. Common changes of state include *freezing* (liquid to solid), *melting* (solid to liquid), *boiling* (liquid to gas), and *condensing* (gas to liquid).

Figure 17 *When you melt cheese, you change the state of the cheese but not its identity.*

Heat During Changes of State Suppose you put an ice cube in a pan and set the pan on a stove burner. Soon the ice will turn to water and then to steam. If you made a graph of the heat involved versus the temperature of the ice during this process, it would look something like the graph below.

As the ice is heated, its temperature increases from –25°C to 0°C. At 0°C, the ice begins to melt. Notice, however, that the temperature of the ice remains 0°C even when energy is still being added. The energy added at this point is used to change the arrangement of the particles, or molecules, in the ice. The temperature of the ice remains constant until all of its particles have dislodged from their positions in the solid. When all of the ice has become liquid water, the water's temperature will start to increase from 0°C to 100°C. At 100°C, the water will begin to turn into steam. Again, the temperature remains constant, and the energy added at the boiling point is used to change the arrangement of the particles of water. The particles of water increase their motion until the water has entirely changed to a gaseous state. When all of the water has become steam, the temperature will again increase as it continues to be heated.

Self-Check

Why do you think you can get a more severe burn from steam than from boiling water? *(See page 564 to check your answer.)*

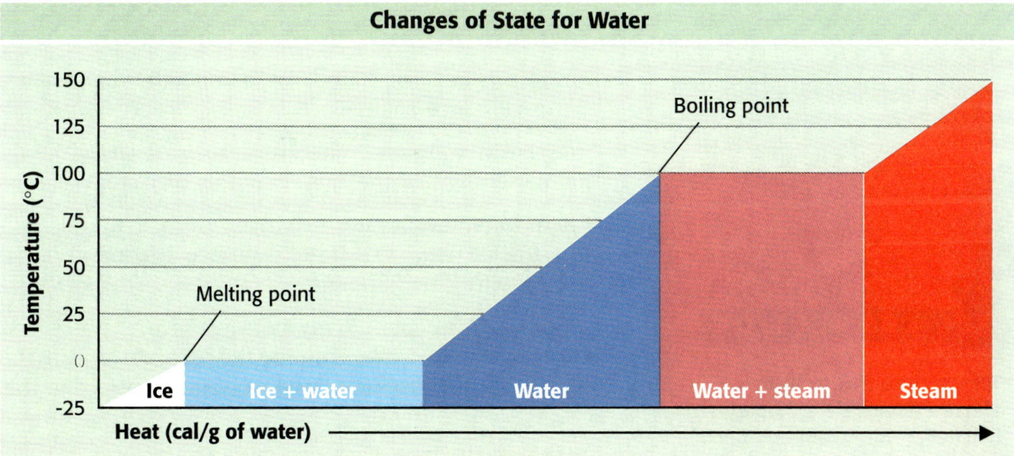

2 Teach

Activity

MATERIALS

For Each Group:
- 3 thermometers
- 3 test tubes
- 10 mL each of water, nail polish remover, and isopropyl alcohol (in the test tubes)

Safety Caution: Caution students to wear safety goggles and gloves for this activity. Remind them that nail polish remover and alcohol should be handled with great care.

Have students insert the thermometers into the liquids and wait for the temperatures to stabilize before taking readings. Have them record the temperatures on a chart. Then have them remove one thermometer, carefully wave it in the air, and take another temperature reading. Instruct them to record the new temperature, then repeat the procedure for the other liquids. Ask students what caused the temperature to decrease as the thermometer was waved around. (The liquid absorbed energy from the thermometer as it evaporated.)

Using the Figure

Draw students' attention to **Figure 19.** Discuss where the two plateaus occur on the graph. (at 0°C and at 100°C)

Challenge students to explain whether ice can be warmer than 0°C and whether liquid water can be warmer than 100°C. (No, energy added at these temperatures causes a change of state, not a temperature increase.)

What do these two temperatures represent? (the melting point and the boiling point of water)

Sheltered English

Weird Science

Potassium compounds that are used in agriculture and industry are obtained from brine water that evaporates, leaving the potassium compounds behind. To speed up the evaporation, a blue dye is added to the salty water to absorb more solar radiation.

Answer to Self-Check

Steam can cause a more severe burn than boiling water because steam contains more energy per unit mass than does boiling water.

3 Extend

Research

Writing | Ask students to find out about French chemist Pierre E. M. Berthelot (1827–1907). Have them find out what contributions he made to the study of chemical changes. (He synthesized many organic compounds, including alcohols, methane, benzene, and acetylene.)

Students can display their results in a concept map, on a poster, or by writing a poem or skit.

4 Close

Quiz

Ask students whether these statements are true or false.

1. When ice changes to a liquid, it absorbs energy. (true)
2. When a liquid evaporates, it absorbs energy. (true)
3. When a vapor condenses to a liquid, energy is given off. (true)
4. When a liquid boils, energy is absorbed. (true)

Alternative Assessment

Concept Mapping Have students make a concept map showing how heat affects matter during a change of state and during a chemical change.

The substances your body needs to survive and grow come from food. Carbohydrates, proteins, and fats are major sources of energy for the body. The energy content of food can be found by burning a dry food sample in a special calorimeter. Both carbohydrates and proteins provide 4 Cal of energy per gram, while fats provide 9 Cal of energy per gram.

Heat and Chemical Changes

Heat is involved not only in changes of state, which are physical changes, but also in *chemical changes,* changes that occur when one or more substances are changed into entirely new substances with different properties. During a chemical change, new substances are formed. For a new substance to form, old bonds between particles must be broken and new bonds created. The breaking and creating of bonds between particles involves energy. Sometimes a chemical change requires thermal energy to be absorbed. For example, photosynthesis is a chemical change in which carbon dioxide and water combine to form sugar and oxygen. In order for this change to occur, energy must be absorbed. That energy is radiated by the sun. Other times, a chemical change, such as the one shown in **Figure 18,** will result in energy being released.

Figure 18 *In a natural-gas fireplace, the methane in natural gas and the oxygen in air change into carbon dioxide and water. As a result of the change, energy is given off, making a room feel warmer.*

across the sciences CONNECTION

Turn to page 243 to learn about a fabric called Diaplex that keeps you warm and dry.

REVIEW

1. During a change of state, why doesn't the temperature of the substance change?
2. Compare the thermal energy of 10 g of ice with the thermal energy of the same amount of water.
3. When water evaporates (changes from a liquid to a gas), the air near the water's surface becomes cooler. Explain why this happens.
4. **Applying Concepts** Many cold packs used for sports injuries are activated by bending the package, causing the substances inside to interact. How is heat involved in this process?

Answers to Review

1. Energy added to or removed from a substance during a change of state rearranges the particles of the substance rather than raises its temperature.
2. Particles of water in the liquid state have more kinetic energy than particles of water in the solid state, so 10 mL of water has more thermal energy than 10 g of ice.
3. Sample answer: For water to evaporate, it must absorb energy. The air near the water's surface transfers energy to the water to make it evaporate. Because the air loses energy, it becomes cooler.
4. Sample answer: When you bend the ice pack, the substances inside interact. That interaction absorbs so much energy that the pack feels colder.

4

Heat Technology

NEW TERMS

insulation

heat engine

thermal pollution

OBJECTIVES

- Analyze several kinds of heating systems.
- Describe how a heat engine works.
- Explain how a refrigerator keeps food cold.
- Give examples of some effects of heat technology on the environment.

You probably wouldn't be surprised to learn that the heater in your home is an example of heat technology. But did you know that automobiles, refrigerators, and air conditioners are also examples of heat technology? It's true! You can travel long distances, food can stay cold, and you can feel comfortable indoors during the summer—all because of heat technology.

Heating Systems

Many homes and buildings have a central heating system that controls the temperature in every room. On the next few pages, you will see some different central heating systems.

Hot-Water Heating Water's high specific heat capacity makes it a good candidate for heating systems. In a hot-water heating system, shown in **Figure 19,** water is heated by the burning of fuel (usually natural gas or fuel oil) in a hot-water heater. The hot water is then pumped through a pipe network that leads to radiators in each room. The hot water heats the radiators, and the radiators then heat the colder air surrounding them. The water returns to the hot-water heater to be heated again. A *steam-heating system* is similar to a hot-water heating system, except that steam is used. An advantage of using steam instead of water is that steam has a higher temperature than hot water. However, it is more difficult to regulate room temperature with a steam-heating system than with a hot-water heating system.

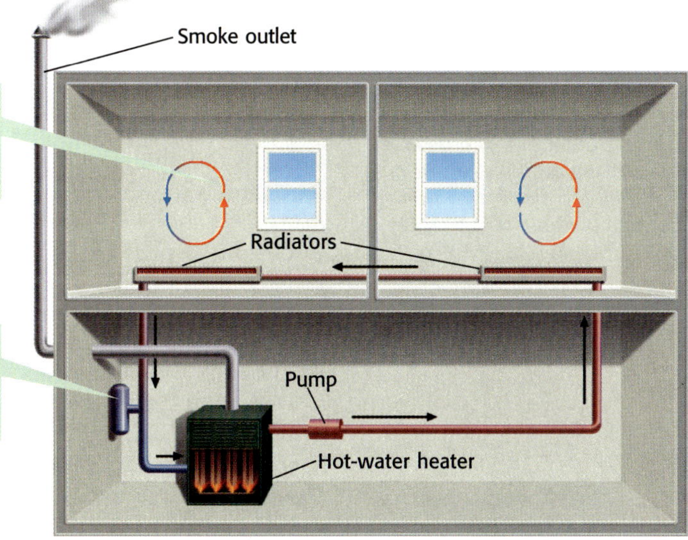

Figure 19
A Hot-Water Heating System

Section 4

Focus

Heat Technology

In this section, students learn about different kinds of heating systems, heat engines, and cooling systems. They also learn about some effects of heat on the environment.

Bellringer

Write the following on the board:

Predict whether leaving the refrigerator door open on a hot summer day will help to cool the kitchen? Explain your answer.

Have students write their responses in their ScienceLog. Review these predictions after students have read pages 235 and 236.

1 Motivate

Discussion

Have students work together to hypothesize about how a refrigerator or an air conditioner works and how heat is involved with an appliance that cools. Have the groups share their hypotheses with the class. Discuss with students some ways people may have cooled their homes before air conditioners were invented and have them imagine what their lives would be like today without heating or air conditioning.

Cross-Disciplinary Focus

History The first heating systems developed by people were probably open fires in caves. When people found a way to make a hole in the side or top of the cave to let the smoke out, a type of fireplace was created. Fireplaces with a chimney tall enough to provide adequate draft for fires were first built in the twelfth century.

Directed Reading Worksheet 9 Section 4

Section 4 Opener–California Standards: PE/ATE 3, 3a, 3b, 6a

2 Teach

READING STRATEGY

Prediction Before students read this section, have them predict the answers to the following questions about heating and cooling systems:

- Where should a heat register or heating vent be placed for maximum effect? (on the floor)
- Where should the cold-air return be placed? (on the floor)
- If you were cooling a house with central air conditioning, where would you place the cold-air register? (on the ceiling) the warm-air return? (on the ceiling)

Students often believe that blankets provide heat. Explain that blankets insulate the body; they slow the escape of thermal energy from the body into the air, and the feeling of warmth results. Electric blankets are an exception.

Homework

Have students investigate the type of heating and cooling systems used in their home. Ask them to draw a diagram of their home showing the placement of the equipment (fireplaces, registers, cold-air intakes, hot-water pipes, radiators, and so on) used to keep their home warm or cool.

Warm-Air Heating Although air has a lower specific heat capacity than water, warm-air heating systems are commonly used in homes and offices in the United States. In a warm-air heating system, shown in **Figure 20,** air is heated in a separate chamber by the burning of fuel (usually natural gas) in a furnace. The warm air travels through a network of ducts to different rooms, which it enters through vents. After transferring its thermal energy to the rooms, the air is cooler, so it sinks and enters a vent near the floor. A fan forces cooled air into the furnace, where it will be heated and returned to the ducts. An air filter allows the air to be cleaned as it gets recirculated throughout the system.

Figure 20
A Warm-Air Heating System

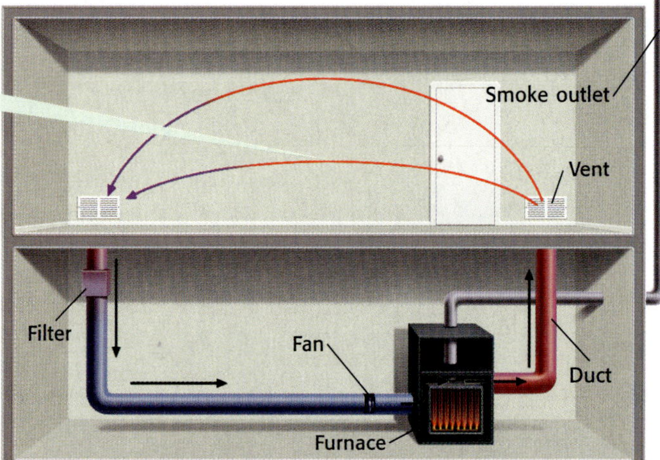

Heating and Insulation Because heat is a transfer of energy from high temperatures to low temperatures, thermal energy has a tendency to be transferred out of a house during cold weather and into a house during hot weather. To keep the house comfortable, a heating system must run almost continuously during the winter, and air conditioners often do the same during the summer. This can be wasteful. That's where insulation comes in. **Insulation** is a substance that reduces the transfer of thermal energy. Insulation, such as the fiberglass insulation shown in **Figure 21,** is made of insulators, materials that do not conduct thermal energy very well. Insulation that is used in walls, ceilings, and floors helps a house stay warm in the winter and cool in the summer.

Do you remember the Earthships described at the beginning of this chapter? The tightly packed aluminum cans in the walls of an Earthship have spaces between them. Air filling these spaces insulates the Earthship. These homes also rely on a solar heating system, which you will learn about on the next page.

Figure 21 *Inside the fibers in this insulation are millions of tiny air pockets. Because air is a good insulator, these air pockets help to prevent thermal energy from flowing into or out of a building.*

Solar Heating The sun radiates an enormous amount of energy that can be used by solar heating systems to heat houses and buildings. *Passive solar heating* systems do not have moving parts. They rely on a building's structural design and materials to use energy from the sun as a means of heating. *Active solar heating* systems do have moving parts. They use pumps and fans to distribute energy from the sun throughout a building. The house shown in **Figure 22** uses both forms of solar heating systems. The large windows on the south side of the house are part of the passive solar heating system. These windows receive maximum sunlight, and energy radiated through the windows heats the rooms. Thick, well-insulated concrete walls absorb energy and heat the house at night or when it is cloudy. In the active solar heating system, water is pumped toward the solar collector, where it is heated. The hot water is then pumped through a pathway of pipes, transferring its energy to the pipes. A fan blowing over the pipes helps the pipes transfer their thermal energy to the air. Warm air is then sent into rooms through vents. Cooler water returns to the water storage tank to be pumped back through the solar collector.

Figure 22 *Passive and active solar heating systems work together to use the sun's energy to heat an entire house.*

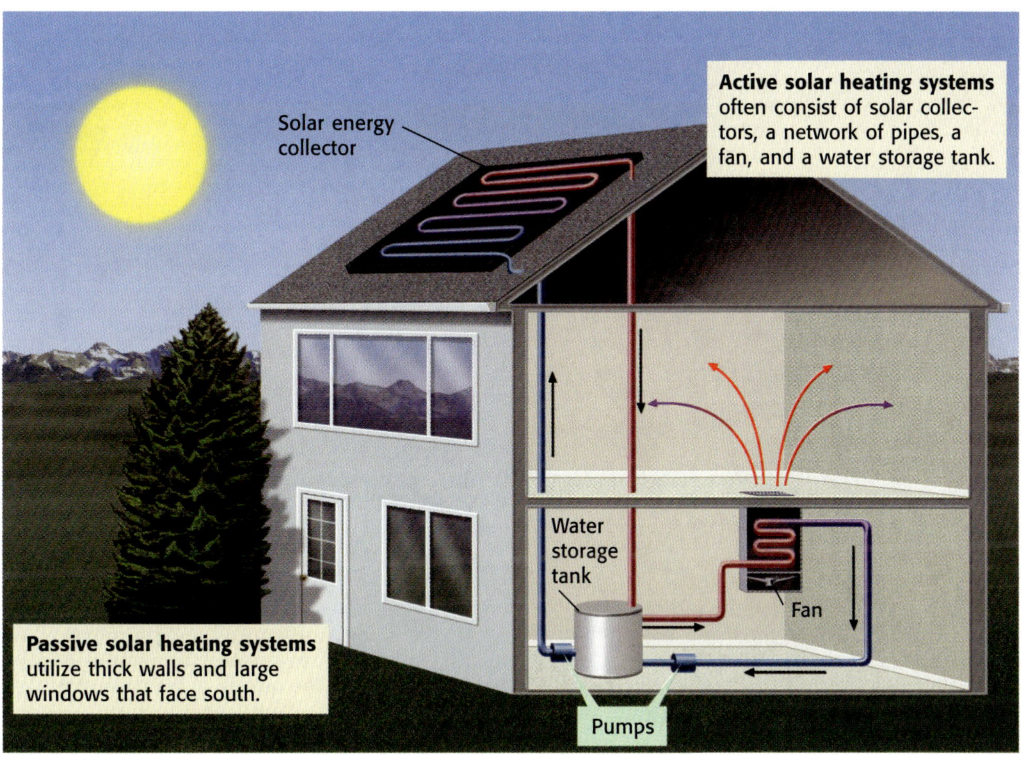

USING THE FIGURE

Draw students' attention to **Figure 22.** Ask which parts of the house are part of the passive solar heating system and which are part of the active solar heating system. (passive: large, south-facing windows and thick walls; active: solar collectors, network of pipes, fan, and water-storage tank)

GROUP ACTIVITY

Provide groups with shoe boxes painted flat black inside and out, jars or cans painted white and black, water, thermometers, and tubing. Challenge students to construct a model of a solar heating system.

MEETING INDIVIDUAL NEEDS

Learners Having Difficulty

Help students draw diagrams of the heating systems shown in **Figures 19, 20,** and **22.** Have them use red arrows to indicate the flow of hot air and blue arrows to indicate the flow of cold air. Sheltered English

Teaching Transparency 121
"Solar Heating Systems"

IS THAT A FACT!

Earth receives enough energy from the sun in 1 minute to meet the planet's energy demands for an entire year. If humans could find better ways to capture and use solar energy, dependence on fossil fuels for energy sources could be reduced.

2 Teach, continued

CROSS-DISCIPLINARY FOCUS

History In 1769, Nicolas-Joseph Cugnot (1725–1804), a French Army engineer, built a three-wheeled, steam-powered tractor. It traveled very slowly (3.6 km/h) and had to stop every 20 minutes to build up a fresh head of steam. Cugnot's tractor was hard to drive and not very practical, but his ideas led others to create better self-propelled vehicles.

USING THE FIGURE

Concept Mapping Ask students to study **Figures 23** and **24.** Have them create a concept map that shows the similarities and differences between an external combustion engine and an internal combustion engine. The concept map should show the source of the energy, what the energy does, where the combustion takes place, and any other features of the two types of engines.

Ask students which type of engine is more efficient and why.

oceanography CONNECTION

Ocean engineers are developing a new technology known as Ocean Thermal Energy Conversion, or OTEC. OTEC uses temperature differences between surface water and deep water in the ocean to do work like a heat engine. Warm surface water vaporizes a fluid, such as ammonia, causing it to expand. Then cool water from ocean depths causes the fluid to condense and contract. The continuous cycle of vaporizing and condensing converts thermal energy into kinetic energy that can be used to generate electrical energy.

Heat Engines

Did you know cars work because of heat? A car has a **heat engine,** a machine that uses heat to do work. In a heat engine, fuel combines with oxygen in a chemical change that produces thermal energy. This process, called *combustion,* is how engines burn fuel. Heat engines that burn fuel outside the engine are called *external combustion engines*. Heat engines that burn fuel inside the engine are called *internal combustion engines*. In both types of engines, fuel is burned to produce thermal energy that can be converted into kinetic energy. This kinetic energy can be used to do work.

External Combustion Engine A simple steam engine, shown in **Figure 23,** is an example of an external combustion engine. Coal is burned to generate thermal energy that will change water to steam. When water changes to steam, it expands. This expansion is used to drive a piston, which can be attached to other mechanisms that do work, such as a flywheel. Modern steam engines, such as those used to generate electricity at a power plant, drive turbines instead of pistons.

Figure 23 An External Combustion Engine

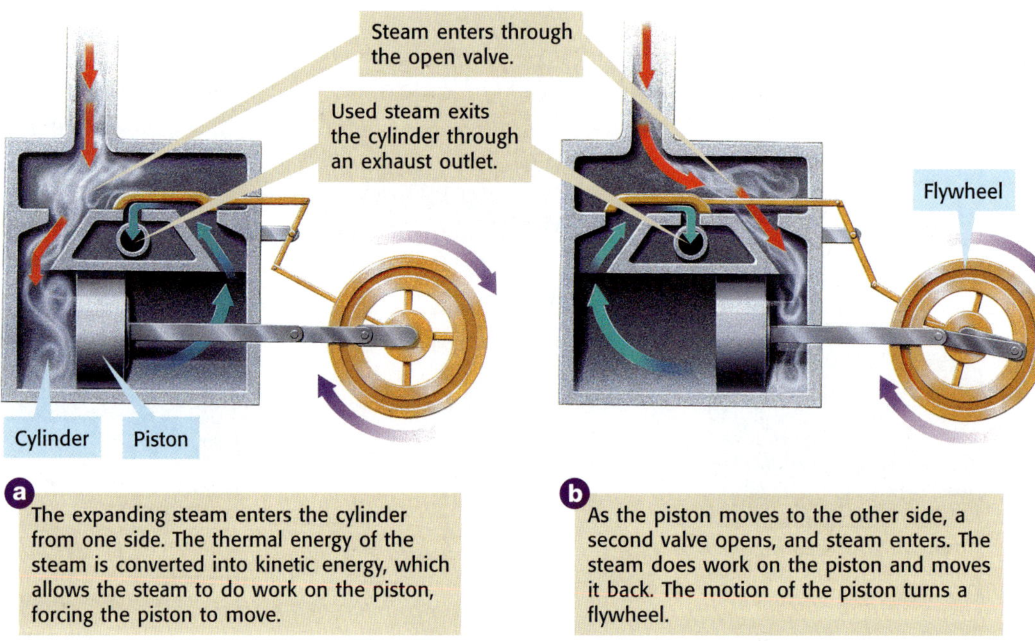

a The expanding steam enters the cylinder from one side. The thermal energy of the steam is converted into kinetic energy, which allows the steam to do work on the piston, forcing the piston to move.

b As the piston moves to the other side, a second valve opens, and steam enters. The steam does work on the piston and moves it back. The motion of the piston turns a flywheel.

234

Science Bloopers

When automobiles were first built, they shared the roads with horses. Horses were often quite frightened by the cars. Uriah Smith, founder of a "horseless carriage" company in Michigan, came up with a solution to this problem: He made an automobile with a wooden, life-size horse head on the front. Unfortunately, this did nothing to quiet the noise of the engine, and horses were still frightened by cars.

Internal Combustion Engine In the six-cylinder car engine shown in **Figure 24,** fuel is burned inside the engine. During the intake stroke, a mixture of gasoline and air enters each cylinder as the piston moves down. Next the crankshaft turns and pushes the piston up, compressing the fuel mixture. This is called the compression stroke. Next comes the power stroke, in which the spark plug uses electrical energy to ignite the compressed fuel mixture, causing the mixture to expand and force the piston down. Finally, during the exhaust stroke, the crankshaft turns and the piston is forced back up, pushing exhaust gases out of the cylinder.

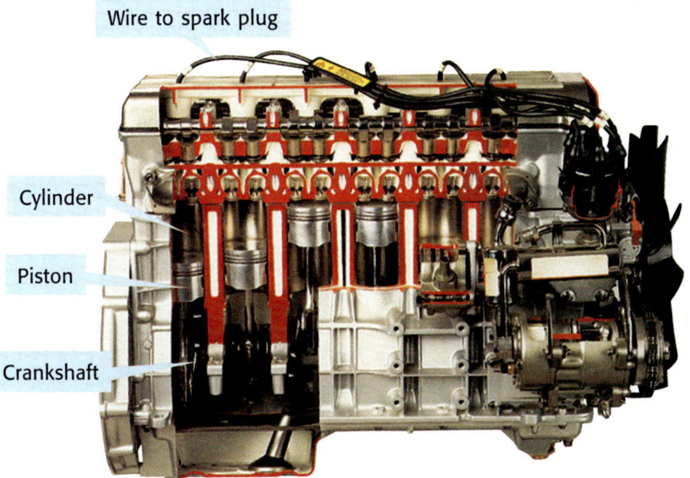

Figure 24 *The continuous cycling of the four strokes in the cylinders converts thermal energy into the kinetic energy required to make the car move.*

Cooling Systems

When it gets hot in the summer, an air-conditioned room can sure feel refreshing. Cooling systems are used to transfer thermal energy out of a particular area so that it feels cooler. An air conditioner, shown in **Figure 25,** is a cooling system that transfers thermal energy from a warm area inside a building or car to an area outside, where it is often even warmer. But wait a minute—doesn't that go against the natural direction of heat—from higher temperatures to lower temperatures? Well, yes. A cooling system moves thermal energy from colder temperatures to warmer temperatures. But in order to do that, the cooling system must do work.

Figure 25 *This air conditioning unit keeps a building cool by moving thermal energy inside the building to the outside.*

235

IS THAT A FACT!

A heat pump is a "refrigerator" that can be run in two directions. When a heat pump is used for cooling, energy is extracted from the air in the house and pumped outside. When the heat pump is used for heating, energy is extracted from the air outside and pumped inside.

MEETING INDIVIDUAL NEEDS

Advanced Learners Encourage interested students to research different types of heat engines, such as external and internal heat engines, the Carnot engine, and Hero's engine. Encourage them to include information on the laws of thermodynamics, perpetual motion machines, and entropy and chaos.

REAL-WORLD CONNECTION

Swamp coolers, or evaporative cooling systems, are used in areas of hot, dry weather, such as the southwestern United States. Swamp coolers work in a manner similar to the way evaporating sweat cools the body. A swamp cooler consists of a simple fan that draws in hot, dry outside air and passes it through wet filters. The evaporation process lowers the temperature of the indoor air, which the fan then distributes throughout the building.

CONNECT TO PHYSICAL SCIENCE

Have students draw a series of cylinders similar to the ones in **Figure 24,** showing the four-stroke process. The strokes should be labeled to indicate the intake stroke, compression stroke, power stroke, and exhaust stroke. Ask students to then write a brief description of the processes that are occurring during each stroke. Use Teaching Transparency 192 to help students understand how each of the four strokes helps convert chemical energy into kinetic energy.

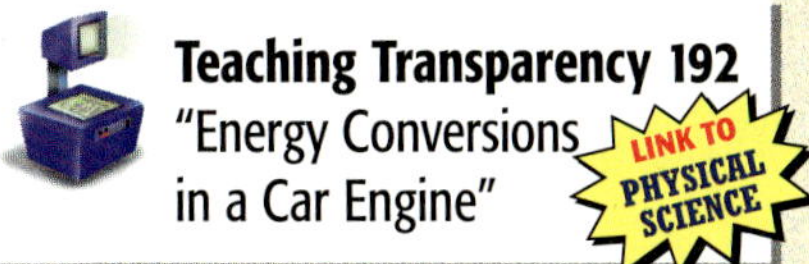

Teaching Transparency 192
"Energy Conversions in a Car Engine"
LINK TO PHYSICAL SCIENCE

3 Extend

Using the Figure

After students have studied **Figure 26,** discuss with them how refrigeration has affected food storage and the kinds of foods we eat. What did refrigeration allow that had never been possible before?

Going Further

Have interested students investigate the controversy about Freon's™ effect on the environment. Students should also research the alternatives to Freon. Explain that Freon used to be a commonly used refrigerant in the United States.

Cross-Disciplinary Focus

History The air conditioning systems we use today evolved from commercial refrigeration systems. In 1902, a young engineer named Willis Carrier helped a printing company having a problem with its color printing. Humidity caused the paper to expand or shrink. The colored inks would not align correctly, which caused fuzzy pictures. Carrier intended to control humidity with his device. To his surprise, the air was not only drier but also cooler. Carrier patented his machine in 1906 and made his first international sale to a silk mill in Japan in 1907. In this country, textile mills in the southern states were among the first to use Carrier's machines. The Carrier Corporation still manufactures air conditioners for homes and businesses today.

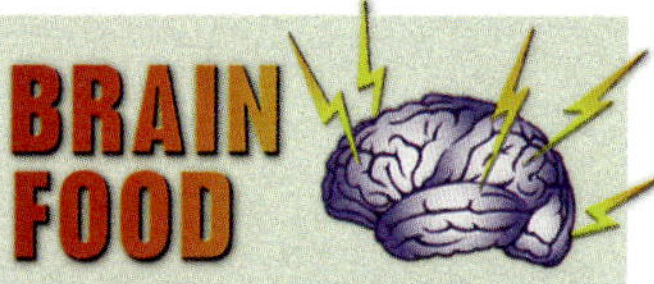

If you had a refrigerator in Antarctica, you would actually have to heat it to keep it running at its normal temperature. Otherwise, it would transfer energy to its surroundings until the refrigerator reached the same temperature as its surroundings. So it would freeze!

Electrical energy is required to do the work of cooling. Electrical energy enters a cooling system through a device called a compressor. The compressor does the work of compressing the refrigerant, a gas that has a boiling point below room temperature. This property of the refrigerant allows it to condense easily.

To keep many foods fresh, you store them in a refrigerator. A refrigerator is another example of a cooling system. **Figure 26** shows how a refrigerator continuously transfers thermal energy from inside the refrigerator to the condenser coils on the outside of the refrigerator. That's why the area near the back of a refrigerator feels warm.

Figure 26 How a Refrigerator Works

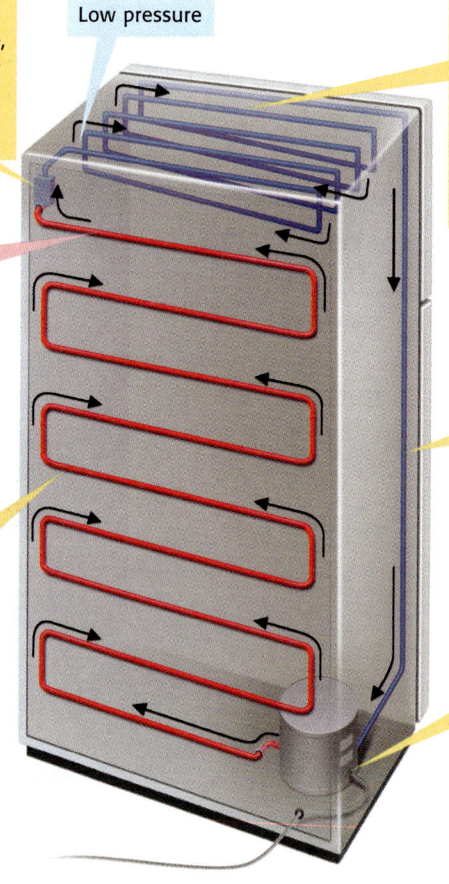

236

Is That a Fact!

A German scientist named Karl von Linde (1842–1934) made the first practical refrigerator, which used ammonia as the refrigerant.

Heat Technology and Thermal Pollution

Heating systems, car engines, and cooling systems all transfer thermal energy to the environment. Unfortunately, too much thermal energy can negatively affect the environment.

One of the negative effects of excess thermal energy is **thermal pollution,** the excessive heating of a body of water. Thermal pollution can occur near large power plants, which are often located near a body of water. Electric power plants burn fuel to produce thermal energy that is used to do the work of generating electrical energy. Unfortunately, it is not possible for all that thermal energy to do work, so some waste thermal energy results. **Figure 27** shows how a cooling tower helps remove this waste thermal energy in order to keep the power plants operating smoothly. In extreme cases, the increase in temperature downstream from a power plant can adversely affect the ecosystem of the river or lake. Some power plants reduce thermal pollution by reducing the temperature of the water before it is returned to the river.

Large cities can exhibit something called a heat island effect when excessive amounts of waste thermal energy are added to the urban environment. This thermal energy comes from automobiles, factories, home heating and cooling, lighting, and even just the number of people living in a relatively small area. The heat island effect can make the temperature of the air in a city higher than that of the air in the surrounding countryside.

Figure 27 *Cool water is circulated through a power plant to absorb waste thermal energy.*

REVIEW

1. Compare a hot-water heating system with a warm-air heating system.
2. What is the difference between an external combustion engine and an internal combustion engine?
3. **Analyzing Relationships** How are changes of state an important part of the way a refrigerator works?

4 Close

Quiz

Ask students whether the following statements are true or false:

1. You can cool the kitchen by leaving the refrigerator door open. (false)
2. Refrigeration is possible because of energy absorbed and released during changes in state. (true)
3. A radiator heats a room by heating the air, which circulates in convection currents. (true)

Alternative Assessment

Refrigerators and air conditioners seem to produce colder temperatures rather than warmer temperatures. Have students explain how heat is involved in the lowering of temperatures. Then have students make a list of household objects that are useful because they radiate or absorb thermal energy.

Answers to Review

1. Accept all reasonable responses. (A description of a hot-water heating system can be found on page 231, and a description of a warm-air heating system can be found on page 232.)
2. In an external combustion engine, fuel is burned outside the engine. In an internal combustion engine, fuel is burned inside the engine.
3. Sample answer: When the compressed liquid refrigerant passes through the expansion valve, it changes into a gas. During this change of state, the refrigerant absorbs thermal energy from the interior of the refrigerator, keeping it cold. (A description of the changes of state in a refrigerator can be found in Figure 26, on page 236.)

Section 4 Review–California Standards: PE/ATE 6a

Chapter Highlights

VOCABULARY DEFINITIONS

SECTION 1

temperature a measure of how hot (or cold) something is; specifically, a measure of the average kinetic energy of the particles in an object

thermal expansion the increase in volume of a substance due to an increase in temperature

absolute zero the lowest possible temperature (0 K, −273°C)

SECTION 2

heat the transfer of energy between objects that are at different temperatures; energy is always transferred from higher-temperature objects to lower-temperature objects until thermal equilibrium is reached

thermal energy the total kinetic energy of the particles that make up an object

conduction the transfer of thermal energy from one substance to another through direct contact; conduction can also occur within a substance

conductor a substance that conducts thermal energy well

insulator a substance that does not conduct thermal energy well

convection the transfer of thermal energy by the movement of a liquid or a gas

radiation the transfer of thermal energy through space

specific heat capacity the amount of energy needed to change the temperature of 1 kg of a substance by 1°C; specific heat capacity is a characteristic property of a substance

Chapter Highlights

SECTION 1

Vocabulary

temperature *(p. 214)*
thermal expansion *(p. 216)*
absolute zero *(p. 217)*

Section Notes

- Temperature is a measure of the average kinetic energy of the particles of a substance. It is a specific measurement of how hot or cold a substance is.
- Thermal expansion is the increase in volume of a substance due to an increase in temperature. Temperature is measured according to the expansion of the liquid in a thermometer.
- Fahrenheit, Celsius, and Kelvin are three temperature scales.
- Absolute zero—0 K, or −273°C— is the lowest possible temperature.
- A thermostat works according to the thermal expansion of a bimetallic strip.

SECTION 2

Vocabulary

heat *(p. 219)*
thermal energy *(p. 220)*
conduction *(p. 221)*
conductor *(p. 222)*
insulator *(p. 222)*
convection *(p. 222)*
radiation *(p. 223)*
specific heat capacity *(p. 224)*

Section Notes

- Heat is the transfer of energy between objects that are at different temperatures.
- Thermal energy is the total kinetic energy of the particles that make up a substance.
- Energy transfer will always occur from higher temperatures to lower temperatures until thermal equilibrium is reached.

Skills Check

Math Concepts

TEMPERATURE CONVERSION To convert between different temperature scales, you can use the equations found on page 217. The example below shows you how to convert a Fahrenheit temperature to a Celsius temperature.

Convert 41°F to °C.

$$°C = \frac{5}{9} \times (°F - 32)$$
$$°C = \frac{5}{9} \times (41°F - 32)$$
$$°C = \frac{5}{9} \times 9 = 5°C$$

Visual Understanding

HEAT—A TRANSFER OF ENERGY Remember that thermal energy is transferred between objects at different temperatures until both objects reach the same temperature. Look back at Figure 7, on page 220, to review what you've learned about heat.

238

Lab and Activity Highlights

Feel the Heat PG 520

Save the Cube! PG 522

Counting Calories PG 523

Datasheets for LabBook (blackline masters for these labs)

SECTION 2

- Conduction, convection, and radiation are three methods of heating.
- Specific heat capacity is the amount of energy needed to change the temperature of 1 kg of a substance by 1°C. Different substances have different specific heat capacities.
- Energy transferred by heat cannot be measured directly. It must be calculated using specific heat capacity, mass, and change in temperature.
- A calorimeter is used to determine the specific heat capacity of a substance.

Labs

Feel the Heat *(p. 520)*
Save the Cube! *(p. 522)*
Counting Calories *(p. 523)*

SECTION 3

Vocabulary

states of matter *(p. 228)*
change of state *(p. 229)*

Section Notes

- A substance's state is determined by how fast its particles are moving.
- Thermal energy transferred during a change of state does not change a substance's temperature. Rather, it causes a substance's particles to be rearranged due to an increase or decrease in their kinetic energy.
- Chemical changes can cause thermal energy to be absorbed or released.

SECTION 4

Vocabulary

insulation *(p. 232)*
heat engine *(p. 234)*
thermal pollution *(p. 237)*

Section Notes

- Central heating systems include hot-water heating systems and warm-air heating systems.
- Solar heating systems can be passive or active.
- Heat engines use heat to do work. External combustion engines burn fuel outside the engine. Internal combustion engines burn fuel inside the engine.
- A cooling system transfers thermal energy from cooler temperatures to warmer temperatures by doing work.
- Transferring excess thermal energy to lakes and rivers can result in thermal pollution.

internet**connect**

GO TO: go.hrw.com

Visit the **HRW** Web site for a variety of learning tools related to this chapter. Just type in the keyword:

KEYWORD: HSTHOT

GO TO: www.scilinks.org

Visit the **National Science Teachers Association** on-line Web site for Internet resources related to this chapter. Just type in the ***sci*LINKS** number for more information about the topic:

TOPIC	*sci*LINKS NUMBER
What Is Temperature?	HSTE555
Thermal Expansion	HSTE560
What Is Heat?	HSTE565
Methods of Heating	HSTE570
Changes of State	HSTE575

VOCABULARY DEFINITIONS, *continued*

SECTION 3

states of matter the physical forms in which a substance can exist

change of state the conversion of a substance from one physical form to another

SECTION 4

insulation a substance that reduces the transfer of thermal energy

heat engine a machine that uses heat to do work

thermal pollution the excessive heating of a body of water

Vocabulary Review Worksheet 9

Blackline masters of these Chapter Highlights can be found in the **Study Guide.**

Lab and Activity Highlights

LabBank

Whiz-Bang Demonstrations, Cool It, Demo 52

Labs You Can Eat, Baked Alaska, Lab 22

EcoLabs & Field Activities, Energy-Efficient Home, EcoLab 19

Long-Term Projects & Research Ideas, Project 60

Chapter Review Answers

Using Vocabulary

1. Temperature is a direct measure of the average kinetic energy of the particles of a substance; thermal energy is the total kinetic energy of the particles of the substance.
2. Heat is the transfer of energy between objects at different temperatures. Thermal energy is energy transferred by heat.
3. A conductor is a material that conducts energy easily. An insulator is a material that does not conduct energy easily.
4. Conduction is the transfer of energy from one substance to another through direct contact. Convection is the transfer of energy by the movement of a gas or a liquid.
5. The states of matter are the physical forms in which a substance can exist. A change of state occurs when a substance changes from one state to another.

Understanding Concepts

Multiple Choice

6. c
7. b
8. b
9. c
10. d
11. a
12. b

Short Answer

13. Temperature is a direct measure of the average kinetic energy of the particles in a substance. The more kinetic energy the particles have, the higher the temperature of the substance.
14. Specific heat capacity is the amount of energy needed to change the temperature of 1 kg of a substance by 1°C. Specific heat capacity determines the rate at which a substance changes temperature. Every substance has a unique specific heat capacity.

Chapter Review

USING VOCABULARY

For each pair of terms, explain the difference in their meanings.

1. temperature/thermal energy
2. heat/thermal energy
3. conductor/insulator
4. conduction/convection
5. states of matter/change of state

UNDERSTANDING CONCEPTS

Multiple Choice

6. Which of the following temperatures is the lowest?
   a. 100°C
   b. 100°F
   c. 100 K
   d. They are the same.
7. Compared with the Pacific Ocean, a cup of hot chocolate has
   a. more thermal energy and a higher temperature.
   b. less thermal energy and a higher temperature.
   c. more thermal energy and a lower temperature.
   d. less thermal energy and a lower temperature.
8. The energy units on a food label are
   a. degrees
   b. Calories
   c. calories
   d. joules
9. Which of the following materials would not be a good insulator?
   a. wood
   b. cloth
   c. metal
   d. rubber
10. The engine in a car is a(n)
    a. heat engine.
    b. external combustion engine.
    c. internal combustion engine.
    d. Both (a) and (c)
11. Materials that warm up or cool down very quickly have a
    a. low specific heat capacity.
    b. high specific heat capacity.
    c. low temperature.
    d. high temperature.
12. In an air conditioner, thermal energy is
    a. transferred from higher to lower temperatures.
    b. transferred from lower to higher temperatures.
    c. used to do work.
    d. taken from air outside a building and transferred to air inside the building.

Short Answer

13. How does temperature relate to kinetic energy?
14. What is specific heat capacity?
15. Explain how heat affects matter during a change of state.
16. Describe how a bimetallic strip works in a thermostat.

240

15. During a change of state, the thermal energy transferred to or from the matter is used to rearrange the particles of the matter. This rearranging involves overcoming the attraction between particles (as when a solid changes to a liquid) or increasing the attraction between particles (as when a liquid changes to a solid).
16. A bimetallic strip is made of two metals that expand and contract at different rates with changes in temperature. If the temperature drops below the thermostat setting, the strip coils up. This causes a glass tube to tilt, and a drop of mercury rolls down the tube to close an electric circuit that turns on the heater. When the temperature rises, the process is reversed.

Chapter 9 Review–California Standards: PE/ATE Q1-5: 3, 3a, 3c; Q6-17: 3, 3a, 3c, 6a

Concept Mapping

17. Use the following terms to create a concept map: thermal energy, temperature, radiation, heat, conduction, convection.

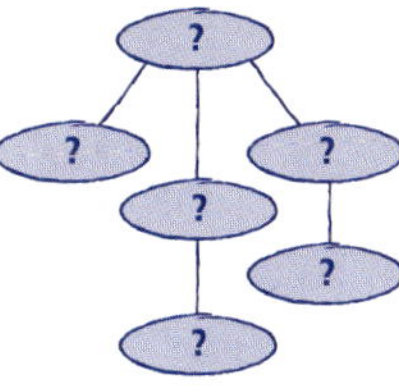

CRITICAL THINKING AND PROBLEM SOLVING

18. Why does placing a jar under warm running water help to loosen the lid on the jar?

19. Why do you think a down-filled jacket keeps you so warm? (Hint: Think about what insulation does.)

20. Would opening the refrigerator cool a room in a house? Why or why not?

21. In a hot-air balloon, air is heated by a flame. Explain how this enables the balloon to float in the air.

MATH IN SCIENCE

22. The weather forecast calls for a temperature of 86°F. What is the corresponding temperature in degrees Celsius? in kelvins?

23. Suppose 1,300 mL of water are heated from 20°C to 100°C. How much energy was transferred to the water? (Hint: Water's specific heat capacity is 4,184 J/kg•°C.)

INTERPRETING GRAPHICS

Examine the graph below, and then answer the questions that follow.

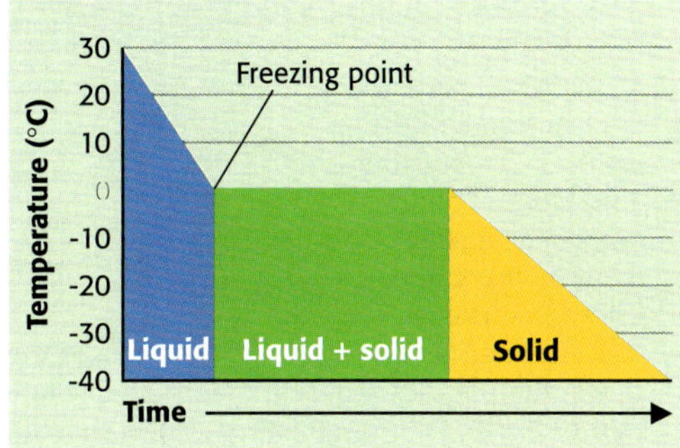

24. What physical change does this graph illustrate?

25. What is the freezing point of this liquid?

26. What is happening at the point where the line is horizontal?

NOW What Do You Think?

Take a minute to review your answers to the ScienceLog questions on page 213. Have your answers changed? If necessary, revise your answers based on what you have learned since you began this chapter.

241

Concept Mapping

17. 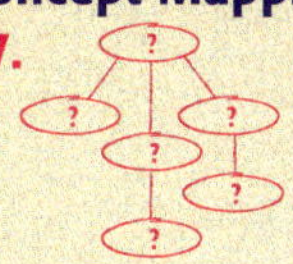 An answer to this exercise can be found at the end of this book.

Critical Thinking and Problem Solving

18. The water warms the lid, causing it to expand so that it can be removed more easily.
19. Inside a down-filled jacket are thousands of air pockets between the feathers. You stay warm because these air pockets slow the transfer of energy from your body to the cooler air outside the jacket.
20. No; a refrigerator transfers energy from its interior into the room. If you open the refrigerator door, its interior warms up, and it has to transfer even more thermal energy away from its interior. This extra thermal energy coming from the back of the refrigerator makes the room warmer.
21. Heating the air increases the kinetic energy of the air particles, causing them to move faster and spread apart. As a result, the warmer air rises, and the balloon floats.

Math in Science

22. 30°C; 303 K
23. Energy transferred = 4,184 J/kg•°C × 1.3 kg × 80°C = 435,136 J

Interpreting Graphics

24. Freezing, a change of state from liquid to a solid
25. 0°C
26. A change of state; energy is being transferred away from the substance and the attraction between particles is increasing.

NOW What Do You Think?

1. Use a thermometer to measure how hot or cold objects are.
2. A given object feels hot or cold depending on how its temperature compares with body temperature. If an object's temperature is higher than body temperature, energy transfers from the object to your body and the object feels hot. If an object's temperature is lower than body body temperature, energy transfers from your body to the object and the object feels cold.
3. Central heating systems, such as hot-water or warm-air heating systems, use a combination of conduction and convection to heat the air in the house.

Concept Mapping Transparency 9

Blackline masters of this Chapter Review can be found in the **Study Guide.**

Science, Technology, and Society
The Deep Freeze

Background

Scientists know that as gases approach absolute zero, they condense into a state of matter called a Bose-Einstein condensate. This state is named for physicists Satyendra Nath Bose and Albert Einstein. At these very low temperatures, almost all particle motion ceases, and the particles overlap one another. In 1999, scientists used a thick Bose-Einstein condensate of sodium atoms to slow the speed of a beam of light to 61 km/h.

Discussion

Why is cryogenics useful to biological researchers? (Scientists can preserve tissues and test the effects of extremely low temperatures on living tissue.)

Science, Technology, and Society

The Deep Freeze

In the dark reaches of outer space, temperatures can drop below −270°C. Perhaps the only place colder is a laboratory here on Earth!

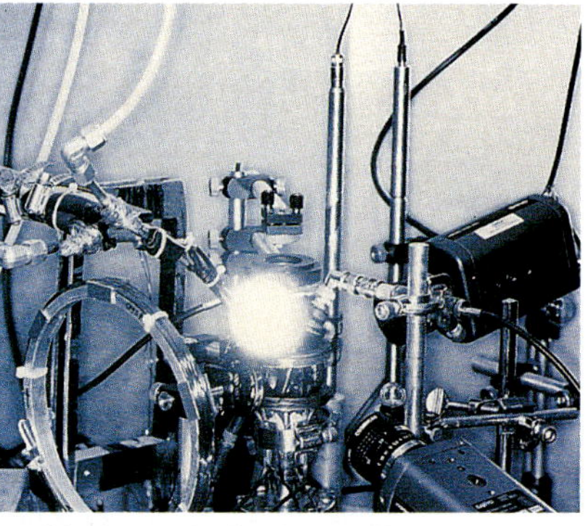

▲ *This laser device is used to cool matter to nearly absolute zero.*

The Quest for Zero

All matter is made up of tiny, constantly vibrating particles. Temperature is a measure of the average kinetic energy of these particles. The colder a substance gets, the less kinetic energy its particles have and the slower the particles move. In theory, at absolute zero (−273°C), all movement of matter should stop. Scientists are working in laboratories to slow down matter so much that the temperature approaches absolute zero.

How Low Can They Go?

Using lasers, along with magnets, mirrors, and supercold chemicals, scientists have cooled matter to within a millionth of a degree of absolute zero. In one method, scientists aim lasers at tiny gas particles inside a special chamber. The lasers hold the particles so still that their temperature approaches −272.999998°C.

To get an idea of what takes place, imagine turning on several garden hoses as high as they can go. Then direct the streams of water at a soccer ball so that each stream pushes the ball from a different angle. If the hoses are aimed properly, the ball won't roll in any direction. That's similar to what happens to the particles in the scientists' experiment.

Cryogenics—Cold Temperature Technology

Supercold temperatures have led to some super-cool technology. Cryosurgery, which is surgery that uses extremely low temperatures, allows doctors to seal off tiny blood vessels during an operation or to freeze diseased cells and destroy them.

Cooling materials to near absolute zero has also led to the discovery of superconductors. Superconductors are materials that lose all of their electrical resistance when they are cooled to a low enough temperature. Imagine the possibilities for materials that could conduct electricity indefinitely without any energy loss. Unfortunately, it takes a great deal of energy to cool such materials. Right now, applications for superconductors are still just the stuff of dreams.

Freezing Fun on Your Own

▶ You can try your hand at cryo-investigation. In three separate plastic containers, place 50 mL of tap water, 50 mL of salt water (50 mL of water plus 15 g salt), and 50 mL of rubbing alcohol (isopropanol). Then put all three containers in your freezer at the same time. Check the containers every 5 minutes for 40 minutes. Which liquid freezes first? How can you explain any differences?

242

Answers to Freezing Fun on Your Own

The tap water should freeze first. The salt water should freeze second. The alcohol should not freeze at all because alcohol's freezing point (−117.3°C) is below the temperature of the freezer. Different liquids freeze at different temperatures. (Remind students not to ingest these substances.)

California Standards: PE/ATE 7, 7b

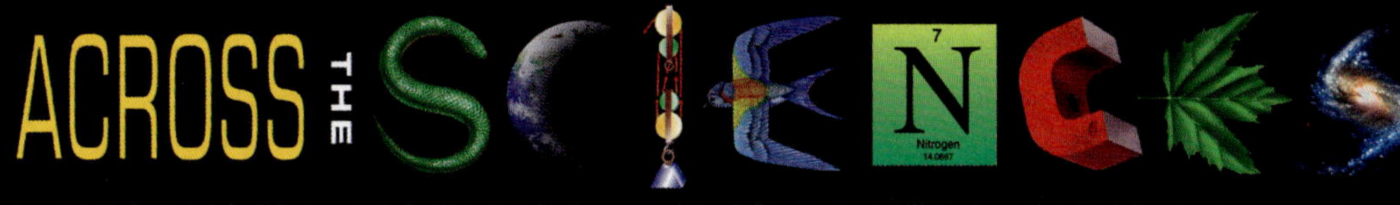

EARTH SCIENCE • PHYSICAL SCIENCE

Diaplex: The Intelligent Fabric

Wouldn't it be great if you had a winter coat that could automatically adjust to keep you cozy regardless of the outside temperature? Well, scientists have developed a new fabric, called Diaplex, that can be used to make such a coat!

With Pores or Without?

Winter adventurers usually wear nylon fabrics to keep warm. These nylon fabrics are laminated with a thin coating that contains thousands of tiny pores, or openings. The pores allow moisture, such as sweat from your body, and excess thermal energy to escape. You might think the pores would let moisture and cold air into the fabric, but that's not the case. Because the pores are so small, the nylon fabric is windproof and waterproof.

Diaplex is also made from laminated nylon, but the coating is different. Diaplex doesn't have pores; it is a solid film. This film makes Diaplex even more waterproof and breathable than other laminated nylon fabrics. So how does it work?

Moving Particles

Diaplex keeps you warm by taking advantage of how particles move. When the air outside is cold, the particles of Diaplex arrange themselves into a solid sheet, forming an insulator and preventing the transfer of thermal energy from your body to colder surroundings. As your body gets warm, such as after exercising, the fabric's particles respond to your body's increased thermal energy. Their kinetic energy increases, and they rearrange to create millions of tiny openings that allow excess thermal energy and moisture to escape.

Donning Diaplex

Diaplex has a number of important advantages over traditional nylon fabrics. Salts in perspiration and ice can clog the pores of traditional nylon fabrics, decreasing their ability to keep you warm and dry. But Diaplex does not have this problem because it contains no pores. Since Diaplex is unaffected by UV light and is machine washable, it is also a durable fabric that is easy to care for.

Anatomy Connection

▶ Do some research to find out how your skin lets thermal energy and moisture escape.

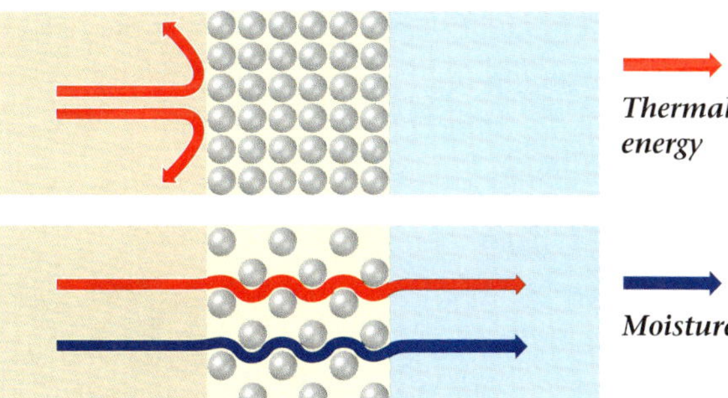

▶ *When your body is cold, the Diaplex garment adjusts to prevent the transfer of thermal energy from your body to its surroundings, and you feel warmer.*

▶ *When your body gets too warm, the Diaplex garment adjusts to allow your body to transfer excess thermal energy and moisture to your surroundings, and you feel cooler.*

243

Answer to Anatomy Connection

Sweat is one way our bodies remove excess thermal energy. Our skin contains about 100 sweat glands per square centimeter. The evaporation of sweat from the skin's surface removes heat from the body much more efficiently than simply radiating heat from the blood into the air. Without sweat, we would have great difficulty cooling our bodies on a hot day or after exercising. Most sweat is about 99 percent water, mixed with small amounts of salts, acids, and waste products.

Across the Sciences
Diaplex

Background

Diaplex™ fabric allows moisture to escape twice as fast as regular microporous fabrics, and it maintains a constant internal temperature of 0°C. This may sound cold, but at temperatures above 0°C, skiers begin to leave their microporous jackets on the slopes. The jackets don't allow enough body heat to escape, and the skiers start to sweat. People who wear Diaplex garments, however, remove layers of clothing far less frequently.

Diaplex works on the principles of micro-Brownian motion, the random, zigzag motion of particles in solution. This phenomenon was first observed by the British botanist Robert Brown in 1827.

Students may find Diaplex intriguing because the molecules of this solid fabric are capable of moving and reconfiguring, properties usually believed to occur only in liquids and gases. As the temperature rises, the molecules of Diaplex become more excited and move more rapidly. Although Diaplex is a solid fabric, the temperature range over which its molecules are active is conveniently the temperature range where we change our clothes the most often.

TIMELINE

UNIT

4

Reshaping the Land

In this unit, you will learn about the way the surface of the Earth changes. There is a constant struggle between the forces that build up Earth's land features and those that break them down. The mountains built by Earth's internal forces are torn down by the actions of weathering and erosion. This timeline shows some of the events that have occurred in this struggle as natural changes in the Earth's features continue to take place.

320 Million years ago

Vast swamps along the western edge of the Appalachian Mountains are buried by sediment and form the largest coal fields in the world.

280 Million years ago

The shallow inland sea that covered much of what is now the midwestern United States fills with sediment and disappears.

1880

Cleopatra's Needle, a granite obelisk, is moved from Egypt to New York City. Within the next 100 years, the weather and pollution severely damage the 3,000-year-old monument.

1930

Carlsbad Caverns National Park is established. It features the nation's deepest limestone cave and one of the largest underground chambers in the world.

1941

Mount Rushmore is completed—an example of purposeful human erosion.

140 Million years ago

The mouth of the Mississippi River is near present-day Cairo, Illinois.

65 Million years ago

Dinosaurs become extinct.

6 Million years ago

The Colorado River begins to carve the Grand Canyon, which today is roughly 2 km deep.

12,000 Years ago

The Great Lakes form at the end of the last ice age.

1775

The Battle of Bunker Hill, a victory for the Colonials, takes place on a drumlin, a tear-shaped mound of sediment that was formed by an ice-age glacier 10,000 years earlier.

1987

An iceberg twice the size of Rhode Island breaks off the edge of Antarctica's continental glacier.

1998

Hong Kong opens a new airport on an artificial island. Almost 150 million metric tons of rock and soil were deposited in the South China Sea to form the 3,000-acre island.

Chapter Organizer

CHAPTER ORGANIZATION	TIME MINUTES	OBJECTIVES	LABS, INVESTIGATIONS, AND DEMONSTRATIONS
Chapter Opener **pp. 246–247**	45	California Standards: PE/ATE 2, 2a, 2b, 7, 7b, 7e	**Investigate!** Gently Down the Stream, p. 247
Section 1 **The Active River**	90	▶ Illustrate the water cycle. ▶ Describe a drainage basin. ▶ Explain the major factors that affect the rate of stream erosion. ▶ Identify the stages of river development. PE/ATE 2, 2a, 2b, 4a; LabBook 4, 7, 7b, 7e	**Demonstration,** p. 249 in ATE **Making Models,** Water Cycle—What Goes Up . . . , p. 524 **Datasheets for LabBook,** Water Cycle—What Goes Up . . . , Datasheet 21
Section 2 **Stream and River Deposits**	90	▶ Describe the different types of stream deposits. ▶ Explain the relationship between rich agricultural regions and river flood plains. PE/ATE 2, 2a–2c	**Demonstration,** Modeling Deposition, p. 255 in ATE
Section 3 **Water Underground**	90	▶ Identify and describe the location of a water table. ▶ Describe the characteristics of an aquifer. ▶ Explain how caves and karst topography form as a result of erosion and deposition. PE/ATE 2, 6, 6a, 6b, 7	**Demonstration,** p. 258 in ATE **QuickLab,** Degree of Permeability, p. 259
Section 4 **Using Water Wisely**	90	▶ Describe the stages of treatment for water at a sewage treatment plant. ▶ Compare a septic system with a sewage treatment plant. ▶ Explain how ground water can be both a renewable and nonrenewable resource. PE/ATE 2, 2b, 2c, 5e, 6, 6b; LabBook 7, 7a, 7b, 7d, 7e	**Interactive Explorations CD-ROM,** Flood Bank *A* ***Worksheet*** *is also available in the* ***Interactive Explorations Teacher's Edition.*** **Discovery Lab,** Clean Up Your Act, p. 526 **Datasheets for LabBook,** Clean Up Your Act, Datasheet 22 **EcoLabs & Field Activities,** The Frogs Are Off Course, Field Activity 12 **Long-Term Projects & Research Ideas,** Project 39

See page **T20** *for a complete correlation of this book with the*

CALIFORNIA SCIENCE CONTENT STANDARDS.

Correlations are also provided at point of use throughout this ATE.

TECHNOLOGY RESOURCES

Guided Reading Audio CD
English or Spanish, Chapter 10

Classroom Management CD-ROM

Test Generator CD-ROM

Interactive Explorations CD-ROM
CD 1, Exploration 8, Flood Bank

Earth Science Videodisc
Water and Erosion: 46567–48921

CNN **Science, Technology & Society,**
Tapping into Yellowstone's Hot Springs, Segment 1

Eye on the Environment, Watch for Flooding, Segment 9
China's Superdam, Segment 10

Science Discovery Videodiscs
Image and Activity Bank with Lesson Plans: Dirty Water
Science Sleuths: The Missing Beach

Chapter 10 • The Flow of Fresh Water

CLASSROOM WORKSHEETS, TRANSPARENCIES, AND RESOURCES	SCIENCE INTEGRATION AND CONNECTIONS	REVIEW AND ASSESSMENT
Directed Reading Worksheet 10 **Science Puzzlers, Twisters & Teasers,** Worksheet 10		
Math Skills for Science Worksheet 6, Checking Division with Multiplication **Transparency 122,** The Water Cycle **Directed Reading Worksheet 10,** Section 1 **Transparency 68,** River Features	**Real-World Connection,** p. 250 in ATE **MathBreak,** Calculating a Stream's Gradient p. 251 **Connect to Physical Science,** p. 251 in ATE **Cross-Disciplinary Focus,** p. 253 in ATE	**Self-Check,** p. 252 **Homework,** p. 252 in ATE **Review,** p. 254 **Quiz,** p. 254 in ATE **Alternative Assessment,** p. 254 in ATE
Directed Reading Worksheet 10, Section 2 **Reinforcement Worksheet 10,** Fresh Water in the United States	**Astronomy Connection,** p. 256	**Self-Check,** p. 256 **Homework,** p. 256 in ATE **Review,** p. 257 **Quiz,** p. 257 in ATE **Alternative Assessment,** p. 257 in ATE
Transparency 123, The Water Table **Directed Reading Worksheet 10,** Section 3 **Transparency 124,** Artesian Formation **Transparency 124,** The Water Table and Wells **Reinforcement Worksheet 10,** Dig It! **Problem Solving Worksheet 10,** Water Crisis at Happy Acres	**Multicultural Connection,** p. 258 in ATE **Real-World Connection,** p. 259 in ATE **Connect to Life Science,** p. 260 in ATE **Environmental Science Connection,** p. 261 **Weird Science:** Bubble, Boil, & Squirt, p. 272	**Self-Check,** p. 260 **Review,** p. 262 **Quiz,** p. 262 in ATE **Alternative Assessment,** p. 262 in ATE
Directed Reading Worksheet 10, Section 4 **Math Skills for Science Worksheet 3,** Multiplying Whole Numbers	**Multicultural Connection,** p. 264 in ATE **Math and More,** p. 265 in ATE **Apply,** p. 266 **Eye on the Environment:** Disaster Along the Delta, p. 273	**Homework,** p. 264 in ATE **Review,** p. 267 **Quiz,** p. 267 in ATE **Alternative Assessment,** p. 267 in ATE

END-OF-CHAPTER REVIEW AND ASSESSMENT

Chapter Review in Study Guide
Vocabulary and Notes in Study Guide
Chapter Tests with Performance-Based Assessment, Chapter 10 Test
Chapter Tests with Performance-Based Assessment, Performance-Based Assessment 10
Concept Mapping Transparency 10

internetconnect

Holt, Rinehart and Winston On-line Resources

go.hrw.com

For worksheets and other teaching aids related to this chapter, visit the HRW Web site and type in the keyword: **HSTDEP**

National Science Teachers Association

www.scilinks.org

Encourage students to use the keywords listed on the Technology Highlights page to access information and resources on the NSTA Web site.

Chapter Resources & Worksheets

Visual Resources

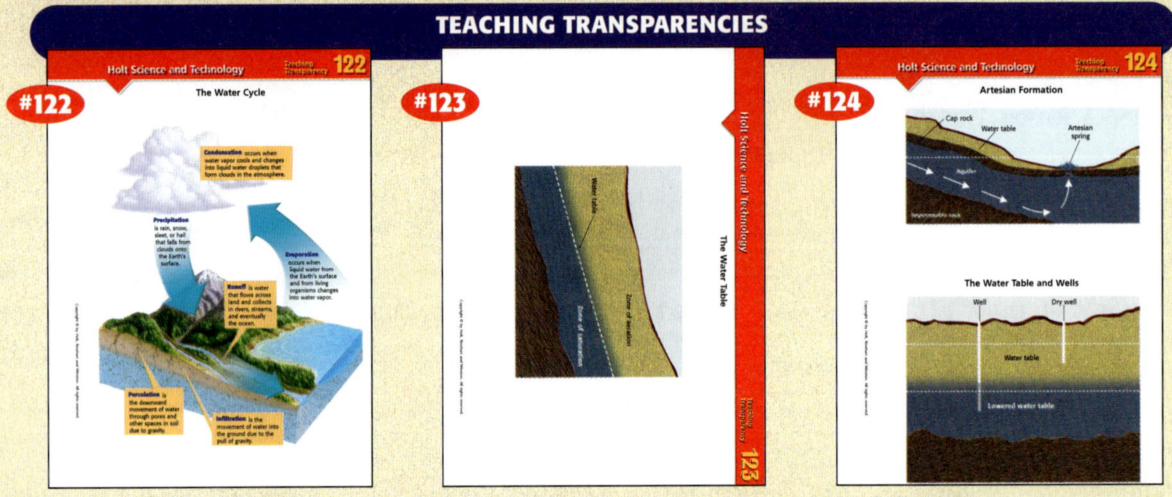

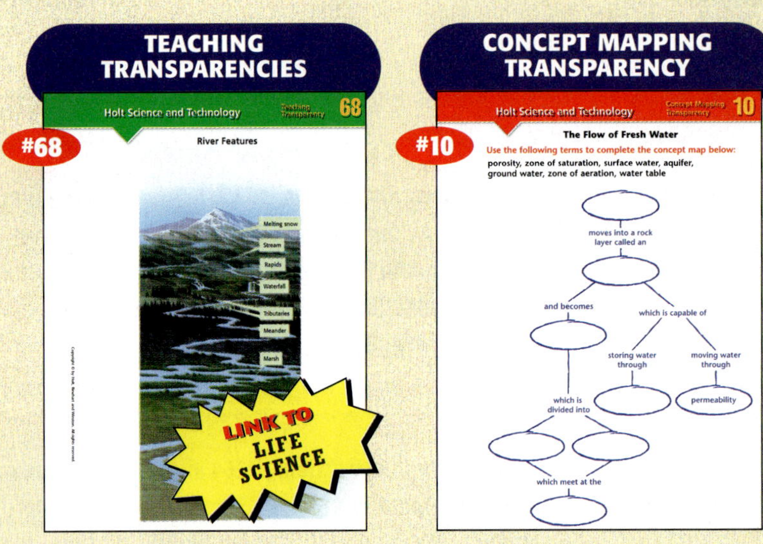

Meeting Individual Needs

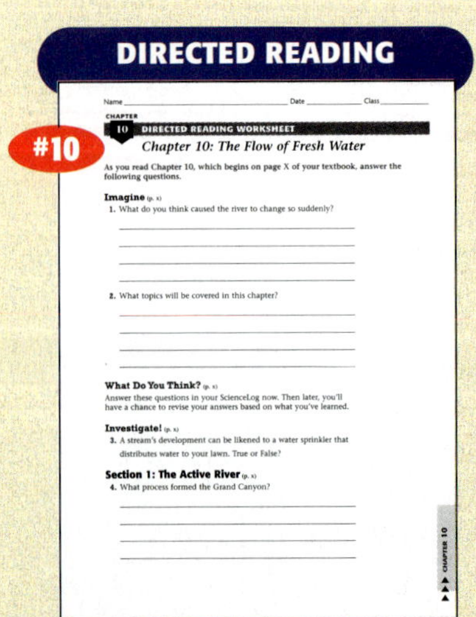

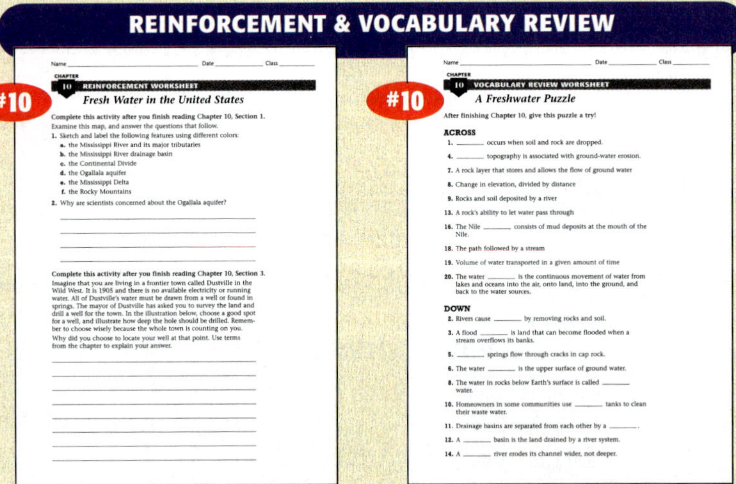

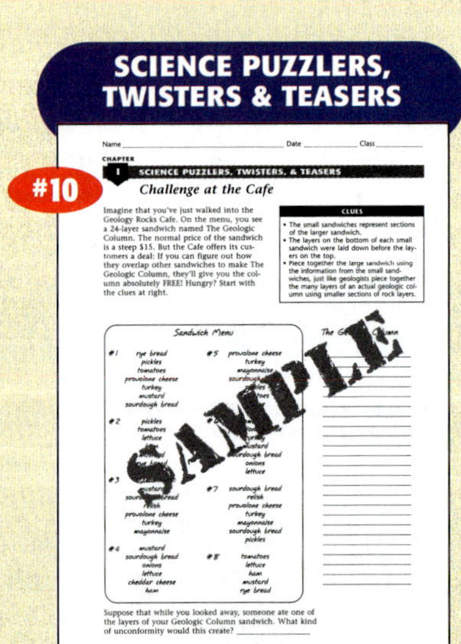

Chapter 10 • The Flow of Fresh Water

Review & Assessment

STUDY GUIDE

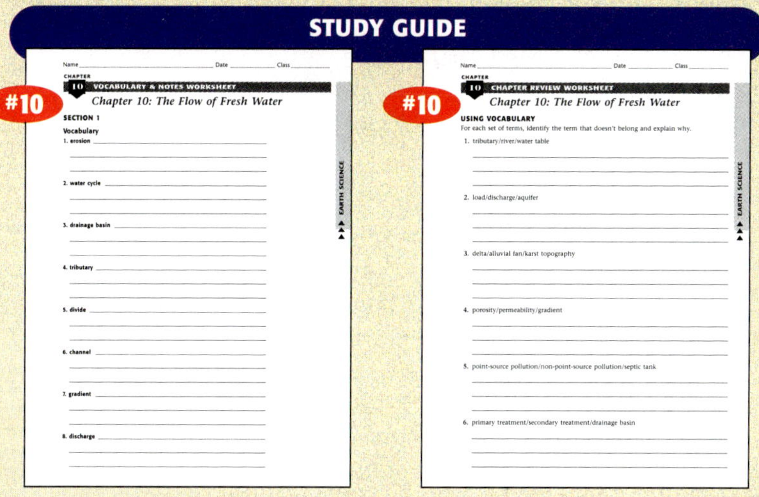

CHAPTER TESTS WITH PERFORMANCE-BASED ASSESSMENT

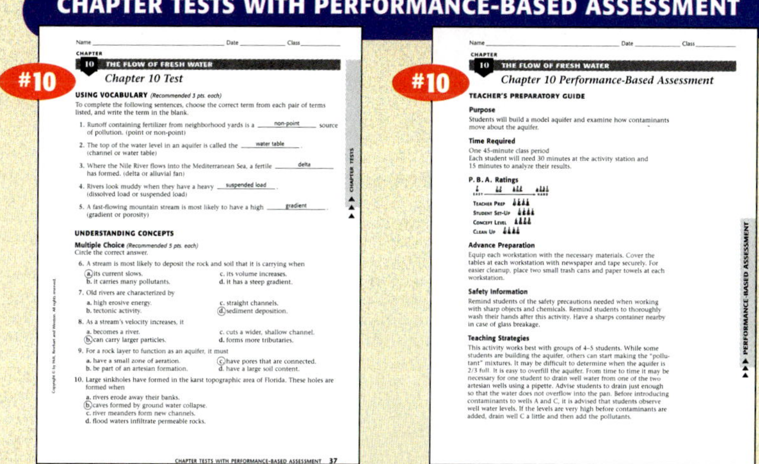

Lab Worksheets

ECOLABS & FIELD ACTIVITIES

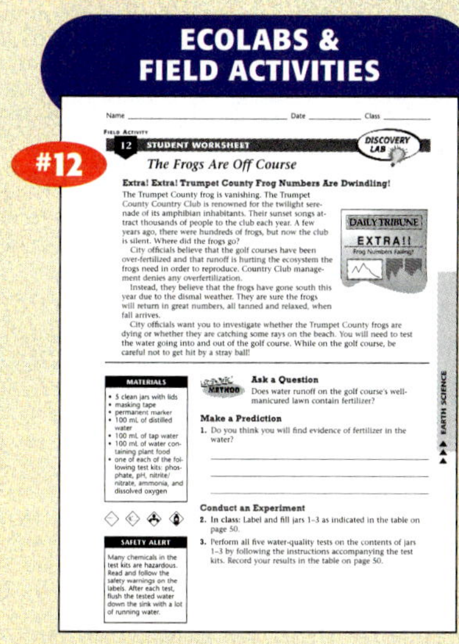

LONG-TERM PROJECTS & RESEARCH IDEAS

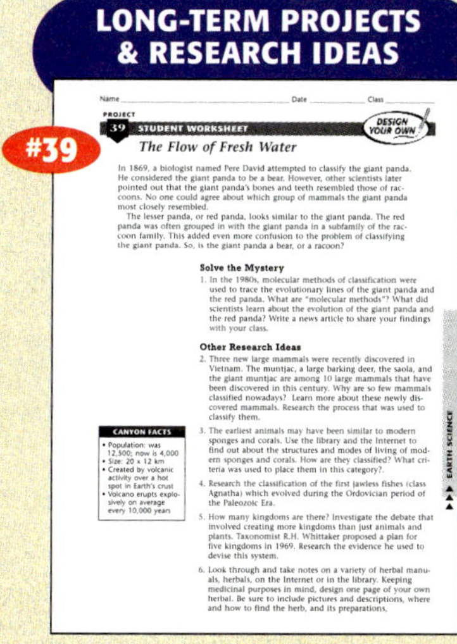

DATASHEETS FOR LABBOOK

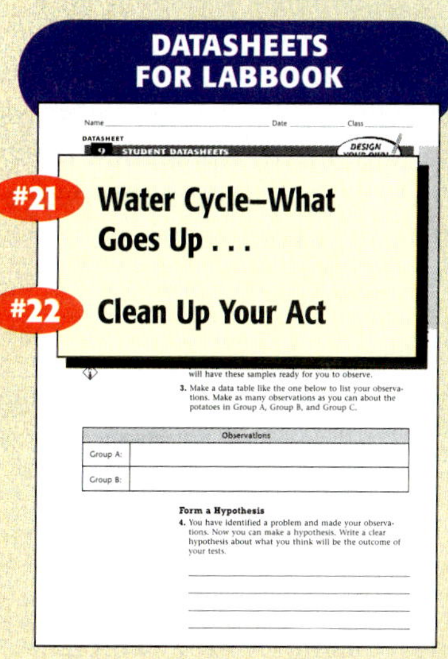

Applications & Extensions

CRITICAL THINKING & PROBLEM SOLVING

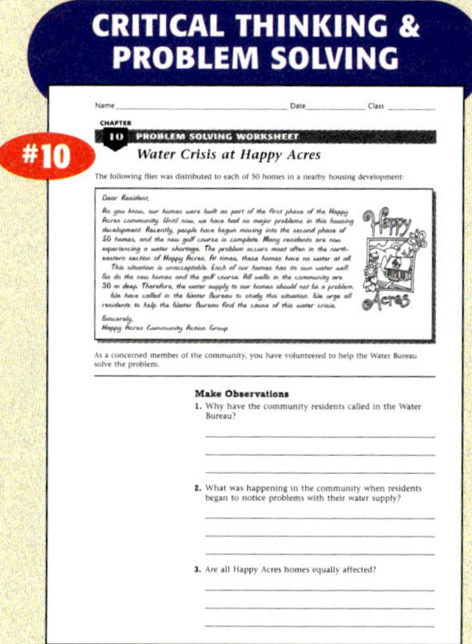

SCIENCE TECHNOLOGY

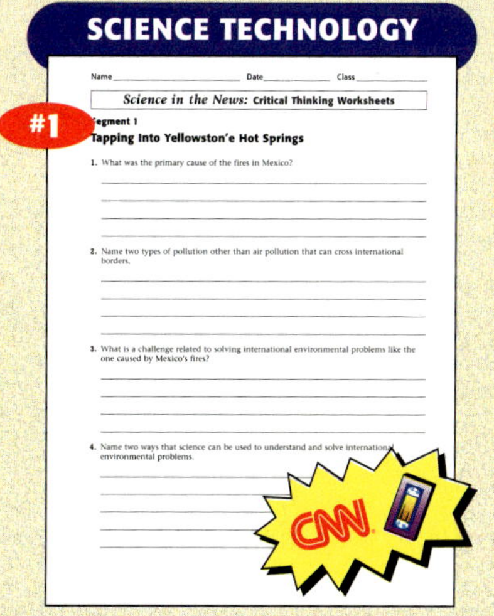

EYE ON THE ENVIRONMENT

#9 #10

Science in the News: Critical Thinking Worksheets

Segment 9

Watch for Flooding

INTERACTIVE EXPLORATIONS

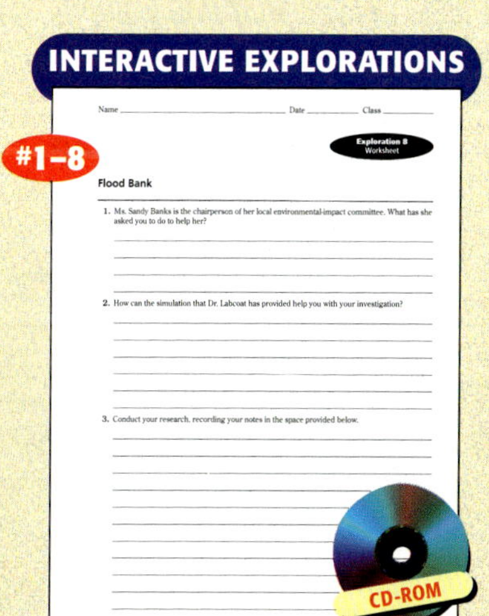

Chapter Background

Section 1

The Active River

▶ William Morris Davis

William Morris Davis (1850–1934) was a famous American geographer who was the first to propose the erosion cycle. Davis theorized that landscapes are initially uplifted. Streams flow rapidly from the uplifted land, cutting into the landscape. Gradually, the landscape's slope is reduced. Eventually, the landscape changes into an old erosional surface that is fairly flat. Davis's theory is not supported by academics today, however. The process of river erosion is approached today from a systems perspective. Each system is composed of different parts that vary from landscape to landscape.

▶ Stream Flow

Streams have two general types of flow—laminar and turbulent. Laminar flow occurs when the stream load moves in a generally parallel flow. This occurs where the water moves slowly and the channel is smooth. Streams with a greater velocity experience turbulent flow. The stream load generally is rolled, lifted, and bounced along, causing much more erosion in the stream channel.

Is That a Fact!

- Geologists have learned that about 300 million years ago, massive rivers may have run down the Appalachian Mountains through river valleys 32 km wide! These rivers drained much of the continent, emptying into the ocean at today's Alabama-Mississippi coastline.

Section 2

Stream and River Deposits

▶ Drainage Patterns

A drainage pattern is the arrangement of river channels in a drainage basin. A drainage pattern is determined by an area's geology and climate. One of the most common patterns, called *dendritic,* is a treelike pattern that forms where rocks and sediments are flat. A *parallel* pattern occurs where there are steep slopes. And a *radial* pattern results when streams flow from a central peak, such as a volcanic mountain.

▶ Deltas

The word *delta* was first used by the Greek historian Herodotus to describe the mouth of a river. In the fifth century B.C., Herodotus was traveling in Egypt when he saw the triangular mouth of the Nile River and named the shape after the Greek letter Δ, delta.

▶ Paleoecology at Work

Paleoecologists study the rock and fossil record to understand what ancient environments were like. For example, paleoecologists learned that a great inland sea once covered the Plains states by studying thick layers of sedimentary rock in the area, such as sandstone, shale, and chalk. Such rocks form only when sediments accumulate in calm waters.

Is That a Fact!

- Over the last 6,000 years, the Mississippi River delta has shifted from east to west several times. Today the river empties to the east, but scientists think that if left alone the river would change its course and head toward a swampy region called the Atchafalaya. Only massive dams keep the Mississippi on its present course. If the river channel changes, the river may no longer pass through New Orleans.

Section 3

Water Underground

▶ Caves as Shelters

The flow of fresh water underground created caves that were just as important to the development of human civilizations as fertile flood plains. Humans have used caves as shelters for hundreds of thousands of years. Evidence suggests that use of caves for shelter coincides with the first controlled use of fire. Hearths that may be 750,000 years old have been found in the cave of l'Escale, in southeastern France.

- In China, excavations in a cave called Chou-k'ou-tien have yielded 400,000-year-old fossilized remains of *Homo erectus.* Evidence of charred animal bones suggests that the inhabitants may have cooked their food.

IS THAT A FACT!

- The largest cave chamber in the world is the Sarawak chamber, in Malaysia. The chamber is 600 m long and has an average width of 450 m.

Section 4

Using Water Wisely

▶ Aquifers

There are two types of aquifers. The first occurs in *consolidated formations,* those formed from solid rock overlaid with permeable rock that is saturated with water. The second kind of aquifer forms in *unconsolidated formations*—loose sand, soil, and gravel. The amount of water contained in an unconsolidated aquifer depends on how tightly the materials are packed. Because of this, sand and gravel, which are coarse-grained, are usually high-yield aquifers, while formations composed of finer-grained soil tend to hold less water.

▶ Acequias in New Mexico

New Mexico gets only an average of 32.5 cm of rain per year, so water conservation is critical. Because wide irrigation ditches lose a great deal of water to evaporation, New Mexicans have relied for centuries on shallow earthen ditches fed by local rivers to supply growing plants with water. Each ditch, called an *acequia,* provides water to a small area. Acequias allow for water to seep into the ground, minimizing evaporation and allowing water to reach plant roots. Water that isn't absorbed by the soil returns to the river, providing water to people downstream to irrigate their fields.

IS THAT A FACT!

- When ground water is depleted so quickly that the system cannot recharge, there can be dramatic consequences. At Edwards Air Force Base, in California, the aquifer has shrunk so quickly that ground settling has led to sinks and fissures. One of the fissures is about 625 m long!
- A comprehensive 1998 study conducted by the Nature Conservancy warns that continued pollution of the nation's 2,100 rivers and streams threatens approximately 40 percent of fresh-water fish species and two-thirds of mussel species with extinction. In addition, the degradation of our fresh-water sources poses a threat to human health and harms the country's $16 billion sport-fishing industry.

For additional background resources, please refer to the ***HST Reference Library.***

CHAPTER 10

The Flow of Fresh Water

Chapter Preview

Section 1
The Active River
- River Systems
- Stream Erosion
- The Stages of a River

Section 2
Stream and River Deposits
- Deposition in Water
- Deposition on Land

Section 3
Water Underground
- Location of Ground Water
- Aquifers
- Springs and Wells
- Underground Erosion and Deposition

Section 4
Using Water Wisely
- Water Pollution
- Renewing Polluted Water
- Where the Water Goes

Directed Reading Worksheet 10

Science Puzzlers, Twisters & Teasers Worksheet 10

Guided Reading Audio CD English or Spanish, Chapter 10

Imagine...

Picture yourself canoeing down a gentle stream on a beautiful sunny afternoon. You can see the gravelly stream bottom through the crystal blue water.

All of a sudden, the silence is broken by the sound of rushing water. You notice that the current has picked up and the water is moving much faster. In the distance you see some large boulders and a waterfall. Unexpectedly, the canoe hits a rock and nearly topples over. You are safe, but your gear is now on a journey of its own. Rather than brave the rapids, you pull your canoe onto shore. You turn around just in time to see your cooler crash against the rocks and tumble over the falls. You think to yourself, "I didn't want tuna for lunch anyway!"

Tired, you walk downstream along the shore, the sound of the rushing falls growing fainter with each step. The stream begins to widen and slow again. Suddenly, you see your cooler washed up on a gravel bar. You run toward it, hoping the canned meat survived. Although badly scraped and empty, the cooler is still usable.

You put your cooler into your canoe and continue your journey downstream, only to again hear the sound of rushing water.

What forces of nature could cause the stream to change so drastically? In this chapter you will learn about river and stream development. You will also learn about how surface water and underground water change the face of our planet.

246

Imagine . . .

Experts have devised an international scale for rating the difficulty of traveling down a river. A river's rapids are rated in an ascending level of difficulty from 1 to 6. The rating is based on factors such as speed, turbulence, hazards, and length. Class 4 rapids may have large waves or holes that cannot be avoided or tight passages that demand fast maneuvers. Class 5 rapids are extremely long, obstructed, or very turbulent and may contain steep chutes with complex routes. Class 5 rapids are so challenging that a rescue mission is considered difficult for expert canoers. Imagine what Class 6 rapids are like!

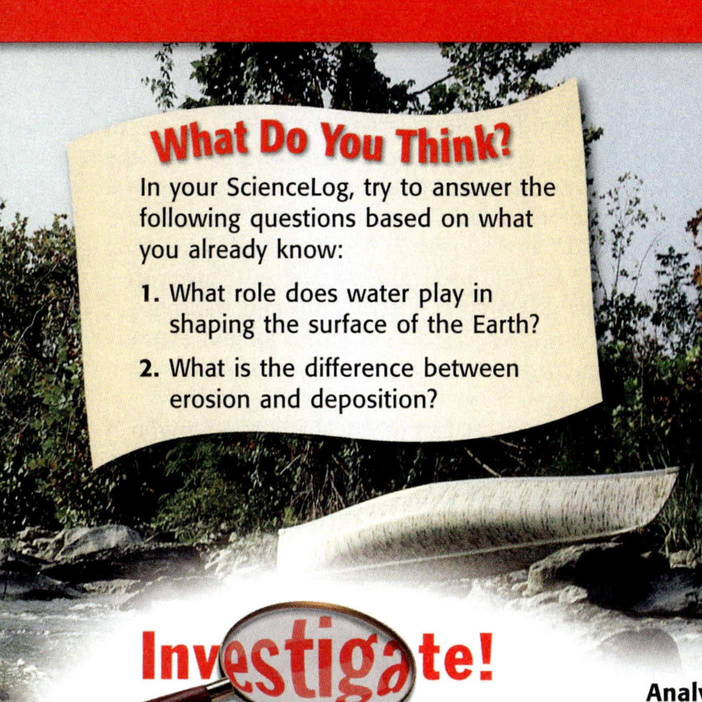

What Do You Think?

In your ScienceLog, try to answer the following questions based on what you already know:

1. What role does water play in shaping the surface of the Earth?
2. What is the difference between erosion and deposition?

Investigate!

Gently Down the Stream

How do streams and river systems develop? Believe it or not, the process is almost as simple as turning on a garden hose and letting the water run on the ground. How is this possible? Do the following investigation to find out.

Procedure

1. Obtain a bucket of **sand** and enough **gravel** to fill the bottom of a rectangular **plastic washtub.**
2. Spread the gravel in a layer at the bottom of the washtub. Place 4–6 cm of sand on top of the gravel. Create a slope by adding more sand to one end of the washtub.
3. Make a small hole in the bottom of a **plastic-foam cup.** Attach the cup to the inside of the tub with a **clothespin.** The cup should be placed at the end that has more sand. Fill the cup with **water,** and observe the water's movement over the sand.
4. Record your observations in your ScienceLog.

Analysis

5. At the start of your experiment, how did the moving water affect the sand?
6. As time passed, how did the moving water affect the sand?
7. How do you think your results might relate to stream development?

Going Further

Perform the same activity, but this time increase the slope of the washtub by tilting one end of the tub. You can do this by placing an ordinary object, such as a block of wood, under one end of the washtub. How does the increase in slope affect the development of the "stream"?

247

What Do You Think?

Accept all reasonable responses.

Students will have a chance to revise their answers in the Chapter Review under NOW What Do You Think?

Investigate!

MATERIALS

For Each Group:

- bucket of sand
- gravel
- rectangular plastic washtub
- plastic-foam cup
- clothespin
- water

Answer to Investigate!

5. The moving water cuts into the sand, forming a groove.
6. As time passes, the moving water cuts deeper into the sand, creating a deeper and wider groove.
7. Accept all reasonable responses. Sample answer: Runoff (water) moves over the land, cutting a gully into the dirt. At first the gully is shallow and narrow, but over time the gully widens and becomes deeper. If there is enough water, the gully eventually becomes a river.

Answer to Going Further

By increasing the slope, students should observe that the water runs faster, creating a deeper groove in a shorter period of time.

Chapter 10 Opener—California Standards: PE/ATE 2, 2a, 2b, 7, 7b, 7e

Section 1

Focus

The Active River

This section introduces the water cycle and discusses the role that rivers play in the movement of fresh water. Students will learn that rivers are changing, dynamic systems that continually shape the land. The section discusses the factors that contribute to rates of stream erosion and concludes with a discussion of the life cycle of rivers.

Bellringer

Have students write a paragraph about an imaginary canoe trip down a river. They could choose the river described in the chapter opener or another river of their choice. Ask students to describe the river's features and hypothesize how those features formed. Sheltered English

1 Motivate

Activity

Discuss the photograph of the Grand Canyon shown in **Figure 1.** Help students compare the size of the canyon with the size of the Empire State Building, which is 381 m tall. Ask students to calculate how many Empire State Buildings it would take to create a stack as deep as the Grand Canyon. (1.6 km deep = 1,600 m; 1,600 ÷ 381 = 4.2)

The Grand Canyon is 29 km wide at its widest point. How many Empire State Buildings laid end-to-end would fit in the canyon's widest point? (29 km = 29,000 m; 29,000 ÷ 381 = 76)

1

The Active River

NEW TERMS

erosion
water cycle
drainage basin
tributary
divide
channel
gradient
discharge
load

OBJECTIVES

- Illustrate the water cycle.
- Describe a drainage basin.
- Explain the major factors that affect the rate of stream erosion.
- Identify the stages of river development.

You are probably familiar with the Grand Canyon, shown in **Figure 1.** But did you know that about 6 million years ago, the area now known as the Grand Canyon was nearly as flat as a pancake? The Colorado River cut down into the rock and formed the Grand Canyon over millions of years by washing billions of tons of soil and rock from its riverbed. This process is a type of *erosion*. **Erosion** is the removal and transport of surface material, such as rock and soil. Rivers are not the only agents of erosion. Wind, rain, ice, and snow can cause erosion as well.

Because of erosion caused by water, the Grand Canyon is now about 1.6 km deep, 3.2 km wide, and 446 km long. In this section, you will learn about stream development, river systems, and the different factors that affect the rate of stream erosion.

Figure 1 *The Grand Canyon is located in northwestern Arizona. It formed over millions of years as running water eroded rock and soil. In some places the canyon is 29 km wide.*

Have you ever wondered how rivers keep flowing and where rivers get their water? The water cycle answers these and other questions. The **water cycle,** shown on the next page, is the continuous movement of water from water sources, such as lakes or oceans, into the air, onto land, into the ground, and back to the water sources. Running-water sources, such as rivers, depend on the water cycle to maintain a constant flow of water.

248

internetconnect

TOPIC: The Grand Canyon
GO TO: www.scilinks.org
*sci*LINKS NUMBER: HSTE255

TOPIC: Rivers and Streams
GO TO: www.scilinks.org
*sci*LINKS NUMBER: HSTE260

Math Skills Worksheet 6 "Checking Division with Multiplication"

Section 1—California Standards: PE/ATE 2, 2a, 2b, 4a; LabBook: 4, 7, 7b, 7e

The Water Cycle

249

2 Teach

 PG 524

Water Cycle—What Goes Up . . .

DEMONSTRATION

Add a teaspoon of brightly colored tempera paint to about half a cup of soil. Place the soil in a funnel lined with filter paper, and place the funnel over a large jar. Tell students that the tempera paint represents nutrients in the soil. Ask students to predict what will happen to the nutrients in the soil when it rains. Demonstrate by slowly pouring water into the funnel. Discuss the important role that rivers play in distributing soil nutrients.

MEETING INDIVIDUAL NEEDS

Learners Having Difficulty

Have students make a scrapbook about rivers. Suggest that they include photographs of streams and rivers and write captions to describe each photo. The captions should incorporate terms such as *gradient, erosion, load, channel,* and *meanders*. Finally, have them hypothesize about the river's speed, load, and erosional capacity. Sheltered English

Teaching Transparency 122 "The Water Cycle"

Directed Reading Worksheet 10 Section 1

IS THAT A FACT!

Under average conditions, the Mississippi River carries about 17,000 m^3 of water every second. A small carry-on suitcase is about .03 m^3, so watching the river go by on an average day is equivalent to watching about 566,666 suitcases pass by you every second!

MISCONCEPTION ALERT

Be sure students realize that water can evaporate from the soil and vegetation as well as from rivers and other bodies of water.

2 Teach, *continued*

Answers to Explore

Tributaries: Musselshell, Yellowstone, Badlands, Heart, Grand, Moreau, Cheyenne, White, Niobrara, Elkhorn, Loup, Platte, Kansas, Ohio, Arkansas, Red

Cities: Bismarck, Omaha, Kansas City, Saint Louis, Memphis, Baton Rouge, New Orleans

Distance: approximately 3,900 km

Hint: Measure the distance with a string, then find the actual distance traveled by using the map's scale.

REAL-WORLD CONNECTION

Meteorologists recognize the power of moving water, and they issue special warnings when there is a danger of floods. Ask students to guess how much moving water it takes to knock an adult off his or her feet: 15 cm, 30 cm, or 1 m. (15 cm)

Ask them how deep the water would have to be to sweep away a car: more than 2 m, at least 1.5 m, or less than 1 m. (less than 1 m)

Demonstrate these water depths using a meterstick, and caution students to be careful around flowing water.

Explore

Imagine that you are planning a rafting trip down the Missouri River to the Mississippi River. On a map of the United States, trace the route of your trip from the Rocky Mountains in Montana to the mouth of the Mississippi River, in Louisiana. What major tributaries would you travel past? What cities would you pass through? Mark them on the map. How many kilometers would you travel on this trip?

River Systems

A river system is a network of streams that drains an area of its runoff. River systems begin to form when an area's precipitation is greater than its evaporation and infiltration. After the ground has soaked up all the water it can hold, the remaining water moves downslope as runoff. Sometimes runoff moving across the land will start to erode a narrow gully. With each passing rain, the water moving through the gully will make the gully wider and deeper.

River systems are divided into regions known as drainage basins, or watersheds. A **drainage basin** is the land drained by a river system, which includes the main river and all of its tributaries. **Tributaries** are smaller streams or rivers that flow into larger ones. The largest drainage basin in the United States is the Mississippi River basin. It has hundreds of tributaries that extend from the Rocky Mountains, in the West, to the Appalachian Mountains, in the East. The Ohio and Missouri Rivers are just two of the main tributaries of the Mississippi River.

A drainage basin is not simply water moving downhill in streams; it is also a system of moving energy and materials. The map in **Figure 2** shows that the Mississippi River drainage basin covers more than one-third of the United States. Other major drainage basins in the United States are the Columbia, Rio Grande, and Colorado River basins.

Drainage basins are separated from each other by an area called a **divide.** A divide is generally an area of higher ground than the basins it separates. On the map below, you can see that the Continental Divide is a major divide in the United States. On which side do you live?

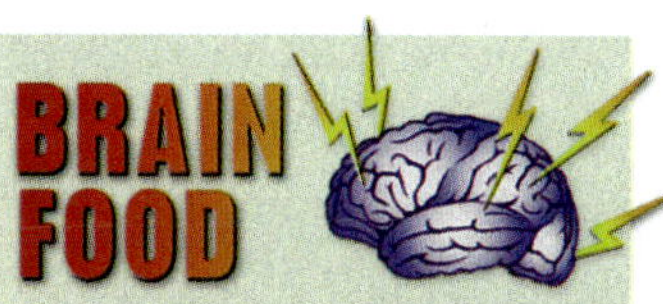

The Amazon River basin, in South America, is the world's largest drainage basin. It has an area of about 6 million square kilometers. That's almost twice as big as the United States' largest drainage basin, the Mississippi River basin!

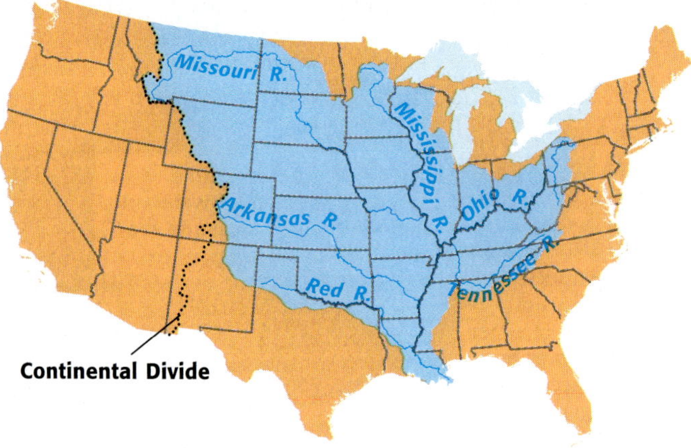

Figure 2 *The Continental Divide runs through the Rocky Mountains. It separates the drainage basins that flow into the Atlantic Ocean and the Gulf of Mexico from those that flow into the Pacific Ocean.*

250

Science Bloopers

In 1935, a dam was constructed in California to prevent sediment from filling Gibraltar Reservoir. This dam created Mono Reservoir. The watershed above Mono Reservoir was burned by forest fires, and people worried that sediment would fill Gibraltar Reservoir before plants had a chance to regrow and hold the soil. Unfortunately, the next 2 years saw record rainfall. Sediment completely filled Mono Reservoir and half-filled Gibraltar Reservoir.

Stream Erosion

When a stream first forms, the water cuts downward, eroding soil and rock to create a channel. A **channel** is the path that a stream follows. At first, stream channels are small and steep. As more rock and soil are transported downstream, the channels become wider and deeper, forming broad valleys. When streams become longer, they are referred to as rivers. Have you ever wondered why some streams are fast, while others are slow? In this section, you will find answers to this and other questions.

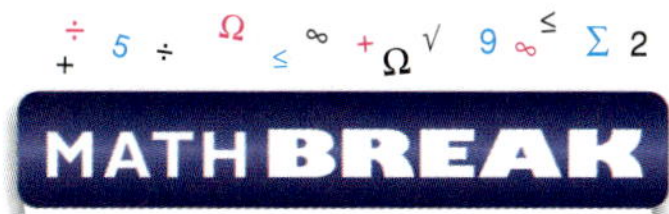

MATHBREAK

Calculating a Stream's Gradient

If a river starts at an elevation of 4,900 m and travels 450 km downstream to a lake that is at an elevation of 400 m, what is the stream's gradient?

Rates of Stream Erosion The rate of stream erosion is determined by various factors, including the stream's speed, discharge, and load. One factor that can affect the speed of a river is its gradient. **Gradient** is a measure of the change in elevation over a certain distance. Gradients are usually measured in meters per kilometer or in feet per mile. The steeper a stream's slope is, or the higher its gradient, the faster the stream will flow. A higher gradient gives a stream more energy to erode rock and soil. For example, a mountain stream has a high gradient, as shown in **Figure 3.** It flows rapidly and has more erosive energy. A stream or river on a flat plain has a low gradient, as shown in **Figure 4.** These rivers tend to flow slowly and have less erosive energy.

Discharge is the volume of water transported by a stream in a given amount of time. The discharge of a stream increases when a major storm occurs or when warm weather rapidly melts snow. As the stream's discharge increases, its erosive energy, speed, and load increase. During a drought or a dry season, the stream's discharge can become a mere trickle. When this occurs, the erosive energy, speed, and load drop dramatically.

Figure 3 *A mountain stream has a high gradient.*

Figure 4 *A river on a flat plain has a low gradient.*

Answer to MATHBREAK

4,900 m − 400 m = 4,500 m

$\frac{4,500 \text{ m}}{450 \text{ km}} = 10 \text{ m/km}$

Discussion

Have students think about watering a garden using a hose. Ask whether they would spray the water at full blast or gently. Would they lay the hose on the ground or hold it at waist level? Refer to this example as you work through the concepts of erosion, gradient, and discharge. Sheltered English

CONNECT TO PHYSICAL SCIENCE

Water flowing downstream can be compared to a rock tumbling down a mountainside. Water's potential energy is constantly being converted into kinetic energy. Ask students to come up with other examples similar to the way water flows.

MISCONCEPTION ALERT

When water flows down a river channel, it does not flow straight down the channel. Water flowing in a river or stream channel moves in a helical or corkscrew motion. This motion causes erosion on the bank where the water is rising and causes deposition on the bank where the water is falling. The helical flow of water helps explain the formation of bends or meanders in the channel.

IS THAT A FACT!

Most river water comes from rainfall and melted snow that flows down from mountains. Why do some rivers continue to flow during a severe drought? These rivers are probably lower than the water table, so their flow is maintained by seepage from ground water.

WEIRD SCIENCE

Stream piracy occurs when one river "steals" another. If the land dividing two streams is eroded, one stream can "capture" the headwaters of the other. The eroding stream eventually pirates all of the other stream's water.

2 Teach, continued

Group Activity

Assign each group of students one of the world's major rivers. Have each group prepare a poster on the river indicating its headwaters and mouth. The poster should also include major tributaries. Have students indicate a change in the river's gradient by shading the area with colored pencils. Encourage students to discover interesting facts about their river, such as the ecosystem the river supports and the river's effects on human populations living near it.

Cooperative Learning

Stream Load To help students learn the differences between the types of loads that streams carry, engage groups of four in this activity. Have groups fill a Mason jar three-quarters full of water. Provide a few small pebbles, a quarter cup of soil, and 3 tbsp of salt for each group. Have students choose which material best represents a stream's bed load (the pebbles), its suspended load (the soil), and its dissolved load (the salt).

Have students add all three materials to the jar and then shake it carefully to simulate a stream's load. After the contents have been thoroughly mixed, ask students to hypothesize how they could remove each material from the jar. (The pebbles settle to the bottom and can be picked out easily. If the water remains still long enough, the sediment will settle to the bottom of the jar. The salt can be removed through evaporation.)

Answer to Self-Check

If a river slowed down, the suspended load would be deposited.

A Stream's Load The rock and soil carried in a stream's water are collectively called the stream's **load.** The size of the particles in the stream's load is affected by the stream's speed. Fast-moving streams can carry large particles. The load also affects the stream's rate of erosion. Rocks and pebbles bounce and scrape along the bottom and sides of the bed. The illustration below shows the three ways a stream can carry its load.

1 A stream can bounce large materials, such as pebbles and boulders, along the stream bed. These rocks are called the **bed load.**

2 A stream can carry small rocks and soil in suspension. This suspended material is carried downstream with the flow of water. These materials, called the **suspended load,** make the river look muddy. When the current slows to a point where the particles can no longer be carried in suspension, the suspended load is deposited.

3 Some material is carried in solution, meaning that the material is dissolved in the water. The **dissolved load** consists of dissolved materials, such as sodium and calcium.

Self-Check

What would happen to a suspended load if the river slowed down? *(See page 564 to check your answer.)*

252

Homework

Writing Have students prepare an *Encyclopedia of Rivers* with a full definition of each new term in the section and at least one illustration for each term.

Q: What is a flood?

A: a river that's too big for its bridges

The Stages of a River

In the early 1900s, William Morris Davis developed a model that identified the stages of river development. According to this model, rivers evolve from a youthful stage to an old-age stage. Davis believed that all rivers erode in the same way and at the same rate. Today, however, scientists support a different model that considers the effects of a river's environment on stream development. For example, because different material erodes at different rates, one river may develop more quickly than another river. Many factors, including climate, gradient, and load, influence the development of a river. Although scientists no longer use Davis's model to explain river development, they still use many of his terms to describe a river. Remember, these terms do not tell the actual age of a river. Instead, they are used to describe the general characteristics of the river.

Figure 5 *This youthful river is located in Yellowstone National Park, Wyoming. The rapids and falls are located where the river flows over hard, resistant rock.*

Youthful Rivers A youthful river, like the one shown in **Figure 5,** erodes its channel deeper rather than wider. The river flows quickly because of its steep gradient. Its sides and channel are steep and straight. The river tumbles over rocks in rapids and waterfalls. Youthful rivers have few tributaries.

Mature Rivers A mature river, as shown in **Figure 6,** erodes its channel wider rather than deeper. The gradient of a mature river is not as steep as that of a youthful river, and there are fewer falls and rapids. A mature river is fed by many tributaries, and because of its good drainage, it has more discharge than a younger river.

Figure 6 *A mature river begins to curve back and forth. The bends in the river's channel are called* meanders.

3 Extend

Reading Strategy

Prediction Guide Write "Young," "Mature," "Old," and "Rejuvenated" on the board. Have students brainstorm about concepts, words, or images related to these terms, and write their suggestions below the terms. Next add the dictionary definitions of the terms. Then discuss how the terms might describe a river. Have students write their ideas in their ScienceLog and then compare their ideas with the descriptions in the text. Sheltered English

Independent Practice

Illustrating River Stages As students read the section on the stages of a river, have them illustrate the stages in their ScienceLog. Encourage students to draw a cross section of the river channel and valley. Students should label the parts of their diagrams and write a brief description of each stage of river development.

Cross-Disciplinary Focus

Writing **History** In the eighteenth and nineteenth centuries, the Mississippi River served as an important trade route for the Midwest. Riverboats carried people and goods up and down the Mississippi River. The riverboats carried resources such as grains, meat, and skins down the river. Have interested students research how the Mississippi River influenced the history of the Midwest or write a short essay on the history of a city built on a Midwestern river, such as Saint Louis, New Orleans, or Kansas City. They should concentrate on how the river was important to the city's growth and development.

4 Close

Quiz

1. How does rainfall or snowmelt affect a river's discharge and its ability to cause erosion? (Rainfall and snowmelt increase a river's discharge and the amount of erosion it can cause.)
2. Explain the three types of materials carried by a river. (bed load: large materials that roll or bounce along a riverbed; suspended load: materials that float suspended in a river; dissolved load: materials dissolved in a river)

Alternative Assessment

Display the Teaching Transparency listed below, and discuss the features labeled. Then divide students into groups, and have them use modeling clay to make a model of a river, incorporating the concepts they have learned in this chapter. Students can use pins with attached labels to indicate river features.

Teaching Transparency 68
"River Features"

LINK TO LIFE SCIENCE

Figure 7 *This old river is located in New Zealand.*

Figure 8 *This rejuvenated river is located in Canyonlands National Park, Utah.*

Old Rivers An old river has a low gradient and extremely low erosive power. Instead of widening and deepening its banks, the river deposits sediment in its channel and along its banks. Old rivers, like the one in **Figure 7,** are characterized by wide, flat *flood plains*, or valleys, and more meanders. Also, an older river has fewer tributaries than a mature river because the smaller tributaries have merged.

Rejuvenated Rivers Rejuvenated rivers occur where the land is raised by the Earth's tectonic forces. When land rises, the river's gradient becomes steeper. The increased gradient of a rejuvenated river allows the river to cut more deeply into the valley floor, as shown in **Figure 8.** Steplike *terraces* often form on both sides of a stream valley as a result of rejuvenation. Terraces are nearly flat portions of the landscape that end at a steep cliff.

REVIEW

1. How does the water cycle help to develop river systems?
2. Describe a drainage basin.
3. What are three factors that affect the rate of stream erosion?
4. **Summarizing Data** How do youthful, mature, and old rivers differ?

254

Answers to Review

1. Answers will vary. Accept all reasonable responses.
2. A drainage basin is the land drained by a river system, including the main river and all of its tributaries.
3. Three factors that affect the rate of stream erosion are a stream's gradient, its discharge, and its load.
4. Youthful rivers are steep and straight, with low discharge due to fewer tributaries. Mature rivers have more curves, tributaries, and discharge than youthful rivers, as well as a lower gradient. Old rivers have less erosive power than other rivers. Old rivers have fewer tributaries than mature rivers do, but these tributaries are larger and they meander more.

Section 1 Review—California Standards: PE/ATE 2, 2a, 2b, 4a

2

Stream and River Deposits

NEW TERMS

deposition
alluvium
delta
alluvial fan
flood plain

OBJECTIVES

- Describe the different types of stream deposits.
- Explain the relationship between rich agricultural regions and river flood plains.

You have learned that flowing rivers can pick up and move soil and rock. Sooner or later, this material must be deposited somewhere. **Deposition** is the process by which material is dropped, or settles. Imagine a mud puddle after a rainy day. If the water is not disturbed, the soil particles will eventually settle and the muddy water will become clear again. Deposition also forms and renews some of the world's most productive soils. People who live in the lower Mississippi River valley depend on the river to bring them new, fertile soil. Before the Aswan Dam was built on the Nile River, the lower Nile River valley, shown in **Figure 9,** was the site of an important agricultural civilization. Every year, the Nile River deposited rich soil in the valley during floods.

Figure 9 *This photograph shows the agricultural communities that lined the Nile River before the Aswan Dam was completed, in 1970. The dam interrupted the annual flooding, altering the landscape and people's livelihood.*

Deposition in Water

After rivers erode rock and soil, they deposit the rock and soil downstream. Rock and soil deposited by streams is called **alluvium.** Alluvium is dropped at places in a river where the speed of the current decreases. Take a look at **Figure 10** to see how this type of deposition occurs.

Figure 10 *Deposition occurs along the inside turns of meanders, often producing sandbars. On the outside turns, where the current flows faster, the meander's banks are eroded and the channel is deepened.*

SECTION 2

Focus

Stream and River Deposits

This section describes the variety of ways that a river's load can be deposited. Students will learn why different patterns of deposition occur, and they will explore the connections between river deposits and agriculture.

Bellringer

Post the following question on the board or overhead projector:

Even though flooding along rivers is potentially harmful, many farmers have traditionally located their farms near rivers. Why? (The flood waters carry rich sediments that contribute to the land's fertility.)

1 Motivate

DEMONSTRATION

Modeling Deposition To show students how moving water separates sediment into different-sized particles, place a handful of soil, sand, and small gravel in a large jar of water. Shake the jar vigorously, and then place it in on your desk. Ask students to describe what happens to the different-sized particles in the jar as time passes. Ask students to compare how the different-sized particles settled. Sheltered English

WEIRD SCIENCE

The Okavango River, in Africa, flows approximately 1,600 km through Angola, Namibia, and Botswana before it empties into the middle of the Kalahari Desert, where it evaporates! The river's delta provides a haven for the desert's plants and animals.

Directed Reading Worksheet 10 Section 2

Section 2–California Standards: PE/ATE 2, 2a, 2b, 2c

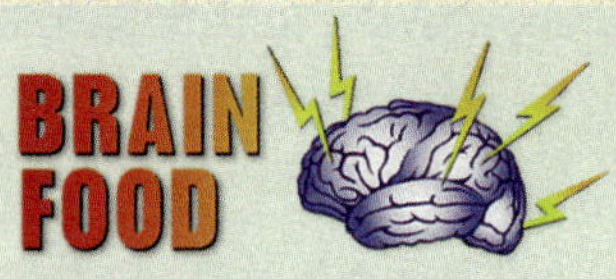

Figure 11 *Miners rushed to California in the 1850s to find gold. They often found it in the bends of rivers in placer deposits.*

Heavy minerals are sometimes deposited at places in a river where the current slows down. This kind of alluvium is called a *placer deposit*. Some placer deposits contain gold, as **Figure 11** shows. During the California gold rush, which began in 1849, many miners panned for gold in the placer deposits of rivers.

The current also slows when a river empties into a large body of water, such as a lake or an ocean. Much of the river's load may be deposited where the river reaches the large body of water, forming a fan-shaped deposit called a **delta.** In **Figure 12** you can see an astronaut's view of the Nile Delta. A delta usually forms on a flat surface and consists mostly of mud. These mud deposits form new land, causing the coastline to grow.

Figure 12 *Sediment is dropped at the mouth of the Nile River, forming a delta.*

If you look back at the map of the Mississippi River drainage basin in Figure 2, you can see where the Mississippi River flows into the Gulf of Mexico. This is where the Mississippi Delta has formed. Each of the fine mud particles in the delta began its journey far upstream. Parts of Louisiana are made up of particles that were transported from as far away as Montana, Minnesota, Ohio, and Illinois.

astronomy CONNECTION

The remains of an ancient riverbed have been discovered on Mars. Satellite images show the deposits of stream channels, which indicate that liquid water once existed on the now dry and frozen planet.

Self-Check

What might cause the current of a river to slow?

(See page 564 to check your answer.)

2 Teach

BRAIN FOOD

Ask students to examine a map of the United States and to note that rivers often serve as state borders. For instance, the Ohio River is the border between Indiana and Kentucky. But meanders can sometimes shift the course of the river. Does the state border then change? To prevent feuding between states, the courts have declared that state boundaries do not change when a river shifts.

Cooperative Learning

PORTFOLIO

Gold Rush Between 1870 and 1898, many prospectors discovered gold in Canada's Yukon Territory. Dreams of getting rich overnight lured people to the Klondike River area in vast numbers.

Have students research the Yukon gold rush. Divide the class into three groups. Have Group 1 prepare a presentation on how the gold deposits formed. Have Group 2 prepare a presentation on how the gold ore became placer deposits in the Klondike River. Have Group 3 prepare a presentation on the geography of the Yukon's river systems.

Students can also find out about life in the gold fields and present their findings using models or posters.

Answer to Self-Check

A river might slow where there is a bend or where the river empties into a large body of water.

Homework

Investigate Your Area Have students find out how your city or county is working to control flooding and erosion along area streams and rivers. Have them write a brief report on a watershed project in their area. You may consider inviting a watershed engineer to speak to the class.

Reinforcement Worksheet 10
"Fresh Water in the United States"

Deposition on Land

When a fast-moving mountain stream flows onto a flat plain, the stream's speed is greatly reduced due to a decrease in the stream's gradient. As the stream slows down, it deposits alluvium where the mountain meets the flat plain, forming an alluvial fan, such as the one shown in **Figure 13. Alluvial fans** are fan-shaped deposits that form on dry land.

During periods of high rainfall or rapid snowmelt, a sudden increase in the volume of water flowing into a stream can cause the stream to overflow its banks, flooding the surrounding land. This land is called a **flood plain.** When a stream floods, a layer of alluvium is deposited across the flood plain. Each flood adds another layer of alluvium.

Flood plains are very rich farming areas because periodic flooding brings new soil to the land. However, flooding can cause extensive property damage. Much farming activity takes place in the Mississippi River valley, a large flood plain with very rich soil. When the Mississippi River flooded in 1993, however, farms were abandoned and whole towns had to be evacuated. The flood was so huge that it caused damage in nine Midwestern states. **Figure 14** shows an area that was flooded just north of St. Louis, Missouri.

Figure 13 *An alluvial fan, such as this one from the Sierra Nevada, in California, forms when a steep-gradient eroding stream changes rapidly into a low-gradient depositing stream.*

Figure 14 *The normal flow of the Mississippi River is shown in black. The area that was flooded when the Mississippi River spilled over its banks in 1993 is shaded red.*

REVIEW

1. What happens to a river's flow that causes alluvium to be deposited?
2. How are alluvial fans and deltas similar? How are they different?
3. Explain why flood plains are good farming areas.
4. **Identifying Relationships** What factors increase the likelihood that alluvium will be deposited?

257

Answers to Review

1. The slowing of a river's flow causes alluvium to be deposited.
2. Deltas and alluvial fans are both fan-shaped deposits formed when a stream slows. Deltas form as rivers enter larger bodies of water, and alluvial fans form on dry land.
3. Flood plains form rich farmland because flood waters periodically deposit new soil on the land.
4. Factors that reduce a river's speed increase the likelihood that alluvium will be deposited.

DEBATE

Flood Management The flooding of the Mississippi River in 1993 spurred a great debate. Some people blamed the severity of the flood on development projects that had destroyed wetlands and the natural flood plain. They argued that parts of the flood plain should be restored to their natural state. Others argued that if the natural habitat were restored, people living and working in the flood plain would be displaced. Others wondered if insurance companies should pay to rebuild houses that were located in flood plains.

Have two groups research the controversy and defend their positions in a class debate.

3 Close

Quiz

1. A river runs down a rapids, eases through a valley for about 3 km, then tumbles down a waterfall into a lake. Where along this path would you most likely find a placer deposit? Why? (in the valley, because heavy minerals are sometimes deposited where currents are slow)
2. Define *flood plain.* (land that is flooded when a river overflows its banks)

ALTERNATIVE ASSESSMENT

Have students use modeling clay to create a model of a delta and an alluvial fan. Ask them to also model the immediate environment around each river feature and use pins with labels to identify the processes involved in the formation of each feature.

Section 2 Review—California Standards: PE/ATE 2, 2a, 2b

SECTION 3

Focus

Water Underground

In this section, students will learn what ground water is and where it is found. The section discusses the formation of aquifers and their importance to agriculture and human populations. Students will learn how wells and springs bring water from aquifers to the surface. The section concludes with a discussion of how the movement of ground water forms caves and karst topography.

Bellringer

Pose the following scenario to students on the board or overhead projector:

A family lives 50 km from the nearest stream or lake and gets water from a well. Where does the water in the well come from? (It comes from water stored underground.)

1) Motivate

DEMONSTRATION

Layer an aquarium with gravel, sand, and potting soil until it is three-quarters full. Pack the material firmly. Add water until you can clearly see areas of aeration and saturation. Ask students to compare this model to **Figure 15.** Using a marker, draw a line for the water table on the glass. Introduce the terms *zone of saturation* and *zone of aeration*, and discuss the difference between the two. Sheltered English

3

NEW TERMS

ground water
water table
aquifer
porosity
permeability
artesian spring
karst topography

OBJECTIVES

- Identify and describe the location of a water table.
- Describe the characteristics of an aquifer.
- Explain how caves and karst topography form as a result of erosion and deposition.

Water Underground

Although we can see surface water in streams and lakes, there is a lot of water flowing underground that we cannot see. The water located within the rocks below the Earth's surface is called **ground water.** Ground water not only is an important resource but also plays an important role in erosion and deposition. In order to understand erosion and deposition by ground water, you must understand where and how ground water collects.

Location of Ground Water

Surface water seeps underground into the soil and rock. Earth scientists divide this underground area into two zones. The upper zone, called the *zone of aeration,* usually is not completely filled with water. The rock and soil that make up the zone of aeration contain air spaces. These air spaces are filled with water only immediately after a rain. Farther down, the water accumulates in an area called the *zone of saturation*. Here the spaces between the rock particles are filled with water.

The zone of aeration and the zone of saturation meet at an underground boundary known as the **water table,** as shown in **Figure 15.** The water table changes with the seasons. It rises during wet seasons and drops during dry seasons. In wet regions the water table can be just beneath the soil's surface or at the surface. But in deserts the water table may be hundreds of meters underground.

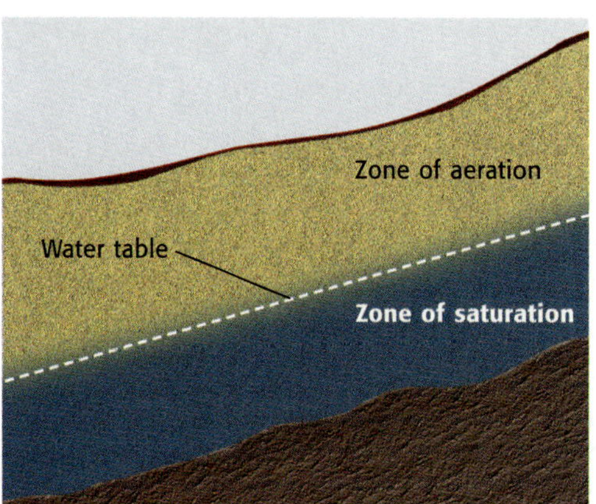

Figure 15 *The water table is the upper surface of the zone of saturation.*

A mud pie the size of a house—where would you see something like that? Turn to page 272 to find out about this huge flying wad of mud.

Aquifers

Some types of rock can hold large quantities of water, while other types can hold little or no water. A rock layer that stores and allows the flow of ground water is called an **aquifer.**

A rock layer must have two characteristics to qualify as an aquifer. First the rock layer must be *porous*, or contain open spaces. A rock's **porosity** is the amount of open space between individual rock particles. Second the rock layer must allow water to pass freely through it, from one pore to another. If the pores are connected, ground water can flow through the rock layer. A rock's ability to let water pass through it is called **permeability.** A rock that tends to stop the flow of water is impermeable.

258

Multicultural CONNECTION

The Maya, one of the early civilizations of the Americas, believed that rain clouds formed in caves and then rose to the sky. Elaborate ceremonies were performed in caves for the rain god. Have interested students find out more about how caves and rituals were important to early Mesoamerican civilizations.

IS THAT A FACT!

Geologists estimate that aquifers hold 50 million cubic kilometers of water worldwide. There is about 20 times more water underground than in all the rivers, lakes, and the atmosphere.

Section 3—California Standards: PE/ATE 2, 6b, 7

The best aquifers are usually formed of sandstone, limestone, or layers of sand and gravel. Some aquifers cover large underground areas and are an important source of water for cities and agriculture. The map in **Figure 16** shows the location of aquifers in the United States. Can you locate one that your town might use?

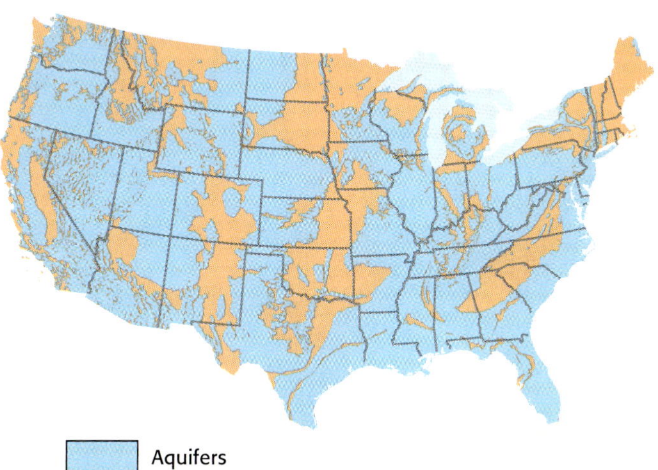

Figure 16 Potential Ground-Water Sources for the Continental United States

Like rivers, aquifers are dependent on the water cycle to maintain a constant flow of water. The ground surface where water enters an aquifer is called the *recharge zone*. The size of the recharge zone varies depending on whether the rock at the surface is permeable or impermeable. In an area that contains a permeable rock layer, the water can seep down into the aquifer. In areas where the aquifer is confined on top by an impermeable rock layer, the recharge zone is restricted to areas where there is a permeable rock layer.

Springs and Wells

Ground-water movement is determined by the slope of the water table. Just like surface water, ground water tends to move downslope, toward lower elevations. If the water table reaches the Earth's surface, water will flow out from the ground, forming a *spring*. Springs are an important source of drinking water. Lakes form in low areas, where the water table is higher than the Earth's surface.

QuickLab

Degree of Permeability

1. Obtain five **plastic-foam cups.**
2. Fill one cup halfway with **soil,** such as garden soil. Pack the soil.
3. Fill a second cup halfway with **sand.** Pack the sand.
4. Poke 5 to 7 holes in the bottom of each cup with a sharpened **pencil.**
5. Fill a third cup with **water.** Hold one of the remaining empty cups under the cup filled with soil. Pour the water into the top cup.
6. Allow the cup to drain for 45 seconds, and then put the cup aside (even if it is still draining). Put the cup filled with water aside.
7. Repeat steps 5 and 6 with the cup of sand. Compare the volumes of the two cups of water. The cup that allowed the most water to pass holds the more permeable sediment.

WEIRD SCIENCE

Only recently have scientists discovered how much fresh water flows into the oceans from ground water. When the tide comes in, sea water seeps into the sediments of coastal land, mixing with the ground water. When the tide recedes, the water mixture is drawn out to sea; the ground water is recharged and the cycle repeats. These findings are significant because pollution in ground water can seriously threaten the oceans.

2 Teach

QuickLab

MATERIALS

- 5 plastic-foam cups
- soil
- sand
- pencil
- water

Teacher Notes: There are no safety precautions required for this experiment. Cover the work area with plastic, and have students wear lab aprons and plastic gloves.

Real-World Connection

Investigate Your Area Ground water is a drinking water source for about 60 percent of the population of the United States. Encourage students to find out where their drinking water comes from. Students can do research in local newspapers to learn about issues affecting the quality of their drinking water and prepare a poster illustrating the path that local ground water follows from a rain cloud to a faucet. If there is time, arrange for a tour of a local water treatment plant.

MISCONCEPTION ALERT

Students may think that ground water creates vast underground lakes or rivers. This happens only rarely. Most ground water moves through spaces in rock and soil similar to the way water is stored in a sponge.

Teaching Transparency 123 "The Water Table"

Directed Reading Worksheet 10 Section 3

2) Teach, *continued*

Using the Figure

Guide students through **Figures 17** and **18.** List the labels on the board. Help students define each term. Explain that ground water can build up above the cap rock when the rock is cracked, thus hiding the aquifer. Have students hypothesize about how a crack could form in the cap rock. (splitting from freezing and thawing, penetration by roots, shifting from earthquakes)

Explain that the pressure driving an artesian spring may come from the weight of rock and sediment overlaying the aquifer. Sheltered English

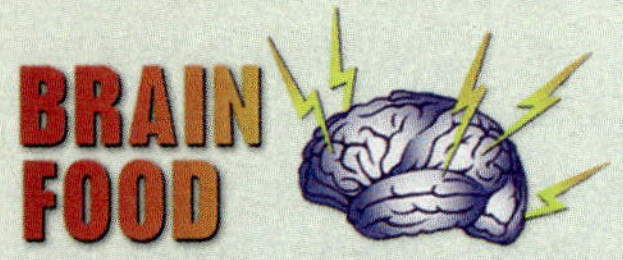

Much of Australia's ground water is stored in artesian formations, such as those fed by a vast underground rock formation called the Great Artesian Basin. Unfortunately, most of the water is too salty for people to drink or use for irrigation. Have students find out how this water could be processed in a desalination plant.

Answer to Self-Check

The impermeable rock layer in the aquifer traps the water in the permeable layer below. This creates the pressure needed to form an artesian spring.

Teaching Transparency 124
"Artesian Formation"
"The Water Table and Wells"

A sloping layer of permeable rock sandwiched between two layers of impermeable rock is called an *artesian formation.* The permeable rock is an aquifer, and the top layer of the impermeable rock is called a *cap rock,* as shown in **Figure 17.** Artesian formations are the source of water for **artesian springs.** Artesian springs are springs that form when cracks occur naturally in the cap rock and the pressurized water in the aquifer flows through the cracks to the surface. Artesian springs are sometimes found in deserts, where they are often the only source of water.

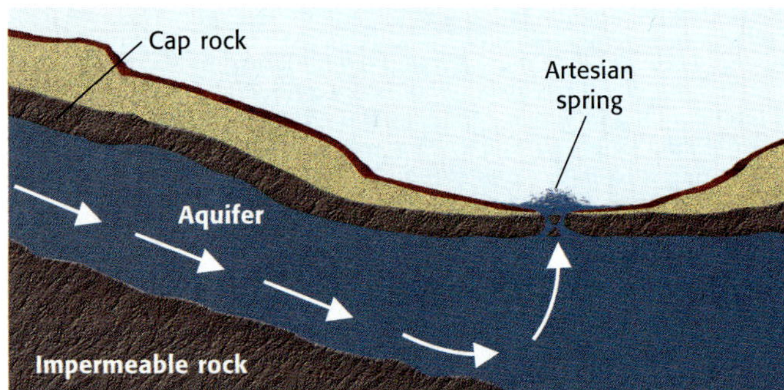

Figure 17 *Artesian springs form when water from an aquifer flows through cracks in the cap rock of an artesian formation.*

A *well* is a human-made hole that is deeper than the level of the water table; wells therefore fill with ground water, as shown in **Figure 18.** If a well is not deep enough, it will dry up when the water table falls below the bottom of the well. Also, if too many wells in an area remove ground water too rapidly, the water table will drop and all the wells will run dry.

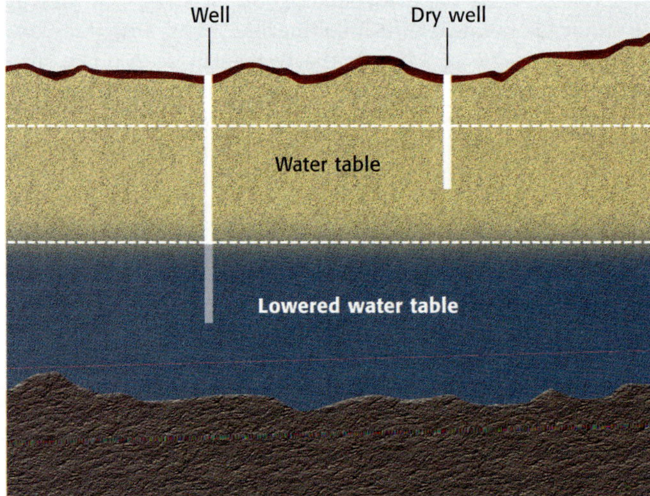

Figure 18 *A good well is drilled deep enough so that when the water table drops, the well still contains water.*

Self-Check

Why is it important that there is a layer of impermeable rock in an artesian formation?

(See page 564 to check your answer.)

260

CONNECT TO LIFE SCIENCE

Elephants that live in the desert of Namibia may travel 4 days to find a water hole. Once there, they might have to dig almost a meter into the sand to reach clear water. Antelopes, such as springbok and eland, and other desert-dwelling animals depend on the elephants to penetrate the water table. Have students research ways in which desert plants and animals have adapted to regions with little surface water.

Underground Erosion and Deposition

Although most ground water moves slowly, its movement still causes erosion and deposition. Unlike a river, which erodes its banks when water moves over rock and soil, ground water erodes certain types of rock by dissolving the rock. Most of the world's caves formed over thousands of years as ground water dissolved limestone. Limestone, made of calcium carbonate, dissolves easily in water, leaving behind spectacular underground features when the water drains. You can see some of these features in **Figure 19.**

Figure 19 *At Carlsbad Caverns, in New Mexico, underground passages and enormous "rooms" have been eroded below the surface of the Earth.*

While caves are formed by erosion, they are often decorated by deposition. Water that drips from a crack in a cave's ceiling leaves behind deposits of calcium carbonate. These deposits of calcium carbonate are a type of limestone called *dripstone*. Water and dissolved limestone can drip downward into a sharp, icicle-shaped dripstone feature known as a stalactite. At the same time, water drops that fall to the cave's floor add to cone-shaped dripstone features known as stalagmites. **Figure 20** shows some dripstone features formed by deposition. Can you name them?

Figure 20 *If water drips long enough, the stalactites and stalagmites can reach each other and join, forming a dripstone column.*

environmental science CONNECTION

Most bat species live in caves. These night-flying mammals navigate by sound and can reach speeds of 95 km/h. Today scientists know that bats play an extremely important role in the environment. Bats are great consumers of insects, and many bat species pollinate plants and distribute seeds.

IS THAT A FACT!

Mount Shasta is a dormant volcano in the Shasta River basin, in California. During snowmelts, the Shasta River doesn't receive much runoff. The snowmelt is absorbed by the porous volcanic slopes and reemerges through springs at the bottom of the river valley.

internetconnect

SCiLINKS NSTA

TOPIC: Water Underground
GO TO: www.scilinks.org
***sci*LINKS NUMBER:** HSTE265

3 Extend

Group Activity

MATERIALS

For Each Group:

- 2 jars
- washing soda (sodium carbonate)
- spoon
- dish
- paper clips
- yarn

Tell students to fill the jars with very warm water and stir a few spoonfuls of washing soda into each jar. Students should stop when the soda no longer dissolves. Set the dish between the jars. Clip paper clips to the ends of the yarn, and lower each end into a different jar. After 2 or 3 days, some of the soda-water mixture will have moved through the yarn by capillary action, and the solution will have dripped onto the plate, forming a stalactite and stalagmite by evaporation.

Going Further

Have students research Mammoth Cave, in Kentucky, to learn more about the unique formations there. Then help them construct a "virtual cave." Have students work in groups to create models of the cave's formations using modeling clay. Different groups can model different sections of the cave. Students can also make an audio tape tour of the cave that tells visitors about the structures, including how they formed.

4 Close

Quiz

1. Define *porosity* and *permeability.* (Porosity is the amount of open space between rock particles. Permeability is the ability of rock to allow water to flow through it.)
2. Describe the rock layers that produce an artesian spring. (A cap rock seals off permeable rock; water is released through a crack in the cap rock.)
3. What is a spring? What is a well? (A spring forms where the water table reaches the surface and water flows out. A well is a human construction that extends below the water table. Water flows into the well's opening and is pumped to the surface.)

Alternative Assessment

Concept Mapping Have students use the following terms to make a concept map:

ground water, water table, aquifer, porosity, permeability, artesian spring, karst topography, sinkhole, spring, well, cave, dripstone

Sheltered English

Reinforcement Worksheet 10
"Dig It!"

Problem Solving Worksheet 10
"Water Crisis at Happy Acres"

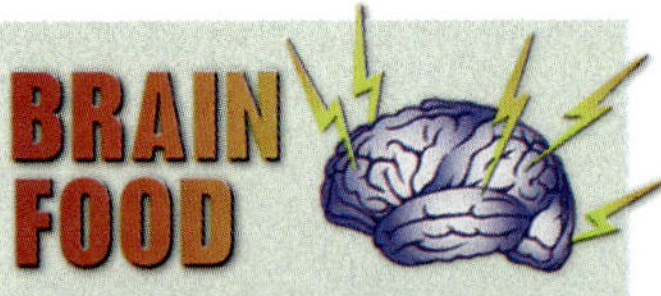

The term *karst topography* comes from a region in central Slovenia called the Karst. This area has many caves, valleys, and underground channels that are formed in limestone.

Areas where the effects of ground-water erosion are noticeable at the surface are said to have **karst topography.** This landscape is decorated by unusual formations associated with ground-water erosion and underground caves. When the water table is lower than the level of a cave, the cave is no longer supported by the water underneath. The roof of the cave can then collapse, leaving a circular depression called a *sinkhole*. Surface streams can "disappear" into sinkholes and then flow through underground caves. Sinkholes often form lakes in areas where the water table is high. Central Florida is covered with hundreds of round sinkhole lakes. Karst valleys form where many sinkholes have grown together, leaving sharp-edged ridges. Spectacular limestone cliffs sometimes form on the edges of large sinkholes and karst valleys. After thousands of years of ground-water erosion, the level of the whole landscape is lowered. **Figure 21** shows how karst topography can affect a landscape.

Figure 21 *Karst topography is found in various regions, including the Mediterranean coast, southern China, and the United States. The photo above shows the effect of ground-water erosion in China. The photo at right shows the effects of a sinkhole in Winter Park, Florida.*

REVIEW

1. What is the water table?
2. What is an aquifer?
3. What are some of the features formed by underground erosion and deposition?
4. **Analyzing Relationships** What is the relationship between the zone of aeration, the zone of saturation, and the water table?

262

Answers to Review

1. The water table is the underground boundary where the zone of aeration and the zone of saturation meet.
2. An aquifer is a rock layer that stores and allows the flow of ground water.
3. Caves, sinkholes, and features of karst topography form by ground water erosion. Stalagmites, stalactites, and dripstone columns form by underground deposition.
4. The water table is the underground boundary where the zone of aeration and the zone of saturation meet.

4 Using Water Wisely

NEW TERMS
point-source pollution
non-point-source pollution
sewage treatment plant
septic tank

OBJECTIVES
- Describe the stages of treatment for water at a sewage treatment plant.
- Compare a septic system with a sewage treatment plant.
- Explain how ground water can be both a renewable and nonrenewable resource.

All living things need water to survive. But there is a limited amount of fresh water available on Earth. Only 3 percent of Earth's water is drinkable. And of the 3 percent that is drinkable, 75 percent is frozen in the polar icecaps. That's more than 100 times the volume of water found in lakes and streams! This frozen water is not readily available for our use. Therefore, it is important that we use our water resources wisely.

Water Pollution

Surface water, such as rivers and lakes, and ground water are often polluted by waste from cities, factories, and farms. One type of pollution is called **point-source pollution** because it comes from one particular point, such as a sewer pipe or a factory drain. Fortunately, laws prohibit much of this type of pollution.

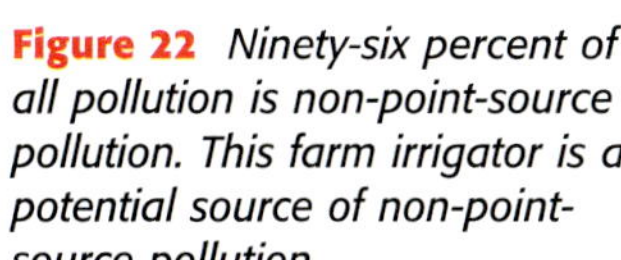

Figure 22 *Ninety-six percent of all pollution is non-point-source pollution. This farm irrigator is a potential source of non-point-source pollution.*

There is growing concern, however, about another type of pollution, called **non-point-source pollution**. This type of pollution, as shown in **Figure 22,** is much more difficult to control because it does not come from a single source. Most non-point-source pollution contaminates rivers and lakes by runoff. The main sources of non-point-source pollution are street gutters, fertilizers, eroded soils and silt from farming and logging, drainage from mines, and salts from irrigation. Some airborne acid pollutants are introduced into freshwater sources through falling rain.

As you know, ground water is an important source of fresh water. In fact, more than half of all household water in the United States comes from ground water. Farms use ground water for irrigation. Because ground water is supplied by water from the Earth's surface, ground water can become contaminated when surface water is polluted. And once polluted, ground water is very difficult and expensive to clean up.

SECTION 4

Focus

Using Water Wisely

This section discusses water pollution, overuse, and treatment. Students learn about the difference between point-source and non-point-source pollution and explore different methods for treating polluted water. The section then discusses trends in domestic, industrial, and agricultural water use and conservation.

Bellringer

Pose the following question on the board or overhead projector:

While hiking, you realize your canteen is almost empty. Why should you not fill it with water from the nearby stream? (Even though the water may look clean, it might contain pollutants or bacteria.)

1 Motivate

DISCUSSION

Ask students to identify all the activities their family does that involve water. Write students' responses on the board. Encourage students to discuss how their lives would be affected if the water supply became depleted or too contaminated to use.

IS THAT A FACT!

According to a 1998 U.S. Geological Survey report, water use in the United States has decreased 2 percent since 1990 and almost 10 percent since 1980, despite an increase in population. The report attributes this to public awareness and community conservation efforts.

Directed Reading Worksheet 10 Section 4

2 Teach

Multicultural CONNECTION

Writing Encourage students to use library or Internet resources to investigate traditional American Indian beliefs about the Earth, including its rivers. Ask them to write a brief report summarizing their findings.

Cooperative Learning

Divide the class into small groups, and challenge each group to create a board game. Tell them that the object of the game is to be the first player to successfully travel through a sewage treatment plant. Provide each group with poster board, plain index cards, and markers. Direct them to create a game board that leads players through the plant and incorporates the concepts they have learned about in this section. Have them use the index cards to write clues and questions directing players' movements through the sewage treatment process. For example, they might write, "If you can define primary treatment, advance to the tank." Have students create written rules, and allow time for the game to be played.

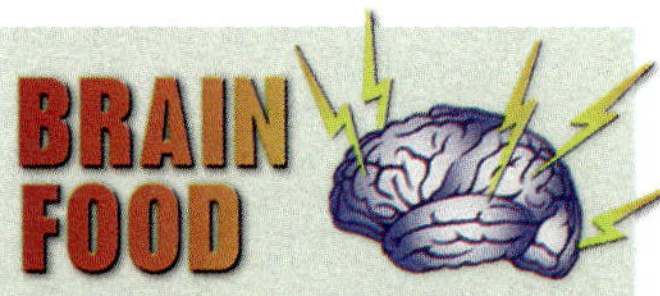

Each year more than 2.5 million people die from waterborne diseases, such as cholera and typhoid. With better sewage treatment, many of these lives could be saved.

Renewing Polluted Water

When you flush the toilet or watch water go down the shower drain, do you ever wonder where this water goes? If you live in a city or large town, the water flows through sewer pipes to a sewage treatment plant. **Sewage treatment plants** are factories that clean the waste matter out of water that comes from the sewer or drains. These plants help protect the environment from water pollution by cleaning polluted water. They also protect us from diseases that are easily transmitted through dirty water.

Cleaning Up Water When water reaches a sewage treatment plant, it is cleaned in two different ways. First it goes through a series of steps known as *primary treatment.* In primary treatment, dirty water is passed through a large screen to catch solid objects, such as paper, rags, and bottle caps. The water is then placed in a large tank, where smaller particles can sink and be filtered out. These particles include things such as food, coffee grounds, and soil. Any floating oils and scum are skimmed off the surface.

At this point, the water is ready for *secondary treatment.* In secondary treatment, the water is sent to an aeration tank, where it is mixed with oxygen and bacteria. The bacteria feed on the wastes and use the oxygen. The water is then sent to another settling tank, where chlorine is added to disinfect the water. The water is finally released into a water source—a stream, a lake, or the ocean. The treated water is often cleaner than the water into which it is released. **Figure 23** shows the major components of a sewage treatment plant.

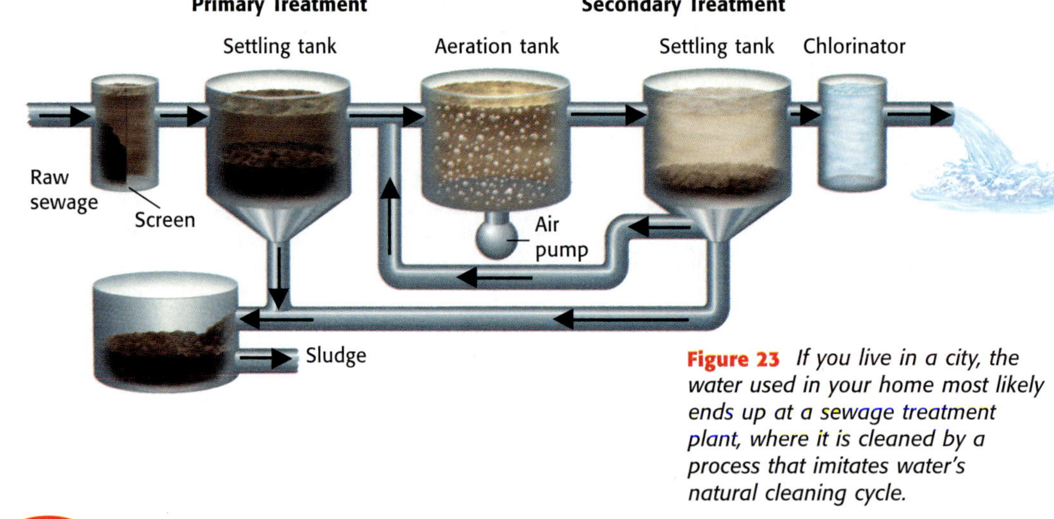

Figure 23 *If you live in a city, the water used in your home most likely ends up at a sewage treatment plant, where it is cleaned by a process that imitates water's natural cleaning cycle.*

264

Homework

Presentation Have students research sources of non-point-source pollution. Ask them to make posters for a community action campaign to reduce non-point-source pollution. Display students' posters in the classroom or around school.

MISCONCEPTION ALERT

Students may think that they cannot do anything to conserve water and prevent pollution. Point out to students that there are many things they can do to contribute to conservation. Tell students that by changing a few habits, they can greatly reduce their water consumption and reduce water pollution.

If you live in an area without a sewage treatment plant, your house probably has a septic tank, such as the one shown in **Figure 24.** A **septic tank** is a large underground tank that collects and cleans waste water from a household. Waste water flows from the house into the tank, where the solids sink to the bottom. Bacteria consume these wastes on the bottom of the tank. The water flows from the tank into a group of buried pipes. The buried pipes distribute the water, enabling it to soak into the ground. This group of pipes is called a *drain field*.

Get your hands dirty and learn about some of the methods used to clean up water. Check out page 526 of the LabBook.

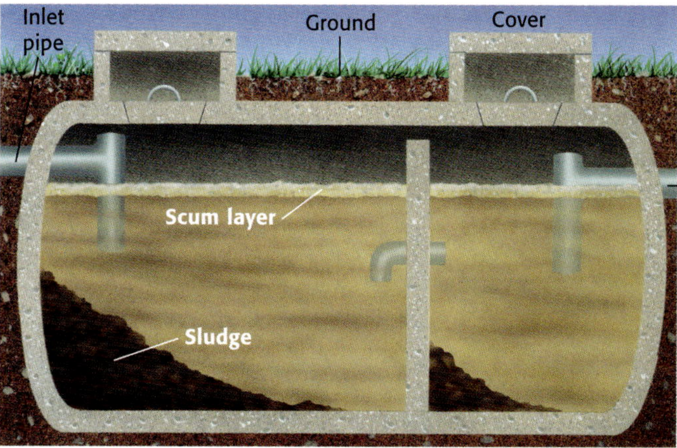

Figure 24 *Most septic tanks must be cleaned out every few years to work properly.*

Where the Water Goes

The chart in **Figure 25** shows how an average household in the United States uses water. Notice that less than 8 percent of the water we use in our homes is used for drinking. The rest is used for flushing toilets, doing laundry, bathing, and watering lawns and plants. Understanding the value of fresh water is the first step to conserving this limited resource.

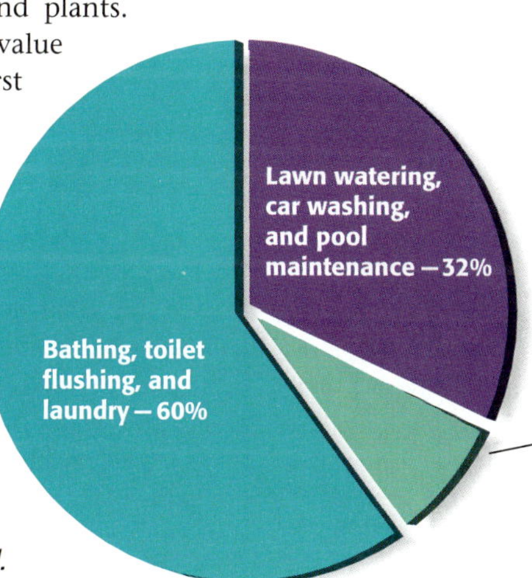

Figure 25 *The average household in the United States uses about 100 gal of water per day. This pie chart shows some common uses of this 100 gal.*

Explore

After studying the chart at left and determining where the majority of water is used, think of some ways that you can decrease the amount of water that you use in your home.

PG 526

Clean Up Your Act

MATH and MORE

Low-flush toilets use about 6 L of water per flush. Standard toilets use 19 L of water per flush. How much water is saved in a week by replacing a standard toilet with a low-flush toilet? Assume the toilet is flushed 10 times a day. (910 L)

How much water would be saved in a year? (47,450 L)

Math Skills Worksheet 3 "Multiplying Whole Numbers"

Answers to Explore

Sample answers: I will make sure the dishwasher is completely full when it is being used. If I'm washing dishes in the sink, I won't let the water run continuously. I'll turn the shower off when lathering up. And I won't do several small loads of laundry if I can do fewer large loads instead.

IS THAT A FACT!

Four major river basins in Pennsylvania are being polluted by runoff from thousands of abandoned coal mines. As a result, more than 4,800 km of stream water and ground water have been contaminated with acidic runoff containing toxic metals. The impact has been enormous; many of the streams are now devoid of fish.

3 Extend

DEBATE

Should Water Conservation Be Enforced? Point out to students that many communities are enacting mandatory water conservation measures. For example, Albuquerque, New Mexico, has adopted a water-conservation policy in an effort to reduce per capita water use by 30 percent. However, some people are opposed to government regulation of water use. Divide the class into two groups, and assign each group a position in the debate. Have students use library or Internet resources to research their position.

COOPERATIVE LEARNING

Divide the class into small groups. Challenge each group to write a public-service announcement to educate the public about the need to conserve water and to avoid polluting ground water. The announcements should include definitions of nonrenewable and renewable resources.
Sheltered English

Answer to APPLY

Answers will vary. Accept all reasonable responses.

internetconnect

TOPIC: Water Pollution and Conservation
GO TO: www.scilinks.org
*sci*LINKS NUMBER: HSTE270

Water in Industry The chart on the previous page shows how fresh water is used in homes. Even more water is required for industry, as shown in **Figure 26.** Water is used to cool power stations, to clean industrial products, to extract minerals, and to create power for factories. Many industries are trying to conserve water by reusing it in their production processes. In the United States, most of the water used in factories is recycled at least once. At least 90 percent of this water can be treated and returned to surface water.

Ground-water supplies also need to be monitored. Although ground water is considered to be a *renewable resource,* a resource that can be replenished, recycling ground water can be a lengthy process. When overused, ground water can sometimes be categorized as a *nonrenewable resource,* a substance that cannot be replaced once it is used. Ground water collects and moves slowly, and water taken from some aquifers might not be replenished for many years. Aquifers are often overused and therefore do not have time to replenish themselves. Like surface water, ground water must be conserved.

Figure 26 **(a)** *The core of a nuclear reactor is cooled by water.* **(b)** *Highly pressurized water is used to dig in mining.* **(c)** *A dam containing water is used to generate hydroelectric power.*

APPLY

How much water do you use when you brush your teeth? Picture yourself at home brushing your teeth. Time how long it takes you to go through the procedure. In your ScienceLog, write down the steps you take, making sure to include how many times you turn on and turn off the faucet. During what percentage of the time spent brushing your teeth is the water running? How do you think you might be wasting water? What are some ways that you could conserve water while brushing your teeth?

IS THAT A FACT!

The Ogallala aquifer, which provides nearly 30 percent of the ground water used for irrigation in the United States, experienced a significant drop in water level between 1940 and 1980. In some areas, the water table dropped 30 m! Since 1980, the decline has slowed. Scientists attribute this improvement to several factors, including more-efficient irrigation techniques.

Water in Agriculture The Ogallala aquifer is the largest known aquifer in North America. The map in **Figure 27** shows that the Ogallala aquifer runs beneath the ground through eight states, from South Dakota to Texas. For the last 100 years, the aquifer has been used heavily for farming. The Ogallala aquifer provides water for approximately one-fifth of the cropland in the United States. Recently, the water table in the aquifer has dropped so low that some scientists say that it would take at least 1,000 years to replenish the aquifer if it were no longer used.

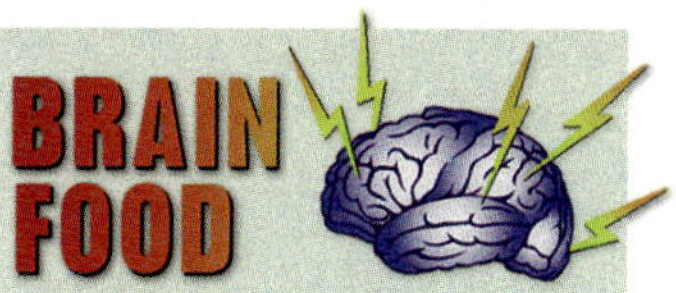

The Ogallala aquifer can hold enough water to fill Lake Huron. At this time, however, the aquifer is being used 25 times as fast as it is being replenished.

Figure 27 *Because the Ogallala aquifer has been such a good source of ground water, it has become overused. The water table has dropped more than 30 m in some areas.*

Water resources are different from other resources. Because water is necessary for life, there is no alternative resource. To protect supplies of ground water, some communities are regulating its use. These communities monitor water levels and discourage use when levels fall below a certain point.

REVIEW

1. What is the difference between point-source and non-point-source pollution?
2. Summarize the process of water treatment in a sewage treatment plant.
3. What is the difference between a renewable resource and a nonrenewable resource?
4. **Summarizing Data** How does a septic tank work?

4 Close

Quiz

1. What are two sources of non-point-source pollution? (street gutters, fertilizers, eroded soils and silt from farming and logging, drainage from mines, and salts from irrigation)
2. How do sewage treatment plants protect the environment? (They clean polluted water before it is returned to a water source.)

Alternative Assessment

Provide students with poster board and markers. Direct them to create posters illustrating how non-point-source pollution can cause contamination of both surface water and ground water. Their diagrams should reflect the understanding that pollution of surface water can spread to ground water. Sheltered English

Interactive Explorations CD-ROM "Flood Bank"

Answers to Review

1. Point-source pollution comes from a single, identifiable source, whereas non-point-source pollution does not.
2. When water enters a sewage plant, it goes through two treatments. In primary treatment, all the solid material is filtered out. In secondary treatment, the water is cleaned by bacteria that feed on the waste and chlorine that kill the bacteria.
3. A renewable resource can be replaced or recycled. Once a nonrenewable resource is used up, it cannot be replaced.
4. Used water from a home flows into an underground tank, where bacteria feed on the solid waste. The rest of the water flows through underground pipes, which distribute it into the surrounding soil.

Section 4 Review—California Standards: PE/ATE 6, 6b

Chapter Highlights

VOCABULARY DEFINITIONS

SECTION 1

erosion the removal and transport of material by wind, water, or ice

water cycle the continuous movement of water from water sources into the air, onto land, into and over the ground, and back to the water sources

drainage basin an area drained by a river system, including the main river and all of its tributaries

tributary a small stream or river that flows into a larger one

divide an area of higher ground that separates drainage basins

channel the path a stream follows

gradient a measure of the change in elevation over a certain distance

discharge the volume of water transported by a stream in a given amount of time

load the rock and soil carried in a stream

SECTION 2

deposition the process by which material is dropped or settles

alluvium rock and soil deposited by streams

delta a fan-shaped deposit of sediment at the mouth of a stream where the stream empties into a large body of water

alluvial fan fan-shaped deposits of sediment that form on dry land

flood plain an area along a river formed from sediments deposited by floods

Chapter Highlights

SECTION 1

Vocabulary

erosion *(p. 248)*
water cycle *(p. 248)*
drainage basin *(p. 250)*
tributary *(p. 250)*
divide *(p. 250)*
channel *(p. 251)*
gradient *(p. 251)*
discharge *(p. 251)*
load *(p. 252)*

Section Notes

- Erosion is the removal and transport of soil and rock.
- The water cycle is the continuous movement of water from water sources into the air, onto land, and back into water sources.
- A drainage basin, or watershed, includes a main river and all of its tributaries.
- The rate of stream erosion is affected by many factors, including the stream's gradient, discharge, speed, and load.
- Gradient is the change in slope over distance.
- Discharge is the volume of water moved by a stream in a given amount of time.
- A stream's load is the amount of material a stream can carry.
- Rivers can be described as youthful, mature, old, or rejuvenated.

Labs

Water Cycle—What Goes Up . . . *(p. 524)*

SECTION 2

Vocabulary

deposition *(p. 255)*
alluvium *(p. 255)*
delta *(p. 256)*
alluvial fan *(p. 257)*
flood plain *(p. 257)*

Section Notes

- Deposition occurs when eroded soil and rock are dropped.
- Alluvium is the material deposited by rivers and streams.
- Deltas are deposits of alluvium at a river's mouth.
- Alluvial fans are deposits of alluvium at the base of a mountain.
- Flood plains are rich farming areas because flooding brings new soils to the area.

Skills Check

Math Concepts

A STREAM'S GRADIENT One factor that can affect the speed of a river is its gradient. The gradient is a measure of the change in elevation over a certain distance. You can use the following equation to calculate a stream's gradient:

$$\text{gradient} = \frac{\text{change in elevation}}{\text{distance}}$$

For example, consider a river that starts at an elevation of 5,500 m and travels 350 km downstream to a lake, which is at an elevation of 2,000 m. By using the formula above, you would find the stream's gradient to be 10 m/km.

$$10\text{ m/km} = \frac{(5{,}500\text{ m} - 2{,}000\text{ m})}{350\text{ km}}$$

Visual Understanding

A STREAM'S LOAD Look back at the diagram on page 252 to review the different types of loads a stream can carry.

A SEWAGE TREATMENT PLANT Study Figure 23 on page 264 to review the two processes used to clean water in a sewage treatment plant.

268

Lab and Activity Highlights

Water Cycle—What Goes Up . . . PG 524

Clean Up Your Act PG 526

Datasheets for LabBook (blackline masters for these labs)

Vocabulary Definitions, *continued*

Section 3

ground water water that is stored in underground caverns or in porous rock below the Earth's surface

water table an underground boundary where the zone of aeration and the zone of saturation meet

aquifer a rock layer that stores and allows the flow of ground water

porosity amount of open space between individual rock particles

permeability a rock's ability to let water pass through it

artesian spring a spring that forms when cracks occur naturally in the cap rock and the pressurized water in the aquifer flows through the cracks to the surface

karst topography areas where the effects of ground water are noticeable at the surface

Section 4

point-source pollution pollution that comes from one particular source area

non-point-source pollution pollution that comes from many sources and that cannot be traced to specific sites

sewage treatment plant a factory that cleans waste matter out of water that comes from sewers or drains

septic tank a large underground tank that collects and cleans waste water from a household

SECTION 3

Vocabulary

ground water *(p. 258)*
water table *(p. 258)*
aquifer *(p. 258)*
porosity *(p. 258)*
permeability *(p. 258)*
artesian spring *(p. 260)*
karst topography *(p. 262)*

Section Notes

- Ground water is located below the Earth's surface. Ground water can dissolve rock, especially limestone.
- The zone of aeration and the zone of saturation meet at a boundary called the water table.
- An aquifer is a porous and permeable rock layer through which ground water flows.
- Karst topography forms when ground water erodes certain types of rock, such as limestone, by dissolving the rock.

SECTION 4

Vocabulary

point-source pollution *(p. 263)*
non-point-source pollution *(p. 263)*
sewage treatment plant *(p. 264)*
septic tank *(p. 265)*

Section Notes

- Sewage is treated in sewage treatment plants and in septic tanks.
- In a sewage treatment plant, water is cleaned in two different ways—primary treatment and secondary treatment.
- While water is generally considered to be a renewable resource, when overused it can sometimes be categorized as a nonrenewable resource.

Labs

Clean Up Your Act *(p. 526)*

internetconnect

GO TO: go.hrw.com

Visit the **HRW** Web site for a variety of learning tools related to this chapter. Just type in the keyword:

KEYWORD: HSTDEP

GO TO: www.scilinks.org

Visit the **National Science Teachers Association** on-line Web site for Internet resources related to this chapter. Just type in the ***sci*LINKS** number for more information about the topic:

TOPIC	*sci*LINKS NUMBER
The Grand Canyon	HSTE255
Rivers and Streams	HSTE260
Water Underground	HSTE265
Water Pollution and Conservation	HSTE270

269

Lab and Activity Highlights

LabBank

EcoLabs & Field Activities, The Frogs Are Off Course, Field Activity 12

Long-Term Projects & Research Ideas, Project 39

Interactive Explorations CD-ROM

CD 1, Exploration 8, "Flood Bank"

Vocabulary Review Worksheet 10

Blackline masters of these Chapter Highlights can be found in the **Study Guide.**

Chapter Review Answers

Using Vocabulary

1. A **water table** is the boundary between the zone of aeration and the zone of saturation. A **tributary** flows into a **river.**
2. An **aquifer** is an underground river. Stream **load** and **discharge** are factors that influence the rate of erosion.
3. **Karst topography** is a type of landscape shaped by ground water erosion. **Deltas** and **alluvial fans** are both fan-shaped alluvial deposits.
4. **Gradient** refers to a stream's slope. **Porosity** and **permeability** are the two characteristics that a rock layer must have to qualify as an aquifer.
5. A **septic tank** is used to collect and clean polluted water. **Point-source** and **non-point-source pollution** are two types of pollution that contaminate surface and ground water.
6. A **drainage basin** is the area that encompasses a river and all of its tributaries. **Primary** and **secondary treatments** are the two different ways that a sewage treatment plant cleans water.

Understanding Concepts

Multiple Choice

7. d
8. c
9. c
10. a
11. d
12. d
13. d
14. c
15. c

Chapter Review

USING VOCABULARY

For each set of terms, identify the term that doesn't belong, and explain why.

1. tributary/river/water table
2. load/discharge/aquifer
3. delta/alluvial fan/karst topography
4. porosity/permeability/gradient
5. point-source pollution/non-point-source pollution/septic tank
6. primary treatment/secondary treatment/drainage basin

UNDERSTANDING CONCEPTS

Multiple Choice

7. Which of the following processes is not part of the water cycle?
   a. evaporation
   b. infiltration
   c. condensation
   d. deposition

8. Which type of stream load makes a river look muddy?
   a. bed load
   b. dissolved load
   c. suspended load
   d. gravelly load

9. What features are common in youthful river channels?
   a. meanders
   b. flood plains
   c. rapids
   d. sandbars

10. Which depositional feature is found at the coast?
   a. delta
   b. flood plain
   c. alluvial fan
   d. placer deposit

11. Karst topography is mainly a product of
   a. erosion by rivers.
   b. river deposition.
   c. water pollution.
   d. erosion by ground water.

12. The largest drainage basin in the United States is the
   a. Amazon.
   b. Columbia.
   c. Colorado.
   d. Mississippi.

13. An aquifer must be
   a. nonporous and nonpermeable.
   b. nonporous and permeable.
   c. porous and nonpermeable.
   d. porous and permeable.

14. Which of the following is a point source of water pollution?
   a. fertilizer from a farming area
   b. runoff from city streets
   c. a waste-water pipe
   d. leaking septic tanks

15. Why is chlorine added to the water in a sewage treatment plant?
   a. to remove large particles
   b. to kill the bacteria that feed on waste in the secondary treatment tanks
   c. to kill harmful germs before releasing the water
   d. to make fine particles settle in the primary treatment tanks

Short Answer

16. What is the relationship between tributaries and rivers?
17. How are aquifers replenished?
18. Why are caves usually found in limestone-rich regions?

270

Short Answer

16. Tributaries flow into rivers and supply them with water.
17. Aquifers are replenished in the recharge zone. This is an area where a permeable rock layer allows water to percolate down into the aquifer.
18. Limestone is made of calcium carbonate, which dissolves easily in water. Ground water dissolves the limestone, producing caves.

Chapter 10 Review—California Standards: PE/ATE Q1–6: 2, 2a, 2b, 6, 6b; Q7–14: 2, 2a, 2b, 2c

Concept Mapping

19. Use the following terms to create a concept map: zone of aeration, zone of saturation, water table, gravity, porosity, permeability.

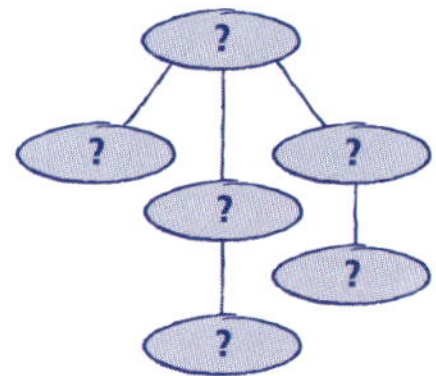

CRITICAL THINKING AND PROBLEM SOLVING

Write one or two sentences to answer the following questions:

20. What role does water play in erosion and deposition?
21. What are the features of a river channel that has a steep gradient?
22. Ground water is hard to pollute. Why is it also hard to clean up?
23. Imagine you are hiking beside a mature stream. What would the stream be like?
24. How can water be considered both a renewable and a nonrenewable resource? Give an example of each case.

MATH IN SCIENCE

25. A sinkhole has formed in a town with a population of 5,000. The town is declared a disaster area, and $2 million is given to the town by the federal government. The local government uses 60 percent of the money for repairs to city property, and the rest is given to the townspeople.
    a. How much would each person receive?
    b. If there are 2,000 families in the town, how much would each family receive?
    c. Would each family receive enough money to help them rebuild a home? If not, how could the money be distributed more fairly?

INTERPRETING GRAPHICS

The hydrograph below illustrates river flow over a period of 1 year. The discharge readings are from the Yakima River, in Washington. The Yakima River flows eastward from the Cascade Mountains to the Columbia River.

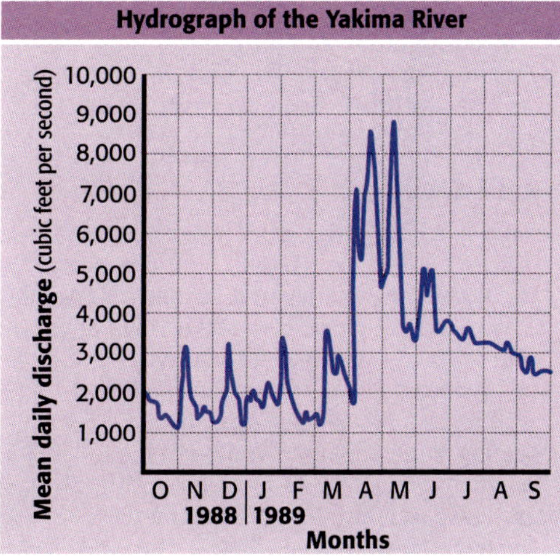

26. In which months is there the highest river discharge?
27. Why is there such a high river discharge during these months?
28. What might cause the peaks in river discharge between November and March?

NOW What Do You Think?

Take a minute to review the answers to the ScienceLog questions on page 247. Have your answers changed? If necessary, revise your answers based on what you have learned since you began this chapter.

271

Concept Mapping

19.  An answer to this exercise can be found at the end of this book.

Critical Thinking and Problem Solving

20. Water flows across a landscape, eroding, transporting, and depositing material. Water is an agent of erosion and deposition.
21. A river channel that has a steep gradient is straight and narrow with rapids, waterfalls, and V-shaped valleys.
22. Once ground water becomes polluted, it is hard to clean up because it is not at the surface, where cleanup is done. Also, it moves very slowly and will therefore take a long time to clean up.
23. A mature river is wide with meanders. It can have a lot of discharge due to its width.
24. Water is a renewable resource when it can be replaced or recycled. Rain is a renewable resource. Water is nonrenewable when it cannot be replenished, as in the Ogallala aquifer.

Math in Science

25. a. $160
    b. $400
    c. Accept all reasonable responses. Sample answer: No; more money should be distributed to the families whose houses were directly affected by the sinkhole.

Interpreting Graphics

26. April and May
27. Accept all reasonable responses. (spring snowmelt from the mountains, high rainfall)
28. winter storms

NOW What Do You Think?

1. Answers will vary. Accept all reasonable responses. Sample answer: Running water erodes the landscape, redistributing sediment.
2. Erosion is the removal and transport of sediment. Deposition is the dropping off of sediment.

Concept Mapping Transparency 10

Blackline masters of this Chapter Review can be found in the **Study Guide.**

Chapter 10 Review—California Standards: PE/ATE Q20–24: 2, 2a, 2b, 6, 6b; Q26–28: 2b; Think: 2, 2a, 2b

Background

Yellowstone National Park, located in northwestern Wyoming and southern Montana, includes more than 10,000 geothermal features. All of these features are the product of Yellowstone's unique geographic position. About half of Yellowstone Park lies on top of three major calderas that formed between 0.6 million and 2 million years ago. A caldera is a circular depression formed when the roof of a magma chamber collapses as a result of a volcanic eruption. The high temperatures from the most recent caldera account for the large number of geothermal features in the park.

Fumaroles are the vents that emit the volcanic gas responsible for forming mud pots.

WEIRD SCIENCE

BUBBLE, BOIL, & SQUIRT

In parts of Yellowstone National Park boiling water blasts into the sky, lakes of strange-colored mud boil and gurgle, and hot gases hiss from the ground. What are these strange geologic features? What causes them? The story begins deep in the Earth.

Old Geysers

One of Yellowstone's main tourist attractions is a *geyser* called Old Faithful. Erupting every 60 to 70 minutes, Old Faithful sends a plume of steam and scalding-hot water as high as 60 m into the air. A geyser is formed when a narrow vent connects one or more underground chambers to Earth's surface. These underground chambers are heated by nearly molten rock. As underground water flows into the vent and chambers, it is heated above 100°C. The superheated water quickly turns to steam and explodes first toward the surface and then into the air. And Old Faithful erupts right on schedule!

Nature's Hot Tub

A *hot spring* is a geyser without pressure. Its vents are wider than a geyser's, and they let the underground water cool a little and flow to the surface rather than erupt in a big fountain. To be called a hot spring, the water must be at least as warm as human body temperature (37°C). Some springs reach temperatures of several hundred degrees Celsius.

Flying Mud Pies

Mud pots form when steam or hot underground water trickles to the surface and chemically weathers and dissolves surface features, such as rocks. The mixture of dissolved rock and water creates a boiling, bubbling pool of sticky liquid clay. But don't get too close! Occasionally, the steam will rise quickly and forcefully enough to make the mud pot behave like a volcano. When it does, a mud pot can toss car-sized gobs of mud high into the air!

Some mud pots become *paint pots* when microorganisms or brightly colored minerals are mixed in. For instance, if there is a lot of iron in the mud, the paint pot will turn reddish brown or yellowish brown. Other minerals and bacteria can make the mud white or bluish in color. Some paint pots may even gurgle up blobs in several different colors.

▲ *Mud Pot in Yellowstone National Park*

What Do You Think?

▶ Some people believe that tapping geothermal energy sources such as geysers could harm the delicate ecology of those sources. Find out about the benefits and the risks of using geothermal energy. What is your opinion?

272

Sample Answer to What Do You Think?

The main advantage of geothermal energy is that, unlike fossil fuels, it doesn't produce pollution and is a renewable resource. Also, geothermal energy plants require less space than normal power plants. However, some scientists believe that using geothermal energy from geysers could disrupt the natural flow of hot springs and possibly disrupt ground-water sources. Some geysers recently used to make electricity have stopped producing steam. Other possible consequences of the disruption of geothermal areas are as follows: the extinction of microorganisms that thrive in hot waters, collapsing calderas, and more-frequent volcanic eruptions.

California Standards: PE/ATE 6, 6a

EYE ON THE ENVIRONMENT

Disaster Along the Delta

As the sun rises over the delta wetlands of the Mississippi River, fishermen test their skills. Long-legged birds step lightly through the marsh, hunting fish or frogs for breakfast. And hundreds of species of plants and animals start another day in this fragile ecosystem. But the delta ecosystem is in danger of being destroyed.

The threat comes from efforts to make the Mississippi more useful. Large portions of the river bottom were dredged to make the river deeper for ship traffic. Underwater channels were built to control flooding. What no one realized was that sediments that were once deposited to form new land now pass through the deep channels and flow out into the ocean.

Those river sediments replaced the land that was lost every year to erosion. Without the sediments, the river can't replace the land lost to erosion. And so the Mississippi River delta is disappearing. By 1995, more than half the wetlands were already gone, swept out to sea by waves along the Louisiana coast.

▲ *The Mississippi River flows from Minnesota through the Midwest to the Gulf of Mexico in the southern United States.*

Sedimental Journey

The Mississippi River journeys 3,766 km to empty 232 million metric tons of sediment into the Gulf of Mexico each year. The end of the Mississippi River delta forms the largest area of wetlands in North America. A *delta* forms when sediments settle at the mouth of a river. At the Mississippi River delta, the sediments build up and form new land along the Louisiana coastline. The area around the delta is called *wetlands.* It has fertile soil, which produces many crops, and a variety of habitats—marsh, freshwater, and saltwater—that support many species of plants and animals.

Taking Action to Preserve the Delta

Since the mid-1980s, local, state, and federal governments, along with Louisiana citizens and businesses, have been working together to monitor and restore the Mississippi River delta. Some projects to protect the delta include filling in canals that divert the sediments and even using old Christmas trees as fences to trap the sediments! With the continued efforts of scientists, government leaders, and concerned citizens, the Mississippi River delta stands a good chance of recovering.

Explore the Delta

▶ Find out more about the industries and organisms that depend on the Mississippi River delta for survival. What will happen to them if we don't take care of the ecosystem?

273

Answers to Explore the Delta

The coastal wetlands provide a habitat for diverse communities of plants and animals, such as fish, shellfish, and birds. The wetlands are the nursery and feeding area for millions of waterfowl. These species and the industries that rely on them, such as fishing and tourism, will suffer greatly if the wetland ecosystems are not protected. If erosion is severe enough, buildings, highways, phone lines, and pipelines will need to be relocated.

EYE ON THE ENVIRONMENT
Disaster Along the Delta

Background

The word *Mississippi* comes from a Native American word that means "big river." The Mississippi River flows for 3,766 km from its source, in Minnesota, to its mouth, in the Gulf of Mexico. More than 2,897 km of the river can be navigated by ships and boats for commercial, transportational, and recreational uses.

The Mississippi River forms part of the boundaries of 10 different states. As it travels to the Gulf of Mexico, other rivers—such as the Ohio and the Missouri—flow into it and increase the volume of water in the Mississippi River.

The Mississippi River delta covers about 33,700 km^2. It continuously nourishes the coastal wetlands that provide a habitat for diverse populations of plants and animals.

The erosion and sinking of land near the Mississippi River delta has seriously disrupted local economies. For instance, the coastal commercial and recreational fishing industries contribute about $2 billion to Louisiana's economy every year and provide about 50,000 to 70,000 jobs for the people of Louisiana. Also, the coastal wetlands provide coastal residents with protection from hurricanes and other storms. Currently, the destruction in this area accounts for 80 percent of the nation's loss of coastal wetlands per year.

California Standards: PE/ATE 2, 2b, 2c, 5e

Chapter Organizer

CHAPTER ORGANIZATION	TIME MINUTES	OBJECTIVES	LABS, INVESTIGATIONS, AND DEMONSTRATIONS
Chapter Opener **pp. 274–275**	45	California Standards: PE/ATE 2c, 7, 7b, 7e	**Investigate!** Making Waves, p. 275
Section 1 **Shoreline Erosion and Deposition**	90	▶ Explain the connection between storms and wave erosion. ▶ Explain how waves break in shallow water. ▶ Describe how beaches form. ▶ Describe types of coastal landforms created by wave action. PE/ATE 2, 2b, 2c, 3a	**Whiz-Bang Demonstrations,** Between a Rock and a Hard Place, Demo 23 **Whiz-Bang Demonstrations,** Rising Mountains, Demo 24
Section 2 **Wind Erosion and Deposition**	90	▶ Explain why areas with fine materials are more vulnerable to wind erosion. ▶ Describe how wind moves sand and finer materials. ▶ Describe the effects of wind erosion. ▶ Describe the difference between dunes and loess. PE/ATE 2, 6b, 7, 7b, 7e; LabBook 7, 7b, 7e, 7g	**QuickLab,** Making Desert Pavement, p. 283 **Making Models,** Dune Movement, p. 530 **Datasheets for LabBook,** Dune Movement, Datasheet 23
Section 3 **Erosion and Deposition by Ice**	90	▶ Summarize why glaciers are important agents of erosion and deposition. ▶ Explain how ice in a glacier flows. ▶ Describe some of the landforms eroded by glaciers. ▶ Describe some of the landforms deposited by glaciers. PE/ATE 2, 2a, 2b, 7f; LabBook 2, 7, 7b, 7e	**Making Models,** Gliding Glaciers, p. 531 **Datasheets for LabBook,** Gliding Glaciers, Datasheet 24 **Discovery Lab,** Creating a Kettle, p. 533 **Datasheets for LabBook,** Creating a Kettle, Datasheet 25
Section 4 **Gravity's Effect on Erosion and Deposition**	90	▶ Explain how slope is related to mass movement. ▶ State how gravity affects mass movement. ▶ Describe different types of mass movement. PE/ATE 2, 2d, 7, 7b, 7e	**QuickLab,** Angle of Repose, p. 294 **Long-Term Projects & Research Ideas,** Project 40

See page **T20** *for a complete correlation of this book with the*

CALIFORNIA SCIENCE CONTENT STANDARDS.

Correlations are also provided at point of use throughout this ATE.

TECHNOLOGY RESOURCES

Guided Reading Audio CD
English or Spanish, Chapter 11

Classroom Management CD-ROM

Earth Science Videodisc
Reshaping the Crust: 44061–51180
Weathering and Erosion: 44062–46566
Glaciers and Erosion: 48922–51180

CNN **Science, Technology & Society,** Battling over the Oregon Inlet, Segment 17
Eye on the Environment, Shrinking Wetlands, Segment 8

Test Generator CD-ROM

Chapter 11 • Agents of Erosion and Deposition

CLASSROOM WORKSHEETS, TRANSPARENCIES, AND RESOURCES	SCIENCE INTEGRATION AND CONNECTIONS	REVIEW AND ASSESSMENT
Directed Reading Worksheet 11 **Science Puzzlers, Twisters & Teasers,** Worksheet 11		
Math Skills for Science Worksheet 31, The Unit Factor and Dimensional Analysis **Directed Reading Worksheet 11,** Section 1 **Science Skills Worksheet 2,** Using Your Senses	**MathBreak,** Counting Waves, p. 277 **Connect to Physical Science,** p. 277 in ATE **Math and More,** p. 277 in ATE **Multicultural Connection,** p. 278 in ATE **Connect to Life Science,** p. 279 in ATE **Eye on the Environment:** Beach Today, Gone Tomorrow, p. 303	**Self-Check,** p. 277 **Review,** p. 281 **Quiz,** p. 281 in ATE **Alternative Assessment,** p. 281 in ATE
Transparency 125, Saltation **Directed Reading Worksheet 11,** Section 2 **Transparency 126,** Migration of Sand Dunes **Critical Thinking Worksheet 11,** A Future in Sand	**Connect to Life Science,** pp. 282, 285 in ATE **Apply,** p. 284 **Multicultural Connection,** p. 284 in ATE **Cross-Disciplinary Focus,** p. 285 in ATE **Life Science Connection,** p. 286 **Science, Technology, and Society:** Boulder Boogie, p. 302	**Self-Check,** p. 283 **Homework,** p. 285 in ATE **Review,** p. 286 **Quiz,** p. 286 in ATE **Alternative Assessment,** p. 286 in ATE
Directed Reading Worksheet 11, Section 3 **Math Skills for Science Worksheet 17,** Using Proportions and Cross-Multiplication **Transparency 127,** Landscape Features Carved by Alpine Glaciers **Reinforcement Worksheet 11,** An Alpine Vacation	**MathBreak,** Speed of a Glacier, p. 289 **Connect to Physical Science,** p. 289 in ATE **Cross-Disciplinary Focus,** p. 291 in ATE **Real-World Connection,** p. 292 in ATE **Cross-Disciplinary Focus,** p. 292 in ATE	**Self-Check,** p. 289 **Homework,** pp. 290, 291 in ATE **Review,** p. 293 **Quiz,** p. 293 in ATE **Alternative Assessment,** p. 293 in ATE
Transparency 175, The Law of Universal Gravitation **Directed Reading Worksheet 11,** Section 4	**Physical Science Connection,** p. 295 **Connect to Physical Science,** p. 295 in ATE **Real-World Connection,** p. 296 in ATE **Connect to Life Science,** p. 296 in ATE **Life Science Connection,** p. 297	**Homework,** p. 295 in ATE **Review,** p. 297 **Quiz,** p. 297 in ATE **Alternative Assessment,** p. 297 in ATE

Holt, Rinehart and Winston On-line Resources

go.hrw.com

For worksheets and other teaching aids related to this chapter, visit the HRW Web site and type in the keyword: **HSTICE**

National Science Teachers Association

www.scilinks.org

Encourage students to use the keywords listed on the Technology Highlights page to access information and resources on the **NSTA** Web site.

END-OF-CHAPTER REVIEW AND ASSESSMENT

Chapter Review in Study Guide
Vocabulary and Notes in Study Guide
Chapter Tests with Performance-Based Assessment, Chapter 11 Test
Chapter Tests with Performance-Based Assessment, Performance-Based Assessment 11
Concept Mapping Transparency 11

Chapter Resources & Worksheets

Visual Resources

TEACHING TRANSPARENCIES

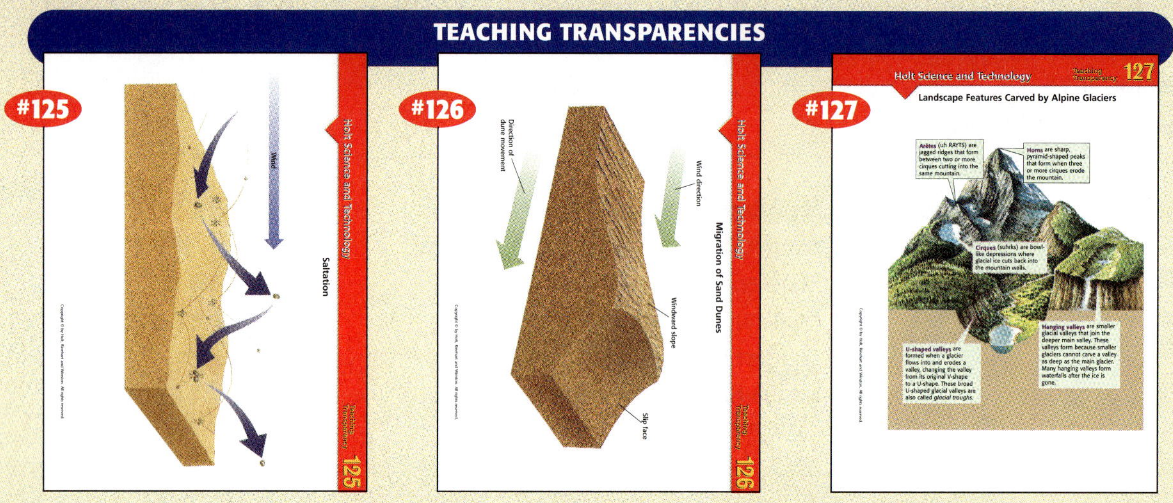

TEACHING TRANSPARENCIES

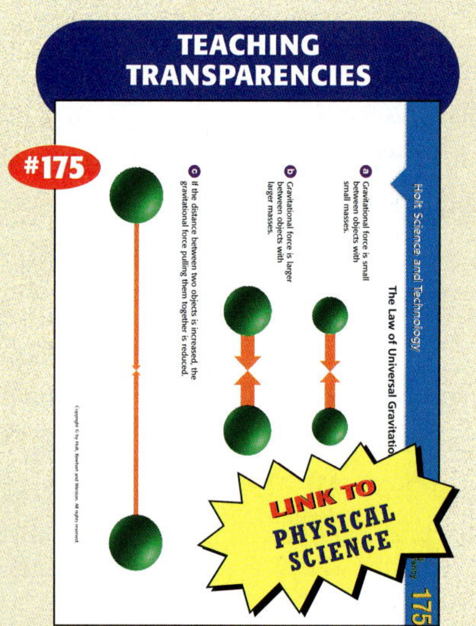

CONCEPT MAPPING TRANSPARENCY

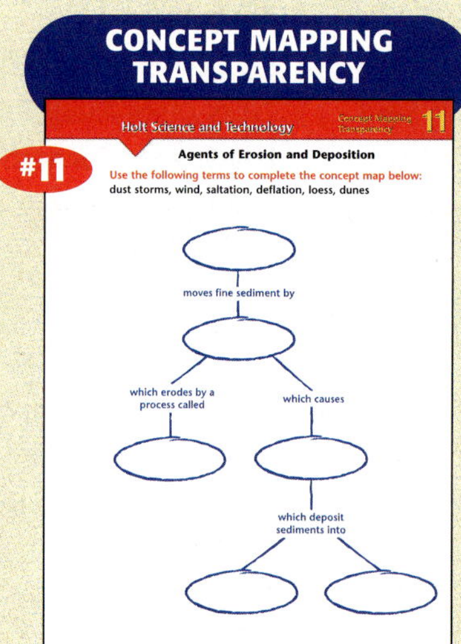

Meeting Individual Needs

DIRECTED READING

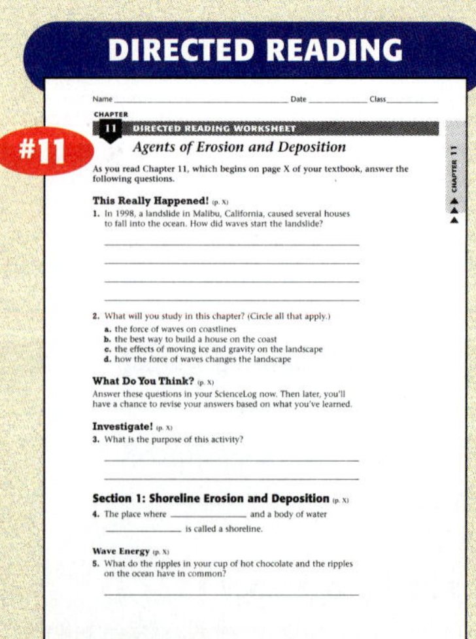

REINFORCEMENT & VOCABULARY REVIEW

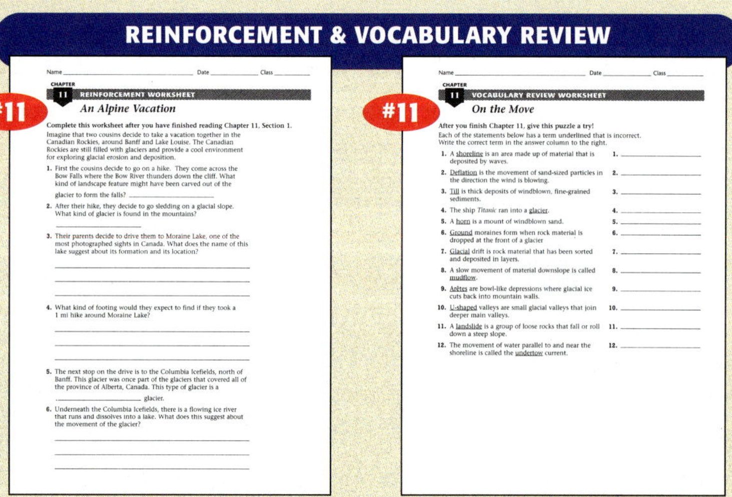

SCIENCE PUZZLERS, TWISTERS & TEASERS

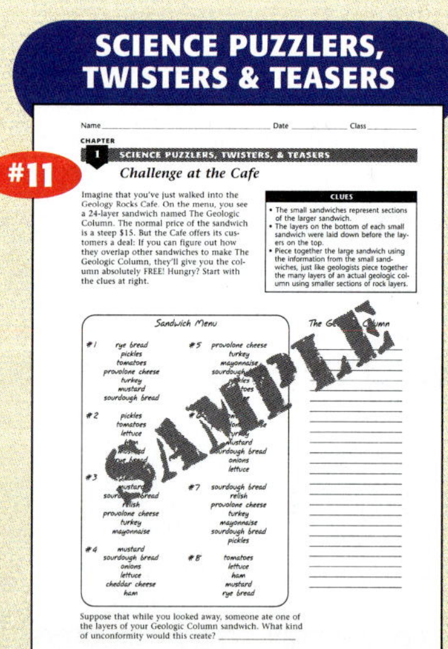

Chapter 11 • Agents of Erosion and Deposition

Review & Assessment

STUDY GUIDE

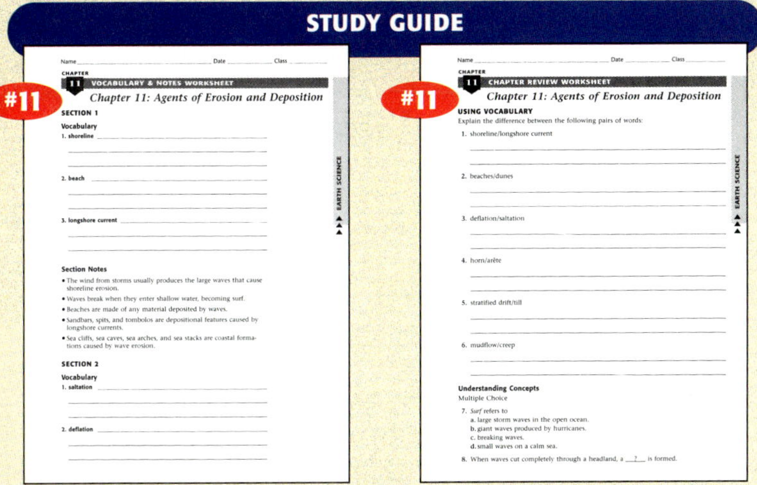

CHAPTER TESTS WITH PERFORMANCE-BASED ASSESSMENT

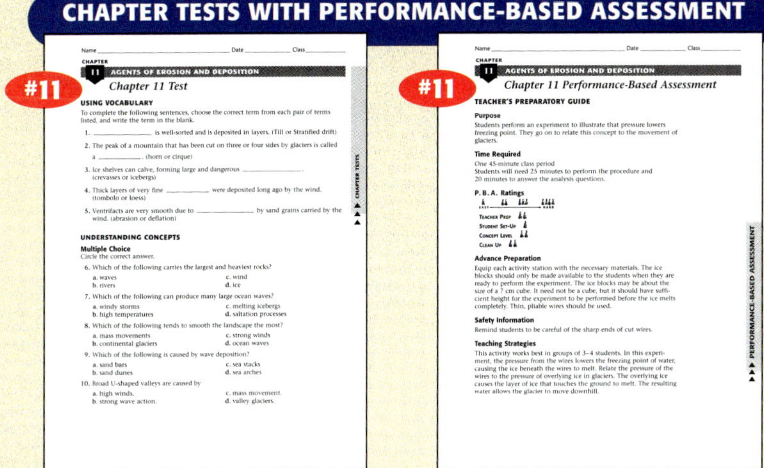

Lab Worksheets

WHIZ-BANG DEMONSTRATIONS

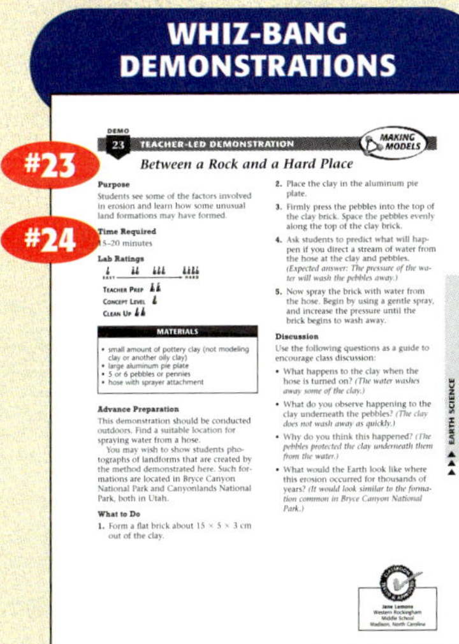

LONG-TERM PROJECTS & RESEARCH IDEAS

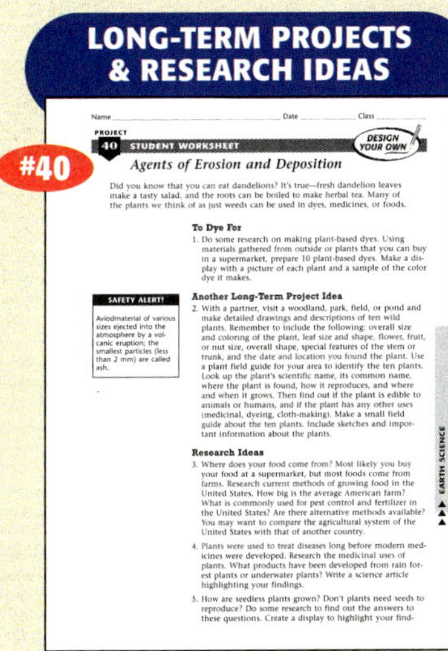

DATASHEETS FOR LABBOOK

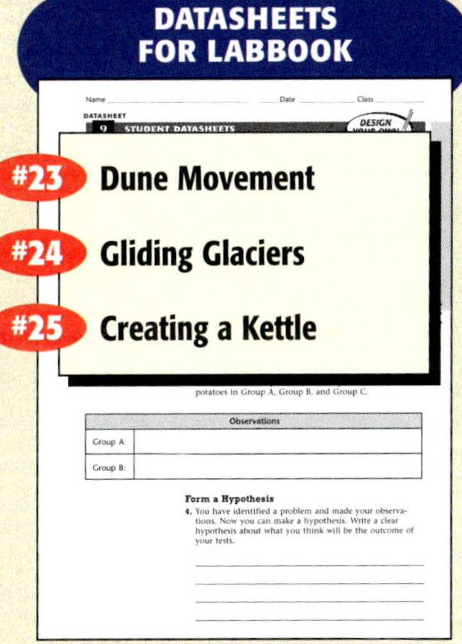

Applications & Extensions

CRITICAL THINKING & PROBLEM SOLVING

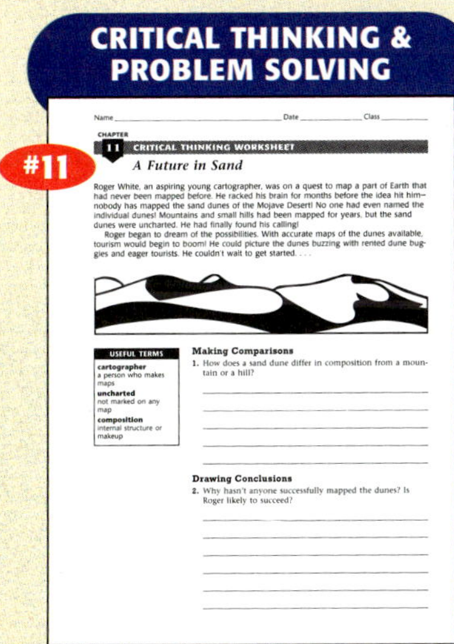

SCIENCE TECHNOLOGY

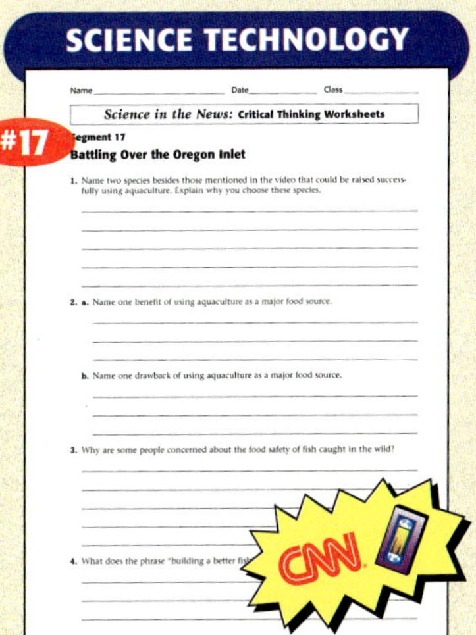

EYE ON THE ENVIRONMENT

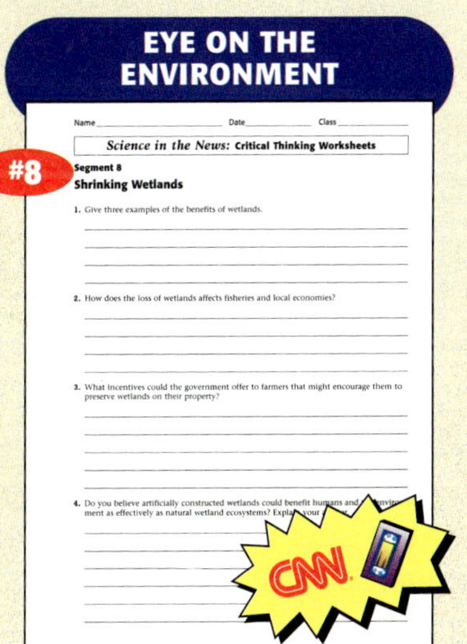

Chapter Background

Section 1

Shoreline Erosion and Deposition

Acrobatic Waves

To understand shoreline erosion, it's helpful to understand the forces acting in a breaking wave. Breaking waves can be thought of as somersaulting water. As waves move toward shallow coastal waters, the wavelengths shorten, crests crowd together, and wave height grows. When a wave becomes too top-heavy, it somersaults over itself, rushing onto the shore. As the water flows back into the ocean, it carries sand and sediment with it.

The Origins of Cape Cod

At the end of the last glacial period—10,000 years ago—glaciers receding across North America helped form Cape Cod, Massachusetts. Cape Cod was initially mounds of outwash debris left behind by the glaciers. These mounds were then surrounded by the rising sea. Over time, currents eroded land and filled in depressions between the islands. Sandbars connected the islands to each other and the mainland. Since that time, Cape Cod has lost 3.2 km of coastline to ocean erosion.

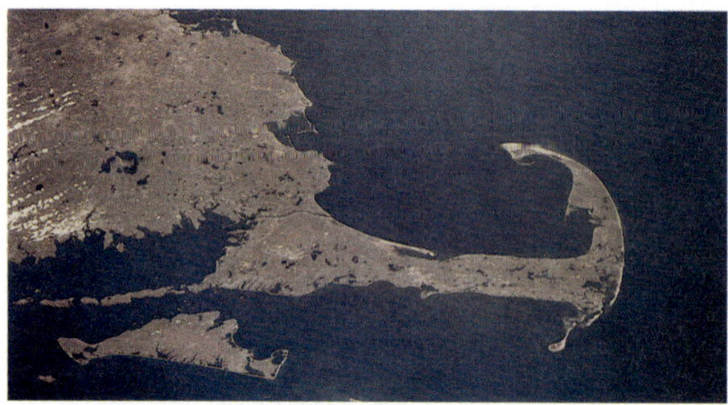

IS THAT A FACT!

- Scientists predict that if the erosion continues at the current rate, Cape Cod will be completely reclaimed by the ocean in 4,000–5,000 years.

Section 2

Wind Erosion and Deposition

The Dust Bowl

The Dust Bowl was a section of the Great Plains of the United States that extended from southeastern Colorado and southwestern Kansas to the panhandles of Texas and Oklahoma and to northeastern New Mexico. In the early 1930s, following years of overcultivation in the 1920s, the region suffered a severe drought. Exposed topsoil was carried away by strong spring winds. Windblown soil sometimes blocked out the sun, and the dirt piled up in drifts like snow. Occasionally, huge dust storms blew across the country and reached the East Coast. The wind erosion was gradually halted when the federal government planted windbreaks and large areas of grasslands were restored. The area had mostly recovered by the early 1940s.

Lost Cities of the Takla Makan Desert

The Takla Makan Desert in China's arid northwest is so inhospitable that its name in the local language means "Go in, and you don't come out." The desert is covered with treacherous dunes of fine, dry sand. Buried under those dunes are the remains of cities that prospered along the ancient Silk Road. The Silk Road was a trade route that connected China to civilizations in the West. NASA's Spaceborne Imaging Radar (SIR-C), which flew on space shuttles twice in 1994, is being used to examine the desert. The radar-imaging technology has already helped archaeologists locate some cities and promises to help them find other ruins.

SECTION 3

Erosion and Deposition by Ice

Glaciers and Drinking Water

About 10 percent of Earth's surface is covered with glaciers. The water frozen in glaciers makes up almost 75 percent of the world's freshwater supply. Arapaho Glacier, a small glacier in Colorado, provides water to more than 75,000 people living in the city of Boulder. Many countries have explored the possibility of obtaining drinking water from glaciers, even by towing icebergs to a nearby harbor!

IS THAT A FACT!

- Glaciers flow at different rates. Most glaciers flow at a rate of 1 m per day or less, but some flow much faster. In 1936, the Black Rapids Glacier, in Alaska, was measured flowing at a rate of 30 m per day.
- If all of Earth's glaciers simultaneously melted, sea level would rise more than 65 m, submerging coastal cities all over the world.

Battles on Siachen Glacier

At 70 km, the Siachen Glacier is one of the world's longest. It's in the Karakoram Range, on the India–Pakistan border. It is also the site of the world's highest battles. Indian and Pakistani soldiers have fought over the disputed territory of Kashmir on peaks as high as 21,000 ft.

The Great Lakes

The Great Lakes were formed by the movement of ice sheets during the Pleistocene epoch. These glaciers advanced over the land, gouging out a series of deep basins. As the glaciers melted, the basins filled with meltwater, and the five Great Lakes were formed.

SECTION 4

Gravity's Effect on Erosion and Deposition

Scree

Mountain stones and boulders loosened by weathering and carried downward by gravity may be deposited in long, loose heaps called scree at the base of a mountain.

IS THAT A FACT!

- When an earthquake measuring 5 on the Richter scale occurred near Mount St. Helens on May 18, 1980, it triggered a landslide of more than 2 km^3 of rock and ice. Immediately afterward, an eruption began, and an explosion of steam and volcanic gases produced a lahar that raced down the mountain at speeds of up to 250 km/h.

For additional background resources, please refer to the ***HST Reference Library.***

CHAPTER 11

Agents of Erosion and Deposition

Chapter Preview

Section 1
Shoreline Erosion and Deposition
- Wave Energy
- Wave Deposits
- Wave Erosion

Section 2
Wind Erosion and Deposition
- Process of Wind Erosion
- Wind-Deposited Materials

Section 3
Erosion and Deposition by Ice
- Glaciers—Rivers of Ice
- Landforms Carved by Glaciers
- Types of Glacial Deposits

Section 4
Gravity's Effect on Erosion and Deposition
- The Forces in Mass Movement

Directed Reading Worksheet 11

Science Puzzlers, Twisters & Teasers Worksheet 11

Guided Reading Audio CD
English or Spanish, Chapter 11

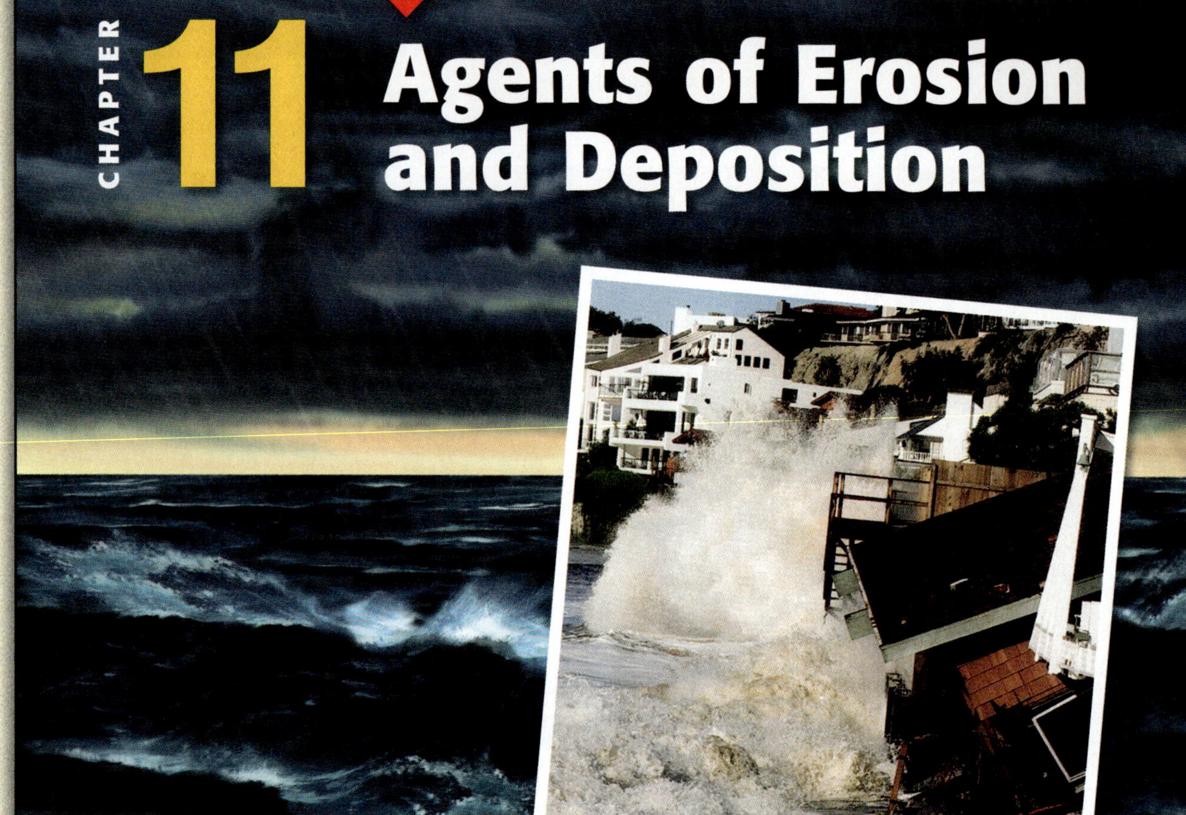

This Really Happened!

The waves struck at the ocean cliffs, releasing their energy as they do every day. But on this day the waves seemed different—larger and more explosive, cutting away at the rock with each crash.

On February 8, 1998, unusually large waves crashed against the cliffs along Broad Beach Road in Malibu, California. Eventually the ocean-eroded cliffs buckled, causing a landslide. One house collapsed into the ocean, while two more dangled on the edge of the cliff's newly eroded face. How did this happen? What made these waves stronger than usual?

This is all part of the ongoing natural process of coastal erosion along the California shoreline and similar shorelines throughout the world. Winter storms create powerful waves that crash into the cliffs, breaking off pieces of rock that fall into the ocean. Sometimes these natural processes are underestimated, and lives and property are put at risk.

In this chapter, you will study the force of waves on coastlines and how this force changes the landscape. You will also study the effects of wind, moving ice, and the pull of gravity on the landscape.

274

This Really Happened!

In years with an El Niño weather pattern, unusually warm water in the Pacific spawns storms that move westward toward the California coast. High winds create large waves that pound the coast, causing erosion. The storms also bring heavy rainfall. In January 1995, parts of California received more than their average annual rainfall in 1 month.

What Do You Think?

In your ScienceLog, try to answer the following questions based on what you already know:

1. What do waves and wind have in common?
2. How do waves, wind, and ice erode and deposit rock materials?

Making Waves

Waves move onto the shore continuously. But have you ever thought about how they affect the shoreline? See for yourself by creating waves of your own.

Procedure

1. Fill a **washtub** with **water** to a depth of 5 cm.
2. Make a beach by adding **sand** to one end of the washtub.
3. In your ScienceLog, sketch the beach profile (side view), and label it "A."
4. Place a **block** at the end of the washtub opposite the beach. Move the block up and down very slowly to create small waves for 2 minutes. Sketch the new beach profile in your ScienceLog, and label it "B."
5. Again place a block at the end of the washtub opposite the beach. Move the block up and down more rapidly to create large waves for 2 minutes. Sketch the new beach profile in your ScienceLog, and label it "C."

Analysis

6. Compare beach profiles A, B, and C. What is happening to the beach?
7. How do small waves and large waves erode the beach differently?
8. What other factors might contribute to beach erosion?

Going Further

On the Internet, explore how coastal erosion affects personal property along the West Coast. Learn about the methods used to slow down coastal erosion.

What Do You Think?

Accept all reasonable responses.

Students will have a chance to revise their answers in the Chapter Review under NOW What Do You Think?

Investigate!

MATERIALS

PER GROUP:
- washtub
- tap water
- sand
- wooden or plastic block

Answers to Investigate!

6. The beach is slowly receding, or eroding.
7. Small waves erode less shoreline than large waves. Therefore, large waves have a greater impact on the shoreline.
8. Accept all reasonable responses. Sample answers: Lack of vegetation increases beach erosion. Wind and storms contribute to beach erosion.

Answer to Going Further

Accept all reasonable responses. Sample answer: Coastal erosion is causing landslides. People's homes are being destroyed. Methods to slow down coastal erosion include beach nourishment and the use of barrier structures and retaining walls.

IS THAT A FACT!

Waves and longshore currents continually move the sand that makes up the barrier islands of the East Coast of the United States. In fact, they have pushed Brigantine Island, near Atlantic City, New Jersey, 1.3 km to the north!

WEIRD SCIENCE

The disappearance of the town of Broadwater, located on Hog Island, in the Chesapeake Bay, is a striking example of the power of ocean waves. Waves eroded the sandy land on which the town existed, and Broadwater is no longer there!

Chapter 11 Opener–California Standards: PE/ATE 2c, 7, 7b, 7e

SECTION 1

Focus

Shoreline Erosion and Deposition

This section explores how wave action sculpts and builds shorelines. Students first focus on the formation of beaches and offshore landforms by deposition and then learn how waves erode the shoreline. Students explore the formation of sea cliffs, sea stacks, sea arches, and sea caves, and learn how waves work to erode cliffs, creating headlands and wave-cut terraces.

Bellringer

Writing Ask students to think about where sand comes from. Have them write a short poem in their ScienceLog about how ocean waves create sand from rock.

1 Motivate

ACTIVITY

Explain to students that shorelines are dynamic, changing environments because ocean waves and currents continually erode and redeposit sand. Have each student draw a "filmstrip" illustrating the changes that could occur in the history of a beach.

Encourage students to illustrate the processes that cause these changes and to write a caption that explains each frame and the time interval that elapses between scenes. Students can present their filmstrips to the class.

1

NEW TERMS
shoreline
beach
longshore current

OBJECTIVES
- Explain the connection between storms and wave erosion.
- Explain how waves break in shallow water.
- Describe how beaches form.
- Describe types of coastal landforms created by wave action.

Shoreline Erosion and Deposition

What images pop into your head when you hear the word *beach*? You probably picture sand, blue ocean as far as the eye can see, balmy breezes, and waves. In this section you will learn how all those things relate to erosion and deposition along the shoreline. A **shoreline** is where land and a body of water meet. *Erosion,* as you may recall, is the breakdown and movement of materials. *Deposition* takes place when these materials are dropped. Waves can be powerful agents of erosion and deposition, as you will soon learn.

Wave Energy

Have you ever noticed the tiny ripples created by your breath when you blow on a cup of hot chocolate to cool it? Similarly, the wind moves over the ocean surface, producing ripples called *waves*. The size of a wave depends on how hard the wind is blowing and the length of time the wind blows. The harder and longer the wind blows, the bigger the wave is. Try it the next time you drink cocoa.

The wind that comes from severe winter storms and summer hurricanes generally produces the large waves that cause shoreline erosion. Waves may travel hundreds or even thousands of kilometers from a storm before reaching the shoreline. Some of the largest waves to reach the California coast are produced by storms as far away as Alaska and Australia. Thus, the California surfer in **Figure 1** can ride a wave produced by a storm on the other side of the Pacific Ocean.

Figure 1 *Waves produced by storms on the other side of the Pacific Ocean propel this surfer toward a California shore.*

276

MISCONCEPTION ALERT

It is a popular misconception that a wave is a moving wall of water. Water actually moves up and down rather than forward as wave energy travels through it.

Section 1–California Standards: PE/ATE 2, 2b, 2c, 3a

Wave Trains On your imaginary visit to the beach, do you remember seeing just one wave? Of course not; waves don't move alone. They travel in groups called *wave trains*. As wave trains move away from their source, they travel through the ocean water without interruption. When they reach shallow water, they change form and begin to break. The ocean floor crowds the lower part of the wave, shortening the wave length and increasing the wave height. This results in taller, more closely spaced waves. When the top of the wave becomes so tall that it cannot support itself, it begins to curl and break. These breaking waves are known as *surf*. Now you know how surfers got their name.

Figure 2 *Because waves travel in wave trains, they break at regular intervals, such as every 10 to 20 seconds.*

If you've ever heard a surf report, it might have sounded like this: "10- to 12-foot waves from the southwest at 12-second intervals." This type of report gives the wave height, the direction the wave is moving, and the wave period. The *wave period,* as shown in **Figure 2,** is the time interval between breaking waves. Wave periods are usually 10 to 20 seconds long.

The Pounding Surf One reason waves are so effective at picking up, transporting, and depositing material is that they are continually breaking. Another reason is that a tremendous amount of energy is released when waves break, as shown in **Figure 3.** A crashing wave can break solid rock or throw broken rocks back against the shore. The rushing water in breaking waves can easily wash into cracks in rock, helping to break off large boulders or fine grains of sand. The loose sand picked up by the waves polishes and wears down coastal rocks. Waves can also move sand and small rocks and deposit them in other locations, forming beaches.

MATH BREAK

Counting Waves

How many waves do you think reach a shoreline in a day if the wave period is 10 seconds?
(Hint: Calculate how many waves occur in a minute, in an hour, and in a day.)

Figure 3 *Breaking waves crash against the rocky shore, releasing their energy.*

Self-Check

Would a large wave or a small wave have more erosive energy? Why? *(See page 564 to check your answer.)*

277

Answer to Self-Check

A large wave has more erosive energy than a small wave because a large wave releases more energy when it breaks.

2 Teach

CONNECT TO PHYSICAL SCIENCE

The waves in lakes and oceans are a form of energy traveling through a medium—water. Other energy waves, such as sound waves, also require a medium through which to travel. Some waves, however, such as light and radio waves, can travel through a vacuum.

MATH and MORE

Have students calculate how many waves would reach a shoreline in 24 hours with periods of 15 and 20 seconds. (With a 15-second period, 5,760 waves would reach the shore. With a 20-second period, 4,320 waves would reach the shore.)

Math Skills Worksheet 31 "The Unit Factor and Dimensional Analysis"

Answer to MATHBREAK

In 1 minute, six waves occur. In 1 hour, 360 waves occur. In 1 day, 8,640 waves occur.

$60 \div 10 = 6$ waves

$6 \times 60 = 360$ waves

$360 \times 24 = 8,640$ waves

Directed Reading Worksheet 11 Section 1

2 Teach, continued

Using the Figure

Draw students' attention to **Figure 5.** Point out that when water strikes the shoreline at an angle and then retreats in a direction perpendicular to the shore, material is moved along the beach in a zigzag pattern. Inform students that this is known as *beach* or *longshore drift.*

Encourage students to use the Internet or reference texts in their school library to learn more about longshore drift. Ask students to prepare labeled diagrams in their ScienceLog illustrating the phenomenon. Sheltered English

Multicultural Connection

The Polynesians are considered some of the greatest navigators of the ancient world. Polynesians visited and inhabited more than 10,000 islands throughout the South Pacific. They navigated not by using maps but by carefully observing stars, winds, and waves. On cloudy nights, they navigated by listening to the way the waves rocked and slapped against their dugout canoes. The Polynesians understood how wave patterns could indicate the direction of land or the presence of dangerous reefs or sandbars. Encourage students to discover more about Polynesian cultures in the past and present.

Science Skills Worksheet 2 "Using Your Senses"

Figure 4 *Beaches are made of different types of material deposited by waves.*

Wave Deposits

Waves carry an assortment of materials, including sand, rock fragments, and shells. Often this material is deposited on the shore. But as you will learn, this is not always the case.

Beaches You would probably recognize a beach if you saw one. But technically, a **beach** is any area of the shoreline made up of material deposited by waves. Some beach material arrives on the shoreline by way of rivers. Rivers erode mountains, hills, and higher ground. Some of the eroded material is then carried by the river to the ocean and deposited where the river enters the sea. Later, ocean waves interacting with currents move and redeposit the material along the shoreline. Other beach material is eroded from areas located near the shoreline.

Not all beaches are the same. Compare the beaches shown in **Figure 4.** Notice that the colors and textures vary. This is because the type of material found on a beach depends on its source. Light-colored sand is the most common beach material. Much of this sand comes from the quartz in continental rock. But not all beaches are made of light-colored sand. For instance, on many tropical islands, beaches are made of fine white coral material, and some Florida beaches are made of tiny pieces of broken seashells. In Hawaii, there are black sand beaches made of eroded volcanic lava. In areas where stormy seas are common, beaches are made of pebbles and larger rocks.

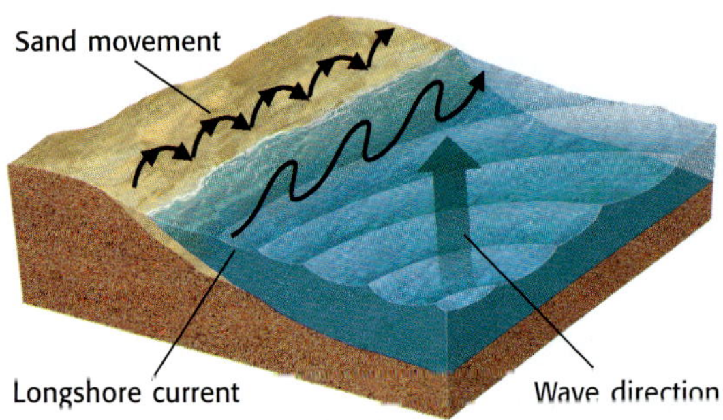

Figure 5 *When waves strike the shoreline at an angle, sand migrates along the beach in a zigzag path.*

Wave Angle Makes a Difference The movement of sand along a beach depends on the angle at which the waves strike the shore. Most waves approach the beach at a slight angle and retreat in a direction more perpendicular to the shore. This moves the sand in a zigzag pattern along the beach, as you can see in **Figure 5.**

278

Science Humor

Q: Why does the beach think the ocean is friendly?

A: because it waves all the time

Offshore Deposits Waves moving at an angle to the shoreline push water along the shore, creating longshore currents. A **longshore current** is a movement of water parallel to and near the shoreline. Sometimes waves erode material from the shoreline, and a longshore current transports and deposits it offshore, creating landforms in open water. Some of these landforms are shown in **Figure 6.**

Figure 6 Three Common Types of Offshore Deposits

A **sandbar** is an underwater or exposed ridge of sand, gravel, or shell material.

A **barrier spit,** like Cape Cod, Massachusetts, occurs when an exposed sandbar is connected to the shoreline.

A **tombolo** is an offshore island connected to the shore by deposited material. Morro Rock, in California, is an offshore volcano that is now connected to the shore by a ridge of beach sand.

Wave Erosion

Wave erosion produces a variety of features along a shoreline. *Sea cliffs,* like the ones in **Figure 7,** are formed when waves erode and undercut rock, producing steep slopes. Waves strike the base of the cliff, wearing away the soil and rock and making the cliff steeper. The rate at which the sea cliffs erode depends on the hardness of the rock and the energy delivered by the wave. Sea cliffs made of hard rock, such as granite, erode very slowly. Other sea cliffs, such as those made of soft sedimentary rock, erode rapidly, especially during storms.

Figure 7 *Ocean-view homes built on sedimentary rock are often threatened as cliffs erode.*

CONNECT TO LIFE SCIENCE

Beaches and intertidal zones can be a challenging place for organisms to live. Beaches offer little protection from predators, and the intertidal zone is periodically pounded by waves and exposed to the sun. Most of the organisms that live in these areas have special adaptations for survival. Have students research how different organisms are adapted for living in these environments.

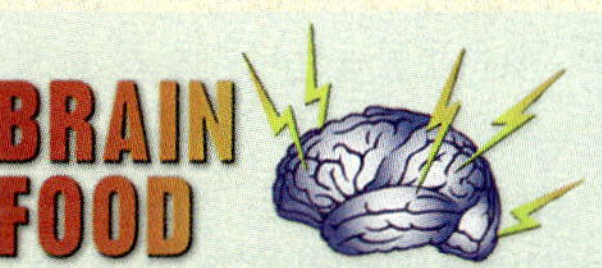

Despite the numerous changes wrought by the sea, people still live and vacation as close to the water as possible. Inevitably, property is damaged. Government loan subsidies to these property owners cost taxpayers millions of dollars a year. Encourage students to consider the costs and benefits of erosion prevention. What solutions to the problem would they propose? How would they finance their plans? Allow time for them to share their ideas with the class.

3 Extend

Group Activity

Coastal Features Board Game

To reinforce section concepts, divide the class into small groups, and challenge each to create a board game. Tell students that the object of the game is for players to visit as many coastal landforms as they can. Provide each group with poster board, plain index cards, and markers. Direct them to create a game board that leads players along a coastline, encountering the features they have learned about. Have students use the index cards to write questions and clues to direct players' movements along the "coast." For example, they might write, "If you can describe how the sea arch formed, you may move ahead to the sea stack. If not, lose a turn." Have groups create written game rules, exchange games, and play again. Sheltered English

Going Further

Have students research and model different methods that have been used to control shoreline erosion. Encourage students to discover which methods have been effective and which have failed. Students can also develop their own plans for minimizing erosion and present them to the class.

TOPIC: Wave Erosion
GO TO: www.scilinks.org
*sci*LINKS NUMBER: HSTE280

Much of the erosion responsible for landforms you might see along the shoreline takes place during storms. Large waves generated by storms release far more energy on the shoreline than normal waves. This energy is so powerful that it is capable of removing huge chunks of rock. The following illustrations show some of the major landscape features that result from wave erosion.

Coastal Landforms Created by Wave Erosion

Sea stacks are offshore columns of resistant rock that were once connected to a sea cliff or headland. In these instances, waves have eroded the sea cliffs and headland, leaving behind isolated columns of rock.

Sea arches form when wave action continues to erode a sea cave, cutting completely through the headland.

Sea caves form when waves cut large holes into fractured or weak rock along the base of sea cliffs. Sea caves are common in limestone cliffs, where the rock is usually quite soft.

280

Weird Science

Sometimes, even when the weather is clear and calm, huge waves, called *rogue waves,* unexpectedly appear. These waves are responsible for damaging or sinking several ships a year. Rogue waves are a poorly understood phenomenon of the high seas. One reason so little is known about them is that their random nature makes them hard to study.

The state of Louisiana is shrinking! Find out why on page 303.

A **headland** is a finger-shaped projection that occurs when cliffs formed of hard rock erode more slowly than surrounding rock. On many shorelines, hard rock will form headlands, and the softer rock will form beaches or bays. Thus, the coastline will alternate between small, pocket-shaped beaches and rocky headlands. This type of shoreline is very common on the West Coast of the United States.

A **wave-cut terrace** forms when a sea cliff is worn back, producing a nearly level platform beneath the water at the base of the cliff. Here the waves break down the materials eroded from the sea cliffs. As the waves cause the cliff to retreat, rocks eroded from the base of the cliff scrape the wave-cut terrace until it is almost flat.

REVIEW

1. What is the source of energy for waves?
2. What are some ways that waves shape the shoreline?
3. Explain how beaches form and why all beaches are not the same.
4. **Summarizing Data** Describe the way beach sand is moved along the shoreline.

4 Close

Quiz

1. What is a wave period? (It is the time it takes for two waves to pass a fixed point.)
2. What determines the way sand moves on a beach? (the direction in which waves strike the shore)
3. Describe how sea stacks, sea caves, and headlands are formed. (Sea stacks are columns of resistant rock left behind when a headland erodes. Sea caves form when waves erode large holes in fractured or weak rock at the base of sea cliffs. A headland forms when cliffs made of hard rock erode more slowly than the surrounding rock; this results in a finger-shaped projection.)

Alternative Assessment

Have students work independently to make a model of several land features created by waves. Ask them to present their models to the class and explain how the water strikes the shore to create the landforms. Have them brainstorm about what organisms, if any, would live on the landforms they modeled.

Answers to Review

1. Wind is the source of wave energy.
2. Sample answer: Waves erode rock, creating headlands and undercutting sea cliffs, sea caves, stacks, and sea arches. Waves also deposit material, forming landforms such as beaches, spits, sandbars, and tombolos.
3. Beaches are usually made of geological material eroded from areas of higher elevation. Rivers deposit this material in oceans. Waves and currents then redeposit the material along the shoreline to form beaches. All beaches are not the same because source materials vary.
4. Beach sand is moved by waves and by longshore currents. If the waves arrive at the shore at an angle, and retreat perpendicular to the shoreline, sand is deposited in a zigzag pattern. Longshore currents move sand in the direction they flow, parallel to the shore.

Section 1 Review–California Standards: PE/ATE 2, 2c

SECTION 2

Focus

Wind Erosion and Deposition

In this section, students learn about the effects of wind erosion. They will explore the three major processes of wind erosion: saltation, deflation, and abrasion. Section 2 explains how the wind deposits materials, such as sand and loess. Students also learn about the migration of sand dunes.

Bellringer

Ask students to answer the following question in their ScienceLog:

What causes wind? (Students should understand that wind is caused by heat from the sun. The sun heats the Earth unevenly; the unequal energy distribution causes pressure differences which, in turn, cause air to move.)

1) Motivate

DISCUSSION

Wind Erosion Engage students in a discussion about the ways wind shapes the Earth's surface. Encourage them to compare the wind with waves. (They should recognize that both change the Earth's shape by erosion and deposition.)

Ask students to think of examples of the wind's effects on landscapes they have observed. (Answers might include the formation of sand dunes, wind-weathered surfaces, and so on.)

Point out that this section will explore the ways in which wind acts to erode and deposit materials on Earth.

2

NEW TERMS

saltation
deflation
abrasion
dune
loess

OBJECTIVES

- Explain why areas with fine materials are more vulnerable to wind erosion.
- Describe how wind moves sand and finer materials.
- Describe the effects of wind erosion.
- Describe the difference between dunes and loess.

Wind Erosion and Deposition

Most of us at one time or another have been frustrated by a gusty wind that blew an important stack of papers all over the place. Remember how fast and far the papers traveled, and how it took forever to pick them up because every time you caught up with them they were on the move again? If you are familiar with this scene, then you already know how wind erosion works. Certain locations are more vulnerable to wind erosion than others. Areas with fine, loose rock material that have little protective plant cover can be significantly affected by the wind. Plant roots anchor sand and soil in place, reducing the amount of wind erosion. The landscapes most commonly shaped by wind processes are deserts and coastlines.

Have you ever tried to track a moving rock? Sounds silly, but people are keeping tabs on some rocks that keep sneaking around behind their backs. To find out more, turn to page 302.

Process of Wind Erosion

Wind moves material in different ways. In areas where strong winds occur, material is moved by saltation. **Saltation** is the movement of sand-sized particles by a skipping and bouncing action in the direction the wind is blowing. As you can see in **Figure 8**, the wind causes the particles to bounce. When bouncing sand particles knock into one another, some particles bounce up in the air and fall forward, striking other sand particles. The impact may in turn cause these particles to roll forward or bounce up in the air.

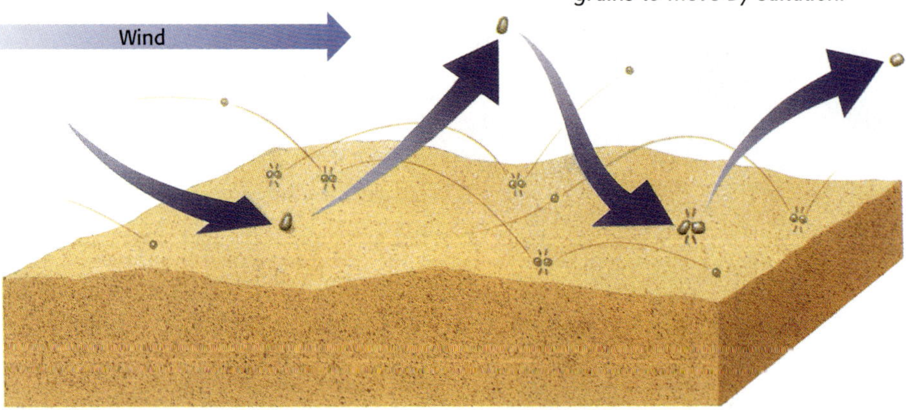

Figure 8 *The wind causes sand grains to move by saltation.*

282

CONNECT TO LIFE SCIENCE

Point out to students that many desert animals have special adaptations to protect themselves from windblown sand. For example, some lizards have transparent eyelids that shield their eyes from blowing sand while still allowing them to see.

Encourage students to use their school library to learn more about animal adaptations that protect against blowing sand. Have them prepare brief oral reports to share their findings with the class.

Section 2–California Standards: PE/ATE 2, 6b, 7, 7b, 7e; LabBook: 7, 7b, 7e, 7g

Two other major processes of wind erosion are *deflation* and *abrasion*. **Deflation** is the lifting and removal of fine sediment by wind. During deflation, wind removes the top layer of fine sediment or soil, leaving behind rock fragments that are too heavy to be lifted by the wind. This hard, rocky surface, consisting of pebbles and small broken rocks, is known as *desert pavement*. An example is shown in **Figure 9.**

Figure 9 *Desert pavement, such as that found in the Painted Desert, in Arizona, forms when wind removes all the fine materials.*

Have you ever blown on a layer of dust while cleaning off a dresser? If you have, you might have noticed that in addition to your face getting dirty, a little scooped-out depression formed in the dust. Similarly, where there is little vegetation, wind may scoop out depressions in the sand. These depressions, like the one shown in **Figure 10,** are known as *deflation hollows*.

Figure 10 *Deflation hollows may begin as depressions less than 1 m across. But continued wind erosion can cause them to become hundreds of meters wide and many meters deep.*

QuickLab

Making Desert Pavement

1. Spread out a mixture of sediments across a **board** or **table** outdoors. Make sure you have a combination of **dust, sand,** and **gravel.**
2. Place an **electric fan** at one end of the board or table.
3. Put on **safety goggles** and a **filter mask.** Aim the fan across the sediment. Start the fan on its lowest speed. Record your observations in your ScienceLog.
4. Turn the fan to a medium speed and then to the highest speed to imitate a wind storm in the desert. Again record your observations.
5. What is the relationship between the wind speed and the sediment size that is moved?
6. Does the remaining sediment fit the definition of desert pavement?

Self-Check

Why do deflation hollows form in areas where there is little vegetation? *(See page 564 to check your answer.)*

283

Answer to Self-Check

The roots of plants anchor sediment in place. Deflation hollows form in areas where there is little vegetation because there is nothing to anchor the sediment in place; the sediment blows away.

2 Teach

QuickLab

MATERIALS

For Each Group:
- table or board
- dust
- sand
- gravel
- electric fan

Safety Caution: Remind students to review all safety cautions and icons before beginning this activity. Because of the risk of eye injury and particle inhalation, students must wear both protective goggles and a filter mask during this lab.

Answers to QuickLab

5. The faster the wind speed, the larger the sediment size that can be moved.
6. Answers may vary. Accept all reasonable responses.

Using the Figure

Direct students' attention to **Figure 9.** Ask them to identify and describe the process that removes the fine sediment. (deflation)

Encourage them to compare the appearance of the desert pavement pictured with that of the desert pavement they created in the QuickLab. Sheltered English

Teaching Transparency 125 "Saltation"

Directed Reading Worksheet 11 Section 2

Answer to APPLY

Deflation caused the Dust Bowl.

Multicultural CONNECTION

The term *hammada* refers to areas of desert pavement. The term is Arabic in origin, as is much of the terminology used to describe desert features. This is because many of Earth's deserts are located in Arabic-speaking countries. Challenge students to use the Internet or reference texts to compile a list of terms that describe desert features. (Terms with Arabic origins include *erg,* which describes sandy desert; *reg,* which are loose stones; *barchan,* which are crescent-shaped dunes; and *seif,* which are sword-shaped dunes.)

PG 530

Dune Movement

Meeting Individual Needs

Learners Having Difficulty

Students may have difficulty visualizing how rock can be abraded by sand. Demonstrate the abrasiveness of sand by briskly rubbing quartz sandpaper on a softer rock specimen, and allow students to observe the changes. Remind them that sandblasting is used in many industrial applications to "erode" away hard surfaces.

Sheltered English

Teaching Transparency 126
"Migration of Sand Dunes"

When a long period without rain, known as a *drought,* occurs, areas that are farmed or overgrazed can suffer extensive soil loss and dense dust storms. The removal of plants exposes the soil, making it more vulnerable to wind erosion. Dust storms occur when strong winds lift large amounts of dust into the atmosphere. During the 1930s, a section of the Great Plains suffered severe wind erosion and dust storms. This area became known as the *Dust Bowl.* The dust darkened the skies so much that street lights were left on during the day in Midwestern cities. In areas where the conditions were even worse, people had to string ropes from their houses to their barns so they wouldn't get lost in the dense dust. The dust was so bad that people slept with damp cloths over their face to keep from choking. Describe the major erosional process that caused the Dust Bowl.

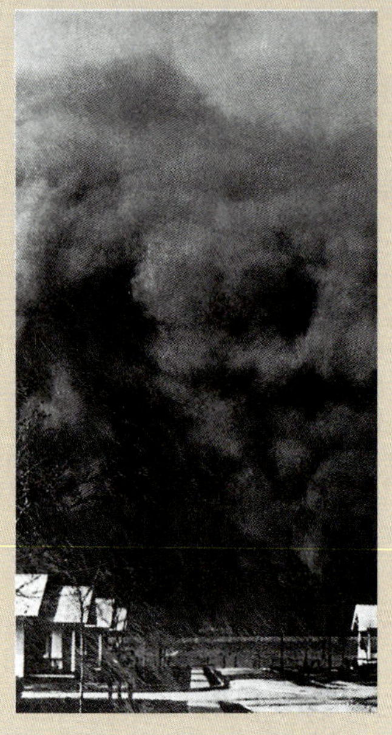

Abrasion is the grinding and wearing down of rock surfaces by other rock or sand particles. Abrasion commonly occurs in areas where there are strong winds, loose sand, and soft rocks. The blowing of millions of sharp sand grains creates a sandblasting effect that helps to erode, smooth, and polish rocks. These wind-polished rocks are called *ventifacts.* The polished side of a ventifact faces the wind.

Turn on a hair dryer—no, not to style your hair, but to find out how dunes migrate. Check out page 530 of the LabBook.

Wind-Deposited Materials

Like a stack of papers blowing in the wind, all the material carried by the wind is eventually deposited downwind. The amount and size of particles the wind can carry depend on wind speed. The faster the wind blows, the more material and the heavier the particles it can carry. As wind speed slows, heavier particles are deposited first.

Dunes When the wind hits an obstacle, such as a plant or a rock, it slows down. As the wind slows, it deposits, or drops, the heavier material. As the material collects, it creates an additional obstacle. This obstacle causes even more material to be deposited, forming a mound. Eventually even the original obstacle becomes buried. The mounds of wind-deposited sand are called **dunes.** Dunes are common in deserts and along the shores of lakes and oceans.

284

The unusual rock formations known as pedestals or mushroom rocks are commonly thought to be the products of abrasion by wind-borne particles. Actually, the base of these rock formations erodes because of salt crystallization and weathering in the humid environment.

IS THAT A FACT!

Sand dunes migrate because persistent wind causes grains of sand to blow up the windward slope to the crest of the dune and then fall. This continuous movement of sand can cause dunes to move more than 24 m a year!

Dunes tend to move in the direction of strong prevailing winds. Different wind conditions produce dunes in various shapes and sizes. A dune usually has a gently sloped side and a steeply sloped side, or *slip face,* as shown in **Figure 11.** In most cases, the gently sloped side faces the wind. The wind is constantly transporting material up this side of the dune. As sand moves over the crest, or peak, of the dune, it slides down the slip face, creating a steep slope.

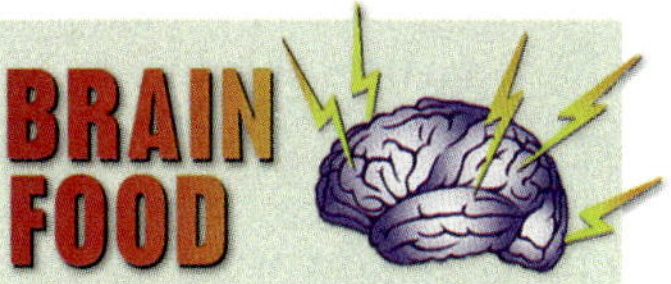

The largest sand dunes ever recorded were found in east-central Algeria in the Sahara. These dunes measured about 4.8 km long and 430 m high.

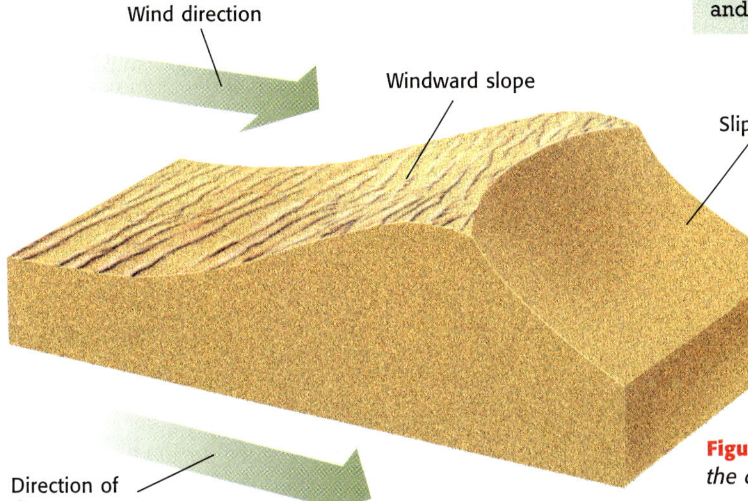

Figure 11 *Dunes migrate in the direction of the wind.*

Disappearing Dunes

Dunes provide homes for hundreds of plant and animal species, including the desert tortoise. This tortoise, found in the Mojave and Sonoran Deserts of the southwestern United States, is able to live where ground temperatures are very hot. It escapes the heat by digging burrows in the sand dunes. The desert tortoise has a problem, though. Dune buggies and other motorized vehicles are destroying the dunes. Dunes are easily disturbed and are vulnerable to erosion. Motorized off-road vehicles break down dunes, destroying habitat for the tortoise as well as many other animal and plant species. For this reason, state and federal wildlife and land-management agencies have taken an active role in helping protect habitat for the desert tortoise and other sensitive desert species by making some areas off-limits to off-road vehicles.

285

Homework

Create a Diagram Challenge students to make diagrams similar to **Figure 11** illustrating why the gently sloping side of a dune usually faces windward. Have them clearly indicate the direction in which the wind and the sand are moving, and have them write a caption summarizing the phenomenon. (The diagrams should indicate that when moving sand meets an obstacle, it falls to the ground and forms a dune. The wind, however, continues to move forward, causing the sand to form a slope against the obstacle. Wind continues to blow sand up the slope to its apex, whereupon the sand falls, creating a sharper slope on the other side.)

3 Extend

Going Further

Encourage students to learn about the many different kinds of dunes that can form when windblown sand meets obstacles. Have them make posters illustrating the types of dunes and indicating the wind patterns that create them. Ask students to explore the differences between beach dunes and desert dunes. Display the posters in the classroom.

Connect to Life Science

Writing Encourage interested students to use library or Internet resources to investigate the living organisms that make sand dunes their home. Have them select one plant or animal and write a brief report describing its habitat, its predators and/or prey, and the adaptations it has made to live in the sand-dune environment. Sheltered English

Cross-Disciplinary Focus

Language Arts Remind students that drought and dust storms plagued the Great Plains in the 1930s. Encourage them to read about the effects of the Dust Bowl in selections from John Steinbeck's *The Grapes of Wrath.* Have them prepare book reports describing how the Joad family was affected economically and psychologically by this event.

4 Close

Quiz

1. Why is sand more likely to move by saltation than silt? (Dust and silt are much lighter than sand; they can be lifted and carried away more easily, rather than falling back to the ground.)
2. How does the process of deflation form desert pavement? (Deflation lifts and carries away lighter materials, while the heavier stones remain as desert pavement.)
3. Describe how dunes form. (When wind encounters an obstacle, it slows down, depositing some of the heavier material it is carrying. Gradually, this material grows to become a mound and then a dune.)

Alternative Assessment

Concept Mapping Have students use section vocabulary to construct a concept map that explores the ways wind can shape the Earth's surface.

Critical Thinking Worksheet 11
"A Future in Sand"

internet**connect**

TOPIC: Wind Erosion
GO TO: www.scilinks.org
***sci*LINKS NUMBER:** HSTE285

life science CONNECTION

The sidewinder adder is a poisonous snake that lives in the dunes of the Namib Desert, in southwestern Africa. It is called a sidewinder because of the way it rolls its body to one side as it moves across the sand. This motion allows the snake to move above the loose, sliding sand. Its close cousin, the sidewinder rattlesnake, found in the deserts of the southwestern United States, uses a similar motion to move. The sidewinder adder's scales look like sand grains. When hiding and waiting for prey, it buries itself in the sand with only its eyes showing above the surface like two dark sand grains.

Loess Wind can deposit material much finer than sand. Thick deposits of this windblown, fine-grained sediment are known as **loess** (LOH es). Loess is very fine and feels much like the talcum powder you use after a shower.

Because wind carries fine-grained material much higher and farther than it carries sand, loess deposits are sometimes found far away from their source. A large area of China is covered completely with loess. This windblown sediment is thought to have originated in the Gobi Desert of Mongolia.

Many loess deposits came from glacial sources during the last ice age. Loess is present in much of the midwestern United States, along the eastern edge of the Mississippi Valley, and in eastern Oregon and Washington. Huge bluffs of loess are found in Mississippi, as shown in **Figure 12.**

Loess deposits can easily be prepared for growing crops and are responsible for the success of many of the grain-growing areas of the world. Outside the United States, these "breadbaskets" are found in Argentina, Ukraine, central Europe, New Zealand, and China.

Figure 12 *The thick loess deposits found in Mississippi contribute to the state's fertile soil.*

REVIEW

1. What areas have the greatest amount of wind erosion and deposition? Why?
2. Explain the process of saltation.
3. What is the difference between a dune and a loess deposit?
4. **Analyzing Relationships** Explain the relationship between deflation and dune movement.

286

Answers to Review

1. Deserts and coastlines experience the greatest amount of wind erosion and deposition because they are composed of fine, loose material and have little vegetation to anchor the sediment in place.
2. Saltation is the movement of sand by wind in a bouncing and skipping fashion. The wind lifts sand particles into the air. When the particles land, they hit other particles, causing them to bounce forward.
3. Dunes are made of sand. Loess is made of finer materials that are the size of dust particles. Loess can be carried much higher and farther by wind than can sand.
4. Deflation removes dune sediment. The material is then carried by the wind and redeposited elsewhere, creating another dune.

3

Erosion and Deposition by Ice

NEW TERMS

glacier
iceberg
crevasse
horn
cirque
arête
hanging valley
U-shaped valley
glacial drift
stratified drift
till

OBJECTIVES

- Summarize why glaciers are important agents of erosion and deposition.
- Explain how ice in a glacier flows.
- Describe some of the landforms eroded by glaciers.
- Describe some of the landforms deposited by glaciers.

Can you imagine an ice cube the size of a football stadium? Well, glaciers can be even bigger than that. A **glacier** is an enormous mass of moving ice. Because glaciers are very heavy and have the ability to move across the Earth's surface, they are capable of eroding, moving, and depositing large amounts of rock materials. And while you will never see a glacier chilling a punch bowl, you might one day visit some of the spectacular landscapes carved by glacial activity.

Glaciers—Rivers of Ice

Glaciers form in areas so cold that snow stays on the ground year-round. Areas like these, where you can chill a can of juice by simply carrying it outside, are found at high elevations and in polar regions. Because the average temperature is freezing or near freezing, snow piles up year after year. Eventually, the weight of the snow on top causes the deep-packed snow to become ice crystals, forming a giant ice mass. These ice packs then become slow-moving "rivers of ice" as they are set in motion by the pull of gravity on their extraordinary mass.

Types of Glaciers There are two main types of glaciers, *alpine* and *continental*. **Figure 13** shows an alpine glacier. As you can see, this type of glacier forms in mountainous areas. One common type of alpine glacier is a *valley glacier.* Valley glaciers form in valleys originally created by stream erosion. These glaciers flow slowly downhill, widening and straightening the valleys into broad U-shapes as they travel downward. *Piedmont glaciers,* another type of alpine glacier, form at the base of mountain ranges.

Figure 13 *Alpine glaciers start as snowfields in mountainous areas.*

287

SECTION 3

Focus

Erosion and Deposition by Ice

This section examines how glaciers form and how they shape the Earth's surface. Students will learn to identify different types of glaciers and understand how they move. Finally, students will focus on the changes to the Earth's landscape caused by ice erosion and deposition.

Bellringer

Tell students that 14,000 years ago, much of North America was covered in a thick layer of ice called a *continental glacier,* which moved as far as southern Illinois. Humans were living in North America at the time. Have students imagine they encounter this glacier as an early human, and write a paragraph in their ScienceLog about the experience.

1 Motivate

GROUP ACTIVITY

Glacier Game Give groups of students a world map, two dice, and string to explore the causes and effects of glacial movement. Have each group brainstorm six causes and six effects of glacial movement; these will become 12 possible moves in a glacier game. With each roll of the dice, the group's glacier (represented by a line of string on the map) will either advance or recede. For example, a roll of 5 might mean, "Volcanic eruption triggers global cooling, glacier advances 100 km." The winning group will be the first to have their glacier advance to your hometown.

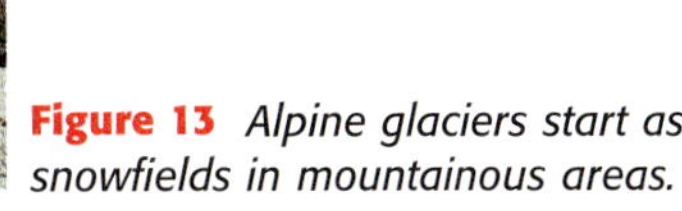

WEIRD SCIENCE

Glaciers are very noisy. As they move and stretch, they howl, shriek, pop, groan, and make explosive noises. These sounds can be so loud that they have kept high-altitude mountaineers awake at night!

Directed Reading Worksheet 11 Section 3

Section 3–California Standards: PE/ATE 2, 2a, 2b, 7f; LabBook: 2, 7, 7b, 7e

2 Teach

Answers to Explore

Sample Answer: The iceberg that struck the *Titanic* traveled approximately 2,000 km from Greenland to Newfoundland. Accept all reasonable responses for the mapping portion of Explore.

Guided Practice

Have students compare in writing the process of making a snowball with that of forming glacial ice. Students should understand that snowflakes are compressed together when both snowballs and glaciers are formed. When a snowball is made, heat from a person's hands partially melts the snow. As the snowball is squeezed, the snowball becomes denser and harder. Alpine glaciers form in a similar way, but pressure comes from the snow pack above. Because temperatures always remain below freezing in Antarctica, ice sheets form as lower layers of snow are compressed by the weight of overlying layers. Sheltered English

Explore

How far do you think the iceberg that struck the *Titanic* drifted before the two met that fateful night in 1912? Plot on a map of the North Atlantic Ocean the route of the *Titanic* from Southampton, England, to New York. Then plot a possible route of the drifting iceberg from Greenland to where the ship sank, just south of the Canadian island province of Newfoundland.

Not all glaciers are true "rivers of ice." In fact, some glaciers continue to get larger, spreading across entire continents. These glaciers, called continental glaciers, are huge continuous masses of ice. **Figure 14** shows the largest type of this glacier, a *continental ice sheet.* Ice sheets can cover millions of square kilometers with ice. The continent of Antarctica is almost completely covered by one of the largest ice sheets in the world, as you can see below. This ice sheet is approximately one and a half times the size of the United States. It is so thick—more than 4,000 m in places—that it buries everything but the highest mountain peaks.

Figure 14 *Antarctica contains approximately 91 percent of all the glacial ice on the planet.*

A continental ice sheet usually has a dome-shaped center of snow and ice accumulation. Ice flows from the center to the outer edges of the ice sheet and beyond. An area where the ice is attached to the ice sheet but is resting on open water is called an *ice shelf.* The largest ice shelf is the Ross Ice Shelf, shown in **Figure 15,** which is attached to the ice sheet that covers Antarctica. This ice shelf covers an area of ocean about the size of Texas.

Figure 15 *Icebergs break off the Ross Ice Shelf into the Ross Sea.*

Large pieces of ice that break off an ice shelf and drift into the ocean are called **icebergs.** The process by which an iceberg forms is called *calving.* Calving can be a spectacular event, with huge pieces of ice falling into the sea producing giant splashes and waves. Because most of an iceberg is below the surface of the water, it can be a hazard for ships that cannot see how far the iceberg extends. In the North Atlantic Ocean near Newfoundland, the *Titanic* struck an iceberg that calved off the Greenland ice sheet.

288

Is That a Fact!

How do snowflakes become massive blocks of glacial ice? As the snow melts and is compacted, the grains become more dense. As snow packs to a greater density, the air spaces among ice crystals are pressed out. Eventually, the ice recrystallizes to a stage between flakes and ice called *firn.* Over time, with more pressure from overlying layers of snow, the firn will recrystallize again to become glacial ice.

Movement of Glaciers When enough ice builds up on a slope, the ice begins to move downhill. The thickness of the ice and the steepness of the slope determine how fast a glacier will move. Thick glaciers move faster than thin glaciers, and the steeper the slope is, the faster the glacier will move. Glaciers move by two different methods. Glaciers move when the weight of the ice causes the ice at the bottom to melt. The water from the melted ice allows the glacier to move forward, like a partially melted ice cube moving across your kitchen counter. Glaciers also move when solid ice crystals within the glacier slip over each other, causing a slow forward motion. However, scientists have found that the rate of movement is not the same for all parts of the glacier. This process is similar to placing a deck of cards on a table and then tilting the table. The top cards will slide farther than the lower cards. Like the cards, the upper part, or surface, of the glacier flows faster than the glacier's base. Also, the center of the glacier flows faster than its sides and base. This is because friction caused by contact of the glacier's sides and base with the rock surface slows the flow rate.

As a glacier flows forward, sometimes crevasses occur. A **crevasse,** as shown in **Figure 16,** is a large crack that forms where the glacier picks up speed or flows over a high point. Crevasses form because the ice cannot stretch quickly, and it cracks. Crevasses can be dangerous for people who are traveling across glaciers because a bridge layer of snow can hide them from view.

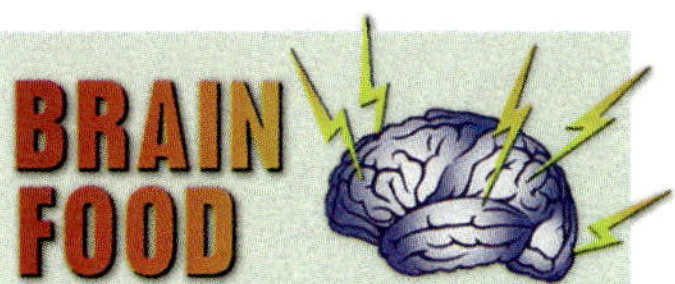

Many icebergs now being calved by Alaskan glaciers are made of millions of snowflakes that fell at about the time Columbus arrived in the Americas.

Speed of a Glacier

An alpine glacier is estimated to be moving forward at 5 m per day. Calculate how long it will take for the ice to reach a road and campground located 0.5 km from the front of the advancing glacier.

1 km = 1,000 m

Figure 16 *Crevasses can be dangerous for mountain climbers who must cross glaciers.*

How are ice crevasses related to glacier flow? *(See page 564 to check your answer.)*

289

CONNECT TO PHYSICAL SCIENCE

Point out to students that while most glaciers move only a few meters a year, certain conditions can cause *glacial surge.* When glaciers surge, or flow rapidly, they may travel 30 m in a day. Encourage students to use the Internet or library resources to investigate glacial surges. Have them explain in writing why this phenomenon occurs. (Students should understand that friction between the glacier and land is reduced, allowing gravity to pull the ice downhill faster. Before and during a glacial surge, meltwater does not drain away from the glacier; instead it builds up beneath the ice. The water decreases the friction between the glacier and the land below, permitting the glacier to flow more rapidly.)

RETEACHING

You may wish to demonstrate for students the comparison made on this page between a sliding deck of cards and one type of glacial flow. This process is called *internal plastic flow.*

Answer to MATHBREAK

(0.5 km × 1,000 m/km) ÷ 5 m = 100 days

Math Skills Worksheet 17
"Using Proportions and Cross-Multiplication"

IS THAT A FACT!

When metal pipes are drilled through a glacier's layers, they eventually bend in the direction of flow, demonstrating that glacial layers tend to move at different speeds. One cause of this is friction—layers in closest contact with Earth are often slowed by friction.

Answer to Self-Check

When a moving glacier picks up speed or flows over a high point, a crevasse may form. This occurs because the ice cannot stretch quickly while it is moving and therefore cracks.

2 Teach, continued

Group Activity

Making Models Divide the class into pairs, and ask each pair to select a landscape feature created by glaciers. Provide modeling clay for students to make a model of the feature. Have each pair present its model to the class and demonstrate how the feature was formed using another color of clay to represent the glacier. Sheltered English

Homework

Investigate Your Area If you live in an area that has been affected by glaciers, ask the class to find evidence of glacial erosion and deposition in your area. If not, ask each student to select a landform created by glacial activity and use atlases or other resources to learn where these features are found. For example, the Matterhorn, in Switzerland, is an example of a *horn*. Have students locate their feature on a classroom map and present a short report on what they learned.

Landforms Carved by Glaciers

Alpine glaciers and continental glaciers produce landscapes that are very different from one another. Alpine glaciers carve out rugged features in the mountain rocks through which they flow. Continental glaciers smooth the landscape by scraping and removing features that existed before the ice appeared, flattening even some of the highest mountains. **Figure 17** and **Figure 18** show the very different landscapes that each glacial type produces.

Figure 17 *Continental glaciers smooth and flatten the landscape.*

Figure 18 *The hard ice of alpine glaciers carved out this rugged landscape.*

290

Is That a Fact!

During the last glacial period, the northern part of North America was covered by as much as 4,000 m of ice. The weight of the ice pushed the North American continent down by almost 400 m. Since the ice sheet melted about 10,000 years ago, the continent has risen over 300 m. The continent is still rising at a rate of about 2 cm per year. This process is known as isostatic rebound.

Alpine glaciers carve out large amounts of rock material, creating spectacular landforms. These glaciers are responsible for landscapes such as the Rocky Mountains and the Alps. **Figure 19** shows the kind of landscape that is sculpted by alpine glacial erosion and revealed after the ice melts back.

Figure 19 **Landscape Features Carved by Alpine Glaciers**

Horns are sharp, pyramid-shaped peaks that form when three or more cirques erode the mountain.

Cirques (suhrks) are bowl-like depressions where glacial ice cuts back into the mountain walls.

Arêtes (uh RAYTS) are jagged ridges that form between two or more cirques cutting into the same mountain.

Hanging valleys are smaller glacial valleys that join the deeper main valley. These valleys form because smaller glaciers cannot carve a valley as deep as the main glacier. Many hanging valleys form waterfalls after the ice is gone.

U-shaped valleys are formed when a glacier flows into and erodes a valley, changing the valley from its original V-shape to a U-shape. These broad U-shaped glacial valleys are also called *glacial troughs.*

291

Creating a Kettle

READING STRATEGY

Activity Draw students' attention to **Figure 19.** Challenge them to write new captions to describe each landscape feature carved by glaciers. Sheltered English

CROSS-DISCIPLINARY FOCUS

History Encourage students to research Camp Century, a city built by the United States government inside the Greenland ice sheet. Ask them to research the purpose of the project, the discoveries scientists made, the obstacles faced by the engineers, and the problems that eventually led to the abandonment of the project. Have them write brief reports about their findings. (Students will find that the purpose of Camp Century was twofold: to learn about glaciers and life in the extreme Arctic environment and to protect the United States from attack—missiles were concealed in ice tunnels. The biggest problem the engineers encountered was the need to continually dig their way into the camp because new snow kept accumulating and the glacial layers shifted. Each year, the camp was pressed about a half-meter farther into the glacial ice by new snow.)

Homework

Preparing Tables Have students work independently to create tables summarizing the characteristics and formation of the following landforms: arêtes, horns, hanging valleys, and cirques. Have them keep the tables to use as study guides for the Chapter Review.

Teaching Transparency 127
"Landscape Features Carved by Alpine Glaciers"

3 Extend

REAL-WORLD CONNECTION

Glaciers throughout the world provide fresh water that helps regulate the flow of large rivers and recharge aquifers. Scientists are concerned, however, that a permanent increase in global temperatures would alter this naturally controlled process. If the 13,800,000 km^2 Antarctic ice sheet melted, sea level could rise 60 m, with devastating effects. Coastal towns and cities would be flooded, and some islands would disappear. Have students draw a map of what the coastline of the United States would look like if the sea level rose 60 m.

COOPERATIVE LEARNING

Divide the class into small groups, and ask them to imagine an Earth untouched by glaciers. Have them work together to make a poster showing such a planet. Encourage them to consider not only Earth's landscape but also the living things inhabiting it. Ask students to share their posters with the class.

Figure 20 *Striations, such as these seen in Central Park, in New York City, are evidence of glacial erosion.*

While many of the erosional features created by glaciers are unique to alpine glaciers, alpine and continental glaciers share some common features. For example, when a glacier erodes the landscape, the glacier picks up rock material and carries it away. This debris is transported on the glacier's surface as well as beneath and within the glacier. Many times, rock material is frozen into the glacier's bottom. As the glacier moves, the rock pieces scrape and polish the surface rock. Larger rocks embedded in the glacier gouge out grooves in the surface rock. As you can see in **Figure 20,** these grooves, called *striations,* help scientists determine the direction of ice flow.

Types of Glacial Deposits

When a glacier melts, all the material it has been carrying is dropped. **Glacial drift** is the general term used to describe all material carried and deposited by glaciers. Glacial drift is divided into two main types, based on whether the material is sorted or unsorted.

Outwash plain

Kettle

Figure 21 *Stratified drift is deposited to form various types of landscape features.*

Esker

Stratified Drift Rock material that has been sorted and deposited in layers by water flowing from the melted ice is called **stratified drift.** Various types of stratified drift are shown in **Figure 21.** Many streams are created by the meltwater from the glacier. These streams carry an abundance of sorted material, which is deposited in front of the glacier in a broad area called an *outwash plain.* Sometimes a block of ice is left in the outwash plain when the glacier retreats. During the time it takes for the ice to melt, sediment builds up around the block of ice. After the ice has melted, a depression called a *kettle* is left. Kettles commonly fill with water, forming a lake or pond.

Some meltwater streams flow in tunnels along the bottom of the melting glacier. The meltwater moves through crevasses and cracks in the ice, creating tunnels that run downhill. Through these tunnels, the streams transport sand and gravel, which are later deposited in long, narrow, winding ridges called *eskers.* When the glacier melts back, the esker is revealed.

292

CROSS-DISCIPLINARY FOCUS

Geography The spectacular fjords of Norway are underwater valleys carved by glaciers. During the Pleistocene era, glaciers traveled beyond the coastline, digging trenches in the ocean floor. When they retreated to the coast, sea water flooded the valleys that the glaciers had formed.

In September 1991, a melting glacier deposited an unusual load in Italy near its border with Austria: the frozen body of a 5,300-year-old man!

Till Deposits The second type of glacial drift, **till,** is unsorted rock material that is deposited directly by the ice when it melts. *Unsorted* means that the till is made up of different sizes of rock material, ranging from large boulders to fine glacial silt. As a glacier flows, it carries different sizes of rock fragments. When the glacier melts, the unsorted material is deposited on the ground surface. The most common till deposits are *moraines.* Moraines generally form ridges along the edges of glaciers. They are produced when glaciers carry material to the front of the ice and along the sides of the ice. As the ice melts away, the sediment and rock it was carrying are dropped, forming the different types of moraines. The various types of moraines are shown in **Figure 22.**

Figure 22 *Moraines provide clues to where glaciers once were located.*

4 Close

Quiz

1. What are the differences between continental ice sheets and alpine glaciers? (Continental ice sheets are large and tend to expand across entire continents. Alpine glaciers are smaller and form in mountainous areas.)
2. What is the difference between icebergs and ice shelves? (Ice shelves are attached on one side to an ice sheet but rest on open water; icebergs are large pieces of ice that break off ice shelves into the ocean.)
3. What causes crevasses to form? (As glaciers move forward, crevasses may form when a glacier picks up speed or travels over a high point. The ice cannot stretch to accommodate its movement, so it cracks.)

REVIEW

1. How does glaciation change the appearance of mountains?
2. Explain why continental glaciers smooth the landscape and alpine glaciers create a rugged landscape.
3. What do moraines indicate?
4. **Applying Concepts** How can a glacier deposit both sorted and unsorted material?

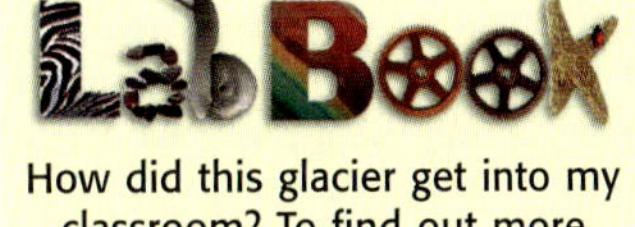

How did this glacier get into my classroom? To find out more about glaciers and erosion, turn to page 531 of the LabBook.

Answers to Review

1. Glaciers create unique mountain features, such as horns, cirques, arêtes, and broad U-shaped valleys.
2. Continental glaciers smooth the landscape because they cover it entirely and scrape away older surface features. Alpine glaciers create rugged landscapes because they cover only portions of mountains. Moving downhill, they cut into the mountains, creating dramatic features that were not there before.
3. Moraines indicate that a glacier once flowed through and dropped its sediment load in a given area.
4. Meltwater streams flowing through a glacier carry sorted material. Unsorted material is deposited when a glacier melts entirely.

ALTERNATIVE ASSESSMENT

Have students work independently to create a small glacier handbook that includes illustrations and descriptions of 10 terms used in this section. Their books should include examples of stratified drift, outwash plains, kettles, eskers, till, and moraines.

Reinforcement Worksheet 11
"An Alpine Vacation"

Section 3 Review–California Standards: PE/ATE 2

SECTION 4

Focus

Gravity's Effect on Erosion and Deposition

This section introduces gravity as an agent of erosion and deposition. Students learn that mass movements caused by gravity are affected by the material's size, weight, shape, and moisture content and by the slope on which the material rests. Students then learn about landslides, mudslides, and volcanic lahars. The section also examines the effect of slow mass movements, such as creep.

Bellringer

Write the following sentence on the board or overhead projector:

Watch for falling rocks!

Ask students to describe in their ScienceLog places where a warning sign like this would be necessary. Ask students to consider what factors contribute to make a rockfall zone.

1 Motivate

DISCUSSION

Ask students to review the three processes of erosion and deposition that they have learned about so far: shoreline erosion, wind erosion, and glacial erosion. Then ask students how rocks move from mountaintops to valleys. Tell them that gravity is an important force influencing erosion and deposition. Explain that although events like rockfalls and mudslides occur rapidly, most erosion and deposition occurs very slowly as gravity pulls material downward.

4

Gravity's Effect on Erosion and Deposition

NEW TERMS

mass movement
rock fall
landslide
mudflow
creep

OBJECTIVES

- Explain how slope is related to mass movement.
- State how gravity affects mass movement.
- Describe different types of mass movement.

Waves, wind, and ice are all agents of erosion and deposition that you can see. And though you can't see it and might not be aware of it, gravity is also an agent of erosion and deposition constantly at work on the Earth's surface. Gravity not only influences the movement of water, such as waves, streams, and ice, but also causes rocks and soil to move downslope. **Mass movement** is the movement of any material, such as rock, soil, or snow, downslope. Mass movement is controlled by the force of gravity and can occur rapidly or slowly.

The Forces in Mass Movement

All mass movement occurs on slopes as a result of gravitational pull. If dry sand is piled up, it will move downhill until the slope becomes stable. The *angle of repose* is the steepest angle, or slope, at which loose material will not slide downslope. This is demonstrated in **Figure 23.** The angle of repose is different for each type of sediment. As with any material, loose rock and sediment will not move unless the angle of the material is steeper than the angle of repose.

The effect of gravity on the surface material depends on many of the surface material's characteristics, such as its size, weight, shape, and moisture level. Another factor that influences mass movement is the slope on which the surface material rests. The steeper the slope is, the more likely it is that mass movement will occur.

QuickLab

Angle of Repose

1. Pour a **container** of **dry sand** onto a lab table.
2. With a **protractor,** measure the slope of the sand, or the *angle of repose.*
3. Pour another beaker of sand on top of the first pile.
4. Measure the angle of repose again for the new pile.
5. Which pile is more likely to collapse? Why?

Figure 23 *If the angle of a slope on which material rests is less than the angle of repose, the material will stay in place. If the angle is greater than the angle of repose, the material will move downslope.*

294

QuickLab

MATERIALS

- beaker
- dry sand
- protractor

Answer to QuickLab

5. The second pile is more likely to collapse because it has a steeper slope, which was created by the addition of sediment. The steeper the slope, the more likely mass movement will occur.

Section 4–California Standards: PE/ATE 2, 2d, 7, 7b, 7e

Rapid Mass Movement The most destructive mass movements occur suddenly and rapidly. Rapid mass movement occurs when material, such as rock and soil, moves downslope quickly. A rapid mass movement can be very dangerous, destroying everything in its path. While driving along a mountain road, you might have noticed signs that warn of falling rock. A **rock fall** happens when a group of loose rocks falls down a steep slope, as seen in **Figure 24.** Steep slopes are sometimes created to make room for a road in mountainous areas. Loosened and exposed rocks above the road tend to fall as a result of gravity. The rocks in a rock fall can range in size from small fragments to large boulders.

Another type of rapid mass movement is a *landslide.* A **landslide** is the sudden and rapid movement of a large amount of material downslope. A *slump* is an example of one kind of landslide. Slumping occurs when a block of material moves downslope over a curved surface, as seen in **Figure 25.**

physical science CONNECTION

Gravity is one of the major forces that cause rocks and soil to move from one place to another. Gravity is the force of attraction between objects. The more mass an object has, the more attraction there is between it and other objects.

Figure 24 *If enough rock falls from a mountain, a pile forms at the base of the slope. This pile of rock debris is called a* talus slope.

Figure 25 *A slump is a type of landslide that occurs when a small block of land becomes detached and slides downhill.*

295

2 Teach

Homework

Research Have students research lahars. The Mount St. Helens eruption in 1980, for example, produced tremendously destructive lahars of ash and melted snow. Volcanoes all over the world have created significant lahars or have the potential for major lahars. Have students select one volcano and prepare a hazard report detailing the lahar potential and possible effects on populated areas.

CONNECT TO PHYSICAL SCIENCE

Use the Teaching Transparency listed below to discuss the force of gravity. Have students write a paragraph in their ScienceLog describing the effects of Earth's gravity on matter. (Students should recognize that gravity is a force of attraction between two masses. The larger the masses are and the closer they are to one another, the stronger gravity is. Because Earth is so massive, it exerts a strong gravitational pull on objects near its surface.)

Teaching Transparency 175 "The Law of Universal Gravitation"

LINK TO PHYSICAL SCIENCE

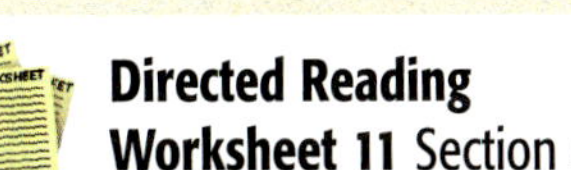

Directed Reading Worksheet 11 Section 4

SCIENTISTS AT ODDS

Long run-out landslides have been the focus of much scientific debate because they appear to defy the laws of physics. Long run-out slides occur when massive amounts of rock, perhaps half a mountainside, suddenly give way. Moving at tremendous speeds (more than 160 km/h), these slides behave more like a liquid than a rock. Scientists know that there is more than just the force of gravity involved in these landslides because they can travel 20 times the height that they fall. In 1903, a long run-out landslide in Frank, Canada, traveled 1 km uphill!

3 Extend

Activity

Making Models Provide students with poster board and markers. Have them each create a diagram of one form of mass movement, such as a landslide, mudslide, or creep. Direct them to label relevant parts of their diagrams and to write captions that explain the phenomenon illustrated. Encourage students to share their posters with the class.

Meeting Individual Needs

Learners Having Difficulty
Ask students to prepare a demonstration that compares mass movements of different materials on varying slopes. Provide a cookie sheet, dry sand, small pebbles, and gravel. Have them raise one end of the cookie sheet about 2 cm. Ask students to use a protractor to measure the angle of repose for each material. Have students repeat the procedure after moistening the materials, and ask them to make conclusions about the effect of water saturation on mass movement.
Sheltered English

Real-World Connection

Lack of vegetative cover contributes to the frequency and severity of mudslides. Tree roots stabilize the soil and absorb ground water. Deforestation accelerates erosion of slopes. In 1995, there were 260 landslides in British Columbia's Clayquot Sound region during the rainy season. Only about 33 were in unlogged areas. As a class, find out more about the connections between large-scale logging operations and recent mudslides.

A **mudflow** is a rapid movement of a large mass of mud. Mudflows, which are like giant moving mud pies, occur when a large amount of water mixes with soil and rock. The water causes the slippery mass of mud to flow rapidly downslope. Mudflows most commonly occur in mountainous regions when a long dry season is followed by heavy rains. As you can see in **Figure 26,** a mudflow can carry trees, houses, cars, and other objects that lie in its path.

Figure 26 *When heavy rains saturate mountain slopes, mudflows occur. This photo shows one of the many mudflows that have occurred in California during rainy winters.*

Figure 27 *Lahars are extremely dangerous due to their size and speed. This lahar overtook the city of Kyushu, in Japan.*

The most dangerous mudflows occur as a result of volcanic eruptions. Mudflows of volcanic origin are called *lahars*. Lahars can move at speeds of more than 80 km/h and are as thick as concrete. In mountains with snowy peaks, a volcanic eruption can suddenly melt a great amount of ice, causing a massive and rapid lahar, as shown in **Figure 27.** The water from the ice liquefies the soil and volcanic ash, sending a hot mudflow downslope. Other lahars are caused by heavy rains on volcanic ash.

Slow Mass Movement Sometimes you don't even notice mass movement occurring. While rapid mass movements are visible and dramatic, slow mass movements happen a little at a time. However, because slow mass movements occur more frequently, more material is moved collectively over time.

Connect to Life Science

In 1980, six successive storms caused devastating mudslides in California. The storms dropped 33 cm of rain, transforming the soil into a sea of oozing mud. Soil on slopes oozed out from under the foundations of houses, sending them crashing into canyons and valleys. Twenty-four people were killed, and millions of dollars in damage was done. Many believe that the mudslides were so massive because the area was recently logged.

Although most slopes appear to be stable, they are actually undergoing slow mass movement, as shown in **Figure 28.** The extremely slow movement of material downslope is called **creep.** Many factors contribute to creep. Water breaks up rock particles, allowing them to move freely. The roots of growing plants act as a wedge, forcing rocks and soil particles apart. Burrowing animals, such as gophers and groundhogs, loosen rock and soil particles.

Since trees need light to grow, they usually grow straight upward, toward the sun. However, if the soil on a slope is creeping downhill, the trees will develop bent trunks. The trunks bend because the trees continue to grow upward even as their roots and trunks are tilted downhill. Trees with a "pistol butt" shape show that mass movement is happening on a slope.

Figure 28 *Tilted fence posts and bent tree trunks are evidence that creep is occurring.*

Another kind of slow mass movement, called *solifluction,* occurs in arctic and alpine climates where the subsoil is permanently frozen. In the spring and summer, only the upper layer of soil thaws, while the ground below remains frozen. The moisture from the thawing soil layer cannot move into the frozen soil below; therefore, the surface layer becomes saturated with water. As a result, the surface layer of soil becomes muddy and moves downslope. This type of mass movement can also occur in warmer regions where the subsoil consists of clay. Clay acts like the permanently frozen layer, preventing water from moving into the subsurface layer.

REVIEW

1. In your own words, explain why slump occurs.
2. What factors increase the potential for mass movement?
3. How do slope and gravity affect mass movement?
4. **Analyzing Relationships** Some types of mass movement are considered dangerous to humans. Which types are most dangerous? Why?

4 Close

Quiz

1. What is the relationship between the angle of repose and the slope required for mass movement to occur? (Mass movement will occur only if the angle of the material is steeper than the angle of repose.)
2. What is creep? (Creep is the slow movement of surface material downslope.)
3. Does slow mass movement or rapid mass movement move more material down a slope? Why? (Slow mass movement, such as creep, occurs more frequently than rapid mass movement, so it moves more material over time.)

Alternative Assessment

Divide the class into small groups, and challenge each group to write a public-service announcement designed to educate the public about the dangers of one form of mass movement. Instruct them to focus on the causes and consequences of these phenomena. Allow time for each group to perform its announcement for the class.

TOPIC: Mass Movement
GO TO: www.scilinks.org
***sci*LINKS NUMBER:** HSTE295

Answers to Review

1. Slump occurs when a block of material moves downslope over a curved surface.
2. Steep slopes, heavy rainfall or snowfall, volcanic eruptions, and alternating freezing and thawing temperatures increase the chances that mass movement will occur.
3. Mass movement occurs on slopes as a result of gravitational pull. The effect of gravity depends on the characteristics of the surface material. The steeper the slope, the more likely mass movement will occur.
4. Answers may vary. Accept all reasonable responses. Rapid mass movements are the most dangerous type of mass movement because a large amount of material moves rapidly and without warning.

Chapter Highlights

VOCABULARY DEFINITIONS

SECTION 1

shoreline the boundary between land and a body of water

beach any area of the shoreline made up of material deposited by waves

longshore current the movement of water parallel to and near the shoreline

SECTION 2

saltation the movement of sand-sized particles by a skipping and bouncing action in the direction the wind is blowing

deflation the lifting and removal of fine sediment by wind

abrasion the grinding and wearing down of rock surfaces by other rock or sand particles

dune a mound of wind-deposited sand

loess thick deposits of windblown, fine-grained sediments

Vocabulary Review Worksheet 11

Blackline masters of these Chapter Highlights can be found in the **Study Guide.**

Chapter Highlights

SECTION 1

Vocabulary

shoreline *(p. 276)*
beach *(p. 278)*
longshore current *(p. 279)*

Section Notes

- The wind from storms usually produces the large waves that cause shoreline erosion.
- Waves break when they enter shallow water, becoming surf.
- Beaches are made of any material deposited by waves.
- Sandbars, spits, and tombolos are depositional features caused by longshore currents.
- Sea cliffs, sea caves, sea arches, and sea stacks are coastal formations caused by wave erosion.

SECTION 2

Vocabulary

saltation *(p. 282)*
deflation *(p. 283)*
abrasion *(p. 284)*
dune *(p. 284)*
loess *(p. 286)*

Section Notes

- Wind is an important agent of erosion and deposition in deserts and along coastlines.
- Saltation is the process of the wind bouncing sand grains downwind along the ground.
- Deflation is the removal of materials by wind. If deflation removes all fine rock materials, a barren surface called desert pavement is formed.
- Abrasion is the grinding and wearing down of rock surfaces by other rock or sand particles.
- Dunes are formations caused by wind-deposited sand.
- Loess is wind-deposited silt, and it forms soil material good for farming.

Labs

Dune Movement *(p. 530)*

Skills Check

Math Concepts

WAVE PERIOD Waves travel in intervals that are usually between 10 and 20 seconds apart. Use the following equation to calculate how many waves reach the shore in 1 minute:

$$\text{number of waves per minute} = \frac{60 \text{ seconds}}{\text{waves period (seconds)}}$$

After you find out how many waves reach the shore in 1 minute, you can figure out how many waves occur in an hour or even a day. For example, consider a wave period of 15 seconds. Using the formula above, you find that 4 waves occur in 1 minute. To find out how many waves occur in 1 hour, multiply 4 by 60. To find out how many waves occur in 1 day, multiply 240 by 24.

$$\text{number of waves per day} = \frac{60}{15} \times 60 \times 24 = 5{,}760$$

Visual Understanding

U-SHAPED VALLEYS AND MORE Look back at the illustration on page 291 to review the different types of landscape features carved by alpine glaciers.

298

Lab and Activity Highlights

Dune Movement PG 530

Gliding Glaciers PG 531

Creating a Kettle PG 533

Datasheets for LabBook (blackline masters for these labs)

SECTION 3

Vocabulary

glacier *(p. 287)*
iceberg *(p. 288)*
crevasse *(p. 289)*
horn *(p. 291)*
cirque *(p. 291)*
arête *(p. 291)*
hanging valley *(p. 291)*
U-shaped valley *(p. 291)*
glacial drift *(p. 292)*
stratified drift *(p. 292)*
till *(p. 293)*

Section Notes

- Masses of moving ice are called glaciers.
- There are two main types of glaciers—alpine glaciers and continental glaciers.
- Glaciers move when the ice that comes into contact with the ground melts and when ice crystals slip over one another.
- Alpine glaciers produce rugged, erosive landscape features, such as cirques, arêtes, and horns.
- Continental glaciers smooth the landscape.
- There are two main types of glacial deposits—stratified drift and till.
- Some of the landforms deposited by glaciers include outwash plains, eskers, and moraines.

Labs

Gliding Glaciers *(p. 531)*
Creating a Kettle *(p. 533)*

SECTION 4

Vocabulary

mass movement *(p. 294)*
rock fall *(p. 295)*
landslide *(p. 295)*
mudflow *(p. 296)*
creep *(p. 297)*

Section Notes

- Mass movement is the movement of material downhill due to the force of gravity.
- The angle of repose is the steepest slope at which loose material will remain at rest.
- Rock falls, landslides, and mudflows are all types of rapid mass movement.
- Creep and solifluction are types of slow mass movement.

internetconnect

GO TO: go.hrw.com

Visit the **HRW** Web site for a variety of learning tools related to this chapter. Just type in the keyword:

KEYWORD: HSTICE

GO TO: www.scilinks.org

Visit the **National Science Teachers Association** on-line Web site for Internet resources related to this chapter. Just type in the ***sci*LINKS** number for more information about the topic:

TOPIC: Wave Erosion	***sci*LINKS NUMBER:** HSTE280
TOPIC: Wind Erosion	***sci*LINKS NUMBER:** HSTE285
TOPIC: Glaciers	***sci*LINKS NUMBER:** HSTE290
TOPIC: Mass Movement	***sci*LINKS NUMBER:** HSTE295
TOPIC: Wetlands	***sci*LINKS NUMBER:** HSTE300

299

Lab and Activity Highlights

LabBank

Whiz-Bang Demonstrations
- Between a Rock and a Hard Place, Demo 23
- Rising Mountains, Demo 24

Long-Term Projects & Research Ideas, Project 40

VOCABULARY DEFINITIONS, *continued*

SECTION 3

glacier an enormous mass of moving ice

iceberg a large piece of ice that breaks off an ice shelf and drifts into the ocean

crevasse a large crack that forms where a glacier picks up speed or flows over a high point

horn a sharp pyramid-shaped peak that forms when three or more cirques erode a mountain

cirque a bowl-like depression where glacial ice cuts back into mountain walls

arête a jagged ridge that forms between two or more cirques cutting into the same mountain

hanging valley a small glacial valley that joins the deeper main valley

U-shaped valley a valley that forms when a glacier flows into and erodes a valley, changing the valley from its original V shape to a U shape

glacial drift all material carried and deposited by glaciers

stratified drift rock material that has been sorted and deposited in layers by water flowing from the melted ice of a glacier

till unsorted rock material that is deposited directly by glacial ice when it melts

SECTION 4

mass movement the movement of any material downslope

rock fall a group of loose rocks that fall down a steep slope

landslide a sudden and rapid movement of a large amount of material downslope

mudflow the rapid movement of a large mass of mud/rock and soil mixed with a large amount of water that flows downhill

creep the extremely slow movement of material downslope

Chapter Review Answers

Using Vocabulary

1. The shoreline is the area where land and a body of water meet. A longshore current is a movement of water parallel to and near the shoreline.
2. A beach is an area of the shoreline made up of material deposited by waves. A dune is a deposit of windblown sand that can be found on a beach.
3. Deflation is the lifting and removal of material by the wind. Saltation is the movement of sand in the direction the wind is blowing by a skipping and bouncing action.
4. Horns are sharp, pyramid-shaped peaks that are carved by glaciers when several cirques form. Arêtes are jagged ridges that form between two or more cirques that cut into the same mountain.
5. Stratified drift is sorted glacial drift. Till is unsorted glacial drift.
6. A mudflow is a rapid mass movement. Creep is a slow mass movement.

Understanding Concepts

Multiple Choice

7. c
8. c
9. c
10. c
11. d
12. b
13. a
14. b
15. a
16. c

Short Answer

17. When waves reach shallow water, the lower part of the wave is crowded by the ocean floor. The wave becomes taller, eventually growing so tall that it cannot support itself. When it reaches this point, it curls and breaks.
18. Storms generally produce larger waves, which have greater erosive energy. These waves are capable of removing chunks of rock from the coastline.
19. Sometimes people remove native vegetation from an area to make room for agricultural land. The plants anchor the soil in place. By removing the plants, they make the area more vulnerable to wind erosion.
20. Sand dunes move in the direction of the prevailing winds.
21. Glaciers are effective agents of erosion and deposition because they are very large and heavy and move across the Earth's surface.
22. Tilted fence posts and bent tree trunks are evidence of creep.

Chapter Review

USING VOCABULARY

Explain the difference between the words in the following pairs:

1. shoreline/longshore current
2. beaches/dunes
3. deflation/saltation
4. horn/arête
5. stratified drift/till
6. mudflow/creep

UNDERSTANDING CONCEPTS

Multiple Choice

7. *Surf* refers to
   a. large storm waves in the open ocean.
   b. giant waves produced by hurricanes.
   c. breaking waves.
   d. small waves on a calm sea.

8. When waves cut completely through a headland, a __?__ is formed.
   a. sea cave
   b. sea cliff
   c. sea stack
   d. sea arch

9. A narrow strip of sand that is formed by wave deposition and is connected to the shore is called a __?__
   a. marine terrace.
   b. sandbar.
   c. spit.
   d. headland.

10. A wind eroded rock is called a
   a. deflation hollow.
   b. desert pavement.
   c. ventifact.
   d. dust bowl.

11. Where is the world's largest ice sheet located?
   a. Greenland
   b. Canada
   c. Alaska
   d. Antarctica

12. The process of calving forms __?__
   a. continental ice sheets.
   b. icebergs.
   c. U-shaped valleys.
   d. moraines.

13. What term describes all types of glacial deposits?
   a. drift
   b. loess
   c. till
   d. outwash

14. Which of the following is not a landform created by an alpine glacier?
   a. cirque
   b. deflation hollow
   c. horn
   d. arête

15. What is the term for a mass movement that occurs in climates where the subsoil is permanently frozen?
   a. solifluction
   b. slump
   c. creep
   d. lahar

16. Which of the following is a slow mass movement?
   a. mudflow
   b. landslide
   c. creep
   d. rock fall

Short Answer

17. Why do waves break when they get near the shore?
18. What role do storms play in coastal erosion?
19. How do humans increase the erosion caused by dust storms?

300

Chapter 11 Review–California Standards: PE/ATE Q1–6: 2, 2c, 2d; Q7–23: 2, 2d, 3a

20. How do sand dunes move?

21. Why are glaciers such effective agents of erosion and deposition?

22. List some evidence for creep.

Concept Mapping

23. Use the following terms to create a concept map: deflation, dust storm, saltation, dune, loess.

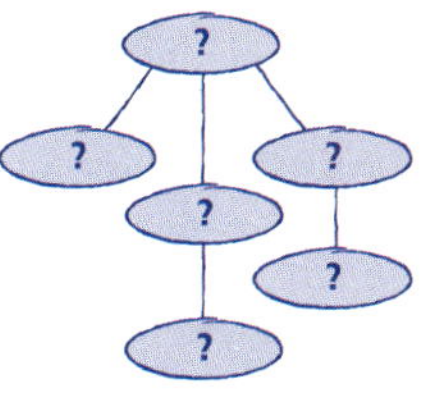

CRITICAL THINKING AND PROBLEM SOLVING

Write one or two sentences to answer the following questions:

24. What role does wind play in the processes of erosion and deposition?

25. What are the main differences between alpine glaciers and continental glaciers?

26. Describe the different types of moraines.

27. What kind of mass movement occurs continuously, day after day? Why can't you see it?

MATH IN SCIENCE

28. While standing on a beach, you can estimate a wave's speed in kilometers per hour. This is done by counting the seconds between each arriving wave crest to determine the wave period and then multiplying the wave period by 3.5. Calculate the speed of a wave with a 10-second period.

INTERPRETING GRAPHICS

The following graph illustrates coastal erosion and deposition occurring at an imaginary beach over a period of 8 years.

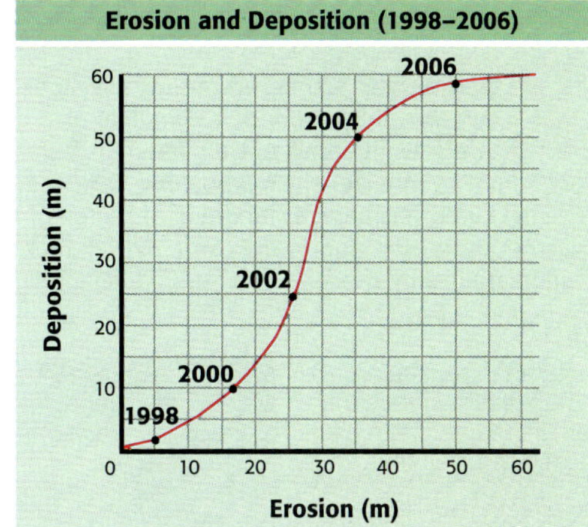

29. What is happening to the beach over time?

30. In what year does the amount of erosion that has occurred along the shoreline equal the amount of deposition?

31. Based on the erosion and deposition data for 2000, what might happen to the beach in the years to follow?

NOW What Do You Think?

Take a minute to review your answers to the ScienceLog questions on page 275. Have your answers changed? If necessary, revise your answers based on what you have learned since you began this chapter.

NOW WHAT DO YOU THINK?

1. Answers may vary. Waves and wind both erode and deposit sediment.
2. Answers may vary.

Concept Mapping Transparency 11

Blackline masters of this Chapter Review can be found in the **Study Guide.**

Concept Mapping

23.  An answer to this exercise can be found at the end of this book.

CRITICAL THINKING AND PROBLEM SOLVING

24. Wind removes sediment through saltation and deflation and deposits it in a different area. Wind also erodes the surface of material, such as rocks, through abrasion.
25. Alpine glaciers are generally smaller than continental glaciers. Alpine glaciers carve out rugged landscapes, while continental glaciers smooth the landscape. Alpine glaciers form in the mountains, and continental glaciers spread across a continent.
26. Lateral moraines are the till that is deposited on the side of the glaciers. Medial moraines form when the lateral moraines of two glaciers are pushed together. Terminal moraines are the till that is deposited at the front of a glacier. Ground moraines are the material left beneath the glacier.
27. Creep happens every day. You can't see it happening because it is a slow mass movement.

MATH IN SCIENCE

28. $10 \times 3.5 = 30.5$ km/h

INTERPRETING GRAPHICS

29. At first, more soil is being eroded than deposited. The area is losing beach. After 2002, more soil is being deposited than eroded. The beach is getting larger.
30. 2002
31. In 2000, more sand is being eroded than deposited; the coastline is losing land. This would lead you to believe that the coastline would continue shrinking. But by 2002, the coastline stops losing land and begins growing. The most recent data indicates that the coastline will continue growing.

Science, Technology, and Society

Boulder Boogie

Background

Previous researchers of this topic have used trace parallelism as evidence that rocks are moved while they are embedded in a rigid ice sheet. The trails of a pair of rocks, named Jacki and Julie, showed remarkable congruence when Messina analyzed the data to determine the distance between the rocks. Although their movement across the Racetrack appeared to be a type of synchronized ballet, the rocks converged as they twirled around. If the rocks were stuck in ice, they would remain the same distance apart; if the ice sheet shattered, the rocks would diverge. When Messina measured the convergence between Jacki and Julie, she ruled out the rigid-ice-sheet theory.

Teaching Strategies

Point out that rain makes the surface of the lake bed slippery, allowing the rocks to be moved more easily. To demonstrate this, you may wish to have students experiment with wet and dry clay to compare the friction between the two surfaces.

Boulder Boogie

Karen weighs 320 kg. When no one's looking, she slides around, leaving lots of tracks. But Karen's not a person. In fact, she's not even alive—she's a boulder! Over the years, Karen has moved hundreds of meters across the desert floor. How can a 320 kg rock slide around by itself?

▲ *A mystery in Death Valley: What moved this rock across the desert floor?*

▲ *New technology is helping Paula Messina study the paths of the "dancing rocks."*

Slipping and Sliding

Karen is one of the mysterious dancing rocks of Death Valley. These rocks slide around—sometimes together, sometimes alone. There are nearly 200 of them, and they range in size from small to very large. No one has seen them move, but their trails show where they've been.

The rocks are scattered across a dry lake bed, called the Racetrack, in Death Valley, California. The Racetrack is very flat and has almost no plants or wildlife. Several times a year, powerful storms rip across the lake bed, bringing plenty of rain, wind, and sometimes snow. The Racetrack's clay surface becomes slippery, and that's apparently when the rocks dance.

Puzzles and Clues

What could push a 320 kg boulder hundreds of yards across the mud? With the help of technology, scientists like Paula Messina are finally getting some answers. Messina uses a global positioning system (GPS) receiver and a geographic information system (GIS) to study the rocks. Using GPS satellites, Messina is able to map the movements of the rocks. Her measurements are more accurate than ever before. This new device measures the locations within centimeters! A computer equipped with GIS software constructs maps that allow her to study how the rock movement relates to the terrain. Messina's investigations with this equipment have led her to conclude that wind is probably pushing the rocks.

But how does the wind push such massive rocks? Messina thinks the gaps in the mountains at one end of the valley funnel high-speed winds down onto the slippery clay surface, pushing the rocks along. And why do some rocks move while others nearby do not? This mystery will keep Messina returning to Death Valley for years.

Search and Find

► Go to the library or the Internet, and research the many uses for GPS devices. Make a list in your ScienceLog of all the uses for GPS devices you find.

Answers to Search and Find

Students' answers will vary but might include one of the following: for marine navigation, for aviation, to find ancient trails, or to find water.

EYE ON THE ENVIRONMENT

Beach Today, Gone Tomorrow

Beaches are fun, right? But what if you went to the coast and found that the road along the beach had washed away? It could happen. In fact, erosion is stripping away beaches from islands and coastlines around the world.

An Island's Beaches

The beaches of Anguilla, a small Caribbean island, are important to the social, economic, and environmental well-being of the island and its inhabitants. Anguilla's sandy shores protect coastal areas from wave action and provide habitats for coastal plants and animals. The shores also provide important recreational areas for tourists and local residents. When Hurricane Luis hit Anguilla in 1995, Barney Bay was completely stripped of sand. But Anguilla's erosion problems started long before Luis hit the island. Normal ocean wave action had already washed away some beaches.

Back in the United States

Louisiana provides a good example of coastal problems in the United States. Louisiana has 40 percent of the nation's coastal wetlands. As important as these wetlands are, parts of the Louisiana coast were disappearing at a rate of 65 to 90 km^2 per year. That's a football field every 15 minutes! At that rate of erosion, Louisiana's new coastline would be 48 km inland by the year 2040!

Save the Sand

The people of Louisiana and Anguilla have acted to stop the loss of their coastlines. But many of their solutions are only temporary. Waves, storms, and human activity continue to erode coastlines. What can be done about beach erosion?

Scientists know that beaches and wetlands come and go to a certain extent. Erosion is part of a natural cycle. Scientists must first determine how much erosion is normal for a particular area and how much is the result of human activities or some unusual process. The next step is to preserve or stabilize existing sand dunes, preserve coastal vegetation, and plant more shrubs, vines, grasses, and trees. The people of Louisiana and Anguilla have learned a lot from their problems and are taking many of these steps to slow further erosion. If steps are taken to protect valuable coastal areas, beaches will be there when you go on vacation.

▲ *This is what Barney Bay looked like in 1995 before and after Hurricane Luis.*

Extending Your Knowledge

► What are barrier islands? How are they related to coastal erosion? On your own, find out more about barrier islands and why it is important to preserve them.

EYE ON THE ENVIRONMENT

Beach Today, Gone Tomorrow

Background

State and federal agencies, as well as concerned Louisiana citizens and businesses, have been taking steps in the right direction to preserve the Louisiana coast. A joint effort is being made to rebuild and restore the wetlands. Rebuilding methods include using sediments from near-shore sandbars to create wetlands and refilling canals, which were previously sending loose sediment directly to the ocean.

TOPIC: Wetlands
GO TO: www.scilinks.org
***sci*LINKS NUMBER:** HSTE300

Answer to Extending Your Knowledge

Barrier islands are long, narrow islands formed by the deposition of sediment. Louisiana's barrier islands formed as a result of the Mississippi River changing course. As one delta was abandoned, a new one formed, and a series of islands developed at the end of the old delta. According to some experts, Louisiana's barrier islands are eroding so rapidly that they will disappear by the end of this century. These islands protect the coast from devastating winds and waves created by offshore storms. If the barrier islands were to completely disappear, Louisiana could lose an additional 48 km of shoreline. Experts suggest that the most effective means to preserve Louisiana's barrier islands would be to nourish them. Beach nourishment involves the transport of sand from other areas in order to replenish the area lost to erosion.

California Standards: PE/ATE 2c

Chapter Organizer

CHAPTER ORGANIZATION	TIME MINUTES	OBJECTIVES	LABS, INVESTIGATIONS, AND DEMONSTRATIONS
Chapter Opener **pp. 304–305**	45	California Standards: PE/ATE 5b, 5e, 7	**Investigate!** Who Eats Whom? p. 305
Section 1 **Everything Is Connected**	90	▶ Distinguish between the biotic and abiotic environment. ▶ Explain how populations, communities, ecosystems, and the biosphere are related. ▶ Explain how the abiotic environment relates to communities. PE/ATE 5, 5a–5c, 5e, 7, 7b, 7c; LabBook 7, 7c, 7e	**QuickLab,** The Human Population, p. 307 **Skill Builder,** Capturing the Wild Bean, p. 534 **Datasheets for LabBook,** Capturing the Wild Bean, Datasheet 26
Section 2 **Living Things Need Energy**	90	▶ Describe the functions of producers, consumers, and decomposers in an ecosystem. ▶ Distinguish between a food chain and a food web. ▶ Explain how energy flows through a food web. ▶ Distinguish between an organism's habitat and its niche. PE/ATE 5, 5a–5e	**EcoLabs & Field Activities,** Survival Is Just a Roll of the Dice, EcoLab 5 **Whiz-Bang Demonstrations,** Voracious Fly Catcher, Demo 11
Section 3 **Types of Interactions**	135	▶ Distinguish between the two types of competition. ▶ Give examples of predators and prey. ▶ Distinguish between mutualism, commensalism, and parasitism. ▶ Define *coevolution,* and give an example. PE/ATE 5, 5a–5e; LabBook 7, 7d, 7e	**Interactive Explorations CD-ROM,** What's Bugging You? *A **Worksheet** is also available in the **Interactive Explorations Teacher's Edition.*** **Making Models,** Adaptation: It's a Way of Life, p. 536 **Datasheets for LabBook,** Adaptation: It's a Way of Life, Datasheet 27 **Long-Term Projects & Research Ideas,** Project 18

See page **T20** *for a complete correlation of this book with the*

CALIFORNIA SCIENCE CONTENT STANDARDS.

Correlations are also provided at point of use throughout this ATE.

TECHNOLOGY RESOURCES

Guided Reading Audio CD
English or Spanish, Chapter 12

Classroom Management CD-ROM

Interactive Explorations CD-ROM
CD 2, Exploration 1, What's Bugging You?

CNN **Eye on the Environment,** Hummingbird Mites, Segment 3

Test Generator CD-ROM

Science Discovery Videodiscs
Image and Activity Bank with Lesson Plans: Balanced Ecosystems
Science Sleuths: Neo-Cassava: The Tropical Miracle

Chapter 12 • Interactions of Living Things

CLASSROOM WORKSHEETS, TRANSPARENCIES, AND RESOURCES	SCIENCE INTEGRATION AND CONNECTIONS	REVIEW AND ASSESSMENT
Directed Reading Worksheet 12 **Science Puzzlers, Twisters & Teasers,** Worksheet 12		
Transparency 128, The Five Levels of Environmental Organization **Directed Reading Worksheet 12,** Section 1	**Multicultural Connection,** p. 307 in ATE **Multicultural Connection,** p. 308 in ATE **Connect to Environmental Science,** p. 308 in ATE **Eye on the Environment:** Alien Invasion, p. 327	**Review,** p. 309 **Quiz,** p. 309 in ATE **Alternative Assessment,** p. 309 in ATE
Transparency 5, Energy for Cells **Directed Reading Worksheet 12,** Section 2 **Math Skills for Science Worksheet 22,** Working with Percentages and Proportions **Transparency 129,** Energy Pyramid **Reinforcement Worksheet 12,** Weaving a Food Web **Critical Thinking Worksheet 12,** A Struggle to Survive	**Connect to Life Science,** p. 310 in ATE **Real-World Connection,** p. 311 in ATE **Math and More,** p. 312 in ATE **MathBreak,** Energy Pyramids, p. 313	**Self-Check,** p. 311 **Self-Check,** p. 312 **Review,** p. 315 **Quiz,** p. 315 in ATE **Alternative Assessment,** p. 315 in ATE
Directed Reading Worksheet 12, Section 3 **Reinforcement Worksheet 12,** Symbiotic Relationships	**Real-World Connection,** p. 319 in ATE **Multicultural Connection,** p. 320 in ATE **Apply,** p. 321 **Health Watch:** An Unusual Guest, p. 326	**Self-Check,** p. 317 **Review,** p. 321 **Quiz,** p. 321 in ATE **Alternative Assessment,** p. 321 in ATE

Holt, Rinehart and Winston On-line Resources

go.hrw.com

For worksheets and other teaching aids related to this chapter, visit the HRW Web site and type in the keyword: **HSTINT**

National Science Teachers Association

www.scilinks.org

Encourage students to use the keywords listed on the Technology Highlights page to access information and resources on the **NSTA** Web site.

END-OF-CHAPTER REVIEW AND ASSESSMENT

Chapter Review in Study Guide
Vocabulary and Notes in Study Guide
Chapter Tests with Performance-Based Assessment, Chapter 12 Test
Chapter Tests with Performance-Based Assessment, Performance-Based Assessment 12
Concept Mapping Transparency 12

Chapter Resources & Worksheets

Visual Resources

TEACHING TRANSPARENCIES

#128 #129

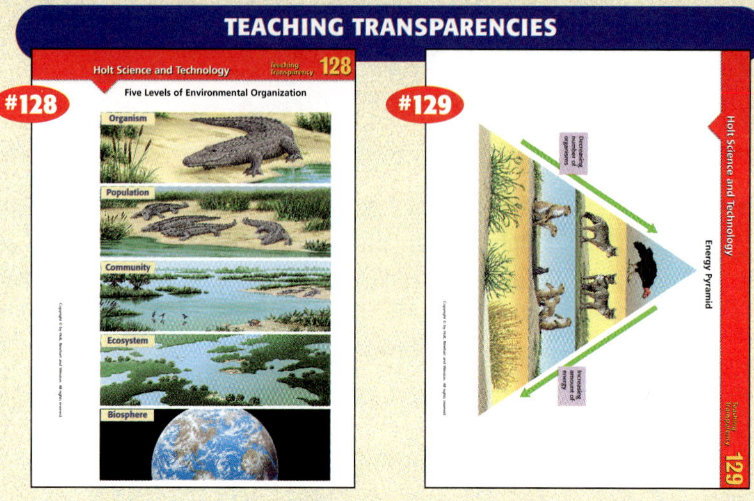

TEACHING TRANSPARENCIES

#5

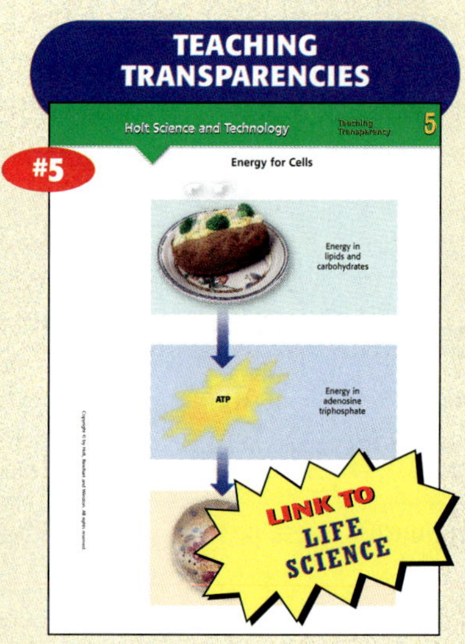

CONCEPT MAPPING TRANSPARENCY

#12

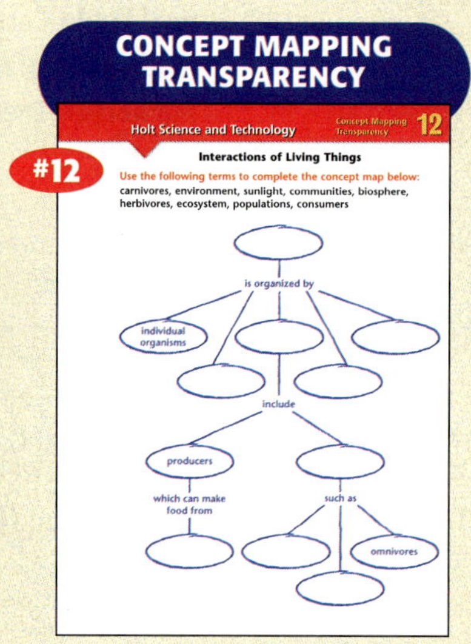

Meeting Individual Needs

DIRECTED READING

#12

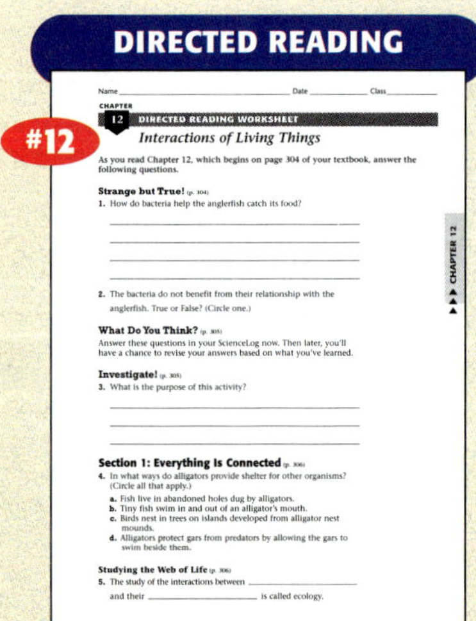

REINFORCEMENT & VOCABULARY REVIEW

#12 #12

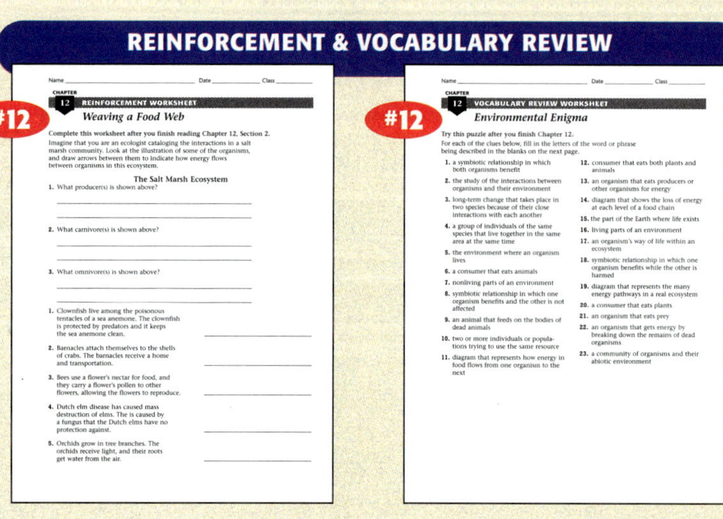

SCIENCE PUZZLERS, TWISTERS & TEASERS

#12

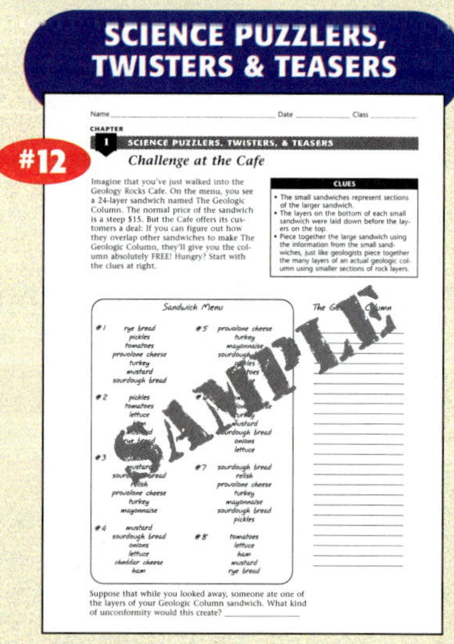

Review & Assessment

STUDY GUIDE

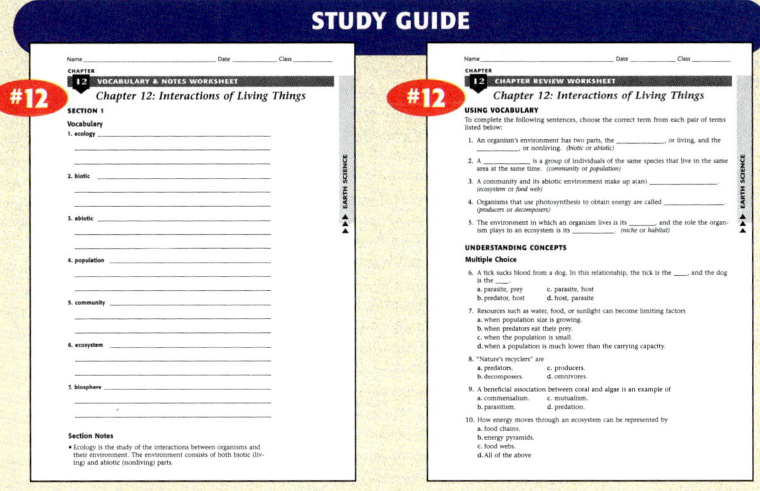
#12 Chapter 12: Interactions of Living Things — Vocabulary & Notes Worksheet

#12 Chapter 12: Interactions of Living Things — Chapter Review Worksheet

CHAPTER TESTS WITH PERFORMANCE-BASED ASSESSMENT

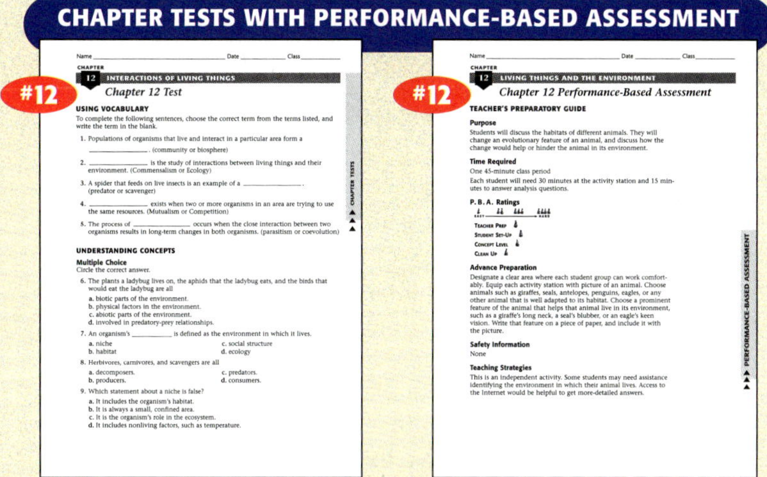
#12 Chapter 12 Test — Interactions of Living Things

#12 Chapter 12 Performance-Based Assessment — Living Things and the Environment

Lab Worksheets

ECOLABS & FIELD ACTIVITIES

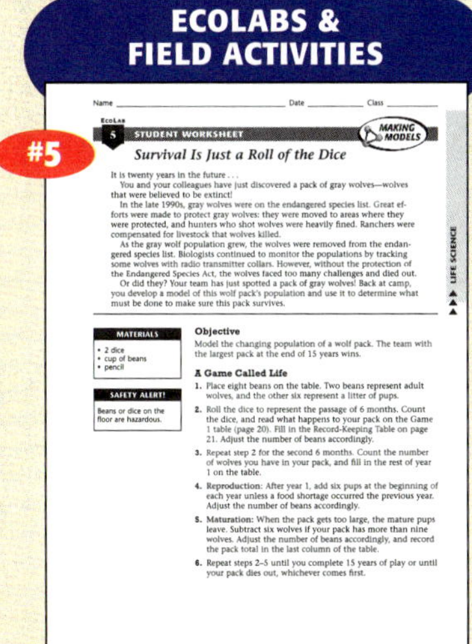
#5 Survival Is Just a Roll of the Dice

WHIZ-BANG DEMONSTRATIONS

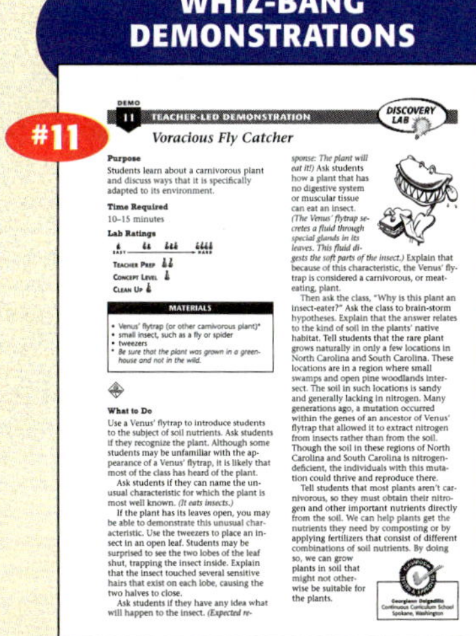
#11 Voracious Fly Catcher

LONG-TERM PROJECTS & RESEARCH IDEAS

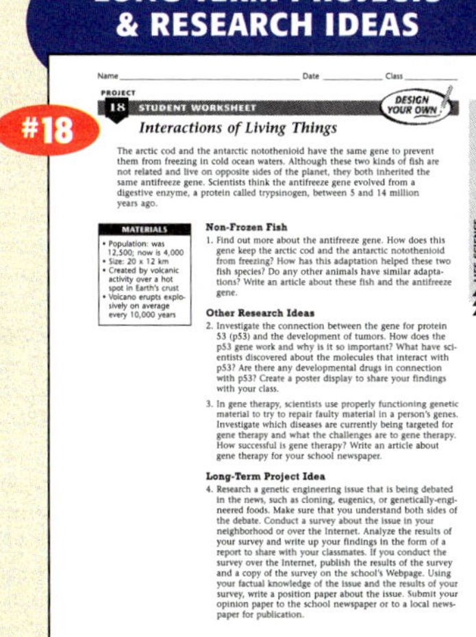
#18 Interactions of Living Things

DATASHEETS FOR LABBOOK

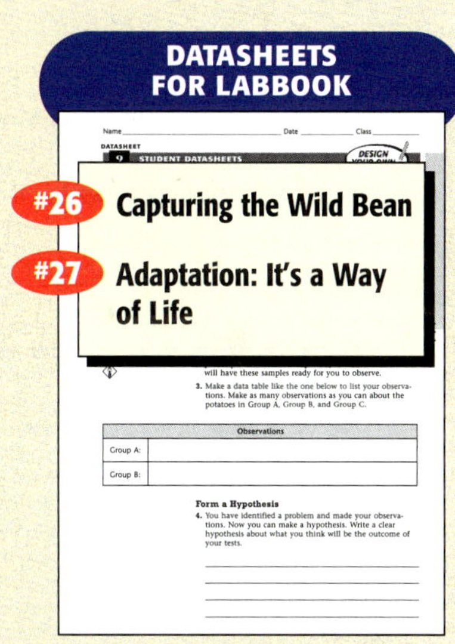
#26 Capturing the Wild Bean

#27 Adaptation: It's a Way of Life

Applications & Extensions

CRITICAL THINKING & PROBLEM SOLVING

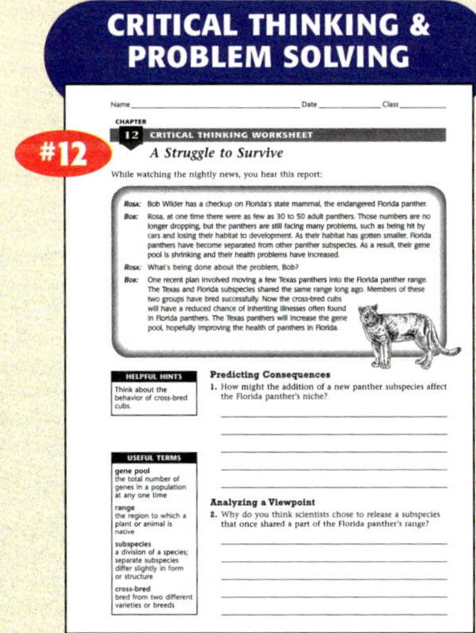
#12 A Struggle to Survive

EYE ON THE ENVIRONMENT

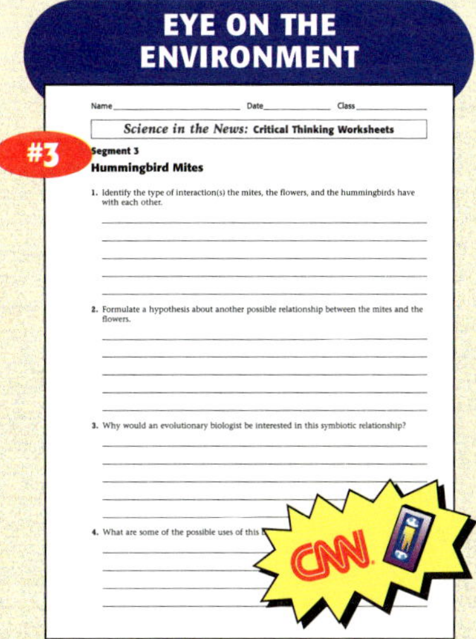
#3 Science in the News: Critical Thinking Worksheets — Segment 3 Hummingbird Mites

INTERACTIVE EXPLORATIONS

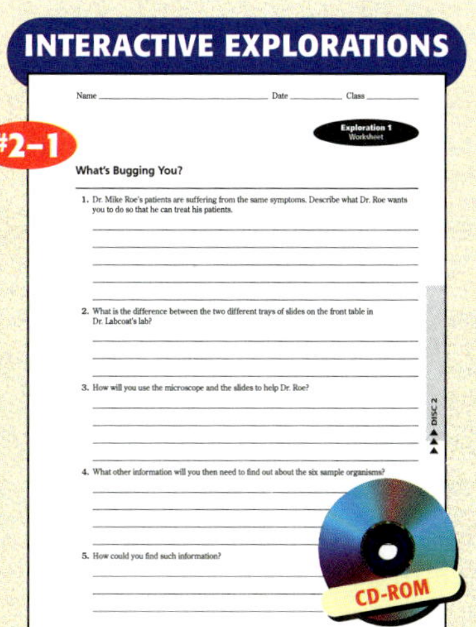
#2–1 What's Bugging You?

Chapter Background

Section 1

Everything Is Connected

▶ Indicator Species

An indicator species is a plant or animal that, by its presence in a particular area, indicates the environmental conditions of the site. This information tells scientists what other species might thrive in the locale. For example, mosses usually indicate acidic soil, which would limit the types of plants that can survive in the same area. This, in turn, affects the variety of herbivores and other animals that can live there.

▶ Ecology

Ecology as an academic discipline can be traced to Theophrastus (c. 372–287 B.C.), a student of Aristotle (384–322 B.C.). Theophrastus offered the first descriptions of the relationships between organisms and the living and nonliving parts of their environment. The term *ecology* was coined in 1866 by Ernst Haeckel (1834–1919), a German zoologist. *Oekologie*, the German word for ecology, comes from the Greek *oikos*, which means "household, home, or place to live."

Is That a Fact!

- The Australian mallee fowl regulates the temperature of its nest mound with the help of other organisms. A healthy population of fungus and bacteria inhabit the leaf-and-twig mound built by the birds. As the bacteria decompose the leaves, they give off heat. When the temperature reaches 34°C (the birds can tell by sticking their beak into the mound), it's egg-laying time! The birds work hard to keep the mound and their eggs at a constant temperature by adding more material or digging ventilation shafts. They can also fight off potential predators while their eggs remain warm in the mound.

Section 2

Living Things Need Energy

▶ Systems Ecology

Some early ecologists focused on communities and populations, but others looked at the energy transfer between organisms. Today the study of energy transfer is called systems ecology. It involves analysis of the flow of energy and the recycling of nutrients within an ecosystem to answer the question, "How does the ecosystem function?" The use of modern materials and techniques, such as radioisotopes, computer science, and applied mathematics, has enabled scientists to quantify the movement of nutrients and energy through ecosystems.

Is That a Fact!

- The coral reef is the most productive habitat on Earth, followed by the tropical rain forest, the temperate forest, the savanna, cultivated land, the open sea, and the semidesert.
- Kelp is a marine alga, often called seaweed, anchored to the ocean floor. It is a primary producer. Sea urchins and many other organisms eat it. Kelp also provides shelter for animals such as bronze kelp perch. Sea otters sometimes wrap themselves in a blade of kelp to keep from drifting while they nap.
- Blades of the Pacific giant kelp can grow up to 120 m, taller than the Statue of Liberty.
- Some animals build a home within their habitat. The trapdoor spider digs a burrow in the ground and constructs a "trap door" of silk and mud with

silk hinges. It waits until an insect walks by, then quickly opens the door and grabs its prey. Trapdoor spiders inject venom into their prey, but they are harmless to people.

- Different habitats provide different materials for animals to use when constructing their home. These homes have different names. A squirrel's nest of leaves and sticks is called a drey. A badger's burrow is called a sett. A river otter's burrow in a river bank is called a holt.

Section 3

Types of Interactions

Mimicry

Batesian mimicry was named for Henry Walter Bates (1825–1892), who described it in 1862. The mimic assumes the form of its model to take advantage of the model's defenses. For example, the viceroy butterfly looks just like the unappetizing monarch, which birds avoid. The snake caterpillar's movements resemble those of a real snake and thus help prevent attack by predators fearful of snakes.

- In 1878, Fritz Müller (1821–1897) described Müllerian mimicry, in which the resemblance of two species gives them mutual defense benefits. Both the sand wasp and the yellow jacket can sting. A predator that avoids one will avoid the other.
- Camouflage, a prey adaptation illustrated by the praying mantis's resemblance to a leaf, is a form of mimicry.

Joke's on You: Prey Adaptations

The killdeer is a ground-nesting bird that will distract a predator from its nest or chicks with a "broken-wing" display. It will limp and drag a wing on the ground, making itself appear to be an easy catch. But because it is actually quite healthy, it always stays one step ahead of the predator.

Plants and Ants

Symbiotic relationships between animals and plants are often a marvel to behold. There are plants called epiphytes that have coevolved with ants. The plants provide knobby, chambered tubers in which the ants live. The excrement from the ants provides vital nutrition for the plant.

- Some tree-dwelling tropical ants collect and plant seeds in gardens they tend in their tree homes. The ants nourish the seeds with feces they collect and bring to the garden. The plants then grow and provide the ants with food.

- Other ants live inside the stems of rattan palms. When one of these palms, the ant-filled Korthalsa, is touched, the ants inside the plant begin smashing their mandibles (jaws) together, creating a hissing, whispering, or rattling noise. No one is quite sure of the function of this activity, but it may serve to deter interested animals from further disturbing the plant.
- In West Africa, stinging ants protect the *Barteria,* the small tree in which the ants live. The sting of this ant can numb a human for several days and can penetrate even the tough skin of an elephant.

The Bacteria House

Humans benefit from the mutualistic relationship we have with the *Escherichia coli* that live inside of us. As many as 100 trillion bacteria live in each of our digestive systems, 400 species living in an intricate ecological balance. We provide the bacteria with food and comfortable growing conditions, and they help us digest our food and provide us with nutrients.

For additional background resources, please refer to the **HST Reference Library.**

CHAPTER 12

Interactions of Living Things

Chapter Preview

Directed Reading Worksheet 12

Science Puzzlers, Twisters & Teasers Worksheet 12

Guided Reading Audio CD
English or Spanish, Chapter 12

CHAPTER 12

Interactions of Living Things

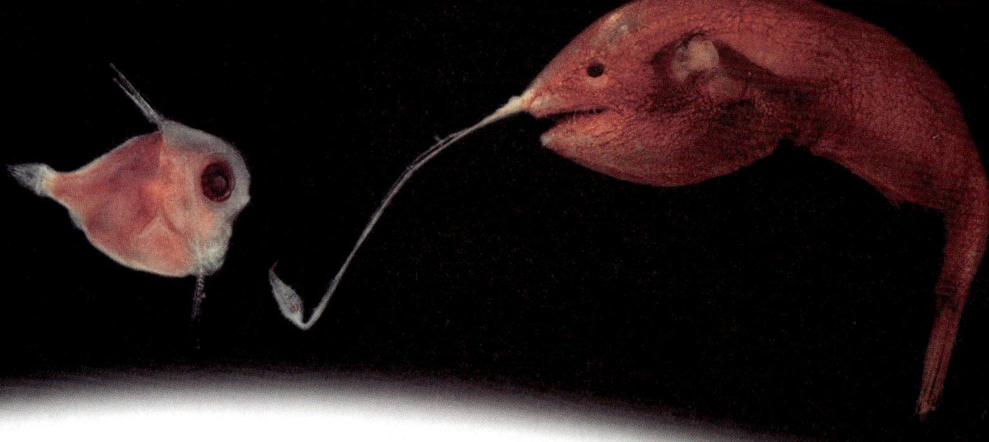

Strange but True!

A small fish swims through the darkest part of the ocean in search of its next meal. Food is scarce at this depth, but suddenly a glowing morsel comes into view. The tiny fish swims quickly to it, but just as the little fish is about to nab its meal, large jaws rimmed with needle-sharp teeth appear out of nowhere. Before the fish can escape, it is swallowed whole.

This is how the deep-sea anglerfish—the one with the needle-sharp teeth—catches its food. The anglerfish has a unique way of fooling unsuspecting prey. The anglerfish is equipped with its own "fishing pole," a special branchlike body part that hangs over its head, and bait. The bait is a small mass of bacteria attached to the tip of the "fishing pole" that glow in the dark. The anglerfish is only about 7 cm long and is hard to see in the murky depths of the ocean. Fish attracted to the bright bait do not notice the lurking anglerfish until it is too late.

The anglerfish and the glowing bacteria are involved in a relationship that benefits both of them. In exchange for providing the anglerfish with a lure to catch fish, the bacteria get to live in a protected and mobile home. In this chapter you will learn more about the diverse ways living things interact with each other and with their environment. Some of these relationships are almost too strange to believe!

304

Strange but True!

The anglerfish uses bacteria to catch its food. Leaf-cutting ants use fungi to make food. The ants, as many as 2 million in one colony, cut tiny pieces of leaves that they transport back to their nest mounds. Then the ants chew the leaves to create a pasty fertilizer for their fungus gardens, which they maintain in the 2,000 (on average) chambers of their colony. The fungi convert the cellulose, which the ants cannot eat, to carbohydrates. The ants then eat the fungi.

What Do You Think?

In your ScienceLog, try to answer the following questions based on what you already know:

1. Imagine a deer living in a meadow. What does the deer eat? What eats the deer? When the deer dies, what happens to its remains?
2. What is the source of energy for plants?

Investigate!

Who Eats Whom?

In this activity, you will learn how certain organisms interact when finding (or becoming) the next meal. You will need **five index cards,** which you can obtain from your teacher.

Procedure

1. On each index card, print the name of one of the organisms shown at right. All these organisms live in the cold ocean water near Antarctica.
2. Arrange the cards on your desk to show who eats whom. (Hint: Algae are small organisms that use the sun's energy to make food. Therefore, the algae card belongs at the bottom of your arrangement.)
3. Draw your card arrangement in your ScienceLog, beginning with the algae card.
4. In its natural habitat, which organism exists in the greatest number? Arrange the cards in order of most to fewest individuals.

Analysis

5. How does the arrangement of who eats whom compare with the arrangement of the number of individuals?
6. What might happen to the other organisms if the algae were removed from this group? What might happen if the killer whales were removed?
7. Are there any organisms in this group that eat more than one kind of food? How would you change the order of your cards to reflect this information?

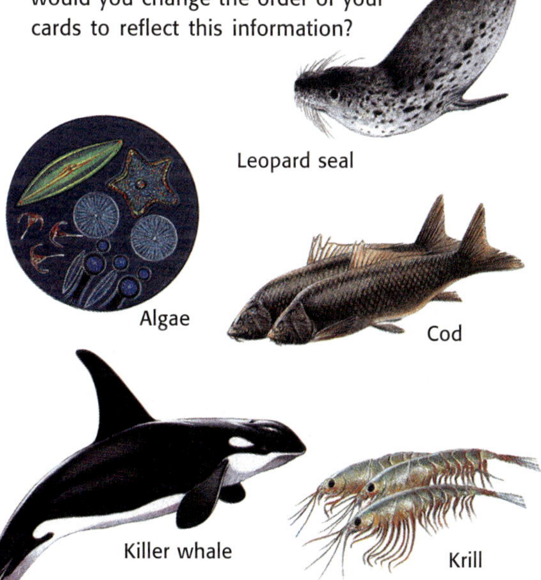

What Do You Think?

Accept all reasonable responses.

Students will have a chance to revise their answers in the Chapter Review under NOW What Do You Think?

Investigate!

MATERIALS
For Each Group:
• 3 × 5 in. index cards

Answers to Investigate!

4. Algae, the most abundant organisms, are at the bottom of the food chain.
5. At the bottom of the arrangement are the algae, the most numerous organisms. Next are krill. There are fewer krill than algae. Cod are third, then leopard seals. Finally, the killer whale is at the top of this food chain.
6. In this food chain, the krill feed only on the algae. If the algae were removed, the krill would die out. The cod would then die out because there would be no krill for them to eat. The leopard seals would have no cod to eat and would therefore starve, and the killer whales would in turn starve. If the killer whales were removed, the leopard seals might overpopulate and eat all of the cod until there were no more. The leopard seals might then suffer a massive starvation. Also, if there were no more cod, krill might overpopulate and eliminate the algae. Removing either the bottom organism or the top organism of a food chain results in great harm to the environment.
7. Cod eat algae and krill; leopard seals eat both krill and cod; killer whales eat krill, cod, and leopard seals. This is a true food web, and it contains more than the five organisms that are shown here. Accept any arrangement of cards that indicate that there are several predator-prey relationships. Your best students may arrange the cards in trophic levels.

IS THAT A FACT!

A blue whale eats about 3.5 metric tons of krill every day.

Chapter 12 Opener—California Standards: PE/ATE 5b, 5e, 7

SECTION 1

Focus

Everything Is Connected

In this section, students will learn that ecology is the study of interactions between organisms and their environment. Students will also learn to identify the biotic and abiotic parts of an environment and how environments are organized into populations, communities, and ecosystems.

Bellringer

Use the board or an overhead projector to display these two sentences as students enter:

People are a part of nature. People are not a part of nature.

Ask students to consider the meanings of these statements and explain them in their ScienceLog.

1 Motivate

DISCUSSION

The *fynbos* is a region in South Africa that contains more than 8,500 native plants, two-thirds of which live nowhere else. Non-native plants are now threatening the survival of the fynbos by out-competing the local plants for resources such as light, space, and water. Research has shown that there is a connection between the health of the fynbos and the well-being of the people nearby. Ask students the following question:

Should the non-native plants be removed from the fynbos? That would be very expensive and difficult. What other options are there?

1

Everything Is Connected

NEW TERMS

- ecology
- biotic
- abiotic
- population
- community
- ecosystem
- biosphere

OBJECTIVES

- Distinguish between the biotic and abiotic environment.
- Explain how populations, communities, ecosystems, and the biosphere are related.
- Explain how the abiotic environment relates to communities.

Look at **Figure 1** below. An alligator drifts in a weedy Florida river, watching a long, thin fish called a gar. The gar swims too close to the alligator. Suddenly, in a rush of snapping jaws and splashing water, the gar becomes a meal for the alligator.

It is clear that these two organisms have just interacted with one another. But organisms have many interactions other than simply "who eats whom." For example, alligators dig underwater holes to escape from the heat. Later, after the alligators abandon these holes, fish and other aquatic organisms live in them when the water level gets low during a drought. Alligators also build nest mounds in which to lay their eggs, and they enlarge these mounds each year. Eventually, the mounds become small islands where trees and other plants grow. Herons, egrets, and other birds build their nests in the trees. It is easy to see that alligators affect many organisms, not just the gars that they eat.

Studying the Web of Life

All living things are connected in a web of life. Scientists who study the connections among living things specialize in the science of ecology. **Ecology** is the study of the interactions between organisms and their environment.

An Environment Has Two Parts An organism's environment is anything that affects the organism. An environment consists of two parts. The **biotic** part of the environment is all of the organisms that live together and interact with one another. The **abiotic** part of the environment includes all of the physical factors—such as water, soil, light, and temperature—that affect organisms living in a particular area. Take another look at **Figure 1.** How many biotic parts can you see? How many abiotic parts?

Figure 1 *The alligator affects, and is affected by, many organisms in its environment.*

Teaching Transparency 128 "The Five Levels of Environmental Organization"

Directed Reading Worksheet 12 Section 1

IS THAT A FACT!

Alligators often dig deep holes in the ground. These holes fill up with water and remain full, even during dry winters. Other animals rely heavily on these holes when fresh water is scarce. In Florida, cattle ranchers have used these water sources for their livestock during droughts.

Section 1—California Standards: PE/ATE 5, 5a, 5b, 5c, 5e, 7, 7b, 7c; LabBook: 7, 7c, 7e

Organization in the Environment At first glance, the environment may look anything but organized. To ecologists, however, the environment can be organized into different levels, as shown in **Figure 2.** The first level contains the individual organism. The second level contains individuals in a population. The next three levels contain populations organized into a community, communities organized into an ecosystem, and ecosystems organized into the biosphere. Turn the page and examine **Figure 3** to see these levels in a salt marsh.

Figure 2 **The Five Levels of Environmental Organization**

QuickLab

The Human Population

1. Using a **sheet of graph paper,** a **pencil,** and a **ruler,** draw and label a graph as shown below.

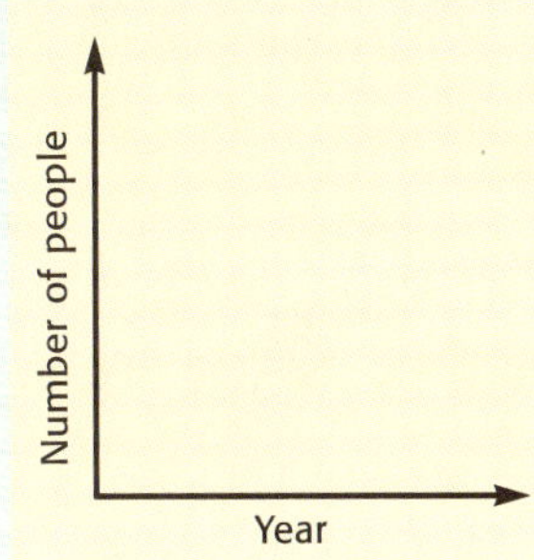

2. Plot the following points on your graph:
   (1800, 1 billion people)
   (1930, 2 billion people)
   (1960, 3 billion people)
   (1975, 4 billion people)
   (1987, 5 billion people)
   (1999, 6 billion people)
3. Draw a line connecting the points.
4. Answer the following questions in your ScienceLog.
   a. What does the curve that you have drawn indicate about human population growth?
   b. Do you think the human population can continue to grow indefinitely? Why or why not?

2 Teach

Answers to QuickLab

3. Students' drawings should match the following:

4. a. exponential growth
   b. Answers will vary but should indicate that the human population will run out of food, water, and other resources and will stop growing.

Using the Figure

Have students redraw **Figure 2** using a field mouse as the base of the five levels of ecological organization. Tell students to include at least five different populations (field mice, worms, raccoons, meadow plants, owls, snakes, grasshoppers) in the community level. Have them divide the parts of the ecosystem into biotic and abiotic categories.

Multicultural CONNECTION

The Yanomami are a tribe living in remote rain-forest jungles of Venezuela and Brazil. The Yanomami in Venezuela have had very little contact with outsiders and are one of the few cultures remaining in the world in which people are still an integral part of an intact natural ecosystem. The Yanomami and their land in Venezuela are protected as an international biosphere reserve. Outsiders must get written permission to visit, but even these few visits have given the Yanomami a taste of the outside world. Many observers question how long the Yanomami hunting and gathering culture can last.

2 Teach, continued

Multicultural CONNECTION

In Hawaii, officials of the Ethnobotanical Garden are working with scientists to develop wetland habitats that will support makaloa, a wetland sedge once used by Hawaiians to weave mats. The wetlands will be part of a waste-water treatment system and will support the resurgence of makaloa. Encourage interested students to research the weaving traditions of Hawaii and to present their findings to the class.

RETEACHING

Ask students to list biotic and abiotic factors in their neighborhood. Write these factors on the board. Then ask students to describe how biotic factors change when abiotic factors change. (For example, if it rains a lot, plants grow more. If there is a drought, plants wither and leaves turn brown.) Sheltered English

internetconnect

SCILINKS NSTA
TOPIC: Organization in the Environment
GO TO: www.scilinks.org
***sci*LINKS NUMBER:** HSTE585

Populations A salt marsh is a coastal area where grasslike plants grow. A **population** is a group of individuals of the same species that live together in the same area at the same time. For example, all of the seaside sparrows that live together in a salt marsh are members of a population. The individuals in the population compete with one another for food, nesting space, and mates.

Communities A **community** consists of all the populations of different species that live and interact in an area. The various animals and plants you see below form a salt-marsh community. The different populations in a community depend on each other for food, shelter, and many other things.

Ecosystems An **ecosystem** is made up of communities of organisms and their abiotic environment. An ecologist studying the salt-marsh ecosystem would examine how the ecosystem's organisms interact with each other and how temperature, precipitation, and soil characteristics affect the organisms. For example, the rivers and streams that empty into the salt marsh carry nutrients, such as nitrogen from the land. These nutrients influence how the cordgrass and algae grow.

Figure 3 *Examine the picture of a salt marsh below. See if you can find examples of each level of organization in this environment.*

CONNECT TO ENVIRONMENTAL SCIENCE

Wetland communities are more than plant and animal habitats. Wetlands are also natural water-filtration systems that reduce levels of contaminants in municipal waste water. Wetlands also aid in soil formation, the replenishment of ground water, shoreline stabilization, and erosion prevention. In Arizona, California, Hawaii, New Mexico, and Nevada, engineers and biologists have constructed artificial wetlands to study these processes.

The Biosphere The **biosphere** is the part of Earth where life exists. It extends from the deepest parts of the ocean to very high in the atmosphere, where tiny insects and plant spores drift, and it includes every ecosystem. Ecologists study the biosphere to learn how organisms interact with the abiotic environment—Earth's gaseous atmosphere, water, soil, and rock. The water in the abiotic environment includes both fresh water and salt water as well as water that is frozen in polar icecaps and glaciers.

REVIEW

1. What is ecology?
2. Give two examples each of biotic and abiotic factors in the salt-marsh ecosystem.
3. Using the salt-marsh example, distinguish between populations, communities, ecosystems, and the biosphere.
4. **Analyzing Relationships** What do you think would happen to the other organisms in the salt-marsh ecosystem if the cordgrass were to suddenly die?

309

Answers to Review

1. Ecology is the study of the interactions of organisms with each other and with their environment.
2. Biotic factors include all living organisms in the salt marsh. Abiotic factors include all nonliving things in the salt marsh.
3. A population of seaside sparrows lives in a community, which includes all the populations around it. This community lives in a salt-marsh ecosystem, which is defined by a certain geographical location and a certain climate. This ecosystem exists within the biosphere, which is the part of Earth where life exists, including our atmosphere.
4. All the other organisms depend directly or indirectly on cordgrass for food. Without cordgrass, all of the other organisms would probably die out or move into other areas.

3 Extend

Going Further

Writing Have students write a brief report about the effects of temperature on alligator eggs; about the effects of rain, or the lack of rain, on the animals that live in Serengeti National Park, in Tanzania, and the Masai Mara, in Kenya; or about the salinity of the Dead Sea and its effects on organisms that live there.

4 Close

Quiz

1. A caterpillar, a deer, and a rabbit all want to drink from the same puddle, eat the same plant, and bask in the same spot of sunshine. Are they competing members of a population? Why or why not? (No; each is a different species. Therefore, they are competing members of a community.)
2. Using the salt marsh example, explain why ecologists state that saving a large animal, such as the heron or egret, can also save an ecosystem? (The heron and the egret can survive only if the salt marsh remains intact to provide shelter and food for the organisms that the birds need to eat.)

Alternative Assessment

Have students find and draw pictures to create a poster that shows at least five biotic and five abiotic factors of either an aquatic or a terrestrial ecosystem. Sheltered English

SECTION 2

Focus

Living Things Need Energy

In this section students will learn how producers, consumers, and decomposers obtain energy to survive. They will also learn the difference between a food chain and a food web and how energy is transferred among members of a food chain or a food web. Finally, students will learn to define *habitat* and *niche.*

Bellringer

Inform students that a plant called Indian pipe is completely white—it has no chlorophyll or chloroplasts. Can this plant still be a producer? If not, where does it get the energy it needs to survive? Have students write their answer in their ScienceLog. (This plant is a consumer. It lives off the roots of rotting trees with the help of a fungus.)

1) Motivate

ACTIVITY

Before reading this section, students should define *producer* and *consumer* in their ScienceLog, using prior knowledge. They should also define *carnivore, omnivore,* and *herbivore* in their own words. After reading the section, students should revise their definitions.

internetconnect

SCILINKS NSTA
TOPIC: Producers, Consumers, and Decomposers
GO TO: www.scilinks.org
*sci*LINKS NUMBER: HSTE590

2

NEW TERMS

producer	decomposer
consumer	food chain
herbivore	food web
carnivore	energy pyramid
omnivore	habitat
scavenger	niche

OBJECTIVES

- Describe the functions of producers, consumers, and decomposers in an ecosystem.
- Distinguish between a food chain and a food web.
- Explain how energy flows through a food web.
- Distinguish between an organism's habitat and its niche.

Living Things Need Energy

All living things need energy to survive. For example, black-tailed prairie dogs, which live in the grasslands of North America, eat grass and seeds to get the energy they need. They use this energy to grow, move, heal injuries, and reproduce. In fact, everything a prairie dog does requires energy. The same is true for the plants that grow in the grasslands where the prairie dogs live. Coyotes that stalk prairie dogs, as well as the bacteria and fungi that live in the soil, all need energy.

The Energy Connection

Organisms in a prairie or any community can be divided into three groups based on how they obtain energy. These groups are producers, consumers, and decomposers. Examine **Figure 4** to see how energy passes through these groups in an ecosystem.

Producers Organisms that use sunlight directly to make food are called **producers.** They do this using a process called photosynthesis. Most producers are plants, but some algae and bacteria are also producers. Grasses are the main producers in a prairie ecosystem. Examples of producers in other ecosystems include cordgrass and algae in a salt marsh and trees in a forest. Algae are the main producers in the sea.

Figure 4 *Follow the pathway of energy as it moves from the sun through the ecosystem.*

310

CONNECT TO LIFE SCIENCE

This section discusses how organisms obtain energy. Use Teaching Transparency 5 to illustrate how cells use energy.

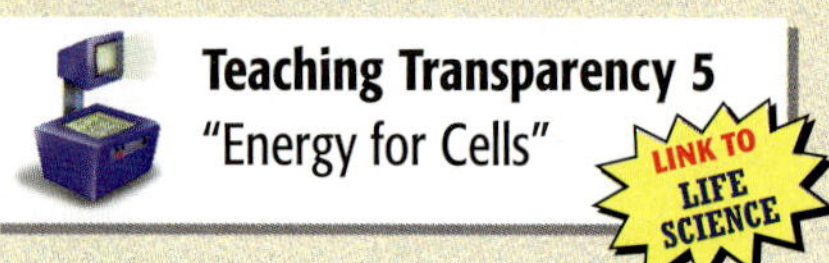

Section 2—California Standards: PE/ATE 5, 5a, 5b, 5c, 5d, 5e

Consumers Organisms that eat producers or other organisms for energy are called **consumers.** They cannot use the sun's energy directly like producers can. Instead, consumers must eat producers or other animals to obtain energy. There are several kinds of consumers. A **herbivore** is a consumer that eats plants. Herbivores in the prairie ecosystem include grasshoppers, gophers, prairie dogs, bison, and pronghorn antelope. A **carnivore** is a consumer that eats animals. Carnivores in the prairie ecosystem include coyotes, hawks, badgers, and owls. Consumers known as **omnivores** eat a variety of organisms, both plants and animals. The grasshopper mouse is an example of an omnivore in the prairie ecosystem. It eats insects, scorpions, lizards, and grass seeds. **Scavengers** are animals that feed on the bodies of dead animals. The turkey vulture is a scavenger in the prairie ecosystem. Examples of scavengers in aquatic ecosystems include crayfish, snails, clams, worms, and crabs.

Decomposers Organisms that get energy by breaking down the remains of dead organisms are called **decomposers.** Bacteria and fungi are examples of decomposers. These organisms extract the last bit of energy from dead organisms and produce simpler materials, such as water and carbon dioxide. These materials can then be reused by plants and other living things. Decomposers are an essential part of any ecosystem because they are nature's recyclers.

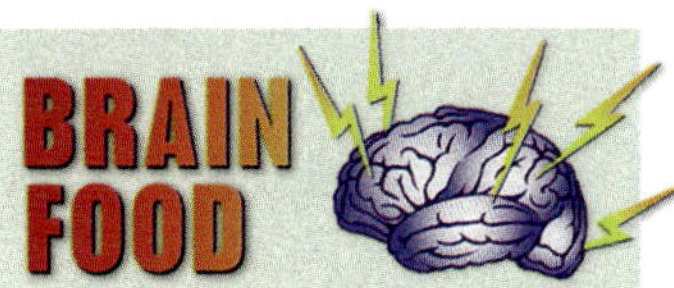

Prairie dogs are not really dogs. They are rodents. They are called dogs because their warning calls sound like the barking of dogs.

Self-Check

Are you a herbivore, a carnivore, or an omnivore? Explain. *(See page 564 to check your answer.)*

Turkey vultures have an acute sense of smell. A biologist once put decaying carcasses in metal containers, hid the containers in the California foothills, and used a fan to diffuse the odor. Turkey vultures were soon soaring overhead. Engineers once pumped ethyl mercaptan, which smells like rotting flesh, into natural-gas lines. They located leaks by watching for turkey vultures attracted to the pipeline.

2 Teach

Real-World Connection

Having survived for 300 million years, the common cockroach may be the most successful and well-adapted scavenger of all time. Cockroaches scavenged dinosaur leftovers long before they survived on the crumbs and kitchen scraps of humans. Dead skin and fingernails are a real treat for them; leftover food is a delicacy. If these tasty morsels aren't available, cockroaches can survive on such unlikely food sources as shoe polish, paint, and soap.

Answer to Self-Check

Humans are omnivores. An omnivore eats both plants and animals. Humans can eat meat and vegetables as well as animal products, such as milk and eggs, and plant products, such as grains and fruit. Remind students that humans also eat fungus (mushrooms) and bacteria (in yogurt)!

Using the Figure

Have students write new captions in their ScienceLog for **Figure 4.** Have students draw a similar diagram following the transfer of energy within an aquatic ecosystem. Sheltered English

Misconception Alert

The North American black bear and the grizzly are not carnivores. They are omnivores. Besides eating mammals and fish, both bears eat berries and roots. Black bears also eat pine cones, acorns, and insects. Grizzlies sometimes even eat grass.

Directed Reading Worksheet 12 Section 2

2 Teach, continued

Answer to Self-Check

A food chain shows how energy moves in one direction from one organism to the next. A food web shows that there are many energy pathways between organisms.

MATH and MORE

There are 12,000 units of the sun's energy available to grass at the base of an energy pyramid. Grass stores in its tissues 10 percent of the available energy, so that energy becomes available to the next consumer, a rabbit. The rabbit, a consumer of grass, stores 10 percent of the energy that was stored in the grass. A coyote, a consumer of rabbits, stores 10 percent of the energy that was stored in the rabbit. Calculate the units of food energy stored in the grass, the rabbit, and the coyote.

The grass stores 10 percent of the sun's energy:

$0.1 \times 12{,}000 = 1{,}200$ units of energy stored in the grass

The rabbit stores 10 percent of the grass' stored energy:

$0.1 \times 1{,}200 = 120$ units of energy stored in the rabbit

The coyote stores 10 percent of the rabbit's stored energy:

$0.1 \times 120 = 12$ units of energy stored in the coyote

Math Skills Worksheet 22 "Working with Percentages and Proportions"

Self-Check

How is a food web different from a food chain? *(See page 564 to check your answer.)*

Food Chains and Food Webs

Figure 4, on pages 310–311, shows a **food chain,** which represents how the energy in food molecules flows from one organism to the next. But because few organisms eat just one kind of organism, simple food chains rarely occur in nature. The many energy pathways possible are more accurately shown by a **food web.** **Figure 5** shows a simple food web for a forest ecosystem.

Find the fox and the rabbit in the figure below. Notice that the arrow goes from the rabbit to the fox, showing that the rabbit is food for the fox. The rabbit is also food for the owl. Neither the fox nor the owl is ever food for the rabbit. Energy moves from one organism to the next in a one-way direction even in a food web. Any energy not immediately used by an organism is stored in its tissues. Only the energy stored in an organism's tissues can be used by the next consumer.

Figure 5 *Energy moves through an ecosystem in complex ways. Most consumers eat a variety of foods and can be eaten by a variety of other consumers.*

internet connect

TOPIC: Food Chains and Food Webs
GO TO: www.scilinks.org
***sci*LINKS NUMBER:** HSTE595

Customer: Waiter! Waiter! There's a fly in my soup!

Waiter: Don't worry, sir, the spider in your salad will get it!

Energy Pyramids

A grass plant uses most of the energy it obtains from the sun for its own life processes. Only a very small amount of energy stored in the tissues of the grass plant is left over for prairie dogs and other animals that eat the grass. Therefore, prairie dogs have to eat a lot of grass to get the energy they need. Likewise, each prairie dog uses most of the energy it obtains from eating grass and stores only a little of it in its tissues. Because of this, a coyote must eat many prairie dogs to survive. There must be many more prairie dogs in the community than there are coyotes that eat prairie dogs. Likewise, the coyote uses most of the energy it obtains from its diet of insects, gophers, and prairie dogs.

The loss of energy at each level of the food chain can be represented by an **energy pyramid,** as shown in **Figure 6.** You can see that the energy pyramid has a large base and becomes smaller at the top. The amount of available energy is reduced at higher levels because most of the energy is either used by the organism or given off as heat. Only energy stored in the tissues of an organism can be transferred to the next level.

Figure 6 *The pyramid represents energy. As you can see, more energy is available at the base of the pyramid than at its top.*

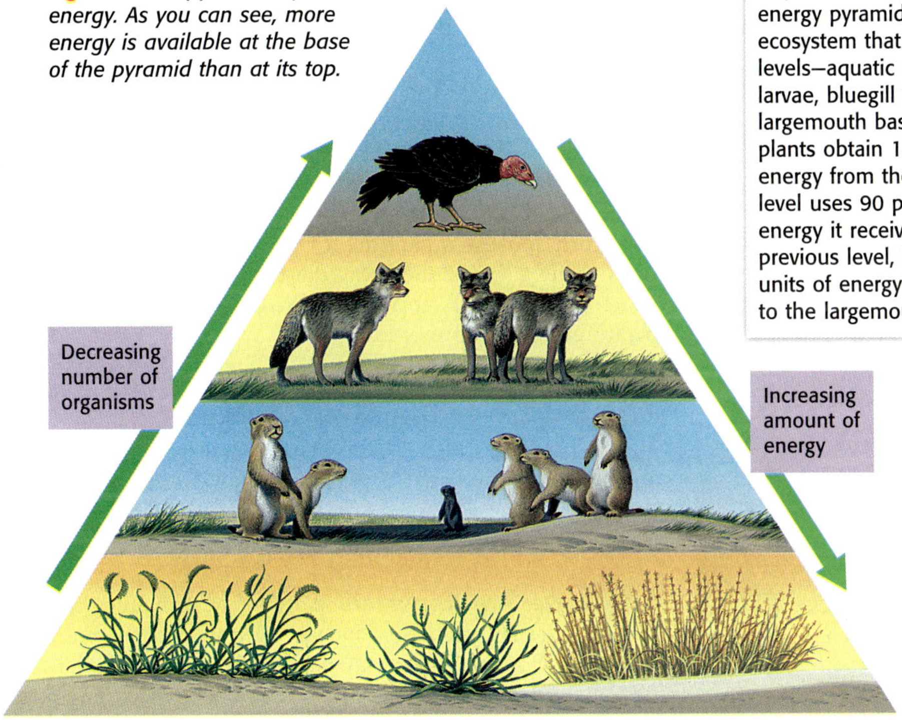

Decreasing number of organisms

Increasing amount of energy

Explore

Draw a large circle on a **sheet of paper.** Write the names of the eight members of a prairie ecosystem listed below around the circle.

vulture	grasshopper
coyote	gopher
hawk	grass
mouse	prairie dog

Now draw arrows from each organism to the organisms that eat it.

MATH BREAK

Energy Pyramids

In your ScienceLog, draw an energy pyramid for a river ecosystem that contains four levels—aquatic plants, insect larvae, bluegill fish, and a largemouth bass. The aquatic plants obtain 10,000 units of energy from the sun. If each level uses 90 percent of the energy it receives from the previous level, how many units of energy are available to the largemouth bass?

IS THAT A FACT!

In 1989, the Nature Conservancy purchased 30,000 acres of grassland in Oklahoma. The conservancy's goal is "the restoration of a functioning tall-grass prairie ecosystem." The land has been grazed by cattle but never plowed; the restoration will allow the more than 700 prairie plant species to reestablish themselves. A healthy prairie is also home to 300 bird species, 80 mammal species, and millions of insect species. Biologists have reintroduced bison, whose grazing is an integral part of the prairie food web.

Answer to Explore

Grass is a producer and is eaten primarily by herbivores (the gopher, mouse, and prairie dog), omnivores (the coyote), and scavengers (the vulture). The mouse, prairie dog, and gopher are eaten by the hawk, coyote, and vulture. The grasshopper may be eaten by the mouse, prairie dog, gopher, and coyote. Everything is eaten by the vulture as carrion or dead material. The vulture is eaten only by decomposers, which are not shown.

ACTIVITY

Writing **Inferring Information** Chipmunks, tree squirrels, and flying squirrels are all related animals that eat seeds. Yet each has its own niche, or way of life, that serves to limit the amount of competition between the species.

Have students describe in writing, to the best of their knowledge, the niche, or way of life, for each of these seed eaters.

(**Chipmunks** live underground, collect small seeds, and store these seeds in cheek pouches until depositing them in an underground storage area.

Tree squirrels live in trees, collect larger seeds and nuts one at a time, and bury them in the ground.

Flying squirrels are active only at night; live in trees; eat large and small seeds, fruits, and insects; and glide from tree to tree using flaps of skin.)

Answer to MATHBREAK

10 units of energy

Teaching Transparency 129 "Energy Pyramid"

3 Extend

Meeting Individual Needs

Advanced Learners By 1970, peregrine falcon populations had been decimated by the effects of DDT. Professor Tom Cade of Cornell University established the Peregrine Fund for the captive breeding and release of peregrine falcons. Cade's release program and other programs placed the birds in urban environments, such as Chicago and Seattle. Have students investigate the peregrine falcon restoration programs and prepare a report that includes answers to the following questions: What is the peregrine falcon's natural habitat? What is its niche? How do cities provide a suitable habitat for the peregrine falcon?

Activity

Poster Project An organism's habitat may be large, as in the habitat of the gray wolf, or quite small, as in the habitat of planaria. For stationary animals, such as the mussel, the habitat can be as small as a group of rocks in the tidal zone of the ocean. The habitat of a blue whale may be nearly as large as the ocean itself. Have interested students make a poster depicting the components of four distinct habits of four very different animals. Sheltered English

Figure 7 *Members of the U.S. Fish and Wildlife Service are moving a caged wolf to a location in Yellowstone National Park.*

Wolves and the Energy Pyramid

A single species can be very important to the flow of energy in an environment. Gray wolves, for example, are a consumer species that can control the populations of many of the other species in their environment. The diet of gray wolves can include anything from a lizard to an elk.

Gray wolves were once common throughout much of the United States. However, as the wilderness was settled, populations of gray wolves declined until they were almost wiped out. Once the wolves were gone, certain other species, such as elk, were no longer controlled. The overpopulation of elk in some areas led to overgrazing and starvation.

Gray wolves were recently restored to the United States at Yellowstone National Park as shown in **Figure 7.** The U.S. Fish and Wildlife Service hopes this action will restore the natural energy flow in this wilderness area. Not everyone approves of this program, however. Ranchers near Yellowstone are concerned about the safety of their livestock.

Habitat and Niche

An organism's **habitat** is the environment in which it lives. The wolf's habitat was originally very extensive. It included forests, grasslands, deserts, and the northern tundra. Today the wolf's habitat in North America is much smaller. It includes wilderness areas in portions of Montana, Washington, Minnesota, Michigan, and Wisconsin, and parts of Canada. Gray wolves are able to find food and survive best in these wilderness areas.

An organism's way of life within an ecosystem is its **niche.** An organism's niche includes its habitat, its food, its predators, and the organisms it competes with. An organism's niche also includes how the organism affects and is affected by abiotic factors in its environment, such as temperature, light, and moisture.

Figure 8 *Wolves feed mainly on large herbivores, such as elk, moose, and deer.*

The Niche of the Gray Wolf

A complete description of a species' niche is very complex. To help you distinguish between habitat and niche, the following is a short description of parts of the niche of the gray wolf.

Gray Wolves Are Consumers Wolves are carnivores. Their diet includes large animals, such as deer, moose (shown in **Figure 8**), reindeer, sheep, and elk, as well as small animals, such as birds, lizards, snakes, and fish.

Reinforcement Worksheet 12 "Weaving a Food Web"

Critical Thinking Worksheet 12 "A Struggle to Survive"

Weird Science

In certain tropical areas, the dry season can last several months. Some frogs, such as the African bullfrog, burrow into the mud before the mud dries out. Then the frog sheds several intact layers of skin, which harden and form a waterproof covering. Only the frog's nostrils are exposed, so it can breathe. When the rains return, the frog breaks through the moist soil and returns to the surface.

Gray Wolves Have a Social Structure Wolves live and hunt in packs, which are groups of about six animals that are usually members of the same family. Each member of the pack has a particular rank within the pack. The pack has two leaders, as shown in **Figure 9,** that help defend the pack against enemies, such as other wolf packs or bears.

Gray Wolves Nurture and Teach Their Young A female wolf, shown in **Figure 10,** has five to seven pups and nurses her babies for about two months. The entire pack help bring the pups food and baby-sit when the parents are away from the den. It takes about 2 years for the young wolves to learn to hunt. At that time, some young wolves leave the pack to find mates and start their own pack.

Gray Wolves Are Needed in the Food Web If wolves become reestablished at Yellowstone National Park, they will reduce the elk population by killing the old, injured, and diseased elk. This in turn will allow more plants to grow, which will allow animals that eat the plants, such as snowshoe hares, and the animals that eat the hares, such as foxes, to increase in number.

Figure 9 *A pack of gray wolves is led by a pair called the alpha male and the alpha female.*

Figure 10 *In small wolf packs, only the alpha female has pups. They are well cared for, however, by all the males and females in the pack.*

REVIEW

1. How are producers, consumers (herbivores, carnivores, and scavengers), and decomposers linked in a food chain?
2. How do food chains link together to form a food web?
3. Distinguish between an organism's habitat and its niche using the prairie dog as an example.
4. **Applying Concepts** Is it possible for an inverted energy pyramid to exist, as shown in the figure at right? Explain why or why not.

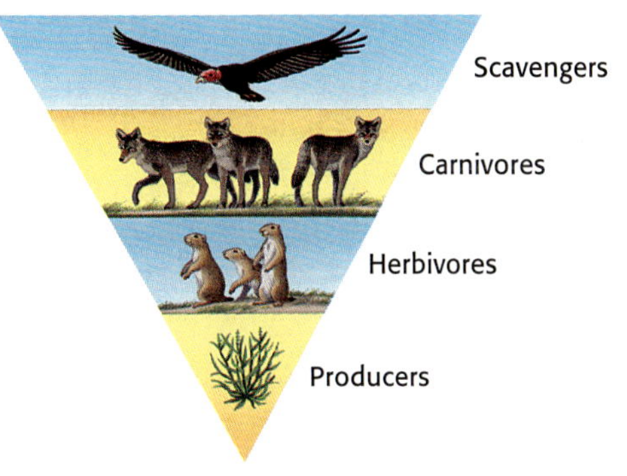

4 Close

Quiz

1. How might an omnivore be a link both at the beginning of a food web and near the end? (An omnivore can be at the beginning because it eats plants. It can be near the end because it also eats other consumers.)
2. Is your attendance at school a characteristic of your habitat or your niche? (Niche; being a student is one of the things I do within my habitat. It is part of my way of life.)

ALTERNATIVE ASSESSMENT

Writing Have students write an eight-step recipe for a decomposer's dinner. Tell students the first ingredient is the sun.

Answers to Review

1. Producers convert sunlight into food. Herbivores and carnivores are both consumers. Herbivores eat producers, and carnivores eat herbivores. Scavengers eat the bodies of dead animals. Decomposers break down the remains of dead animals and extract the last bit of energy from them.
2. Food chains show how energy is passed through an ecosystem from producers to decomposers. A food web shows how all the food chains of an ecosystem are linked.
3. The prairie is a prairie dog's habitat. What it affects and what affects it make up its niche.
4. No; the widest part of the pyramid has the most energy, and the pointed top has the least. An ecosystem cannot support the greatest energy level with the level that has the least energy.

Section 2 Review—California Standards: PE/ATE 5, 5a, 5b, 5c, 5d, 5e

Section 3

Focus

Types of Interactions

In this section, students will learn about the types of interactions that organisms have with each other and with their environment. Students will learn to distinguish the two types of competition and to identify predator and prey species. They will also learn to recognize mutualism, commensalism, and parasitism. Finally, students will learn to define *coevolution*.

Bellringer

On the board or overhead projector, write the following:

In your ScienceLog, make a list of predators that are also prey. (Answers may include salamanders, frogs, shrews, snakes, lizards, and weasels.) Sheltered English

1) Motivate

Discussion

In India, the chital, a small deer, has trouble finding enough grass to eat during the dry season. The deer rely on help from a type of monkey to get enough to eat. Ask students:

Can you guess how the monkeys help the deer? (This particular monkey is a messy and finicky eater, dropping leaves as it feeds in the trees. The deer then gobble up the food.)

Which species benefit from this relationship? (It seems that only the deer benefit.)

Now tell students that the deer have keen eyesight, hearing, and sense of smell. They therefore help warn the monkeys of predators. Now which species do you think benefit? (Both species benefit.)

3

NEW TERMS

carrying capacity, limiting factor, competition, prey, predator, symbiosis, mutualism, commensalism, parasitism, parasite, host, coevolution

OBJECTIVES

- Distinguish between the two types of competition.
- Give examples of predators and prey.
- Distinguish between mutualism, commensalism, and parasitism.
- Define *coevolution,* and give an example.

Types of Interactions

Look at the seaweed forest shown in **Figure 11** below. How many populations can you see? Notice that some populations, such as the seaweed, are made of many individuals. Other populations have far fewer individuals. Interactions between populations influence the size of each population.

Figure 11 *This seaweed forest is home to a large number of interacting species.*

Where on Earth could this bird live? Find out on page 536 of your LabBook.

Interactions with the Environment

Most living things produce more offspring than will survive. A female frog, for example, might lay hundreds of eggs in a small pond. In a few months, the population of frogs in that pond will be about the same as it was the year before. Why won't the pond become overrun with frogs? An organism, such as a frog, interacts with biotic or abiotic factors in its environment that can control the size of its population.

Limiting Factors Populations cannot grow indefinitely because the environment contains only so much food, water, living space, and other needed resources. When one or more of those resources becomes scarce, it is said to be a **limiting factor.** For example, food becomes a limiting factor when a population becomes too large for the amount of food available. Any single resource can be a limiting factor to population size.

PG 536

Adaptation: It's a Way of Life

Green herons make interesting use of the biotic and abiotic parts of their environment in Japan. They will drop sticks and even bread crumbs into the water to attract fish. Sometimes they catch a fish just 2–3 seconds after they drop the bait.

Section 3—California Standards: PE/ATE 5, 5a, 5b, 5c, 5d, 5e; LabBook: 7, 7d, 7e

Carrying Capacity The largest population that a given environment can support over a long period of time is known as the environment's **carrying capacity.** When a population grows larger than its carrying capacity, limiting factors in the environment cause the population to get smaller. For example, after a very rainy growing season in an environment, plants may produce a large crop of leaves and seeds. This may cause a herbivore population to grow large because of the unlimited food supply. If the next year has less rainfall than usual, there won't be enough food to support the large herbivore population. In this way, a population may temporarily exceed the carrying capacity. But a limiting factor will cause the population to die back. The population will return to a size that the environment can support over a long period of time.

Self-Check

1. Explain how water can limit the growth of a population.
2. Describe how the carrying capacity for deer in a forest ecosystem might be affected by weather.

(See page 564 to check your answers.)

Interactions Among Organisms

Populations contain interacting individuals of a single species, such as a group of rabbits feeding in the same area. Communities contain interacting populations of several species, such as a coral reef community with many species trying to find living space. Ecologists have described four main ways species and individuals affect each other: competition, predators and prey, certain symbiotic relationships, and coevolution.

Competition

When two or more individuals or populations try to use the same limited resource, such as food, water, shelter, space, or sunlight, it is called **competition.** Because resources are in limited supply in the environment, their use by one individual or population decreases the amount available to other organisms.

Competition can occur among individuals *within* a population. The elk population in Yellowstone National Park are herbivores that compete with each other for the same food plants in the park. This is a big problem for this species in winter. Competition can also occur *between* populations of different species. The different species of trees in **Figure 12** are competing with each other for sunlight and space.

Figure 12 *Some of the trees in this forest grow tall in order to reach sunlight, reducing the amount of sunlight available to shorter trees nearby.*

2 Teach

Answers to Self-Check

1. If an area has only enough water to support 10 organisms, any additional organisms will cause some to go without water and move away or die.
2. Weather favorable for growing the food the deer eat will allow the forest to support more deer.

DISCUSSION

Examining Cycles The lynx relies primarily upon the snowshoe hare for food. Ask students:

How will an abundance of plant food affect the hare population? (The population will increase.)

What will then happen to the lynx population? (It will also increase.)

What will happen when the hares begin to run out of food? (Hares will grow weak from hunger and will be easily caught by lynxes. The lynx population will grow until so many hares are killed that the lynxes also begin to die off.)

How can the hare and lynx populations recover? (The plants must recover from the overbrowsing.)

Explain that observers have documented 10-year cycles of peaks and crashes in the lynx and snowshoe hare populations for the past 200 years. Studies have shown that snowshoe hares have the same population cycles when no lynxes are present. Lynx population cycles, however, are dependent on the availability of hares.

Directed Reading Worksheet 12 Section 3

MISCONCEPTION ALERT

While it's true that all members of an ecosystem have important roles, some members are more important than others to the overall health of the ecosystem. Such species are called keystone species. Like removing the keystone that holds up the other stones in an arch, removing a keystone species can cause the whole system to collapse. This occurred when the sea otter was hunted to near extinction in the kelp forests of the Pacific Ocean. With the otters gone, nothing was left to eat the sea urchins, which multiplied and ate all the kelp. The kelp was home to dozens of animals, all of which disappeared, along with most of the sea urchins. When the otter was reintroduced, all these organisms returned!

2 Teach, continued

Cooperative Learning

Divide students into six groups. Then divide each group into subgroups of two or three, and designate each subgroup as Predator or Prey. Instruct each Predator group to name a prey animal and the adaptation it uses to catch the prey. (speed, talons, strength)

Tell each Prey group to name a predator animal and its adaptations to evade capture. (camouflage, speed, protective armor, flight)

Have students write down the adaptations and share their information with the other groups. Sheltered English

Misconception Alert

The phrase *balance of nature* does not imply that the components of an environment are static. Populations are in balance when their sizes are stable. That stability is the result of constant interactions between individuals of a population, between populations in a community, and between populations and environmental factors.

Predators and Prey

Many interactions among species occur because one organism eats another. The organism that is eaten is called the **prey.** The organism that eats the prey is called the **predator.** When a bird eats a worm, the worm is the prey and the bird is the predator.

Figure 13 *The goldenrod spider is difficult for its insect prey to see. Can you see it?*

Predator Adaptations In order to survive, predators must be able to catch their prey. Predators have a wide variety of methods and abilities for doing this. The cheetah, for example, is able to run at great speed to catch its prey. Other predators, such as the goldenrod spider, shown in **Figure 13,** ambush their prey. This spider blends in so well with the goldenrod flower that all it has to do is wait for its next insect meal to arrive.

Figure 14 *Experienced predators know better than to eat the fire salamander! This colorful animal will make an unlucky predator very sick.*

Prey Adaptations Prey organisms have their own methods and abilities to keep from being eaten. Prey are able to run away, stay in groups, or camouflage themselves. Some prey organisms are poisonous to predators. They may advertise their poison with bright colors to warn predators to stay away. The fire salamander, shown in **Figure 14,** sprays a poison that burns. Predators quickly learn to recognize its warning coloration.

Many animals run away from predators. Prairie dogs run to their underground burrows when a predator approaches. Many small fishes, such as anchovies, swim in groups called schools. Antelopes and buffaloes stay in herds. All the eyes, ears, and noses of the individuals in the group are watching, listening, and smelling for predators. This behavior increases the likelihood of spotting a potential predator.

Some prey species hide from predators by using camouflage. Certain insects resemble leaves so closely that you would never guess they are animals. Can you find the mantis in **Figure 15**?

Figure 15 *This mantis goes out on a limb to hide from predators.*

Weird Science

Pancake tortoises live on rocky hillsides in Africa. They are very flat and can wedge themselves into cracks in the rocks for protection from predators. Their bottom shells are pliable and can "inflate" so that a predator can't pry the tortoises out.

Symbiosis

Some species have very close interactions with other species. **Symbiosis** is a close, long-term association between two or more species. The individuals in a symbiotic relationship can benefit from, be unaffected by, or be harmed by the relationship. Often, one species lives in or on the other species. The thousands of symbiotic relationships that occur in nature are often classified into three groups: mutualism, commensalism, and parasitism.

Figure 16 *Coral animals and certain algae are an example of mutualism. In the smaller photo above, you can see the gold-colored algae inside the coral animal.*

Mutualism A symbiotic relationship in which both organisms benefit is called **mutualism.** For example, you and a species of bacteria that lives in your intestines benefit each other! The bacteria get a plentiful food supply from you, and in return you get vitamins that the bacteria produce.

Another example of mutualism occurs between coral and algae. The living corals near the surface of the water provide a home for the algae. The algae produce food through photosynthesis that is used by the corals. When a coral animal dies, its skeleton serves as a foundation for other corals. Over a long period of time these skeletons build up large, rock-like formations that lie just beneath the surface of warm, sunny seas, as shown in **Figure 16.**

Commensalism A symbiotic relationship in which one organism benefits and the other is unaffected is called **commensalism.** One example of commensalism is the relationship between sharks and remoras. **Figure 17** shows a shark with a remora attached to its body. Remoras "hitch a ride" and feed on scraps of food left by sharks. The remoras benefit from this relationship, while sharks are unaffected.

Figure 17 *The remora attached to the shark benefits from the relationship. The shark is neither benefited nor harmed.*

319

Q: What is a parasite's favorite party?

A: a louse-warming party

Real-World Connection

As a simple exercise to help students understand the differences between mutualism, commensalism, and parasitism, ask students to think about their relationships with other species in the environment. Interactions with pets, livestock, backyard animals, or annoying insects shed light on these relationships. Are any of these interaction mutualism? parasitism? commensalism?

Reteaching

The honey guide, a small African bird, lives up to its name. The bird sings in an attempt to lure all nearby creatures to a nest of honeybees it has found. Animals have learned to listen for this bird! Baboons, mongooses, ratels (or honey badgers), and even people will follow the bird to claim the honey. Out of harm's way, the bird waits for the leftovers: bee larvae. The bird's unique digestive system allows it to eat wax as well. Ask students the following questions:

Which animals in this story are in a mutualistic relationship? (The bird and the animals that eat the honey.)

Which animals are prey, and which are predators? (The bees are prey. All the other animals are predators.) Sheltered English

MISCONCEPTION ALERT

You will often hear the word *symbiosis* used when *mutualism* is meant. Mutualism is one type of symbiosis; commensalism and parasitism are the other two types.

3 Extend

MEETING INDIVIDUAL NEEDS

Learners Having Difficulty Reinforce the concept of symbiosis by presenting the following examples and asking students to categorize the relationship:

1. Acacia ants live on the bullhorn acacia tree, which provides the ants' food and shelter. The ants deter browsing animals who want to eat the tree. (mutualism)
2. Plants called epiphytes, such as algae, lianas, and certain orchids, live on other plants, which provide only a substrate. Epiphytes absorb sunlight, water, and nutrients with their own structures and make their own food. (commensalism)
3. There is a tiny wasp that lays its eggs in a variety of insects, such as caterpillars, spiders, aphids, and flies. The wasp larvae feed on the host insect, eventually killing it. (parasitism)

Sheltered English

DEBATE

Bird Behavior The brown-headed cowbird is a parasite. It lays its eggs in the nests of other birds, which incubate the cowbird's eggs and raise the chicks. Some of the host species are smaller than the cowbird. Their own chicks cannot compete with the cowbird chicks for food and sometimes starve. Some people view the cowbird as a pest that harms other bird species. Others note that it has an adaptation that ensures its survival, no different from any other competitive advantage. Have students discuss these two points of view.

Parasitism A symbiotic association in which one organism benefits while the other is harmed is called **parasitism.** The organism that benefits is called the **parasite.** The organism that is harmed is called the **host.** The parasite gets nourishment from its host, which is weakened in the process. Sometimes a host organism becomes so weak that it dies. Some parasites, such as ticks, live outside the host's body. Other parasites, such as tapeworms, live inside the host's body.

Figure 18 *The tomato hornworm is being parasitized by young wasps. Do you see their cocoons?*

Figure 18 shows a bright green caterpillar called a tomato hornworm. A female wasp laid tiny eggs on the caterpillar. When the eggs hatch, each young wasp will burrow into the caterpillar's body. The young wasps will actually eat the caterpillar alive! In a short time, the caterpillar will be almost completely consumed and die. When that occurs, the mature wasps will fly away.

In this example of parasitism, the host dies. Most parasites, however, do not kill their hosts. Can you think of reasons why?

Figure 19 *This tropical tree and these ants have coevolved. The ants are shown collecting food made by the tree and storing the food in the ant's shelter, also made by the tree.*

Coevolution

Symbiotic relationships and other interactions among organisms in an ecosystem may cause coevolution. **Coevolution** is a long-term change that takes place in two species because of their close interactions with one another.

Coevolution sometimes occurs between herbivores and the plants on which they feed. For example, the ants shown in **Figure 19** have coevolved with a tropical tree called the acacia. The ants protect the tree on which they live by attacking any other herbivore that approaches the tree. The plant has coevolved special structures on its stems that produce food for the ants. The ants live in other structures also made by the tree.

In Africa, billions of dollars a year are spent to destroy a parasitic plant that lives off important crops such as sorghum. The parasite weakens the plant, preventing it from producing its much-needed grains. Recently, a sorghum plant that is resistant to the parasite was developed. Ethiopian farmers were so eager to get started again that they smuggled the new seeds in from Sudan before their own government approved the seeds.

In 1859, settlers released 12 rabbits in Australia. There were no predators or parasites to control the rabbit population, and there was plenty of food. The rabbit population increased so fast that the country was soon overrun by rabbits. To control the rabbit population, the Australian government introduced a virus that makes rabbits sick. The first time the virus was used, more than 99 percent of the rabbits died. The survivors reproduced, and the rabbit population grew large again. The second time the virus was used, about 90 percent of the rabbits died. Once again, the rabbit population increased. The third time the virus was used, only about 50 percent of the rabbits died. Biologists tested the rabbits and the virus and determined that they were coevolving. Suggest what changes might have occurred in the rabbits and the virus.

Coevolution and Flowers Some of the most amazing examples of coevolution are between flowers and their pollinators. (An organism that carries pollen from flower to flower is called a *pollinator.*) When the pollinator travels to the next flower to feed, some of the pollen is left behind on the female part of the flower, and more pollen is picked up. Because of pollination, reproduction can take place in the plant. Organisms such as bees, bats, and hummingbirds are attracted to a flower because of its colors, odors, and nectar.

During the course of evolution, hummingbird-pollinated flowers, for example, developed nectar with just the right amount of sugar for their pollinators. The hummingbird's long, thin tongue and beak coevolved to fit into the flowers so they could reach the nectar. As the hummingbird, like the one shown in **Figure 20,** feeds on the nectar, its head and body become smeared with pollen.

Figure 20 *The bird is attracted to the flower's nectar and picks up the flower's pollen as it feeds.*

REVIEW

1. Briefly describe one example of a predator-prey relationship. Identify the predator and the prey.
2. Name and define the three kinds of symbiosis.
3. **Analyzing Relationships** Explain the probable relationship between the giant *Rafflesia* flower, shown at right, which smells like rotting meat, and the carrion flies that buzz around it. HINT: *carrion* means "rotting flesh."

Answers to Review

1. Accept any answer in which one animal (the predator) is eating another (the prey).
2. *mutualism*—a symbiotic relationship in which both organisms benefit

   commensalism—a symbiotic relationship in which one organism benefits and the other is unaffected

   parasitism—a symbiotic association in which one organism benefits while the other is harmed
3. The probable relationship between *Rafflesia* and carrion flies is a symbiotic mutualism brought about by coevolution.

4 Close

Quiz

1. Explain the difference between mutualism and coevolution. (Mutualism is a close, long-term association between two organisms in which both benefit. Coevolution is the gradual change in two organisms' physical characteristics as a result of a symbiotic relationship.)
2. Can a predator ever be the prey for another species? (Yes; field mice eat insects and are sometimes eaten by snakes and hawks. Small fish are consumed by larger fish, which are eaten by even larger fish.)

Alternative Assessment

Concept Mapping Have students organize the following terms into a concept map:

competition, predator, individuals, population, symbiosis, commensalism, prey, mutualism, interactions

Answer to APPLY

Viruses that kill all of their hosts have no place to live. The viruses in Australia that changed to become less virulent and avoided killing rabbits had more hosts to occupy. The rabbits, on the other hand, began to produce more survivors with immunity. The survivors bred, producing a more immune population of rabbits.

Reinforcement Worksheet 12 "Symbiotic Relationships"

Interactive Explorations CD-ROM "What's Bugging You?"

Section 3 Review—California Standards: PE/ATE 5, 5a, 5b, 5c

Chapter Highlights

VOCABULARY DEFINITIONS

SECTION 1

ecology the study of the interactions between organisms and their environment

biotic living factors in the environment

abiotic nonliving factors in the environment

population a group of individuals of the same species that live together in the same area at the same time

community all of the populations of different species that live and interact in an area

ecosystem a community of organisms and their nonliving environment

biosphere the part of the Earth where life exists

SECTION 2

producer organisms that use sunlight directly to make sugar

consumer organisms that eat producers or other organisms for energy

herbivore a consumer that eats plants

carnivore a consumer that eats animals

omnivore a consumer that eats a variety of organisms

scavenger an animal that feeds on the bodies of dead animals

decomposer an organism that gets energy by breaking down the remains of dead organisms and consuming or absorbing the nutrients

food chain a diagram that represents how the energy in food molecules flows from one organism to the next

food web a complex diagram representing the many energy pathways in a real ecosystem

energy pyramid a diagram shaped like a triangle showing the loss of energy at each level of the food chain

Chapter Highlights

SECTION 1

Vocabulary

ecology *(p. 306)*
biotic *(p. 306)*
abiotic *(p. 306)*
population *(p. 308)*
community *(p. 308)*
ecosystem *(p. 308)*
biosphere *(p. 309)*

Section Notes

- Ecology is the study of the interactions between organisms and their environment. The environment consists of both biotic (living) and abiotic (nonliving) parts.

- Ecologists study organisms, populations, communities, ecosystems, and the biosphere. A population is a group of the same species living in the same place at the same time. A community is all the populations of different species living together. An ecosystem is a community and its abiotic environment. The biosphere consists of all of Earth's ecosystems.

Labs

Capturing the Wild Bean *(p. 534)*

SECTION 2

Vocabulary

producer *(p. 310)*
consumer *(p. 311)*
herbivore *(p. 311)*
carnivore *(p. 311)*
omnivore *(p. 311)*
scavenger *(p. 311)*
decomposer *(p. 311)*
food chain *(p. 312)*
food web *(p. 312)*
energy pyramid *(p. 313)*
habitat *(p. 314)*
niche *(p. 314)*

Section Notes

- Producers are organisms that obtain their energy directly from sunlight. Consumers are organisms that eat other organisms to obtain energy. Decomposers are bacteria and fungi that break down the remains of dead organisms to obtain energy.

☑ Skills Check

Math Concepts

ENERGY PYRAMIDS Try calculating the MathBreak on page 313 as if each unit of energy were $1.00. If you have $10,000.00, but you spend 90 percent, how much do you have left to leave in your will? ($1,000.00) If your heir spends 90 percent of that, how much can your heir leave? ($100.00) After four generations, how much will the inheritance be? ($1.00) Not much, huh? That's why there are very few large organisms at the top of the energy pyramid.

Visual Understanding

FOOD WEBS Several food pathways are shown in the food web in Figure 5 on page 312. However, an actual food web in a forest ecosystem is much more complex because hundreds of species live in a forest. Find the mouse in Figure 5. How many organisms feed on the mouse? How many organisms feed on the earwigs? What might happen to this forest ecosystem if these animals were eliminated?

322

Lab and Activity Highlights

Capturing the Wild Bean PG 534

Adaptation: It's a Way of Life PG 536

Datasheets for LabBook (blackline masters for these labs)

SECTION 2

- A food chain shows how energy flows from one organism to the next.
- Because most organisms eat more than one kind of food, there are many energy pathways possible; these are represented by a food web.
- Energy pyramids demonstrate that most of the energy at each level of the food chain is used up at that level and is unavailable for organisms higher on the food chain.
- An organism's habitat is the environment in which it lives. An organism's niche is its role in the ecosystem.

SECTION 3

Vocabulary

limiting factor *(p. 316)*
carrying capacity *(p. 317)*
competition *(p. 317)*
prey *(p. 318)*
predator *(p. 318)*
symbiosis *(p. 319)*
mutualism *(p. 319)*
commensalism *(p. 319)*
parasitism *(p. 320)*
parasite *(p. 320)*
host *(p. 320)*
coevolution *(p. 320)*

Section Notes

- Population size changes over time.
- Limiting factors slow the growth of a population. The largest population that an environment can support over a long period of time is called the carrying capacity.
- When one organism eats another, the organism that is eaten is the prey, and the organism that eats the prey is the predator.
- Symbiosis is a close, long-term association between two or more species. There are three general types of symbiosis: mutualism, commensalism, and parasitism.
- Coevolution involves the long-term changes that take place in two species because of their close interactions with one another.

Labs

Adaptation: It's a Way of Life *(p. 536)*

internet connect

GO TO: go.hrw.com

Visit the **HRW** Web site for a variety of learning tools related to this chapter. Just type in the keyword:

KEYWORD: HSTINT

GO TO: www.scilinks.org

Visit the **National Science Teachers Association** on-line Web site for Internet resources related to this chapter. Just type in the *sci*LINKS number for more information about the topic:

TOPIC	sciLINKS NUMBER
Biotic and Abiotic Factors	HSTE580
Organization in the Environment	HSTE585
Producers, Consumers, and Decomposers	HSTE590
Food Chains and Food Webs	HSTE595
Habitats and Niches	HSTE600

323

VOCABULARY DEFINITIONS, *continued*

habitat the environment where an organism lives

niche an organism's way of life and its relationships with its abiotic and biotic environment

SECTION 3

limiting factor a needed resource that is in limited supply

carrying capacity the largest population that a given environment can support over a long period of time

competition two or more species or individuals trying to use the same limited resource

prey an organism that is eaten by another organism

predator an organism that eats other organisms

symbiosis a close, long-term association between two or more species

mutualism a symbiotic relationship in which both organisms benefit

commensalism a symbiotic relationship in which one organism benefits and the other is unaffected

parasitism a symbiotic association in which one organism benefits while the other is harmed

parasite an organism that feeds on another living creature, usually without killing it

host an organism on which a parasite lives

coevolution long-term changes that take place in two species because of their close interactions with one another

Lab and Activity Highlights

LabBank

Whiz-Bang Demonstrations, Voracious Fly Catcher, Demo 11

EcoLabs & Field Activities, Survival Is Just a Roll of the Dice, EcoLab 5

Long-Term Projects & Research Ideas, Project 18

Interactive Explorations CD-ROM

CD 2, Exploration 1, "What's Bugging You?"

Vocabulary Review Worksheet 12

Blackline masters of these Chapter Highlights can be found in the **Study Guide.**

Chapter Review Answers

Using Vocabulary

1. biotic, abiotic
2. population
3. ecosystem
4. producers
5. habitat, niche

Understanding Concepts

Multiple Choice

6. c
7. a
8. b
9. c
10. d
11. a
12. d
13. b

Short Answer

14. The wolf's habitat includes wilderness areas in portions of Montana, Washington, Minnesota, Michigan, Wisconsin, and parts of Canada. Part of a wolf's niche is being a predator of large herbivores. Wolves remove the old and sick members of large herds of deer, moose, reindeer, sheep, and elk.
15. Trees might compete for sunlight, water, or space.
16. Limiting factors generally define an environment's carrying capacity. Populations cannot grow indefinitely because the environment contains a fixed amount of food, water, living space, and other needed resources. Each of these resources is a limiting factor. If only one of them is in short supply, the environment's carrying capacity is lowered for a specific species.
17. Coevolution is a long-term change that takes place in two species because of their close interactions with one another.

Chapter Review

USING VOCABULARY

To complete the following sentences, choose the correct term from each pair of terms listed below:

1. An organism's environment has two parts, the __?__, or living, and the __?__, or nonliving. *(biotic* or *abiotic)*
2. A __?__ is a group of individuals of the same species that live in the same area at the same time. *(community* or *population)*
3. Communities and their abiotic environments make up a(an) __?__. *(ecosystem* or *food web)*
4. Organisms that use photosynthesis to obtain energy are called __?__. *(producers* or *decomposers)*
5. The environment in which an organism lives is its __?__, and the role the organism plays in an ecosystem is its __?__. *(niche* or *habitat)*

UNDERSTANDING CONCEPTS

Multiple Choice

6. A tick sucks blood from a dog. In this relationship, the tick is the __?__, and the dog is the __?__.
   a. parasite, prey
   b. predator, host
   c. parasite, host
   d. host, parasite
7. Resources such as water, food, or sunlight are more likely to be limiting factors
   a. when population size is growing.
   b. when predators eat their prey.
   c. when the population is small.
   d. when a population is much lower than the carrying capacity.
8. "Nature's recyclers" are
   a. predators.
   b. decomposers.
   c. producers.
   d. omnivores.
9. A beneficial association between coral and algae is an example of
   a. commensalism.
   b. parasitism.
   c. mutualism.
   d. predation.
10. How energy moves through an ecosystem can be represented by
    a. food chains.
    b. energy pyramids.
    c. food webs.
    d. All of the above
11. The base of an energy pyramid represents which organisms in an ecosystem?
    a. producers
    b. carnivores
    c. herbivores
    d. scavengers
12. Which of the following is the correct order in a food chain?
    a. sun → producers → herbivores → scavengers → carnivores
    b. sun → consumers → predators → parasites → hosts
    c. sun → producers → decomposers → consumers → omnivores
    d. sun → producers → herbivores → carnivores → scavengers
13. Remoras and sharks have a relationship best described as
    a. mutualism.
    b. commensalism.
    c. predator and prey.
    d. parasitism.

Short Answer

14. Briefly describe the habitat and niche of the gray wolf.
15. What might different species of trees in a forest compete for?
16. How do limiting factors affect the carrying capacity of an environment?
17. What is coevolution?

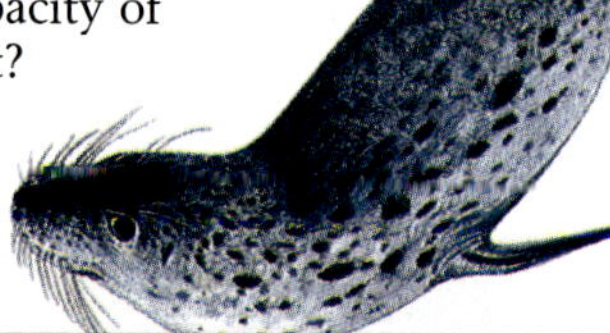

324

Concept Mapping

18. 
An answer to this exercise can be found at the end of this book.

Critical Thinking and Problem Solving

19. An ecosystem with no decomposers could not exist very long because the ecosystem would soon become buried under the bodies of its dead organisms. Decomposers recycle dead material back into the ecosystem.

Concept Mapping Transparency 12

Chapter 12 Review—California Standards: PE/ATE Q1–5: 5, 5a, 5c, 5e; Q6–18: 5, 5a, 5b, 5c, 5e

Concept Mapping

18. Use the following terms to create a concept map: individual organisms, producers, populations, ecosystems, consumers, herbivores, communities, carnivores, the biosphere.

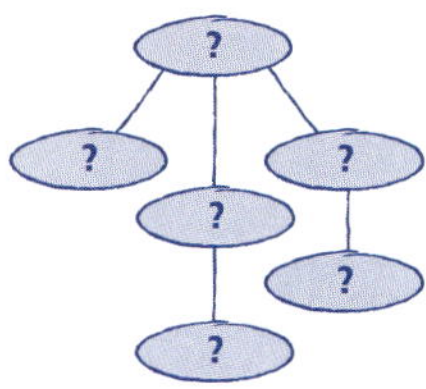

CRITICAL THINKING AND PROBLEM SOLVING

Write one or two sentences to answer the following questions:

19. Could a balanced ecosystem contain producers and consumers but no decomposers? Why or why not?
20. Some biologists think that certain species, such as alligators and wolves, help maintain biological diversity in their ecosystems. Predict what might happen to other species, such as gar fish or herons, if alligators were to become extinct in the Florida Everglades.
21. Does the Earth have a carrying capacity for humans? Explain your answer.
22. Explain how biodiversity is important in a community of interacting species. Give an example.

MATH IN SCIENCE

23. The plants in each square meter of an ecosystem obtained 20,810 Calories of the sun's energy by photosynthesis per year. The herbivores in that ecosystem ate all of the plants, but they only obtained 3,370 Calories of energy. How much energy did the plants use for their own life processes?

INTERPRETING GRAPHICS

Examine the following graph, which shows the population growth of a species of *Paramecium,* a slipper-shaped, single-celled microorganism, over a period of 18 days. Food was occasionally added to the test tube in which the paramecia were grown. Answer the following questions:

24. What is the carrying capacity of the test tube as long as food is added?
25. Predict what will happen to the population if the researcher stops adding food to the test tube.
26. What keeps the number of *Paramecium* at a steady level?
27. Predict what might happen if the amount of water is doubled and the food supply stays the same.

***Paramecium caudatum* Growth**

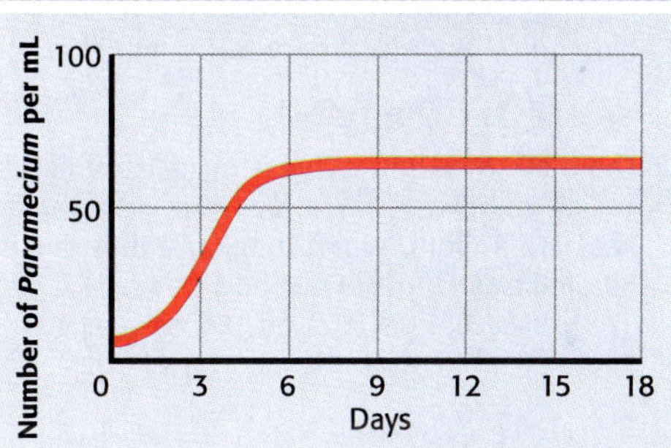

NOW What Do You Think?

Take a minute to review your answers to the ScienceLog questions on page 305. Have your answers changed? If necessary, revise your answers based on what you have learned since you began this chapter.

325

20. A predator, such as the alligator, removes the weak, old, or sick individuals from its prey population and contributes to the health of that population. If alligators became extinct in the Everglades, gars and herons might soon overpopulate. They would weaken their own food sources and possibly contribute to the extinction of other species.
21. The Earth does have a carrying capacity for humans. We have extended our carrying capacity by growing more crops and controlling our environments to make previously uninhabitable areas livable. But we will eventually reach a carrying capacity that we cannot exceed.
22. Biodiversity in a community provides many ways for species to interact and many energy pathways. The benefits of this can be seen in the following example: If there is only one species of fish in a pond and it dies out, the roles fish fill in the system would be empty. If there are many species of fishes and one species dies out, there are more options for the system to adjust and change quickly.

Math in Science

23. 17,440 Cal

Interpreting Graphics

24. about 65
25. The population will crash due to starvation.
26. The limiting factors, such as food supply, limit growth.
27. Any single factor can be limiting. Space may be increased, but unless food is increased, the carrying capacity is the same.

Now What Do You Think?

1. The deer eats the grass, tree leaves, and acorns. Wolves are common predators of deer. When the deer dies, it becomes food for scavengers and is eventually recycled back into the environment by decomposers.
2. the sun

Blackline masters of this Chapter Review can be found in the **Study Guide.**

Chapter 12 Review–California Standards: PE/ATE Q19–22: 5, 5a, 5b, 5d, 5e; Q23: 5, 5a; Q24–27: 5, 5b, 5e; Think: 5, 5a, 5b

Health Watch
An Unusual Guest

Background

Mites are not always benign guests. They are responsible for the devastation of honeybee populations in the United States. In the last few decades, tracheal mites and varroa mites have cut the number of domesticated colonies in half. There are almost no wild honeybees left in the United States.

The honeybee is a hardworking and important participant in agriculture. Apples and other orchard fruits require the honeybee for pollination. Domesticated honeybees enable the production of $10 billion worth of crops as well as produce $250 million worth of honey.

Scientists and beekeepers are trying various solutions to the mite infestations. Some chemicals seem to help. More promising solutions are found in new strains of honeybees bred to be resistant to mites, and some honeybees have developed the ability to groom mites off each other.

An Unusual Guest

What has a tiny tubelike body and short stumpy legs and lives upside down in your eyebrows and eyelashes? Would you believe a small animal? It's called a follicle mite, and humans are its host organism. Like all large animals, human beings are hosts to an interesting variety of smaller creatures. They live in or on our bodies and share our bodies' resources. But none of our guests is stranger than *D. folliculorum*—the follicle mite. They feed on oil and dead cells from your skin.

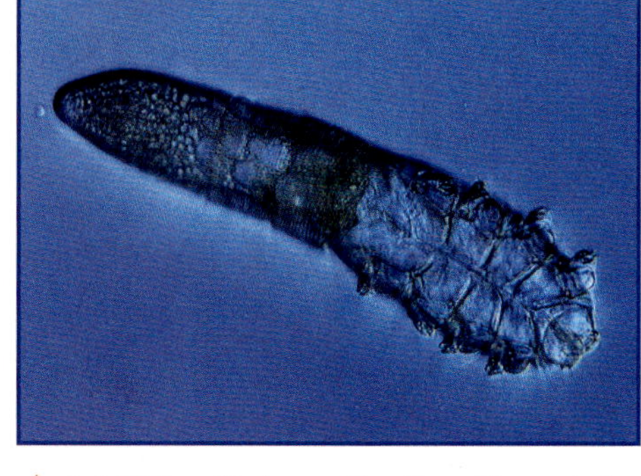

▲ *A follicle mite is smaller than the period at the end of this sentence.*

What Are They?

There are a couple of types of follicle mites. Follicle mites are arachnids—relatives of spiders. They are about 0.4 mm long, and they live in hair follicles all over your body. Usually they like to live in areas around the nose, cheek, forehead, chin, eyebrows, and eyelashes.

Follicle Mites Don't Bite

Are follicle mites harmful? These tiny guests are almost always harmless and they seldom live on children and adolescents. You probably wouldn't even know they were there. Studies reveal that between 97% and 100% of all adults have one or both kinds of mites. Except in rare cases, follicle mites in adults are also pretty harmless.

Some Health Concerns

Although follicle mites rarely cause problems, they are sometimes responsible for an acnelike condition around the nose, eyebrows, and eyelashes. A large number of mites (up to 25) may live in the same follicle. This can cause an inflammation of the follicle. The follicle does not swell like acne; instead it becomes red and itchy.

Mites living in eyelashes and on eyelids can irritate those areas. The inflammation causes itchy eyelids or eyebrows. But such inflammations are rare, and the condition clears up very quickly when suitable medication is applied. So while follicle mites may be one of the strangest guests living on human skin, they are almost never a problem.

Other Companions

Many tiny organisms make their home in humans' bodies. Bacteria within the body may help maintain proper pH levels. Even *E. coli,* a type of bacteria that can cause severe health problems, lives in the human colon. Without *E. coli,* a person would be unable to produce enough vitamin K or folic acid.

On Your Own

▶ Do some more research on follicle mites. Search for *Demodex folliculorum* or *Demodex brevis.* Find out more about some of the other strange organisms that rely on humans' bodies for food and shelter. Report on your findings, or write a story from the organism's point of view.

326

Answer to On Your Own

If you can find a copy of the book *Furtive Fauna: A Field Guide to the Creatures Who Live On You,* by Roger M. Knutson, you and your students will have more than enough information about follicle mites, tooth amoebas, bedbugs, ticks, and other organisms that find humans a wonderful place to live. There are a number of sites on the Internet that will provide additional information and links. (Use keywords such as follicle mites, Demodex, and human parasites.)

California Standards: PE/ATE 5, 5b

EYE ON THE ENVIRONMENT

Alien Invasion

A group of tiny aliens left their ship in Mobile, Alabama. Their bodies were red and shiny, and they walked on six legs. The aliens looked around and then quietly crawled off to make homes in the new land.

Westward Ho!

In 1918, fire ants were accidentally imported into the United States by a freighter ship from South America. In the United States, fire ants have no natural predators or competitors. In addition, these ants are extremely aggressive, and their colonies can harbor many queens, instead of just one queen, like many other ant species. With all these advantages, it is not surprising that the ants have spread like wildfire. By 1965, fire-ant mounds were popping up on the southeastern coast and as far west as Texas. Today they are found in at least 10 southern states and may soon reach as far west as California.

▲ *Three types of fire ants are found in a colony: the queen, workers, and males. Notice how the queen ant dwarfs the worker ants.*

Jaws of Destruction

Imported fire ants have done a lot of damage as they have spread across the United States. Because they are attracted to electrical currents, they chew through wire insulation, causing shorts in electrical circuits. The invaders have also managed to disturb the natural balance of native ecosystems. In some areas, they have killed off 70 percent of the native ant species and 40 percent of other native insect species. Each year, about 25,000 people seek medical attention for painful fire-ant bites.

Fighting Fire

Eighty years after the fire ants' introduction into the United States, the destructive ants continue to multiply. About 157 chemical products, including ammonia, gasoline, extracts from manure, and harsh pesticides, are registered for use against fire ants, but most have little or no success. Unfortunately, many of these remedies also harm the environment. By 1995, the government had approved only one fire-ant bait for large-scale use.

An Ant-Farm Census

▶ How many total offspring does a single fire-ant queen produce if she lives for 5 years and produces 1,000 eggs a day? If a mound contains 300,000 ants, how many mounds is this?

327

Answers to An Ant Farm Census

A typical queen may produce over 1.8 million eggs in her life:

1,000 eggs/day × 365 days/year × 5 years = 1,825,000 eggs.

Point out that a queen may not produce eggs every day.

You might also want to explain to the students that by dividing by 300,000 ants per mound, this number is equal to just over six mounds, or more than one new mound every year!

EYE ON THE ENVIRONMENT
Alien Invasion

Background

In combating the spread of fire ants, people must be careful not to harm the environment. In the 1960s, ground-up corncobs and soybean oil were mixed with an ant poison and sprayed over huge areas of land. Studies have since shown that the poison used is toxic to many species. In addition, many researchers speculate that this strategy may have backfired because fire ants can recover from disasters much more quickly than other types of ants. After an area was treated with insecticides, the first ants that were able to reinhabit it were fire ants. Similar scenarios occurred in many different areas. As a result of these treatments, fire ants have become a serious ecological problem in many areas.

Discussion

Discuss with students some safe and natural ways that they can eliminate ants around their home. For instance, they can squeeze fresh lemon or lime juice into holes or cracks in their homes and then leave the peels where they have seen ants. They can also scatter aromatic substances, such as mint, red pepper, or paprika, around spots where ants enter homes. These substances repel ants.

UNIT 5

Oceanography

In this unit, you will learn about the Earth's oceans and the vast landscapes they cover. Together, the oceans form the largest single feature on the planet. In fact, they cover approximately 70 percent of the Earth's surface. Now that's a lot of water! Not only do the oceans serve as home for countless living organisms, but they also affect life on land. You will learn more about the oceans in this unit as well as in the timeline presented here. Take a deep breath, and dive in!

1851

Herman Melville's novel *Moby-Dick* is published.

1872

The HMS *Challenger* begins its four-year voyage. Its discoveries lay the foundation for the science of oceanography.

1977

Thermal vent communities of creatures that exist without sunlight are discovered on the ocean floor.

1978

Louise Brown, the first "test-tube baby," is born in England.

1986

Commercial whaling is officially banned by the International Whaling Commission, but some whaling continues.

1914

The Panama Canal is completed, linking the Atlantic Ocean with the Pacific Ocean.

1927

Charles Lindbergh completes the first nonstop solo airplane flight over the Atlantic Ocean.

1938

A coelacanth is discovered in the Indian Ocean near South Africa. Called a fossil fish, the coelacanth was thought to have been extinct for 60 million years.

1943

Jacques Cousteau and Émile Gagnon invent the Aqualung, a breathing device that allows divers to freely explore the silent world of the oceans.

1960

Jacques Piccard and Don Walsh dive to a record 10,910 m below sea level in their bathyscaph *Trieste.*

1990

The tunnel under the English Channel is completed, making train and auto travel between Great Britain and France possible.

1998

Ben Lecomte of Austin, Texas, successfully swims across the Atlantic Ocean from Massachusetts to France, a distance of 6,015 km. His record-breaking feat took 74 days.

Chapter Organizer

CHAPTER ORGANIZATION	TIME MINUTES	OBJECTIVES	LABS, INVESTIGATIONS, AND DEMONSTRATIONS
Chapter Opener pp. 330–331	45	California Standards: PE/ATE 7, 7e	**Investigate!** Exit Only? p. 331
Section 1 Earth's Oceans	135	▶ Name the major divisions of the global ocean. ▶ Describe the history of Earth's oceans. ▶ Summarize the properties and other aspects of ocean water. ▶ Summarize the interaction between the ocean and the atmosphere. PE/ATE 1, 1a, 2b, 3a, 4a, 4d, 7, 7b, 7d	
Section 2 The Ocean Floor	90	▶ Identify the two major regions of the ocean floor. ▶ Classify subdivisions and features of the two major regions of the ocean floor. ▶ Describe technologies for studying the ocean floor. PE/ATE 1, 1a, 1e, 2a, 4a, 7, 7f; LabBook 7, 7b, 7c, 7e	**Making Models,** Probing the Depths, p. 538 **Datasheets for LabBook,** Probing the Depths, Datasheet 28
Section 3 Life in the Ocean	90	▶ Identify and describe the three groups of marine organisms. ▶ Identify and describe the benthic and pelagic environments. ▶ Classify the zones of the benthic and pelagic environments. PE/ATE 5, 5c–5e	**Interactive Explorations CD-ROM,** Sea Sick *A **Worksheet** is also available in the **Interactive Explorations Teacher's Edition.***
Section 4 Resources from the Ocean	90	▶ List two methods of harvesting the ocean's living resources. ▶ List nonliving resources in the ocean. ▶ Describe the ocean's energy resources. PE/ATE 6, 6a–6c, 7, 7a, 7b, 7e	**QuickLab,** How Much Fresh Water Is There? p. 351 **Inquiry Labs,** Surf's Up! Lab 11
Section 5 Ocean Pollution	90	▶ List different types of ocean pollution ▶ Explain how to prevent or minimize different types of ocean pollution. ▶ Outline what is being done to control ocean pollution. PE/ATE LabBook 7, 7a, 7b, 7e	**Discovery Lab,** Investigating an Oil Spill, p. 540 **Datasheets for LabBook,** Investigating an Oil Spill, Datasheet 29 **EcoLabs & Field Activities,** EcoLab 13 **Whiz-Bang Demonstrations,** Fowl Play, Demo 25 **Long-Term Projects & Research Ideas,** Project 41

*See page **T20** for a complete correlation of this book with the*

CALIFORNIA SCIENCE CONTENT STANDARDS.

Correlations are also provided at point of use throughout this ATE.

TECHNOLOGY RESOURCES

Guided Reading Audio CD
English or Spanish, Chapter 13

Classroom Management CD-ROM

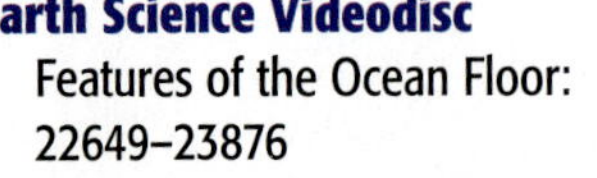
Earth Science Videodisc
Features of the Ocean Floor: 22649–23876

CNN **Multicultural Connections,** Segment 9
Scientists in Action, Segment 17 and 18

Test Generator CD-ROM

Interactive Explorations CD-ROM
CD 2, Exploration 2, Sea Sick

Chapter 13 • Exploring the Oceans

CLASSROOM WORKSHEETS, TRANSPARENCIES, AND RESOURCES	SCIENCE INTEGRATION AND CONNECTIONS	REVIEW AND ASSESSMENT
Science Puzzlers, Twisters & Teasers, Worksheet 13 **Directed Reading Worksheet 13**		
Transparency 130, Divisions of the Global Oceans **Directed Reading Worksheet 13,** Section 1 **Transparency 131,** Ocean Salinity **Transparency 132,** The Ocean and the Water Cycle	**Connect to Physical Science,** p. 333 in ATE **Connect to Physical Science,** p. 335 in ATE **Cross-Disciplinary Focus,** p. 336 in ATE **Multicultural Connection,** p. 337 in ATE	**Self-Check,** p. 333 **Review,** p. 336 **Review,** p. 338 **Quiz,** p. 338 in ATE **Alternative Assessment,** p. 338 in ATE
Directed Reading Worksheet 13, Section 2 **Math Skills for Science Worksheet 3,** Multiplying Whole Numbers; **Worksheet 15,** Multiplying and Dividing Fractions **Transparency 133,** How Sonar Works	**Connect to Physical Science,** p. 340 in ATE **Math and More,** p. 340 in ATE **Cross-Disciplinary Focus,** pp. 341, 342 in ATE **MathBreak,** Depths of the Deep, p. 342 **Across the Sciences:** Exploring Ocean Life, p. 362	**Self-Check,** p. 341 **Homework,** p. 341 in ATE **Review,** p. 343 **Quiz,** p. 343 in ATE **Alternative Assessment,** p. 343 in ATE
Transparency 134, The Three Groups of Marine Life **Directed Reading Worksheet 13,** Section 3 **Transparency 32,** Natural Selection in Four Steps **Reinforcement Worksheet 13,** The Ocean's Environment	**Life Science Connection,** p. 345 **Multicultural Connection,** p. 345 in ATE **Connect to Life Science,** p. 346 in ATE **Connect to Life Science,** p. 347 in ATE	**Homework,** p. 345 in ATE **Review,** p. 347 **Quiz,** p. 347 in ATE **Alternative Assessment,** p. 347 in ATE
Directed Reading Worksheet 13, Section 4 **Reinforcement Worksheet 13,** The Oceans and Us **Critical Thinking Worksheet 13,** Chain Reaction	**Real-World Connection,** pp. 349, 350 in ATE **Connect to Physical Science,** p. 351 in ATE **Eye on the Environment:** Putting Fresh Water Problems on Ice, p. 363	**Homework,** pp. 350, 351 in ATE **Review,** p. 352 **Quiz,** p. 352 in ATE **Alternative Assessment,** p. 352 in ATE
Directed Reading Worksheet 13, Section 5	**Environmental Science Connection,** p. 354 **Math and More,** p. 355 in ATE **Connect to Environmental Science,** p. 355 in ATE **Apply,** p. 356	**Homework,** p. 354 in ATE **Review,** p. 357 **Quiz,** p. 357 in ATE **Alternative Assessment,** p. 357 in ATE

Holt, Rinehart and Winston On-line Resources

go.hrw.com

For worksheets and other teaching aids related to this chapter, visit the HRW Web site and type in the keyword: **HSTOCE**

National Science Teachers Association

www.scilinks.org

Encourage students to use the keywords listed on the Technology Highlights page to access information and resources on the **NSTA** Web site.

END-OF-CHAPTER REVIEW AND ASSESSMENT

Chapter Review in Study Guide

Vocabulary and Notes in Study Guide

Chapter Tests with Performance-Based Assessment, Chapter 13 Test, Performance-Based Assessment 13

Concept Mapping Transparency 13

Chapter Resources & Worksheets

Visual Resources

TEACHING TRANSPARENCIES

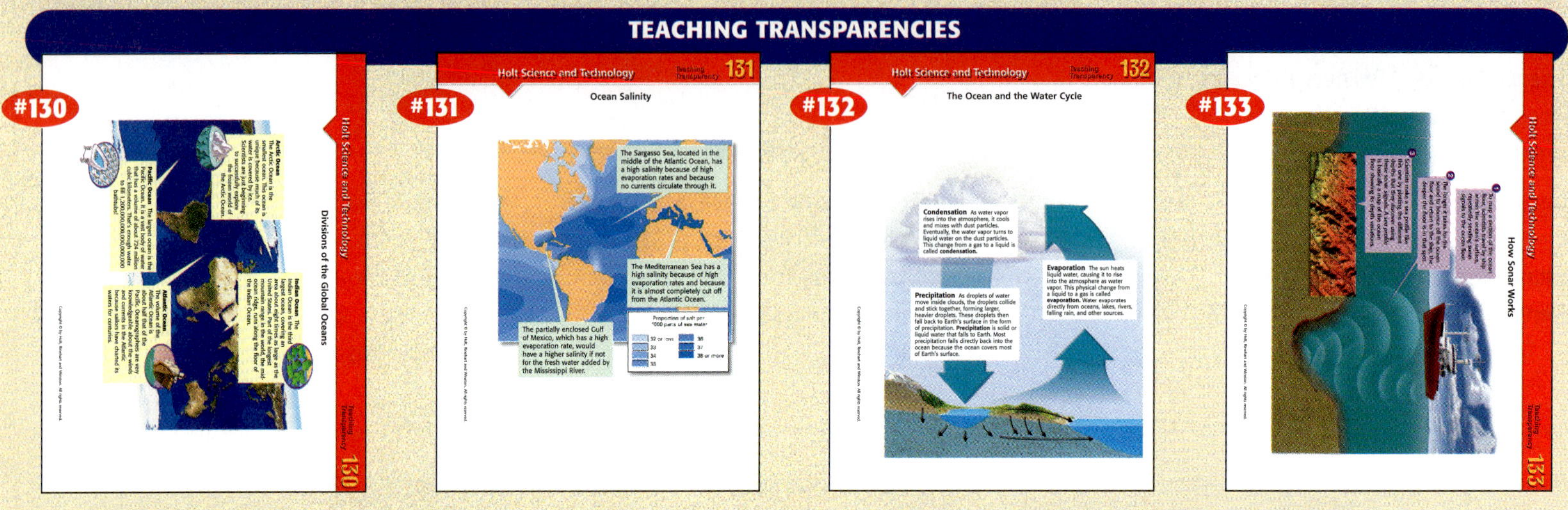

TEACHING TRANSPARENCIES

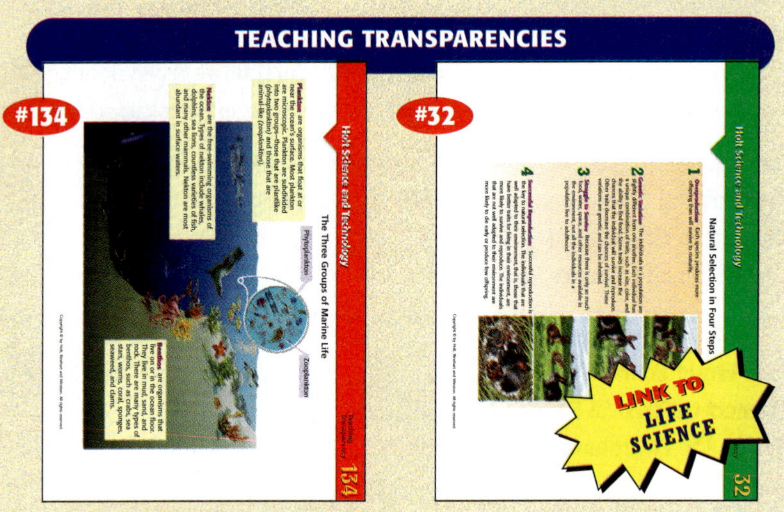

CONCEPT MAPPING TRANSPARENCY

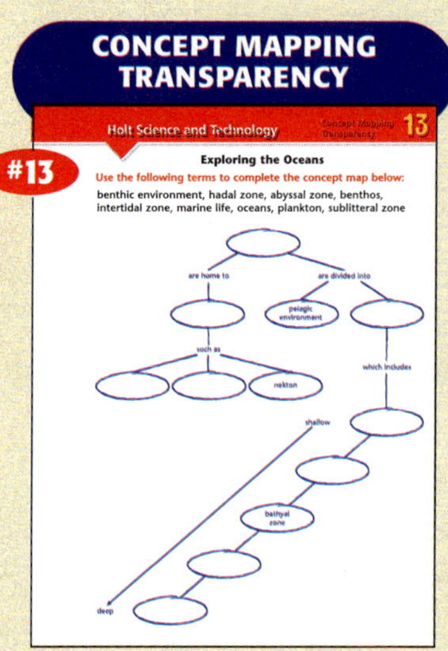

Meeting Individual Needs

DIRECTED READING

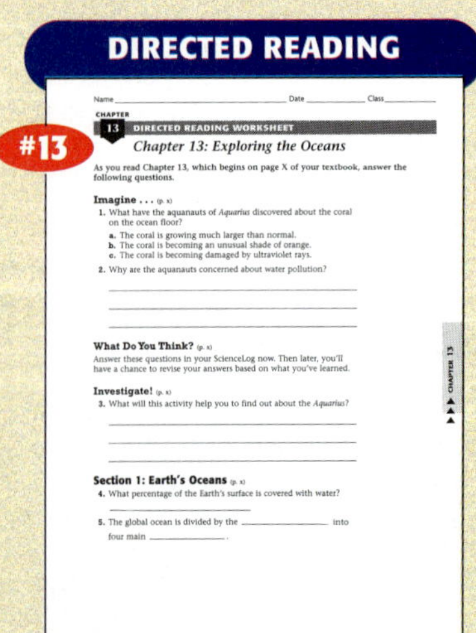

REINFORCEMENT & VOCABULARY REVIEW

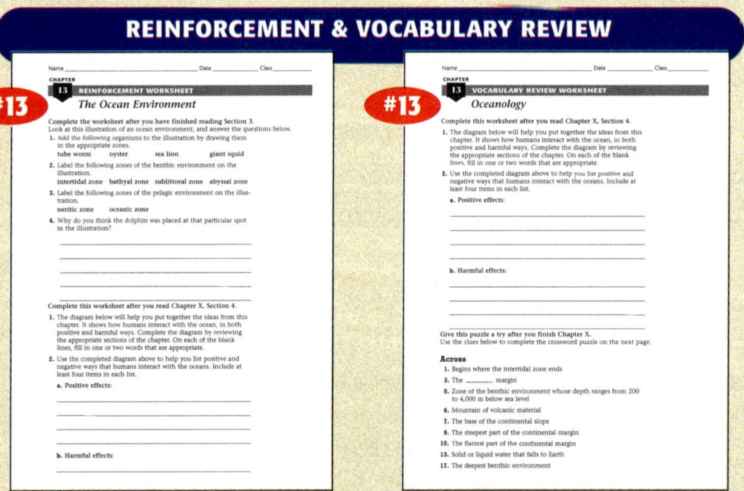

SCIENCE PUZZLERS, TWISTERS & TEASERS

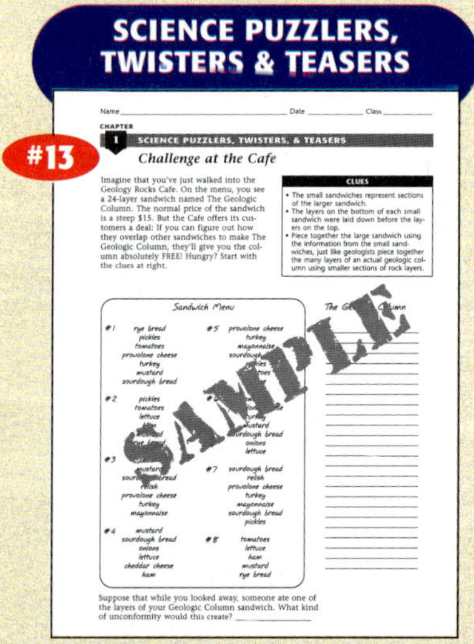

Review & Assessment

STUDY GUIDE

#13

#13

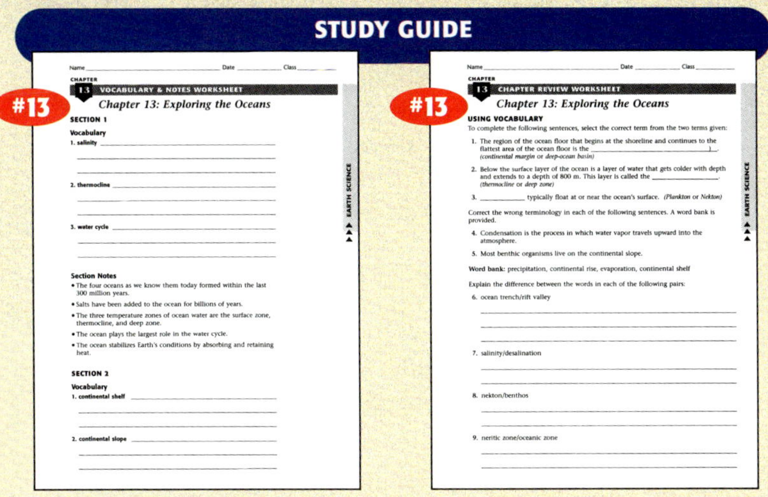

Chapter 13 Vocabulary & Notes Worksheet

Chapter 13: Exploring the Oceans

Chapter 13 Chapter Review Worksheet

Chapter 13: Exploring the Oceans

CHAPTER TESTS WITH PERFORMANCE-BASED ASSESSMENT

#13

#13

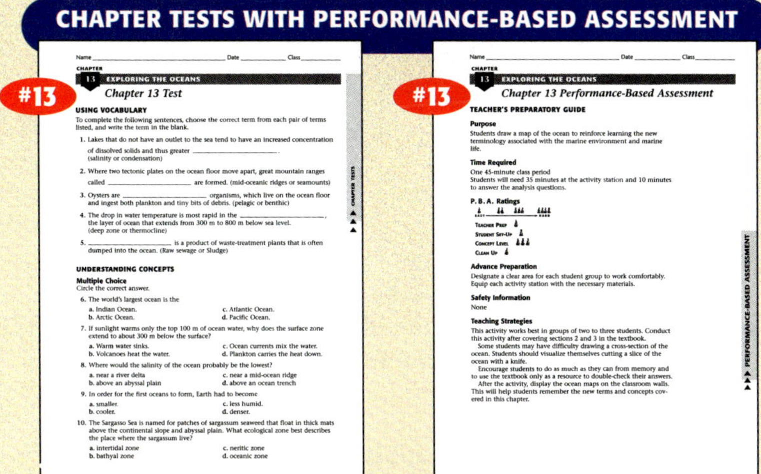

Chapter 13 Exploring the Oceans

Chapter 13 Test

Chapter 13 Exploring the Oceans

Chapter 13 Performance-Based Assessment

Lab Worksheets

INQUIRY LABS

#11

LONG-TERM PROJECTS & RESEARCH IDEAS

#41

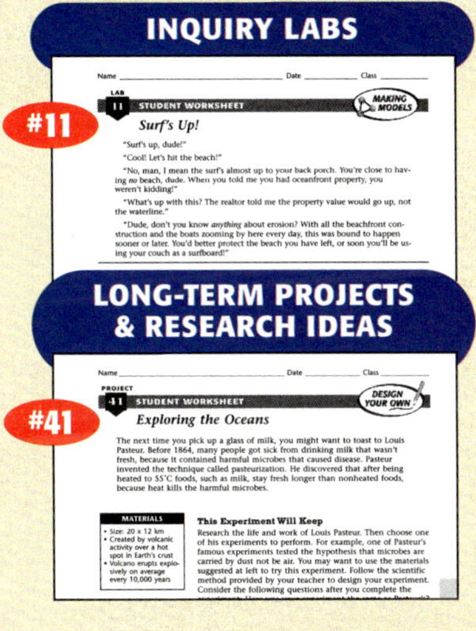

Lab 11 Student Worksheet

Surf's Up!

Project 41 Student Worksheet

Exploring the Oceans

ECOLABS & FIELD ACTIVITIES

#13

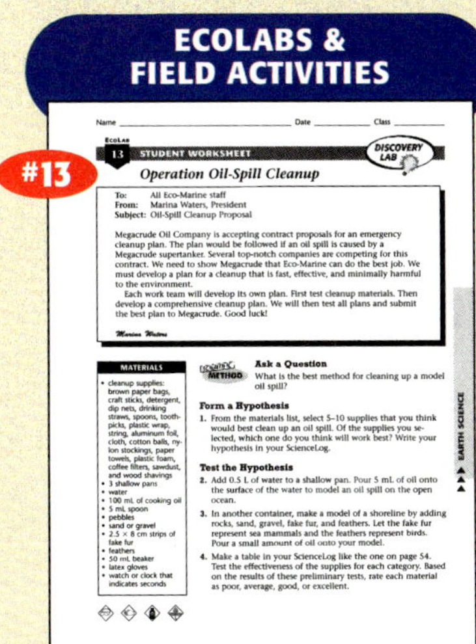

EcoLab 13 Student Worksheet

Operation Oil-Spill Cleanup

WHIZ-BANG DEMONSTRATIONS

#25

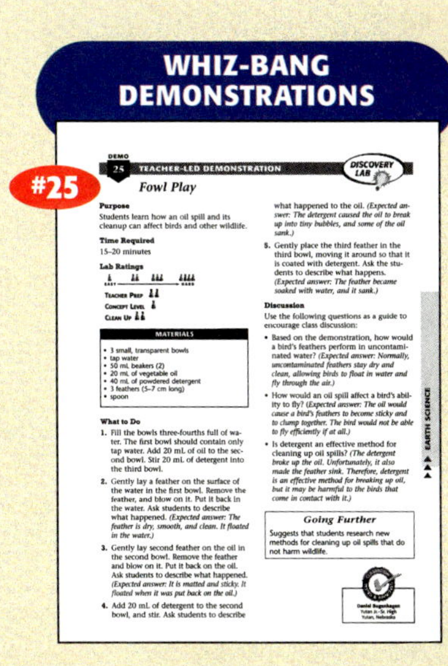

Demo 25 Teacher-Led Demonstration

Fowl Play

DATASHEETS FOR LABBOOK

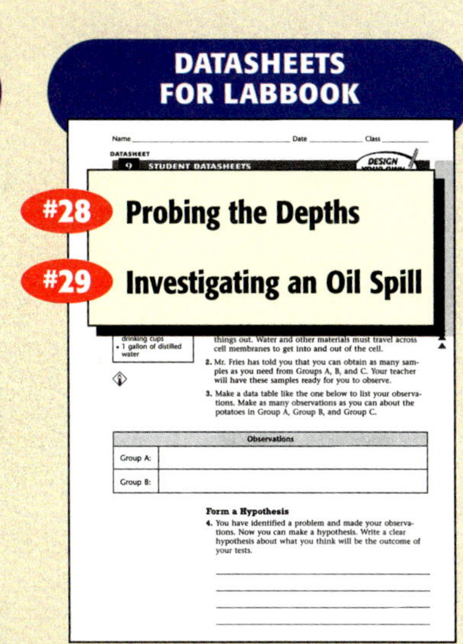

#28 Probing the Depths

#29 Investigating an Oil Spill

Applications & Extensions

CRITICAL THINKING & PROBLEM SOLVING

#13

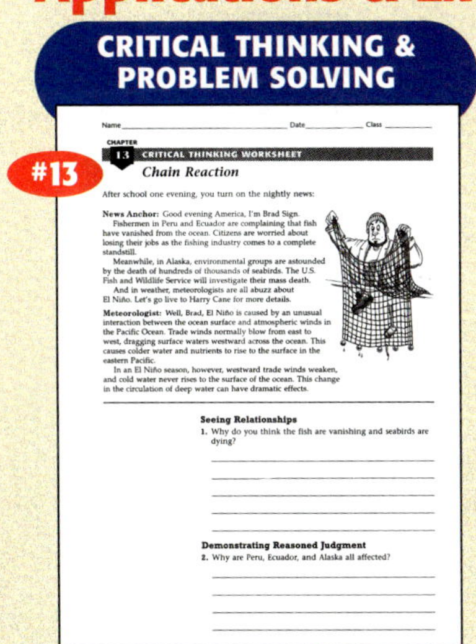

Chapter 13 Critical Thinking Worksheet

Chain Reaction

MULTICULTURAL CONNECTIONS

#9

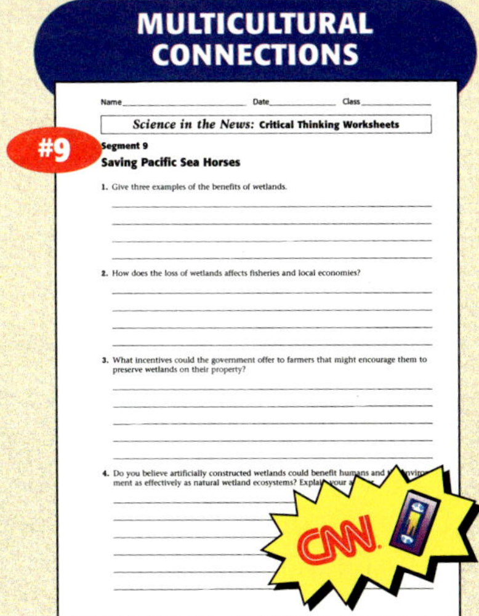

Science in the News: Critical Thinking Worksheets

Segment 9

Saving Pacific Sea Horses

SCIENTISTS IN ACTION

#17

#18

Science in the News: Critical Thinking Worksheets

Segment 17

Deep Flight

INTERACTIVE EXPLORATIONS

#2–2

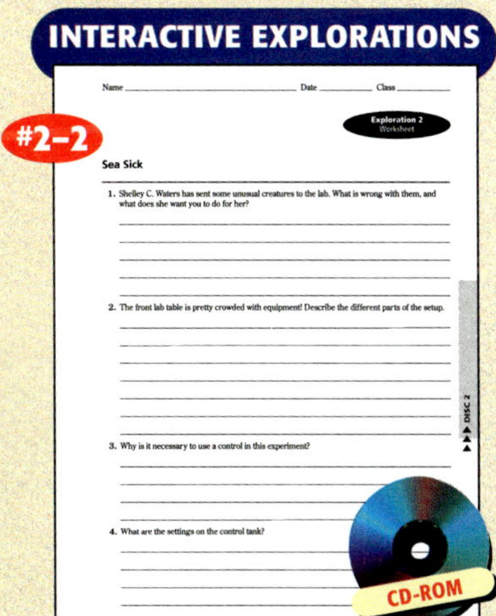

Exploration 2 Worksheet

Sea Sick

CD-ROM

Chapter Background

Section 1

Earth's Oceans

▶ The Global Ocean

Historically, the global ocean was divided into five oceans: the Atlantic, Pacific, Indian, Arctic, and Antarctic Oceans. Today, most oceanographers agree that the Antarctic Ocean is actually the southernmost section of the Atlantic, Pacific, and Indian Oceans.

▶ The Mariana Trench

In 1960, the *Trieste,* a small submarine designed to explore the ocean to great depths, set out on a voyage that until then had only been imagined: it descended into the Mariana Trench, the deepest known place on the Earth. As its inventor, Auguste Picard, and a companion descended, they were surprised to feel abrupt changes between the ocean's temperature layers. Every time the vessel reached the boundary between two layers, it seemed to stop as though it had reached the ocean floor.

IS THAT A FACT!

- The average depth of each ocean is as follows:
  Arctic: 1,038 m
  Atlantic: 3,735 m
  Indian: 3,872 m
  Pacific: 4,188 m

- The average depth for all the oceans is about 3,200 m.

Section 2

The Ocean Floor

▶ The Renewal of a Planet

During missions such as *Alvin*'s, oceanographers are able to witness the creation of solid earth and the forces that drive plate movement. By observing molten rock welling up into the ocean, they have seen how new seafloors form and have gained a better understanding of how and why the continents drift apart. Trained to "read" rock formations, these scientists use their observations to further our understanding of how Earth formed, as well as what we might expect in the future.

IS THAT A FACT!

- The oceans' deep-water sound channels carry sound waves for hundreds of kilometers. Whales and other marine animals take advantage of these properties for long-range communication and to search for food. Whales communicate with clicks, whistles, squeaks, and songs that convey information. Scientists aren't sure what these songs mean, but they do know that whales can communicate at distances as great as 1,600 km!

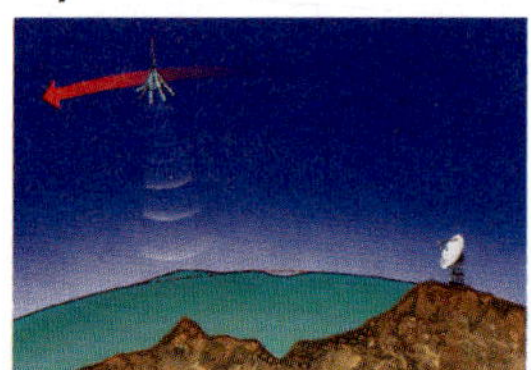

Section 3

Life in the Ocean

▶ A World of Its Own

In 1977, scientists aboard *Alvin* witnessed an astonishing new world around deep-sea vents. Exploring hydrothermal vents 320 km off the Galápagos Islands, these explorers saw an amazing multitude of unusual marine populations—giant clams and worms, fish, and crabs—gathered in an abyssal oasis.

- Using a special claw attachment, scientists harvested samples of the marine life they found. When they analyzed their specimens, they were in for a surprise—the water smelled like rotten eggs! This smell came from hydrogen sulfide dissolved in the water around the vents.

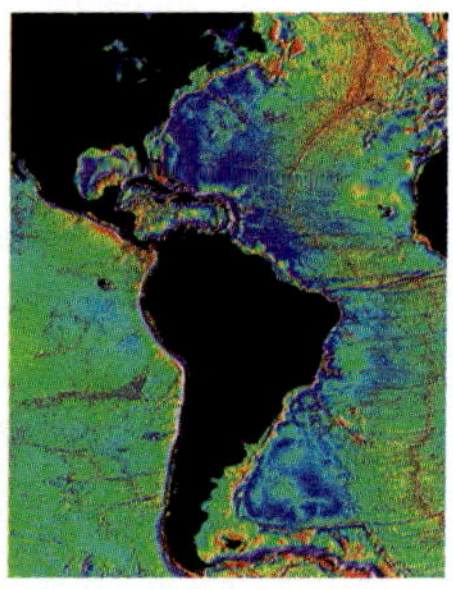

- The scientists discovered that certain marine bacteria thrive on the hydrogen sulfide released by vents in the ocean floor. These bacteria are food for the other marine creatures and they are part of a food chain that does not rely on photosynthesis for energy.

Creatures of the Dark

The most imaginative science-fiction author would be hard pressed to conceive of creatures as bizarre as the organisms inhabiting the deep sea. Living in perpetual darkness, some—such as the cookie-cutter shark—are bioluminescent. Others lack any organs or structures for vision or photosensitivity. Many benthic (ocean bottom) animals look more like plants than animals. Some exhibit such unique methods of feeding, reproduction, and movement that they are difficult to classify under our current system.

IS THAT A FACT!

- The word *plankton* comes from the Greek *planktos,* meaning "wandering." Because plankton float at or near the ocean's surface, they "wander" with the ocean currents. Interestingly, tiny plankton are the sole sustenance of two of the largest marine animals—the blue whale and the basking shark.

Section 4

Resources from the Ocean

Food for Thought

Fish are an invaluable ocean resource, providing a significant percentage of the world's protein needs every year. About 75 million tons of fish are harvested from the ocean each year. But many fish populations have been depleted by overfishing.

- Concerned that too few fish will remain to breed, scientists determine the maximum sustainable yield, or the amount of fish that can be harvested each year without jeopardizing future catches. Using the scientists' guidelines, governments sometimes impose fishing restrictions to manage fish populations. Many people are working to ensure that the world can continue to count on fish for food.

Sea Thermal Plants

Harnessing tidal and wave energy is not the only way to get electrical power from the ocean. Since 1979, the United States government has operated an Ocean Thermal Energy Conversion (OTEC) plant off the coast of Hawaii, where the temperature differential between surface and deeper water layers is converted into electrical energy.

Section 5

Ocean Pollution

Thermal Pollution

Pesticides, oil, sludge, and trash are not the only harmful pollutants released into our oceans. Power plants can cause thermal pollution by releasing heated water into the sea. Thermal pollution may result in only a 1- or 2-degree temperature difference in the area near the heat source, but that can have profound effects on the ecology. Fish populations may migrate away from the affected area, and overgrowth of other organisms, or "algal blooms," may occur.

Close Quarters

Closed-in seas are particularly vulnerable to damage from ocean pollution. The shores and adjacent waters of the Mediterranean, Baltic, and Adriatic Seas have been fouled with city sewage, factory waste, and fertilizer and pesticide runoff from farms. Their open waters have been affected by dumping and oil spills.

For additional background resources, please refer to the ***HST Reference Library.***

CHAPTER 13

Exploring the Oceans

Chapter Preview

Section 1
Earth's Oceans
- Divisions of the Global Ocean
- How Did the Oceans Form?
- Characteristics of Ocean Water
- The Ocean and the Water Cycle
- A Global Thermostat

Section 2
The Ocean Floor
- Exploring the Ocean Floor
- Revealing the Ocean Floor
- Viewing the Ocean Floor from Above

Section 3
Life in the Ocean
- The Three Groups of Marine Life
- The Benthic Environment
- The Pelagic Environment

Section 4
Resources from the Ocean
- Living Resources
- Nonliving Resources

Section 5
Ocean Pollution
- Sources of Ocean Pollution
- Saving Our Ocean Resources

Science Puzzlers, Twisters & Teasers Worksheet 13

Guided Reading Audio CD
English or Spanish, Chapter 13

CHAPTER 13

Exploring the Oceans

A glimpse of the future in the next frontier—the ocean floor

Imagine . . .

You are living at the bottom of the ocean, surrounded by colorful creatures swimming gracefully around you. Inside glass domes are entire cities of people who mine rich mineral deposits, farm fish and other aquatic life, and study the mysteries of Earth's vast, unexplored oceans.

Scientists are bringing that vision one step closer to reality inside an undersea home off the coast of Key Largo, Florida. There, at a depth of 19 m, scientists called *aquanauts* live and work inside *Aquarius,* an underwater laboratory and living facility.

Inside *Aquarius*, which is about as big as a bus, research teams conduct missions that can last up to 7 days. The purpose of the missions is to study North America's largest living coral-reef system. The scientists' only lifeline is a buoy on the surface of the water. The buoy enables air to be pumped into *Aquarius* and data, such as video images, to be transmitted back to shore.

The aquanauts have made some important discoveries. They have found evidence that ultraviolet rays from the sun are damaging the sensitive coral that live on the ocean floor.

Aquanauts are taking the next step toward underwater living. Aquarius *may not be a high-rise, but it lays the foundation for human colonization of the ocean floor.*

330

Imagine . . .

The first human seafloor habitat was built by marine explorer Jacques Cousteau. Launched in 1962, the Conshelf (Continental Shelf Station) project was based in the Mediterranean Sea. Aquanauts Albert Falco and Claude Wesley lived for a week in an underwater station called *Diogenes* while they studied the ocean floor.

Some people think that these ultraviolet rays are able to reach the coral because air pollution is destroying the atmosphere's protective ozone layer. Water pollution also appears to be harming marine organisms. This concerns the aquanauts, who are extracting natural chemicals from these organisms that may provide cures for certain human diseases.

In this chapter you'll learn more about the Earth's oceans. You'll find out how scientists are exploring Earth's final frontier, uncovering its secrets, and protecting its valuable resources for the next generation.

What Do You Think?

In your ScienceLog, try to answer the following questions based on what you already know:

1. How have Earth's oceans changed over time?
2. Name two ways scientists study the ocean without going underwater.
3. Name two valuable resources that are taken from the ocean.

Exit Only?

How do aquanauts enter and leave *Aquarius*? Believe it or not, the simplest way is through a hole in the lab's floor. You might think water would come in through the hole, but it doesn't. People inside *Aquarius* can breathe freely and can come and go through the hole at any time. How is this possible? Do the following investigation to find out.

Procedure

1. Fill a large **bowl** about two-thirds full of **water.**
2. Turn a clear plastic **cup** upside down.
3. Slowly guide the cup straight down into the water, being careful not to tip the cup.
4. Record your observations in your ScienceLog.

Analysis

5. How far into the cup does the water go?
6. How does the air inside the cup affect the water below the cup?
7. Relate your findings to the hole in the bottom of the underwater research lab.

Going Further

Perform the same experiment, but this time tip the cup slightly to one side after you have submerged it. What does this demonstrate about the limits of the hole-in-the-floor design?

331

What Do You Think?

Accept all reasonable responses.

Students will have a chance to revise their answers in the Chapter Review under NOW What Do You Think?

Investigate!

MATERIALS

For Each Group:

- large bowl
- small, clear plastic cup

Teacher Notes: A cylindrical cup (one that does not taper) is best for this activity.

Answers to Investigate!

5. The water should not go very far into the cup.
6. The air inside the cup keeps the water below it from filling the space inside the cup.
7. Like the air in the cup keeps the water from filling the cup, the air in the underwater research lab keeps water from coming through the hole in the bottom of the lab.

Answers to Going Further

Students will find that if the cup is tipped, water will enter it. This demonstrates that the hole in the lab floor must be level. Otherwise water will come through the hole.

Directed Reading Worksheet 13

SECTION 1

Focus

Earth's Oceans

In this section students learn how the global ocean is divided as well as how the oceans formed. They explore the properties of ocean water, including factors that affect salinity, temperature zones, and surface temperature changes. Finally, they learn how the ocean interacts with the atmosphere and the land via the water cycle.

Bellringer

Have students predict the percentage of land and water on Earth. Show students a photo of Earth from outer space, and ask them to list some of the planet's most obvious features. Tell students that water covers 71 percent of Earth's surface and that liquid water is very rare in our solar system. Discuss the significance of Earth's abundant water resources.
Sheltered English

1) Motivate

ACTIVITY

Discuss the divisions of the global ocean shown on this page, noting the volume of the Pacific Ocean. The volume of the Atlantic Ocean is about 322 million cubic kilometers, the volume of the Indian Ocean is about 292 million cubic kilometers, and the volume of the Arctic Ocean is about 12 million cubic kilometers. Have students use graduated cylinders filled with water to demonstrate these ratios. (The Pacific Ocean would be 724 mL, the Atlantic Ocean would be 322 mL, the Indian Ocean would be 292 mL, and the Arctic Ocean would be 12 mL.)

1 Earth's Oceans

NEW TERMS
salinity
thermocline
water cycle

OBJECTIVES
- Name the major divisions of the global ocean.
- Describe the history of Earth's oceans.
- Summarize the properties and other aspects of ocean water.
- Summarize the interaction between the ocean and the atmosphere.

Earth stands out from the other planets in our solar system primarily for one reason—71 percent of the Earth's surface is covered with water. Most of Earth's water is found in the global ocean, which is divided by the continents into four main oceans. This is shown in the figure below. The ocean is a unique body of water that plays many roles in regulating Earth's environment. Read on to learn more about one of our most important resources—the ocean.

Divisions of the Global Ocean

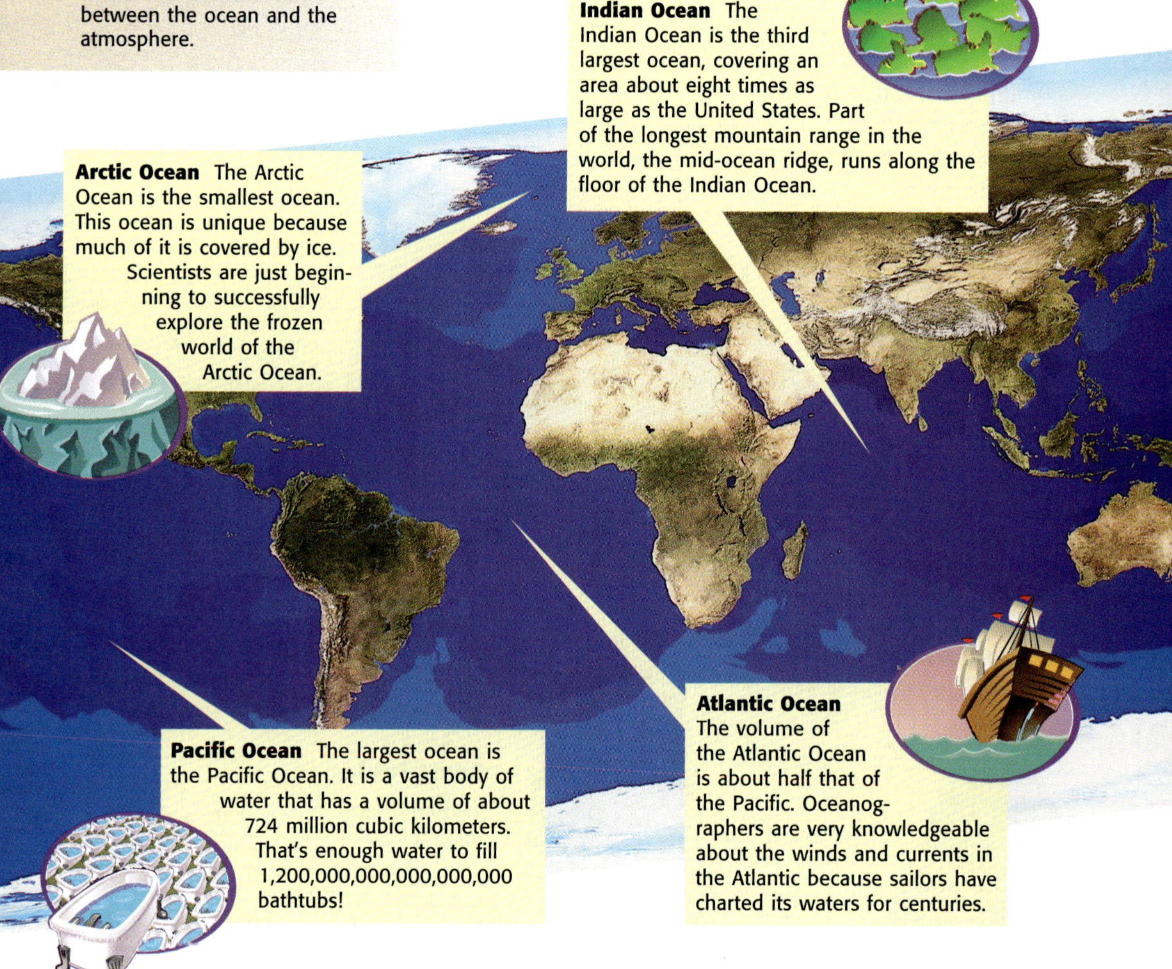

332

Teaching Transparency 130 "Divisions of the Global Oceans"

Directed Reading Worksheet 13 Section 1

IS THAT A FACT!

The global ocean covers nearly 376 million square kilometers. The entire North American continent, by comparison, covers only a little more than 24 million square kilometers.

Section 1–California Standards: PE/ATE 1, 1a, 2b, 3a, 4a, 4d, 7, 7b, 7d

How Did the Oceans Form?

About four and a half billion years ago, the Earth was a very different place. There were no oceans. Volcanoes spewed lava, ash, and gases all over the planet, which was much hotter than it is today. The volcanic gases, including water vapor, began to form Earth's atmosphere. While the atmosphere developed, the Earth was cooling. Between 3.5 billion and 3 billion years ago, the Earth cooled enough for water vapor to condense and fall as rain. The rain began filling the lower levels of Earth's surface, and the first oceans began to form.

Earth's oceans have changed a lot throughout history. Scientists who study oceans have learned much about the oceans' history, as shown in the diagram below.

Self-Check

Examine the diagram below. If North America and South America continue to drift westward and Asia continues to drift eastward, what will eventually happen? *(See page 564 to check your answer.)*

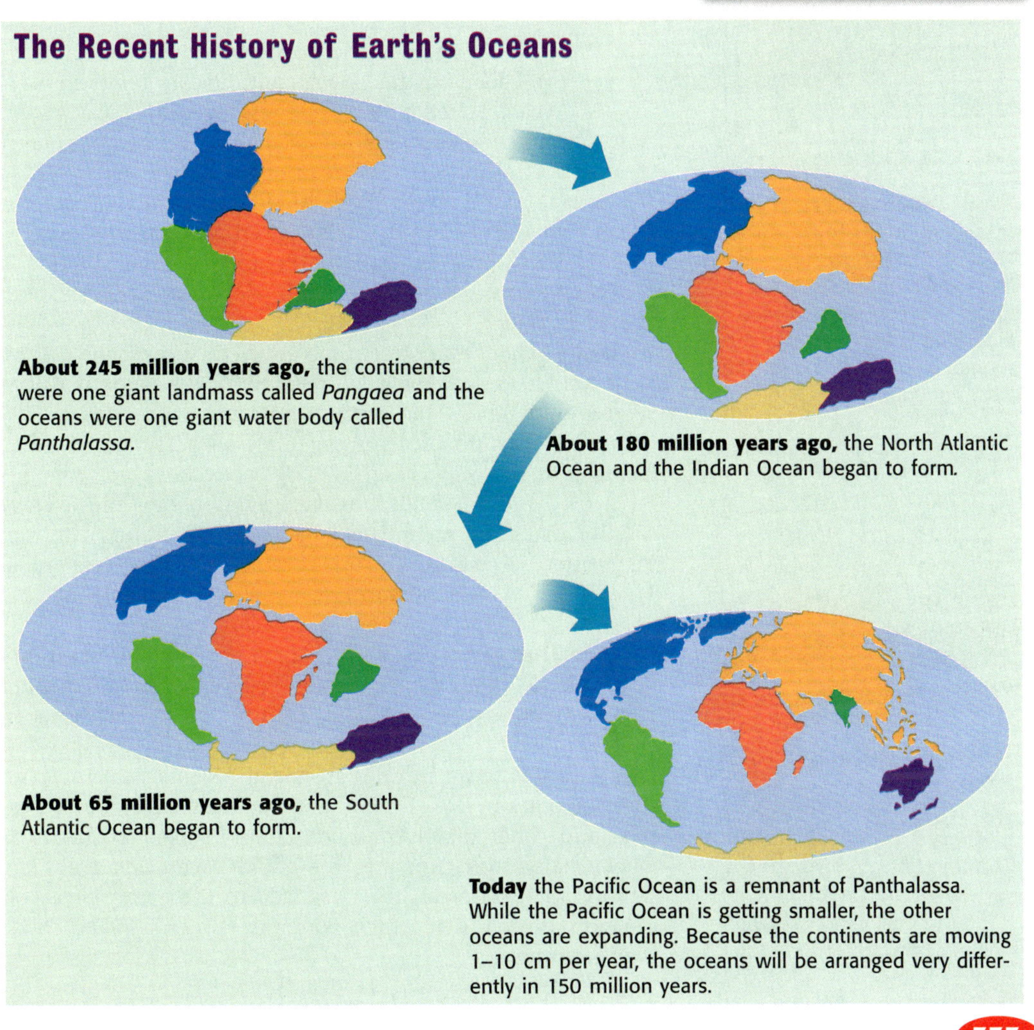
The Recent History of Earth's Oceans

About 245 million years ago, the continents were one giant landmass called *Pangaea* and the oceans were one giant water body called *Panthalassa.*

About 180 million years ago, the North Atlantic Ocean and the Indian Ocean began to form.

About 65 million years ago, the South Atlantic Ocean began to form.

Today the Pacific Ocean is a remnant of Panthalassa. While the Pacific Ocean is getting smaller, the other oceans are expanding. Because the continents are moving 1–10 cm per year, the oceans will be arranged very differently in 150 million years.

2 Teach

Reading Strategy

Mnemonics Encourage students to create a mnemonic device that will help them remember the names of the world's oceans. For example, they might write, **A**unt **P**atty **A**te **I**nchworms in order to recall **A**tlantic, **P**acific, **A**rctic, and **I**ndian. Have students share their ideas with the class.

Misconception Alert

Students might find the terms *sea* and *ocean* confusing. In some cases the words are interchangeable, but other times the terms mean different things. Parts of the global ocean that are partly or completely surrounded by land are known as seas. The Mediterranean Sea, partly surrounded by land, is an example of a sea that is part of the global ocean. Seas that are completely landlocked, such as the Caspian Sea, are not part of the global ocean. Have students identify landlocked seas and the global ocean on a map.

Connect to Physical Science

Explain to students that condensation is a physical change from a gas to a liquid. In the atmosphere, the amount of water vapor that the air can hold is dependent on temperature. As temperature decreases, the air can hold less water vapor, and the water vapor condenses, forming clouds. Ask students to consider other examples of condensation in their lives. (Examples might include condensation on the side of a soda can, dew in the morning, or a foggy mirror in the bathroom.)

Scientists at Odds

When Earth cooled about 3 billion years ago, the rains that resulted lasted for thousands of years. But some scientists do not believe all the water on Earth came from condensation as Earth cooled. Instead, they argue that some of the water came from "cosmic rain"—comets that struck Earth in its early history.

Answer to Self-Check

If North America and South America continue to drift westward and Asia continues to drift eastward, the continents will eventually collide on the other side of the Earth.

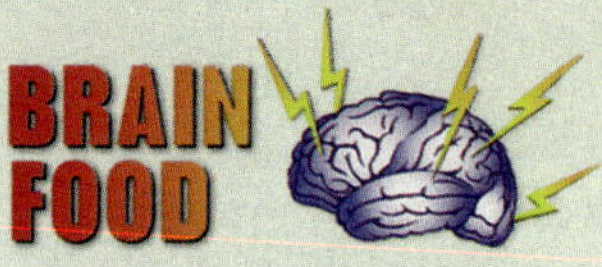

BRAIN FOOD

To help students conceptualize the concentration of gold in sea water, point out that 3 to 4 billion metric tons of ocean water contains about 11 to 14 kg of gold. On land, some mining companies use a bacteria called *Thiobacillus ferrooxidans* to extract gold from mine wastes. Have students find out more about this process and whether it could be used to recover gold from the oceans.

MISCONCEPTION ALERT

In **Figure 1,** students may notice that the percentages of some of the elements dissolved in ocean water are particularly low. This does not necessarily mean these elements are not abundant in the ocean. Organisms, such as diatoms and coral, remove dissolved minerals containing some of these elements and use them to make hard body parts.

Characteristics of Ocean Water

You know that ocean water is different from the water that flows from the faucet of your kitchen sink. For one thing, ocean water is not safe to drink. But there are other characteristics that make ocean water special. Read on to learn about ocean water's characteristics.

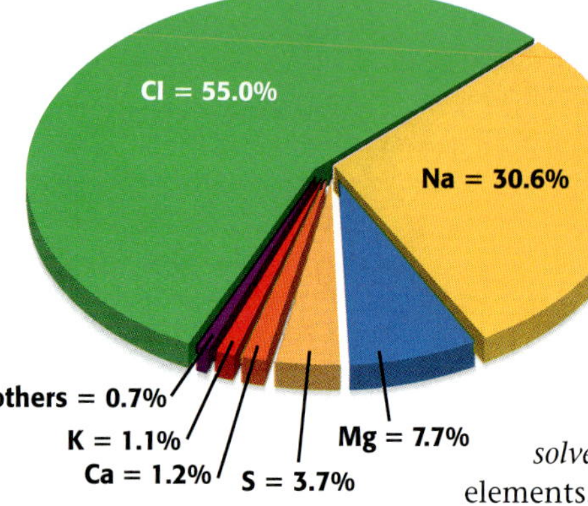

Figure 1 Percentages of Dissolved Solids in Ocean Water *This pie chart shows the relative abundance of the dissolved solids in ocean water. Notice that the two elements that form sodium chloride are by far the most abundant.*

Ocean Water Is Salty Have you ever swallowed a mouthful of water while swimming in the ocean? It sure had a nasty taste, didn't it? You know the ocean is salty, but tasting it firsthand can be a shock. Most of the salt in the ocean is the same kind of salt that we sprinkle on our food. Scientists call this salt *sodium chloride.*

The ocean is so salty because salt has been added to the ocean continuously for billions of years. Here's how it happens. Rivers and streams *dissolve* minerals on land into elements and compounds of elements. The running water carries these dissolved solids to the ocean. At the same time, water is *evaporating* from the ocean, but the dissolved solids stay in the ocean. The most abundant dissolved solid in the ocean is sodium chloride, a compound of the elements sodium (Na) and chlorine (Cl), as shown in **Figure 1.**

If more water evaporates than enters the ocean, the ocean's salinity increases. **Salinity** is a measure of the amount of dissolved solids in a given amount of liquid. Salinity is usually measured as grams of dissolved solids per kilogram of water. Think of it this way: 1 kg (1,000 g) of ocean water contains 35 g of dissolved solids on average; therefore, the average salinity of ocean water is 35 parts per thousand. This can be written as 35‰. In other words, if you evaporated 1 kg of ocean water, about 35 g of solids would remain.

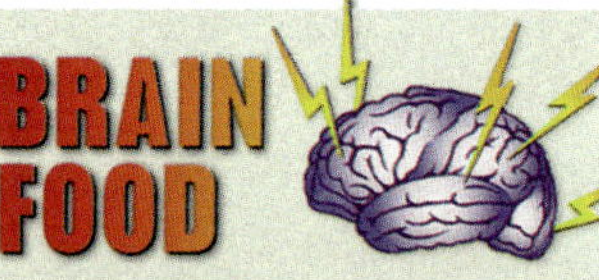

Did you know that there are about 9 million tons of gold dissolved in the ocean? Too bad the gold's concentration is only 0.000004 mg per kilogram of sea water. Mining the gold from the water would be difficult, and the cost of extraction would be greater than the gold's value.

Factors That Affect Salinity Some areas of the ocean are saltier than others. Coastal water in areas with hotter, drier climates typically have a higher salinity than coastal water in cooler, more humid areas. This is because less fresh water runs into the ocean in drier areas and because heat increases the evaporation rate. Evaporation removes water but leaves salts and other dissolved solids behind. Also, coastal areas where major rivers run into the ocean have a relatively low salinity. In these areas, the rivers add to the ocean large volumes of fresh water, which contains fewer dissolved solids than sea water.

334

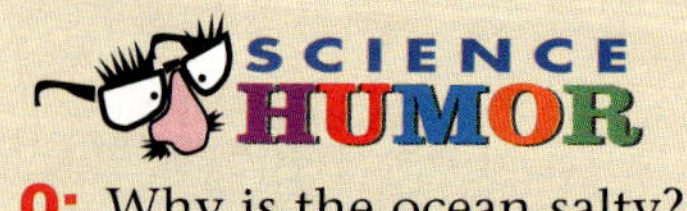

Q: Why is the ocean salty?

A: because fish don't like pepper

Another factor that affects ocean salinity is water movement. Surface water in some areas of the ocean, such as bays, gulfs, and seas, circulates less than surface water in other parts. Areas in the open ocean that have no currents running through them can also be slow moving. **Figure 2** shows how salinity variations relate to many factors.

Temperature Zones The temperature of ocean water decreases as the depth of the water increases. However, this does not occur gradually from the ocean's surface to its bottom. Water in the ocean can be divided into three layers according to temperature. As you can see in the graph below, the water at the top is much warmer than the average temperature of the ocean.

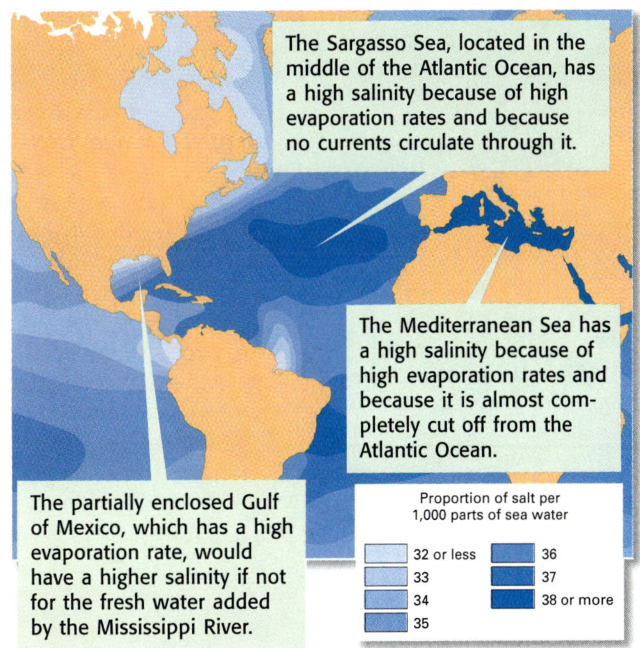

Figure 2 *Salinity varies in different parts of the ocean because of variations in evaporation, circulation, and freshwater inflow.*

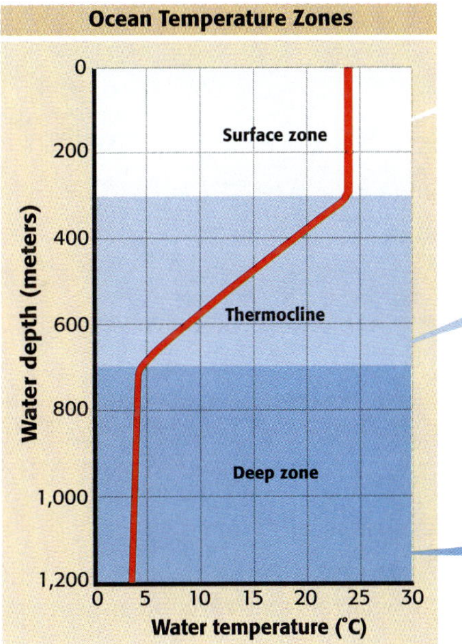

Surface zone
The surface zone is the warm, top layer of ocean water. Sunlight penetrates the top 100 m of the surface zone, heating it with solar energy. Surface currents mix the heated water with cooler water below, which causes the surface zone to extend to 300 m below sea level.

Thermocline
The **thermocline** is a layer of water extending from 300 m below sea level to about 700 m below sea level. In this zone, water temperature drops with increased depth faster than it does in the other two zones. The water in the thermocline is colder and denser than the water in the surface zone.

Deep zone
This bottom layer extends from the base of the thermocline to the bottom of the ocean. The temperature in this zone averages a chilling 2°C, which is 4°C above the freezing point of salt water.

335

MEETING INDIVIDUAL NEEDS

Learners Having Difficulty To help students visualize the temperature zones of the ocean, ask them to make cross-section diagrams of the ocean, labeling the surface zone, thermocline, and deep zone. Have them write captions for their drawings that explain the relationship between temperature and depth. Sheltered English

CONNECT TO PHYSICAL SCIENCE

Sound waves travel faster in warm water than in cold water. A technique called acoustic thermometry of ocean climate (ATOC) measures the time it takes for sound to travel a known distance through the ocean. Using this method, oceanographers can determine the average temperature of the ocean water with great accuracy.

MISCONCEPTION ALERT

Although the graph of ocean temperature zones only extends to a depth of 1,200 m, the ocean is much deeper than 1,200 m in most places, and the deep zone extends all the way to the bottom of the ocean. The rate at which temperature decreases with depth is constant throughout the deep zone.

IS THAT A FACT!

The deepest water in the ocean is colder than 0°C, but it remains liquid because of its salinity and the increased pressures at that depth.

The Amazon River feeds so much fresh water into the Atlantic Ocean that the ocean water has different salinity and color almost 160 km from shore!

Teaching Transparency 131 "Ocean Salinity"

2 Teach, continued

Group Activity

Making Models Using balloons and permanent markers, students can model how latitude affects ocean surface temperatures. Have them clearly label the poles and equator on their balloons and indicate surface water temperatures between the two. Have them use colored pens to draw bands around their balloons. They should construct a key for their colors, correlating warmer temperatures with the colors closest to the equator. After they color in the shapes of the continents, students can present their models to the class.

Cross-Disciplinary Focus

Geography Encourage students to use atlases or globes to locate the four main oceans. Remind them that these oceans are separated by land. Suggest that students draw a map of the oceans that indicates modern or ancient trade routes and illustrate it with drawings of animals that are unique to each ocean. Students might also make a chart in which they compare all of the oceans by size, average temperature, depth, and other characteristics.

Surface Temperature Changes Temperatures in the surface zone vary with latitude and the time of year. Surface temperatures range from 1°C near the poles to about 24°C near the equator. Areas of the ocean along the equator are warmer because they receive more sunlight per year than areas closer to the poles.

The time of year also affects surface-zone temperatures in most regions. For example, the sun's rays in the Northern Hemisphere are more direct during the summer than during the winter. Therefore, the surface zone absorbs more heat energy during the summer. If you live near the coast, you may know firsthand how different a dip in the ocean feels in December than it feels in July. **Figure 3** shows how surface-zone temperatures vary depending on the time of year. The left image shows the region's winter temperatures, and the right image shows the region's summer temperatures.

Figure 3 *These satellite images show that the surface temperatures in this part of the northern Pacific Ocean are colder during the winter (left) than during the summer (right).*

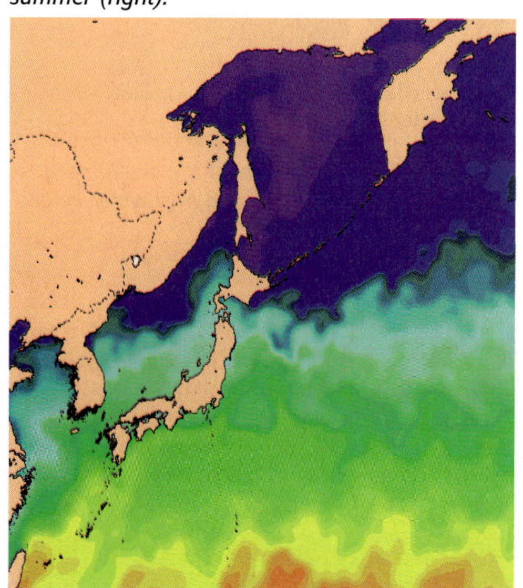

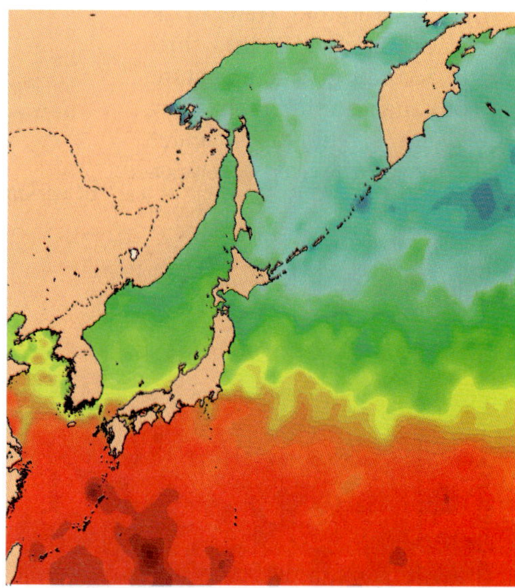

Cool — Warm

Review

1. Name the major divisions of the global ocean.
2. Explain how Earth's first oceans formed.
3. **Summarizing Data** List three factors that affect salinity in the ocean and three factors that affect ocean temperatures. Explain how each factor affects salinity or temperature.

336

Answers to Review

1. The major divisions of the global ocean are the Pacific Ocean, the Atlantic Ocean, the Indian Ocean, and the Arctic Ocean.
2. Between 3.5 billion and 3 billion years ago, the Earth cooled enough for water vapor in the atmosphere to condense and fall as rain. The rain began filling the lower levels of Earth's surface, and the first oceans began to form. (Answers that name comets as the source for water for Earth's first oceans are acceptable.)
3. factors affecting salinity: type of climate, addition or removal of fresh water, and water movement; factors affecting temperature: water depth, latitude, and the time of year

Section 1 Mid-section Review–California Standards: PE/ATE 1, 1a

The Ocean and the Water Cycle

If you could sit on the moon and look down at Earth, what would you see? You would notice that Earth's surface is made up of three basic components—water, land, and air. All three are involved in an ongoing process called the water cycle, as shown below. The **water cycle** is a cycle that links all of Earth's solid, liquid, and gaseous water together. The ocean is an important part of the water cycle because nearly all of Earth's water is found in the ocean.

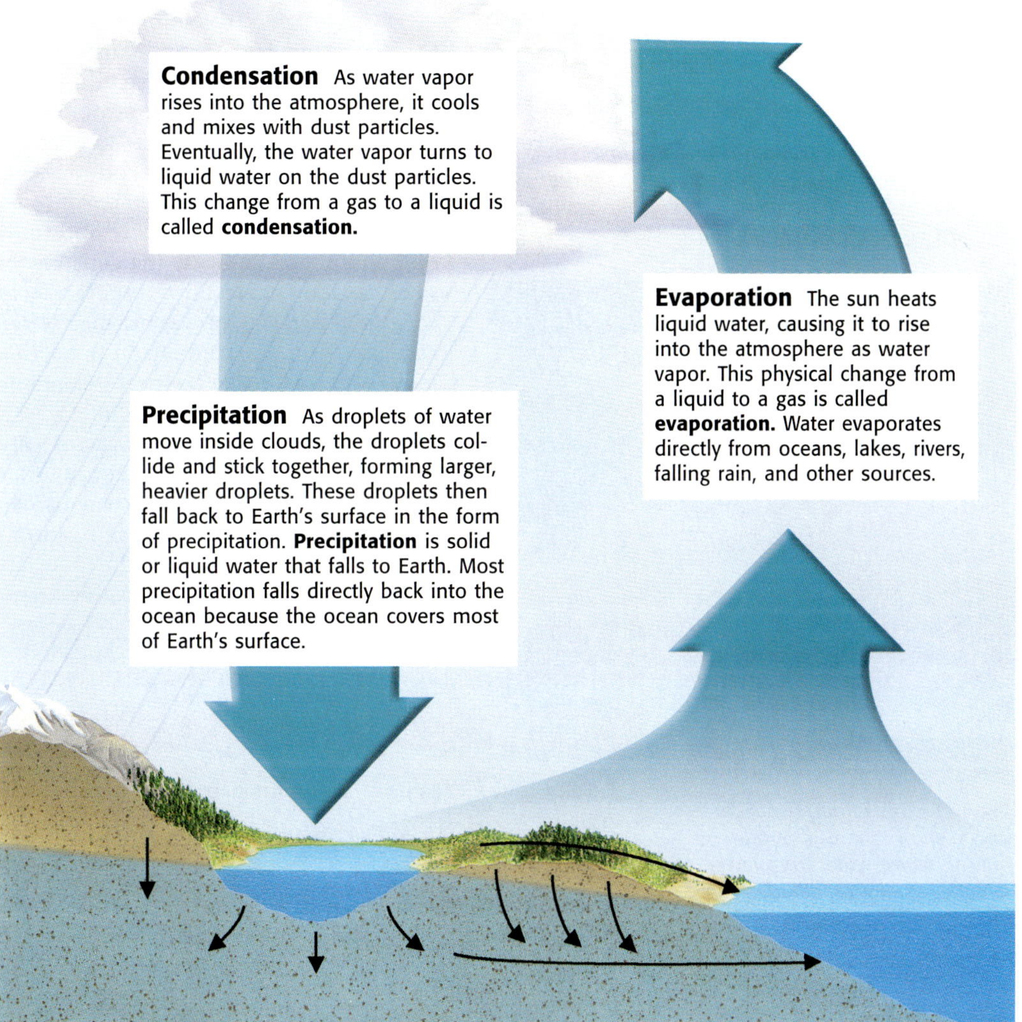

IS THAT A FACT!

Twelve thousand years ago much of Earth's water was frozen in glaciers and icecaps, and the Atlantic coast was miles farther out than it is today. Divers exploring the Chesapeake Bay found a mound of oyster shells—the remains of a long-ago picnic—almost 40 m below sea level!

Teaching Transparency 132
"The Ocean and the Water Cycle"

3 Extend

MEETING INDIVIDUAL NEEDS

Advanced Learners Divide the class into small groups, and provide each with a small dish or bowl, a plastic bag with twist-tie, and water. Challenge them to create a model demonstrating the water cycle. (Students might place the dish, filled with water, into the bag and seal it. As water evaporates from the dish, it will condense on the inner surface of the bag, eventually falling as "rain." Allow time for each group to explain its model to the class.)

GOING FURTHER

Challenge students to explain why the oceans are a crucial influence on the world's weather. (The oceans receive and absorb a large portion of the sun's energy. This energy raises the temperature of the oceans, which influences the atmosphere. Winds create currents, which carry warm water to colder areas, and vice versa, affecting local climates. Finally, solar energy evaporates an enormous amount of sea water, which eventually returns to Earth as precipitation.)

About 3,000 years ago, Greek maps of the world had the Mediterranean Sea in the center of a flat world. Oceans surrounded the lands around the Mediterranean Sea. Ask students: Why do you think the Greeks drew the Mediterranean Sea at the center of their maps? (Their known world centered around it.)

In what ways were their maps considered accurate? (The Greek maps had fairly accurate details of local coastlines and topography.)

4 Close

MISCONCEPTION ALERT

Sea level is not the same worldwide. Tides alter the ocean's depth constantly. Pacific Ocean trade winds blow westward, causing the ocean level to be about a half meter higher on the western side of the Pacific. Sea level is also higher at the equator than at the poles because the warm equatorial waters expand and the centrifugal force of Earth's rotation causes the middle of the planet to bulge.

Quiz

1. How is the global ocean divided, and what are the divisions? (It is divided by the continents into four main oceans, the Pacific, the Atlantic, the Indian, and the Arctic.)
2. How do scientists think the oceans are likely to change in the future? (They predict that the oceans will change in size and shape as the continents move apart.)

Alternative Assessment

Encourage students to examine the illustration on page 333. Have them prepare a timeline detailing the history of Earth's oceans. Challenge students to predict how the oceans will change during the next 150 million years. Students can illustrate their timelines with drawings of each stage of Earth's history.

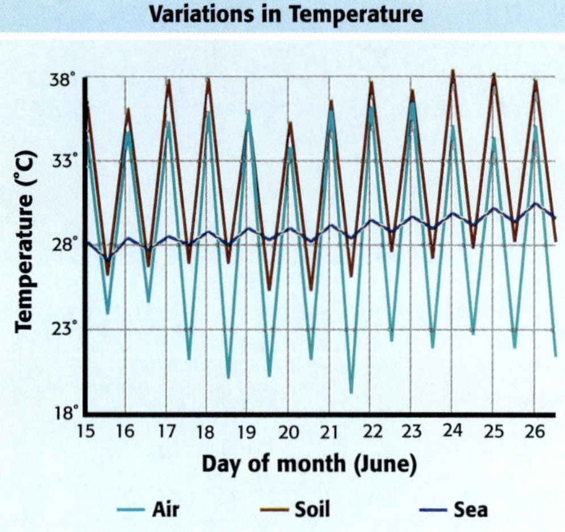

Figure 4 *This chart compares the fluctuation of the soil and air temperatures in Castle Hayne, North Carolina, with the fluctuation of the ocean temperature just off North Carolina's coast.*

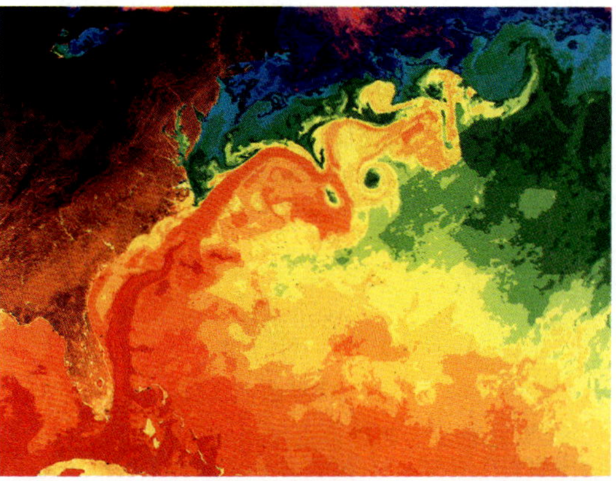

Figure 5 *This infrared satellite image shows the Gulf Stream moving warm water from lower latitudes to higher latitudes.*

A Global Thermostat

The ocean plays a vital role in maintaining conditions favorable for life on Earth. Perhaps the most important function of the ocean is to absorb and retain heat from sunlight. This function regulates temperatures in the atmosphere.

As you can see in **Figure 4,** the ocean absorbs and releases heat much more slowly than dry land does. If it were not for this function of the ocean, the average air temperature on Earth would vary from above 100°C during the day to below –100°C at night. In addition to causing this major temperature fluctuation, the rapid exchange of heat between the atmosphere and the Earth's surface would cause sudden changes in weather and violent weather patterns. Life as we know it could not exist with these unstable conditions.

The ocean also regulates temperatures on a more local scale. At the equator, the sun's rays are more direct, which causes equatorial waters to be warmer than waters at higher latitudes. Currents in the oceans move water, as well as the heat it contains, around the Earth, as shown in **Figure 5.** This circulation of warm water causes some coastal lands to have warmer climates than they would have without the currents. The British Isles, for example, have a warmer climate than most regions at the same latitude because of the warm water of the Gulf Stream.

REVIEW

1. Why is the ocean an important part of the water cycle?
2. Between which two steps of the water cycle does the ocean fit?
3. **Making Inferences** Explain why St. Louis, Missouri, has colder winters and warmer summers than San Francisco, California, even though the two cities are at about the same latitude.

338

Answers to Review

1. The ocean is an important part of the water cycle because nearly all of Earth's water is found in the ocean.
2. The ocean fits between precipitation and evaporation in the water cycle.
3. San Francisco is on the coast of the Pacific Ocean. Because the coastal waters absorb and slowly release heat from sunlight, San Francisco has less severe temperature fluctuations. St. Louis, however, is far from the ocean and does not receive heat from it. Even though St. Louis is at about the same latitude as San Francisco, not having the ocean nearby contributes to much more severe temperature fluctuations in St. Louis.

Section 1 Review–California Standards: PE/ATE 4a, 4d

2

The Ocean Floor

NEW TERMS

continental shelf
continental slope
continental rise
abyssal plain
mid-ocean ridge
rift valley
seamount
ocean trench

OBJECTIVES

- Identify the two major regions of the ocean floor.
- Classify subdivisions and features of the two major regions of the ocean floor.
- Describe technologies for studying the ocean floor.

What lies at the bottom of the ocean? How deep is the ocean? These are questions that were once unanswerable. But humans have learned a lot about the ocean floor, especially in the last few decades. Using state-of-the-art technology, scientists have discovered a wide variety of landforms on the ocean floor. Scientists have also determined accurate depths for almost the entire ocean floor.

Exploring the Ocean Floor

One of the ways scientists are learning more about the ocean floor is by exploring it. You probably already know that most humans who explore the subsurface ocean do so in submarines. But some parts of the ocean are so deep that humans must use special underwater vessels to travel there.

Perhaps the most familiar underwater vessel used by scientists is a minisub called *Alvin. Alvin* is a 7 m long vessel that can reach some of the deepest parts of the ocean. Scientists have used *Alvin* for many underwater missions, including searches for sunken ships, the recovery of a lost hydrogen bomb, and explorations of landforms on the sea floor.

Although the use of *Alvin* has enabled scientists to make some amazing discoveries, scientists are developing new vessels for exploration of the deep ocean. One modern vessel in ocean technology is an underwater airplane called *Deep Flight,* shown in **Figure 6.** This vessel moves through the water much like an airplane moves through the air. Future models of *Deep Flight* will be designed to transport pilots to the deepest part of the ocean, which is more than 11,000 m deep.

Turn to page 362 to meet the most famous underwater explorer who ever lived.

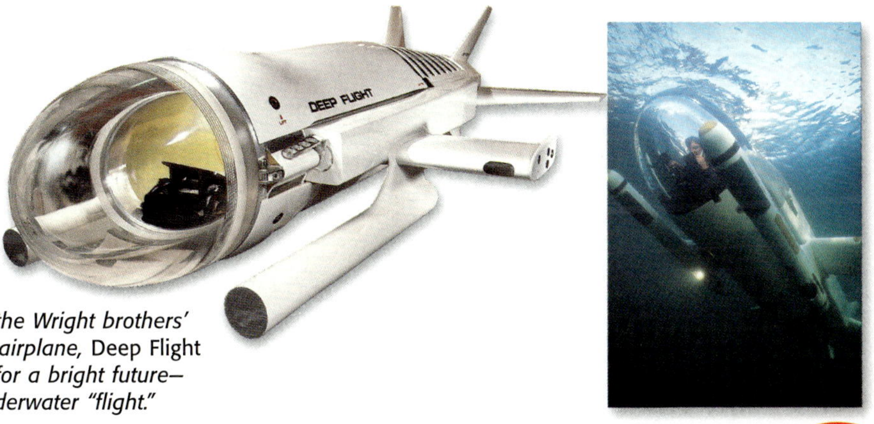

Figure 6 *Like the Wright brothers' first successful airplane,* Deep Flight *sets the stage for a bright future—this time in underwater "flight."*

SECTION 2

Focus

The Ocean Floor

In this section, students learn about the regional divisions of the ocean floor and the geographic features of each division. They learn how technology has facilitated exploration of the ocean floor, and they learn about the methods used to survey the ocean floor, including sonar and satellites.

Bellringer

Before students read this section, have them explore their ideas about the ocean floor by telling them to pretend they have walked off the edge of North America and into the depths of the Atlantic Ocean. As they walk along the ocean floor toward Europe, what would they see? Have each student make a drawing of the ocean floor that he or she would see along the way. Sheltered English

1 Motivate

DISCUSSION

It has been said that scientists know more about the surface of the moon than about the ocean floor. Most of what scientists know about the ocean floor comes from sonar reading and sample dredging. Ask students what kinds of technology would help scientists learn more about the deep-ocean floor.

Directed Reading Worksheet 13 Section 2

IS THAT A FACT!

The same explorer who led the first voyage around the world also attempted to determine the depth of the ocean. In 1520, Ferdinand Magellan weighted a 370 m rope with lead, and lowered it into the ocean. Unfortunately, his rope was not long enough to reach the ocean floor. It was not until 1773 that a successful measurement was made. Using Magellan's techniques, explorers found that the depth of the ocean near Norway is about 1,250 m.

Section 2–California Standards: PE/ATE 1, 1a, 1e, 2a, 4a, 7, 7f; LabBook: 7, 7b, 7c, 7e

2 Teach

PG 538

Probing the Depths

CONNECT TO PHYSICAL SCIENCE

To show how water pressure changes with depth, take a milk carton and punch three holes in its side: one near the top, one halfway down the side, and one near (but not at) the bottom. Put one piece of tape over all three holes, and fill the carton with water. Remove the tape quickly. Have students observe the streams of water. Ask them to explain what they are seeing.

(The water stream at the bottom of the carton shot out the farthest, with the greatest force. This is because the water above exerted pressure on the water at the bottom of the carton.)

MATH and MORE

Water pressure increases with depth. For every 10 m of depth, the pressure increases by 1 atmosphere (atm). For example, at a depth of 10 m, the pressure is 2 atm, or twice the pressure of the atmosphere at sea level. Ask students:

What is the pressure at 20 m? (3 atm)

50 m? (6 atm)

100 m? (11 atm)

What is the pressure at the bottom of the Mariana Trench? (greater than 1200 atm)

Math Skills Worksheet 3 "Multiplying Whole Numbers"

LabBook

Want to survey the ocean floor? Turn to page 538 in the LabBook to bring the ocean floor to your desktop.

Revealing the Ocean Floor

What if you were an explorer assigned to map uncharted areas on the planet? You might think there were not many uncharted areas left because most of the land had already been explored. But what about the bottom of the ocean? Most of the Earth's surface is hidden by water. What if you could operate *Deep Flight*? You would have a fish's eye view of the land under the ocean. What would it look like? You might think you would see a huge empty bowl, but in fact you would see the world's longest mountain chain and canyons deeper than the Grand Canyon.

As you began your descent into the underwater realm, you would notice that the land under the ocean is divided into two major regions—the *continental margin,* which is made of continental crust, and the *deep-ocean basin,* which is made of oceanic crust. It may help to imagine the ocean as a giant swimming pool; the continental margin is the shallow end and slope of the pool, and the deep-ocean basin is the deep end of the pool. **Figure 7** shows how these two regions are subdivided.

Figure 7 *The continental margin is subdivided into three depth zones, and the deep-ocean basin consists of one depth zone with several features.*

340

Q: What lies on the bottom of the ocean and trembles?

A: a nervous wreck

Underwater Real Estate As you can see, the continental margin is subdivided into the continental shelf, the continental slope, and the continental rise based on depth and changes in slope. The deep-ocean basin consists of the abyssal plain, with features such as mid-ocean ridges, rift valleys, and ocean trenches that form near the boundaries of Earth's *tectonic plates*. On parts of the abyssal plain that are not near plate boundaries, thousands of seamounts are found on the ocean floor.

Explore

To get an idea of how deep parts of the ocean are, use an encyclopedia to find out how deep the Grand Canyon is. Compare this depth with that of the Mariana Trench, which is more than 11,000 m deep!

Self-Check

How do the locations of rift valleys and ocean trenches differ? *(See page 564 to check your answer.)*

Mid-ocean ridges are mountain chains formed where *tectonic plates* pull apart. This pulling motion creates cracks in the ocean floor called *rift zones.* Directly below rift zones, molten rock called *magma* rises from below the crust and erupts through the cracks as *lava.* The lava then cools as it enters the water, becoming new oceanic crust. As plates on either side of rift zones continue to pull apart, more magma rises to fill in the spaces. Heat from the magma causes the crust on either side of the rifts to expand, forming the ridges.

Seamounts are individual mountains of volcanic material that are scattered across the abyssal plain. They form where magma pushes its way through or between tectonic plates. If a seamount builds up above sea level, it becomes a volcanic island. The Hawaiian Islands formed this way.

Ocean trenches are seemingly bottomless crevices in the deep-ocean basin. These narrow features sometimes reach thousands of kilometers in length and are the deepest places on Earth. Ocean trenches form where one oceanic plate is forced underneath a continental plate or another oceanic plate.

As mountains build up, a **rift valley** forms between them in the rift zone.

341

Answer to Self-Check

Rift valleys form where tectonic plates pull apart, and ocean trenches form where one oceanic plate is forced underneath a continental plate or another oceanic plate.

CROSS-DISCIPLINARY FOCUS

Art Draw students' attention to **Figure 7** and have them draw, label, and color their own picture of the depth zones of the ocean floor. Point out the canyon in the continental slope. This is a *submarine canyon.* Most of the sediment that makes up the continental rise travels down from the continental shelf through submarine canyons. Be sure that students have divided the continental margin into the continental shelf, continental slope, and continental rise. They should identify the features of the deep-ocean basin as mid-ocean ridges, seamounts, rift valleys, and ocean trenches. In addition, students can indicate the temperature of the ocean water at each depth by using different colors. Sheltered English

Homework

Concept Mapping Remind students that volcanic seamounts that rise above the ocean surface become volcanic islands. Have them research other ways islands form. Have students prepare a concept map of the different ways that islands form. They should find that some islands are formed by the growth of coral; some are formed by wind, longshore currents, and waves (barrier islands); and some are continental islands (Great Britain, Madagascar).

3 Extend

Reteaching

Have students review **Figure 7**, which shows zones and features of the ocean floor. Ask students to choose any two zones or features and describe them in their own words. If describing features, students should include how the features form. Students should also tell why they like each feature or zone. Sheltered English

Cross-Disciplinary Focus

Language Arts Tell students that the 1870 publication of *Twenty Thousand Leagues Under the Sea,* by Jules Verne, revived an interest in undersea exploration. Have students read sections of Verne's book aloud in class. Point out that the story inspired engineers to solve the problems plaguing submarines, enabling scientists to reach greater depths in their exploration of the sea.

Answers to MATHBREAK

1. D = 1,500 m
2. D = 10,500 m
3. D = 3,975 m

Explain why the constant $\frac{1}{2}$ is in the equation in the MATHBREAK. The time represented by t is the two-way travel time of sound waves. Without using the constant $\frac{1}{2}$, the equation would give the distance to the ocean floor and back to the ship instead of the distance to the floor only.

MathBreak

Depths of the Deep

The depths in a sea profile are calculated using the following simple formula:

$$D = \frac{1}{2}t \times v$$

D is the depth of the ocean floor, t is the time it takes for the sound to reach the bottom and return to the surface, and v equals the speed of sound in water (1,500 m/s). Calculate D for the following three parts of the ocean floor:

1. a mid-ocean ridge (t = 2 s)
2. an ocean trench (t = 14 s)
3. an abyssal plain (t = 5.3 s)

Viewing the Ocean Floor from Above

In spite of the great success of underwater exploration, sending scientists into deep water is still risky. Fortunately, there are ways to survey the underwater realm from the surface and from high above in space. Read on to learn about two technologies—sonar and satellites—that enable scientists to study the ocean floor without going below the surface.

Seeing by Sonar *Sonar*, which stands for "sound navigation and ranging," is a technology based on the echo-ranging behavior of bats. Scientists use sonar to determine the ocean's depth by sending high-frequency sound pulses from a ship down into the ocean. The sound travels through the water, bounces off the ocean floor, and returns to the ship. The deeper the water is, the longer the round trip takes. Scientists then calculate the depth by multiplying half the travel time by the speed of sound in water (about 1,500 m/s). This process is shown in the illustration below.

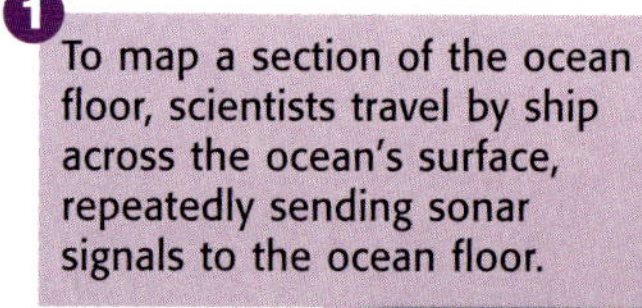

1 To map a section of the ocean floor, scientists travel by ship across the ocean's surface, repeatedly sending sonar signals to the ocean floor.

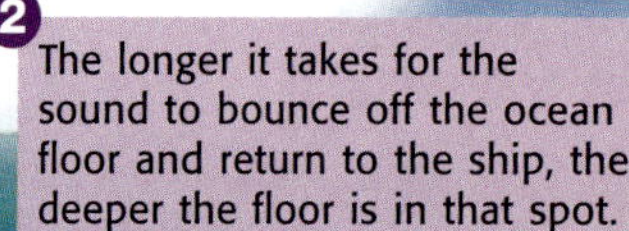

2 The longer it takes for the sound to bounce off the ocean floor and return to the ship, the deeper the floor is in that spot.

3 Scientists make a sea profile like this one by plotting the different depths that they discover using these sonar signals. A *sea profile* is basically a map of the ocean floor showing its depth variations.

342

Teaching Transparency 133 "How Sonar Works"

Math Skills Worksheet 15 "Multiplying and Dividing Fractions"

internetconnect

TOPIC: The Ocean Floor
GO TO: www.scilinks.org
***sci*LINKS NUMBER:** HSTE310

Weird Science

Though many people know that whales and dolphins communicate by sound, few are aware that shrimp do the same thing. They emit a sound similar to that of bacon frying to locate one another and food sources!

Oceanography via Satellite In the 1970s, scientists began studying Earth from satellites in orbit around the Earth. In 1972, *Landsat 1* orbited the Earth and sent back information about Earth's natural resources. In 1978, scientists launched the satellite *Seasat.* This satellite focused on the ocean, sending images back to Earth that allowed scientists to measure the direction and speed of ocean currents and detect changes in the polar icecaps.

Geosat, once a top-secret military satellite, has been used to measure slight changes in the height of the ocean's surface. Different underwater features, such as mountains and trenches, affect the height of the water above them. For example, the height of the ocean surface is higher over mountains than over the abyssal plains, thus reflecting the underwater topography of the ocean floor. Scientists measure the different heights of the ocean surface and use the measurements to make highly detailed maps of the ocean floor. As illustrated in **Figure 8,** oceanographers can make maps that cover a lot more territory by using satellites than by using ship-based sonar readings.

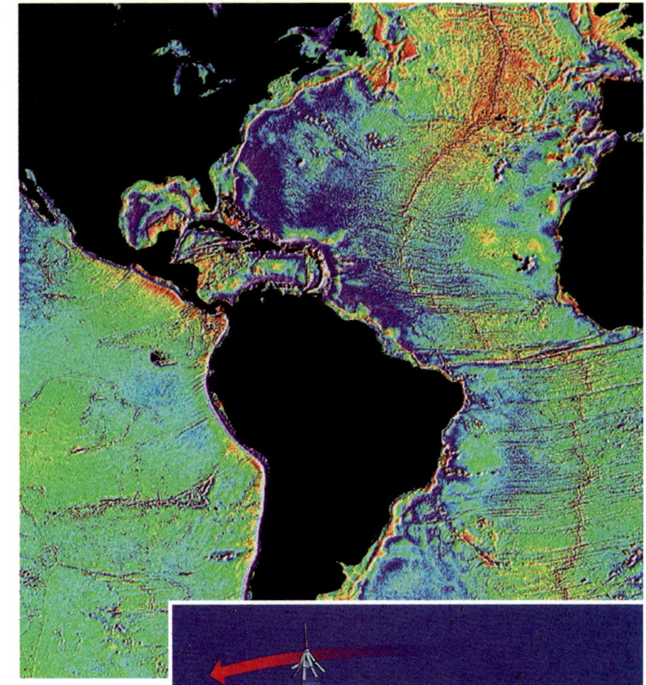

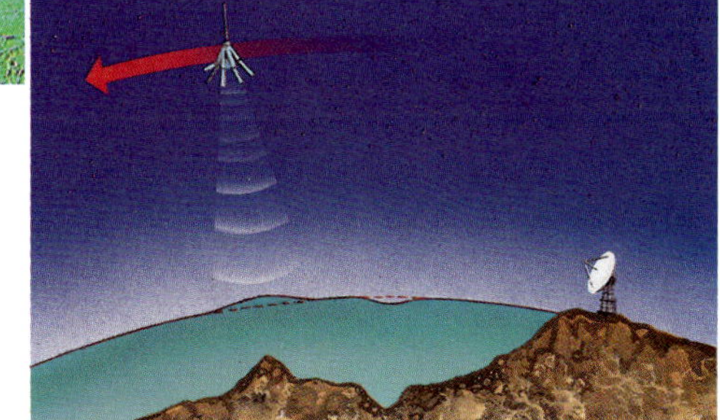

Figure 8 *The map above was generated by satellite measurements of different heights of the ocean surface.*

REVIEW

1. Name the two major regions of the ocean floor.
2. List the subdivisions of the continental margin.
3. List three technologies for studying the ocean floor, and explain how they are used.
4. **Interpreting Graphics** What part of the ocean floor would the sea profile at right represent?

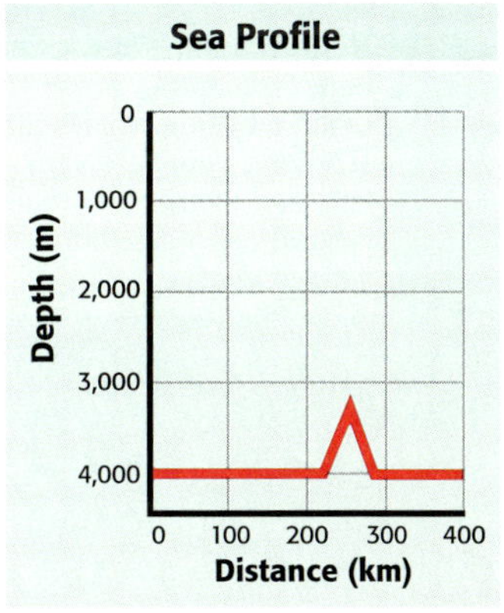

4 Close

Quiz

1. Which features of the abyssal plain form at the boundaries of tectonic plates? (mid-ocean ridges, rift valleys, ocean trenches)
2. How is the depth of the ocean measured? (It is measured using sonar. Scientists calculate the depth by multiplying half the time it takes a sound wave to hit the ocean floor and return to the surface by the speed of sound in water.)

ALTERNATIVE ASSESSMENT

Encourage students to imagine that they are oceanographers on a deep-sea mission aboard *Alvin.* Have them work in groups to make a model of the ocean floor, including all the features from this section. The model can be a cross-section similar to **Figure 7** or a view from above.

Sheltered English

Answers to Review

1. the continental margin and the deep-ocean basin
2. the continental shelf, continental slope, and continental rise
3. Answers may include underwater vessels, such as *Alvin* and *Deep Flight,* sonar, and satellites. (Some technologies not mentioned in the text are acceptable.) Scientists visit the ocean floor in underwater vessels. Sonar is used to determine the ocean's depth and the topography of the ocean floor. Satellites are used to measure the direction and speed of ocean currents, detect changes in the polar icecaps, and measure changes in the height of the ocean surface that reflect the topography of the ocean floor.
4. The abyssal plain; the sharp rise and fall in the profile represents a seamount or part of a mid-ocean ridge.

Section 2 Review–California Standards: PE/ATE 1, 1a

SECTION 3

Focus

Life in the Ocean

This section introduces a system for classifying marine organisms based on where they live and how they move. Students also learn to describe ecological zones of the ocean and give examples of organisms inhabiting each zone.

Bellringer

Before they read this section, have students imagine they are marine biologists who must classify marine life into three groups. Challenge them to identify the criteria they would use in their classification systems.

1 Motivate

GROUP ACTIVITY

Classifying Divide the class into small groups. Ask them to classify as many items in the classroom as they can based on the following categories:

- height at which the items are located
- what the items are used for

Teaching Transparency 134 "The Three Groups of Marine Life"

Directed Reading Worksheet 13 Section 3

3

Life in the Ocean

NEW TERMS

plankton
nekton
benthos
benthic environment
pelagic environment

OBJECTIVES

- Identify and describe the three groups of marine organisms.
- Identify and describe the benthic and pelagic environments.
- Classify the zones of the benthic and pelagic environments.

The ocean contains a wide variety of life-forms, many of which we know little about. Trying to study them can be quite a challenge for scientists. To make things easier, scientists classify marine organisms into three main groups. Scientists also divide the ocean into two main environments based on the types of organisms that live in them. These two main environments are further subdivided into ecological zones based on locations of different organisms.

The Three Groups of Marine Life

The three main groups of marine life are plankton, nekton, and benthos. Marine organisms are placed into one of these three groups according to where they live and how they move. Carefully examine the figure below to understand the differences between these groups.

Phytoplankton

Zooplankton

Plankton are organisms that float at or near the ocean's surface. Most plankton are microscopic. Plankton are subdivided into two groups—those that are plantlike *(phytoplankton)* and those that are animal-like *(zooplankton)*.

Nekton are the free-swimming organisms of the ocean. Types of nekton include whales, dolphins, sea lions, countless varieties of fish, and many other mammals. Nekton are most abundant in surface waters.

Benthos are organisms that live on or in the ocean floor. They live in mud, sand, and rock. There are many types of benthos, such as crabs, sea stars, worms, coral, sponges, seaweed, and clams.

344

SCIENTISTS AT ODDS

Before the late 1870s, scientists widely believed the "azoic theory" of James Forbes and Alexander Agassiz. This theory argued that no life existed below the shallow depths of the oceans. Sir Wyville Thomson, one of Darwin's shipmates on the HMS *Challenger,* disputed this theory, citing examples brought up from the ocean depths during the HMS *Challenger* voyage. He published his results in *Depths of the Sea,* the first general textbook on oceanography.

The Benthic Environment

In addition to being divided into zones based on depth, the ocean floor is divided into ecological zones based on where different types of benthos live. These zones are grouped into one major marine environment—the benthic environment. The **benthic environment,** or bottom environment, is the ocean floor and all the organisms that live on or in it.

Intertidal Zone The shallowest benthic zone, the *intertidal zone,* is located between the low-tide and high-tide limits. Twice a day, the intertidal zone transforms. As the tide flows in, the zone is covered with ocean water, and as the tide retreats, the intertidal zone is exposed to the air and sun.

Intertidal organisms must be able to live both underwater and on exposed land. Some organisms attach themselves to rocks and reefs to avoid being washed out to sea during low tide, as shown in **Figure 9.** Clams, oysters, barnacles, and crabs have tough shells that give them protection against strong waves during high tide and against harsh sunlight during low tide. Some animals can burrow in sand or between rocks. Plants such as seaweed have strong *holdfasts* (rootlike structures) that allow them to grow in this zone.

Coral reefs, found in shallow marine waters, have the largest concentration of life in the ocean. Layers of skeletons from animals called *corals* form the reefs, which are the largest animal structures on Earth. Many other organisms live on, around, and even in coral reefs.

Figure 9 *Organisms such as sea anemones and starfish attach themselves to rocks and reefs. These organisms must be able to survive wet and dry conditions.*

Sublittoral Zone The *sublittoral zone* begins where the intertidal zones ends, at the low-tide limit, and extends to the edge of the continental shelf. This benthic zone is more stable than the intertidal zone; the temperature, water pressure, and amount of sunlight remain fairly constant. Consequently, sublittoral organisms, such as corals, shown in **Figure 10,** do not have to cope with as much change as intertidal organisms. Although the sublittoral zone extends down 200 m below sea level, plants and most animals stay in the upper 100 m, where sunlight reaches the ocean floor.

Figure 10 *Corals, like many other types of organisms, can live in both the sublittoral zone and the intertidal zone. However, they are more common in the sublittoral zone.*

345

Writing Stories of mermaids and sea monsters abound in many different cultures. In some legends, mermaids were good and helped shipwrecked sailors. In others, mermaids lured ships and sailors into dangerous waters. Sea monsters, on the other hand, were always bad, sinking ships and killing sailors. Discuss with students why they think these legends were told. Have them research a legend and write one of their own.

2 Teach

READING STRATEGY

Mnemonics Ask students to create a mnemonic device that will remind them of the zones of the benthic environment. For example, they might write **I**sabel **S**ent **B**art **A**way from **H**ome to remind them that the zones are **I**ntertidal, **S**ublittoral, **B**athyal, **A**byssal, and **H**adal. Ask them to share their mnemonic devices with the class. Sheltered English

MISCONCEPTION ALERT

Many people think that rain forests produce most of Earth's oxygen. Actually, ocean phytoplankton are the most productive photosynthesizers on the planet.

Homework

Have students draw imaginary organisms that would live in all five of the benthic zones. Students should describe each plant or animal and explain its particular adaptations for living in that zone. Their drawings and descriptions should include the following:

- how they obtain food
- how they avoid predation
- how they withstand the water pressure and temperature at the depth where they live

Encourage students to share their drawings and explanations with the class. Sheltered English

3 Extend

COOPERATIVE LEARNING

Divide the class into groups of five, and provide each group with poster board and markers. Ask them to draw a cross-sectional illustration of the ocean and label the following features:

benthic environment, intertidal zone, sublittoral zone, bathyal zone, abyssal zone, hadal zone

Have each group member illustrate the organisms found in one of the five zones. (Each group should illustrate all of the five zones.) Instruct each group to elect a spokesperson to present the poster to the class.

RESEARCH

Have students select one of the benthic zones to investigate further. Ask them to focus on the adaptations that organisms living there have developed that enable them to exist in that zone. Students can present their findings in a concept map, poster, or comic book. Sheltered English

CONNECT TO LIFE SCIENCE

Because food is so scarce in the deeper parts of the ocean, its inhabitants have special adaptations to ensure their survival. Some gulper eels, for example, have huge jaws and elastic stomachs that allow them to eat fish larger than themselves. Show students photographs of some of these organisms, and use Teaching Transparency 32 to discuss the process of natural selection.

Teaching Transparency 32
"Natural Selection in Four Steps"
LINK TO LIFE SCIENCE

Figure 11 *Octopuses are one of the animals common to the bathyal zone.*

Bathyal Zone The *bathyal zone* extends from the edge of the continental shelf to the abyssal plain. The depth of this zone ranges from 200 m to 4,000 m below sea level. Because of the lack of sunlight at these depths, plant life is scarce in this part of the benthic environment. Animals in this zone include sponges, *brachiopods,* sea stars, *echinoids,* and octopuses, such as the one shown in **Figure 11.**

Figure 12 *Tube worms can tolerate higher temperatures than any other organism. These animals survive in water as hot as 81°C.*

Abyssal Zone No plants and very few animals live in the *abyssal zone*, which is on the abyssal plain. Among the abyssal animal types are crabs, sponges, worms, and sea cucumbers. Many of these organisms, such as the tube worms shown in **Figure 12,** live around hot-water vents called *black smokers*. The abyssal zone can reach 6,000 m in depth. Scientists know very little about this benthic zone because it is so deep and dark.

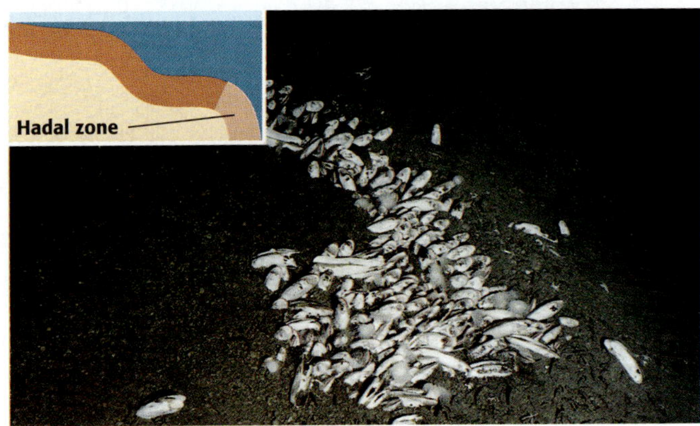

Figure 13 *These clams are one of the few types of organisms known to live in the hadal zone.*

Hadal Zone The deepest benthic zone is the *hadal zone*. This zone consists of the floor of the ocean trenches and any organisms found there. Scientists know even less about the hadal zone than they do about the abyssal zone. So far, scientists have discovered a type of sponge, a few species of worms, and a type of clam, which is shown in **Figure 13.**

346

Q: What's the best way to catch a fish?

A: Have someone throw it to you.

The Pelagic Environment

The **pelagic environment,** or water environment, includes the entire volume of water in the ocean and the marine organisms that live above the ocean floor. There are two major zones in the pelagic environment—the *neritic zone* and the *oceanic zone.*

Figure 14 *Many marine mammals, such as this dolphin, live in the neritic zone.*

Neritic Zone The neritic zone includes the volume of water that covers the continental shelf. This warm, shallow pelagic zone contains the largest concentration of marine life. This is due in part to an abundance of sunlight and in part to the many benthos below the neritic zone that serve as a food supply. Fish, plankton, and marine mammals, such as the one in **Figure 14,** are just a few of the animal groups found here. Most seafood is harvested from the neritic zone.

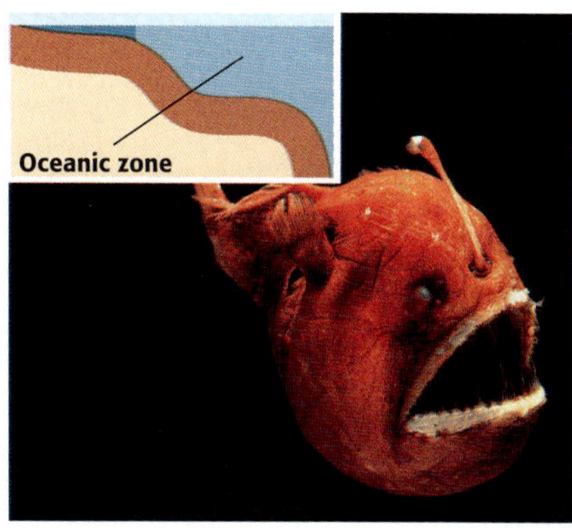

Figure 15 *The anglerfish lives deep in the oceanic zone.*

Oceanic Zone The oceanic zone includes the volume of water that covers the entire sea floor except for the continental shelf. In the deeper parts of the oceanic zone, the water temperature is colder and the pressure is much greater than in the neritic zone. Also, organisms are more spread out in the oceanic zone than in the neritic zone. While many of the same organisms found in the neritic zone cross the vast expanse of the upper regions, some strange animals lurk in the darker depths. For example, the anglerfish, shown in **Figure 15,** is a tricky predator that uses a natural lure attached to its head to attract prey. And the *Gigantura,* a fish with long, tubular eyes and flexible skin, can expand its body to swallow animals larger than itself! Other animals in the deeper parts of this zone include giant squids and some whale species.

REVIEW

1. List and briefly describe the three main groups of marine organisms.
2. Name the two ocean environments. List the zones of each environment.
3. **Making Predictions** How would the ocean's ecological zones change if sea level dropped 300 m?

CONNECT TO LIFE SCIENCE

Sea skaters are the only insects known to live directly on the surface of the open ocean. The insects have waxy hairs on their feet that repel water and help them travel on the surface of the water. They are predators that hunt prey swimming beneath the surface by spearing them with sharp mouth parts. Ask students to think about why other insects do not live in the open ocean.

4 Close

Quiz

1. Why do scientists know little about the abyssal and hadal zones? (Because these zones are so deep and dark, scientists know very little about them.)
2. Where do most marine organisms live? (in the neritic zone)

Alternative Assessment

Challenge students to write science-fiction stories about exploring the abyssal zone of the benthic environment. Have them describe the difficulties of exploring that zone, and encourage them to use their imagination to describe creatures they might find there.

Answers to Review

1. plankton, nekton, and benthos; plankton float at or near the surface, nekton swim freely, and benthos live on or in the ocean floor.
2. the benthic environment and the pelagic environment; the zones of the benthic environment are the intertidal, sublittoral zone, bathyal, abyssal, and hadal zones; the zones of the pelagic environment are the neritic and oceanic zones.
3. Answers will vary. If sea level dropped 300 m, the shoreline would move down to the continental slope. This would cause an overall shift of ecological zones as many marine organisms are restricted to certain depths.

Reinforcement Worksheet 13 "The Ocean's Environment"

Interactive Explorations CD-ROM "Sea Sick"

Section 3 Review–California Standards: PE/ATE 5c, 5e

Section 4

Focus

Resources from the Ocean

In this section, students learn about the ocean's living and nonliving resources, focusing on the methods used to obtain them. Students are asked to consider the importance of the ocean's resources and steps that have been taken to prevent overfishing.

Bellringer

Before they read this section, write the following sentences on the board and challenge students to identify four items or activities that involve resources that can be obtained from the sea.

"Tabitha drove her car to the market to buy a tuna steak for dinner. When she got home, she poured herself a glass of water, then fired up her gas grill, and cooked the tuna."

1) Motivate

Group Activity

Divide the class into small groups. Have them imagine a world with no ocean resources. Ask them to brainstorm to come up with a list of activities that would no longer be possible. Examples might include eating certain types of seafood, shipping goods by sea, or deep-sea diving. Have each group share its list with the class and discuss the importance of ocean resources.

4

Resources from the Ocean

NEW TERMS

desalination

OBJECTIVES

- List two methods of harvesting the ocean's living resources.
- List nonliving resources in the ocean.
- Describe the ocean's energy resources.

The ocean offers a seemingly endless supply of resources. Food, raw materials, energy, and drinkable water all are harvested from the ocean. And there are probably undiscovered resources in unexplored regions of the ocean. As human populations have grown, however, the demand for these resources has increased while the availability has decreased.

Living Resources

People have been harvesting marine plants and animals for food for thousands of years. Many civilizations formed in coastal regions that were rich enough in marine life to support growing human populations. Read on to learn how humans harvest marine life today.

Fishing the Ocean Harvesting food from the ocean is a multibillion-dollar industry. Of all the seafood taken from the ocean, fish are the most abundant. Almost 75 million tons of fish is harvested each year. With improved technology, such as sonar and drift nets, fishermen have become better at locating and taking fish from the ocean. **Figure 16** illustrates how drift nets are used. In recent years, many people have become concerned that we are overfishing the ocean—taking more fish than can be naturally replaced. Also, a few years ago, the public became aware that animals other than fish, especially dolphins and turtles, were accidentally being caught in drift nets. Today the fishing industry is making efforts to prevent overfishing and damage to other wildlife from drift nets.

Figure 16 *Drift nets are fishing nets that cover kilometers of ocean. Fishermen can harvest entire schools of fish in one drift net.*

348

Directed Reading Worksheet 13 Section 4

IS THAT A FACT!

Modern factory ships not only catch fish but also process, package, and freeze them. In one day, these vessels can process about 600 tons of fish!

Section 4—California Standards: PE/ATE 6, 6a, 6b, 6c, 7, 7a, 7b, 7e

Farming the Ocean As overfishing reduces fish populations and laws regulating fishing become stricter, it is becoming more difficult to supply our demand for fish. To compensate for this, many ocean fish, such as salmon and turbot, are being captively bred in fish farms. Fish farming requires several holding ponds, each containing fish at a certain level of development. **Figure 17** shows a holding pond in a fish farm. When the fish are old enough, they are harvested and packaged for shipping.

Figure 17 *Consuming fish raised in a fish farm helps reduce the number of fish harvested from the ocean.*

Fish are not the only seafood harvested in a farmlike setting. Shrimp, oysters, crabs, and mussels are raised in enclosed areas near the shore. Mussels and oysters are grown attached to ropes, as shown in **Figure 18.** Huge nets line the nursery area, preventing the animals from being eaten by their natural predators.

Many species of algae, commonly known as seaweed, are also harvested from the ocean. For example, kelp, a seaweed that grows as much as 33 cm a day, is harvested and used as a thickener in jellies, ice cream, and similar products that have a smooth, gel-like composition. The next time you enjoy your favorite chocolate-ripple ice cream, remember that without seaweed, it would be a runny mess! Seaweed is rich in protein, and several species of seaweed are staples of the Japanese diet. For example, the rolled varieties of sushi, a Japanese dish, are wrapped in seaweed.

Figure 18 *In addition to fish, there are many other types of seafood, such as these mussels, that are raised in farms.*

349

2 Teach

Reading Strategy

Prediction Guide Before students read the passage about living ocean resources, ask them to write an answer for the following question:

What are two problems you think might be associated with fishing the oceans? (Sample answers: overfishing, pollution, accidentally catching other animals in drift nets)

Debate

Fishing the Ocean Lead students in a debate about the costs and benefits of fishing the oceans. Fish are an important source of protein, but overfishing threatens entire ecosystems. Also, fishing is a major source of employment in the world. But many scientists agree that strong restrictions limiting fishing are important. Help students research and debate these issues, and discuss alternatives to traditional fishing, such as fish farming.

Real-World Connection

In the United States, more than 50 percent of the population lives and works within 80 km of the sea, even though coastal areas account for only 11 percent of the nation's land area.

Science Bloopers

Because starfish eat oysters, oyster fishermen have always battled starfish. In this war, when fishermen pulled up a starfish with a clump of oysters, they cut up the starfish and tossed it overboard. Then scientists pointed out that starfish can regenerate from their parts and that by cutting them up, the fishermen were actually making more starfish!

2 Teach, continued

Real-World Connection

Have students make a list of all their daily activities that rely on petroleum. Answers might include taking a hot shower, using a hair dryer, cooking breakfast, driving to school, turning on lights, or washing and drying clothes. Allow time for students to share their lists with classmates, then encourage them to brainstorm about ways they might reduce their reliance on fossil fuels.

Group Activity

Divide the class into small groups, and encourage each to select a different ocean resource. Have them work together to write a public service announcement designed to convince the public of the resource's value to people. Have them include ways people can help conserve the resource. Ask students to present their announcements to the class.

Cross-Disciplinary Focus

Language Arts Read Samuel Taylor Coleridge's "The Rime of the Ancient Mariner" in class. Discuss the lines:

> "Water, water, everywhere,
> Nor any drop to drink."

Ask students:

- Where does most drinking water come from? (lakes, rivers, underground)
- How can ocean water be made drinkable? (by desalination)

You may wish to revisit this poem as you discuss ocean pollution in the next section.

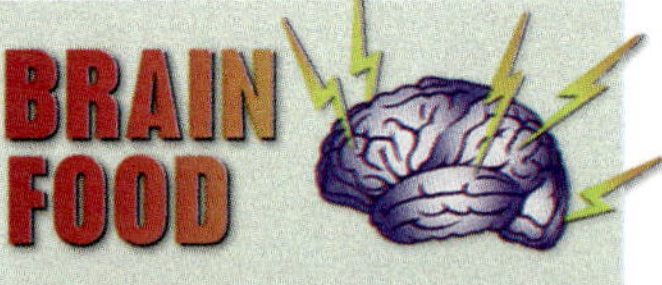

Did you know that the United States imports more oil than any other nation? Because oil is a nonrenewable resource, scientists continue to research alternatives to fossil fuels, such as solar energy and wind-generated electricity.

Nonliving Resources

Humans harvest many types of nonliving resources from the ocean. These resources provide raw materials, drinkable water, and energy for our expanding population. Some resources are easily obtained, while others are rare or difficult to harvest.

Oil and Natural Gas Modern civilization continues to be very dependent on oil and natural gas as major sources of energy. Oil and natural gas are *nonrenewable resources,* which means that they are used up faster than they can be replenished naturally. However, drilling for oil and gas on the ocean floor as well as on land is still profitable. Much of Earth's oil and gas began to form beneath the sea millions of years ago when dead organisms on the ocean floor were covered by sediment. This organic matter was crushed and buried deep beneath the surface by the overlying sediment. Heat was generated during this process, and the animal and plant matter eventually turned into oil or natural gas. These two resources are trapped under layers of impermeable rock. Petroleum engineers must drill through this rock in order to reach the resources.

But how do petroleum engineers know where to drill? Ships with seismic equipment are used for this purpose. Special devices send powerful pulses of sound to the ocean floor. The pulses travel through the water and penetrate the rocks below. The pulses are then reflected back toward the ship, where they are recorded by electronic equipment and analyzed by a computer. The computer readings indicate how rock layers are arranged below the ocean floor. Petroleum geologists look for readings that indicate arrangements that might trap oil and gas, such as the reading in **Figure 19.** They then recommend drilling in a spot that could contain a lot of oil or gas.

Figure 19 *Petroleum geologists look at seismic readings to decide where on the ocean floor to drill for oil and gas. This reading shows some promise!*

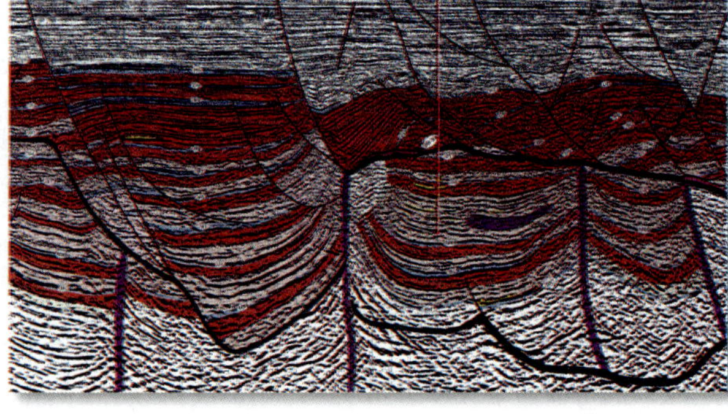

Homework

Research Help students research the dangers and drawbacks of petroleum drilling and petroleum use. They should look for information about how heavily the world economy depends on petroleum products and why people should be finding cheap, reliable alternative fuels.

Fresh Water and Desalination In some areas of the world where fresh water is limited, people desalinate ocean water. **Desalination** is the process of evaporating sea water so that the water and the salt separate. As the water cools and condenses, it is collected and processed for human use. But desalination is not as simple as it sounds, and it is very costly. Countries with an adequate amount of annual rainfall rely on the fresh water provided by precipitation and therefore do not need costly desalination plants. But some countries located in arid regions of the world must build desalination plants to provide an adequate supply of fresh water. Saudi Arabia, located in the desert region of the Middle East, has one of the largest desalination plants in the world. Look at a world map, and try to identify other areas that might depend on desalination.

Sea-Floor Minerals Scientists are very interested in mineral nodules that are lying on the ocean floor. These nodules are made mostly of manganese, which can be used to make certain types of steel. They also contain iron, copper, nickel, and cobalt. Other nodules are made of phosphates, which are used in making fertilizer.

Nodules are formed from dissolved substances in sea water that stick to solid objects, such as pebbles. As more substances stick to the coated pebble, a nodule begins to grow. Manganese nodules range from the size of a marble to the size of a soccer ball. The nodules were discovered nearly 130 years ago when HMS *Challenger,* a British exploration ship, dredged them up while exploring the Pacific Ocean. The photograph in **Figure 20** shows a number of nodules scattered across the ocean floor. It is believed that 15 percent of the ocean floor is covered with these nodules. However, they are located in the deeper parts of the ocean, and mining them is costly and difficult.

How Much Fresh Water Is There?

1. Fill a large **beaker** with 1,000 mL of **water.** This represents all the water on Earth.
2. Carefully pour 970 mL from the beaker into a **graduated cylinder.** This represents the amount of water in the ocean.
3. Pour another 20 mL from the beaker into a **second graduated cylinder.** This represents the amount of water frozen in icecaps and glaciers.
4. Pour another 5 mL into a **third graduated cylinder.** This represents nonconsumable water on land.
5. Take a look at the leftover water. This represents Earth's supply of fresh water.

Put freshwater problems on ice! Turn to page 363 to find out how.

Figure 20 *These manganese nodules could make you wealthy if you knew an affordable way to mine them.*

3 Extend

QuickLab

MATERIALS

For Each Student:
- large beaker
- three graduated cylinders

CONNECT TO PHYSICAL SCIENCE

Explain that the mineral nodules shown in **Figure 20** form much like pearls or rock candy—a solid precipitates out of a chemical solution and adheres to a particle. This particle could be nearly anything—a small pebble or even a piece of shell. The nodules grow larger in a process called accretion as more solids precipitate out of the solution. Students could model accretion by making rock candy with a supersaturated sugar solution and a piece of string.

Homework

Graphing Help students use references to find out how much of the world's energy needs are met by the following:

oil, natural gas, coal, tidal energy, wave energy, hydroelectric energy, solar energy, and wind energy

Have students prepare pie charts or bar graphs of their findings.

WEIRD SCIENCE

Methane exists in tremendous amounts in seafloor sediments, but it doesn't exist as a gas. It exists as an ice called *methane hydrate*. The conditions are right for methane hydrate to exist at depths greater than 500 m below sea level. These methane deposits are estimated to be twice as abundant as all natural gas, petroleum, and coal deposits combined. In the future, methane hydrate may be a valuable energy resource, but engineers have not yet discovered how to mine it.

internetconnect

SCILINKS NSTA
TOPIC: Ocean Resources
GO TO: www.scilinks.org
***sci*LINKS NUMBER:** HSTE320

4 Close

Quiz

1. Explain some of the ecological risks of using drift nets. (Using drift nets can lead to overfishing, which depletes fish populations. Drift nets also accidentally trap other marine animals such as dolphins and turtles.)
2. What are nonrenewable resources? Give two examples. (Nonrenewable resources are resources that are used up faster than they can be replenished naturally. Natural gas and oil are nonrenewable resources.)
3. What is desalination, and why is it done? (Desalination is the process of evaporating sea water so that the water and the salt separate. Desalination provides fresh water for human use.)

Alternative Assessment

Challenge students to make drawings that demonstrate how tidal energy is harnessed. Encourage them to explain the process to the class, using their drawings as visual aids. Their drawings and explanations should reflect the understanding that water must rush through a narrow channel and move turbines to generate electricity.

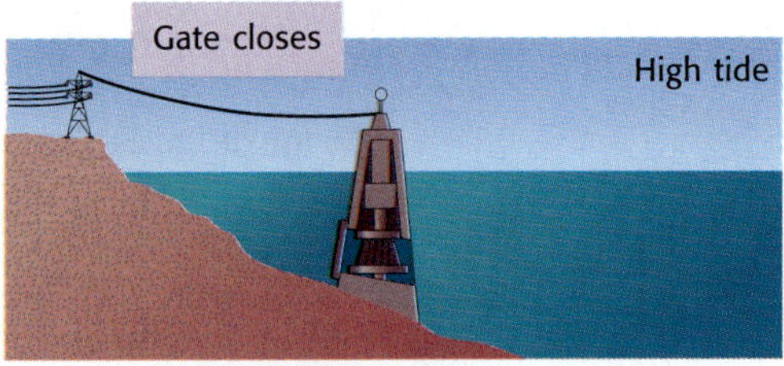

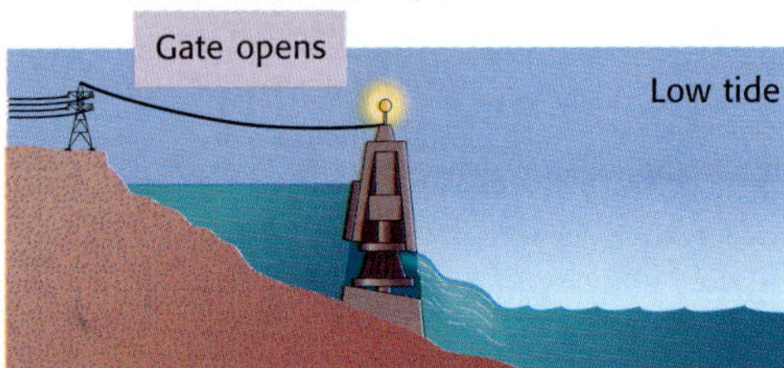

Figure 21 *As the tide rises, water enters a bay behind a dam. The gates then close at high tide. The gates remain closed as the tide lowers. At low tide, the gates open, and the water rushes through the dam, moving the turbines, which in turn create electricity.*

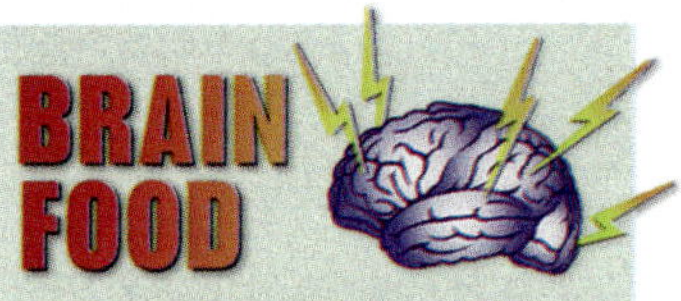

The difference between high and low tide in the Bay of Fundy, in New Brunswick, Canada, can be greater than 15 m! This tidal range is the world's largest.

Tidal Energy The ocean creates several types of energy resources simply because of its constant movement. The gravitational pull of the sun and moon causes the ocean to rise and fall as tides. *Tidal energy,* energy generated from the movement of tides, is an excellent alternative source of energy. If the water during high tide can be rushed through a narrow coastal passageway, the water's force can be powerful enough to generate electricity. **Figure 21** shows how this works. Tidal energy is a clean, inexpensive, and renewable resource once the dam is built. A *renewable resource* can be replenished, in time, after being used. Unfortunately, tidal energy is practical only in a few areas of the world, where the coastline has shallow, narrow channels. For example, the coastline at Cook Inlet, in Alaska, is perfect for generating tidal power.

Wave Energy Have you ever stood on the beach and watched as waves crashed onto the shore? This constant motion, which has been occurring since the oceans formed billions of years ago, is an energy resource. Wave energy, like tidal energy, is a clean, renewable resource.

Recently, computer programs have been developed to analyze the energy of waves. Researchers have located certain areas of the world where wave energy can generate enough electricity to make it worthwhile to build power plants. Wave energy in the North Sea is strong enough to produce power for parts of Scotland and England.

REVIEW

1. List two methods of harvesting the ocean's living resources.
2. Name four nonliving resources in the ocean.
3. **Interpreting Graphics** Take another look at Figure 21. As the tide is rising, will the gate be open or closed? How might this affect the turbines?

Reinforcement Worksheet 13
"The Oceans and Us"

Critical Thinking Worksheet 13
"Chain Reaction"

Answers to Review

1. Two methods of harvesting the ocean's resources are fishing and farming the ocean.
2. Any four of the following nonliving resources are acceptable: oil, natural gas, fresh water, minerals, tidal energy, and wave energy.
3. As the tide is rising, the gate will be open. The turbines may turn while the water passes through the dam from the open ocean. (A specific answer might state that the turbines may turn the opposite direction that they turn when water rushes through from behind the dam into the open ocean.)

Section 4 Review–California Standards: PE/ATE 6, 6b

Ocean Pollution

NEW TERMS
non-point source pollution

OBJECTIVES
- List different types of ocean pollution.
- Explain how to prevent or minimize different types of ocean pollution.
- Outline what is being done to control ocean pollution.

Humans have used the ocean for waste disposal for hundreds, if not thousands, of years. This has harmed the organisms that live in the oceans as well as animals that depend on marine organisms. People are also affected by polluted oceans. Fortunately, we are becoming more aware of ocean pollution, and we are learning from our mistakes.

Sources of Ocean Pollution

There are many sources of ocean pollution. Some of these sources are easily identified, but others are more difficult to pinpoint. Read on to find out where different types of ocean pollution come from and how they affect the ocean.

Trash Dumping People dump trash in many places, including the ocean. In the 1980s, scientists became alarmed by the kind of trash that was washing up on beaches. Bandages, vials of blood, and syringes (needles) were found among the waste. Some of the blood in the vials even contained the AIDS virus. The Environmental Protection Agency (EPA) began an investigation and discovered that hospitals in the United States produce an average of 3 million tons of medical waste each year. And where does some of this trash end up? You guessed it—in the ocean. Because of stricter laws, much of this medical waste is now buried in sanitary landfills. However, dumping trash in the deeper part of the ocean is still a common practice in many countries.

Figure 22 *This barge is headed out to the open ocean, where it will dump the trash it carries.*

Q: How do you know the ocean is friendly?

A: because it waves all the time

Directed Reading Worksheet 13 Section 5

Section 5

Focus

Ocean Pollution

In this section, students learn about the sources and effects of ocean pollution. They also learn about the strategies that are used to minimize ocean pollution. The section examines the effects and cleanup of a major oil spill, and discusses national and international action to reduce ocean pollution.

Bellringer

Ask students to write a few sentences about how ocean pollution could affect their lives. Then have students list the ways they contribute to ocean pollution in their daily lives.

1) Motivate

Activity

Cleaning Up an Oil Spill Give each pair of students a pan of water. Pour about 5 mL of vegetable oil into each pan. Have students think of ways to remove the oil from the pan *without pouring out the water.* Students can experiment with methods such as absorbing the oil with a paper towel or scooping it out with a spoon. Discuss the results of students' efforts. Tell them that this problem is similar to dealing with a petroleum spill in the ocean. Ask students what other factors would be important to containing an oil spill in the ocean. (wind, currents, waves, the size of the spill)

Section 5–California Standards: PE/ATE LabBook: 7, 7a, 7b, 7e

2 Teach

MEETING INDIVIDUAL NEEDS

Learners Having Difficulty Draw students' attention to the photographs of non-point source pollutants in **Figure 23.** Ask them to think about their daily lives and to list ways they might be contributing to non-point source pollution. Ask them to help you list ways that they could reduce their contribution to non-point source pollution.

Homework

Investigate Your Area Inform students that many manufacturers are developing products designed to be less harmful to the environment. Ask students to visit the detergent aisle of a grocery store to compare products. Have them prepare a list of products claiming to be environmentally friendly and their primary ingredients. Encourage students to use Internet or library resources to determine whether the ingredients listed could be harmful to the environment. Allow time for students to share their findings with the class.

In Austin, Texas, sludge is used to make a compost called *Dillo Dirt.* (*Dillo* refers to *armadillo,* a small aardvark-like mammal common in Texas.) Instead of polluting the Gulf of Mexico, Austinites are using sludge to grow beautiful and beneficial gardens.

Sludge Dumping By 1990, the United States alone had discharged 38 trillion liters of treated sludge into the waters along its coasts. What is sludge, and why is it so bad? To answer this question, we need to define *raw sewage.*

Raw sewage refers to all the liquid and solid wastes that are flushed down toilets and poured down drains. After collecting in sewer drains, raw sewage is sent through a treatment plant, where it undergoes a cleaning process that removes the solid waste. Once the liquid is sufficiently treated, it is released into nearby waterways. The remaining solid waste, which is called *sludge,* still contains toxins and bacteria that can cause diseases. In many areas, people dump sludge into the ocean several kilometers offshore, intending for it to settle to and stay on the ocean floor. Unfortunately, this sludge does not always stay on the ocean floor. Sometimes currents stir the sludge up and move it closer to shore. This can pollute beaches and kill marine life. Many countries have banned sludge dumping, but it continues to occur in many areas of the world.

Non-Point Source Pollution Did you know that every time you wash a car or fertilize your lawn you contribute to ocean pollution? Unfortunately, it's true. We usually think of water pollution as coming from large factories, but you may be surprised to know that most of the pollution comes from everyday citizens doing everyday things. This type of pollution, which is shown in **Figure 23,** is called **non-point source pollution** because you cannot pinpoint its exact source. But if the source of pollution is everyday activities at people's homes, how does the pollution get into the ocean? All waste water and runoff eventually enter a body of water, usually a stream. Every stream leads to a river, and every river leads to the ocean.

Figure 23 *Non-point source pollution contributes significantly to ocean pollution. What can you do to cut down on non-point source pollution?*

354

IS THAT A FACT!

The world's first major oil spill occurred on March 18, 1967. The tanker *Torrey Canyon* ran aground off the coast near Cornwall, England. The ship spilled about 870,000 barrels of oil, more than three times the oil spilled by the *Exxon Valdez.*

Oil Spills Because oil is in such high demand across the world, large tankers must transport billions of barrels of it across the oceans. If not handled properly, these transports can quickly turn disastrous. In 1989, the United States experienced a large oil spill in Prince William Sound, a waterway on the Alaskan coast. The *Exxon Valdez,* a supertanker, struck a reef and spilled more than 260,000 barrels of crude oil. The effect of this accident on wildlife was catastrophic. Many animals were covered in oil and started dying immediately. Animals that fed on these oil-contaminated animals also died. Many Alaskans who made their living from fishing lost their businesses and, in some cases, their traditional way of life. Although many animals were saved, as shown in **Figure 24,** and the Exxon Oil Company spent $2.5 billion to try to clean up the mess, Alaska's wildlife and economy will continue to suffer for decades.

Figure 24 *Many oil-covered animals were rescued and cleaned after the* Exxon Valdez *spill.*

Today many oil companies are using new technology to safeguard against oil spills. Tankers are now being built with two hulls instead of one. This prevents oil from spilling into the ocean if the outside hull of the ship is damaged. **Figure 25** illustrates the design of a double-hulled tanker.

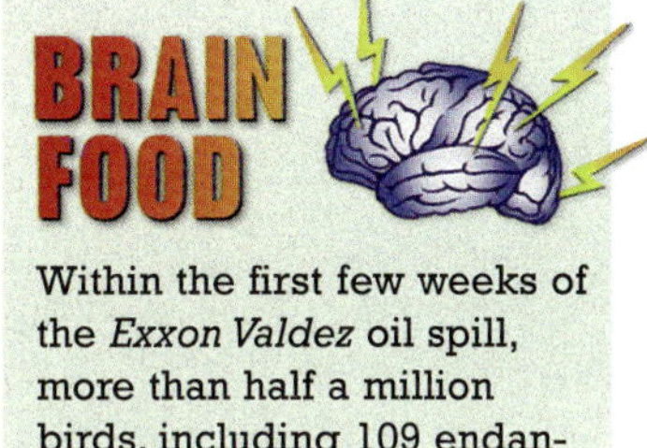

Within the first few weeks of the *Exxon Valdez* oil spill, more than half a million birds, including 109 endangered bald eagles, were covered with oil and drowned. Almost half the sea otters in the area also died either from drowning or from being poisoned by the oil.

Figure 25 *If the outside hull of a double-hulled tanker is punctured, the oil will still be contained within the inside hull.*

CONNECT TO ENVIRONMENTAL SCIENCE

The Oil Pollution Act of 1990 was a direct response to the *Exxon Valdez* oil spill. The controversial bill had been debated for 14 years; it passed swiftly in the aftermath of the disaster. Under the law, all oil tankers operating in United States waters must be double-hulled by 2015. Compliance has been slow, however; many oil companies have been reluctant to replace the aging boats in their fleets with hundred-million-dollar double-hulled ships. As of 1999, of the 3,294 oil tankers operating worldwide, only 876 were double-hulled.

MATH and MORE

Challenge students to use library resources to find out which nations contribute the most to ocean pollution. Have them construct pie graphs to show their results and write a short essay explaining the trends they observe.

DISCUSSION

Nuclear Wastes and the Ocean Remind students that the ocean tends to separate into layers because temperature and salinity differences create layers with different densities.

Point out that the world community is confronted with the dilemma of nuclear waste disposal. One proposed solution is to bury weighted barrels of waste in the sediment of the ocean floor. Encourage students to consider the implications of such a strategy. As nuclear waste decays, it releases heat. What would happen if water contaminated by nuclear waste heated the deep zone?

COOPERATIVE LEARNING

Divide the class into small groups. Ask each group to imagine that they are the campaign managers for a candidate trying to become the city manager of a coastal town. Tell them that they must convince voters that they are concerned for the environmental health of the ocean and have a realistic plan to preserve the beaches and marine life. Have them write a campaign speech outlining the sources of pollution and the solutions they propose. Ask one student from each group to present the speech to the class. Allow the class to vote for the most convincing candidate.

PG 540

Investigating an Oil Spill

Activity

Divide the class into small groups. Provide each group with poster board and markers. Direct each group to work together to create a poster designed to educate the public about the need for clean water. Ask them to focus on ways people can minimize the pollution of our oceans. Consider displaying the posters around the school to educate students and teachers. As an extension, have students draft a letter to a United States Congress member that outlines each group's ideas.

Sheltered English

Research

Help students find information to investigate the environmental impact of one of the following: building marinas where salt marshes once stood, using dynamite to catch fish (common in the Pacific and particularly harmful to coral reefs), and destroying coral reefs to obtain construction materials.

Encourage students to focus on the effects of these human behaviors on other organisms, and challenge them to suggest alternatives.

Why worry about a few drops of oil? You might be surprised that a little goes a long way. Turn to page 540 in the LabBook to learn more.

Saving Our Ocean Resources

Although humans have done much to harm the ocean's resources, we have also begun to do more to save them. From international treaties to volunteer cleanups, efforts to conserve the ocean's resources are making an impact around the world.

Nations Take Notice When ocean pollution reached an all-time high, many countries recognized the need to work together to solve the problem. In 1989, 64 countries ratified a treaty that prohibits the dumping of mercury, cadmium compounds, certain plastics, oil, and high-level radioactive wastes into the ocean. Many other international agreements restricting ocean pollution have been made, but enforcing them is often difficult.

In spite of efforts to protect the ocean, waste dumping and oil spills still occur, and contaminated organisms continue to wash ashore. Why are the laws not working as well as they should? Enforcing these laws takes money and human resources, and many agencies are lacking in both.

Action in the United States The United States, like many other countries, has taken additional measures to control local pollution. In 1992, Congress passed the Clean Water Act, which put the EPA in charge of issuing permits for any dumping of trash into the ocean. Later that year, a stricter law was passed. The U.S. Marine Protection, Research, and Sanctuaries Act prohibits the dumping of any material that would affect human health or welfare, the marine environment or ecosystems, or businesses that depend on the ocean.

Get together with your classmates and divide yourselves into three groups: Nation A, Nation B, and Nation C. All three nations are located near the ocean, and all three nations share borders. Nation A has a very rich supply of oil, which it transports around the world. Nation B currently depends on nuclear energy and has many nuclear power plants near its shores. Nation B has no place on land to store radioactive waste from its nuclear power plants. Nation C sells nuclear technology to Nation B, buys oil from Nation A, and has the world's most diverse coastal ecosystem. The three nations must form a treaty to safeguard against ocean pollution without seriously harming any of their economies. Can you do it?

356

Answers to APPLY

Although there are no specific answers, students should consider the following factors:

1. Nation A and Nation C must keep each other satisfied because they depend on the sale of oil from Nation A to Nation C.
2. Nation B and Nation C must keep each other satisfied because Nation B buys nuclear technology from Nation C.
3. Nation C must protect its coastal ecosystem, but Nation C also depends on Nation A's transport of oil and Nation B's use of nuclear energy, both of which can potentially threaten the coastal ecosystem.

Figure 26 *The Adopt-a-Beach program in Texas has been a huge success.*

Citizens Take Charge Citizens of many countries have demanded that their governments do more to solve the growing problem of ocean pollution. Because of public outcry, the United States now spends more than $130 million each year monitoring the oceans. United States citizens have also begun to take the matter into their own hands. In the early 1980s, citizens began organizing beach cleanups. One of the largest cleanups is the semiannual Adopt-a-Beach program, shown in **Figure 26,** that originated with the Texas Coastal Cleanup campaign. Millions of tons of trash have been gathered from the beaches, and people are being educated about the hazards of ocean dumping.

Though governments pass laws against ocean dumping, keeping the oceans clean is everyone's responsibility. The next time you and your family visit the beach, make sure the only items you leave behind on the sand are hermit crabs, shells, and maybe a few sand dollars.

REVIEW

1. List three types of ocean pollution. How can each of these types be prevented or minimized?
2. Which type of ocean pollution is most common?
3. **Summarizing Data** List and describe three measures that governments have taken to control ocean pollution.

Answers to Review

1. Any of the following are acceptable: trash dumping, sludge dumping, non-point source pollution, and oil spills. Trash can be dumped in sanitary landfills, sludge can be used to make compost, people can reduce non-point source pollution by changing daily behaviors, and tankers with double hulls can be used to transport oil. All of these types of pollution can be prevented or minimized through legislation, education, and actions by citizens.
2. non-point source pollution
3. Three measures taken by governments to control ocean pollution are described on page 356.

DEBATE

Clean Water Legislation
Challenge groups of students to research legislation intended to control ocean pollution. Students might learn more about the Clean Water Act, the MARPOL Act, or the U.S. Marine Protection, Research, and Sanctuaries Act, all of which limit dumping. Groups should debate the pros and cons of each bill.

4 Close

Quiz

1. Why do oil spills pose a long-term risk? (The oil gets into the food chain, affecting wildlife for decades.)
2. Why is sludge dumping a threat to marine and human life? (Sludge dumping can cause diseases, kill marine organisms, and pollute beaches.)

ALTERNATIVE ASSESSMENT

Concept Mapping Have students recall the sources of ocean pollution discussed in this section, the effects of pollution on oceans and wildlife, and the actions being taken by nations and individuals to limit and reduce pollution. Ask them to prepare a concept map that organizes and compares this information. Challenge students to propose additional suggestions for pollution prevention.

Chapter Highlights

Vocabulary Definitions

Section 1

salinity a measure of the amount of dissolved solids in a given amount of liquid

thermocline a layer of ocean water in which water temperature drops with increased depth faster than in other layers of the ocean

water cycle the continuous movement of water from water sources into the air, onto land, into and over the ground, and back to the water sources

Section 2

continental shelf the flattest part of the continental margin

continental slope the steepest part of the continental margin

continental rise the base of the continental slope

abyssal plain the broad, flat portion of the deep-ocean basin

mid-ocean ridge a long mountain chain that forms on the ocean floor where tectonic plates pull apart; usually extends along the center of ocean basins

rift valley a valley that forms in a rift zone between mountains

seamount an individual mountain of volcanic material on the abyssal plain

ocean trench a seemingly bottomless crevice in the deep-ocean basin that forms where one oceanic plate is forced underneath a continental plate or another oceanic plate

Chapter Highlights

Section 1

Vocabulary

salinity *(p. 334)*
thermocline *(p. 335)*
water cycle *(p. 337)*

Section Notes

- The four oceans as we know them today formed within the last 300 million years.
- Salts have been added to the ocean for billions of years.
- The three temperature zones of ocean water are the surface zone, thermocline, and deep zone.
- The ocean plays the largest role in the water cycle.
- The ocean stabilizes Earth's conditions by absorbing and retaining heat.

Section 2

Vocabulary

continental shelf *(p. 340)*
continental slope *(p. 340)*
continental rise *(p. 340)*
abyssal plain *(p. 340)*
mid-ocean ridge *(p. 341)*
rift valley *(p. 341)*
seamount *(p. 341)*
ocean trench *(p. 341)*

Section Notes

- The ocean floor is divided into zones based on depth and slope.
- The continental margin consists of the continental shelf, the continental slope, and the continental rise.
- The deep-ocean basin consists of the abyssal plain, with features such as mid-ocean ridges, rift valleys, seamounts, and ocean trenches.
- In addition to directly studying the ocean floor, scientists indirectly study the ocean floor using sonar and satellites.

Labs

Probing the Depths *(p. 538)*

Skills Check

Math Concepts

PERCENTAGES Percentages are a way of describing the parts within a whole. Percentages are expressed in hundredths. Take another look at Figure 1 on page 334. The pie chart shows the percentages of dissolved solids in ocean water. The amount of chlorine (Cl) dissolved in the ocean is 55 percent. This means that 55 of every 100 parts of dissolved solids in the ocean are chlorine.

Visual Understanding

RETAINING HEAT The ocean retains heat better than air or dry land. Look at Figure 4 on page 338. Notice how the line representing sea temperatures varies little from day to day. On the other hand, the lines representing air and soil temperatures vary significantly from day to day.

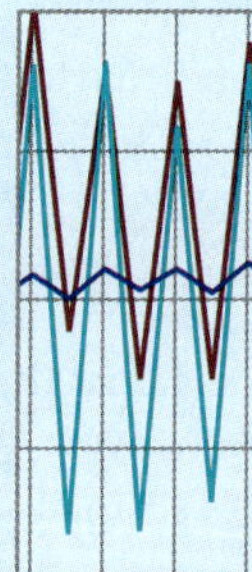

358

Lab and Activity Highlights

Probing the Depths PG 538

Investigating an Oil Spill PG 540

Datasheets for LabBook
(blackline masters for these labs)

SECTION 3

Vocabulary

plankton *(p. 344)*
nekton *(p. 344)*
benthos *(p. 344)*
benthic environment *(p. 345)*
pelagic environment *(p. 347)*

Section Notes

- There are three main groups of marine life—plankton, nekton, and benthos.
- The two main ocean environments—the benthic and pelagic environments—are divided into ecological zones based on the locations of organisms that live in the environments.

SECTION 4

Vocabulary

desalination *(p. 351)*

Section Notes

- Humans depend on the ocean for living and nonliving resources.
- Ocean farms raise fish and other marine life to help feed growing human populations.
- Nonliving ocean resources include oil and natural gas, fresh water, minerals, and tidal and wave energy.

SECTION 5

Vocabulary

non-point source pollution *(p. 354)*

Section Notes

- Types of ocean pollution include trash dumping, sludge dumping, non-point source pollution, and oil spills.
- Non-point source pollution cannot be traced to specific points of origin.
- Efforts to save ocean resources include international treaties and volunteer cleanups.

Labs

Investigating an Oil Spill *(p. 540)*

internet connect

GO TO: go.hrw.com

Visit the **HRW** Web site for a variety of learning tools related to this chapter. Just type in the keyword:

KEYWORD: HSTOCE

GO TO: www.scilinks.org

Visit the **National Science Teachers Association** on-line Web site for Internet resources related to this chapter. Just type in the ***sci*LINKS** number for more information about the topic:

TOPIC	*sci*LINKS NUMBER
Exploring Earth's Oceans	HSTE305
The Ocean Floor	HSTE310
Life in the Oceans	HSTE315
Ocean Resources	HSTE320
Jacques Cousteau: Ocean Explorer	HSTE325

359

VOCABULARY DEFINITIONS, *continued*

SECTION 3

plankton very small organisms floating at or near the ocean's surface that form the base of the oceans' food web

nekton free-swimming organisms of the ocean

benthos organisms that live on or in the ocean floor

benthic environment the ocean floor and all the organisms that live on or in it; also known as the bottom environment

pelagic environment the entire volume of water in the ocean and the marine organisms that live above the ocean floor; also known as the water environment

SECTION 4

desalination the process of evaporating sea water so that the water and the salt separate

SECTION 5

non-point source pollution pollution that comes from many sources and that cannot be traced to specific sites

Vocabulary Review Worksheet 13

Blackline masters of these Chapter Highlights can be found in the **Study Guide.**

Lab and Activity Highlights

LabBank

Inquiry Labs, Surf's Up! Lab 11

Whiz-Bang Demonstrations, Fowl Play, Demo 25

EcoLabs & Field Activities, Operation Oil-Spill Cleanup, EcoLab 13

Long-Term Projects & Research Ideas, Project 41

Interactive Explorations CD-ROM

CD 2, Exploration 2, "Sea Sick"

Chapter Review Answers

Using Vocabulary

1. continental shelf
2. thermocline
3. Plankton
4. *Desalination* is the process of evaporating sea water so that the water and salt separate.
5. Types of *benthos* include sea stars and clams.
6. An ocean trench forms where one oceanic plate is forced underneath a continental plate or another oceanic plate, while a rift valley forms in a rift zone, where tectonic plates pull apart.
7. Salinity is a measure of the amount of dissolved solids in a given amount of liquid, while desalination is the process of evaporating sea water so that the water and the salt separate.
8. Nekton are free-swimming marine organisms, while benthos are marine organisms that live on or in the ocean floor.
9. The pelagic environment is made up of the water in the ocean and all the organisms that live in the water, while the benthic environment is made up of the ocean floor and all the organisms that live on or in the ocean floor.

Understanding Concepts

Multiple Choice

10. b
11. c
12. d
13. c
14. a

Chapter Review

USING VOCABULARY

To complete the following sentences, choose the correct term from each pair of terms listed below:

1. The region of the ocean floor that is closest to the shoreline is the __?__. *(continental shelf* or *continental slope)*

2. Below the surface layer of the ocean is a layer of water that gets colder with depth and extends to a depth of 700 m. This layer is called the __?__. *(thermocline* or *benthic environment)*

3. __?__ typically float at or near the ocean's surface. *(Plankton* or *Nekton)*

Correct the wrong terminology in each of the following sentences. A word bank is provided.

4. The water cycle is the process of evaporating sea water so that the water and salt separate.

5. Types of nekton include sea stars and clams.

Word bank: nonpoint source pollution, plankton, desalination, benthos

Explain the difference between the words in each of the following pairs:

6. ocean trench/rift valley

7. salinity/desalination

8. nekton/benthos

9. pelagic environment/benthic environment

UNDERSTANDING CONCEPTS

Multiple Choice

10. The largest ocean is the
    a. Indian Ocean.
    b. Pacific Ocean.
    c. Atlantic Ocean.
    d. Arctic Ocean.

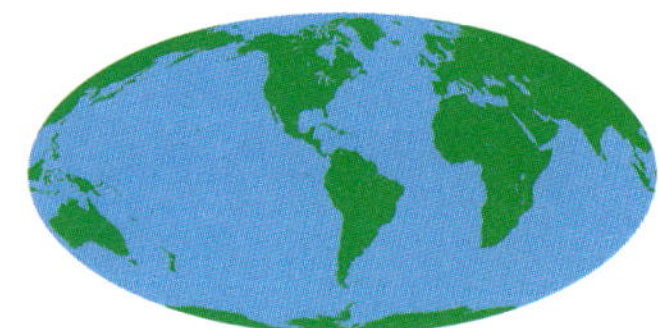

11. The average salinity of ocean water is
    a. 45‰.
    b. 24‰.
    c. 35‰.
    d. None of the above

12. Which of the following affects the ocean's salinity?
    a. fresh water added by rivers
    b. currents
    c. evaporation
    d. All of the above

13. Most precipitation falls
    a. on land.
    b. into lakes and rivers.
    c. into the ocean.
    d. in rain forests.

14. Which benthic zone has a depth range between 200 m and 4,000 m?
    a. bathyal zone
    b. abyssal zone
    c. hadal zone
    d. sublittoral zone

Chapter 13 Review–California Standards: PE/ATE Q1–9; 1a, 4a; Q10–18: 1, 1a, 1c, 4a

Short Answer

15. Why does coastal water in areas with hotter, drier climates typically have a higher salinity than coastal water in cooler, more humid areas?

16. What is the difference between the abyssal plain and the abyssal zone?

17. How do the continental shelf, the continental slope, the continental rise, and the continental margin relate to each other?

Concept Mapping

18. Use the following terms to create a concept map: marine life, plankton, nekton, benthos, benthic environment, pelagic environment.

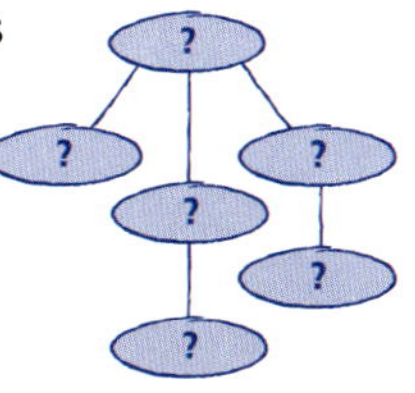

CRITICAL THINKING AND PROBLEM SOLVING

Write one or two sentences to answer the following questions:

19. Other than obtaining fresh water, what benefit comes from desalination?

20. Explain the difference between a sea profile and a seismic reading.

MATH IN SCIENCE

21. Imagine that you are in the kelp-farming business and that your kelp grows 33 cm per day. You begin harvesting when your plants are 50 cm tall. During the first seven days of harvest, you cut 10 cm off the top of your kelp plants each day. How tall would your kelp plants be after the seventh day of harvesting?

INTERPRETING GRAPHICS

Examine the image below, and answer the questions that follow:

Ecological Zones of the Ocean

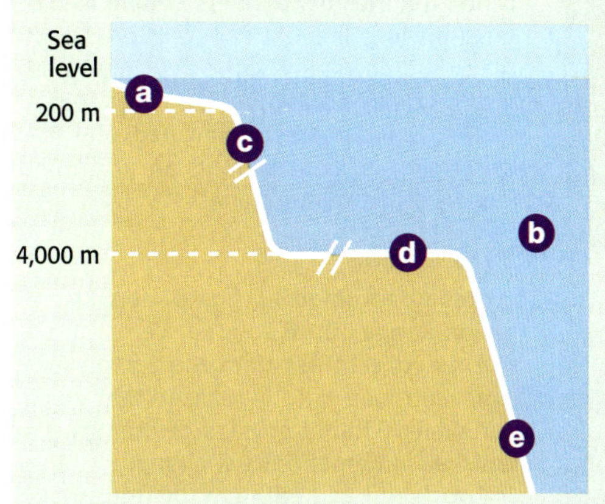

22. At which point *(a, b, c, d, or e)* would you most likely find an anglerfish?

23. At which point would you most likely find tube worms?

24. Which ecological zone is at point *c*? Which depth zone is at point *c*?

25. Name a type of organism you might find at point *e*.

NOW What Do You Think?

Take a minute to review your answers to the ScienceLog questions on page 331. Have your answers changed? If necessary, revise your answers based on what you have learned since you began this chapter.

361

Short Answer

15. because less fresh water runs into the ocean in drier areas and because heat increases the evaporation rate
16. The abyssal plain is the flattest part of the ocean floor. The abyssal zone is an ecological zone that consists of the abyssal plain and all the organisms that live on or in it.
17. The continental shelf, the continental slope, and the continental rise are sections of the continental margin. Also, the continental rise is part of the continental slope.

Concept Mapping

18. 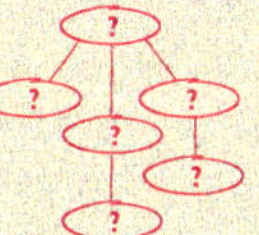 An answer to this exercise can be found at the end of this book.

Critical Thinking and Problem Solving

19. Salt is left behind. Salt can be used for many things.
20. A sea profile shows what the contour of the ocean floor looks like, while a seismic reading shows what rocks beneath the ocean floor look like. (Seismic readings can show the contour of the ocean floor too.)

Math in Science

21. 50 cm + 7(33 cm − 10 cm) = 211 cm

Interpreting Graphics

22. *b*
23. *d*
24. ecological zone = bathyal zone, depth zone = continental slope
25. Accept any one of the following: clams, sponges, and worms.

NOW What Do You Think?

1. The oceans have changed in both size, shape, and salinity over time. Other changes that are not covered in this chapter include changes in marine life, water chemistry, and sea level.
2. Technologies that scientists use to study the ocean without going under that are mentioned in this chapter include sonar, satellites, seismic technology, and dredging.
3. Answers will vary. Some resources mentioned in this chapter include fish, oil, natural gas, fresh water, minerals from nodules, tidal energy, and wave energy.

Concept Mapping Transparency 13

Blackline masters of this Chapter Review can be found in the **Study Guide.**

Chapter 13 Review–California Standards: PE/ATE Think: 6b

Across the Sciences

Exploring Ocean Life

Teaching Strategy

In addition to being an inventor and an explorer, Jacques Cousteau was a commentator on the twentieth century and its environmental problems. He was criticized as being a populist because he brought information to the public in common language instead of in academic terms. Help the class find information about his condemnation of French nuclear testing or his controversial opinions on overpopulation and animal testing.

You may want to show your students some of Cousteau's inspired documentaries. Some of his full-length features include *The Silent World, World Without Sun,* and *Voyage to the Edge of the World.* Tapes of his many television series *(The Undersea World of Jacques Cousteau, Cousteau Odyssey,* and *Cousteau Amazon)* may also be available at a public library.

Answer to Write About It

Students should be able to find a great deal of information about ocean pollution and overfishing. Many articles have been published in the various science magazines, and there are a large number of government and nonprofit Web sites that deal with these issues.

ACROSS THE SCIENCES

EARTH SCIENCE • LIFE SCIENCE

Exploring Ocean Life

Jacques Cousteau, born in France in 1910, opened the eyes of countless people to the sea. During his long life, Cousteau explored Earth's oceans and documented the amazing variety of life they contained. Jacques Cousteau was an explorer, environmentalist, inventor, and teacher who inspired millions with his joy and wonder at the watery part of our planet.

Early Dives

Cousteau performed his first underwater diving mission at age 10. At summer camp he was asked to collect trash from the camp's lake. The young Cousteau quickly realized that working underwater without goggles or breathing equipment was a tremendous challenge.

Cousteau had another early underwater experience when he visited Southeast Asia. He saw people diving into the water to catch fish with their bare hands. This fascinated Cousteau. Even at a young age, he was thinking about how to make equipment that would let a person breathe underwater.

▲ *Cousteau in front of the* Calypso II

Underwater Flight

As a young man, Cousteau and some friends developed the aqualung, a self-contained breathing system for underwater exploration. As someone who had often dreamed of flying, Cousteau was thrilled with his invention. After one of his first dives, Cousteau explained, "I experimented with all possible maneuvers—loops, somersaults, and barrel rolls. . . . Delivered from gravity and buoyancy, I flew around in space."

Using the aqualung and other underwater equipment he developed, Cousteau began making underwater films. In 1950, he bought a boat named *Calypso,* which became his home and floating laboratory. For the next 40 years, through his films and television series, Cousteau brought what he called "the silent world" of the oceans and seas to living rooms everywhere.

A Protector of Life

Cousteau was long an outspoken defender of the environment. "When I saw all this beauty under the sea, I fell in love with it. And finally, when I realized to what extent the oceans were threatened, I decided to campaign as vigorously as I could against everything that threatened what I loved."

Jacques Cousteau died in 1997 at age 87. Before his death, he dedicated the *Calypso II,* a new research vessel, to the children of the world.

Write About It

▶ Ocean pollution and overfishing are subjects of intense debate. Think about these issues, and discuss them with your classmates. Then write an essay in which you try to convince readers of your point of view.

362

internetconnect

SCILINKS NSTA

TOPIC: Jacques Cousteau: Ocean Explorer
GO TO: www.scilinks.org
***sci*LINKS NUMBER:** HSTE325

EYE ON THE ENVIRONMENT

Putting Freshwater Problems on Ice

Imagine how different your life would be if you couldn't get fresh water. What would you drink? How would you clean things? The Earth has enough fresh water to supply 100 billion liters to each person, yet water shortages affect millions of people every day. So what's the problem?

The Ice-Water Planet

Three-quarters of Earth's fresh water is frozen in polar icecaps. Plenty of fresh water is there, but people can't use water that is frozen and thousands of kilometers away.

The ice sheet that covers Antarctica is thousands of meters thick and is almost twice the size of the United States. Hundreds of huge chunks break off its edges every year. These icebergs, which are made up entirely of frozen fresh water, float away into the sea and eventually melt. Water from 1 year's worth of these icebergs would be enough to supply all of southern California for more than a century. So why not use it?

Obvious but Not Easy

Transporting icebergs to areas that need fresh water is harder than it sounds. For one thing, many of the icebergs are huge. The largest ever recorded was about the size of Connecticut. Even small icebergs may be 2 km long and 1 km wide.

Researchers have considered many methods of transporting icebergs. Most of the ideas involve pushing or towing icebergs through the water. A few ideas involve attaching engines and propellers directly to the icebergs.

However, because icebergs are so large, it takes a long time to move them. And when an iceberg finally does get somewhere, a considerable amount of it has melted. To prevent melting, insulating materials could be wrapped around an iceberg.

▲ *Icebergs such as this one might provide water in the future.*

A Worthy Investment

Lakes and groundwater still provide the cheapest fresh water in most areas. However, if there is no lake, river, or well water available, icebergs may then be a reasonable option to consider. Even though transporting icebergs is difficult, it may still be worthwhile to try. Irrigating 100 km^2 of desert with water from icebergs might cost as much as $1 million, but purifying enough sea water to irrigate that amount of desert could cost over $1 billion.

People in arid regions have spent considerable time on iceberg research. So far, no one has set up a program for harvesting icebergs. But someday water from icebergs may flow from our household faucets.

An Icy Investigation

▶ Float an ice cube in a bowl of cold water, and record the time it takes the cube to melt. Then try to insulate other ice cubes with different materials, such as cloth, plastic wrap, and aluminum foil. Which material works best? How could this material be used on real icebergs?

363

EYE ON THE ENVIRONMENT

Putting Freshwater Problems on Ice

Background

Icebergs form in both the Northern and Southern Hemispheres, but they are typically very different in size and appearance. Icebergs in the Northern Hemisphere, such as those that break off from the ice sheet covering Greenland, tend to be spiky and irregularly shaped. Icebergs in the Southern Hemisphere are much larger and usually have a fairly flat top.

People first considered the possibility of using icebergs as a water source many years ago. Just after 1900, Antarctic icebergs were towed by steamships to Callao, Peru. In addition to using icebergs for fresh water, people have proposed using them for air conditioning, as a source of gourmet ice cubes, and even as giant aircraft carriers.

Answers to An Icy Investigation

Answers will vary. Students may find that some materials prevent the ice cubes from melting as quickly as they would if they were unprotected. Students should propose realistic ways of using their materials on icebergs.

California Standards: PE/ATE 6, 6b, 7, 7e

Chapter Organizer

CHAPTER ORGANIZATION	TIME MINUTES	OBJECTIVES	LABS, INVESTIGATIONS, AND DEMONSTRATIONS
Chapter Opener **pp. 364–365**	45	California Standards: PE/ATE 1, 1e, 4a, 4d, 7, 7e	**Investigate!** When Two *Whirls* Collide, p. 365
Section 1 **Currents**	90	▶ Describe surface currents, and list the three factors that control them. ▶ Describe deep currents. ▶ Illustrate the factors involved in deep-current movement. ▶ Explain how currents affect climate. PE/ATE 4, 4a, 4d, 4e, 5e, 7, 7c; LabBook 7, 7b, 7e, 7h	**Interactive Explorations CD-ROM,** Latitude Attitude *A **Worksheet** is also available in the **Interactive Explorations Teacher's Edition.*** **Skill Builder,** Up from the Depths, p. 542 **Datasheets for LabBook,** Up from the Depths, Datasheet 30 **Whiz-Bang Demonstrations,** Spin Cycle, Demo 26
Section 2 **Waves**	90	▶ Identify wave components, and explain how they relate to wave movement. ▶ Describe how ocean waves form and how they move. ▶ Classify types of waves. ▶ Analyze types of dangerous waves. PE/ATE 1, 1e, 2, 2d, 2e, 3a, 4, 4a	**Demonstration,** p. 374 in ATE **QuickLab,** Do the Wave, p. 379
Section 3 **Tides**	90	▶ Explain tides and their relationship with the Earth, the sun, and the moon. ▶ Classify different types of tides. ▶ Analyze the relationship between tides and coastal land. PE/ATE 3a, 4, 4a, 5b, 7c; LabBook 7, 7b, 7e	**Making Models,** Turning the Tides, p. 544 **Datasheets for LabBook,** Turning the Tides, Datasheet 31 **Long-Term Projects & Research Ideas,** Project 42

See page **T20** *for a complete correlation of this book with the*

CALIFORNIA SCIENCE CONTENT STANDARDS.

Correlations are also provided at point of use throughout this ATE.

TECHNOLOGY RESOURCES

Guided Reading Audio CD
English or Spanish, Chapter 14

Classroom Management CD-ROM

Test Generator CD-ROM

Interactive Explorations CD-ROM
CD 3, Exploration 4, Latitude Attitude

CNN. **Scientists in Action,** Mapping El Niño Erosion, Segment 20

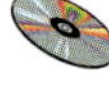

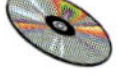

Science Discovery Videodiscs
Science Sleuths: The Mystery Fog

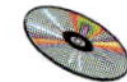

Earth Science Videodisc
Tides: 23877–29491

Chapter 14 • The Movement of Ocean Water

CLASSROOM WORKSHEETS, TRANSPARENCIES, AND RESOURCES	SCIENCE INTEGRATION AND CONNECTIONS	REVIEW AND ASSESSMENT
Directed Reading Worksheet 14 **Science Puzzlers, Twisters & Teasers,** Worksheet 14	**Careers:** Seismologist—Hiroo Kanamori, p. 388	
Directed Reading Worksheet 14, Section 1 **Transparency 135,** Earth's Surface Currents **Math Skills for Science Worksheet 25,** What Is Scientific Notation? **Transparency 136,** How Deep Currents Form **Transparency 137,** Circulation of Deep and Surface Currents	**Real-World Connection,** p. 366 in ATE **Cross-Disciplinary Focus,** p. 367 in ATE **Connect to Life Science,** p. 367 in ATE **Real-World Connection,** p. 368 in ATE **Physical Science Connection,** p. 369 **Math and More,** p. 370 in ATE **Connect to Life Science,** p. 371 in ATE **Cross-Disciplinary Focus,** p. 372 in ATE **Real-World Connection,** p. 373 in ATE	**Self-Check,** p. 367 **Review,** p. 369 **Homework,** pp. 369, 371 in ATE **Review,** p. 373 **Quiz,** p. 373 in ATE **Alternative Assessment,** p. 373 in ATE
Transparency 138, Wave Period and Speed **Directed Reading Worksheet 14,** Section 2 **Transparency 139,** Deep-Water Waves Become Shallow-Water Waves **Math Skills for Science Worksheet 11,** What Is a Fraction? **Transparency 195,** Wave Speed, Wavelength, and Frequency **Reinforcement Worksheet 14,** Waves to Your Pen Pal	**MathBreak,** Wave Speed, p. 375 **Math and More,** p. 375 in ATE **Real-World Connection,** p. 376 in ATE **Environmental Science Connection,** p. 377 **Math and More,** p. 377 in ATE **Connect to Environmental Science,** p. 377 in ATE **Connect to Meteorology,** p. 378 in ATE **Apply,** p. 379	**Homework,** p. 377 in ATE **Review,** p. 379 **Quiz,** p. 379 in ATE **Alternative Assessment,** p. 379 in ATE
Directed Reading Worksheet 14, Section 3 **Critical Thinking Worksheet 14,** Tides of Trouble **Transparency 140,** Tidal Variations **Reinforcement Worksheet 14,** But What About the Tides?	**Health Watch:** Red Tides, p. 389	**Homework,** p. 382 in ATE **Review,** p. 383 **Quiz,** p. 383 in ATE **Alternative Assessment,** p. 383 in ATE

internet connect

Holt, Rinehart and Winston On-line Resources

go.hrw.com

For worksheets and other teaching aids related to this chapter, visit the HRW Web site and type in the keyword: **HSTH2O**

National Science Teachers Association

www.scilinks.org

Encourage students to use the keywords listed on the Technology Highlights page to access information and resources on the **NSTA** Web site.

END-OF-CHAPTER REVIEW AND ASSESSMENT

Chapter Review in Study Guide
Vocabulary and Notes in Study Guide
Chapter Tests with Performance-Based Assessment, Chapter 14 Test
Chapter Tests with Performance-Based Assessment, Performance-Based Assessment 14
Concept Mapping Transparency 14

Chapter Resources & Worksheets

Visual Resources

TEACHING TRANSPARENCIES

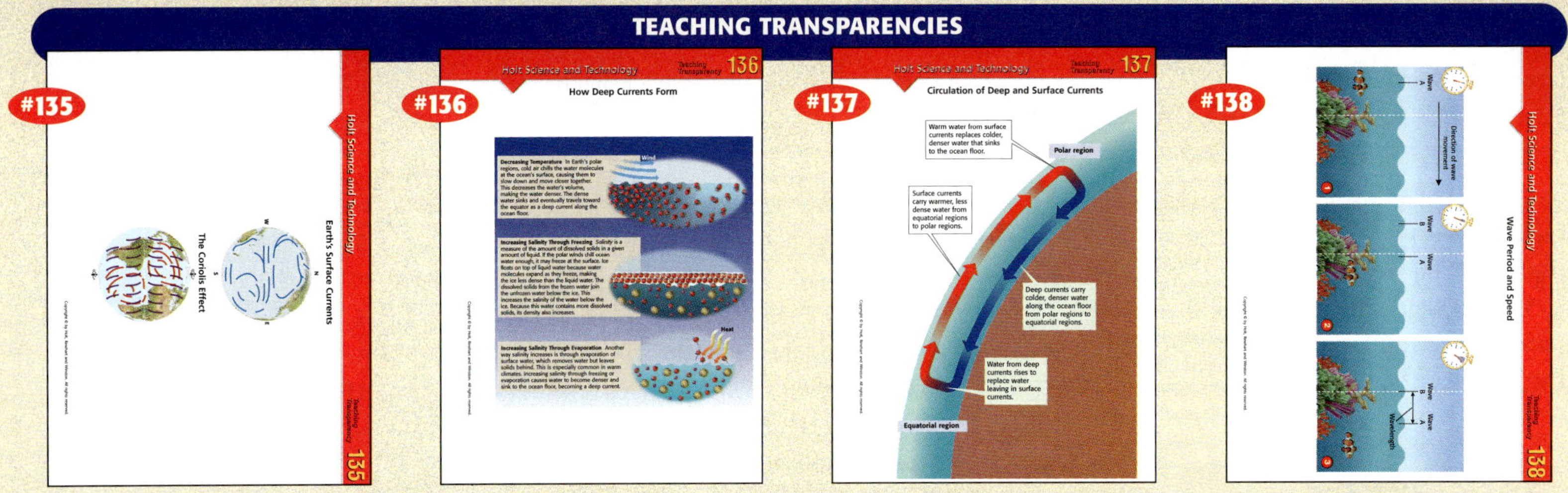

TEACHING TRANSPARENCIES

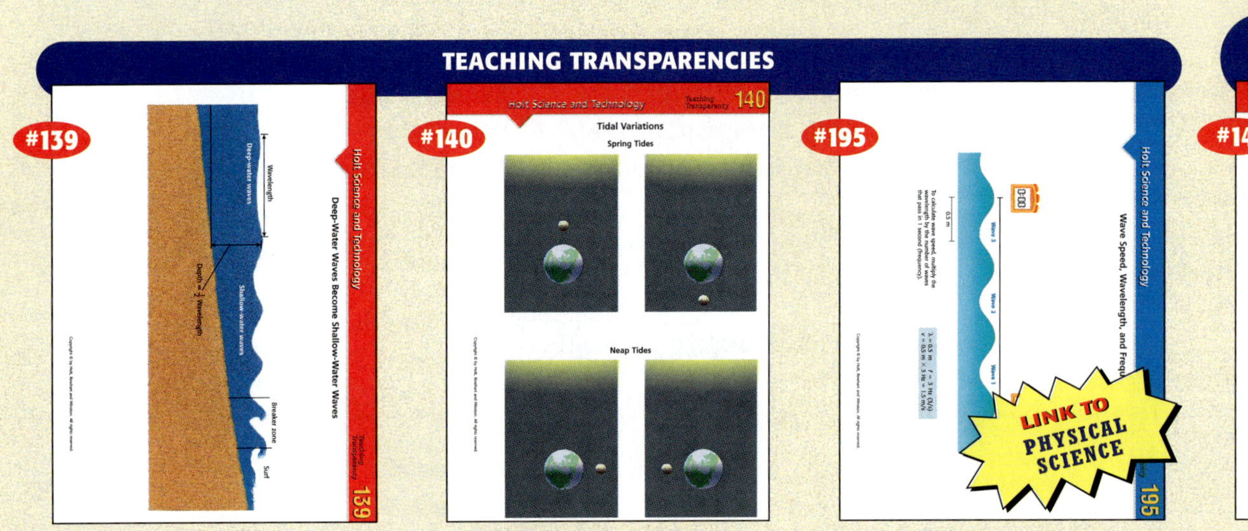

CONCEPT MAPPING TRANSPARENCY

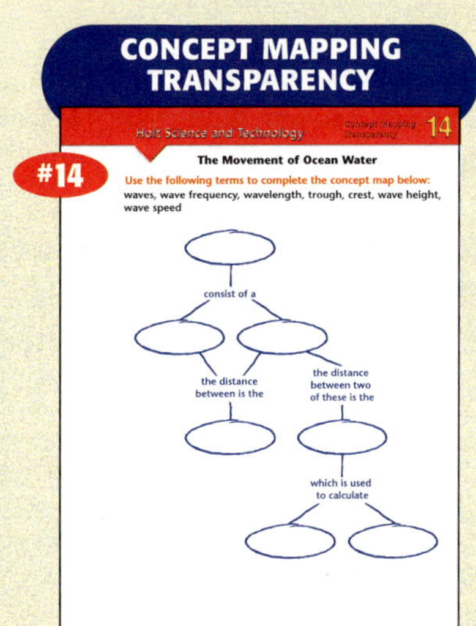

Meeting Individual Needs

DIRECTED READING

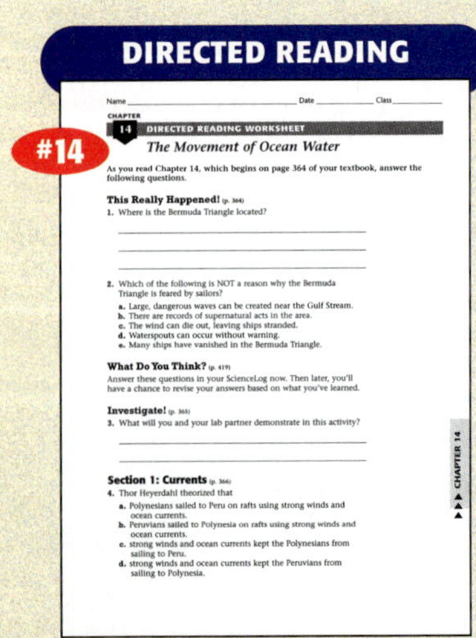

REINFORCEMENT & VOCABULARY REVIEW

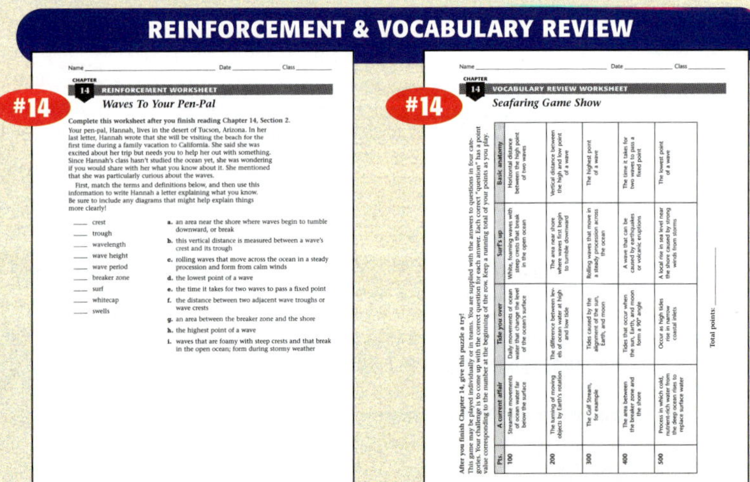

SCIENCE PUZZLERS, TWISTERS & TEASERS

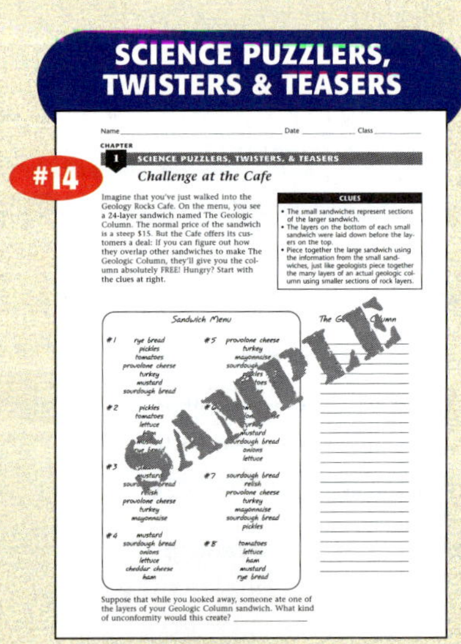

Chapter 14 • The Movement of Ocean Water

Review & Assessment

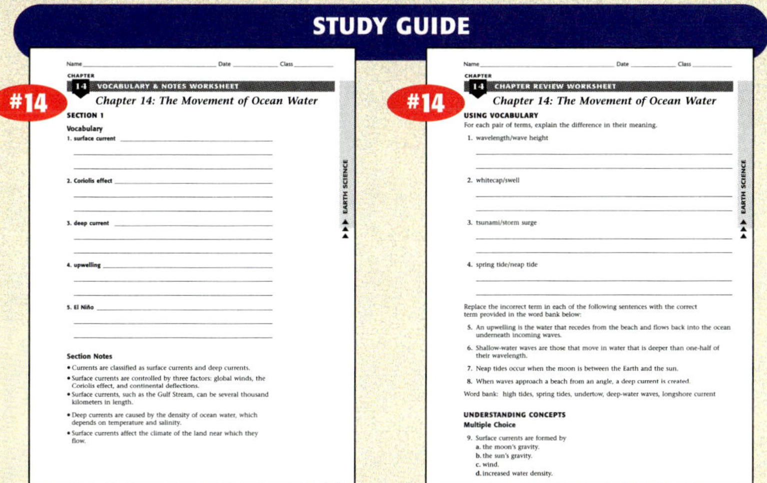
STUDY GUIDE

#14 VOCABULARY & NOTES WORKSHEET
Chapter 14: The Movement of Ocean Water

#14 CHAPTER REVIEW WORKSHEET
Chapter 14: The Movement of Ocean Water

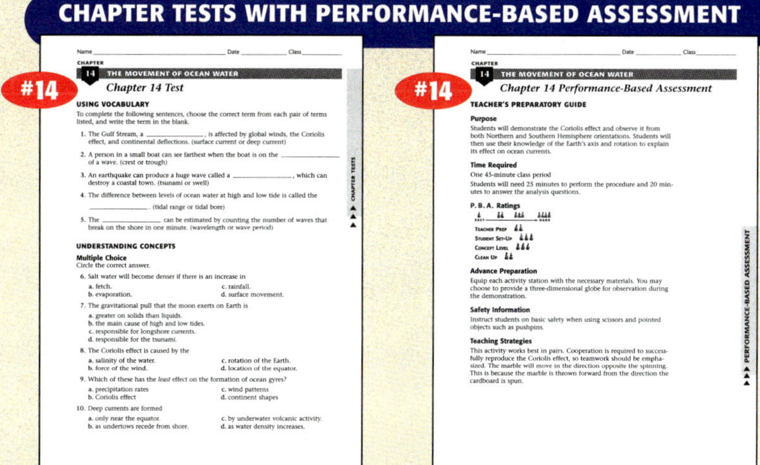
CHAPTER TESTS WITH PERFORMANCE-BASED ASSESSMENT

#14 THE MOVEMENT OF OCEAN WATER
Chapter 14 Test

#14 THE MOVEMENT OF OCEAN WATER
Chapter 14 Performance-Based Assessment

Lab Worksheets

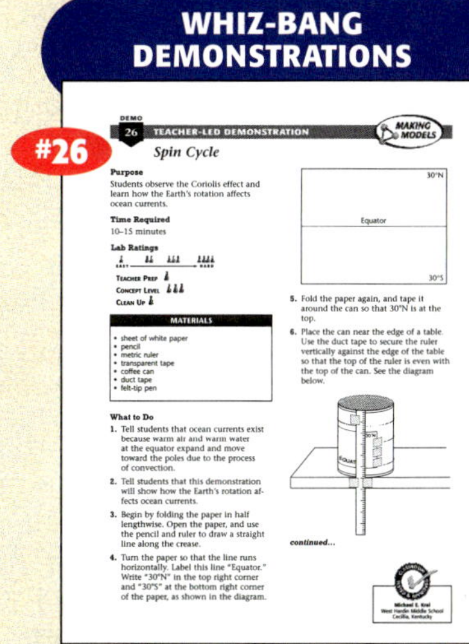
WHIZ-BANG DEMONSTRATIONS

#26 TEACHER-LED DEMONSTRATION
Spin Cycle

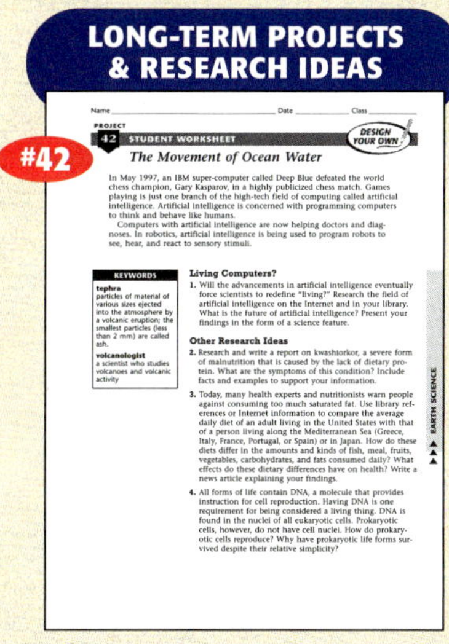
LONG-TERM PROJECTS & RESEARCH IDEAS

#42 STUDENT WORKSHEET
The Movement of Ocean Water

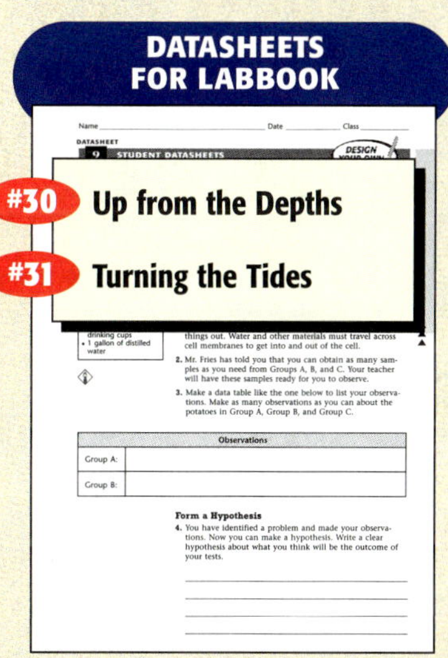
DATASHEETS FOR LABBOOK

#30 Up from the Depths

#31 Turning the Tides

Applications & Extensions

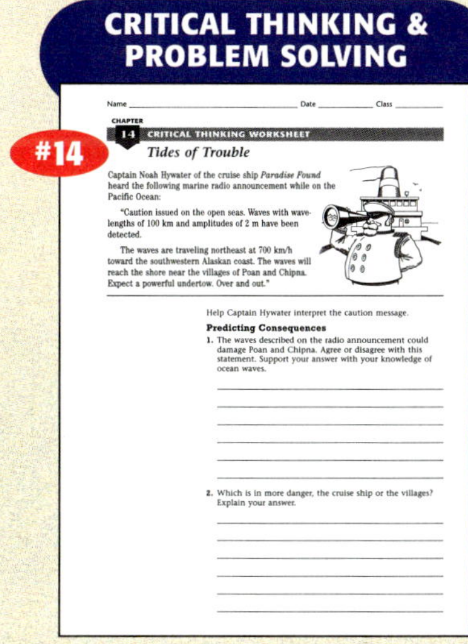
CRITICAL THINKING & PROBLEM SOLVING

#14 CRITICAL THINKING WORKSHEET
Tides of Trouble

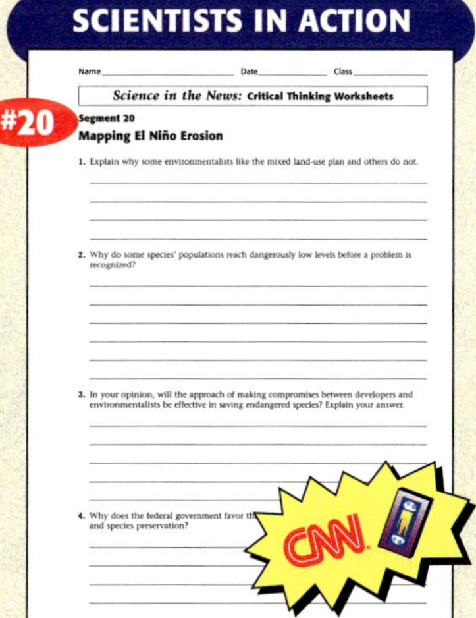
SCIENTISTS IN ACTION

#20 Science in the News: Critical Thinking Worksheets
Segment 20
Mapping El Niño Erosion

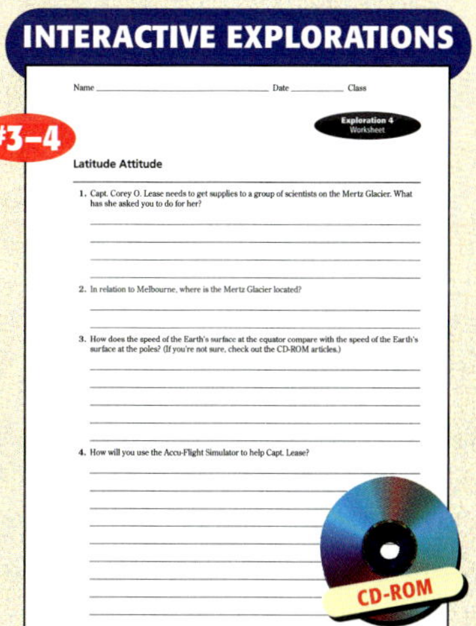
INTERACTIVE EXPLORATIONS

#3–4 Exploration 4 Worksheet
Latitude Attitude

Chapter Background

Section 1

Currents

▶ Solar Radiation

One of the fundamental energy sources for all ocean currents is solar radiation. Uneven heating of the Earth by the sun creates differences in air pressure. These differences create wind, which drives surface currents. The sun's heat also creates temperature differences in ocean water, driving deep currents.

▶ The *Ra II* Expedition

On May 17, 1970, Thor Heyerdahl's *Ra II* expedition attempted to demonstrate that mariners from ancient Egypt could have reached the New World. The eight-man expedition successfully reached its destination in the Barbados on July 12, 1970.

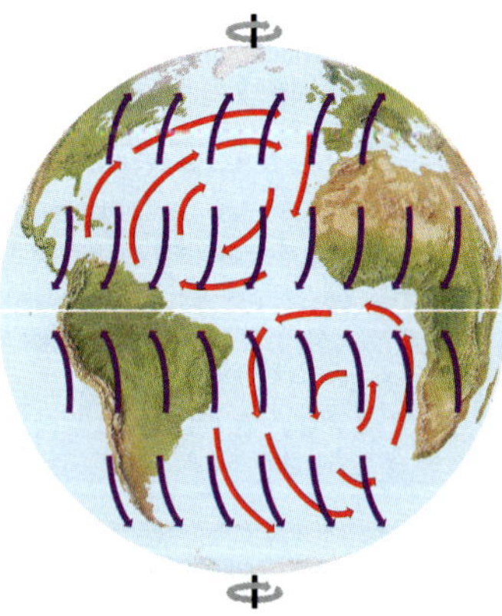

▶ Gaspard Coriolis

The Coriolis effect was named after Gaspard Coriolis (1792–1843), a French engineer. Coriolis was the first to attribute the deflection of surface currents across the surface of Earth to a hypothetical force. It was not until later that the force was identified as Earth's rotation.

Is That a Fact!

- The strongest and largest ocean current is the Antarctic Circumpolar Current, which is estimated to flow at a rate of 125 million cubic meters per second.
- One of the fastest ocean currents is the Somali Current, in the western Indian Ocean, which flows at a speed of 14.5 km/h.
- The Weddell Sea, where the Antarctic Bottom Water is thought to originate, has the clearest water of any sea. Its clarity has been recorded to a depth of nearly 80 m. In other words, water collected from the upper 80 m of the Weddell Sea is as clear as you would find in a glass of distilled water.

Section 2

Waves

▶ Swells

Swells are generated in the open ocean by wind and can travel thousands of kilometers to shore. These long-wavelength waves have periods of 10 to 30 seconds. When swells reach shallower water, their height increases, causing them to fall forward. When this occurs, the waves are called breakers.

Tsunamis

Tsunami is a Japanese word that means "harbor wave." Japan has experienced many devastating tsunamis throughout history. The subduction of tectonic plates generates the seismic energy necessary to cause tsunamis. Because the Japanese islands are on the edge of deep water and the coastline is rugged, with many small harbors, tsunamis have been particularly destructive. The deep water close to the Japanese islands keeps tsunami wave heights short until the waves are very close to shore; when the waves enter shallow water, they suddenly grow taller. The narrow shape of many Japanese harbors causes tsunamis to grow even taller.

- Tsunamis have the potential to be the most destructive of ocean waves. Their speed averages 500 km/h, and their period ranges from 5 to 60 minutes. Because the wave height of a tsunami is usually less than 2 m in the open ocean, they often pass unnoticed beneath ships.
- The earthquakes that produce destructive tsunamis are generally greater than 6.5 on the Richter scale. Most occur in the Pacific Ocean, where there is a high level of seismic activity near plate boundaries.

Section 3

Tides

Perigean Spring Tides

On March 7, 1993, a full moon appeared on the same day that the moon was closest to Earth in its orbit (or its perigee). This event produced extraordinarily high and low tides, called *perigean spring tides*. During perigean spring tides, high tides rise higher than normal onto beaches, while low tides expose parts of the ocean floor that are normally submerged.

Is That a Fact!

- The sun exerts only about half the tidal force on Earth that the moon does. This is because the distance between Earth and the sun is much greater than the distance between Earth and the moon.

- High tide that occurs on the side of Earth that faces the moon is called a *direct high tide*. High tide that occurs on the side of Earth opposite the moon is called an *indirect high tide*.
- The Great Lakes also experience tides. Although the tidal range is small compared with that of the oceans, the size and depth of the five lakes make small fluctuations in water level noticeable.

For additional background resources, please refer to the **HST Reference Library.**

CHAPTER 14

The Movement of Ocean Water

Chapter Preview

Section 1
Currents
- Surface Currents
- Deep Currents
- Surface Currents and Climate

Section 2
Waves
- Anatomy of a Wave
- Wave Formation and Movement
- Specifics of Wave Movement
- Types of Waves
- Storm Surges

Section 3
Tides
- The Lure of the Moon
- Tidal Variations
- Tides and Topography

Directed Reading Worksheet 14

Science Puzzlers, Twisters & Teasers Worksheet 14

Guided Reading Audio CD English or Spanish, Chapter 14

This Really Happened!

On February 3, 1963, the ocean tanker SS *Marine Sulphur Queen* sailed eastward around the Florida Keys bound for Virginia. Soon after the ship entered the Atlantic, all radio contact with it was lost. Coast Guard rescuers who tried to locate the ship found only life jackets, oil cans, and debris in the area of the tanker's last known position. No survivors were ever found. Several explanations for the *Queen*'s disappearance were offered, but very little evidence supported any of them. The only certainty was that the ship entered the Bermuda Triangle, never to be heard from again.

The Bermuda Triangle is a part of the Atlantic Ocean extending from the Florida coast to Bermuda and Puerto Rico. Many ships have sailed into this area only to vanish. Is there an explanation for this?

In the western part of the triangle, a wide ocean current called the Gulf Stream is squeezed into the narrow area between Florida and the Great Bahama Banks as it flows northward. Winds blowing southward across the ocean surface in this area sometimes create large, dangerous waves when they meet the Gulf Stream. The Bermuda Triangle also has a reputation for unpredictable weather. Many sailors have been stranded there without wind for their sails. Strong thunderstorms and *waterspouts,* which are like tornadoes on the surface of the ocean, occur with little warning. To make matters worse, the ocean floor beneath the triangle is a maze of deep trenches that can hide a shipwreck.

The Bermuda Triangle

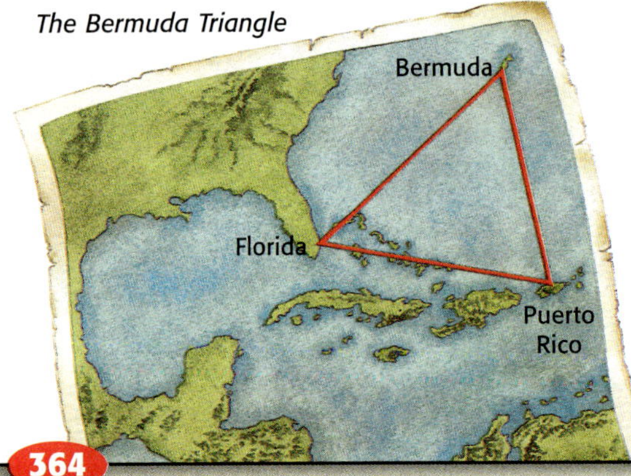

364

This Really Happened!

Sailing through the Bermuda Triangle is difficult because strong currents interact with the variable ocean-floor topography, which features shoals, deep trenches, and reefs, that cause turbulence. Students may be interested in researching scientific theories regarding the Bermuda Triangle. Encourage them to distinguish between theories that are based on scientific evidence and theories that are only speculation.

While many people link the Bermuda Triangle to the supernatural, the disappearance of ships there is probably best explained by scientific facts—dangerous waves and weather are capable of sinking ships. In this chapter you will learn about waves and other movements of ocean water.

What Do You Think?

In your ScienceLog, try to answer the following questions based on what you already know:

1. What factors control ocean currents?
2. What causes the ocean tides?

When Two *Whirls* Collide

Ocean currents in the Northern Hemisphere flow in a clockwise direction, while ocean currents in the Southern Hemisphere flow in a counterclockwise direction. In certain parts of the ocean, however, southern currents flow across the equator into the Northern Hemisphere and begin flowing clockwise. In this activity you and your lab partner will demonstrate how two currents flowing in opposite directions affect one another.

Procedure

1. Fill a large **tub** 5 cm full with **water.**
2. Add 10 drops of **red food coloring** to the water on one end of the tub.
3. Add 10 drops of **blue food coloring** to the water at the other end of the tub.
4. Using a **pencil,** quickly stir the water at the end of the tub with the red food coloring in a clockwise direction while your partner stirs the water at the other end in a counterclockwise direction. Stir both ends steadily for about 5 seconds.
5. In your ScienceLog, draw what you see happening in the tub immediately after you stop stirring. (Both ends should still be swirling.)

Analysis

6. How did the blue water and the red water interact?
7. How does this relate to the ocean currents in the Northern and Southern Hemispheres?

365

What Do You Think?

Accept all reasonable responses.

Students will have a chance to revise their answers in the Chapter Review under NOW What Do You Think?

Investigate!

MATERIALS
For Each Pair of Students:
• large tub
• water
• red food coloring
• blue food coloring
• 2 pencils

Teacher Notes: To avoid moving the tub after it is filled with water, put the tub in position before the water is added. Although food coloring is nontoxic and washes out of clothing, students should be careful not to spill the food coloring on their skin or clothes.

A cake pan similar in size to the tub can be used for this activity. Water depth should be about 5 cm. Advise students to observe the experiment closely—the desired result happens quickly and lasts only a few seconds.

Explore what happens with different types of tubs. Does the depth of the tub change the results?

Answers to Investigate!

6. When the blue or red water left its circle of moving water, it crossed the middle of the tub, joined the other colored water, and began circling with the other colored water in the opposite direction.
7. Currents in the Northern Hemisphere circle in the opposite direction as currents in the Southern Hemisphere do. When a current crosses the equator, it joins other currents and eventually circles in the direction opposite the direction it was circling before.

Chapter 14 Opener—California Standards: PE/ATE 4a, 4d, 7, 7e

SECTION 1

Focus

Currents

This section discusses the causes and characteristics of surface and deep currents in the ocean. Students will learn about the different factors related to ocean currents and explore the ways currents and climate are related.

Read excerpts from Thor Heyerdahl's *Kon-Tiki* (1950) or *The Ra Expeditions* (1971) to students. Display a large map of the world that shows the different ocean currents. After showing students the origination and destination points for Heyerdahl's voyages, discuss which currents he would have used to reach his destinations. Sheltered English

1) Motivate

REAL-WORLD CONNECTION

Have students discuss the characteristics of rivers. Ask students to compare rivers to ocean currents. Lead students to the understanding that rivers and currents are very different but share some important similarities. For example, both are long moving bodies of water. However, rivers flow due to the pull of gravity and are usually confined between banks. Ocean currents are driven by the wind or by temperature and salinity differences.

Directed Reading Worksheet 14 Section 1

1

NEW TERMS

surface current
Coriolis effect
deep current
upwelling
El Niño

OBJECTIVES

- Describe surface currents, and list the three factors that control them.
- Describe deep currents.
- Illustrate the factors involved in deep-current movement.
- Explain how currents affect climate.

Currents

Imagine that you are stranded on a desert island. You stuff a distress message into a bottle and throw it into the ocean, hoping it will find its way to someone who will send help. What are the forces that would send your bottle across the ocean, bobbing up and down as it traveled? Is there any way to predict where your bottle may land?

Earlier this century, a Norwegian explorer named Thor Heyerdahl tried to answer similar questions that involved human migration across the ocean. Heyerdahl theorized that the inhabitants of Polynesia originally sailed from Peru on rafts powered only by the wind and ocean currents. Unable to convince scientists of his theory, he decided to prove it. In 1947, Heyerdahl and a crew of five people set sail from Peru on a handcrafted raft. The raft, shown in **Figure 1,** was named the *Kon-Tiki,* after the Peruvian sun god.

Figure 1 *The handcrafted* Kon-Tiki *was made mainly from materials that would have been available to ancient Peruvians.*

BRAIN FOOD

There are two ways to send a message in a bottle via the Internet. You can request that a real, biodegradable bottle be tossed into the sea from various parts of the world, or you can send a virtual message in a bottle that will eventually wash up on somebody's "E-mail beach."

On the 97th day of their expedition, Heyerdahl and his crew landed on an island in Polynesia. The Humboldt and South Equatorial Currents had carried the raft westward more than 6,000 km across the South Pacific. This supported Heyerdahl's theory that ocean-surface currents carried the ancient Peruvians across the Pacific to Polynesia. But how did Heyerdahl know the direction of the currents? What forces created these currents? To answer these questions about ocean currents, and others you may have, let's examine what causes ocean currents, the different types of ocean currents, and how ocean currents affect climate.

IS THAT A FACT!

No metal was used in the construction of the *Kon-Tiki*. The wood raft was made of thick Peruvian balsa logs and featured a bamboo cabin set in the center, a large steering oar at the stern, and five centerboards. Two masts were used to support the rectangular sail. Although it crashed into a reef when it finally reached Polynesia, the *Kon-Tiki* was restored and is currently on display at a museum in Oslo, Norway.

Section 1—California Standards: PE/ATE 4, 4a, 4d, 4e, 7, 7c; LabBook: 7, 7b, 7e, 7h

Surface Currents

Surface currents are streamlike movements of water that occur at or near the surface of the ocean. Some surface currents are several thousand kilometers in length, traveling across entire oceans. The Gulf Stream, one of the longest surface currents, transports 25 times more water than all the rivers in the world. Surface currents are controlled by three factors: global winds, the Coriolis effect, and continental deflections. These three factors keep surface currents flowing continuously in distinct patterns around the Earth.

Global Winds Have you ever blown gently on a cup of hot chocolate? You may have noticed ripples moving across the surface. These ripples are caused by a tiny surface current created by your breath. In much the same way, winds blowing across the Earth's surface create surface currents in the ocean. Surface currents can reach depths of several hundred meters and widths of more than 1,000 km. That's quite a bit larger than the current in your cup of hot chocolate!

Wind has the power to move large quantities of water. Different winds cause currents to flow in different directions. Near the equator, the winds blow ocean water east to west, but closer to the poles, ocean water is blown west to east, as shown in **Figure 2.** Merchant ships often use these currents to travel more quickly back and forth across the oceans.

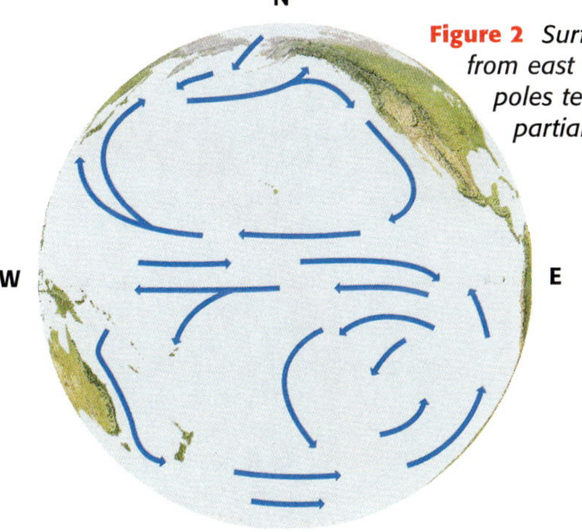

Figure 2 *Surface currents near the equator generally flow from east to west, but surface currents closer to the poles tend to flow from west to east. This pattern is partially a result of global wind patterns.*

Self-Check

Take another look at Figure 2. As Heyerdahl made his journey in 1947, from what direction would he have noticed the wind blowing? *(See page 564 to check your answer.)*

Answer to Self-Check

It may help students to look at a globe when answering the Self-Check. The Polynesian Islands are very small islands in the South Pacific, and students may not know where Peru is located in South America. Because he was traveling from Peru to a Polynesian island to the west, Heyerdahl would have noticed the wind blowing from the east.

2 Teach

Reading Strategy

Prediction Guide Before students read the passage describing the three causes of surface currents, ask them what they think might cause currents on the surface of oceans. Students will discover the answers as they continue reading Section 1.

Cross-Disciplinary Focus

Language Arts Ask students to copy passages from novels that describe the ocean and its currents. Students can share these passages in class and discuss whether or not they are scientifically accurate.

Connect to Life Science

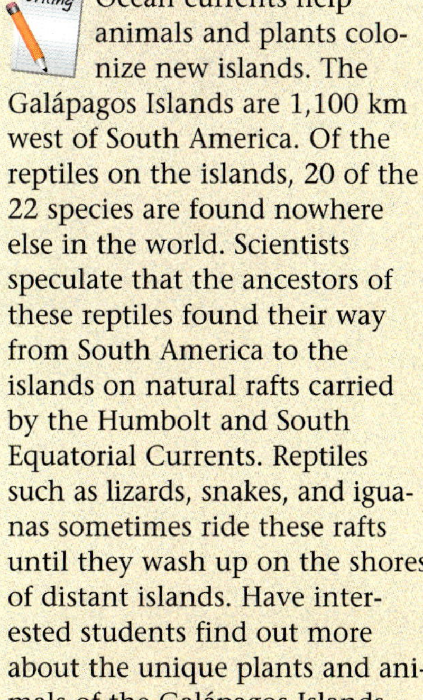

Writing | Ocean currents help animals and plants colonize new islands. The Galápagos Islands are 1,100 km west of South America. Of the reptiles on the islands, 20 of the 22 species are found nowhere else in the world. Scientists speculate that the ancestors of these reptiles found their way from South America to the islands on natural rafts carried by the Humbolt and South Equatorial Currents. Reptiles such as lizards, snakes, and iguanas sometimes ride these rafts until they wash up on the shores of distant islands. Have interested students find out more about the unique plants and animals of the Galápagos Islands.

2 Teach, continued

Reteaching

For students having difficulty understanding the Coriolis effect, use a turntable to demonstrate the concept.

1. Cover the surface of the turntable with a circle of paper cut to fit.
2. Turn the turntable platter so that it is spinning. Explain to students that the spinning turntable represents the rotating Earth.
3. Instruct a student to attempt to draw a straight line from the center of the turntable to the edge. A curved line will be formed. The curved line represents the curved path of surface currents due to Earth's rotation.

Sheltered English

Real-World Connection

In 1990, a Korean ship carrying a load of athletic shoes was bound for the United States. During a storm, 80,000 athletic shoes were washed overboard. This accident turned out to be a big bonus to oceanographers. The shoes, which were picked up by currents in the North Pacific, started to show up on the shores of Hawaii and northwestern North America. Oceanographers were pleased because the shoes traveled the same route that was predicted by computer models of the ocean currents. Have students look at a map of global ocean currents and identify the currents that carried the shoes to these shores.

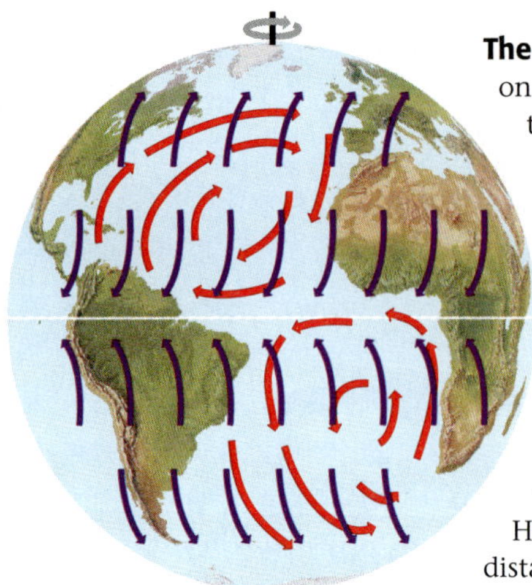

Figure 3 *The rotation of the Earth causes ocean currents (red arrows) and global winds (purple arrows) to move in opposite directions on either side of the equator.*

The Coriolis Effect You already know that the Earth rotates on its axis, but have you ever thought about how this rotation affects the Earth's surface? The Earth's rotation causes surface currents to move in curved paths rather than in straight lines. The turning of moving objects, such as ocean currents, by the Earth's rotation is called the **Coriolis effect.** The Coriolis effect acts on any object turning on an axis. For example, if you try to roll a ball straight across a turning merry-go-round, its path will turn before it reaches the other side. The Coriolis effect also causes global winds to blow in curved paths. **Figure 3** shows that ocean currents in the Northern Hemisphere turn clockwise, while ocean currents in the Southern Hemisphere turn counterclockwise. When water travels a great distance across the ocean, the Coriolis effect is much stronger.

Continental Deflections If the Earth's surface were covered only with water, surface currents would travel freely across the globe in a very uniform pattern. However, we know that this is not the case—continents rise above sea level over roughly one-third of the Earth's surface. When surface currents meet continents, they *deflect,* or change direction. Notice in **Figure 4** how the Brazil Current deflects southward as it meets the east coast of South America.

Explore

Some people think the Coriolis effect can be seen in sinks; that is, water draining from sinks turns clockwise in the Northern Hemisphere and counterclockwise in the Southern Hemisphere. Is this true? Research this question at the library, on the Internet, and in your sinks and tubs at home.

Figure 4 *If South America were not in the way, the Brazil Current would probably flow farther west.*

368

Misconception Alert

It is a common misconception that the direction in which water drains (clockwise versus counterclockwise) is determined by the Coriolis effect. Allow students to discover this themselves by directing them to do the Explore on this page.

Is That a Fact!

The Earth's rotation affects ocean currents directly by causing currents to circle in opposite directions on either side of the equator. Earth's rotation also affects the wind patterns, which in turn drive surface currents.

Taking Temperatures All three factors—global winds, the Coriolis effect, and continental deflections—work together to form a pattern of surface currents on Earth. But currents are also affected by the temperature of the water in which they arise. Warm-water currents begin near the equator and carry warm water to other parts of the ocean. Cold-water currents begin closer to the poles and carry cool water to other parts of the ocean. As you can see on the map in **Figure 5,** all the oceans are connected, and both warm-water and cold-water currents travel from one ocean to another.

While winds are responsible for ocean currents, the sun is the initial energy source of the currents. Because the sun heats the Earth more in some places than in others, convection currents are formed, which cause winds to blow.

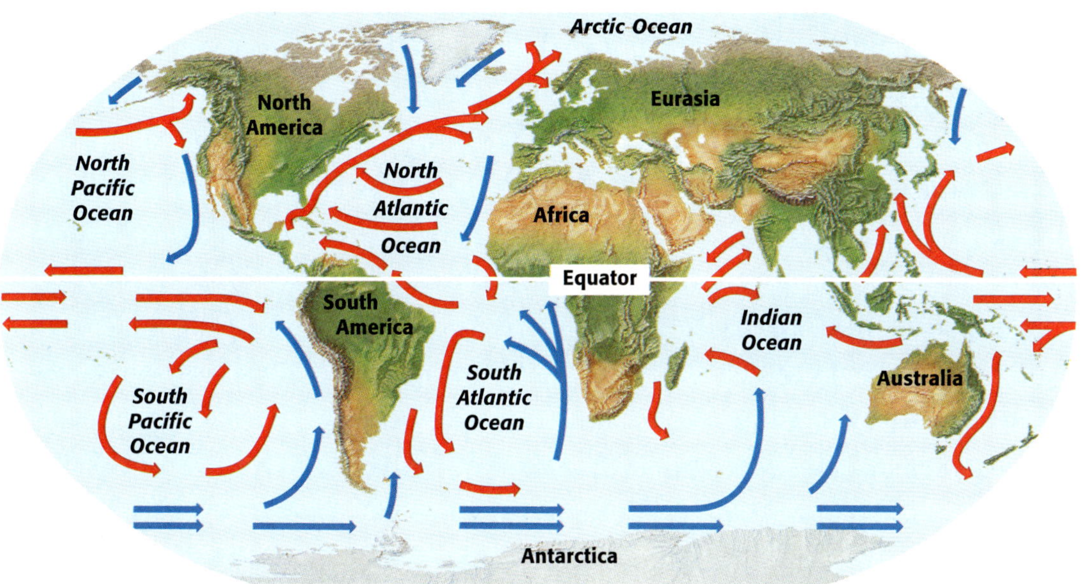

Figure 5 *This map shows Earth's surface currents. Warm-water currents are shown as red arrows, and cold-water currents are shown as blue arrows.*

REVIEW

1. List the three factors that control surface currents.
2. Explain how the Earth's rotation affects the patterns of surface currents.
3. **Inferring Conclusions** If there were no land on Earth's surface, what would the pattern of surface currents look like? Explain.

Answers to Review

1. The three factors that control surface currents are global winds, the Coriolis effect, and continental deflections.
2. The Earth's rotation causes the Coriolis effect. The Coriolis effect is seen in the pattern of the ocean's surface currents—surface currents in the Northern Hemisphere turn clockwise, and surface currents in the Southern Hemisphere turn counterclockwise.
3. If there were no land on Earth's surface, surface currents would not deflect sharply, as they do when they approach continents. The pattern of surface currents would reflect more-gradual turns.

MEETING INDIVIDUAL NEEDS

Learners Having Difficulty
Refer to **Figure 5** to point out that the currents in the Southern Hemisphere turn counterclockwise and the currents in the Northern Hemisphere turn clockwise. Using a globe, show the direction of ocean currents in various areas around the world. Note for students that a current in the South Atlantic Ocean crosses the equator and joins the clockwise-turning currents. Discuss how this process was modeled in the Investigate! activity at the beginning of this chapter. Sheltered English

Homework

Research Have students choose two coastal cities that are separated by an ocean. Ask students to describe in their ScienceLog the currents they would use to sail from one city to the other. Students should use **Figure 5** as a reference for determining which currents they would use. Students can use an atlas or another reference tool to find the names of their currents. They can write their entries in the form of a ship's log.

Teaching Transparency 135
"Earth's Surface Currents"

 PG 542

Up from the Depths

READING STRATEGY

Prediction Guide Before students read the section on deep currents, ask them to respond to the following questions:

Do global winds directly cause deep currents? (no)

Can ocean currents be caused by differences in water temperature? (yes)

Can ocean currents be caused by differences in salinity? (yes)

MATH and MORE

Review scientific notation with students. Tell them there are approximately 1.7×10^{19} water molecules in one drop of sea water and 1×10^{44} water molecules in the Mediterranean Sea. Have students help you write these two numbers to show how large they are. For reference, tell students that there are 17 times as many molecules in a drop of water than there are insects on Earth.

Math Skills Worksheet 25
"What Is Scientific Notation?"

Turn to page 542 in the LabBook to demonstrate how temperature and salinity affect ocean water.

Deep Currents

Deep currents are streamlike movements of ocean water far below the surface. Unlike surface currents, deep currents are not directly controlled by wind or the Coriolis effect. Instead, they form in parts of the ocean where water density increases. *Density* is the ratio of the mass of a substance to its volume. Two main factors—temperature and salinity—combine to affect the density of ocean water, as shown below. As you can see, both decreasing the temperature of ocean water and increasing the water's salinity increase the water's density.

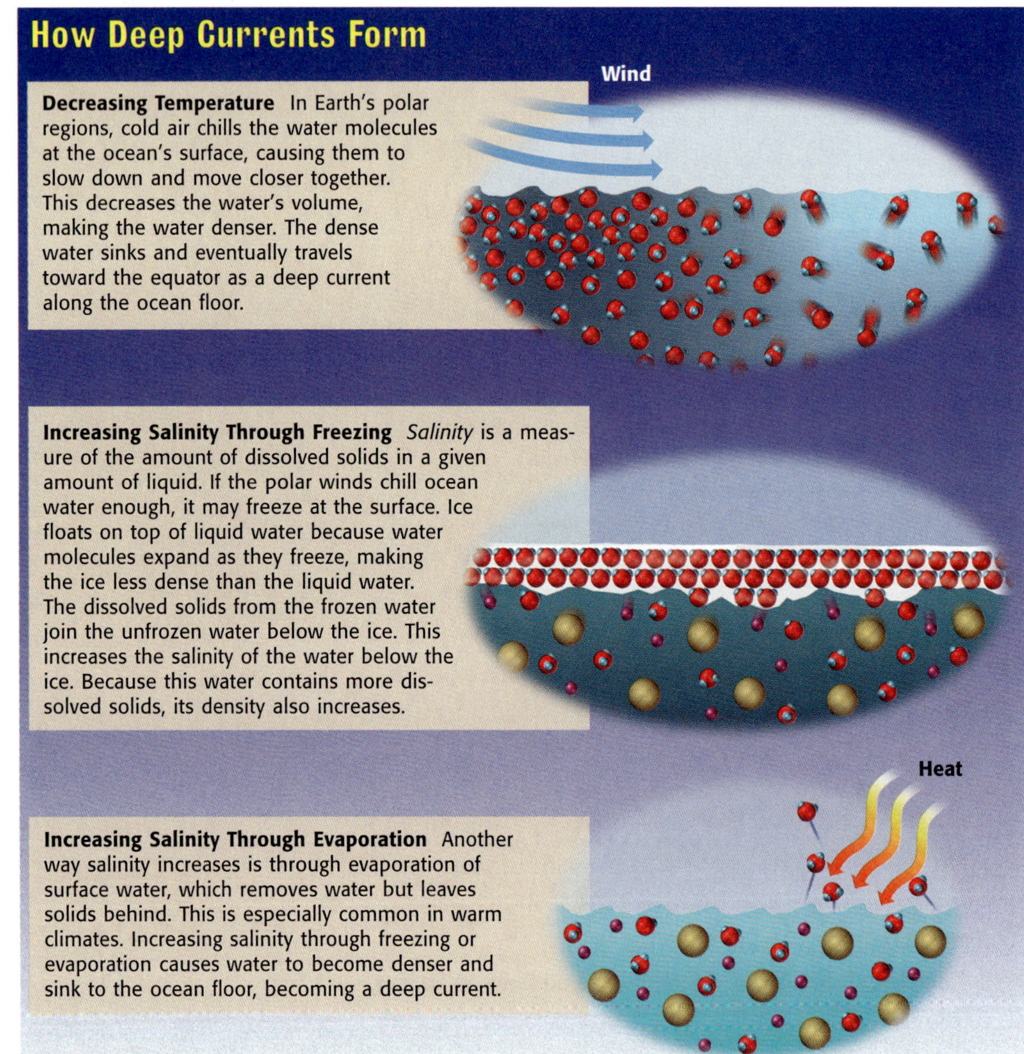

Decreasing Temperature In Earth's polar regions, cold air chills the water molecules at the ocean's surface, causing them to slow down and move closer together. This decreases the water's volume, making the water denser. The dense water sinks and eventually travels toward the equator as a deep current along the ocean floor.

Increasing Salinity Through Freezing *Salinity* is a measure of the amount of dissolved solids in a given amount of liquid. If the polar winds chill ocean water enough, it may freeze at the surface. Ice floats on top of liquid water because water molecules expand as they freeze, making the ice less dense than the liquid water. The dissolved solids from the frozen water join the unfrozen water below the ice. This increases the salinity of the water below the ice. Because this water contains more dissolved solids, its density also increases.

Increasing Salinity Through Evaporation Another way salinity increases is through evaporation of surface water, which removes water but leaves solids behind. This is especially common in warm climates. Increasing salinity through freezing or evaporation causes water to become denser and sink to the ocean floor, becoming a deep current.

370

MISCONCEPTION ALERT

Remind students that molecules aren't made of little colored balls—the balls in the illustration on this page are models that represent molecules. The red and blue balls that are attached to one another represent water molecules, and the other balls represent dissolved solids.

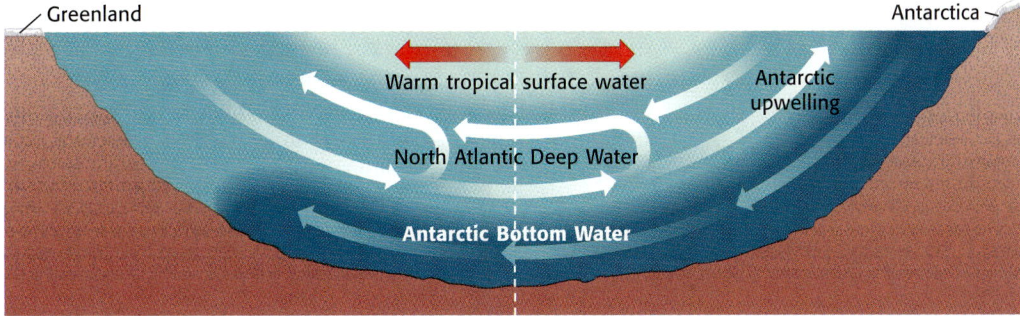

Figure 6 *This cross section shows that the less-dense North Atlantic Deep Water, which forms in the Arctic Ocean near Greenland, flows on top of the denser Antarctic Bottom Water when the two currents meet.*

Movement of Deep Currents The movement of deep currents as they travel along the ocean floor is very complex. Differences in temperature and salinity, and therefore in density, cause variations in deep currents. For example, the deepest current, the Antarctic Bottom Water, is denser than the North Atlantic Deep Water. Both currents spread out across the ocean floor as they flow toward the same equatorial region. But when the currents meet, the North Atlantic Deep Water actually flows on top of the denser Antarctic Bottom Water, as shown in **Figure 6.** The Antarctic Bottom Water is so dense that it moves incredibly slowly—it takes 750 years for water in this current to make it from Antarctica's coastal waters to the equator!

Currents Trading Places Now that you understand how deep currents form and how they move along the ocean floor, you can learn how they trade places with surface currents. To see how this works, study **Figure 7.**

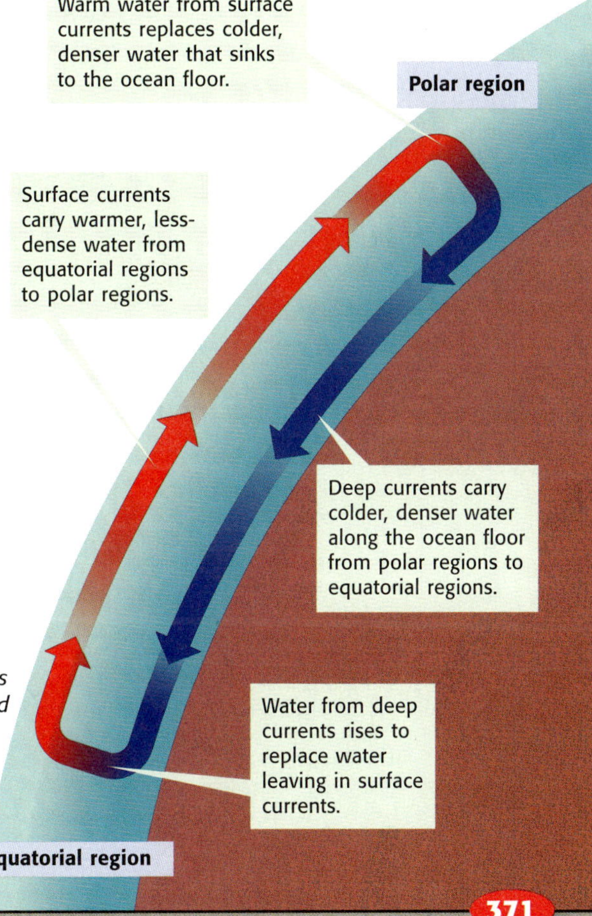

Figure 7 *This cross section shows the movement of warm water and cold water between polar and equatorial regions.*

371

Using the Figure

Figure 6 and **Figure 7** may appear to contradict one another. Explain to students that **Figure 6** is a detailed diagram showing the interaction of specific currents, while **Figure 7** is a generalized description of a cycle involving deep currents and surface currents. Make sure students realize that colder water becomes warmer near the equator and that warmer water becomes colder near the poles.

Connect to Life Science

Deep currents that reach the equator rise to the surface. This water brings with it nutrients that allow plankton to grow. The massive amounts of plankton in turn support large fish populations. The western coasts of both South America and North America are incredibly rich sources of fish. Populations in these coastal areas depend on the fishing industry as a major source of income and food. Encourage interested students to find out about different species of commercial fish harvested off the western coasts of North and South America.

Teaching Transparency 136
"How Deep Currents Form"

Teaching Transparency 137
"Circulation of Deep and Surface Currents"

Homework

Graphing Have students select two pairs of cities on opposite sides of a continent. All the cities should be at approximately the same latitude. One city from each pair should be located on the coast, and the other for each pair should be less than 300 km inland. For example, they could choose San Francisco and Fresno, California, and Norfolk and Roanoke, Virginia. Have students find the average high and low temperatures for each city. Next, have students find the average ocean temperature at the coastal cities. Have students plot the temperatures on a bar graph. Ask students to explain how ocean temperature affects the climate of the coastal cities.

3 Extend

Cross-Disciplinary Focus

History Early in American history, Benjamin Franklin noticed that mail ships took much longer to travel from England to America than from America to England. He then discovered that ships from England were sailing against the Gulf Stream. Franklin revolutionized ocean navigation by designing charts that helped sailors avoid sailing against major surface currents.

Brain Food

Hurricanes are large tropical storms that originate in either the Atlantic or the Caribbean. Hurricanes are created when warm water builds storm clouds, resulting in a massive low-pressure cell. Hurricanes generally make landfall on the East Coast of the United States, and they have reached as far north as Maine. On the West Coast, a hurricane has never made landfall in California. Ask students:

Why does the California Current, shown in **Figure 8,** protect California from hurricanes? (Because it is a cold-water current; the water off the coast of California is not warm enough to generate storm clouds or a low-pressure cell.)

Surface Currents and Climate

Surface currents greatly affect the climate in many parts of the world. Some surface currents warm or cool coastal areas year-round. Other surface currents sometimes change their circulation pattern. This causes changes in the atmosphere that disrupt the climate in many parts of the world.

Currents That Stabilize Climate Although surface currents are generally much warmer than deep currents, their temperatures do vary. Surface currents are classified as warm-water currents or cold-water currents. Look back at Figure 5 to see where each type is located. Because they are warm or cold, surface currents affect the climate of the land near the area where they flow. For example, warm-water currents create warmer climates in coastal areas that would otherwise be much cooler. Likewise, cold-water currents create cooler climates in coastal areas that would otherwise be much warmer. **Figure 8** shows how a warm-water current and a cold-water current affect coastal climates.

Figure 8 *Both warm-water currents, such as the Gulf Stream, and cold-water currents, such as the California Current, can affect the climate of coastal regions.*

372

Misconception Alert

El Niño is not a storm or any kind of weather pattern. It is a periodic change in the location of warm and cool surface waters in the Pacific Ocean. However, El Niño does ultimately cause local weather conditions that differ from typical conditions.

Current Variations—El Niño The surface currents in the tropical region of the Pacific Ocean usually travel with the trade winds from east to west. This builds up warm water in the western Pacific and causes upwelling in the eastern Pacific. **Upwelling** is a near-shore process in which cold, nutrient-rich water from the deep ocean rises to the surface to replace warm surface water that is blown farther out to sea by prevailing winds. But every 2 to 7 years, the South Pacific trade winds relax and move less surface water to the western Pacific. This reduces upwelling along the coast of South America, causing surface water temperatures there to rise. Gradually, this warming spreads westward. This periodic change in the location of warm and cool surface waters in the Pacific Ocean is called **El Niño.** El Niño not only affects surface waters but also alters the interaction between the ocean and the atmosphere, causing changes in the atmosphere's circulation. Global climatic changes are the end result.

BRAIN FOOD

El Niño means "The Child" in Spanish. The term originally referred to a warm current that arrived each year during the Christmas season off the coast of Ecuador and Peru.

Effects of El Niño Scientists are concerned about the global climatic changes caused by El Niño because the changes alter weather patterns. These changing weather patterns cause disasters, such as flash floods and mudslides in areas of the world that normally receive little rain. **Figure 9** shows homes destroyed by a mudslide in Southern California, an area that usually receives little rainfall. While some regions flood, regions that usually receive a lot of rain may experience droughts, which can lead to crop failures. For example, the country of Indonesia (located in the Pacific Ocean along the equator) depends on annual monsoon rains for growing crops. During an El Niño season, these rains are blown over the middle of the Pacific Ocean, missing Southeast Asia altogether.

Figure 9 *In 1997, an El Niño caused excessive rain in Southern California. These homes were destroyed by rain-generated mudslides.*

REVIEW

1. How do temperature and salinity relate to deep-current movement?
2. Why is the climate in Scotland relatively mild even though the country is located at a high latitude?
3. **Applying Concepts** Many marine organisms depend on upwelling to bring nutrients to the surface. How might an El Niño affect Peruvians' way of life?

373

Answers to Review

1. Decreasing the water's temperature or increasing its salinity will increase its density. As water gets denser, it sinks and becomes a deep current that moves along the ocean floor.
2. Because the Gulf Stream brings warm water from the tropics to Scotland's shore, the retained heat in the water helps warm the air in Scotland.
3. El Niño prevents upwelling from occurring along the coast of Peru. Without upwelling, nutrients from deep water do not rise to the surface. Marine organisms that depend on the nutrients for food may die. Peruvians who depend on these organisms may suffer. For example, if fish die, the fishing industry will suffer.

REAL-WORLD CONNECTION

El Niño has far-reaching effects on many countries. Many areas have been devastated as a result of El Niño–related floods, storms, and droughts. Have students search for news stories describing some of the effects of El Niño in recent years. Encourage students to contrast these reports with the positive effects of El Niño, such as extended growing seasons.

4 Close

Quiz

Ask students to give two characteristics and one example of each type of current. Allow for various answers.

1. Sample answer: Surface currents occur at the surface of the ocean and are influenced by the Coriolis effect; the Gulf Stream is an example.
2. Sample answer: Deep currents occur deep in the ocean and are influenced by differences in water density; the Antarctic Bottom Water is an example.

ALTERNATIVE ASSESSMENT

Ask students to imagine they are planning a voyage around the world. They can choose any route they wish, but they must sail with the currents. Have them map out their selected route, showing the names of the currents, their point of origin, and point of destination.

Interactive Explorations, CD-ROM "Latitude Attitude"

Section 1 Review—California Standards: PE/ATE 4, 4d, 4e, 5e

SECTION 2

Focus

Waves

This section describes the characteristics of waves. Students will explore wave formation and movement. They will also learn how to identify different types of waves and measure different wave features. Finally, the section discusses dangerous movements of ocean water.

Bellringer

Illustrate the following scenario on the board or overhead projector:

You are floating in the ocean 1 km from shore, which is north of you. There is a surface current flowing east. Are you more likely to travel north with the waves toward the shore or east with the surface current? (east, because wave energy travels through the water but the water doesn't travel with the waves)

Tell students that Section 2 will help explain this answer.

1 Motivate

DEMONSTRATION

Arrange chairs in a long row, and have students sit in the chairs. Then have them stand and sit in succession to form a "human wave." Ask them to discuss and then demonstrate how the shape and motion of the wave could be changed. (Examples include standing and sitting more quickly to decrease the wave period or stretching their arms over their heads as they stand and bringing them down to their sides as they sit to increase the wave height.) Sheltered English

2

NEW TERMS

crest, trough, wavelength, wave height, wave period, breaker zone, surf, whitecap, swells, tsunami, storm surge

OBJECTIVES

- Identify wave components, and explain how they relate to wave movement.
- Describe how ocean waves form and how they move.
- Classify types of waves.
- Analyze types of dangerous waves.

Waves

We all know what ocean waves look like. Even if you've never been to the seashore, you've most likely seen waves on television. But what are ocean waves? How do they form and move? Are all waves the same? And what do they do besides drop shells and sand dollars on the beach? Let us examine ocean waves so that we can answer these questions.

Anatomy of a Wave

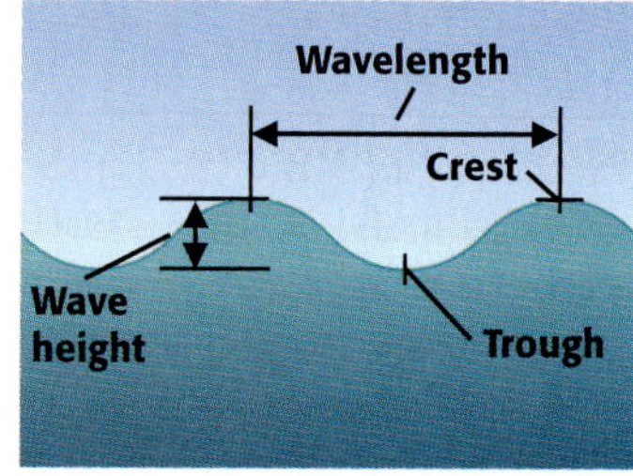

Waves are made up of two main components—crests and troughs. A **crest** is the highest point of a wave, and a **trough** is the lowest point. Envision a thrilling roller coaster designed with many rises and dips. The top of a rise on a roller-coaster track is similar to the crest of a wave, and the bottom of a dip in the track resembles the trough of a wave. The distance between two adjacent wave crests or wave troughs is a **wavelength.** The vertical distance between a wave's crest and its trough is a **wave height.**

Wave Formation and Movement

If you have watched ocean waves before, you may have noticed that water appears to move across the ocean's surface. However, this movement is only an illusion. Most waves form as wind blows across the water's surface, transferring energy to the water. As the energy moves through the water, so do the waves. But the water itself stays behind, rising and falling in circular movements. Notice in **Figure 10** that the floating bottle remains in the same spot as the waves travel from left to right. The circle of moving water that the bottle moves with has a diameter that is equal to the height of the waves that created it. Underneath this circle are smaller circles of moving water. The diameters of these circles get smaller with depth because wave energy decreases with depth. Wave energy only reaches to a certain depth. Below that depth, the water is not affected by wave energy.

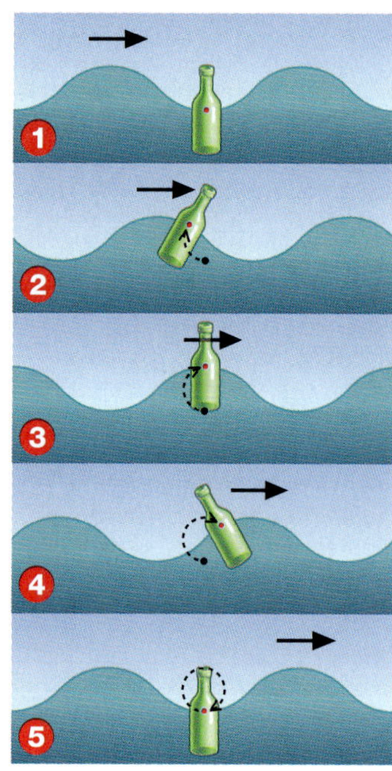

Figure 10 *Like the bottle in this figure, water remains in the same place as waves travel through it.*

374

Draw this diagram to show students how the circular motion of water in waves decreases in size as depth increases.

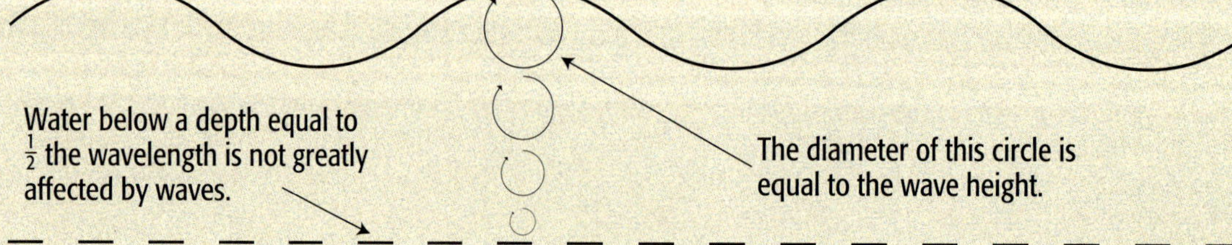

Section 2—California Standards: PE/ATE 1, 1e, 2, 2d, 2e, 3a, 4, 4a

Specifics of Wave Movement

Waves not only come in different sizes but also travel at different speeds. To calculate wave speed, scientists must know the wavelength and the wave period. **Wave period** is the time it takes for two waves to pass a fixed point, as shown in **Figure 11.** Dividing wavelength by wave period gives you wave speed, as shown below.

$$\frac{\text{wavelength (m)}}{\text{wave period (s)}} = \text{wave speed (m/s)}$$

For any given wavelength, an increase in wave period will decrease the wave speed, and a decrease in wave period will increase the wave speed.

MATH BREAK

Wave Speed

Imagine you are in a rowboat on the open ocean. You count 4 waves traveling right under your boat in 10 seconds. You estimate the wavelength to be 3 m. What is the wave speed?

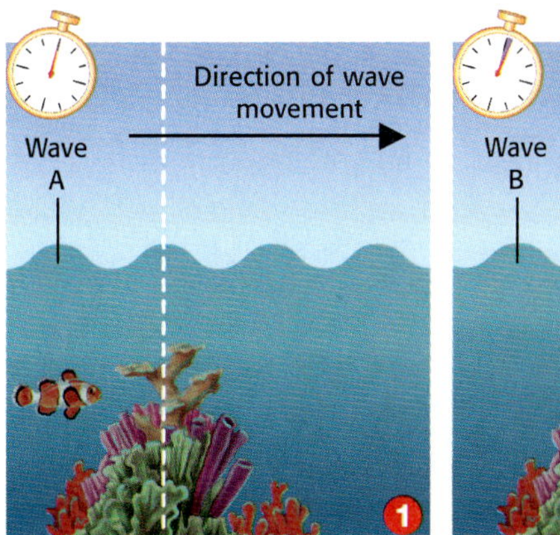

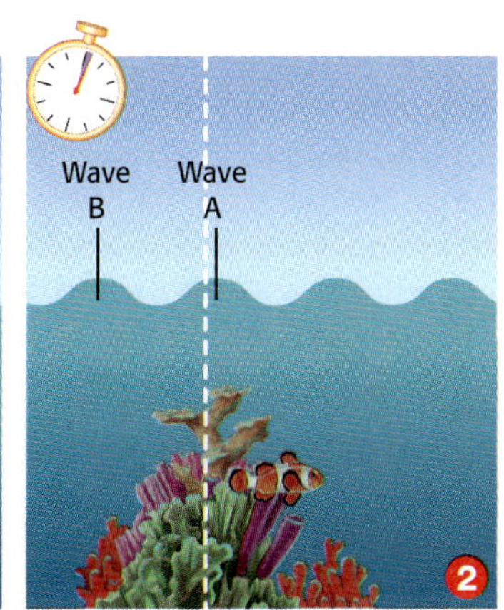

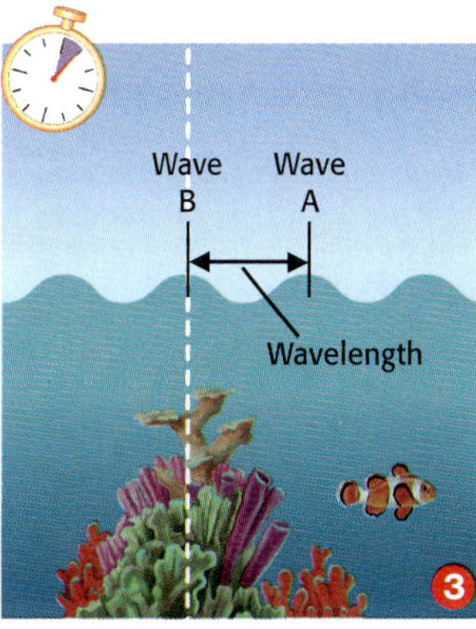

Figure 11 *Notice in frame 1 that the waves are moving from left to right. In frame 2, the clock begins running as Wave A passes the reef's peak. The clock stops in frame 3 as Wave B passes the reef's peak. The time shown on the clock (5 seconds) represents the wave period.*

Ocean waves travel in the direction the wind blows. If the wind is constantly blowing, wavelength, wave height, and the energy of the waves increase. Wave height depends on the *fetch,* the distance the wind is able to blow and waves are able to travel without interruption. The greater the fetch is, the higher the waves are.

Types of Waves

As you learned earlier in this section, wind forms most ocean waves. However, waves can form by other mechanisms. Underwater earthquakes and landslides as well as impacts by cosmic bodies can form different types of waves. The sizes of the different types of waves can vary, but most move the same way. Depending on their size and the angle at which they hit the shore, waves can generate a variety of near-shore events, some of which can be dangerous to humans.

internetconnect

TOPIC: Ocean Waves
GO TO: www.scilinks.org
***sci*LINKS NUMBER:** HSTE340

TOPIC: Tsunamis
GO TO: www.scilinks.org
***sci*LINKS NUMBER:** HSTE345

2 Teach

MATH and MORE

Ask students how they would estimate wavelength and wave period if they were in a boat at sea. What visual marks might they use? Make sure students understand that wave period and wave speed are inversely proportional. That is, for a given wavelength, an increase in wave period means a decrease in wave speed. Have students work through several examples in their ScienceLog to see the relationships between the three wave measurements:

- The value of the wavelength is greater than the value of the wave period. (speed is greater than 1 m/s)
- The value of the wavelength is equal to the value of the wave period. (speed is equal to 1 m/s)
- The value of the wavelength is less than the value of the wave period. (speed is less than 1 m/s)

Answer to MATHBREAK

The wave speed is 0.6 m/s.

Teaching Transparency 138 "Wave Period and Speed"

Directed Reading Worksheet 14 Section 2

2 Teach, *continued*

READING STRATEGY

Activity Have students reproduce **Figures 12** and **13** in their ScienceLog. As you read the section, pause at each term, and have them label the terms in their diagram. Make sure students understand each new term before proceeding.
Sheltered English

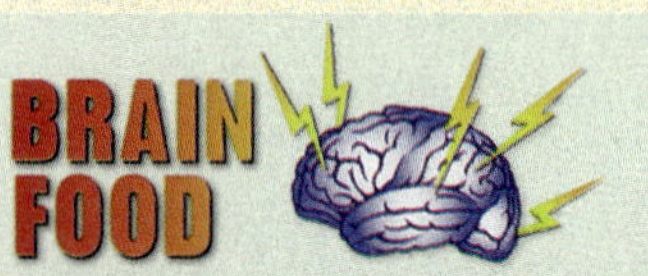

Ask the class why sighting a line of offshore breakers might cause sailors to consider turning their boats around. (Breaking waves could signal a submerged sandbar or reef. A ship could run aground if it encounters such an obstacle.)

REAL-WORLD CONNECTION

Discuss with students what they should do if they are ever caught in an undertow. Explain that instead of trying to swim against the current, they should swim parallel to the shore. This will get them out of the undertow. They can then swim to shore. Diagram this scenario for students, and have them show you the proper direction to swim.

Teaching Transparency 139
"Deep-Water Waves Become Shallow-Water Waves"

Deep-Water Waves and Shallow-Water Waves Have you ever wondered why waves increase in height as they approach the shore? The answer has to do with the depth of the water. *Deep-water waves* are waves that move in water that is deeper than one-half of their wavelength. But as the waves move closer to shore, the water becomes shallower. When the waves reach water that is shallower than one-half of their wavelength, they begin to interact with the ocean floor. These waves are called *shallow-water waves*.

As deep-water waves become shallow-water waves, the water particles slow down and build up, forcing more water between wave crests and increasing wave height. Gravity eventually pulls the high wave crests down, causing them to crash into the ocean floor as *breakers*. The near-shore area where waves first begin to tumble downward, or break, is called the **breaker zone.** Waves continue to break as they move from the breaker zone to the shore. The area between the breaker zone and the shore is called the **surf. Figure 12** illustrates how deep-water waves become shallow-water waves that eventually break.

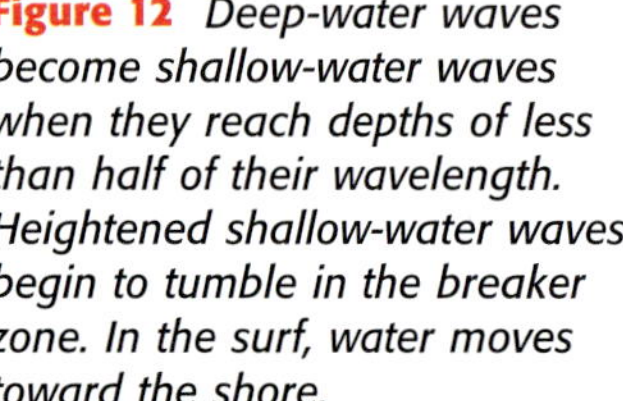

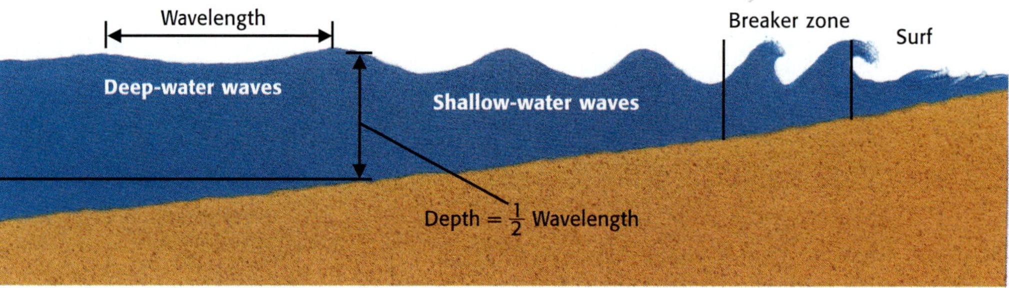

Figure 12 *Deep-water waves become shallow-water waves when they reach depths of less than half of their wavelength. Heightened shallow-water waves begin to tumble in the breaker zone. In the surf, water moves toward the shore.*

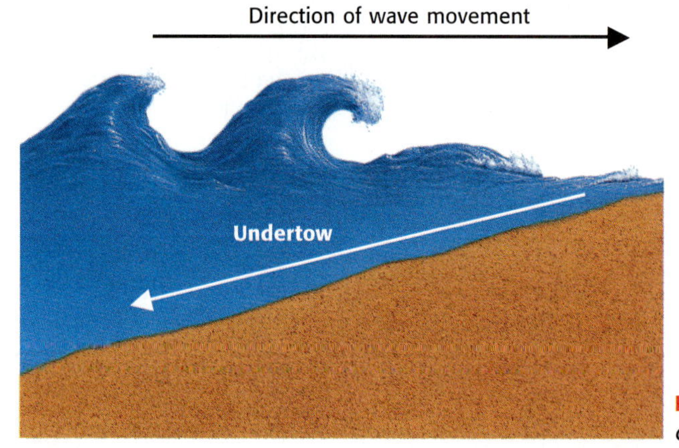

When waves crash on the beach head-on, the water they moved through flows back to the ocean underneath new incoming waves. This receding movement of water, which carries sand, rock particles, and plankton away from the shore, is called an *undertow*. **Figure 13** illustrates the back-and-forth movement of water at the shore.

Figure 13 *Head-on waves create an undertow.*

Q: What do two oceans say when they meet?

A: long time no sea

When waves hit the shore at an angle, they cause water to move along the shore in a current called a *longshore current*. This process is shown in **Figure 14.** Longshore currents are responsible for most sediment transport in beach environments. This movement of sand and other sediment both tears down and builds up the coastline. Unfortunately, longshore currents also carry trash and other types of ocean pollution, spreading it along the shore.

Figure 14 *Longshore currents form where waves approach beaches at an angle.*

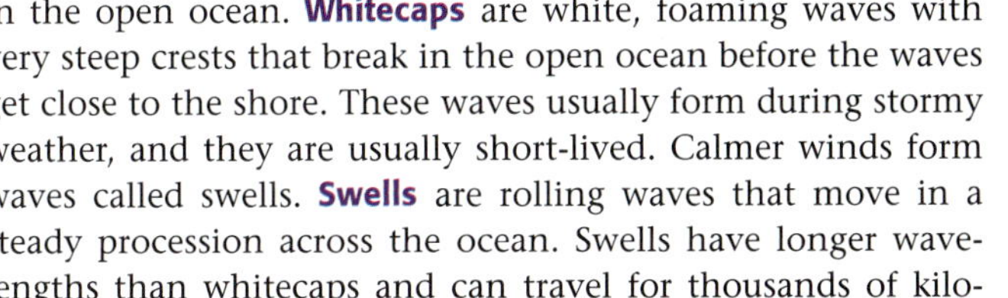

Open-Ocean Waves Sometimes waves called whitecaps form in the open ocean. **Whitecaps** are white, foaming waves with very steep crests that break in the open ocean before the waves get close to the shore. These waves usually form during stormy weather, and they are usually short-lived. Calmer winds form waves called swells. **Swells** are rolling waves that move in a steady procession across the ocean. Swells have longer wavelengths than whitecaps and can travel for thousands of kilometers. **Figure 15** shows how whitecaps and swells differ.

Not far offshore from Galveston Island, Texas, engineers use huge suction machines to collect sand from the ocean floor. This sand is then blown onto the shoreline, rebuilding the beaches that have been eroded by longshore currents.

Figure 15 *Whitecaps, shown in the photo above, break in the open ocean, while swells, shown in the photo at right, roll gently in the open ocean.*

MATH and MORE

Whitecaps are usually caused by strong winds. When the wind blows more than 13 km/h, wave height increases faster than wavelength. When wave height is more than one-seventh of the wavelength, whitecaps form. If the wavelength is 3 m, what is the minimum wave height for whitecaps to form? (about 43 cm)

If the wavelength is 10 m, what is the minimum wave height for whitecaps to form? (about 1.43 m)

If whitecaps begin to form when the wave height reaches 4 m, what is the wavelength? (about 28 m)

Math Skills Worksheet 11 "What Is a Fraction?"

Homework

Writing Surfing originated in the South Seas about 2,500 years ago. Polynesian sailors who couldn't get their boats through the rough waves near the shore would surf to land. It is now a recreational sport practiced all over the world.

Have students write a report about the history of surfing. Their report should include an explanation of the characteristics that make specific locations around the world ideal for surfing.

CONNECT TO ENVIRONMENTAL SCIENCE

Discuss the Environmental Science Connection in the text. Students may be interested to know that this process is also done on other islands along the Texas coast as well as along the Atlantic Coast from New Jersey to South Carolina. There is controversy over rebuilding beaches because some people believe the natural erosion of beaches should not be tampered with. However, the net loss of sediment on many barrier islands is great due to artificial dams that prevent rivers from bringing more sediment to the coastal islands.

3 Extend

CONNECT TO METEOROLOGY

The sciences of oceanography and meteorology are combined in the duties of the National Oceanic and Atmospheric Administration (NOAA). Founded in 1970, this federal agency forecasts weather and monitors potentially destructive natural events, such as hurricanes, floods, and tsunamis. Interested students can write to NOAA or visit their Web site for more information.

GOING FURTHER

Writing Have students research a tsunami that occurred in recent history and write a brief newspaper-style article about it. Students could learn about the tsunami that struck the Pacific coast of Nicaragua in 1992 or the one that devastated Papau New Guinea in 1998. Encourage students to read their articles to the class.

Turn to page 388 to learn about a scientist who studies earthquakes that cause tsunamis.

Tsunamis Professional surfers often travel to Hawaii to catch some of the highest waves in the world. But even the best surfers would not be able to handle a giant tsunami. **Tsunamis** are waves that form when a large volume of ocean water is suddenly moved up or down. This movement can be caused by underwater earthquakes, volcanic eruptions, landslides, underwater explosions, or the impact of a cosmic body, such as a meteorite or comet. The majority of tsunamis occur in the Pacific Ocean because of the greater number of earthquakes in that region. **Figure 16** shows how an earthquake can generate a tsunami.

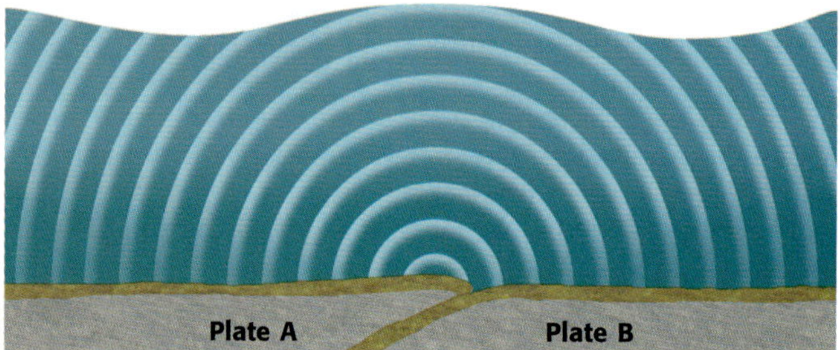

Figure 16 *Tectonic Plate B moves suddenly under Plate A, causing an upward shift in the ocean floor. This shift creates an earthquake that releases energy into the ocean. The energy pushes a large volume of water upward, creating a series of dangerous tsunamis.*

Although tsunami wavelengths can be more than 150 km, tsunamis behave much like wind-generated waves. When tsunamis near continents, they slow down and their wavelengths shorten as they interact with the ocean floor. As tsunamis get closer together, the water is compressed into a smaller space, increasing their wave height. Tsunamis can reach more than 30 m in height as they slam into the coast, destroying just about everything in their path. The powerful undertow created by a tsunami can be as destructive as the tsunami itself. **Figure 17** shows a coastal community devastated by a tsunami.

Figure 17 *Imagine the strength of the tsunami that carried this boat so far inland!*

378

WEIRD SCIENCE

In 1946, the crew of a freighter anchored offshore near Hilo, Hawaii, were astounded to witness an enormous tsunami crash on the shore, crushing buildings, felling trees, and carrying boats, piers, and rocks ashore. Moments before, the wave had passed beneath the freighter unnoticed!

IS THAT A FACT!

The highest recorded tsunami was 64 m (210 ft) high; it struck Kamchatka, Siberia, in 1737.

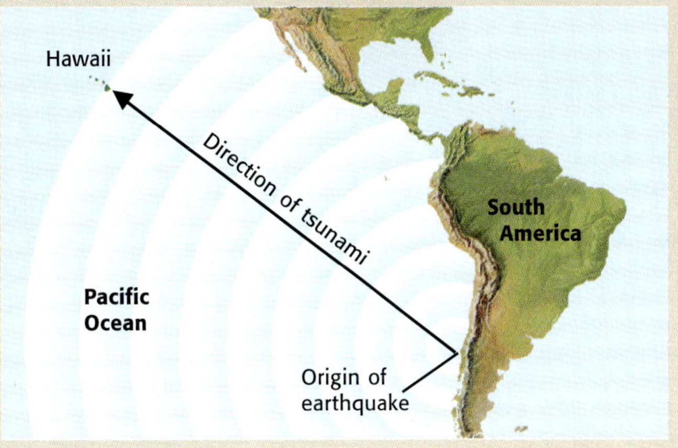

On May 22, 1960, an earthquake off the coast of South America generated a tsunami that completely crossed the Pacific Ocean. Ten thousand kilometers away from the origin of the earthquake, the tsunami hit the city of Hilo on the coast of Hawaii, causing extensive damage. If the tsunami traveled at a speed of 188 m/s, how long after the earthquake occurred did the tsunami reach Hilo? If the residents of Hilo heard about the earthquake as soon as it happened, do you think they had enough warning time? What might be done to ensure that this amount of time would be sufficient warning for a tsunami?

Storm Surges

A **storm surge** is a local rise in sea level near the shore that is caused by strong winds from a storm, such as a hurricane. Winds form a storm surge by blowing water into a big pile under the storm. As the storm moves onto shore, so does the giant mass of water beneath it. Storm surges often disappear as quickly as they form, making them difficult to study. Storm surges contain a lot of energy and can reach about 8 m in height. This often makes them the most destructive part of hurricanes.

REVIEW

1. Explain how water moves as waves travel through it.
2. Where do deep-water waves become shallow-water waves?
3. Name five events that can cause a tsunami.
4. **Doing Calculations** Look again at Figure 11. If the wave speed is 0.8 m/s, what is the wavelength?

QuickLab

Do the Wave

1. Tie one end of a thin piece of **rope** to a doorknob.
2. Tie a **ribbon** around the rope halfway between the doorknob and the other end of the rope.
3. Holding the rope at the untied end, quickly move the rope up and down, and observe the ribbon.
4. How does the movement of the rope and ribbon relate to the movement of water and deep-water waves?
5. Repeat step 3, but move the rope higher and lower this time.
6. How does this affect the waves in the rope?

4 Close

Answers to APPLY

The tsunami reached Hilo almost 15 hours after the earthquake occurred. Fifteen hours may seem like a long time, but evacuating people from a coastal area is a major task. It is important for people who live along the coast to be educated about tsunamis. To better prepare for tsunamis, people could make an evacuation plan, perform evacuation drills, and set aside nonperishable food and medical supplies for emergency use.

Quiz

Concept Mapping Have students create a concept map linking section concepts and vocabulary.

ALTERNATIVE ASSESSMENT

Using the wave characteristics described in this section, have students construct diagrams of different types of waves with varied characteristics. Use the transparency below to review wave characteristics with students. The diagrams should be made on poster board so they can be shared with the class and displayed in the classroom.

Teaching Transparency 195
"Wave Speed, Wavelength, and Frequency"

Reinforcement Worksheet 14
"Waves to Your Pen Pal"

Answers to Review

1. Water at and near the surface rises and falls in circular movements as waves move through the water.
2. Deep-water waves become shallow-water waves in water that is shallower than one-half the wavelength of the deep-water waves.
3. Five events that can cause a tsunami are underwater earthquakes, volcanic eruptions, landslides, underwater explosions, and the impact of a cosmic body.
4. The wavelength is 4 m.

SECTION 3

Focus

Tides

The gravitational attraction of the moon and the sun creates tides on Earth. Students will learn how the position of Earth in relation to the moon and the sun creates different kinds of tides. They will also learn about the effects of coastal topography on tidewaters.

Bellringer

Measure 0.75 m toward the ceiling from a spot in the center of a wall, and mark this point with a piece of tape. Beside the measurement, write "average high tide." Then measure 0.75 m below the center spot, and label it "average low tide." Ask students, "What do you think is the greatest tidal range in the world?"

After students have guessed, tell them that the world's greatest tidal range occurs in the Bay of Fundy, between Nova Scotia and Maine. There, the tidal range can be more than 15 m. Be prepared to show students how high 15 m (or 10 times the example on the wall) is. Sheltered English

1) Motivate

ACTIVITY

If possible, plan a visit to a coastal area. Beforehand, have the class research intertidal zones and the organisms that inhabit these areas. If a visit to the coast is not possible, have students research intertidal organisms and their survival strategies and share their findings with the class.

3

NEW TERMS

tides
tidal range
spring tides
neap tides
tidal bore

OBJECTIVES

- Explain tides and their relationship with the Earth, the sun, and the moon.
- Classify different types of tides.
- Analyze the relationship between tides and coastal land.

Tides

You haved learned how winds and earthquakes can move ocean water. But there are less-obvious forces that continually move ocean water in regular patterns called tides. **Tides** are daily movements of ocean water that change the level of the ocean's surface. Tides are influenced by the sun and the moon, and they occur in a variety of cycles.

Gravitational forces from both the sun and the moon continuously pull on the Earth. Although the moon is much smaller than the sun, the moon's gravity is the dominant force behind Earth's tides.

The Lure of the Moon

The phases of the moon and their relationship to the tides were first discovered more than 2,000 years ago by a Greek explorer named Pytheas. But Pytheas and other early investigators could not explain the relationship. A scientific explanation was not given until 1687, when Sir Isaac Newton's theories on the principle of gravitational pull were published. The gravity of the moon pulls on every particle of the Earth, but the pull is much more noticeable in liquids than in solids. This is because liquids move more easily. Even the liquid in an open soft drink is slightly pulled by the moon's gravity.

High Tide and Low Tide How high tides get and how often they occur depend on the position of the moon as it revolves around the Earth. The moon's pull is strongest on the part of the Earth directly facing the moon. When that part happens

380

MISCONCEPTION ALERT

Students may think that water flows horizontally toward or away from the shore due to tides. As students read this section, make sure they understand that low tide occurs in an area because the water is actually pulled away from the area. This decreases the volume of water in that location and causes the water level to lower and the shoreline to move seaward.

Section 3—California Standards: PE/ATE 3a, 4, 4a, 7c; LabBook: 7, 7b, 7e to be a portion of the ocean, the water there bulges toward the moon. At the same time, water on the opposite side of the Earth bulges due to the motion of the Earth and the moon around each other. These bulges are called *high tides*. Notice in **Figure 18** how the position of the moon causes the water to bulge. Also notice that when high tides occur, water is drawn away from the area between the high tides, causing *low tides* to form.

Puzzled about why high tide also occurs on the side of the Earth opposite the moon? Turn to page 544 to see how you can find out for yourself.

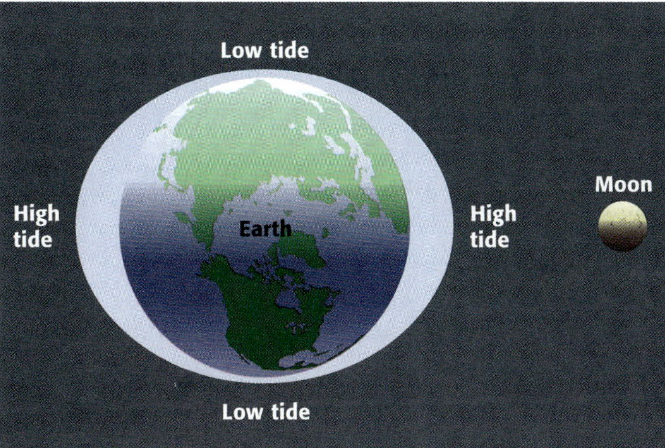

Figure 18 *High tide occurs on the part of Earth that is closest to the moon. At the same time, high tide also occurs on the opposite side of Earth.*

The rotation of the Earth and the revolving of the moon around the Earth determine when tides occur. If the Earth rotated at the same speed that the moon revolves around the Earth, tides would continuously occur at the same spots on Earth. But the moon revolves around the Earth much more slowly than the Earth rotates. **Figure 19** shows that it takes 24 hours and 50 minutes for a spot on Earth that is facing the moon to rotate so that it is facing the moon again.

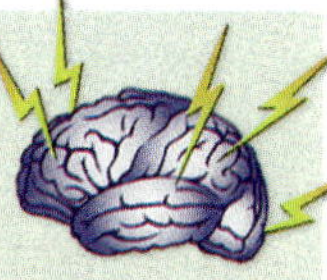

BRAIN FOOD

Even dry land has tides. For example, the land in Oklahoma moves up and down several centimeters throughout the day, corresponding with the tides. Tides on the solid part of Earth's surface are usually about one-third the size of ocean tides.

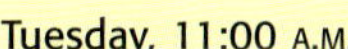

Tuesday, 11:00 A.M.

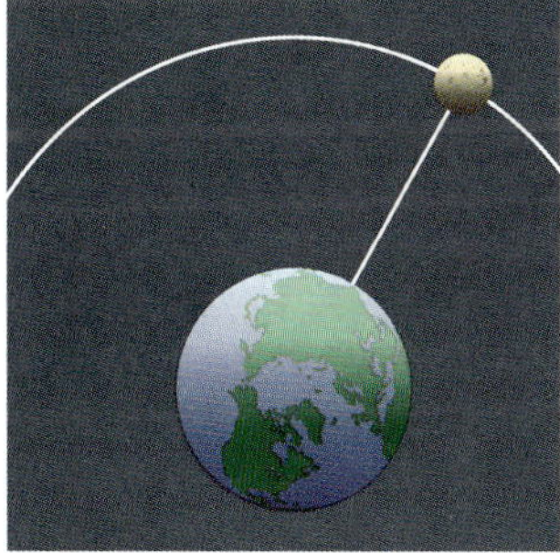

Wednesday, 11:50 A.M.

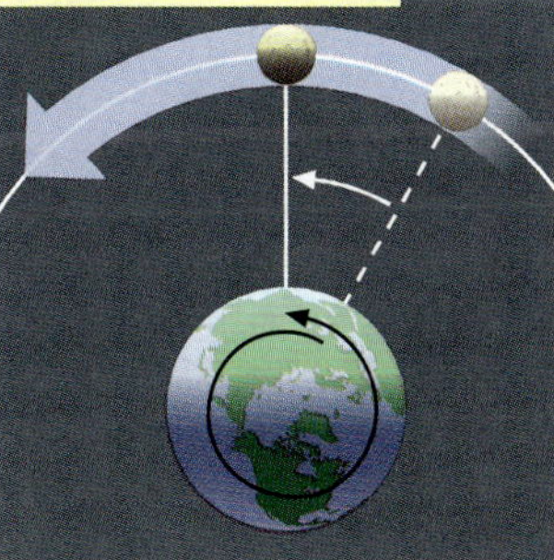

Figure 19 *Tides occur at different spots on Earth because the Earth rotates more quickly than the moon revolves around the Earth.*

2 Teach

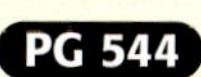

PG 544

Turning the Tides

USING THE FIGURE

Remind students that the Earth rotates at a much faster speed than the moon orbits. In **Figure 19,** point out that the distance the moon traveled is much shorter than the distance the spot on Earth facing the moon traveled. The spot on the Earth made more than a full rotation around the Earth's axis.

RETEACHING

Help students understand the hypothetical scenario discussed in the text (the moon revolving around the Earth at the same speed Earth rotates). Have students imagine the moon attached to a pole that is anchored to the Earth. In this scenario, the moon would turn with the Earth as the Earth rotates. The moon would always be facing the same spot on the Earth, so high tide would always occur at that spot and at the spot on the opposite side of the Earth. Make sure students realize this is not the case and that because the moon's revolution and the Earth's rotation occur at different speeds, the location of tides vary constantly.

SCIENTISTS AT ODDS

The cause of tides was a hotly debated topic in the sixteenth and seventeenth centuries. Galileo suggested that there was a connection between tides and the Earth's motion. To Galileo, tides proved beyond all doubt that Earth was moving. He argued that because Earth's waters are moving, Earth must be moving too. Johannes Kepler, another prominent scientist of the time, argued that the tides were linked to the moon's phases. Galileo made such a convincing argument that Kepler's ideas were dismissed. It was not until much later that scientists accepted that the gravitational forces exerted by the moon and the sun as well as the Earth's rotation are responsible for the tides.

Directed Reading Worksheet 14 Section 3

3 Extend

Meeting Individual Needs

Learners Having Difficulty Use this demonstration to show how tides are caused.

1. Use a small ball to represent the moon, a globe to represent Earth, and a large ball to represent the sun.
2. Ask a volunteer to help you show how the moon and Earth revolve around the sun.
3. Remind students that the moon and the sun are both "pulling" on Earth.
4. Point out that the moon's "pull" is greater than the sun's. Regions on Earth that are in a straight line from the moon experience high tides.
5. Point out that regions on Earth that face 90° away from the moon experience low tides.

Have students repeat the demonstration for each other to strengthen their understanding. Then ask students to read the text that explains spring tides and neap tides. Challenge students to use the globe and balls to demonstrate how spring tides and neap tides are caused.

Sheltered English

Homework

Graphing Help students look in the newspaper or on the Internet to find daily tidal information for a certain area for 1 month. Record the high- and low-tide measurements on a large chart that can be displayed in the classroom. At the end of the month, determine when spring tide and neap tide occurred. Compare these dates with the full, new, and quarter moon dates on a calendar, and have students graph this data to explain why the dates correspond.

Tidal Variations

The sun also affects tides. The sun is much larger than the moon, but it is also much farther away. As a result, the sun's influence on tides is less powerful than the moon's influence. The combined forces of the sun and the moon on the Earth result in tidal ranges that vary based on the positions of all three bodies. A **tidal range** is the difference between levels of ocean water at high tide and low tide.

Figure 20 *During spring tides, the gravitational forces of the sun and moon pull on the Earth either from the same direction (left) or from opposite directions (right).*

Spring Tides When the sun, Earth, and moon are in alignment with one another, spring tides occur. **Spring tides** are tides with maximum daily tidal range that occur during the new and full moons. Spring tides occur every 14 days. The first time spring tides occur is when the moon is between the sun and Earth. The second time spring tides occur is when the moon and the sun are on opposite sides of the Earth. **Figure 20** shows the positions of the sun and moon during spring tides.

Figure 21 *During neap tides, the sun and moon are at right angles with respect to the Earth. This arrangement minimizes their gravitational effect on the Earth.*

Neap Tides When the sun, Earth, and moon form a 90° angle, as shown in **Figure 21,** neap tides occur. **Neap tides** are tides with minimum daily tidal range that occur during the first and third quarters of the moon. Neap tides occur halfway between the occurrence of spring tides. When neap tides occur, the gravitational forces on the Earth by the sun and the moon work against each other—they do not pull along the same line as they do during spring tides.

Critical Thinking Worksheet 14 "Tides of Trouble"

The moon also creates tides in our atmosphere called lunar winds. Lunar winds move eastward in the morning and westward in the evening. Although these tides travel only 0.08 km/h, they can be detected by studying slight fluctuations in weather patterns.

Tides and Topography

Tides can be accurately predicted once the tidal range has been measured at a certain point over a period of time. This information can be useful for people who live near the coast, as illustrated in **Figure 22.**

Figure 22 *It's a good thing the people on the beach (left) knew when high tide occurred (right). These photos show the Bay of Fundy, in New Brunswick, Canada. The Bay of Fundy has the greatest tidal range on Earth.*

In some coastal areas with narrow inlets, movements of water called tidal bores occur. A **tidal bore** is a body of water that rushes up through a narrow bay, estuary, or river channel during the rise of high tide, causing a very sudden tidal rise. Sometimes tidal bores form waves that rush up the inlets, as shown in **Figure 23.** Tidal bores occur in coastal areas of China, the British Isles, France, and Canada.

Figure 23 *Surf's up! These people are riding a wave created by a tidal bore.*

REVIEW

1. At what two spots on Earth does high tide occur?
2. Which tides have minimum tidal range? Which tides have maximum tidal range?
3. What causes tidal bores?
4. **Applying Concepts** How many days pass between minimum and maximum tidal range in any given area? Explain.

Answers to Review

1. High tide occurs at the spot on Earth directly facing the moon and at the spot on Earth directly opposite the spot facing the moon.
2. Neap tides have minimum tidal range, and spring tides have maximum tidal range.
3. Tidal bores are caused by high tide rising in a narrow coastal inlet.
4. Seven days pass between minimum and maximum tidal range in any given area. Spring tides occur every 14 days, and neap tides occur midway between the occurrence of spring tides. Neap tides also occur every 14 days. Therefore, midway between the cycle of each type of tide, the other type occurs. The two types of tides alternate every 7 days.

RESEARCH

Making Models Tidal energy is one of the oldest renewable resources used by human civilizations. Tidal mills were used in England and France more than 900 years ago. Today, there are tidal power plants on the coast of France; on the Barents Sea, in Russia; and at Royal, Nova Scotia, in Canada. Have students research and make models of tidal energy plants.

4 Close

Quiz

1. How are high and low tides alike? (Answers will vary. Both depend on the position of the moon as it revolves around Earth.)
2. Why do spring tides exhibit such extremes of range? (When the moon, the sun, and Earth are aligned, as they are during spring tides, the tidal pull is maximized.)

ALTERNATIVE ASSESSMENT

Draw a random configuration of the sun, the moon, and Earth. Have students copy the drawing onto a sheet of paper. Then ask them to draw the tidal bulges caused by that configuration. Finally, have students draw the positions of the sun, moon, and Earth during spring and neap tides.

Teaching Transparency 140
"Tidal Variations"

Reinforcement Worksheet 14
"But What About the Tides?"

Chapter Highlights

Vocabulary Definitions

Section 1

surface current a streamlike movement of water that occurs at or near the surface of the ocean

Coriolis effect the turning of moving objects, such as ocean currents or winds, by the Earth's rotation

deep current a streamlike movement of ocean water far below the surface

upwelling a near-shore process in which cold, nutrient-rich water from the deep ocean rises to the surface to replace warm surface water that is blown farther out to sea by prevailing winds

El Niño a periodic change in the location of warm and cool surface waters in the Pacific Ocean

Section 2

crest the highest point of a wave

trough the lowest point of a wave

wavelength the distance between one point on a wave and the corresponding point on an adjacent wave in a series of waves; for example, the distance between two adjacent crests or compressions

wave height the vertical distance between a wave's crest and its trough

wave period the time it takes for two waves to pass a fixed point

breaker zone the near-shore area where waves first begin to tumble downward, or break

Chapter Highlights

Section 1

Vocabulary

surface current *(p. 367)*
Coriolis effect *(p. 368)*
deep current *(p. 370)*
upwelling *(p. 373)*
El Niño *(p. 373)*

Section Notes

- Currents are classified as surface currents and deep currents.
- Surface currents are controlled by three factors: global winds, the Coriolis effect, and continental deflections.
- Surface currents, such as the Gulf Stream, can be several thousand kilometers in length.
- Deep currents form where the density of ocean water increases. Water density depends on temperature and salinity.
- Surface currents affect the climate of the land near which they flow.

Labs

Up from the Depths *(p. 542)*

Section 2

Vocabulary

crest *(p. 374)*
trough *(p. 374)*
wavelength *(p. 374)*
wave height *(p. 374)*
wave period *(p. 375)*
breaker zone *(p. 376)*
surf *(p. 376)*
whitecap *(p. 377)*
swells *(p. 377)*
tsunami *(p. 378)*
storm surge *(p. 379)*

Section Notes

- Waves are made up of two main components—crests and troughs.
- Waves are usually created by the transfer of the wind's energy across the surface of the ocean.

Skills Check

Math Concepts

TWO OUT OF THREE The wave equation on page 375 has three variables. If you know two of these variables, you can figure out the third. Take a look at the examples below.

1. wave speed = 0.6 m/s, wave period = 10 s
   wavelength = wave speed × wave period = 6 m
2. wave speed = 0.6 m/s, wavelength = 6 m
   $$\text{wave period} = \frac{\text{wavelength}}{\text{wave speed}} = 10\text{ s}$$

Visual Understanding

BREAKING WAVES Before shallow-water waves break, their wave height increases and their wavelength decreases. Look at Figure 12 on page 376 again. Notice that the waves are taller and that their crests are closer together near the breaker zone.

384

Lab and Activity Highlights

Up from the Depths PG 542

Turning the Tides PG 544

Datasheets for LabBook (blackline masters for these labs)

SECTION 2

- Waves travel through water near the water's surface, while the water itself rises and falls in circular movements.
- Waves travel in the direction the wind blows. If the wind blows over a long distance, the wavelength becomes very large and the waves travel quickly.
- Wind-generated waves are classified as deep-water and shallow-water waves.
- Tsunamis are dangerous waves that can be very destructive to coastal communities.

SECTION 3

Vocabulary

tides *(p. 380)*
tidal range *(p. 382)*
spring tides *(p. 382)*
neap tides *(p. 382)*
tidal bore *(p. 383)*

Section Notes

- Tides are caused by the gravitational forces of the moon and sun tugging on the Earth.
- The moon's gravity is the main force behind tides.
- The relative positions of the sun and moon with respect to Earth cause different tidal ranges.
- Maximum tidal range occurs during spring tides.
- Minimum tidal range occurs during neap tides.
- Tidal bores occur as high tide rises in narrow coastal inlets.

Labs

Turning the Tides *(p. 544)*

internetconnect

GO TO: go.hrw.com

Visit the **HRW** Web site for a variety of learning tools related to this chapter. Just type in the keyword:

KEYWORD: HSTH20

GO TO: www.scilinks.org

Visit the **National Science Teachers Association** on-line Web site for Internet resources related to this chapter. Just type in the ***sci*LINKS** number for more information about the topic:

TOPIC	*sci*LINKS NUMBER
TOPIC: Ocean Currents	***sci*LINKS NUMBER:** HSTE330
TOPIC: El Niño	***sci*LINKS NUMBER:** HSTE335
TOPIC: Ocean Waves	***sci*LINKS NUMBER:** HSTE340
TOPIC: Tsunamis	***sci*LINKS NUMBER:** HSTE345
TOPIC: The Tides	***sci*LINKS NUMBER:** HSTE350

385

Vocabulary Definitions, *continued*

surf the area between the breaker zone and the shore

whitecap a white, foaming wave with a very steep crest that breaks in the open ocean before the wave gets close to the shore

swells rolling waves that move in a steady procession across the ocean

tsunami a wave that forms when a large volume of ocean water is suddenly moved up or down

storm surge a local rise in sea level near the shore that is caused by strong winds from a storm, such as a hurricane

Section 3

tides daily movements of ocean water that change the level of the ocean's surface

tidal range the difference between levels of ocean water at high tide and low tide

spring tides tides with maximum daily tidal ranges that occur during the new and full moons

neap tides tides with minimum daily tidal ranges that occur during the first and third quarters of the moon

tidal bore a body of water that rushes up through a narrow bay, estuary, or river channel during the rise of high tide, causing a very sudden tidal rise

Vocabulary Review Worksheet 14

Blackline masters of these Chapter Highlights can be found in the **Study Guide.**

Lab and Activity Highlights

LabBank

Whiz-Bang Demonstrations, Spin Cycle, Demo 26

Long-Term Projects & Research Ideas, Project 42

Interactive Explorations CD-ROM

CD 3, Exploration 4, "Latitude Attitude"

Chapter Review Answers

Using Vocabulary

1. A wavelength is the distance between two adjacent wave crests or wave troughs, while a wave height is the vertical distance between a wave's crest and its trough.
2. Whitecaps are waves that break in the open ocean, while swells are waves that roll gently.
3. A tsunami is a wave created when a large volume of ocean water is suddenly moved up or down, while a storm surge is a local rise in sea level near the shore that is caused by winds from a storm.
4. Spring tides occur when the sun, the Earth, and the moon are aligned; neap tides occur when the sun, the Earth, and the moon form a 90 degree angle. Tidal range is greatest during spring tide and lowest during neap tide.
5. Surface currents are directly controlled by wind.
6. El Niño reduces upwelling along the coast of South America.
7. Spring tides occur when the moon is between the Earth and the sun.
8. Tidal range is the difference between levels of ocean water at high tide and low tide.

Understanding Concepts

Multiple Choice

9. c
10. d
11. d
12. b
13. c
14. a

Chapter Review

USING VOCABULARY

For each pair of terms, explain the difference in their meaning.

1. wavelength/wave height
2. whitecap/swell
3. tsunami/storm surge
4. spring tide/neap tide

Replace the incorrect term in each of the following sentences with the correct term provided in the word bank below:

5. Deep currents are directly controlled by wind.
6. The Coriolis effect reduces upwelling along the coast of South America.
7. Neap tides occur when the moon is between the Earth and the sun.
8. A tidal bore is the difference between levels of ocean water at high tide and low tide.

Word bank: breaker zone, spring tides, tsunamis, surface currents, tidal range, El Niño.

UNDERSTANDING CONCEPTS

Multiple Choice

9. Surface currents are formed by
   a. the moon's gravity.
   b. the sun's gravity.
   c. wind.
   d. increased water density.

10. Deep currents form when
    a. cold air decreases water density.
    b. warm air increases water density.
    c. the ocean surface freezes and solids from the water underneath are removed.
    d. salinity increases.

11. When waves come near the shore,
    a. they speed up.
    b. they maintain their speed.
    c. their wavelength increases.
    d. their wave height increases.

12. Longshore currents transport sediment
    a. out to the open ocean.
    b. along the shore.
    c. during low tide only.
    d. during high tide only.

13. Whitecaps break
    a. in the surf.
    b. in the breaker zone.
    c. in the open ocean.
    d. as their wavelength increases.

14. Tidal range is greatest during
    a. spring tide.
    b. neap tide.
    c. a tidal bore.
    d. the day only.

Concept Mapping Transparency 14

Blackline masters of this Chapter Review can be found in the **Study Guide.**

Short Answer

15. Explain the relationship between upwelling and El Niño.

16. Explain what happens when the North Atlantic Deep Water meets the Antarctic Bottom Water.

17. Describe the relative positions of the Earth, the moon, and the sun during neap tide. Where do high tide and low tide occur during this time?

18. Explain the difference between the breaker zone and the surf.

Concept Mapping

19. Use the following terms to create a concept map: wind, deep currents, sun's gravity, types of ocean-water movement, surface currents, tides, increasing water density, waves, moon's gravity.

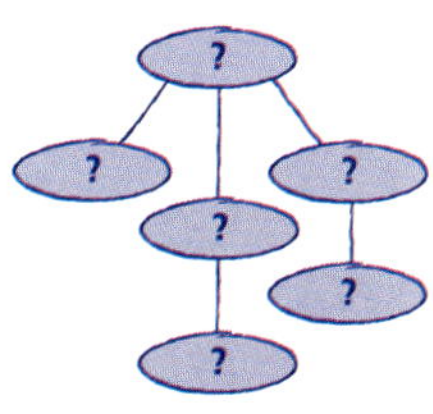

CRITICAL THINKING AND PROBLEM SOLVING

Write one or two sentences to answer the following questions:

20. What would happen to surface currents if the Earth reversed its rotation? Be specific.

21. How would you explain a bottle moving across the water in the same direction the waves are traveling?

22. You and a friend are planning a fishing trip to the ocean. Your friend tells you that the fish bite more in his secret fishing spot during low tide. If low tide occurred at the spot at 7 A.M. today and you are going to fish there in one week, at what time will low tide occur in that spot?

MATH IN SCIENCE

23. If a barrier island that is 1 km wide and 10 km long loses 1.5 m of its width per year to erosion by longshore current, how long will it take for the island to lose one-fourth of its width?

INTERPRETING GRAPHICS

Study the diagram below, and answer the questions that follow.

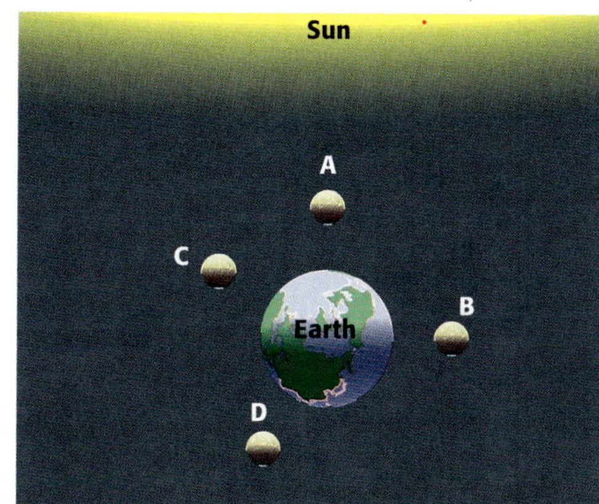

24. At which position (**A**, **B**, **C**, or **D**) would the moon be during a neap tide?

25. At which position (**A**, **B**, **C**, or **D**) would the moon be during a spring tide?

26. Would tidal range be greater with the moon at position **C** or position **D**? Why?

NOW What Do You Think?

Take a minute to review your answers to the ScienceLog questions on page 365. Have your answers changed? If necessary, revise your answers based on what you have learned since you began this chapter.

387

Short Answer

15. When El Niño occurs, warm surface water remains along the Pacific coast of South America. This prevents upwelling from occurring along the coast.

16. The North Atlantic Deep Water flows on top of the Antarctic Bottom Water.

17. During neap tide, the sun, the moon, and the Earth form a right angle, with the Earth in the middle. High tide occurs on the side of the Earth facing the moon and on the side opposite the moon. Low tide occurs on the side of the Earth facing the sun and on the side opposite the sun.

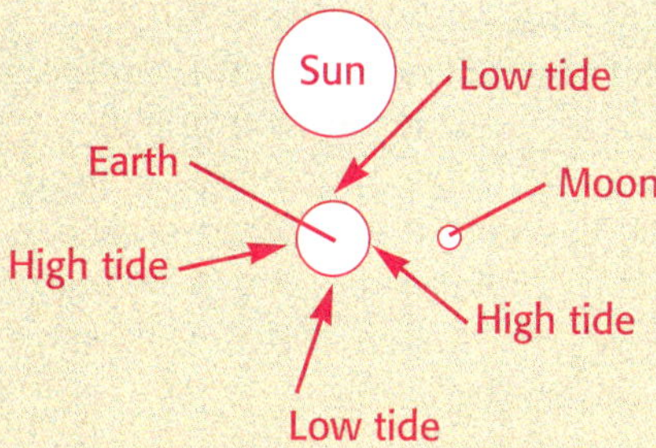

18. The breaker zone is where waves first begin to tumble downward. The surf is the zone between the breaker zone and the shore. In the surf, water moves toward the shore.

Concept Mapping

19. 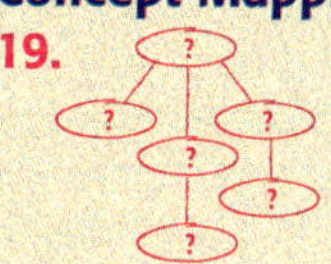 An answer to this exercise can be found at the end of this book.

Critical Thinking and Problem Solving

20. Surface currents in the Northern Hemisphere would rotate counterclockwise, and surface currents in the Southern Hemisphere would rotate clockwise.

21. There would have to be a surface current moving in the same direction as the waves are traveling.

22. 12:50 P.M. (1:15 A.M. is also acceptable.)

Math in Science

23. about 167 years

Interpreting Graphics

24. B

25. A

26. D; when the Earth-moon system is viewed from above the Earth's North Pole, the path of the moon around the Earth appears counterclockwise. In this case, the moon would be very near a spring-tide position at position D and very near a neap-tide position at position C.

NOW What Do You Think?

1. Factors that control ocean currents include wind, the Earth's rotation, water density, water salinity, water temperature, and continental deflections.

2. Gravitational forces from the sun and moon and the motion of the Earth and the moon around each other cause the ocean tides.

Chapter 14 Review—California Standards: PE/ATE Q20-22: 4; Q23: 2, 2c; Think: 4, 4a

CAREERS

Seismologist–Hiroo Kanamori

Background

Seismologists study earthquakes. Then why don't we call them earthquake-ologists? Well, the word *seismology* comes from the Greek language, and in Greek, *seismos* means "to shake"!

Dr. Kanamori recently received the Buchner Medal for his outstanding achievements in seismology. He bridged the gap between seismology and physics by developing an earthquake scale called the "moment magnitude scale." It rates earthquakes by the minimum energy released and is consistent with the Richter scale.

CAREERS

SEISMOLOGIST

As a seismologist, **Hiroo Kanamori** studies how earthquakes occur and tries to reduce their impact on our society. He also analyzes the effects of earthquakes on oceans and how earthquakes cause tsunamis (tsoo NAH mes). He has discovered that even weak earthquakes can create tsunamis.

Since most tsunamis are caused by underwater earthquakes, scientists can monitor earthquakes to predict when and where a tsunami will hit land. But the predictions are not always accurate. Very weak earthquakes should not create powerful tsunamis, yet they do. Kanamori calls these special events *tsunami earthquakes,* and he has learned how to predict when tsunamis will form.

A tsunami can be more dangerous than an earthquake. When people feel the tremors created when the plates slide, they don't always realize that a large tsunami may be on the way. Because of this, people don't expect a tsunami and don't leave the area.

Measuring Tsunami Earthquakes

As tectonic plates grind against each other, they send out seismic waves. These waves travel through the earth's crust and can be recorded by a sensitive machine. But when the plates grind very slowly, only long period seismic waves are recorded. When Kanamori sees a long period wave, he knows that a tsunami will form.

"The speed of the average tsunami is about 800 kilometers per hour, which is much slower than the speed of the long period waves at 15,000 kilometers per hour. So these special seismic waves arrive at distant recording stations much earlier than a tsunami," explains Kanamori. This important fact lets scientists like Kanamori warn people in the tsunami's path so they can leave the area.

An Interesting Career

Kanamori finds his work very rewarding. "It is always good to see how what we learned in the classroom can solve our real-life problems," he explains. "We can see how physics and mathematics work to explain seemingly complex natural events, such as earthquakes, volcanoes, and tsunamis."

A Challenge

► The depth of an ocean influences how fast a tsunami travels. To investigate, fill a 0.5 m long tub with 5 cm of water. Tap the tub. How long does it take for the wave to go back and forth? Add more water, and tap it again. Did the wave move faster or slower?

► *Monster waves are well-known in many communities along the Pacific coast.*

388

Answers to A Challenge

The wave moves faster as the water gets deeper. Ask students what happens to the speed of a tsunami wave as it approaches a shoreline. (The tsunami wave slows down as it approaches the shoreline.) Point out that as a tsunami wave slows down, it becomes taller.

California Standards: PE/ATE 1, 1e

Red Tides

Imagine going to the beach only to find that the ocean water has turned red and fish are floating belly up all over the place. This is not an imaginary scene. It really happens. What could cause such widespread damage to the ocean? Single-cell algae, that's what!

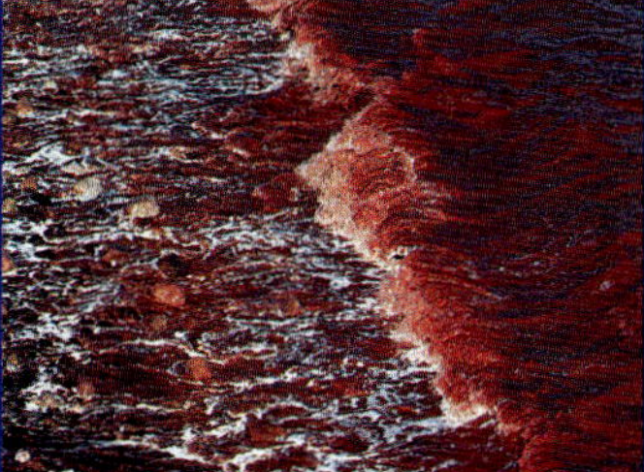

▲ *Harmful algal blooms are caused by algae like the one shown above right.*

Blooming Algae

When certain algae grow rapidly, they clump together on the ocean's surface in an algal bloom that changes the color of the water. People called these algal blooms red tides because the blooms often turned the water red or reddish-brown. They also believed that tidal conditions caused the blooms. Scientists now call these algae explosions harmful algal blooms (HABs) because HABs are not always red, and they are not directly related to tides. The blooms are harmful because certain species of algae produce toxins that can poison fish, shellfish, and people.

Scientists also have learned that the ocean's natural currents may carry HABs hundreds of miles along a coastline. For example, in 1987, the Gulf Stream off the Atlantic coast of Florida carried a toxic bloom up the coast to North Carolina.

Troublesome Toxins

Some people who ate tainted shellfish from the North Carolina coast in 1987 suffered from muscular aches, anxiety, sweating, dizziness, diarrhea, vomiting, and abdominal pain. Some algae toxins can even kill people who eat the tainted seafood. Another HAB occurred in 1987 in Nova Scotia, Canada. Four people died from eating contaminated shellfish, and another 150 people suffered from symptoms such as dizziness, headaches, seizures, short-term memory loss, and comas.

In the 1990s, Texas, Maryland, Alaska, and many other coastal states experienced HABs. However, the problem is not confined to North America. Throughout the 1990s, HABs caused health problems in South Africa, Argentina, India, New Zealand, and France.

No Signs to Read

Fish and shellfish are major sources of protein for people all over the world. Unfortunately, there are no outward signs when seafood is contaminated. The toxins don't change the flavor, and cooking the seafood doesn't eliminate the toxins. Sometimes a HAB rides into an area on an ocean current, causing fish to die and people to become ill before authorities are aware of the problem.

Fortunately, scientists all over the world are working on ways to monitor and even predict HABs. As a result, people eventually may be able to eat fish and shellfish without worrying about toxic algae.

Find Out More

▶ Some people think that human activities are causing more HABs than occurred in the past. Other people disagree. Find out more about this issue, and have a class debate about the role humans play in creating HABs.

389

Health Watch
Red Tides

Background

Of the 4,400 phytoplankton species, a mere 50 to 60 can produce toxins. Even a small dose of the toxin of certain species can prove fatal.

The best way for consumers to reduce the chances of buying poisoned seafood is to shop at a reputable seafood store. Seafood purchased in this way has passed through a government-run system that monitors ocean-water quality and toxin levels. Supermarkets are another safe option, as is ordering seafood at a reputable restaurant.

Answers to Find Out More

At present, no definitive study links HABs to human activities; all information is still speculation. Activities considered to be either directly or indirectly related to the cause of HABs include overfishing, global warming, and ocean-nutrient fluctuations due to coastal development and water runoff.

Some scientists suggest that the increase in reported HAB events might be explained by the existence of better detection methods and the fact that more people are witnessing the events. These scientists are not so quick to claim that new species are being introduced in areas where they have not previously been detected.

Perhaps students will be able to find some specific studies linking human activities to HABs that would serve to sway the debate in support of such arguments.

California Standards: PE/ATE 5b

TIMELINE

UNIT 6

Weather and Climate

In this unit, you will learn more about the ocean of air in which we live. You will learn about the atmosphere and how it affects conditions on the Earth's surface. The constantly changing weather is always a good topic for conversation. It is also the subject of the science of meteorology. Forecasting the weather is not an easy task. Climate, on the other hand, is much more predictable. This timeline shows some of the events that have occurred as scientists have tried to better understand weather and climate.

1281
A sudden typhoon destroys a fleet of Mongolian ships about to reach Japan. This "divine wind," or *kamikaze* in Japanese, saves the country from invasion and conquest.

1656
Saturn's rings are recognized as such. Galileo had seen them in 1612, but his telescope was not strong enough to make them out as rings.

1945
First atmospheric test of an atomic bomb takes place near Alamogordo, New Mexico.

1974
Chlorofluorocarbons (CFCs) are recognized as harmful to the ozone layer.

1982
Weather information becomes available 24 hours a day, 7 days a week on commercial television.

1714

Gabriel Fahrenheit builds the first mercury thermometer.

1749

Benjamin Franklin explains how updrafts of air are caused by the sun's heating of the local atmosphere.

1778

Karl Sheele and Antoine Lavoisier separately conclude that air is mostly made of oxygen and nitrogen.

1838

John James Audubon publishes *The Birds of America.*

1938

The cause of ice ages as a periodic result of the Earth's motion through space is determined by Yugoslav scientist Milutin Milankovitch.

1985

Scientists discover an ozone hole over Antarctica.

1986

The world's worst nuclear accident takes place at Chernobyl, Ukraine, spreading radiation through the atmosphere as far as the western United States.

1999

The first nonstop balloon trip around the world is successfully completed when Brian Jones and Bertrand Piccard land in Egypt.

Chapter Organizer

CHAPTER ORGANIZATION	TIME MINUTES	OBJECTIVES	LABS, INVESTIGATIONS, AND DEMONSTRATIONS
Chapter Opener **pp. 392–393**	45	California Standards: PE/ATE 7, 7b, 7e	**Investigate!** Better Part of Air, p. 393
Section 1 **Characteristics of the Atmosphere**	90	▶ Discuss the composition of the Earth's atmosphere. ▶ Explain why pressure changes with altitude. ▶ Explain how temperature changes with altitude. ▶ Describe the layers of the atmosphere. PE/ATE 3a, 4b, 7, 7b, 7e; LabBook 7, 7b, 7e	**Demonstration,** Air Pressure, p. 394 in ATE **Discovery Lab,** Under Pressure! p. 550 **Datasheets for LabBook,** Under Pressure! Datasheet 34 **Whiz-Bang Demonstrations,** Blue Sky, Demo 27
Section 2 **Heating of the Atmosphere**	90	▶ Describe what happens to radiation that reaches the Earth. ▶ Summarize the processes of radiation, conduction, and convection. ▶ Explain how the greenhouse effect contributes to global warming. PE/ATE 3, 3a, 3c, 3d, 4, 4a, 4b, 4d, 4e, 7, 7a, 7b, 7e; LabBook 7, 7a, 7b, 7e	**Demonstration,** p. 401 in ATE **Design Your Own,** Boiling Over! p. 546 **Datasheets for LabBook,** Boiling Over! Datasheet 32 **EcoLabs & Field Activities,** That Greenhouse Effect! Field Activity 14
Section 3 **Atmospheric Pressure and Winds**	90	▶ Explain the relationship between air pressure and wind direction. ▶ Describe the global patterns of wind. ▶ Explain the causes of local wind patterns. PE/ATE 4, 4a, 4d, 4e, 7, 7b, 7e; LabBook 7, 7b, 7e	**Demonstration,** Air Movement, p. 404 in ATE **QuickLab,** Full of "Hot Air," p. 406 **Discovery Lab,** Go Fly a Bike! p. 548 **Datasheets for LabBook,** Go Fly a Bike! Datasheet 33
Section 4 **The Air We Breathe**	90	▶ Describe the major types of air pollution. ▶ Name the major causes of air pollution. ▶ Explain how air pollution can affect human health. ▶ Explain how air pollution can be reduced. PE/ATE 2d, 4a, 6, 6a	**Demonstration,** Acid Rock! p. 413 in ATE **Interactive Explorations CD-ROM,** Moose Malady *A **Worksheet** is also available in the **Interactive Explorations Teacher's Edition.*** **Long-Term Projects & Research Ideas,** Project 43

See page **T20** *for a complete correlation of this book with the*

CALIFORNIA SCIENCE CONTENT STANDARDS.

Correlations are also provided at point of use throughout this ATE.

TECHNOLOGY RESOURCES

Guided Reading Audio CD
English or Spanish, Chapter 15

Classroom Management CD-ROM

Interactive Explorations CD-ROM
CD 2, Exploration 3, Moose Malady

Earth Science Videodiscs
Global Winds: 29493–33634
Local Winds: 33668–36238

CNN **Eye on the Environment,** Global Warming, Segment 13
CO_2 and the Arctic Ozone, Segment 14

Multicultural Connections, China Coal, Segment 3

Scientists in Action, Tracking Mercury in the Everglades, Segment 15

Test Generator CD-ROM

Chapter 15 • The Atmosphere

CLASSROOM WORKSHEETS, TRANSPARENCIES, AND RESOURCES	SCIENCE INTEGRATION AND CONNECTIONS	REVIEW AND ASSESSMENT
Directed Reading Worksheet 15 **Science Puzzlers, Twisters & Teasers,** Worksheet 15		
Directed Reading Worksheet 15, Section 1 **Transparency 18,** Photosynthesis and Respiration: What's the Connection? **Transparency 141,** Profile of the Earth's Atmosphere **Reinforcement Worksheet 15,** Earth's Amazing Atmosphere	**Physical Science Connection,** p. 395 **Connect to Life Science,** p. 395 in ATE **Apply,** p. 397 **Connect to Physical Science,** p. 398 in ATE **Multicultural Connection,** p. 398 in ATE	**Self-Check,** p. 396 **Review,** p. 399 **Quiz,** p. 399 in ATE **Alternative Assessment,** p. 399 in ATE
Directed Reading Worksheet 15, Section 2 **Transparency 142,** Radiation and the Atmosphere **Transparency 143,** Radiation, Convection, and Conduction **Transparency 144,** The Greenhouse Effect	**Life Science Connection,** p. 403	**Homework,** p. 401 in ATE **Review,** p. 403 **Quiz,** p. 403 in ATE **Alternative Assessment,** p. 403 in ATE
Directed Reading Worksheet 15, Section 3 **Math Skills for Science Worksheet 13,** Improper Fractions and Mixed Numbers **Transparency 145,** Sea and Land Breezes	**Multicultural Connection,** p. 405 in ATE **Environmental Science Connection,** p. 407 **Math and More,** p. 408 in ATE **Multicultural Connection,** p. 408 in ATE **MathBreak,** Calculating Groundspeed, p. 409	**Homework,** p. 407 in ATE **Review,** p. 409 **Quiz,** p. 409 in ATE **Alternative Assessment,** p. 409 in ATE
Directed Reading Worksheet 15, Section 4 **Transparency 146,** The Formation of Smog **Critical Thinking Worksheet 15,** The Extraordinary GBG5K	**Connect to Physical Science,** p. 412 in ATE **Multicultural Connection,** p. 412 in ATE **Cross-Disciplinary Focus,** p. 414 in ATE **Health Watch:** Particles in the Air, p. 420 **Scientific Debate:** A Cure for Air Pollution? p. 421	**Review,** p. 415 **Quiz,** p. 415 in ATE **Alternative Assessment,** p. 415 in ATE

Holt, Rinehart and Winston On-line Resources

go.hrw.com

For worksheets and other teaching aids related to this chapter, visit the HRW Web site and type in the keyword: **HSTATM**

National Science Teachers Association

www.scilinks.org

Encourage students to use the keywords listed on the Technology Highlights page to access information and resources on the **NSTA** Web site.

END-OF-CHAPTER REVIEW AND ASSESSMENT

Chapter Review in Study Guide

Vocabulary and Notes in Study Guide

Chapter Tests with Performance-Based Assessment, Chapter 15 Test

Chapter Tests with Performance-Based Assessment, Performance-Based Assessment 15

Concept Mapping Transparency 15

Chapter Resources & Worksheets

Visual Resources

TEACHING TRANSPARENCIES

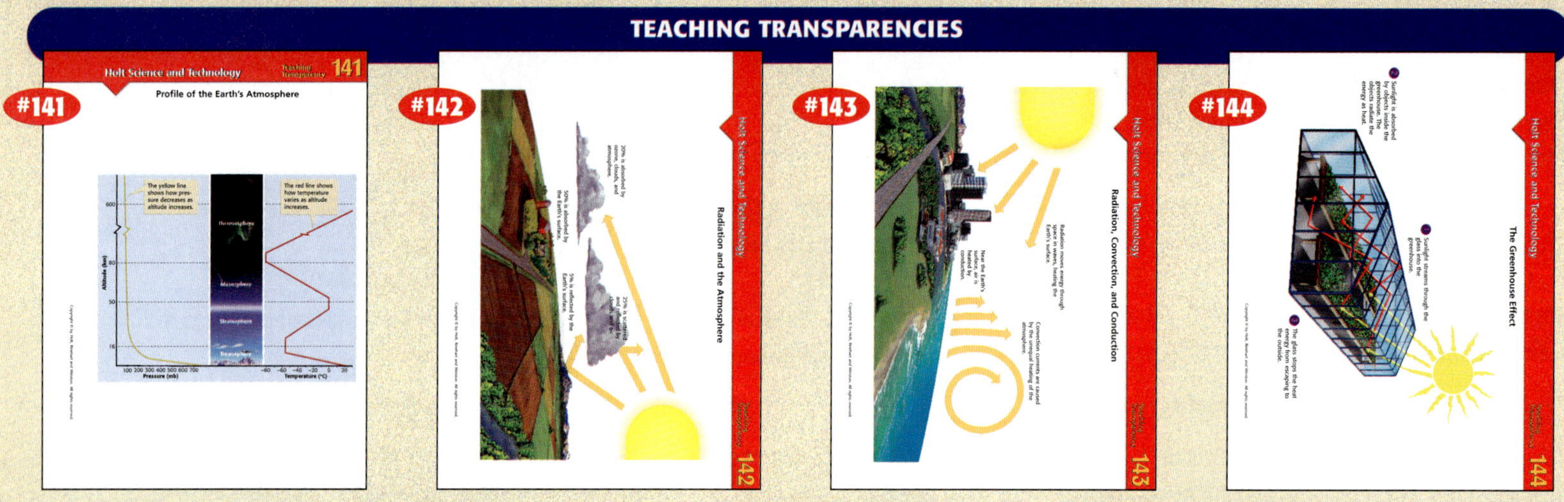

TEACHING TRANSPARENCIES

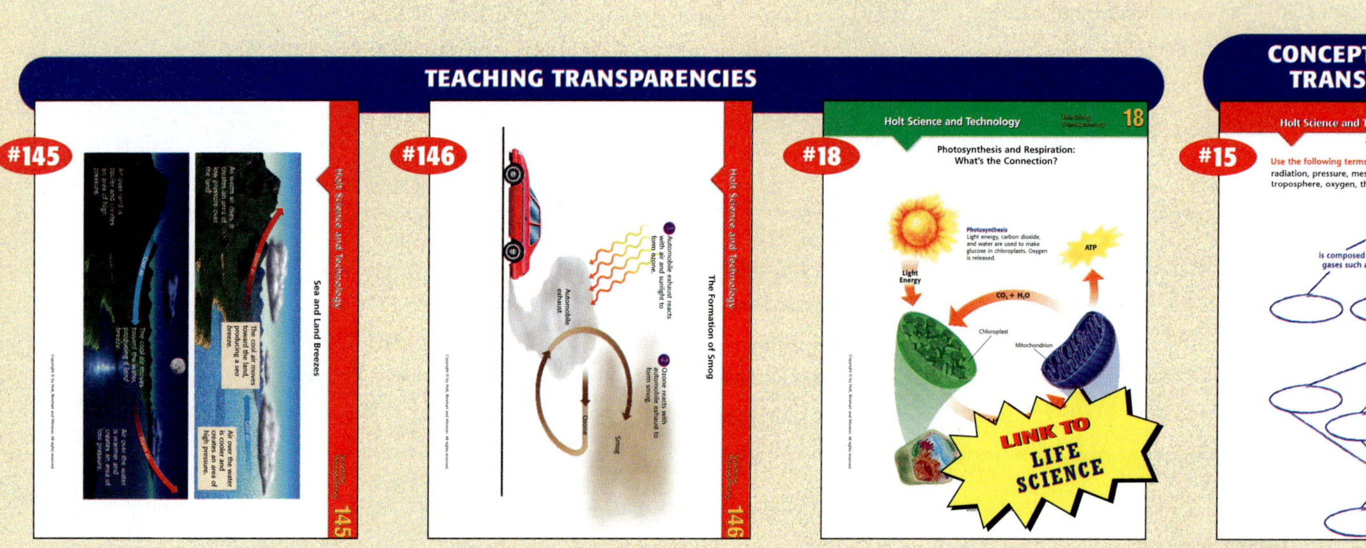

CONCEPT MAPPING TRANSPARENCY

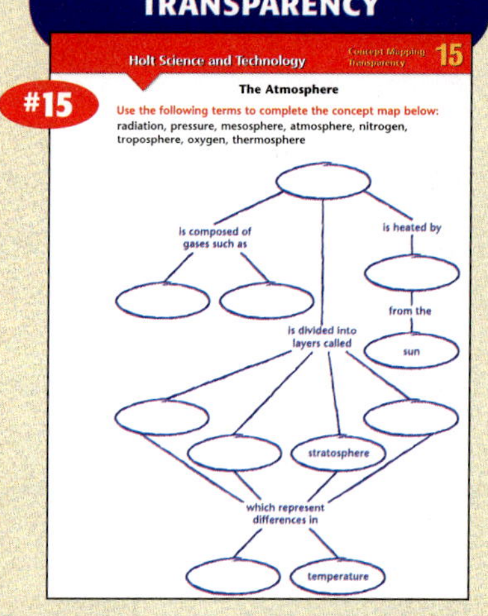

Meeting Individual Needs

DIRECTED READING

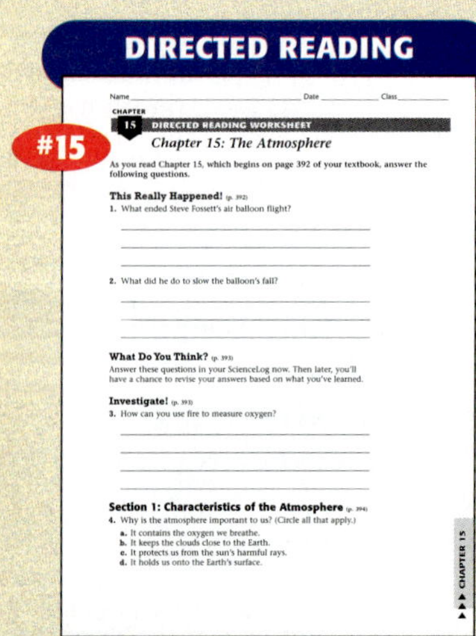

REINFORCEMENT & VOCABULARY REVIEW

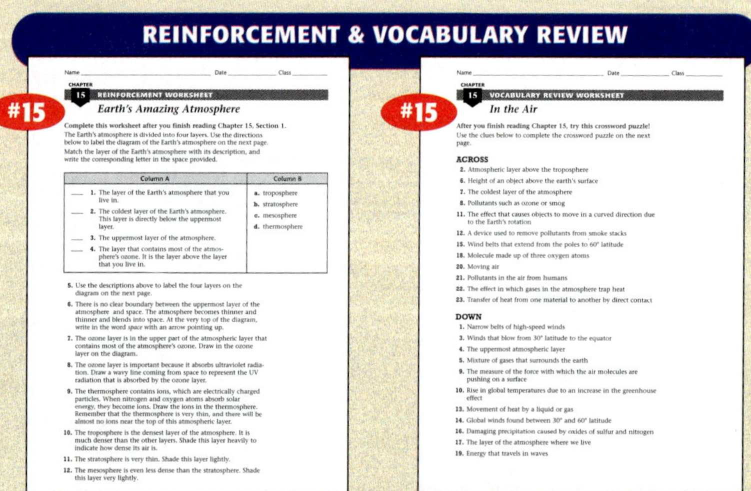

SCIENCE PUZZLERS, TWISTERS & TEASERS

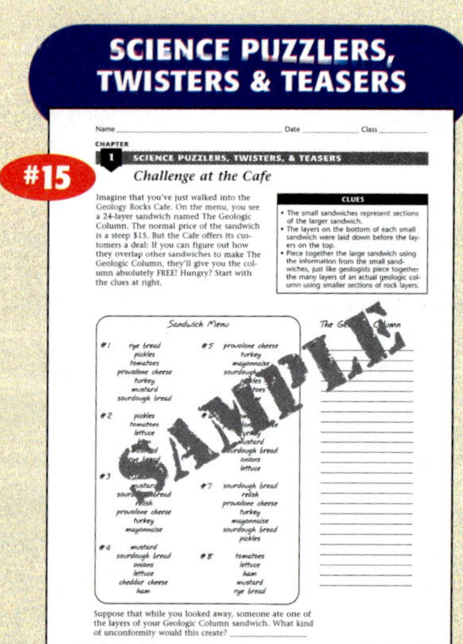

Chapter 15 • The Atmosphere

Review & Assessment

STUDY GUIDE

#15

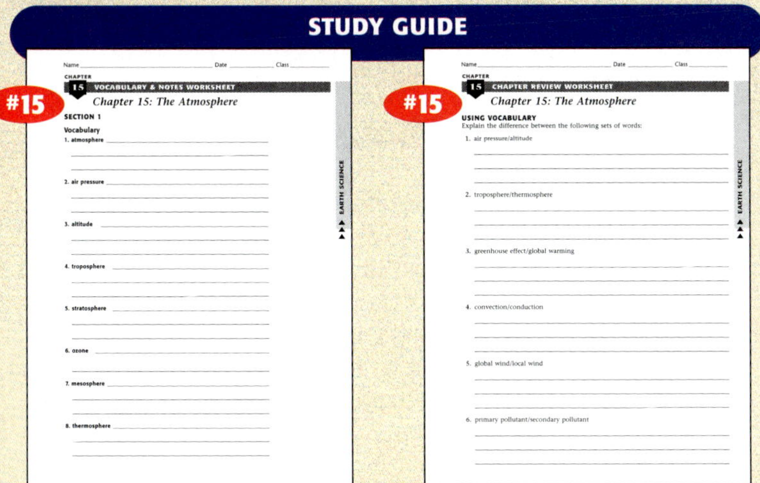
CHAPTER 15 VOCABULARY & NOTES WORKSHEET
Chapter 15: The Atmosphere

#15

CHAPTER 15 CHAPTER REVIEW WORKSHEET
Chapter 15: The Atmosphere

CHAPTER TESTS WITH PERFORMANCE-BASED ASSESSMENT

#15

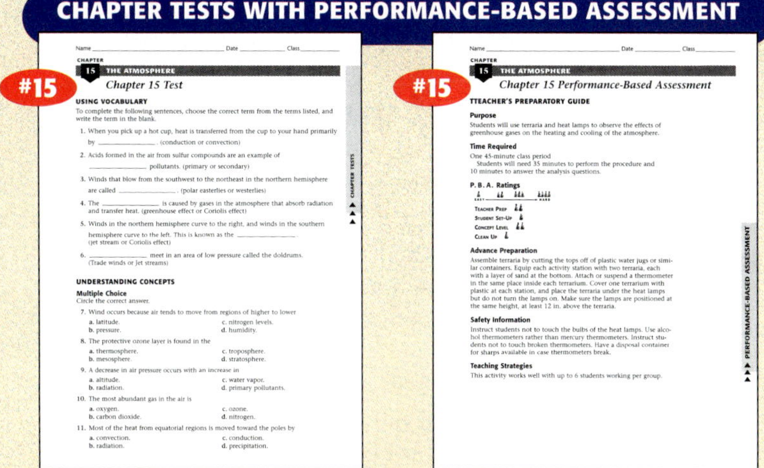
CHAPTER 15 THE ATMOSPHERE
Chapter 15 Test

#15

CHAPTER 15 THE ATMOSPHERE
Chapter 15 Performance-Based Assessment

Lab Worksheets

ECOLABS & FIELD ACTIVITIES

#14

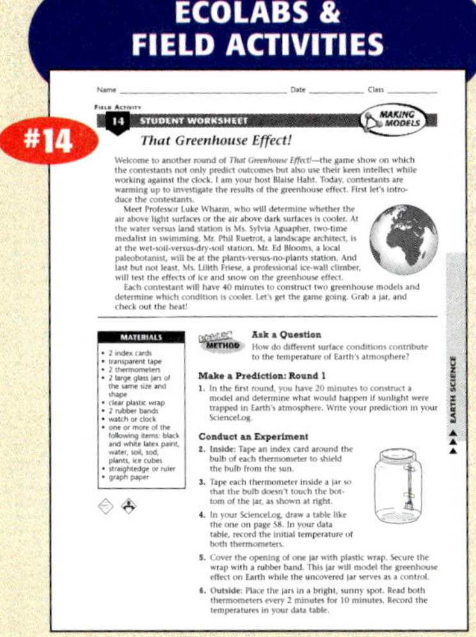
FIELD ACTIVITY 14 STUDENT WORKSHEET
That Greenhouse Effect!

WHIZ-BANG DEMONSTRATIONS

#27

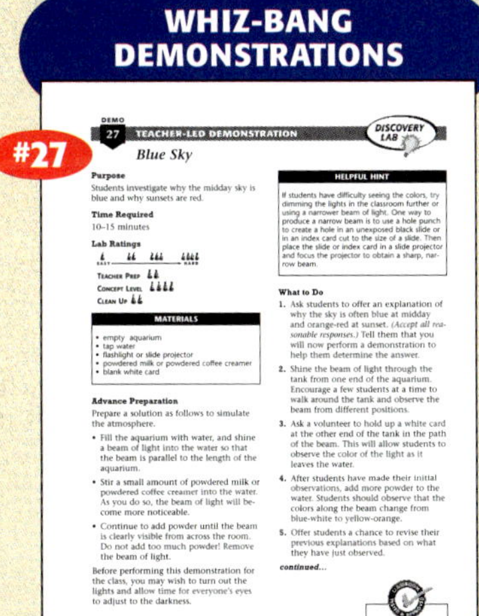
DEMO 27 TEACHER-LED DEMONSTRATION
Blue Sky

LONG-TERM PROJECTS & RESEARCH IDEAS

#43

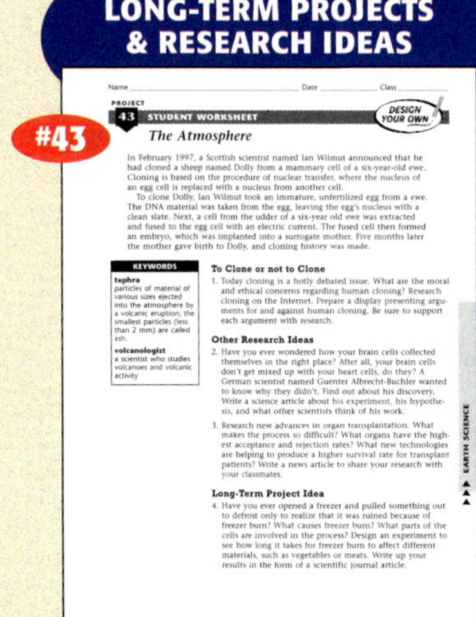
PROJECT 43 STUDENT WORKSHEET
The Atmosphere

DATASHEETS FOR LABBOOK

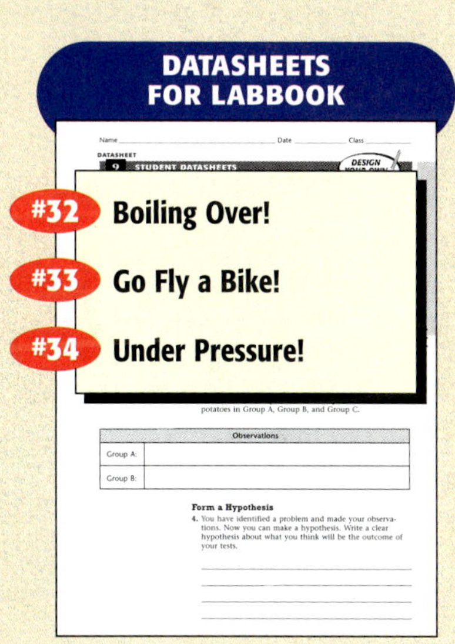

#32 Boiling Over!

#33 Go Fly a Bike!

#34 Under Pressure!

Applications & Extensions

CRITICAL THINKING & PROBLEM SOLVING

#15

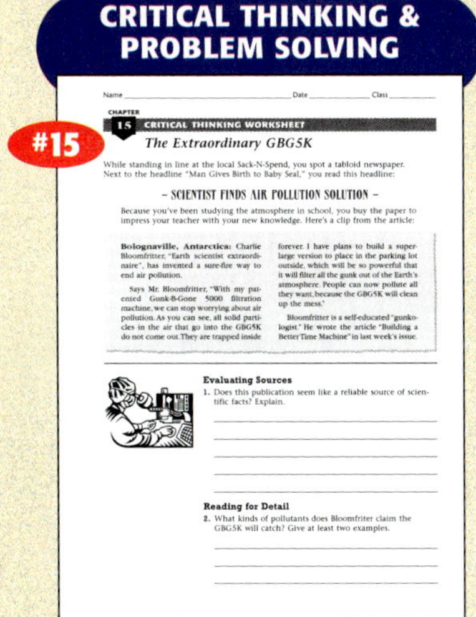
CHAPTER 15 CRITICAL THINKING WORKSHEET
The Extraordinary GBG5K

MULTICULTURAL CONNECTIONS

#3

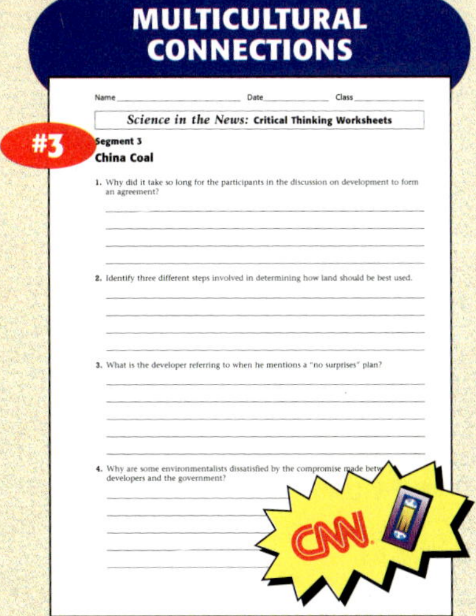
Science in the News: Critical Thinking Worksheets
Segment 3
China Coal

EYE ON THE ENVIRONMENT

#13

Science in the News: Critical Thinking Worksheets
Segment 13
Global Warming

#14

SCIENTISTS IN ACTION

#15

Science in the News: Critical Thinking Worksheets
Segment 15
Tracking Mercury in the Everglades

INTERACTIVE EXPLORATIONS

#2–3

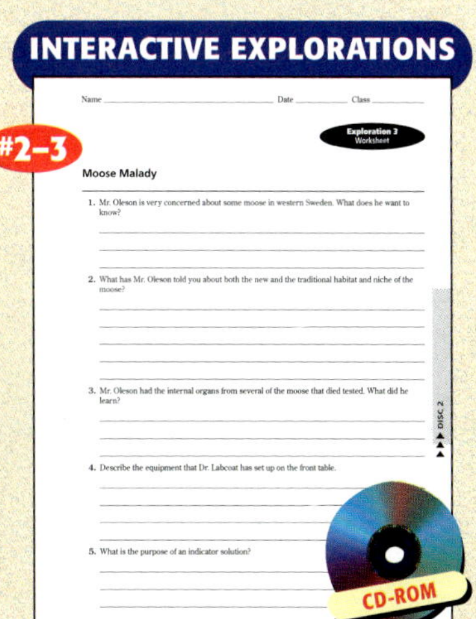
Exploration 3 Worksheet
Moose Malady

CD-ROM

Chapter Background

Section 1

Characteristics of the Atmosphere

▶ Take a Deep Breath!

Near the Earth's surface, the atmosphere consists of 78.08 percent nitrogen, 20.95 percent oxygen, 0.93 percent argon, 0.03 percent carbon dioxide, and traces of water vapor. Earth's primitive atmosphere was quite different than it is today, consisting of about 79 percent water vapor, 11–12 percent carbon dioxide, 6 percent sulfur dioxide, 1 percent nitrogen, less than 1 percent hydrogen, and traces of other gases. Scientists theorize that about 95 percent of the oxygen present in today's atmosphere formed as a byproduct of photosynthesis. As simple organisms evolved in Earth's primitive atmosphere, some of them evolved the ability to produce their own food via photosynthesis.

▶ Radio Days

Fadeouts of radio communications are due to sudden ionospheric disturbances, known as SIDs. These storms can last 15 to 30 minutes and are caused by violent solar outbursts that release electrically charged particles.

IS THAT A FACT!

- The Earth's troposphere contains almost 90 percent of the atmosphere's total mass. In the troposphere, temperature decreases at an average rate of 6.4°C/km with increasing altitude.

Section 2

Heating of the Atmosphere

▶ Cloudy with a Chance of . . .

Clouds reflect incoming solar radiation very effectively. The amount of solar radiation a cloud can reflect depends on its thickness. A cloud less than 50 m thick can reflect up to 40 percent of incoming solar radiation, while a cloud more than 5,000 m thick can reflect 80 percent or more. The average reflectivity of clouds is about 55 percent.

▶ Greenhouse Gases

Water vapor, carbon dioxide, ozone, methane, and chlorofluorocarbons are often called greenhouse gases. These gases transmit incoming short-wave radiation from the sun and absorb much of the outgoing long-wave radiation from the Earth's surface.

▶ Global Warming—An Idea Before Its Time!

Since the 1970s, global warming has been a topic of concern. However, a global warming model was proposed as early as 1896 by a Swedish physicist and chemist named Svante Arrhenius. Arrhenius theorized that the carbon dioxide released from burning coal would increase the intensity of Earth's greenhouse effect and lead to global warming. In 1954, it was first suggested that deforestation increases the amount of CO_2 in the atmosphere. Since then, numerous scientific studies have examined the effects of carbon dioxide on the temperature of Earth's atmosphere.

Section 3

Atmospheric Pressure and Winds

▶ Gustave Coriolis

Gustave Gaspard Coriolis was a French mathematician and engineer who lived and worked in Paris from

1792 to 1843. His most well-known contribution to science is a paper published in 1835 that introduces the Coriolis force. In "On the Equations of Relative Motion of Systems of Bodies," Coriolis proves that an inertial force (the Coriolis force) acts on a rotating object at a right angle to the object's motion. The Coriolis force causes matter to be deflected from its original path. This force determines the general direction of global winds and open-ocean circulation, as well as the rotational movements of severe weather, such as hurricanes.

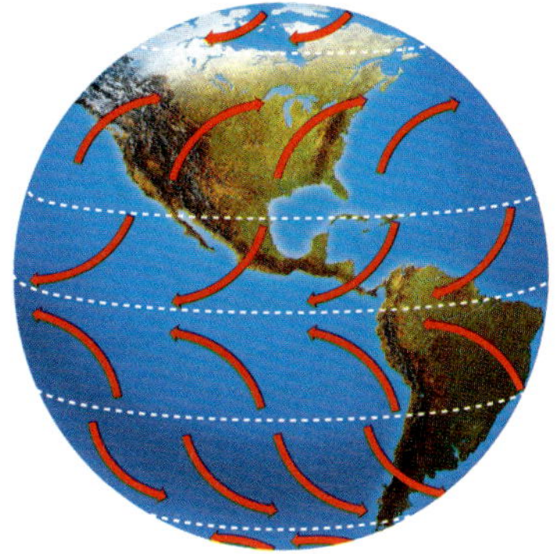

IS THAT A FACT!

- When airplanes fly north or south, pilots have to make corrections to counteract the Coriolis effect.

▶ Jet Streaks

Jet streaks are winds within jet streams that flow faster than the adjacent winds. Jet streaks influence storm formation and associated precipitation. Rising jet streaks and the low-pressure area that forms beneath them present favorable conditions for storms to form. Sinking jet streaks inhibit storm formation and precipitation.

IS THAT A FACT!

- The speed of jet streams ranges from about 92 km/h to more than 483 km/h!

SECTION 4

The Air We Breathe

▶ Vog and Laze

Two pollution problems associated with volcanic activity at Earth's surface are vog and laze. Vog is volcanic smog that forms when the sulfur dioxide released during an eruption reacts with sunlight, dust particles, water vapor, and oxygen to form various sulfur compounds, including sulfur dioxide. When Kilauea began to erupt in 1983, it sent about 2,000 tons of sulfur dioxide into the air each day.

- Laze is lava haze, a form of pollution that forms when lava flows react with ocean water. The extreme temperature of the lava causes sea water to vaporize. Physical and chemical interactions create white plumes of hydrochloric acid and concentrated salt water that can threaten the health of people living near volcanoes.

▶ Allowance Trading System

An important part of the EPA's Acid Rain Program is the allowance trading system, which is designed to reduce sulfur-dioxide emissions. In this system, one ton of sulfur dioxide (SO_2) emission is equivalent to one allowance. There are a limited number of allowances allocated for each year. Companies can buy, sell or trade allowances freely, but if they exceed their allowances, they must pay a punitive fine. The system allows a company to determine the most cost-effective ways to comply with the Clean Air Act. It can reduce emissions by using technology that conserves energy, by using renewable energy sources, or by updating its pollution-control devices and using low-sulfur fuels.

- Sulfur dioxide allowances are inexpensive and can be bought from the EPA by private citizens, schools, and community and environmental organizations. Purchasing one allowance will reduce a company's allowable SO_2 emissions in a given year by one ton.

For additional background resources, please refer to the ***HST Reference Library.***

CHAPTER 15

The Atmosphere

Chapter Preview

Section 1
Characteristics of the Atmosphere
- Composition of the Atmosphere
- Atmospheric Pressure and Temperature
- Layers of the Atmosphere

Section 2
Heating of the Atmosphere
- Energy in the Atmosphere
- The Greenhouse Effect

Section 3
Atmospheric Pressure and Winds
- Why Air Moves
- Types of Winds

Section 4
The Air We Breathe
- Air Quality
- Types of Air Pollution
- Sources of Human-Caused Air Pollution
- The Air Pollution Problem
- Cleaning Up Our Act

Directed Reading Worksheet 15

Science Puzzlers, Twisters & Teasers Worksheet 15

Guided Reading Audio CD
English or Spanish, Chapter 15

CHAPTER 15 The Atmosphere

This Really Happened!

On August 17, 1998, Steve Fossett was well on his way to making the first around-the-world balloon flight. It was his fourth attempt, and after 10 days and 22,910 km he had already traveled two-thirds of the way. At the time, this was farther than any other balloonist had traveled in history. But something happened in the dark morning hours that ended Fossett's flight and nearly cost him his life.

While floating over the Pacific Ocean at 8,839 m above sea level, Fossett noticed a row of thunderstorms below. Suddenly his balloon, the *Solo Spirit,* hit an unexpected air disturbance and was sucked downward at a rate of more than 420 km/h. Knowing he was in danger, Fossett climbed out of his bubble hatch and cut loose the heavy tanks of fuel and oxygen to slow the balloon's fall. He then prepared himself for the crash.

When Fossett regained consciousness, his capsule was upside down, half-full of water, and on fire. With a satellite radio beacon to give his location and a small life boat, Fossett scrambled out of the capsule to await his rescue.

392

This Really Happened!

In addition to its world circumnavigation attempt, the *Solo Spirit* also conducted scientific research. Fossett measured various conditions of the Earth's atmosphere, including temperature and pressure. Months later, in 1999, a Swiss-British team successfully piloted a hot-air balloon around the world. Bertrand Piccard, a pilot on that mission, came from a family of adventurers. His grandfather, Auguste Piccard, was the first to travel to the stratosphere in a hot-air balloon. Bertrand Piccard's father, Jacques Piccard, traveled in the submarine *Trieste* nearly 11,000 m to the bottom of the Mariana Trench. That adventure is discussed in the Background of the chapter "Exploring the Oceans."

Fossett experienced firsthand how unpredictable our atmosphere can be. He was fortunate to have survived. The atmosphere can be unpredictable and dangerous, but it also provides us with gases needed for our survival on Earth. In this chapter you will learn how the Earth's atmosphere affects you and how you affect it.

What Do You Think?

In your ScienceLog, try to answer the following questions based on what you already know:

1. What is air made of?
2. How is the atmosphere organized?
3. What is wind and how does it move?

Investigate!

Better Part of Air

You might wonder how Steve Fossett got his hot air balloon to rise. When you heat a balloon, the air inside the balloon becomes less dense, causing the balloon to rise. When you want to land, you just cool the air to make it more dense, causing the balloon to sink. But with a given mass at the same pressure, what takes up more volume, warm air or cool air? You can find out by doing this simple experiment.

Procedure

1. Using **adhesive putty,** place a **candle** in the center of an **aluminum pie plate.**
2. Fill the pie plate almost one-quarter full with **water.**
3. Light the candle, and place the open end of a **beaker** over it. Notice the level of the water inside the beaker.
4. After the candle goes out, record your observations in your ScienceLog.

Analysis

5. What is happening to the air temperature when the candle goes out?
6. Why does the water rise in the beaker?
7. What takes up more volume, warm air or cool air? Explain.
8. How does the change in air temperature affect a hot air balloon compared with a glass beaker?

What Do You Think?

Accept all reasonable responses.

Students will have a chance to revise their answers in the Chapter Review under NOW What Do You Think?

Investigate!

MATERIALS

For Each Group:
- adhesive putty
- candle
- aluminum pie plate
- water
- beaker

Safety Caution: Remind students to review all safety cautions and icons before beginning this lab activity.

Teacher Notes: Make sure the candle fits entirely into the overturned beaker and that the candle is taller than the height of the water that will enter the beaker.

Students may think that the water rises because the oxygen in the air is being burned off. This activity does not measure change in air composition; it demonstrates change in air density and volume.

Answers to Investigate!

5. The air temperature begins to cool when the candle goes out.
6. The water rises in the beaker because the air cools.
7. Warm air takes up more volume than cool air. Cool air is more dense, so it takes up less volume.
8. Warm air is less dense and takes up more volume, so it fills the balloon, making it rigid. The hot air in the glass takes up more volume, preventing the water from rising in the beaker.

SCIENTISTS AT ODDS

The British clergyman and chemist Joseph Priestley (1733–1804) is usually credited with discovering oxygen, in 1774. In his well-known experiment, Priestley obtained a colorless gas when he heated mercuric oxide. A candle burned remarkably well in this "new species of air." However, it was Carl Scheele (1742–1786), a Swedish chemist and pharmacist, who first observed oxygen, around 1773. Scheele delayed publishing his account, and Priestley has since been credited with the discovery.

Chapter 15 Opener–California Standards: PE/ATE 7, 7b, 7e

Section 1

Focus

Characteristics of the Atmosphere

This section defines the atmosphere and explains its basic characteristics. First it discusses the combination of gases that compose the atmosphere. Then it explains the roles of pressure and temperature. Finally, this section discusses the four layers of the Earth's atmosphere.

Bellringer

Have students list the ways that the atmosphere is different from outer space in their ScienceLog. Tell students that a little more than a century ago, many scientists believed that the Earth's atmosphere blended with a hypothetical substance called *ether* that filled the entire universe. In 1887, the physicist A. A. Michelson demonstrated that the universe is not filled with ether.

1 Motivate

Demonstration

Air Pressure Fill a paper cup with water, and push a square piece of cardboard firmly against the cup's mouth with one hand. Hold the cardboard in place as you position the cup over a volunteer's hand. Ask the class to predict what will happen when you invert the cup. Quickly invert the cup, being careful to keep the cardboard in place. The cardboard should stay in place, and the water should stay in the cup. Explain that this demonstration illustrates that the atmosphere exerts pressure in all directions.

NOTE: Practice this demonstration over a sink before doing it in front of the class.

1

NEW TERMS

atmosphere, air pressure, altitude, troposphere, stratosphere, ozone, mesosphere, thermosphere

OBJECTIVES

- Discuss the composition of the Earth's atmosphere.
- Explain why pressure changes with altitude.
- Explain how temperature changes with altitude.
- Describe the layers of the atmosphere.

Characteristics of the Atmosphere

If you were lost in the desert, you could survive for a few days without food and water. But you wouldn't last more than 5 minutes without the *atmosphere*. The **atmosphere** is a mixture of gases that surrounds the Earth. In addition to containing the oxygen we need to breathe, it protects us from the sun's harmful rays. But the atmosphere is always changing. Every breath we take, every tree we plant, and every motor vehicle we ride in affects the composition of our atmosphere. Later you will find out how the atmosphere is changing. But first you need to learn about the atmosphere's composition and structure.

Composition of the Atmosphere

Figure 1 shows the relative amounts of the gases that make up the atmosphere. Besides gases, the atmosphere also contains small amounts of solids and liquids. Tiny solid particles, such as dust, volcanic ash, sea salt, dirt, and smoke, are carried in the air. Next time you turn off the lights at night, shine a flashlight and you will see some of these tiny particles floating in the air.

Figure 1 *Two gases—nitrogen and oxygen—make up 99 percent of the air we breathe.*

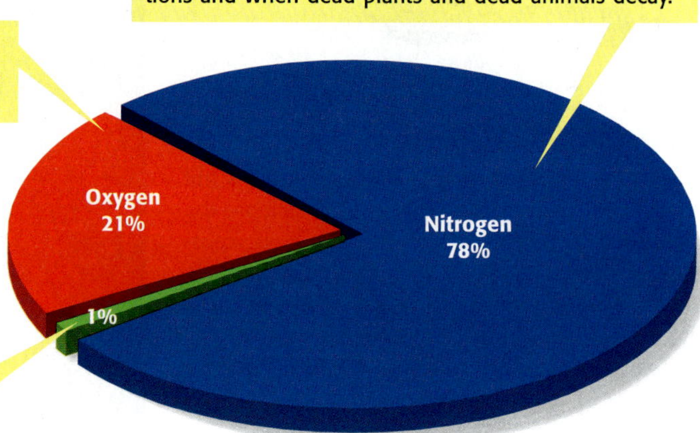

Nitrogen is the most abundant gas in the atmosphere. It is released into the atmosphere by volcanic eruptions and when dead plants and dead animals decay.

Oxygen, the second most common gas in the atmosphere, is produced mainly by plants.

The **remaining 1 percent** of the atmosphere is made up of argon, carbon dioxide, water vapor, and other gases.

394

Directed Reading Worksheet 15 Section 1

An experiment in 1664 demonstrated the force exerted by the Earth's atmosphere. Most of the air was removed from a hollow sphere whose halves had been sealed together with an airtight gasket. Sixteen horses were needed to pull the metal hemispheres apart!

Section 1—California Standards: PE/ATE 3a, 4b, 7, 7b, 7e; LabBook: 7, 7b, 7e

The most common liquid in the atmosphere is water. Liquid water is found as water droplets in clouds. When the water droplets become too big and heavy for the clouds to hold, they fall as rain. Remember that liquid water is different from water vapor. Water vapor, which is also found in the atmosphere, is a gas and is not visible.

Water is the only substance that exists as a liquid, a solid, and a gas in the Earth's atmosphere.

Atmospheric Pressure and Temperature

Have you ever been in an elevator in a tall building? If you have, you probably remember the "popping" in your ears as you went up or down. As you move up or down in an elevator, the air pressure outside your ears changes, while the air pressure inside your ears stays the same. **Air pressure** is the measure of the force with which the air molecules push on a surface. Your ears pop when the pressure inside and outside of your ears suddenly becomes equal. Air pressure changes throughout the atmosphere. Temperature and the kinds of gases present also change. Why do these changes occur? Read on to find out.

Pressure Think of air pressure as a human pyramid, as shown in **Figure 2.** The people at the bottom of the pyramid can feel all the weight and pressure of the people on top. The person on top doesn't feel any weight because there isn't anyone above. The atmosphere works in a similar way.

The Earth's atmosphere is held around the planet by gravity. Gravity pulls the gas molecules in the atmosphere toward the Earth's surface, giving them weight. This weight causes the air to push against the Earth's surface. As you move farther away from the Earth's surface, air pressure decreases because fewer gas molecules are pushing on you. **Altitude** is the height of an object above the Earth's surface. As altitude increases, air pressure decreases.

Figure 2 *Like the bottom row of the human pyramid, the lower atmosphere has more molecules pushing on it and therefore experiences greater pressure than the upper atmosphere.*

2 Teach

READING STRATEGY

Prediction Guide Before students read this page, ask them the following questions:

- Which gas—oxygen or nitrogen—is the major component of Earth's air? (nitrogen)
- Does air contain anything other than gases? (Yes; it contains solids, such as dust, and liquids, such as water.)

GROUP ACTIVITY

It's a Gas! Have small groups demonstrate how oxygen enters the atmosphere. Suggested materials include a freshwater plant, such as *Elodea,* a small plastic storage beaker, a funnel, a test tube, and water. Tell students to immerse the plant in the water-filled beaker and then cover the beaker with the inverted funnel. Have them place a water-filled test tube over the funnel's spout and let the setup sit in a well-lighted area for a few days. After this time, students will observe gas bubbles in the test tube. Inform them that the bubbles they see are made of oxygen gas. Sheltered English

MISCONCEPTION ALERT

Make sure students realize that water vapor is *invisible.* The "steam" they observe coming out of a pot of boiling water is composed of water droplets that form as water vapor cools and condenses on particles in the air.

CONNECT TO LIFE SCIENCE

Use Teaching Transparency 18 to show students how photosynthesis and respiration are linked to gas exchange between organisms and the atmosphere. Photosynthesizing plants use carbon dioxide, water, and light energy to produce oxygen. During respiration, animals consume oxygen and release carbon dioxide, water, and energy.

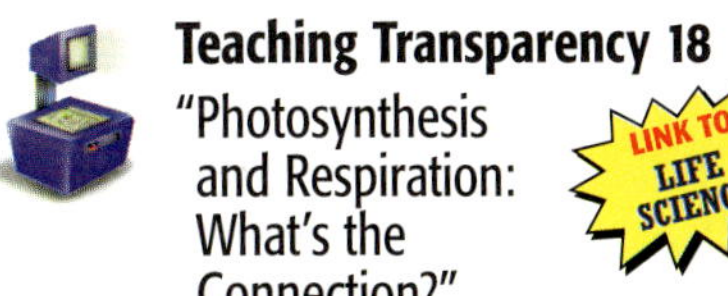

Teaching Transparency 18
"Photosynthesis and Respiration: What's the Connection?"

2 Teach, continued

MEETING INDIVIDUAL NEEDS

Learners Having Difficulty
Students might benefit from using a dictionary to learn the prefixes of the following words:

troposphere, stratosphere, mesosphere, thermosphere

Students will learn that *trop-* means "change" or "turn," *strat-* means "layer," *meso-* means "middle," and *therm-* means "heat." Students should also note that *sphere* means "globe" or "ball." Have students use these meanings to remember the layers of the atmosphere. Sheltered English

USING THE FIGURE

Have students refer to **Figure 3** to answer these questions:

- Which layer of the atmosphere is closest to Earth? (the troposphere)
- How does temperature change within the stratosphere? (For the first few kilometers, the temperature remains fairly constant. Then the temperature begins rising steeply, and levels off again toward the top of the layer.)
- Which atmospheric layer is coldest? (the mesosphere)
- Approximately how thick is the Earth's atmosphere? (about 600 km)

Students may notice that the iridescent cloud in the thermosphere is the aurora borealis and that the white layer at the top of the stratosphere is the ozone layer.

Teaching Transparency 141
"Profile of the Earth's Atmosphere"

Self-Check
Does air become more or less dense as you climb a mountain? Why? *(See page 564 to check your answer.)*

Air Temperature Air temperature also changes as you increase altitude. As you pass through the atmosphere, air temperature changes between warmer and colder conditions. The temperature differences result mainly from the way solar energy is absorbed as it moves downward through the atmosphere. Some parts of the atmosphere are warmer because they contain gases that absorb solar energy. Other parts do not contain these gases and are therefore cooler.

Layers of the Atmosphere

Based on temperature changes, the Earth's atmosphere is divided into four layers—the troposphere, stratosphere, mesosphere, and thermosphere. **Figure 3** illustrates the four atmospheric layers, showing their altitude and temperature. As you can see, each layer has unique characteristics.

Figure 3 Profile of the Earth's Atmosphere

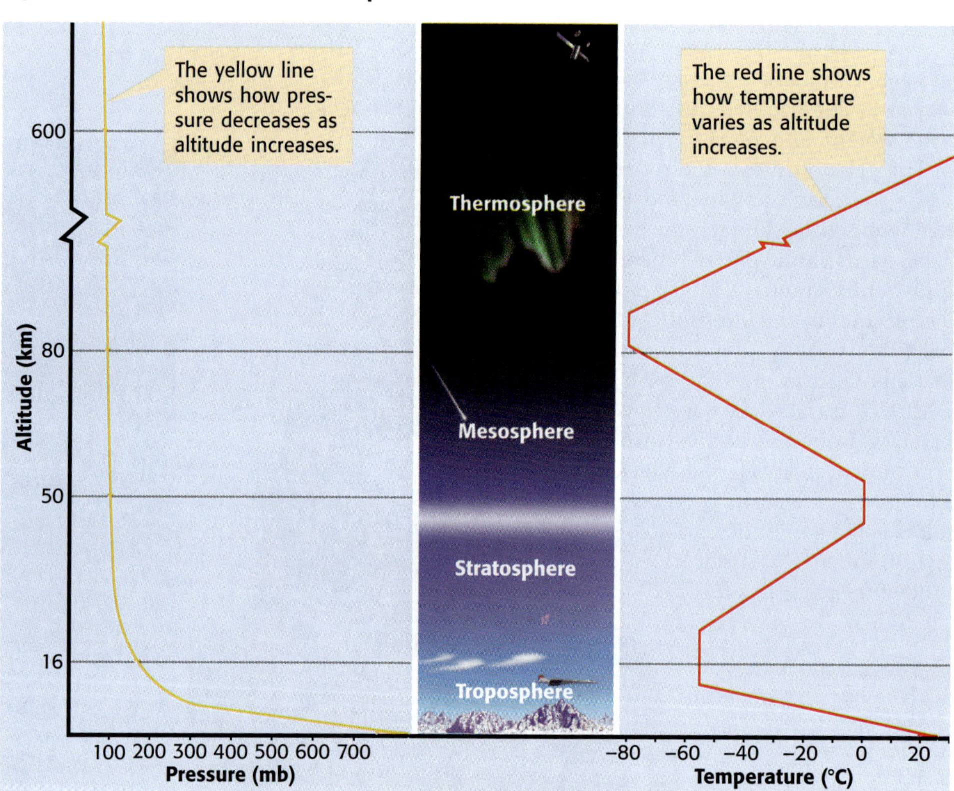

396

Answer to Self-Check
As you climb a mountain, the air becomes less dense because there are fewer molecules to absorb heat. So even though cold air is generally more dense than warm air, it is less dense at higher elevations.

IS THAT A FACT!
The oxygen in the Earth's current atmosphere is produced primarily from phytoplankton (tiny, drifting sea plants) and land plants that release oxygen during photosynthesis.

Troposphere The **troposphere,** which lies next to the Earth's surface, is the lowest layer of the atmosphere. The troposphere is also the densest atmospheric layer, containing almost 90 percent of the atmosphere's total mass. Almost all of Earth's carbon dioxide, water vapor, clouds, air pollution, weather, and life-forms are found in the troposphere. In fact, the troposphere is the layer in which you live. **Figure 4** shows the effects of altitude on temperature in the troposphere.

Stratosphere The atmospheric layer above the troposphere is called the **stratosphere.** In the stratosphere, the air is very thin and contains little moisture. The lower stratosphere is extremely cold, measuring about –60°C. In the stratosphere, the temperature rises with increasing altitude. This occurs because of ozone. **Ozone** is a molecule that is made up of three oxygen atoms, as shown in **Figure 5.** Almost all of the ozone in the atmosphere is contained in the *ozone layer* of the stratosphere. Ozone absorbs solar energy in the form of ultraviolet radiation, warming the air. By absorbing the ultraviolet radiation, the ozone layer also protects life at the Earth's surface.

Figure 4 *Snow and ice can remain year-round on a high mountain while forests grow on its lower slopes and base. That is because as altitude increases, the atmosphere thins, losing its ability to absorb and transfer heat.*

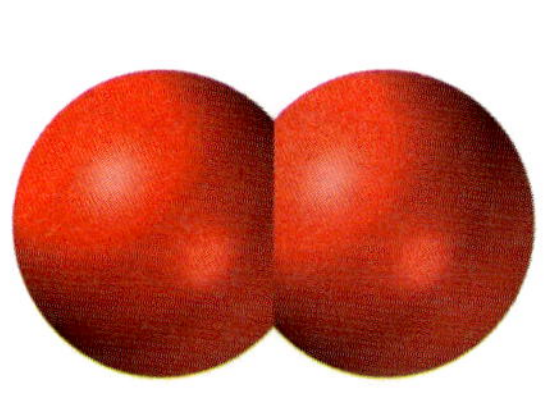

Oxygen gas (O_2)

Ozone (O_3)

Figure 5 *While ozone is made up of three oxygen atoms, the oxygen in the air you breathe is made up of two oxygen atoms.*

People protect themselves from the sun's damaging rays by applying sunblock. Exposure of unprotected skin to the sun's ultraviolet rays over a long period of time can cause skin cancer. The breakdown of the Earth's ozone layer is thinning the layer, which allows some harmful ultraviolet radiation to reach the Earth's surface. Sunblocks contain different ratings of SPFs, or skin protection factors. What do the SPF ratings mean?

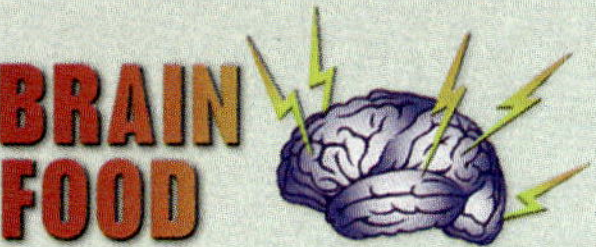

Explain that airplane pilots use instruments, such as altimeters and temperature gauges, to track the changing conditions of the Earth's atmosphere. For example, a pressure altimeter uses atmospheric pressure as an indication of altitude. Have students think about the relationship between pressure and altitude. Then pose the following question:

> Suppose a pilot is flying a plane at an altitude of 9,100 m. If standard air pressure at this elevation is 12 mb (millibars). Would the pilot's altimeter indicate a higher or a lower altitude if the actual barometric pressure were lower than 12 mb? (higher altitude)

Inform students that to compensate for these variations, pilots adjust their altimeter before and during flights.

Under Pressure!

Answer to APPLY

Answers may vary. Sample answer: SPF indicates how many times longer you can stay in the sun without being burned.

MISCONCEPTION ALERT

The amount of stratospheric ozone protecting Earth is smaller than most people realize. If the ozone layer were brought to sea-level pressure and temperature, it would range from 2.5 mm to 3.5 mm thick! (The ozone layer is thinner above the poles than above the equator.)

3 Extend

Guided Practice

On the board, make a table entitled "The Atmosphere." Include the following headings:

Layer, Pressure Range, Temperature Range, and Other Important Information

Have volunteers contribute information for each section of the table. Sheltered English

Connect to Physical Science

Explain that heat energy is the energy of particles in motion, temperature is a measure of how fast the particles are moving, and heat is the transfer of heat energy between objects of different temperature. To clarify these concepts, have students imagine a sink full of hot water. Ask them to pretend that they have removed a cup of the hot water from the sink. Students should agree that both volumes of water have the same temperature at this point. Explain that the heat energy in the sink is greater than the heat energy in the cup because the sink contains more water (and therefore more particles in motion) than the cup.

Using the Figure

Have students use the illustrations in **Figure 6** to compare how energy is transferred in the thermosphere with how it is transferred in the troposphere.

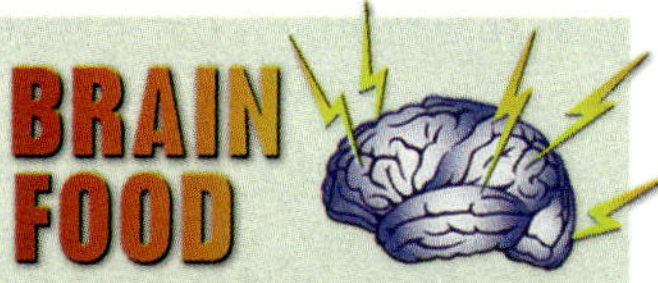

Large continent-sized windstorms were detected by the *Upper Atmosphere Research Satellite.* The effect these winds have on weather at the Earth's surface is currently being studied.

Mesosphere Above the stratosphere is the mesosphere. The **mesosphere** is the coldest layer of the atmosphere. As in the troposphere, the temperature drops with increasing altitude. Temperatures can be as low as –93°C at the top of the mesosphere. Scientists have recently discovered large wind storms in the mesosphere with winds reaching speeds of more than 320 km/h.

Thermosphere The uppermost atmospheric layer is the **thermosphere.** Here temperature again increases with altitude because many of the gases are absorbing solar radiation. Temperatures in this layer can reach 1,700°C. When you think of an area with high temperatures, you probably think of a place that is very hot. While the thermosphere has very high temperatures, it isn't hot. Temperature and heat are not the same thing. Temperature is a measure of the average energy of particles in motion. A high temperature means that the particles are moving very fast. Heat, on the other hand, involves the transfer of energy between objects at different temperatures. But in order to transfer energy, particles must touch one another. The air in the thermosphere is very thin, meaning particles are far apart. So even though the particles are moving very fast, they rarely transfer energy because the particles rarely collide. **Figure 6** illustrates how the density of particles affects the heating of the atmosphere.

Figure 6 *Temperatures in the thermosphere are higher than those in the troposphere, but the air particles are too far apart for heat to be transferred.*

The **thermosphere** contains relatively few particles, all of which are moving fast. The temperature of this layer is high due to the speed of its particles, but because the particles aren't close enough together to touch one another, the thermosphere does not give off much heat.

The **troposphere** contains more particles, all of which travel at a slower speed. The temperature of this layer is lower than that of the thermosphere. But because the particles are bumping into one another, the troposphere transfers much more heat.

internet connect

TOPIC: Composition of the Atmosphere
GO TO: www.scilinks.org
***sci*LINKS NUMBER:** HSTE355

Different cultures have different explanations for the shimmering lights known as the aurora borealis. Inuit groups thought of the aurora borealis as the torches of spirits that guided souls from Earth to paradise. Have students find out about other myths concerning the aurora borealis.

In the upper part of the thermosphere, nitrogen and oxygen atoms absorb harmful solar energy, such as X rays and gamma rays. This absorption not only contributes to the thermosphere's high temperatures but also causes the gas particles to become electrically charged. Electrically charged particles are called ions; therefore, this part of the thermosphere is referred to as the *ionosphere*. Sometimes these ions radiate energy as light of different colors, as shown in **Figure 7.**

Figure 7 *Aurora borealis (northern lights) and aurora australis (southern lights) occur in the ionosphere. The auroras generally occur near the poles between 65° and 90° north and south latitude.*

The ionosphere also reflects certain radio waves, such as AM radio waves. If you have ever listened to an AM radio station, you can be sure that the ionosphere had something to do with how clear it sounded. When conditions are right, an AM radio wave can travel around the world after being reflected off the ionosphere. These radio signals bounce off the ionosphere and are sent back to Earth.

There is no definite boundary between the atmosphere and space. In the upper thermosphere, the air becomes thinner and thinner, eventually blending into space.

REVIEW

1. Explain why pressure decreases but temperature varies as altitude increases.
2. What causes air pressure.
3. How can the thermosphere have high temperatures but not be hot?
4. **Analyzing Relationships** Identify one characteristic of each layer of the atmosphere, and explain how that characteristic affects life on Earth.

Answers to Review

1. Farther away from the Earth's surface, air pressure decreases because there are fewer gas molecules pushing down. Temperature varies due to the way solar energy is absorbed as it moves through the atmosphere.
2. Air pressure is caused by gravity.
3. In the thermosphere, few particles are moving fast, but because they are far apart, they cannot transfer energy.
4. The gases in the troposphere make life on Earth possible. The stratosphere contains the ozone layer, which protects life at the Earth's surface from ultraviolet radiation. The mesosphere is the coldest layer of the atmosphere. The thermosphere contains the ionosphere, which absorbs harmful solar energy and reflects certain radio waves.

4 Close

Quiz

1. What are the two main gases in Earth's atmosphere? (nitrogen and oxygen)
2. What is atmospheric pressure? (Atmospheric pressure is the force exerted by molecules of air on a surface.)
3. Name the layers of the atmosphere, starting with the one closest to Earth. (troposphere, stratosphere, mesosphere, thermosphere)
4. What is the ozone layer, and why is it important to Earth? (The ozone layer is a layer of ozone molecules in the stratosphere. The layer filters ultraviolet radiation from the sun and prevents much of this radiation from reaching Earth.)
5. Explain how density affects heat transfer in the air. (The less dense the air is, the less effective it is at transferring heat. Particles that are farther apart, or less densely packed, are less likely to collide with other particles. Particles must collide with one another in order to transfer heat.)

Alternative Assessment

Writing **Poetry** Have each student write a poem that creatively yet accurately describes one layer of Earth's atmosphere. Allow time for volunteers to read their poem aloud or display the poem for others to read on their own.

PORTFOLIO

Reinforcement Worksheet 15
"Earth's Amazing Atmosphere"

Section 1 Review–California Standards: PE/ATE 3a

Section 2

Focus

Heating of the Atmosphere

In this section, students learn that the sun is the principal energy source for our planet. They also discover that energy is transferred in one of three ways—by conduction, convection, or radiation. The section concludes with a discussion of the greenhouse effect and global warming.

Bellringer

Have students suppose that they will be vacationing in two unique spots—the Sahara Desert and the Antarctic ice sheet. Have them decide whether white or black clothing would be best for each location. Ask students to explain their choices. (Because of its high reflectivity, white would be best for the hot desert. Because of its ability to absorb energy, black clothing would be the wiser choice for the ice sheet.)

1 Motivate

Activity

Get a small table lamp that operates with an incandescent bulb. Remove the shade, turn the lamp on, and put the lamp on your desk or a tabletop. Ask students to hypothesize about how the temperature around the bulb varies. Have two volunteers measure the air temperature 5 cm from the bulb's top and 5 cm from its side. Have students discuss possible reasons why the air above the bulb is hotter than the air to its side.

2

Heating of the Atmosphere

NEW TERMS

radiation
conduction
convection
greenhouse effect
global warming

OBJECTIVES

- Describe what happens to radiation that reaches the Earth.
- Summarize the processes of radiation, conduction, and convection.
- Explain how the greenhouse effect contributes to global warming.

Have you ever walked barefoot across a sidewalk on a sunny day? If so, your foot felt the warmth of the hot pavement. How did the sidewalk become so warm? Solar energy was changed into heat. The Earth's atmosphere is also heated in several ways by the transfer of energy from the sun. In this section you will find out what happens to the solar energy as it enters the Earth's atmosphere, how the energy is transferred through the atmosphere, and why it seems to be getting hotter every year.

Energy in the Atmosphere

The Earth receives energy from the sun in the form of radiation. **Radiation** is energy that is transferred as waves. Although the sun releases a huge amount of radiation, the Earth receives only about two-billionths of this energy. Yet even this small amount of radiation contains a very large amount of energy. **Figure 8** shows what happens to all this radiation once it enters the atmosphere.

When radiation is absorbed, its energy is changed into heat. For example, when you stand in the sun on a cool day, you can feel the sun's rays warming your body. Your skin

Figure 8 *The radiation absorbed by the land, water, and atmosphere is changed into heat.*

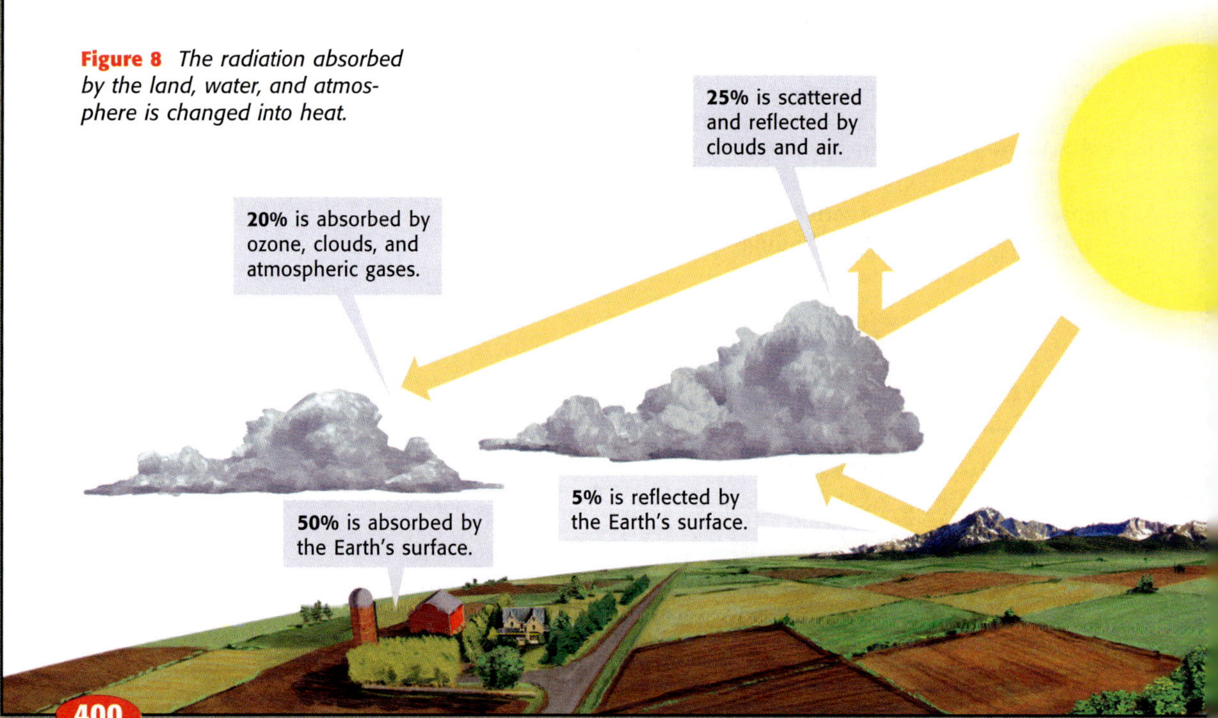

400

Directed Reading Worksheet 15 Section 2

Is That a Fact!

The sun is a medium-sized star that radiates energy through space. About 0.02 percent of solar radiation reaches the Earth. But without the sun's radiant energy, Earth would have little or no cloud cover and winds, and life would not exist.

Section 2–California Standards: PE/ATE 3, 3a, 3c, 3d, 4, 4a, 4b, 4d, 4e, 7, 7a, 7b, 7e; LabBook: 7, 7a, 7b, 7e absorbs the radiation, causing your skin's molecules to move faster. You feel this as an increase in temperature. The same thing happens when radiation is absorbed by the Earth's surface. Energy in the form of heat from the Earth's surface can then be transferred to the atmosphere by two major methods: conduction and convection.

Conduction **Conduction** is the transfer of heat from one material to another by direct physical contact. Think back to the example about walking barefoot on a hot sidewalk. Conduction occurs when heat is transferred from the sidewalk to your foot. Heat always flows from a warm area to a cold area. Just as your foot is heated by the sidewalk, the air is heated by land and ocean surfaces. When air molecules come into direct contact with a warm surface, heat is transferred to the atmosphere.

Convection Most heat in the atmosphere moves by *convection*. **Convection** is the transfer of heat by the circulation or movement of a liquid or gas. For instance, as air is heated, it becomes less dense and rises. Cool air is more dense and sinks. As the cool air sinks, it pushes the warm air up. The cold air is eventually heated by the ground and again begins to rise. This continual process of warm air rising and cool air sinking creates a circular movement of air, called a *convection current,* as shown in **Figure 9.**

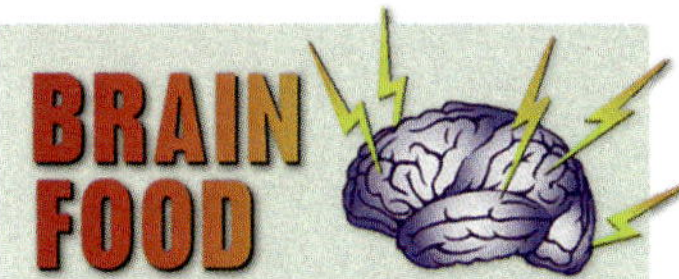

If the Earth is continually absorbing solar energy and changing it to heat energy, why doesn't the Earth get hotter and hotter? The reason is that much of this heat energy is lost to space. This is especially true on cloudless nights.

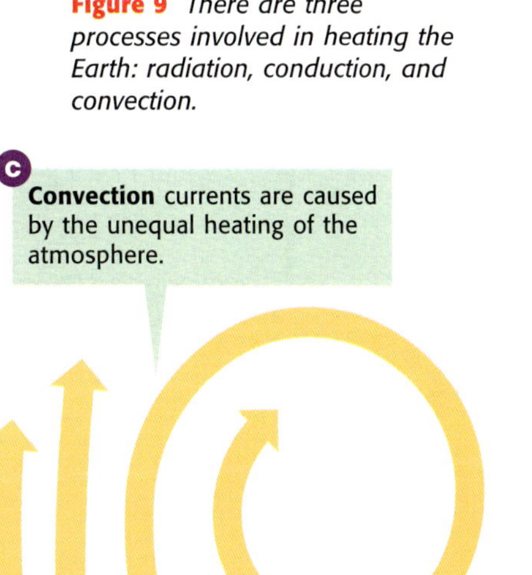

Figure 9 *There are three processes involved in heating the Earth: radiation, conduction, and convection.*

2 Teach

Activity

Make some popcorn the "old-fashioned" way, using a hot plate or stovetop, oil, and popcorn kernels. As you pop the snack, have volunteers explain how the processes of convection, conduction, and radiation are involved. Point out that a kernel pops when the liquid water stored inside changes to water vapor and expands suddenly. Share the treat with students if time allows. Make sure students with allergies to corn do not eat the popcorn. Sheltered English

Demonstration

Use heat-resistant gloves, a hot plate, a transparent coffee decanter, water, and confetti to demonstrate convection. Fill the decanter about three-fourths full of water. Sprinkle the confetti into the water, and mix it slightly so that it settles to the bottom. Put on the heat-resistant gloves, and hold the decanter so that only one-half of it is on the hot plate. Heat the water. Have students observe the confetti rise along the edge that is in contact with the heat source, move along the top of the water, and descend back toward the bottom of the decanter along the cooler side.

Homework

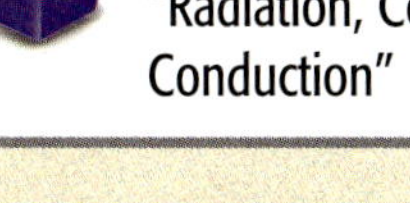

Have students write several paragraphs that compare and contrast various methods used to heat buildings. Suggest that they consider radiators, steam heating systems, heating systems that use furnaces, and solar heating systems. Make sure that students correctly use the terms *radiation, convection,* and *conduction* in their descriptions.

Teaching Transparency 142 "Radiation and the Atmosphere"

Teaching Transparency 143 "Radiation, Convection, and Conduction"

3 Extend

Group Activity

Model Greenhouses

MATERIALS

For Each Group:
- large jar with lid
- thermometer
- small piece of modeling clay

Have students work in small groups to make model greenhouses by placing the thermometer inside the jar and anchoring it with modeling clay. Next have them seal the jar with the lid.

Have each group put its model in a different sunny spot. Students should observe and record changes in temperature every day for 1 week. Students can compare the temperatures they record with the temperatures in a control jar without a lid. Help students infer that radiant energy enters a greenhouse and is converted to heat energy and that the glass prevents most of the heat energy from escaping.

Sheltered English

TOPIC: Energy in the Atmosphere
GO TO: www.scilinks.org
***sci*LINKS NUMBER:** HSTE360

TOPIC: The Greenhouse Effect
GO TO: www.scilinks.org
***sci*LINKS NUMBER:** HSTE365

BRAIN FOOD

Annual average surface temperatures in the Northern Hemisphere have been higher in the 1990s than at any other time in the past 600 years.

The Greenhouse Effect

As you have already learned, only 20 percent of the radiation that enters the Earth's atmosphere is absorbed by gases in the atmosphere and changed into heat. But these gases capture energy in other ways. When land and water absorb radiation, their molecules move faster, increasing their temperature. This energy is transferred to gas molecules in the atmosphere before it can escape into space. As a result, the atmosphere warms up. The Earth's heating process, in which the gases in the atmosphere absorb radiation and change that energy into heat, is known as the **greenhouse effect.** This term is used because the Earth's atmosphere works much like a greenhouse, as shown in **Figure 10.**

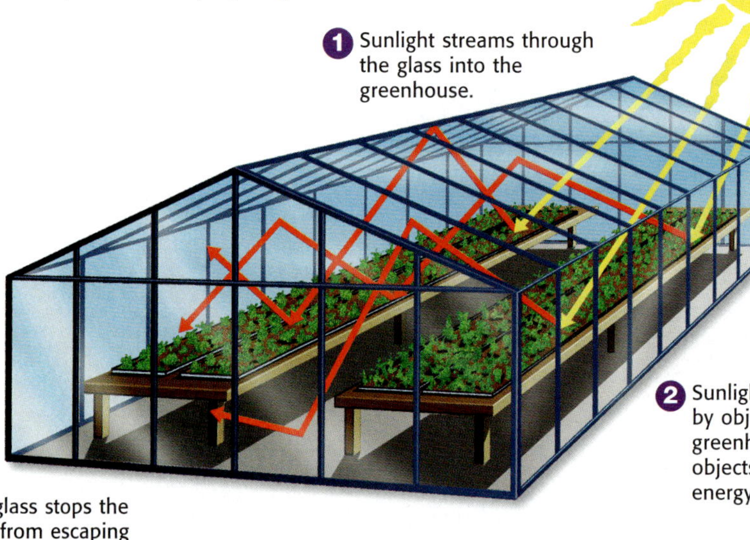

Figure 10 *The gases in the atmosphere act like a layer of glass. Both glass and the gases in the atmosphere allow solar energy to pass through. But glass and some of the gases in the atmosphere absorb heat and stop it from escaping to space.*

Global Warming Not every gas in the atmosphere traps heat. Those that do trap heat are called *greenhouse gases.* In recent decades, many scientists have become concerned that an increase of these gases, particularly carbon dioxide, may be causing an increase in the greenhouse effect. These scientists have hypothesized that a rise in carbon dioxide as a result of human activity has led to increased global temperatures. A rise in average global temperatures is called **global warming.** If there were an increase in the greenhouse effect, global warming would result.

402

Scientists at Odds

While there is little argument about the accuracy of the greenhouse-effect model, there is much debate in the scientific community over whether the recent rise in global temperatures is due to global warming or a normal fluctuation in global temperatures. Scientists agree that the use of fossil fuels and CFCs as well as deforestation contribute to global warming in the greenhouse-effect model, but there is debate over which is the predominant cause. Have interested students learn more about global warming and stage a class debate over some of these issues.

If the average global temperatures continue to rise, the ice-caps could melt, causing a rise in sea level that could flood coastal areas. A rise in global temperatures could also cause climate and weather changes. Later in this chapter you will learn about the human activities that are contributing to an increase in greenhouse gases.

Keeping the Earth Livable For the Earth to remain livable, the amount of solar energy received and the amount of heat energy returned to space must be equal. As you saw in Figure 8, about 30 percent of the incoming radiation is reflected back into space. Most of the 70 percent that is absorbed by the Earth and its atmosphere is sent back into space in the form of heat. The balance between incoming radiation and outgoing heat is known as the *radiation balance*. If greenhouse gases, such as carbon dioxide, continue to increase in the atmosphere, the radiation balance may be affected. Some of the energy that once escaped into space could be trapped. The Earth's temperatures would continue to rise, causing major changes in plant and animal communities.

Some scientists argue that the Earth had warmer periods before humans ever walked the planet, so global warming may be a natural process. Nevertheless, many of the world's nations have signed a treaty to reduce activities that increase greenhouse gases in the atmosphere. Another step that is being taken to reduce high carbon dioxide levels in the atmosphere is the planting of millions of trees by volunteers, as shown in **Figure 11.**

life science CONNECTION

Did you know that if you lived in Florida, your fingernails and toenails would grow faster than if you lived in Minnesota? Studies by scientists at Oxford University, in England, showed that the average fingernail growth in the tropics is 1 mm/day, while in more temperate regions it is 0.8 mm/day. The study showed that warm weather helps tissue growth, while cold weather slightly slows it.

Figure 11 *Plants take in harmful carbon dioxide and give off oxygen, which we need to breathe.*

REVIEW

1. Describe three things that can happen to radiation when it reaches the Earth's atmosphere?
2. How is energy transferred through the atmosphere?
3. What is the greenhouse effect?
4. **Inferring Relationships** How does the process of convection rely on conduction?

4 Close

PG 546

Boiling Over!

Quiz

1. What is radiation? (Radiation is energy transferred as waves.)
2. A metal spoon left in a bowl of hot soup feels hot. Which process—radiation, conduction, or convection—is mainly responsible for heating the spoon? (conduction)
3. What is a convection current? (the continual, circular movement of warm and cool particles in a liquid or gas)
4. How does a greenhouse stay warm? (Sunlight goes through the glass. Objects in the structure absorb some of the radiant energy. In turn, the objects radiate this energy as heat. The glass prevents the heat from escaping. Heat builds up and warms the greenhouse.)

ALTERNATIVE ASSESSMENT

Writing Have students write a paragraph in their ScienceLog that compares and contrasts radiation, conduction, and convection.

Answers to Review

1. Answers will vary. Sample answer: Radiation can be absorbed by the Earth's surface. Radiation can be absorbed by ozone, clouds, and the atmosphere. Radiation can be reflected by the Earth's surface and clouds.
2. Answers will vary. Sample answer: Energy is transferred through the atmosphere through radiation, conduction, and convection.
3. The greenhouse effect is the Earth's natural heating process, by which gases in the atmosphere absorb radiation and transfer energy in the form of heat.
4. The air directly above the Earth's surface is heated by conduction. This warm air is then circulated through the atmosphere by convection currents.

Section 2 Review–California Standards: PE/ATE 3, 3c, 3d, 4d

SECTION 3

Focus

Atmospheric Pressure and Winds

This section explains what wind is and how it is created by differences in atmospheric pressure. Students will also learn about different types of wind, including trade winds, jet streams, and local winds.

Bellringer

Tell students that **Figure 13** is an idealized model. Air doesn't actually follow the lines shown. Tell them that the Earth rotates west to east. Have students predict how this rotation would affect the movement of winds.

1 Motivate

DEMONSTRATION

Air Movement This demonstration will show students how air moves from areas of high pressure to areas of low pressure. An area of high pressure can be created by filling a plastic container with ice. An area of low pressure can be created by heating a hot plate. Place the container of ice and the hot plate approximately 30 cm from each other. Make sure the container of ice is slightly higher than the hot plate so students can better observe the movement of air. Light a splint or long match, and let it burn for a few seconds. Blow out the splint or match over the ice, and place the smoking end close to the ice. Observe the movement of the smoke. The smoke should move from the ice to the hot plate (from an area of high pressure to an area of low pressure).

3

NEW TERMS

wind
Coriolis effect
trade winds
westerlies
polar easterlies
jet streams

OBJECTIVES

- Explain the relationship between air pressure and wind direction.
- Describe the global patterns of wind.
- Explain the causes of local wind patterns.

Atmospheric Pressure and Winds

Sometimes it cools you. Other times it scatters tidy piles of newly swept trash. Still other times it uproots trees and flattens buildings, as shown in **Figure 12.** **Wind** is moving air. In this section you will learn about air movement and about the similarities and differences between different kinds of winds.

Figure 12 *In 1998, the winds from Hurricane Mitch reached speeds of 288 km/h, destroying entire towns in Honduras.*

Why Air Moves

Wind is created by differences in air pressure. These differences in air pressure are generally caused by the unequal heating of the Earth. For example, because the Earth receives more direct solar energy at the equator than at the poles, the air at the equator is warmer and less dense. This warm, less-dense air rises. As it rises it creates an area of low pressure. At the poles, however, the same amount of solar energy that the equator receives is spread over a larger area. Thus, the air is colder and more dense. Colder, more-dense air is heavier and sinks. This cold, sinking air creates areas of high pressure. Pressure differences in the atmosphere at the equator and at the poles cause air to move. Because air moves from areas of high pressure to areas of low pressure, winds generally move from the poles to the equator, as shown in **Figure 13.**

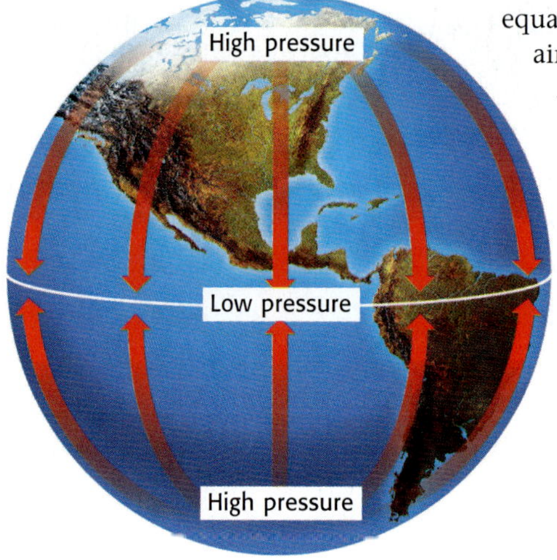

Figure 13 *Surface winds blow from polar high-pressure areas to equatorial low-pressure areas.*

404

SCIENCE HUMOR

Q: What did the air molecule at sea level say to the air molecule on a mountaintop when asked how things were going?

A: Not too well—I'm under a lot of pressure!

Section 3–California Standards: PE/ATE 4, 4a, 4d, 4e, 7, 7b, 7e; LabBook: 7, 7b, 7e

The speed of the wind is determined by the pressure difference between the area of high pressure and the area of low pressure. The greater the pressure difference is, the faster the wind moves.

Pressure Belts You may be imagining wind moving in one huge, circular pattern, from the poles to the equator. In fact, the pattern is much more complex. As warm air rises over the equator, it begins to cool. Eventually, it stops rising and moves toward the poles. At about 30° north and 30° south latitude, some of the cool air begins to sink. This cool, sinking air causes a high pressure belt near 30° north and 30° south latitude.

At the poles, cold air sinks. As this air moves away from the poles and along the Earth's surface, it begins to warm. As the air warms, the pressure drops, creating a low-pressure belt around 60° north and 60° south latitude. The circular patterns caused by the rising and sinking of air are called *convection cells,* as shown in **Figure 14.**

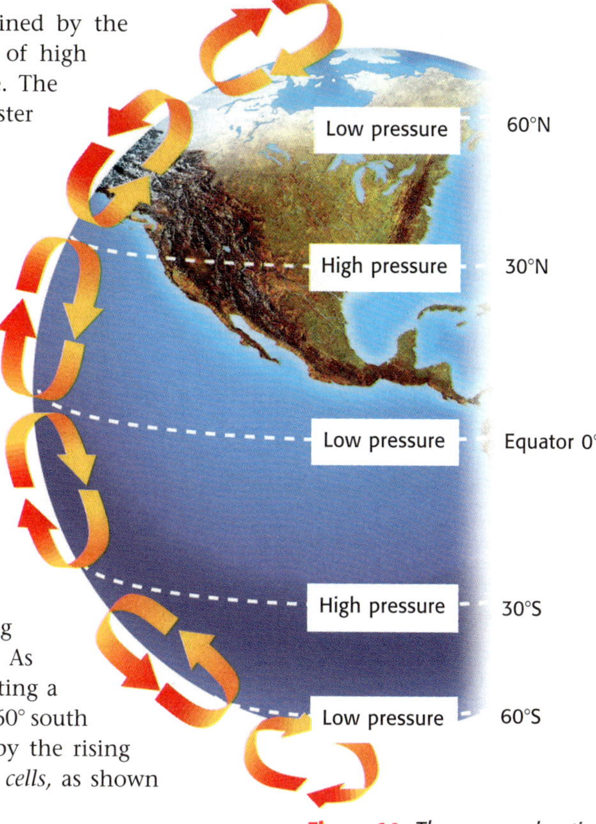

Figure 14 *The uneven heating of the Earth produces pressure belts. These belts occur at about every 30° of latitude.*

Coriolis Effect Winds don't blow directly north or south. The movement of wind is affected by the rotation of the Earth. The Earth's rotation causes wind to travel in a curved path rather than in a straight line. The curving of moving objects, such as wind, by the Earth's rotation is called the **Coriolis effect.** Because of the Coriolis effect, the winds in the Northern Hemisphere curve to the right, and those in the Southern Hemisphere curve to the left.

To better understand how the Coriolis effect works, imagine rolling a marble across a Lazy Susan while it is spinning. What you might observe is shown in **Figure 15.**

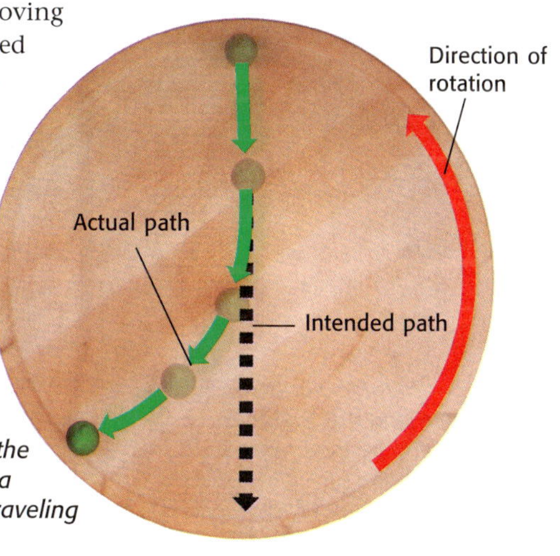

Figure 15 *Because of the Lazy Susan's rotation, the path of the marble curves instead of traveling in a straight line. The Earth's rotation affects objects traveling on or near its surface in much the same way.*

In addition to being observed in ocean and atmospheric currents, the Coriolis effect can also be observed in river systems. Rivers in the Northern Hemisphere erode their right banks more than their left banks. Because the Mississippi River and the Yukon River flow roughly north-south in sections, they are good examples of this effect.

Multicultural CONNECTION

Changes in atmospheric pressure are often said to affect fish. Egyptian fishermen notice that mullet move with the wind to prevent getting stuck in muddy water. According to Caribbean lore, a container of shark oil will grow cloudy when a hurricane is imminent. Have students do some research to find out about other organisms that might indicate changes in wind, air pressure, and other atmospheric phenomena.

MEETING INDIVIDUAL NEEDS

Learners Having Difficulty Try the following activity to help students who have problems understanding the Coriolis effect. You will need a globe, some flour, an eyedropper, red food coloring, and water. Mix a few drops of food coloring with water, and fill the eyedropper with the solution. Dust the globe thoroughly with flour. If the flour doesn't stick, mist the globe lightly with tap water, and sprinkle the flour over the globe. Enlist a volunteer to slowly spin the globe counterclockwise to simulate Earth's rotation. Have another volunteer slowly drop water from the dropper from the top of the globe, at the North Pole. Students will observe that the water is deflected westward in the Northern Hemisphere. Have students demonstrate the Coriolis effect in the Southern Hemisphere by turning the globe upside down and rotating it counterclockwise. Sheltered English

Directed Reading Worksheet 15 Section 3

2 Teach, *continued*

QuickLab

MATERIALS

- large clear-plastic container
- cold water
- packaging string (about 30 cm long)
- small glass bottle with a narrow neck
- hot water
- red food coloring

Answers to QuickLab

6. The red warm water should rise. This activity models the circulation of air in the atmosphere. If the container were filled with cold water, the colored water would sink.

USING THE FIGURE

Have students use **Figure 16** to answer the following questions:

Where are the trade winds? (the winds that blow from 30° north and south latitudes to the equator)

Describe the motion of the trade winds in the Southern Hemisphere. (They move from the southeast to the northwest.)

How do the westerlies flow in the Northern Hemisphere? (The westerlies flow from the southwest to the northeast.)

What is the name of the windless zone that lies between the trade winds? (the doldrums)

TOPIC: Atmospheric Pressure and Winds
GO TO: www.scilinks.org
***sci*LINKS NUMBER:** HSTE370

QuickLab

Full of "Hot Air"

1. Fill a **large clear-plastic container** with **cold water.**
2. Tie the end of a **string** around the neck of a **small bottle.**
3. Fill the small bottle with **hot water,** and add a few drops of **red food coloring** until the water has changed color.
4. Without tipping the small bottle, lower it into the plastic container until it rests on the bottom.
5. Observe what happens.
6. What process does this activity model? What do you think will happen if you fill the small bottle with cold water instead? Try It!

Types of Winds

There are two main types of winds: local winds and global winds. Both types are caused by the uneven heating of the Earth's surface and by pressure differences. *Local winds* generally move short distances and can blow from any direction. *Global winds* are part of a pattern of air circulation that moves across the Earth. These winds travel longer distances than local winds, and they each travel in a specific direction. **Figure 16** shows the location and movement of major global wind systems. First let's review the different types of global winds, and later in this section we will discuss local winds.

Trade Winds In both hemispheres, the winds that blow from 30° latitude to the equator are called **trade winds.** Because the Coriolis effect makes the trade winds curve to the right in the Northern Hemisphere, they move from the northeast to the southwest. In the Southern Hemisphere, the trade winds curve to the left and move from the southeast to the northwest. Early traders used the trade winds to sail from Europe to the Americas, hence the name.

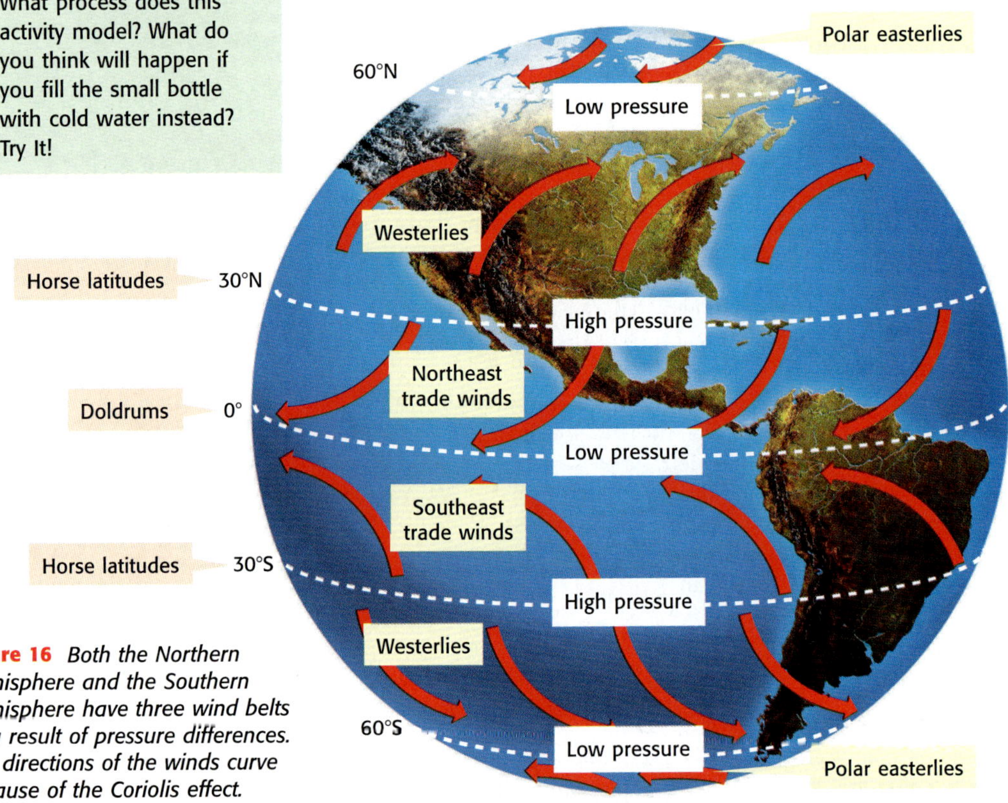

Figure 16 *Both the Northern Hemisphere and the Southern Hemisphere have three wind belts as a result of pressure differences. The directions of the winds curve because of the Coriolis effect.*

406

Science Bloopers

During a World War I naval engagement off the Falkland Islands, British gunners were astonished to see that their artillery shells were landing a hundred yards to the left of German ships. The gunners had made corrections for the Coriolis effect at 50 degrees north latitude, not 50 degrees south of the equator. Consequently, their shells fell at a distance from the target equal to twice the Coriolis deflection!

The trade winds of the Northern and Southern Hemispheres meet in an area of low pressure around the equator called the *doldrums*. In the doldrums there is very little wind because of the warm rising air. *Doldrums* comes from an Old English word meaning "foolish." Sailors were considered foolish if they got their ship stuck in these areas of little wind.

At about 30° north and 30° south latitude, sinking air creates an area of high pressure. This area is called the *horse latitudes*. Here the winds are weak. Legend has it that the name horse latitudes was given to these areas when sailing ships carried horses from Europe to the Americas. When the ships were stuck in this area due to lack of wind, horses were sometimes thrown overboard to save drinking water for the sailors.

Westerlies The **westerlies** are wind belts found in both the Northern and Southern Hemispheres between 30° and 60° latitude. The westerlies flow toward the poles in the opposite direction of the trade winds. In the Northern Hemisphere, the westerlies blow from the southwest to the northeast. In the Southern Hemisphere, they blow from the northwest to the southeast. The westerlies helped early traders return to Europe. Sailing ships, like the one in **Figure 17**, were designed to best use the wind to move the ship forward.

Figure 17 *This ship is a replica of Columbus's* Santa Maria, *which traveled back to Spain with news of the New World.*

Polar Easterlies The **polar easterlies** are wind belts that extend from the poles to 60° latitude in both hemispheres. The polar easterlies are formed from cold, sinking air moving from the poles toward 60° north and 60° south latitude. The polar easterlies blow from the northeast to the southwest in the Northern Hemisphere. In the Southern Hemisphere, these winds blow from the southeast to the northwest.

environmental science CONNECTION

Humans have been using wind power for thousands of years. Today wind energy is being tapped to produce electricity. In California, electricity is produced at wind farms. Wind farms are made up of hundreds of wind turbines that look like giant airplane propellers attached to a tower. Together these wind turbines can produce enough electricity for an entire town. However, these types of farms work only in areas where the wind blows most of the time.

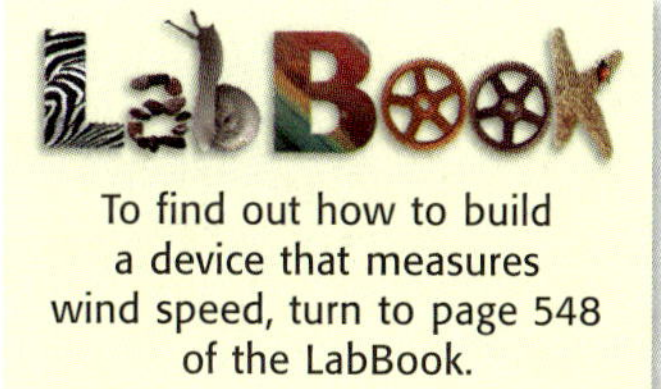

To find out how to build a device that measures wind speed, turn to page 548 of the LabBook.

DISCUSSION

After students study **Figure 16,** have them speculate about how the westerlies got their name. When students realize that their name indicates they blow from the west, inform them that winds are often named for the direction from which they flow. Have students verify this fact by noting the direction from which polar easterlies flow.

Sheltered English

MEETING INDIVIDUAL NEEDS

Advanced Learners Challenge interested students to explore the following question:

If we understand so much about the workings of the atmosphere, why can't we accurately predict weather from one week to the next?

Students will discover that scientists think the answer has to do with the chaotic nature of weather systems. Chaotic systems are so sensitive that slight variations at one point can result in huge changes later on. The behavior of chaotic systems is therefore very difficult to predict over more than a short period of time.

PG 548

Go Fly a Bike!

IS THAT A FACT!

Because the air descending over the horse latitudes has lost most of its moisture, the land around these latitudes receives very little precipitation. In fact, the Earth's largest deserts are in these areas.

Homework

Have students watch or listen to a weather broadcast. Tell them to write down the meteorologist's comments about the local weather. Then have them write their interpretation of the forecast based on what they have learned about the atmosphere.

3 Extend

Using the Figure

Have students refer to **Figure 19** to answer the questions below.

How does air temperature over landmasses and adjacent bodies of water change between day and night? (During the day, the air is cooler over water. At night, the air is cooler over land.)

Explain the circulation pattern that occurs during a sea breeze. (The wind moves from the water toward the land.)

MATH and MORE

Challenge students to solve the following problem:

A pilot flying 950 km to Chicago is worried about a storm that will hit the city in 2 hours. The plane can fly at 500 km/h. A jet stream flowing in the opposite direction is moving at 250 km/h. If the plane must spend 10 minutes in the jet stream in order to climb above it, can the pilot make it to Chicago before the storm hits?

(Yes; the pilot can beat the storm:

$(500 \text{ km/h} \times 1\frac{5}{6} \text{ h}) + (250 \text{ km/h} \times \frac{1}{6} \text{ h}) = 958 \text{ km in 2 hours}$)

Math Skills Worksheet 13 "Improper Fractions and Mixed Numbers"

Teaching Transparency 145 "Sea and Land Breezes"

Figure 18 *The large pressure differences between cold air from the poles and warm air from the middle latitudes produce fast-moving jet streams.*

Jet Streams The **jet streams** are narrow belts of high-speed winds that blow in the upper troposphere and lower stratosphere over both the Northern Hemisphere and the Southern Hemisphere, as shown in **Figure 18.** These winds often change speed and can reach maximum speeds of 500 km/h. Unlike other global winds, the jet streams do not follow regular paths around the Earth, but change both their latitude and altitude.

Knowing the position of the jet stream is important to both meteorologists and airline pilots. Because the jet stream controls the movement of storms, meteorologists can track a storm if they know the location of the jet stream. By flying in the direction of the jet stream, pilots can save time and fuel. On the other hand, pilots flying against the jet stream will use more fuel and take longer to reach their destination.

Local Winds Local winds are influenced by the geography of an area. An area's geography, such as a lake or a mountain, sometimes produces temperature differences that cause local winds like land and sea breezes, as shown in **Figure 19.** During the day, land heats up faster than water. The land heats the air above it. At night, land cools faster than water, cooling the air above the land.

Figure 19 **Sea and Land Breezes**

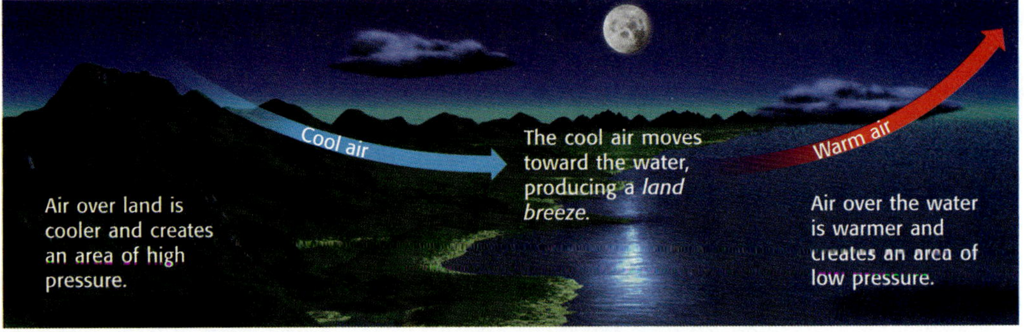

Multicultural Connection

The *chinook,* or "snow eater," is a wind that blows in the northwestern United States and western Canada. American Indians gave the chinook its name because of its ability to melt large amounts of snow very quickly. Originating as moist air blowing off the Pacific Ocean, it heats up and loses moisture over the Rocky Mountains. When it reaches the Northwest, the chinook is warm and dry enough to melt large amounts of snow. Have interested students research other local winds, such as the *sirocco,* that have a profound impact on people's lives.

Mountain and valley breezes are another example of local winds caused by an area's geography. Campers in mountain areas may feel a warm afternoon change into a cold night soon after the sun sets. The illustrations in **Figure 20** show you why.

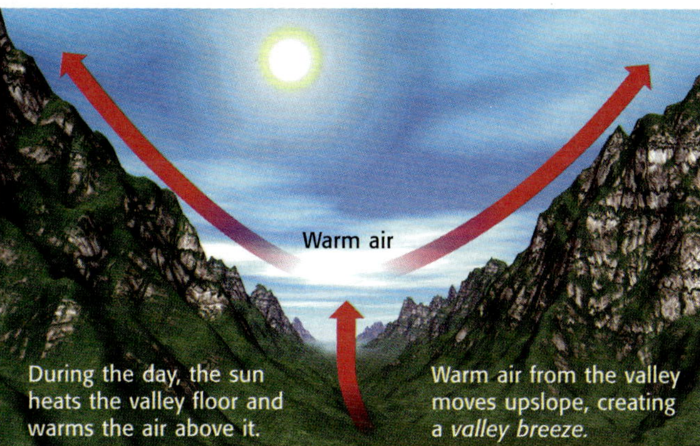

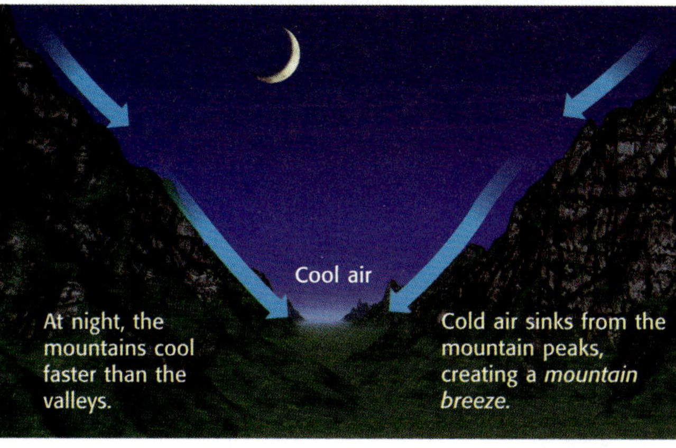

Figure 20 *During the day, a gentle breeze blows up the slopes. At night, cold air flows downslope and settles in the valley.*

MATH BREAK

Calculating Groundspeed
An airplane has an airspeed of 500 km/h and is moving into a 150 km/h head wind due to the jet stream. What is the actual groundspeed of the plane? Over a 3-hour flight, how far would the plane actually travel? (Hint: To calculate actual ground-speed, subtract head-wind speed from airspeed.)

REVIEW

1. How does the Coriolis effect affect wind movement?
2. What causes winds?
3. Compare and contrast global winds and local winds.
4. **Applying Concepts** Suppose you are vacationing at the beach. It is daytime and you want to go swimming in the ocean. You know the beach is near your hotel, but you don't know what direction it is in. How might the local wind help you find the ocean?

Answers to Review

1. The Coriolis effect prevents winds from blowing directly north or south. Due to the Coriolis effect, winds in the Northern Hemisphere curve to the right, and winds in the Southern Hemisphere curve to the left.
2. Winds are caused by the unequal heating of the Earth's surface and by pressure differences.
3. Local winds travel short distances and can blow from any direction. Global winds travel long distances and travel in specific directions.
4. During the day, a sea breeze is caused by the cooler air over the water moving toward the land. Following the direction the sea breeze blows from would lead you to the ocean.

Answers to MATHBREAK

500 km/h − 150 km/h = 350 km/h
3 h × 350 km/h = 1,050 km

4) Close

Quiz

1. What is wind? (air that flows between air masses of different pressures and temperatures)
2. Describe the general movement of wind over the Earth. (Winds generally move from the poles to the equator.)
3. What is the Coriolis effect? (the deflection of moving objects due to Earth's rotation)
4. Compare and contrast the trade winds and the westerlies in the Northern Hemisphere. (Both are global wind systems that curve due to the Coriolis effect. Both result from differences in air pressure and temperature. The trade winds, which lie between the equator and 30° north latitude, blow from the northeast to the southwest. The westerlies lie between 30° and 60° north latitude and blow from the southwest to the northeast.)
5. What are two kinds of breezes that result from local topography? (mountain and valley breezes)

ALTERNATIVE ASSESSMENT

Concept Mapping Have students create a concept map using the vocabulary and concepts in this section.

Section 3 Review–California Standards: PE/ATE 4, 4a, 4d

SECTION 4

Focus

The Air We Breathe

This section defines and discusses air pollution. Students learn the difference between primary and secondary pollutants and explore sources of human-caused air pollution. Students then learn about some broader impacts of air pollution, such as acid precipitation and the ozone hole. Finally, students learn about the health effects of air pollution and what people can do to limit pollution.

Bellringer

Bring a filter mask to class. Have each student make a list of three situations in which one might wear such a mask. For example, surgeons wear such masks to prevent the transfer of disease-causing microbes, and sandblasters wear masks to avoid inhaling dust and paint chips. Tell students that some people living in areas with heavily polluted air wear such masks to protect themselves from impurities in the air they breathe.

1) Motivate

DISCUSSION

Explain that the air inside buildings may be polluted by a variety of sources. Ask students to list possible sources of indoor air pollution. If students have difficulty coming up with examples, lead them to conclude that chalk dust, cooking oils, carpets, insulation, tobacco smoke, paints, glues, copier machines, space heaters, gas appliances, and fireplaces are just a few sources of indoor air pollution.

4

NEW TERMS

primary pollutants
secondary pollutants
acid precipitation
scrubber

OBJECTIVES

- Describe the major types of air pollution.
- Name the major causes of air pollution.
- Explain how air pollution can affect human health.
- Explain how air pollution can be reduced.

The Air We Breathe

Air pollution, as shown in **Figure 21,** is not a new problem. By the middle of the 1700s, many of the world's large cities suffered from poor air quality. Most of the pollutants were released from factories and homes that burned coal for heat. Even 2,000 years ago, the Romans were complaining about the bad air in their cities. At that time the air was thick with the smoke from fires and the smell of open sewers. So you see, cities have always been troubled with air pollution. In this section you will learn about the different types of air pollution, their sources, and what the world is doing to reduce them.

Figure 21 *The air pollution in Mexico City is sometimes so dangerous that some people wear surgical masks when they go outside.*

Air Quality

Even "clean" air is not perfectly clean. It contains many pollutants from natural sources. These pollutants include dust, sea salt, volcanic gases and ash, smoke from forest fires, pollen, swamp gas, and many other materials. In fact, natural sources produce a greater amount of pollutants than humans do. But we have adapted to many of these natural pollutants.

Most of the air pollution mentioned in the news is a result of human activities. Pollutants caused by human activities can be solids, liquids, or gases. Human-caused air pollution, such as that shown in Figure 21, is most common in cities. As more people move to cities, urban air pollution increases.

410

Directed Reading Worksheet 15 Section 4

Q: What did the person say to the polluted air?

A: You take my breath away!

Section 4–California Standards: PE/ATE 6, 6a

Types of Air Pollution

Air pollutants are generally described as either *primary pollutants* or *secondary pollutants*. **Primary pollutants** are pollutants that are put directly into the air by human or natural activity. **Figure 22** shows some examples of primary air pollutants.

Figure 22 *Exhaust from vehicles, ash from volcanic eruptions, and soot from smoke are all examples of primary pollutants.*

Secondary pollutants are pollutants that form from chemical reactions that occur when primary pollutants come in contact with other primary pollutants or with naturally occurring substances, such as water vapor. Many secondary pollutants are formed when a primary pollutant reacts with sunlight. Ozone and smog are examples of secondary pollutants. As you read at the beginning of this chapter, ozone is a gas in the stratosphere that is helpful and absorbs harmful rays from the sun. Near the ground, however, ozone is a dangerous pollutant that affects the health of all organisms. Ozone and smog are produced when sunlight reacts with automobile exhaust, as illustrated in **Figure 23.**

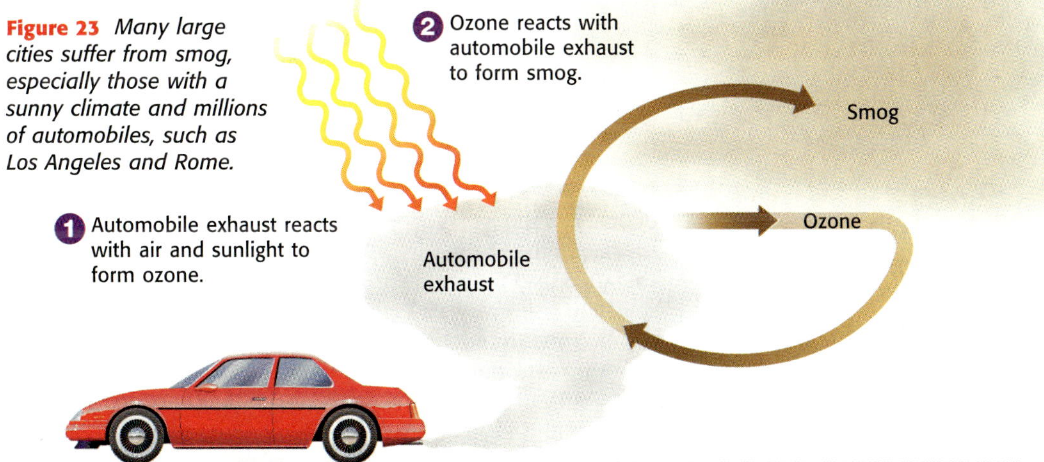

Figure 23 *Many large cities suffer from smog, especially those with a sunny climate and millions of automobiles, such as Los Angeles and Rome.*

411

IS THAT A FACT!

In addition to forming as a reactant when certain pollutants are exposed to sunlight, ozone also forms during thunderstorms. The electrical discharge known as lightning provides the energy. In fact, the distinct smell people notice after an intense thunderstorm is due to the formation of ozone.

2 Teach

GUIDED PRACTICE

List the following pollutants on the board or on an overhead projector:

house dust, pollen, volcanic ash, soot, smog, ground-level ozone, acid rain

Beside the list, make a two-column table with the following column headings:

Primary Pollutants, Secondary Pollutants

Help students classify each pollutant as either a primary pollutant (house dust, pollen, volcanic ash, and soot) or a secondary pollutant (ground-level ozone, smog, and acid rain). Sheltered English

MISCONCEPTION ALERT

Many people believe that polluted air must be visibly smoky or brown or black in color. Stress that some of the most dangerous air pollutants are those that can't be seen with the naked eye. Challenge students to use the Internet to find out about the various pollutants monitored by the Environmental Protection Agency and other organizations that monitor air quality. Have students compile their results in a table that lists the acceptable amounts allowed in the air, the normal levels in your community, and the health problems associated with each pollutant.

Teaching Transparency 146 "The Formation of Smog"

2 Teach, continued

CONNECT TO PHYSICAL SCIENCE

Explain to students that much of the human-caused air pollution results from incomplete combustion. *Combustion,* another word for burning, is the process by which substances combine with oxygen rapidly, producing heat. Byproducts are produced when a substance does not burn completely, as in an automobile engine. Many of these byproducts, such as carbon monoxide, are harmful to living organisms.

RESEARCH

Writing Radon is a naturally occurring gas that results from the decay of uranium particularly in igneous rocks, such as granite. Have interested students research the air pollution and health problems associated with radon. Encourage students to assess the potential for significant radon concentrations in your community. Have students write a short informative essay based on their findings. PORTFOLIO

Figure 24 *In the United States, transportation produces 70 percent of the carbon monoxide found in the atmosphere.*

Sources of Human-Caused Air Pollution

Human-caused air pollution comes from a variety of sources. The major source of air pollution today is transportation, as shown in **Figure 24.** Cars contribute about 60 percent of the human-caused air pollution in the United States. The oxides that come from car exhaust, such as nitrogen oxide, contribute to smog and acid rain. *Oxides* are chemical compounds that contain oxygen and other elements.

Industrial Air Pollution Many industrial plants and electric power plants burn fossil fuels to get their energy. But burning fossil fuels causes large amounts of oxides to be released into the air, as shown in **Figure 25.** In fact, the burning of fossil fuels in industrial and electric power plants is responsible for 96 percent of the sulfur oxides released into the atmosphere.

Some industries also produce chemicals that form poisonous fumes. The chemicals used by oil refineries, chemical manufacturing plants, dry-cleaning businesses, furniture refinishers, and auto-body shops can add poisonous fumes to the air.

Figure 25 *This power plant burns coal to get its energy and releases sulfur oxides and particulates into the atmosphere.*

Figure 26 *Household cleaners, air fresheners, and smoke from cooking all contribute to indoor air pollution.*

Indoor Air Pollution Air pollution is not limited to the outdoors. Our homes, schools, and buildings have air pollution too. Sometimes the air inside a building is even worse than the air outside. As shown in **Figure 26,** many of the products that you use every day contribute to air pollution. Industrial compounds found in carpets, paints, building materials, and furniture also pollute the air, especially when they are new.

In buildings where the windows are tightly sealed to reduce air leaks and keep electric bills low, pollutants can sometimes reach higher levels inside than outside.

412

Multicultural CONNECTION

Scientists have found high levels of airborne contaminants in the breast milk of Inuit women in Greenland and Arctic Canada. Researchers think the contaminants arrived in these remote areas by a process called global distillation. In this process, contaminants are redistributed around the globe by atmospheric currents. They tend to concentrate in northern areas for the same reason that water vapor condenses on cold glass: gaseous substances tend to condense at colder temperatures.

The Air Pollution Problem

Air pollution is both a local and global concern. As you have already learned, local air pollution, such as smog, generally affects large cities. Air pollution becomes a global concern when local pollution moves away from its source. How does this happen? What effect does it have? You will soon find out.

Winds can move pollutants from one place to another, sometimes reducing the amount of pollution in the source area but increasing it in another place. For example, the prevailing winds carry air pollution created in the midwestern United States hundreds of miles to Canada. One such form of this pollution is acid precipitation.

Acid precipitation is precipitation, such as rain, sleet, or snow, that contains acids from air pollution. When fossil fuels are burned, they release oxides of sulfur and nitrogen into the atmosphere. When these oxides combine with water droplets in the atmosphere, they form sulfuric acid and nitric acid, which fall as precipitation. Acid precipitation has many negative effects on the environment, as shown in **Figure 27.**

Figure 27 *Acid precipitation can kill living things, such as fish and trees, by making their environment too acidic to live in. Acid rain can also damage buildings by chemically weathering the concrete and limestone.*

The Ozone Hole Other global concerns brought about by air pollution include the warming of our planet, mentioned earlier in this chapter, and the ozone hole in the stratosphere. Remember, the ozone layer in the stratosphere protects you from the sun's harmful ultraviolet rays. In the 1970s, scientists determined that some chemicals released into the atmosphere react with ozone in the ozone layer. The reaction results in a breakdown of ozone into oxygen, which does not block ultraviolet rays. The loss of ozone creates an ozone hole, which allows more ultraviolet rays to reach the Earth's surface. During the 1980s, scientists found that the ozone layer above the South Pole had thinned by 50 to 98 percent. **Figure 28** shows a satellite image of the ozone hole.

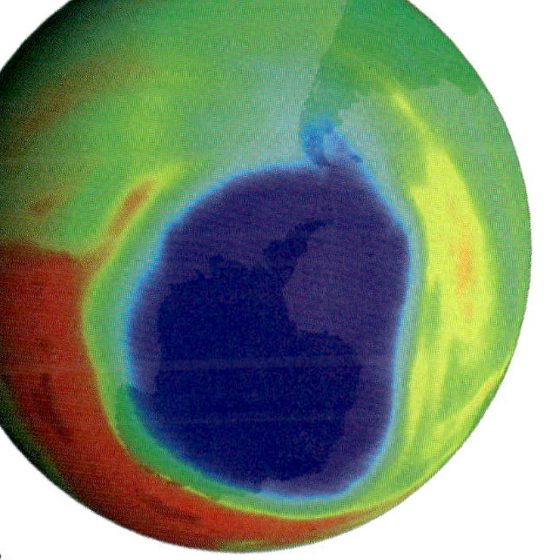

Figure 28 *This satellite image, taken in 1998, shows that the ozone hole, the area with the dark blue border, is still growing.*

INDEPENDENT PRACTICE

Writing Have interested students find out how the ozone hole has changed since it was first measured. Have students graph the values on both a yearly and seasonal basis and describe any trends they see. Have them compile their findings into a short report.

DEMONSTRATION

Acid Rock! Demonstrate how acid rain affects limestone or marble. Put some limestone or marble chips into a beaker of vinegar. Let the chips sit a few days, and have students note any differences in the surface of the chips and in the acid solution. (Students should observe that the surface of the chips is pitted. The solution will be cloudy.)

One reason the ozone layer is thinner over Antarctica involves a strange type of cloud. During winter in Antarctica, the stratosphere over the continent receives little light, and temperatures can be below –80°C. In these conditions, chemicals in the air freeze and form *polar stratospheric clouds*. When light hits the clouds in spring, it catalyzes ozone-destroying reactions in cloud droplets, drastically reducing ozone concentrations over Antarctica.

3 Extend

RETEACHING

Have students try to answer the questions below without referring to their textbook.

How do primary air pollutants differ from secondary ones? (Primary pollutants enter the atmosphere from human activities and natural events. Secondary pollutants form when primary pollutants react with other primary pollutants or with naturally occurring substances in the air.)

How does smog form? (Smog forms when sunlight reacts with automobile exhaust to create ozone. Ozone then reacts with automobile exhaust to create smog.)

How does acid precipitation form? (Acid precipitation forms when fossil fuels are burned, releasing oxides of nitrogen and sulfur into the air. These oxides combine with moisture in the air to form acids that fall to Earth in rain, snow, sleet, and hail.)

Answer to Explore

Answers will vary. Accept all reasonable responses.

CROSS-DISCIPLINARY FOCUS

Health Have students find out about respiratory diseases that can be aggravated by air pollution, such as asthma. Have students compile their findings into tables that list the diseases, their symptoms, how they are treated, the age groups most commonly afflicted, and the relationship between the diseases and air pollutants.

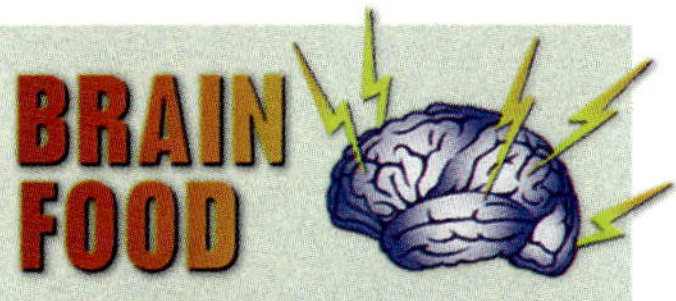

Nonsmoking city dwellers are three to four times more likely to develop lung cancer than nonsmoking people in rural areas.

Effects on Human Health You step outside and notice a smoky haze. When you take a deep breath, your throat tingles and you begin to cough. Air pollution like this affects many cities around the world. For example, on March 17, 1992, in Mexico City, all children under the age of 14 were prohibited from going to school because of extremely high levels of air pollution. This is an extreme case, but daily exposure to small amounts of air pollution can cause serious health problems. Children, elderly people, and people with allergies, lung problems, and heart problems are especially vulnerable to the effects of air pollution. **Figure 29** illustrates some of the effects that air pollution has on the human body.

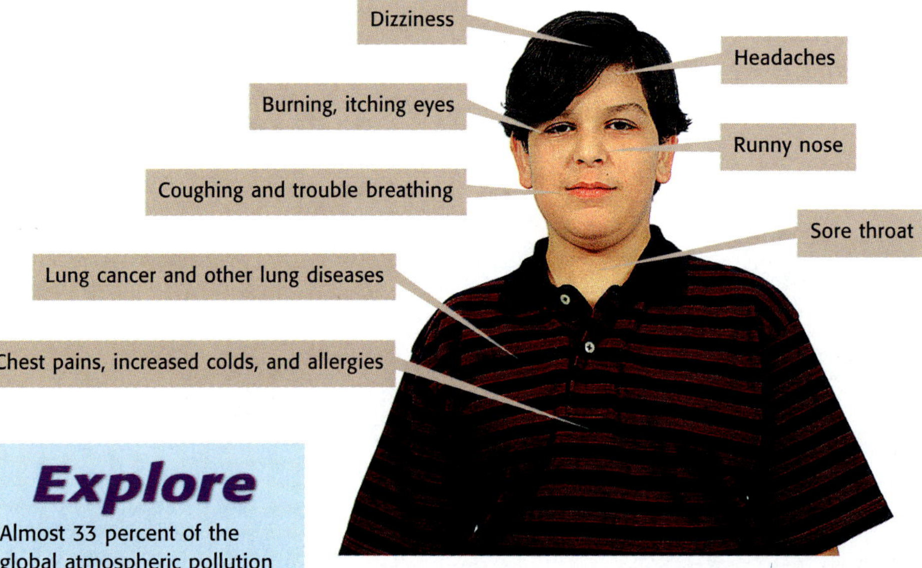

Figure 29 *The Environmental Protection Agency blames air pollution for at least 2,000 new cases of cancer each year.*

Explore

Almost 33 percent of the global atmospheric pollution from carbon dioxide is caused by industrial plants and power plants that burn coal or other fossil fuels. We rely on these sources of power for a better way of life, but our use of them is polluting our air and worsening our quality of life. Use your school library or the Internet to find out about some other sources of electric power. What special problems does each source of energy bring with it?

Cleaning Up Our Act

Is all this talk about bad air making you a little choked up? Don't worry, help is on the way! In the United States, progress has been made in cleaning up the air. One reason for this progress is the Clean Air Act, which was passed by Congress in 1970. The Clean Air Act is a law that gives the Environmental Protection Agency (EPA) the authority to control the amount of air pollutants that can be released from any source, such as cars and factories. The EPA also checks air quality. If air quality worsens, the EPA can set stricter standards. What are car manufacturers and factories doing to improve air quality? Read on to find out.

414

Controlling Air Pollution from Vehicles The EPA has required car manufacturers to meet a certain standard for the exhaust that comes out of the tailpipe on cars. New cars now have devices that remove most of the pollutants from the car's exhaust as it exits the tailpipe. Car manufacturers are also making cars that run on fuels other than gasoline. Some of these cars run on hydrogen and natural gas, while others run on batteries powered by solar energy. The car shown in **Figure 30** is electric.

Are electric cars the cure for air pollution? Turn to page 421 and decide for yourself.

Figure 30 *Instead of having to refuel at a gas station, an electric car is plugged in to a recharging outlet.*

Controlling Air Pollution from Industry The Clean Air Act requires many industries to use *scrubbers*. A **scrubber,** shown in **Figure 31,** is a device that attaches to smokestacks to remove some of the more harmful pollutants before they are released into the air. One such scrubber is used in coal-burning power plants in the United States to remove ash and other particles from the smokestacks. Scrubbers prevent 22 million metric tons of ash from being released into the air each year.

Although we have a long way to go, we're taking steps in the right direction to keep the air clean for future generations.

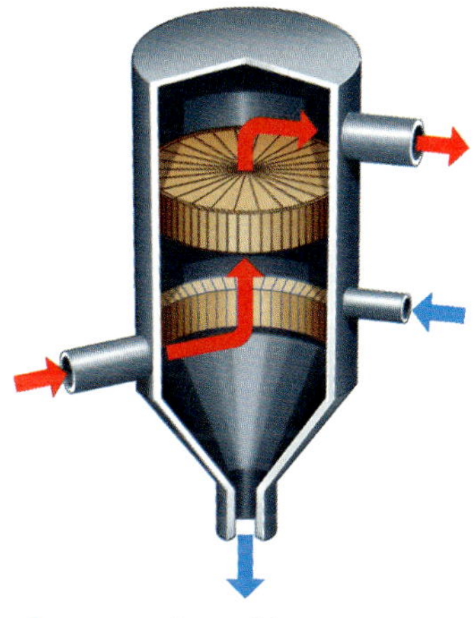

Figure 31 *A scrubber moves gases through a spray of water that dissolves many of the pollutants the gases contain.*

REVIEW

1. How can the air inside a building be more polluted than the air outside?
2. Why might it be difficult to establish a direct link between air pollution and health problems?
3. How has the Clean Air Act helped to reduce air pollution?
4. **Applying Concepts** How is the water cycle affected by air pollution?

4 Close

Quiz

1. Classify each of the following as either a primary or secondary air pollutant: smog, tobacco smoke, chalk dust, and acid rain. (Tobacco smoke and chalk dust are primary pollutants, while smog and acid rain are secondary pollutants.)
2. What are the three sources of outdoor air pollution? (motor vehicles, industries, electric power plants)
3. What are two health problems that can result from breathing polluted air? (dizziness, headaches, burning, itchy eyes, runny nose, coughing, shortness of breath, sore throat, lung cancer and other respiratory diseases, chest pain, colds, and allergies)
4. Explain how scrubbers help reduce air pollution. (Scrubbers spray water on gases, dissolving many pollutants before they are released into the atmosphere.)

Alternative Assessment

Have students use each of the following terms in a sentence that correctly conveys the meaning of the term:

air quality, smog, acid precipitation, industrial pollutants, ozone hole, electric car, and scrubber

Answers to Review

1. Indoor air is polluted by household cleaners, air fresheners, smoke from cooking, as well as industrial compounds found in carpets, paints, building materials, and furniture.
2. Answers will vary. Accept all reasonable responses.
3. The Clean Air Act gives the EPA the authority to control the amount of air pollutants that can be released from any source. The EPA also monitors air quality; if the air quality worsens, the EPA can set stricter standards.
4. Rainwater can become more acidic as a result of air pollution.

Critical Thinking Worksheet 15
"The Extraordinary GBG5K"

Interactive Explorations CD-ROM "Moose Malady"

Section 4 Review–California Standards: PE/ATE 4a

Chapter Highlights

Vocabulary Definitions

Section 1

atmosphere a mixture of gases that surrounds a planet, such as Earth

air pressure the measure of the force with which air molecules are pushing on a surface

altitude the height of an object above the Earth's surface

troposphere the lowest layer of the atmosphere

stratosphere the atmospheric layer above the troposphere

ozone a gas molecule that is made up of three oxygen atoms and that absorbs ultraviolet radiation from the sun

mesosphere the coldest layer of the atmosphere

thermosphere the uppermost layer of the atmosphere

Section 2

radiation the transfer of energy as electromagnetic waves

conduction the transfer of heat from one material to another by physical contact

convection the transfer of heat by the circulation or movement of a liquid or gas

greenhouse effect the natural heating process of a planet, such as the Earth, by which gases in the atmosphere trap thermal energy

global warming a rise in average global temperatures

Chapter Highlights

SECTION 1

Vocabulary

atmosphere *(p. 394)*
air pressure *(p. 395)*
altitude *(p. 395)*
troposphere *(p. 397)*
stratosphere *(p. 397)*
ozone *(p. 397)*
mesosphere *(p. 398)*
thermosphere *(p. 398)*

Section Notes

- The atmosphere is a mixture of gases.
- Nitrogen and oxygen are the two most abundant atmospheric gases.
- Throughout the atmosphere, there are changes in air pressure, temperature, and gases.
- Air pressure decreases as altitude increases.
- Temperature differences in the atmosphere are a result of the way solar energy is absorbed as it moves downward through the atmosphere.
- The troposphere is the lowest and densest layer of the atmosphere. All weather occurs in the troposphere.
- The stratosphere contains the ozone layer, which protects us from harmful radiation.
- The mesosphere is the coldest layer of the atmosphere.
- The uppermost atmospheric layer is the thermosphere.

Labs

Under Pressure! *(p. 550)*

SECTION 2

Vocabulary

radiation *(p. 400)*
conduction *(p. 401)*
convection *(p. 401)*
greenhouse effect *(p. 402)*
global warming *(p. 402)*

Section Notes

- The Earth receives energy from the sun in the form of radiation.
- Radiation that reaches the Earth's surface is absorbed or reflected.
- Heat is transferred through the atmosphere by conduction and convection.
- The greenhouse effect is caused by gases in the atmosphere that trap heat that is reflected off and radiated from the Earth's surface.

Labs

Boiling Over! *(p. 546)*

☑ Skills Check

Math Concepts

FLYING AGAINST THE JET STREAM The groundspeed of an airplane can be affected by the jet stream. The jet stream can push an airplane toward its final destination or slow it down. To find the groundspeed of an airplane, you either add or subtract the wind speed, depending on whether the airplane is moving with or against the jet stream. For example, if an airplane is traveling at an airspeed of 400 km/h and is moving with a 100 km/h jet stream, you would add the jet stream speed to the airspeed of the airplane to calculate the groundspeed.

$$400 \text{ km/h} + 100 \text{ km/h} = 500 \text{ km/h}$$

To calculate the groundspeed of an airplane traveling at 400 km/h that is moving into a 100 km/h jet stream, you would subtract the jet-stream speed from the airspeed of the airplane.

$$400 \text{ km/h} - 100 \text{ km/h} = 300 \text{ km/h}$$

Visual Understanding

GLOBAL WINDS Study Figure 16 on page 406 to review the global wind belts that result from air pressure differences.

416

Lab and Activity Highlights

Under Pressure! PG 550

Boiling Over! PG 546

Go Fly a Bike! PG 548

Datasheets for LabBook (blackline masters for these labs)

SECTION 3

Vocabulary

wind *(p. 404)*
Coriolis effect *(p. 405)*
trade winds *(p. 406)*
westerlies *(p. 407)*
polar easterlies *(p. 407)*
jet streams *(p. 408)*

Section Notes

- At the Earth's surface, winds blow from areas of high pressure to areas of low pressure.
- Pressure belts exist approximately every 30° of latitude.
- The Coriolis effect makes wind curve as it moves across the Earth's surface.
- Global winds are part of a pattern of air circulation across the Earth and include the trade winds, the westerlies, and the polar easterlies.
- Local winds move short distances, can blow in any direction, and are influenced by geography.

Labs

Go Fly a Bike! *(p. 548)*

SECTION 4

Vocabulary

primary pollutants *(p. 411)*
secondary pollutants *(p. 411)*
acid precipitation *(p. 413)*
scrubber *(p. 415)*

Section Notes

- Air pollutants are generally classified as primary or secondary pollutants.
- Human-caused pollution comes from a variety of sources, including factories, cars, and homes.
- Air pollution can heighten problems associated with allergies, lung problems, and heart problems.
- The Clean Air Act has reduced air pollution by controlling the amount of pollutants that can be released from cars and factories.

internetconnect

GO TO: go.hrw.com

Visit the **HRW** Web site for a variety of learning tools related to this chapter. Just type in the keyword:

KEYWORD: HSTATM

GO TO: www.scilinks.org

Visit the **National Science Teachers Association** on-line Web site for Internet resources related to this chapter. Just type in the ***sci*LINKS** number for more information about the topic:

TOPIC	*sci*LINKS NUMBER
Composition of the Atmosphere	HSTE355
Energy in the Atmosphere	HSTE360
The Greenhouse Effect	HSTE365
Atmospheric Pressure and Winds	HSTE370
Air Pollution	HSTE375

417

Vocabulary Definitions, *continued*

Section 3

wind moving air

Coriolis effect the turning of moving objects, such as ocean currents or winds, by the Earth's rotation

trade winds the winds that blow from 30° latitude to the equator

westerlies wind belts found in both the Northern and Southern Hemispheres between 30° and 60° latitude

polar easterlies wind belts that extend from the poles to 60° latitude in both hemispheres

jet streams narrow belts of high-speed winds that blow in the upper troposphere and the lower stratosphere over both the Northern and Southern Hemispheres

Section 4

primary pollutants pollutants that are put directly into the air by human or natural activity

secondary pollutants pollutants that form from chemical reactions that occur when primary pollutants come into contact with other primary pollutants or with naturally occurring substances, such as water vapor

acid precipitation precipitation that contains acids due to air pollution

scrubber a device that attaches to smokestacks to remove some of the more harmful pollutants before they are released into the air

Lab and Activity Highlights

LabBank

Whiz-Bang Demonstrations, Blue Sky, Demo 27

EcoLabs & Field Activities, That Greenhouse Effect! Field Activity 14

Long-Term Projects & Research Ideas, Project 43

Interactive Explorations CD-ROM

CD 2, Exploration 3, "Moose Malady"

Vocabulary Review Worksheet 15

Blackline masters of these Chapter Highlights can be found in the **Study Guide.**

Chapter Review Answers

Using Vocabulary

1. Air pressure is the measure of the force with which the air molecules are pushing on a surface. Altitude is the height of an object above the Earth's surface.
2. The troposphere is the lowest layer of the Earth's atmosphere. The thermosphere is the uppermost atmospheric layer.
3. The greenhouse effect is the Earth's natural heating process, by which gases absorb radiation and transfer energy in the form of heat. Global warming is a rise in average global temperatures due to an increase in the greenhouse effect.
4. Convection is the transfer of heat by the circulation of a liquid or gas. Conduction is the transfer of energy as heat from one material to another by direct physical contact.
5. Global winds are a part of air circulation that moves across the Earth. Local winds generally move short distances and can blow from any direction.
6. Primary pollutants are pollutants that are put directly into the air by human or natural activity. Secondary pollutants form from chemical reactions that occur when primary pollutants come in contact with other primary pollutants or with natural occurring substances.

Understanding Concepts

Multiple Choice

7. b
8. c
9. b
10. c
11. a
12. b
13. d
14. a
15. b
16. d

Chapter Review

USING VOCABULARY

Explain the difference between the following sets of words:

1. air pressure/altitude
2. troposphere/thermosphere
3. greenhouse effect/global warming
4. convection/conduction
5. global wind/local wind
6. primary pollutant/secondary pollutant

UNDERSTANDING CONCEPTS

Multiple Choice

7. What is the most abundant gas in the air that we breathe?
   - a. oxygen
   - b. nitrogen
   - c. hydrogen
   - d. carbon dioxide

8. The major source of oxygen for the Earth's atmosphere is
   - a. sea water.
   - b. the sun.
   - c. plants.
   - d. animals.

9. The bottom layer of the atmosphere, where almost all weather occurs, is the
   - a. stratosphere.
   - b. troposphere.
   - c. thermosphere.
   - d. mesosphere.

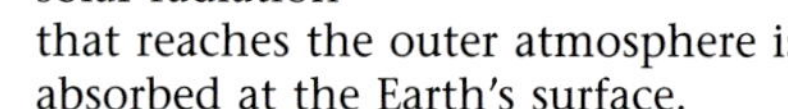

10. About __?__ percent of the solar radiation that reaches the outer atmosphere is absorbed at the Earth's surface.
    - a. 20
    - b. 30
    - c. 50
    - d. 70

11. The ozone layer is located in the
    - a. stratosphere.
    - b. troposphere.
    - c. thermosphere.
    - d. mesosphere.

12. How does most heat energy in the atmosphere move?
    - a. conduction
    - b. convection
    - c. advection
    - d. radiation

13. The balance between incoming radiation and outgoing heat energy is called __?__.
    - a. convection
    - b. conduction
    - c. greenhouse effect
    - d. radiation balance

14. Most of the United States is located in which prevailing wind belt?
    - a. westerlies
    - b. northeast trade winds
    - c. southeast trade winds
    - d. doldrums

15. Which of the following is not a primary pollutant?
    - a. car exhaust
    - b. acid precipitation
    - c. smoke from a factory
    - d. fumes from burning plastic

Chapter 15 Review–California Standards: PE/ATE Q1–6: 3, 3c, 3d, 4, 4a; Q7–21: 3, 3c, 3d, 4, 4a, 4b, 4d

16. The Clean Air Act
  a. controls the amount of air pollutants that can be released from any source.
  b. requires cars to run on fuels other than gasoline.
  c. requires many industries to use scrubbers.
  d. (a) and (c) only

Short Answer

17. Why does the atmosphere become less dense as altitude increases?

18. Explain why air rises when it is heated.

19. What causes temperature changes in the atmosphere.

20. What are secondary pollutants, and how are they formed? Give an example.

Concept Mapping

21. Use the following terms to create a concept map: altitude, air pressure, temperature, atmosphere.

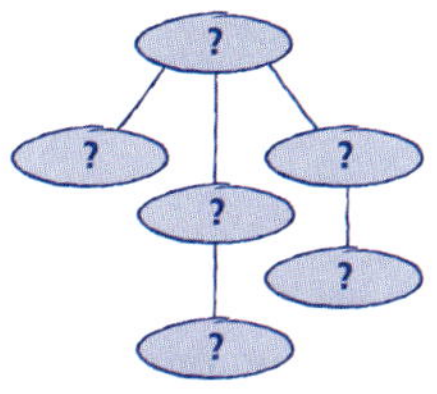

CRITICAL THINKING AND PROBLEM SOLVING

Write one or two sentences to answer the following questions:

22. What is the relationship between the greenhouse effect and global warming?

23. How do you think the Coriolis effect would change if the Earth were to rotate twice as fast? Explain.

24. Without the atmosphere, the Earth's surface would be very different. What are several ways that the atmosphere affects the Earth?

MATH IN SCIENCE

25. Wind speed is measured in miles per hour and in knots. One mile (statute mile or land mile) is 5,280 ft. One nautical mile (or sea mile) is 6,076 ft. Speed in nautical miles is measured in knots. Calculate the wind speed in knots if the wind is blowing at 25 mi/h.

INTERPRETING GRAPHICS

Use the wind-chill chart to answer the questions below.

Wind-Chill Chart

		Actual thermometer reading (°F)				
Wind Speed		**40**	**30**	**20**	**10**	**0**
Knots	**mph**	**Equivalent temperature (°F)**				
Calm		40	30	20	10	0
4	**5**	37	27	16	6	−5
9	**10**	28	16	4	−9	−21
13	**15**	22	9	−5	−18	−36
17	**20**	18	4	−10	−25	−39
22	**25**	16	0	−15	−29	−44
26	**30**	13	−2	−18	−33	−48
30	**35**	11	−4	−20	−35	−49

26. If the wind speed is 20 mi/h and the temperature is 40°F, how cold will the air seem?

27. If the wind speed is 30 mi/h and the temperature is 20°F, how cold will the air seem?

NOW What Do You Think?

Take a minute to review your answers to the ScienceLog questions on page 393. Have your answers changed? If necessary, revise your answers based on what you have learned since you began this chapter.

419

NOW What Do You Think?

1. Air is made of nitrogen, oxygen, argon, carbon dioxide, water vapor, and other trace gases.
2. The atmosphere is organized in layers based on temperature differences.
3. Wind is moving air. Wind is created by differences in air pressure. Air moves from areas of high temperature to areas of low pressure.

Concept Mapping Transparency 15

Blackline masters of this Chapter Review can be found in the **Study Guide.**

Short Answer

17. As altitude increases, there are fewer gas molecules. Gravity pulls much of the atmosphere's gas molecules close to the Earth's surface.
18. Air rises as it is heated because it becomes less dense.
19. The temperature differences in the atmosphere result mainly from the way solar energy is absorbed as it moves downward through the atmosphere. Some layers are warmer because they contain gases that absorb solar energy.
20. Secondary pollutants form when a primary pollutant reacts with other primary pollutants or with naturally occurring substances. Smog and ozone are examples of secondary pollutants.

Concept Mapping

21. 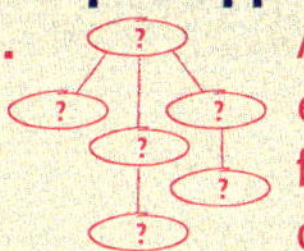 An answer to this exercise can be found in the back of this book.

Critical Thinking and Problem Solving

22. An increase in the greenhouse effect can result in global warming.
23. The Coriolis effect would be more pronounced if the Earth rotated twice as fast. Winds are affected by the rotation of the Earth; if the speed were increased, the curvature would be more pronounced.
24. Answers will vary. Accept all reasonable responses. Sample answer: The atmosphere protects living organisms from harmful rays from the sun. Without the atmosphere, these harmful rays would reach the Earth's surface.

Math in Science

25. 22 knots

Interpreting Graphics

26. 18°F
27. −18°F

Chapter 15 Review–California Standards: PE/ATE Q22–24: 3d, 4; Q25: 4a; Q26–28: 4a; Think: 4, 4a

HEALTH WATCH
Particles in the Air

Background

Particulate matter is one of the major forms of air pollution, along with carbon monoxide (a toxic gas), sulfur dioxides (which contribute to acid rain, smog, and human respiratory problems), and volatile organic compounds, or VOCs (organic chemicals that vaporize and produce toxic fumes).

Particulates are often formed during mechanical processes that break down materials. These include blasting, drilling, and grinding. Some organic matter, such as certain bacteria, are also considered particulates.

The growing problem of particulate pollution has been addressed by the federal government as well as by many local governments and communities. The Clean Air Act, passed by Congress in 1970, sets maximum emission levels for automobiles and industrial sources of pollution. New filtering technology has also helped industries to reduce the amount of particulates being released into the atmosphere.

- In most cases, the majority of the particulates found indoors in dust are particles of human skin.
- Certain types of asbestos are particularly dangerous as particulates. When inhaled, these asbestos fibers scar the lungs, inhibiting breathing and eventually causing cancer.

Particles in the Air

Take a deep breath. You have probably just inhaled thousands of tiny specks of dust, pollen, and other particles. These particles, called particulates, are harmless under normal conditions. But if concentrations of particulates get too high or if they consist of harmful materials, they are considered to be a type of air pollution.

Because many particulates are very small, our bodies' natural filters, such as nasal hairs and mucous membranes, cannot filter all of them out. When inhaled, particulates can cause irritation in the lungs. Over time, this irritation can lead to diseases such as bronchitis, asthma, and emphysema. The danger increases as the level of particulates in the air increases.

▲ *When the ash from Mount St. Helens settled from the air, it created scenes like this one.*

Where There's Smoke...

Unfortunately, dust and pollen are not the only forms of particulates. Many of the particulates in the air come from the burning of various materials. For example, when wood is burned, it releases particles of smoke, soot, and ash into the air. Some of these are so small that they can float in the air for days. The burning of fuels such as coal, oil, and gasoline also creates particulates. The particulates from these sources can be very dangerous in high concentrations. That's why particulate concentrations are one measure of air quality. Large concentrations of particulates are visible in the air. Along with other pollutants, particulates are what make polluted air look brown or yellowish brown. But don't be fooled—even air that appears clean can be polluted.

Eruptions of Particulates

Volcanoes can be the source of incredible amounts of particulates. For example, when Mount St. Helens erupted in 1980, it launched thousands of tons of ash into the surrounding air. The air was so thick with ash that the area became as dark as night. For several hours, the ash completely blocked the light from the sun. When the ash finally settled from the air, it covered the surrounding landscape like a thick blanket of snow. This layer of ash killed plants and livestock for several kilometers around the volcano. One theory to explain the extinction of dinosaurs is that a gargantuan meteorite hit the Earth with such velocity that the resulting impact created enough dust to block out the sun for years. During this dark period, plants were unable to grow and therefore could not support the normal food chains. Consequently, the dinosaurs died out.

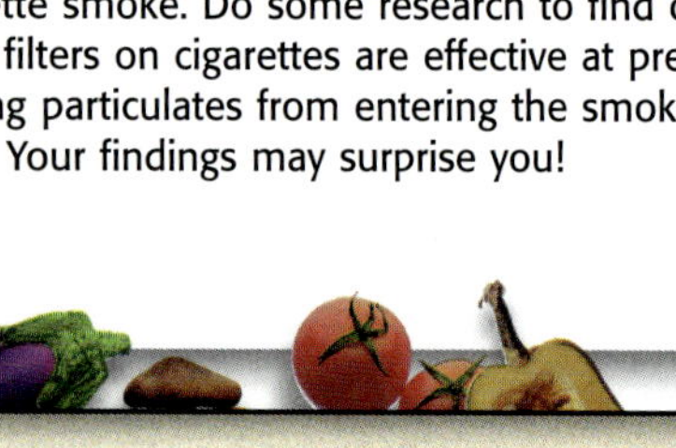

Do Filters Really Filter?

▶ Since the burning of most substances creates particulates, there must be particulates in cigarette smoke. Do some research to find out if the filters on cigarettes are effective at preventing particulates from entering the smoker's body. Your findings may surprise you!

420

Answers to Do Filters Really Filter?

Cigarette filters absorb some of the particulates found in cigarette smoke, but not all of them. A filter that prevented all particulates from entering the lungs would be much too difficult to inhale through.

California Standards: PE/ATE 2d, 6a

SCIENTIFICDEBATE

A Cure for Air Pollution?

Automobile emissions are responsible for at least half of all urban air pollution and a quarter of all carbon dioxide released into the atmosphere. Therefore, the production of a car that emits no polluting gases in its exhaust is a significant accomplishment. The only such vehicle currently available is the electric car. Electric cars are powered by batteries, so they do not produce exhaust gases. Supporters believe that switching to electric cars will reduce air pollution in this country. But critics believe that taxpayers will pay an unfair share for this switch and that the reduction in pollution won't be as great as promised.

▲ *Will a switch to electric cars such as this one reduce air pollution?*

Electric Cars Will Reduce Air Pollution

Even the cleanest and most modern cars emit pollutants into the air. Supporters of a switch to electric cars believe the switch will reduce pollution in congested cities. But some critics suggest that a switch to electric cars will simply move the source of pollution from a car's tailpipe to the power plant's smokestack. This is because most electricity is generated by burning coal.

In California, electric cars would have the greatest impact. Here most electricity is produced by burning natural gas, which releases less air pollution than burning coal. Nuclear plants and dams release no pollutants in the air when they generate electricity. Solar power and wind power are also emission-free ways to generate electricity. Supporters argue that a switch to electric cars will reduce air pollution immediately and that a further reduction will occur when power plants convert to these cleaner sources of energy.

Electric Cars Won't Solve the Problem

Electric cars are inconvenient because the batteries have to be recharged so often. The batteries also have to be replaced every 2 to 3 years. The nation's landfills are already crowded with conventional car batteries, which contain acid and metals that may pollute ground water. A switch to electric cars would aggravate this pollution problem because the batteries have to be replaced so often.

Also, electric cars will likely replace the cleanest cars on the road, not the dirtiest. A new car may emit only one-tenth of the pollution emitted by an older model. If an older car's pollution-control equipment does not work properly, it may emit 100 times more pollution than a new car. But people who drive older, poorly maintained cars probably won't be able to afford expensive electric cars. Therefore, the worst offenders will stay on the road, continuing to pollute the air.

Analyze the Issue

▶ Do you think electric cars are the best solution to the air pollution problem? Why or why not? What are some alternative solutions for reducing air pollution?

421

Scientific Debate
A Cure for Air Pollution?

Background

Electric vehicles have been around for more than 150 years. Their first commercial use was in 1897, when New York City established a fleet of electric taxis. In the years 1899 and 1900 electric vehicles in America outsold all other types of cars. The 1902 Wood's Phaeton had a range of 29 km (18 mi), a top speed of 23 km/h (14 mph), and a price of $2,000.

Answers to Analyze the Issue

Answers will vary. Alternative solutions for reducing air pollution might include educating people about the seriousness of air pollution problems and providing incentives for people to use mass transportation. Other ideas might include alternative fuel sources and more-efficient use of the resources we have. Students might also note that slowing the rate of deforestation would help reduce air pollution significantly.

California Standards: PE/ATE 6, 6a

Chapter Organizer

CHAPTER ORGANIZATION	TIME MINUTES	OBJECTIVES	LABS, INVESTIGATIONS, AND DEMONSTRATIONS
Chapter Opener pp. 422–423	45	California Standards: PE/ATE 7, 7b, 7e	**Investigate!** Cloud in a Bottle, p. 423
Section 1 Water in the Air	120	▶ Explain how water moves through the water cycle. ▶ Define *relative humidity*. ▶ Explain the dew point and its relation to condensation. ▶ Describe the three major cloud forms. ▶ Describe the four major types of precipitation. PE/ATE 4, 4a, 4e, 6b, 7, 7b; LabBook 7, 7b	**Demonstration,** Water Is in the Air, p. 424 in ATE **QuickLab,** Out of Thin Air, p. 427 **Demonstration,** Hail Formation, p. 430 in ATE **Discovery Lab,** Let It Snow! p. 555 **Datasheets for LabBook,** Let It Snow! Datasheet 36 **Whiz-Bang Demonstrations,** It's Raining Again, Demo 29
Section 2 Air Masses and Fronts	90	▶ Explain how air masses are characterized. ▶ Describe the four major types of air masses that influence weather in the United States. ▶ Describe the four major types of fronts. ▶ Relate fronts to weather changes. PE/ATE 4, 4a, 4e	**Demonstration,** Condensation, p. 432 in ATE **Whiz-Bang Demonstrations,** When Air Bags Collide, Demo 28
Section 3 Severe Weather	90	▶ Explain what lightning is. ▶ Describe the formation of thunderstorms, tornadoes, and hurricanes. ▶ Describe the characteristics of thunderstorms, tornadoes, and hurricanes. PE/ATE 4e, 7	**Demonstration,** p. 436 in ATE **Inquiry Labs,** When Disaster Strikes, Lab 12
Section 4 Forecasting the Weather	90	▶ Describe the different types of instruments used to take weather measurements. ▶ Explain how to interpret a weather map. ▶ Explain why weather maps are useful. PE/ATE 7, 7b; LabBook 7, 7b	**Demonstration,** p. 442 in ATE **Skill Builder,** Watching the Weather, p. 552 **Datasheets for LabBook,** Watching the Weather, Datasheet 35 **Making Models,** Gone with the Wind, p. 556 **Datasheets for LabBook,** Gone with the Wind, Datasheet 37 **EcoLabs & Field Activities,** Rain Maker or Rain Faker? Field Activity 15 **Long-Term Projects & Research Ideas,** Project 44

See page **T20** *for a complete correlation of this book with the*

CALIFORNIA SCIENCE CONTENT STANDARDS.

Correlations are also provided at point of use throughout this ATE.

TECHNOLOGY RESOURCES

Guided Reading Audio CD
English or Spanish, Chapter 16

Classroom Management CD-ROM

Test Generator CD-ROM

CNN. **Eye on the Environment,** Hazy Days, Segment 1

Science Discovery Videodiscs
Image and Activity Bank with Lesson Plans: Tracking Tornadoes, Tracking a Hurricane

CLASSROOM WORKSHEETS, TRANSPARENCIES, AND RESOURCES	SCIENCE INTEGRATION AND CONNECTIONS	REVIEW AND ASSESSMENT
Directed Reading Worksheet 16 **Science Puzzlers, Twisters & Teasers,** Worksheet 16		
Directed Reading Worksheet 16, Section 1 **Transparency 147,** Cloud Types Based on Form and Altitude	**Connect to Physical Science,** p. 424 in ATE **MathBreak,** Relating Relative Humidity, p. 425 **Connect to Life Science,** p. 425 in ATE **Multicultural Connection,** p. 426 in ATE **Real-World Connection,** p. 428 in ATE **Connect to Physical Science,** p. 430 in ATE	**Self-Check,** p. 425 **Review,** p. 427 **Homework,** p. 429 in ATE **Review,** p. 431 **Quiz,** p. 431 in ATE **Alternative Assessment,** p. 431 in ATE
Directed Reading Worksheet 16, Section 2 **Transparency 148,** Air Masses in North America	**Multicultural Connection,** p. 433 in ATE	**Review,** p. 435 **Quiz,** p. 435 in ATE **Alternative Assessment,** p. 435 in ATE
Transparency 199, How Lightning Forms **Directed Reading Worksheet 16,** Section 3 **Transparency 149,** How a Tornado Forms **Transparency 150,** A Cross Section of a Hurricane **Reinforcement Worksheet 16,** Precipitation Situations	**Physical Science Connection,** p. 437 **Connect to Physical Science,** p. 437 in ATE **Cross-Disciplinary Focus,** p. 439 in ATE **Astronomy Connection,** p. 441 **Holt Anthology of Science Fiction,** *All Summer in a Day*	**Homework,** p. 439 in ATE **Review,** p. 441 **Quiz,** p. 441 in ATE **Alternative Assessment,** p. 441 in ATE
Directed Reading Worksheet 16, Section 4 **Math Skills for Science Worksheet 35,** Using Temperature Scales **Critical Thinking Worksheet 16,** Commanding the Sky	**Connect to Life Science,** p. 443 in ATE **Math and More,** p. 444 in ATE **Careers:** Meteorologist–Cristy Mitchell, p. 450	**Review,** p. 445 **Quiz,** p. 445 in ATE **Alternative Assessment,** p. 445 in ATE

Holt, Rinehart and Winston On-line Resources

go.hrw.com

For worksheets and other teaching aids related to this chapter, visit the HRW Web site and type in the keyword: **HSTWEA**

National Science Teachers Association

www.scilinks.org

Encourage students to use the keywords listed on the Technology Highlights page to access information and resources on the **NSTA** Web site.

END-OF-CHAPTER REVIEW AND ASSESSMENT

Chapter Review in Study Guide
Vocabulary and Notes in Study Guide
Chapter Tests with Performance-Based Assessment, Chapter 16 Test, Performance-Based Assessment 16
Concept Mapping Transparency 16

Chapter Resources & Worksheets

Visual Resources

TEACHING TRANSPARENCIES

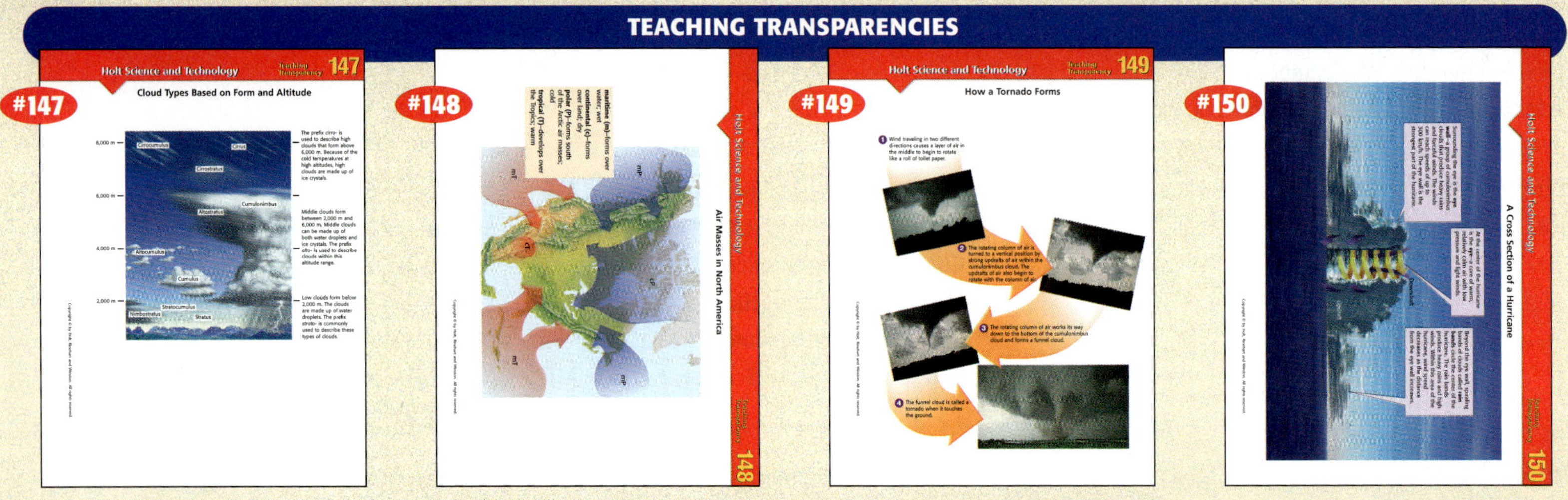

TEACHING TRANSPARENCIES

CONCEPT MAPPING TRANSPARENCY

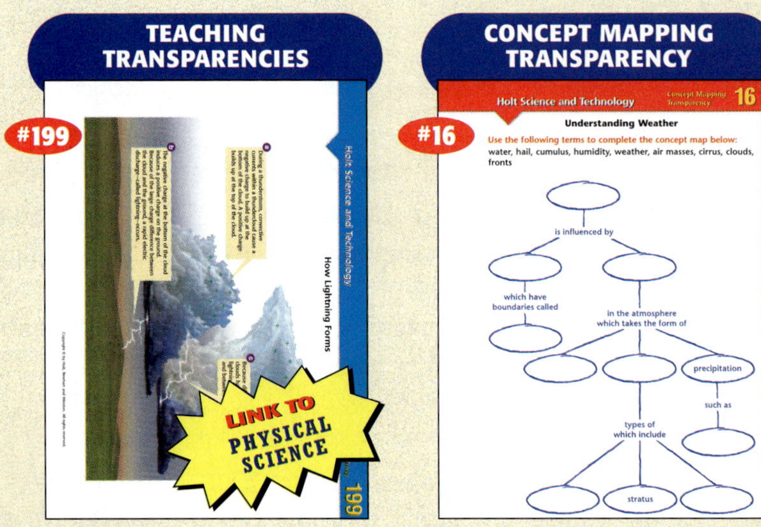

Meeting Individual Needs

DIRECTED READING

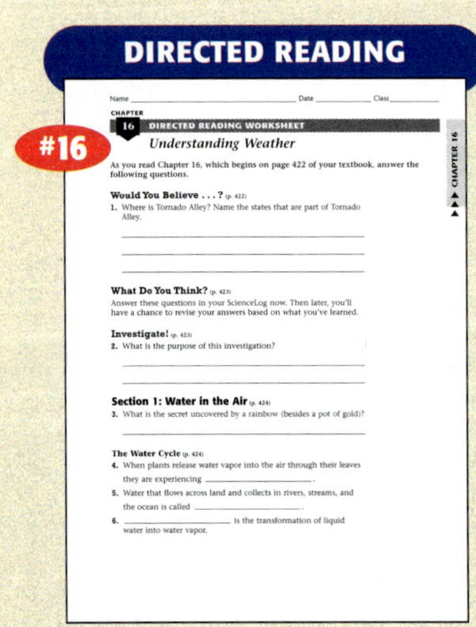

REINFORCEMENT & VOCABULARY REVIEW

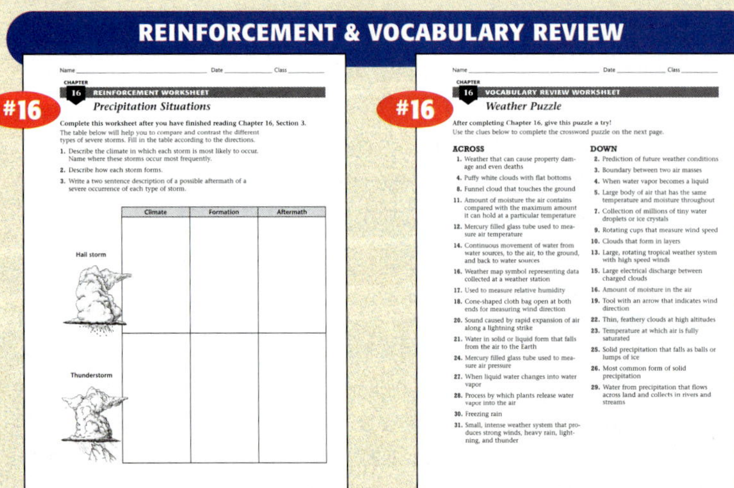

SCIENCE PUZZLERS, TWISTERS & TEASERS

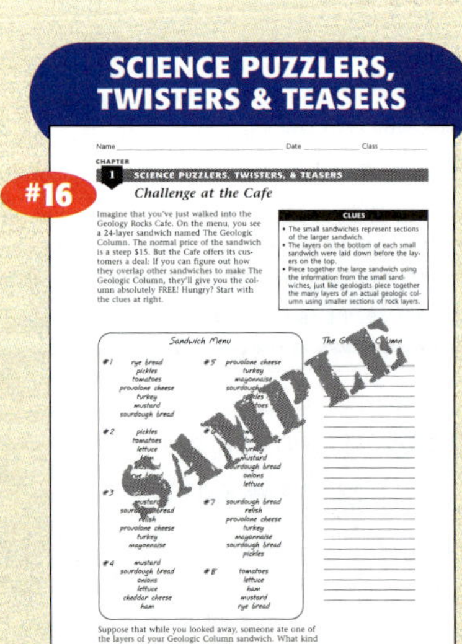

Chapter 16 • Understanding Weather

Review & Assessment

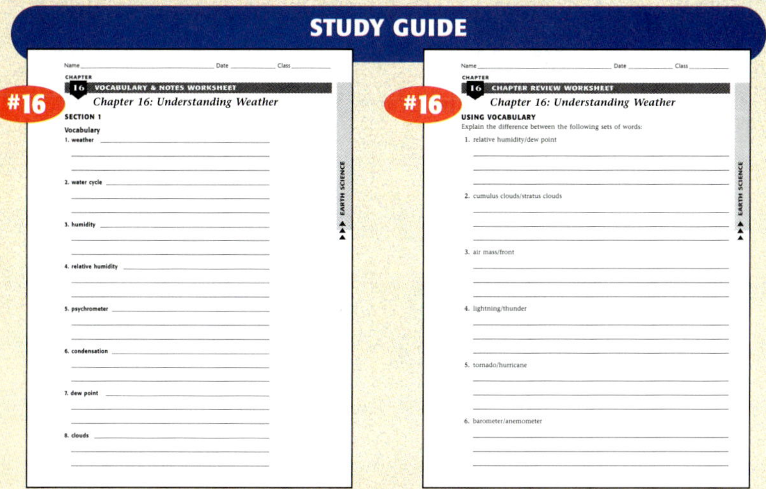

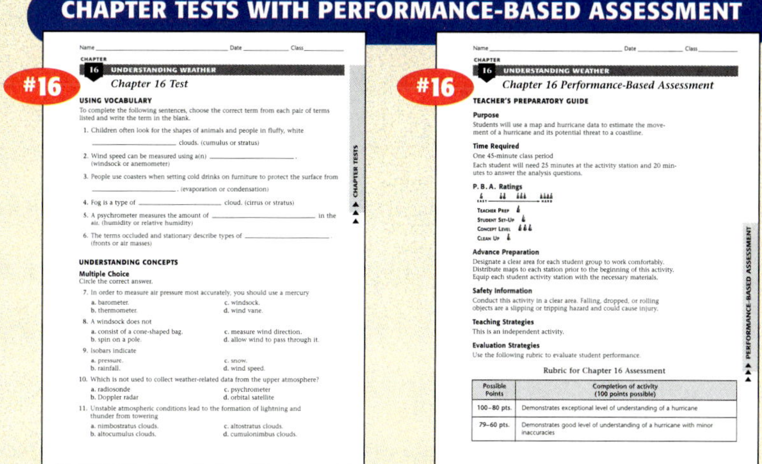

Lab Worksheets

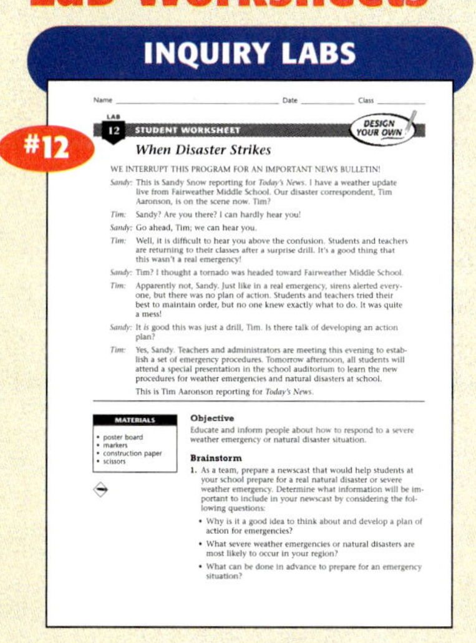

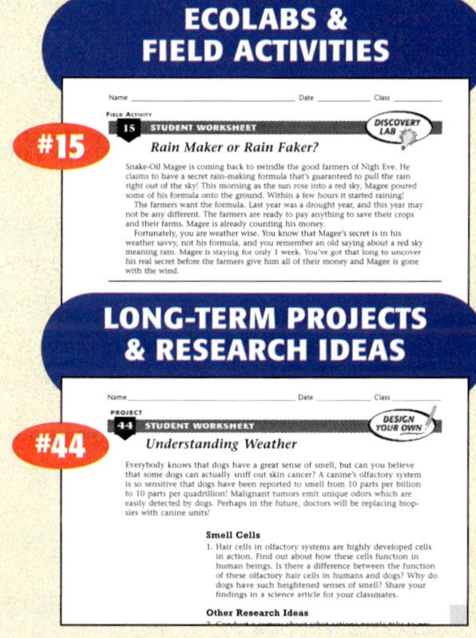

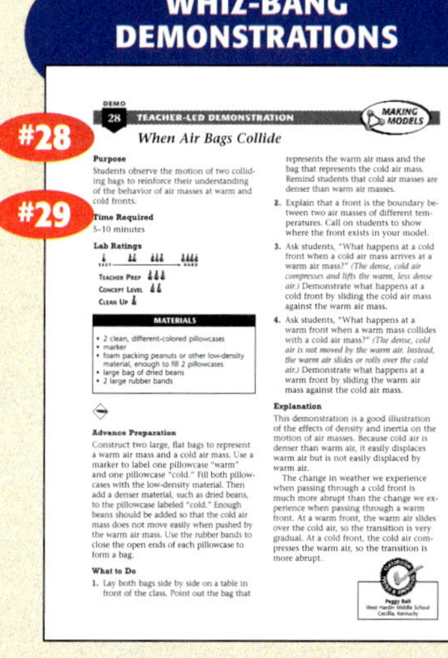

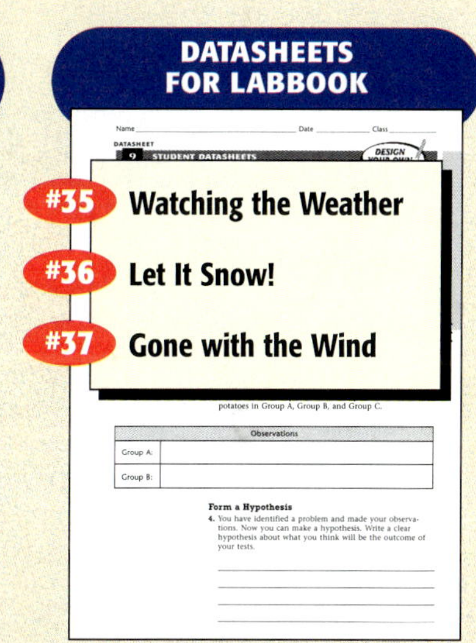

Applications & Extensions

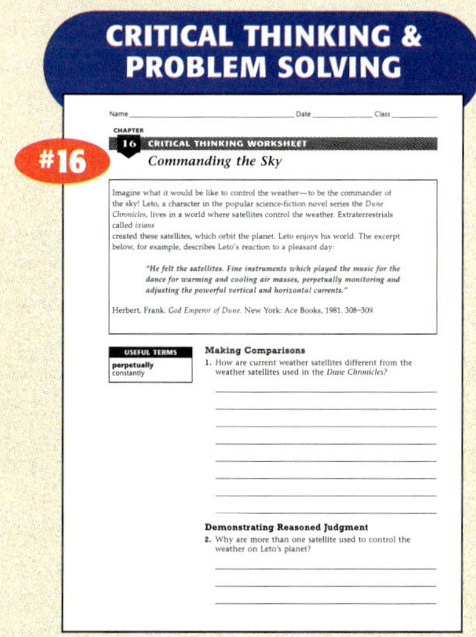

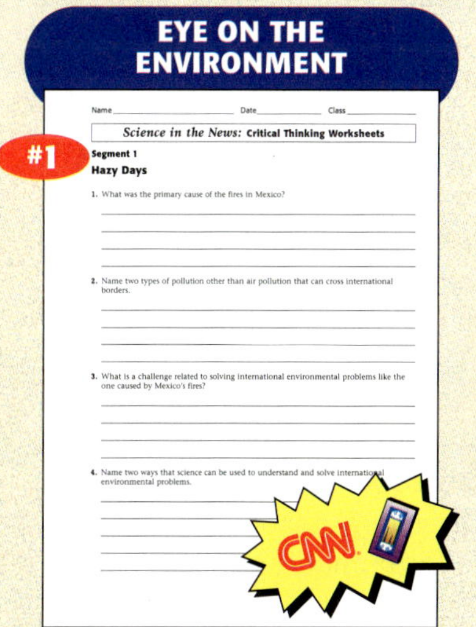

Chapter Background

Section 1

Water in the Air

Earth's Water Cycle
Although the atmosphere contains only about 0.001 percent of the total volume of water on the planet (about 1.46×10^9 km^3), it is an essential link between land masses and bodies of water on Earth.

- The rate at which water evaporates into Earth's atmosphere is about 5.1×10^{17} L per year.
- About 78 percent of all precipitation falls over Earth's oceans. Of the 22 percent that falls on land, about 65 percent returns to the air by evaporation.

Clouds
Clouds may be composed of water droplets, ice crystals, or a combination of the two. For example, cirrus clouds are made of only ice crystals; stratus clouds are made of only water droplets; and altostratus clouds are mixtures of ice and liquid water. Cumulonimbus clouds, which produce snowflakes and hail, consist of water droplets near the bottom of the clouds and ice crystals in the upper parts of the clouds.

Precipitation
Because of differences in condensation rates within the cloud, the millions of droplets of water that make up a cloud are not all the same size. Larger drops collide and merge with smaller drops to form raindrops.

IS THAT A FACT!

- Hailstones as big as grapefruits have fallen to Earth during some severe storms.

Section 2

Air Masses and Fronts

Fronts
A weather front separating two air masses always slopes upward over a colder air mass because the colder air is denser.

- As a warm front approaches, the first clouds to appear in the sky are the high clouds: cirrus, cirrostratus, and cirrocumulus. As the front moves closer, medium-height clouds appear. As the front moves even closer, low clouds appear. As the front approaches, the temperature and air pressure drop, and in the Northern Hemisphere, winds blow from the northeast. Nimbostratus clouds bring drizzly precipitation, which may fall within 24 hours of the first cloud sighting.
- When a cold front enters an area, cumulonimbus clouds produce thunderstorms, heavy rain, or snow along the front. After the cold front passes through an area, winds change direction and barometric pressure rises. Behind the front, temperatures usually fall, bringing cool, clear weather to the area.

Section 3

Severe Weather

Tornadoes

Meteorologists rate tornado intensity using the Fujita Tornado Intensity Scale. An F0 tornado is a relatively weak storm that may damage chimneys, tree branches, and billboard signs. An F1 tornado is a moderate storm that can peel the surfaces off roofs, overturn mobile homes, and push moving cars off roads. F2 and F3 tornadoes cause considerable to severe damage by tearing roofs off houses, overturning railroad cars, and uprooting mature trees. An F4 tornado is a devastating storm that levels houses and other buildings and tosses cars into the air. The most severe tornado is an F5 storm, which can lift houses off their foundations and carry them great distances, carry cars over 100 m, and strip the bark off trees.

Hurricanes

On the Saffir-Simpson scale, hurricanes fall into five categories. Category 1 hurricanes have sustained winds between 119 and 153 km/h and usually cause relatively minimal damage. Category 2 hurricanes cause moderate damage with winds ranging between 154 and 177 km/h. Category 3 hurricanes cause extensive damage with winds that blow between 178 and 209 km/h. Category 4 hurricanes, like Hurricane Andrew, which struck Florida in 1992, have sustained winds between 210 and 250 km/h. Category 5 hurricanes, classified as catastrophic storms, have sustained winds of more than 250 km/h.

IS THAT A FACT!

- A hurricane is called a *willy-willy* in Australia, a *taino* in Haiti, a *baguio* in the Philippines, and a *cordonazo* in western Mexico.

Section 4

Forecasting the Weather

Weather-Prediction Methods

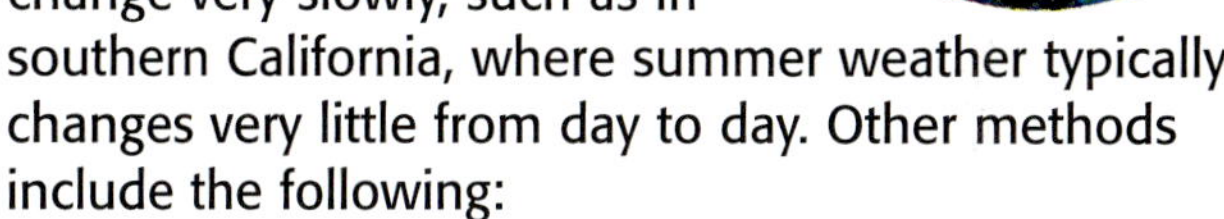

One of the simplest methods for weather prediction, the persistence method, assumes that the atmospheric conditions at the time of a weather forecast will not change in the near future. It is fairly accurate in areas where weather patterns change very slowly, such as in southern California, where summer weather typically changes very little from day to day. Other methods include the following:

- The trends method involves determining high and low pressure areas, the velocity of weather fronts, and areas of clouds and precipitation. A forecaster then uses this data to predict where these weather phenomena will be in the future. This method of weather prediction works well only when weather systems maintain constant velocities for a long period of time.
- The climatology method involves averaging weather data that has accumulated over many years to make a forecast. This method is accurate when weather patterns are similar to those expected for a given time of year.
- The numerical weather-prediction (NWP) method uses complex computer programs to generate models of probable air temperature, barometric pressure, wind velocity, and precipitation. A meteorologist then analyzes how he or she thinks the features predicted by the computer will interact to produce the day's weather. One shortcoming of this method is that it requires very accurate, comprehensive data. If initial weather conditions are not known, the prediction of how the system will change might not be accurate. Despite its flaws, the NWP method is one of the most reliable methods available.

*For additional background resources, please refer to the **HST Reference Library.***

CHAPTER 16

Understanding Weather

Chapter Preview

Section 1
Water in the Air
- The Water Cycle
- Humidity
- The Process of Condensation
- Clouds
- Precipitation

Section 2
Air Masses and Fronts
- Air Masses
- Fronts

Section 3
Severe Weather
- Thunderstorms
- Tornadoes
- Hurricanes

Section 4
Forecasting the Weather
- Weather Forecasting Technology
- Weather Maps

Directed Reading Worksheet 16

Science Puzzlers, Twisters & Teasers Worksheet 16

Guided Reading Audio CD
English or Spanish, Chapter 16

CHAPTER 16 Understanding Weather

Would You Believe . . .

In May of 1997, a springtime tornado wreaked havoc on Jarrell, Texas. The Jarrell tornado was one of the rarest and most powerful tornadoes, with winds estimated at more than 410 km/h. The twister peeled the asphalt from paved roads, stripped fields of corn bare, and destroyed an entire neighborhood.

North America experiences more tornadoes than any other continent—averaging about 700 per year. Most of these tornadoes hit an area in the central United States called Tornado Alley. Tornado Alley covers most of the Great Plains, extending from Texas across Oklahoma, Kansas, southern Nebraska, Iowa, and South Dakota. But what causes these tornadoes, and why is the Great Plains area so vulnerable?

In the spring and early summer, cold, dry air from the North Pole clashes with warm, moist air from the Tropics. This clash forces the warm air to rise and become unstable. When there is a large contrast between the two clashing air masses, the chances that a tornado will form are increased.

Tornado Alley experiences more tornadoes than any other area because its flatness and location on the Earth's

422

Would You Believe . . .

In the past four decades, more tornadoes have struck Texas than any other state. Because of Texas's position within Tornado Alley, many Texans know what to do before, during, and after a tornado strikes. However, tornadoes strike with little warning, often giving people only minutes to seek shelter. The town of Jarrell, Texas, was caught in the path of a tornado that struck in May 1997. The storm took at least 27 lives and left a swath of destruction a half-kilometer wide and more than 11 km long.

surface make it possible for warm and cold air masses to collide with one another.

In this chapter you will learn about what causes weather, the different types of air masses, and how weather can suddenly turn violent.

What Do You Think?

In your ScienceLog, try to answer the following questions based on what you already know:

1. Name some different types of clouds. How are they different?
2. What causes weather?

Investigate!

Cloud in a Bottle

Some tornadoes, like the one that struck the town of Jarrell, Texas, are classified as violent tornadoes. Only 2 percent of the tornadoes that occur in the United States fall into the violent category. You have already learned that tornadoes can occur when two different air masses collide, but how do tornadoes form? Tornadoes form from clouds. And how do clouds form? Try this simple experiment to find out.

Procedure 

1. Pour some **water** into a **large clear-plastic bottle.** Rinse the water around, and then pour it out.
2. Light a long **match** at the mouth of the bottle. Blow it out and then insert it inside the bottle, holding it there for several seconds.
3. After removing the match, put your mouth over the opening and blow into the bottle several times. Have your partner observe and record what happens as you blow into the bottle. Record what happens in your ScienceLog.

Analysis

4. Describe what happened after you blew into the bottle.
5. What role did water play in this lab?
6. What role did smoke play in this lab?
7. Write your explanation for the formation of the cloud in the bottle. See if your explanation matches the explanation found in this chapter.

What Do You Think?

Accept all reasonable responses.

Students will have a chance to revise their answers in the Chapter Review under NOW What Do You Think?

Investigate!

MATERIALS

FOR EACH GROUP:
- water
- large clear-plastic bottle
- long match

Safety Caution: Remind students to review all safety cautions and icons before beginning this lab activity. Students with asthma or respiratory ailments should be the recorder in this lab. Caution students not to inhale the smoke. Tell students to be careful when using matches. Have them douse the match with water before throwing it into a sink or container that you provide. Also insist that students tie back long hair and loose clothing during this investigation.

Teacher Notes: If students have difficulty seeing the cloud, have them shine the beam of a flashlight through the bottle.

Answers to Investigate!

4. A cloud formed in the bottle
5. Answers may vary. Sample answer: Water vapor condenses on the smoke to form a cloud.
6. Water vapor requires a surface on which to condense to form a cloud. The smoke particles provide the surface.
7. Answers may vary.

SCIENCE HUMOR

Q: What did the giant's mother tell her daydreaming son?

A: Get your head out of the clouds!

SECTION 1

Focus

Water in the Air

This section begins with a discussion of the water cycle. It then covers humidity and the process of condensation. Students learn about clouds, including their various forms. Finally, the section discusses precipitation.

Bellringer

Place two glasses on your desk for students to observe: one filled with ice water and one filled with warm water.

Ask students to speculate about why water droplets form on the outside of the cold container. Does the water seep through the glass? Does it come from the air? Why don't the water beads form on the warm container? Tell them that they will learn the answers in this section.
Sheltered English

1 Motivate

DEMONSTRATION

Water Is in the Air Fill a glass container with ice water. Add a few drops of food coloring to the water to distinguish it from liquid water that condenses on the glass surface. Allow the glass to sit for a few minutes. Have students describe what they observe and explain how this demonstration proves that water is in the air.

1

NEW TERMS

weather	dew point
water cycle	cloud
humidity	cumulus clouds
relative humidity	stratus clouds
psychrometer	cirrus clouds
condensation	precipitation

OBJECTIVES

- Explain how water moves through the water cycle.
- Define *relative humidity.*
- Explain the dew point and its relation to condensation.
- Describe the three major cloud forms.
- Describe the four major types of precipitation.

Water in the Air

There might not be a pot of gold at the end of a rainbow, but rainbows hold another secret that you might not be aware of. Rainbows are evidence that the air contains water. Water droplets break up sunlight into the different colors that you can see in a rainbow. Water can exist in the air as a solid, liquid, or gas. Ice, a solid, is found in clouds as snowflakes. Liquid water exists in clouds as water droplets. And water in gaseous form exists in the air as water vapor. Water in the air affects the weather. **Weather** is the condition of the atmosphere at a particular time and place. In this section you will learn how water affects the weather.

The Water Cycle

Water in liquid, solid, and gaseous states is constantly being recycled through the water cycle. The **water cycle** is the continuous movement of water from water sources, such as lakes and oceans, into the air, onto and over land, into the ground, and back to the water sources. Look at **Figure 1** below to see how water moves through the water cycle.

Condensation occurs when water vapor cools and changes back into liquid droplets. This is how clouds form.

Evaporation occurs when liquid water changes into water vapor, which is a gas.

Transpiration is the process by which plants release water vapor into the air through their leaves.

Precipitation occurs when rain, snow, sleet, or hail falls from the clouds onto the Earth's surface.

Runoff is water, usually from precipitation, that flows across land and collects in rivers, streams, and eventually the ocean.

Figure 1 *In the water cycle, water is returned to the Earth's surface through precipitation.*

CONNECT TO PHYSICAL SCIENCE

Energy from the sun moves water through the water cycle. Sunlight provides the energy for condensation, evaporation, transpiration, and precipitation.

Section 1–California Standards: PE/ATE 4, 4a, 4e, 6b, 7, 7b; LabBook: 7, 7b

Humidity

Have you ever spent a long time styling your hair before school and had a bad hair day anyway? You walked outside and—wham—your straight hair became limp, or your curly hair became frizzy. Most bad hair days can be blamed on humidity. **Humidity** is the amount of water vapor or moisture in the air. And it is the moisture in the air that makes your hair go crazy, as shown in **Figure 2.**

Figure 2 *When there is more water in the air, your hair absorbs moisture and becomes longer.*

As water evaporates, the humidity of the air increases. But air's ability to hold water vapor depends on air temperature. As temperature increases, the air's ability to hold water also increases. **Figure 3** shows the relationship between air temperature and air's ability to hold water.

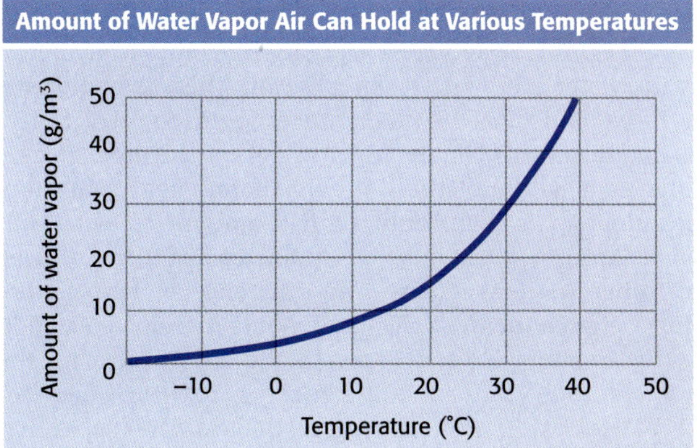

Figure 3 *This graph shows that warmer air can hold more water vapor than cooler air.*

Self-Check

How does humidity relate to the water cycle? *(Turn to page 564 to check your answer.)*

Relative Humidity **Relative humidity** is the amount of moisture the air contains compared with the maximum amount it can hold at a particular temperature. Relative humidity is given as a percentage. When air holds all the water it can at a given temperature, the air is said to be *saturated.* Saturated air has a relative humidity of 100 percent. But how do you find the relative humidity of air that is not saturated? If you know the maximum amount of water vapor air can hold at a particular temperature and you know how much water vapor the air is actually holding, you can calculate the relative humidity.

Suppose that 1 m^3 of air at a certain temperature can hold 24 g of water vapor. However, you know that the air actually contains 18 g of water vapor. You can calculate the relative humidity using the following formula:

$$\frac{\text{(present) } 18 \text{ g/m}^3}{\text{(saturated) } 24 \text{ g/m}^3} \times 100 = \text{(relative humidity) } 75\%$$

MATHBREAK

Relating Relative Humidity

Assume that 1 m^3 of air at 25°C holds 11 g of water vapor. Calculate the relative humidity of the air using the value for saturated air shown in Figure 3.

2 Teach

Meeting Individual Needs

Learners Having Difficulty

Use two small, identical sponges and a beaker of water to demonstrate air's ability to hold water. Explain that one of the dry sponges represents warm, dry air. Warm air can hold more water because it is less dense. Like the dry sponge, warm air can absorb more water because there is more space available. Dip the second sponge into the beaker, and put the sponge on a table. Lead students to conclude that this sponge represents saturated air; there is no room for any more water.

Ask students why they put their wet clothes in a dryer that uses warm air rather than in the refrigerator. (Students should conclude that the warm air in a clothes dryer will remove more moisture from the clothes.) Sheltered English

Using the Figure

Refer students to **Figure 3** and ask which variable is the independent variable. (temperature) Which is the dependent variable? (amount of water vapor)

Answer to Self-Check

Evaporation occurs when liquid water changes into water vapor and returns to the air. Humidity is the amount of water vapor in the air.

Answer to MATHBREAK

$(11 \text{ g/m}^3 \div 20 \text{ g/m}^3) \times 100 = 55\%$

Directed Reading Worksheet 16 Section 1

Connect to Life Science

When the air is humid, hair becomes frizzy. Hair is made of a protein called keratin. Each hair fiber has a scaly outer cuticle, which you can feel by running your fingers up and down a single hair. The scales allow moisture to enter the inner part of the hair fiber. When the air is humid, hair absorbs moisture and becomes longer, making it frizzy. Hair dries out and becomes shorter when the air is dry. Because humidity can cause hair length to change by as much as 2.5 percent, a device called a hair hygrometer can very accurately measure changes in humidity. Have students design and create their own hair hygrometers.

2 Teach, continued

INDEPENDENT PRACTICE

After students have read this page, have them complete the following sentences:

- If the humidity is low, a ___________ amount of water will evaporate from a wet-bulb thermometer and the ____________ between the wet-bulb reading and the dry-bulb reading of the psychrometer will be high. (large, temperature difference)
- If the dry bulb reads 10°C, and the difference between the thermometers is 8°C, the relative humidity is ___________. (15 percent)

MEETING INDIVIDUAL NEEDS

Advanced Learners Have small groups of students devise and carry out an activity to determine the relative humidity at different locations on the same day. Tell them to use the following materials: two identical thermometers, gauze, string, and room-temperature water. Suggest that they create a wet-bulb thermometer by tying a small piece of gauze to the bottom of one thermometer and saturating the covered end with water. Have students record their data in a table. Their data should include information about location, observable weather conditions, time of day, and the duration of the trial.

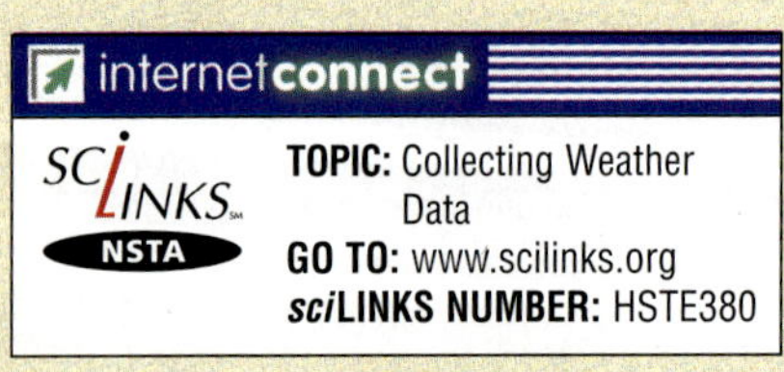

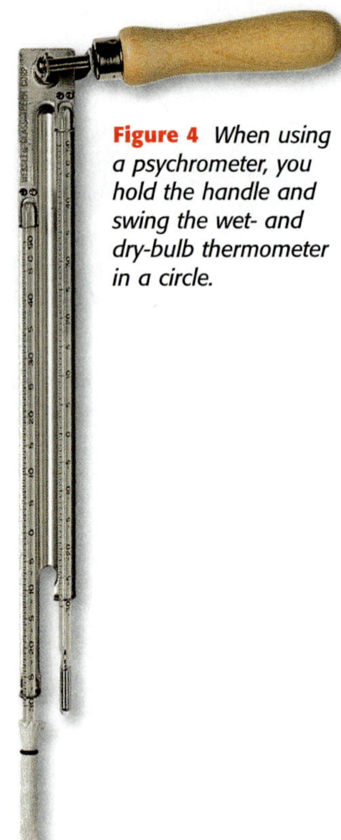

Figure 4 *When using a psychrometer, you hold the handle and swing the wet- and dry-bulb thermometer in a circle.*

If the temperature stays the same, relative humidity changes as water vapor enters or leaves the air. The more water vapor that is in the air at a particular temperature, the higher the relative humidity is. Relative humidity is also affected by changes in temperature. If the amount of water vapor in the air stays the same, the relative humidity decreases as the temperature rises and increases as the temperature drops.

Measuring Relative Humidity A **psychrometer** is an instrument used to measure relative humidity. As you can see in **Figure 4,** a psychrometer consists of two thermometers. The bulb of one thermometer is covered with a damp cloth. This thermometer is called a wet-bulb thermometer. The other thermometer is a dry-bulb thermometer. The dry-bulb thermometer measures air temperature.

As air passes over the wet-bulb thermometer, the water in the cloth begins to evaporate. Evaporation requires heat energy. So as the water evaporates from the cloth, heat is withdrawn from the wet-bulb and the thermometer begins to cool. If there is less humidity in the air, the water will evaporate more quickly and the temperature of the wet-bulb thermometer will drop. If the humidity is high, only a small amount of water will evaporate from the wet-bulb thermometer and there will be little change in temperature. The difference in temperature readings between the wet-bulb and dry-bulb thermometers indicates the amount of water vapor in the air. The greater the difference is between the two readings, the less water vapor that is in the air and the lower the humidity is.

Relative humidity can be determined using a table such as the one in **Figure 5.** The numbers across the top of the table represent the differences between the wet-bulb and dry-bulb temperatures in degrees Celsius. The numbers along the left side of the table indicate the dry-bulb temperature readings in degrees Celsius.

Relative Humidity (in percentage)

Dry-bulb reading (°C)	Difference between wet-bulb reading and dry-bulb reading (°C)									
	1	2	3	4	5	6	7	8	9	10
0	81	64	46	29	13					
2	84	68	52	37	22	7				
4	85	71	57	43	29	16				
6	86	73	60	48	35	24	11			
8	87	75	63	51	40	29	19	8		
10	88	77	66	55	44	34	24	15	6	
12	89	78	68	58	48	39	29	21	12	
14	90	79	70	60	51	42	34	26	18	10
16	90	81	71	63	54	46	38	30	23	15
18	91	82	73	65	57	49	41	34	27	20
20	91	83	74	66	59	51	44	37	31	24
22	92	83	76	68	61	54	47	40	34	28
24	92	84	77	69	62	56	49	43	37	31
26	92	85	78	71	64	58	51	46	40	34
28	93	85	78	72	65	59	53	40	42	37
30	93	86	79	73	67	61	55	50	44	39

Figure 5 *Locate the column that shows the difference between the wet-bulb and dry-bulb readings. Then locate the row that lists the temperature reading on the dry-bulb thermometer. The value where the column and row intersect is the relative humidity.*

426

Multicultural CONNECTION

Before modern weather instruments were invented, natives on the Chiloé Islands, off the coast of Chile, used shells of the crab *Lithodes antarcticus* to measure relative humidity. A dry shell, normally light gray in color, shows red patches when humidity increases. It will become completely red if the humidity continues to rise, as during the rainy season. Australian Aborigines used dry kelp to predict rain. Some kelps contain magnesium chloride, which absorbs water vapor from the air. The kelp will feel damp long before it actually begins to rain.

The Process of Condensation

You have probably seen water droplets form on the outside of a glass of ice water, as shown in **Figure 6.** Did you ever wonder where those water droplets came from? The water came from the surrounding air, and droplets formed because of condensation. **Condensation** is the process by which a gas, such as water vapor, becomes a liquid. Before condensation can occur, the air must be saturated; it must have a relative humidity of 100 percent. Condensation occurs when saturated air cools further.

Air can become saturated when water vapor is added to the air through evaporation or transpiration. Air can also become saturated, as in the case of the glass of ice water, when it cools to its dew point. The **dew point** is the temperature to which air must cool to be completely saturated. The ice in the glass of water causes the air surrounding the glass to cool to its dew point.

Before it can condense, water vapor must also have a surface to condense on. On the glass of ice water, water vapor condenses on the sides of the glass. Another example you may already be familiar with is water vapor condensing on grass, forming small water droplets called *dew,* as shown in **Figure 7.**

Figure 6 *Condensation occurred when the air next to the glass cooled to below its dew point.*

Figure 7 *Dew is most likely to form on cool, clear nights when there is little wind.*

REVIEW

1. What is the difference between humidity and relative humidity?
2. What are two ways that air can become saturated with water vapor?
3. What does a relative humidity of 75 percent mean?
4. How does the water cycle contribute to condensation?
5. **Analyzing Relationships** What happens to relative humidity as the air temperature drops below the dew point?

QuickLab

Out of Thin Air

1. Take a **plastic container,** such as a jar or drinking glass, and fill it almost to the top with room-temperature **water.**
2. Observe the outside of the can or container. Record your observations.
3. Add one or two **ice cubes,** and watch the outside of the container for any changes.
4. What happened to the outside of the container?
5. What is the liquid?
6. Where did the liquid come from? Why?

Reteaching

Ask students to create a chart with two columns titled "Evaporation" and "Condensation." Have them list as many examples of evaporation and condensation as they can think of.

QuickLab

MATERIALS

For Each Group:

- plastic container, such as a jar or drinking glass
- water
- ice cubes

Answers to QuickLab

4. Liquid droplets formed on the outside of the container.
5. The liquid is water.
6. The liquid formed when the water vapor next to the glass condensed. The air cooled to below its dew point and could no longer hold any water, so the water vapor condensed on the glass.

Answers to Review

1. Humidity is the amount of water vapor in the air. Relative humidity is the amount of water vapor the air contains compared with the maximum amount it can hold at a given temperature.
2. Air can become saturated if water evaporates into the air or if the air temperature drops.
3. The air is holding 75 percent of the amount of water it can hold at a given temperature.
4. Before condensation can occur, the air must be saturated. Evaporation, a part of the water cycle, adds water to the air.
5. As the air temperature drops below the dew point, relative humidity increases to the point that the air becomes saturated with moisture and condensation occurs.

Section 1 Mid-section Review–California Standards: PE/ATE 4a, 4e

2 Teach, continued

Reading Strategy

Activity After students read this page, have them arrange the following steps in logical order:

- Water vapor condenses on smoke, dust, salt, and other small particles suspended in air. (4)
- Water vapor is added to the air. (2)
- Warm air rises and cools. (1)
- Air eventually becomes saturated. (3)
- Millions of droplets of liquid water collect to form a cloud. (5)

Using the Figure

Have students carefully study **Figures 8, 9,** and **10.** Challenge them to determine one method of cloud classification based on their observations of the photographs. (In addition to being classified by altitude, as described on the following page, clouds are also classified according to shape.)

Activity

Cloud Models On a posterboard, have students use cotton balls to make models of different types of clouds at different altitudes. Sheltered English

Real-World Connection

What appears to be white smoke from an airplane's engine as it crosses the sky is not smoke at all. Condensation trails, or contrails, form when the combustion of the aircraft's fuel causes water vapor to condense along the airplane's exhaust tail.

Clouds

Some look like cotton balls, some look like locks of hair, and others look like blankets of white blocking out the sun. But what *are* clouds and how do they form? And why are there so many different-looking clouds? A **cloud** is a collection of millions of tiny water droplets or ice crystals. Clouds form as warm air rises and cools. As the rising air cools, it becomes saturated. This is because cooler air cannot hold as much water vapor as warm air. At saturation—that is, 100 percent relative humidity—the water vapor changes to a liquid or a solid depending on the air temperature. In order for water vapor to change physical states, it needs a surface on which to change. These surfaces, called *condensation nuclei,* are small particles, such as dust, smoke, and salt, suspended in the air. At higher temperatures, water vapor condenses on small particles as tiny water droplets. At temperatures below freezing, water vapor changes directly to a solid, forming ice crystals.

Figure 8 *Cumulus clouds look like piles of cotton balls.*

Figure 9 *Although stratus clouds are not as tall as cumulus clouds, they cover more area.*

Kinds of Clouds Although there are many different-looking clouds, all clouds are classified according to three basic types—cumulus, stratus, and cirrus. **Cumulus** (KYOO myoo luhs) **clouds,** as shown in **Figure 8,** are puffy, white clouds that tend to have flat bottoms. Cumulus clouds form when warm air rises. These clouds generally indicate fair weather. However, when these clouds get larger they produce thunderstorms. A cumulus cloud that produces thunderstorms is called a *cumulonimbus cloud.* As a rule, when *-nimbus* or *nimbo-* is part of a cloud's name, it means that precipitation might fall from the cloud.

Stratus (STRAT uhs) **clouds,** as shown in **Figure 9,** are clouds that form in layers. Stratus clouds cover large areas of the sky, often blocking out the sun. These clouds are caused by a gentle lifting of a large body of air into the atmosphere. *Nimbostratus clouds* are stratus clouds that usually produce light to heavy, continuous rain. When water vapor condenses near the ground, it forms a stratus cloud called *fog.*

As you can see in **Figure 10, cirrus** (SIR uhs) **clouds** are thin, feathery, white clouds found at high altitudes. Cirrus clouds form when the wind is strong. Cirrus clouds may indicate approaching bad weather if they thicken and lower in altitude.

Clouds are also classified by the altitude at which they form. The illustration in **Figure 11** shows the three altitude groups used to categorize clouds.

Figure 10 *Cirrus clouds are made of ice crystals because they form at high altitudes where the temperature is below freezing.*

Figure 11 Cloud Types Based on Form and Altitude

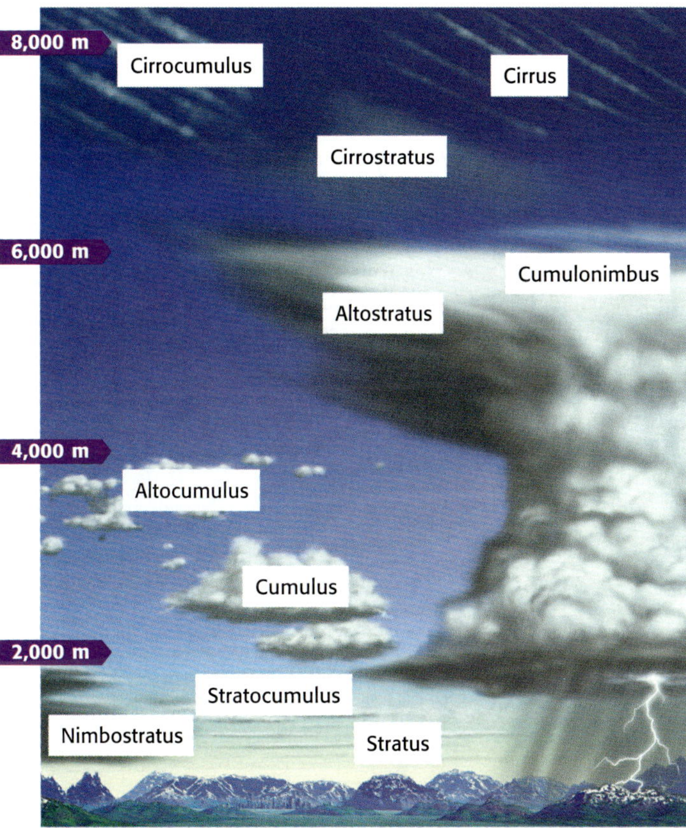

The prefix *cirro-* is used to describe high clouds that form above 6,000 m. Because of the cold temperatures at high altitude, high clouds are made up of ice crystals.

Middle clouds form between 2,000 m and 6,000 m. Middle clouds can be made up of both water droplets and ice crystals. The prefix *alto-* is used to describe clouds within this altitude range.

Low clouds form below 2,000 m. These clouds are made up of water droplets. The prefix *strato-* is commonly used to describe these types of clouds.

429

MEETING INDIVIDUAL NEEDS

Learners Having Difficulty Challenge students to use the adjectives and word parts used to classify clouds to generate a list of possible cloud types. Students' lists should include the following names:

cirrus, cirrostratus, cirrocumulus, altocumulus, altostratus, stratus, stratocumulus, nimbostratus, cumulus, cumulonimbus

INDEPENDENT PRACTICE

Concept Mapping Have students construct a concept map using section concepts and terms. Tell them that their map should explain the relative location of clouds in the atmosphere and how they are formed.

Homework

Reporting on Fog Have students research and write a short paper on fog. Tell them that their paper should explain the relationship between fog and clouds. It should also discuss where, how, and why fog forms. Challenge students to explain the factors that contribute to the famous fogs of San Francisco or London.

Teaching Transparency 147 "Cloud Types Based on Form and Altitude"

The weather was really a pain,
and our clothes were already stained.
Light rain came right at us
from clouds—call them stratus—
and soiled our clothes yet again!

3 Extend

CONNECT TO PHYSICAL SCIENCE

Explain that a water molecule has a positive end and a negative end. Opposite charges attract, so the positive end of one water molecule attracts the negative end of another. This attraction helps explain why small water droplets that collide are able to form relatively large raindrops.

DEMONSTRATION

Hail Formation Melt three or four different-colored crayons or candles in separate containers over a hot plate. Dip a thick, weighted string into one color of wax, blow it dry, and repeat with each different color. After you have built up several layers, cut the wax widthwise. Display the concentric ringed formation to the class. Ask students what kind of precipitation forms in a similar manner. (hail)

Sheltered English

GOING FURTHER

Writing Meteorologists sometimes use a technique known as cloud seeding to cause or increase precipitation. Have students research and write a report about this technique. After they have gathered their information, have small groups debate the pros and cons of artificially stimulating precipitation.

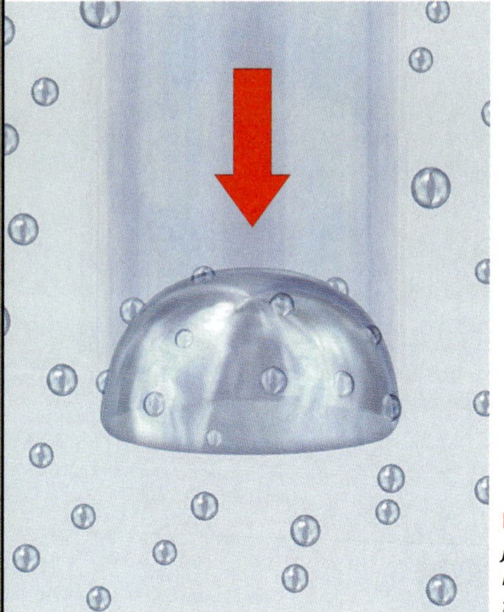

Precipitation

Water vapor that condenses to form clouds can eventually fall to the ground as precipitation. **Precipitation** is water, in solid or liquid form, that falls from the air to the Earth. There are four major forms of precipitation—rain, snow, sleet, and hail.

Rain, the most common form of precipitation, is liquid water that falls from the clouds to Earth. A cloud produces rain when its water droplets become large enough to fall. A cloud droplet begins as a water droplet smaller than the period at the end of this sentence. Before a cloud droplet falls as precipitation, it must increase in size to about 100 times its normal diameter. **Figure 12** illustrates how a water droplet increases in size until it is finally large enough to fall as precipitation.

Figure 12 *Cloud droplets get larger by colliding and joining with other droplets. Eventually the water droplets become too heavy to remain suspended in the cloud and fall as precipitation.*

Snow, Sleet, and Hail The most common form of solid precipitation is *snow.* Snow forms when temperatures are so cold that water vapor changes directly to a solid. Snow can fall as individual ice crystals or combine to form snowflakes, like the one shown in **Figure 13.**

Sleet, also called freezing rain, forms when rain falls through a layer of freezing air. The rain freezes, producing falling ice. Sometimes rain does not freeze until it hits a surface near the ground. When this happens, the rain changes into a layer of ice called *glaze,* as shown in **Figure 14.**

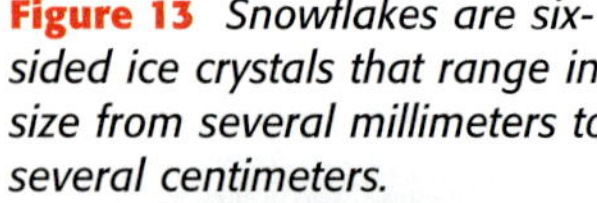

Figure 13 *Snowflakes are six-sided ice crystals that range in size from several millimeters to several centimeters.*

Figure 14 *Glaze ice forms as rain freezes on surfaces near the ground.*

430

WEIRD SCIENCE

The largest hailstone ever recorded fell on Coffeyville, Kansas, on September 3, 1970. The hailstone was the size of a softball, and weighed 1.7 lb.

Hail, as shown in **Figure 15,** is solid precipitation that falls as balls or lumps of ice. Hail usually forms in cumulonimbus clouds. Updrafts of air in the clouds carry raindrops to high altitudes in the cloud, where they freeze. As the frozen raindrops fall, they collide and combine with water droplets. Another updraft of air can send the hail up again high into the cloud. Here the water drops collected by the hail freeze, forming another layer of frozen ice. If the upward movement of air is strong enough, the hail can accumulate many layers of ice. Eventually, the hail becomes too heavy and falls to the Earth's surface. Hail is usually associated with warm weather and most often occurs during the spring and summer months.

Figure 15 *Hail is one of the most destructive forms of precipitation. The impact of large hailstones can damage property and crops.*

Measuring Precipitation A *rain gauge* is an instrument for measuring the amount of rainfall. Although there are many types of rain gauges, a rain gauge typically consists of a funnel and a cylinder, as shown in **Figure 16.** Rain falls into the funnel and collects in the cylinder. Markings on the cylinder indicate how much rain has fallen.

Snow is measured by both depth and water content. The depth of snow is measured using a measuring stick. The snow's water content is determined by melting the snow and measuring the amount of water. The amount of liquid water resulting from a snowmelt depends on the type of snow. Dry snow produces much less water than wet snow. For example, as much as 20 cm of dry snow is needed to produce 1 cm of liquid water. But only 6 cm of wet snow is needed to produce the same amount of water.

Figure 16 *Rain gauges measure only the precipitation that falls in a particular place.*

REVIEW

1. How do clouds form?
2. Why are some clouds formed from water droplets, while others are made up of ice crystals?
3. Describe how rain forms.
4. **Applying Concepts** How can rain and hail fall from the same cumulonimbus cloud?

4 Close

Quiz

1. Compare and contrast the processes of condensation and evaporation in the water cycle. (Both are processes in Earth's water cycle that involve a change of the state of water. They differ in that condensation occurs when water vapor changes to a liquid, while evaporation occurs when liquid water changes to a gas.)
2. What name would you give a lacy, layered cloud above 6,000 m? (cirrostratus)
3. Compare and contrast snow, sleet, and hail. (All are forms of solid precipitation that fall from clouds. Snow forms when water vapor changes to a solid. Sleet forms when rain falls through a layer of freezing air. Hail forms when raindrops are carried by winds to higher altitudes in a cloud, where they freeze and accumulate layers.)

Alternative Assessment

Have students make a table of the types of precipitation, how they form, and how we measure them.

Let It Snow!

Answers to Review

1. Clouds form as warm air rises and cools. As the air cools, it becomes saturated. If there are surfaces available, the water vapor changes physical states to liquid droplets or solid ice crystals, forming a cloud.
2. At higher temperatures, water vapor condenses on surfaces as tiny water droplets. When temperatures are below freezing, water vapor changes directly to ice crystals.
3. Rain forms when a cloud's water droplets become too heavy to remain suspended in the cloud. The droplets grow by colliding and joining with other droplets.
4. Hail forms when raindrops are carried by updrafts of air to higher altitudes in clouds, where the raindrops freeze. Some raindrops may not be caught in the updrafts and will fall to the ground as rain.

Section 1 Review–California Standards: PE/ATE 4, 4a, 4e

SECTION 2

Focus

Air Masses and Fronts

In this section, students learn what air masses are and how they affect weather in the United States. Students also learn about the boundaries of air masses—known as *fronts*—and the results of air-mass interactions.

Bellringer

Show students a weather map that has a frontal boundary. Tell them to think about the weather reports they may have seen on television. Then ask them to describe the type of weather they think is associated with frontal boundaries.

1) Motivate

DEMONSTRATION

Condensation Students may have a difficult time understanding how hot and cold air masses stay separated as they move. Tell students that air at different temperatures has different densities. In this respect, air behaves much like water. To demonstrate how temperature can separate liquid masses, fill a large beaker or jar with hot water and a small beaker with cold water. Add several drops of blue food coloring to the cold water to make it visible. Slowly pour the cold water down the side of the jar. Ask students to describe what they see, and encourage them to explain their observations.

Sheltered English

2

NEW TERMS

air mass

front

OBJECTIVES

- Explain how air masses are characterized.
- Describe the four major types of air masses that influence weather in the United States.
- Describe the four major types of fronts.
- Relate fronts to weather changes.

Air Masses and Fronts

Have you ever wondered how the weather can change so fast? One day the sun is shining and you are wearing shorts, and the next day it is so cold you need a coat. Changes in weather are caused by the movement and interaction of air masses. An **air mass** is a large body of air that has similar temperature and moisture throughout. In this section you will learn about air masses and how their interaction influences the weather.

Air Masses

An air mass gets its moisture and temperature characteristics from the area over which it forms. These areas are called *source regions*. For example, an air mass that develops over the Gulf of Mexico is warm and wet because this area is warm and has a lot of water that evaporates into the air. There are many types of air masses, each associated with a particular source region. And each of these masses can be identified by its moisture and temperature characteristics. The characteristics of these air masses are represented on maps with a two-letter symbol, as shown in **Figure 17.** The first letter indicates the moisture characteristics of the air mass, and the second symbol represents the temperature characteristics of the air mass.

Figure 17 *This map shows the source regions for air masses that influence weather in North America. Air masses keep their moisture and temperature characteristics as they move over the Earth's surface.*

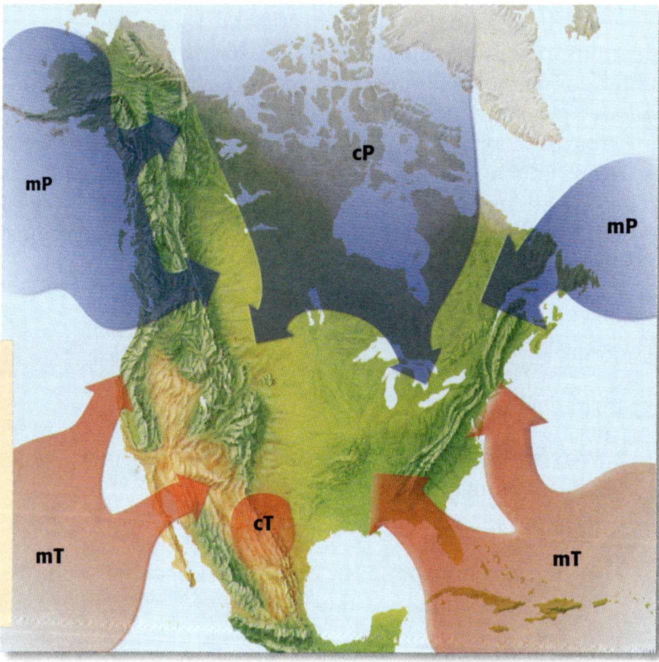

maritime (m)–forms over water; wet

continental (c)–forms over land; dry

polar (P)–forms south of the Arctic air masses; cold

tropical (T)–develops over the Tropics; warm

432

Directed Reading Worksheet 16 Section 2

internet**connect**

SCILINKS NSTA

TOPIC: Air Masses and Fronts
GO TO: www.scilinks.org
***sci*LINKS NUMBER:** HSTE385

Figure 18 *A cP air mass generally moves southeastward across Canada and into the northern United States.*

Cold Air Masses Most of the cold winter weather in the United States is influenced by three polar air masses. One of these air masses develops over land, while the other two form over oceans. The source regions for these air masses are Canada, the North Pacific Ocean, and the North Atlantic Ocean.

A continental polar air mass develops over land in northern Canada. In the winter, this air brings extremely cold weather to the United States, as shown in **Figure 18.** In the summer, it generally brings cool, dry weather.

A maritime polar air mass that forms over the North Pacific Ocean mostly affects the Pacific Coast. This air mass is very wet, but not as cold as the air mass that develops over Canada. In the winter, this air mass brings rain and snow to the Pacific Coast. In the summer, it brings cool, foggy weather.

A maritime polar air mass that forms over the North Atlantic Ocean usually affects New England and eastern Canada. In the winter, it produces cold, cloudy weather with precipitation. In the summer, the air mass brings cool weather with fog.

Warm Air Masses Four warm air masses influence the weather in the United States. Three of these air masses develop over water, while only one forms over land. The source regions for these air masses are the Atlantic Ocean, the Pacific Ocean, the Gulf of Mexico, and the desert region of Mexico and the southwestern United States.

A maritime tropical air mass that develops over warm areas in the North Pacific Ocean is lower in moisture content and weaker than the maritime polar air mass. As a result, southern California receives less precipitation than the rest of California.

Other maritime tropical air masses develop over the warm waters of the Gulf of Mexico and the North Atlantic Ocean. These air masses move north across the East Coast and into the Midwest. In the summer, they bring hot and humid weather, thunderstorms, and hurricanes, as shown in **Figure 19.** In the winter, they bring mild, often cloudy weather.

Figure 19 *People in Houston, Texas, experience the many thunderstorms brought by mT air masses from the Gulf of Mexico.*

433

2 Teach

DISCUSSION

Air Masses and You Have students use **Figure 17** to determine which type of air mass is mainly responsible for the weather in your area. Have students describe the general temperatures and humidity typical of your area. Then have students compare their observations with the information in this section.

Multicultural CONNECTION

Local weather patterns are heavily influenced by air masses, which tend to bring predictable weather. All cultures have names for familiar weather patterns. For example, in Tunisia, Africa, weather forecasters often predict "hot and *chili*" conditions. This forecast may not make sense to people elsewhere, but to a Tunisian, *chili* refers to a hot wind blowing from the North African desert. Similarly, in parts of the eastern United States, people refer to the hot, dry, and relatively windless weeks of August as the Indian summer. Have interested students research the names and characteristics of typical weather patterns in other countries.

Teaching Transparency 148
"Air Masses in North America"

IS THAT A FACT!

Air masses can extend upward for thousands of kilometers and can reach the top of the troposphere—an altitude of 10 to 16 km!

2 Teach, *continued*

READING STRATEGY

Prediction Guide Ask students to answer true or false to the following questions before they read the rest of this section.

Cold air is denser than warm air. (true)

Interactions between cold and warm air masses create specific weather conditions. (true)

MEETING INDIVIDUAL NEEDS

Learners Having Difficulty Perform the following demonstration to show students how cold and warm fronts form. Obtain a pair of surgical gloves. Use magic markers to color one glove red and the other glove blue. When the gloves are completely dry, put them on. Tell students that the blue glove represents a cold air mass and the red glove represents a warm air mass. To show how a cold front forms, hold your hands in front of you, and move your "blue hand" toward your "red hand." Just before they touch, slide your blue hand under your red hand and push your red hand up. To simulate the formation of a warm front, keep your blue hand stationary, and move your red hand toward your blue hand. As your hands touch, slide your red hand up and over your blue hand. Sheltered English

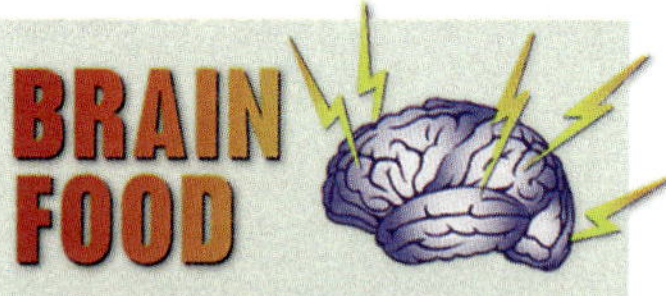

The term *front* was first used to describe weather systems during World War I in Europe. Meteorologists in Norway thought the boundaries between different air masses were much like the opposing armies on the battle front.

A continental tropical air mass forms over the deserts of northern Mexico and the southwestern United States. This air mass influences weather in the United States only during the summer. It generally moves northeastward, bringing clear, dry, and very hot weather.

Fronts

Air masses with different characteristics, such as temperature and humidity, do not usually mix. So when two different air masses meet, a boundary forms between them. This boundary is called a **front.** Weather at a front is usually cloudy and stormy. **Figure 20** illustrates the four different types of fronts—cold fronts, warm fronts, stationary fronts, and occluded fronts. Fronts are usually associated with weather in the middle latitudes, where there are both cold and warm air masses. Fronts do not occur in the Tropics because only warm air masses exist there.

Figure 20 **Different Types of Fronts**

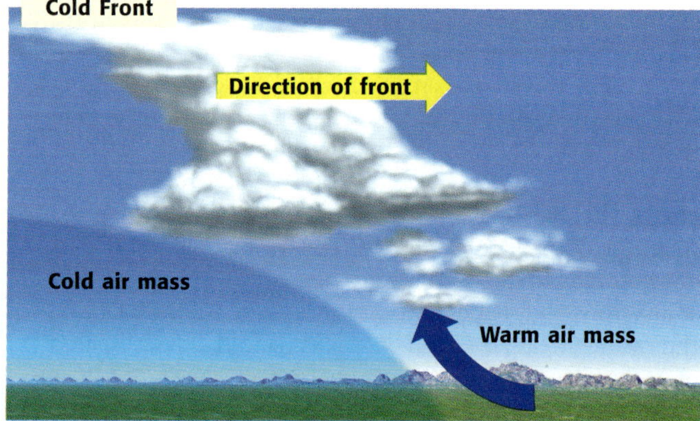

A **cold front** forms when a cold air mass meets and displaces a warm air mass. Because the moving cold air is more dense, it moves under the less-dense warm air, pushing it up. Cold fronts can move fast, producing large cumulonimbus clouds with thunderstorms, heavy rain, or snow. Cooler weather usually follows a cold front.

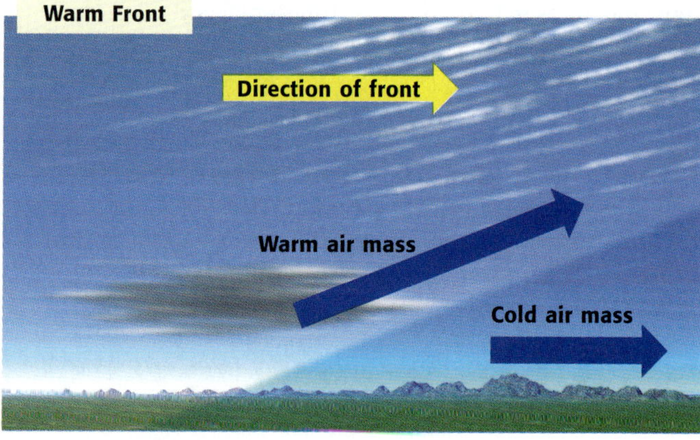

A **warm front** forms when a warm air mass meets and overrides a cold air mass. The warm, less-dense air moves over the cold, denser air. These fronts generally bring nimbostratus clouds and drizzly precipitation. After the front passes, weather conditions are clear and warm.

IS THAT A FACT!

Air masses tend to move toward areas of low pressure. Fronts are caused when two different air masses converge.

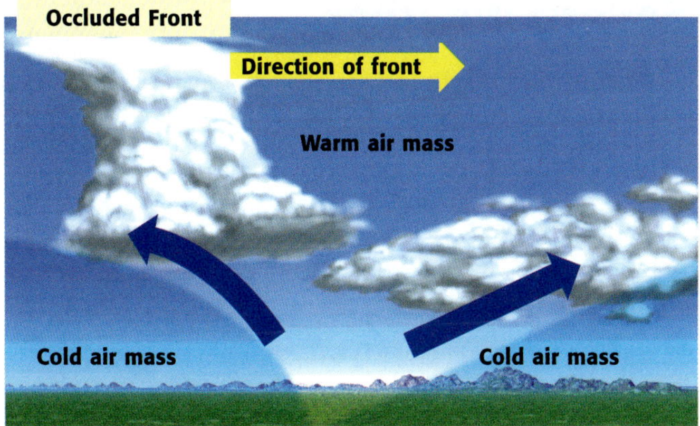

An **occluded front** forms when a faster-moving cold front overtakes a slower-moving warm front and forces the warm air up. The cold front then continues advancing until it meets a cold air mass that is warmer. The cold front then forces this air mass to rise. An occluded front has cooler temperatures and large amounts of precipitation.

A **stationary front** forms when a cold air mass meets a warm air mass and little horizontal movement occurs. The weather associated with a stationary front is similar to that produced by a warm front.

REVIEW

1. What are the characteristics that define air masses?
2. What are the major air masses that influence the weather in the United States?
3. What are fronts, and what causes them?
4. What kind of front forms when a cold air mass displaces a warm air mass?
5. **Analyzing Relationships** Explain why the Pacific Coast has cool, wet winters and warm, dry summers.

Answers to Review

1. temperature and moisture
2. maritime tropical, maritime polar, continental tropical, and continental polar
3. Fronts are boundaries that form between two different air masses. Boundaries form because air masses with different moisture and temperature characteristics do not mix well.
4. a cold front
5. In the winter, the Pacific Coast's climate is governed by a maritime polar air mass that brings wet weather and cool temperatures. In the summer, the Pacific Coast's climate is governed by a maritime tropical air mass that brings warm temperatures and little moisture.

3 Extend

Research

Have students research weather lore to find out if it has a scientific basis. For example, students could research the saying, "Red sky at night, sailor's delight; red sky at morning, sailors take warning."

4 Close

Quiz

1. If a continental polar air mass moves over Ohio in the summer, what will the weather be like? (cool and dry)
2. Why does the continental tropical air mass that forms over northern Mexico bring clear, dry, hot weather? (It forms over the desert, which is hot and contains relatively little moisture.)
3. Explain how a cold front develops. (A cold front develops when a cold air mass moves under a warm air mass, forcing the warmer air upward.)
4. What kind of weather is associated with a stationary front? (It will probably be cloudy and rainy as long as the front lies over an area. After the front passes, the weather will usually clear up.)

Alternative Assessment

Have students list five places in the United States they have visited or would like to visit and the air masses that affect the weather in those places.

Section 2 Review–California Standards: PE/ATE 4, 4e

SECTION 3

Focus

Severe Weather

In this section, students learn about the conditions that form thunderstorms, tornadoes, and hurricanes. The discussion of thunderstorms includes an explanation of lightning and thunder, while the discussion of tornadoes and hurricanes includes information on the incredible damage these storms cause.

Bellringer

Show students a picture of a thunderstorm. Then have them write a one-paragraph description of a thunderstorm in their ScienceLog. Tell them to focus on the characteristics that distinguish thunderstorms from other forms of weather.

1) Motivate

DEMONSTRATION

Perform this demonstration to simulate the forces involved in creating thunder. Inflate a balloon with air, and tie it closed. Explain that thunder occurs when lightning superheats air, causing the gases to expand rapidly. The air in the balloon is under pressure, so it will also expand rapidly if the pressure is suddenly released. The rapid expansion of air causes vibrations that we hear as sound. Hold up a pin or needle, pause, and pop the balloon with a flourish.

3

NEW TERMS

severe weather
thunderstorms
lightning
thunder
tornado
hurricane

OBJECTIVES

- Explain what lightning is.
- Describe the formation of thunderstorms, tornadoes, and hurricanes.
- Describe the characteristics of thunderstorms, tornadoes, and hurricanes.

Severe Weather

Weather in the mid-latitudes can change from day to day. These changes result from the continual shifting of air masses. Sometimes a series of storms will develop along a front and bring severe weather. **Severe weather** is weather that can cause property damage and even death. Examples of severe weather include thunderstorms, tornadoes, and hurricanes. In this section you will learn about the different types of severe weather and how each type forms.

Thunderstorms

Thunderstorms, as shown in **Figure 21,** are small, intense weather systems that produce strong winds, heavy rain, lightning, and thunder. As you learned in the previous section, thunderstorms can occur along cold fronts. But that's not the only place they develop. There are only two atmospheric conditions required to produce thunderstorms: the air near the Earth's surface must be warm and moist, and the atmosphere must be unstable. The atmosphere is unstable when the surrounding air is colder than the rising air mass. As long as the air surrounding the rising air mass is colder, the air mass will continue to rise.

Thunderstorms occur when warm, moist air rises rapidly in an unstable atmosphere. When the warm air reaches its dew point, the water vapor in the air condenses, forming cumulus clouds. If the atmosphere is extremely unstable, the warm air will continue to rise, causing the cloud to grow into a dark, cumulonimbus cloud. These clouds can reach heights of over 15 km.

Figure 21 *A typical thunderstorm produces approximately 470 million liters of water and enough electricity to provide power to the entire United States for 20 minutes.*

internet connect

TOPIC: Severe Weather
GO TO: www.scilinks.org
***sci*LINKS NUMBER:** HSTE390

Trees have exploded when struck by lightning. Why? Lightning causes the sap in the tree to vaporize (turn from a liquid to a gas). The steam expands rapidly as it is heated, causing the tree to explode.

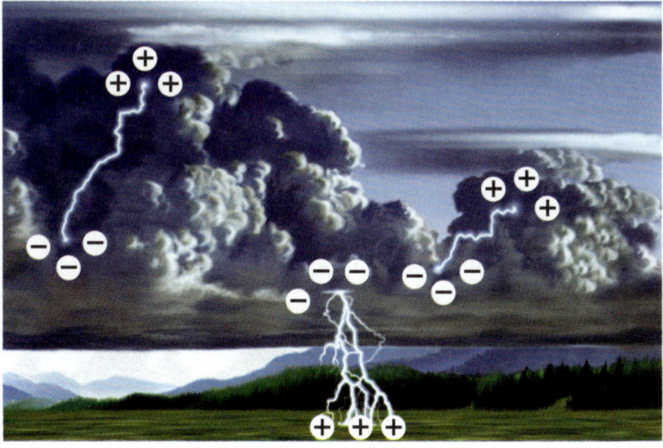

Figure 22 *The upper part of a cloud usually carries a positive electrical charge, while the lower part of the cloud carries mainly negative charges.*

How would you feel if your entire summer was crammed into 1 day every few years? Turn to page 451 to find out how one person felt.

Lightning Thunderstorms are very active electrically. **Lightning** is a large electrical discharge that occurs between two oppositely charged surfaces, as shown in **Figure 22.** Have you ever touched someone after scuffing your feet on the carpet and received a mild shock? If so, you have experienced how lightning forms. While walking around, friction between the floor and your shoes builds up an electrical charge in your body. When you touch someone else, the charge is released.

When lightning strikes, energy is released. This energy transfers heat to the air and causes the air to expand rapidly and send out sound waves. **Thunder** is the sound that results from the rapid expansion of air along the lightning strike.

physical science CONNECTION

Have you ever wondered why you don't see lightning and hear thunder at the same time? Well, there's an easy explanation. Light travels faster than sound. The light reaches you almost instantly, but the sound travels only 1 km every 3 seconds. The closer the lightning is to where you are, the sooner you will hear the thunder.

Severe Thunderstorms Only about 10 percent of thunderstorms are considered severe. Severe thunderstorms produce one or more of the following conditions—high winds, hail, flash floods, and tornadoes. Hailstorms damage crops, dent the metal on cars, and break windows. Sudden flash flooding due to heavy rains causes millions of dollars in property damage annually and is the biggest cause of weather-related deaths.

Lightning, which occurs with all thunderstorms, is responsible for thousands of forest fires each year in the United States. Lightning also kills or injures hundreds of people a year in the United States. **Figure 23** shows how easily lightning can strike an object at the Earth's surface.

Figure 23 *Lightning often strikes the highest object in an area.*

437

2 Teach

MISCONCEPTION ALERT

Inform students that the old saying, "Lightning never strikes twice in the same place," is not true. Lightning has struck the same place, and even the same person, more than once. Ray Sullivan, retired National Park Ranger, has been hit seven times by lightning. Luckily, he has survived the strikes.

CONNECT TO PHYSICAL SCIENCE

Benjamin Franklin performed his most famous experiment, in which he flew a kite in a thunderstorm, in 1752. During this experiment, Franklin discovered that lightning is a form of electricity. Use Teaching Transparency 199 to illustrate how lightning forms.

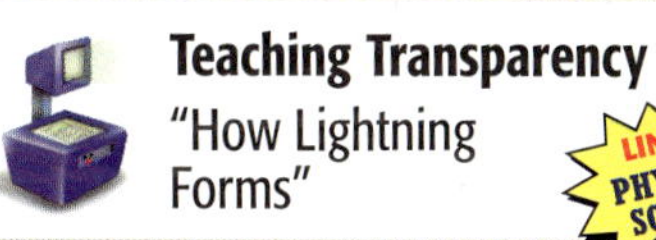

Teaching Transparency 199 "How Lightning Forms" LINK TO PHYSICAL SCIENCE

Directed Reading Worksheet 16 Section 3

IS THAT A FACT!

Benjamin Franklin invented the lightning rod, a device that protects structures and their inhabitants from the potential effects of lightning strikes. Lightning strikes a metal pole and travels through an insulated cable to a metal rod buried in the ground.

2 Teach, continued

Group Activity

Making Models Have pairs of students work together to model a tornado vortex. Supply each pair with a clean, empty jar with its lid, water, food coloring, a teaspoon of liquid dish soap, and a teaspoon of vinegar. Have students fill the jars about three-quarters full of water. Instruct them to add a few drops of food coloring, the soap, and the vinegar. Instruct them to cap the jar tightly and shake it vigorously. Once the solution is mixed, tell students to give the jars a quick twist with a flick of the wrist. Students will observe that a vortex will form and lengthen.

Sheltered English

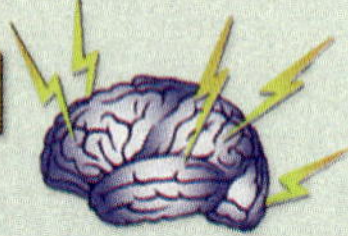

Brain Food

Most tornadoes develop from thunderstorms at the leading edge of a cold front. Ask students how this situation would contribute to the formation of tornadoes? (The cool air wedges under the warm air, forcing it to rise rapidly and become unstable. When there is a large difference between the contrasting air masses, the chance of a tornado forming is increased.)

Tornadoes

Tornadoes are produced in only 1 percent of all thunderstorms. A **tornado** is a small, rotating column of air that has high wind speeds and low central pressure and that touches the ground. A tornado starts out as a funnel cloud that pokes through the bottom of a cumulonimbus cloud and hangs in the air. It is called a tornado when it makes contact with the Earth's surface. **Figure 24** shows the development of a tornado.

Figure 24 How a Tornado Forms

1 Wind traveling in two different directions causes a layer of air in the middle to begin to rotate like a roll of toilet paper.

2 The rotating column of air is turned to a vertical position by strong updrafts of air within the cumulonimbus cloud. The updrafts of air also begin to rotate with the column of air.

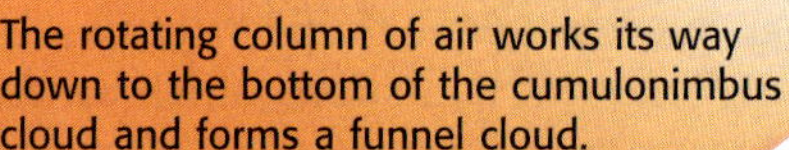

3 The rotating column of air works its way down to the bottom of the cumulonimbus cloud and forms a funnel cloud.

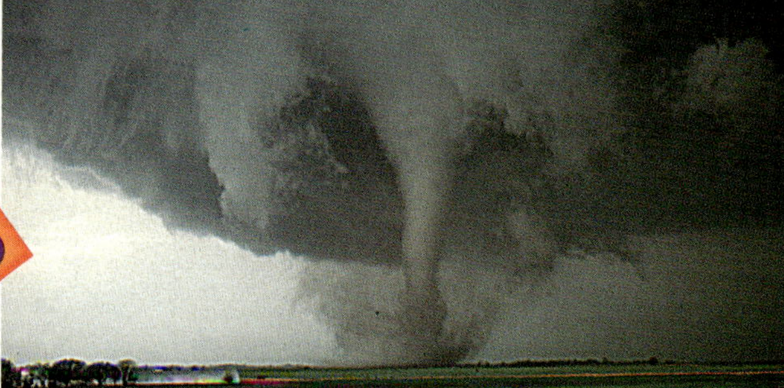

4 The funnel cloud is called a tornado when it touches the ground.

Teaching Transparency 149
"How a Tornado Forms"

Weird Science

People have reported seeing "naked" chickens after tornadoes strike rural areas. A likely explanation is that tornadoes cause chickens to shed their feathers, or molt. Chickens often molt when attacked. As the chickens molt, the strong tornado winds blow their feathers off.

About 75 percent of the world's tornadoes occur in the United States. The majority of these tornadoes happen in the spring and early summer when cold, dry air from Canada collides with warm, moist air from the tropics. The length of a tornado's path of destruction can vary, but it is usually about 8 km long and 10–60 m wide. Although most tornadoes last only a few minutes, they can cause a lot of damage. This is due to their strong spinning winds. The average tornado has wind speeds of between 120 and 180 km/h, but rarer, more violent tornadoes can have spinning winds of up to 500 km/h. The winds of tornadoes have been known to uproot trees and destroy buildings, as shown in **Figure 25.** Tornadoes are capable of picking up heavy objects, such as houses, cars, and store signs, and hurling them through the air.

Figure 25 *The tornado that hit Kissimmee, Florida, in 1998 had wind speeds of up to 416 km/h.*

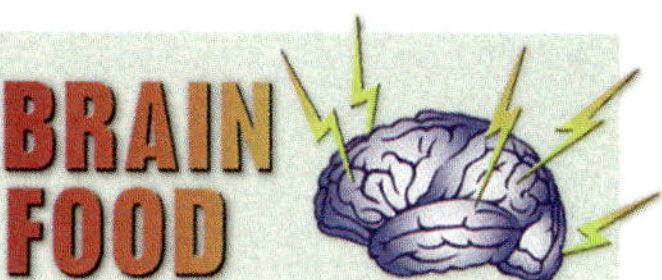

Did you know that fish have been known to fall from the sky? Some scientists think the phenomenon of raining fish is caused by waterspouts. A waterspout is a tornado that occurs over water. When the funnel comes into contact with the surface of the water, it causes the water to spray several meters upward.

Hurricanes

A **hurricane,** as shown in **Figure 26,** is a large, rotating tropical weather system with wind speeds of at least 119 km/h. Hurricanes are the most powerful storms on Earth. Hurricanes have different names in other parts of the world. In the western Pacific Ocean, they are called *typhoons*. Hurricanes that form over the Indian Ocean are called *cyclones*.

Hurricanes generally form in the area between 5° and 20° north and south latitude over warm, tropical oceans. At higher latitudes, the water is too cold for hurricanes to form. Hurricanes vary in size from 160 km to up to 1,500 km in diameter, and they can travel for thousands of miles.

Figure 26 **Hurricane Fran Photographed from Space**

Cooperative Learning

Have students work in pairs or small groups to design a poster or other graphic display that compares and contrasts thunderstorms, tornadoes, and hurricanes. Then have the groups display their posters around the class for others to enjoy.

Cross-Disciplinary Focus

History Hurricanes played a significant role in early American history. In 1609, a fleet of ships with settlers from England bound for Virginia was blown off course by a hurricane. Some of the ships landed in Bermuda instead, and the settlers started the first European colony there.

Homework

Disaster Plan Have students find out how to protect themselves during a thunderstorm, tornado, or hurricane. Using their findings, have each student draw up a disaster plan for severe weather. The plan should include general information as well as things that might be specific to their families, such as what to do with the family pet(s), how to assist a person who uses a wheelchair or walker, and so on. Suggest that students review the plan with their family.

Is That a Fact!

Before 1950 hurricanes were named or identified by their latitude and longitude. In the 1950s meteorologists began assigning names to hurricanes. Today, the names are assigned in advance for six-year cycles. The names are submitted by countries potentially in the path of hurricanes and approved by the World Meteorological Organization.

3 Extend

Research

Writing | Tell students that creating severe weather takes a lot of energy. Have them research the relationship between energy and storm formation. For example, as a warm air mass rises, energy from water condensation helps fuel hurricanes. Challenge students to research these concepts in books, magazines, and the Internet, and compile their findings into a short report.

Group Activity

Have students work in groups to learn about a hurricane of their choosing. Have them find out where the storm formed, its path, the damage it did, and how people coped with the damage. Ask them to focus on the people involved in the hurricane, from the meteorologists to relief workers. Have each group present the information they gather as a series of simulated newscasts.

Teaching Transparency 150
"A Cross Section of a Hurricane"

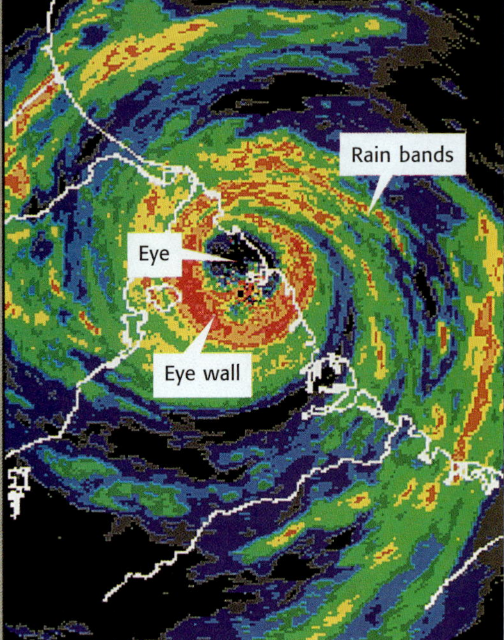

Figure 27 *The photo above gives you a bird's-eye view of a hurricane.*

Formation of a Hurricane A hurricane begins as a group of thunderstorms moving over tropical ocean waters. Winds traveling in two different directions collide, causing the storm to rotate over an area of low pressure. Because of the Coriolis effect, the storm turns counterclockwise in the Northern Hemisphere and clockwise in the Southern Hemisphere.

Hurricanes get their energy from the condensation of water vapor. Once formed, the hurricane is fueled through contact with the warm ocean water. Moisture is added to the warm air by evaporation from the ocean. As the warm, moist air rises, the water vapor condenses, releasing large amounts of heat energy. The hurricane continues to grow as long as it is over its source of warm, moist air. When the hurricane moves into colder waters or over land, it begins to die because it has lost its source of energy. **Figure 27** and **Figure 28** show two views of a hurricane.

Figure 28 *The view below shows how a hurricane would look if you cut it in half and looked at it from the side. The arrows indicate the flow of air.*

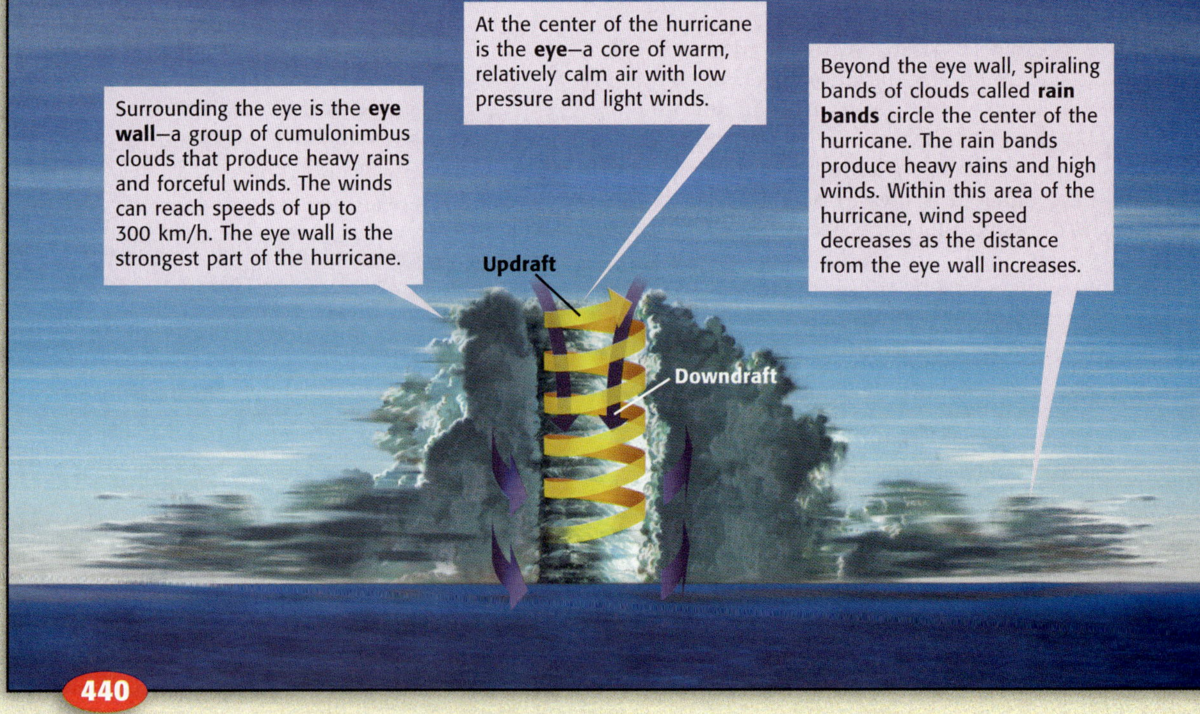

440

Science Bloopers

The Seminole Indians of Florida have used their own observations of nature to successfully predict severe weather. In one instance, their observations of plants and animals indicated that a hurricane was approaching. Though the weather bureau predicted the storm would miss the area, the Seminoles evacuated—and were spared the storm's destruction. In another instance, meteorologists were so sure of their predictions that heavy equipment was moved from the area so that it would be available later to help relief efforts. The Seminoles thought otherwise and remained in the area. The hurricane never reached Florida.

Damage Caused by Hurricanes Hurricanes can cause a lot of damage when they move near or onto land. The speed of the steady winds of most hurricanes ranges from 120 km/h to 150 km/h, and they can reach speeds as high as 300 km/h. Hurricane winds can knock down trees and telephone poles and can damage and destroy buildings and homes.

While high winds cause a great deal of damage, most hurricane damage is caused by flooding associated with heavy rains and storm surges. A *storm surge* is a wall of water that builds up over the ocean due to the heavy winds and low atmospheric pressure. The wall of water gets bigger and bigger as it nears the shore, reaching its greatest height when it crashes onto the shore. Depending on the strength of the hurricane, a storm surge can be 1 m to 5 m high. A storm surge can affect a 65 km–160 km stretch of coastline. Flooding causes tremendous damage to property and lives when a storm surge moves onto shore. Flooding can be increased by the heavy rains that usually accompany hurricanes, as shown in **Figure 29.**

The weather on Jupiter is more exciting than that on Earth. Wind speeds reach up to 540 km/h. Storms last for decades, and one—the Great Red Spot of Jupiter—has been swirling around since it was first discovered, in 1664. The Great Red Spot has a diameter of more than one and a half times that of the Earth. It is like a hurricane that has lasted more than 300 years.

Figure 29 *In 1998, the flooding associated with Hurricane Mitch devastated Central America. Whole villages were swept away by the flood waters and mudslides. Total rainfall for the storm was reported to be as high as 190 cm in some areas. Thousands of people were killed, and damages were estimated to be more than $5 billion.*

REVIEW

1. What is lightning?
2. Describe how tornadoes develop. What is the difference between a funnel cloud and a tornado?
3. Why do hurricanes form only over certain areas?
4. **Inferring Relationships** What happens to a hurricane as it moves over land? Why?

4 Close

Quiz

1. What is the relationship between lightning and thunder? (Lightning is an electrical discharge that forms between clouds or between a cloud and the ground. The air around the lightning bolt expands rapidly, producing sound waves that we call thunder.)
2. Explain why tornadoes often destroy buildings in their path. (Buildings are often destroyed by the enormous force exerted by tornado winds and by the strong updrafts that accompany them.)
3. Why don't hurricanes form over land? (A hurricane gets its energy from enormous volumes of warm, moist air, which are not present over landmasses.)

Alternative Assessment

Concept Mapping Have students make a severe-weather concept map. Tell them that their map should illustrate how thunderstorms, tornadoes, and hurricanes form and what their characteristics are.

Reinforcement Worksheet 16
"Precipitation Situations"

Answers to Review

1. Lightning is a large electrical discharge that occurs between two oppositely charged surfaces.
2. A tornado develops when wind traveling in two different directions causes the air in the middle to rotate. The rotating column of air is turned upright by updrafts that begin spinning with it. The rotating air works its way down to the bottom of the cloud and forms a funnel cloud. When the funnel cloud touches the ground, it is called a tornado.
3. Hurricanes form only over warm, tropical oceans because a hurricane requires the heat and moisture from water to fuel it.
4. A hurricane dissipates as it moves over land because it loses its energy source.

Section 3 Review–California Standards: PE/ATE 4e

SECTION 4

Focus

Forecasting the Weather

In this section, students will learn how we use instruments such as thermometers, barometers, weather balloons, and radar to forecast and report the weather. Students will also learn how meteorologists use weather maps to depict the data they gather.

Bellringer

Pose this question to students:

If you did not have the benefit of the weather forecast on the news, radio, or television, how would you forecast the weather? (Answers will vary. Possible answers include looking at the sky for signs and noticing the direction and intensity of the winds.)

1) Motivate

DEMONSTRATION

Air Pressure and Barometers

Students have learned that thunderstorms and hurricanes are low-pressure storm systems. Low pressure usually indicates stormy weather, and high pressure usually indicates clear weather. Show students a barometer, and tell them that barometers are still widely used in weather forecasting. Show students how to read a barometer and how to use the moveable pointer to track whether air pressure is increasing or decreasing. Sheltered English

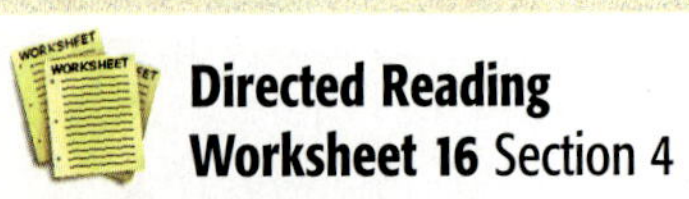

Directed Reading Worksheet 16 Section 4

4

NEW TERMS

weather forecast
thermometer
barometer
windsock
wind vane
anemometer
station model
isobars

OBJECTIVES

- Describe the different types of instruments used to take weather measurements.
- Explain how to interpret a weather map.
- Explain why weather maps are useful.

Forecasting the Weather

Have you ever left your house in the morning wearing a short-sleeved shirt, only to need a sweater in the afternoon? At some time in your life, you have been caught off guard by the weather. Weather affects how you dress and your daily plans, so it is important that you get accurate weather forecasts. A **weather forecast** is a prediction of weather conditions over the next 3 to 5 days. Meteorologists observe and collect data on current weather conditions in order to provide reliable predictions. In this section you will learn about some of the methods used to collect weather data and how those data are displayed.

Weather Forecasting Technology

In order for meteorologists to accurately forecast the weather, they need to measure various atmospheric conditions, such as air pressure, humidity, precipitation, temperature, wind speed, and wind direction. Meteorologists use special instruments to collect data on weather conditions both near and far above the Earth's surface. You have already learned about two tools that meteorologists use near the Earth's surface—psychrometers, which are used to measure relative humidity, and rain gauges, which are used to measure precipitation. Read on to learn about other methods meteorologists use to collect data.

Measuring Air Temperature A **thermometer** is a tool used to measure air temperature. A common type of thermometer uses a liquid sealed in a narrow glass tube, as shown in **Figure 30.** When air temperature increases, the liquid expands and moves up the glass tube. As air temperature decreases, the liquid shrinks and moves down the tube.

Air temperature is measured in both degrees Celsius and degrees Fahrenheit. In the United States, television weather forecasters generally report air temperature in degrees Fahrenheit.

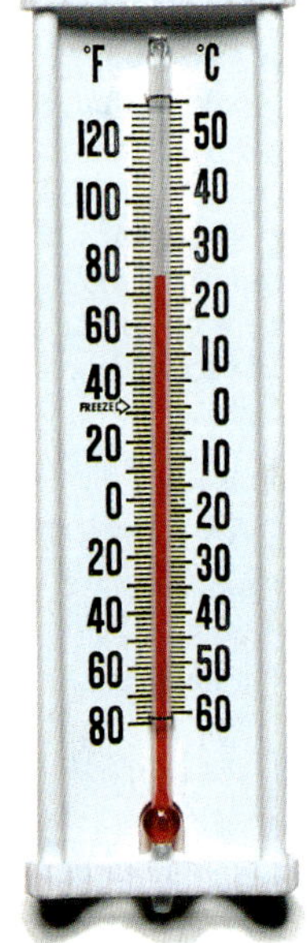

Figure 30 *A liquid thermometer is usually filled with alcohol that is colored red, or mercury, which is silver.*

TOPIC: Forecasting the Weather
GO TO: www.scilinks.org
***sci*LINKS NUMBER:** HSTE395

Measuring Air Pressure A **barometer** is an instrument used to measure air pressure. The mercurial barometer, as shown in **Figure 31,** provides the most accurate method of measuring air pressure. A mercurial barometer consists of a glass tube sealed at one end that is placed in a container full of mercury. The air pressure pushes on the mercury inside the container, causing the mercury to move up the glass tube. The greater the air pressure is, the higher the mercury will rise.

Figure 31 *In a mercurial barometer, the mercury in the tube stops rising when the air pressure inside the glass tube is equal to the air pressure outside.*

Measuring Wind Direction and Wind Speed Wind direction can be measured using a **windsock** or a **wind vane.** A windsock, as shown in **Figure 32,** is a cone-shaped cloth bag open at both ends. The wind enters through the wide end and leaves through the narrow end. Therefore, the wide end points into the wind.

A wind vane is shaped like an arrow with a large tail and is attached to a pole. The wind pushes the tail of the wind vane, spinning it on the pole until the arrow points into the wind.

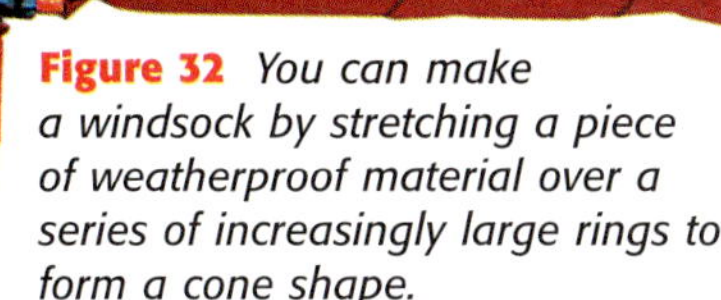

Figure 32 *You can make a windsock by stretching a piece of weatherproof material over a series of increasingly large rings to form a cone shape.*

Wind speed is measured by a device called an **anemometer.** An anemometer, as shown in **Figure 33,** consists of three or four cups connected by spokes to a pole. The wind pushes on the hollow sides of the cups, causing them to rotate on the pole. The motion sends a weak electrical current that is measured and displayed on a dial.

Figure 33 *The faster the wind speed is, the faster the cups of the anemometer spin.*

Measuring Weather in the Upper Atmosphere You have learned how weather conditions are recorded near the Earth's surface. But in order for meteorologists to better understand weather patterns, they must collect data from higher altitudes. Studying weather at higher altitudes requires the use of more-sophisticated equipment.

443

CONNECT TO LIFE SCIENCE

Middle ear barotrauma is an earache caused by a difference in pressure between the air and a person's middle ear. Although airplane cabins are pressurized, passengers still feel the pressure decrease as the plane climbs and increase as it descends. The trauma occurs when the Eustachian tube, a passageway between the middle ear and the throat, fails to open wide enough to equalize the pressure. Chewing gum, yawning, or simply swallowing often alleviates the condition.

2 Teach

MAKING MODELS

Windsocks

MATERIALS

FOR EACH STUDENT:
- old bed sheet, pillow cases, or fabric remnants
- scissors
- stapler
- dowels, 1 m long
- wire
- wire cutters

Safety Caution: Warn students to be careful when handling wire pieces because the ends may be sharp.

Before students arrive, cut the wire into pieces long enough to bend into a 20 cm diameter circle and still wrap the ends around one end of the dowel. Instruct students to do the following:

1. Draw a square with 63 cm sides on the fabric.
2. Draw a line from each lower corner to the midpoint of the top, forming a large triangle.
3. Cut out this triangle with scissors.
4. Fold the triangle so the sides meet and overlap about 1 cm. Staple the edges together and cut off the tip of the triangle.
5. Bend the wire into a 20 cm diameter circle, and wrap the extra wire around the end of the dowel.
6. Roll the bottom edge of the windsock around the wire and staple it.
7. Take the windsock outside, and use a directional compass to determine the direction of the wind.

PG 556

Gone with the Wind

3 Extend

Group Activity

Doppler radar is a type of radar that uses the Doppler effect to determine the direction and speed of weather systems. Radar, an acronym for *ra*dio *d*etection *a*nd *r*anging, is a device that determines the speed and location of weather systems by bouncing radio waves off them. The Doppler effect is the shift in wave frequency detected by an observer due to the motion of the wave source relative to the observer. For example, an ambulance siren may emit sound waves at a uniform rate. But as the ambulance passes you, you may notice that the pitch drops. The reason is that the sound waves seem to be compressed as the ambulance approaches you and spread out as it speeds away. Doppler radar bounces radio waves off weather systems. The reflected waves are used to determine if the system is moving toward or away from the radar source and at what speed it is moving. Challenge students to illustrate the Doppler effect so that the concept makes sense to them, perhaps by making a poster or demonstrating the effect using water waves.

MATH and MORE

Have students use the formulas below to convert 32°F, 72°F, and 5°F into degrees Celsius. Then have them convert 100°C, 45°C, and 21°C into degrees Fahrenheit.

$C = (F - 32) \times \frac{5}{9}$

$F = (C \times \frac{9}{5}) + 32$

(0°C, 22.2°C, −15°C, 212°F, 113°F, 69.8°F)

Math Skills Worksheet 35
"Using Temperature Scales"

Figure 34 *Radiosondes have radio transmitters that send measurements to stations on the ground.*

Weather balloons carry electronic equipment called *radiosondes* to measure weather conditions as high as 30 km above the Earth's surface. Radiosondes, as shown in **Figure 34,** measure temperature, air pressure, and relative humidity.

Radar is used to find the location, movement, and intensity of precipitation. Radar can also detect what form of precipitation a weather system is carrying. Radar is often used for monitoring severe weather systems, such as hurricanes. You might be familiar with a type of radar called Doppler radar. Many television weather reports use Doppler radar to show the direction, velocity, and intensity of precipitation, as shown in **Figure 35.**

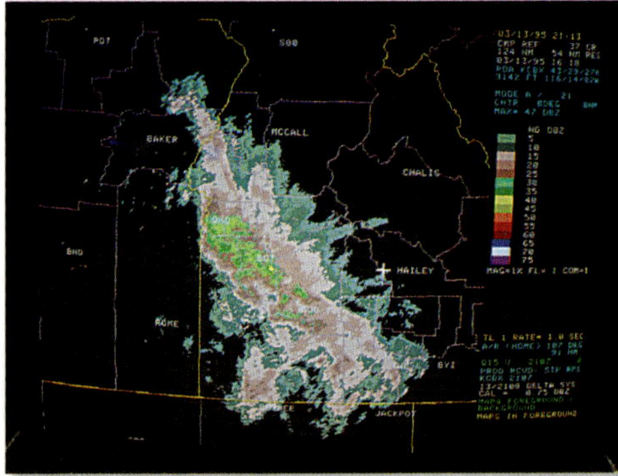

Figure 35 *Doppler radar is used to detect funnel clouds and tornadoes. Using Doppler radar, meteorologists can predict a tornado up to 20 minutes before it touches the ground.*

Explore

Throughout history, people have predicted approaching weather by interpreting natural signs. Animals and plants are usually more sensitive to changes in the atmosphere, such as air pressure, humidity, and temperature, than humans. To find out more about natural signs, research this topic at the library or on the Internet. Try searching using key words and phrases such as "weather and animals" or "weather and plants." Write a short paper on your findings to share with the class.

Weather satellites orbiting the Earth provide weather information that cannot be obtained from the ground. These satellites take images of the swirling clouds you see on television weather reports. Satellites can not only measure wind speeds and humidity but also determine temperatures at various altitudes, from the tops of clouds down to ground level and ocean surfaces.

Weather Maps

As you have learned, meteorologists base their forecasts on information gathered from many sources. In the United States, the National Weather Service (NWS) and the National Oceanic and Atmospheric Administration (NOAA) collect and analyze weather data. The NWS produces weather maps based on information gathered from about 1,000 weather stations across the United States. On these maps, each station is represented by a station model. A **station model,** as shown in **Figure 36,** is a small circle, which shows the location of the weather station, with a set of symbols and numbers surrounding it, which represent the weather data.

Answers to Explore

Answers will vary.

IS THAT A FACT!

Bats use the Doppler effect to locate prey and to navigate. Bats emit high-frequency sounds that bounce off objects. If the objects are moving, the wave frequency changes. If the frequency doesn't change, then the bat knows the object is stationary.

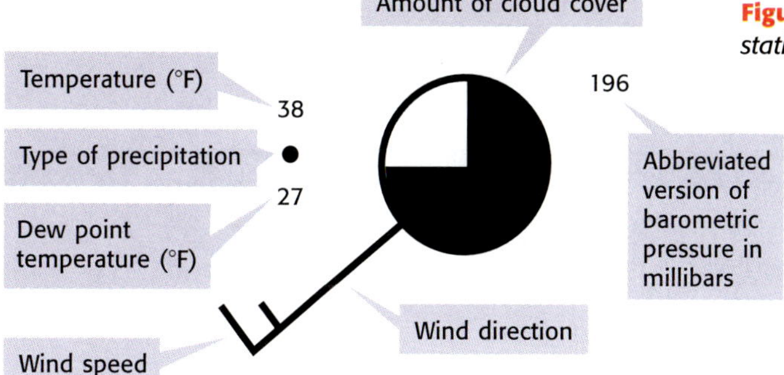

Figure 36 *Weather conditions at a station are represented by symbols.*

Figure 37 *Can you identify the different fronts on the weather map?*

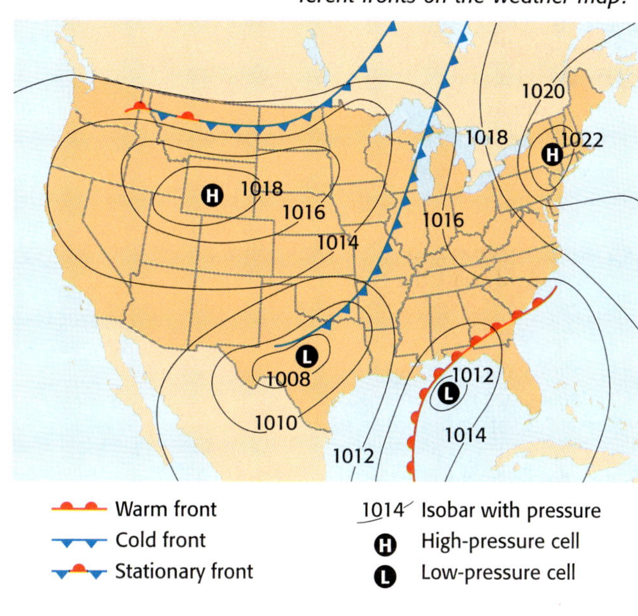

Weather maps also include lines called isobars. Isobars are similar to contour lines on a topographical map, except **isobars** are lines that connect points of equal air pressure rather than equal elevation. Isobar lines that form closed circles represent areas of high or low pressure. These areas are usually marked on a map with a capital *H* or *L*. Fronts are also labeled on weather maps. Weather maps, like the one shown in **Figure 37,** provide useful information for making accurate weather forecasts.

REVIEW

1. What are three methods meteorologists use to collect weather data?
2. What are weather maps based on?
3. What does a station model represent?
4. **Inferring Conclusions** Why would a meteorologist compare a new weather map with one 24 hours old?

To learn more about station models and their symbols, turn to page 552 in the LabBook.

Answers to Review

1. Answers will vary. Sample answer: weather balloons, Doppler radar, and weather satellites
2. Weather maps are based on weather data gathered from weather stations across the United States.
3. A station model represents the location of the weather station and the weather data collected there.
4. Answers may vary. Sample answer: Meteorologists would compare a new weather map with one 24 hours old to see how fast a front is moving.

4 Close

Quiz

1. Would water be a useful fluid to use in a thermometer? Explain. (No, water would not be a good thermometer fluid because it expands when it freezes.)
2. What advantage do weather satellites have over ground-based weather stations? (Satellites can gather weather data from much higher altitudes than land-based instruments can.)
3. Why are so many station models used to gather weather data in the United States? (Because the country is so large, and Earth's atmosphere is constantly changing, we need data from many stations to make accurate forecasts.)

Alternative Assessment

Have students use the weather report from their local newspaper over a 1-week period to construct a picture of local weather conditions. Then tell them to analyze their findings by applying what they have learned in this chapter.

PG 552

Watching the Weather

Critical Thinking Worksheet 16
"Commanding the Sky"

Chapter Highlights

VOCABULARY DEFINITIONS

SECTION 1

weather the condition of the atmosphere at a particular time and place

water cycle the continuous movement of water from water sources into the air, onto land, into and over the ground, and back to the water sources

humidity the amount of water vapor or moisture in the air

relative humidity the amount of moisture the air contains compared with the maximum amount it can hold at a particular temperature

psychrometer an instrument used to measure relative humidity

condensation the change of state from a gas to a liquid

dew point the temperature at which air must cool to be completely saturated

cloud a collection of millions of tiny water droplets or ice crystals

cumulus clouds puffy, white clouds that tend to have flat bottoms

stratus clouds clouds that form in layers

cirrus clouds thin, feathery white clouds found at high altitudes

precipitation water in liquid or solid form that moves from the atmosphere to the land and ocean

SECTION 2

air mass a large body of air that has the same temperature and moisture throughout

front the boundary that forms between two different air masses

Vocabulary Review Worksheet 16

Chapter Highlights

SECTION 1

Vocabulary

weather *(p. 424)*
water cycle *(p. 424)*
humidity *(p. 425)*
relative humidity *(p. 425)*
psychrometer *(p. 426)*
condensation *(p. 427)*
dew point *(p. 427)*
cloud *(p. 428)*
cumulus clouds *(p. 428)*
stratus clouds *(p. 428)*
cirrus clouds *(p. 429)*
precipitation *(p. 430)*

Section Notes

- Water is continuously moving and changing state as it moves through the water cycle.
- Humidity is the amount of water vapor or moisture in the air. Relative humidity is the amount of moisture the air contains compared with the maximum amount it can hold at a particular temperature.
- Water droplets form because of condensation.
- Dew point is the temperature at which air is saturated.
- Condensation occurs when the air next to a surface cools to below its dew point.
- Clouds are formed from condensation on dust and other particles above the ground.
- There are three major cloud forms—cumulus, stratus, and cirrus.
- There are four major forms of precipitation—rain, snow, sleet, and hail.

Labs

Let It Snow! *(p. 555)*

SECTION 2

Vocabulary

air mass *(p. 432)*
front *(p. 434)*

Section Notes

- Air masses form over source regions. An air mass has similar temperature and moisture content throughout.
- Four major types of air masses influence weather in the United States—maritime polar, maritime tropical, continental polar, continental tropical.
- A front is a boundary between contrasting air masses.
- There are four types of fronts—cold fronts, warm fronts, occluded fronts, and stationary fronts.
- Specific types of weather are associated with each front.

Skills Check

Math Concepts

RELATIVE HUMIDITY Relative humidity is the amount of moisture the air is holding compared with the amount it can hold at a particular temperature. The relative humidity of air that is holding all the water it can at a given temperature is 100 percent, meaning it is saturated. You can calculate relative humidity with the following equation:

$$\frac{\text{(present) g/m}^3}{\text{(saturated) g/m}^3} \times 100 = \text{relative humidity}$$

Visual Understanding

HURRICANE HORSEPOWER Hurricanes are the most powerful storms on Earth. A cross-sectional view helps you identify the different parts of a hurricane. The diagram on page 440 shows a side view of a hurricane.

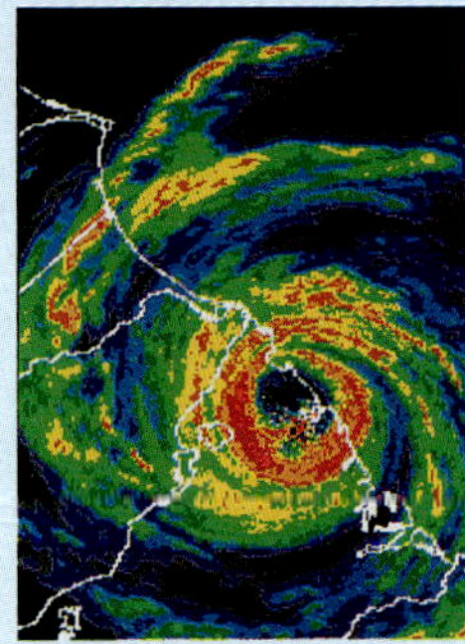

446

Lab and Activity Highlights

Watching the Weather PG 552

Let It Snow! PG 555

Gone with the Wind PG 556

Datasheets for LabBook (blackline masters for these labs)

SECTION 3

Vocabulary

severe weather *(p. 436)*
thunderstorms *(p. 436)*
lightning *(p. 437)*
thunder *(p. 437)*
tornado *(p. 438)*
hurricane *(p. 439)*

Section Notes

- Severe weather is weather that can cause property damage and even death.
- Thunderstorms are small, intense storm systems that produce lightning, thunder, strong winds, and heavy rain.
- Lightning is a large electrical discharge that occurs between two oppositely charged surfaces.
- Thunder is the sound that results from the expansion of air along a lightning strike.
- A tornado is a rotating funnel cloud that touches the ground.
- Hurricanes are large, rotating, tropical weather systems that form over the tropical oceans.

SECTION 4

Vocabulary

weather forecast *(p. 442)*
thermometer *(p. 442)*
barometer *(p. 443)*
windsock *(p. 443)*
wind vane *(p. 443)*
anemometer *(p. 443)*
station model *(p. 444)*
isobars *(p. 445)*

Section Notes

- Radiosondes, radar, and weather satellites take weather measurements at high altitudes.
- Meteorologists present weather data gathered from stations as station models on weather maps.

Labs

Watching the Weather *(p. 552)*
Gone with the Wind *(p. 556)*

internet**connect**

GO TO: go.hrw.com

Visit the **HRW** Web site for a variety of learning tools related to this chapter. Just type in the keyword:

KEYWORD: HSTWEA

GO TO: www.scilinks.org

Visit the **National Science Teachers Association** on-line Web site for Internet resources related to this chapter. Just type in the ***sci*LINKS** number for more information about the topic:

TOPIC: Collecting Weather Data	***sci*LINKS NUMBER:** HSTE380
TOPIC: Air Masses and Fronts	***sci*LINKS NUMBER:** HSTE385
TOPIC: Severe Weather	***sci*LINKS NUMBER:** HSTE390
TOPIC: Forecasting the Weather	***sci*LINKS NUMBER:** HSTE395

447

VOCABULARY DEFINITIONS, *continued*

SECTION 3

severe weather weather that causes property damage and possible death

thunderstorms small, intense storm systems that produce strong winds, heavy rain, lightning, and thunder

lightning the large electrical discharge that occurs between two oppositely charged surfaces

thunder the sound that results from the rapid expansion of air along a lightning strike

tornado a small, rotating column of air with high wind speeds and low central pressure that touches the ground

hurricane a large rotating tropical weather system with wind speeds equal to or greater than 119 km/h

SECTION 4

weather forecast a prediction of future weather conditions

thermometer a tool used to measure air temperature

barometer an instrument used to measure air pressure

windsock an instrument used to measure wind direction

wind vane an instrument used to measure wind direction

anemometer an instrument used to measure wind speed

station model a small circle showing the location of a weather station along with a set of symbols and numbers surrounding it that represent weather data

isobars lines that connect points of equal air pressure

Lab and Activity Highlights

LabBank

Whiz-Bang Demonstrations
- It's Raining Again, Demo 29
- When Air Bags Collide, Demo 28

Inquiry Labs, When Disaster Strikes, Lab 12

EcoLabs & Field Activities, Rain Maker or Rain Faker? Field Activity 15

Long-Term Projects & Research Ideas, Project 44

Blackline masters of these Chapter Highlights can be found in the **Study Guide.**

Chapter Review Answers

Using Vocabulary

1. Relative humidity is the amount of water vapor the air contains relative to the maximum amount it can hold at a given temperature. Dew point is the temperature to which air must cool to be saturated.
2. Cumulus clouds are puffy, white clouds that have a flat bottom. Stratus clouds are clouds that form in layers.
3. An air mass is a large body of air that has the same moisture and temperature throughout. A front is the boundary that forms where two different air masses meet.
4. Lightning is a large electrical discharge that occurs between two oppositely charged surfaces. Thunder is the sound that results from the rapid expansion of air along a lightning strike.
5. A tornado is a small, rotating column of air with high wind speed that touches the ground. A hurricane is a large, rotating tropical weather system with wind speeds equal to or greater than 119 km/h.
6. A barometer measures air pressure. An anemometer measures wind speed.

Understanding Concepts

Multiple Choice

7. c
8. d
9. c
10. d
11. b
12. d
13. a
14. c
15. b
16. c

Chapter Review

USING VOCABULARY

Explain the difference between the following sets of words:

1. relative humidity/dew point
2. cumulus clouds/stratus clouds
3. air mass/front
4. lightning/thunder
5. tornado/hurricane
6. barometer/anemometer

UNDERSTANDING CONCEPTS

Multiple Choice

7. The process of liquid water changing to gas is called
   a. precipitation.
   b. condensation.
   c. evaporation.
   d. water vapor.

8. What is the relative humidity of air at its dew-point temperature?
   a. 0%
   b. 50%
   c. 75%
   d. 100%

9. Which of the following is not a type of condensation?
   a. fog
   b. cloud
   c. snow
   d. dew

10. High clouds made of ice crystals are called __?__ clouds.
    a. stratus
    b. cumulus
    c. nimbostratus
    d. cirrus

11. Large thunderhead clouds that produce precipitation are called __?__ clouds.
    a. nimbostratus
    b. cumulonimbus
    c. cumulus
    d. stratus

12. Strong updrafts within a thunderhead can produce
    a. snow.
    b. rain.
    c. sleet.
    d. hail.

13. A maritime tropical air mass contains
    a. warm, wet air.
    b. cold, moist air
    c. warm, dry air.
    d. cold, dry air..

14. A front that forms when a warm air mass is trapped between cold air masses and forced high up into the atmosphere is called a
    a. stationary front.
    b. warm front.
    c. occluded front.
    d. cold front.

15. A severe storm that forms as a rapidly rotating funnel cloud is called a
    a. hurricane.
    b. tornado.
    c. typhoon.
    d. thunderstorm.

16. The lines on a weather map connecting points of equal atmospheric pressure are called
    a. contour lines.
    b. highs.
    c. isobars.
    d. lows.

Short Answer

17. Explain the relationship between condensation and the dew point.

Chapter 16 Review–California Standards: PE/ATE Q1–6: 4e; Q7–21: 4a, 4e

18. Describe the conditions along a stationary front.

19. What are the characteristics of an air mass that forms over the Gulf of Mexico?

20. Explain how a hurricane develops.

Concept Mapping

21. Use the following terms to create a concept map: evaporation, relative humidity, water vapor, dew, psychrometer, clouds, fog.

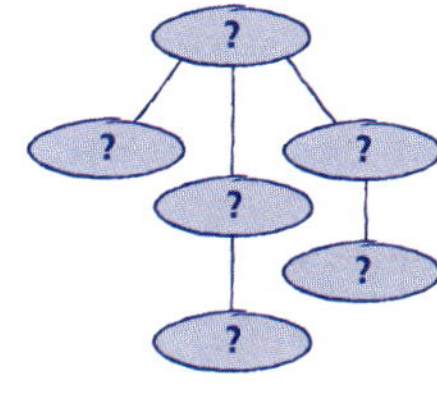

CRITICAL THINKING AND PROBLEM SOLVING

Write one or two sentences to answer the following questions:

22. If both the air temperature and the amount of water vapor in the air change, is it possible for the relative humidity to stay the same? Explain.

23. What can you assume about the amount of water vapor in the air if there is no difference between the wet- and dry-bulb readings of a psychrometer?

24. List the major similarities and differences between hurricanes and tornadoes.

MATH IN SCIENCE

You always see lightning before you hear thunder. That's because light travels at about 300,000,000 m/s, while sound travels only 330 m/s. One way you can determine how close you are to the thunderstorm is by counting how many seconds there are between the lightning and thunder. Usually, it takes thunder about 3 seconds to cover 1 km. Answer the following questions based on this estimate.

25. If you hear thunder 12 seconds after you see the flash of lightning, how far away is the thunderstorm?

26. If you hear thunder 36 seconds after you see the flash of lightning, how far away is the thunderstorm?

INTERPRETING GRAPHICS

Use the weather map below to answer the questions that follow.

Warm front
Cold front
Stationary front

27. Where are thunderstorms most likely to occur? Explain your answer.

28. What are the weather conditions like in Tulsa, Oklahoma? Explain your answer.

NOW What Do You Think?

Take a minute to review your answers to the ScienceLog questions on page 423. Have your answers changed? If necessary, revise your answers based on what you have learned since you began this chapter.

449

UNDERSTANDING CONCEPTS

Short Answer

17. The air must cool to below its dew point before condensation can occur.

18. Stationary fronts generally bring drizzly precipitation. After the front passes, the weather is generally clear and warm.

19. An air mass that forms over the Gulf of Mexico is warm and wet.

20. A hurricane begins as a group of thunderstorms moving over tropical ocean waters. Winds traveling in two different directions collide, causing the storm to rotate over an area of low pressure. The hurricane is fueled by the condensation of water vapor.

Concept Mapping

21. 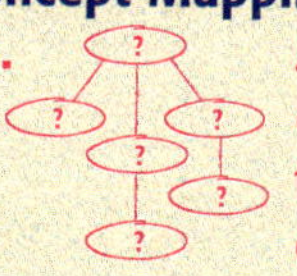 An answer to this exercise can be found at the end of this book.

CRITICAL THINKING AND PROBLEM SOLVING

22. Yes; for example, if both the air temperature and water vapor increased, the relative humidity might remain the same.

23. The air is saturated with water.

24. Answers may vary. Sample answer: Both begin as a result of thunderstorms and are centered around low pressure. Hurricanes occur over water, and tornadoes generally occur over land.

MATH IN SCIENCE

25. $(12 \text{ s} \div 3 \text{ s}) \times 1 \text{ km} = 4 \text{ km}$

26. $(36 \text{ s} \div 3 \text{ s}) \times 1 \text{ km} = 12 \text{ km}$

INTERPRETING GRAPHICS

27. Thunderstorms are most likely to occur in Boston because a cold front is approaching.

28. Tulsa is experiencing a stationary front. It is probably receiving drizzly precipitation.

NOW WHAT DO YOU THINK

1. Answers may vary.
2. Weather is caused by the movement and interaction of air masses.

Concept Mapping Transparency 16

Blackline masters of this Chapter Review can be found in the **Study Guide.**

CAREERS
Meteorologist–Cristy Mitchell

Teaching Strategies

Tell the students to imagine that they are meteorologists studying another planet in the solar system. Ask:

As a meteorologist, what features would you look for to get information about the climate and the weather? (Students should recognize that climates are strongly influenced by major geographic features. A planet's rotation affects prevailing wind patterns. Other features to look for include mountains, deserts, and large bodies of water.)

Discussion

1. Weather stations operate around the clock, 7 days a week. Do you think you would enjoy the night work and rotating shifts that are part of a meteorologist's job? (Some students may think this is exciting, while others may prefer a 9-to-5 job.)
2. There is an old saying: "You can talk about the weather, but you can't do anything about it." How might this relate to a meteorologist's job? (Although scientists like Cristy Mitchell observe the powerful forces of nature, they cannot do anything to stop them. However, issuing accurate weather warnings can save people's lives.)

CAREERS

METEOROLOGIST

Predicting floods, observing the path of a tornado, watching the growth of a hurricane, and issuing flood warnings are all in a day's work for **Cristy Mitchell.** As a meteorologist for the National Weather Service, Mitchell spends each working day observing the powerful forces of nature.

When asked what made her job interesting, Mitchell replied, "There's nothing like the adrenaline rush you get when you see a tornado coming! I would say that witnessing the powerful forces of nature is what really makes my job interesting."

Meteorology is the study of natural forces in Earth's atmosphere. Perhaps the most familiar field of meteorology is weather forecasting. However, meteorology is also used in air-pollution control, agricultural planning, and air and sea transportation. Meteorologists also study trends in Earth's climate, such as global warming and ozone depletion.

Collecting the Data

Meteorologists collect data on air pressure, temperature, humidity, and wind velocity. By applying what they know about the physical properties of the atmosphere and analyzing the mathematical relationships in the data, they are able to forecast the weather.

Meteorologists use a variety of tools, such as computers, to collect the data they need to make accurate weather forecasts. Mitchell explained, "The computer is an invaluable tool for me. Through it, I receive maps and detailed information, including temperature, wind speed, air pressure, and general sky conditions for a specific region."

In addition to using computers, Mitchell also uses radar and satellite imagery to show regional and national weather. Meteorologists also use computerized models of the world's atmosphere to help forecast the weather.

Find Out for Yourself

▶ Use the library or the Internet to find information about hurricanes, tornadoes, or thunderstorms. How do meteorologists define these storms? What trends in air pressure, temperature, and humidity do meteorologists use to forecast storms?

▲ *This photograph of Hurricane Elena was taken from the space shuttle* Discovery *in September 1985.*

450

Answers to Find Out for Yourself

Students' answers will vary depending upon which topic they choose to research.

Science Fiction

"All Summer in a Day"

by Ray Bradbury

It is raining, just like it has been for 7 long years. That is 2,555 days of nonstop rain. For the men, women, and children who came to build a civilization on Venus, constant rain is a fact of life. But there is one special day—a day when it stops raining and the sun shines gloriously. This day comes about only once every 7 years. And today is that day!

At school the students have been looking forward to this day for weeks. In one class they've read about how the sun is like a lemon, and how hot it is. They've written stories and poems about what it might be like to see the sun.

And now that the day has finally arrived, all of the children in that class are peering through the window, searching for the sun. The children are 9 years old, and all of them but Margot have lived on Venus all their lives. None of them remember the day 7 years ago when the rain stopped. They only recall stories about the sunshine, and now they just can't wait to see it for themselves!

But Margot is different. She longs to see the sun even more than the others. The reason makes the other kids jealous. And jealous kids can be cruel. . . .

What happens to Margot? Find out for yourself by reading Ray Bradbury's "All Summer in a Day" in the *Holt Anthology of Science Fiction.*

451

Science Fiction

"All Summer in a Day"

by Ray Bradbury

Often, a memory can be sustaining; other times, it might be crippling. A priceless experience teaches Margot's classmates a lesson in understanding the power of memory.

Teaching Strategy

Reading Level This is a relatively short story that should not be difficult for the average student to read and comprehend.

Background

About the Author Ray Bradbury is one of the world's most celebrated writers. He was born in the small town of Waukegan, Illinois, in 1920. He moved from place to place as a young boy while his father looked for steady work. Eventually, Bradbury and his family ended up in Los Angeles. There he began a writing career that has spanned over 60 years!

Bradbury has earned top honors in the field of literature, including the World Fantasy Award for lifetime work and the Grand Master Award from Science Fiction Writers of America. An unusual honor came when an astronaut named a crater on the moon Dandelion Crater after Ray Bradbury's novel, *Dandelion Wine.*

Much of Bradbury's writing is rich in descriptive detail, and often he writes stories that combine science fiction with comments about the way people behave.

Further Reading Students can check out some of Ray Bradbury's other classic stories in the following collections. Or they can visit the library to scan the wide range of Bradbury's publications.

The Veldt, Creative Education, Inc., 1987

The Foghorn, Creative Education, Inc., 1987

S is for Space, Doubleday, 1966

Chapter Organizer

CHAPTER ORGANIZATION	TIME MINUTES	OBJECTIVES	LABS, INVESTIGATIONS, AND DEMONSTRATIONS
Chapter Opener pp. 452–453	45	California Standards: PE/ATE 4, 4b, 7, 7b, 7e	**Investigate!** What's Your Angle? p. 453
Section 1 What Is Climate?	90	▶ Explain the difference between weather and climate. ▶ Identify the factors that determine climates. PE/ATE 4, 4a, 4b, 4d, 4e, 7, 7b, 7c, 7e, 7f	**QuickLab,** A Cool Breeze, p. 457 **Whiz-Bang Demonstrations,** How Humid Is It? Demo 30
Section 2 Climates of the World	90	▶ Locate and describe the three major climate zones. ▶ Describe the different biomes found in each climate zone. PE/ATE 4, 4b, 4e, 5, 5b, 5d, 5e, 7c; LabBook 7, 7a, 7b, 7d, 7e, 7h	**Demonstration,** Mock Permafrost, p. 467 in ATE **Discovery Lab,** For the Birds, p. 559 **Datasheets for LabBook,** For the Birds, Datasheet 39 **Skill Builder,** Biome Business, p. 562 **Datasheets for LabBook,** Biome Business, Datasheet 40
Section 3 Changes in Climate	135	▶ Describe how the Earth's climate has changed over time. ▶ Summarize the different theories that attempt to explain why the Earth's climate has changed. ▶ Explain the greenhouse effect and its role in global warming. PE/ATE 1, 1a, 1e, 4, 4a, 4b, 6a; LabBook 7, 7c, 7e, 7h	**Demonstration,** The Greenhouse Effect, p. 469 in ATE **Skill Builder,** Global Impact, p. 558 **Datasheets for LabBook,** Global Impact, Datasheet 38 **Long-Term Projects & Research Ideas,** Project 45

See page **T20** *for a complete correlation of this book with the*

CALIFORNIA SCIENCE CONTENT STANDARDS.

Correlations are also provided at point of use throughout this ATE.

TECHNOLOGY RESOURCES

Guided Reading Audio CD
English or Spanish, Chapter 17

Classroom Management CD-ROM

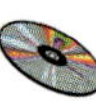
Science Discovery Videodiscs
Image and Activity Bank with Lesson Plans: Exploring Antarctica, Global Warming

CNN **Eye on the Environment,** A Climate Conference, Segment 27

Scientists in Action, Ice Age Discoveries, Segment 23

Test Generator CD-ROM

Chapter 17 • Climate

CLASSROOM WORKSHEETS, TRANSPARENCIES, AND RESOURCES	SCIENCE INTEGRATION AND CONNECTIONS	REVIEW AND ASSESSMENT
Directed Reading Worksheet 17 **Science Puzzlers, Twisters & Teasers,** Worksheet 17		
Directed Reading Worksheet 17, Section 1 **Transparency 151,** Seasons, Latitude, and the Tilt of the Earth **Transparency 152,** Basic Properties of Air **Transparency 153,** An Example of the Rain Shadow Effect	**Multicultural Connection,** p. 454 in ATE **Connect to Geography,** p. 455 in ATE **Math and More,** p. 455 in ATE **Multicultural Connection,** p. 457 in ATE **Across the Sciences:** Blame "The Child," p. 478	**Self-Check,** p. 456 **Homework,** p. 457 in ATE **Review,** p. 459 **Quiz,** p. 459 in ATE **Alternative Assessment,** p. 459 in ATE
Transparency 154, Climate Zones of the Earth **Transparency 154,** The Earth's Land Biomes **Directed Reading Worksheet 17,** Section 2 **Transparency 51,** Transpiration **Math Skills for Science Worksheet 37,** Rain-Forest Math **Science Skills Worksheet 18,** Finding Useful Sources **Reinforcement Worksheet 17,** A Tale of Three Climates	**Math and More,** p. 461 in ATE **Connect to Environmental Science,** p. 461 in ATE **Life Science Connection,** p. 462 **Real-World Connection,** p. 462 in ATE **Real-World Connection,** p. 463 in ATE **Connect to Environmental Science,** p. 464 in ATE **Connect to Environmental Science,** p. 465 in ATE **Life Science Connection,** p. 467 **Physical Science Connection,** p. 468	**Self-Check,** p. 462 **Homework,** pp. 462, 465, 466 in ATE **Review,** p. 463 **Review,** p. 468 **Quiz,** p. 468 in ATE **Alternative Assessment,** p. 468 in ATE
Directed Reading Worksheet 17, Section 3 **Transparency 155,** The Milankovitch Theory of the Causes of the Ice Ages **Critical Thinking Worksheet 17,** Cyberspace Heats Up **Science Skills Worksheet 4,** Understanding Bias	**Real-World Connection,** p. 471 in ATE **Cross-Disciplinary Focus,** p. 471 in ATE **Multicultural Connection,** p. 471 in ATE **MathBreak,** The Ride to School, p. 472 **Connect to Life Science,** p. 472 in ATE **Apply,** p. 473 **Science, Technology, and Society:** Some Say Fire, Some Say Ice..., p. 479	**Self-Check,** p. 470 **Review,** p. 473 **Quiz,** p. 473 in ATE **Alternative Assessment,** p. 473 in ATE

internetconnect

Holt, Rinehart and Winston On-line Resources

go.hrw.com

For worksheets and other teaching aids related to this chapter, visit the HRW Web site and type in the keyword: **HSTCLM**

National Science Teachers Association

www.scilinks.org

Encourage students to use the keywords listed on the Technology Highlights page to access information and resources on the **NSTA** Web site.

END-OF-CHAPTER REVIEW AND ASSESSMENT

Chapter Review in Study Guide
Vocabulary and Notes in Study Guide
Chapter Tests with Performance-Based Assessment, Chapter 17 Test
Chapter Tests with Performance-Based Assessment, Performance-Based Assessment 17
Concept Mapping Transparency 17

Chapter Resources & Worksheets

Visual Resources

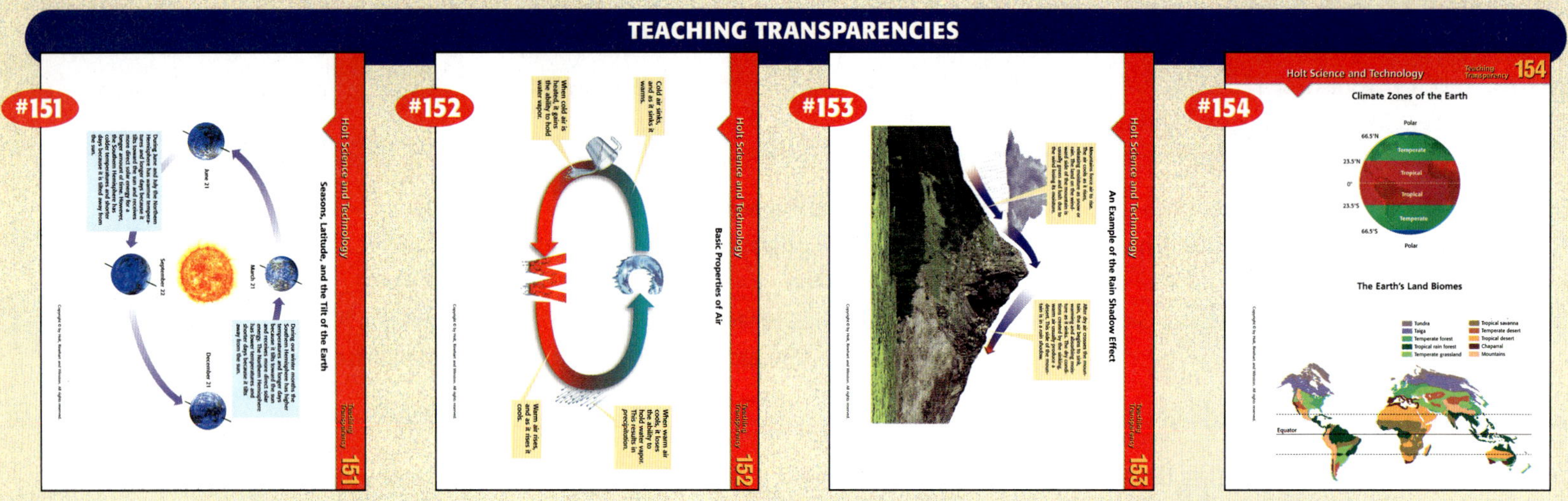

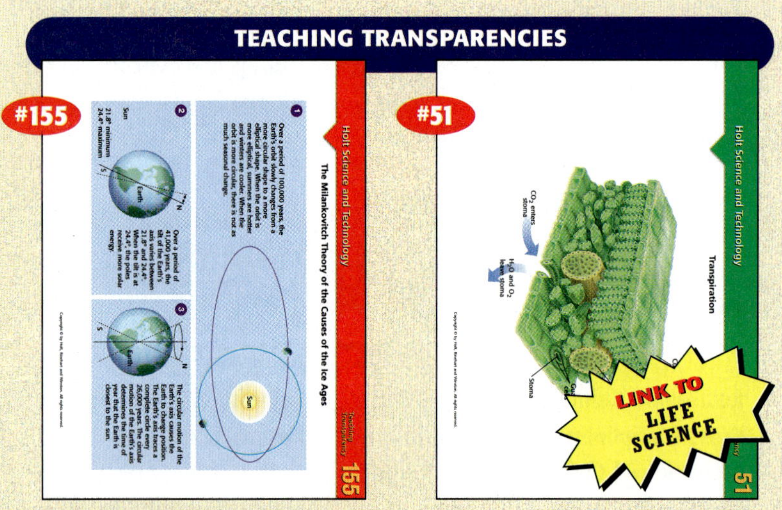

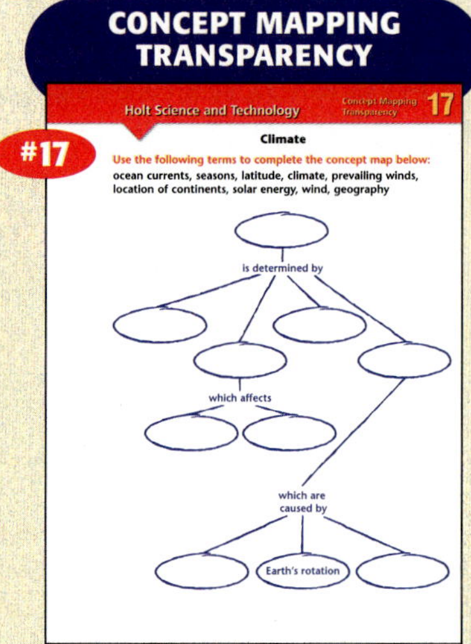

Meeting Individual Needs

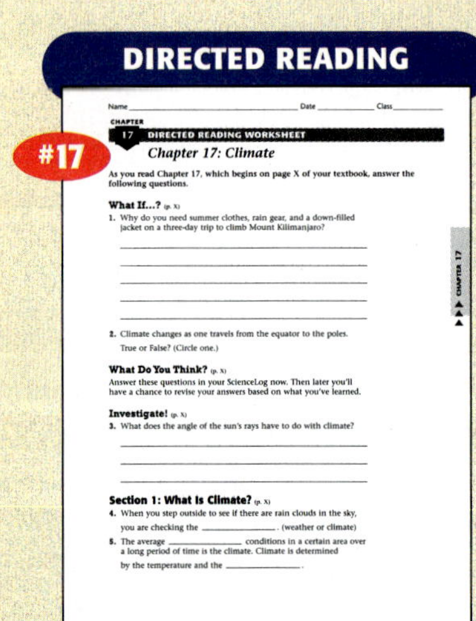

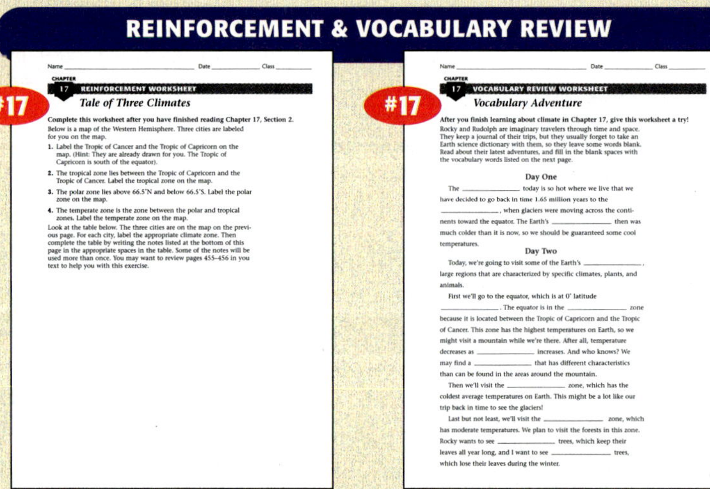

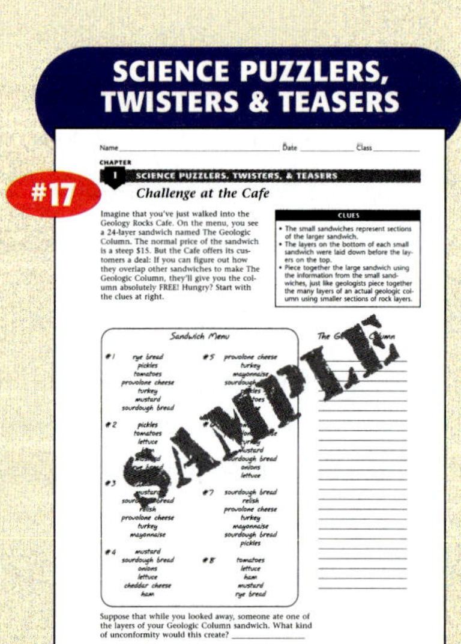

Review & Assessment

STUDY GUIDE

#17

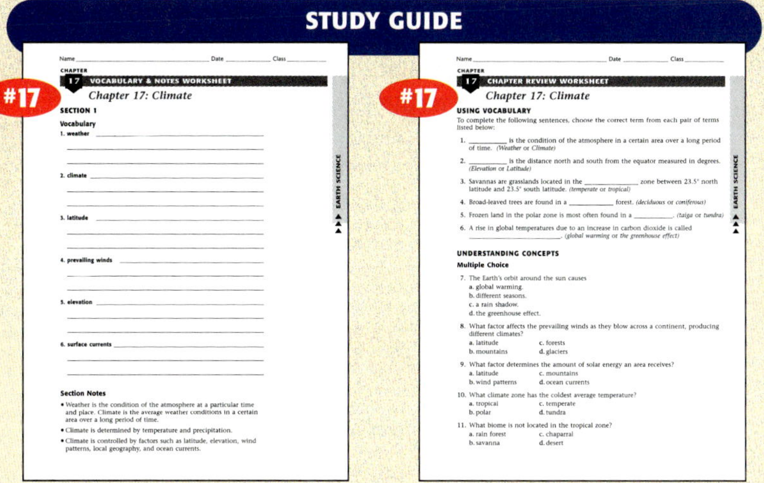
Name ______ Date ______ Class ______

CHAPTER 17 VOCABULARY & NOTES WORKSHEET

Chapter 17: Climate

SECTION 1

Vocabulary

1. weather

2. climate

3. latitude

4. prevailing winds

5. elevation

6. surface currents

Section Notes

- Weather is the condition of the atmosphere at a particular time and place. Climate is the average weather conditions in a certain area over a long period of time.
- Climate is determined by temperature and precipitation.
- Climate is controlled by factors such as latitude, elevation, wind patterns, local geography, and ocean currents.

EARTH SCIENCE

#17

Name ______ Date ______ Class ______

CHAPTER 17 CHAPTER REVIEW WORKSHEET

Chapter 17: Climate

USING VOCABULARY

To complete the following sentences, choose the correct term from each pair of terms listed below:

1. ______ is the condition of the atmosphere in a certain area over a long period of time. *(Weather or Climate)*
2. ______ is the distance north and south from the equator measured in degrees. *(Elevation or Latitude)*
3. Savannas are grasslands located in the ______ zone between 23.5° north latitude and 23.5° south latitude. *(temperate or tropical)*
4. Broad-leaved trees are found in a ______ forest. *(deciduous or coniferous)*
5. Frozen land in the polar zone is most often found in a ______. *(taiga or tundra)*
6. A rise in global temperatures due to an increase in carbon dioxide is called ______. *(global warming or the greenhouse effect)*

UNDERSTANDING CONCEPTS

Multiple Choice

7. The Earth's orbit around the sun causes
a. global warming.
b. different seasons.
c. a rain shadow.
d. the greenhouse effect.
8. What factor affects the prevailing winds as they blow across a continent, producing different climates?
a. latitude c. forests
b. mountains d. glaciers
9. What factor determines the amount of solar energy an area receives?
a. latitude c. mountains
b. wind patterns d. ocean currents
10. What climate zone has the coldest average temperature?
a. tropical c. temperate
b. polar d. tundra
11. What biome is not located in the tropical zone?
a. rain forest c. chaparral
b. savanna d. desert

EARTH SCIENCE

CHAPTER TESTS WITH PERFORMANCE-BASED ASSESSMENT

#17

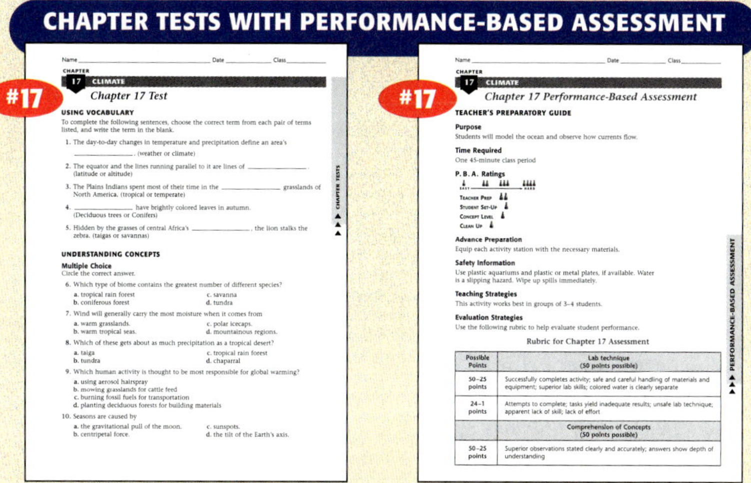
Name ______ Date ______ Class ______

CHAPTER 17 CLIMATE

Chapter 17 Test

USING VOCABULARY

To complete the following sentences, choose the correct term from each pair of terms listed, and write the term in the blank.

1. The day-to-day changes in temperature and precipitation define an area's ______. (weather or climate)
2. The equator and the lines running parallel to it are lines of ______. (latitude or altitude)
3. The Plains Indians spent most of their time in the ______ grasslands of North America. (tropical or temperate)
4. ______ have brightly colored leaves in autumn. (Deciduous trees or Conifers)
5. Hidden by the grasses of central Africa's ______, the lion stalks the zebra. (taiga or savanna)

UNDERSTANDING CONCEPTS

Multiple Choice

Circle the correct answer.

6. Which type of biome contains the greatest number of different species?
a. tropical rain forest c. savanna
b. coniferous forest d. tundra
7. Wind will generally carry the most moisture when it comes from
a. warm grasslands. c. polar icecaps.
b. warm tropical seas. d. mountainous regions.
8. Which of these gets about as much precipitation as a tropical desert?
a. taiga c. tropical rain forest
b. tundra d. chaparral
9. Which human activity is thought to be most responsible for global warming?
a. using aerosol hairspray
b. mowing grasslands for cattle feed
c. burning fossil fuels for transportation
d. planting deciduous forests for building materials
10. Seasons are caused by
a. the gravitational pull of the moon. c. sunspots.
b. centripetal force. d. the tilt of the Earth's axis.

CHAPTER TESTS

#17

Name ______ Date ______ Class ______

CHAPTER 17 CLIMATE

Chapter 17 Performance-Based Assessment

TEACHER'S PREPARATORY GUIDE

Purpose

Students will model the ocean and observe how currents flow.

Time Required

One 45-minute class period

P. B. A. Ratings

Teacher Prep · Student Set-Up · Concept Level · Clean Up

Advance Preparation

Equip each activity station with the necessary materials.

Safety Information

Use plastic aquariums and plastic or metal plates, if available. Water is a slipping hazard. Wipe up spills immediately.

Teaching Strategies

This activity works best in groups of 3–4 students.

Evaluation Strategies

Use the following rubric to help evaluate student performance.

Rubric for Chapter 17 Assessment

Possible Points	Lab technique (50 points possible)
50–25 points	Successfully completes activity; safe and careful handling of materials and equipment; superior lab skills; colored water is clearly separate
24–1 points	Attempts to complete; tasks yield inadequate results; unsafe lab technique, apparent lack of skill; lack of effort
	Comprehension of Concepts (50 points possible)
50–25 points	Superior observations stated clearly and accurately; answers show depth of understanding

PERFORMANCE-BASED ASSESSMENT

Lab Worksheets

WHIZ-BANG DEMONSTRATIONS

#30

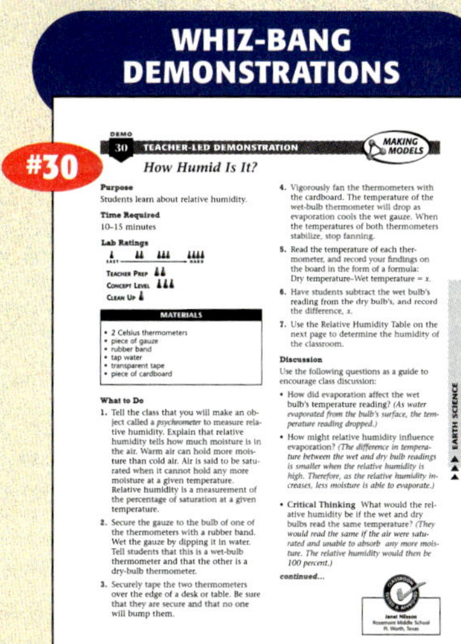
DEMO 30 TEACHER-LED DEMONSTRATION — MAKING MODELS

How Humid Is It?

Purpose

Students learn about relative humidity.

Time Required

10–15 minutes

Lab Ratings

Teacher Prep · Concept Level · Clean Up

MATERIALS

- 2 Celsius thermometers
- piece of gauze
- rubber band
- tap water
- transparent tape
- piece of cardboard

What to Do

1. Tell the class that you will make an object called a *psychrometer* to measure relative humidity. Explain that relative humidity tells how much moisture is in the air. Warm air can hold more moisture than cold air. Air is said to be saturated when it cannot hold any more moisture at a given temperature. Relative humidity is a measurement of the percentage of saturation at a given temperature.
2. Secure the gauze to the bulb of one of the thermometers with a rubber band. Wet the gauze by dipping it in water. Tell students that this is a wet-bulb thermometer and that the other is a dry-bulb thermometer.
3. Securely tape the two thermometers over the edge of a desk or table. Be sure that they are secure and that no one will bump them.
4. Vigorously fan the thermometers with the cardboard. The temperature of the wet-bulb thermometer will drop as evaporation cools the wet gauze. When the temperatures of both thermometers stabilize, stop fanning.
5. Read the temperature of each thermometer, and record your findings on the board in the form of a formula: Dry temperature–Wet temperature = *x*.
6. Have students subtract the wet bulb's reading from the dry bulb's, and record the difference, *x*.
7. Use the Relative Humidity Table on the next page to determine the humidity of the classroom.

Discussion

Use the following questions as a guide to encourage class discussion:

- How did evaporation affect the wet bulb's temperature reading? *(As water evaporated from the bulb's surface, the temperature reading dropped.)*
- How might relative humidity influence evaporation? *(The difference in temperature between the wet and dry bulb readings is smaller when the relative humidity is high. Therefore, as the relative humidity increases, less moisture is able to evaporate.)*
- Critical Thinking What would the relative humidity be if the wet and dry bulbs read the same temperature? *(They would read the same if the air were saturated and unable to absorb any more moisture. The relative humidity would then be 100 percent.)*

continued...

EARTH SCIENCE

LONG-TERM PROJECTS & RESEARCH IDEAS

#45

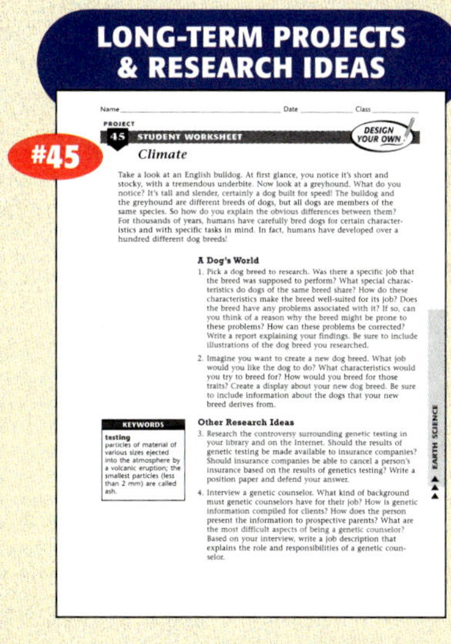
Name ______ Date ______ Class ______

PROJECT 45 STUDENT WORKSHEET — DESIGN YOUR OWN

Climate

Take a look at an English bulldog. At first glance, you notice it's short and stocky, with a tremendous underbite. Now look at a greyhound. What do you notice? It's tall and slender, certainly a dog built for speed! The bulldog and the greyhound are different breeds of dogs, but all dogs are members of the same species. So how do you explain the obvious differences between them? For thousands of years, humans have carefully bred dogs for certain characteristics and with specific tasks in mind. In fact, humans have developed over a hundred different dog breeds!

A Dog's World

1. Pick a dog breed to research. Was there a specific job that the breed was supposed to perform? What special characteristics do dogs of the same breed share? How do these characteristics make the breed well-suited for its job? Does the breed have any problems associated with it? If so, can you think of a reason why the breed might be prone to these problems? How can these problems be corrected? Write a report explaining your findings. Be sure to include illustrations of the dog breed you researched.
2. Imagine you want to create a new dog breed. What job would you like the dog to do? What characteristics would you try to breed for? How would you breed for those traits? Create a display about your new dog breed. Be sure to include information about the dogs that your new breed derives from.

KEYWORDS

tephra
particles of material of various sizes ejected into the atmosphere by a volcanic eruption; the smallest particles (less than 2 mm) are called ash

Other Research Ideas

3. Research the controversy surrounding genetic testing in your library and on the Internet. Should the results of genetic testing be made available to insurance companies? Should insurance companies be able to cancel a person's insurance based on the results of genetics testing? Write a position paper and defend your answer.
4. Interview a genetic counselor. What kind of background must genetic counselors have for their job? How is genetic information compiled for clients? How does the person present the information to prospective parents? What are the most difficult aspects of being a genetic counselor? Based on your interview, write a job description that explains the role and responsibilities of a genetic counselor.

EARTH SCIENCE

DATASHEETS FOR LABBOOK

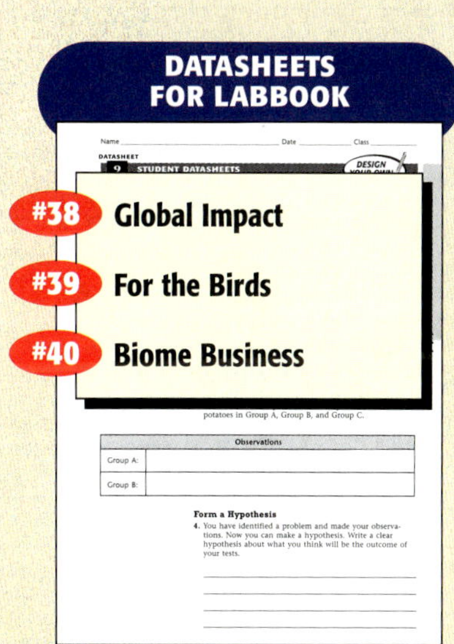
Name ______ Date ______ Class ______

DATASHEET 9 STUDENT DATASHEETS — DESIGN YOUR OWN

potatoes in Group A, Group B, and Group C.

Observations	
Group A:	
Group B:	

Form a Hypothesis

4. You have identified a problem and made your observations. Now you can make a hypothesis. Write a clear hypothesis about what you think will be the outcome of your tests.

#38 Global Impact

#39 For the Birds

#40 Biome Business

Applications & Extensions

CRITICAL THINKING & PROBLEM SOLVING

#17

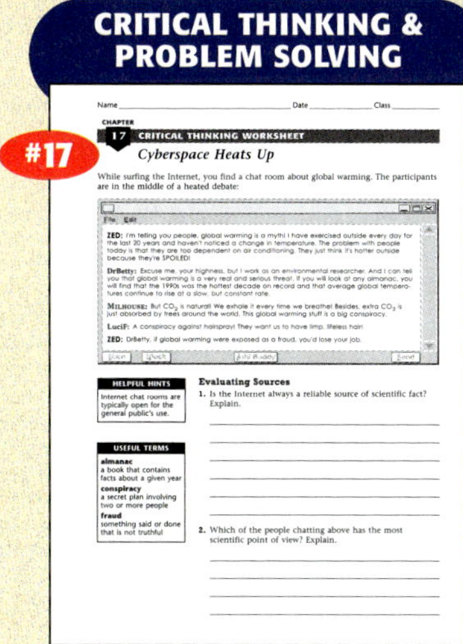
Name ______ Date ______ Class ______

CHAPTER 17 CRITICAL THINKING WORKSHEET

Cyberspace Heats Up

While surfing the Internet, you find a chat room about global warming. The participants are in the middle of a heated debate:

HELPFUL HINTS

Internet chat rooms are typically open for the general public's use.

USEFUL TERMS

almanac
a book that contains facts about a given year

conspiracy
a secret plan involving two or more people

fraud
something said or done that is not truthful

Evaluating Sources

1. Is the Internet always a reliable source of scientific fact? Explain.
2. Which of the people chatting above has the most scientific point of view? Explain.

EYE ON THE ENVIRONMENT

#27

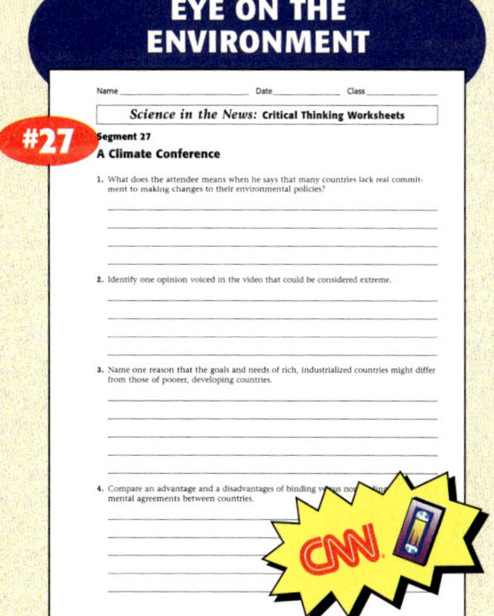
Name ______ Date ______ Class ______

Science in the News: Critical Thinking Worksheets

Segment 27

A Climate Conference

1. What does the attendee mean when he says that many countries lack real commitment to making changes to their environmental policies?
2. Identify one opinion voiced in the video that could be considered extreme.
3. Name one reason that the goals and needs of rich, industrialized countries might differ from those of poorer, developing countries.
4. Compare an advantage and a disadvantages of binding ... mental agreements between countries.

SCIENTISTS IN ACTION

#23

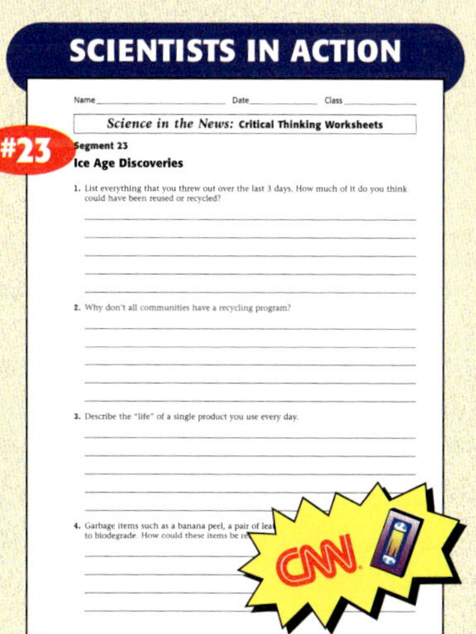
Name ______ Date ______ Class ______

Science in the News: Critical Thinking Worksheets

Segment 23

Ice Age Discoveries

1. List everything that you threw out over the last 3 days. How much of it do you think could have been reused or recycled?
2. Why don't all communities have a recycling program?
3. Describe the "life" of a single product you use every day.
4. Garbage items such as a banana peel, a pair of ... to biodegrade. How could these items be ...

Chapter Background

Section 1

What Is Climate?

Climatology

The study of climate can be traced back to Greek scientists of the sixth century B.C. In fact, the word *climate* comes from the Greek word *klíma,* meaning "an inclination," such as the angle of the sun's rays. Climatology can be divided into three branches—global climatology, regional climatology, and physical climatology. Global climatology investigates the general circulation of wind and water currents around Earth. Regional climatology studies the characteristic weather patterns and related phenomena of a particular region. Physical climatology analyzes statistics concerning climatic factors such as temperature, moisture, wind, and air pressure.

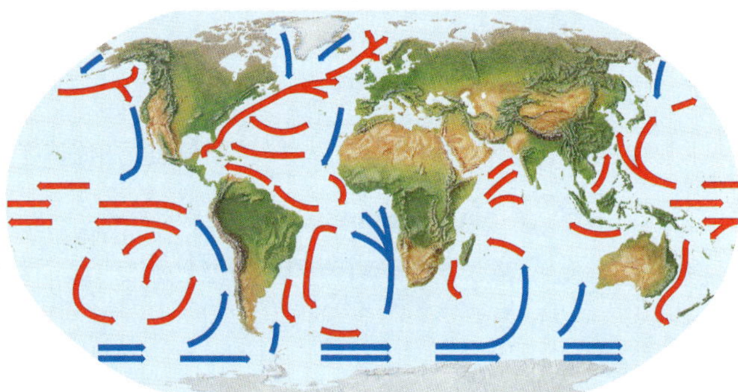

Global Winds

Global winds are patterns of air circulation that travel across the Earth. These winds include the trade winds, the prevailing westerlies, and the polar easterlies.

- In both hemispheres, the trade winds blow from 30° latitude to the equator. The Coriolis effect makes the trade winds curve to the right in the Northern Hemisphere, moving northeast to southwest. In the Southern Hemisphere, the trade winds curve to the left and move from southeast to northwest.

- The westerlies are found in both the Northern and Southern Hemispheres between 30° and 60° latitude. In the Northern Hemisphere, the westerlies blow from the southwest to the northeast. In the Southern Hemisphere, they blow from the northwest to the southeast.

- The polar easterlies extend from the poles to 60° latitude in both hemispheres. The polar easterlies blow from the northeast to the southwest in the Northern Hemisphere. In the Southern Hemisphere, these winds blow from the southeast to the northwest.

Section 2

Climates of the World

Climate Classification

Because climate is a complicated and somewhat abstract concept, more than 100 classification models have been devised, which vary according to the data on which the classifications are based. For instance, there have been attempts to classify climates according to factors such as soil formation, rock weathering, and even effects on human comfort!

Polar
66.5°N
Temperate
23.5°N
Tropical
0°
Tropical
23.5°S
Temperate
66.5°S
Polar

- In 1966, Werner Terjung, an American geographer, developed a physiological climate classification. This system categorized climates according to their effects on people's comfort levels. The system focused on four factors that might affect human comfort—temperature, relative humidity, wind speed, and solar radiation.

The Köppen System

The most widely used climate classification system is the Köppen system. This system, named for Wladimir Köppen, the German botanist and climatologist who developed it, uses vegetation regions and average weather statistics to classify local climates. Each vegetation region is characterized by the natural vegetation that is predominant there. Critics have found fault with the Köppen system because it considers only average monthly temperatures and precipitation, ignoring other factors, such as winds, cloud cover, and daily temperature extremes.

Section 3

Changes in Climate

Pangaea

In 1620, the British philosopher Francis Bacon noted that Africa and South America looked as if they could fit together like puzzle pieces. But it was not until the early twentieth century that the German meteorologist Alfred Wegener proposed a theory that all the continents were once one landmass. Wegener's hypothesis was supported by the existence of similar plant and animal fossils on different continents. Although his theory was initially ridiculed, Wegener was vindicated after World War II when sea-floor spreading and a mechanism for continental drift were discovered.

Is That a Fact!

- Pangaea, the name Wegener gave to the supercontinent, is Greek for "all lands."

The Greenhouse Effect

Gases such as carbon dioxide, methane, and chlorofluorocarbons (CFCs) are known as greenhouse gases because they "trap" heat in Earth's atmosphere by absorbing infrared radiation that would otherwise be emitted into space. Normal amounts of greenhouse gases, with the exception of CFCs (which are artificial chemicals), are necessary for life on Earth because they keep Earth's average temperature at 15°C. Without them, Earth would be frozen; the average temperature would be about −18°C.

- CFCs are manufactured chemicals that contain chlorine, fluorine, and carbon. Before 1978, when the United States banned the use of CFCs, they were widely used as propellants in aerosol cans. They are also a component of plastic foam and of a coolant used in air conditioners. CFCs are extremely potent; one molecule of a CFC can absorb about 10,000 times more heat than a molecule of carbon dioxide.
- There is much less methane in the air than carbon dioxide. However, per molecule, methane absorbs 20 times more infrared radiation than carbon dioxide, and its concentration in the atmosphere is increasing. Methane is a natural product of animal digestion. A significant amount of the methane released into the atmosphere is produced by livestock. Methane is also produced as microorganisms decompose organic material.

Is That a Fact!

- In 1958, a geochemist named Charles Keeling climbed to the top of Mauna Loa, in Hawaii, to install a device to measure CO_2 levels in our atmosphere. Since that time, CO_2 levels in our atmosphere have risen more that 12 percent.

*For additional background resources, please refer to the **HST Reference Library**.*

CHAPTER 17

Climate

Chapter Preview

Directed Reading Worksheet 17

Science Puzzlers, Twisters & Teasers Worksheet 17

Guided Reading Audio CD
English or Spanish, Chapter 17

CHAPTER 17 Climate

What If . . . ?

The brochure boasts of the most adventurous summer camp in the world. You can't wait to lace up your hiking boots and head for the outdoors. But before you fly halfway around the world, you check the recommended supply list: light summer clothes, sunscreen, rain gear, heavy down-filled jacket, ski mask, and thick gloves. Wait a minute! You are traveling to only one destination, so why are you required to bring such a wide variety of clothes? On further investigation, you learn that your outdoor adventure advertises the opportunity to "climb the climates of the world in just three days."

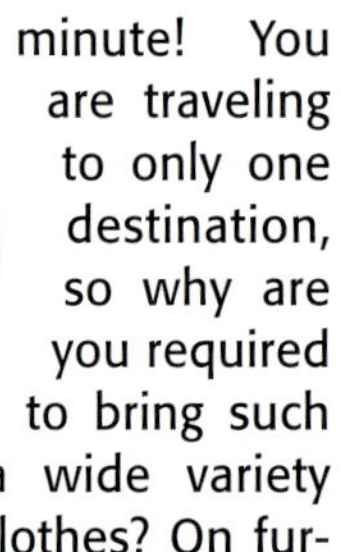

Your destination is Africa's tallest mountain, Kilimanjaro, which is 5,895 m above sea level. But you can leave your heavy climbing gear at home because the summit is a slight 51.2 km slope that can be reached without the aid of special equipment.

The trek starts at 2,700 m above sea level, where you spend the first day hiking through a hot, sweltering rain forest. Day two finds you treading through a grassy meadow that slopes up the side of the first peak, called Mawensii. On the third day, you start to get cold. The frozen ground crunches under your feet. Within 2 hours your feet feel like blocks of ice, and breathing is difficult. You finally reach the summit just as the clouds part, revealing steam rising off the rain forest 3,000 m below. Maybe the trip was worth the effort after all!

Climate changes as elevation increases, just as it changes from the equator to the poles. In this chapter you will learn what factors affect climate, how climate is influenced by human and natural activity, and what type of environment is found in which climate.

What If . . . ?

Kilimanjaro is 3° south of the equator. In 1848, when European missionaries reported that Kilimanjaro was a snow-capped peak, people didn't believe them. As altitude increases, temperature drops—on average, about 0.7°C per 100 m. Temperatures are cold enough at Kilimanjaro's highest peak, Kibo, to maintain a permanent icecap on the mountain.

IS THAT A FACT!

The name Kilimanjaro comes from the Swahili name for the mountain, *Kilima Njaro,* which means "shining mountain."

What Do You Think?

In your ScienceLog, try to answer the following questions based on what you already know:

1. What is the difference between weather and climate?
2. List ways in which human influences such as pollution and technology can affect climate.

What's Your Angle?

Because the Earth is round, the sun's solar rays strike the Earth's surface at different angles. Therefore, different amounts of solar energy reach the Earth's surface at different places. The area around the equator receives the direct rays of the sun. The energy is more concentrated because it is spread over a smaller area. This results in high temperatures. At the poles, the sun's rays strike the surface at a lower angle. The energy is therefore less concentrated, resulting in low temperatures. Try this simple experiment to find out how the amount of solar energy received at the equator differs from the amount received at the poles.

Procedure 

1. Plug in a **lamp**, and position it 30 cm from a **globe.**
2. Point the lamp so that the light shines directly on the globe's equator, as shown in the diagram.
3. Using **adhesive putty,** attach one **thermometer** to the globe's equator and another **thermometer** to the globe's north pole.
4. Record the temperature reading of each thermometer in your ScienceLog.
5. Turn on the lamp, and let the light shine on the globe for 3 minutes.
6. When the time is up, turn off the lamp, and record the temperature reading of each thermometer again in your ScienceLog.

Analysis

7. Was there a difference between the starting temperatures and the final temperatures? Explain your results.
8. Was there a difference between the final temperature at the globe's north pole and that at the globe's equator? If so, what was it?
9. How does this experiment relate to solar radiation striking the Earth?
10. Based on the experiment, what temperature changes would you expect if you traveled from the equator to the polar regions?

What Do You Think?

Accept all reasonable responses.

Students will have a chance to revise their answers in the Chapter Review under NOW What Do You Think?

Investigate!

MATERIALS
For Each Group:
• lamp
• globe
• adhesive putty
• 2 thermometers

Safety Caution: Remind students to review all safety cautions and icons before beginning this lab activity. Students should not touch the lamp's bulb while it is on or immediately after it has been turned off.

Teacher Notes: If you have time, encourage students to repeat the experiment, positioning one thermometer at the equator and one at the South Pole. Have them compare their results.

Answers to Investigate!

7. Yes; the starting temperatures were cooler than the final temperatures. This was because the light bulb served as a source of heat, warming the thermometers and the surface to which they were taped.
8. The final temperature at the globe's North Pole was cooler than the final temperature at the globe's equator. This is because the globe's equator received more direct heat from the light bulb than the globe's North Pole received.
9. In this experiment, the light bulb represents the sun. As with the globe, the equator on the Earth's surface receives more direct energy than the North Pole or South Pole.
10. You would expect that the temperatures would cool as you moved away from the equator toward the poles.

Chapter 17 Opener–California Standards: PE/ATE 4, 4b, 7, 7b, 7e

SECTION 1

Focus

What Is Climate?

In this section, students learn the difference between weather and climate. They examine how latitude, prevailing winds, geography, and ocean currents affect an area's climate.

Bellringer

Have students imagine they have entered a contest for a free trip to a place with a perfect climate. To win, they need to describe in 25 words or less their idea of a perfect climate. Sheltered English

1) Motivate

DISCUSSION

Tell students that in the early 1900s, a geographer named Ellsworth Huntington conducted research to see if he could determine the ideal climate for human beings—the type of climate that would result in optimal physical and mental well-being. He concluded that a climate with considerable daily and seasonal weather changes and an average temperature of 18°C was ideal. Ask students whether they agree or disagree with Huntington and why.

Directed Reading Worksheet 17 Section 1

1

NEW TERMS

weather
climate
latitude
prevailing winds
elevation
surface currents

OBJECTIVES

- Explain the difference between weather and climate.
- Identify the factors that determine climates.

What Is Climate?

You have just received a call from a friend who is coming to visit you tomorrow. He is wondering what clothing to bring and wants to know about the current weather in your area. You step outside, check to see if there are rain clouds in the sky, and note the temperature. But what if your friend asked you about the climate in your area? What is the difference between weather and climate?

The best way to distinguish between weather and climate is to think in terms of time. **Weather** is the condition of the atmosphere at a particular time and place. A typical weather report might read, "Today will be hot and humid, with a 20 percent chance of rain." Weather conditions vary from day to day. **Climate,** on the other hand, is the average weather conditions in a certain area over a long period of time. Climate is determined by two main factors, temperature and precipitation. Study the world map in **Figure 1,** and see if you can describe the climate in northern Africa.

Figure 1 *How does the climate in northern Africa differ from the climate where you live?*

454

Multicultural CONNECTION

Weather and climate have inspired a great number of rhymes, greetings, sayings, and other folklore. For example, in the hot, wet climate of Venezuela, indigenous people sometimes greet each other by saying, "How have the mosquitoes used you?" Russia's cold climate inspired the saying, "There's no bad weather, only bad clothing." Invite students to interview friends and relatives or research weather and climate folklore in another country. Have them share their findings with the class.

Section 1–California Standards: PE/ATE 4, 4b, 4d, 4e, 7, 7b, 7e, 7f

As you can see in **Figure 2,** if you were to take a trip around the world, or even across the United States, you would experience different climates. For example, if you visited the Texas coast in the summer, you would find it hot and humid. But if you visited interior Alaska during the summer, it would probably be much cooler and less humid. Why are the climates so different? The answer is complicated. It includes factors such as latitude, wind patterns, geography, and ocean currents.

Figure 2 *Summer in Texas is very different from summer in Alaska.*

Latitude

Think of the last time you looked at a globe. Do you recall the thin horizontal lines that circle the globe? These horizontal lines are called lines of latitude. **Latitude** is the distance north or south, measured in degrees, from the equator. In general, the temperature of an area depends on its latitude. The higher the latitude is, the colder the climate is. For example, the two coldest places on Earth, the North Pole and the South Pole, are at 90° north and south of the equator, respectively. On the other hand, the equator, which has a latitude of 0°, is hot.

Why are there such temperature differences at different latitudes? The answer has to do with solar energy. Solar energy heats the Earth. Latitude determines the amount of solar energy a particular area receives. You can see how this works in **Figure 3.** Notice that the sun's rays hit the area around the equator directly, at nearly a 90° angle. At this angle, a small area of the Earth's surface receives more direct solar energy, resulting in high temperatures. Near the poles, however, the sun's rays strike the surface at a lesser angle than at the equator. This lesser angle spreads the same amount of solar energy over a larger area, resulting in lower temperatures.

Figure 3 *The sun's rays strike the Earth's surface at different angles because the surface is curved.*

455

2 Teach

CONNECT TO GEOGRAPHY

Monsoons are recurrent global weather patterns that dramatically affect the populations, economies, and environment of South Asia. The wet summer monsoon usually begins mid-June, when temperatures rise sharply in Asia's interior, causing the air above the land to warm and rise. This creates a low pressure area that draws warm, moist air inland from the Indian and Pacific oceans. This moisture-laden air cools as it moves across the continent, and heavy rains, thunderstorms, and flooding occur. The heaviest rains occur where this air mass meets the foothills of the Himalayas. During a winter monsoon, the interior of Asia cools rapidly. This cool, dense air creates an immense high pressure center, forcing cool, dry air to flow outward toward the oceans. As the air mass travels, it warms and becomes even drier. This results in warm, dry winters. Encourage students to find out more about the effect of monsoons on the environment, economy, and people of South Asia.

MATH and MORE

Each degree or line of latitude is approximately 111 km, and there are 180 lines of latitude circling the Earth. Have students calculate the circumference of the Earth at the poles. (111 km/line × 180 = 19,980) Then multiply by 2, because the Earth is a sphere. (39,960 km)

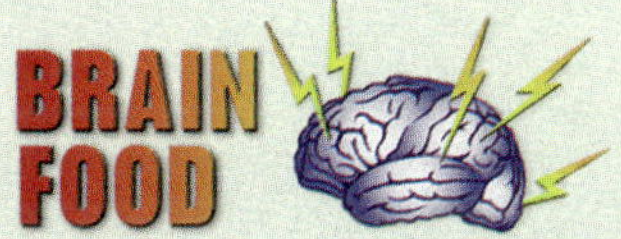

Show students a world map. Ask them to name a location where they have lived or visited or where friends or relatives live. Write the locations and their latitudinal positions on the board. Ask students to help you list some observations about the climate in each area.

TOPIC: What Is Climate?
GO TO: www.scilinks.org
***sci*LINKS NUMBER:** HSTE405

2 Teach, *continued*

COOPERATIVE LEARNING

Ask two volunteers to act as the Earth and the sun. Give the "sun" a flashlight and the "Earth" a globe with a half-meridian mounting. Turn off the lights, and have the volunteers sit on the floor. Ask the "sun" to shine the flashlight on the globe, and ask the "Earth" to slowly spin the globe. Have the class notice which parts of the globe are most exposed to the light. Next, have the "Earth" make a complete revolution slowly around the "sun" while at the same time rotating the globe. Make sure that the volunteer always keeps the axis of the globe oriented in the same direction. Stop the "Earth" at each season so students can observe the flashlight's rays on the two hemispheres. If necessary, repeat this activity with other volunteers. Sheltered English

MISCONCEPTION ALERT

Some students may equate the seasons with certain times of the year. Remind them that summer in the Northern Hemisphere is winter in the Southern Hemisphere.

Answer to Self-Check

Australia has summer during our winter months, December–February.

Teaching Transparency 151
"Seasons, Latitude, and the Tilt of the Earth"

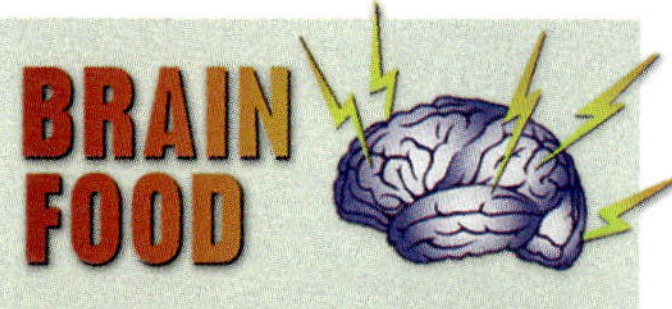

The polar regions receive almost 24 hours of daylight each day in the summer and almost 24 hours of darkness each day in the winter.

Seasons and Latitude In most places in the United States, the year consists of four seasons. Winter is probably cooler than summer where you live. But there are places in the world that do not have such seasonal changes. For example, areas near the equator have approximately the same temperatures and same amount of daylight year-round. **Figure 4** shows how latitude determines the seasons.

Figure 4 *The Earth is tilted on its axis at a 23.5° angle. This tilt affects how much solar energy an area receives as the Earth moves around the sun.*

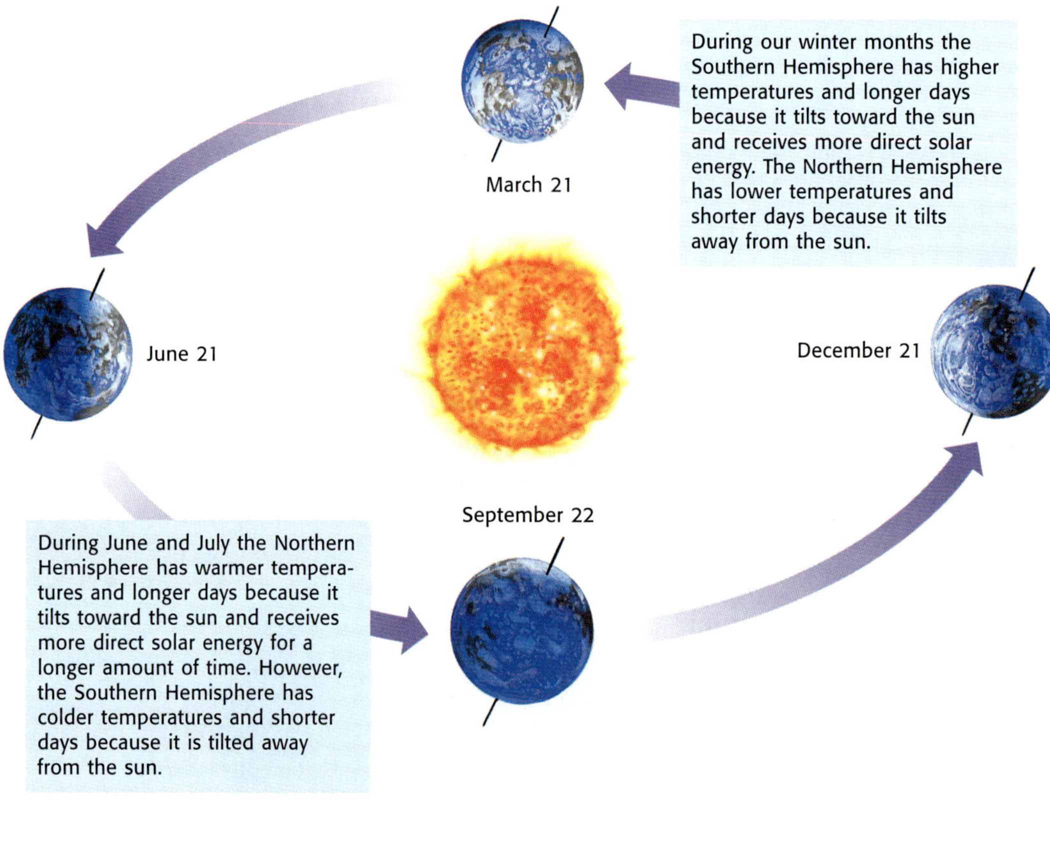

Self-Check

During what months does Australia have summer? (See page 564 to check your answer.)

456

IS THAT A FACT!

Tutunendo, Colombia, is the rainiest place in the world. It averages almost 12 m of rain per year. Cherrapunji, India, received more than 9 m of rain in 1 month. It is the most rainfall ever recorded in a month. The hottest day ever recorded occurred in Libya, where it reached 58°C (136°F) in 1922. Antarctica holds the record as the coldest place on Earth, with temperatures reaching –89°C (–128°F).

Prevailing Winds

Prevailing winds are winds that blow mainly from one direction. These winds influence an area's moisture and temperature. Before you learn how the prevailing winds affect climate, take a look at **Figure 5** to learn about some of the basic properties of air.

Figure 5 *Because warm air is less dense, it tends to rise. Cooler, denser air tends to sink.*

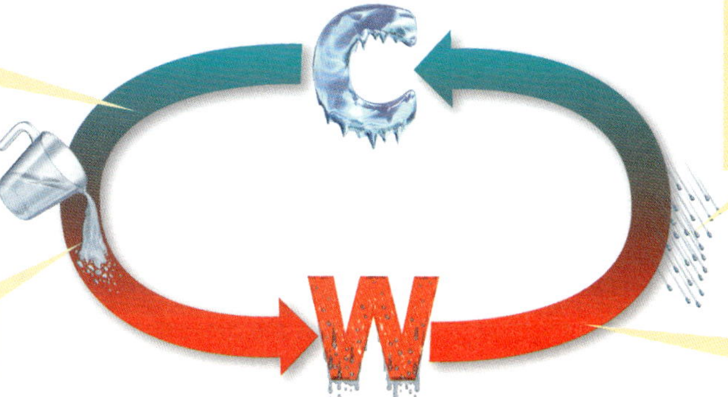

Prevailing winds affect the amount of precipitation that a region receives. If the prevailing winds form from warm air, they will carry moisture. If the prevailing winds form from cold air, they will probably be dry. Precipitation is more likely to occur when the prevailing winds are warm and moist.

The amount of moisture in prevailing winds is also affected by whether the winds blow across land or across a large body of water. Winds that travel across large bodies of water, such as the ocean, absorb moisture. Winds that travel across land tend to be dry. Even if a region borders the ocean, the area might be dry if the prevailing winds blow across the land, as shown in **Figure 6.**

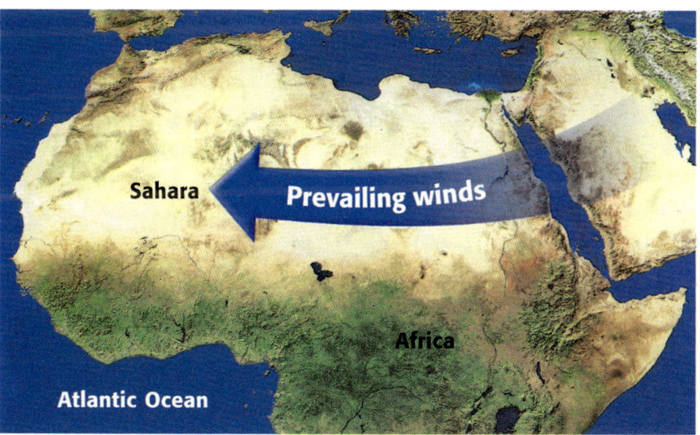

Figure 6 *The Sahara Desert, in northern Africa, is extremely dry because the prevailing winds blow across the continent from east to west and is formed from cold, sinking air.*

QuickLab

A Cool Breeze

1. Hold a **thermometer** next to the top edge of a **cup of water** containing **two ice cubes.** Read the temperature next to the cup.
2. Have your lab partner fan the surface of the cup with a **paper fan.** Read the temperature again. Has the temperature changed? Why? Record your answer in your ScienceLog.

QuickLab

MATERIALS

For Each Pair of Students:
- thermometer
- cup of water
- 2 ice cubes
- paper fan

Answers to QuickLab

2. The temperature dropped after someone fanned the surface of the cup. This is because the fanned air traveling across the cup's surface picked up cold air from the ice, thereby changing the air temperature (wind-chill).

Homework

Using Maps Have students look at a map and find five cities at about the same latitude in a single continent. They should research the annual rainfall for each city and the direction of the prevailing winds. Students can create a bar graph showing the differences in rainfall for each city and attempt to explain the patterns they notice by identifying physical features on the map. If their data contradicts what they have learned in this section, ask them to suggest explanations.

Teaching Transparency 152
"Basic Properties of Air"

Multicultural CONNECTION

Charles Edward Anderson was the first African American to receive a Ph.D. in meteorology. Anderson began his career in meteorology during World War II. He was a captain in the Air Force and served as a weather officer for the Tuskegee Airmen Regiment. He earned his Ph.D. in 1960 from the Massachusetts Institute of Technology. His work focused on cloud physics, the forecasting of severe storms, and weather on other planets.

3 Extend

Answers to Explore

Mountain ranges: the Sierra Nevada, Rocky Mountains, Appalachians. The Sierra Nevada exhibits the biggest variance from one side of the mountain to the other; there is green vegetation on one side and a desert on the other. The prevailing wind is blowing from the west.

USING THE FIGURE

Remind students that winds traveling across large bodies of water, such as the ocean, absorb moisture. Have students study **Figure 7**, and then ask them to consider which side of the mountain is likely to be closer to a large body of water. (the left side) Sheltered English

GOING FURTHER

Have students find out which prevailing winds affect climate in the United States and in which direction they blow. Students can compile their findings in a short report that explains how a particular prevailing wind influences climate in a region.

Teaching Transparency 153
"An Example of the Rain Shadow Effect"

Explore

Using a topographical map, locate the mountain ranges in the United States. Does climate vary from one side of a mountain range to the other? If so, what does this tell you about the climatic conditions on either side of the mountain? From what direction are the prevailing winds blowing?

Geography

Mountains can influence an area's climate by affecting both temperature and precipitation. For example, Kilimanjaro, the tallest mountain in Africa, has snow-covered peaks year-round, even though it is only about 3° (320 km) south of the equator. Temperatures on Kilimanjaro and in other mountainous areas are affected by elevation. **Elevation** is the height of surface landforms above sea level. As the elevation increases, the atmosphere becomes less dense. As the atmosphere becomes less dense, its ability to absorb and hold heat is reduced and the temperature decreases.

Mountains also affect the climate of nearby areas by influencing the distribution of precipitation. **Figure 7** shows how the climates on two sides of a mountain can be very different.

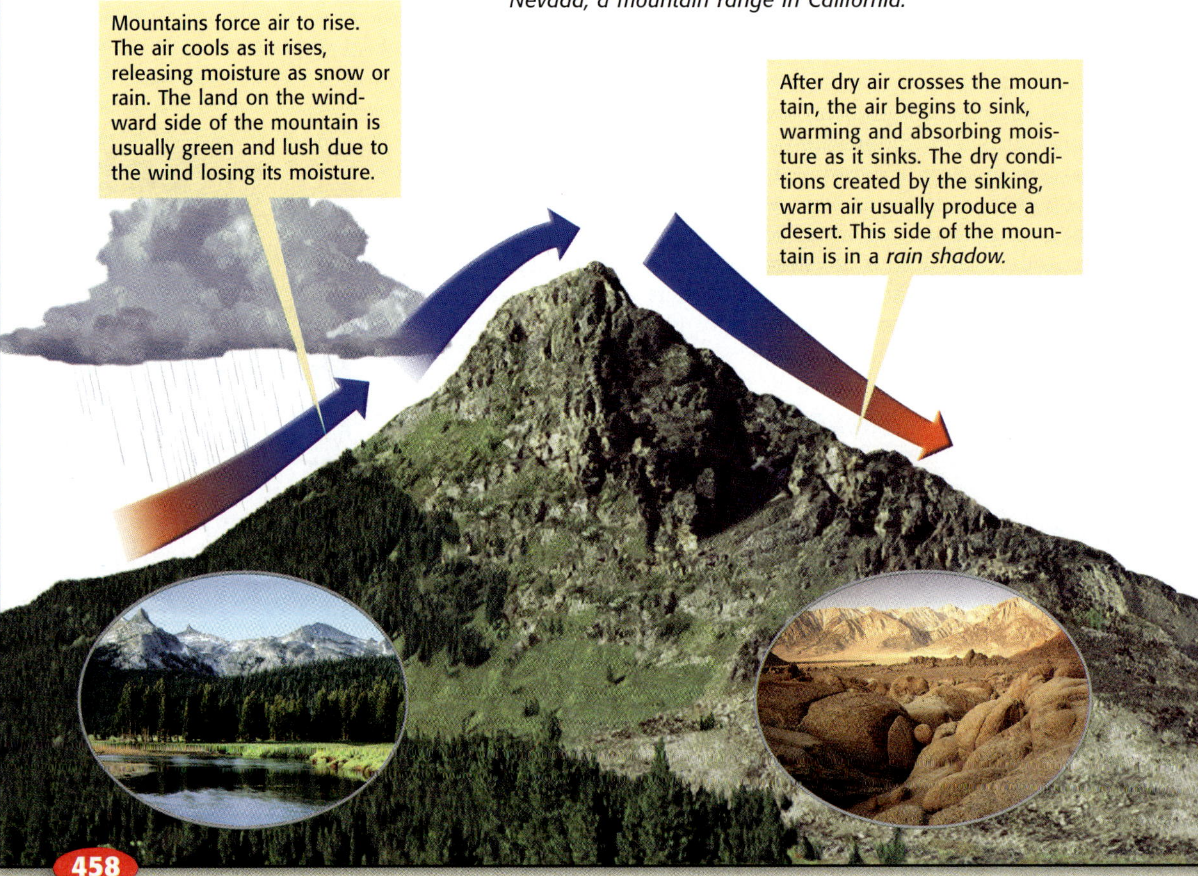

Figure 7 *As the prevailing winds blow across a continent, mountains act as barriers, forcing changes in the condition of the wind. The inset photos show both sides of the Sierra Nevada, a mountain range in California.*

458

SCIENCE HUMOR

Western and eastern Oregon have very different climates because the Cascade Mountains divide the state. Oregonians living east of the Cascades complain, "It's so dry, the jackrabbits carry canteens." West of the Cascades, people say, "It's so wet, folks don't tan, they rust!"

IS THAT A FACT!

Large lakes, such as the Great Lakes, in the United States and Canada, and Lake Victoria, in east-central Africa, also affect climate. The lake effect helps keep the surrounding land cooler in the summer and warmer in the winter.

Ocean Currents

Because of water's ability to absorb and release heat, the circulation of ocean surface currents has an enormous effect on an area's climate. **Surface currents,** which can be either warm or cold, are streamlike movements of water that occur at or near the surface of the ocean. **Figure 8** shows the pattern of the major warm and cold ocean currents.

The movement of surface currents is affected by three factors—wind, the Earth's rotation, and the location of continents. As surface currents move, they carry warm or cool water to different locations. The surface temperature of the water affects the temperature of the air above it. Warm currents heat the surrounding air and cause warmer temperatures, while cool currents cool the surrounding air and cause cooler temperatures. For example, the Gulf Stream current carries warm water northward off the east coast of North America past Iceland, an island country located just below the Arctic Circle. The warm water from the Gulf Stream heats the surrounding air, creating warmer temperatures in southern Iceland. Temperatures in Iceland are milder than in its neighboring country, Greenland, where the climate is not influenced by the Gulf Stream.

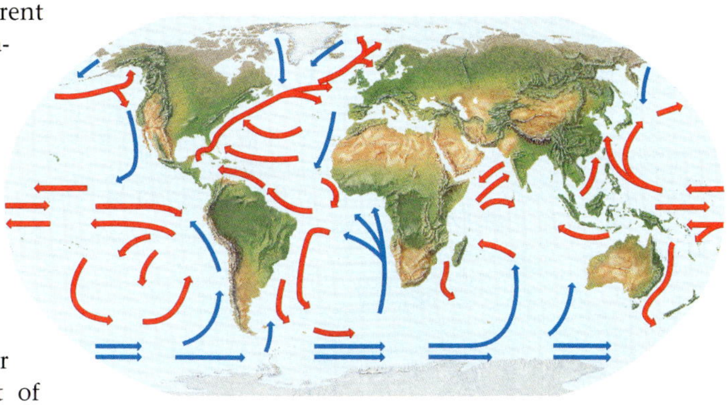

Figure 8 *The red arrows represent the movement of warm ocean currents. The blue arrows represent the movement of cold ocean currents.*

REVIEW

1. What is the difference between weather and climate?
2. How do mountains affect climate?
3. Describe how air temperature is affected by ocean currents.
4. **Analyzing Relationships** How would seasons be different if the Earth did not tilt on its axis?

What is El Niño? Can it affect our health? Turn to page 478 to find out.

4 Close

Quiz

1. Why are the poles colder than the equator? (At the poles, the sun's rays strike the Earth's surface at a lesser angle than at the equator; the same amount of solar energy is spread over a larger area.)
2. Is precipitation more likely to occur when the prevailing winds are formed from warm air or when they are formed from cold air? (warm air)

Alternative Assessment

Climate Game Organize students into several teams to play a simulated popular game show. Have one team act as the game-show host and think of statements that reinforce section concepts, such as, "This determines how much solar energy an area receives." Have the other teams compete to formulate questions that the statements answer. Remind the "contestants" that they must phrase their answers in the form of a question. In the example above, the question could be "What is the Earth's tilt?"

Answers to Review

1. Weather is the condition of the atmosphere at a particular time and place. Climate is the average weather conditions in a certain area over a long period of time.
2. Mountains can influence an area's temperature and precipitation. Temperature is affected by elevation. The windward side of a mountain receives much more precipitation than the rain-shadow side.
3. The surface temperature of water affects the temperature of the air above it. As the surface currents move, they carry warm or cool water to different locations. This heats or cools the surrounding air.
4. If the Earth did not tilt on its axis, there would be no seasons. The same amount of solar radiation would reach the Earth year-round.

Section 1 Review–California Standards: PE/ATE 4, 4a, 4d

SECTION 2

Focus

Climates of the World

In this section, students learn the location and the characteristics of the three major climate zones and the different types of biomes that are found in each zone.

Bellringer

Ask students to describe in their Sciencelog differences between the plant life where they live and the plant life in an area they have visited. Ask students to think about how climate influences the vegetation in these areas. Sheltered English

1) Motivate

ACTIVITY

Have each student choose a country to focus on for this section. Students should record the area's latitude and geographic characteristics in their ScienceLog. Tell students to imagine they are on a fact-finding mission concerning the area's climate, the people that live there, and the plant and animal life of the region. Have them record evidence about the area's climate as they read the section.

Teaching Transparency 154
"Climate Zones of the Earth"
"The Earth's Land Biomes"

Directed Reading Worksheet 17 Section 2

2 Climates of the World

NEW TERMS

biome
tropical zone
temperate zone
deciduous
evergreens
polar zone
microclimates

OBJECTIVES

- Locate and describe the three major climate zones.
- Describe the different biomes found in each climate zone.

Have you ever wondered why the types of plants and animals in one part of the world are different from those found in another part? One reason involves climate. Plants and animals that have adapted to one climate may not be able to live in another climate. For instance, frogs do not live in Antarctica. **Figure 9** illustrates the three major climate zones of Earth—tropical, temperate, and polar. Each zone has a temperature range that relates to its latitude. However, in each of these zones there are several types of climates due to differences in the geography and the amount of precipitation. Because of the various climates in each zone, there are different biomes. A **biome** is a large region characterized by a specific type of climate and the plants and animals that live there. **Figure 10** shows the distribution of the Earth's land biomes. In this section we will review each of the three major climate zones and the biomes that are found in each zone.

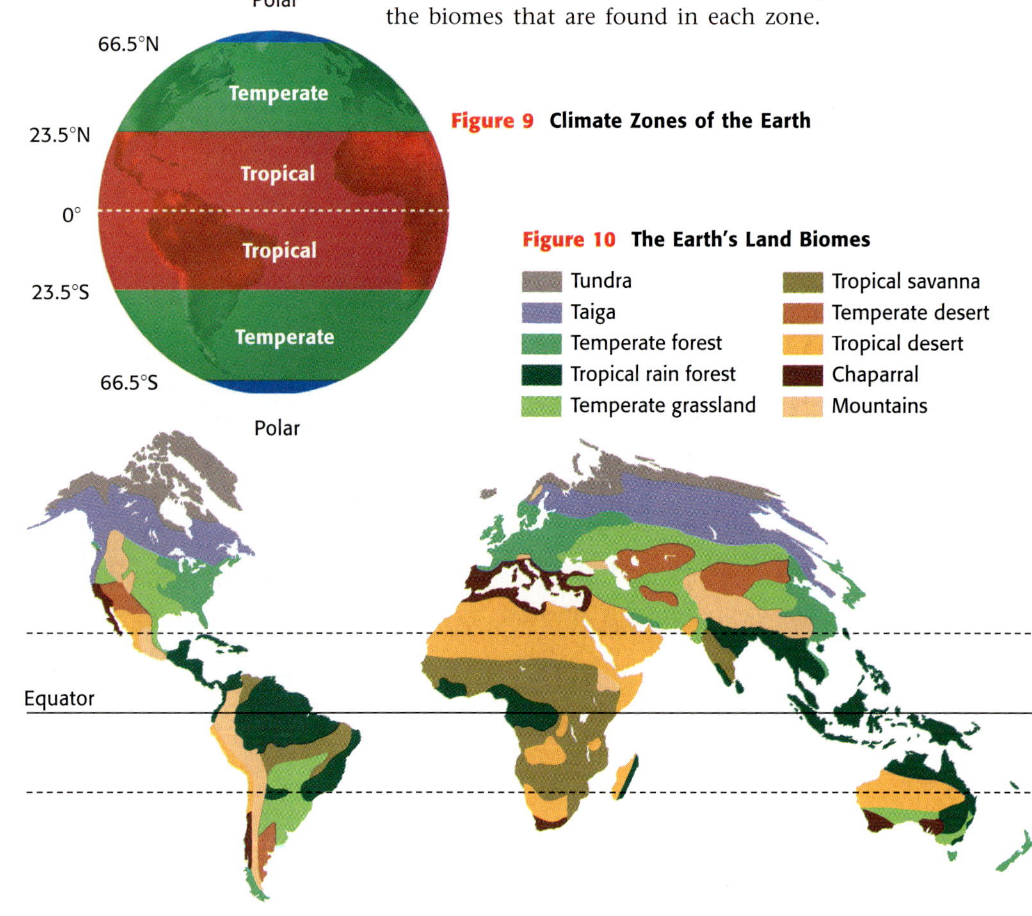

Figure 9 Climate Zones of the Earth

Figure 10 The Earth's Land Biomes

WEIRD SCIENCE

In addition to having land biomes, Earth also has marine biomes. It is impossible to distinguish biomes in the oceans by latitude, however. Marine biomes are determined by water depth. Some of the animals that inhabit the deeper biomes have very interesting adaptations. For example, the anglerfish, which lives in total darkness, has a clever hunting strategy: a luminescent "lure" trails from the fish's jaw and attracts prey within reach of its enormous, sharp teeth.

Section 2–California Standards: PE/ATE 4, 4b, 4e, 5, 5b, 5d, 5e, 7c; LabBook: 7, 7a, 7b, 7d, 7e, 7h

The Tropical Zone

The **tropical zone,** or the *Tropics,* is the warm zone located around the equator, as shown in **Figure 11.** This zone extends from the tropic of Cancer to the tropic of Capricorn. As you have learned, latitudes in this zone receive the most solar radiation. Temperatures are therefore usually hot, except at high elevations. Within the tropical zone there are three types of biomes—tropical rain forest, tropical desert, and tropical savanna. **Figure 12** shows the distribution of these biomes.

Figure 11 The Earth's Tropical Zone

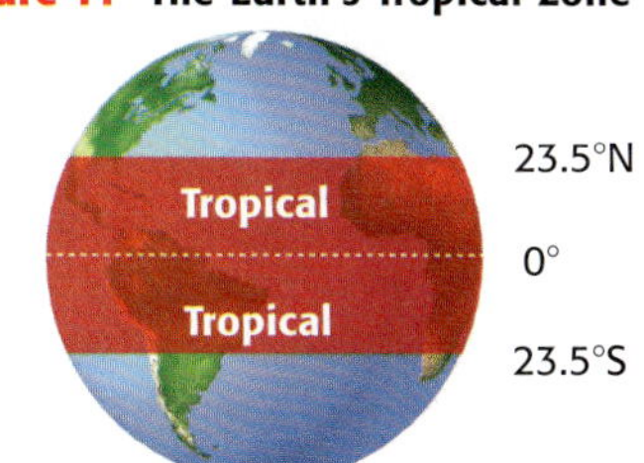

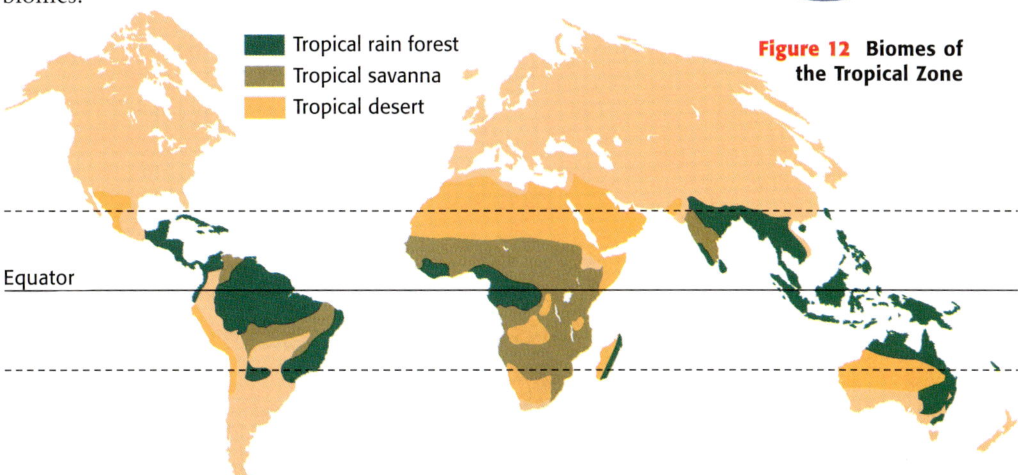

Figure 12 Biomes of the Tropical Zone

Tropical Rain Forest Tropical rain forests are always warm and wet. Because they are located near the equator, they receive strong sunlight year-round, causing little difference between seasons. Tropical rain forests contain the greatest number of plant and animal species of any biome. But in spite of the lush vegetation, shown in **Figure 13,** the soil in rain forests is poor. The rapid decay of plants and animals returns nutrients to the soil, but these nutrients are quickly absorbed and used by the plants. The nutrients that are not immediately used by the plants are washed away by the heavy rains, leaving soil that is thin and nutrient poor.

Figure 13 *In tropical rain forests, many of the trees form aboveground roots that grow horizontally from the trees to provide extra support for the trees in the thin soil.*

Avg. Temperature Range: 25°C–28°C (77°F–82°F)
Avg. Yearly Precipitation: 200 cm or more
Soil Characteristics: thin and nutrient poor
Vegetation: mahogany, ebony, rosewood, and balsa trees; vines, ferns, and bamboo
Animals: monkeys, lemurs, parrots, snakes, tree frogs, bats, pigs, small antelopes, tigers, jaguars, and leopards

461

2 Teach

READING STRATEGY

Prediction Guide Have students consider the following statements:

- Some deserts are cold. (true)
- The polar zone has below-freezing temperatures year-round. (false)

MATH and MORE

Rain forests actually "recycle" much of their rain. In the Amazon rain forest about three-quarters of all rainfall comes from the evaporation of water and the process of *transpiration* (the release of water vapor through leaf pores, or stoma). Use Transparency 51 to discuss this process. How much rain is "recycled" if an Amazon rain forest gets 650 cm of rain annually? (488 cm)

Teaching Transparency 51 "Transpiration"

LINK TO LIFE SCIENCE

CONNECT TO ENVIRONMENTAL SCIENCE

As much as 130,000 km² of tropical rain forest is currently being deforested each year. At this rate the tropical rain forests will be gone in 30 years. Much of the rain forest is being converted to grassland for grazing or is being logged. The loss of the forest has a great influence on local and global climates.

Math Skills Worksheet 37 "Rain-Forest Math"

MISCONCEPTION ALERT

It's not a jungle out there. The popular image of a tropical rain forest is of dense jungle undergrowth, but this occurs only along rivers or places that humans have cleared. Students may also confuse rain forests with forests in monsoon-climate regions. While rain forests have a fairly steady rate of precipitation, monsoon forests have a rainy season and a dry season. Rainfall during the rainy season may be measured in meters. During the dry season, the monsoon forest may receive little or no rainfall for many months. In fact, many monsoon-forest plants have some of the same adaptations for dry conditions that desert plants have.

2 Teach, *continued*

REAL-WORLD CONNECTION

Deserts are expanding at an accelerating rate. In the last 100 years, the estimated area of land occupied by deserts rose from 9.4 percent to 23.3 percent. Many factors have contributed to this, including climatic shifts, overgrazing, and overuse of the land through inefficient agricultural practices.

COOPERATIVE LEARNING

Many people believe that conditions in the desert biomes are so extreme that they are nearly devoid of life. In fact, there are many different kinds of deserts that can support thriving ecological communities. Have students choose a tropical or temperate desert and create a poster display to teach the class about its location, the organisms that inhabit the desert, and other facts about the desert. Students could study the Gobi Desert, the Sahara Desert, the Great Sandy Desert, the Sonoran Desert, the Patagonian Desert, the Namib Desert, or another desert of their choice.

Homework

Research Draw students' attention to an important distinction between the vegetation in Old World and New World tropical deserts. Cactus is a succulent found in the New World. Euphorbia is a succulent found in the Old World. Have students find photographs of these types of plants and share them with the class.

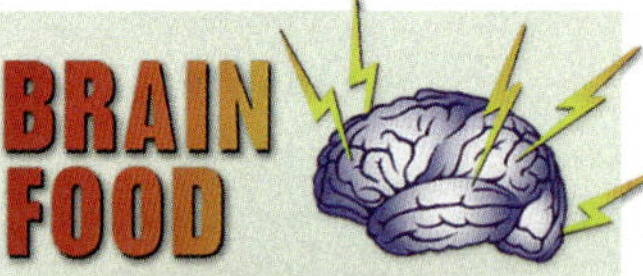

Most desert rodents, such as the kangaroo rat, hide in burrows during the day and are active at night, when the temperatures are cooler.

Tropical Deserts A desert is an area that receives less than 25 cm of rainfall per year. Because of this low yearly rainfall, deserts are the driest places on Earth. A typical desert, shown in **Figure 14,** has large areas of barren rock and soil and contains very little vegetation. Deserts can be divided into hot deserts and cold deserts. The majority of hot deserts, such as the Sahara, in Africa, are tropical deserts. Hot deserts are caused by cool sinking air masses. Daily temperatures in tropical deserts vary from very hot daytime temperatures (50°C) to cool nighttime temperatures (20°C). Winters in hot deserts are usually mild. Because of the dryness, the soil is poor in organic matter, which fertilizes the soil. The dryness makes it hard to break down dead organic matter.

Avg. Temperature Range: 16°C–50°C (61°F–120°F)
Avg. Yearly Precipitation: 0–25 cm
Soil Characteristics: poor in organic matter
Vegetation: succulents (cactus and euphorbia), shrubs, thorny trees
Animals: kangaroo rats, lizards, scorpions, snakes, birds, bats, toads

Some desert animals, such as the spadefoot toad, survive the scorching summer heat by burying themselves in the ground and sleeping through the dry season.

Figure 14 *Plants called succulents have adapted to dry conditions by developing fleshy stems and leaves to store water and a waxy coating to prevent water loss. A cactus is a type of succulent.*

Self-Check

If desert soil is so nutrient rich, why are deserts not suitable for agriculture? *(See page 564 to check your answer.)*

Answer to Self-Check

Because of the dryness, desert soil is poor in organic matter, which fertilizes the soil. Without this natural fertilizer, crops would not be able to grow.

IS THAT A FACT!

The world's largest desert, the Sahara, covers more than 9 million square kilometers—about the size of the United States. In contrast, the largest desert in the United States, is the Mojave Desert. It covers 38,900 km^2, nearly twice the size of New Jersey.

Tropical Savannas Tropical savannas, sometimes referred to as grasslands, are dominated by tall grasses, with trees scattered here and there. **Figure 15** is a photo of an African savanna. The climate is usually very warm, with a dry season that lasts four to eight months followed by short periods of rain. Savanna soils are generally nutrient poor, but grass fires, which are common during the dry season, leave the soils nutrient enriched. Many plants have adapted to fire and use it to reproduce. Grasses sprout from their roots after the upper part of the plant is burned. The seeds of some plant species require fire in order to grow. For example, some species need fire to break open the seed's outer skin. Only after this skin is broken can the seed grow. Other species drop their seeds at the end of fire season. The heat from the fire triggers the plants to drop their seeds into the newly enriched soil.

Avg. Temperature Range: 27°C–32°C (80°F–90°F)

Avg. Yearly Precipitation: 100 cm

Soil Characteristics: generally nutrient poor

Vegetation: tall grasses (3–5 m), trees, thorny shrubs

Animals: gazelles, rhinoceroses, giraffes, lions, hyenas, ostriches, crocodiles, elephants

Figure 15 *The grass of a tropical savanna is 3–5 m tall, much taller than that of a temperate grassland.*

REVIEW

1. What are the soil characteristics of a tropical rain forest?
2. In what way has savanna vegetation adapted to fire?
3. **Summarizing Data** How do each of the tropical biomes differ?

Meeting Individual Needs

Learners Having Difficulty

Help students learn the characteristics of each of the nine biomes by having them make a graphic organizer for each climate zone. Have them match the appropriate biomes with each climate zone folder. Each biome should have its own fact sheet complete with information about temperature, precipitation, soil, plants, and animals. Students can also paste photographs taken from magazines that show plants and animals that inhabit each biome. Sheltered English

Real-World Connection

Some of the large mammals of the savanna, such as the elephant, are losing habitat because of the increase in grazing by domestic animals and the effects of hunting. Encourage students to find out more about conservation efforts in parks that are in tropical savannas.

Misconception Alert

Is a biome an ecosystem? A biome is a large region that is defined by the characteristic plants and animals that inhabit it. Biologists studying the interrelationship between these organisms and their environment identify many different ecosystems within a biome. An ecosystem can be as a large as an entire biome or as small as the community of microorganisms in a human stomach.

Answers to Review

1. The soil in a tropical rain forest is thin and nutrient poor. Nutrients are rapidly returned to the soil, but these nutrients are quickly absorbed and used by the plants. The remaining nutrients are washed away by heavy rains.
2. Many plants require fire to reproduce. The seeds of some plants require fire to break open the seed's outer skin so the plant can grow. The heat from the fire triggers other plants to drop their seeds into the newly enriched soil.
3. Answers will vary. Accept all reasonable responses. The tropical biomes differ in the amount of precipitation they receive and the range of temperatures that occur. This in turn affects the vegetation, the soil type, and the animals.

Section 2 Mid-section Review–California Standards: PE/ATE 5d

2 Teach, continued

READING STRATEGY

Prediction Guide If your community is in the continental United States, with the exception of northern Alaska, point out to students that they live in the temperate climate zone. The temperate climate zone is made up of four biomes: temperate forest, temperate grassland, chaparral, and temperate desert.

Write the following sentence on the board and have students copy it into their ScienceLog:

"I think we live in the ________ biome because ________."

Have them complete the sentence with the name of the biome and some ideas that support their prediction.

MISCONCEPTION ALERT

You don't need to travel to the tropics to find a rain forest. Western Washington state is home to the largest temperate rain forest in the world. Moss-covered trees more than 500 years old stand 60 m tall and are 5 m in diameter. The ground is covered by moss, ferns, salmonberries, and the thorny Hercules's club. The growth is not as diverse as the tropical forests, but it is every bit as lush. It receives 380 cm of rain a year! Have students find out more about this remarkable ecosystem and the efforts to preserve it.

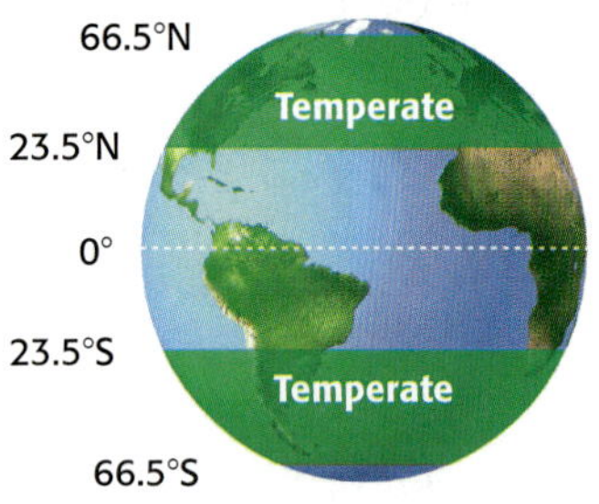

Figure 16 **The Earth's Temperate Zone**

The Temperate Zone

The **temperate zone,** as shown in **Figure 16,** is the climate zone between the Tropics and the polar zone. Temperatures in the temperate zone tend to be moderate. The continental United States is in this zone and includes the following four biomes: temperate forest, temperate grassland, chaparral, and temperate desert. **Figure 17** shows the distribution of the biomes found in the temperate zone.

Figure 17 **Biomes of the Temperate Zone**

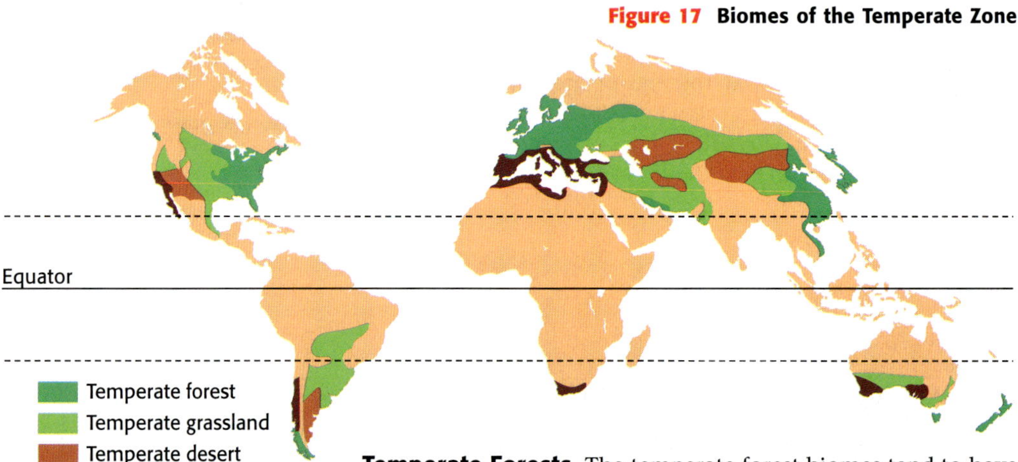

Temperate Forests The temperate forest biomes tend to have very high amounts of rainfall and seasonal temperature differences. Because of these distinct seasonal changes, summers are usually warm and winters are usually cold. The largest temperate forests are deciduous, such as the one shown in **Figure 18.** **Deciduous** trees are trees that lose their leaves when the weather becomes cold. These trees tend to be broad-leaved. The soils in deciduous forests are usually quite fertile because of the high organic content contributed by decaying leaves that drop every winter.

Another type of temperate forest is the evergreen forest. **Evergreens** are trees that keep their leaves year-round. Evergreens can be either broad-leaved trees or needle-leaved trees, such as pine trees. Mixed forests of broad-leaved and needle-leaved trees can be found in humid climates, such as Florida, where winter temperatures rarely fall below freezing.

Figure 18 *Deciduous trees have leaves that change color and drop when temperatures become cold.*

Avg. Temperature Range: 0°C–28°C (32°F–82°F)
Avg. Yearly Precipitation: 76–250 cm
Soil Characteristics: very fertile, organically rich
Vegetation: deciduous and evergreen trees, shrubs, herbs
Animals: deer, bears, boars, badgers, squirrels, wolves, wild cats, red foxes, owls, and many other birds

464

CONNECT TO ENVIRONMENTAL SCIENCE

The settlement of humans in the temperate forests has greatly fragmented these areas. Much of the temperate forest has been converted to agricultural land or logged. Fragmentation has a negative impact on many plants and animals that have certain habitat requirements. In fact fragmentation has led to the extinction of many species. The temperate forest has also been impacted by air pollution resulting from industrial activity. Acid precipitation and ozone has damaged entire forests, either killing the trees or making them more susceptible to disease.

Temperate Grasslands Temperate grasslands, such as those shown in **Figure 19,** occur in regions that receive too little rainfall for trees to grow. This biome has warm summers and cold winters. The temperate grasslands are known by many local names—the *prairies* of North America, the *steppes* of Eurasia, the *veldt* of Africa, and the *pampas* of South America. Grasses are the most common type of vegetation found in this biome. Because grasslands have the most fertile soils of all biomes, much of the temperate grassland has been plowed to make room for croplands.

Avg. Temperature Range: −6°C–26°C (21°F–78°F)

Avg. Yearly Precipitation: 38–76 cm

Soil Characteristics: most fertile soils of all biomes

Vegetation: grasses

Animals: large grazing animals, including the bison of North America, the kangaroo of Australia, and the antelope of Africa

Figure 19 *The world's grasslands once covered about 42 percent of Earth's total land surface. Today they occupy only about 12 percent of the Earth's surface.*

Chaparrals Chaparral regions, as shown in **Figure 20,** have cool, wet winters and hot, dry summers. The vegetation is mainly evergreen shrubs, which are short, woody plants with thick, waxy leaves. The waxy leaves are adaptations that help prevent water loss in dry conditions. These shrubs grow in rocky, nutrient-poor soil. Like tropical-savanna vegetation, chaparral vegetation has adapted to fire. In fact, some plants, such as chamise, can grow back from their roots after a fire.

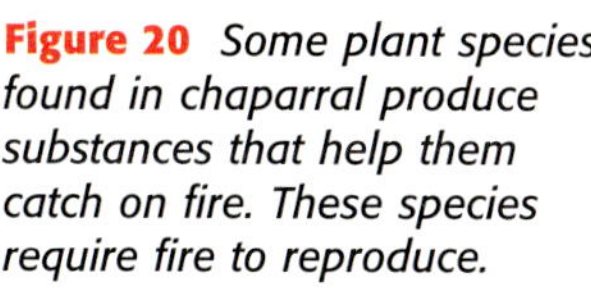

Avg. Temperature Range: 11°C–26°C (51°F–78°F)

Avg. Yearly Precipitation: 48–56 cm

Soil Characteristics: rocky, nutrient-poor soils

Vegetation: evergreen shrubs, scrubby trees, herbs

Animals: ground squirrels, deer, elk, mountain lions, coyotes, wolves

Figure 20 *Some plant species found in chaparral produce substances that help them catch on fire. These species require fire to reproduce.*

MEETING INDIVIDUAL NEEDS

Learners Having Difficulty

Tell students that the word *chaparral* comes from the Spanish word *chaparro,* which is a dwarf evergreen oak tree similar to the evergreen scrub oaks characteristic of some chaparrals. If you have Spanish-speaking students in your class, invite them to pronounce *chaparro* for the class. You might also tell students that the word *chaps* comes from the word *chaparro* and that chaps protect horseback riders' legs from the shrubby, scratchy vegetation of these areas.

Sheltered English

CONNECT TO ENVIRONMENTAL SCIENCE

Air pollution has a significant effect on chaparral vegetation. Ozone and other pollutants affect the vegetation, such as coastal sage scrub, making it less able to recover from the frequent fires.

Homework

Research Direct students' attention to **Figure 19,** and have them read the caption. A substantial part of North America's grasslands are now cropland. Have students find out what crops are most frequently grown in North American grassland biomes. Encourage them to find out why these crops grow particularly well there. Students can also include "before" and "after" drawings with captions describing native grasses and cultivated crops. (Students should discover that corn and wheat grow in the grasslands biome. They should also discover that these grain crops grow well in grasslands biomes because they are grasses.)

IS THAT A FACT!

Some grasses have defensive adaptations against grazing animals. Cordgrass, also known as rip gut, is found in marshy grassland areas and has sharp, hooklike barbs on its leaves that can easily cut an animal's mouth or a person's hands.

Science Skills Worksheet 18
"Finding Useful Sources"

2 Teach, continued

BRAIN FOOD

Chile's arid northern desert is one of the driest places on Earth. It receives so little rainfall that the yearly average is listed as "immeasurable." Surprisingly, people live there. They get drinking water by harvesting the fog. The village of Chungungo has built 75 fog-catching nets that supply 11,000 L of clean water a day. The nets, which look like giant volleyball nets, are positioned in the hills above the town. As the mountain fog passes through the nets, beads of water collect and are channeled to a large pipeline that supplies the village with water. Scientists believe this technology could be used in 30 other countries to supply safe and inexpensive water for drinking and agriculture.

Homework

Graphing Have students construct a bar graph that compares the average yearly precipitation ranges for the nine biomes discussed in the text. Have them use their graph to determine which biomes receive the most rain, which biomes receive the least rain, and which biome has the widest variation in annual precipitation. Suggest that students obtain yearly precipitation records for your region and compare them with the information in their graph.

Temperate Deserts The temperate desert biomes, like the one shown in **Figure 21,** tend to be cold deserts. Like all deserts, cold deserts receive less than 25 cm of rainfall annually. Temperate deserts can be very hot in the daytime, but—unlike hot deserts—they tend to be very cold at night.

Avg. Temperature Range: 1°C–50°C (34°F–120°F)
Avg. Yearly Precipitation: 0–25 cm
Soil Characteristics: poor in organic matter
Vegetation: succulents (cactus), shrubs, thorny trees
Animals: kangaroo rats, lizards, scorpions, snakes, birds, bats, toads

Figure 21 *The Great Basin Desert is in the rain shadow of the Sierra Nevada.*

The temperatures sometimes drop below freezing. This large change in temperature between day and night is caused by low humidity and cloudless skies. These conditions allow for a large amount of energy to reach, and thus heat, the Earth's surface during the day. However, these same characteristics allow the heat to escape at night, causing temperatures to drop. You probably rarely think of snow and deserts together, but temperate deserts often receive light snow during the winter.

Temperate deserts are dry because they are generally located inland, far away from a moisture source, or are located on the rain-shadow side of a mountain range.

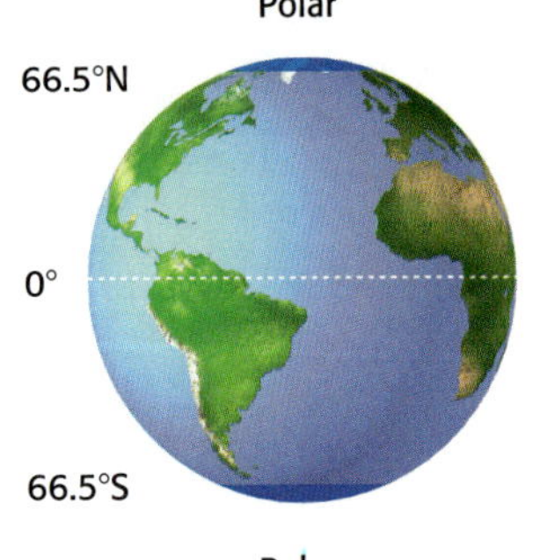

Figure 22 The Earth's Polar Zone

The Polar Zone

The **polar zone** includes the northernmost and southernmost climate zones, as shown in **Figure 22.** Polar climates have the coldest average temperatures. The temperatures in the winter stay below freezing, and the temperatures during the summer months remain chilly. **Figure 23,** on the next page, shows the distribution of the biomes found in the polar zone.

466

WEIRD SCIENCE

Lichens are primitive organisms that thrive in the polar zone. Some lichens in the Arctic have been determined to be 4,500 years old. To protect themselves from the cold, some lichens live 2 cm inside rocks! Despite their ability to survive in extremely harsh arctic conditions, most lichens have an extremely low tolerance for sulfur dioxide air pollution. As a result, they are usually not found in industrialized areas.

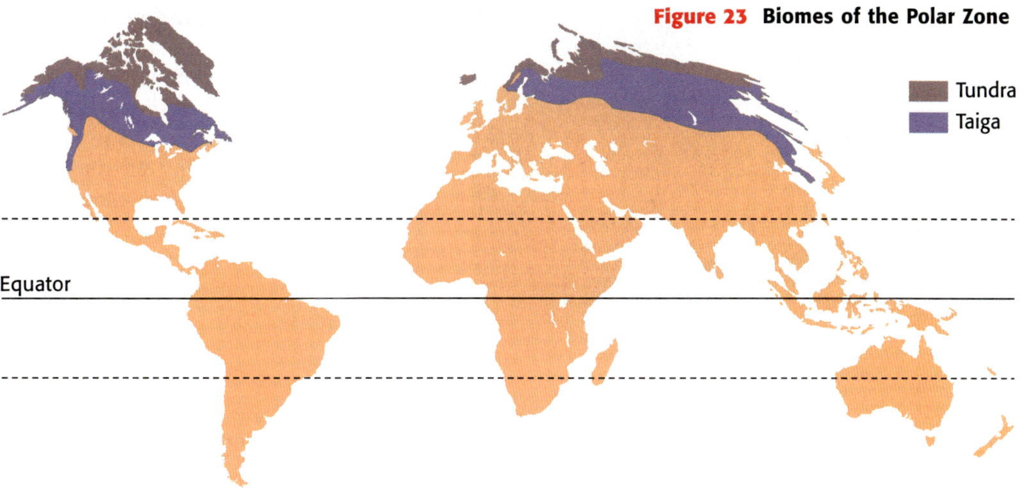

Figure 23 Biomes of the Polar Zone

Tundra Next to deserts, the tundra, as shown in **Figure 24,** is the driest place on Earth. This biome has long, cold winters with almost 24 hours of night and short, cool summers with almost 24 hours of daylight. In the summer, only the top meter of soil thaws. Underneath the thawed soil lies a permanently frozen layer of soil, called *permafrost.* This frozen layer prevents the water in the thawed soil from draining. Because of the poor drainage, the upper soil layer is muddy and is therefore an excellent breeding ground for insects, such as mosquitoes. Many birds migrate to the tundra during the summer to feed on the insects.

Subfreezing climates contain almost no decomposing bacteria. The well-preserved body of John Torrington, a member of an expedition that explored the Northwest Passage in Canada in the 1840s, was uncovered in 1984, appearing much as it did when he died, more than 140 years earlier.

Avg. Temperature Range: −27°C–5°C (−17°F–41°F)

Avg. Yearly Precipitation: 0–25 cm

Soil Characteristics: frozen

Vegetation: mosses, lichens, sedges, and dwarf trees

Animals: rabbits, lemmings, reindeer, caribou, musk oxen, wolves, foxes, birds, and polar bears

Figure 24 *In the tundra, mosses and lichens cover rocks. Dwarf trees grow close to the ground to protect themselves from strong winds and to absorb heat from the Earth's sunlit surface.*

467

Biome Business

DEMONSTRATION

Mock Permafrost Prepare for the demonstration by punching five holes in the bottom of two coffee cans and filling each can one-third full with potting soil. Slowly add water to one can until it begins to drain through the bottom; the soil should be moist but not saturated. Allow the excess water to drain, and pack the soil firmly. Place that can in a freezer for 6 to 8 hours. Bring the two cans to class, and have students gather at a sink. Hold the can with the unfrozen soil over the sink, and slowly pour a glass of water onto the soil. Repeat with the frozen can. Discuss with students why muddy or "marshy" areas form in the frozen soil and why the soil did not drain.

GROUP ACTIVITY

Have groups write a brochure for a summer camp in the biome of their choice. Suggest that they include information about the environment that will entice people to come and helpful tips about how to prepare for the area's climate.

WEIRD SCIENCE

Conical hills, called pingos, form in the arctic tundra when frozen ground water trapped under the permafrost is forced up due to pressure. As the frozen ground water rises, it pushes the layer of frozen ground over it upward. Pingos can be up to 46 m high and 400 m across.

MISCONCEPTION ALERT

Students may think that the tundra is a relatively small and barren area of land. Actually, 1/10 of the Earth's land is tundra, and about 600 species of plants are native to the biome. Ninety-nine percent of those plants are perennials; the growing season is too short for annuals, which need time to produce flowers and seeds.

4 Close

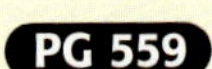

LabBook PG 559
For the Birds

Quiz

1. What are the three major climate zones? (the tropical zone, the temperate zone, and the polar zone)
2. Can a climate zone contain more than one biome? (A climate zone may contain several different biomes.)
3. What is a microclimate? (a small region with unique climate characteristics)

ALTERNATIVE ASSESSMENT

Concept Mapping Have students create a concept map that shows how each of the nine biomes is influenced by precipitation and temperature.

RESEARCH

Have students research the various microclimates that can be found on either side of Mount Shasta, in California. Have them find out which plants and animals are dominant at different elevations. They may want to present their findings in a color-coded diagram of the mountain with a key that explains the main characteristics of each microclimate.

Reinforcement Worksheet 17
"A Tale of Three Climates"

Figure 25 *The taiga is the major source of wood for paper.*

Taiga (Northern Coniferous Forest) Just south of the tundra lies the taiga biome. The taiga, as shown in **Figure 25,** has long, cold winters and short, warm summers. Like the tundra, the soil during the winter is frozen. The majority of the trees are evergreen needle-leaved trees called *conifers,* such as pine, spruce, and fir trees. The needles and bendable branches allow these trees to shed heavy snow before they can be damaged. Conifer needles contain acidic substances. When the needles die and fall to the soil, they make the soil acidic. Most plants cannot grow in acidic soil, and therefore the forest floor is bare except for some mosses and lichens.

Microclimates

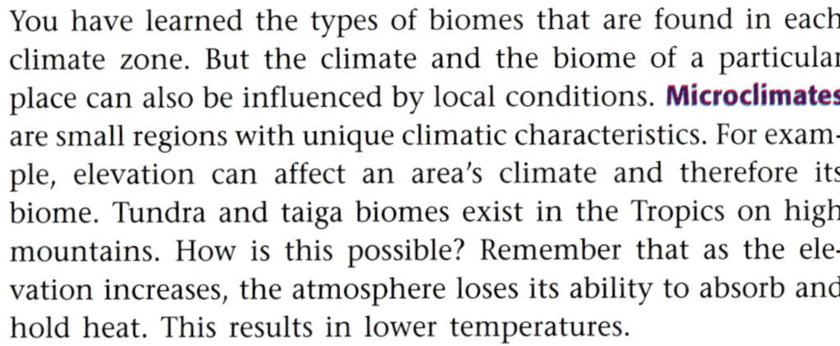

You have learned the types of biomes that are found in each climate zone. But the climate and the biome of a particular place can also be influenced by local conditions. **Microclimates** are small regions with unique climatic characteristics. For example, elevation can affect an area's climate and therefore its biome. Tundra and taiga biomes exist in the Tropics on high mountains. How is this possible? Remember that as the elevation increases, the atmosphere loses its ability to absorb and hold heat. This results in lower temperatures.

Cities are also microclimates. In a city, temperatures can be 1°C to 2°C warmer than the surrounding rural areas. This is because buildings and pavement made of dark materials absorb solar radiation instead of reflecting it. There is also less vegetation to take in the sun's rays. This absorption of the sun's rays by buildings and pavement heats the surrounding air and causes temperatures to rise.

physical science CONNECTION

Roof temperatures can get so hot that you can fry an egg on them! In a study of roofs on a sunny day when the air temperature was 13°C, scientists recorded roof temperatures ranging from 18°C to 61°C depending on color and material of the roof.

To find out more about microclimates, turn to page 559 of the LabBook.

REVIEW

1. Describe how tropical deserts and temperate deserts differ.
2. List and describe the three major climate zones.
3. **Inferring Conclusions** Rank each biome according to how suitable it would be for growing crops. Explain your reasoning.

Answers to Review

1. Answers will vary. Sample answer: Tropical deserts are hot deserts, and temperate deserts are cold deserts. Winters in tropical deserts are usually mild, but temperate deserts often receive light snow during winter.
2. The three climate zones are the tropical zone, the temperate zone, and the polar zone. The tropical climate zone receives the most direct solar radiation; therefore the temperatures are generally hot. Temperatures in the temperate zone tend to be moderate. The temperate zone experiences seasonal variations, such as warm summers and cold winters. During winter, the temperatures in the polar zone stay below freezing. During the summer, temperatures remain cold as well.
3. Answers will vary.

Section 2 Review–California Standards: PE/ATE 5d, 5e

3

Changes in Climate

NEW TERMS
ice age
global warming
greenhouse effect

OBJECTIVES
- Describe how the Earth's climate has changed over time.
- Summarize the different theories that attempt to explain why the Earth's climate has changed.
- Explain the greenhouse effect and its role in global warming.

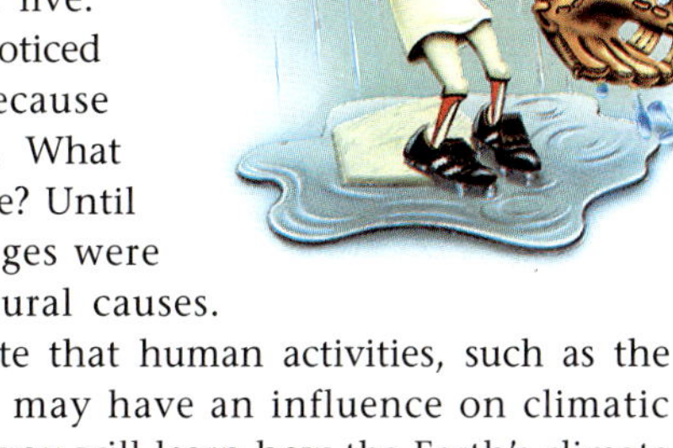

As you know, the weather constantly changes—sometimes several times in one day. Saturday, your morning baseball game was canceled because of rain, but by that afternoon the sun was shining. Now think about the climate where you live. You probably haven't noticed a change in climate, because climates change slowly. What causes climates to change? Until recently, climatic changes were connected only to natural causes. However, studies indicate that human activities, such as the burning of fossil fuels, may have an influence on climatic change. In this section, you will learn how the Earth's climate has changed. You will also see how natural and human factors may influence climatic change.

Ice Ages

The geologic record indicates that the Earth's climate has been much colder than it is today. In fact, much of the Earth was covered by sheets of ice during certain periods. An **ice age** is a period during which ice collects at the poles and moves repeatedly outward from the poles toward the equator. Scientists have found evidence of many major ice ages throughout the Earth's geologic history. The most recent ice age began about 1.65 million years ago. During an ice age, there are periods of cold, when much of the Earth's surface is covered by ice, and periods of warmth, when the ice melts. These periods are called glacial and interglacial periods. During *glacial periods,* the enormous sheets of ice advance, getting bigger and covering a larger area. Because much of the Earth's water is frozen during glacial periods, sea level drops. **Figure 26** shows that during the last glacial period, which began 115,000 years ago and ended 10,000 years ago, huge sheets of ice covered much of the northern United States.

Figure 26 *During the last glacial period, the Great Lakes were covered by an enormous block of ice that was 1.5 km high.*

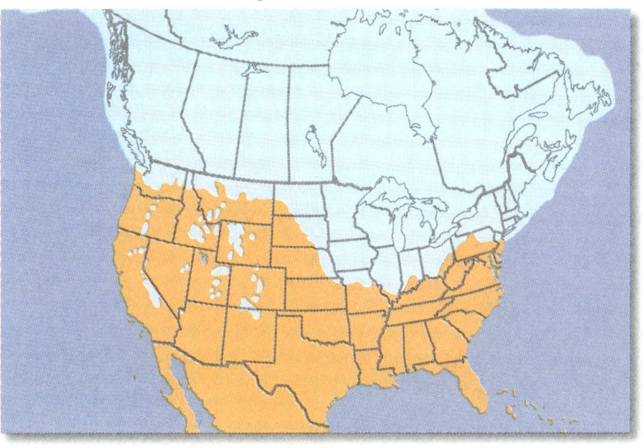

469

SECTION 3

Focus

Changes in Climate

This section describes significant changes in the Earth's climate. Students learn how different theories attempt to explain the cause of ice ages. Students also learn about the greenhouse effect and how the human production of greenhouse gases may contribute to global warming.

Bellringer

Have students imagine that the climate of the area where they live has changed so that it is now warmer than it used to be. Have students write down five different ways they think the area would be affected by warmer temperatures.

1 Motivate

DEMONSTRATION

The Greenhouse Effect Tell students that the glass windows in a greenhouse are similar to the Earth's atmosphere. The glass allows radiant energy to enter but prevents heat energy from escaping. Have students place a thermometer in a plastic bag on a sunny windowsill. Place another thermometer next to the plastic bag. After a few minutes, have a student read the two thermometers and compare the differences in temperature.
Sheltered English

Directed Reading Worksheet 17 Section 3

MISCONCEPTION ALERT

Students may be confused about the difference between an ice age and a glacial period. An ice age is the gradual cooling of the planet over thousands of years. During this time, glaciers repeatedly spread outward from the Earth's poles toward the equator. Ice ages are characterized by glacial periods (when glaciers spread) and interglacial periods (when glaciers retreat). Glacial periods can happen rather quickly—often in less than 30 years. Ice cores indicate that sudden glaciation periods could be caused by changes in major ocean currents or by volcanic eruptions.

2 Teach

MEETING INDIVIDUAL NEEDS

Advanced Learners Have students find out why scientists study the dust concentrations and gas composition of glacial ice in places such as Antarctica and Greenland. Have them explain why these and other data provide evidence about the last glacial period and other ice ages. Suggest that students share their findings with the class by giving an oral presentation.

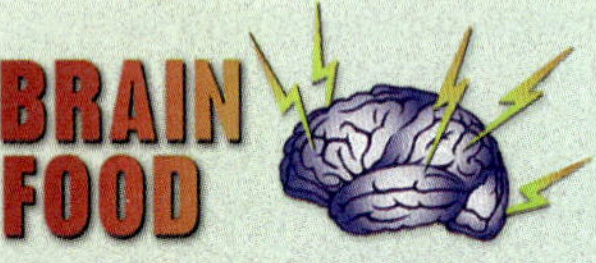

Scientists have proposed a theory that the fallout from a nuclear war would result in disastrous climatic changes. The fallout, consisting of billions of tons of dust and ash ejected into the atmosphere, would act as a shield, blocking out so much of the sun's rays that it would cause periods of darkness and below-freezing temperatures possibly lasting a year or longer. This scenario is described as a "nuclear winter." Discuss with students the similarities between the nuclear-winter theory and the theory that suggests glaciation is caused by catastrophic events such as massive volcanic eruptions.

Interglacial periods are warmer times that occur between glacial periods. During an interglacial period, the ice begins to melt back, or retreat. As the ice melts, the sea level rises again. The last interglacial period began 10,000 years ago and is still occurring. Why does this periodic change in temperature occur? Will the Earth experience another glacial period in the future? To answer these questions, let's examine the theories that scientists have been debating for the past 200 years.

Causes of Ice Ages There are many theories about the causes of ice ages. Each theory attempts to explain the gradual cooling that leads to the development of enormous ice sheets that periodically cover large areas of the Earth's surface. The *Milankovitch theory* explains why an ice age isn't just one long cold spell but instead alternates between cold and warm periods. Milutin Milankovitch, a Yugoslavian scientist, proposed that changes in the Earth's orbit and in the tilt of the Earth's axis cause ice ages, as illustrated in **Figure 27.**

Figure 27 *According to the Milankovitch theory, the amount of solar radiation the Earth receives varies due to three kinds of changes in the Earth's orbit.*

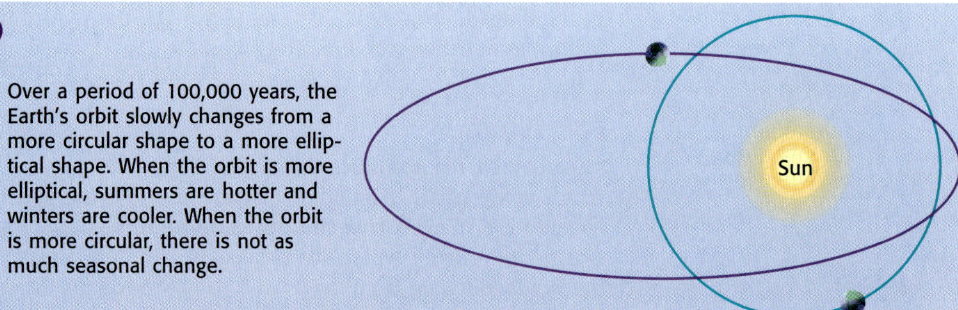

2

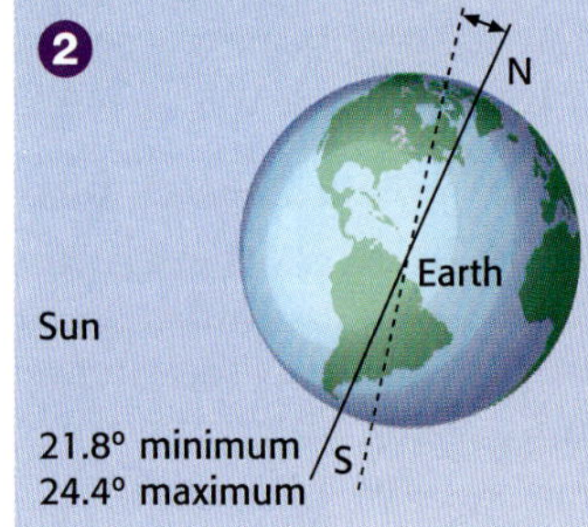

Over a period of 41,000 years, the tilt of the Earth's axis varies between 21.8° and 24.4°. When the tilt is at 24.4°, the poles receive more solar energy.

3

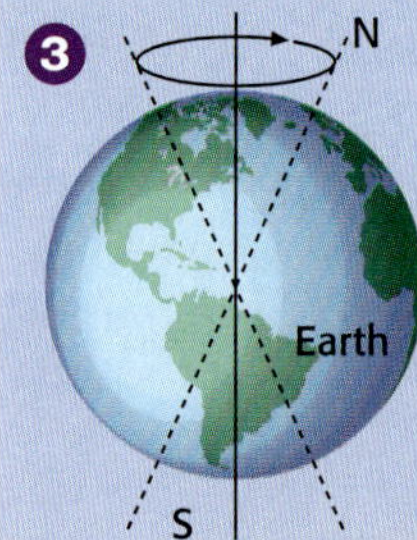

The circular motion of the Earth's axis causes the Earth to change position. The Earth's axis traces a complete circle every 26,000 years. The circular motion of the Earth's axis determines the time of year that the Earth is closest to the sun.

Self-Check

How do you think the Earth's elliptical orbit affects the amount of solar radiation that reaches the surface? *(See page 564 to check your answer.)*

470

Teaching Transparency 155
"The Milankovitch Theory of the Causes of the Ice Ages"

Answer to Self-Check

(Point out that the elliptical orbit of the Earth shown in **Figure 27** is exaggerated for effect. The change in orbits from circular to more elliptical is actually very slight.) The Earth's elliptical orbit causes increased seasonal differences. When the Earth's orbit is more elliptical, summers are hotter because the Earth is closer to the sun and receives more solar radiation. However, winters are cooler because the Earth is farther from the sun and receives less solar radiation.

During the last glacial period, animals that live in the northern part of North America, such as the Arctic fox, wolf, grizzly bear, and caribou, were living in Oklahoma, Missouri, and Texas!

There are many natural factors that can affect global climate. Some of these factors are thought to have contributed to the Earth's cooling that led to the ice ages. Catastrophic events, such as volcanic eruptions, can influence climate. Volcanic eruptions send large amounts of dust, ash, and smoke into the atmosphere. Once in the atmosphere, the dust, smoke, and ash particles act as a shield, blocking out so much of the sun's rays that the Earth cools. **Figure 28** shows how dust particles from a volcanic eruption block the sun.

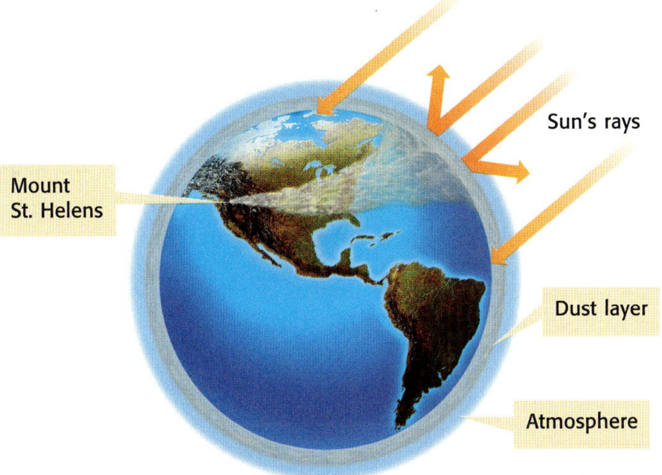

Figure 28 *Volcanic eruptions, such as the one that occurred at Mount St. Helens, shown above, produce dust that reflects sunlight, as shown at left.*

Changes in the sun's energy output also affect global climate. When the sun is radiating a lot of energy, temperatures increase. But when the sun's energy output decreases, temperatures drop.

The Earth's climate is further influenced by plate tectonics and continental drift. One theory proposes that ice ages occur when the continents are positioned closer to the polar regions. For example, approximately 250 million years ago, all the continents were connected near the South Pole in one giant landmass called Pangaea, as shown in **Figure 29.** During this time, ice covered a large area of the Earth's surface. As Pangaea broke apart, the continents moved toward the equator, and the ice age ended. During the last ice age, many large landmasses were positioned in the polar zones. Antarctica, northern North America, Europe, and Asia all were covered with large sheets of ice.

Pangaea

Figure 29 *Much of Pangaea—the part that is now Africa, South America, India, Antarctica, Australia, and Saudi Arabia—was covered by continental ice sheets.*

BRAIN FOOD

When the climate starts to cool, ice sheets grow and creep over the Earth. Ice sheets act as reflectors, reflecting solar radiation away from the Earth, causing it to cool even more. The more the Earth cools, the larger glaciers grow.

REAL-WORLD CONNECTION

Tell students that washing clothes in cold water instead of hot water can reduce the amount of carbon dioxide released into the atmosphere. This is because fossil fuels are used to heat the water. For example, a household that uses cold water to do two loads of laundry a week releases about 225 kg *less* carbon dioxide into the atmosphere each year. Have students calculate what the annual reduction in released carbon dioxide would be if the family of every student in the class used cold water for laundry.

CROSS-DISCIPLINARY FOCUS

History Archaeological evidence suggests that North America was originally settled by people who walked here from Asia between 15,000 and 25,000 years ago. At that time, sea levels were as much as 150 m lower, exposing the land between Alaska and Siberia. The sea level was lower because the ice sheets that spread across the Northern Hemisphere contained vast amounts of water. Have students write a short report about other human migrations thought to be caused by climate change.

Multicultural CONNECTION

It is difficult for scientists to predict climate changes because weather data has been accurately recorded for less than 200 years. However, the meteorological records of the Chinese date back to 1216 B.C. While these records do not indicate temperature, they do record rainfall, sleet, snow, humidity, and wind direction. There are also comments on unusually warm or cool temperatures. Have interested students research the reasons for collecting the data and find out how it is used today.

3 Extend

Answers to MATHBREAK

Answers will vary.

Given: The distance from home to school is 3 mi.

3 mi (1.6 km/mi) = 4.8 km

4.8 km/day (20 day/month) = 96 km/month

96 ÷ 20 = 4.8 gal of gas

4.8 gal (9 kg/gal) = 43.2 kg of carbon dioxide

CONNECT TO LIFE SCIENCE

There are many consequences of global warming. One consequence is the spread of tropical diseases, such as malaria and dengue fever. Both of these diseases are carried by a specific species of mosquito. These mosquitoes have a minimum temperature at which they can survive and breed. Ask students to create a temperature map for the world and identify the areas that are most likely to have a problem with these diseases.

PG 558

Global Impact

Critical Thinking Worksheet 17 "Cyberspace Heats Up"

Science Skills Worksheet 4 "Understanding Bias"

MATHBREAK

The Ride to School

Find out how much carbon dioxide is released into the atmosphere each month from the car or bus that transports you to school.

1. Figure out the distance from your home to school.
2. From this figure, calculate how many kilometers you travel to and from school, in a car or bus, per month.
3. Divide this number by 20. This represents approximately how many gallons of gas are used during your trips to school.
4. If burning 1 gal of gasoline produces 9 kg of carbon dioxide, how much carbon dioxide is released?

Global Warming

Is the Earth really experiencing global warming? **Global warming** is a rise in average global temperatures that can result from an increase in the greenhouse effect. To understand how global warming works, you must first learn about the greenhouse effect.

Greenhouse Effect The **greenhouse effect** is the Earth's natural heating process, in which gases in the atmosphere trap heat. Think about the case illustrated in **Figure 30.** It's a hot summer day, and you are about to go for a ride in the car with your brother. As you crawl into the back seat, you notice that it feels hotter inside the car than outside. Then you sit down and—ouch!—burn yourself on the seat. If you have experienced this, then you already know something about the greenhouse effect. The Earth's atmosphere performs the same function as the glass windows in a car.

Figure 30 *Sunlight streams into the car through the clear glass windows. The seats absorb the radiant energy and change it into heat energy. The heat is then trapped in the car.*

Greenhouse gases allow sunlight to pass through the atmosphere. It is absorbed by the Earth's surface and reradiated as heat energy. Greenhouse gases absorb the heat as it moves out of the atmosphere. An increase in the greenhouse effect occurs when there is an increase in greenhouse gases in the atmosphere. Many scientists hypothesize that the rise in global temperatures is due to an increase of carbon dioxide, a greenhouse gas, as a result of human activity. Most evidence indicates that the increase in carbon dioxide is caused by the burning of fossil fuels, such as coal, oil, and natural gas, which releases carbon dioxide into the atmosphere. But the burning of fossil fuels is not the only reason for the increase in carbon dioxide.

LabBook

Are global temperatures really on the rise? Turn to page 558 of the LabBook to find out.

SCIENTISTS AT ODDS

Svante Arrhenius was the first scientist to propose that the global climate was changing as a result of human activities. He put forth his theory in 1905. Other scientists ridiculed his ideas. It was not until much later that scientists took a serious look at the effects of carbon dioxide on the global climate.

internetconnect

TOPIC: Changes in Climate
GO TO: www.scilinks.org
***sci*LINKS NUMBER:** HSTE415

TOPIC: Modeling Earth's Climate
GO TO: www.scilinks.org
***sci*LINKS NUMBER:** HSTE420

A city just received a warning from the Environmental Protection Agency for exceeding the automobile fuel emissions standards. If you were the city manager, what suggestions would you make to reduce the amount of automobile emissions?

Another contributing factor might be deforestation. *Deforestation* is the process of clearing forests, as shown in **Figure 31.** In many countries around the world, forests are being burned to clear land for agriculture. All types of burning release carbon dioxide into the atmosphere, thereby increasing the greenhouse effect. Plants use carbon dioxide to make food. As plants are removed from the Earth, the carbon dioxide that would have been used by the plants builds up in the atmosphere.

Figure 31 *Clearing land by burning leads to increased levels of carbon dioxide in the atmosphere.*

Consequences of Global Warming If the average global temperature continues to rise, some regions of the world might experience flooding. Warmer temperatures could cause the icecaps to melt, raising the sea level and flooding low-lying areas, such as the coasts.

Areas that receive little rainfall, such as deserts, might receive even less due to increased evaporation. Scientists predict that the Midwest, an agricultural area, could experience warmer, drier conditions. A change in climate such as this could harm crops. But farther north, such as in Canada, weather conditions for farming would improve.

REVIEW

1. How has the Earth's climate changed over time? What might have caused these changes?
2. Explain how the greenhouse effect warms the Earth.
3. What are two ways that humans contribute to the increase in carbon dioxide levels in the atmosphere?
4. **Analyzing Relationships** How will the warming of the Earth affect agriculture in different parts of the world?

Answers to Review

1. Throughout time the climate has been colder and warmer than today. The cooling and warming of the Earth's surface might have been caused by changes in the Earth's orbit; catastrophic events, such as volcanic eruptions; and the movement of the continents by plate tectonics and continental drift.
2. Greenhouse gases allow sunlight to pass through the atmosphere, where it is absorbed by the Earth's surface and reradiated as heat energy. The greenhouse gases absorb the heat energy as it moves out of the atmosphere.
3. burning fossil fuels and deforestation
4. The warming of the Earth would change the climate. Areas that were suitable for farming might become warmer and drier.

4 Close

Answers to APPLY

Answers will vary. Students might suggest reducing the number of automobiles on the road. This could be done by establishing incentives for people who carpool or bicycle to work. The city could build a lane solely for those that carpool so they can avoid the congestion of rush-hour traffic. Another solution would be to develop a more efficient mass-transit system. More buses and reduced fares could encourage people to use mass transit rather than drive cars.

Quiz

1. Why does the sea level fall during glacial periods? (because much of Earth's water is frozen during a glacial period)
2. How might a major volcanic eruption have brought about an ice age? (Dust, smoke, and ash from a volcanic eruption enters the atmosphere and acts as a shield, blocking out much of the sun's rays and causing the Earth to cool.)
3. How might global warming affect coastal areas? (The warmer temperatures could cause polar icecaps to melt, which would raise the sea level and cause flooding in coastal areas.)

Alternative Assessment

Have students make a collage about global cooling or warming. They can include images of how they think the Earth would appear and descriptions of the likely causes of climate change. Sheltered English

Section 3 Review–California Standards: PE/ATE 1, 1e, 4, 4a, 4b

Chapter Highlights

VOCABULARY DEFINITIONS

SECTION 1

weather the condition of the atmosphere at a particular time and place

climate the average weather conditions in a certain area over a long period of time

latitude the distance north or south from the equator; measured in degrees

prevailing winds winds that blow mainly from one direction

elevation the height of surface landforms above sea level; the height of an object above sea level

surface currents a streamlike movement of water that occurs at or near the surface of the ocean

Chapter Highlights

SECTION 1

Vocabulary

weather *(p. 454)*
climate *(p. 454)*
latitude *(p. 455)*
prevailing winds *(p. 457)*
elevation *(p. 458)*
surface currents *(p. 459)*

Section Notes

- Weather is the condition of the atmosphere at a particular time and place. Climate is the average weather conditions in a certain area over a long period of time.
- Climate is determined by temperature and precipitation.
- Climate is controlled by factors such as latitude, elevation, wind patterns, local geography, and ocean currents.
- The amount of solar energy an area receives is determined by the area's latitude.
- The seasons are a result of the tilt of the Earth's axis and its path around the sun.
- The amount of moisture carried by prevailing winds affects the amount of precipitation that falls.
- As elevation increases, temperature decreases.
- Mountains affect the distribution of precipitation. The dry side of the mountain is called the rain shadow.
- As ocean currents move across the Earth, they redistribute warm and cool water. The temperature of the surface water affects the air temperature.

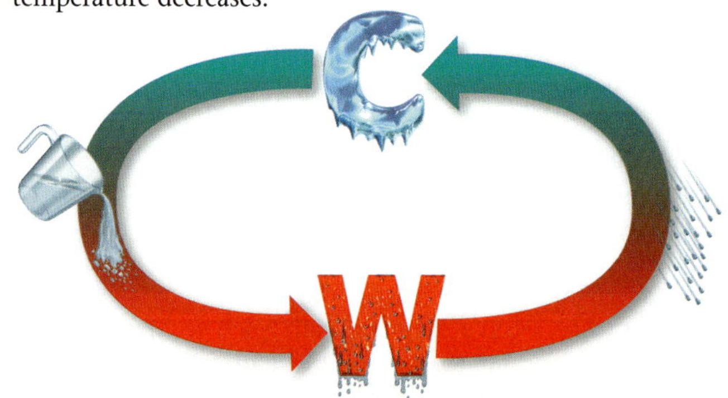

Skills Check

Visual Understanding

THE SEASONS Seasons are determined by latitude. The diagram on page 456 shows how the tilt of the Earth affects how much solar energy an area receives as the Earth moves around the sun.

THE RAIN SHADOW The illustration on page 458 shows how the climates on two sides of a mountain can be very different. A mountain can affect the climate of areas nearby by influencing the amount of precipitation these areas receive.

LAND BIOMES OF THE EARTH Look back at Figure 10 on page 460 to review the distribution of the Earth's Land Biomes.

474

Lab and Activity Highlights

For the Birds PG 559

Biome Business PG 562

Global Impact PG 558

Datasheets for LabBook
(blackline masters for these labs)

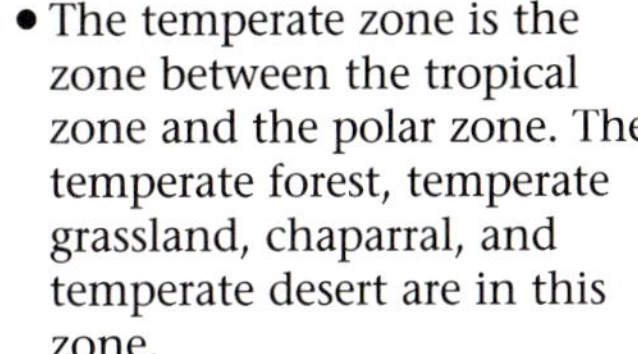

SECTION 2

Vocabulary

biome *(p. 460)*
tropical zone *(p. 461)*
temperate zone *(p. 464)*
deciduous *(p. 464)*
evergreens *(p. 464)*
polar zone *(p. 466)*
microclimates *(p. 468)*

Section Notes

- The Earth is divided into three climate zones according to latitude—the tropical zone, the temperate zone, and the polar zone.
- The tropical zone is the zone around the equator. The tropical rain forest, tropical desert, and tropical savanna are in this zone.
- The temperate zone is the zone between the tropical zone and the polar zone. The temperate forest, temperate grassland, chaparral, and temperate desert are in this zone.
- The polar zones are the northernmost and southernmost zones. The taiga and tundra are in this zone.

Labs

For the Birds *(p. 559)*
Biome Business *(p. 562)*

SECTION 3

Vocabulary

ice age *(p. 469)*
global warming *(p. 472)*
greenhouse effect *(p. 472)*

Section Notes

- Explanations for the occurrence of ice ages include changes in the Earth's orbit, volcanic eruptions, changes in the sun's energy output, and plate tectonics and continental drift.
- Some scientists believe that global warming is occurring as a result of an increase in carbon dioxide from human activity.
- If global warming continues, it could drastically change climates, causing either floods or drought.

Labs

Global Impact *(p. 558)*

internetconnect

GO TO: go.hrw.com

Visit the **HRW** Web site for a variety of learning tools related to this chapter. Just type in the keyword:

KEYWORD: HSTCLM

GO TO: www.scilinks.org

Visit the **National Science Teachers Association** on-line Web site for Internet resources related to this chapter. Just type in the ***sci*LINKS** number for more information about the topic:

TOPIC: What Is Climate? ***sci*LINKS NUMBER:** HSTE405
TOPIC: Climates of the World ***sci*LINKS NUMBER:** HSTE410
TOPIC: Changes in Climate ***sci*LINKS NUMBER:** HSTE415
TOPIC: Modeling Earth's Climate ***sci*LINKS NUMBER:** HSTE420

475

Lab and Activity Highlights

LabBank

Whiz-Bang Demonstrations, How Humid Is It? Demo 30

Long-Term Projects & Research Ideas, Project 45

VOCABULARY DEFINITIONS, *continued*

SECTION 2

biome a large region characterized by a specific type of climate and certain types of plant and animal communities

tropical zone the warm zone located around the equator

temperate zone the climate zone between the tropics and the polar zone

deciduous describes trees that have leaves that change color in autumn and that fall off in winter

evergreens trees that keep their leaves year-round

polar zone the northernmost and southernmost climate zone

microclimate a small region with unique climatic characteristics

SECTION 3

ice age a period during which ice collects at the poles and moves outward from the poles toward the equator

global warming a rise in average global temperatures

greenhouse effect the natural heating process of a planet, such as the Earth, by which gases in the atmosphere trap thermal energy

Vocabulary Review Worksheet 17

Blackline masters of these Chapter Highlights can be found in the **Study Guide.**

Chapter Review Answers

Using Vocabulary

1. Climate
2. Latitude
3. tropical
4. deciduous
5. tundra
6. global warming

Understanding Concepts

Multiple Choice

7. b
8. b
9. a
10. b
11. c
12. a
13. d
14. b

Short Answer

15. Higher latitudes receive less solar radiation because the sun's rays strike the Earth's surface at a lesser angle than at the equator. This lesser angle spreads the same amount of solar energy over a larger area, resulting in lower temperatures.
16. The amount of precipitation an area receives can depend on whether the region's prevailing winds form from a warm air mass or from a cold air mass. If the winds form from a warm air mass, they will probably carry moisture. If the winds form from a cold air mass, they will probably be dry. Precipitation is more likely to occur when the prevailing winds are warm and moist.
17. Tropical rain forests contain the greatest number of plant and animal species because they receive strong sunlight year-round and sufficient precipitation.
18. Plants have adapted by developing fleshy leaves to store water and a waxy coating to prevent water loss. Animals are more active at night, when temperatures are cooler, and burrow during the day.
19. Both the tundra and desert biomes receive very little precipitation.

Concept Mapping

20. 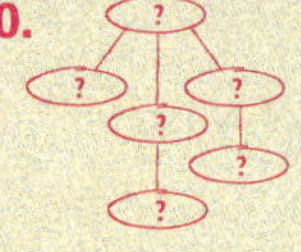

An answer to this exercise can be found at the end of this book.

Chapter Review

USING VOCABULARY

To complete the following sentences, choose the correct term from each pair of terms listed below:

1. __?__ is the condition of the atmosphere in a certain area over a long period of time. *(Weather* or *Climate)*
2. __?__ is the distance north and south from the equator measured in degrees. *(Elevation* or *Latitude)*
3. Savannas are grasslands located in the __?__ zone between 23.5° north latitude and 23.5° south latitude. *(temperate* or *tropical)*
4. Broad-leaved trees are found in a __?__ forest. *(deciduous* or *coniferous)*
5. Frozen land in the polar zone is most often found in a __?__. *(taiga* or *tundra)*
6. A rise in global temperatures due to an increase in carbon dioxide is called __?__. *(global warming* or *the greenhouse effect)*

UNDERSTANDING CONCEPTS

Multiple Choice

7. The Earth's orbit around the sun causes
   a. global warming.
   b. different seasons.
   c. a rain shadow.
   d. the greenhouse effect.

8. What factor affects the prevailing winds as they blow across a continent, producing different climates?
   a. latitude
   b. mountains
   c. forests
   d. glaciers
9. What factor determines the amount of solar energy an area receives?
   a. latitude
   b. wind patterns
   c. mountains
   d. ocean currents
10. What climate zone has the coldest average temperature?
    a. tropical
    b. polar
    c. temperate
    d. tundra
11. What biome is not located in the tropical zone?
    a. rain forest
    b. savanna
    c. chaparral
    d. desert
12. What biome contains the greatest number of plant and animal species?
    a. rain forest
    b. temperate forest
    c. grassland
    d. tundra
13. Which of the following is not a theory for the cause of ice ages?
    a. the Milankovitch theory
    b. volcanic eruptions
    c. plate tectonics
    d. the greenhouse effect
14. Which of the following is thought to contribute to global warming?
    a. wind patterns
    b. deforestation
    c. ocean surface currents
    d. microclimates

476

Concept Mapping Transparency 17

Chapter 17 Review–California Standards: PE/ATE Q7–20: 1, 1a, 1e, 4b, 5e

VOCABULARY

Short Answer

15. Why do higher latitudes receive less solar radiation than lower latitudes?
16. How does wind influence precipitation patterns?
17. Why do tropical rain forests contain the greatest number of plant and animal species on the planet?
18. How have desert plants and animals adapted to this biome?
19. How are tundra and deserts similar?

Concept Mapping

20. Use the following terms to create a concept map: climate, global warming, deforestation, greenhouse effect, flooding.

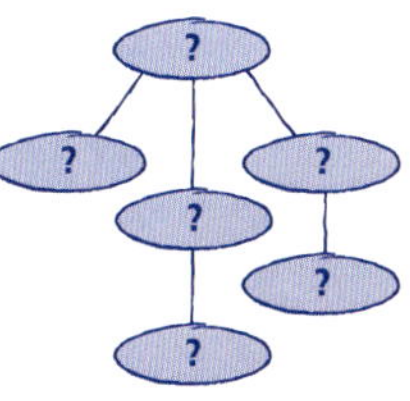

CRITICAL THINKING AND PROBLEM SOLVING

Write one or two sentences to answer the following questions:

21. Explain how ocean surface currents are responsible for milder climates.
22. In your own words, explain how a change in the Earth's orbit can affect the Earth's climates as proposed by Milutin Milankovitch.
23. Explain why the climate differs drastically on each side of the Rocky Mountains.
24. What are some steps you and your family can take to reduce the amount of carbon dioxide that is released into the atmosphere?

MATH IN SCIENCE

25. If the air temperature near the shore of a lake measures 24°C, and if the temperature increases by 0.05°C every 10 m traveled away from the lake, what would the air temperature be 1 km from the lake?

INTERPRETING GRAPHICS

The following illustration shows the Earth's orbit around the sun.

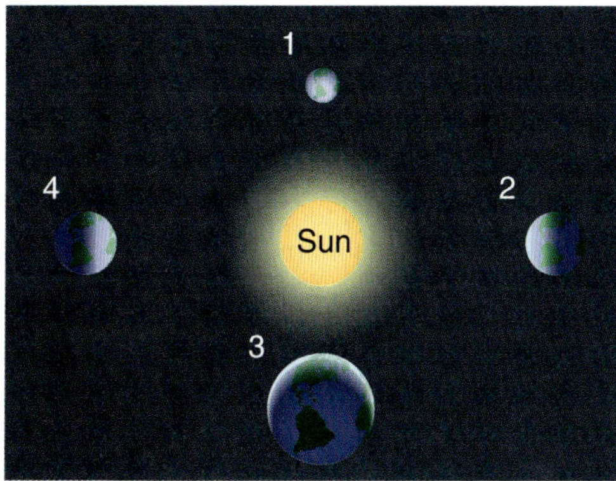

26. At what position, **1**, **2**, **3**, or **4**, is it spring in the Southern Hemisphere?
27. At what position does the South Pole receive almost 24 hours of daylight?
28. Explain what is happening in each climate zone in both the Northern Hemisphere and Southern Hemisphere at position **4**.

NOW What Do You Think?

Take a minute to review your answers to the ScienceLog questions on page 453. Have your answers changed? If necessary, revise your answers based on what you have learned since you began this chapter.

477

NOW What Do You Think?

1. Weather is the condition of the atmosphere at a certain time or place. Climate is the average weather conditions over a long period of time.
2. Pollution created by technology might cause an area to become warmer. This is because the carbon dioxide released into the atmosphere traps heat.

Blackline masters of this Chapter Review can be found in the **Study Guide.**

Critical Thinking and Problem Solving

21. Warmer surface currents heat the surrounding air, and colder surface currents cool the surrounding air. A warm surface current might bring warmer temperatures to a cold area. A cold surface current might cool an area that is generally hot.
22. Answers will vary. Sample answer: A change in the Earth's orbit can affect the Earth's climates by limiting or increasing the amount of solar radiation the Earth receives.
23. The climate differs on each side of the Rocky Mountains because the mountains affect the distribution of precipitation. The windward side receives more precipitation because as the warm air is forced to rise, it releases precipitation. As the dry air crosses the mountain, it sinks, warming and absorbing the moisture.
24. Answers will vary.

Math in Science

25. 1 km = 1,000 m
    1,000 m ÷ 10 m = 100
    100 × .05°C = 5°C
    24°C + 5°C = 29°C

Interpreting Graphics

26. 3
27. 2
28. In the tropical zone temperatures are warm. The temperate zone in the Northern Hemisphere is experiencing summer. The temperate zone in the Southern Hemisphere is experiencing winter. Deciduous trees have shed their leaves. The polar zone in the Northern Hemisphere is experiencing almost 24 hours of daylight. Temperatures are cool, and the top meter of soil is thawing. The polar zone in the Southern Hemisphere is experiencing almost 24 hours of night. Temperatures are extremely cold, and the soil is frozen.

Across the Sciences
Blame "The Child"

Background
Another pattern in the global weather system is called the southern oscillation. In 1924, the British mathematician Gilbert Walker described a see-saw pattern in tropical Pacific air pressure. He found that when air pressure is low around Australia, it is high to the east, in Tahiti. Conversely, when air pressure is high in Australia, it is low in Tahiti. This see-saw effect is called the southern oscillation.

By the 1970s, scientists realized that El Niño and the southern oscillation are part of a huge oceanic-atmospheric system that affects the weather in many parts of the world.

ACROSS THE SCIENCES

EARTH SCIENCE • LIFE SCIENCE

Blame "The Child"

El Niño, which is Spanish for "the child," is the name of a weather event that occurs in the Pacific Ocean. Every 3 to 5 years, the interaction between the ocean surface and atmospheric winds creates El Niño. This event influences weather patterns in many regions of the world.

Difficult Breathing
For Indonesia and Malaysia, El Niño meant droughts and forest fires in 1998. Thousands of people in these countries suffered from respiratory ailments from breathing the smoke caused by these fires. Heavy rains in San Francisco created extremely high mold-spore counts. These spores cause problems for people with allergies. The spore count in February in San Francisco is usually between 0 and 100. In 1998, the count was often higher than 8,000!

Rodent Invasion
In areas where El Niño creates heavy rains, the result is lush vegetation. This lush vegetation provides even more food and shelter for rodents. As the rodent population increases, so does the threat of the diseases they spread. In states like Arizona, Colorado, and New Mexico, this means there is a greater chance among humans of contracting hantaviral pulmonary syndrome (HPS).

HPS is carried by deer mice and remains in their urine and feces. People are infected when they inhale dust contaminated with mouse feces or urine. Once infected, a person experiences flulike symptoms that can sometimes lead to fatal kidney or lung disease.

More Rodents and Insects
Heavy rains near Los Angeles might encourage a rodent-population explosion in the mountains east of the city. If so, there could be an increase in the number of rodents infected with bubonic plague. More infected rodents means more infected fleas, which carry bubonic plague to humans.

Ticks and mosquitoes could also increase in number. These insects can spread disease too. For example, ticks can carry Lyme disease, ehrlichiosis, babesiosis, and Rocky Mountain spotted fever. Mosquitoes can spread malaria, dengue fever, encephalitis, and Rift Valley fever.

If this flea carries bubonic plague bacteria, just one bite can infect a person.

What About Camping?
Because all of these diseases can be fatal to humans, people must take precautions. Camping in the great outdoors increases the risk of infection. Campers should steer clear of rodents and their burrows. Don't forget to dust family pets with flea powder, and don't let them roam free. Try to remember that an ounce of prevention is worth a pound of cure.

Find Out More
▶ How do you think El Niño affects the fish and mammals that live in the ocean? Write your answer in your ScienceLog, and then do some research to see if you are correct.

478

Answer to Find Out More
Due to a shortage of phytoplankton, El Niño forces fish to find food in other areas. For example, mako sharks, which normally live in warm tropical waters, were found in the chilly waters of Monterey Bay, California. Birds such as pelicans might end up in areas that are far from their normal habitat. This was the case in Arica, Chile, in August 1997, when the number of local pelicans grew from 200 to 4,000 in just a few weeks. The population surge was believed to be caused by El Niño. If food is not available, El Niño can cause starvation among some species. Such was the case for the Galápagos penguin, whose numbers decreased by 50 percent due to weather caused by El Niño and La Niña.

California Standards: PE/ATE 4e

Science, Technology, and Society

Some Say Fire, Some Say Ice . . .

The Earth's climate has undergone many drastic changes. For example, 6,000 years ago in the part of North Africa that is now a desert, hippos, crocodiles, and early Stone Age people shared shallow lakes that covered the area. Grasslands stretched as far as the eye could see.

Scientists have known for many years that Earth's climate has changed. What they didn't know was why. Using supercomputers and complex computer programs, scientists may now be able to explain why North Africa's lakes and grasslands became a desert. And that information may be useful for predicting future heat waves and ice ages.

Climate Models

Scientists who study Earth's atmosphere have developed climate models to try to imitate Earth's climate. A climate model is like a very complicated recipe with thousands of ingredients. These models do not make exact predictions about future climates, but they do estimate what might happen.

What ingredients are included in a climate model? One important ingredient is the level of greenhouse gases (especially carbon dioxide) in the atmosphere. Land and ocean water temperatures from around the globe are other ingredients. So is information about clouds, cloud cover, snow, and ice cover. And in more recent models, scientists have included information about ocean currents.

A Challenge to Scientists

Earth's atmosphere-ocean climate system is extremely complex. One challenge for scientists is to understand all the system's parts. Another is to understand how those parts work together. But understanding Earth's climate system is critical. An accurate climate model should help scientists predict heat waves, floods, and droughts.

Even the best available climate models must be improved. The more information scientists can include in a climate model, the more accurate the results. Today data are available from more locations, and scientists need more-powerful computers to process all the data.

As more-powerful computers are developed to handle all the data in a climate model, scientists' understanding of Earth's climate changes will improve. This knowledge should help scientists better predict the impact human activities have on global climate. And these models could help scientists prevent some of the worst effects of climate change, such as global warming or another ice age.

▲ *This meteorologist is using a high-powered supercomputer to do climate modeling.*

A Challenge for You

▶ Earth's oceans are a major part of the climate model. Find out some of the ways oceans affect climate. Do you think human activities are changing the oceans?

Science, Technology, and Society

Some Say Fire, Some Say Ice . . .

Teaching Strategies

There are many sites on the Internet that contain information about and graphic displays of global and regional climate models. A search using the keywords "climate models" should produce plenty of information for you and your students.

Answers to A Challenge for You

Student answers will vary. Sample answer: Oceans affect climate by circulating warm waters in currents, absorbing carbon dioxide, producing oxygen, contributing to El Niño and La Niña, and providing water for the water cycle.

LabBook

Contents

Exploring, inventing, and investigating are essential to the study of science. However, these activities can also be dangerous. To make sure that your experiments and explorations are safe, you must be aware of a variety of safety guidelines.

You have probably heard of the saying, "It is better to be safe than sorry." This is particularly true in a science classroom where experiments and explorations are being performed. Being uninformed and careless can result in serious injuries. Don't take chances with your own safety or with anyone else's.

Following are important guidelines for staying safe in the science classroom. Your teacher may also have safety guidelines and tips that are specific to your classroom and laboratory. Take the time to be safe.

Safety Rules!

Start Out Right

Always get your teacher's permission before attempting any laboratory exploration. Read the procedures carefully, and pay particular attention to safety information and caution statements. If you are unsure about what a safety symbol means, look it up or ask your teacher. You cannot be too careful when it comes to safety. If an accident does occur, inform your teacher immediately, regardless of how minor you think the accident is.

If you are instructed to note the odor of a substance, wave the fumes toward your nose with your hand. Never put your nose close to the source.

Safety Symbols

All of the experiments and investigations in this book and their related worksheets include important safety symbols to alert you to particular safety concerns. Become familiar with these symbols so that when you see them, you will know what they mean and what to do. It is important that you read this entire safety section to learn about specific dangers in the laboratory.

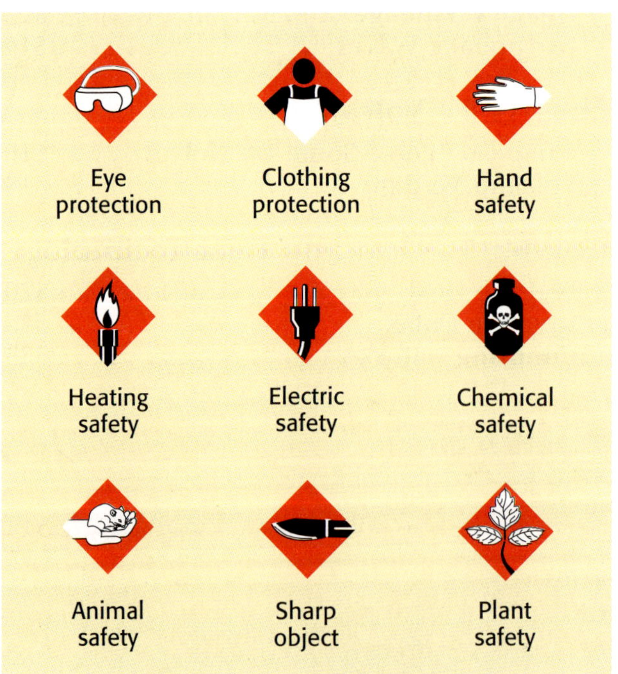

Eye Safety 

Wear safety goggles when working around chemicals, acids, bases, or any type of flame or heating device. Wear safety goggles any time there is even the slightest chance that harm could come to your eyes. If any substance gets into your eyes, notify your teacher immediately, and flush your eyes with running water for at least 15 minutes. Treat any unknown chemical as if it were a dangerous chemical. Never look directly into the sun. Doing so could cause permanent blindness.

Avoid wearing contact lenses in a laboratory situation. Even if you are wearing safety goggles, chemicals can get between the contact lenses and your eyes. If your doctor requires that you wear contact lenses instead of glasses, wear eye-cup safety goggles in the lab.

Neatness

Keep your work area free of all unnecessary books and papers. Tie back long hair, and secure loose sleeves or other loose articles of clothing, such as ties and bows. Remove dangling jewelry. Don't wear open-toed shoes or sandals in the laboratory. Never eat, drink, or apply cosmetics in a laboratory setting. Food, drink, and cosmetics can easily become contaminated with dangerous materials.

Certain hair products (such as aerosol hair spray) are flammable and should not be worn while working near an open flame. Avoid wearing hair spray or hair gel on lab days.

Safety Equipment

Know the locations of the nearest fire alarms and any other safety equipment, such as fire blankets and eyewash fountains, as identified by your teacher, and know the procedures for using them.

Sharp/Pointed Objects 

Use knives and other sharp instruments with extreme care. Never cut objects while holding them in your hands. Place objects on a suitable work surface for cutting.

Be extra careful when using any glassware. When adding a heavy object to a graduated cylinder, tilt the cylinder so the object slides slowly to the bottom.

Heat   

Wear safety goggles when using a heating device or a flame. Whenever possible, use an electric hot plate as a heat source instead of an open flame. When heating materials in a test tube, always angle the test tube away from yourself and others. In order to avoid burns, wear heat-resistant gloves whenever instructed to do so.

Chemicals    

Wear safety goggles when handling any potentially dangerous chemicals, acids, or bases. If a chemical is unknown, handle it as you would a dangerous chemical. Wear an apron and safety gloves when working with acids or bases or whenever you are told to do so. If a spill gets on your skin or clothing, rinse it off immediately with water for at least 5 minutes while calling to your teacher.

Never mix chemicals unless your teacher tells you to do so. Never taste, touch, or smell chemicals unless you are specifically directed to do so. Before working with a flammable liquid or gas, check for the presence of any source of flame, spark, or heat.

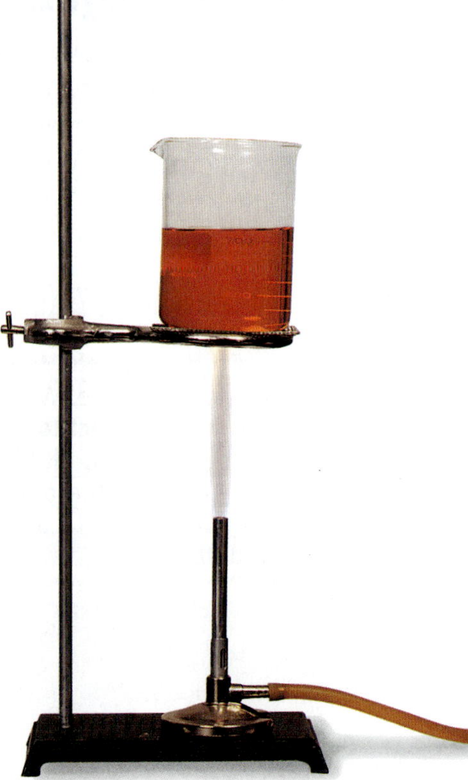

Electricity 

Be careful with electrical cords. When using a microscope with a lamp, do not place the cord where it could trip someone. Do not let cords hang over a table edge in a way that could cause equipment to fall if the cord is accidentally pulled. Do not use equipment with damaged cords. Be sure your hands are dry and that the electrical equipment is in the "off" position before plugging it in. Turn off and unplug electrical equipment when you are finished.

484

Animal Safety 

Always obtain your teacher's permission before bringing any animal into the school building. Handle animals only as your teacher directs. Always treat animals carefully and with respect. Wash your hands thoroughly after handling any animal.

Plant Safety 

Do not eat any part of a plant or plant seed used in the laboratory. Wash hands thoroughly after handling any part of a plant. When in nature, do not pick any wild plants unless your teacher instructs you to do so.

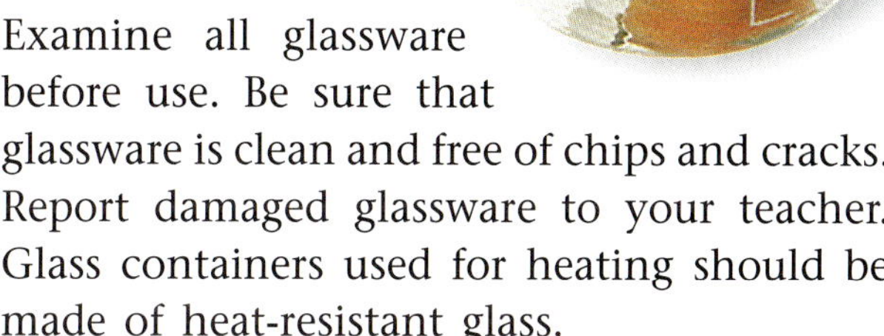

Glassware

Examine all glassware before use. Be sure that glassware is clean and free of chips and cracks. Report damaged glassware to your teacher. Glass containers used for heating should be made of heat-resistant glass.

485

Using the Scientific Method

Teacher's Notes

Time Required

One 45-minute class period

Lab Rating

TEACHER PREP ▲▲
STUDENT SET-UP ▲▲▲
CONCEPT LEVEL ▲▲
CLEAN UP ▲▲

MATERIALS

The materials listed on the student page are enough for a pair of students. Students can also work in groups of four. In that case, two students should assume the role of model builders, and the two others should assume the role of core samplers.

Safety Caution

Remind students to review all safety cautions and icons before beginning this lab activity.

Lab Notes

Provide each student group with three pieces of 1.3 cm PVC pipe cut slightly longer than the height of their models.

Jan Nelson
East Valley Middle School
East Helena, Montana

Using the Scientific Method

Geologists often use a technique called *core sampling* to learn what underground rock layers look like. This technique involves drilling several holes in the ground in different places and taking samples of the underground rock or soil. Geologists then compare the samples from each hole to construct a diagram that shows the bigger picture.

In this activity, you will model the process geologists use to diagram underground rock layers. You will first use modeling clay to form a rock-layer model. You will then exchange models with a classmate, take core samples, and draw a diagram of your classmate's layers.

Materials

- 3 colored pencils or markers
- nontransparent pan or box
- modeling clay in three colors
- 1.3 cm PVC pipe
- plastic knife

SCIENTIFIC METHOD

Ask a Question

1. Can unseen features be revealed by sampling parts of the whole?

Form a Hypothesis

2. Form a hypotheses on whether taking core samples from several locations will give a good indication of the entire hidden feature.

Test the Hypothesis

3. To test your hypothesis, you will take core samples from a model of underground rock layers, draw a diagram of the entire rock-layer sequence, and then compare your drawing with the actual model.

Build a Model

The model rock layers should be formed out of view of the classmates who will be taking the core samples.

4. Form a plan for your rock layers, and sketch the layers in your ScienceLog. Your sketch should include the three colors in several layers of varying thicknesses.
5. In the pan or box, mold the clay into the shape of the lowest layer in your sketch.
6. Repeat step 5 for each additional layer of clay. You now have a rock-layer model. Exchange models with a classmate.

California Standards: PE /ATE 7, 7a, 7b, 7e

Collect Data

7. Choose three places on the surface of the clay to drill holes. The holes should be far apart and in a straight line. (You do not need to remove the clay from the pan or box.)
8. Use the PVC pipe to "drill" a vertical hole in the clay at one of the chosen locations by slowly pushing the pipe through all the layers of clay. Slowly remove the pipe.
9. Remove the core sample from the pipe by gently pushing the clay out of the pipe with an unsharpened pencil.
10. Draw the core sample in your ScienceLog, and record your observations. Be sure to use a different color of pencil or marker for each layer.
11. Repeat steps 8–10 for the next two core samples. Make sure your drawings are side by side in your ScienceLog in the same order as the samples in the model.

Analyze the Results

12. Look at the pattern of rock layers in each of your core samples. Think about how the rock layers between the core samples might look. Then construct a diagram of the rock layers.
13. Complete your diagram by coloring the rest of the rock layers.

Draw Conclusions

14. Use the plastic knife to cut the clay model along a line connecting the three holes and remove one side of the model. The rock layers should now be visible.
15. How well does your rock-layer diagram match the model? Explain.
16. Is it necessary to revise your diagram from step 13? If so, how?
17. Do your conclusions support your hypothesis? Why or why not?

Going Further
What are two ways that the core-sampling method could be improved?

Answers

15. The rock-layer diagram provides a general overview of the layers. It may not be as specific as the model or provide all the details from the model.
16. Answers will vary. If the core samples are significantly different from the diagram, students should modify their diagram.
17. Answers will depend on student hypotheses.

Going Further

Answers could include: more core samples could be taken, the core samples could be taken in specific areas, the core samples could be larger or closer together, or smaller areas could be combined for an overall picture of the layers.

Datasheets for LabBook
Datasheet 1

Science Skills Worksheet 10
"Doing a Lab Write-up"

Science Skills Worksheet 24
"Using Models to Communicate"

Round or Flat?
Teacher's Notes

Time Required
One 45-minute class period

Lab Ratings

TEACHER PREP 2
STUDENT SET-UP 3
CONCEPT LEVEL 3
CLEAN UP 2

MATERIALS

The materials listed on the student page are enough for a group of 3–4 students.

Safety Caution
Remind students to review all safety cautions before beginning this lab activity.

Preparation Notes
Obtain inflated basketballs from your school's physical education instructor. It may be necessary to ask students to bring basketballs from home. Begin the activity by reminding students that *circumference* is the distance around a circle or sphere.

You may also need to review the use of protractors with students before performing this activity.

Round or Flat?

SKILL BUILDER

Eratosthenes thought he could measure the circumference of the Earth. He came up with the idea while reading that a deep vertical well in southern Egypt was entirely lit up by the sun at noon once each year. He realized that for this to happen, the sun must be directly over the well at that moment! But at the same moment, in a city just north of this well, a tall monument cast a shadow. Eratosthenes reasoned that the sun could not be directly over both the monument and the well at noon on the same day. In this experiment, you will test his idea and see for yourself how his experiment works.

Materials
- basketball
- 2 books or notebooks
- modeling clay
- 2 unsharpened pencils
- metric ruler
- meterstick
- masking tape
- flashlight or small lamp
- string, 10 cm long
- protractor
- tape measure
- calculator (optional)

SCIENTIFIC METHOD

Ask a Question
1. How could I use Eratosthenes' experiment to measure the size of the Earth?

Conduct an Experiment
2. Set the basketball on a table, and place a book or notebook on either side to hold the ball in place. The ball represents the Earth.
3. Use modeling clay to attach a pencil to the "equator" of the ball so that it sticks directly outward.
4. Attach the second pencil to the ball 5 cm above the first pencil. This second pencil should also stick directly outward, as shown on the next page.

488

Explain that Eratosthenes' experiment worked because he set up a ratio. It may be necessary to review ratios before performing this activity. The formula Eratosthenes used is as follows:

$$\frac{\text{Distance around ball}}{\text{Distance between sticks}} = \frac{360° \text{ in the sphere}}{\text{Angle of shadow with stick}}$$

California Standards: PE/ATE 7, 7b, 7e

5. Use a meterstick to measure 1 m away from the ball. Mark this position with masking tape, and label it "sun." Place the flashlight here.
6. When your teacher turns out the lights, turn on your flashlight, and point it so that the pencil on the equator does not cast a shadow. Ask a partner to hold the flashlight in this position. The second pencil should cast a shadow on the ball.
7. Tape one end of the string to the top of the second pencil. Hold the other end of the string against the ball at the far edge of the shadow. Make sure that the string is taut, but be careful not to pull the pencil over.
8. Use a protractor to measure the angle between the string and the pencil. Record this angle in your ScienceLog.
9. Use the following formula to calculate the *experimental circumference* of the ball:

$$\text{Circumference} = \frac{360° \times 5 \text{ cm}}{\text{angle between pencil and string}}$$

Record this circumference in your ScienceLog.

10. Wrap the tape measure around the ball's "equator" to measure the *actual circumference* of the ball. Record this circumference in your ScienceLog.

Analyze the Results

11. In your ScienceLog, compare the experimental circumference with the actual circumference.
12. What could have caused your experimental circumference to be different from the actual value?
13. What are some of the advantages and disadvantages of taking measurements this way?

Draw Conclusions

14. Was this an effective method for Eratosthenes to measure the Earth's circumference? Explain your answer.

Going Further

You can calculate the circumference of Earth by doing Eratosthenes' experiment with other schools around the world during the fall and spring equinoxes. To find out more, search for "Eratosthenes' experiment" on the Internet. The experiment is conducted each year.

Answers

11. Students are likely to find that the experimental and actual circumference are not equal, but the two values should be close.
12. Answers may vary. Factors that affect this measurement include a slant of the pencils and human error in measurement.
13. Because it is impossible to use a tape measure to determine the circumference of the Earth, this procedure offers a good approximation. One disadvantage is that the measurements are not exact.
14. Yes, because it gives a value that is close to the actual value.

Datasheets for LabBook Datasheet 2

Science Skills Worksheet 12 "Working with Hypotheses"

Barry L. Bishop
San Rafael Junior High
Ferron, Utah

Orient Yourself!
Teacher's Notes

Time Required
Two 45-minute class periods, one period to learn the use of a compass and the second to follow the orienteering course

Lab Ratings

TEACHER PREP 3
STUDENT SET-UP 1
CONCEPT LEVEL 3
CLEAN UP 1

MATERIALS

The materials listed on the student page are enough for a group of 3–4 students.

Preparation Notes
Find a suitable outdoor location for a simple orienteering course, and choose five control points for students to map. For example, you may wish to use several pieces of equipment in the playground, the flagpole, a tree, and a small hill. Be sure to mark each control point with either a specific color or a code word that students can collect or note on their maps when they reach each point.

Next, draw a map that includes the control points and the cardinal directions. Label a sixth spot as the starting point. Each group of students will need a copy of this map.

Orient Yourself!

You have been invited to attend an orienteering event with your neighbors. In orienteering events, participants use maps and compasses to find their way along a course. There are several control points that each participant must reach. The object is to reach each control point and then the finish line. Orienteering events are often timed competitions. In order to find the fastest route through the course, the participants must read the map and use their compass correctly. Being the fastest runner does not necessarily guarantee finishing first. You also must choose the most direct route to follow.

Your neighbors participate in several orienteering events each year. They always come home raving about how much fun they had. You would like to join them, but you will need to learn how to use your compass first.

Materials
- magnetic compass
- course map
- ruler
- 2 colored pencils or markers

SCIENTIFIC METHOD

Procedure
1. Together as a class, go outside to the orienteering course your teacher has made.
2. Hold your compass flat in your hand. Turn the compass until the N is pointing straight in front of you. (The needle in your compass will always point north.) Turn your body until the needle lines up with the N on your compass. You are now facing north.
3. Regardless of which direction you want to face, you should always align the end of the needle with the N on your compass. If you are facing south, the needle will be pointing directly toward your body. When the N is aligned with the needle, the S will be directly in front of you, and you will be facing south.
4. Use your compass to face east. Align the needle with the N. Where is the E? Turn to face that direction. When the needle and the N are aligned and the E is directly in front of you, you are facing east.
5. In an orienteering competition, you will need to know how to determine which direction you are traveling. Now, face any direction you choose.

Before groups begin exploring the orienteering course, have students perform steps 1–6 individually. It may take as much as an entire class period for students to feel confident using a compass.

David Jones
Andrew Jackson Middle School
Cross Lanes, West Virginia

California Standards: PE/ATE 7, 7b, 7f

6. Do not move, but rotate the compass to align the needle on your compass with the N. What direction are you facing? You are probably not facing directly north, south, east, or west. If you are facing between north and west, you are facing northwest. If you are facing between north and east, you are facing northeast.

7. Find a partner or partners to follow the course your teacher has made. Get a copy of the course map from your teacher. It will show several control points. You must stop at each one. You will need to follow this map to find your way through the course. Find and stand at the starting point.

8. Face the next control point on your map. Rotate your compass to align the needle on your compass with the N. What direction are you facing?

9. Use the ruler to draw a line on your map between the two control points. Write the direction between the starting point and the next control point on your map.

10. Walk toward the control point. Keep your eyes on the horizon, not on your compass. You might need to go around obstacles such as a fence or building. Use the map to find the easiest way around.

11. Record the color or code word you find at the control point next to the control point symbol on your map.

12. Repeat steps 8–11 for each control point. Follow the points in order as they are labeled. For example, determine the direction from control point 1 to control point 2. Be sure to include the direction between the final control point and the starting point.

Analysis

13. The object of an orienteering competition is to arrive at the finish line first. The maps provided at these events do not instruct the participants to follow a specific path. In one form of orienteering, called "score orienteering," competitors may find the control points in any order. Look at your map. If this course were used for a score-orienteering competition, would you change your route? Explain.

14. If there is time, follow the map again. This time, use your own path to find the control points. Draw this path and the directions on your map in a different color. Do you believe this route was faster? Why?

Going Further

Do some research to find out about orienteering events in your area. The Internet and local newspapers may be good sources for the information. Are there any events that you would like to attend?

Answers

13. Answers will vary. Students should realize that the path shown on the map did not instruct them to follow the most direct route. They should propose a more direct route to follow. Their proposal should include the direction from one control point to the next.

14. This route should be faster. Students should realize that in an orienteering event, participants generally need to determine the most direct route. Some students may also realize that sometimes the most direct route is not the quickest. For example, there may be obstacles in the way (like hills or lakes) that could slow participants down. Orienteering maps include these landmarks as well.

Datasheets for LabBook
Datasheet 3

Science Skills Worksheet 13
"Designing an Experiment"

Topographic Tuber
Teacher's Notes

Time Required
One 45-minute class period

Lab Ratings

TEACHER PREP 🧪🧪
STUDENT SET-UP 🧪
CONCEPT LEVEL 🧪🧪🧪
CLEAN UP 🧪

MATERIALS
The materials listed on the student page are enough for groups of 2–3 students. Modeling clay may be used in place of the potatoes. Students can mold the clay into a variety of shapes and compare their topographic maps.

Preparation Notes
It may be easier for students to see the waterline if you add a few drops of food coloring to the water before they add it to the container.

Before the activity, select several oddly shaped root vegetables from your local grocery store. Choose vegetables that have var ied contour and shape. Sweet potatoes, for example, are available year-round and have many irregular shapes. If you cannot find naturally occurring root vegetables that have odd shapes, shape potatoes with a knife and peeler. You will then need to cut the potatoes in half lengthwise.

Topographic Tuber

Imagine that you live on top of a tall mountain and often look down on the lake below. Every summer, an island appears. You call it Sometimes Island because it goes away again during heavy fall rains. This summer you begin to wonder if you could make a topographic map of Sometimes Island. You don't have fancy equipment to make the map, but you have an idea. What if you place a meterstick with the 0 m mark at the water level in the summer? Then as the expected fall rains come, you could draw the island from above as the water rises. Would this idea really work?

Materials
- clear plastic storage container with transparent lid
- transparency marker
- metric ruler
- potato, cut in half
- water
- tracing paper

SCIENTIFIC METHOD

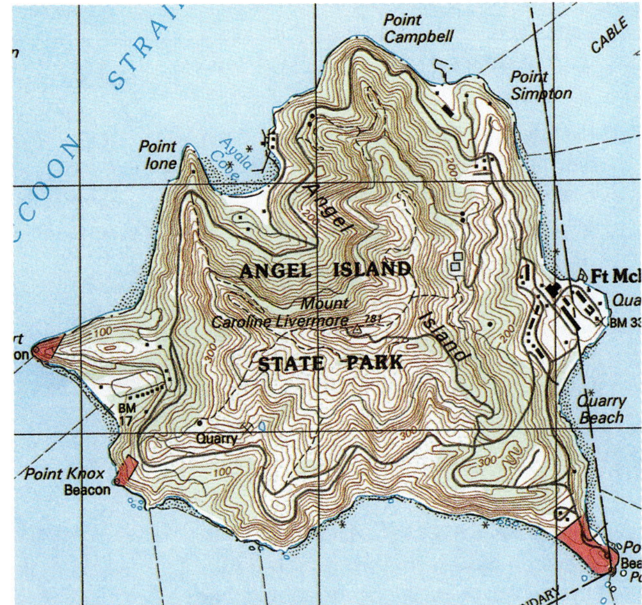

Ask a Question
1. How do I make a topographic map?

Conduct an Experiment
2. Place a mark at the storage container's base. Label this mark "0 cm" with a transparency marker.
3. Measure and mark 1 cm increments up the side of the container until you reach the top of the container. Label these marks "1 cm," "2 cm," "3 cm," and so on.
4. Place the potato flat side down in the center of the container.
5. Pour water into the container until it reaches the line labeled "1 cm."
6. Place the lid on the container, and seal it. Part of the potato will be sticking out above the water. Viewing the potato from above, use the transparency marker to trace the part of the potato that touches the top of the water.
7. The scale for your map will be 1 cm = 10 m. Draw a 2 cm line in the bottom right-hand corner of the lid. Place hash marks at 0 cm, 1 cm, and 2 cm. Label these marks "0 m," "10 m," and "20 m."

Lab Notes
Only islands that are at sea level begin at an elevation of 0 m. In order to calculate the elevation of an island that forms in a lake, you must add the number of meters the lake is above sea level.

Michael E. Kral
West Hardin Middle School
Cecilia, Kentucky

California Standards: PE/ATE 7, 7b, 7f

8. Label the elevation of the contour line you drew in step 6. According to the scale, the elevation is 10 m.
9. Remove the lid. Carefully pour water into the container until it reaches the line labeled "2 cm."
10. Place the lid on the container, and seal it. Viewing the potato from above, trace the part of the potato that touches the top of the water at this level.
11. Use the scale to calculate the elevation of this line. Label the elevation on your drawing.
12. Repeat steps 9–11, adding 1 cm to the depth of the water each time. Stop when the potato is completely covered.
13. Remove the lid, and set it on a tabletop. Place tracing paper on top of the lid. Trace the contours from the lid onto the paper. Label the elevation of each contour line. Congratulations! You have just made a topographic map!

Analyze the Results

14. What is the contour interval of this topographic map?
15. By looking at the contour lines, how can you tell which parts of the potato are steeper?

Draw Conclusions

16. Do all topographic maps have a 0 m elevation contour line as a starting point? How would this affect a topographic map of Sometimes Island? Explain your answer.
17. Would this be an effective way to make a topographic map of Sometimes Island? Why or why not?
18. What is the elevation of the highest point on your map?

Going Further

Place all of the potatoes on a table or desk at the front of the room. Your teacher will mix up the potatoes as you trade topographic maps with another group. By reading the topographic map you just received, can you pick out the matching potato?

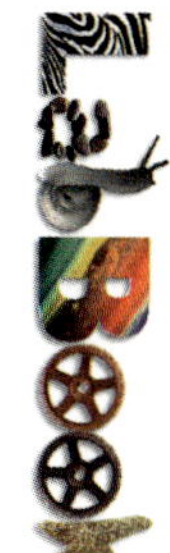

Answers

14. The contour interval of the topographic map is 10 m.
15. Steeper parts of the root will have contour lines that are closer together. Elevation is indicated by numbers on the contour lines.
16. No; all topographic maps do not need to start with a 0 m elevation contour line because they might not show an area at sea level. A topographic map of Sometimes Island made in this fashion would not show the land at sea level or the part of the island underneath the water.
17. No; flooding an island is not an effective way of mapping it.
18. Answers will vary according to the size and shape of the potatoes.

Datasheets for LabBook
Datasheet 4

Mysterious Minerals
Teacher's Notes

Time Required
One 45-minute class period

Lab Ratings

TEACHER PREP 2
STUDENT SET-UP 2
CONCEPT LEVEL 2
CLEAN UP 1

MATERIALS

The materials listed on the student page are sufficient for each student. Students may also work in groups of 3–4. You will need one streak plate per student or group. A class should be able to share 3–5 streak plates.

Safety Caution
Remind students to review all safety cautions and icons before beginning this lab activity. Students need to be careful with glass microscope slides. Broken slides are likely to have sharp edges.

Preparation Notes
Students are not determining the absolute hardness of the mineral samples. Instead they are comparing the hardness of the samples with that of glass.

Your sample minerals should include pyrite, galena, hematite, magnetite, orthoclase (feldspar), quartz, muscovite, gypsum, hornblende (amphibole), garnet, biotite, and graphite.

Mysterious Minerals

Imagine sitting on a rocky hilltop, gazing at the ground below you. You can see dozens of different types of rocks. How can scientists possibly identify the countless variations? It's a mystery!

In this activity you'll use your powers of observation and a few simple tests to determine the identities of rocks and minerals. Take a look at the Mineral Identification Key on the next page. That key will help you use clues to discover the identity of several minerals.

Materials
- several sample minerals
- glass microscope slides
- streak plate
- safety gloves
- iron filings

Procedure
1. In your ScienceLog, create a data chart like the one below.
2. Choose one mineral sample, and locate its column in your data chart.
3. Follow the Mineral Identification Key to find the identity of your sample. When you are finished, record the mineral's name and primary characteristics in the appropriate column in your data chart. **Caution:** Put on your gloves when scratching the glass slide.
4. Select another mineral sample, and repeat steps 3 and 4 until your data table is complete.

Analysis
5. Were some minerals easier to identify than others? Explain.
6. A streak test is a better indicator of a mineral's true color than visual observation. Why isn't a streak test used to help identify every mineral?
7. In your ScienceLog, summarize what you learned about the various characteristics of each mineral sample you identified.

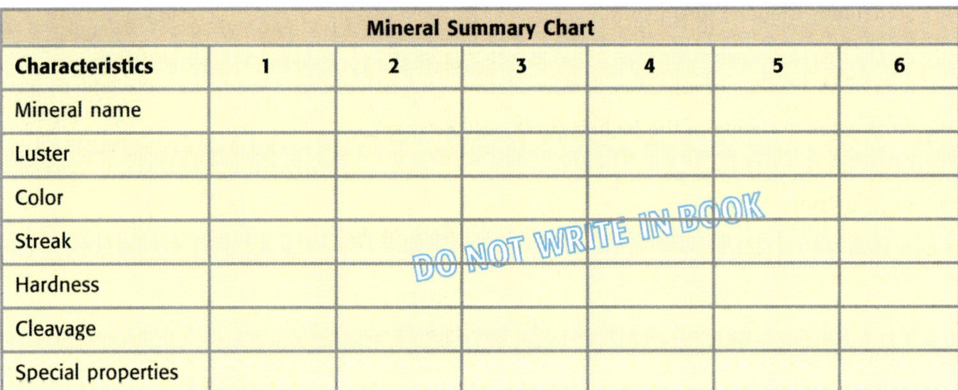

Mineral Summary Chart						
Characteristics	**1**	**2**	**3**	**4**	**5**	**6**
Mineral name						
Luster						
Color						
Streak						
Hardness						
Cleavage						
Special properties						

494

David Jones
Andrew Jackson Middle School
Cross Lanes, West Virginia

California Standards: PE/ATE 7, 7b, 7e

Mineral Identification Key
1. a. If your mineral has a metallic luster, **GO TO STEP 2.** **b.** If your mineral has a nonmetallic luster, **GO TO STEP 3.**
2. a. If your mineral is black, **GO TO STEP 4.** **b.** If your mineral is yellow, it is **PYRITE.** **c.** If your mineral is silver, it is **GALENA.**
3. a. If your mineral is light in color, **GO TO STEP 5.** **b.** If your mineral is dark in color, **GO TO STEP 6.**
4. a. If your mineral leaves a red-brown line on the streak plate, it is **HEMATITE.** **b.** If your mineral leaves a black line on the streak plate, it is **MAGNETITE.** Test your sample for its magnetic properties by holding it near some iron filings.
5. a. If your mineral scratches the glass microscope slide, **GO TO STEP 7.** **b.** If your mineral does not scratch the glass microscope slide, **GO TO STEP 8.**
6. a. If your mineral scratches the glass slide, **GO TO STEP 9.** **b.** If your mineral does not scratch the glass slide, **GO TO STEP 10.**
7. a. If your mineral shows signs of cleavage, it is **ORTHOCLASE FELDSPAR.** **b.** If your mineral does not show signs of cleavage, it is **QUARTZ.**
8. a. If your mineral shows signs of cleavage, it is **MUSCOVITE.** Examine this sample for twin sheets. **b.** If your mineral does not show signs of cleavage, it is **GYPSUM.**
9. a. If your mineral shows signs of cleavage, it is **HORNBLENDE.** **b.** If your mineral does not show signs of cleavage, it is **GARNET.**
10. a. If your mineral shows signs of cleavage, it is **BIOTITE.** Examine your sample for twin sheets. **b.** If your mineral does not show signs of cleavage, it is **GRAPHITE.**

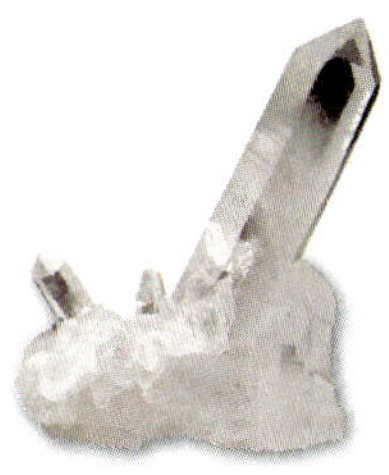

Going Further

Using your textbook and other reference books, research other methods of identifying different types of minerals. Based on your findings, create a new identification key. Give it to a friend along with a few sample minerals, and see if your friend can unravel the mystery!

495

Lab Notes

Each test in this lab tells the student more about the sample and narrows the possibilities. For example, the fact that a particular mineral sample does not have a streak eliminates hematite as a possibility but indicates that quartz is a possibility.

- It is possible for minerals that are softer than glass to leave a mark on glass. If the glass wipes clean and no scratch remains, then students will know that the mineral is softer than glass.
- Garnet is typically red but it can also be pale green.

Answers

5. Students will find that some minerals required fewer steps to identify than others. For example, pyrite and galena are identified in two steps. Students may also find that they recognize some of the minerals and that the identification key is there merely to verify the identity.
6. For a mineral to leave a streak on the streak plate, the plate must be harder than the mineral. Therefore, extremely hard minerals do not leave a streak. Alternatively, some minerals that are softer than a streak plate leave behind a colorless streak.

Going Further

Scientists test other characteristics of minerals as well. These characteristics may include density, crystal form, reaction to acids, optical properties, fluorescence, and radioactivity. Students should create an identification key that is very similar to the one provided in the lab, but their key should include different characteristics.

Datasheets for LabBook Datasheet 5

Is It Fool's Gold?—A Dense Situation

Teacher's Notes

Time Required

One 45-minute class period

Lab Ratings

TEACHER PREP 2
STUDENT SET-UP 3
CONCEPT LEVEL 2
CLEAN UP 1

MATERIALS

Materials listed on the student page are sufficient for a group of 2–4 students. If your mineral samples are small, the change in volume may be difficult to detect. In that case, replace the beaker in steps 6–7 with a graduated cylinder.

Preparation Notes

Students may need to review density and specific gravity prior to performing this activity.

Lab Notes

- Density is conventionally described as g/cm^3, not g/mL.
- Because specific gravity is the ratio of a substance's density to the density of water (1g/cm^3), the value will be the same for density. The difference is that specific gravity is a number, and density is a number with the units g/cm^3.
- Due to impurities, the density of some minerals is given in ranges. The larger number for gold represents pure gold; lower numbers indicate the presence of impurities. The density of pure silver is 10.5 g/cm^3; depending on impurities, that number can be higher or lower.
- Ideally, the values for specific gravity and density obtained in this lab will be identical. Discrepancies will likely result from differences in precision. Students should learn that all scientific measurements involve some margin of error.

SKILL BUILDER

Is It Fool's Gold?—A Dense Situation

Have you heard of fool's gold? Maybe you've seen a piece of it. This notorious mineral was often passed off as real gold. There are, however, simple tests you can do to keep from being tricked. Minerals can be identified by their properties. Some properties, such as color, vary between different samples of the same mineral. Other properties, such as density and specific gravity, remain consistent from one sample to another. In this activity, you will try to verify the identity of some mineral samples.

Materials

- spring scale
- ring stand
- pyrite sample
- galena sample
- balance
- string
- 400 mL beaker
- 400 mL of water

Ask a Question

1. How can I determine if an unknown mineral is not gold or silver?

Make Observations

2. Copy the data table below into your ScienceLog. Use it to record your observations.

Observation Chart		
Measurement	**Galena**	**Pyrite**
Mass in air (g)		
Weight in air (N)		
Beginning volume of water (mL)	DO NOT WRITE IN BOOK	
Final volume of water (mL)		
Volume of mineral (mL)		
Weight in water (N)		

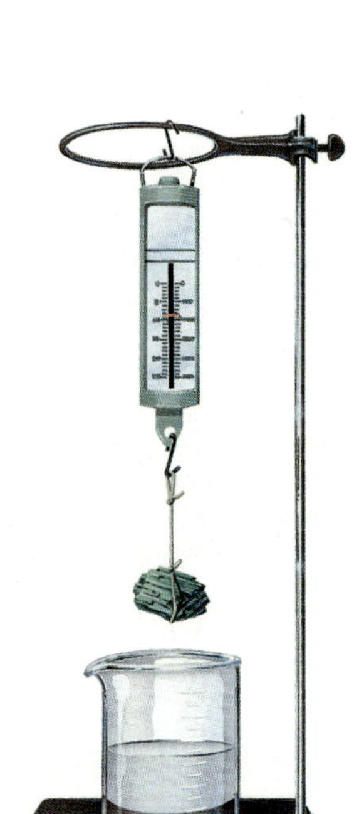

3. Find the mass of each sample by laying the mineral on the balance. Record the mass of each in your data table.
4. Attach the spring scale to the ring stand.
5. Tie a string around the sample of galena, leaving a loop at the loose end. Suspend the galena from the spring scale, and find its weight in air. Do not remove the sample from the spring scale yet. Enter these data in your data table.

Norman Holcomb
Marion Local Schools
Maria Stein, Ohio

6. Fill a beaker halfway with water. Record the beginning volume of water in your data table.
7. Carefully lift the beaker around the galena until the mineral is completely submerged. Be careful not to splash any water out of the beaker! Be sure the mineral does not touch the beaker.
8. Record the new volume and weight in your data table.
9. Subtract the original volume of water from the new volume to find the amount of water displaced by the mineral. This is the volume of the mineral sample itself. Record this value in your data table.
10. Repeat steps 5–9 for the sample of pyrite.

Analyze the Results

11. Copy the data table below into your ScienceLog. **Note:** 1 mL = 1 cm^3
12. Use the following equations to calculate the density and specific gravity of each mineral, and record your answers in your data table.

$$\text{Density} = \frac{\text{mass in air}}{\text{volume}}$$

$$\text{Specific gravity} = \frac{\text{weight in air}}{\text{weight in air} - \text{weight in water}}$$

Mineral	Density (g/cm^3)	Specific gravity
Silver	10.5	10–12
Galena		
Pyrite		
Gold	19.3	15.3–19.3

Draw Conclusions

13. The density of pure gold is 19.3 g/cm^3. How can you use this information to prove that your sample of pyrite is not gold?
14. The density of pure silver is 10.5 g/cm^3. How can you use this information to prove that your sample of galena is not silver?
15. If you found a gold-colored nugget, how could you find out if the nugget was real gold or fool's gold?

Going Further
Sugar cubes dissolve in water. Explain how you would find the density of a sugar cube.

Answers

12.

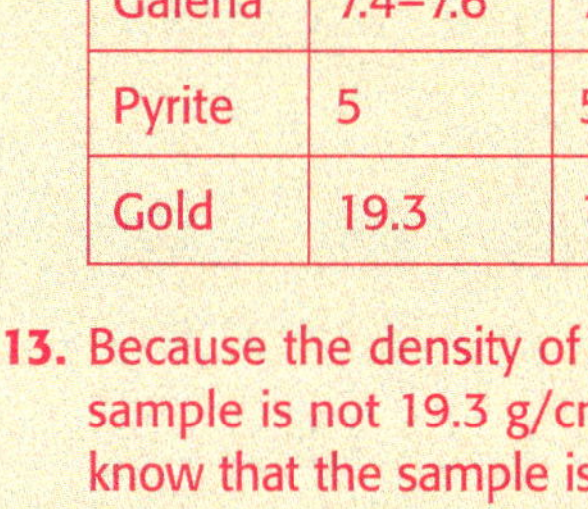

Mineral	Density (g/cm^3)	Specific gravity
Silver	10.5	10–12
Galena	7.4–7.6	7.4–7.6
Pyrite	5	5
Gold	19.3	15.3–19.3

13. Because the density of your sample is not 19.3 g/cm^3, you know that the sample is not pure gold. You cannot use the density of your sample to prove that the sample is a certain substance—only to prove that it is not a pure sample of that substance.
14. Because the density of your sample is not 10.5 g/cm^3, you know that the sample is not pure silver. Your sample could contain silver mixed with other minerals.

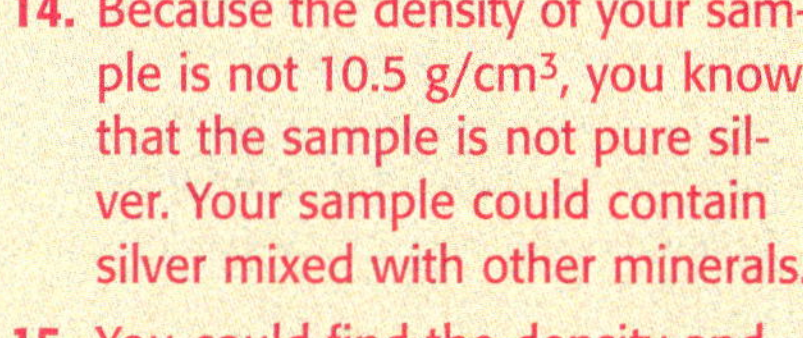

15. You could find the density and specific gravity of your gold-colored nugget. If it is pure gold, the density will be 19.3 g/cm^3 and the specific gravity will be 19.3. If your sample does not have this density and specific gravity, it is not pure gold. If it does have this density and specific gravity, it could be gold, but you would have to perform more tests to prove it.

Datasheets for LabBook Datasheet 6

Going Further

To find the volume of a cube, students can multiply length times width times height. The mass divided by the volume equals the density of the sugar cube. Additionally, you may substitute another liquid for the water. For example, sugar does not dissolve in oil.

Crystal Growth
Teacher's Notes

Time Required
Two 45-minute class periods

Lab Ratings

TEACHER PREP 2
STUDENT SET-UP 2
CONCEPT LEVEL 2
CLEAN UP 1

MATERIALS

The materials listed are enough for a group of 4–5 students working cooperatively. Using a higher proportion of magnesium sulfate crystals to water will take significantly longer.

Safety Caution
Remind students to review all safety cautions and icons before beginning this lab activity.

Preparation Notes
Samples of igneous rocks may be obtained locally or through various science supply catalogs.

Gordon Zibelman
Drexel Hill Middle School
Drexel Hill, Pennsylvania

Crystal Growth

Magma forms deep below the Earth's surface at depths of 25 to 160 km and at extremely high temperatures. Some magma reaches the surface and cools quickly. Other magma gets trapped in cracks or magma chambers beneath the surface and cools very slowly. In both cases, the magma forms crystals as it cools and solidifies. The size of the crystals found in igneous rocks gives geologists clues about where and how the crystals formed.

When magma cools slowly, large, well-developed crystals form. On the other hand, when magma erupts onto the surface, heat is lost rapidly to the air or water. There is not enough time for large crystals to grow.

In this experiment, you will demonstrate how the rate of cooling affects the size of crystals in igneous rocks by cooling crystals of magnesium sulfate at two different rates.

Materials

- heat-resistant gloves
- 400 mL beaker
- 200 mL of tap water
- hot plate
- Celsius thermometer
- magnesium sulfate ($MgSO_4$) (Epsom salts)
- hand lens
- pointed laboratory scoop
- medium test tube
- distilled water
- watch or clock
- aluminum foil
- test-tube tongs
- dark marker
- masking tape
- basalt
- pumice
- granite

SCIENTIFIC METHOD

Make a Prediction

1. Suppose you have two solutions that are identical in every way except for temperature. How will the temperature of a solution affect the size of the crystals and the rate at which they form?

Make Observations

2. Put on your gloves, apron, and goggles.
3. Fill the beaker halfway with tap water. Place the beaker on the hot plate, and let it begin to warm. The temperature of the water should be between 40°C and 50°C. **Caution:** Make sure the hot plate is away from the edge of the lab table.
4. Examine two or three crystals of the magnesium sulfate with your hand lens. In your ScienceLog, describe the color, shape, luster, and other interesting features of the crystals.
5. Draw a sketch of the magnesium sulfate crystals in your ScienceLog.

Conduct an Experiment

6. Use the pointed laboratory scoop to fill the test tube about halfway with the magnesium sulfate. Add an equal amount of distilled water.

California Standards: PE/ATE 1d, 7, 7a, 7b, 7d, 7e, 7h

7. Hold the test tube in one hand, and use one finger from your other hand to tap the test tube gently. Observe the solution mixing as you continue to tap the test tube.
8. Place the test tube in the beaker of hot water, and heat it for approximately 3 minutes. **Caution:** Be sure to direct the opening of the test tube away from you and other students.
9. While the test tube is heating, shape your aluminum foil into two small boatlike containers by doubling the foil and turning up each edge.
10. If all the magnesium sulfate is not dissolved after 3 minutes, tap the test tube again, and heat it for 3 more minutes. **Caution:** Use the test-tube tongs to handle the hot test tube.
11. With a marker and a piece of masking tape, label one of your aluminum boats "Sample 1", and place it on the hot plate. Turn the hot plate off.
12. Label the other aluminum boat "Sample 2," and place it on the lab table.
13. Using the test-tube tongs, remove the test tube from the beaker of water, and evenly distribute the contents to each of your foil boats. Carefully pour the hot water in the beaker down the drain. Do not move or disturb either of your foil boats.

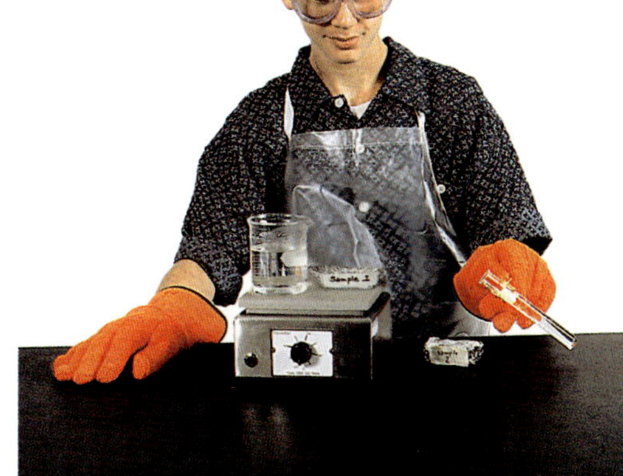

14. Copy the table below into your ScienceLog. Using the hand lens, carefully observe the foil boats. Record the time it takes for the first crystals to appear.
15. If crystals have not formed in the boats before class is over, carefully place the boats in a safe place. You may then record the time in days instead of in minutes.
16. When crystals have formed in both boats, use your hand lens to examine the crystals carefully.

Crystal-Formation Table

Crystal formation	Time	Size and appearance of crystals	Sketch of crystals
Sample 1			
Sample 2			

Lab Notes

Some volcanic rocks contain both large and small crystals. This is because the magma cooled for a period of time before erupting. This period of time was long enough for some minerals to crystallize but too short for other minerals to form.

Datasheets for LabBook
Datasheet 7

Answers

17. Answers will vary. Students may predict that the crystal would grow where it was warm but at a slower rate than where it was cool.
18. Because the original crystals were small, students may conclude that they formed quickly.
20. Accept all reasonable sketches.
21. See the chart at the bottom of the page.

Going Further

Volcanic rocks that form in the air as the result of a violent volcanic eruption would cool quickly, so they would have small crystals. Volcanic rocks that form from lava oozing out of a volcano would cool more slowly, so they would have larger crystals.

Science Skills Worksheet 27
"Interpreting Your Data"

Analyze the Results

17. Was your prediction correct? Explain.
18. Compare the size and shape of the crystals in Samples 1 and 2 with the size and shape of the crystals you examined in step 4. How long do you think the formation of the original crystals must have taken?

Draw Conclusions

19. Granite, basalt, and pumice are all igneous rocks. The most distinctive feature of each is the size of their crystals. Different igneous rocks form when magma cools at different rates. Examine a sample of each with your hand lens.
20. Copy the table below into your ScienceLog, and sketch each rock sample.
21. Use what you have learned in this activity to explain how each rock sample formed and how long it took for the crystals to form. Record your answers in your table.

Igneous Rock Observations

	Granite	Basalt	Pumice
Sketch			
How did the rock sample form?		DO NOT WRITE IN BOOK	
Rate of cooling			

Going Further

Describe the size and shape of the crystals you would expect to find when a volcano erupts and sends material into the air and when magma oozes down the volcano's slope.

500

21.

	Granite	Basalt	Pumice
How did the rock sample form?	when magma cools slowly beneath the Earth's surface	when lava cools quickly on the Earth's surface	when magma is ejected from a volcano during a violent eruption
Rate of cooling	cools slowly; large crystals	cools quickly; small crystals	cools very quickly; very small or no crystals

Let's Get Sedimental

Superposition makes a lot of sense. Consider the following statement: "In an undisturbed column of sedimentary rock, the oldest rock has to be on the bottom." You cannot drop sediment on top of something that isn't there any more than you can sit on a chair that isn't there. But notice the word *undisturbed.* That means the layers of sediment today look exactly like they did when they first settled—there has been no folding and no flipping over. But how do we determine if sedimentary rocks are undisturbed? The best way is to be sure that the top of the layer still points up. This experiment will show you how to read rock features that say, in effect, "This side up." Then you can look for the signs at a real outcrop.

Materials

- sand
- gravel
- soil (clay-rich, if available)
- 3 L mixing bowl
- plastic pickle jar or 3 L plastic soda bottle with a cap
- water
- scissors
- dropper pipet
- magnifying lens

Procedure

1. Thoroughly mix the sand, gravel, and soil together, and fill the plastic container about one-third full of the mixture.
2. Add water until the container is two-thirds full. Twist the cap back onto the container, and shake the container vigorously until all of the sediment is mixed in the rapidly moving water.

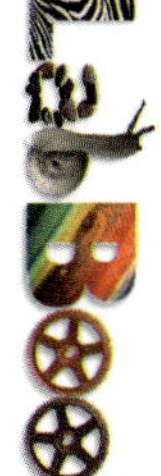

3. Place the container on a tabletop. Using the scissors, carefully cut the top off the container a few centimeters above the water, as shown at right. This will promote evaporation.
4. Do not disturb the container. Allow the water to evaporate. (You may accelerate the process by carefully using the dropper pipet to siphon off some of the clear water after allowing the container to sit for at least 24 hours.)
5. Immediately after you set the bottle on the desk, describe what you see from above and through the sides of the bottle. Do this at least once each day. Record your observations in your ScienceLog.
6. After the sediment has dried and hardened, describe its surface in your ScienceLog.
7. Carefully lay the container on its side, and cut a strip of plastic out of the side to expose the sediments in the bottle. You may find it easier if you place pieces of clay on either side of the bottle to stabilize it.

501

Let's Get Sedimental Teacher's Notes

Time Required

Two 45-minute class periods

Lab Ratings

TEACHER PREP 1
STUDENT SET-UP 2
CONCEPT LEVEL 2
CLEAN UP 3

MATERIALS

The materials listed are enough for a group of 3–4 students. You may substitute smaller plastic bottles. The amount of sand, gravel, and soil depends on the size of the jar. Each group will need enough of these materials to fill the bottle two-thirds full with a mixture of sand, gravel, and soil.

Safety Caution

Remind students to review all safety cautions and icons before beginning this lab activity. Students should be extremely careful when cutting the sides from the plastic bottles.

Preparation Notes

If the students use larger plastic bottles, it may take several days for the sediment to dry completely. It may be a good idea to ask the students to follow steps 1–5 as an introduction to the chapter. The class can then finish the procedure when the sediment has dried and you have covered all of the concepts.

Helen Schiller
Northwood Middle School
Taylors, South Carolina

Lab Notes

This lab illustrates the sedimentary (depositional) process of *sorting.* When sediment is suspended in water, the largest, heaviest particles will settle out first, followed by the finer, lighter particles. This process allows scientists and students studying sedimentary rock layers to determine the original orientation of the rock.

California Standards: PE/ATE 7, 7b, 7d, 7e, 7h

Answers

9. Students should understand that the finest sediments should be at the top layers. This sequence can indicate the top of a sedimentary outcrop.

10. Students might find mud cracks and peels on the top layer. Scientists would not expect to find these features in the bottom of an undisturbed column of sedimentary rock.

11. If features that scientists expect to find only in the top layer are found elsewhere, this indicates that the column has been disturbed. Scientists carefully observe the layers for these features so they can determine the original order of the layers.

12. Each layer should show finer particles at the top. This pattern may be seen only from the side.

13. Students should see the same grading effect at the boundaries. The changes within each layer will be gradual, but the changes between different layers in the "rock" column may be more dramatic.

Going Further

Answers will vary. Students should realize that finding the bottom layer would help because in an undisturbed column the bottom layer is down. Students also should realize that the bottom of the new layer would fill in gaps in the top of the column in their container. For example, any cracks would be filled with the new sediment. This may appear as a wall or partition extending from the bottom of the new layer.

Datasheets for LabBook
Datasheet 8

8. Brush away the loose material from the sediment, and gently blow on the surface until it is clean. Examine the surface, and record your observations in your ScienceLog.

Analysis

9. Do you see anything through the side of the bottle that could help you determine if a sedimentary rock is undisturbed? Explain.

10. What structures do you see on the surface of the sediment that you would not expect to find at the bottom?

11. Explain how these features might be used to identify the top of the sedimentary bed in a real outcrop and to decide if the bed has been disturbed.

12. Did you see any structures on the side of the container that might indicate which direction is up?

13. After removing the side of the bottle, use the magnifying glass to examine the boundaries between the gravel, sand, and silt. What do you see? Do the size and type of sediment change quickly or gradually?

Going Further

Explain why the following statement is true: "If the top of a layer can't be found, finding the bottom of it works just as well." Imagine that a layer was deposited directly above the layers in your container. Describe the bottom of this layer.

Metamorphic Mash

Metamorphism is a complex process that takes place deep within the Earth, where the temperature and pressure would turn a human into a crispy pancake. The effects of this extreme temperature and pressure are obvious in some metamorphic rocks. One of these effects is the reorganization of mineral grains within the rock fabric. In this activity, you will investigate the process of metamorphism without being charred, flattened, or buried.

Materials

- modeling clay
- sequins or other small flat objects
- plastic knife
- small pieces of very stiff cardboard or plywood

Procedure

1. Flatten the clay into a layer about 1 cm thick. Sprinkle the surface with sequins.
2. Roll the corners of the clay toward the middle to form a neat ball.
3. Carefully use the plastic knife to cut the ball in half. In your ScienceLog, describe the position and location of the sequins inside the ball.
4. Put the ball back together, and use the sheets of cardboard or plywood to flatten the ball until it is about 2 cm thick.
5. Using the plastic knife, slice open the slab of clay in several places. In your ScienceLog, describe the position and location of the sequins in the slab.

Analysis

6. What physical process does flattening the ball represent?
7. Describe any changes in the position and location of the sequins that occurred as the clay ball was flattened into a slab.
8. How are the sequins oriented in relation to the force you put on the ball to flatten it?
9. Do you think the orientation of the mineral grains in a foliated metamorphic rock tells you anything about the rock? Defend your answer.

Going Further

Suppose you find a foliated metamorphic rock that has grains running in two distinct directions. Use what you have learned in this activity to offer a possible explanation for this observation.

Metamorphic Mash Teacher's Notes

Time Required

One 45-minute class period

Lab Ratings

TEACHER PREP: 1
STUDENT SET-UP: 1
CONCEPT LEVEL: 2
CLEAN UP: 2

MATERIALS

The materials listed in the student page are enough for one student.

Safety Caution

Remind students to review all safety cautions and icons before beginning this lab activity.

Answers

3. The sequins should be lying in a random pattern. Any layering is left over from rolling the ball.
5. The sequins are all horizontal.
6. the pressure that creates metamorphic rock
7. Before the ball was flattened, the sequins were in a random pattern. Once the ball was flattened, they lined up perpendicular to the pressure.
8. The sequins are aligned perpendicular to the force.
9. Because the grains line up at right angles to the pressure, they are perpendicular to the strongest stress.

Going Further

Two pressures acting on the rock at different times must have pushed on the rock in different directions.

CLASSROOM TESTED & APPROVED

Dwight Patton
Carrol T. Welch Middle School
Horizon City, Texas

Datasheets for LabBook
Datasheet 9

California Standards: PE/ATE 7, 7b, 7d, 7e

Make A Water Wheel
Teacher's Notes

Time Required
One or two 45-minute class periods

Lab Ratings

TEACHER PREP 1
STUDENT SET-UP 3
CONCEPT LEVEL 1
CLEAN UP 1

MATERIALS

The materials listed are best for a group of 3–4 students.

Safety Caution
Remind students to review all safety cautions and icons before beginning this lab activity.

Preparation Notes
One week before the activity, have students bring in empty, 1 gal plastic milk and distilled-water jugs. (Be sure that the milk jugs are thoroughly rinsed.) You can also get these from a plastic recycling drop-off center. Do not use plastic jugs that once contained harmful chemicals. Also have students bring in empty 2 L soda bottles. Obtain corks from a craft store, or collect them yourself. Some restaurants will save corks for you from opened wine bottles if you ask ahead of time. You may wish to have extra corks on hand; some corks become dry, brittle, and crumbly. Skewers can be obtained at a grocery store; they usually come in packages of 200 and are inexpensive. Pick off the rough fibers from the skewers to reduce the friction.

SKILL BUILDER

Make a Water Wheel

Lift Enterprises is planning to build a water wheel that will lift objects like a crane does. City planners feel that this would make very good use of the energy supplied by the river that flows through town. Development of the water wheel is in the early stages. The president of the company has asked you to modify the basic water-wheel design so that the final product will lift objects more quickly.

Materials
- index card
- metric ruler
- scissors
- safety razor (for teacher)
- large plastic milk jug
- permanent marker
- 5 thumbtacks
- cork
- glue
- 2 wooden skewers
- hole punch
- modeling clay
- transparent tape
- 20 cm of thread
- coin
- 2 L bottle filled with water
- watch or clock that indicates seconds

Ask a Question
1. What factors influence the rate at which a water wheel lifts a weight?

Form a Hypothesis
2. In your ScienceLog, change the question above into a statement giving your "best guess" as to what factors will have the greatest effect on your water wheel.

Build a Model
3. Measure and mark a 5 × 5 cm square on an index card. Cut the square out of the card.
4. Fold the square in half to form a triangle.
5. Measure and mark a line 8 cm from the bottom of the plastic jug. Use scissors to cut along this line. (Your teacher may need to use a safety razor to start this cut for you.) Keep both sections of the jug.

6. Use the permanent marker to trace four triangles onto the flat parts of the top section of the plastic jug. Use the paper triangle you made in step 4 as a template. Cut the triangles out of the plastic to form four fins.
7. Use a thumbtack to attach one corner of each plastic fin to the round edge of the cork, as shown at right. Make sure the fins are equally spaced around the cork.

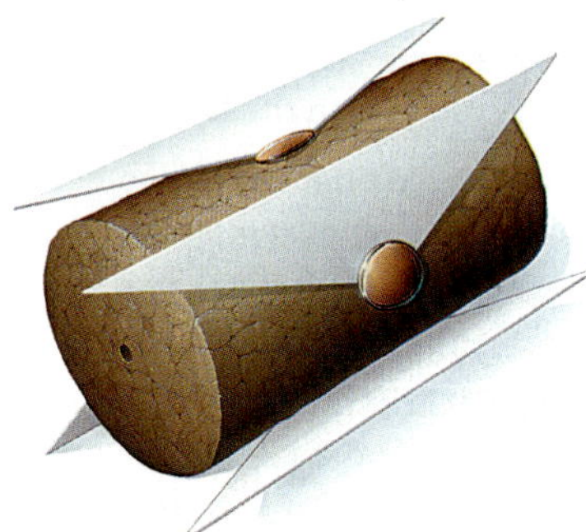

8. Press a thumbtack into one of the flat sides of the cork. Jiggle the thumbtack to widen the hole in the cork, and then remove the thumbtack.
9. Repeat step 8 on the other side of the cork.

Lab Notes
If the coin is lowered instead of raised in step 16, instruct students to unwrap the thread, wrap it in the other direction around the clay, and repeat step 16. You may wish to have a class competition to see which wheel can lift the weight the fastest.

Tracy Jahn
Berkshire Jr.–Sr. High
Canaan, New York

California Standards: PE/ATE 7, 7b, 7e

10. Place a drop of glue on the end of a skewer, and insert the skewer into one of the holes in the end of the cork. Insert the second skewer into the hole in the other end.

11. Use a hole punch to carefully punch two holes in the bottom section of the plastic jug. Punch each hole 1 cm from the top edge of the jug, directly across from one another.

12. Carefully push the skewers through the holes, and suspend the cork in the center of the jug.

13. Attach a small ball of clay to the end of each skewer. The clay balls should be the same size.

14. Tape one end of the thread to one skewer on the outside of the jug next to the clay ball. Wrap the thread around the clay ball three times. (As the water wheel turns, the thread should continue to wrap around the clay. The other ball of clay balances the weight and helps to keep the water wheel turning smoothly.)

15. Tape the free end of the thread to a coin. Wrap the thread around the coin once, and tape it again. You are now ready to test your hypothesis.

Test the Hypothesis

16. Slowly and carefully pour water from the 2 L bottle onto the fins so that the water wheel spins. What happens to the coin? Record your observations in your ScienceLog.

17. Lower the coin back to the starting position. Add more clay to the skewer to increase the diameter of the wheel. Repeat step 16. Did the coin rise faster or slower this time?

18. Lower the coin back to the starting position. Modify the shape of the clay, and repeat step 16. Does the shape of the clay affect how quickly the coin rises? Explain your answer.

19. What happens if you remove two of the fins from opposite sides? What happens if you add more fins? Modify your water wheel to find out.

20. Experiment with another fin shape. How does a different fin shape affect how quickly the coin rises?

Analyze the Results

21. What factors influence how quickly you can lift the coin?

Draw Conclusions

22. What recommendations would you make to Lift Enterprises to improve its water wheel?

Going Further

Design and build your own water wheel using the materials from this activity. Decide how many fins to use and what shape the fins should be. As a class, hold a competition to see which wheel can lift the most weight.

Answers

16. The coin rises.
17. The coin rises faster with more clay.
18. If the clay is shaped so that the thread has to wrap around a bulge, the coin will rise faster. If the clay is shaped so that the thread has to wrap around a narrow part, the coin will rise slower.
19. Fewer fins cause the wheel to turn slower, causing the coin to rise slower. More fins cause the wheel to turn faster, causing the coin to rise faster.
20. Generally, fins that catch more water will cause the wheel to turn faster, causing the coin to rise faster.
21. The shape and amount of clay and the number and shape of the fins influence how quickly the wheel is able to lift the coin.
22. Recommendations should include that the following will allow the water wheel to lift objects more quickly: more fins, fin shapes that catch more water, and wrapping the rope or cable around a large diameter.

Datasheets for LabBook Datasheet 10

Power of the Sun
Teacher's Notes

Time Required
One or two 45-minute class periods

Lab Ratings

TEACHER PREP ▲▲
STUDENT SET-UP ▲
CONCEPT LEVEL ▲▲
CLEAN UP ▲

MATERIALS

The materials listed for this lab are enough for a group of 2–3 students.

Safety Caution
Remind students to review all safety cautions and icons before beginning this lab activity. Before beginning this lab, you may wish to review the concept of ratios with students. Instruct students to not look directly at the sun. Also caution them not to squeeze the aluminum too hard around the thermometer to avoid crushing the thermometer bulb. Also tell students not to force the thermometers through the holes if the holes are too small.

Preparation Notes
Prepare the lids by punching a hole in the center of each lid with a nail and hammer. Flatten the jagged edges against the inside of the lid with the hammer. Each hole should be big enough to accommodate a thermometer. Cut 2 × 8 cm strips of aluminum from the bottom of a pie plate. Make sure there are no sharp burrs left on the edges of the strips.

Power of the Sun

DISCOVERY LAB

The sun radiates energy in every direction. Like the sun, the energy radiated by a light bulb spreads out in all directions. But how much energy an object receives depends on how close that object is to the source. As you move farther from the source, the amount of energy you receive decreases. For example, if you measure the amount of energy that reaches you from a light and then move three times farther away, you will discover that nine times less energy will reach you at your second position. Energy from the sun travels as light energy. When light energy is absorbed by an object it is converted into heat energy. *Power* is the rate at which one form of energy is converted to another, and it is measured in *watts.* Because power is related to distance, nearby objects can be used to measure the power of far-away objects. In this lab you will calculate the power of the sun using an ordinary 100-watt light bulb.

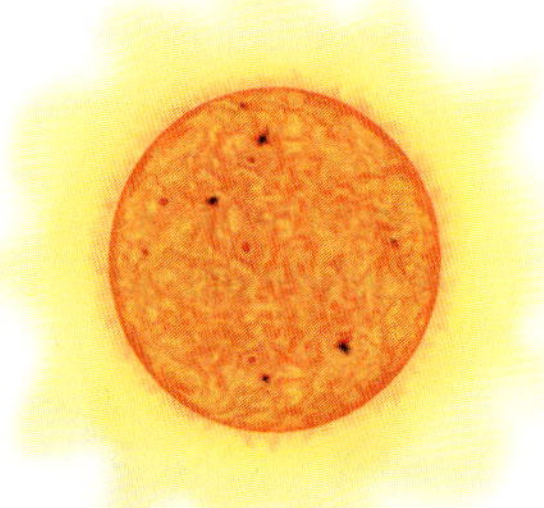

Materials
- protective gloves
- aluminum strip, 2 × 8 cm
- pencil
- black permanent marker
- Celsius thermometer
- mason jar, cap, and lid with hole in center
- modeling clay
- desk lamp with a 100 W bulb and removable shade
- metric ruler
- watch or clock that indicates seconds
- scientific calculator

Procedure
1. Gently shape the piece of aluminum around a pencil so that it holds on in the middle and has two wings, one on either side of the pencil.
2. Bend the wings outward so that they can catch as much sunlight as possible.
3. Use the marker to color both wings on one side of the aluminum strip black.
4. Remove the pencil and place the aluminum snugly around the thermometer near the bulb.
   Caution: Do not press too hard—you do not want to break the thermometer! Wear protective gloves when working with the thermometer and the aluminum.
5. Carefully slide the top of the thermometer through the hole in the lid. Place the lid on the jar so that the thermometer bulb is inside the jar, and screw down the cap.
6. Secure the thermometer to the jar lid by molding clay around the thermometer on the outside of the lid. The aluminum wings should be in the center of the jar.
7. Read the temperature on the thermometer. Record this as room temperature.
8. Place the jar on a windowsill in the sunlight. Turn the jar so that the black wings are angled toward the sun.
9. Watch the thermometer until the temperature reading stops rising. Record the temperature in your ScienceLog.
10. Remove the jar from direct sunlight, and allow it to return to room temperature.

Gordon Zibelman
Drexel Hill Middle School
Drexel Hill, Pennsylvania

California Standards: PE/ATE 4b, 7, 7b, 7e

11. Remove any shade or reflector from the lamp. Place the lamp at one end of a table.
12. Place the jar about 30 cm from the lamp. Turn the jar so that the wings are angled toward the lamp.
13. Turn on the lamp, and wait about 1 minute.
14. Move the jar a few centimeters toward the lamp until the temperature reading starts to rise. When the temperature stops rising, compare it with the reading you took in step 9.
15. Repeat step 14 until the temperature matches the temperature you recorded in step 9.
16. If the temperature reading rises too high, move the jar away from the lamp and allow it to cool. Once the reading has dropped to at least 5°C below the temperature you recorded in step 9, you may begin again at step 12.
17. When the temperature in the jar matches the temperature you recorded in step 9, record the distance between the center of the light bulb and the thermometer bulb in your ScienceLog.

Analysis

18. The thermometer measured the same amount of energy absorbed by the jar at the distance you measured to the lamp. In other words, your jar absorbed as much energy from the sun at a distance of 150 million kilometers as it did from the 100 W light bulb at the distance you recorded in step 17.
19. Use the following formula to calculate the power of the sun (be sure to show your work):

$$\frac{\text{power of the sun}}{(\text{distance to the sun})^2} = \frac{\text{power of the lamp}}{(\text{distance to the lamp})^2}$$

Hint: $(\text{distance})^2$ means that you multiply the distance by itself. If you found that the lamp was 5 cm away from the jar, for example, the $(\text{distance})^2$ would be 25.

Hint: Convert 150,000,000 km to 15,000,000,000,000 cm.

20. Review the discussion of scientific notation in the Math Refresher found in the Appendix at the back of this book. You will need to understand this technique for writing large numbers in order to compare your calculation with the actual figure. For practice, convert the distance to the sun given in step 19 to scientific notation.

$15{,}000{,}000{,}000{,}000 \text{ cm} = 1.5 \times 10^{\underline{?}} \text{ cm}$

21. The sun emits 3.7×10^{26} W of power. Compare your answer in step 19 with this value. Was this a good way to calculate the power of the sun? Explain.

Answers

19. Answers will vary. Ask students to show their calculations.
20. 13 (1.5×10^{13})
21. Answers will vary. If students performed the lab correctly, their numbers should be close to 3.7×10^{26} W.

Datasheets for LabBook Datasheet 11

Math Skills Worksheet 25 "What Is Scientific Notation?"

Math Skills Worksheet 26 "Multiplying and Dividing in Scientific Notation"

Convection Connection
Teacher's Notes

Time Required

One 45-minute class period

Lab Ratings

Teacher Prep 1
Student Set-Up 3
Concept Level 2
Clean Up 2

MATERIALS

The materials listed on the student page are enough for a group of 2–3 students.

Safety Caution

Remind students to review all safety cautions and icons before beginning this lab activity.

Preparation Notes

Because of the volume of water being used, you may wish to set up the blocks and hot plates ahead of time. Also, breezes and drafts may move the craft sticks, so eliminate or reduce as many of these variables as possible.

Datasheets for LabBook
Datasheet 12

Terry J. Rakes
Elmwood Jr. High
Rogers, Arkansas

MAKING MODELS

Convection Connection

Some scientists think convection currents within the Earth's mantle are responsible for the movement of tectonic plates. Because these convection currents cannot be observed, scientists use models to simulate the process. In this activity, you will make your own model to simulate tectonic-plate movement.

Materials

- heat-resistant gloves
- 2 small hot plates
- rectangular aluminum pan
- wooden blocks
- cold water
- 2 craft sticks
- pencil
- metric ruler
- food coloring
- 3 thermometers

Procedure

1. Place two hot plates side by side in the center of your lab table. Be sure they are safely away from the edge of the table.
2. Place the pan on top of the hot plates. Slide the wooden blocks under the pan to support the ends. Make sure the pan is level and secure.
3. Fill the pan with cold water. The water should be at least 4 cm deep. Turn on the hot plates, and put on your gloves.
4. After a minute or two, tiny bubbles will begin to rise in the water above the hot plates. Gently place two craft sticks on the water's surface.
5. Use the pencil to align the sticks parallel to the short ends of the pan. The sticks should be about 3 cm apart and near the center of the pan.
6. As soon as the sticks begin to move, place a drop of food coloring in the water at the center of the pan. Observe what happens to the food coloring.
7. With the help of a partner, hold one thermometer bulb just under the water at the center of the pan. Hold the other two thermometers just under the water near the ends of the pan. Record the temperatures.
8. When you are finished, turn off the hot plates. After the water has completely cooled, carefully empty the water into a sink.

Analysis

9. Based on your observations of the motion of the food coloring, how does the temperature of the water affect the direction the water moves?
10. How does the motion of the craft sticks relate to the motion of the water?
11. How does this model relate to plate tectonics and the movement of the continents?

508

Answers

9. The warmer water moves up, and the cooler water moves down.
10. The moving water pushed the sticks away from each other and toward the edges of the pan. (In some cases, the sticks may move together.)
11. Convection currents within the Earth's mantle may move tectonic plates in the same way the convecting water moved the craft sticks. The convection currents in this model were created by the hot plates warming the water. In the mantle, convection currents are caused by heat from deep within the Earth.

California Standards: PE/ATE 1, 1b, 1c, 7, 7b, 7e

Oh, the Pressure!

MAKING MODELS

When scientists want to understand natural processes, such as mountain formation, they often make models to help them. Models are useful in studying how rocks react to the forces of plate tectonics. In a short amount of time, a model can demonstrate geological processes that take millions of years. Do the following activity to find out how folding and faulting occur in the Earth's crust.

Materials

- modeling clay in 4 different colors
- 5 × 15 cm strip of poster board
- soup can or rolling pin
- newspaper
- colored pencils
- plastic knife
- 5 × 5 cm squares of poster board (2)

SCIENTIFIC METHOD

Ask a Question

1. How do synclines, anticlines, and faults form?

Conduct an Experiment

2. Use modeling clay of one color to form a long cylinder, and place the cylinder in the center of the glossy side of the poster-board strip.
3. Mold the clay to the strip. Try to make the clay layer the same thickness all along the strip; you can use the soup can or rolling pin to even it out. Pinch the sides of the clay so that it is the same width and length as the strip. Your strip should be at least 15 cm long and 5 cm wide.

Daniel Bugenhagen
Yutan Jr.—Sr. High
Yutan, Nebraska

LabBook

Oh, the Pressure!
Teacher's Notes

Time Required

One 45-minute class period

Lab Ratings

TEACHER PREP 3
STUDENT SET-UP 2
CONCEPT LEVEL 3
CLEAN UP 3

MATERIALS

The materials listed on the student page are enough for a group of 3–4 students. Modeling clay can be substituted for the modeling dough.

Safety Caution

Remind students to review all safety cautions and icons before beginning this lab activity.

Lab Notes

Modeling clay may be substituted for homemade modeling dough in this activity. In step 3, students may find it easier to trim each layer of clay with the plastic knife before stacking the layers together.

Datasheets for LabBook
Datasheet 13

California Standards: PE/ATE 1, 1e, 7, 7b, 7d, 7e

Preparation Notes

The night before the activity, prepare enough modeling dough for each class using the recipe below. The recipe provides enough dough for each group. Combine the following ingredients in a large saucepan over low heat in the order that they are listed:

- 2 cups cold water
- $\frac{1}{3}$ cup cooking oil
- 1 cup salt
- 4 teaspoons cream of tartar
- 2 cups flour
- Food coloring

Constantly stir the mixture until the modeling dough forms a ball. Turn the modeling dough out onto a floured surface. Use a ruler to divide the dough into fourths. When the dough cools slightly, add 15–20 drops of food coloring to each quarter. Fold and knead to evenly distribute the color throughout the dough. Place the dough in an airtight container, such as an 8 oz yogurt container. If you freeze it, the modeling dough will last for months.

Just before the activity, cover all workspaces with newspaper and secure the newspapers in place. If the dough gets dry, rinse your hands and continue to mold the dough.

4. Flip the strip over on the newspaper your teacher has placed across your desk. Carefully peel the strip from the modeling clay.
5. Repeat steps 2–4 with the other colors of modeling clay. Each member of your group should have a turn molding the clay. Each time you flip the strip over, stack the new clay layer on top of the previous one. When you are finished, you should have a block of clay made of four layers.
6. Lift the block of clay and hold it parallel to and just above the tabletop. Push gently on the block from opposite sides, as shown below.

7. Use the colored pencils to draw the results of step 6 in your ScienceLog. Use the terms *syncline* and *anticline* to label your diagram. Draw arrows to show the direction that each edge of the clay was pushed.
8. Repeat steps 2–5 to form a second block of clay.
9. Cut the second block of clay in two at a 45° angle as seen from the side of the block.
10. Press one poster-board square on the angled end of each of the block's two pieces. The poster board represents a fault. The two angled ends represent a hanging wall and a footwall. The model should resemble the one in the photograph on the next page.

11. Keeping the angled edges together, lift the blocks and hold them parallel to and just above the tabletop. Push gently on the two blocks until they move. Record your observations in your Sciencelog.
12. Now hold the two pieces of the clay block in their original position, and slowly pull them apart, allowing the hanging wall to move downward. Record your observations.

Analyze the Results

13. What happened to the first block of clay in step 6? What kind of force did you apply to it?
14. What happened to the pieces of the second block of clay in step 11? What kind of force did you apply to them?
15. What happened to the pieces of the second block of clay in step 12? Describe the forces that acted on the block and how the pieces of the block reacted.

Draw Conclusions

16. Summarize how the forces you applied to the blocks of clay relate to the way tectonic forces affect rock layers. Be sure to use the terms *fold, fault, anticline, syncline, hanging wall, footwall, tension,* and *compression* in your summary.

Lab Notes

Students should realize that stress is equivalent to pressure or force. Explain to them that rocks can undergo stress without deforming. When the stress becomes too much or when it operates for such a long time that the rocks become folded or faulted, deformation, or *strain,* occurs. Stress and the result of stress are two different things.

Answers

13. The first block got shorter and taller. The layers of clay became folded due to compression.
14. One of the pieces (the hanging wall) slid above the other piece (the footwall) due to compression.
15. One of the pieces (the footwall) moved up relative to the other piece (the hanging wall) due to tension.
16. The conclusion should be a complete summary of this activity, indicating the direction of pressure at each step. Any diagrams should be correctly labeled, and students should show a good understanding of the terms *syncline, fold, fault, anticline, hanging wall, footwall, tension,* and *compression.*

Quake Challenge
Teacher's Notes

Time Required
One 45-minute class period

Lab Ratings

Teacher Prep: 2
Student Set-Up: 1
Concept Level: 2
Clean Up: 1

MATERIALS

The materials listed on the student page are enough for two students.

Preparation Notes
Make the gelatin 24 hours in advance to ensure that it has set sufficiently. Cut the gelatin squares ahead of time, and place each square on a piece of wax paper. For steps 8 and 9, you will need to create a gelatin square large enough to place all the student structures on. This allows each group's structure to be evaluated on its own merit. Keep the gelatin refrigerated until it's ready to be used.

Helen Schiller
Northwood Middle School
Taylors, South Carolina

Quake Challenge

In many parts of the world, it is important that buildings be built with earthquakes in mind. Each building must be designed so that the structure is protected during an earthquake. Architects have improved the design of buildings a lot since 1906, when an earthquake destroyed much of San Francisco. In this activity you will use marshmallows and toothpicks to build a structure that can withstand a simulated earthquake. In the process, you will discover some of the ways a building can be built to withstand an earthquake.

Materials
- 10 marshmallows
- 10 toothpicks
- square of gelatin, approximately 8 × 8 cm
- paper plate

Ask a Question
1. What features help a building withstand an earthquake? How can I use this information to build my structure?

Form a Hypothesis
2. Brainstorm with a classmate to design a structure that will resist the simulated earthquake. Sketch your design in your ScienceLog. Write two or three sentences to describe your design.

Test the Hypothesis
3. Follow your design to build a structure using the toothpicks and marshmallows.
4. Set your structure on a square of gelatin.
5. Shake the square of gelatin to test whether your building will remain standing during a quake. Do not pick up the gelatin.
6. If your first design does not work well, change it until you find a design that does. Try to determine why your building is falling so that you can improve your design each time.
7. Sketch your final design in your ScienceLog.
8. After you have tested your final design, place your structure on the gelatin square on your teacher's desk

512

California Standards: PE/ATE 7, 7a, 7e

9. When every group has added a structure to the teacher's gelatin, your teacher will simulate an earthquake by shaking the gelatin. Watch to see which buildings withstand the most severe quake.

Analyze the Results

10. Which buildings were still standing after the final earthquake? What features made them more stable?
11. How would you change your design to make your structure more stable?

Communicate Results

12. This was a simple model of a real-life problem for architects. Based on this activity, what advice would you give to those who design buildings in earthquake-prone areas?

Answers

10. Structures that had a wide base generally withstood the earthquake. Structures that incorporated triangles into the design also were successful.
11. Accept all reasonable answers.
12. Buildings designed in earthquake-prone areas should have wide and flexible foundations. The building should also be reinforced to prevent collapsing.

Datasheets for LabBook
Datasheet 14

Earthquake Waves
Teacher's Notes

Time Required
One 45-minute class period

Lab Ratings

Teacher Prep
Student Set-Up
Concept Level
Clean Up

MATERIALS

The materials listed in the student page are enough for two students.

Safety Caution
Remind students to review all safety cautions and icons before beginning this lab activity.

Preparation Notes
Be sure that students understand how to calculate the distance from each city to the epicenter of the earthquake in step 6. These distances must be correct to accurately determine the epicenter of the earthquake on the map.

Emphasize to students that the circles on the map must intersect or come very close to intersecting in order to determine the epicenter of the earthquake. If the circles do not come close to intersecting, tell students that they must check their calculations.

SKILL BUILDER

Earthquake Waves

The energy from an earthquake travels as seismic waves in all directions through the Earth. Seismologists can use the properties of certain types of seismic waves to find the epicenter of an earthquake.

P waves travel more quickly than S waves and are always detected first. The average speed of P waves in the Earth's crust is 6.1 km/s. The average speed of S waves in the Earth's crust is 4.1 km/s. The difference in arrival time between P waves and S waves is called *lag time.*

In this activity you will use the S-P-time method to determine the location of an earthquake's epicenter.

Materials
- calculator (optional)
- compass
- metric ruler

Procedure

1. The illustration below shows seismographic records made in three cities following an earthquake. These traces begin at the left and show the arrival of P waves at time zero. The second set of waves on each record represents the arrival of S waves.

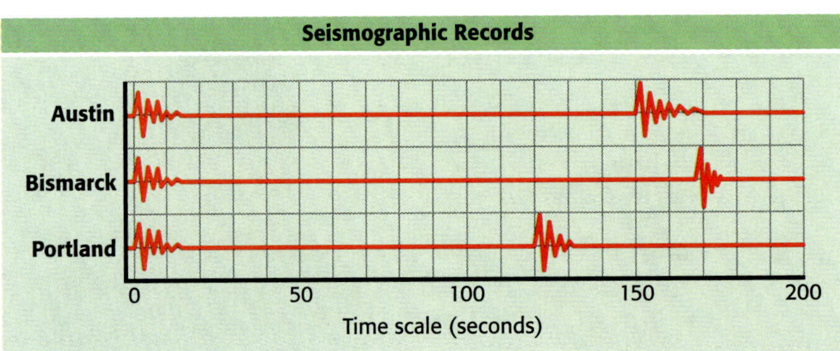

2. Copy the data table on the next page into your ScienceLog.
3. Use the time scale provided with the seismographic records to find the lag time between the P waves and the S waves for each city. Remember, the lag time is the time between the moment when the first P wave arrives and the moment when the first S wave arrives. Record this data in your table.
4. Use the following equation to calculate how long it takes each wave type to travel 100 km:

   100 km ÷ average speed of the wave = time

Janel Guse
West Central Middle School
Hartford, South Dakota

California Standards: PE/ATE 1g, 7, 7b, 7c, 7e, 7g

5. To find lag time for earthquake waves at 100 km, subtract the time it takes P waves to travel 100 km from the time it takes S waves to travel 100 km. Record the lag time in your ScienceLog.

6. Use the following formula to find the distance from each city to the epicenter:

$$\text{distance} = \frac{\text{measured lag time (s)} \times 100 \text{ km}}{\text{lag time for 100 km (s)}}$$

In your Data Table, record the distance from each city to the epicenter.

Epicenter Data Table		
City	Lag time (seconds)	Distance to the epicenter (km)
Austin, TX		
Bismarck, ND	DO NOT WRITE IN BOOK	
Portland, OR		

7. Trace the map below into your ScienceLog.

8. Use the scale to adjust your compass so that the radius of a circle with Austin at the center is equal to the distance between Austin and the epicenter of the earthquake.

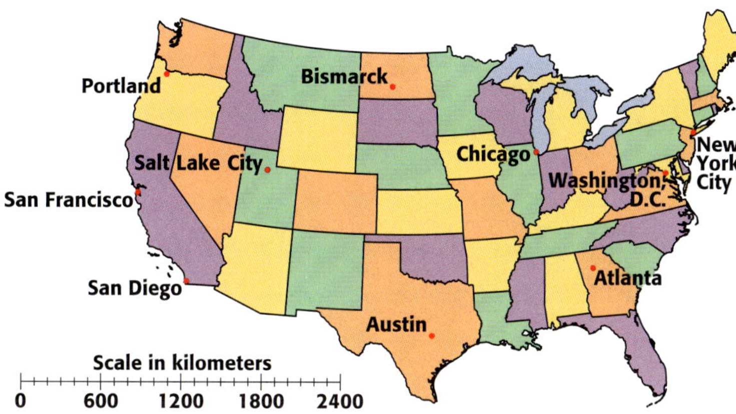

9. Put the point of your compass at Austin on your copy of the map, and draw a circle.

10. Repeat steps 8 and 9 for Bismarck and Portland. The epicenter of the earthquake is located near the point where the three circles meet.

Analysis

11. Which city is closest to the epicenter?

12. Why do seismologists need measurements from three different locations to find the epicenter of an earthquake?

Answers

3. Austin: 150 seconds
Bismarck: 168 seconds
Portland: 120 seconds

6. Austin: 1,875 km; Bismarck: 2,100 km; Portland: 1,500 km

11. San Diego, California

12. Seismologists need measurements from three different cities to ensure that the location is accurate. The first two circles intersect in two places. When a third circle is used, all three circles intersect in only one place.

Datasheets for LabBook
Datasheet 15

Science Skills Worksheet 26
"Grasping Graphing"

Some Go "Pop," Some Do Not
Teacher's Notes

Time Required
One 45-minute class period

Lab Ratings

TEACHER PREP
STUDENT SET-UP
CONCEPT LEVEL
CLEAN UP

MATERIALS

The materials listed on the student page are enough for one student.

Preparation Notes
From the unit, students should be aware that volcanoes with a high water and silica content tend to erupt explosively. They should use this information to analyze the data in this activity. You may also wish to inform students that, in general, quietly erupting volcanoes are derived from basaltic crust, while explosively erupting volcanoes are derived from granitic crust. Oceanic crust is basaltic and low in silica. Continental crust is granitic and high in silica.

DISCOVERY LAB

Some Go "Pop," Some Do Not

Volcanic eruptions range from mild to violent. When volcanoes erupt, the materials left behind provide information to scientists studying the Earth's crust. Mild, or nonexplosive, eruptions produce thin, runny lava that is low in silica. During nonexplosive eruptions, lava simply flows down the side of the volcano. Explosive eruptions, on the other hand, do not produce much lava. Instead, the explosions hurl ash and debris into the air. The materials left behind are light in color and high in silica. These materials help geologists determine the composition of the crust underneath the volcanoes.

Materials
- graph paper
- metric ruler
- red, yellow, and orange colored pencils or markers

Procedure
1. Copy the map below onto graph paper. Take care to line the grid up properly.
2. Locate each volcano from the list on the next page by drawing a circle with a diameter of about 1 cm in the proper location on your copy of the map. Use the latitude and longitude grids to help you.
3. Review all the eruptions for each volcano. For each explosive eruption, color the circle red. For each quiet volcano, color the circle yellow. For volcanoes that have erupted in both ways, color the circle orange.

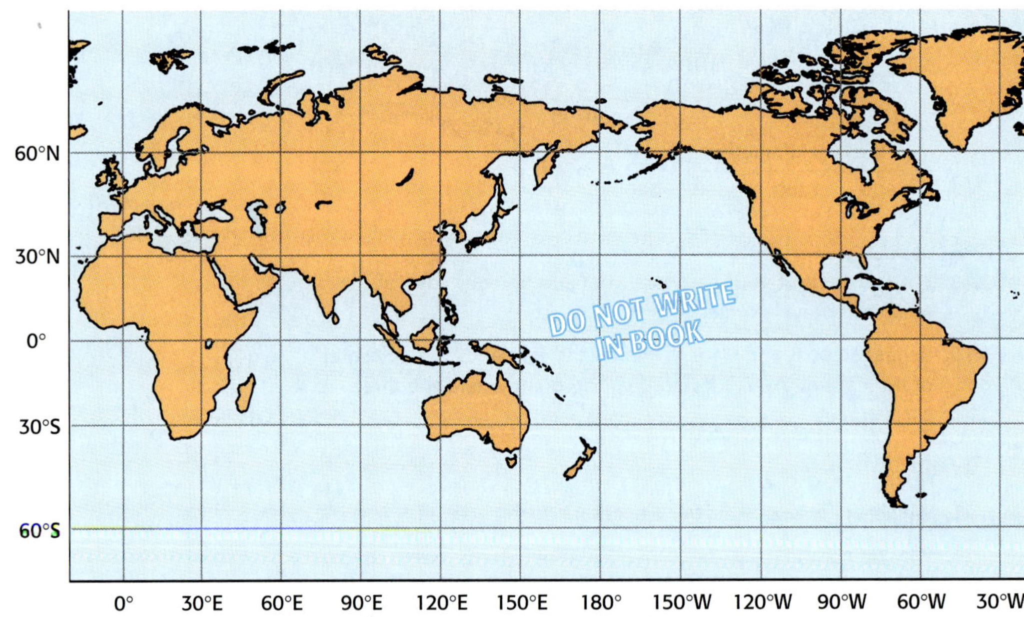

Lab Notes
In a very simple way, this lab models how the composition of magma can evolve. For example, basaltic (mafic) magma can evolve into granitic (felsic) magma through chemical differentiation processes. Scientists often use measurements of trace elements in the resulting rock to "fingerprint" the source of magma from which volcanic rocks formed.

C. John Graves
Monforton Middle School
Bozeman, Montana

Volcanic Activity Chart		
Volcano name	**Location**	**Description**
Mount St. Helens	46°N 122°W	An explosive eruption blew the top off the mountain. Light-colored ash covered thousands of square kilometers. Another eruption sent a lava flow down the southeast side of the mountain.
Kilauea	19°N 155°W	One small eruption sent a lava flow along 12 km of highway.
Rabaul caldera	4°S 152°E	Explosive eruptions have caused tsunamis and have left 1–2 m of ash on nearby buildings.
Popocatépetl	19°N 98°W	During one explosion, Mexico City closed the airport for 14 hours because huge columns of ash made it too difficult for pilots to see. Eruptions from this volcano have also caused damaging avalanches.
Soufriere Hills	16°N 62°W	Small eruptions have sent lava flows down the hills. Other explosive eruptions have sent large columns of ash into the air.
Long Valley caldera	37°N 119°W	Explosive eruptions have sent ash into the air.
Okmok	53°N 168°W	Recently, there have been slow lava flows from this volcano. Twenty-five hundred years ago, ash and debris exploded from the top of this volcano.
Pavlof	55°N 161°W	Eruption clouds have been sent 200 m above the summit. Eruptions have sent ash columns 10 km into the air. Occasionally, small eruptions have caused lava flows.
Fernandina	42°N 12°E	Eruptions have ejected large blocks of rock from this volcano.
Mount Pinatubo	15°N 120°E	Ash and debris from an explosive eruption destroyed homes, crops, and roads within 52,000 km^2 around the volcano.

Analysis

4. According to your map, where are volcanoes that always have nonexplosive eruptions located?
5. Where are volcanoes that always erupt explosively located?
6. Where are volcanoes that erupt in both ways located?
7. If volcanoes get their magma from the crust below them, what can you say about the silica content of Earth's crust under the oceans?
8. What is the composition of the crust under the continents? How do we know?
9. What is the source of materials for volcanoes that erupt in both ways? How do you know?
10. Do the locations of volcanoes that erupt in both ways make sense based on your answers to questions 7 and 8? Explain.

Going Further

Volcanoes are present on other planets. If a planet had only nonexplosive volcanoes on its surface, what would we be able to infer about the planet? If a planet had volcanoes that ranged from nonexplosive to explosive, what might that tell us about the planet?

Answers

4. Nonexplosive volcanoes are usually located on oceanic crust.
5. Explosive volcanoes are usually located on continental crust.
6. Volcanoes that erupt in both ways are usually located near boundaries between oceanic and continental crust.
7. The crust under the oceans must be low in silica. Students may also know that the crust is likely to be made of basalt.
8. Continental crust is generally high in silica. Students may also know that the crust is likely to be made of granite.
9. The volcanoes that erupt in both ways must be near the boundary between the oceanic crusts and the continental crusts. The crust must have both basalt and granite.
10. The volcanoes that erupt in both ways are located near continents and oceans. Students should be able to understand that two different crusts must meet in this area and that both granitic (felsic) and basaltic (mafic) magma is generated there.

Going Further

Answers should reflect the idea that the crust on planets with nonexplosive volcanoes must be low in silica compared to Earth. Students may then realize that planets with only this type of volcano must have basaltic crust. If a planet has all three types of volcanoes, it must have both basaltic and granitic crust.

Datasheets for LabBook
Datasheet 16

Volcano Verdict
Teacher's Notes

Time Required

One 45-minute class period

Lab Ratings

TEACHER PREP 2
STUDENT SET-UP 3
CONCEPT LEVEL 2
CLEAN UP 2

MATERIALS

The materials listed in the student page are sufficient for a pair of students.

Safety Caution

Remind students to review all safety cautions and icons before beginning this lab activity. Students should wear goggles and aprons for this activity.

Preparation Notes

You may want to combine this activity with an activity involving a tiltmeter. Emphasize to students that a gas-emissions tester is just one tool used by volcanologists. These scientists must compare the data gathered through many tests before drawing any conclusions. Other tools include seismographs or satellites that record infrared images of volcanoes over a period of time.

Volcano Verdict

You will need to pair up with a partner for this exploration. You and your partner will act as geologists who work in a city located near a volcano. City officials are counting on you to predict when the volcano will erupt next. You and your partner have decided to use limewater as a gas-emissions tester. You will use this tester to measure the levels of carbon dioxide emitted from a simulated volcano. The more active the volcano is, the more carbon dioxide it releases.

Materials

- 1 L of limewater
- 9 oz clear plastic cup
- graduated cylinder
- 100 mL of water
- 140 mL of white vinegar
- 16 oz drink bottle
- modeling clay
- flexible drinking straw
- 15 mL of baking soda
- 2 sheets of bathroom tissue
- coin
- box or stand for plastic cup

Procedure

1. Put on your safety goggles, and carefully pour limewater into the plastic cup until the cup is three-fourths full. This is your gas-emissions tester.
2. Now build a model volcano. Begin by pouring 50 mL of water and 70 mL of vinegar into the drink bottle.
3. Form a plug of clay around the short end of the straw, as shown below. The clay plug must be large enough to cover the opening of the bottle. Be careful not to get the clay wet.
4. Sprinkle 5 mL of baking soda along the center of a single section of bathroom tissue. Then roll the tissue and twist the ends so that the baking soda can't fall out.

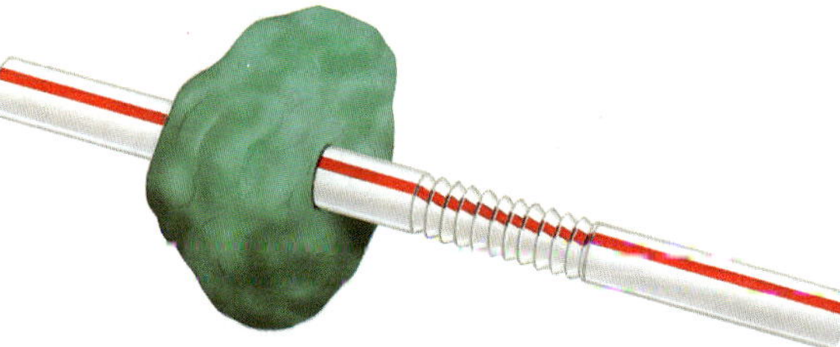

518

Lab Notes

Scientists base their predictions of eruptions on several different kinds of evidence. If a variety of evidence indicates an eruption is imminent, they will recommend evacuation. They are much less likely to make this kind of recommendation if only one kind of evidence suggests an eruption is possible.

Gordon Zibelman
Drexel Hill Middle School
Drexel Hill, Pennsylvania

California Standards: PE/ATE 7, 7b, 7e

5. Drop the tissue into the drink bottle, and immediately put the short end of the straw inside the bottle, making a seal with the clay.
6. Put the other end of the straw into the limewater, as shown at right.
7. You have just taken your first measurement of gas levels from the volcano. Record your observations in your ScienceLog.
8. Imagine that it is several days later and you need to test the volcano again to collect more data. Before you continue, toss a coin. If it lands heads up, go to step 9a. If it lands tails up, go to step 9b. Write the step you take in your ScienceLog.

9a. Repeat steps 1–7. This time add 2 mL of baking soda to the vinegar and water. **Note:** You must use fresh water, vinegar, and limewater. Describe your observations in your ScienceLog. Go to step 10.

9b. Repeat steps 1–7. This time add 8 mL of baking soda to the vinegar and water. **Note:** You must use fresh water, vinegar, and limewater. Describe your observations in your ScienceLog. Go to step 10.

Analysis

10. How do you explain the difference in the appearance of the limewater from one trial to the next?
11. What do your measurements indicate about the activity in the volcano?
12. Based on your results, do you think it would be necessary to evacuate the city?
13. How would a geologist use a gas-emissions tester to forecast volcanic eruptions?

Answers

10. If the students followed step 9a, they should conclude that the volcano released less gas in the second trial. If the students performed step 9b, they should conclude that the volcano released more gas in the second trial.
11. The answer to this question depends on which steps the students followed. If the students performed step 9a and used 2 mL of baking soda in the second trial, they should conclude that the volcano is not likely to erupt in the immediate future because it released less gas during the second trial. If the students performed step 9b with 8 mL of baking soda, on the other hand, they should conclude that the volcano is likely to erupt. More gas was released during the second trial, and therefore the pressure must be building.
12. If the students followed step 9a, they should conclude that the city does not need to be evacuated. If they performed step 9b, they should conclude that the city may need to be evacuated.
13. A geologist would use a gas-emissions tester in conjunction with other tests to determine if pressure is building within a volcano. As the pressure builds, the volcano is more and more likely to erupt.

Datasheets for LabBook
Datasheet 17

Feel the Heat
Teacher's Notes

Time Required
One or two 45-minute class periods

Lab Ratings

TEACHER PREP 3
STUDENT SET-UP 2
CONCEPT LEVEL 3
CLEAN UP 2

MATERIALS

Materials listed are for each group of 2–4 students.

Safety Caution
Caution students to review all safety cautions and icons before beginning this activity. Remind students that a thermometer should never be used for stirring. The container of hot water should be located where it cannot spill on students. Caution students to handle the nails carefully.

Procedure Notes
Heat water before class. Do not let the water temperature exceed 60°C. You may want to keep a large container of water heating on a hot plate. For step 4, the nails are set aside for about 5 minutes so that they will warm up to the same temperature as the water.

Answer
1. Accept all reasonable predictions.

Feel the Heat

Heat is the transfer of energy between objects at different temperatures. Energy moves from objects at higher temperatures to objects at lower temperatures. If two objects are left in contact for a while, the warmer object will cool down, and the cooler object will warm up until they eventually reach the same temperature. In this activity, you will combine equal masses of water and iron nails at different temperatures to determine which has a greater effect on the final temperature.

Materials
- rubber band
- 10–12 nails
- metric balance
- 30 cm of string
- 9 oz plastic-foam cups (2)
- hot water
- 100 mL graduated cylinder
- cold water
- thermometer
- paper towels

Make a Prediction
1. When you combine substances at two different temperatures, will the final temperature be closer to the initial temperature of the warmer substance, the colder substance, or halfway in between? Write your prediction in your ScienceLog.

Conduct an Experiment/Collect Data
2. Copy the table below into your ScienceLog.

Data Collection Table

Trial	Mass of nails (g)	Volume of water that equals mass of nails (mL)	Initial temp. of water and nails (°C)	Initial temp. of water to which nails will be transferred (°C)	Final temp. of water and nails combined (°C)
1					
2		DO NOT WRITE IN BOOK			

3. Use the rubber band to bundle the nails together. Find and record the mass of the bundle. Tie a length of string around the bundle, leaving one end 15 cm long.
4. Put the bundle of nails into one of the cups, letting the string dangle outside the cup. Fill the cup with enough hot water to cover the nails, and set it aside for at least 5 minutes.
5. Use the graduated cylinder to measure enough cold water to exactly equal the mass of the nails (1 mL of water = 1 g). Record this volume in the table.
6. Measure and record the temperature of the hot water with the nails and the temperature of the cold water.

Datasheets for LabBook
Datasheet 18

Dennis Hanson
Big Bear Middle School
Big Bear Lake, California

California Standards: PE/ATE 3, 7, 7a, 7b, 7d, 7e

7. Use the string to transfer the bundle of nails to the cup of cold water. Use the thermometer to monitor the temperature of the water-nail mixture. When the temperature stops changing, record this as the final temperature in the table.
8. Empty the cups, and dry the nails.
9. For Trial 2, repeat steps 3 through 8, but this time switch the hot and cold water. Record all your measurements.

Analyze the Results

10. In Trial 1, you used equal masses of cold water and nails. Did the final temperature support your initial prediction? Explain.
11. In Trial 2 you used equal masses of hot water and nails. Did the final temperature support your initial prediction? Explain.
12. In Trial 1, which material—the water or the nails—changed temperature the most after you transferred the nails? What about in Trial 2? Explain your answers.

Draw Conclusions

13. The cold water in Trial 1 gained energy. Where did the energy come from?
14. How does the energy gained by the nails in Trial 2 compare with the energy lost by the hot water in Trial 2? Explain.
15. Which material seems to be able to hold energy better? Explain your answer.
16. Specific heat capacity is a property of matter that tells how much energy is required to change the temperature of 1 kg of a material by 1°C. Which material in this activity has a higher specific heat capacity (changes temperature less for the same amount of energy)?
17. Would it be better to have pots and pans made from a material with a high specific heat capacity or a low specific heat capacity? Explain your answer. (Hint: Do you want the pan or the food in the pan to absorb all the energy from the stove?)

Communicate Results

18. Share your results with your classmates. Discuss how you would change your prediction to include your knowledge of specific heat capacity.

Answers

10. Answers will vary depending on the initial prediction.
11. Answers will vary depending on the initial prediction.
12. The nails changed temperature more in both trials. Explanations should include references to initial and final temperatures.
13. from the heated nails
14. The energy gained by the nails should be about the same as the energy lost by the hot water (there might be some difference due to energy transfer to the cup and air). The energy changes are the same because energy is conserved. Any energy gained by the nails must come from somewhere, in this case from the water.
15. The water appears to hold energy better. Students' explanations should include that the temperature of the water changed less than the temperature of an equal mass of iron.
16. water
17. Pots and pans should be made from a material with a low specific heat capacity so that more energy from the stove will be transferred to the food than to the pots and pans.
18. Accept all reasonable answers. Sample revised prediction: The final temperature would be closer to the original temperature of the substance with the higher specific heat capacity.

Save the Cube! Teacher's Notes

Time Required

One or two 45-minute class periods

Lab Ratings

TEACHER PREP 3
STUDENT SET-UP 2
CONCEPT LEVEL 3
CLEAN UP 1

MATERIALS

Use incandescent lights, a hair dryer, or hot plates (low setting) to prepare a "thermal zone." Use the lowest setting on the hot plate so the plastic bags do not melt. Provide a large assortment of materials to protect the ice cubes, including white paper, cotton balls, plastic-foam packing peanuts, bubble wrap, tape, aluminum foil, and rubber bands.

Safety Caution

Caution students to wear heat-resistant gloves if working near a hot plate.

Procedure Notes

Set up the thermal zone before class. Have students find and record the masses of the empty cup and empty bag before they obtain their ice cubes.

Datasheets for LabBook Datasheet 19

DESIGN YOUR OWN

Save the Cube!

The biggest enemy of an ice cube is the transfer of thermal energy—heat. Energy can be transferred to an ice cube in three ways: conduction (the transfer of energy through direct contact), convection (the transfer of energy by the movement of a liquid or gas), and radiation (the transfer of energy through space). Your challenge in this activity is to design a way to protect an ice cube as much as possible from all three types of energy transfer.

Materials

- small plastic bag
- ice cube
- assorted materials provided by your teacher
- empty half-pint milk carton
- metric balance
- small plastic or paper cup

Procedure

1. The guidelines for your design are as follows: You must use a plastic bag to hold the ice cube and any water from its melting. You may use any of the available materials to protect the ice cube. The ice cube, bag, and protection must be small enough to all fit inside the milk carton.
2. Write a description of your proposed design in your ScienceLog. Be sure to describe how your design protects against each type of energy transfer.
3. Find the mass of the empty cup, and record it in your ScienceLog. Then find and record the mass of an empty plastic bag.
4. Place an ice cube in the bag. Quickly find and record their mass together.
5. Quickly wrap the bag (and the ice cube inside) with the protection. Remember that the package must fit in the milk carton.
6. Place your protected ice cube in the "thermal zone" set up by your teacher. After 10 minutes, carefully remove the protected cube from the thermal zone, and remove the protection from the plastic bag and ice cube.
7. Open the bag. Pour any water into the cup. Find and record the mass of the cup and water together.
8. Find and record the mass of the water by subtracting the mass of the empty cup from the mass of the cup and water.
9. Find and record the mass of the ice cube by subtracting the mass of the empty bag from the mass of the bag and ice cube.
10. Find the percentage of the ice cube that melted using the following equation:

$$\% \text{ melted} = \frac{\text{mass of water}}{\text{mass of ice cube}} \times 100$$

11. Record your percentage in your ScienceLog and on the board.

Analysis

12. Describe how well your design protected against each type of energy transfer compared with other designs in your class. How could you improve your design?
13. Why is a white plastic-foam cooler so useful for keeping ice frozen?

522

Answers

12. Answers will vary but should provide an accurate assessment of results and reasonable ideas for design improvement.
13. Answers should address how the cooler minimizes the effects of all three types of energy transfer (radiation, convection, and conduction).

David Sparks
Redwater Junior High
Redwater, Texas

California Standards: PE/ATE 3, 3a, 3c, 3d, 7, 7b, 7d, 7e

Counting Calories

Energy transferred by heat is often expressed in units called calories. In this lab, you will build a model of a device called a calorimeter. Scientists often use calorimeters to measure the amount of energy that can be transferred by a substance. In this experiment, you will construct your own calorimeter and test it by measuring the energy released by a hot penny.

Materials

- small plastic-foam cup with lid
- thermometer
- large plastic-foam cup
- water
- 100 mL graduated cylinder
- tongs
- heat source
- penny
- stopwatch

Procedure

1. Copy the table below into your ScienceLog.

Data Collection Table									
Seconds	0	15	30	45	60	75	90	105	120
Water temp. (°C)	DO NOT WRITE IN BOOK								

2. Place the lid on the small plastic-foam cup, and insert a thermometer through the hole in the top of the lid. (The thermometer should not touch the bottom of the cup.) Place the small cup inside the large cup to complete the calorimeter.
3. Remove the lid from the small cup, and add 50 mL of room-temperature water to the cup. Measure the water's temperature, and record the value in the 0 seconds column of the table.
4. Using tongs, heat the penny carefully. Add the penny to the water in the small cup, and replace the lid. Start your stopwatch.
5. Every 15 seconds, measure and record the temperature. Gently swirl the large cup to stir the water, and continue recording temperatures for 2 minutes (120 seconds).

Analysis

6. What was the total temperature change of the water after 2 minutes?
7. The number of calories absorbed by water is the mass of the water (in grams) multiplied by the temperature change (in °C) of the water. How many calories were absorbed by the water? (Hint: 1 mL of water = 1 g of water.)
8. In terms of heat, explain where the calories to change the water temperature came from.

523

Counting Calories Teacher's Notes

Time Required

One 45-minute class period

Lab Ratings

TEACHER PREP 2
STUDENT SET-UP 1
CONCEPT LEVEL 2
CLEAN UP 1

MATERIALS

The materials listed are for each group of 2–3 students.

Safety Caution

Caution students to wear goggles and an apron and to use care when working near the heat source. Remind students never to use a thermometer for stirring. Advise students not to overheat the penny.

Preparation Notes

You may wish to model the proper method of heating the penny before students begin the lab. Remind students that a calorie is the amount of energy needed to raise the temperature of 1 g of water by 1°C.

CLASSROOM TESTED & APPROVED

John Zambo
E. Ustach Middle School
Modesto, California

Answers

6. Answers should be the final temperature (at 120 seconds) minus the initial temperature (at 0 seconds).
7. The number of calories absorbed by the water equals temperature change (step 6) times the mass of the water (50 g).
8. The calories came from the penny. The penny heated the water by transferring energy to it.

Datasheets for LabBook
Datasheet 20

California Standards: PE/ATE 3, 7, 7b

Water Cycle—What Goes Up . . .
Teacher's Notes

Time Required
One 45-minute class period

Lab Rating

TEACHER PREP 1
STUDENT SET-UP 1
CONCEPT LEVEL 2
CLEAN UP 1

MATERIALS
The materials listed on the student page are enough for a group of 4–5 students.

Safety Caution
Remind students to review all safety cautions and icons before beginning this lab activity. Students should be cautioned when using a hot plate. Care should also be exercised in using the glassware. Appropriate methods should be used to dispose of broken glass.

Norman Holcomb
Marion Local Schools
Maria Stein, Ohio

Water Cycle—What Goes Up . . .

Why does a bathroom mirror "fog up"? What happens when water "dries up"? Where does rain come from, and why doesn't it just "run out"? These questions relate to the major parts of the water cycle—condensation, evaporation, and precipitation. In this activity, you will make a model of the water cycle and watch water as it moves through the model.

Materials
- graduated cylinder
- 50 mL of tap water
- heat-resistant gloves
- beaker
- hot plate
- glass plate or watch glass
- tongs or forceps

Procedure

1. Use the graduated cylinder to pour 50 mL of water into the beaker. Note the water level in the beaker.
2. Put on your gloves, and place the beaker securely on the hot plate. Turn on the heat to medium, and bring the water to a boil.
3. While waiting for the water to boil, practice picking up and handling the glass plate or watch glass with the tongs. Hold the glass plate a few centimeters above the beaker, and tilt it so that the lowest edge of the glass is still above the beaker.
4. Observe the glass plate as the water in the beaker heats. In your ScienceLog, write down the changes you see in the beaker, in the air above the beaker, and on the glass plate held over the beaker. Write down any changes you see in the water.
5. Continue until you have observed steam rising off the water, the glass plate above the beaker becoming foggy, and water dripping from the glass plate.
6. Carefully set the glass plate on a counter or other safe surface as directed by your teacher.
7. Turn off the hot plate, and allow the beaker to cool. Move the hot beaker with gloves or tongs if directed to do so by your teacher.
8. Copy the illustration shown on the next page into your ScienceLog. On your sketch, draw and label the water cycle as it occurred in your model. Include arrows and labels for condensation, evaporation, and precipitation.

California Standards: PE/ATE 4, 7, 7b, 7e

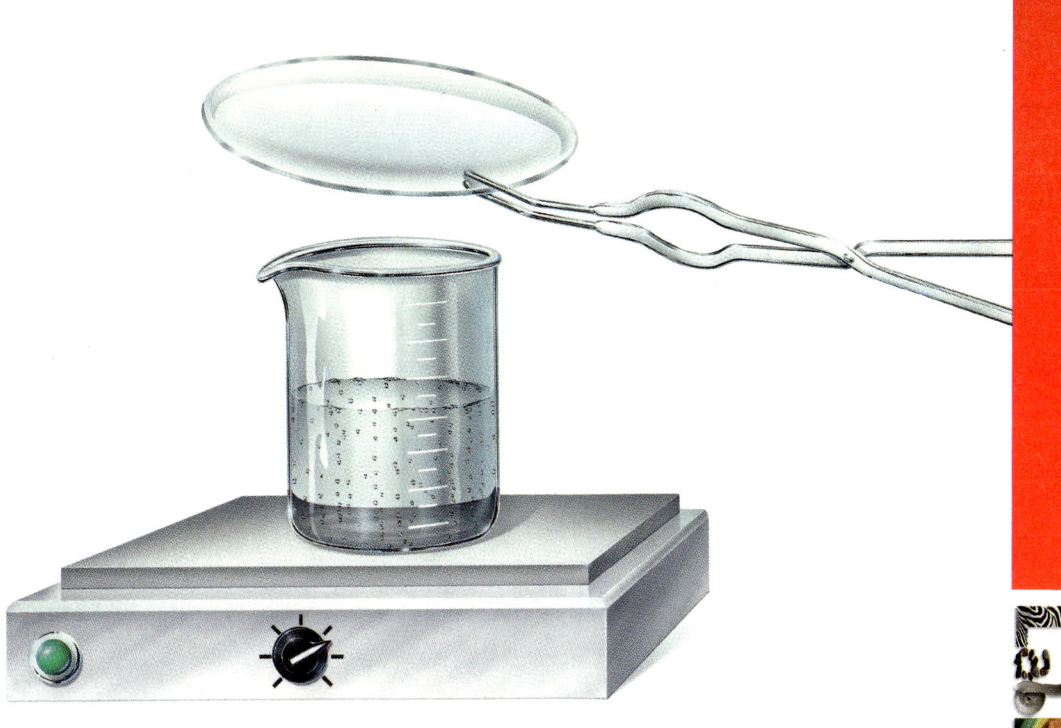

Analysis

9. Compare the water level in the beaker now with the water level at the beginning of the experiment. Was there a change? Explain why or why not.
10. If you had used a scale or balance to measure the mass of the water in the beaker before and after this activity, would the mass have changed? Why or why not?
11. How is your model similar to the Earth's water cycle? On your sketch of the illustration above, label where the processes shown in the model mimic the Earth's water cycle.
12. When you finished this experiment, the water in the beaker was still hot. What stores much of the heat in the Earth's water cycle?

Going Further

As rainwater runs over the land, the rainwater picks up minerals and salts. Do these minerals and salts evaporate, condense, and precipitate as part of the water cycle? Where do they go?

If the average global temperature on Earth gets warmer, how would you expect sea levels to change, and why? What if the average global temperature cools?

Answers

8. Answer is at the bottom of the page.
9. The water level is less at the end of the experiment than at the beginning of the experiment because some of the water escaped in the form of steam.
10. The mass would have changed slightly. Because some of the steam escaped, the mass of the water in the beaker would be reduced.
11. The model is similar to the Earth's water cycle because there was precipitation, condensation, and evaporation. Accept all reasonable depictions of the water cycle.
12. Some of the heat is stored in the atmosphere. Also, the oceans and the Earth's land surface store heat.

Going Further

- No; the minerals and salts are not included in the water cycle. Once the water evaporates, the minerals and salts are left behind as deposits.
- If the average global temperature gets warmer, the sea level may rise because the polar icecaps would melt. If the average global temperature gets cooler, the sea level may decrease as more water is frozen.

8. Student sketches should illustrate the water cycle illustrated below:

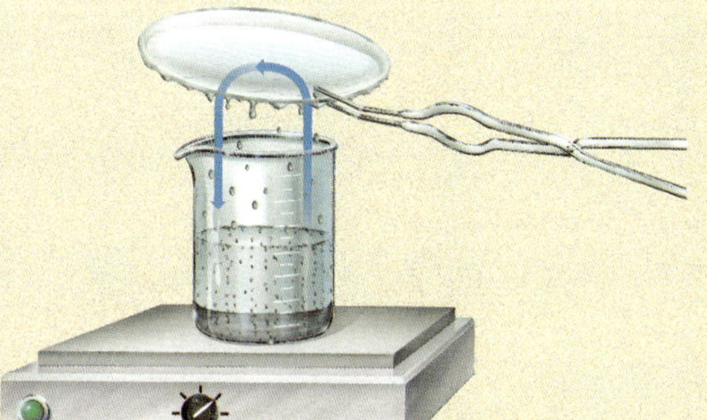

Datasheets for LabBook Datasheet 21

Science Skills Worksheet 23 "Science Drawing"

Clean Up Your Act
Teacher's Notes

Time Required
Two 45-minute class periods

Lab Rating

Teacher Prep: 2
Student Set-Up: 2
Concept Level: 2
Clean Up: 1

MATERIALS

The materials listed on the student page are enough for a group of 4–5 students. To keep results consistent with all lab groups, each group should have the same size gravel and the same size sand. Also, the layers of sand and gravel should be the same dimensions in each group.

Safety Caution
Remind students to review all safety cautions and icons before beginning this lab activity.

Kenneth Creese
White Mountain Jr. High
Rock Springs, Wyoming

Clean Up Your Act

When you wash dishes, the family car, the bathroom sink, or your clothes, you wash them with water. But have you ever wondered how water gets clean? Two major methods of purifying water are filtration and evaporation. In this activity you will use both of these methods to test how well they remove pollutants from water. You will test detritus (decaying plant matter), soil, vinegar, and detergent. Your teacher may also ask you to test other pollutants.

Form a Hypothesis

1. Form a hypothesis about whether filtration and evaporation will clean each of the four pollutants from the water and how well they might do it. Then use the procedures below to test your hypothesis.

Method 1: Filtration

Filtration is a common method of removing various pollutants from water. It requires very little energy—gravity pulls water down through the layers of filter material. See how well this energy-efficient method works to clean your sample of polluted water.

Conduct an Experiment

2. Put on your gloves and goggles. Use scissors to cut the bottom out of the empty soda bottle carefully.
3. Carefully punch four or five small holes through the plastic cap of the bottle using a small nail and hammer. Screw the plastic cap onto the bottle.
4. Turn the bottle upside down, and set its neck in a ring on a ring stand, as shown on the next page. Put a handful of gravel into the inverted bottle. Add a layer of activated charcoal, followed by thick layers of sand and gravel. Place a 400 mL beaker under the neck of the bottle.
5. Fill each of the large beakers with 1,000 mL of clean water. Set one beaker aside to serve as the control. Add three or four spoonfuls of each of the following pollutants to the other beaker: detritus, soil, household vinegar, and dishwashing detergent.

Materials

- scissors
- plastic 2 L soda bottle with cap
- small nail
- hammer
- ring stand with ring
- gravel
- activated charcoal
- sand
- 400 mL beakers (2)
- 2,000 mL of water
- 1,000 mL beakers (2)
- detritus (grass and leaf clippings)
- soil
- household vinegar
- dishwashing detergent
- hand lens
- 2 plastic spoons
- pH test strips
- Erlenmeyer flask
- one-hole rubber stopper with a glass tube
- 1.5 m of plastic tubing
- heat-resistant gloves
- hot plate
- sealable plastic sandwich bag
- ice

California Standards: PE/ATE 7, 7a, 7b, 7d, 7e

Collect Data

6. Copy the table below into your ScienceLog, and record your observations for each beaker in the columns labeled "Before cleaning."
7. Observe the color of the water in each beaker.
8. Use a hand lens to examine the water for visible particles.
9. Smell the water, and note any unusual odors.
10. Stir the water in each beaker rapidly with a plastic spoon, and check for suds. Use a different spoon for each sample.
11. Use a pH test strip to find the pH of the water.
12. Gently stir the clean water, and then pour half of it through the filtration device.
13. Observe the water in the collection beaker for color, particles, odors, suds, and pH. Be patient. It may take several minutes for the water to travel through the filtration device.
14. Record your observations in the appropriate "After filtration" column in your table.
15. Repeat steps 12–14 using the polluted water.

Results Table

	Before cleaning (clean water)	Before cleaning (polluted water)	After filtration (clean water)	After filtration (polluted water)	After evaporation (clean water)	After evaporation (polluted water)
Color						
Particles						
Odor						
Suds						
pH						

DO NOT WRITE IN BOOK

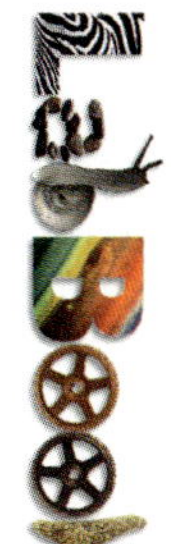

Preparation Notes

Varying the thickness of the layers can contribute to a variation in the results. Specify the thickness of each layer so that the results between groups are comparable. The layers can be the following dimensions: 7 cm of gravel, 2.5 cm of charcoal, 10 cm of sand, 10 cm of gravel, and 1 cm of sand. You may adjust the layers according to your class size or the size of the bottles.

For variations, try different sizes of gravel or different textures of sand. Both will affect how many particles travel through the filter. If you place a few drops of food coloring in the water, students can watch the progress of the water as it passes through the filter.

You may decide that it is easier and safer for you to perform step 2 of Method 1, cutting the soda bottles, before class. You may also wish to perform steps 19–20 of Method 2 ahead of time. Some students may find it difficult to attach the plastic tubing to the glass tube or to slide the glass tube into the rubber stopper.

Datasheets for LabBook
Datasheet 22

Answers

16. The filtered water was lighter in color than the unfiltered water. The water was still not as clear as the clean water. The color of the clean water stayed about the same.

17. No; the filtration method did not remove all of the particles from the polluted water. Many of the particles were able to penetrate the filter, but there were fewer particles than before the filtration.

18. The pH of the water changed slightly. The final pH of the polluted water was not the same as the clean water. After the polluted water was filtered, its pH was still slightly more acidic than the clean water.

Analyze the Results

16. How did the color of the polluted water change after the filtration? Did the color of the clean water change?

17. Did the filtration method remove all of the particles from the polluted water? Explain.

18. How much did the pH of the polluted water change? Did the pH of the clean water change? Was the final pH of the polluted water the same as the pH of the clean water before cleaning? Explain.

Method 2: Evaporation

Cleaning water by evaporation is more expensive than cleaning water by filtration. Evaporation requires more energy, which can come from a variety of sources. In this activity, you will use an electric hot plate as the energy source. See how well this method works to clean your sample of polluted water.

Conduct an Experiment

19. Fill an Erlenmeyer flask with about 250 mL of the clean water, and insert the rubber stopper and glass tube into the flask.

20. Wearing goggles and gloves, connect about 1.5 m of plastic tubing to the glass tube.

21. Set the flask on the hot plate, and run the plastic tubing up and around the ring and down into a clean, empty 400 mL collection beaker.

22. Fill the sandwich bag with ice, seal the bag, and place the bag on the ring stand. Be sure the plastic bag and the tubing touch, as shown below.

23. Bring the water in the flask to a slow boil. As the water vapor passes by the bag of ice, the vapor will condense and drip into the collection beaker.

Collect Data

24. Observe the water in the collection beaker for color, particles, odor, suds, and pH. Record your observations in the appropriate "After evaporation" column in your data table.
25. Repeat steps 23–24 using the polluted water.

Analyze the Results

26. How did the color of the polluted water change after evaporation? Did the color of the clean water change after evaporation?
27. Did the evaporation method remove all of the particles from the polluted water? Explain.
28. How much did the pH of the polluted water change? Did the pH of the final clean water change? Was the final pH of the polluted water the same as the pH of the clean water before it was cleaned? Explain.

Draw Conclusions

29. Which method—filtration or evaporation—removed the most pollutants from the water? Explain your reasoning.
30. Describe any changes that occurred in the clean water during this experiment.
31. What do you think are the advantages and disadvantages of each method?
32. Explain how you think each material (sand, gravel, and charcoal) used in the filtration system helped clean the water.
33. List areas of the country where you think each method of purification would be the most and the least beneficial. Explain your reasoning.

Going Further

Do you think either purification method would remove oil from water? If time permits, repeat your experiment using several spoonfuls of cooking oil as the pollutant.

Filtration is only one step in the purification of water at water-treatment plants. Research other methods used to purify public water supplies.

529

Answers

26. After the evaporation process, the polluted water was the same color as the color of the clean water before cleaning. The color of the clean water did not change.
27. No particles were visible in the polluted water after the evaporation method. The particles in the polluted water were left behind when the water evaporated.
28. Answers may vary, depending on the clean-water source. Generally, the pH of the two samples should be very close or the same.
29. The evaporation method removed the most pollutants in the water. The pollutants are left behind when the water evaporates.
30. The clean water picked up some particles as it traveled through the filter. It was not as clean after the filtration as it had been before the filtration.
31. The advantages of the filtration method include: it is easy to do; it can be done with large amounts of water; and it works relatively quickly. However, the filtration method doesn't remove all of the pollutants.

    The evaporation method removes more of the pollutants. Two disadvantages of the evaporation method are that it is time consuming and expensive, especially with large amounts of water.
32. The sand filtered out some of the larger particles and some of the soap. The gravel also removed the large particles. The charcoal removed most of the smaller particles, the odors, and some of the soap.
33. Answers will vary.

Going Further

- Oil is removed from the water in both methods. The filtration method is relatively quicker than the evaporation method.
- Other methods of water purification include: reverse osmosis; settling ponds; chemical additives, such as chlorine; and other filtration layers.

Dune Movement
Teacher's Notes

Time Required
30 minutes

Lab Ratings

TEACHER PREP 1
STUDENT SET-UP 2
CONCEPT LEVEL 1
CLEAN UP 2

MATERIALS
The materials listed in the student page are enough for two students.

Safety Caution
Remind students to review all safety cautions and icons before beginning this lab activity.

Preparation Notes
You might want to have students do this activity outside, in an area where an electrical outlet is available.

Datasheets for LabBook
Datasheet 23

Larry Tackett
Andrew Jackson Middle School
Cross Lanes, West Virginia

MAKING MODELS

Dune Movement

Have you ever heard news reporters talk about a hurricane or a thunderstorm that eroded a beach? Wind is always moving the sand along a beach. However, big storms produce strong winds that erode a beach and sand dunes more quickly than usual. Wind moves the sand by a process called *saltation.* The sand skips and bounces along the ground in the direction the wind is blowing. As the sand is blown across the beach, the dunes change. In this activity, you will investigate the effect wind has on a model sand dune.

Materials
- marker
- metric ruler
- shallow cardboard box
- fine sand
- paper bag, large enough to hold half the box
- filter mask
- hair dryer
- watch or clock that indicates seconds

Procedure
1. Use the marker to draw and label vertical lines 5 cm apart along one side of the box.
2. Fill the box about halfway with sand. Brush the sand into a dune shape about 10 cm from the end of the box.
3. Use the lines you drew along the edge of the box to measure the location of the dune's peak to the nearest centimeter.
4. Slide the box into the paper bag until only about half the box is exposed, as shown below.
5. Put on your safety goggles and filter mask. Hold the hair dryer so that it is level with the peak of the dune and about 10–20 cm from the open end of the box.
6. Turn on the hair dryer at the lowest speed, and direct the air toward the model sand dune for 1 minute.
7. Record the new location of the model dune in your ScienceLog.
8. Repeat steps 5 and 6 three times. After each trial, measure and record the location of the dune's peak.

Analysis
9. How far did the dune move during each trial?
10. How far did the dune move overall?
11. How might the dune's movement be affected if you were to turn the hair dryer to the highest speed?

Going Further
Flatten the sand. Place a barrier, such as a rock, in the sand. Position the hair dryer level with the top of the sand's surface. How does the rock affect the dune's movement?

Answers
9. Answers will vary. A typical answer would be about 0.5 to 1.0 cm.
10. Answers will vary. A typical answer would be about 5 to 10 cm.
11. Answers will vary. A typical answer would be that the sand would be blown until it hits the bag or the dune would move farther. It may also be expected that much of the sand would be blown out of the box completely.

Going Further
The dune forms on the downwind side of the barrier. The rock slows the migration of the dune.

California Standards: PE/ATE 7, 7b, 7e, 7g

Gliding Glaciers

A glacier is large moving mass of ice. Glaciers are responsible for shaping many of the Earth's natural features. Glaciers are set in motion by the pull of gravity. As a glacier moves it changes the landscape, eroding the surface over which it passes.

Slip-Sliding Away

The material that is carried by a glacier erodes the Earth's surface, gouging out grooves called *striations.* Different materials have varying effects on the landscape. By creating a model glacier, you will demonstrate the effects of glacial erosion by various materials.

Materials

- 3 empty margarine containers
- sand
- gravel
- metric ruler
- water
- freezer
- rolling pin
- modeling clay
- small towel
- 3 bricks
- 3 pans
- graduated cylinder
- timer

Procedure

1. Fill one margarine container with sand to a depth of 1 cm. Fill another margarine container with gravel to a depth of 1 cm. Leave the third container empty. Fill the containers with water.
2. Put the three containers in a freezer, and leave them overnight.
3. Retrieve the containers from the freezer, and remove the three ice blocks from the containers.
4. Use a rolling pin to flatten the modeling clay.
5. Hold the plain ice block firmly with a towel, and press as you move it along the length of the clay. Do this three times. In your ScienceLog, sketch the pattern the ice block makes in the clay.
6. Repeat steps 4 and 5 with the ice block that contains sand. Sketch the pattern this ice block makes in the clay.
7. Repeat steps 4 and 5 with the ice block that contains gravel. Sketch the pattern this ice block makes in the clay.

Analysis

8. Did any material from the clay become mixed with the material in the ice blocks? Explain.
9. Was any material deposited on the clay surface? Explain.
10. What glacial features are represented in your clay model?
11. Compare the patterns formed by the three model glaciers. Do the patterns look like features carved by alpine glaciers or by continental glaciers? Explain.

LabBook

Gliding Glaciers
Teacher's Notes

Time Required

Two 45-minute class periods plus a 15-minute activity ahead of time

Lab Ratings

TEACHER PREP: 1
STUDENT SET-UP: 2
CONCEPT LEVEL: 1
CLEAN UP: 1

MATERIALS

The materials listed in the student page are enough for one student or a pair of students. These materials could also be used for larger groups or classes of students. For example, students may use ice cubes and a smaller amount of clay, sand, and gravel.

Preparation Notes

Students should review the entire section on glaciers in this chapter prior to performing this activity. For the second part of the lab, students might have to refreeze ice blocks overnight or make three more ice blocks. If new ice blocks are made, the sand and gravel can be omitted.

Answers

8. Answers will vary. A typical answer would be that small amounts of the surface material became mixed with the ice.
9. Answers will vary. A typical answer would be that small amounts of the material in the ice were deposited on the clay surface.
10. Answers will vary. Typical answers will include moraines, striations, and outwash plains.
11. Accept all reasonable, justified answers. Alpine glaciers leave rugged features behind as they flow. Continental glaciers smooth the landscape.

Datasheets for LabBook
Datasheet 24

Bert Sherwood
Socorro Middle School
El Paso, Texas

California Standards: PE/ATE 2, 7, 7b, 7e

Answers

17. The ice block with two bricks on it produced the most water.
18. The bricks represent layers of ice.
19. The bottom of the ice block melted first. This is because the weight of the bricks on top causes the ice on the bottom to melt.
20. The investigation models the melting rate of glaciers. The weight of the glacier causes the bottom to melt. The bottom of glaciers that are heavier melt faster, thus causing the glacier to move faster.

Going Further

Replace the clay with different materials, such as soft wood or sand. How does each ice block affect the different surface materials? What types of surfaces do the different materials represent?

Slippery When Wet

As the layers of ice build up and the glacier gets larger, the glacier will eventually begin to melt. The water from the melted ice allows the glacier to move forward. In this activity, you'll learn about the effect of pressure on the melting rate of a glacier.

Procedure

12. Place one ice block upside down in each pan.
13. Place one brick on top of one of the ice blocks. Place two bricks on top of another ice block. Leave the third ice block alone.
14. After 15 minutes, remove the bricks from the ice blocks.
15. Measure the amount of water that has melted from each ice block using the graduated cylinder.
16. Record your findings in your ScienceLog.

Analysis

17. Which ice block produced the most water?
18. What did the bricks represent?
19. What part of the ice block melted first? Explain.
20. How could you relate this investigation to the melting rate of glaciers? Explain.

Creating a Kettle

As glaciers recede, they leave huge amounts of rock material behind. Sometimes receding glaciers form moraines by depositing some of the rock material in ridges. At other times, glaciers leave chunks of ice that form depressions called *kettles.* These depressions may form ponds or lakes. In this activity, you will create your own kettle and discover how they are formed by glaciers.

Materials

- small tub
- sand
- 4–5 ice cubes of various sizes
- metric ruler

Ask a Question

1. How are kettles formed?

Conduct an Experiment

2. Fill the tub three-quarters full with sand.
3. In your ScienceLog, describe the size and shape of the ice cubes.
4. Push the ice cubes to various depths in the sand.
5. Put the tub where it won't be disturbed overnight.

Make Observations

6. Look for the ice cubes the next day. Closely observe the sand around the area where you left each ice cube.
7. What happened to the ice cubes?
8. Use a metric ruler to measure the depth and diameter of the indentation left by the ice cubes.

Analyze the Results

9. How does this model relate to the size and shape of a natural kettle?
10. In what ways are your model kettles similar to real ones? How are they different?

Draw Conclusions

11. Based on your model, what can you conclude about the formation of kettles by receding glaciers?

Janel Guse
West Central Middle School
Hartford, South Dakota

Datasheets for LabBook
Datasheet 25

California Standards: PE/ATE 2, 7, 7b, 7e

Creating a Kettle
Teacher's Notes

Time Required

One 45-minute class period plus 30 minutes during a second day

Lab Ratings

TEACHER PREP 1
STUDENT SET-UP 1
CONCEPT LEVEL 1
CLEAN UP 1

MATERIALS

The materials listed on the student page are enough for a group of 4–5 students.

Answers

9. The model is similar. The simulated kettle is the size of the ice cube. A real kettle hole is the size of the block of ice that breaks off. The shape is determined by the shape of the ice.
10. The ice melted slowly to form the holes in the model and in real kettles. The materials and debris surrounding the model hole are different from that surrounding a real kettle. In addition, a real kettle would not be as uniform as the shape of the model hole.
11. Accept all reasonable responses. Kettles form from the slow melting of ice left behind when a glacier recedes.

Capturing the Wild Bean
Teacher's Notes

Time Required
One 45-minute class period

Lab Ratings

TEACHER PREP ♟♟
STUDENT SET-UP ♟♟
CONCEPT LEVEL ♟♟
CLEAN UP ♟

MATERIALS

The materials listed on the student page are enough for a group of 4–5 students. Large, dried beans of any kind will work well in this exercise.

Safety Caution
Remind students to review all safety cautions and icons before beginning this lab activity.

Lab Notes
Explain to students that this is a very common method used in field biology by scientists who need to count a population that is on the move, such as a flock of migratory birds. Explain that scientists always mark their captures in a way that neither harms the organism nor alters its behavior.

Capturing the Wild Bean

When wildlife biologists study a group of organisms in an area, one of the things they need to know is how many organisms there are in the area. Occasionally, biologists worry that a certain organism is outgrowing the environment's carrying capacity. Other times, scientists need to know if an organism is becoming rare so steps can be taken to protect it. However, animals can be difficult to count because they can move around and hide. Because of this, biologists have developed methods to estimate the number of animals in a specific area. One of these counting methods is called the mark-recapture method.

In this activity, you will enter the territory of the wild pinto bean to get an estimation of the number of beans that live in their paper-bag habitat.

Materials
- small paper lunch bag
- pinto beans
- permanent marker
- pencil
- calculator

Procedure
1. Prepare a data table in your ScienceLog like the one below.

Mark-Recapture Data Table				
Number of animals in first capture	Total number of animals in recapture	Number of marked animals in recapture	Calculated estimate of population	Actual total population
	DO NOT WRITE IN BOOK			

2. Your teacher will provide you with a paper bag containing an unknown number of beans. Carefully reach into the bag and remove a handful of beans.
3. Count the number of beans you have "captured," and record this number in your data table under "Number of animals in first capture."

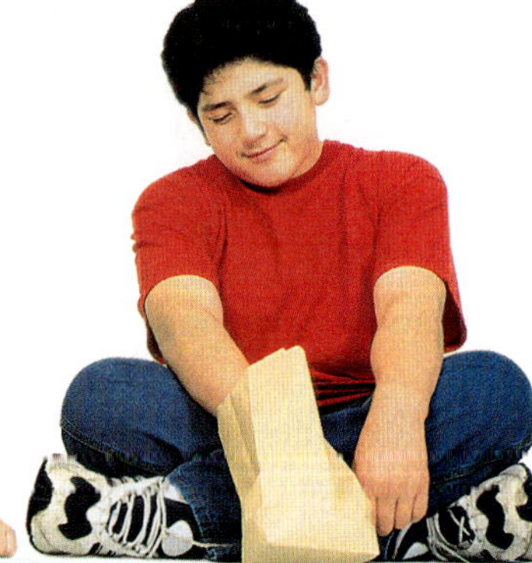

Datasheets for LabBook
Datasheet 26

Science Skills Worksheet 30
"Hints for Oral Presentations"

Jason Marsh
Montevideo High and Country School
Montevideo, Minnesota

4. Use the permanent marker to carefully mark each bean that you have just counted. Allow the marks to dry completely. When you are certain that all the marks are dry, place the marked beans back into the bag.
5. Gently mix the beans in the bag so the marks won't rub off. Once again, reach into the bag, "capture," and remove a handful of beans.
6. Count the total number of beans in your "recapture." Record this number in your data table under "Total number of animals in recapture."
7. Count the number of beans in your recapture that have marks on them from the first capture. Record this number in your data table under "Number of marked animals in recapture."
8. Calculate your estimation of the total number of beans in the bag using the following equation:

$$\frac{\text{total number of beans in recapture} \times \text{total number of beans marked}}{\text{number of marked beansin recapture}} = \text{calculated estimate of population}$$

Enter this number in your data table under "Calculated estimate of population."

9. Replace all the beans in the bag. Then empty the bag on your work table. Be careful that no beans escape! Count each bean as you place them one at a time back into the bag. Record the number in your data table under "Actual total population."

Analysis

10. How close was your estimate to the actual number of beans?
11. If your estimate was not close to the actual number of beans, how might you change your mark-recapture procedure? If you did not recapture any marked beans, what might be the cause?

Going Further
How could you use the mark-recapture method to estimate the population of turtles in a small pond? Explain your procedure.

Answers

10. Have students evaluate their estimate. Ask them if they think their estimate was close enough to the actual number of beans in the bag.
11. If estimates were not close, there was probably a sampling error. Explain to students that the larger the sample, the closer the estimate. When a marked bean is not recaptured, it usually means the sample was too small and the bean simply got lost among the unmarked beans. This is a sampling error, and it happens in the field often when a population is much larger than the scientists originally thought. When that happens, the scientists have learned something: the population is very large, and they must increase their sample size accordingly.

Math Skills Worksheet 39
"Random Samples: Estimating Population"

Going Further

Students should state the size of the pond and form a reasonable hypothesis, including how many animals should be in the sample size. Students should describe a way to capture turtles without harming them. They should recommend a marking method that will not harm the turtles or alter the turtles' behavior.

The turtles should be returned in their environment immediately and given a day or two to recover from the trauma.

Important: students should recognize the need for the recapture size to be the same size as the original capture size.

Adaptation: It's a Way of Life
Teacher's Notes

Time Required

One or two 45-minute class periods

Lab Ratings

TEACHER PREP 2
STUDENT SET-UP 2
CONCEPT LEVEL 2
CLEAN UP 1

MATERIALS

The materials listed on the student page are enough for a group of 4–5 students. Materials for this activity can include recycled materials, glue, buttons, pipe cleaners, poster paints and brushes, and any number of other art or craft supplies. Have students bring in as much as they can for their own project and to share.

Lab Notes

This lab provides an opportunity for students to exercise a great deal of creativity and to expand their understanding of adaptations. Most students will probably enjoy choosing the adaptations and inventing a niche where those adaptations are useful. Help them understand that environments and adaptations usually evolve together in the natural world, not one before the other. You may want to make sets of the adaptations and put them in a container for students to draw from. Doing this may lessen duplication in the classroom. Someone might be challenged to design a flying decomposer with armor!

Adaptation: It's a Way of Life

Since the beginning of life on Earth, species have had special characteristics called adaptations that have helped them survive changes in environmental conditions. Changes in a species' environment include climate changes, habitat destruction, or the extinction of prey. These things can cause a species to die out unless the species has a characteristic that helps it survive. For example, a species of bird may have an adaptation for eating sunflower seeds and ants. If the ant population dies out, the bird can still eat seeds and can therefore survive.

In this activity, you will explore several adaptations and design an organism with adaptations you choose. Then you will describe how these adaptations help the organism survive.

Materials

- poster board
- colored markers
- scissors
- magazines for cutouts
- other arts-and-crafts materials

Procedure

1. Study the chart below. Choose one adaptation from each column. For example, an organism might be a scavenger that burrows underground and has spikes on its tail!

Adaptations		
Diet	**Type of transportation**	**Special adaptation**
carnivore	flies	uses sensors to detect heat
herbivore	glides through the air	is active only at night and has excellent night vision
omnivore	burrows underground	changes colors to match its surroundings
scavenger	runs fast	has armor
decomposer	swims	has horns
	hops	can withstand extreme temperature changes
	walks	secretes a terrible and sickening scent
	climbs	has poison glands
	floats	has specialized front teeth
	slithers	has tail spikes
		stores oxygen in its cells so it does not have to breathe continuously
		one of your own invention

536

Datasheets for LabBook
Datasheet 27

Alonda Droege
Pioneer Middle School
Steilacom, Washington

California Standards: PE/ATE 7, 7e

2. Design an organism that has the three adaptations you have chosen. Use poster board, colored markers, picture cutouts, or craft materials of your choosing to create your organism.
3. Write a caption on your poster describing your organism. Describe its appearance, its habitat, its niche, and how its adaptations help it survive. Give your animal a two-part "scientific" name based on its characteristics.
4. Display your creation in your classroom. Share with classmates how you chose the adaptations for your organism.

Analysis

5. What does your imaginary organism eat?
6. In what environment or habitat would your organism be most likely to survive—in the desert, tropical rain forest, plains, icecaps, mountains, or ocean? Explain your answer.
7. Is your creature a mammal, a reptile, an amphibian, a bird, or a fish? What modern organism (on Earth today) or ancient organism (extinct) is your imaginary organism most like? Explain the similarities between the two organisms. Do some research outside of the lab, if necessary, to find out about a real organism that your imaginary organism may be similar to.
8. If a sudden climate change occurred, such as daily downpours of rain in a desert, would your imaginary organism survive? What adaptations for surviving such a change does it have?

Going Further

Call or write to an agency such as the U.S. Fish and Wildlife Service to get a list of endangered species in your area. Choose an organism on that list. Describe the organism's niche and any special adaptations it has that help it survive. Find out why it is endangered and what is being done to protect it.

Examine the illustration of the animal at right. Based on its physical characteristics, describe its habitat and niche. Is this a real animal?

Answers

5.–7. All answers will depend on the adaptations that the student chose and the organism the student invented. Students should relate one or more adaptations to the kinds of food the organism eats, where the animal lives, or what kind of animal it is.

8. Several adaptations can be given, but expect a few to say their animals don't survive.

Going Further

This is a good activity to expand your study of the environment. Students can relate problems in the area where they live to adaptations. Often, people wonder why an organism doesn't just "adapt" to changes in its environment. This is a good opportunity to learn firsthand why that can't happen within the span of a single generation and why organisms become endangered.

Probing the Depths
Teacher's Notes

Time Required
One 45-minute class period

Lab Ratings

TEACHER PREP 1
STUDENT SET-UP 2
CONCEPT LEVEL 2
CLEAN UP 1

MATERIALS

The materials listed on the student page are enough for each student or for a group of 2–4 students.

Safety Caution
Remind students to review all safety cautions and icons before beginning this lab activity.

Preparation Notes
You may wish to ask students to provide their own shoe boxes. It may be safer and easier if you punch the holes along the center of the lids for the students prior to class. You may use corrugated cardboard instead of modeling clay. Shape the cardboard into steps and ridges to model changes in depth. With this type of model, students should use unsharpened pencils and use the eraser end of the pencil to measure depths.

Probing the Depths

In the 1870s, the crew of the ship the HMS *Challenger* used a wire and a weight to discover and map some of the deepest places in the world's oceans. Scientists tied a wire to a weight and dropped the weight overboard. When the weight reached the bottom of the ocean, they hauled the weight back up to the surface and measured the length of the wet wire. In this way, they were eventually able to map the ocean floor.

In this activity, you will model this traditional method of mapping by making a map of an ocean-floor model.

Materials
- modeling clay
- shoe box and lid
- scissors
- 8 unsharpened pencils
- metric ruler

Procedure

1. Use the clay to make a model ocean floor in the shoe box. Give the floor some mountains and valleys.
2. Cut eight holes in a line along the center of the lid. The holes should be just big enough to slide a pencil through. Close the box.
3. Exchange boxes with another student or group of students. Do not look into the box.
4. Copy the data table below into your ScienceLog. Also make a copy of the graph on the next page.

Ocean Depth Chart

Hole position	Original length of probe	Amount of probe showing	Depth in centimeters	Depth in meters (cm × 200)
1				
2				
3				
4				
5				
6				
7				
8				

DO NOT WRITE IN BOOK

5. Measure the length of the probe (pencil) in centimeters. Record the length in your data table.

538

Tracy Jahn
Berkshire Jr.-Sr. High
Canaan, New York

California Standards: PE/ATE 7, 7b, 7c, 7e

6. Gently insert the probe into the first hole position in the box until it touches the bottom. Do not force the probe down; this could affect your reading.
7. Making sure the probe is straight up and down, measure the length of probe showing above the lid. Record your data in the data table.
8. Use the following formula to calculate the depth in centimeters:

original length of probe	−	amount of probe showing	=	depth in cm

9. Use the scale 1 cm = 200 m to convert the depth in centimeters to meters to better represent real ocean depths. Add the data to your table.
10. Transfer the data to your graph for position 1.
11. Repeat steps 6–10 for the additional positions in the box.
12. After plotting all the points onto your graph, connect the points with a smooth curve.
13. Put a pencil in each of the holes in the shoe box. Compare the rise and fall of the set of pencils with your graph.

Depth of Shoe Box

Depth in meters: 0, 50, 100, 150, 200, 250, 300

Position: 1, 2, 3, 4, 5, 6, 7, 8

DO NOT WRITE IN BOOK

Analysis

14. What was the depth of your deepest point? your shallowest point?
15. Did your graph resemble the ocean-floor model, as shown by the pencils? If not, why not?
16. What difficulties might scientists have when measuring the real ocean floor? Do they ever get to "open the box"? Explain.

Going Further

At the beginning of the twentieth century, scientists discovered that sound waves can be used to measure the depth of the ocean. By knowing the speed of sound and measuring the time it takes for the sound to travel to the bottom of the ocean and back, scientists can calculate the depth of the ocean. Do you think the speed of sound in water is constant (never changing)? If it does change, what might cause the change? How might the change affect the depth readings sonar provides?

539

Answers

14. Answers will vary. Make sure students understand that the less of the probe that is seen, the deeper the model is in that spot.
15. Answers will vary. Accept all reasonable responses. Discrepancies between the model and the graph may be attributed to incorrectly plotting the points, failing to keep the probe vertical, or pushing the probe into the clay.
16. Scientists may encounter many difficulties in measuring the ocean floor. Students may note that the extreme depths of the ocean makes it more difficult to use this method to map the ocean floor. Students may also note that scientists are often unable to "open the box" to check their measurements; that is, the ocean is too deep in places or too vast to fully explore.

Going Further

Students should realize that ocean water varies in temperature and salinity. Either variable may affect water density, which affects the speed of sound in water. Deeper water tends to be colder, more saline, and denser than more shallow water. The speed of sound tends to be faster in deeper water. This difference needs to be considered in order to make accurate depth readings.

Datasheets for LabBook Datasheet 28

Science Skills Worksheet 25 "Introduction to Graphs"

Investigating an Oil Spill

Teacher's Notes

Time Required

One 45-minute class period

Lab Ratings

TEACHER PREP ▲▲▲
STUDENT SET-UP ▲
CONCEPT LEVEL ▲▲
CLEAN UP ▲▲▲

MATERIALS

The materials listed on the student page are sufficient for a group of 2–4 students. You may also choose to perform this activity as a demonstration to limit your use of oil.

Safety Caution

Remind students to review all safety cautions and icons before beginning this lab activity. Machine oil releases a strong odor. Use it only in well-ventilated areas.

Preparation Notes

Light machine oil may be replaced by cooking oil to demonstrate the same principle. If you choose to use machine oil, be sure there is sufficient ventilation in your classroom.

Disposal Information

Always follow federal, state, and local guidelines when disposing of oil. Pour cooking oil into a container of sand and put it in the trash.

Investigating an Oil Spill

Have you ever wondered why it is important to bring used motor oil to a recycling center rather than simply pouring it down the nearest drain or sewer? Or have you ever wondered why an oil spill of only a few thousand liters into an ocean containing many millions of liters of water can cause so much damage? The reason has to do with the fact that a little oil goes a long way.

Materials

- safety gloves
- large pan (at least 22 cm in diameter)
- water
- pipet
- 15 mL light machine oil
- metric ruler
- graduated cylinder
- calculator (optional)

Observing Oil and Water

You may have heard the expression "Oil and water don't mix." This is true—oil dropped on water will spread out thinly over the surface of the water. In this activity, you'll learn exactly how far oil can spread when it is in contact with water.

Procedure

1. Fill the pan two-thirds full with water. Be sure to wear your goggles and gloves.
2. Using the pipet, carefully add one drop of oil to the water in the middle of the pan. **Caution:** Machine oil is poisonous. Keep materials that have contacted oil out of your mouth and eyes.
3. Observe what happens to the drop of oil for the next few seconds. Record your observations in your ScienceLog.
4. Using a metric ruler, measure the diameter of the oil slick to the nearest centimeter.
5. Determine the area of the oil slick in square centimeters by using the formula for finding the area of a circle ($A = \pi r^2$). The radius (r) is equal to the diameter you measured in step 4 divided by 2. Multiply the radius by itself to get the square of the radius (r^2). Pi (π) is equal to 3.14.

Example
If your diameter is 10 cm,
$r = 5$ cm, $r^2 = 25$ cm^2, $\pi = 3.14$
$A = \pi r^2$
$A = 3.14 \times 25$ cm^2
$A = 78.5$ cm^2

6. Record your answers in your ScienceLog.

David Sparks
Redwater Jr. High
Redwater, Texas

California Standards: PE/ATE 7, 7a, 7b, 7e

Analysis

7. What happened to the drop of oil when it came in contact with the water? Did this surprise you?
8. What total surface area was covered by the oil slick? (Be sure to show your calculations.)
9. What does this experiment tell you about the density of oil compared with the density of water? Explain.

Going Further
Can you devise a way to clean the oil from the water? Get permission from your teacher before testing your cleaning method.
Do you think oil behaves the same way in ocean water? Devise an experiment to test your hypothesis.

Finding the Number of Drops in a Liter

"It's only a few drops," you may think as you spill something toxic on the ground. But those drops eventually add up. Just how many drops does it take to make a difference? In this activity, you'll learn just what an impact a few drops can have.

Procedure

10. Using a clean pipet, count the number of water drops it takes to fill the graduated cylinder to 10 mL. Be sure to add the drops slowly so you get an accurate count.
11. Since there are 1,000 mL in a liter, multiply the number of drops in 10 mL by 100. This gives you the number of drops in a liter.

Analysis

12. How many drops of water from your pipet does it take to fill a 1 L container?
13. What would happen if someone spilled 4 L of oil into a lake?

Going Further
Find out how much oil supertankers contain. Can you imagine the size of an oil slick that would form if one of these tankers spilled its oil?

Answers

7. When the drop of oil touched the water, it spread out. This may surprise some students, who could expect the two substances to mix or the oil to sink.
8. Answers will vary. Students should show their work to illustrate that they understand the mathematical principles involved.
9. This experiment shows that oil is less dense than water. Because oil is less dense than water, it floats on water.

Going Further

- Answers will vary. One possibility is to use detergent to change the surface tension and remove the oil.
- To test the effect of oil on ocean water, students could repeat the activity, using salt water instead of tap water.

12. Answers will vary. The answer depends on the number of drops the students count in 10 mL of water. They should show their work to illustrate that they understand the mathematical principles involved.
13. The oil would spread to cover a large area. Students will not be able to determine the exact area for such an oil slick, but they should understand that the oil will spread significantly and pollute much of the lake.

Datasheets for LabBook
Datasheet 29

Up from the Depths
Teacher's Notes

Time Required
One 45-minute class period

Lab Ratings

TEACHER PREP
STUDENT SET-UP
CONCEPT LEVEL
CLEAN UP

MATERIALS

The materials listed on the student page are enough for a group of 4–5 students. Note that the food coloring is used only to distinguish the water layers. If any color is unavailable, you may substitute with the color of your choice. You may find it simpler to make a roll of plastic wrap available to the class. Groups can then take a piece when they reach the appropriate steps.

Safety Caution
Remind students to review all safety cautions and icons before beginning this lab activity.

Answers
13. The warm, red water remained on top of the cold, blue water. There was very little mixing (if any), and there was no turning over.
15. The cold, blue water did not remain on top of the warm, red water. There was very little mixing (if any), and the water definitely turned over.

Up from the Depths

Every year, the water in certain parts of the ocean "turns over." This means that the water at the bottom rises to the top and the water at the top falls to the bottom. This yearly change brings fresh nutrients from the bottom of the ocean to the fish living near the surface. That makes it a great time for fishing! However, the water in some parts of the ocean never turns over. You will use this activity to find out why.

Some parts of the ocean are warmer at the bottom, and some are warmer at the top. Sometimes the saltiest water is at the bottom; sometimes it is not. You will investigate how these factors help determine whether the water will turn over.

Materials
- 400 mL beakers (5)
- tap water
- blue and red food coloring
- spoon
- bucket of ice
- watch or clock
- hot plate
- heat-resistant gloves
- 4 pieces of plastic wrap, approximately 30 × 20 cm
- salt

Ask a Question
1. Why do some parts of the ocean turn over, while others do not?

Conduct an Experiment
2. Label the beakers 1 through 5. Fill beakers 1 through 4 with tap water.
3. Add a drop of blue food coloring to the water in beakers 1 and 2. Stir.
4. Place beaker 1 in the bucket of ice for 10 minutes.
5. Add a drop of red food coloring to the water in beakers 3 and 4. Stir.
6. Set beaker 3 on a hot plate turned to a low setting for 10 minutes.
7. Add one spoonful of salt to the water in beaker 4, and stir.
8. While beaker 1 is cooling and beaker 3 is heating, copy the data table on the next page into your ScienceLog.
9. Pour half of the water in beaker 1 into beaker 5. Return beaker 1 to the bucket of ice.
10. Tuck a sheet of plastic wrap into beaker 5 so that the plastic rests on the surface of the water and lines the upper half of the beaker.

542

Gordon Zibelman
Drexel Hill Middle School
Drexel Hill, Pennsylvania

California Standards: PE/ATE 7, 7b, 7e, 7h

Observations Chart	
Mixture of water	**Observations**
Warm water placed above cold water	
Cold water placed above warm water	
Salty water placed above fresh water	
Fresh water placed above salty water	

11. Put on your gloves. Slowly pour half of the water in beaker 3 into the plastic-lined upper half of beaker 5 to form two layers of water. Return beaker 3 to the hot plate, and remove your gloves.
12. Very carefully pull on one edge of the plastic wrap and remove it so that the warm, red water rests on the cold, blue water. **Caution:** The plastic wrap may be warm.

Make Observations

13. Wait about 5 minutes, and then observe the layers in beaker 5. Did one layer remain on top of the other? Was there any mixing or turning over? Record your observations in your data table.
14. Empty and rinse beaker 5 with clean tap water.
15. Repeat the procedure in steps 9–14, this time with warm, red water from beaker 3 on the bottom and cold, blue water from beaker 1 on top. (Use gloves when pouring warm water.)
16. Again repeat the procedure used in steps 9–14, this time with blue tap water from beaker 2 on the bottom and red, salty water from beaker 4 on top.
17. Repeat the procedure used in steps 9–14 a third time, this time with red, salty water from beaker 4 on the bottom and blue tap water from beaker 2 on top.

Analyze the Results

18. Compare the results of all four trials. Explain why the water turned over in some of the trials but not in all of them.

Draw Conclusions

19. What is the effect of temperature and salinity on the density of water?
20. What makes the temperature of ocean water decrease? What could make the salinity of ocean water increase?
21. What explanations can you give for the fact that some parts of the ocean turn over in the spring, while some do not?

Going Further

Suggest a method for setting up a model that tests the combined effects of temperature and salinity on the density of water. Consider using more than two water samples and dyes.

16. The red, salty water did not remain on top of the blue tap water. There was little mixing, and the water turned over.
17. The blue tap water remained on top of the red, salty water. There was little mixing, and the water did not turn over.
18. In each case, the denser water sank to the bottom. Cold water is denser than warm water. When put in a beaker with warm water, the cold water either stayed at the bottom or sank to the bottom. Salt water is denser than fresh water. When put in a beaker with fresh water, the salt water either stayed at the bottom or sank to the bottom.
19. The density of water increases as its temperature decreases—cold water is denser than warm water. The density of water increases as its salinity increases—salt water is denser than fresh water.
20. The temperature of water can decrease due to seasonal temperature fluctuations or cold wind blowing across the water's surface. Currents can also carry cooler water to an area. The salinity of water can increase when evaporation occurs or when ice forms on the water's surface. These processes leave salts behind and make the remaining liquid water denser.
21. Parts of the ocean that turn over do so because their density changes due to variations in salinity or temperature. Parts of the ocean that do not turn over must not experience significant variations in salinity or temperature.

Going Further

The following combinations could be used:

Top	Bottom
Salt/cold	Fresh/warm
Salt/warm	Fresh/cold
Fresh/cold	Salt/warm
Fresh/warm	Salt/cold

Datasheets for LabBook
Datasheet 30

Turning the Tides
Teacher's Notes

Time Required
One 45-minute class period

Lab Ratings

TEACHER PREP
STUDENT SET-UP
CONCEPT LEVEL
CLEAN UP

MATERIALS

The materials listed on the student page are enough for a group of 2–4 students.

Safety Caution
Remind students to review all safety cautions and icons before beginning this lab activity. Students should wear safety goggles for this activity. Be sure that students have enough space to spin the system.

Preparation Notes
You will need to put a mark at the center of all of the cardboard disks. Students will need to draw the radius of the circle from the center to the edge of the disk. Encourage students to draw this line along the corrugations of the cardboard. Otherwise, several other steps will be made more difficult. The cardboard disks are not to scale with the Earth and moon. They are used to show how a two-body system, such as the Earth-moon system, rotates. The disks must be different sizes. The large disks may be 10 cm in diameter, and the smaller disks may be 5 cm in diameter.

Turning the Tides

Daily tides are caused by two "bulges" on the ocean's surface—one on the side of the Earth facing the moon and the other on the opposite side. The bulge on the side facing the moon is caused by the moon's gravitational pull on the water. But the bulge on the opposite side is slightly more difficult to explain. Whereas the moon pulls the water on one side of the Earth, the combined rotation of the Earth and the moon "pushes" the water on the opposite side of the Earth. The sun also affects the tides, but because it is so far away from Earth, the sun's pull on the water is considerably weaker than the moon's. In this activity, you will model the motion of the Earth and the moon to investigate the tidal bulge on the side of Earth facing away from the moon.

Materials
- 2 disks of corrugated cardboard, one large and one small, with centers marked
- white glue
- piece of dowel, 2/3 cm in diameter and 36 cm long
- 5 cm length of string
- stapler with staples
- 1 × 1 cm piece of cardboard
- sharp pencil

Procedure
1. Draw a line from the center of each disk along the folds in the cardboard to the edge of the disk. This line is the radius.
2. Place a drop of white glue on one end of the dowel. Lay the larger disk flat, and align the dowel with the line for the radius you drew in step 1. Insert about 2.5 cm of the dowel into the edge of the disk.
3. Add a drop of glue to the other end of the dowel, and push that end into the smaller disk, again along its radius. The setup should look like a large two-headed lollipop, as shown below. This is a model of the Earth-moon system.
4. Staple the string to the edge of the large disk on the side opposite the dowel. Staple the cardboard square to the other end of the string. This smaller piece of cardboard represents the Earth's oceans that face away from the moon.

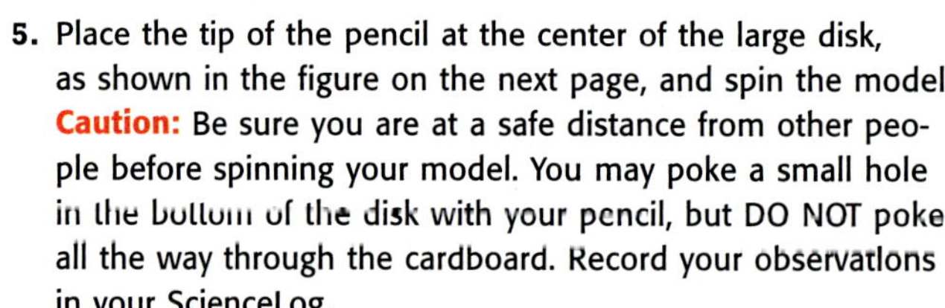

5. Place the tip of the pencil at the center of the large disk, as shown in the figure on the next page, and spin the model. **Caution:** Be sure you are at a safe distance from other people before spinning your model. You may poke a small hole in the bottom of the disk with your pencil, but DO NOT poke all the way through the cardboard. Record your observations in your ScienceLog.

544

Tracy Jahn
Berkshire Jr.-Sr. High
Canaan, New York

California Standards: PE/ATE 7, 7b, 7e

6. Now find your model's *center of mass.* This is the point at which the model can be balanced on the end of the pencil. **Hint:** It might be easier to find the center of mass using the eraser end. Then use the sharpened end of the pencil to balance the model. This balance point should be just inside the edge of the larger disk.
7. Place the pencil at the center of mass, and spin the model around the pencil. Again, you may wish to poke a small hole in the disk. Record your observations in your ScienceLog.

Analysis

8. What happened when you tried to spin the model around the center of the large disk? This model, called the Earth-centered model, represents the incorrect view that the moon orbits the center of the Earth.
9. What happened when you tried to spin the model around its center of mass? This point, called the *barycenter,* is the point around which both the Earth and the moon rotate.
10. In each case, what happened to the string and cardboard square when the model was spun?
11. Which model—the Earth-centered model or the barycentric model—explains why the Earth has a tidal bulge on the side opposite the moon? Explain.

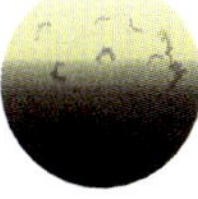

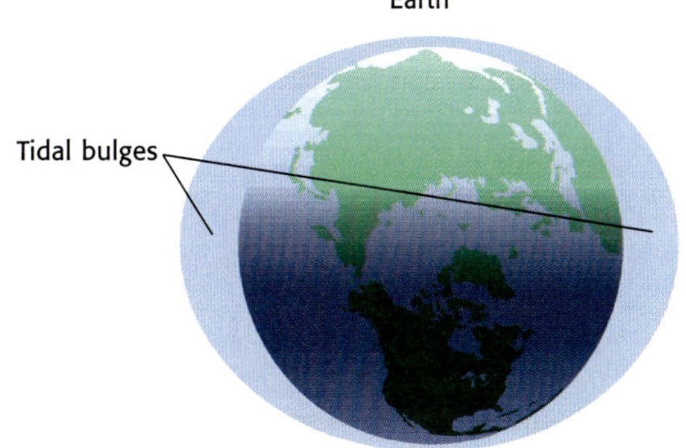

Answers

8. *Sample answer:* When I tried to spin the model around the center of the large disk, I could not get the model to balance on the pencil.
9. *Sample answer:* I was able to balance the model at the barycenter. The model spun, and the small piece of cardboard on the string swung outward.
10. The cardboard square just hung down when I tried to swing the setup around the center of the large disk; I was unable to make the model spin. When I spun the model around its barycenter, the square swung away from the model in a circle.
11. The barycentric model explains why the Earth has a bulge on the side opposite the moon. The side of the Earth opposite the side facing the moon acts in much the same way the small square of cardboard does in this model. As the Earth-moon system rotates, the side of the Earth facing away from the moon bulges outward.

Datasheets for LabBook Datasheet 31

Boiling Over!
Teacher's Notes

Time Required
One 45-minute class period

Lab Ratings

Teacher Prep: 1
Student Set-Up: 3
Concept Level: 2
Clean Up: 1

MATERIALS

The materials listed on the student page are enough for a group of 3–4 students.

Safety Caution
Remind students to review all safety cautions and icons before beginning this lab activity.

Preparation Notes
Begin the activity by leading a discussion of how thermometers work. Have students observe a regular thermometer. Ask students what parts are involved to make a thermometer work. (a receptacle containing the fluid referred to as the bulb, a tube, and air in the tube)

Datasheets for LabBook
Datasheet 32

Boiling Over!

Safety Industries, Inc., would like to offer the public safer alternatives to the mercury thermometer. Many communities have complained that the glass thermometers are easy to break, and people are concerned about mercury poisoning. As a result, we would like your team of inventors to come up with a workable prototype that uses water instead of mercury. Safety Industries would like to offer a contract to the team that comes up with the best substitute for a mercury thermometer. In this activity, you will design and test your own water thermometer. Good luck!

Ask a Question
1. What conditions cause the liquid to rise in a thermometer? How can I use this information to build a thermometer?

Form a Hypothesis
2. Brainstorm with a classmate to design a thermometer that requires only water. Sketch your design in your ScienceLog. Write a one-sentence hypothesis that describes how your thermometer will work.

Test the Hypothesis
3. Follow your design to build a thermometer using only materials from the materials list. Like a mercury thermometer, your thermometer will need a bulb and a tube. However, the liquid in your thermometer will be water.
4. To test your design, place the aluminum pie pan on a hot plate. Carefully pour water into the pan until it is halfway full. Allow the water to heat.
5. Put on your gloves, and carefully place the "bulb" of your thermometer in the hot water. Observe the water level in the tube. Does it rise?
6. If the water level does not rise, adjust your design as necessary, and repeat steps 3–5. When the water level does rise, sketch your final design in your ScienceLog.
7. After you finalize your design, you must calibrate your thermometer with a laboratory thermometer by taping an index card to the thermometer tube so that the entire part of the tube protruding from the "bulb" of the thermometer touches the card.

Materials
- heat-resistant gloves
- aluminum pie pan
- hot plate
- water
- assorted containers, such as plastic bottles, soda cans, film canisters, medicine bottles, test tubes, balloons, and yogurt containers with lids
- assorted tubes, such as clear inflexible plastic straws or 5 mm diameter plastic tubing, 30 cm long
- modeling clay
- food coloring
- pitcher
- transparent tape
- index card
- Celsius thermometer
- a paper cone-shaped filter or funnel
- 2 large plastic-foam cups
- ice cubes
- metric ruler

546

Daniel Bugenhagen
Yutan Jr.–Sr. High
Yutan, Nebraska

California Standards: PE/ATE 7, 7a, 7b, 7e

8. Place the cone-shaped filter or funnel into the plastic-foam cup. Carefully pour hot water from the hot plate into the filter or funnel. Be sure that no water splashes or spills.
9. Place your own thermometer and a laboratory thermometer in the hot water. Mark the water level on the index card as it rises. Observe and record the temperature on the laboratory thermometer, and write this value on the card beside the mark.
10. Repeat steps 8–9 with warm water from the faucet.
11. Repeat steps 8–9 with ice water.
12. Divide the markings on the index card into equally sized increments, and write the corresponding temperatures on the index card.

Analyze the Results

13. How effective is your thermometer at measuring heat?
14. Compare your thermometer design with other students' designs. How would you modify your design to make your thermometer measure temperature even better?

Draw Conclusions

15. Take a class vote to see which design should be chosen for a contract with Safety Industries. Why was this thermometer chosen? How did it differ from other designs in the class?

General Design

A water thermometer has a receptacle containing water and air with a tube protruding from the receptacle. A trick to getting the water thermometer to work well is to allow a lot of air in the "bulb" because it will heat up faster than it would if there were more water than air. As the air heats, it expands, pushing the water upward in the tube. One way to build such a thermometer is to put a straw in a soda can and to seal the opening of the can with modeling clay so that water can escape only by moving upward, out of the straw. A sample design is shown below.

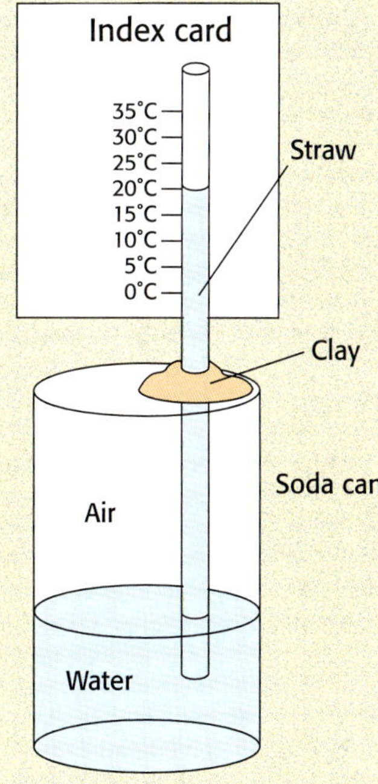

Answers

13. Answers will vary. Accept all reasonable responses.
14. Answers will vary. Accept all reasonable responses.
15. Accept all reasonable responses.

Science Skills Worksheet 1
"Being Flexible"

Science Skills Worksheet 5
"Using Logic"

Go Fly a Bike!
Teacher's Notes

Time Required
One 45-minute class period

Lab Ratings

TEACHER PREP
STUDENT SET-UP
CONCEPT LEVEL
CLEAN UP

MATERIALS

The materials listed on the student page are enough for a group of 3–4 students.

Safety Caution
Remind students to review all safety cautions and icons before beginning this lab activity.

Preparation Notes
Conduct this activity on a day when the wind is blowing, but not when the wind speed is greater than 50 km/h. Use straight, plastic straws. Before the activity, explain that an *anemometer* is a device that measures wind speed. It works because the wind pushes the cups at the same speed that the wind is moving.

Datasheets for LabBook
Datasheet 33

Go Fly a Bike!

Your friend Daniel just invented a bicycle that can fly! Trouble is, the bike can fly only when the wind speed is between 3 m/s and 10 m/s. If the wind is not blowing hard enough, the bike won't get enough lift to rise into the air, and if the wind is blowing too hard, the bike is difficult to control. Daniel needs to know if he can fly his bike today. Can you build a device that can estimate how fast the wind is blowing?

Materials
- scissors
- 5 small paper cups
- metric ruler
- hole punch
- 2 straight plastic straws
- colored marker
- small stapler
- thumbtack
- sharp pencil with an eraser
- modeling clay
- masking tape
- watch or clock that indicates seconds

Ask a Question
1. How can I construct a device to measure wind speed?

Construct an Anemometer
2. Cut off the rolled edges of all five paper cups. This will make them lighter, so that they can spin more easily.
3. Measure and place four equally spaced markings 1 cm below the rim of one of the paper cups.
4. Use the hole punch to punch a hole at each mark so that the cup has four equally spaced holes. Use the sharp pencil to carefully punch a hole in the center of the bottom of the cup.
5. Push a straw through two opposite holes in the side of the cup.
6. Repeat step 5 for the other two holes. The straws should form an X.
7. Measure 3 cm from the bottom of the remaining paper cups, and mark each spot with a dot.
8. At each dot, punch a hole in the paper cups with the hole punch.
9. Color the outside of one of the four cups.
10. Slide a cup on one of the straws by pushing the straw through the punched hole. Rotate the cup so that the bottom faces to the right.
11. Fold the end of the straw, and staple it to the inside of the cup directly across from the hole.
12. Repeat steps 10–11 for each of the remaining cups.
13. Push the tack through the intersection of the two straws.

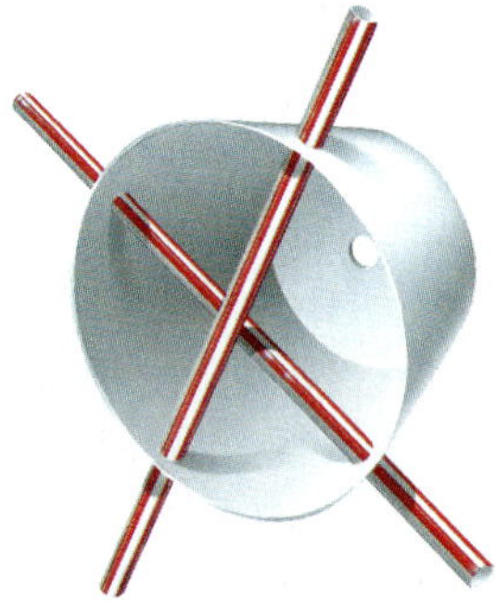

548

Terry J. Rakes
Elmwood Jr. High
Rogers, Arkansas

California Standards PE/ATE: 7, 7b, 7e

14. Push the eraser end of a pencil through the bottom hole in the center cup. Push the tack as far as it will go into the end of the eraser.
15. Push the sharpened end of the pencil into some modeling clay to form a base. This will allow the device to stand up without being knocked over, as shown at right.
16. Blow into the cups so that they spin. Adjust the tack so that the cups can freely spin without wobbling or falling apart. Congratulations! You have just constructed an anemometer.

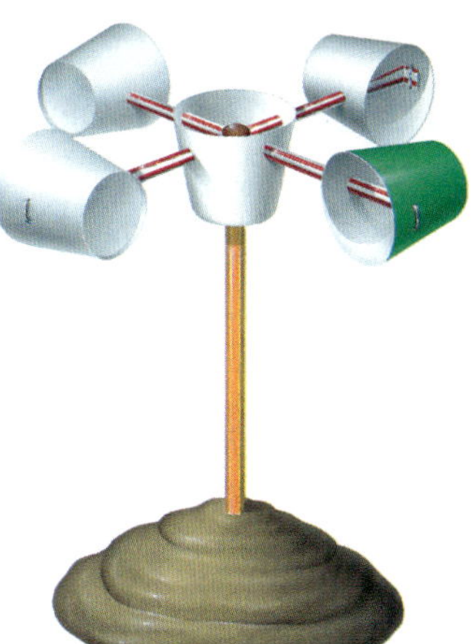

Conduct an Experiment

17. Find a suitable area outside to place the anemometer vertically on a surface away from objects that would obstruct the wind, such as buildings and trees.
18. Mark the surface at the base of the anemometer with masking tape. Label the tape "starting point."
19. Hold the colored cup over the starting point while your partner holds the watch.
20. Release the colored cup. At the same time, your partner should look at the watch or clock. As the cups spin, count the number of times the colored cup crosses the starting point in 10 seconds.

Analyze the Results

21. How many times did the colored cup cross the starting point in 10 seconds?
22. Divide your answer in step 21 by 10 to get the number of revolutions in 1 second.
23. Measure the diameter of your anemometer (the distance between the outside edges of two opposite cups) in centimeters. Multiply this number by 3.14 to get the circumference of the circle made by the cups of your anemometer.
24. Multiply your answer from step 23 by the number of revolutions per second (step 22). Multiply that answer by 100 to get wind speed in meters per second.
25. Compare your results with those of your classmates. Did you get the same result? What could account for any slight differences in your results?

Draw Conclusions

26. Could Daniel fly his bicycle today? Why or why not?

Answers

21. Answers will vary, depending on your current local weather conditions.
22. Answers will vary according to each student's response to question 21.
23. Answers will vary according to the length of the straws and the size of the cups used.
24. Answers will vary.
25. Each group's anemometer should provide similar results. Differences may be caused by inconsistent wind speed. If students did not answer question 20 precisely, their results will be slightly different from other groups.
26. If the wind speed is between 3 and 10 m/s, Danny could fly his bicycle. Otherwise, the weather would be too windy or too still for the bicycle to work.

Under Pressure! Teacher's Notes

Time Required

One 45-minute class period plus 15 minutes each day for 3–4 days

Lab Ratings

TEACHER PREP 2
STUDENT SET-UP 3
CONCEPT LEVEL 2
CLEAN UP 2

MATERIALS

The materials listed on the student page are enough for a group of 2–4 students.

Safety Caution

Remind students to review all safety cautions and icons before beginning this lab activity.

Do not allow students to make a mercury barometer. Mercury fumes are dangerous.

Preparation Notes

A few weeks before the activity, collect daily weather newspaper clippings. A week before the activity, have students bring in large coffee cans. Jars can substitute for coffee cans in this experiment.

Under Pressure!

You are planning a picnic with your friends, so you look in the newspaper for the weather forecast. The temperature this afternoon should be in the low 80s. This sounds quite comfortable! But you notice that the newspaper's forecast also includes the barometer reading. What does the reading tell you? In this activity, you will build your own barometer and discover what this instrument can tell you.

Materials

- balloon
- scissors
- large empty coffee can with 10 cm diameter
- masking tape or rubber band
- drinking straw
- transparent tape
- index card

Ask a Question

1. How can I construct a device that measures changes in atmospheric pressure?

Conduct an Experiment

2. Stretch and inflate the balloon. Let the air out. This will allow your barometer to be more sensitive to changes in atmospheric pressure.
3. Cut off the end of the balloon that you put in your mouth to inflate it. Stretch the balloon snugly over the mouth of the coffee can. Attach the balloon to the can with the tape or the rubber band.
4. Cut one end of the straw at an angle to form a pointer.

Datasheets for LabBook Datasheet 34

Science Skills Worksheet 2 "Using Your Senses"

Terry J. Rakes
Elmwood Jr. High
Rogers, Arkansas

California Standards: PE/ATE 7, 7b, 7e

5. Place the straw with the pointer pointed away from the center of the stretched balloon so that 5 cm of the end of the straw hangs over the edge of the can, as shown at right. Tape the straw to the balloon.
6. Tape the index card to the can near the straw. Congratulations! You have just constructed a barometer!
7. Find a suitable area outside to place the barometer. Record the location of the straw for 3–4 days by marking it on the index card.

Analyze the Results

8. What factors affect how your barometer works? Explain your answer.
9. What does an upward movement of the straw indicate?
10. What does a downward movement of the straw indicate?

Draw Conclusions

11. Compare your results with the barometric pressures listed in your local newspaper. What kind of weather is associated with high pressure? What kind of weather is associated with low pressure?

Going Further

Now you can calibrate your barometer! Gather the weather section from your local newspaper for the same 3 or 4 days that you were testing your barometer. Find the barometer reading in the newspaper for each day, and record it beside that day's mark on your index card. Divide the markings on the index card into regular increments, and write the corresponding barometric pressures on the card.

Answers

8. Temperature and pressure will affect how the barometer works. At higher temperatures, air pressure decreases, relieving pressure on the balloon and making the straw point downward. At lower temperatures, the air pressure increases, increasing pressure on the balloon and making the straw point upward.
9. An upward movement of the straw means that the atmospheric pressure is increasing. Pressure is pushing on top of the balloon, causing the pointer to rise.
10. A downward movement of the straw means that the atmospheric pressure is decreasing.
11. Clear, dry days are associated with high pressure. Cloudy, rainy, or humid days are associated with low pressure. A sudden drop in air pressure usually indicates that a storm is on the way.

Watching the Weather
Teacher's Notes

Time Required
One 45-minute class period

Lab Ratings

TEACHER PREP 1
STUDENT SET-UP 1
CONCEPT LEVEL 2
CLEAN UP 1

MATERIALS

There are no materials required in this lab. Have students complete the lab individually.

Watching the Weather

SKILL BUILDER

Imagine that you own a private consulting firm that helps people plan for big occasions, such as weddings, parties, and celebrity events. One of your duties is making sure the weather doesn't put a damper on your clients' plans. In order to provide the best service possible, you have taken a crash course in reading weather maps. Will the celebrity golf match have to be delayed on account of rain? Will the wedding ceremony have to be moved inside so the blushing bride doesn't get soaked? It is your job to say "yea" or "nay."

Procedure

1. Study the station model and legend shown on the next page. You will use the legend to interpret the weather map on the final page of this activity.
2. Weather data is represented on a weather map by a station model. A station model is a small circle that shows the location of the weather station along with a set of symbols and numbers around the circle that represent the data collected at the weather station. Study the table below.

Weather-Map Symbols

Weather conditions		Cloud cover		Wind speed (mph)	
••	Light rain	○	No clouds	◎	Calm
∴	Moderate rain	⦶	One-tenth or less	⟋	3–8
⁘	Heavy rain	◔	Two- to three-tenths	⟋	9–14
,	Drizzle	◕	Broken	⟋⟋	15–20
**	Light snow	◐	Nine-tenths	⟋⟋	21–25
⁂	Moderate snow	●	Overcast	⟋⟋⟋	32–37
⩊	Thunderstorm	⊗	Sky obscured	⟋⟋⟋⟋	44–48
∾	Freezing rain	**Special Symbols**		◢	55–60
∞	Haze	▲▲▲▲	Cold front	◢⟋	66–71
≡	Fog	●●●●	Warm front		
		H	High pressure		
		L	Low pressure		
		꩜	Hurricane		

Gordon Zibelman
Drexel Hill Middle School
Drexel Hill, Pennsylvania

California Standards: PE/ATE 4e, 7

Station Model

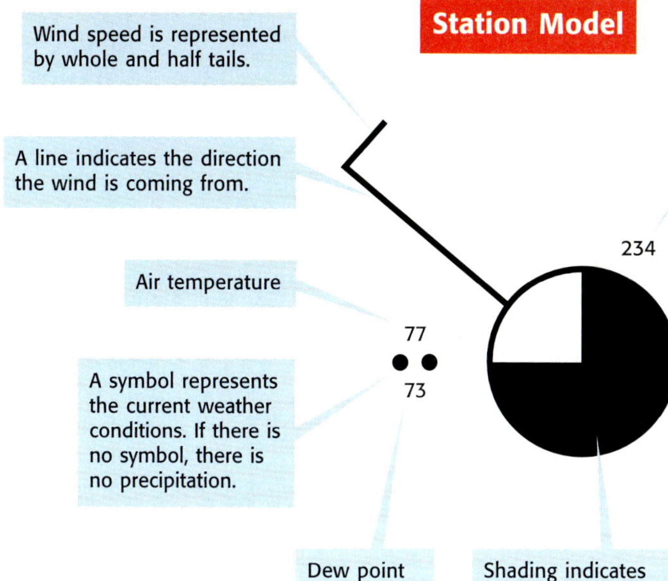

Atmospheric pressure in millibars (mbar). This number has been shortened on the station model. To read the number properly you must follow a few simple rules.

- If the first number is greater than 5, place a 9 in front of the number and a decimal point between the last two digits.
- If the first number is less than or equal to 5, place a 10 in front of the number and a decimal point between the last two digits.

Interpreting Station Models

The station model below is for Boston, Massachusetts. The current temperature in Boston is 42°F, and the dew point is 39°F. The barometric pressure is 1011.0 mbar. The sky is overcast, and there is a moderate rainfall. The wind is coming from the southwest at 15–20 mph.

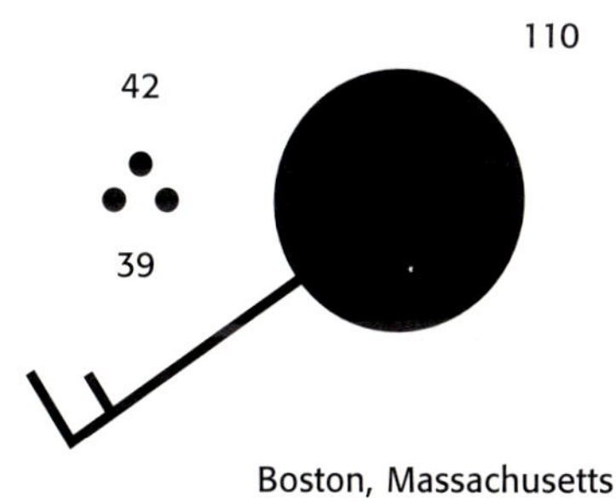

Boston, Massachusetts

Lab Notes

You may want to go over the different weather symbols with students and discuss how to convert the abbreviated form of atmospheric pressure to its actual measure. Before the lab, have students review the different kinds of fronts. Students may enjoy creating a weather report based on the weather report provided in this lab. Students can present this report to the class as a "live" studio show or through a video tape they create in their own time.

Datasheets for LabBook Datasheet 35

Answers

3. It's the winter. A cold front is coming through. Temperatures are pretty low everywhere.
4. The temperature is 42°F. The barometric pressure is 1024.6 mb. The dewpoint is 36°F. There is broken cloud cover. There is a light rain, and the wind is from the northwest at 3–8 mph.
5. As the cold front approaches, the wind is generally from the south, the barometric pressure is low, and temperatures are warmer. As the cold front passes, the wind is from the northwest, the pressure rises, and temperatures are much cooler.
6. The temperature is 45°F. The barometric pressure is 965.41 mb, the dewpoint is 38°F, the sky is obscured, there is a thunderstorm, and the wind is from the south at 21–25 mph.

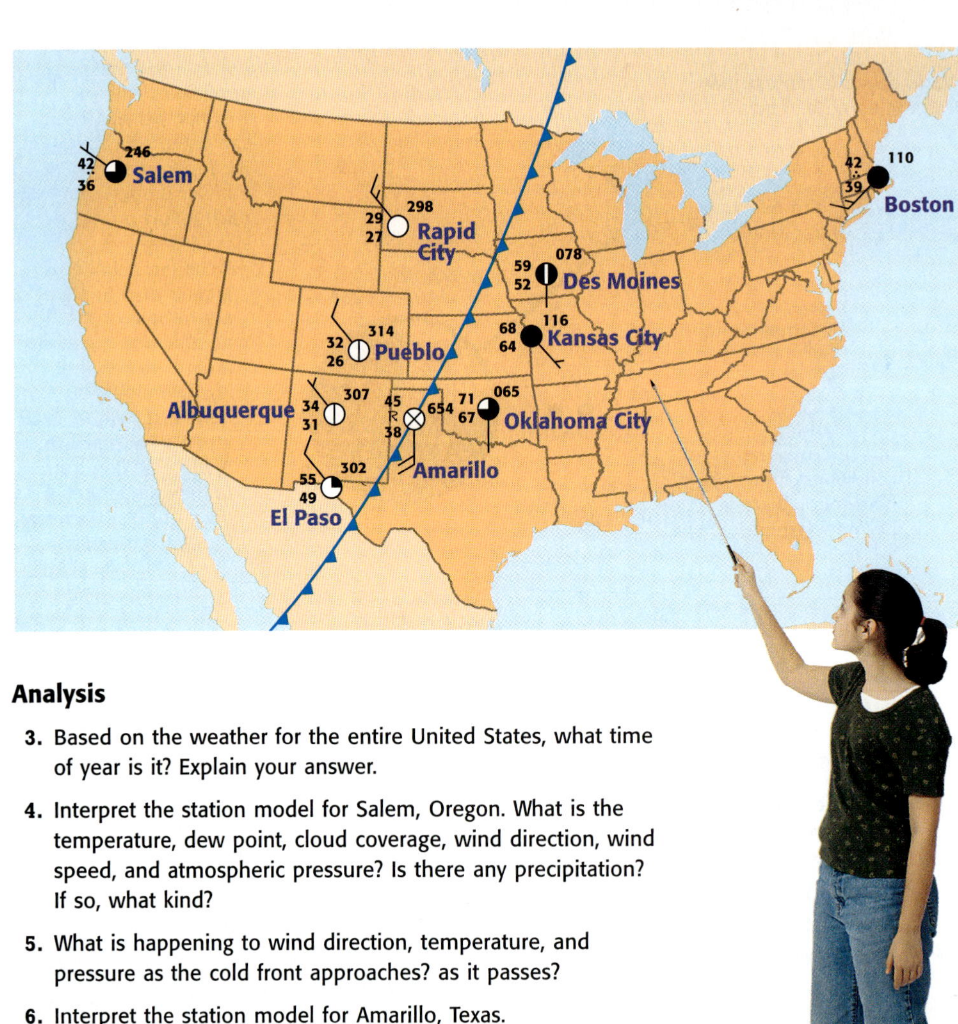

Analysis

3. Based on the weather for the entire United States, what time of year is it? Explain your answer.
4. Interpret the station model for Salem, Oregon. What is the temperature, dew point, cloud coverage, wind direction, wind speed, and atmospheric pressure? Is there any precipitation? If so, what kind?
5. What is happening to wind direction, temperature, and pressure as the cold front approaches? as it passes?
6. Interpret the station model for Amarillo, Texas.

Let It Snow!

DISCOVERY LAB

While an inch of rain might be good for your garden, 7 or 8 cm could cause an unwelcome flood. But what about snow? How much snow is too much? A blizzard might drop 40 cm of snow overnight. Sure it's up to your knees, but how does this much snow compare with rain? This activity will help you find out.

Materials

- 150 mL of shaved ice
- 100 mL beaker
- metric ruler
- heat-resistant gloves
- hot plate
- graduated cylinder

Procedure

1. Pour 50 mL of shaved ice into your beaker. Do not pack the ice into the beaker. This ice will represent your snowfall.
2. Use the ruler to measure the height of the snow in the beaker.
3. Turn on the hot plate to a low setting. **Caution:** Wear heat-resistant gloves and goggles when working with the hot plate.
4. Place the beaker on the hot plate, and leave it there until all of the snow melts.
5. Pour the water into the graduated cylinder, and record the height and volume of the water in your ScienceLog.
6. Repeat steps 1–5 two more times.

Analysis

7. What was the difference in height before and after the snow melted in each of your three trials? What was the average difference?
8. Why did the volume change after the ice melted?
9. In this activity, what was the ratio of snow height to water height?
10. Use the ratio you found in step 9 to calculate how much water 50 cm of this snow would produce. Use the following equation to help.

$$\frac{\text{measured height of snow}}{\text{measured height of water}} = \frac{\text{50 cm of snow}}{\text{? cm of water}}$$

11. Why is it important to know the water content of a snowfall?

Going Further

Shaved ice isn't really snow. Research to find out how much water real snow would produce. Does every snowfall produce the same ratio of snow height to water depth?

Let It Snow!
Teacher's Notes

Time Required

One 45-minute class period

Lab Ratings

TEACHER PREP: 1
STUDENT SET-UP: 2
CONCEPT LEVEL: 1
CLEAN UP: 1

MATERIALS

The materials listed are best for a group of 3–4 students.

Safety Caution

Remind students to review all safety cautions and icons before beginning this lab activity.

Answers

7. Answers will vary according to the water content of the ice or snow sample.
8. The volume changed because the water changed from a solid to a liquid.
9. Answers will vary.
10. Answers will vary
11. Answers will vary. The water content of a snowfall—whether it is relatively wet or relatively dry—affects how much flooding may occur as the snow melts. A "wetter" snow has more water per volume and may cause more flooding than a "drier" snow.

Going Further

Every snowfall does not produce the same ratio of snow height to water depth. The ratio of snow height to water depth is dependent on whether the snow is wet or dry.

CLASSROOM TESTED & APPROVED

Walter Woolbaugh
Manhattan School System
Manhattan, Montana

Datasheets for LabBook
Datasheet 36

California Standards: PE/ATE 7, 7b

Gone with the Wind
Teacher's Notes

Time Required
One 45-minute class period

Lab Ratings

TEACHER PREP 1
STUDENT SET-UP 2
CONCEPT LEVEL 2
CLEAN UP 1

MATERIALS
This activity works best in groups of 2–3 students.

Safety Caution
Remind students to review all safety cautions and icons before beginning this lab activity.

Preparation Notes
You might want to watch your local weather station in order to schedule this experiment on a windy day. Use a magnetic compass to find magnetic north. Then use masking tape or chalk to mark the sidewalk or parking lot with an arrow pointing toward magnetic north. Before the activity, ask students if they have ever seen a weather vane. Also have them list several reasons why knowing the wind direction might be helpful.

MAKING MODELS

Gone with the Wind

Pilots at the Fly Away Airport need your help—fast! Last night, lightning destroyed the orange windsock. This windsock helped pilots measure which direction the wind was blowing. But now the windsock is gone with the wind, and an incoming airplane needs to land. The pilot must know what direction the wind is blowing and is counting on you to make a device that can measure wind direction.

Materials
- paper plate
- drawing compass
- metric ruler
- protractor
- index card
- scissors
- stapler
- straight plastic straw
- sharpened pencil
- thumbtack or pushpin
- magnetic compass
- small rock

SCIENTIFIC METHOD

Ask a Question
1. How can I measure wind direction?

Conduct an Experiment
2. Find the center of the plate by tracing around its edge with a drawing compass. The pointed end of the compass should poke a small hole in the center of the plate.
3. Use a ruler to draw a line across the center of the plate.
4. Use a protractor to help you draw a second line through the center of the plate. This new line should be at a 90° angle to the line you drew in step 3.
5. Moving clockwise, label each line *N, E, S,* and *W.*
6. Use a protractor to help you draw two more lines through the center of the plate. These lines should be at a 45° angle to the lines you drew in steps 3 and 4.
7. Moving clockwise from *N,* label these new lines *NE, SE, SW,* and *NW.* The plate now resembles the face of a magnetic compass. This will be the base of your wind-direction indicator. It will help you read the direction of the wind at a glance.

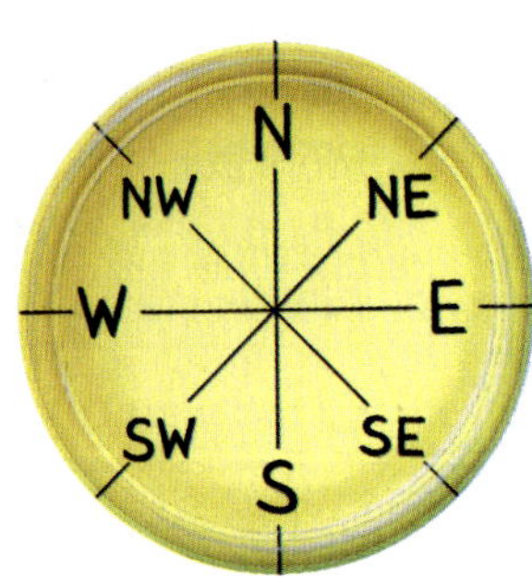

Walter Woolbaugh
Manhattan School System
Manhattan, Montana

California Standards: PE/ATE 7, 7b

8. Measure and mark a 5 × 5 cm square on an index card. Cut the square out of the card. Fold the square in half to form a triangle.
9. Staple an open edge of the triangle to the straw so that one point of the triangle touches the end of the straw.
10. Hold the pencil at a 90° angle to the straw. The eraser should touch the balance point of the straw. Push a thumbtack or pushpin through the straw and into the eraser. The straw should spin without falling off.
11. Find a suitable area outside to measure the wind direction. The area should be clear of trees and buildings.
12. Press the sharpened end of the pencil through the center hole of the plate and into the ground. The labels on your paper plate should be facing the sky, as shown below.
13. Use a compass to find magnetic north. Rotate the plate so that the *N* on the plate points north. Place a small rock on top of the plate so that it does not turn.
14. Watch the straw as it rotates. The triangle will point in the direction the wind is blowing.

Analyze the Results

15. From what direction is the wind coming?
16. In what direction is the wind blowing?

Draw Conclusions

17. Would this be an effective way for pilots to measure wind direction? Why or why not?
18. What improvements would you suggest to Fly Away Airport to measure wind direction more accurately?

Going Further

Use this tool to measure and record wind direction for several days. What changes in wind direction occur as a front approaches? as a front passes?

Review magnetic declination in the chapter titled "Maps as Models of the Earth." How might magnetic declination affect your design for a tool to measure wind direction?

Answers

15. Answers will vary.
16. Answers will vary.
17. Answers will vary. Accept all reasonable responses.
18. Answers will vary. Accept all reasonable responses.

Going Further

Answers will vary. (Wind direction varies according to the type of front that is moving through.) Sample answer: You have to adjust the weather vane to account for the difference between magnetic north and true north.

Answers will vary. The adjustment will vary depending on where you live.

Datasheets for LabBook
Datasheet 37

Science Skills Worksheet 24
"Using Models to Communicate"

Global Impact
Teacher's Notes

Time Required
One 45-minute class period

Lab Ratings

TEACHER PREP 1
STUDENT SET-UP 3
CONCEPT LEVEL 2
CLEAN UP 1

MATERIALS
The materials listed in the student page are enough for each student.

Preparation Notes
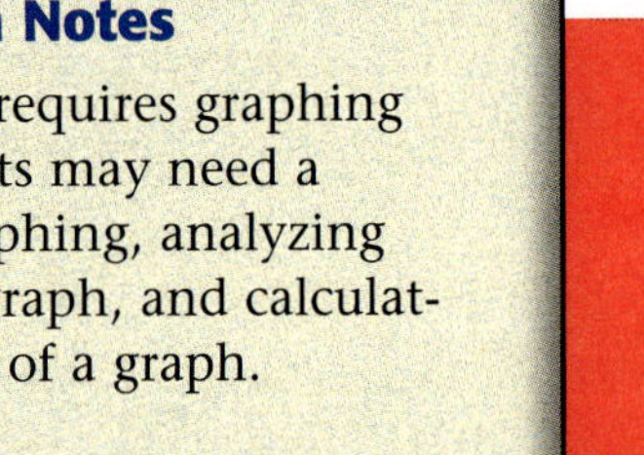
This activity requires graphing skills. Students may need a review of graphing, analyzing data from a graph, and calculating the slope of a graph.

Datasheets for LabBook Datasheet 38

Science Skills Worksheet 26 "Grasping Graphing"

Janel Guse
West Central Middle School
Hartford, South Dakota

Global Impact

SKILL BUILDER

For years scientists have debated the topic of global warming. Is the temperature of the Earth actually getting warmer? Sample sizes are a very important factor in any scientific study. In this activity, you will examine a chart to determine if the data indicate any trends. Be sure to notice how much the trends seem to change as you analyze different sets of data.

Materials
- 4 colored pencils
- metric ruler

Procedure
1. Look at the chart below. It shows average global temperatures recorded over the last 100 years.
2. Draw a graph in your ScienceLog. Label the horizontal axis "Time," and mark the grid in 5-year intervals. Label the vertical axis "Temperature (°C)," with values ranging from 13°C to 15°C.
3. Starting with 1900, use the numbers in red to plot the temperature in 20-year intervals. Connect the dots with straight lines.
4. Using a ruler, estimate the overall slope of temperatures, and draw a red line to represent the slope.
5. Using different colors, plot the temperatures at 10-year intervals and 5-year intervals on the same graph. Connect each set of dots, and draw the average slope for each set.

Analysis
6. Examine your completed graph, and explain any trends you see in the graphed data. Was there an increase or a decrease in average temperature over the last 100 years?
7. What differences did you see in each set of graphed data? what similarities?
8. What conclusions can you draw from the data you graphed in this activity?
9. What would happen if your graph were plotted in 1-year intervals? Try it!

Average Global Temperatures

Year	°C	Year	°C	Year	°C	Year	°C	Year	°C	Year	°C
1900	**14.0**	1917	13.6	1934	14.0	1951	14.0	1968	13.9	**1985**	**14.1**
1901	13.9	1918	13.6	**1935**	**13.9**	1952	14.0	1969	14.0	1986	14.2
1902	13.8	1919	13.8	1936	14.0	1953	14.1	**1970**	**14.0**	1987	14.3
1903	13.6	**1920**	**13.8**	1937	14.1	1954	13.9	1971	13.9	1988	14.4
1904	13.5	1921	13.9	1938	14.1	**1955**	**13.9**	1972	13.9	1989	14.2
1905	**13.7**	1922	13.9	1939	14.0	1956	13.8	1973	14.2	**1990**	**14.5**
1906	13.8	1923	13.8	**1940**	**14.1**	1957	14.1	1974	13.9	1991	14.4
1907	13.6	1924	13.8	1941	14.1	1958	14.1	**1975**	**14.0**	1992	14.1
1908	13.7	**1925**	**13.8**	1942	14.1	1959	14.0	1976	13.8	1993	14.2
1909	13.7	1926	14.1	1943	14.0	**1960**	**14.0**	1977	14.2	1994	14.3
1910	**13.7**	1927	14.0	1944	14.1	1961	14.1	1978	14.1	**1995**	**14.5**
1911	13.7	1928	14.0	**1945**	**14.0**	1962	14.0	1979	14.1	1996	14.4
1912	13.7	1929	13.8	1946	14.0	1963	14.0	**1980**	**14.3**	1997	14.4
1913	13.8	**1930**	**13.9**	1947	14.1	1964	13.7	1981	14.4	1998	14.5
1914	14.0	1931	14.0	1940	14.0	**1965**	**13.8**	1982	14.1	1999	
1915	**14.0**	1932	14.0	1949	13.9	1966	13.9	1983	14.3	**2000**	
1916	13.8	1933	13.9	**1950**	**13.8**	1967	14.0	1984	14.1	2001	

558

Answers
6. Students will notice that the temperatures fluctuated over the last 100 years but have gradually increased in the last 30 years.
7. The larger the sample size, the more precise your analysis will be. You notice that in the larger samples, temperatures are constantly fluctuating. A smaller sample doesn't always adequately display what is really happening with the data. For instance, the average temperature for a certain year might not be representative for the entire decade. The smaller the data set, the more your outcome is subject to error. There were very few similarities among the graphs.
8. You can conclude that a larger data set gives you a more complete picture of what is happening. Global temperatures have gradually increased in the twentieth century.
9. Global temperatures would appear to fluctuate more.

California Standards: PE/ATE 7, 7c, 7e, 7h

For the Birds

You and a partner have a new business building birdhouses. But your first clients have told you that birds do not want to live in the birdhouses you have made. The clients want their money back unless you can solve the problem. You need to come up with a solution right away!

You remember reading an article about microclimates in a science magazine. Cities often heat up because the pavement and buildings absorb so much solar radiation. Maybe the houses are too warm! How can the houses be kept cooler?

You decide to investigate the roofs; after all, changing the roofs would be a lot easier than building new houses. In order to help your clients and the birds, you decide to test different roof colors and materials to see how these variables affect a roof's ability to absorb the sun's rays.

One partner will test the color, and the other partner will test the materials. You will then share your results and make a recommendation together.

Materials

- 4 pieces of cardboard
- black, white, and light-blue tempera paint
- 4 Celsius thermometers
- watch or clock
- beige or tan wood
- beige or tan rubber

Part One: Color Test

Ask a Question

1. What color would be the best choice for the roof of a birdhouse?

Form a Hypothesis

2. In your ScienceLog, write down the color you think will keep a birdhouse coolest.

Test the Hypothesis

3. Paint one piece of cardboard black, another piece white, and a third light blue.
4. After the paint has dried, take the three pieces of cardboard outside, and place a thermometer on each piece.
5. In an area where there is no shade, place each piece at the same height so that all three receive the same amount of sunlight. Leave the pieces in the sunlight for 15 minutes.
6. Leave a fourth thermometer outside in the shade to measure the temperature of the air.

559

For the Birds
Teacher's Notes

Time Required

One 45-minute class period

Lab Ratings

TEACHER PREP ▲
STUDENT SET-UP ▲▲
CONCEPT LEVEL ▲▲
CLEAN UP ▲▲

MATERIALS

The materials listed on the student page are enough for a group of 4–5 students.

Safety Caution

Remind students to review all safety cautions and icons before beginning this lab activity.

Preparation Notes

As an alternative to painting the rubber in the *Going Further* section, have the students use the soles of athletic shoes. They come in a variety of colors and are readily available.

Datasheets for LabBook
Datasheet 39

Larry Tackett
Andrew Jackson Middle School
Cross Lanes, West Virginia

California Standards: PE/ATE 7, 7a, 7b, 7d, 7e, 7h

Answers

8. No, they were different. The black and blue pieces of cardboard, particularly the black one, were higher in temperature.
9. The temperature of the black cardboard was much higher than the outside temperature. Accept all other reasonable answers for the temperatures of the other colors in relation to the outside temperature.
10. Students' answers will vary. Accept all reasonable responses.

7. In your ScienceLog, record the reading of the thermometer on each piece of cardboard. Also record the outside temperature.

Analyze the Results

8. Did each of the three thermometers record the same temperature after 15 minutes? Explain.
9. Were the temperature readings on each of the three pieces of cardboard the same as the reading for the outside temperature? Explain.

Draw Conclusions

10. How do your observations compare with your hypothesis?

Part Two: Material Test

Ask a Question

11. Which material would be the best choice for the roof of a birdhouse?

Form a Hypothesis

12. In your ScienceLog, write down the material you think will keep a birdhouse coolest.

Test the Hypothesis

13. Take the rubber, wood, and the fourth piece of cardboard outside, and place a thermometer on each.
14. In an area where there is no shade, place each material at the same height so that they all receive the same amount of sunlight. Leave the materials in the sunlight for 15 minutes.
15. Leave a fourth thermometer outside in the shade to measure the temperature of the air.
16. In your ScienceLog, record the temperature of each material. Also record the outside temperature.

560

Analyze the Results

17. Did each of the thermometers on the three materials record the same temperature after 15 minutes? Explain.
18. Were the temperature readings on the rubber, wood, and cardboard the same as the reading for the outside temperature? Explain.

Draw Conclusions

19. How do your observations compare with your hypothesis?

Part Three: Sharing Information

Communicate Results

After you and your partner have finished your investigations, take a few minutes to share your results. Then work together to design a new roof.

20. Which material would you use to build the roofs for your birdhouses? Why?
21. Which color would you use to paint the new roofs? Why?

Going Further

Make three different-colored samples for each of the three materials. When you measure the temperatures for each sample, how do the colors compare for each material? Is the same color best for all three materials? How do your results compare with what you concluded in Part Three of this activity? What's more important, color or material?

Answers

17. No, they were different. The temperature of the rubber was higher than that of the other two materials.
18. No, the temperature of the rubber was higher than the outside temperature. Accept all other reasonable answers for the other materials.
19. Answers will vary. Accept all reasonable answers.
20. The wood would be the coolest. The cardboard would be a second alternative.
21. The white roof would be the coolest. The light blue roof would be a second alternative.

Going Further

Answers will vary. Accept all reasonable interpretations of the data collected.

Science Skills Worksheet 11
"Understanding Variables"

Biome Business
Teacher's Notes

Time Required
One 45-minute class period

Lab Ratings

Teacher Prep 1
Student Set-Up 1
Concept Level 3
Clean Up 1

MATERIALS

Student groups will need a general map to identify their biome location.

Preparation Notes
Remind students not to use seasonal terms such as spring and fall because some of the biomes in the Southern Hemisphere may experience seasons opposite those of the Northern Hemisphere.

Datasheets for LabBook
Datasheet 40

David Sparks
Redwater Jr. High
Redwater, Texas

SKILL BUILDER

Biome Business

You have just been hired as an assistant to a world-famous botanist. Your duties include collecting vegetation samples to study the effects of human activity on different plant species. Unfortunately, you were hired at the last minute, and no one has explained tomorrow's plan to you. You have been provided with climatographs for three biomes. A *climatograph* is a graph that shows the temperature and precipitation patterns for an area for a year. Each climatograph has two axes. The right axis indicates the temperature of the biome, while the left axis indicates the precipitation. You can use the information provided in the graphs to determine the type of climate in each biome. You also have a general map of the biomes, but nothing is labeled. Using this information, you must figure out what the environment will be like so that you can prepare yourself.

In this activity you will use climatographs and maps to determine where you will be traveling. You can find the exact locations by tracing the general maps and matching them to Figure 10 in the Climate chapter. Good luck!

Biome A

Procedure

1. Look at each climatograph. The shaded areas show the average precipitation for the biome. The red line shows the average temperature.
2. Use the climatographs to determine the climate patterns for each biome. Compare the maps with the general map in Figure 10 to find the exact location of each region.

Analysis

3. Describe the precipitation patterns of each biome by answering the following questions:
   a. When does it rain the most in this biome?
   b. Do you think the biome is relatively dry, or do you think it rains a lot?
4. Describe the temperature patterns of each biome by answering the following questions:
   a. What are the warmest months of the year?
   b. Does the biome seem to have temperature cycles, like seasons, or is the temperature almost always the same?
   c. Do you think the biome is warm or cool? Explain.
5. Name each biome.
6. Where is each biome located?

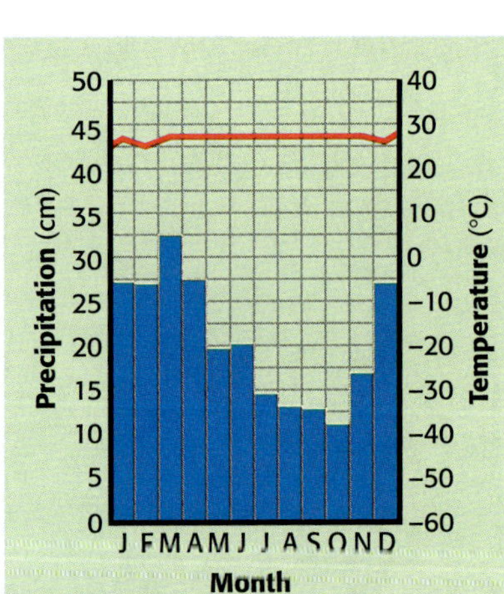

California Standards: PE/ATE 7, 7b, 7e

Biome B

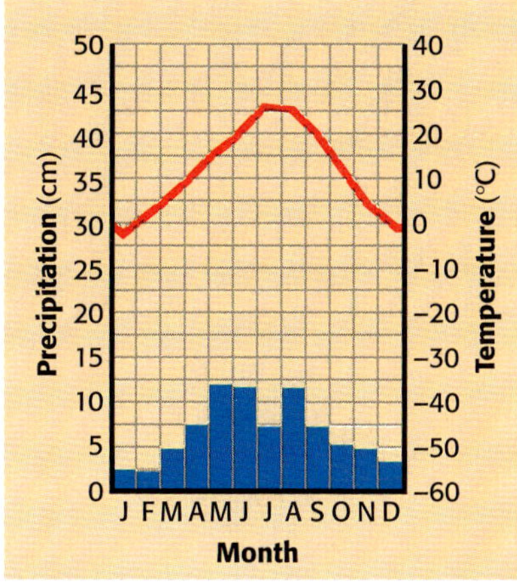

Biome C

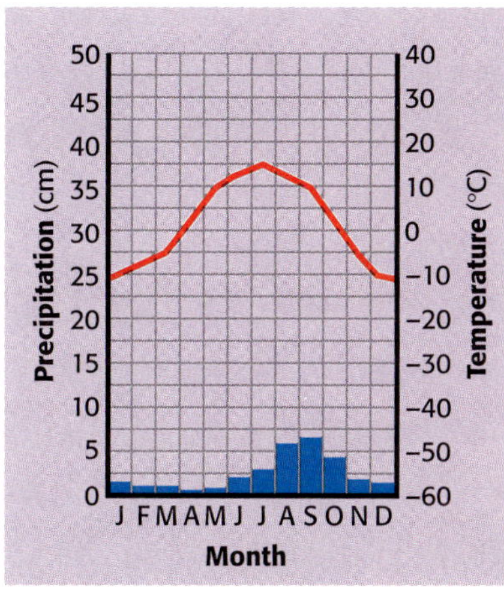

Going Further

In a cardboard box no bigger than a shoe box, build a model of one of the biomes that you investigated. Include things to represent the biome, such as the plants and animals that inhabit the area. Use magazines, photographs, colored pencils, plastic figurines, clay, or whatever you like. Be creative!

Answers

3. a. In Biome A, the rain falls throughout the year but is heaviest in November and December.
In Biome B, the rain is heaviest in September and October.
In Biome C, the rain is heaviest in May and August.

b. Biome A is very rainy and wet. Biomes B and C are relatively dry, except for a few months.

4. a. Biome A has a relatively constant temperature throughout the year.
Biomes B and C experience their warmest months from June to August.

b. Biome A has a constant temperature throughout the year.
Biomes B and C experience seasonal cycles.

c. Biome A is warm and the temperature is high year-round. Biome B has a cooler climate and the climatograph shows cooler temperatures year-round.
Biome C has a moderate climate in the early and late months of the year, but the temperature is quite hot in the middle months of the year.

5. Biome A = a tropical rain forest
Biome B = a taiga
Biome C = a temperate grassland

6. Biome A = the west coast of Africa near the equator
Biome B = northern Asia
Biome C = midwestern United States

Self-Check

Self-Check Answers

Chapter 2—Maps as Models of the Earth

Page 36: The Earth rotates around the geographic poles.

Page 42: The measurements would be more accurate on a globe; there would be a certain amount of distortion on a world map.

Page 47: If the lines are close together, then the mapped area is steep. If the lines are far apart, the mapped area has a gradual slope or is flat.

Chapter 3—Minerals of the Earth's Crust

Page 69: These minerals form wherever salt water has evaporated.

Chapter 4—Rocks: Mineral Mixtures

Page 88: From fastest-cooled to slowest-cooled, the rocks in Figure 10 are: basalt, rhyolite, gabbro, and granite.

Page 96: Geologists have discovered that rocks can indeed undergo both regional and contact metamorphism. If a rock is buried and regionally metamorphosed when magma intrudes, the effects of contact metamorphism will be superimposed on the effects of regional metamorphism.

Chapter 5—Energy Resources

Page 123: Both devices harness energy from falling water.

Chapter 6—Plate Tectonics

Page 153: When folding occurs, sedimentary rock strata bend but do not break. When faulting occurs, sedimentary rock strata break along a fault, and the fault blocks on either side move relative to each other.

Chapter 7—Earthquakes

Page 169: Convergent motion creates reverse faults, while divergent motion creates normal faults. Convergent motion produces deep, strong earthquakes, while divergent motion produces shallow, weak earthquakes.

Page 176: 120

Chapter 8—Volcanoes

Page 201: 1. Solid rock may become magma when pressure is released, when the temperature rises above its melting point, or when its composition changes. 2. Magma forms in the lower crust and upper mantle, at depths between 25 and 160 km.

Chapter 9—Heat and Heat Technology

Page 227: Two substances can have the same temperature but different amounts of thermal energy. Unlike thermal energy, temperature does not depend on mass. A small amount of a substance at a particular temperature will have less thermal energy than a large amount of the substance at the same temperature.

Page 229: Steam can cause a more severe burn than boiling water because steam contains more energy per unit mass than does boiling water.

Chapter 10—The Flow of Fresh Water

Page 252: If a river slowed down, the suspended load would be deposited.

Page 256: A river might slow where there is a bend or where the river empties into a large body of water.

Page 260: The impermeable rock layer in the aquifer traps the water in the permeable layer below. This creates the pressure needed to form an artesian spring.

Chapter 11—Agents of Erosion and Deposition

Page 277: A large wave has more erosive energy than a small wave because a large wave releases more energy when it breaks.

Page 283: The roots of plants anchor sediment in place. Deflation hollows form in areas where there is little vegetation because there is nothing to anchor the sediment in place; the sediment blows away.

Page 289: When a moving glacier picks up speed or flows over a high point, a crevasse may form. This occurs because the ice cannot stretch quickly while it is moving and therefore cracks.

Chapter 12—Interactions of Living Things

Page 311: Humans are omnivores. An omnivore eats both plants and animals. Humans can eat meat and vegetables as well as animal products, such as milk and eggs, and plant products, such as grains and fruit. Humans also eat fungus (mushrooms) and bacteria (in yogurt)!

Page 312: A food chain shows how energy moves in one direction from one organism to the next. A food web shows that there are many energy pathways between organisms.

Page 317: 1. If an area has only enough water to support 10 organisms, any additional organisms will cause some to go without water and move away or die. 2. Weather favorable for growing the food the deer eat will allow the forest to support more deer.

Chapter 13—Exploring the Oceans

Page 333: If North America and South America continue to drift westward and Asia continues to drift eastward, the continents will eventually collide on the other side of the Earth.

Page 341: Rift valleys form where tectonic plates pull apart, and ocean trenches form where one oceanic plate is forced underneath a continental plate or another oceanic plate.

Chapter 14—The Movement of Ocean Water

Page 367: Because he was traveling from Peru to a Polynesian island to the west, Heyerdahl would have noticed the wind blowing from the east.

Chapter 15—The Atmosphere

Page 396: As you climb a mountain, the air becomes less dense because there are fewer molecules to absorb heat. So even though cold air is generally more dense than warm air, it is less dense at higher elevations.

Chapter 16—Understanding Weather

Page 425: Evaporation occurs when liquid water changes into water vapor and returns to the air. Humidity is the amount of water vapor in the air.

565

Self-Check

Chapter 17—Climate

Page 456: Australia has summer during our winter months, December–February.

Page 462: Because of the dryness, desert soil is poor in organic matter, which fertilizes the soil. Without this natural fertilizer, crops would not be able to grow.

Page 470: The Earth's elliptical orbit causes increased seasonal differences. When the Earth's orbit is more elliptical, summers are hotter because the Earth is closer to the sun and receives more solar radiation. However, winters are cooler because the Earth is farther from the sun and receives less solar radiation.

CONTENTS

567

Concept Mapping: A Way to Bring Ideas Together

What Is a Concept Map?

Have you ever tried to tell someone about a book or a chapter you've just read and found that you can remember only a few isolated words and ideas? Or maybe you've memorized facts for a test, and then weeks later discover you're not even sure what topics those facts cover.

In both cases, you may have understood the ideas or concepts by themselves but not in relation to one another. If you could somehow link the ideas together, you would probably understand them better and remember them longer. This is something a concept map can help you do. A concept map is a way to see how ideas or concepts fit together. It can help you see the "big picture."

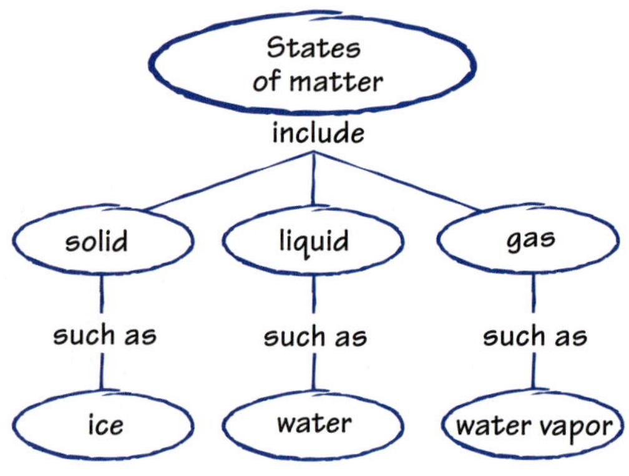

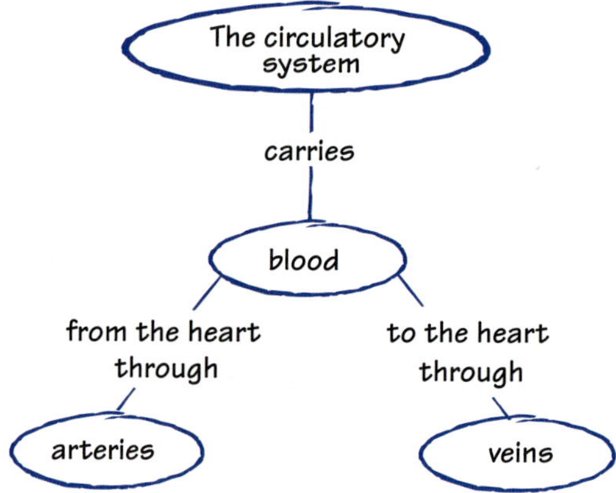

How to Make a Concept Map

1. **Make a list of the main ideas or concepts.**

   It might help to write each concept on its own slip of paper. This will make it easier to rearrange the concepts as many times as necessary to make sense of how the concepts are connected. After you've made a few concept maps this way, you can go directly from writing your list to actually making the map.

2. **Spread out the slips on a sheet of paper, and arrange the concepts in order from the most general to the most specific.**

   Put the most general concept at the top and circle it. Ask yourself, "How does this concept relate to the remaining concepts?" As you see the relationships, arrange the concepts in order from general to specific.

3. **Connect the related concepts with lines.**

4. **On each line, write an action word or short phrase that shows how the concepts are related.**

   Look at the concept maps on this page, and then see if you can make one for the following terms:

   plants, water, photosynthesis, carbon dioxide, sun's energy

   The answer is provided at right, but don't look at it until you try the concept map yourself.

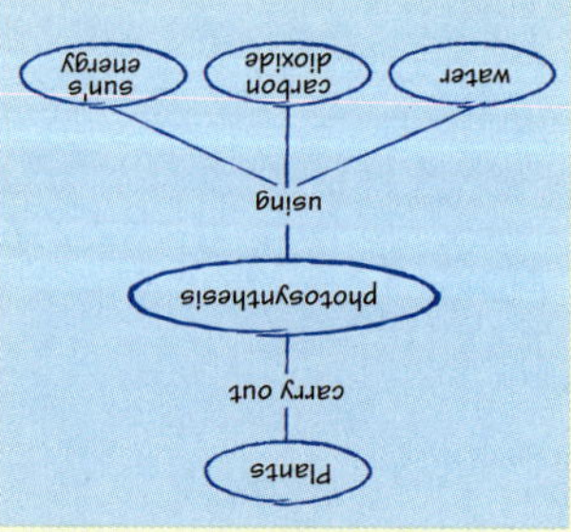

SI Measurement

The International System of Units, or SI, is the standard measuring system for all scientists. Using the same standards of measurement makes it easier for scientists to communicate with one another.

SI works by combining prefixes and base units. Each base unit can be used with different prefixes to define smaller and larger quantities. The table below lists common SI prefixes.

SI Prefixes

Prefix	Abbreviation	Factor	Example
kilo-	k	1,000	kilogram, 1 kg = 1000 g
hecto-	h	100	hectoliter, 1 hL = 100 L
deca-	da	10	decameter, 1 dam = 10 m
		1	meter, liter
deci-	d	0.1	decigram, 1 dg = 0.1 g
centi-	c	0.01	centimeter, 1 cm = 0.01 m
milli-	m	0.001	milliliter, 1 mL = 0.001 L
micro-	µ	0.000001	micrometer, 1 µm = 0.000001 m

SI Conversion Table

SI units	From SI to English	From English to SI
Length		
kilometer (km) = 1,000 m	1 km = 0.621 mi	1 mi = 1.069 km
meter (m) = 100 cm	1 m = 3.281 ft	1 ft = 0.305 m
centimeter (cm) = 0.01 m	1 cm = 0.394 in.	1 in. = 2.540 cm
millimeter (mm) = 0.001 m	1 mm = 0.039 in.	
micrometer (µm) = 0.000 001 m		
nanometer (nm) = 0.000 000 001 m		
Area		
square kilometer (km^2) = 100 hectares	1 km^2 = 0.386 mi^2	1 mi^2 = 2.590 km^2
hectare (ha) = 10,000 m^2	1 ha = 2.471 acres	1 acre = 0.405 ha
square meter (m^2) = 10,000 cm^2	1 m^2 = 10.765 ft^2	1 ft^2 = 0.093 m^2
square centimeter (cm^2) = 100 mm^2	1 cm^2 = 0.155 in.^{2}	1 in.^{2} = 6.452 cm^2
Volume		
liter (L) = 1,000 mL = 1 dm^3	1 L = 1.057 fl qt	1 fl qt = 0.946 L
milliliter (mL) = 0.001 L= 1 cm^3	1 mL = 0.034 fl oz	1 fl oz = 29.575 mL
microliter (µL) = 0.000 001 L		
Mass		
kilogram (kg) = 1,000 g	1 kg = 2.205 lb	1 lb = 0.454 kg
gram (g) = 1,000 mg	1 g = 0.035 oz	1 oz = 28.349 g
milligram (mg) = 0.001 g		
microgram (µg) 0.000 001 g		

569

Temperature Scales

Temperature can be expressed with three different scales: Fahrenheit, Celsius, and Kelvin. The SI unit for temperature is the kelvin (K). Although 0 K is much colder than 0°C, a change of 1 K is equal to a change of 1°C.

Three Temperature Scales

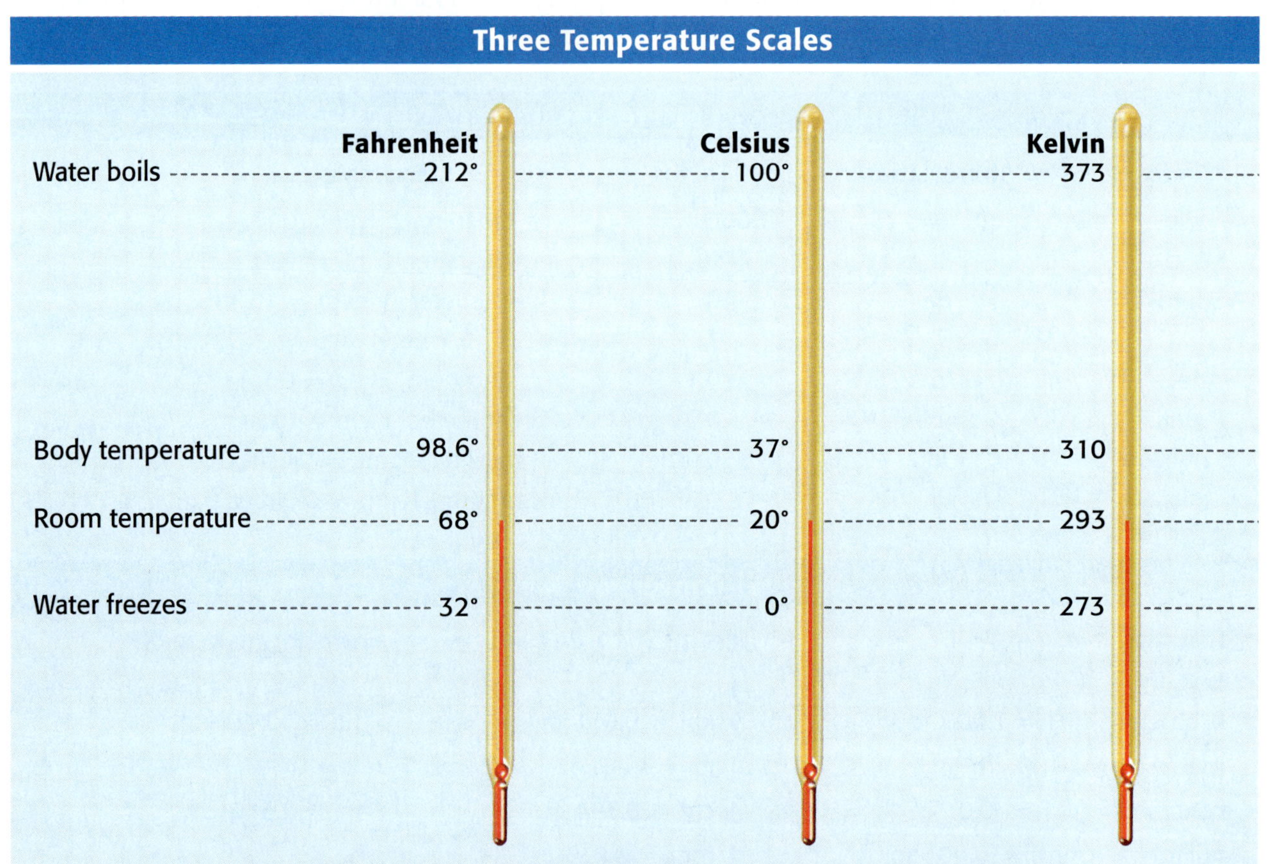

Temperature Conversions Table

To convert	Use this equation:	Example
Celsius to Fahrenheit °C ⟶ °F	$°F = \left(\frac{9}{5} \times °C\right) + 32$	Convert 45°C to °F. $°F = \left(\frac{9}{5} \times 45°C\right) + 32 = 113°F$
Fahrenheit to Celsius °F ⟶ °C	$°C = \frac{5}{9} \times (°F - 32)$	Convert 68°F to °C. $°C = \frac{5}{9} \times (68°F - 32) = 20°C$
Celsius to Kelvin °C ⟶ K	$K = °C + 273$	Convert 45°C to K. $K = 45°C + 273 = 318\ K$
Kelvin to Celsius K ⟶ °C	$°C = K - 273$	Convert 32 K to °C. $°C = 32\ K - 273 = -241°C$

Measuring Skills

Using a Graduated Cylinder

When using a graduated cylinder to measure volume, keep the following procedures in mind:

1. Make sure the cylinder is on a flat, level surface.
2. Move your head so that your eye is level with the surface of the liquid.
3. Read the mark closest to the liquid level. On glass graduated cylinders, read the mark closest to the center of the curve.

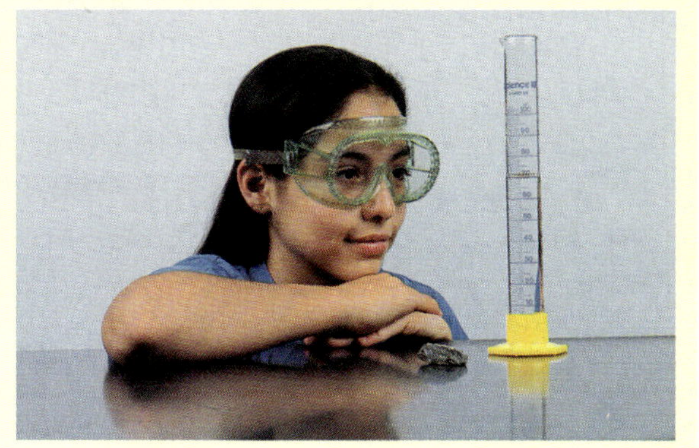

Using a Meterstick or Metric Ruler

When using a meterstick or metric ruler, keep the following procedures in mind:

1. Place the ruler firmly against the object you are measuring.
2. Align one edge of the object exactly with the zero end of the ruler.
3. Look at the other edge of the object to see which of the marks on the ruler is closest to that edge. **Note:** Each small slash between the centimeters represents a millimeter, which is one-tenth of a centimeter.

Using a Triple-Beam Balance

When using a triple-beam balance, keep the following procedures in mind:

1. Make sure the balance is on a level surface.
2. Place all of the countermasses at zero. Adjust the balancing knob until the pointer rests at zero.
3. Place the object you wish to measure on the pan. **Caution:** Do not place hot objects or chemicals directly on the balance pan.
4. Move the largest countermass along the beam to the right until it is at the last notch that does not tip the balance. Follow the same procedure with the next-largest countermass. Then move the smallest countermass until the pointer rests at zero.
5. Add the readings from the three beams together to determine the mass of the object.
6. When massing crystals or powders, use a piece of filter paper. First mass the paper. Then add the crystals or powder to the paper and remass. The actual mass of the crystals or powder is the total mass minus the mass of the paper. When massing liquids, first mass the empty container. Then mass the liquid and container together. The mass of the liquid is the total mass minus the mass of the container.

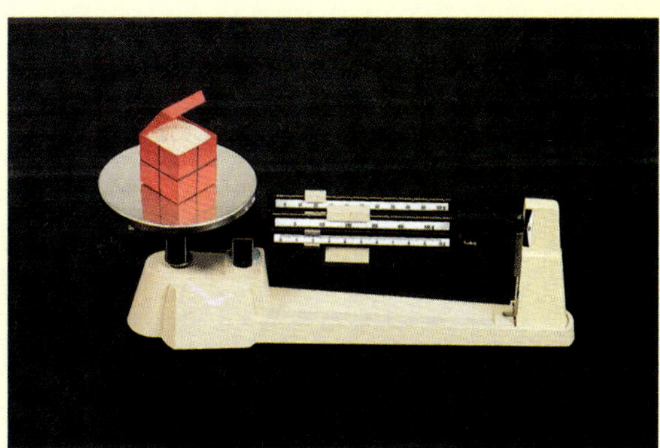

Scientific Method

The steps that scientists use to answer questions and solve problems is often called the **scientific method.** The scientific method is not a rigid procedure. Scientists may use all of the steps or just some of the steps of the scientific method. They may even repeat some of the steps. The goal of a scientific method is to come up with reliable answers and solutions.

Six Steps of a Scientific Method

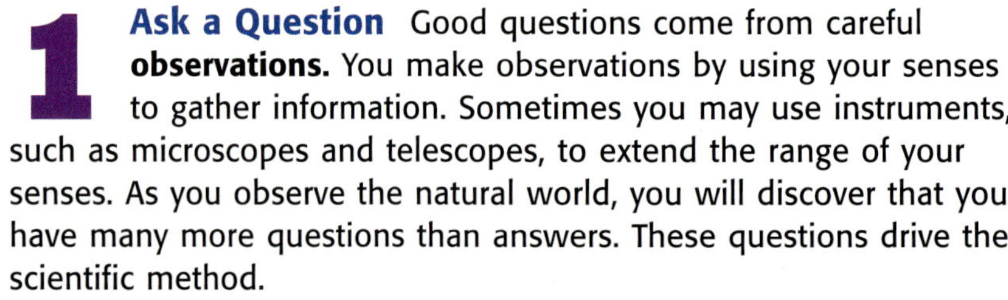

1 Ask a Question Good questions come from careful **observations.** You make observations by using your senses to gather information. Sometimes you may use instruments, such as microscopes and telescopes, to extend the range of your senses. As you observe the natural world, you will discover that you have many more questions than answers. These questions drive the scientific method.

Questions beginning with *what, why, how,* and *when* are very important in focusing an investigation, and they often lead to a hypothesis. (You will learn what a hypothesis is in the next step.) Here is an example of a question that could lead to further investigation.

Question: How does acid rain affect plant growth?

2 Form a Hypothesis After you come up with a question, you need to turn the question into a **hypothesis.** A hypothesis is a clear statement of what you expect the answer to your question to be. Your hypothesis will represent your best "educated guess" based on your observations and what you already know. A good hypothesis is one that is testable. If observations and information cannot be gathered or if an experiment cannot be designed to test your hypothesis, it is untestable, and the investigation can go no further.

Here is a hypothesis that could be formed from the question, "How does acid rain affect plant growth?"

Hypothesis: Acid rain causes plants to grow more slowly.

Notice that the hypothesis provides some specifics that lead to methods of testing. The hypothesis can also lead to predictions. A **prediction** is what you think will be the outcome of your experiment or data collection. Predictions are usually stated in an "if . . . then" format. For example, **if** meat is kept at room temperature, **then** it will spoil faster than meat kept in the refrigerator. More than one prediction can be made for a single hypothesis. Here is a sample prediction for the hypothesis that acid rain causes plants to grow more slowly.

Prediction: If a plant is watered with only acid rain (which has a pH of 4), then the plant will grow at half its normal rate.

3 **Test the Hypothesis** After you have formed a hypothesis and made a prediction, you should test your hypothesis. There are different ways to do this. Perhaps the most familiar way is to conduct a **controlled experiment.** A controlled experiment tests only one factor at a time. A controlled experiment has a **control group** and one or more **experimental groups.** All the factors for the control and experimental groups are the same except one factor, which is called the **variable.** By changing only one factor (the variable), you can see the results of just that one change.

Sometimes, the nature of an investigation makes a controlled experiment impossible. For example, dinosaurs have been extinct for millions of years, and the Earth's core is surrounded by thousands of meters of rock. It would be difficult if not impossible to conduct controlled experiments on such things. Under such circumstances, a hypothesis may be tested by making detailed observations. Taking measurements is one way of making observations.

Test Your Hypothesis

4 **Analyze the Results** After you have completed your experiments, made your observations, and collected your data, you must analyze all the information you have gathered. Tables and graphs are often used in this step to organize the data.

Analyze the Results

5 **Draw Conclusions** Based on the analysis of your data, you should conclude whether or not your results support your hypothesis. If your hypothesis is supported, you (or others) might want to repeat the observations or experiments to verify your results. If your hypothesis is not supported by the data, you may have to check your procedure for errors. You may even have to reject your hypothesis and make a new one. If you cannot draw a conclusion from your results, you may have to try the investigation again or carry out further observations or experiments.

Draw Conclusions

Do they support your hypothesis?

No

Yes

6 **Communicate Results** After any scientific investigation, you should report your results. By doing a written or oral report, you let others know what you have learned. They may want to repeat your investigation to see if they get the same results. Your report may even lead to another question, which in turn may lead to another investigation.

Scientific Method in Action

A scientific method is not a "straight line" of steps. It contains loops in which several steps may be repeated over and over again, while others may not be necessary. For example, sometimes scientists will find that testing one hypothesis raises new questions and new hypotheses to be tested. And sometimes, testing the hypothesis leads directly to a conclusion. Furthermore, the steps in a scientific method are not always used in the same order. Follow the steps in the diagram below, and see how many different directions a scientific method can take you.

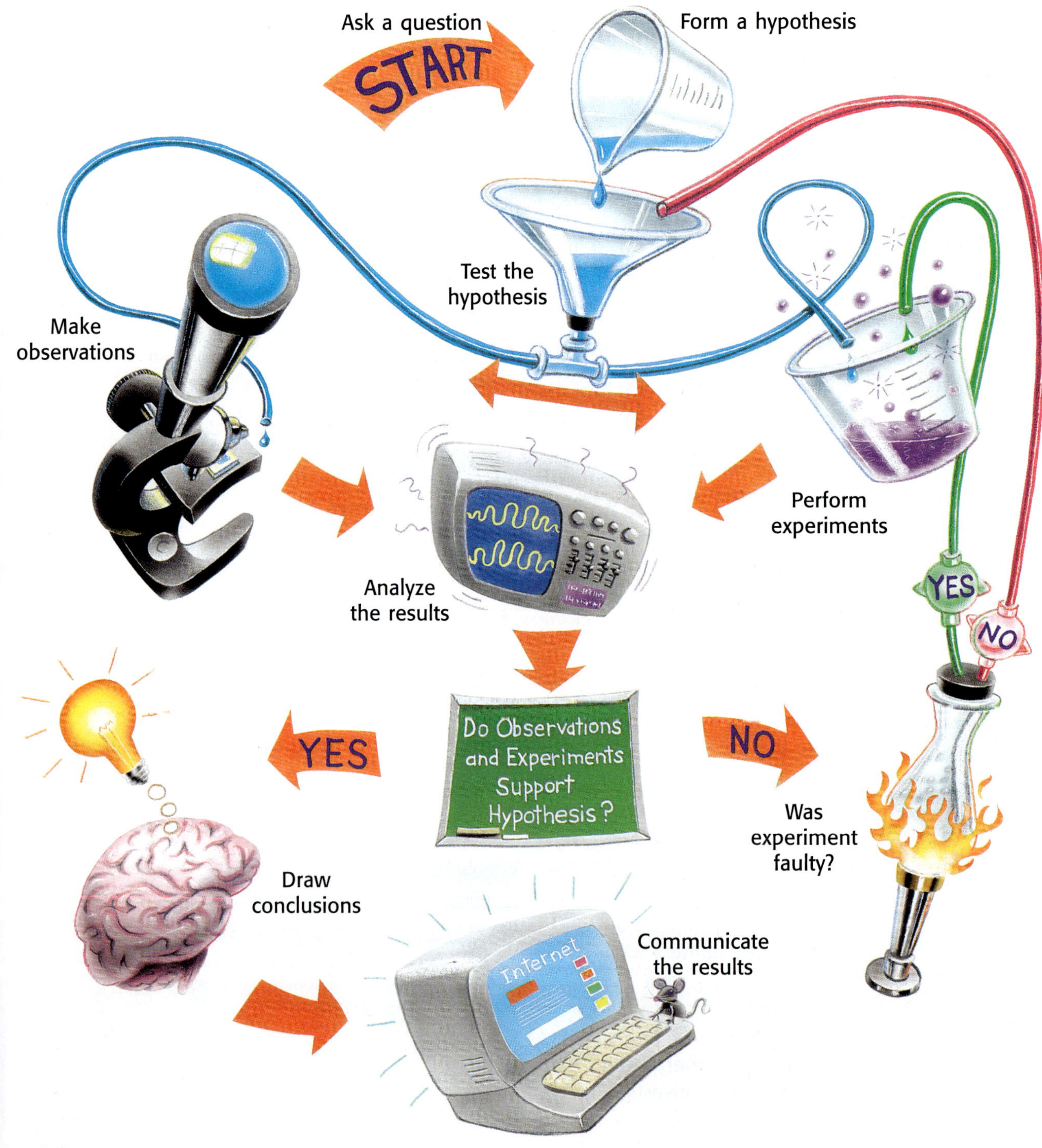

574

Making Charts and Graphs

Circle Graphs

A circle graph, or pie chart, shows how each group of data relates to all of the data. Each part of the circle represents a category of the data. The entire circle represents all of the data. For example, a biologist studying a hardwood forest in Wisconsin found that there were five different types of trees. The data table at right summarizes the biologist's findings.

Wisconsin Hardwood Trees

Type of tree	Number found
Oak	600
Maple	750
Beech	300
Birch	1,200
Hickory	150
Total	3,000

How to Make a Circle Graph

1. In order to make a circle graph of this data, first find the percentage of each type of tree. To do this, divide the number of individual trees by the total number of trees and multiply by 100.

$$\frac{\text{600 Oak}}{\text{3,000 Trees}} \times 100 = 20\%$$

$$\frac{\text{750 Maple}}{\text{3,000 Trees}} \times 100 = 25\%$$

$$\frac{\text{300 Beech}}{\text{3,000 Trees}} \times 100 = 10\%$$

$$\frac{\text{1,200 Birch}}{\text{3,000 Trees}} \times 100 = 40\%$$

$$\frac{\text{150 Hickory}}{\text{3,000 Trees}} \times 100 = 5\%$$

2. Now determine the size of the pie shapes that make up the chart. Do this by multiplying each percentage by 360°. Remember that a circle contains 360°.

$20\% \times 360° = 72°$ $\quad 25\% \times 360° = 90°$

$10\% \times 360° = 36°$ $\quad 40\% \times 360° = 144°$

$5\% \times 360° = 18°$

3. Then check that the sum of the percentages is 100 and the sum of the degrees is 360.

$20\% + 25\% + 10\% + 40\% + 5\% = 100\%$

$72° + 90° + 36° + 144° + 18° = 360°$

4. Use a compass to draw a circle and mark its center.

5. Then use a protractor to draw angles of 72°, 90°, 36°, 144°, and 18° in the circle.

6. Finally, label each part of the graph and choose an appropriate title.

A Community of Wisconsin Hardwood Trees

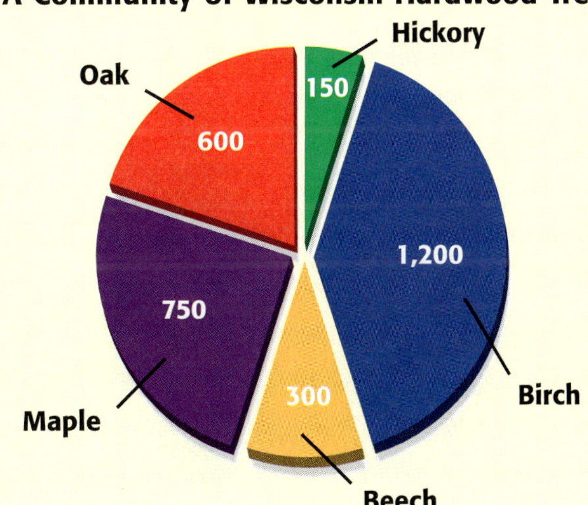

Appendix

Line Graphs

Population of Appleton, 1900–1990	
Year	**Population**
1900	1,800
1920	2,500
1940	3,200
1960	3,900
1980	4,600
2000	5,300

Line graphs are most often used to demonstrate continuous change. For example, Mr. Smith's science class analyzed the population records for their hometown, Appleton, between 1900 and 2000. Examine the data at left.

Because the year and the population change, they are the *variables*. The population is determined by, or dependent on, the year. Therefore, the population is called the **dependent variable,** and the year is called the **independent variable.** Each set of data is called a **data pair.** To prepare a line graph, data pairs must first be organized in a table like the one at left.

How to Make a Line Graph

1. Place the independent variable along the horizontal (x) axis. Place the dependent variable along the vertical (y) axis.
2. Label the x axis "Year" and the y axis "Population." Look at your largest and smallest values for the population. Determine a scale for the y axis that will provide enough space to show these values. You must use the same scale for the entire length of the axis. Find an appropriate scale for the x axis too.
3. Choose reasonable starting points for each axis.
4. Plot the data pairs as accurately as possible.
5. Choose a title that accurately represents the data.

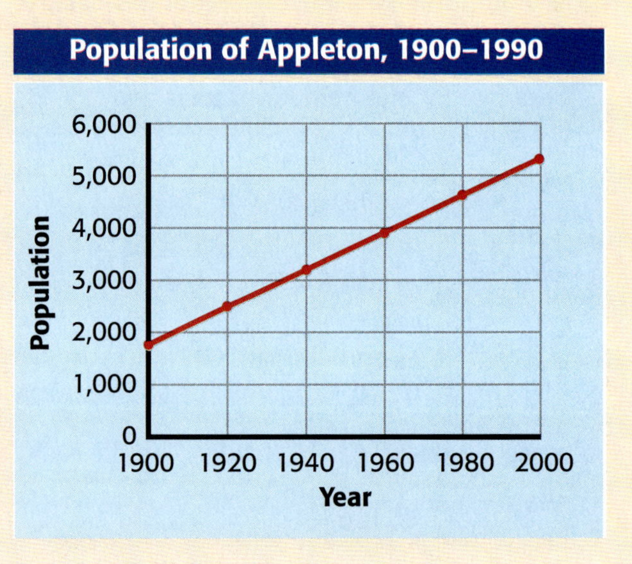

How to Determine Slope

Slope is the ratio of the change in the y axis to the change in the x axis, or "rise over run."

1. Choose two points on the line graph. For example, the population of Appleton in 2000 was 5,300 people. Therefore, you can define point a as (2000, 5,300). In 1900, the population was 1,800 people. Define point b as (1900, 1,800).
2. Find the change in the y axis.
   (y at point a) − (y at point b)
   5,300 people − 1,800 people = 3,500 people
3. Find the change in the x axis.
   (x at point a) − (x at point b)
   2000 − 1900 = 100 years
4. Calculate the slope of the graph by dividing the change in y by the change in x.

$$\text{slope} = \frac{\text{change in } y}{\text{change in } x}$$

$$\text{slope} = \frac{3{,}500 \text{ people}}{100 \text{ years}}$$

$$\text{slope} = 35 \text{ people per year}$$

In this example, the population in Appleton increased by a fixed amount each year. The graph of this data is a straight line. Therefore, the relationship is **linear.** When the graph of a set of data is not a straight line, the relationship is **nonlinear.**

Using Algebra to Determine Slope

The equation in step 4 may also be arranged to be:

$$y = kx$$

where y represents the change in the y axis, k represents the slope, and x represents the change in the x axis.

$$\text{slope} = \frac{\text{change in } y}{\text{change in } x}$$

$$k = \frac{y}{x}$$

$$k \times x = \frac{y \times x}{x}$$

$$kx = y$$

Bar Graphs

Bar graphs are used to demonstrate change that is not continuous. These graphs can be used to indicate trends when the data are taken over a long period of time. A meteorologist gathered the precipitation records at right for Hartford, Connecticut, for April 1–15, 1996, and used a bar graph to represent the data.

Precipitation in Hartford, Connecticut April 1–15, 1996

Date	Precipitation (cm)	Date	Precipitation (cm)
April 1	0.5	April 9	0.25
April 2	1.25	April 10	0.0
April 3	0.0	April 11	1.0
April 4	0.0	April 12	0.0
April 5	0.0	April 13	0.25
April 6	0.0	April 14	0.0
April 7	0.0	April 15	6.50
April 8	1.75		

How to Make a Bar Graph

1. Use an appropriate scale and reasonable starting point for each axis.
2. Label the axes, and plot the data.
3. Choose a title that accurately represents the data.

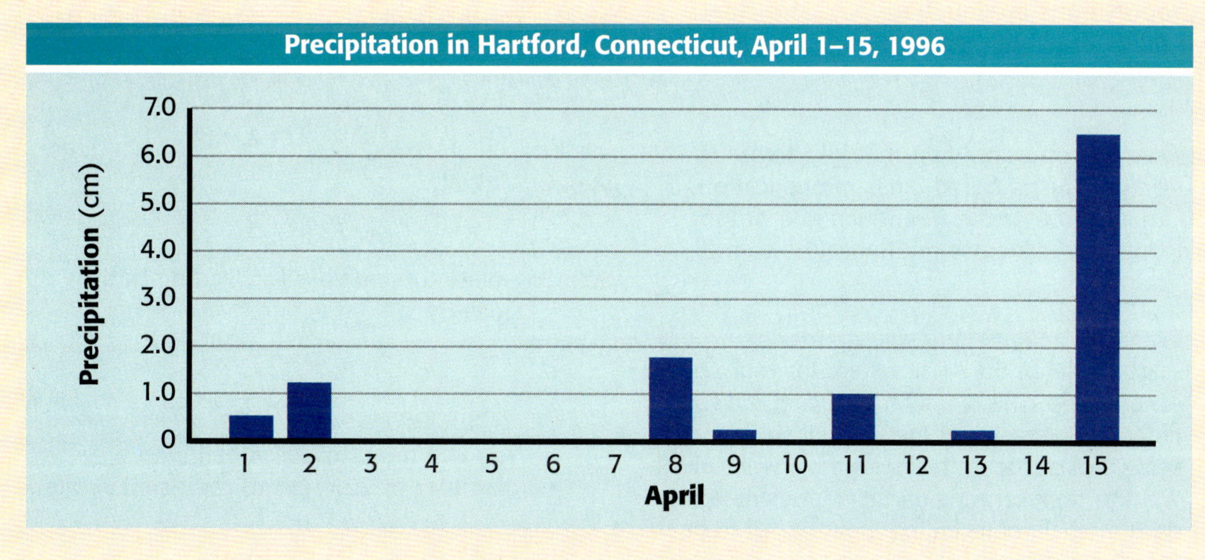

Appendix

Appendix

Math Refresher

Science requires an understanding of many math concepts. The following pages will help you review some important math skills.

Averages

An **average,** or **mean,** simplifies a list of numbers into a single number that *approximates* their value.

Example: Find the average of the following set of numbers: 5, 4, 7, 8.

Step 1: Find the sum.

$$5 + 4 + 7 + 8 = 24$$

Step 2: Divide the sum by the amount of numbers in your set. Because there are four numbers in this example, divide the sum by 4.

$$\frac{24}{4} = 6$$

The average, or mean, is **6.**

Ratios

A **ratio** is a comparison between numbers, and it is usually written as a fraction.

Example: Find the ratio of thermometers to students if you have 36 thermometers and 48 students in your class.

Step 1: Make the ratio.

$$\frac{\text{36 thermometers}}{\text{48 students}}$$

Step 2: Reduce the fraction to its simplest form.

$$\frac{36}{48} = \frac{36 \div 12}{48 \div 12} = \frac{3}{4}$$

The ratio of thermometers to students is **3 to 4,** or $\frac{3}{4}$. The ratio may also be written in the form 3:4.

Proportions

A **proportion** is an equation that states that two ratios are equal.

$$\frac{3}{1} = \frac{12}{4}$$

To solve a proportion, first multiply across the equal sign. This is called cross-multiplication. If you know three of the quantities in a proportion, you can use cross-multiplication to find the fourth.

Example: Imagine that you are making a scale model of the solar system for your science project. The diameter of Jupiter is 11.2 times the diameter of the Earth. If you are using a plastic-foam ball with a diameter of 2 cm to represent the Earth, what diameter does the ball representing Jupiter need to be?

$$\frac{11.2}{1} = \frac{x}{2\text{ cm}}$$

Step 1: Cross-multiply.

$$\frac{11.2}{1} \times \frac{x}{2}$$

$$11.2 \times 2 = x \times 1$$

Step 2: Multiply.

$$22.4 = x \times 1$$

Step 3: Isolate the variable by dividing both sides by 1.

$$x = \frac{22.4}{1}$$

$$x = 22.4\text{ cm}$$

You will need to use a ball with a diameter of **22.4 cm** to represent Jupiter.

Percentages

A **percentage** is a ratio of a given number to 100.

Example: What is 85 percent of 40?

Step 1: Rewrite the percentage by moving the decimal point two places to the left.

.85

Step 2: Multiply the decimal by the number you are calculating the percentage of.

$$0.85 \times 40 = 34$$

85% of 40 is **34**

Decimals

To **add** or **subtract decimals,** line up the digits vertically so that the decimal points line up. Then add or subtract the columns from right to left, carrying or borrowing numbers as necessary.

Example: Add the following numbers: 3.1415 and 2.96.

Step 1: Line up the digits vertically so that the decimal points line up.

$$\begin{array}{r} 3.1415 \\ +\ 2.96 \\ \hline \end{array}$$

Step 2: Add the columns from right to left, carrying when necessary.

$$\begin{array}{r} {\scriptstyle 1\ 1} \\ 3.1415 \\ +\ 2.96 \\ \hline 6.1015 \end{array}$$

The sum is **6.1015**

Fractions

Numbers tell you how many; **fractions** tell you *how much of a whole.*

Example: Your class has 24 plants. Your teacher instructs you to put 5 in a shady spot. What fraction does this represent?

Step 1: Write a fraction with the total number of parts in the whole as the denominator.

$$\frac{?}{24}$$

Step 2: Write the number of parts of the whole being represented as the numerator.

$$\frac{5}{24}$$

$\mathbf{\frac{5}{24}}$ of the plants will be in the shade.

Reducing Fractions

It is usually best to express a fraction in simplest form. This is called *reducing* a fraction.

Example: Reduce the fraction $\frac{30}{45}$ to its simplest form.

Step 1: Find the largest whole number that will divide evenly into both the numerator and denominator. This number is called the greatest common factor (GCF).

factors of the numerator 30: 1, 2, 3, 5, 6, 10, 15, 30

factors of the denominator 45: 1, 3, 5, 9, 15, 45

Step 2: Divide both the numerator and the denominator by the GCF, which in this case is 15.

$$\frac{30}{45} = \frac{30 \div 15}{45 \div 15} = \frac{2}{3}$$

$\frac{30}{45}$ reduced to its simplest form is $\mathbf{\frac{2}{3}}$.

579

Appendix

Adding and Subtracting Fractions

To **add** or **subtract fractions** that have the **same denominator,** simply add or subtract the numerators.

Examples:

$$\frac{3}{5} + \frac{1}{5} = ? \text{ and } \frac{3}{4} - \frac{1}{4} = ?$$

Step 1: Add or subtract the numerators.

$$\frac{3}{5} + \frac{1}{5} = \frac{4}{} \text{ and } \frac{3}{4} - \frac{1}{4} = \frac{2}{}$$

Step 2: Write the sum or difference over the denominator.

$$\frac{3}{5} + \frac{1}{5} = \frac{4}{5} \text{ and } \frac{3}{4} - \frac{1}{4} = \frac{2}{4}$$

Step 3: If necessary, reduce the fraction to its simplest form.

$$\mathbf{\frac{4}{5}} \text{ cannot be reduced, and } \frac{2}{4} = \mathbf{\frac{1}{2}}$$

To **add** or **subtract fractions** that have **different denominators,** first find a common denominator (LCD).

Examples:

$$\frac{1}{2} + \frac{1}{6} = ? \text{ and } \frac{3}{4} - \frac{2}{3} = ?$$

Step 1: Write the equivalent fractions with a common demominator.

$$\frac{3}{6} + \frac{1}{6} = ? \text{ and } \frac{9}{12} - \frac{8}{12} = ?$$

Step 2: Add or subtract.

$$\frac{3}{6} + \frac{1}{6} = \frac{4}{6} \text{ and } \frac{9}{12} - \frac{8}{12} = \frac{1}{12}$$

Step 3: If necessary, reduce the fraction to its simplest form.

$$\frac{4}{6} = \mathbf{\frac{2}{3}}, \text{ and } \mathbf{\frac{1}{12}} \text{ cannot be reduced}$$

Multiplying Fractions

To **multiply fractions,** multiply the numerators and the denominators together, and then reduce the fraction to its simplest form.

Example:

$$\frac{5}{9} \times \frac{7}{10} = ?$$

Step 1: Multiply the numerators and denominators.

$$\frac{5}{9} \times \frac{7}{10} = \frac{5 \times 7}{9 \times 10} = \frac{35}{90}$$

Step 2: Reduce.

$$\frac{35}{90} = \frac{35 \div 5}{90 \div 5} = \mathbf{\frac{7}{18}}$$

Dividing Fractions

To **divide fractions**, first rewrite the divisor (the number you divide *by*) upside down. This is called the reciprocal of the divisor. Then you can multiply and reduce if necessary.

Example:

$$\frac{5}{8} \div \frac{3}{2} = ?$$

Step 1: Rewrite the divisor as its reciprocal.

$$\frac{3}{2} \rightarrow \frac{2}{3}$$

Step 2: Multiply.

$$\frac{5}{8} \times \frac{2}{3} = \frac{5 \times 2}{8 \times 3} = \frac{10}{24}$$

Step 3: Reduce.

$$\frac{10}{24} = \frac{10 \div 2}{24 \div 2} = \mathbf{\frac{5}{12}}$$

Scientific Notation

Scientific notation is a short way of representing very large and very small numbers without writing all of the place-holding zeros.

Example: Write 653,000,000 in scientific notation.

Step 1: Write the number without the place-holding zeros.

653

Step 2: Place the decimal point after the first digit.

6.53

Step 3: Find the exponent by counting the number of places that you moved the decimal point.

6.53000000

The decimal point was moved eight places to the left. Therefore, the exponent of 10 is positive 8. Remember, if the decimal point had moved to the right, the exponent would be negative.

Step 4: Write the number in scientific notation.

$\mathbf{6.53 \times 10^8}$

Area

Area is the number of square units needed to cover the surface of an object.

Formulas:

Area of a square = side × side

Area of a rectangle = length × width

Area of a triangle = $\frac{1}{2}$ base × height

Examples: Find the areas.

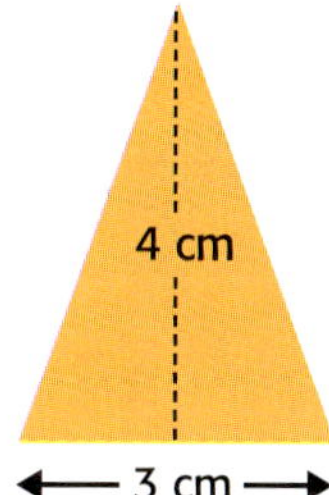

Triangle

Area = $\frac{1}{2}$ × base × height

Area = $\frac{1}{2}$ × 3 cm × 4 cm

Area = **6 cm²**

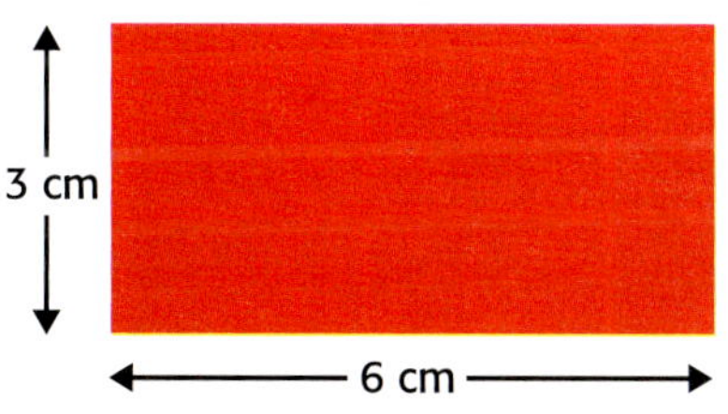

Rectangle

Area = length × width

Area = 6 cm × 3 cm

Area = $\mathbf{18\ cm^2}$

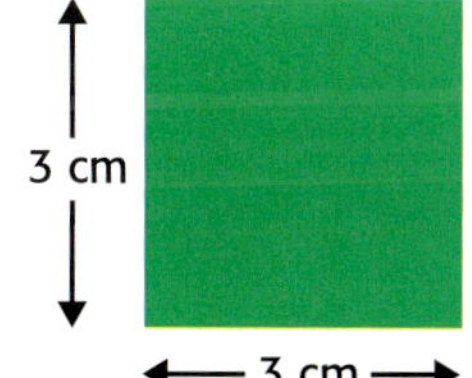

Square

Area = side × side

Area = 3 cm × 3 cm

Area = $\mathbf{9\ cm^2}$

Volume

Volume is the amount of space something occupies.

Formulas:

Volume of a cube = side × side × side

Volume of a prism = area of base × height

Examples: Find the volume of the solids.

Cube

Volume = side × side × side

Volume = 4 cm × 4 cm × 4 cm

Volume = $\mathbf{64\ cm^3}$

4 cm

4 cm

4 cm

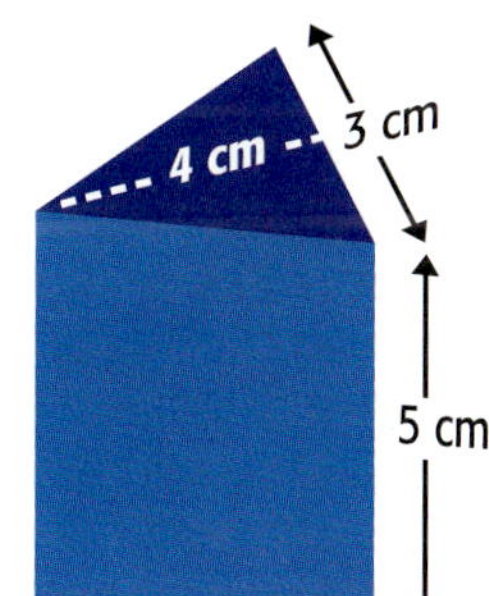

Prism

Volume = area of base × height

Volume = (area of triangle) × height

Volume = $\left(\frac{1}{2} \times 3\text{ cm} \times 4\text{ cm}\right) \times 5\text{ cm}$

Volume = $6\text{ cm}^2 \times 5\text{ cm}$

Volume = $\mathbf{30\ cm^3}$

Periodic Table of the Elements

Each square on the table includes an element's name, chemical symbol, atomic number, and atomic mass.

Atomic number	6
Chemical symbol	C
Element name	Carbon
Atomic mass	12.0

The background color indicates the type of element. Carbon is a nonmetal.

The color of the chemical symbol indicates the physical state at room temperature. Carbon is a solid.

Background

- Metals (blue)
- Metalloids (green)
- Nonmetals (yellow)

Chemical symbol

- Solid (red)
- Liquid (dark blue)
- Gas (green)

	Group 1	Group 2	Group 3	Group 4	Group 5	Group 6	Group 7	Group 8	Group 9
Period 1	1 H Hydrogen 1.0								
Period 2	3 Li Lithium 6.9	4 Be Beryllium 9.0							
Period 3	11 Na Sodium 23.0	12 Mg Magnesium 24.3							
Period 4	19 K Potassium 39.1	20 Ca Calcium 40.1	21 Sc Scandium 45.0	22 Ti Titanium 47.9	23 V Vanadium 50.9	24 Cr Chromium 52.0	25 Mn Manganese 54.9	26 Fe Iron 55.8	27 Co Cobalt 58.9
Period 5	37 Rb Rubidium 85.5	38 Sr Strontium 87.6	39 Y Yttrium 88.9	40 Zr Zirconium 91.2	41 Nb Niobium 92.9	42 Mo Molybdenum 95.9	43 Tc Technetium (97.9)	44 Ru Ruthenium 101.1	45 Rh Rhodium 102.9
Period 6	55 Cs Cesium 132.9	56 Ba Barium 137.3	57 La Lanthanum 138.9	72 Hf Hafnium 178.5	73 Ta Tantalum 180.9	74 W Tungsten 183.8	75 Re Rhenium 186.2	76 Os Osmium 190.2	77 Ir Iridium 192.2
Period 7	87 Fr Francium (223.0)	88 Ra Radium (226.0)	89 Ac Actinium (227.0)	104 Rf Rutherfordium (261.1)	105 Db Dubnium (262.1)	106 Sg Seaborgium (263.1)	107 Bh Bohrium (262.1)	108 Hs Hassium (265)	109 Mt Meitnerium (266)

A row of elements is called a period.

A column of elements is called a group or family.

Lanthanides	58 Ce Cerium 140.1	59 Pr Praseodymium 140.9	60 Nd Neodymium 144.2	61 Pm Promethium (144.9)	62 Sm Samarium 150.4
Actinides	90 Th Thorium 232.0	91 Pa Protactinium 231.0	92 U Uranium 238.0	93 Np Neptunium (237.0)	94 Pu Plutonium 244.1

These elements are placed below the table to allow the table to be narrower.

This zigzag line reminds you where the metals, nonmetals, and metalloids are.

Group 10	Group 11	Group 12	Group 13	Group 14	Group 15	Group 16	Group 17	Group 18
								2 **He** Helium 4.0
			5 **B** Boron 10.8	6 **C** Carbon 12.0	7 **N** Nitrogen 14.0	8 **O** Oxygen 16.0	9 **F** Fluorine 19.0	10 **Ne** Neon 20.2
			13 **Al** Aluminum 27.0	14 **Si** Silicon 28.1	15 **P** Phosphorus 31.0	16 **S** Sulfur 32.1	17 **Cl** Chlorine 35.5	18 **Ar** Argon 39.9
28 **Ni** Nickel 58.7	29 **Cu** Copper 63.5	30 **Zn** Zinc 65.4	31 **Ga** Gallium 69.7	32 **Ge** Germanium 72.6	33 **As** Arsenic 74.9	34 **Se** Selenium 79.0	35 **Br** Bromine 79.9	36 **Kr** Krypton 83.8
46 **Pd** Palladium 106.4	47 **Ag** Silver 107.9	48 **Cd** Cadmium 112.4	49 **In** Indium 114.8	50 **Sn** Tin 118.7	51 **Sb** Antimony 121.8	52 **Te** Tellurium 127.6	53 **I** Iodine 126.9	54 **Xe** Xenon 131.3
78 **Pt** Platinum 195.1	79 **Au** Gold 197.0	80 **Hg** Mercury 200.6	81 **Tl** Thallium 204.4	82 **Pb** Lead 207.2	83 **Bi** Bismuth 209.0	84 **Po** Polonium (209.0)	85 **At** Astatine (210.0)	86 **Rn** Radon (222.0)
110 **Uun** Ununnilium (271)	111 **Uuu** Unununium (272)	112 **Uub** Ununbium (277)						

The names and symbols of elements 110–112 are temporary. They are based on the atomic number of the element. The official name and symbol will be approved by an international committee of scientists.

63 **Eu** Europium 152.0	64 **Gd** Gadolinium 157.3	65 **Tb** Terbium 158.9	66 **Dy** Dysprosium 162.5	67 **Ho** Holmium 164.9	68 **Er** Erbium 167.3	69 **Tm** Thulium 168.9	70 **Yb** Ytterbium 173.0	71 **Lu** Lutetium 175.0
95 **Am** Americium (243.1)	96 **Cm** Curium (247.1)	97 **Bk** Berkelium (247.1)	98 **Cf** Californium (251.1)	99 **Es** Einsteinium (252.1)	100 **Fm** Fermium (257.1)	101 **Md** Mendelevium (258.1)	102 **No** Nobelium (259.1)	103 **Lr** Lawrencium (262.1)

A number in parentheses is the mass number of the most stable isotope of that element.

Physical Science Refresher

Atoms and Elements

Every object in the universe is made up of particles of some kind of matter. **Matter** is anything that takes up space and has mass. All matter is made up of elements. An **element** is a substance that cannot be separated into simpler components by ordinary chemical means. This is because each element consists of only one kind of atom. An **atom** is the smallest unit of an element that has all of the properties of that element.

Atomic Structure

Atoms are made up of small particles called subatomic particles. The three major types of subatomic particles are **electrons, protons,** and **neutrons.** Electrons have a negative electrical charge, protons have a positive charge, and neutrons have no electrical charge. The protons and neutrons are packed close to one another to form the **nucleus.** The protons give the nucleus a positive charge. The electrons of an atom move in a region around the nucleus known as an **electron cloud.** The negatively charged electrons are attracted to the positively charged nucleus. An atom may have several energy levels in which electrons are located.

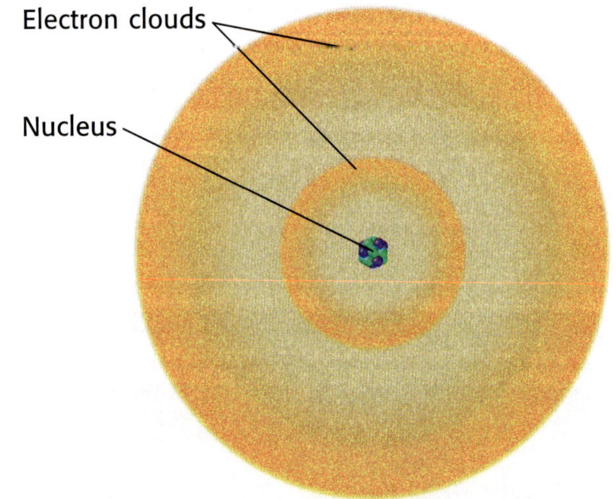

Atomic Number

To help in the identification of elements, scientists have assigned an **atomic number** to each kind of atom. The atomic number is equal to the number of protons in the atom. Atoms with the same number of protons are all the same kind of element. In an uncharged, or electrically neutral, atom there are an equal number of protons and electrons. Therefore, the atomic number also equals the number of electrons in an uncharged atom. The number of neutrons, however, can vary for a given element. Atoms of the same element that have different numbers of neutrons are called **isotopes.**

Periodic Table of the Elements

In the periodic table, the elements are arranged from left to right in order of increasing atomic number. Each element in the table is in a separate box. Each element has one more electron and one more proton than the element to its left. Each horizontal row of the table is called a **period.** Changes in chemical properties across a period correspond to changes in the elements' electron arrangements. Each vertical column of the table, known as a **group,** lists elements with similar properties. The elements in a group have similar chemical properties because they have the same number of electrons in their outer energy level. For example, the elements helium, neon, argon, krypton, xenon, and radon all have similar properties and are known as the noble gases.

Molecules and Compounds

When the atoms of two or more elements are joined chemically, the resulting substance is called a **compound.** A compound is a new substance with properties different from those of the elements that compose it. For example, water (H_2O) is a compound formed when atoms of hydrogen (H) and oxygen (O) combine. The smallest complete unit of a compound that has all of the properties of that compound is called a **molecule.** A chemical formula indicates the elements in a compound. It also indicates the relative number of atoms of each element present. The chemical formula for water is H_2O, which indicates that each water molecule consists of two atoms of hydrogen and one atom of oxygen. The subscript number is used after the symbol for an element to indicate how many atoms of that element are in a single molecule of the compound.

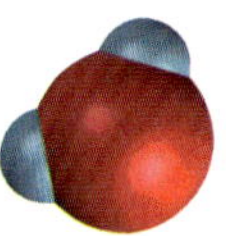

Acids, Bases, and pH

An ion is an atom or group of atoms that has an electrical charge because it has lost or gained one or more electrons. When an acid, such as hydrochloric acid (HCl), is mixed with water, it separates into ions. An **acid** is a compound that produces hydrogen ions (H^+) in water. The hydrogen ions then combine with a water molecule to form a hydronium ion (H_3O^+). A solution that contains hydronium ions is an acidic solution. A **base,** on the other hand, is a substance that produces hydroxide ions (OH^-) in water.

To determine whether a solution is acidic or basic, scientists use pH. The **pH** is a measure of the hydronium ion concentration in a solution. The pH scale ranges from 0 to 14. The middle point, pH = 7, is neutral, neither acidic nor basic. Acids have a pH less than 7; bases have a pH greater than 7. The lower the number is, the more acidic the solution. The higher the number is, the more basic the solution.

Chemical Equations

A chemical reaction occurs when a chemical change takes place. (In a chemical change, new substances with new properties are formed.) A chemical equation is a useful way of describing a chemical reaction by means of chemical formulas. The equation indicates what substances react and what the products are. For example, when carbon and oxygen combine, they can form carbon dioxide. The equation for the reaction is as follows: $C + O_2 \rightarrow CO_2$.

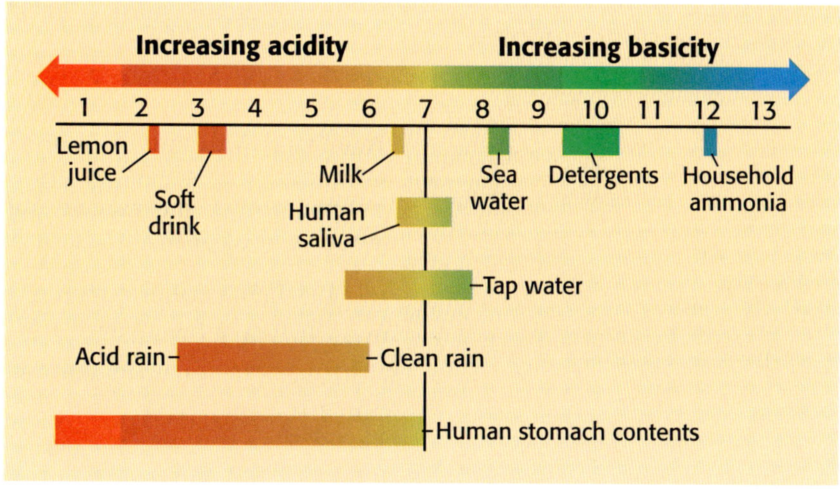

Physical Laws and Equations

Law of Conservation of Energy

The law of conservation of energy states that energy can be neither created nor destroyed.

The total amount of energy in a closed system is always the same. Energy can be changed from one form to another, but all the different forms of energy in a system always add up to the same total amount of energy, no matter how many energy conversions occur.

Law of Universal Gravitation

The law of universal gravitation states that all objects in the universe attract each other by a force called gravity. The size of the force depends on the masses of the objects and the distance between them.

The first part of the law explains why a bowling ball is much harder to lift than a table-tennis ball. Because the bowling ball has a much larger mass than the table-tennis ball, the amount of gravity between the Earth and the bowling ball is greater than the amount of gravity between the Earth and the table-tennis ball.

The second part of the law explains why a satellite can remain in orbit around the Earth. The satellite is carefully placed at a distance great enough to prevent the Earth's gravity from immediately pulling it down but small enough to prevent it from completely escaping the Earth's gravity and wandering off into space.

Newton's Laws of Motion

Newton's first law of motion states that an object at rest remains at rest and an object in motion remains in motion at constant speed and in a straight line unless acted on by an unbalanced force.

The first part of the law explains why a football will remain on a tee until it is kicked off or until a gust of wind blows it off.

The second part of the law explains why a bike's rider will continue moving forward after the bike tire runs into a crack in the sidewalk and the bike comes to an abrupt stop until gravity and the sidewalk stop the rider.

Newton's second law of motion states that the acceleration of an object depends on the mass of the object and the amount of force applied.

The first part of the law explains why the acceleration of a 4 kg bowling ball will be greater than the acceleration of a 6 kg bowling ball if the same force is applied to both.

The second part of the law explains why the acceleration of a bowling ball will be larger if a larger force is applied to it.

The relationship of acceleration (a) to mass (m) and force (F) can be expressed mathematically by the following equation:

$$\text{acceleration} = \frac{\text{force}}{\text{mass}} \quad \text{or} \quad a = \frac{F}{m}$$

This equation is often rearranged to the form:

$$\text{force} = \text{mass} \times \text{acceleration}$$

or

$$F = m \times a$$

Newton's third law of motion states that whenever one object exerts a force on a second object, the second object exerts an equal and opposite force on the first.

This law explains that a runner is able to move forward because of the equal and opposite force the ground exerts on the runner's foot after each step.

Useful Equations

Average speed

$$\text{Average speed} = \frac{\text{total distance}}{\text{total time}}$$

Example: A bicycle messenger traveled a distance of 136 km in 8 hours. What was the messenger's average speed?

$$\frac{136 \text{ km}}{8 \text{ h}} = 17 \text{ km/h}$$

The messenger's average speed was **17 km/h.**

Average acceleration

$$\text{Average acceleration} = \frac{\text{final velocity} - \text{starting velocity}}{\text{time it takes to change velocity}}$$

Example: Calculate the average acceleration of an Olympic 100 m dash sprinter who reaches a velocity of 15 m/s south at the finish line. The race was in a straight line and lasted 10 s.

$$\frac{15 \text{ m/s} - 0 \text{ m/s}}{10 \text{ s}} = 1.5 \text{ m/s/s}$$

The sprinter's average acceleration is **1.5 m/s/s south.**

Net force

Forces in the Same Direction

When forces are in the same direction, add the forces together to determine the net force.

Example: Calculate the net force on a stalled car that is being pushed by two people. One person is pushing with a force of 13 N northwest and the other person is pushing with a force of 8 N in the same direction.

$$13 \text{ N} + 8 \text{ N} = 21 \text{ N}$$

The net force is **21 N northwest.**

Forces in Opposite Directions

When forces are in opposite directions, subtract the smaller force from the larger force to determine the net force.

Net force (cont'd)

Example: Calculate the net force on a rope that is being pulled on each end. One person is pulling on one end of the rope with a force of 12 N south. Another person is pulling on the opposite end of the rope with a force of 7 N north.

$$12 \text{ N} - 7 \text{ N} = 5 \text{ N}$$

The net force is **5 N south.**

Density

$$\text{Density} = \frac{\text{Mass}}{\text{Volume}}$$

Example: Calculate the density of a sponge with a mass of 10 g and a volume of 40 mL.

$$\frac{10 \text{ g}}{40 \text{ mL}} = 0.25 \text{ g/mL}$$

The density of the sponge is **0.25 g/mL.**

Pressure

Pressure is the force exerted over a given area. The SI unit for pressure is the pascal, which is abbreviated Pa.

$$\text{Pressure} = \frac{\text{Force}}{\text{Area}}$$

Exampe: Calculate the pressure of the air in a soccer ball if the air exerts a force of 10 N over an area of 0.5 m^2.

$$\text{Pressure} = \frac{10 \text{ N}}{0.5 \text{ m}^2} = 20 \text{ N/m}^2 = 20 \text{ Pa}$$

The pressure of the air inside of the soccer ball is **20 Pa.**

Concentration

$$\text{Concentration} = \frac{\text{Mass of solute}}{\text{Volume of solvent}}$$

Example: Calculate the concentration of solution in which 10 g of sugar is dissolved in 125 mL of water.

$$\frac{10 \text{ g of sugar}}{125 \text{ mL of water}} = 0.08 \text{ g/mL}$$

The concentration of this solution is **0.08 g/mL.**

Properties of Common Minerals

	Mineral	Color	Luster	Streak	Hardness
Silicate Minerals	**Beryl**	deep green, pink, white, bluish green, or light yellow	vitreous	none	7.5–8
	Chlorite	green	vitreous to pearly	pale green	2–2.5
	Garnet	green or red	vitreous	none	6.5–7.5
	Hornblende (Amphibole)	dark green, brown, or black	vitreous or silky	none	5–6
	Muscovite	colorless, gray, or brown	vitreous or pearly	white	2–2.5
	Olivine	olive green	vitreous	none	6.5–7
	Orthoclase	colorless, white, pink, or other colors	vitreous to pearly	white or none	6
	Plagioclase	blue gray to white	vitreous	white	6
	Quartz	colorless or white; any color when not pure	vitreous or waxy	white or none	7
Nonsilicate Minerals	**Native Elements**				
	Copper	copper-red	metallic	copper-red	2.5–3
	Diamond	pale yellow or colorless	vitreous	none	10
	Graphite	black to gray	submetallic	black	1–2
	Carbonates				
	Aragonite	colorless, white, or pale yellow	vitreous	white	3.5–4
	Calcite	colorless or white to tan	vitreous	white	3
	Halides				
	Fluorite	light green, yellow, purple, bluish green, or other colors	vitreous	none	4
	Halite	colorless or gray	vitreous	white	2.5–3
	Oxides				
	Hematite	reddish brown to black	metallic to earthy	red to red-brown	5.6–6.5
	Magnetite	iron black	metallic	black	5–6
	Sulfates				
	Anhydrite	colorless, bluish, or violet	vitreous to pearly	white	3–3.5
	Gypsum	white, pink, gray, or colorless	vitreous, pearly, or silky	white	1–2.5
	Sulfides				
	Galena	lead gray	metallic	lead gray to black	2.5
	Pyrite	brassy yellow	metallic	greenish, brownish, or black	6–6.5

Appendix

Density (g/cm^3)	Cleavage, Fracture, Special Properties	Common Uses
2.6–2.8	1 cleavage direction; irregular fracture; some varieties fluoresce in ultraviolet light	gemstones, ore of the metal beryllium
2.6–3.3	1 cleavage direction; irregular fracture	
4.2	no cleavage; conchoidal to splintery fracture	gemstones, abrasives
3.2	2 cleavage directions; hackly to splintery fracture	
2.7–3	1 cleavage direction; irregular fracture	electrical insulation, wallpaper, fireproofing material, lubricant
3.2–3.3	no cleavage; conchoidal fracture	gemstones, casting
2.6	2 cleavage directions; irregular fracture	porcelain
2.6–2.7	2 cleavage directions; irregular fracture	ceramics
2.6	no cleavage; conchoidal fracture	gemstones, concrete, glass, porcelain, sandpaper, lenses
8.9	no cleavage; hackly fracture	wiring, brass, bronze, coins
3.5	4 cleavage directions; irregular to conchoidal fracture	gemstones, drilling
2.3	1 cleavage direction; irregular fracture	pencils, paints, lubricants, batteries
2.95	2 cleavage directions; irregular fracture; reacts with hydrochloric acid	minor source of barium
2.7	3 cleavage directions; irregular fracture; reacts with weak acid, double refraction	cements, soil conditioner, whitewash, construction materials
3.2	4 cleavage directions; irregular fracture; some varieties fluoresce or double refract	hydrochloric acid, steel, glass, fiberglass, pottery, enamel
2.2	3 cleavage directions; splintery to conchoidal fracture; salty taste	tanning hides, fertilizer, salting icy roads, food preservation
5.25	no cleavage; splintery fracture; magnetic when heated	iron ore for steel, gemstones, pigments
5.2	2 cleavage directions; splintery fracture; magnetic	iron ore
2.89–2.98	3 cleavage directions; conchoidal to splintery fracture	soil conditioner, sulfuric acid
2.2–2.4	3 cleavage directions; conchoidal to splintery fracture	plaster of Paris, wallboard, soil conditioner
7.4–7.6	3 cleavage directions; irregular fracture	batteries, paints
5	no cleavage; conchoidal to splintery fracture	dyes, inks, gemstones

Glossary

A

abiotic nonliving factors in the environment (306)

abrasion the grinding and wearing down of rock surfaces by other rock or sand particles (284)

absolute zero the lowest possible temperature (0 K, –273°C) (217)

abyssal (uh BIS uhl) **plain** the broad, flat portion of the deep-ocean basin (340)

acid precipitation precipitation that contains acids due to air pollution (116, 413)

active solar heating a solar-heating system consisting of solar collectors and a network of pipes that distributes energy from the sun throughout a building (233)

aerial photograph a photograph taken from the air (43)

air mass a large body of air that has the same temperature and moisture throughout (432)

air pressure the measure of the force with which air molecules are pushing on a surface (395)

alluvial (uh LOO vee uhl) **fan** fan-shaped deposits of sediment that form on dry land (257)

alluvium (uh LOO vee uhm) rock and soil deposited by streams (255)

altitude the height of an object above the Earth's surface (395)

anemometer (AN uh MAHM uht uhr) an instrument used to measure wind speed (443)

anticline a bowl-shaped fold in sedimentary rock layers (152)

aquifer (AHK wuh fuhr) a rock layer that stores and allows the flow of ground water (258)

arête (uh RAYT) a jagged ridge that forms between two or more cirques cutting into the same mountain (291)

artesian (ahr TEE zhuhn) **spring** a spring that forms when cracks occur naturally in the cap rock and the pressurized water in the aquifer flows through the cracks to the surface (260)

asthenosphere (as THEN uh SFIR) the partially molten layer of the upper mantle on which the tectonic plates of the lithosphere move (138)

astronomy the study of all physical objects beyond Earth (9)

atmosphere a mixture of gases that surrounds a planet, such as Earth (394)

atom the smallest particle into which an element can be divided and still retain all of the properties of that element (61)

azimuthal (AZ uh MOOTH uhl) **projection** a map projection that is made by transferring the contents of the globe onto a plane (42)

B

barometer an instrument used to measure air pressure (443)

beach an area of the shoreline made up of material deposited by waves (278)

benthic environment the ocean floor and all the organisms that live on or in it; also known as the bottom environment (345)

benthos organisms that live on or in the ocean floor (344)

bimetallic (BIE muh TAL ik) **strip** a strip made by stacking two different metals in a long thin strip; because the different metals expand at different rates when they get hot, a bimetallic strip can coil and uncoil with changes in temperature; bimetallic strips are used in devices such as thermostats (218)

biomass organic matter, such as plants, wood, and waste, that contains stored energy (124)

biome a large region characterized by a specific type of climate and certain types of plant and animal communities (460)

biosphere the part of the Earth where life exists (309)

biotic living factors in the environment (306)

breaker zone the near-shore area where waves first begin to tumble downward, or break (376)

C

caldera a circular depression that forms when a magma chamber empties and causes the ground above to sink (199)

calorie the amount of energy needed to change the temperature of 0.001 kg of water by 1°C; 1 calorie is equivalent to 4.184 J (226)

calorimeter (KAL uh RIM uht uhr) a device used to determine the specific heat capacity of a substance (226)

cardinal directions north, south, east, and west (35)

carnivore a consumer that eats animals (311)

carrying capacity the largest population that a given environment can support over a long period of time (317)

change of state the conversion of a substance from one physical form to another (229)

channel the path a stream follows (251)

chemical change a change that occurs when one or more substances are changed into entirely new substances with different properties; cannot be reversed using physical means (230)

cinder cone volcano a small, steeply sloped volcano that forms from moderately explosive eruptions of pyroclastic material (198)

cirque (suhrk) a bowl-like depression where glacial ice cuts back into mountain walls (291)

cirrus (SIR uhs) **clouds** thin, feathery white clouds found at high altitudes (429)

cleavage (KLEEV IJ) the tendency of a mineral to break along flat, parallel surfaces (65)

climate the average weather conditions in a certain area over a long period of time (454)

cloud a collection of millions of tiny water droplets or ice crystals (428)

coal a solid fossil fuel formed underground from buried, decomposed plant material (112)

coevolution (KOH EV uh LOO shuhn) long-term changes that take place in two species because of their close interactions with one another (320)

combustion the burning of fuel; specifically, the process in which fuel combines with oxygen in a chemical change that produces thermal energy (234)

commensalism (kuh MEN suhl IZ uhm) a symbiotic relationship in which one organism benefits and the other is unaffected (319)

community all of the populations of different species that live and interact in an area (308)

competition two or more species or individuals trying to use the same limited resource (317)

composite volcano a volcano made of alternating layers of lava and pyroclastic material; also called *stratovolcano* (198)

composition the makeup of a rock; describes either the minerals or elements present in it (85)

compound a pure substance composed of two or more elements that are chemically combined; forms when atoms of two or more different elements become chemically bonded (61)

compression stress that occurs when opposing forces apply pressure to a given material (151)

condensation the change of state from a gas to a liquid (337, 427)

conduction the transfer of thermal energy from one substance to another through direct contact; conduction can also occur within a substance (221, 401)

conductor a substance that conducts thermal energy well (222)

conic projection a map projection that is made by transferring the contents of the globe onto a cone (42)

consumer an organism that eats producers or other organisms for energy (311)

continental drift the theory that continents can drift apart from one another and that they have done so in the past (143)

continental margin the portion of the Earth's surface beneath the ocean that is made of continental crust (340)

continental rise the base of the continental slope (340)

continental shelf the flattest part of the continental margin (340)

continental slope the steepest part of the continental margin (340)

contour interval the difference in elevation between one contour line and the next (47)

contour lines lines that connect points of equal elevation (46)

convection the transfer of thermal energy by the movement of a liquid or a gas (222, 401)

591

convection current the circular motion of liquids or gases due to density differences that result from temperature differences (222)

convergent boundary the boundary between two colliding tectonic plates (148)

core the central, spherical part of the Earth below the mantle (137)

Coriolis (KOHR ee OH lis) **effect** the turning of moving objects, such as ocean currents or winds, by the Earth's rotation (368, 405)

crater a funnel-shaped pit around the central vent of a volcano (199)

creep the extremely slow movement of material downslope (297)

crest the highest point of a wave (374)

crevasse a large crack that forms where a glacier picks up speed or flows over a high point (289)

crust the thin, outermost layer of the Earth, or the uppermost part of the lithosphere (136)

crystal the solid, geometric form of a mineral produced by a repeating pattern of atoms (61)

cumulus (KYOO myoo luhs) **clouds** puffy, white clouds that tend to have flat bottoms (428)

D

deciduous (dee SIJ oo uhs) describes trees that have leaves that change color in autumn and fall off in winter (464)

decomposer an organism that gets energy by breaking down the remains of dead organisms and consuming or absorbing the nutrients (311)

deep current a streamlike movement of ocean water far below the surface (370)

deep-ocean basin the portion of the Earth's surface beneath the ocean that is made of oceanic crust (340)

deflation the lifting and removal of fine sediment by wind (283)

deformation the change in the shape of rock in response to stress (167)

delta a fan-shaped deposit of sediment at the mouth of a stream where the stream empties into a large body of water (256)

density the amount of matter in a given space; mass per unit volume (66)

deposition the process by which material is dropped or settles (255)

desalination the process of evaporating sea water so that the water and the salt separate (351)

dew point the temperature at which air must cool to be completely saturated (427)

discharge the volume of water transported by a stream in a given amount of time (251)

divergent boundary the boundary between two tectonic plates that are moving away from each other (149)

divide an area of higher ground that separates drainage basins (250)

drainage basin an area drained by a river system, including the main river and all of its tributaries (250)

dune a mound of wind-deposited sand (284)

E

ecology the study of the interactions between organisms and their environment (306)

ecosystem a community of organisms and their nonliving environment (10, 308)

elastic rebound the sudden return of elastically deformed rock to its undeformed shape (167)

element a pure substance that cannot be separated or broken down into simpler substances by ordinary physical or chemical means (60)

elevation the height of surface landforms above sea level; the height of an object above sea level (46, 458)

El Niño a periodic change in the location of warm and cool surface waters in the Pacific Ocean (373)

energy pyramid a diagram shaped like a triangle showing the loss of energy at each level of the food chain (313)

energy resource a natural resource that can be converted by humans into other forms of energy in order to do useful work (111)

epicenter the point on the Earth's surface directly above an earthquake's starting point (172)

equator an imaginary circle halfway between the poles that divides the Earth into the Northern and Southern Hemispheres (37)

592

erosion the removal and transport of material by wind, water, or ice (248)

evaporation the change from a liquid to a vapor (337)

evergreens trees that keep their leaves year-round (464)

external combustion engine a heat engine that burns fuel outside the engine, such as a steam engine (234)

extrusive (eks TROO siv) the type of igneous rock that forms when lava or pyroclastic material cools and solidifies on the Earth's surface (90)

F

fault a break in the Earth's crust along which blocks of the crust slide relative to one another; due to tectonic forces (153, 166)

fault block a block of the Earth's crust that moves relative to another block along a fault (153)

fault-block mountain a mountain that forms when faulting causes large blocks of the Earth's crust to drop down relative to other blocks (156)

felsic describes relatively light-colored, light-weight igneous rocks that are rich in silicon, aluminum, sodium, and potassium (88)

flood plain an area along a river formed from sediments deposited by floods (257)

focus the point inside the Earth where an earth-quake begins (172)

fold a type of plastic deformation in rock layers that gives the layers a wavelike appearance (152)

folded mountain a mountain that forms when rock formations bend and fold due to stresses in the Earth's crust (155)

folding the bending of rock layers due to pressure caused by movements in the Earth's crust (152)

foliated the texture of metamorphic rock in which the mineral grains are aligned like the pages of a book (98)

food chain a diagram that represents how the energy in food molecules flows from one organ-ism to the next (312)

food web a complex diagram representing the many energy pathways in a real ecosystem (312)

footwall the fault block that is below a fault (153)

fossil fuel a nonrenewable energy resource that forms in the Earth's crust over millions of years from the buried remains of once-living organisms (111)

fracture the tendency of a mineral to break along curved or irregular surfaces (65)

front the boundary that forms between two different air masses (434)

G

gap hypothesis states that sections of active faults that have had relatively few earthquakes are likely to be the sites of strong earthquakes in the future (176)

gasohol a mixture of gasoline and alcohol that is burned as a fuel (124)

gems precious stones of natural origin; rare min-eral crystals prized for their beauty and geometric form (71)

geology the study of the solid Earth (6)

geothermal energy energy resulting from the heating of the Earth's crust (125)

glacial drift all material carried and deposited by glaciers (292)

glacier an enormous mass of moving ice (287)

global warming a rise in average global tempera-tures (18, 402, 472)

gradient a measure of the change in elevation over a certain distance (251)

greenhouse effect the natural heating process of a planet, such as the Earth, by which gases in the atmosphere trap thermal energy (223, 402, 472)

ground water water that is stored in under-ground caverns or in porous rock below the Earth's surface (258)

H

habitat the environment where an organism lives (314)

hanging valley a small glacial valley that joins the deeper main valley (291)

hanging wall the fault block that is above a fault (153)

hardness the resistance of a mineral to being scratched (66)

heat the transfer of energy between objects that are at different temperatures; energy is always transferred from higher-temperature objects to lower-temperature objects until thermal equilibrium is reached (219)

heat engine a machine that uses heat to do work (234)

herbivore a consumer that eats plants (311)

horn a sharp pyramid-shaped peak that forms when three or more cirques erode a mountain (291)

host an organism on which a parasite lives (320)

hot spot a place within a tectonic plate that sits directly above a rising column of magma called a mantle plume (203)

humidity the amount of water vapor or moisture in the air (425)

hurricane a large rotating tropical weather system with wind speeds equal to or greater than 119 km/h (439)

hydroelectric energy electricity produced by falling water (123)

hypothesis a possible explanation or answer to a question (14)

I

ice age a period during which ice collects at the poles and moves outward repeatedly from the poles toward the equator (469)

iceberg a large piece of ice that breaks off an ice shelf and drifts into the ocean (288)

igneous rock rock that forms when magma, lava, or pyroclastic material cools and solidifies (84)

index contour a darker contour line that is usually every fifth line and is labeled by elevation (47)

inner core the solid, dense, spherical center of the Earth (139)

insulation a substance that reduces the transfer of thermal energy (232)

insulator a substance that does not conduct thermal energy well (222)

internal combustion engine a heat engine that burns fuel inside the engine, for example, an automobile engine (235)

intrusive (in TROO siv) the type of igneous rock that forms when magma cools and solidifies beneath Earth's surface (89)

isobars lines that connect points of equal air pressure (445)

J

jet streams narrow belts of high-speed winds that blow in the upper troposphere and the lower stratosphere over both the Northern and Southern Hemispheres (408)

K

karst topography areas where the effects of ground water are noticeable at the surface (262)

kilocalorie the unit of energy equal to 1,000 calories; the kilocalorie can also be referred to as the Calorie, which is the unit of energy listed on food labels (226)

L

landslide a sudden and rapid movement of a large amount of material downslope (295)

latitude the distance north or south from the equator; measured in degrees (37, 455)

lava magma that erupts onto the Earth's surface (84, 194)

lightning the large electrical discharge that occurs between two oppositely charged surfaces (437)

limiting factor a needed resource that is in limited supply (316)

lithosphere the outermost, rigid layer of the Earth that consists of the crust and the rigid, uppermost part of the mantle (138)

load the rock and soil carried in a stream (252)

loess (LOH ESS) thick deposits of windblown, fine-grained sediments (286)

longitude the distance east or west from the prime meridian; measured in degrees (38)

longshore current the movement of water parallel to and near the shoreline (279)

luster the way the surface of a mineral reflects light (64)

M

mafic (MAYF ik) describes relatively dark-colored, heavy igneous rocks that are rich in iron, magnesium, and calcium (88)

magma the hot liquid that forms when rock partially or completely melts; may include mineral crystals (83, 194)

magnetic declination the angle of correction for the difference between geographic north and magnetic north (36)

magnetic reversal the process by which the Earth's north and south magnetic poles periodically change places (146)

mantle the layer of the Earth between the crust and the core (137)

map a model or representation of the Earth's surface (34)

mass the amount of matter that something is made of; its value does not change with the object's location (24)

mass movement the movement of any material downslope (294)

Mercator projection a map projection that results when the contents of the globe are transferred onto a cylinder (41)

mesosphere literally, the "middle sphere"—the rigid, lower part of the mantle between the asthenosphere and the outer core (139); *also* the coldest layer of the atmosphere (398)

metamorphic rock rock that forms when the texture or composition of preexisting rock changes due to heat or pressure (84)

meteorology the study of the entire atmosphere (8)

meter the basic unit of length in the SI system (23)

microclimate a small region with unique climatic characteristics (468)

mid-ocean ridge a long mountain chain that forms on the ocean floor where tectonic plates pull apart; usually extends along the center of ocean basins (145, 341)

mineral a naturally formed, inorganic solid with a crystalline structure (60)

model a representation of an object or system (19)

Moho a place within the Earth where the speed of seismic waves increases sharply; marks the boundary between the Earth's crust and mantle (181)

monocline a fold in sedimentary rock layers in which the layers are horizontal on both sides of the fold (152)

mudflow the rapid movement of a large mass of mud/rock and soil mixed with a large amount of water that flows downhill (296)

mutualism (MYOO choo uhl IZ uhm) a symbiotic relationship in which both organisms benefit (319)

N

natural gas a gaseous fossil fuel (112)

natural resource any natural substance, organism, or energy form that living things use (108)

neap tides tides with minimum daily tidal ranges that occur during the first and third quarters of the moon (382)

nekton (NEK TAHN) free-swimming organisms of the ocean (344)

niche an organism's way of life and its relationships with its abiotic and biotic environment (314)

nonfoliated the texture of metamorphic rock in which mineral grains show no alignment (99)

nonpoint-source pollution pollution that comes from many sources and that cannot be traced to specific sites (263, 354)

nonrenewable resource a natural resource that cannot be replaced or that can be replaced only over thousands or millions of years (109)

nonsilicate mineral a mineral that does not contain compounds of silicon and oxygen (63)

normal fault a fault in which the hanging wall moves down relative to the footwall (153)

nuclear energy the form of energy associated with changes in the nucleus of an atom; an alternative energy resource (118)

O

observation any use of the senses to gather information (14)

oceanography the study of the ocean (7)

ocean trench a seemingly bottomless crevice in the deep-ocean basin that forms where one oceanic plate is forced underneath a continental plate or another oceanic plate (341)

omnivore a consumer that eats a variety of organisms (311)

ore a mineral deposit large enough and pure enough to be mined for a profit (70)

outer core the liquid layer of the Earth's core between the mesosphere and the inner core (139)

ozone a gas molecule that is made up of three oxygen atoms and that absorbs ultraviolet radiation from the sun (397)

P

parasite an organism that feeds on another living creature, usually without killing it (320)

parasitism (PAR uh SIET IZ uhm) a symbiotic association in which one organism benefits while the other is harmed (320)

passive solar heating a solar-heating system that relies on thick walls and large windows to use energy from the sun as a means of heating (233)

pelagic (pi LAJ ik) **environment** the entire volume of water in the ocean and the marine organisms that live above the ocean floor; also known as the water environment (347)

permeability (PUHR mee uh BIL uh tee) a rock's ability to let water pass through it (258)

petroleum an oily mixture of flammable organic compounds from which liquid fossil fuels and other products are separated; crude oil (111)

physical change a change that affects one or more physical properties of a substance; most physical changes are easy to undo (229)

plankton very small organisms floating at or near the ocean's surface that form the base of the oceans' food web (344)

plate tectonics the theory that the Earth's lithosphere is divided into tectonic plates that move around on top of the asthenosphere (147)

point-source pollution pollution that comes from one particular source area (263)

polar easterlies wind belts that extend from the poles to 60° latitude in both hemispheres (407)

polar zone the northernmost and southernmost climate zone (466)

population a group of individuals of the same species that live together in the same area at the same time (308)

porosity (poh RAHS uh tee) the amount of open space between individual rock particles (258)

precipitation water in liquid or solid form that moves from the atmosphere to the land and ocean (337, 430)

predator an organism that eats other organisms (318)

prevailing winds winds that blow mainly from one direction (457)

prey an organism that is eaten by another organism (318)

primary pollutants pollutants that are put directly into the air by human or natural activity (411)

prime meridian the line of longitude that passes through Greenwich, England; represents 0° longitude (38)

producer an organism that uses sunlight directly to make sugar (310)

psychrometer an instrument used to measure relative humidity (426)

P waves the fastest type of seismic wave; can travel through solids, liquids, and gases; also known as pressure waves and primary waves (170)

pyroclastic material magma and fragments of rock that are ejected into the atmosphere during a violent volcanic eruption (194)

R

radiation the transfer of thermal energy through space (223); *also* the transfer of energy as electromagnetic waves (400)

reclamation the process of returning land to its original state after mining is completed (71)

recycling the use of used or discarded materials that have been reprocessed into new products (110)

reference point a fixed place on the Earth's surface used to describe direction and location (35)

relative humidity the amount of moisture the air contains compared with the maximum amount it can hold at a particular temperature (425)

relief the difference in elevation between the highest and lowest points of an area being mapped (47)

remote sensing gathering information about something without actually being nearby (43)

renewable resource a natural resource that can be used and replaced over a relatively short time (109)

reverse fault a fault in which the hanging wall moves up relative to the footwall (153)

rift a zone of thin, fractured lithosphere that forms between tectonic plates as they separate (202)

rift valley a valley that forms in a rift zone between mountains (341)

rock a naturally formed solid mass made of one or more minerals or noncrystalline materials (80)

rock cycle the continuous process by which one rock type changes into another rock type (82)

rock fall a group of loose rocks that fall down a steep slope (295)

S

salinity a measure of the amount of dissolved solids in a given amount of liquid (334)

saltation the movement of sand-sized particles by a skipping and bouncing action in the direction the wind is blowing (282)

scavenger an animal that feeds on the bodies of dead animals (311)

scientific method a series of steps that scientists use to answer questions and solve problems (13)

scrubber a device that attaches to smokestacks to remove some of the more harmful pollutants before they are released into the air (415)

sea-floor spreading the process by which new oceanic crust forms at mid-ocean ridges as tectonic plates are pulled away from each other (145)

seamount an individual mountain of volcanic material on the abyssal plain (341)

secondary pollutants pollutants that form from chemical reactions that occur when primary pollutants come into contact with other primary pollutants or with naturally occurring substances, such as water vapor (411)

sedimentary rock rock that forms when sediments are compacted and cemented together or when minerals crystallize out of oceans and lakes (84)

seismic (SIEZ mik) **gap** an area along a fault where relatively few earthquakes have occurred (176)

seismic waves waves of energy that travel through the Earth (170)

seismogram a tracing of earthquake motion created by a seismograph (172)

seismograph an instrument located at or near the surface of the Earth that records seismic waves (172)

seismology the study of earthquakes (166)

septic tank a large underground tank that collects and cleans waste water from a household (265)

severe weather weather that causes property damage and possible death (436)

sewage treatment plant a factory that cleans waste matter out of water that comes from sewers or drains (264)

shadow zone an area on the Earth's surface where no direct seismic waves from a particular earthquake can be detected (181)

shield volcano a large, gently sloped volcano that forms from repeated, nonexplosive eruptions of lava (198)

shoreline the boundary between land and a body of water (276)

silica a compound of silicon and oxygen atoms (194)

silicate mineral a mineral that is made mostly of silica, a combination of the elements silicon and oxygen (62)

597

smog a photochemical fog produced by the action of sunlight on air pollutants (117)

solar energy energy from the sun (119)

specific gravity the ratio of an object's density to the density of water (66)

specific heat capacity the amount of energy needed to change the temperature of 1 kg of a substance by 1°C; specific heat capacity is a characteristic property of a substance (224)

spring tides tides with maximum daily tidal ranges that occur during the new and full moons (382)

states of matter the physical forms in which a substance can exist (228)

station model a small circle showing the location of a weather station along with a set of symbols and numbers surrounding it that represent weather data (444)

storm surge a local rise in sea level near the shore that is caused by strong winds from a storm, such as a hurricane (379)

strata layers of sedimentary rock that form from the deposition of sediment (91)

stratification the layering of sedimentary rock (94)

stratified drift rock material that has been sorted and deposited in layers by water flowing from the melted ice of a glacier (292)

stratosphere the atmospheric layer above the troposphere (397)

stratus (STRAT uhs) **clouds** clouds that form in layers (428)

streak the color of a mineral in powdered form (65)

stress the amount force placed on a given material (151)

strike-slip fault a fault in which the two fault blocks move past each other horizontally (154)

strip mining a process in which rock and soil are stripped from the Earth's surface to expose the underlying materials to be mined (115)

subduction zone the region where an oceanic plate sinks down into the asthenosphere at a convergent boundary, usually between continental and oceanic plates (148)

surf the area between the breaker zone and the shore (376)

surface current a streamlike movement of water that occurs at or near the surface of the ocean (367, 459)

S waves the second-fastest type of seismic wave; cannot travel through materials that are completely liquid; also known as shear waves and secondary waves (170)

swells rolling waves that move in a steady procession across the ocean (377)

symbiosis (SIM bie OH sis) a close, long-term association between two or more species (319)

syncline a trough-shaped fold in sedimentary rock layers (152)

T

tectonic plates huge pieces of the lithosphere that move around on top of the asthenosphere (140)

temperate zone the climate zone between the tropics and the polar zone (463)

temperature a measure of how hot (or cold) something is; specifically, a measure of the average kinetic energy of the particles in an object (25, 214)

tension stress that occurs when opposing forces act to stretch a given material (151)

texture the sizes, shapes, and arrangement of particles or grains that a rock is made of (86)

theory a unifying explanation for a broad range of hypotheses and observations that have been supported by testing (19)

thermal energy the total kinetic energy of the particles that make up an object (220)

thermal equilibrium the point at which two objects reach the same temperature; at thermal equilibrium, no net transfer of thermal energy occurs (220)

thermal expansion the increase in volume of a substance due to an increase in temperature (216)

thermal pollution the excessive heating of a body of water (237)

thermocline a layer of ocean water in which water temperature drops with increased depth faster than in other layers of the ocean (335)

thermometer a tool used to measure air temperature (442)

thermosphere the uppermost layer of the atmosphere (398)

thunder the sound that results from the rapid expansion of air along a lightning strike (437)

thunderstorms small, intense storm systems that produce strong winds, heavy rain, lightning and thunder (436)

tidal bore a body of water that rushes up through a narrow bay, estuary, or river channel during the rise of high tide, causing a very sudden tidal rise (383)

tidal range the difference between levels of ocean water at high tide and low tide (382)

tides daily movements of ocean water that change the level of the ocean's surface (380)

till unsorted rock material that is deposited directly by glacial ice when it melts (293)

topographic map a map that shows the surface features of the Earth's surface (46)

tornado a small, rotating column of air with high wind speeds and low central pressure that touches the ground (438)

trade winds the winds that blow from 30° latitude to the equator (406)

transform boundary the boundary between two tectonic plates that are sliding past each other (149)

tributary a small stream or river that flows into a larger one (250)

tropical zone the warm zone located around the equator (461)

troposphere (TROH poh SFIR) the lowest layer of the atmosphere (397)

trough (trahf) the lowest point of a wave (374)

true north the geographic North Pole (36)

tsunami a wave that forms when a large volume of ocean water is suddenly moved up or down (378)

U

upwelling a near-shore process in which cold, nutrient-rich water from the deep ocean rises to the surface to replace warm surface water that is blown farther out to sea by prevailing winds (373)

U-shaped valley a valley that forms when a glacier flows into and erodes a valley, changing the valley from its original V shape to a U shape (291)

V

vent a hole or crack in the Earth's crust through which magma rises to the surface (194)

volcano a mountain that forms when lava or pyroclastic material builds up around a volcanic vent (194)

volume the amount of space that something occupies or the amount of space that something contains (23)

W

water cycle the continuous movement of water from water sources into the air, onto land, into and over the ground, and back to the water sources (248, 337, 424)

water table an underground boundary where the zone of aeration and the zone of saturation meet (258)

wave height the vertical distance between a wave's crest and its trough (374)

wavelength the distance between one point on a wave and the corresponding point on an adjacent wave in a series of waves; for example, the distance between two adjacent crests or compressions (374)

wave period the time it takes for two waves to pass a fixed point (375)

weather the condition of the atmosphere at a particular time and place (424, 454)

weather forecast a prediction of future weather conditions (442)

westerlies wind belts found in both the Northern and Southern Hemispheres between 30° and 60° latitude (407)

whitecap a white, foaming wave with a very steep crest that breaks in the open ocean before the wave gets close to the shore (377)

wind moving air (404)

wind energy energy in wind (122)

windsock an instrument used to measure wind direction (443)

wind vane an instrument used to measure wind direction (443)

Index

Index

A **boldface** number refers to an illustration on that page.

A

B

C

Index

D

E

F

G

H

I

605

N

Index

Q

R

Index

S

T

U

V

W

Z

Credits

Abbreviations used: (t) top, (c) center, (b) bottom, (l) left, (r) right, (bkgd) background

ILLUSTRATIONS

All illustrations, unless noted below, by Holt, Rinehart & Winston.

Table of Contents: Page ix(tl), Dan Stuckenschneider/Uhl Studios Inc; (br), Patrick Gnan; x(tr), Stephen Durke/Washington Artists; (bl), Mike Wepplo; xi(b), Will Nelson/Sweet Reps; xii(tl), Yuan Lee; (bl), Marty Roper/Planet Rep; xiiii(tl), Marty Roper/Planet Rep; (b), Dan Stuckenschneider/Uhl Studios Inc.

Unit One Chapter One Page 4(br), Barbara Hoopes-Ambler; 7(br), Craig Attebery/Jeff Lavaty; 9(b), David Schleinkofer/Mendola Ltd.; 10(tl), Robert Hynes; 12(b), Barbara Hoopes-Ambler; 14(all), 15(all), 16(tl), 16(cl), Carlyn Iverson; 16(b), 17(b), Christy Krames; 18(all), Dan Stuckenschneider/Uhl Studios Inc; 19(br), Stephen Durke/Washington Artists; 20(c), Jared Schneidman/Wilkinson Studios; 22(all), Stephen Durke/Washington Artists; 23(cl), MapQuest.com; 25(tr), Stephen Durke/Washington Artists; 26(cr), Christy Krames; 27(c), Dan Stuckenschneider/Uhl Studios Inc; 28(cr), Geoff Smith/Scott Hull; 29(cr), Sidney Jablonski; 30(c), Dan Stuckenschneider/Uhl Studios Inc.

Chapter Two Page 35(bl), John White/The Neis Group; 37(all), MapQuest.com; 38(tl), MapQuest.com; 39(all), MapQuest.com; 41(all), MapQuest.com; 42(all), MapQuest.com.

Unit Two Chapter Three Page 60(bl), Gary Locke/Suzanne Craig; 61(c), Stephen Durke/Washington Artists; 68(bkgd), Dan Stuckenschneider/Uhl Studios Inc; 70(bl), Jared Schneidman/Wilkinson Studios; 72(all), Stephen Durke/Washington Artists.

Chapter Four Page 81(tr), Marty Roper/Planet Rep; 82(all), 83(all), Dan Stuckenschneider/Uhl Studios Inc; 84(c), The Mazer Corporation; 85(all), Sidney Jablonski; 87(all), Keith Locke; 88(l), Dan Stuckenschneider/Uhl Studios Inc; 89(b), Dan Stuckenschneider/Uhl Studios Inc; 90(bl), Geoff Smith/Scott Hull; 91(bl), The Mazer Corporation; 92(bl), Robert Hynes; 96(b), Dan Stuckenschneider/Uhl Studios Inc; 97(c), Stephen Durke/Washington Artists; 97(b), Dan Stuckenschneider/Uhl Studios Inc; 100(br), Sidney Jablonski; 102(bl), Stephen Durke/Washington Artists; 103(cr), Sidney Jablonski.

Chapter Five Page 106(tl), Dan Stuckenschneider/Uhl Studios Inc; 108(b), Dan Stuckenschneider/Uhl Studios Inc; 110(bl), Blake Thornton/Rita Marie; 113(bl), Dan Stuckenschneider/Uhl Studios Inc; 114(all), Dan Stuckenschneider/Uhl Studios Inc; 115(tr), MapQuest.com; 121(tr), John Huxtable; 125(br), Dan Stuckenschneider/Uhl Studios Inc; 126(cr), Dan Stuckenschneider/Uhl Studios Inc; 126(br), John Huxtable; 129(tr), Sidney Jablonski.

Unit Three Page 133(cr), Terry Kovalcik.

Chapter Six Page 136(b), Dan Stuckenschneider/Uhl Studios Inc; 137(br), Dan Stuckenschneider/Uhl Studios Inc; 138(all), Dan Stuckenschneider/Uhl Studios Inc; 139(b), Dan Stuckenschneider/Uhl Studios Inc; 140(t), Dan Stuckenschneider/Uhl Studios Inc; 141(c), Dan Stuckenschneider/Uhl Studios Inc; 142(cl), Dan Stuckenschneider/Uhl Studios Inc; 143(tr), Dan Stuckenschneider/Uhl Studios Inc; 143(cl), MapQuest.com; 143(bl), 143(br), Stephen Durke/Washington Artists; 144(all), MapQuest.com; 145(all), Dan Stuckenschneider/Uhl Studios Inc; 146(cl), Stephen Durke/Washington Artists; 146(cr), Dan Stuckenschneider/Uhl Studios Inc; 147(b), Dan Stuckenschneider/Uhl Studios Inc; 148(b), 149(b), Dan Stuckenschneider/Uhl Studios Inc; 152(all), Dan Stuckenschneider/Uhl Studios Inc; 153(tr), Marty Roper/Planet Rep; 153(cr), Dan Stuckenschneider/Uhl Studios Inc; 153(br), Dan Stuckenschneider/Uhl Studios Inc; 155(tr), Dan Stuckenschneider/Uhl Studios Inc; 156(t), Tony Morse; 156(b), Dan Stuckenschneider/Uhl Studios Inc; 158(all), Dan Stuckenschneider/Uhl Studios Inc; 159(cr), Marty Roper/Planet Rep.

Chapter Seven Page 164(tr), Tony Morse; 166(bl), MapQuest.com; 167(all), 168(all), Dan Stuckenschneider/Uhl Studios Inc; 169(all), Dan Stuckenschneider/Uhl Studios Inc; 170(all), Stephen Durke/Washington Artists; 171(tr), Sidney Jablonski; 171(cl), Stephen Durke/Washington Artists; 172(bl), Dan Stuckenschneider/Uhl Studios Inc; 173(tr), Sidney Jablonski; 175(b), MapQuest.com; 177(t), Jared Schneidman/Wilkinson Studios; 178(all), Dan Stuckenschneider/Uhl Studios Inc; 179(br), Marty Roper/Planet Rep; 181(all), Dan Stuckenschneider/Uhl Studios Inc; 182(all), Sidney Jablonski; 184(c), Stephen Durke/Washington Artists; 184(br), Sidney Jablonski; 186(br), Dan Stuckenschneider/Uhl Studios Inc; 187(cr), Sidney Jablonski.

Chapter Eight Page 194(tl), Dan Stuckenschneider/Uhl Studios Inc; 197(bl), Geoff Smith/Scott Hull; 198(all), Patrick Gnan; 199(tr), Dan Stuckenschneider/Uhl Studios Inc; 200(br), Dan Stuckenschneider/Uhl Studios Inc; 201(tr), Stephen Durke/Washington Artists; 201(br), MapQuest.com; 202(all), 203(all), 204(all), Dan Stuckenschneider/Uhl Studios Inc; 206(br), Dan Stuckenschneider/Uhl Studios Inc; 207(l), Patrick Gnan; 207(cr), Dan Stuckenschneider/Uhl Studios Inc; 209(tr), Ross Culbert & Lavery.

Chapter Nine Page 214(b), Charles Thomas; 215(all), Stephen Durke/Washington Artists; 216(b), Terry Guyer; 217(tr), Dave Joly; 218(all), Dan Stuckenschneider/Uhl Studios Inc; 220(all), Stephen Durke/Washington Artists/Preface Inc.; 221(all), Stephen Durke/Washington Artists/Preface Inc.; 222(bl), Mark Heine; 223(c), Jared Schneidman/Wilkinson Studios; (br), Geoff Smith/Scott Hull, Scott Hull Assoc.; 226(cr), Stephen Durke/Washington Artists; 228(all), Stephen Durke/Washington Artists; 229(b), Preface Inc.; 231(br), Dan Stuckenschneider/Uhl Studios Inc; 232(cr), Dan Stuckenschneider/Uhl Studios Inc; 233(b), Dan Stuckenschneider/Uhl Studios Inc; 234(all), Dan Stuckenschneider/Uhl Studios Inc; 236(c), Dan Stuckenschneider/Uhl Studios Inc; 237(c), Dan Stuckenschneider/Uhl Studios Inc; 238(c), Dave Joly; 240(br), Dan Stuckenschneider/Uhl Studios Inc; 241(cr), Preface Inc.; 243(all), Stephen Durke/Washington Artists.

Unit Four Page 245(tc), MapQuest.com

Chapter Ten: Page 249(bkgd), Mike Wepplo; 250(br), MapQuest.com; 252(all), Dan Stuckenschneider/Uhl Studios Inc; 255(b), Marty Roper/Planet Rep; 258(cl), Stephen Durke/Washington Artists; 258(bl), Geoff Smith/Scott Hull; 259(tl), MapQuest.com; 260(all), Stephen Durke/Washington Artists; 264(b), John Huxtable; 265(tl), John Huxtable; 265(b), Sidney Jablonski; 267(c), MapQuest.com; 268(c), Mike Wepplo; 271(tr), Sidney Jablonski.

Chapter Eleven Page 274(t), Paul DiMare; 278(bl), Dan Stuckenschneider/Uhl Studios Inc; 280(bkgd), 281(bkgd), Mike Wepplo; 281(tr), 282(cl), Keith Locke; 282(b), Dean Fleming; 284(bl), Geoff Smith/Scott Hull; 285(c), Dan Stuckenschneider/Uhl Studios Inc; 288(cr), Sidney Jablonski; 291(bkgd), Robert Hynes; 301(tr), Sidney Jablonski.

Chapter Twelve Page 305(all), David Beck; 306(b), Will Nelson/Sweet Reps; 307(all), Will Nelson/Sweet Reps; 308(b), John White/The Neis Group; 310(b), Will Nelson/Sweet Reps; 312(b), John White/The Neis Group; 313(b), Will Nelson/Sweet Reps; 315(br), Will Nelson/Sweet Reps; 316(bl), Blake Thornton/Rita Marie; 321(cr), Mike Wepplo; 322(cl), Will Nelson/Sweet Reps; 324(br), David Beck; 325(cr), Rob Schuster.

Unit Five Chapter Thirteen Page 330(t), Rainey Kirk/The Neis Group; 332(all), Geoff Smith/Scott Hull; 333(all), MapQuest.com; 334(tl), Ross Culbert & Lavery; 335(tr), MapQuest.com; 335(b), Ross Culbert & Lavery; 337(bkgd), Mike Wepplo; 338(tl), Sidney Jablonski; 339(cl), Marty Roper/Planet Rep;340(b), 341(b), Dan Stuckenschneider/Uhl Studios Inc; 342(b), Dan Stuckenschneider/Uhl Studios Inc; 343(cr), Craig Attebery/Jeff Lavaty; (br), Ross Culbert & Lavery; 344(all), Yuan Lee; 345(all), 346(all), 347(all), Jared Schneidman/Wilkinson Studios; 352(all), Jared Schneidman/Wilkinson Studios; 355(br), Mark Heine; 358(br), Sidney Jablonski; 360(tr), MapQuest.com; 360(cl), Bill Mayer; 361(tr), Ross Culbert & Lavery.

Chapter Fourteen Page 364(t), John Huxtable; 364(bl), Tony Morse; 366(tr), Dean Fleming; 367(tr), Stephen Durke/Washington Artists; 367(bl), MapQuest.com; 368(all), MapQuest.com; 369(c), MapQuest.com; 370(all), Stephen Durke/Washington Artists; 371(all), Jared Schneidman/Wilkinson Studios; 372(all), MapQuest.com; 374(all), Jared Schneidman/Wilkinson Studios; 375(all), Jared Schneidman/Wilkinson Studios; 376(all), Dean Fleming; 378(cr), Dan Stuckenschneider/Uhl Studios Inc; 379(tr), MapQuest.com; 380(c), Marty Roper/Planet Rep; 381(all), 382(all), Sidney Jablonski; 384(c), Stephen Durke/Washington Artists/Sam Dudgeon/HRW Photo; (bl), Dean Fleming; 385(cr), Marty Roper/Planet Rep; 387(cr), Sidney Jablonski.

Unit Six Page 390(bl), John Huxtable; (br), Annie Bissett; 391(cl), Terry Kovalcik.

Chapter Fifteen Page 394(br), Sidney Jablonski; 395(br), 396(all), 397(cr), 398(all), Stephen Durke/Washington Artists; 400(b), 401(b), Dan Stuckenschneider/Uhl Studios Inc; 402(c), John Huxtable; 404(bl), 405(tr), 406(br), Stephen Durke/Washington Artists; 408(all), 409(all), Stephen Durke/Washington Artists; 411(b), John Huxtable; 415(br), John Huxtable; 417(cl), Stephen Durke/Washington Artists; 419(cr), The Mazer Corporation.

Chapter Sixteen Page 424(b), Robert Hynes; 426(bl), The Mazer Corporation; 429(b), Stephen Durke/Washington Artists; 430(tl), Stephen Durke/Washington Artists; 432(b), MapQuest.com; 434(all), 435(all), Stephen Durke/Washington Artists; 437(tl), 440(b), Paul DiMare; 442(tr), Dan McGeehan/Koralik Associates; 445(cr), MapQuest.com; 449(cr), MapQuest.com.

Chapter Seventeen Page 452(tr), John White/The Neis Group; 455(br), Stephen Durke/Washington Artists; 456(c), Craig Attebery/Jeff Lavaty; 457(tc), Stephen Durke/Washington Artists; 458(b), Dan Stuckenschneider/Uhl Studios Inc; 459(cl), MapQuest.com; 460(cl), Stephen Durke/Washington Artists; 460(b), MapQuest.com; 461(tr), Stephen Durke/Washington Artists; 461(c), MapQuest.com; 461(br), 462(tr), 463(tr), Annie Bissett; 464(tl), Stephen Durke/Washington Artists; 464(c), MapQuest.com; 464(bc), 465(all), 466(tl), Annie Bissett; 466(bl), Stephen Durke/Washington Artists; 467(t), MapQuest.com; 467(br), 468(cl), Annie Bissett; 469(tr), Marty Roper/Planet Rep; 469(bl), MapQuest.com; 470(all), Sidney Jablonski; 471(tl), Dan Stuckenschneider/Uhl Studios Inc; 471(br), MapQuest.com; 472(c), Marty Roper/Planet Rep; 474(cr), Stephen Durke/Washington Artists; 474(bl), Craig Attebery/Jeff Lavaty; 476(tr), Terry Kovalcik; 477(cr), Sidney Jablonski.

LabBook Page 480 (tl), Stephen Durke/Washington Artists; 487(tr), Mark Heine; 488(cl), Marty Roper/Planet Rep; 496(br), Mark Heine; 501(all), Mark Heine; 504(br), Mark Heine; 506(c), Dan Stuckenschneider/Uhl Studios Inc; 514(cl), Sidney Jablonski; 515(c), MapQuest.com; 516(b), MapQuest.com; 518(tl), Marty Roper/Planet Rep; (br), Ralph Garafola; 519(tr), Ralph Garafola; 522(br), Dave Joly; 525(t), Mark Heine; 527(tr), Mark Heine; 537(tr), Blake Thornton/Rita Marie; (br), Lori Anzalone; 538(cr), Dean Fleming; 539(cr), Sidney Jablonski; 541(cr), Geoff Smith/Scott Hull; 544(bc), Mark Heine; 545(b), Sidney Jablonski; 548(br), Mark Heine; 549(tr), Mark Heine; 551(tl), Mark Heine; 554(t), MapQuest.com; 556(tl), Dan McGeehan/Koralik Associates; (br), Mark Heine; 559(cr), Marty Roper/Planet Rep; 562(cr), MapQuest.com; (br), Sidney Jablonski; 563(tl), Sidney Jablonski; (tr), MapQuest.com; (cl), Sidney Jablonski; (cr), MapQuest.com.

Appendix Page 567(cl), Blake Thornton/Rita Marie; 570(t), Terry Guyer; 574(all), Mark Mille/Sharon Langley; 582, 583(all), Kristy Sprott; 584(bl), Stephen Durke/Washington Artists; 585(b), Bruce Burdick.

PHOTOGRAPHY

Cover and Title Page: (tl), Jack Dykinga/Tony Stone Images; (tr), Barry Rosenthal/FPG International; (bl), David Parker/Science Photo Library/Photo Researchers; (br), Geospace/Science Photo Library/Photo Researchers; owl (cover, spine, back, title page) Kim Taylor/Bruce Coleman.

Table of Contents: Page v(tr), E.R. Degginger/Color-Pic, Inc; (cr), K. Segerstrom/USGS; vi (tl), Jean Miele/Stock Market; vii(tr), E.R. Degginger/Color-Pic; (bl), Walter H. Hodge/Peter Arnold; ix(bl), Tom Bean/DRK Photo; xi (tr), Gay Bumgarner/Tony Stone Images; xii(tr), James B. Wood; xii (bl), TOMS/NASA; xix(br), William Manning/Stock Market.

Unit One Page 2(tr), Uwe Fink/University of Arizona, Department of Planetary Sciences, Lunar & Planetary Laboratory; (cl), Ed Reschke/Peter Arnold; (cl), T.A. Wiewandt/DRK Photo; (bl), National Air and Space Museum; (br), K. Segerstrom/USGS; 3(tl), Hulton Getty Images/Liaison International; (tr), Adam Wooleitt/Woodfin Camp & Associates; (cl), Francois Gohier; (bl), Jason Laure/Woodfin Camp & Associates; (br), NASA.

Chapter One Page 4 (c), Dr. David Gillette; 5 (tr), Earth Imaging/Tony Stone Images; (bl), S. Schwabe/The Rob Palwer Blue Holes Foundation; 8(tl), Marit Jentof-Nilsen and Fritz Hasler - NASA Goddard Laboratory for Atmospheres; (bl), NCAR/MMM Blustein; 9(tr), Jean Miele/Stock Market; 11(tr), Mark Howard/Westfall Eco Images; (cr), Annie Griffiths/Westlight; 15(tr), Brian Parker/Tom Stack & Associates; 19(cr), Paul Bagby/NASA; 23(tr), Otis Imboden/National Geographic Image Collection; (c), Alan Schein/Stock Market; 28(cl), Ken Lucas/Visuals Unlimited; 31(br), NASA.

Chapter Two Page 32(cr), Scala/Art Resource, NY; (bl), Victor Boswellings/National Geographic Image Collection; (bkgd), USGS; 34(br), Royal Geographical Society, London/The Bridgeman Art Library International Ltd.; 36(cr), Tom Van Sant/Stock Market; 43(tr), USGS; (br), Aerial Images and SOVINFORMSPUTNIK; 44(c), The American Map Corporation/ADC The Map People; (cl), ADC The Map People; 45(cr), ADC The Map People; (bl), USGS; 47(cl,cr), USGS; 48; USGS 51(cr), Tom Van Sant/Stock Market; 52(tr), Vladimir Pcholkin/FPG International; 53(cr), USGS; 54(bl), NASA/JPL; (br), Courtesy Lower Colorado River Authority, Austin, TX.

Unit Two Page 56(tl), Science Photo Library; (tr), Science VU/Visuals Unlimited; (bl), NASA/International Stock; (br), UPI/Corbis; (br), Thomas Laird/Peter Arnold; 57(tr), SuperStock; (cl), AP Wide World Photos; (cr), Francois Gohier; (bc), NASA/Science Photo Library/Photo Researchers.

Chapter Three Page 58(t), E.R. Degginger/Color-Pic; (t), Mike Husar/DRK Photo; 59(tr), Inga Spence/Tom Stack & Associates; 61(cr), Dr. Rainer Bode/Bode-Verlag Gmb; 62(c,cl), E.R. Degginger/Color-Pic; (bl), Pat Lanza/Bruce Coleman Inc.; 63(top to bottom), (top four), E.R. Degginger/Color-Pic; SuperStock; Ken Lucas/Visuals Unlimited Inc.; 64(tc), Jane Burton/Bruce Coleman Inc.; (tr), Liasion International; Luster Chart (row 1), E.R. Degginger/Color-Pic; John Cancalosi/DRK Photo; (row 2), Biophoto Associates/ Photo Researchers, Inc; E.R. Degginger/Bruce Coleman Inc.; (row 3), E.R. Degginger/ Color-Pic; Biophoto Associates/Photo Researchers; (row 4), E.R. Degginger/Color-Pic; 65(c), E.R. Degginger/Color-Pic; (cr), Erica and Harold Van Pelt/American Museum of Natural History; Fracture Chart(tl,br), Tom Pantages; 66 Harness Scale,(1), Ken Lucas/ Visuals Unlimited Inc, (2,4,5,6), E.R. Degginger/Color-Pic; (3), Dane S. Johnson/Visuals Unlimited Inc.; (7), Carlyn Iverson/Absolute Science Illustration and Photography; (8), Mark A. Schneider/Visuals Unlimited Inc.; (9), Charles D. Winters/Photo Researchers, Inc; (10), Bard Wrisley/Liasion International; 67(tl,bc), E.R. Degginger/Color-Pic; (cr), Tom Pantages; 69(tl,cl), E.R. Degginger/Color-Pic; 70(cl), Kosmatsu Mining Systems; (cr), Wernher Krutein/Liasion International; (br), Index Stock Imagery; 71(cl), Historic Royal Palaces; 73(tr), Historic Royal Palaces; 74(bl), E.R. Degginger/Color-Pic; 76(tc), Ralph Wetmore/Tony Stone Images; (bl), Peter Menzel.

Chapter Four Page 78(t), Ron Ruhoff; (br), Kreb Photography; 80(c), Kenneth Garrett; (cl), Historical Collections, National Museum of Health and Medicine, AFIP; (bc), Fergus O'Brien/FPG International; (br), Peter Cummings/Tom Stack & Associates; 81(c), Breck P. Kent; (cr), NASA/Science Photo Library/Photo Researchers, Inc; (bl), A.F. Kersting; 85(tr,br), E.R. Degginger/Color-Pic; (cl), Walter H. Hodge/Peter Arnold; (bl), Spharry Taylor/Dorling Kindersley; (bcl), Breck P. Kent; (br), E.R. Degginger/Color-Pic; (granite), Pat Lanza/Bruce Coleman Inc.; 86(tc), Dorling Kindersley; (tr), Breck P. Kent; (cl), Breck P. Kent; (cr), E.R. Degginger/Color-Pic; 88(cl), Breck P. Kent; (cr), Breck P. Kent; (bl), Breck P. Kent; (br), E.R. Degginger/Color-Pic; 89(tr), Laurence Parent; 90(tl,cl), Breck P. Kent; (bl), Doug Martin/Photo Researchers; (cr), Peter French/Bruce Coleman Inc.; 91(br), Ed Cooper Photo; 92(tl), Breck P. Kent/Animals Animals Earth Scenes; (tr), Breck P. Kent; (cl), Joyce Photographics/Photo Researchers, Inc; (cr), E.R. Degginger/Color-Pic; (br), Breck P. Kent; 93(tl), Linda Pitkin/Masterfile; (tc), Stephen Frink/The Waterhouse; (tr), NASA; (bl), SuperStock; (bc), Breck P. Kent; (br), Ed Cooper; 94(tl), Franklin P. OSF/Animals Animals Earth Scenes; (cr), Breck P. Kent/Animals Animals Earth Scenes; (bl), Breck P. Kent; 95(bl), E.R. Degginger/Color-Pic; (br), George Wuethner; 97(tl), Dane S. Johnson/ Visuals Unlimited; (tlc), Carlyn Iverson/Absolute Science Illustration and Photography; (tlb), Breck P. Kent; (tr), Breck P. Kent/Animals Animals Earth Scenes; (brt), Breck P. Kent; (brc), Tom Pantages; (br), Breck P. Kent/Animals Animals Earth Scenes; 98(b) Breck P. Kent 99(tl), E.R. Degginger/Color-Pic; (tc), The Natural History Museum, London; (bl), Ray Simons/Photo Researchers; (bc), Breck P. Kent; 100(c), E.R. Degginger/Color-Pic; 101(cr), Doug Sokell/Tom Stack & Associates; 104(tc), Wolfgang Kaehler/Liaison International

Chapter Five Page 106(top to bottom), Florida Tech; Kaku Kurita/Liaison International; Greg Vaughn/Tom Stack & Associates; Kaku Kurita/Liaison International; Mark Burnett/ Photo Researchers; Kaku Kurita/Liaison International; 107(tr), Greg Vaughn/Tom Stack & Associates; 108(cl), John Blaustein/Liaison International; (cr), Mark Lewis/Tony Stone Images; 109(tl), James Randklev/Tony Stone Images; (tc), Luc Cuyvers/Image Bank; (tr), Bruce Hands/Tony Stone Images; (bl), Ed Malles/Liaison International; (bc), John Zoiner Photographer; (br), Tom Lippert/Liaison International; 111(br), Telegraph Colour Library/ FPG International; 112(cr,bl), John Zoiner; 114(tr), Horst Schafer/Peter Arnold; (cr), Paolo Koch/Photo Researchers; (cr), Brian Parker/Tom Stack & Associates; (br), C. Kuhn/ Image Bank; 115(bl), Mark A. Leman/Tony Stone Images; (br), Tim Eagan/Woodfin Camp & Associates; 116(tl), Adam Hart-Davis/Science Photo Library/Photo Researchers; (cl), John Shaw/Tom Stack & Associates; (br), James Stanfield/National Geographic Image Collection; 117(tr), A. Ramey/Woodfin Camp & Associates; 118(bl), Sylvain Coffie/Tony Stone Images; 119(cl), Tom Myers/Photo Researchers; 120(tr), Alex Bartel/Science Photo Library/Photo Researchers; (bl), Joyce Photographics/Photo Researchers; 121(br), Hank Morgan/Science Source/Photo Researchers; 122(tl), Ed Collacott/Tony Stone Images; (bl), Mark Lewis/Liaison International; 123(tr), Craig Sands/National Geographic Image Collection; (bl), Tom Bean; (cr), G.R. Dick Roberts; 125(tr), Luis Castaneda/Image Bank; 128(tl), John Blaustein/Liaison International; 130(tr), SuperStock; (cr), Bedford Recycled Plastic Timbers; (br), Kay Park-Rec Corp.; 131(cr), Culver Pictures Inc.

Unit Three Page 132(tc), Charles Scribner's Sons NY, 1906; (bl), USGS/NASA/Science Source/Photo Researchers; (bc), Steve Winter/National Geographic Society; 133(tl), FPG International; (tr), Culver Pictures Inc.; (cl), Lambert/Archive Photos; (bl), Randy Duchaine/Stock Market; (br), The Robotics Institute Carnegie Mellon University.

Chapter Six Page 134(b), Alex Stewart/Image Bank; (bl), Wally Berg; 137(tr), James Watt/Animals Animals Earth Scenes; (br), World Perspective/Tony Stone Images; 149(tr), Emory Kristof/National Geographic Image Collection ; 150(tl), NASA; (cl), ESA/CE/Eurocontral/Science Photo Library/Photo Researchers; 152(bl), Sylvester Allred/Visuals Unlimited; (br), G.R. Dick Roberts; 154(tl), Tom Bean; (tr), Landform Slides; (c), Michael Collier; (bl), G.R. Dick Roberts; 155(bl), William Manning/Stock Market; 157(tr), Michelle & Tom Grimm/Tony Stone Images; (br), David Falconer/ DRK Photo; 160(br), NASA/Photo Researchers; 162(cl), Bob Krist; 163(tc), Martin Schwarzbach/Photo Deutsches Museum Munchen.

Chapter Seven Page 164(b), Haruyoshi Yamaguchi/SYGMA; 167(tr), Joe Dellingest/ NOAA/USGS; 172(cl), Bob Paz/Caltech; 173(b), Earth Images/Tony Stone Images; 176(bl), Peter Cade/Tony Stone Images; 177(br), A. Ramey/Woodfin Camp & Associates; (bl), Paul Chesley/Tony Stone Images; 183(tr), NASA/JPL; (c), Astronomy online; (cr), SOHO(ESA & NASA); 185(cl), A. Ramey/Woodfin Camp & Associates; 186(tl), Chuck O'Rear/Westlight; 189(cr), David Madison/Bruce Coleman Inc.

Chapter Eight Page 190(t), David Hardy/Science Photo Library/Photo Researchers; (cr), Circus World Museum, Baraboo, Wisconsin; (bl), Library of Congress, LC-USZ62-25077; 192(bl), Robert W. Madden/National Geographic Society; (bc), Ken Sakamoto/ Black Star; (br), Douglas Peebles Photography; 193(tr), Joyce Warren/USGS Photo Library; (bl), SuperStock; (br), Milton Rand/Tom Stack & Associates; 195(cr), Jim Yuskavitch; (bl), Karl Weatherly; (bc), Tui De Roy/Minden Pictures; (br), B. Murton/ Southampton Oceanography Centre/Science Photo Library; 196(tl), Tom Bean/ DRK Photo; (cl), Francois Gohier/Photo Researchers; (cr), Glenn Oliver/Visuals Unlimited Inc.; (br), E.R. Degginger/Color-Pic; 197(cl), Alberto Garcia/SABA; 198(tc), Jeff Greenberg/ Visuals Unlimited; (c), Krafft/Explorer/Science Source/Photo Researchers; (bc), SuperStock; 199(cl), R. & E. Thane/Animals Animals Earth Scenes; (br), NASA/TSADO/Tom Stack & Associates; 204(cl), Andrew Rafkind/Tony Stone Images; 205(tr), Game McGimsey/ USGS Alaska Volcano Observatory; (br), Gilles Bassignac/Liasion International; 206(c), Robert W. Madden/National Geographic Society; 208(tl), Krafft/Explorer/Science Source/ Photo Researchers; (cl), Karl Weatherly; 210(tc), The Robotics Institute Carnegie Mellon University; 211(bl), NASA/Science Photo Library/Photo Researchers.

Chapter Nine Page 212(t), Solar Survival Architecture; 218(tl), Mark Burnett/ Photo Researchers;; 235(cl), Dorling Kindersley LTD; (br), Peter Arnold Inc., NY; 240(tr), Dorling Kindersley LTD; 241(bl), Kees van den Berg/Photo Researchers; 242(tc), Dan Winters/Discover Magazine.

Unit Four Page 244(tc), The Age of Reptiles, a mural by Rudolph F. Zallinger. ©1996, 1975,1985,1989, Peabody Museum of Natural History, Yale University, New Haven, Connecticut, USA; (c), Tom Bean/Tony Stone Images; (bl), Dr. John Murphy; (br), Mike Roemer/Liaison International; 245(tr), John Eastcott/YVA MOMATIUK/DRK Photo; (cl), Stock Montage; (cr), Peter Essick/Aurora & Quanta; (bl), Price, R.-Survi OSF/Animals Animals Earth Scenes; (br), David Wong/South China Morning Post; (br), Telegraph Colour Library/FPG International.

Chapter Ten Page 248(c), Floyd Holdman/Royce Bair & Associates; 251(cr), Ed Reschke/Peter Arnold; (bl), Jim Wark/Peter Arnold; 253(tr), Laurence Parent; (br), Victor Brunelle/Stock Boston; 254(tl), G.R. Dick Roberts; (cl), Galen Rowell/Peter Arnold; 255(cr), Winfield Parks, Jr./National Geographic Image Collection; 256(tl), SuperStock; (cr), Earth Satellite Corporation/Science Photo Library; 257(tr), Martin G. Miller/Visuals Unlimited Inc.; (cr), Earth Satellite Corporation; 261(tl), Richard Reid/ Animals Animals Earth Scenes; (bc), E.R. Degginger/Color-Pic; 262(cl), ChromoSohm/ Sohm/Stock Boston; (cr), Leif Skoogfers/Woodfin Camp & Assoicates; 263(tr), Wayne Lynch/DRK Photo; (bl), Laurance B. Auippy/FPG International; 266(tl), Arthus Bertrand-Explorer/Photo Researchers; (c), George Herben/Visuals Unlimited Inc.; (cl), SuperStock; 269(tc), E.R. Degginger/Color-Pic; 270(tr), TSA/Tom Stack & Associates; (bl), Donald Nausbaum/Tony Stone Images; 272(br), Jeff & Alexa Henry; 273(tr), C.C. Lockwood/DRK Photo.

Chapter Eleven Page 274(cr), Los Angeles Times Photo by Ken Lubas; 276(b), Aaron Chang/Stock Market; 277(tr), Philip Long/Tony Stone Images; (bl), SuperStock; 278(top to bottom), SuperStock; Don Hebert/FPG International; Jonathan Weston/ Adventure Photo & Film; Larry Ulrich; 279(tl), Index Stock; (cl), James Blank; (cr), NASA; (br), Tina Buckman/Index Stock Photographers; 280(tl), G.R. Dick Roberts; (bl), Jeff Foott/Tom Stack & Associates; (br), Jeff Foott/DRK Photo; 281(tl), Breck P. Kent; (cr), John S. Shelton; 283(tl), Breck P. Kent; (b), Tom Bean; 284(tr), Brown Brothers; 285(br), Mickey Gibson/Animals Animals; 286(cl), Michael Fogden/Bruce Coleman; (cr), Peter Arnold; 287(bl), SuperStock; 288(c), Barbara Gerlach/DRK; (bl), Colin Monteath/Hedgehog House New Zealand; 289(bl), Didier Givois Agence Vandystadt/Photo Researchers; 290(tl), Tony Stone Images; (bl), Glenn M. Oliver/ Visuals Unlimited; 292(tl), Breck P. Kent; (c), Norbert Rosing/Animals Animals Earth Scenes; (cl), Keith Gunnar/Bruce Coleman; (bl), Tom Bean; 293(tr), Tom Bean; 295(cr), A. J. Copley/Visuals Unlimted; (bl), G.R. Roberts; 296(tr), Jebb Harris/Orange County Register/SABA; (bl), Mike Yamashita/Woodfin Camp & Associates; 297(tl), John D. Cunningham/Visuals Unlimited; (tc), J & B Photographers/Animals Animals Earth Scenes; 298(cr), Brown Brothers; 299(c), Didier Givois Agence Vandystadt/Photo Researchers; 300(tr), Face of the Earth/Tom Stack & Associates; (bl), Micheal Fredericks/ Animal Animals Earth Scenes; 302(cl), Richard Sisk/Panoramic Images; (cr), Jane Ellen Stevens/Paula Messina; 303(all), Gillian Cambers/UNESCO/Coping with beach erosion, Coastal Management Sourcebooks.

Chapter Twelve Page 304(all), Norbert Wu; 305(tr), Ed Reschke/Peter Arnold; 314(tl), Bruce Babbit/Liasion International; (bl), Rolf Peterson; 315(tr), Laguna Photo/ Liaison International; (cr), Jeff Lepore/Photo Researchers; 316(tr), Jeff Foott/AUSCAPE; 317(bl), Ross Hamilton/Tony Stone Images; 318(tl), Gerald & Buff Corsi/Visuals Unlimited; (cl), Hans Pfletschinger/Peter Arnold; (bl), Michael Fogden & Patricia Fogden/ Corbis; 319(tr), Telegraph Colour Library/FPG International; (tr), Peter Parks/Animals Animals Earth Scenes; 319(bl), Ed Robinson/Tom Stack & Associates; 320(tl), Gay Bumgarner/Tony Stone Images; (cl), Gregory G. Dimijian/Photo Researchers; (bl), Carol Hughes/Bruce Coleman; 321(tr), CSIRO Wildlife & Ecology; (br), David M. Dennis/ Tom Stack & Associates; 323(tr), Gay Bumgarner/Tony Stone Images; 326(tl), Darlyne Murawskings/National Geographic Society; 327(tr), Sanford D. Porter/ U.S. Department of Agriculture.

Unit Five Page 328(tl), Herman Melville: Classics Illustrated/Kenneth Spencer Research Library; (c), Science VU/WHOI-D. Foster/Visuals Unlimited; (bc), Mark Votier/ SYGMA Photo News; 329(tl), NASA; (tr), Peter Scoones/Woodfin Camp &Associates; (cl), Hulton-Deutsch Collection/Corbis; (cr), SAOLA/Wallet-Rosenfeld/Liaison International; (bl), Jeremy Horner/Corbis; (bc), Bassignac/Deville/Gaillar/Liaison International.

Chapter Thirteen Page 330(bc), Tom & Theresa Stack; 332(c), Tom Van Sant, Geosphere Project/Planetary Visions/Science Photo Library; 336(all), Charlie Barron/ NASA SST; 338(cl), O. Brown, R. Evans and M. Carle, University of Miami, Rosenstiel School of Marine and Atmospheric Science, Miami, Florida.; 339(bc), James Wilson/ Woodfin Camp & Associates; (br), Norbert Wu; 342(bl), W. Haxby, Lamont-Doherty Earth Observatory/Science Photo Library; 343(tr), NOAA/NSDS; 345(cr), Jim Zipp/Photo Researchers; 345(br), Mike Bacon/Tom Stack & Associates; 346(tl), James B. Wood; (cl), Al Giddings/Al Giddings Images; (bl), Japan Marine Science and Technology Center; 347(tr), E.R. Degginger/Color-Pic; (cr), Norbert Wu; 348(bl), Bruce Coleman Inc.; 349(tl), Breg Vaughn/Tom Stack & Associates; (br), Taylor Shellfish Farm; 350(br), TGS-NOPEC Geophysical Company; 351(bl), Institute of Oceanographic Sciences/NERC/Science Photo Library; (br), Charles D. Winters/Photo Researchers; 353(b), E.R. Degginger/ Color-Pic; 354(cl), Tony Freeman/PhotoEdit; (br), Ron Chapple/FPG International; 355(tr), Ben Osborne/Tony Stone Images; (bl), Mobil Oil Corporation; 357(all), Information and photograph courtesy of the Texas General Land Office's Texas Adopt-A-Beach Program.; 362(bl), Gilles Bassignac/Liaison International; 363(tr), SuperStock.

Chapter Fourteen Page 366(c), Hulton Getty Images/Liaison International; 373(cr), AP Wide World Photo/San Francisco Examiner, Lacy Atkins; 377(tr), C.C. Lockwood/ Bruce Coleman Inc.; (bl), Darrell Wong/Tony Stone Images; (br), August Upitis/ FPG International; 378(tl), Art Resource, NY; (br), NOAA; 383(tl), VOSCAR the Maine Photographer; (tr), VOSCAR the Maine Photographer; (cr), Russell Higgins; 385(cl), Art Resource, NY; 386(tl), Warren Bolster/Tony Stone Images; (br), Fred Whitehead/ Animals Animals Earth Scenes; 388(tl), Todd Bigelow/Black Star; (br), Warren Bolster/ Tony Stone Images; 389(tc), J.A.L. Cooke/Oxford Scientific Films/Animals Animals Earth Scenes; (tr), David M. Phillips/Animals Animals Earth Scenes.

Unit Six Page 390(tl), Ronald Sheridan/Ancient Art & Architecture Collection; (tr), NASA; (c), SuperStock; (cr), The Huntington Library, Art Collections, and Botanical Gardens, San Marino, California/SuperStock; (bc), Lawrence Livermore Laboratory/ Photo Researchers.

Chapter Fifteen: Page 392(tc), Paul Wager/Associated Press Brisbane Courier Mail; (bkgd), Michael Melford/Image Bank; 397(tr), SuperStock; 398(b), Photodisc; 399(cl), Johnny Johnson/DRK Photo; 403(cl), Renee Lynn/Photo Researchers; 404(tr), AP Photo/ Jame Puebla; 407(cr), A&L Sinibaldi/Tony Stone Images; (bl), Luc Marescot/Liaison International; 408(tl), NASA/Science Photo Library/Photo Researchers; 410(c), Byron Augustin/Tom Stack & Associates; 411(tc), David Weintraub/Photo Researchers; (tr), Argus Potoarchiv/Peter Arnold; (cr), Bruce Forster/Tony Stone Images; 412(tl), Robert Ginn/PhotoEdit; (cr), Phil Schofield/Picture Quest; 413(tr), Gary Parker/Science Photo Library/Photo Researchers; (c), David Woodfall/Tony Stone Images; (cl), Jean Lauzon/ Publiphoto/Photo Researchers; (br), TOMS/NASA; 415(tc), Chromosohm/Sohm/Photo Researchers; (cl), SuperStock; 418(tr), Salaber/Liaison International; (bl), Telegraph

Colour Library/FPG International; 420(tc), Bill Thompson/Woodfin Camp & Associates; 421(tr), Steve Winter/Black Star.

Chapter Sixteen Page 422(cr), Duane A. Laverty/Waco Tribune Herald; (bl), Samuel Barricklow; (bkgd), Ted S. Warren/Austin American-Statesman/Liaison International; (cl), Gerry Ellis/Ellis Nature Photography; 428(cl), Eric Sander/Liaison Intiernational; (bl), NOAA; 429(tr), Joyce Photographics/Photo Researchers; 430(bl), Nuridsany Et Perennou/SS/Photo Researchers; (br), Jim Mone/AP Wide World Photos; 431(tr), Gene E. Moore; 433(tr), Rod Planck/Tom Stack & Associates; (br), Norman Lamer/Stock House; 436(bl), Kent Wood/Peter Arnold; 437(br), Jean-Loup Charmet/Science Photo Library/Photo Researchers; 438(all), Howard B. Bluestein/Photo Researchers ; 439(tr), Red Huber/Orlando Sentinel/SYGMA; (br), rsd/gsfc/nasa; 440(tl), NASA/Science Photo Library/Photo Researchers; 441(cl), Victor R. Caivano/AP Wide World Photo; 443(tr), Tom Pantages; (cl), David Hwang; (br), G.R. Dick Roberts; 444(tl), Tom Bean; (cr), David R. Frazier Photo Library; 446(br), NASA/Science Photo Library/Photo Researchers; 447(c), Jean-Loup Charmet/Science Photo Library/Photo Researchers; 448(tr), Clyde H. Smith/Peter Arnold; 450(tl), Michael Lyon; (br), Salaber/Liaison International.

Chapter Seventeen Page 452(cl), Gunter Ziesler/Peter Arnold; (br), Richard Packwood/Oxford Scienctific Films/Animals Animals Earth Scenes; 454(tl), G.R. Dick Roberts; (tr), Index Stock; (c), Yvamomatiuk & John Eastcott/Woodfin Camp & Associates; (bl), Gary Retherford/Photo Researchers; (br), SuperStock; (bkgd), Tom Van Sant, Geosphere Project/Planetary Visions/Science Photo Library; 455(tc), Michael Newman/PhotoEdit; (cr), Kim Heacox/DRK Photo; 457(bl), Tom Van Sant, Geosphere Project/Planetary Visions/Science Photo Library/Photo Researchers; 458(bl), Larry Ulrich; (br), Paul Wakefield/Tony Stone Images; 461(bc), Michael Fogden/Bruce Coleman Inc.; 462(cl), Thomas A. Wiewandt; (cr), Larry Ulrich; 463(c), Nadine Zuber/Photo Researchers; 464(bl), Carr Clifton/Minden Pictures; 465(cl), Tom Bean/Tony Stone Images; (bc), Fred Hirschmann; 466(tr), Stephen Simpson/FPG International; 467(bl), Harry Wakjer/Alaska Stock; 468(tl), SuperStock; 471(tr), Roger Werth/Woodfin Camp & Associates; 473(tr), Leverett Bradley/Tony Stone Images; (cr), Jaques Janqoux/Tony Stone Images; 475(c), Danilo G. Donadoni/Bruce Coleman Inc.; 476(bl), Richard Pharaoh/International Stock; 478(c), George Bernard/Animals Animals Earth Scenes; 479(br), Hank Morgan/Photo Researchers.

Feature Borders: Unless otherwise noted below, all images copyright ©2001 PhotoDisc/HRW. Pages 30, 211, 243, 362, 478, *Across the Sciences:* all images by HRW. Pages 31, 55, 388, 450, *Careers:* sand bkgd and saturn, Corbis Images; DNA, Morgan Cain & Associates; scuba gear, ©1997 Radlund & Associates for Artville. Pages 131, *Eureka:* copyright ©2001 PhotoDisc/HRW. Pages 130, 189, 273, 303, 327, 363, *Eye on the Environment:* clouds and sea in bkgd, HRW; bkgd grass and red eyed frog, Corbis Images; hawks and pelican, Animals Animals/Earth Scenes; rat, John Grelach/Visuals Unlimited; endangered flower, Dan Suzio/PhotoResearchers, Inc Pages 105, 326, 389, 420, *Health Watch:* dumbell, Sam Dudgeon/HRW Photo; aloe vera and EKG, Victoria Smith/HRW Photo; basketball, ©1997 Radlund & Associates for Artville; shoes and Bubbles, Greg Geisler. Pages 163, 421, *Scientific Debate:* Sam Dudgeon/HRW Photo. Pages 77, 451, *Science Fiction:* saucers, Ian Christopher/Greg Geisler; book, HRW; bkgd, Stock Illustration Source. Pages 54, 104, 162, 210, 242, 302, 479, *Science Technology and Society:* robot, Greg Geisler. Pages 76, 188, 272, *Weird Science:* mite, David Burder/Tony Stone; atom balls, J/B Woolsey Associates; walking stick and turtle, EclectiCollection.

LabBook "LabBook Header" "L", Corbis Images; "a", Letraset Phototone; "b" and "B", HRW; "o" and "k",images copyright ©2001 PhotoDisc/HRW. Page 492(cr), USGS; 495(tl), Ken Lucas/Visuals Unlimited Inc.; (b), James Tallon/Outdoor Exposure; 509(cl), Tom Bean; 512(cr), mgdc/noaa; 553(br), Kuni Stringer/AP Wide World Photos; 555(cr), Jay Malonson/AP Wide World Photos

Sam Dudgeon/HRW Photo Page v(br); vi(bl,cl); viii(tl); xi(tl); xiii(tl); xv(b); xvi (br); xvii(tr,b); xviii(tr); 5(br); 21(cl); 23(cl,cr); 33(cr); 35(cr); 38(bl); 46(tr); 59(tc,b); 60(c); 62(cl); 65(tr,cl,bl,bc); 66(bl); 67(cl,tc,tr, Courtesy of Science Stuff, Austin, TX); 68(c,t,) Courtesy of Science Stuff, Austin, TX,); 69(br); 73(cl); 74(tl); 75(cl); 79(all); 84(br); 85(c,bcr); 86(tl); 92(c); 95(tl); 97(br,tc,c); 98(center 3) 105(tc); 107(br); 110(tr); 117(bl,br); 119(br); 124(tl); 134(tl,tr); 151(c); 165(br); 179(tr); 180(br); 188(c); 212(br); 213(cr); 219(bl); 224(tl); 247(br); 266(bl); 275(b); 294(all); 331(b); 350(bl); 356(br); 365(bl); 367(tr); 374(tr); 391(tl,tr); 393(br); 397(br); 405(br); 412(cl,bl); 414(c); 423(br); 425(tr); 426(tl); 431(br); 442(bl); 453(br); 489(all); 490(br); 491(br); 493(tr); 495(bc,br); 497(tr,br); 498(br); 502(tr); 503(all); 505(br); 507(b); 508(br); 510(cl); 511(tc); 513(all); 516(tr); 523(br); 530(br); 531(br); 532(b,br); 534(all); 535(tr); 539(tr); 540(br); 547(bl); 550(tl); 551(bl); 557(cr); 560(b); 567(t,b); 571(b) Victoria Smith: Page 67(br); 68(tl) Courtesy of Science Stuff/Austin, TX ; 117(cl,cr); 191(br); 427(tr); 486(br); 495(tr) Courtesy of Science Stuff/Austin, TX; 499(all); 521(br); 524(br); 528(b); 545(tr); 554(cr): Andy Christiansen: Page 10 (bl, bc); 24(tl); 40(cl,b); 52(bl); 55(tl); 81(br); 108(c); 110(cl); 246(t); 354 (bl,bc,cr); 356(bkgd); 412(cl); 500(all); 514(br); 529(all); 542(br); 559(br); 561(bl): John Langford: Page x(tl); 215(br); 220(tl,bl); 221(br); 222(cr); 223(tr); 225(tr); 226(bl); 228(tr); 229(tr); 232(bl); 238(br): Peter Van Steen: Page viii(bl); 4(t); 24(cl,cr); 135(bl); 230(cr); 395(br); 571(t): Russell Dian: Page 497(cr): Paul Fraughton: Page 17(cr): Michael Lyon: Page 31(tl) :Ken Karp: Page 98(t): Ken Lax: Page 180(cl): Charlie Winters: Page 495(cr)

Annotated Teacher's Edition Credits

TE Front Matter Page T1(cl), Louis Psihoyos/Matrix International; T2(cl), Image copyright ©2001 PhotoDisc/HRW; T3(c), E.R. Degginger/Color-Pic; (c), DRK Photo; T4(tl), Grant Heilman Photography; T5(br), Trevor Wood/Tony Stone Images; T6(tl), Sam Dudgeon/HRW Photo; (tr), Sam Dudgeon/HRW Photo; T7(tr), Image copyright ©2001 PhotoDisc, Inc./HRW; T8(bl), Ron Ruhoff/Stock Imagery; T9(tr), Bruce Coleman, Inc.; T10(bl), SuperStock; T11(cr), Image copyright ©2001 PhotoDisc/HRW; T12(b), Soames Summerhays/Photo Researchers, Inc.; T13(cr), Image copyright ©2001 PhotoDisc, Inc./HRW; T14(bl), The Stock Market; T15(tr), Sam Dudgeon/HRW Photo; T16(cl), Image copyright ©2001 PhotoDisc/HRW; T17(br), Image copyright ©2001 PhotoDisc/HRW.

Master Materials List: Unless otherwise noted all images © 2001 PhotoDisc/HRW: Page xxii(CD), HRW Photo; xxiii(beans), Corbis Images; (gelatin,marshmellows), Sam Dudgeon/HRW; (paint), Andy Christiansen/HRW; xxiv(salt), Corbis Images;(ball), © 1997 Radlund & Assoc. for Artville; xxv(coin), EyeWire, Inc; (hammer), Sam Dudgeon/HRW; xxvi(minerals,bl), HRW Photos; (coins), EyeWire, Inc; xxvii(tr), Robert Wolf/HRW

Lab Approval Portraits: All photos courtesy of the reviewers

TE Background Illustrations: Page 3F(cr), Stephen Durke; (bl), David Schleinkofer; 57E(tl), Holt, Rinehart & Winston; 77E(bl), David Uhl Studio; 77F(cr), David Uhl Studio; 105F(c), Holt, Rinehart & Winston; 133E(tl), David Uhl Studio; (cl), GeoSystems Global Corporation; 133F(tl), David Uhl Studio; 189E(tr), David Uhl Studio; (bl), David Uhl Studio; 189F(bl), GeoSystems Global Corporation; 211E(tl), Terry Guyer; 211F(bl), Uhl Studios Inc.; 303E(cl), Will Nelson; 329E(tr), Craig Attebery; 363E(bl), GeoSystems Global Corporation; 363F(br), Marty Roper; 391E(cr), John Huxtable; 391F(tl), Stephen Durke; 421E(br), GeoSystems Global Corporation; 451E(cl), Geosystems Global Corporation; (cr), Stephen Durke; (br), Marty Roper; 451F(cl), Geosystems Global Corporation.

TE Background Photography: Page 3E(tr), Marit Jentof-Nilsen and Fritz Hasler/NASA Goddard Laboratory for Atmospheres; (bl), S. Schwabe/The Rob Palwer Blue Holes Foundation; 3F(tl), Earth Imaging/Tony Stone Images; 31E(tl), Andy Christiansen/HRW Photo; (bl), Andy Christiansen/HRW Photo; (br), USGS; 31F(tl), Sam Dudgeon/HRW Photo; (cr), USGS; (bl), USGS; 57E(cr), E. R. Degginger/Color-Pi; 57F(cl), Erica and Harold Van Pelt/American Museum of Natural History; (cr), E. R. Degginger/Color-Pic; (bl), Index Stock Photography; 77E(tl), Breck P. Kent/Animals Animals Earth Scenes; (br), E. R. Degginger/Color-Pic; 77F(tl), Peter Cummings/Tom Stack & Associates; (bl), Sam Dudgeon/HRW Photo; (bc), Breck P. Kent; (br), Dorling Kindersley; 105E(tl), James Randklev/Tony Stone Images; (cr), Mark A. Leman/Tony Stone Images; (bl), Andy Christiansen/HRW Photo; 105F(tr), Luis Castaneda/Image Bank; (cl), Sylvain Coffie/Tony Stone Images; (br), G.R. Dick Roberts; 133F(tr), Sylvester Allred/Visuals Unlimited; (bl), ESA/CE/Eurocontral/Science Photo Library/Photo Researchers; 163E(cr), Bob Paz/Caltech; 163F(tc), Astronomy online; (tr), SOHO/ESA/NASA; (cl), A. Ramey/Woodfin Camp & Associates; 189E(cl), Robert W. Madden/National Geographic Society; 189F(tr), Andrew Rafkind/Tony Stone Images; (cr), Gilles Bassignac/Liasion International; 211E(br), Sam Dudgeon/HRW photo; 211F(tl), John Langford/HRW photo; 245E(tl), Galen Rowell/Peter Arnold; (cr), Earth Satellite Corporation/Science Photo Library; (bl), Laurence Parent; 245F(tl), E. R. Degginger/Color-Pic; (br), SuperStock; 273E(tl), SuperStock; (bl), NASA ; (cr), Brown Brothers; 273F(tl), Didier Givois Agence Vandystadt/Photo Researchers; (cr), A. J. Copley/Visuals Unlimted; (bl), Colin Monteath/Hedgehog House New Zealand; 303E(cr), Laguna Photo/ Liaison International; 303F(tr), Gregory G. Dimijian/Photo Researchers; (bl), Michael Fogden & Patricia Fogden/Corbis; (br), Telegraph Colour Library/FPG International; 329E(tl), Norbert Wu; (cl), James Wilson/Woodfin Camp & Associates; (br), NOAA/NSDS; 329F(br), Ben Osborne/Tony Stone Images; 363E(tl), Hulton Getty/Liaison International; (br), August Upitis/FPG International; 363F(tl), NOAA; (tc), VOSCAR the Maine Photographer; (tr), VOSCAR the Maine Photographer; (bl), Darrell Wong/Tony Stone Images; 391E(cl), Image copyright ©2001 PhotoDisc; (bl), SuperStock; 391F(tr), David Weintraub/Photo Researchers; (bl), NASA/Science Photo Library/Photo Researchers; 421E(tr), Gene E. Moore; (cl), Eric Sandler/NOAA; 421F(tr), NASA/Science Photo Library/Photo Researchers; (cr), Howard Bluestein/Photo Researchers; 451F(tr), Jaques Janqoux/Tony Stone Images; (br), Leverett Bradley/Tony Stone Images.

Acknowledgments continue from page iv.

Alyson Mike
Science Teacher
East Valley Middle School
East Helena, Montana

Michael Minium
Vice President of Program Development
United States Orienteering Federation
Forest Park, Georgia

Jan Nelson
Science Teacher
East Valley Middle School
East Helena, Montana

Dwight Patton
Science Teacher
Carroll T. Welch Middle School
Horizon City, Texas

Terry J. Rakes
Science Teacher
Elmwood Junior High School
Rogers, Arkansas

Steven Ramig
Science Teacher
West Point High School
West Point, Nebraska

Helen P. Schiller
Science Teacher
Northwood Middle School
Taylors, South Carolina

Bert J. Sherwood
Science Teacher
Socorro Middle School
El Paso, Texas

David M. Sparks
Science Teacher
Redwater Junior High School
Redwater, Texas

Larry Tackett
Science Teacher and Dept. Chair
Andrew Jackson Middle School
Cross Lanes, West Virginia

Walter Woolbaugh
Science Teacher
Manhattan Junior High School
Manhattan, Montana

Alexis S. Wright
Middle School Science Coordinator
Rye Country Day School
Rye, New York

John Zambo
Science Teacher
E. Ustach Middle School
Modesto, California

Gordon Zibelman
Science Teacher
Drexel Hill Middle School
Drexel Hill, Pennsylvania

Answers to Concept Mapping Questions

The following pages contain sample answers to all of the concept mapping questions that appear in the Chapter Reviews. Because there is more than one way to do a concept map, your students' answers may vary.

CHAPTER 1 The World of Earth Science

CHAPTER 2 Maps as Models of the Earth

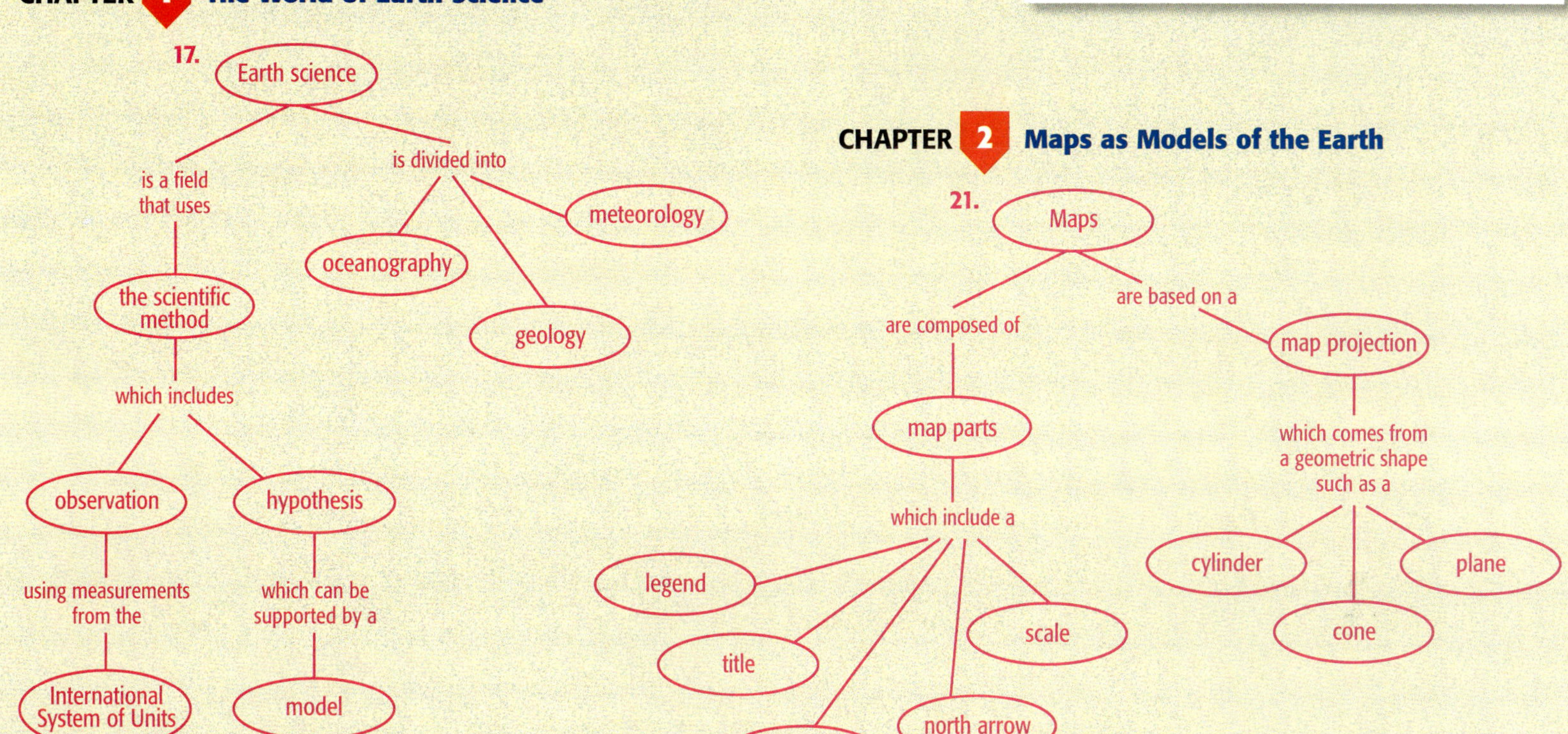

CHAPTER 3 Minerals of the Earth's Crust

CHAPTER 4 Rocks: Mineral Mixtures

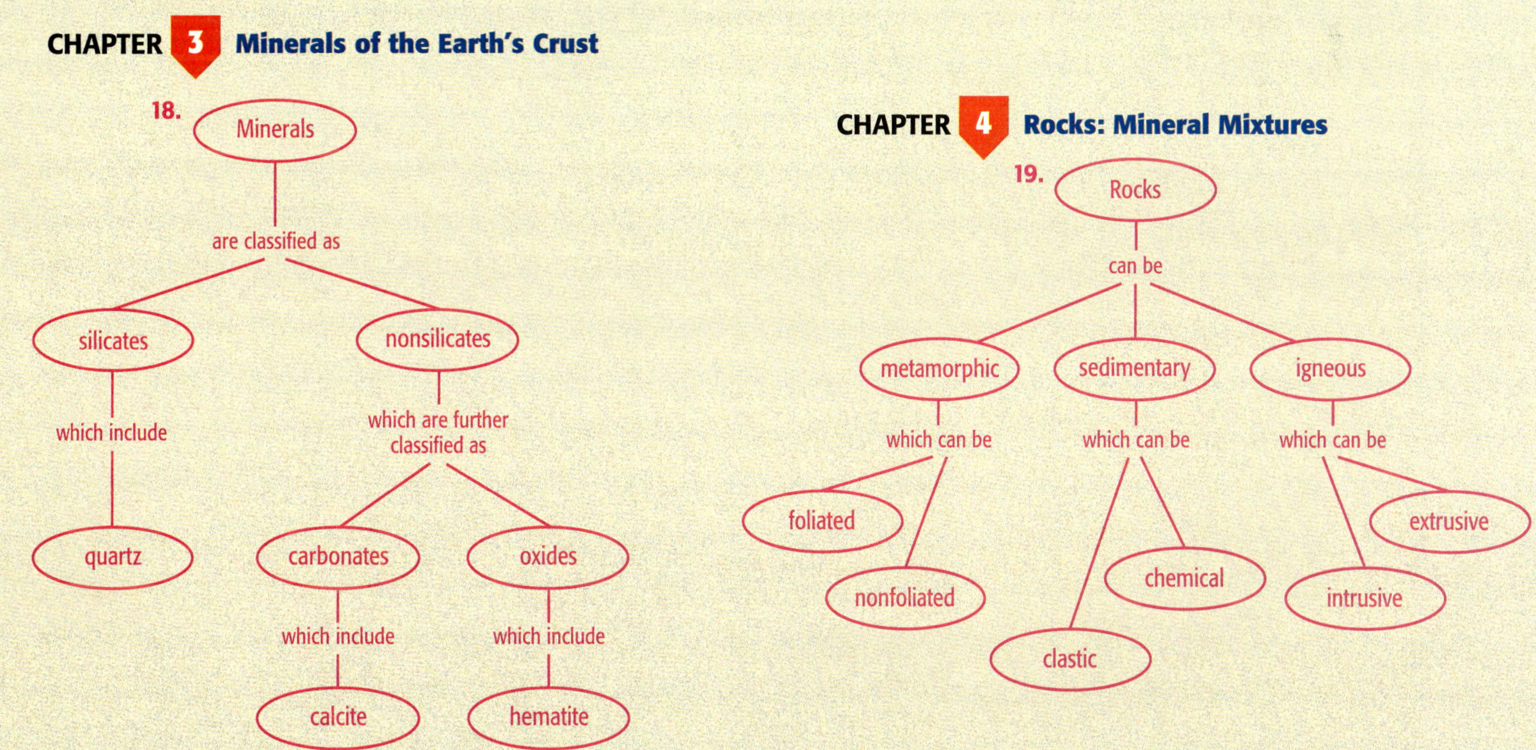

CHAPTER 5 Energy Resources

18.

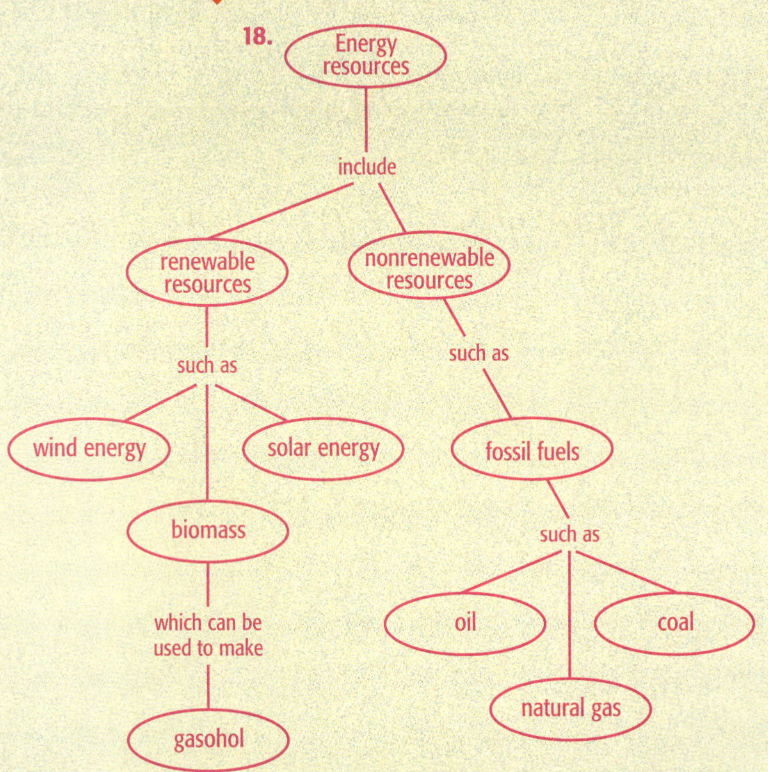

CHAPTER 6 Plate Tectonics

21.

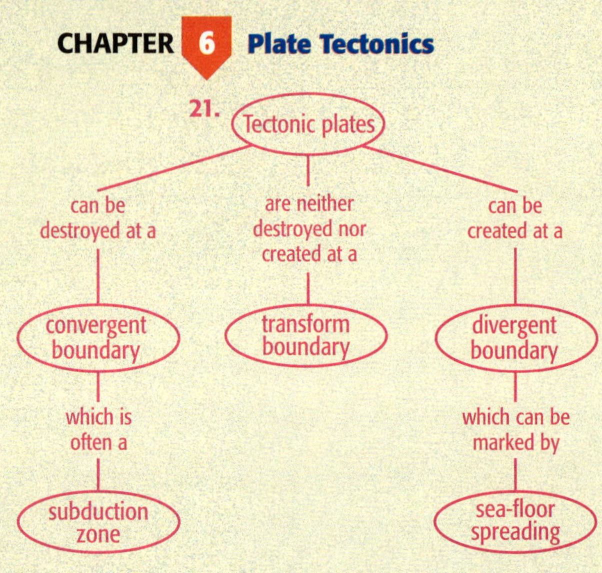

CHAPTER 7 Earthquakes

15.

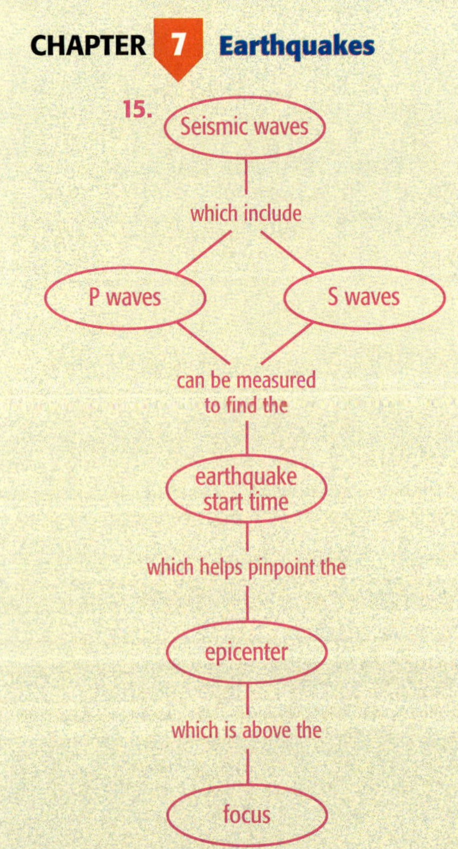

CHAPTER 8 Volcanoes

17.

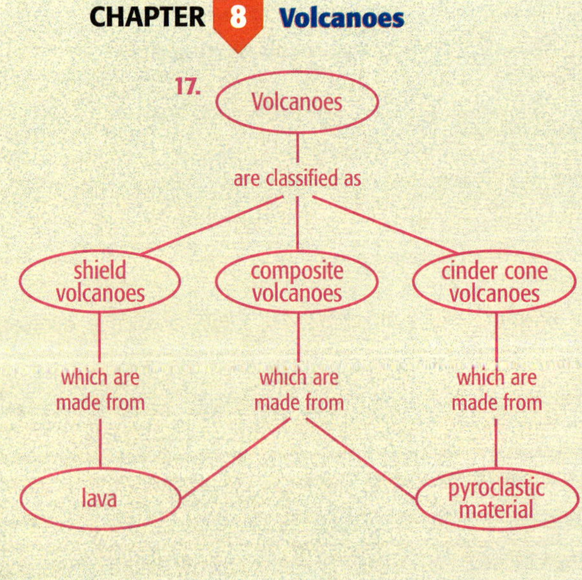

CHAPTER 9 Heat and Heat Technology

17.
Heat
is a transfer of
thermal energy
by
conduction
convection
radiation
due to a difference in
temperature

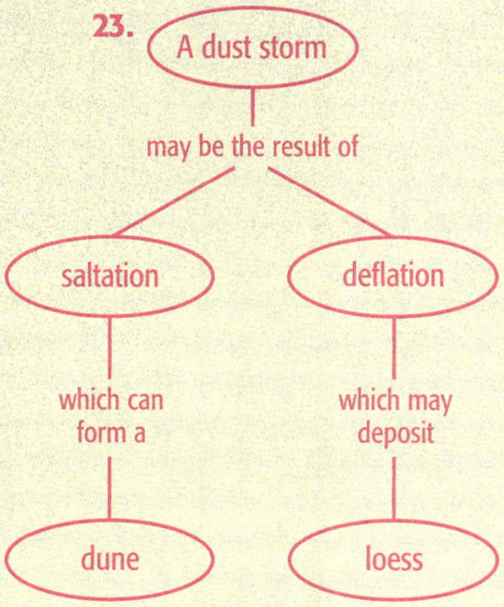

CHAPTER 12 Interactions of Living Things

18.
The biosphere
includes
ecosystems
composed of
communities
composed of
populations
composed of
individual organisms
composed of
producers
consumers
which include
herbivores
carnivores

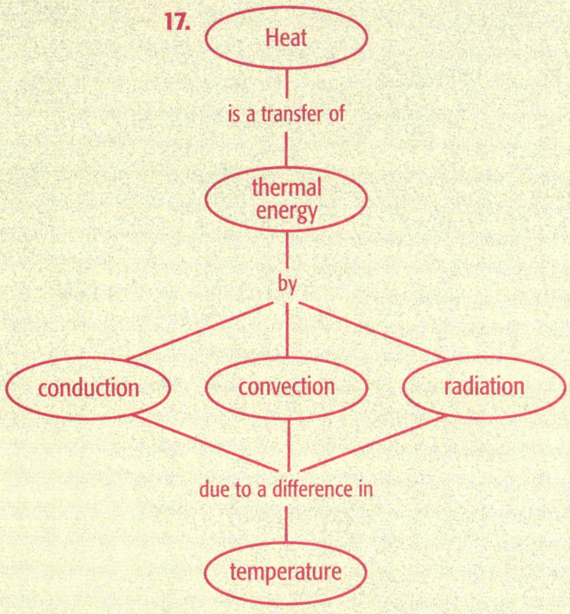

CHAPTER 10 The Flow of Fresh Water

19.
Gravity
moves water down below the
water table
which is the boundary between the
zone of aeration
zone of saturation
whose water content depends on the rock's
permeability
porosity

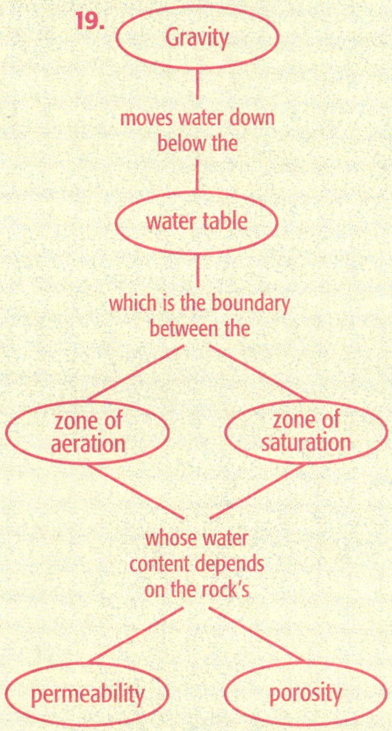

CHAPTER 11 Agents of Erosion and Deposition

23.
A dust storm
may be the result of
saltation
which can form a
dune
deflation
which may deposit
loess

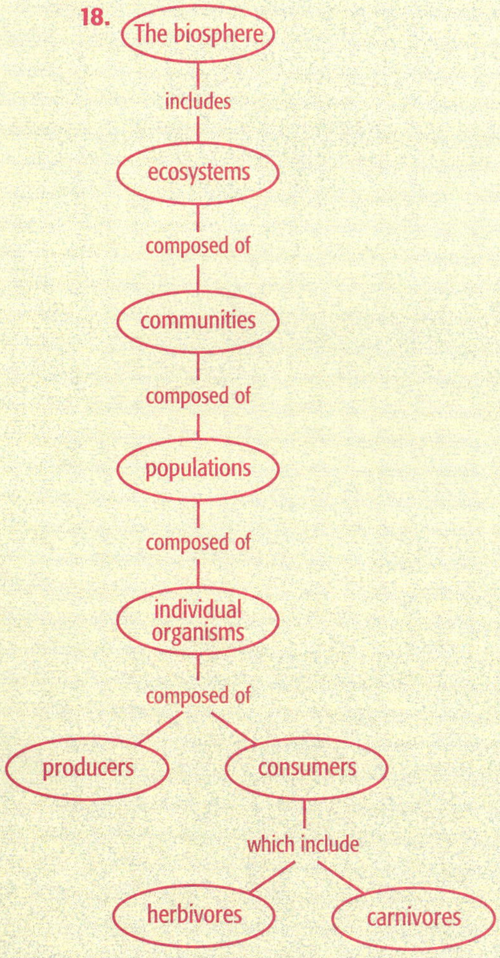

CHAPTER 13 Exploring the Oceans

18.
Marine life
includes
plankton
nekton
which live in the
pelagic environment
benthos
which live in the
benthic environment

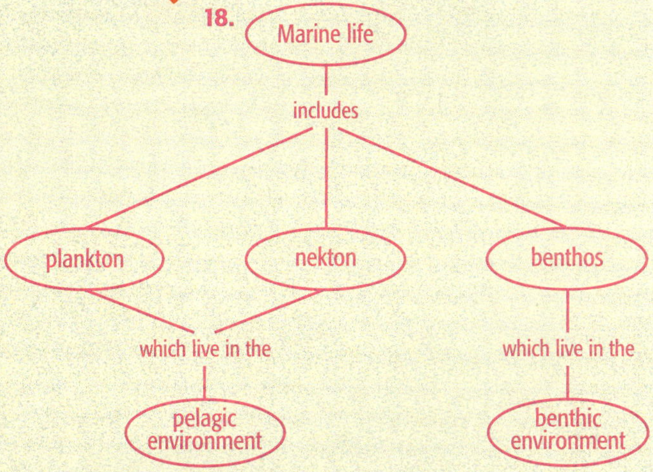

CHAPTER 14 The Movement of Ocean Water

19.

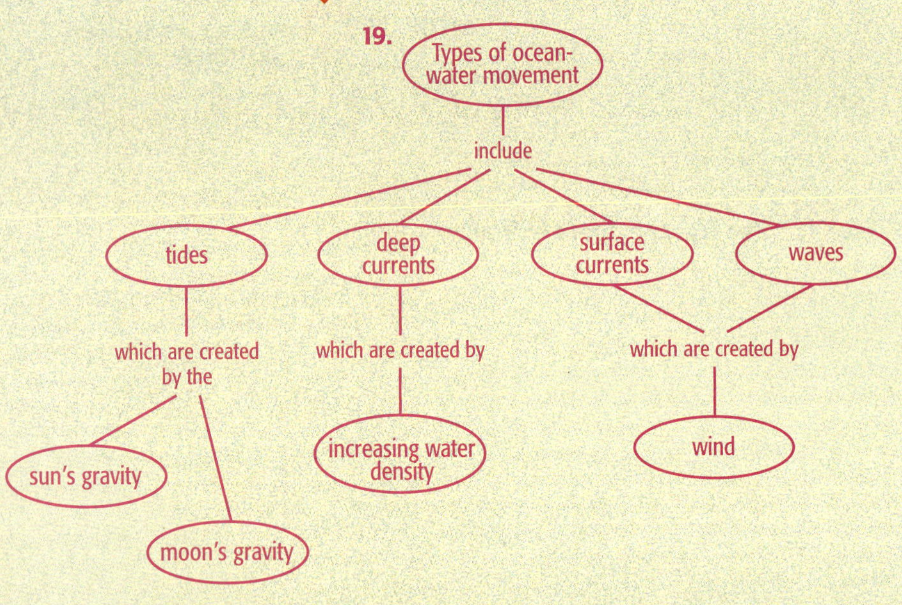

CHAPTER 15 The Atmosphere

21.

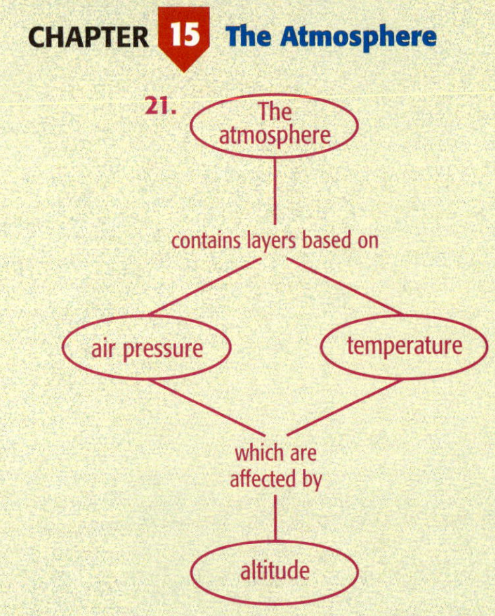

CHAPTER 16 Understanding Weather

21.

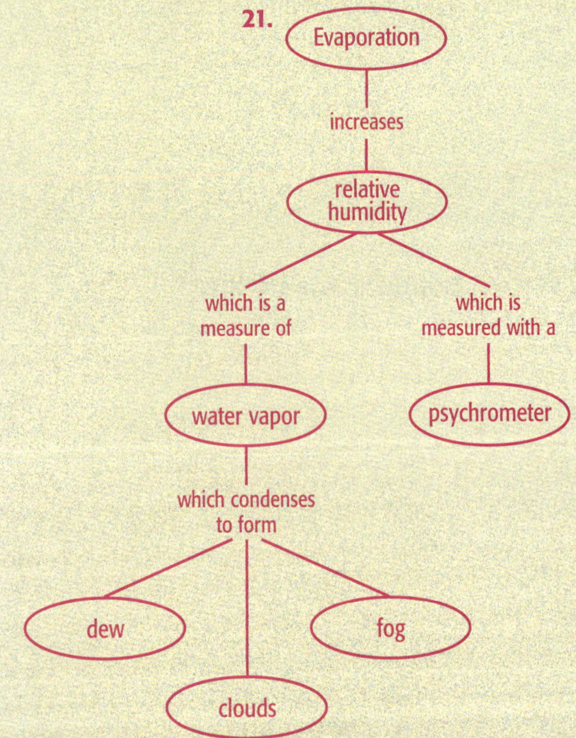

CHAPTER 17 Climate

20.

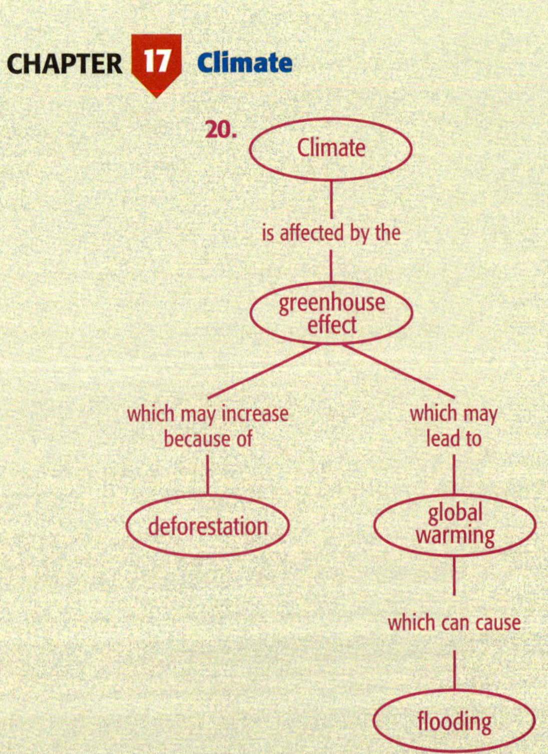